hology

Franklin
Delano Roosevelt

Adolf
Hitler

1935 *Handbook of Social Psychology* Murchison

1936 *The Psychology of Social Norms,* an important early work
      on social norms and social influence Sherif

1939 Early studies on leadership; start of research on group
      dynamics Lewin, Lippitt, White

1946 Early research on impression formation, a key aspect of
      person perception Asch

1947 Establishment of the Research Center for Group
      Dynamics Lewin, Cartwright, White, Zander, French

1950 *The Authoritarian Personality* Adorno, Frenkel-Brunswik,
      Levinson, Sanford

1951 Important research on conformity and group pressure Asch

SOCIAL PSYCHOLOGY
Understanding Human Interaction

FOURTH EDITION

Robert A. Baron
Purdue University

Donn Byrne
State University of New York
at Albany

ALLYN AND BACON, INC.
Boston/London/Sydney/Toronto

Series Editor: Bill Barke
Production Editor: Joanne Dauksewicz

Library of Congress Cataloging in Publication Data

Baron, Robert A.
  Social psychology.

  Accompanied by instructor's manual, test bank, and student guide.
  Bibliography: p.
  Includes index.
  1. Social psychology. I. Byrne, Donn Erwin. II. Title.
HM251.B437   1983   302   83-22319
ISBN 0-205-08054-5
ISBN 0-205-08119-3 (International)

Printed in the United States of America

10 9 8 7 6 5 4 3 2   88 87 86 85 84

Photo research by Laurel Anderson.

Chapter Opening Photo Credits
1. Eric Roth/The Picture Cube.
2. Ulrike Welsch.
3. Ulrike Welsch.
4. Ulrike Welsch.
5. Robert Eckert/Stock, Boston.
6. Ulrike Welsch.
7. Ulrike Welsch.
8. Ulrike Welsch.
9. Patricia H. Gross/Stock, Boston.
10. Ulrike Welsch.
11. Ulrike Welsch.
12. George Malave/Stock, Boston.
13. Shirley Zieberg/Taurus Photos.
14. Ulrike Welsch.
15. Ulrike Welsch.

To Ruth, for all her love, kindness, and understanding.
AND
To Aunt L.E. and Uncle Jack, two very special people.

Brief Contents

CHAPTER ONE ◆ *Understanding Social Behavior: An Introduction*　1

CHAPTER TWO ◆ *Social Perception: Knowing Others . . . and Ourselves*　37

CHAPTER THREE ◆ *Social Cognition: Thinking about (and Making Sense of) the Social World*　81

CHAPTER FOUR ◆ *Attitudes and Attitude Change: Reactions to the Social World*　123

CHAPTER FIVE ◆ *Prejudice and Discrimination: Why All Too Often (and with Little Reason) Differences Count*　167

CHAPTER SIX ◆ *Attraction, Friendship, and Love*　209

CHAPTER SEVEN ◆ *Social Influence: Changing the Behavior of Others*　245

CHAPTER EIGHT ◆ *Prosocial Behavior: Helping, Intervening, and Resisting*　205

CHAPTER NINE ◆ *Aggression: Its Nature, Causes, and Control*　321

CHAPTER TEN ◆ *Social Exchange: Coming to Terms with Others*　365

CHAPTER ELEVEN ◆ *Groups and Individual Behavior: The Consequences of Belonging*　409

CHAPTER TWELVE ◆ *Environment and Behavior: Social Impact of the Physical World*　451

CHAPTER THIRTEEN ◆ *Applying Social Psychology*　487

CHAPTER FOURTEEN ◆ *Personality and Social Behavior: The Role of Individual Differences*　527

CHAPTER FIFTEEN ◆ *Sexuality: The Most Intimate Social Behavior*　563

Contents

Special Features   ix

A Note from the Authors   xi

Acknowledgments   xvi

CHAPTER ONE   ◆   *Understanding Social Behavior: An Introduction*   1

Social Psychology: A Working Definition   6
Social Psychology: A Capsule Memoir   11
Extending the Frontiers: Research Methods in Social
    Psychology   15
Using This Book: A Displaced Preface   29
Summary   32
Glossary   33
For More Information   34

CHAPTER TWO   ◆   *Social Perception: Knowing Others . . . and Ourselves*   37

Nonverbal Communication: "Reading" the Language of
    Expressions, Gazes, and Gestures   41
Attribution: Understanding the Causes of Behavior   54
Self-attribution: Knowing and Understanding Ourselves   70
Summary   78
Glossary   78
For More Information   79

CHAPTER THREE   ◆   *Social Cognition: Thinking about (and Making Sense of) the Social
World*   81

Schemata: Cognitive Frameworks for Understanding the Social
    World   88
Social Cognition: Some Basic Processes   97
Forming Impressions of Others: Social Cognition and the
Integration of Social Information   111

Summary 119
Glossary 120
For More Information 121

CHAPTER FOUR ◆ *Attitudes and Attitude Change: Reactions to the Social World*   123

Attitude Formation: The Role of Learning and Experience 127
Attitude Measurement: Assessing the Unseen, Part 2 130
Changing Attitudes: The Persuasion Approach 135
Changing Attitudes: The Dissonance Approach 150
Attitudes and Behavior: The Essential Link 159
Summary 164
Glossary 165
For More Information 166

CHAPTER FIVE ◆ *Prejudice and Discrimination: Why All Too Often (and with Little Reason) Differences Count*   167

Prejudice and Discrimination: What They Are and How They Are Measured 170
Theoretical Explanations of Prejudice: The Origins of Hate 181
Reducing Prejudice: Some Steps in the Right Directions 188
Prejudice Based on Sex: A Special, Timely Case 191
Sex Roles and Sexual Identity: Masculine, Feminine, or Androgynous? 199
Summary 206
Glossary 206
For More Information 207

CHAPTER SIX ◆ *Attraction, Friendship, and Love*   209

Reacting to Strangers: Proximity, Feelings, and Affiliative Needs 213
Evaluating Acquaintances: Attractiveness, Similarity, and Reciprocity 221
Falling in (and out of) Love 234
Summary 241
Glossary 242
For More Information 243

CHAPTER SEVEN ◆ *Social Influence: Changing the Behavior of Others*   245

Conformity: To Get Along, Often We Must "Go Along" 249
Compliance: To Ask—Sometimes—Is to Receive 264
Obedience: Social Influence by Demand 271
Summary 281
Glossary 282
For More Information 282

CHAPTER EIGHT ◆ *Prosocial Behavior: Helping, Intervening, and Resisting*   205

Responding to an Unexpected Emergency: Helping a Stranger in Distress 288
Intervening to Stop a Wrongdoer As a Prosocial Act 304
Resisting Temptation: The Ability to Sacrifice Immediate Gains 311
Summary 317
Glossary 318
For More Information 319

CHAPTER NINE ◆ *Aggression: Its Nature, Causes, and Control*   321

Aggression: A Social Definition 325
Theoretical Perspectives on Aggression: In Search of the Roots of Violence 326
Social and Situational Determinants of Aggression: External Causes of Violence 330
Individual Determinants of Aggression: Personality, Genes, and Sex 345
Aggression: Its Prevention and Control 352
Summary 360
Glossary 362
For More Information 362

CHAPTER TEN ◆ *Social Exchange: Coming to Terms with Others*   365

Cooperation and Competition: Working with — or against — Others 370
Bargaining and Negotiation: Resolving Interpersonal Conflict 382
Perceived Fairness in Social Exchange: In Search of Social Justice 395
Summary 406
Glossary 407
For More Information 407

CHAPTER ELEVEN ◆ *Groups and Individual Behavior: The Consequences of Belonging*   409

Social Facilitation: When the Presence of Others Counts 413
Deindividuation: Groups, Self-awareness, and the Shattering of Restraint 423
Decision Making in Groups: How (Process) and What (Outcome) 438
Leaders and Followers: Patterns of Influence within Groups 438
Summary 447
Glossary 448
For More Information 449

CHAPTER TWELVE ◆ *Environment and Behavior: Social Impact of the Physical World*   451

The Interpersonal Environment: Responding to the Physical
Presence of Others 455
Negative Aspects of the Physical Environment: When Conditions
Are Stressful 470
Positive Aspects of the Physical Environment: Excitement and
Pleasure in a City 476
Summary 484
Glossary 485
For More Information 486

CHAPTER THIRTEEN ◆ *Applying Social Psychology*   487

The Legal System: Social Psychology in the Courtroom 491
Behavioral Medicine: Health Care and Social Psychology 504
The Workplace: Behavior in Organizations 514
Summary 523
Glossary 524
For More Information 525

CHAPTER FOURTEEN ◆ *Personality and Social Behavior: The Role of Individual
Differences*   527

Personality Traits: Stable Characteristics across Situations 531
Loneliness: Those Who Feel Left out of Social Interactions 540
The Type A – Type B Personality Dimension: Who Succeeds and
Who Survives? 546
Locus of Control: Assigning Responsibility for Life's Outcomes 555
Summary 559
Glossary 560
For More Information 561

CHAPTER FIFTEEN ◆ *Sexuality: The Most Intimate Social Behavior*   563

Changes in Sexuality: Society, Attitudes, and Behavior 566
Sexual Attraction 574
The Effects of Erotic Images on Motivation, Fantasy, and
Behavior 583
Erotophobia-Erotophilia: Attitudes about Sexuality 594
Summary 602
Glossary 603
For More Information 604

Bibliography   607
Name Index   665
Subject Index   679

SPECIAL FEATURES

FOCUS ON RESEARCH

Experimentation: Laboratory or Field? 20

The Role of Facial Feedback: Do We Show What We Feel, Feel What We Show, . . . or Both? 46

Studying Social Cognition: Methods for Measuring the Unseen 86

Cognition and Affect: How Feelings Shape Thought, and Thought Shapes Feelings 116

Message Content and Persuasion: The Role of Recipients' Self-schemata 142

The Physiology of Persuasion: Patterns of Brain Activity during Pro- and Counterattitudinal Messages 146

When Attitude Change Fails: Resistance to Persuasion 152

Stereotypes: An Unsettling Note on Their Self-confirming Nature 174

The Illusion of Outgroup Homogeneity: A Cognitive Basis for Prejudice 186

What Is Physical Attractiveness? 224

Similarity as a Threat: The Need to be Unique 230

Conformity and Private Attitudes: Why Social Support Sometimes Backfires 256

"Low-balling": Changing the Rules in Midgame — and Getting Away with It! 272

Emotions and Attributions as Determinants of Altruism 296

Measuring Human Aggression: Hurt without Harm 332

Violent Pornography: A Special, Dangerous Case 346

Love, Money, or . . . ? The "What" and "When" of Social Exchange 368

Personality and Success in Social Exchange: Beware the High Mach! 392

Social Loafing and Social Impact: Why Groups Are Often Inefficient 420

The Great Man / Great Woman Theory Revisited: Personality and Leadership 442

Jump! Jump! Environmental Influences on Response to a Suicide Threat 466

Initiating Environmental Improvement 516

Personality and Auto Accidents: Characteristics of DWI Offenders 538

Negative Consequences of the Sexual Revolution: Pressure, Parenthood, and Pestilence 572

Sexual Attraction to One's Own Gender: The Determinants of Homosexual Behavior 580

ON THE APPLIED SIDE

Why Study Social Behavior? A Survival-Oriented Reply 8

Social Psychology's Practical Benefits: On the Costs of Being a "Secret Donor" 30

Bias in Causal Attribution: Some Negative Potential Effects 68

Attribution as a Form of Therapy: When a New Causal Framework Can Help 76

Errors in Social Inference: Some Unsettling, Practical Effects 112

Dissonance, Arousal, and Social Drinking 160

Failure of the Equal Rights Amendment: A Social Psychological Perspective 204

Rejection — When Love Is a One-Way Street 238

Modeling: Social Influence and the Enhancement of Human Welfare 278

What to Do about Shoplifters 308

How Can Cheating Be Stopped? 314

Incompatible Responses: Some Potential, Practical Uses 360

Social Exchange: Some Steps in the Right Direction 402

Countering Deindividuation: Some Potentially Useful Steps 430

Where Would You Like to Live? Choosing the Ideal Environment 478

Overpopulation: An Environmental Time Bomb 482

Crime in the Neighborhood: Evaluating a Community Project 502

Time, Schedules, and Circadian Principles 520

Overcoming Shyness and Increasing Sociability 544

Reducing Coronary Heart Disease by Altering Personality Patterns 548

Repeated Exposure to Erotica: Less Arousal but More Callous Attitudes 596

In Search of the Cutting Edge

Every field of science has—or certainly should have—a "cutting edge." That is, each should possess one or more areas in which progress is swift, gains in knowledge are impressive, and major breakthroughs unfold at a heady pace. The absence of such centers of scientific excitement may indicate that stagnation has developed, and woe to any field that finds itself in this state of affairs! Social psychology, of course, is in no danger of confronting the problem of stagnation. Partly because of its great diversity and partly because of its own intrinsic vigor, it currently possesses an active "cutting edge." Indeed, given the scope of progress in several different areas (e.g., social cognition, the application of social psychological knowledge to law and health), it actually appears to possess several "cutting edges" rather than only one. Further, the rapid advances attained in these areas during recent years have contributed greatly to the overall aura of optimism that now pervades our field.

But given that social psychology possesses several centers of rapid scientific progress, where should a text such as this one stand in relation to them? Our answer is simple: *as close to them as it can get.* We believe that an introductory text should do its very best to reflect those areas experiencing maximum growth and advancement—ones that constitute the center of social psychology's current "scientific action." Two major factors lie behind this view. First, we believe that when students are exposed to a new field for the first time, it is crucial that they learn about it as it exists today—not as it was at some point in the past. After all, this will be the only contact with social psychology most students will ever have. In view of this, it seems crucial that they obtain as accurate and up-to-date a picture as possible from their basic course. Second, we feel that any introductory text should communicate the appeal and excitement of its field to students. How better to accomplish this task than through attention to those lines of study currently generating the highest degree of excitement among active researchers? One of our major goals has been that of approaching the "cutting edge" of social psychology as closely as possible—of reflecting recent advances in our field to the best of our ability.

We should hasten to note, however, that this has been only one of the major goals we have sought. Another, and one of equal importance, derives from our belief that social psychology is no longer the "new kid on the block." As of the mid 1980's, it has existed in modern form for several decades. During that time it has made impressive progress and added substantially to our knowledge of the ways in which we think about and behave toward other people. This knowledge rests on firm scientific foundations and is, we believe, both valuable and intellectually stimulating. Thus, it seems crucial that students be exposed to this accumulated knowledge in their first contact with the field. Our second major goal, then, has been that of providing readers with as broad, comprehensive, and accurate a survey of this vast body of enduring social psychological knowledge as possible.

We believe that the two objectives outlined above — adequate representation of the "cutting edge" of our field and provision of a comprehensive summary of its major findings — are useful ones. Further, we believe that many of our colleagues will share our conclusions in this respect. But stating such goals is one thing; attaining them is clearly another. In order to move toward these objectives (and to approach them more closely than in previous editions), we found it necessary to make many changes in our text. These are so numerous and so substantial in scope that the end product is closer to being a new book than a revision. Because past users may find it helpful to know something about the scope and nature of the changes made, however, we will summarize several of them here. Briefly, the alterations we perceive as being most important fall under three distinct headings: (1) *changes in content,* (2) *changes in special features,* and (3) *changes in ancillary materials* accompanying the text.

Changes in Content

Only a few years have passed since the publication of the third edition of our text. Yet, in that time, social psychology has changed in many important ways. In order to take account of these shifts in content and perspective, we have made the following alterations:

Addition of a New Chapter on Social Cognition: First, and perhaps most important, we have inserted a new chapter on social cognition. This unit summarizes major advances made in our understanding of social thought — how we think about other persons. Thus, it includes coverage of such important topics as *schemata* and *prototypes, social inference, person memory,* and the relationship between *affect* and *cognition.* We believe that much of this work falls directly on the "cutting edge" of social psychology, and clearly deserves thorough coverage.

Addition of a New Chapter on Personality and Social Behavior: During the past several years, social psychologists have shown renewed interest in personality — relatively stable individual differences in behavior. This renewed interest has led to the investigation of many fascinating topics (e.g., *loneliness,* the *Type*

A – Type B dimension, locus of control, and the stability of individual behavior). All of these topics, plus several others, are considered in detail.

Coverage of Many New Topics and Progress in Other Areas: In addition to the shifts and advances mentioned above, important progress has occurred in many other areas. In order to represent this important work, we have included coverage of literally dozens of new topics. A small sample of these includes:

The facial feedback hypothesis

Attribution therapy

Information-processing perspective on attitudes

Direct experience and attitude formation

Dissonance and social drinking

Attribution and altruism

Empathy and empathic emotional arousal

Impact of violent pornography

Group size and cooperation

Relative deprivation theory

Social impact theory

Social decision schemes/Social transition schemes

The illusion of outgroup homogeneity

The complexity-extremity effect

Gender-schema theory

Minority influence

Effects of interpersonal rejection

Crime and community size

Improving eyewitness testimony

Stress and loss of personal control

Organizational behavior

Performance appraisal and attribution

Overcoming shyness

Effects of repeated exposure to erotica

Changes in Special Features

The third edition of our text contained a number of special features designed to enhance its usefulness. In the current edition, we have improved and refined several of these (e.g., special labeling of all graphs and figures). In addition, we have added several important new features. These include:

"ON THE APPLIED SIDE" A New Type of Special Insert: Boxes of this type are designed to illustrate the implications and applications of social psychology's findings to important practical problems. In recent years, many of our colleagues have shown increased concern with application. **On the Applied Side** boxes (which appear in every chapter) are designed to highlight this concern and call the practical side of social psychology to students' attention. Additionally, another type of special insert used in the third edition, **Focus on Research,** has been retained.

Careful Citation of All Boxes in the Text: In the past, our own students (and those of many colleagues) have indicated that they were sometimes uncertain about precisely when to read boxed materials. In order to eliminate this source of confusion, all special inserts (both **Focus on Research** and **On the Applied Side** boxes) are now carefully cited in the text. Special comments, printed in **bold face like this,** tell readers when each insert is to be read, and also relate its content to other text materials. We feel that this will be a helpful aid to students.

Inclusion of "Milestones of Social Psychology": The front and back endsheets of our text (those pages inside the front and back covers) now contain a new special feature — various "Milestones" in the development of social psychology. These events were chosen on the basis of input kindly provided by several hundred colleagues. Thus, there is consensus that they are important and helped shape the present form and content of social psychology. Since knowing where one has been can often shed revealing light on where one is going, we feel that such "Milestones" will be of interest both to our colleagues and to students.

Changes in Ancillary Materials Accompanying the Text

Our combined teaching experience totals more than forty years. Thus, we know only too well how time-consuming and challenging it can be teaching undergraduate social psychology. For this reason, we have attempted to provide as much assistance as possible to colleagues faced with this task. Along these lines, our text is accompanied by several ancillary items (all expertly handled by Bem Allen and Gene Smith of Western Illinois University). The most important of these are:

A Comprehensive Test Bank: Over 1500 multiple-choice test items are provided in a separate test bank. These items are cross-referenced to the text and study guide learning objectives. In addition, they are classified by difficulty level, so that instructors can design tests to match the level of their courses and the background of their students.

Instructor's Manual: This aid includes useful information for preparing lectures (e.g., materials not included in the text itself), lists of references from popular sources, and many new class-tested exercises and demonstrations. A set of transparency masters is also included in the instructor's manual. These are a special set of graphs, tables, and charts that can be used to produce overhead transparencies. Such illustrations, in turn, can be of considerable help in the preparation and presentation of lectures.

Student Study Guide: This ancillary, too, has been revised and expanded. It contains detailed study objectives that specify (on a page by page basis) just what students should be learning from the text, a variety of study exercises, and specific tips and aids designed to help students master text materials.

A Concluding Comment — and a Request for Help

These, then, are the major changes we have instituted in the fourth edition of our text. Looking back, we can say now — as we have in the past — that we have spared no effort in our attempts to make *Social Psychology: Understanding Human Interaction* as current and comprehensive as possible, to place it as close to social psychology's "cutting edge" as we knew how. Given the imperfect nature of all human endeavors, though, we're sure that there is still much room for improvement. With this thought in mind, we invite—and eagerly await—your feedback and suggestions. We have always found such input valuable in the past, and would greatly appreciate receiving it now as well. So please, don't hesitate: send your comments whenever (and in whatever form) you wish. Rest assured, they will *not* be ignored!

ROBERT A. BARON
Department of Psychology
Purdue University
West Lafayette, IN 47907

DONN BYRNE
Department of Psychology
SUNY—Albany
Albany, New York 12222

ACKNOWLEDGMENTS

Some Words of Thanks

In a very real sense, each new edition of this text is a major learning experience for both of us. And the people from whom we learn, by and large, are our colleagues. Many have assisted us, and in many different ways. At this point, then, we would like to offer our thanks for their valuable—and highly *valued!*—aid.

First, we wish to express our gratitude to the colleagues who read and commented upon various portions of the manuscript. Their comments and suggestions were both thoughtful and informative. Moreover, they were uniformly kind and constructive; who could possibly ask for more? So, our warm thanks to the people listed below:

Paul Abramson

Robert Arkin

Jack Brigham

Jeff Fisher

Susan Fiske

William Froming

John Harvey

Elaine Hatfield

E. Tory Higgins

Norbert Kerr

Dale Miller

Ron Rogers

Caryl Rusbult

Joy Stapp

Second, we want to offer our thanks to the large number of colleagues, students, and others who were kind enough to provide us with reprints or preprints of their work, to call our attention to interesting new lines of research, and to share their ideas about social psychology and this text with us. Since literally scores of persons helped us in these ways, we could not possibly list all of them here. But we do want to gratefully acknowledge their kindness.

Third, one of us (Robert A. Baron) would like to express his sincere appreciation to Michael Argyle, Jos Jaspers, Peter Collett, David Clarke, and other members of the Department of Experimental Psychology, Oxford University, for their kind hospitality during his visit. Several chapters were prepared while Professor Baron was in residence at Oxford, and the aid of this outstanding group of colleagues is gratefully acknowledged.

Fourth, our special thanks to Susan Fiske for her expert help with respect to the new chapter on social cognition. Her advice and guidance were invaluable in many ways, and we appreciate it very much.

Fifth, it is a distinct pleasure to acknowledge the aid of several outstanding individuals affiliated with our publisher. In this regard, special thanks are certainly due to Joanne Dauksewicz, our production editor most of the way through. Her skill, diligence, kindness, tact, and enthusiasm were major factors in making this one of the smoothest production cycles we have ever experienced. In a word: Joanne, we're really going to miss you! In addition, of course, we appreciate the expert help of our good friend Nancy Murphy, who oversaw the final stages of production in her usual flawless, professional style. And additional thanks are due to Rosalie Briand, Judy Fiske, and Diana Gibney for their hard work on behalf of the project. Last, but of course not least, we are grateful to Megan Brook for an excellent internal design.

Finally, our warm thanks to our editor Bill "Ziggy" Barke. Working with him is always a pleasure, and once again, his enthusiasm, help, and support, have been key ingredients in the final result.

To everyone mentioned here and to dozens of others, too, a very warm and sincere "Thank You!"

CHAPTER 1

Understanding Social Behavior:
An Introduction

Social Psychology:
A Working Definition

Social Psychology Is Scientific in Orientation/Social Psychology Focuses on the Behavior of Individuals/Social Psychology Seeks to Comprehend the Causes of Social Behavior/Social Psychology: Summing Up

Social Psychology:
A Capsule Memoir

The Early Years: Social Psychology Emerges/Decades of Growth: The 1940s, 1950s, and 1960s/The 1970s, 1980s, and Beyond: A Productive Past and a Promising Future

Extending the Frontiers:
Research Methods in Social Psychology

The Experimental Method: Knowledge through Intervention/The Correlational Method: Knowledge through Systematic Observation/Theory: Essential Guide to Research/The Quest for Knowledge and the Rights of Individuals: In Search of an Appropriate Balance

Using This Book: A Displaced Preface

Special Inserts

ON THE APPLIED SIDE
  Why Study Social Behavior? A Survival-Oriented Reply

FOCUS ON RESEARCH
  Experimentation: Laboratory or Field?

ON THE APPLIED SIDE
  *Social Psychology's Practical Benefits:
  On the Costs of Being a "Secret Donor"*

It's 2:15 P.M., and you've been waiting outside the student union building for almost twenty minutes. Pam, your newest flame, was supposed to meet you here at 2:00 P.M., but it's beginning to look as though she's not coming. "What gives with this woman?" you wonder with considerable irritation. "She makes a date and then doesn't show up. It's enough to drive a person crazy. Hot and cold, hot and cold . . . I can't take much more." At this moment, the clock strikes 2:30, rousing you from your thoughts. Looking around one last time, you begin to walk slowly away, heading for a local pub where you plan to drown your sorrow in several mugs of beer. As you stroll dejectedly along, you continue to think about Pam and her puzzling behavior. "Boy," you muse, "this woman is a mystery to me. I'm sure she likes me — I can see it in those big blue eyes. But then she pulls stunts like this. What's going on? Let me see, what could account for her not showing up today. . . . Hmm . . . I guess she might just have forgotten, but that doesn't seem likely. I could be wrong about her liking me a lot — I've made mistakes about that *before. But no, I'm sure she's attracted to me. I can tell from the way she acts when we kiss . . . there's a real spark. . . . Maybe she has some other man in her life and is conflicted about making a switch. . . . Yeah, that's probably it. . . . But she might also just be playing some kind of silly game, trying to get me really going. Oh nuts! What a mess. If only I knew how she really felt, and what she was thinking. Then I'd know just what to do. The way things are, I'm kind of tied up in knots. . . . "*

"Oh, no," you think as you glance up from your desk. "It's that Todd McEwan again. Here comes trouble." Seemingly unaware of your thoughts, Todd greets you with a big smile and cheerfully says hello. For a few minutes, you and Todd engage in small talk. Then, finally, he comes to the point.

"Look, Heather, I need your help. We're way behind on that Hillyard project. How about letting Sam Perkins, Hernando Montez, and Jill Vilnis join our group for a few weeks?"

You are shocked; what a request! "No way," you reply at once. "It's totally out of the question. You know as well as I do that this is the peak of our season. I can't spare all those people. Come on, Todd, be reasonable."

"Well," Todd replies, "if you can't spare all three, how about Hernando just for a couple of days?"

You are greatly relieved; this is more like it. "O.K.," you mutter reluctantly, "I guess we can get along without him for two or three days. But no longer."

At these words, Todd smiles, thanks you, and beats a hasty retreat. After he is gone, you sit quietly for a moment. Then all at once, it hits you: he's done it again! When will you learn? He really set you up beautifully with that "ask for a lot, settle for a little" tactic. Just how many of these strategies for getting one's way from others are there? You're not sure, but one thing seems certain: Todd knows just about all of them. . . .

L ife is complex, and every person's experience tends to be unique. For these reasons, it is unlikely that you have ever faced situations precisely like the ones just described. Yet, despite this fact, you have probably thought about questions similar to those faced by the characters in our stories on many occasions. Like the young man in the first incident you have probably puzzled over the behavior of friends, lovers, and others, seeking to comprehend the true motives behind their actions. And like the young woman in the second tale, you have probably considered the practical question of how to influence others — how to get them to do your bidding or help you in some manner. Interest in these and related matters is hardly surprising, for other persons play a central role in our lives. Thus, it is only natural for us to be deeply concerned with the nature of our relations with them. And please note: in focusing on this general issue, we are in excellent company. Over the centuries, poets, philosophers, playwrights, and novelists have filled countless volumes with their thoughts and speculations about human social affairs. Since many of these persons were brilliant and insightful, their work is often quite impressive. For example, there seem to be basic truths in such age-old principles as "Misery loves company," "It is better to give than to receive," and "Revenge is sweet."

In many cases, though, such informal knowledge seems both confusing and inconsistent. For example, consider the following illustration. The "wisdom of the ages" informs us that prolonged separation may strengthen bonds of affection between two persons: "Absence makes the heart grow fonder." At the same time, though, it tells us that such separation can also produce the opposite effect: "Out of sight, out of mind." Which view is correct? Can both be true? Unfortunately, common sense offers no clear-cut answer. As a second example, consider the recommendations of such informal knowledge with respect to handling provocations from others. On the one hand, we are urged to "turn the other cheek," and so bring aggression to a halt. On the other, we are informed that vengeance and counteraggression are both justified and effective: "An eye for an eye, a tooth for a tooth." Again, can both of these recommendations be useful? Common sense offers no clue. We could go on to list many other examples of a similar, inconsistent nature (e.g., "Birds of a feather flock together," "Opposites attract") but by now the main point is probably clear. Often, common knowledge or the wisdom of the ages provides us with a confusing picture of human social affairs (see Figure 1.1).

At this point, we should hasten to insert a word of caution: we certainly do *not* wish to suggest that such information is totally useless. On the contrary, it is often insightful and can serve as a rich source of suggestions for further study. By itself, however, such knowledge does not provide an adequate basis for understanding the complex nature of our social relations with other persons.

Of course, it is one thing to reject traditional sources of knowledge about social behavior, and quite another to offer alternative means for acquiring such information. How, aside from speculation, insight, and intuition, can this important task be accomplished? One potential answer — and a very successful one, we believe — is provided by the field of **social psychology.** Briefly stated,

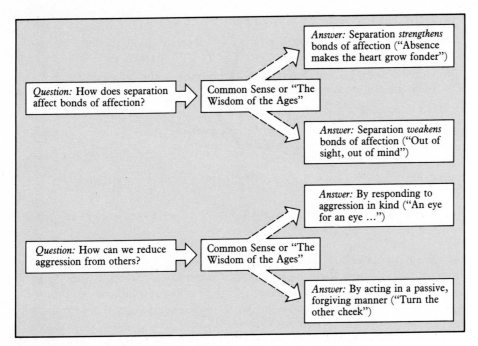

FIGURE 1.1 *Common sense: An uncertain guide to human social behavior.*

As shown here, common sense or the "wisdom of the ages" often paints a confusing and inconsistent picture of the nature of social relations.

this solution is as follows: accurate and useful information about human social relations can be acquired through use of scientific methods. In short, social psychologists contend that we *can* come to understand the complex nature of social behavior, provided we are willing to study it in an essentially scientific manner.

Given the reasonable nature of this suggestion, you may be surprised to learn that a science-oriented approach to the study of social relations is quite new. Indeed, it took root only during this century, and has flourished primarily in the past three or four decades. Despite its recent arrival on the scene, however, social psychology has already made considerable progress. Perhaps the breadth and scope of the new information it has uncovered is best suggested by the following list, which offers a small sample of the topics currently under study by social psychologists:

(1) Does exposure to pornography—and especially pornography containing scenes of violence—cause individuals to adopt callous attitudes toward members of the opposite sex?

(2) Why do some conflicts (e.g., strikes, wars) persist long past the point where participants in them can hope to make any real gains?

(3) Do negative environmental conditions such as air pollution, noise, heat, and crowding adversely affect social behavior as well as personal health?

(4) What makes people fall in — and out of — love?

(5) Why is it easier to remember facts and information about some people we meet than others?

(6) How do people attempt to deal with inequity — the belief that they have been treated unfairly by others?

(7) Does being in a good mood increase our willingness to help others?

(8) What are the causes of prejudice and discrimination? Do these negative forces stem, in part, from basic ways in which we perceive and remember social information?

(9) Does remembering our own attitudes help us to resist attempts at persuasion by others?

(10) What behaviors or characteristics distinguish effective leaders from poor ones?

Even this brief list should suggest that social psychologists have turned their attention — and their use of scientific methods — to a truly wide range of issues. In view of the intriguing nature of many of these topics, we would prefer to turn to them at once. Before doing so, though, it seems useful to pause briefly to provide you with certain background information — knowledge that will assist you in understanding many portions of this book. In the remainder of this chapter, then, we will seek to accomplish three preliminary tasks. First, we will present a formal definition of social psychology. While we don't find definitions any more exciting than you do, we feel that this one will be helpful. Specifically, it will help clarify just what social psychology is, and what it seeks to accomplish. Second, we will offer a brief description of social psychology's history and growth. And third, we will examine the basic methods used by social psychologists in their research. As you will soon see, knowledge of these methods will help you to understand just how the facts and principles presented in later chapters were obtained. (Before proceeding, please read the **On the Applied Side** insert on p. 8. It indicates why, in our opinion, the systematic study of social behavior is both an important and a timely task.)

Social Psychology: A Working Definition

Offering a formal definition of almost any field is a complex task. And in the case of social psychology, the difficulties of this undertaking are increased by the diversity of the field and its rapid changes. Despite the broad sweep of topics they choose to study, though, social psychologists seem to focus most of their attention on the following central task: understanding the behavior of individuals in social situations. In short, they are primarily concerned with comprehending how and why individuals behave, think, and feel as they do in situations involving the presence (actual or symbolic) of other persons. Taking this central concern into account, our working definition of social psychology will be as follows: *Social psychology is the scientific field that seeks to comprehend the nature and causes of individual behavior in social situations.* (Please note, again, that by the term "behavior" we mean feelings and thoughts as well as overt actions.) As is true of most definitions, this one is a bit abstract, so please bear with us for a few moments while we clarify several of its key features.

Social Psychology Is Scientific in Orientation

In the minds of many persons, the term "science" refers primarily (or even exclusively) to specific fields of study such as chemistry, physics, and biology. Such individuals, of course, will find our suggestion that social psychology, too, is scientific somewhat surprising. How can a field that seeks to investigate the origins of love, violence, and everything in between be scientific in the same sense as organic chemistry, astrophysics, or cellular physiology? The answer is surprisingly simple. In reality, the term "science" refers to a general set of methods—techniques that can be used to study an extremely wide range of topics. In deciding whether a given field is scientific in nature, therefore, the crucial question is this: does it make use of such procedures? To the extent that it does, it may be viewed as scientific in orientation; to the extent that it does not, it can be perceived as falling outside the realm of science. When this basic criterion is applied to social psychology, there can be little doubt that it falls into the first of these two categories. In their attempts to understand social behavior, social psychologists do rely heavily on basic methods of science. Thus, while the topics they seek to investigate certainly differ from those in older and more established disciplines, their approach—and so their field—is certainly scientific in orientation.

the scientific method

Social Psychology Focuses on the Behavior of Individuals

Societies may go to war, but it is individual soldiers who take aim at enemy troops, feel anger toward them, and attempt to kill them. Similarly, a given culture may define some sexual practice as acceptable or deviant; yet it is particular individuals (or couples) who decide whether to avoid or adopt it. In short, social behavior—in the final analysis—is performed by specific persons. With this basic fact firmly in mind, social psychologists have chosen to focus the bulk of their attention upon the actions of individuals in social situations (ones involving the real or symbolic presence of others). They realize, of course, that such behavior occurs against a backdrop of group membership and varied social structures. (We will return to this fact later.) But their major interest is understanding the factors that shape and direct the actions of individual human beings in a wide range of social settings.

Social Psychology Seeks to Comprehend the Causes of Social Behavior

In a key sense, this is the most central aspect of our definition: it specifies the very essence of our field. What it means, briefly, is this: social psychologists are primarily concerned with understanding the wide range of conditions that

Why Study Social Behavior?
A Survival-Oriented Reply

In our discussion so far, we have noted that common sense often serves as a confusing and inaccurate guide to human social behavior. Further, we have suggested that more useful knowledge about this topic can be obtained through the application of scientific methods. As yet, however, we have not addressed a closely related issue: Is there a need for such information? In short, should we be concerned—either as individuals or as a civilization—with obtaining systematic knowledge about human social relations?

Our answer, of course, is a definite "Yes!" In fact, we feel that there are several powerful reasons for seeking accurate knowledge of human social behavior—knowledge based on careful scientific inquiry. Perhaps the most compelling of these, however, is suggested by the following question: *What are the most serious problems confronting humanity and threatening its continued survival today?* While different persons might mention different issues in replying, most, we feel, would mention the following: a rising tide of violence, overpopulation, and growing pollution (see Figure 1.2).

Now consider another question: Can these (and other) major problems be solved through purely technological approaches? The answer, we think you'll agree, is definitely "no." Rather, solutions to each of these dangerous problems require shifts in

patterns of human behavior and attitudes, as well as new breakthroughs in engineering and technology. For example, consider overpopulation. Even if totally safe and effective contraceptives are developed, they will have little impact on population growth unless hundreds of millions of human beings decide to use them. Similarly, consider pollution. While new techniques for eliminating toxic wastes are certainly essential, they will not be put to actual use unless millions of individuals (including leaders of industry and governments) decide that the costs of doing so are justified. If, instead, many persons conclude that the dangers of pollution are not sufficient to warrant the major expenses involved in its elimination, even advanced technology for coping with this problem will be of little use. And finally, turning to human violence, it is apparent that neither super weapons nor super defenses will eliminate warfare or atrocities unless they are accompanied by shifts in human attitudes and values concerning such behavior.

In sum, there seem to be powerful grounds for desiring and seeking increased scientific knowledge about human social behavior. Indeed, in our view, advances in such knowledge may ultimately be just as essential as advances in technology in guaranteeing continued human survival in the troubled years ahead.

---

shape the social behavior of individuals—their actions, feelings, and thoughts with respect to other persons. Interest in this issue, in turn, stems from a basic belief: knowledge about these conditions will permit us to both predict social behavior and, perhaps, change it in desirable ways. Thus, it may have important practical as well as scientific outcomes. As you can readily guess, the task of identifying all of the factors that affect our behavior toward others is one of mammoth proportions. Social behavior is shaped by a seemingly endless array of variables, so in this sense, social psychologists truly have their work cut out for them! But while the number of specific factors influencing social reactions is large, it appears that most fall into three major categories. These involve (1) the

FIGURE 1.2   Guaranteeing human survival: Technology alone is not enough.

Unfortunately, problems such as the ones suggested by these photos (e.g., pollution, violence, overpopulation) cannot be solved solely through advances in technology. [Source: Photos by Wide World Photos (top left); Leo Vals / Frederic Lewis Photographs (top right); Mark Godfrey / Archive Pictures, Inc. (bottom).]

behavior and characteristics of other persons, (2) *social cognition* (our thoughts, attitudes, memories, etc., about these individuals), and (3) the *broader social context* in which social behavior occurs.

(That our behavior, feelings, and thoughts are strongly affected by the actions of other persons is obvious.) For example, imagine how you would respond if, while standing in a crowded store, one of the other shoppers began to shout "Fire! Fire!" There is little doubt that your overt actions, your emotional state, and your current thoughts would all be strongly altered. Similarly, imagine that while at a party, you notice an attractive member of the opposite sex gazing longingly in your direction and smiling in a seductive

FIGURE 1.3 *Physical appearance: One strong determinant of social behavior.*

As suggested by this cartoon, we are often strongly affected by the observable characteristics of others (i.e., by their physical appearance, style of dress, etc.). [Source: © 1975 NEA, Inc. Reprinted by permission.]

manner. Again, you might well experience powerful reactions to this person's behavior. In these and countless other situations, we are strongly affected by the overt actions of the persons around us. That we also react to their observable characteristics is equally apparent. For example, we often respond differently to old and young individuals, to attractive and unattractive ones, and to members of our own race and those of another race (see Figure 1.3). Indeed, even seemingly trivial characteristics such as others' style of dress or the ethnic identity of their last names can sometimes strongly alter our feelings, behavior, and thoughts.

But the behavior and characteristics of others represent only part of the total picture. In addition, we are also often strongly affected by **social cognition**—by our own thoughts, beliefs, attitudes, and memories concerning the persons around us. For example, consider a case in which you are asked to choose between two candidates for a promotion or a prize. In this situation you might well go over the qualifications and past behavior of both persons. And then the ways in which you combine and remember such information would strongly affect your final decision. Similarly, imagine that during a conversation with a casual acquaintance, he or she says something that hurts your feelings deeply and intensely. How will you react? Again, cognitions play a major role. If you conclude that the insult was unintended—a mere slip of the tongue—you may try to overlook the annoying comment. But if you decide that it was designed to cause you discomfort, you may grow very angry and seek to respond in kind. In sum, our behavior in social situations is often strongly affected by our thoughts, memories, beliefs, and inferences about others. Thus, you should not be surprised to learn that the investigation of such effects is a major part of modern social psychology.

Finally, we should note once again that social behavior does *not* occur in a social vacuum. Rather, it takes place against a complex backdrop of group membership, social structure, and cultural rules and expectations. These factors, too, can strongly affect its form and nature. It is probably reasonable to state that, in the past, variables falling into this general category have received somewhat less attention from social psychologists than the behavior and charac-

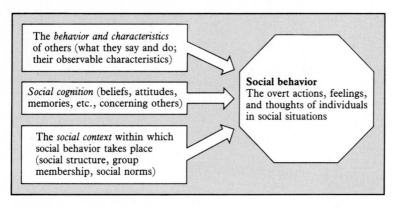

FIGURE 1.4 *Major determinants of social behavior.*

As shown here, social behavior is strongly affected by (1) the behavior and characteristics of others, (2) social cognition, and (3) the broader social context within which it occurs.

teristics of others, or our cognitions about them. But certain aspects of the broader social context *have* been of continuing interest (e.g., social norms), and we will comment on them at several points in this book (see especially Chapter 7).

Social Psychology: Summing Up

To conclude: social psychology focuses mainly on the task of unraveling the causes of social behavior—identifying those factors that, together, shape our feelings, overt actions, and thoughts in social situations (see Figure 1.4). Further, it seeks to accomplish this goal through the use of essentially scientific methods. The remainder of this text will be devoted to the task of summarizing the intriguing—and often surprising—findings uncovered by social psychologists in their studies of social interaction. The information we will present in this respect is quite varied in nature, and we can't predict your specific reactions to all portions of it. However, there is one outcome about which we are quite confident: the knowledge you acquire will arm you with many new insights into your own behavior and that of the people around you. Those who wish to be so enlightened, read on; those who do not, now is the time to turn back!

Social Psychology: A Capsule Memoir

Speculation concerning social behavior has continued for centuries. In view of this fact, any attempt to present a complete survey of all of the historical roots of social psychology would quickly bog us down in endless lists of names and dates. Since we fervently wish to avoid that pitfall, the present discussion will be both brief and limited in scope. Specifically, we will examine the emergence of social psychology as an independent field, its growth during the middle decades of this century, and its current status and trends.

The Early Years: Social Psychology Emerges

Few fields of science mark their beginnings with formal ceremonies. Instead, most develop quietly in a gradual manner, as growing numbers of

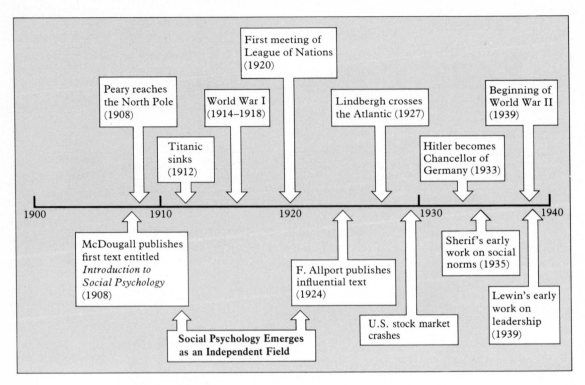

FIGURE 1.5   Social psychology emerges: The broader historical perspective.

The years during which social psychology emerged as an independent field and took its modern form were highly eventful.

scholars shift their attention to certain topics, or develop new methods for studying old ones (Rosenberg & Gara, 1981). This was certainly the pattern for social psychology. No bottles of champagne were uncorked or ribbons cut to mark its entry upon the scientific scene. Accordingly, it is difficult to point to any specific date as the time of its official arrival. As a rough guess, though, the years between 1908 and 1924 seem to qualify as the period when it first emerged as an independent entity. Each of these dates represents a year in which important texts containing the term "social psychology" in their title were published. Yet, comparison of the two volumes is informative. The first, published in 1908 by William McDougall, was based on the view that social behavior stems mainly from a small number of innate tendencies or instincts. This view is currently rejected by almost all social psychologists, so it is easy to see that the field had not assumed its modern form at that time. (We should note, though, that in recent years, interest in the possible role of innate mechanisms or tendencies in social behavior has been revived by *sociobiology*. We will have reason to comment on this new field and its controversial views in later chapters, e.g., Chapter 9).

    The second volume, published in 1924 by Floyd Allport, provides a sharp contrast. In fact, it is much closer in orientation to that of our modern field. Basically, this text argued that social behavior stems from—and is influenced by—many different factors, including the presence of other persons and their specific behaviors. Further, it contained discussions of actual research which had already been performed on topics such as the ability to recognize the emotions of others from their facial expressions, social conformity, and the impact of audiences on task performance. The fact that we will return to each of these topics in later chapters of this book points to the following conclusion: by the middle of the Roaring Twenties social psychology had appeared on the scene and begun to focus on many of the issues and topics it seeks to study today.

The years following publication of Allport's text were marked by rapid growth. New and interesting issues were studied, and systematic methods for investigating them were rapidly developed. Especially important was the work of two major pioneers in the history of social psychology—Muzafer Sherif and Kurt Lewin. Sherif (1935) began the study of *social norms*—rules telling individuals how they ought to behave. We will consider these in more detail in Chapter 7. Lewin and his colleagues (Lewin, Lippitt, & White, 1939) began the systematic study of *leadership* and related *group processes* (see Chapter 11). Further, they urged the adoption of an approach in which careful scientific methods are applied to the study of key social problems—a tradition that has persisted within social psychology until the present time (see Chapter 13). By the end of the 1930s, then, social psychology was clearly an active and growing field. (To get an idea of world events occurring during this period, see Figure 1.5).

Decades of Growth: The 1940s, 1950s, and 1960s

After a pause brought on by World War II, social psychology continued its growth and progress during the late 1940s and 1950s. During this time, it expanded its scope in several directions. One important theme, especially in the 1950s, was the influence of groups and group membership on individual behavior (Paulus, 1980). A second theme focused on the link between various personality traits and social behavior. (Interestingly, this topic has recently experienced a reawakening, although in far more sophisticated terms; see Chapter 14). Perhaps the major event of this period, however, was the development of the theory of **cognitive dissonance** (Festinger, 1957). This framework proposed that human beings dislike inconsistency and will strive to reduce it. Specifically, it argued that we find inconsistency between our attitudes—or inconsistency between our attitudes and our behavior—disturbing, and seek to eliminate it. While these suggestions may not strike you as very surprising, they actually lead to many unexpected predictions. For example, they suggest that offering individuals small rewards for stating views they don't hold may often be much more effective in getting them to change these opinions than offering them larger rewards for engaging in such behavior—a principle often known as the "less leads to more" effect in social psychology. Festinger's theory captured the interest of many of our colleagues and remained a major topic of research for many years. (We will return to this theory in detail in Chapter 4.)

In an important sense, the 1960s can be viewed as the time when social psychology "came into its own." During this turbulent decade, it expanded its scope to include virtually every imaginable aspect of social interaction. The lines of research begun or enlarged in these years are so numerous that we could not possibly list all of them here. But among the topics receiving major attention were the following: *social perception* (how do we form first impressions of others? how do we seek to uncover the motives behind others' behavior?); *aggression* and *violence* (what factors cause this dangerous form of behavior? what techniques can be used to reduce it?); *attraction* and *love* (why do individuals like—or dislike—others? what is the nature of romantic love?); *group decision making* (do groups actually make better and more conservative decisions than individuals?); *equity* and *inequity* (how do people react to unfair treatment at the hands of others?); *prosocial behavior* (why do individuals often fail to offer aid in emergency situations? what factors or conditions encourage such prosocial actions?). As you can see from even this brief list, social psychology moved vigorously into many new issues and areas during the 1960s.

The 1970s, 1980s, and Beyond: A Productive Past and a Promising Future

Surprisingly, the rapid pace of change in our field did not slacken in the 1970s. In fact, one could argue strongly that, if anything, it accelerated. First, many lines of investigation begun in the 1960s were continued and expanded. Second, several new topics rose to prominence, or were investigated from a more sophisticated perspective. Among the most important of these were: *attribution* (how do we infer the causes behind others' behavior, and our own—the reasons why they, and we, behave in certain ways); *sex roles* and *sex discrimination* (how are sex roles and sex role stereotypes acquired? what forces tend to work against achievement by females in many societies?); *environmental psychology* (what is the impact of the physical environment, including heat, noise, crowding, and pollution, upon social behavior?).

In addition, two larger-scale trends begun in the 1970s have expanded in the 1980s. The first of these involves growing interest among many social psychologists in the cognitive processes underlying social interaction (Fiske & Taylor, 1983; Hastie, 1983). The basic idea behind this new approach is both simple and compelling: understanding the ways in which we think about others is central to understanding our relations with them. More concretely, this new perspective—often termed *social cognition*—is concerned with applying ideas and findings about human cognition (e.g., memory, attention, cognitive organization) to key aspects of social behavior. We share the current excitement about this perspective, and fully expect that it will yield major advances in the years ahead. Even more important, since similar cognitive processes may underlie a wide range of social behaviors, findings in social cognition may play a valuable role in helping to integrate previously separate lines of research.

Second, there has been a growing tendency for social psychologists to become concerned with practical matters and applied issues (Bickman, 1981). We will return to some of this work below (see pp. 20–21), so at this point, we simply wish to note that in recent years, increasing numbers of social psychologists have begun to use their unique skills and knowledge to answer questions about the *legal process* (what factors influence jury decision making, and eyewitness testimony?), *personal health* (are there links between psychological stress and personality on the one hand, and illness on the other?), and *organizational concerns* (how can large organizations be made better places in which to work, as well as more efficient?). We find the extension of social psychology into such areas exciting, and look for many practical benefits from this research in the near future.

And where, you might ask, do we go from here? Actually, social psychology has shown itself to be such a flexible and dynamic field that we hesitate to offer any firm predictions. We do expect, though, that the trends described here will continue, at least for several years. Beyond that, any suggestions we might offer would probably be little more than guesses. Primarily for this reason, we are content to sit back and allow the future to unfold by itself. There is one prediction, though, that we *are* quite willing to make—and with some conviction. No matter how social psychology changes in the years ahead, and no matter what topics it chooses to emphasize, it will remain an active, vital field, with much to recommend it.

Extending the Frontiers:
Research Methods in Social Psychology

We trust that by now, you are convinced that social psychology is diverse in scope, and that it focuses on many fascinating topics. Our next task, then, is to describe just how social psychologists investigate various aspects of social interaction. This, in turn, will require three steps. First, we will describe basic methods used in social psychological research—the *experimental* and *correlational* approaches. Next, we will examine the role of *theory* in such research. And third, we will consider some of the complex *ethical issues* that often arise in connection with investigations in social psychology.

The Experimental Method:
Knowledge through Intervention

Because it is generally viewed as the most powerful weapon in social psychology's research "arsenal," we will begin with the experimental method. Unfortunately, our past experience suggests that if you have not learned about it in other courses, you may view this approach as mysterious and complex. Actually, though, this is far from the case. In its basic logic, experimentation is surprisingly simple. To help you understand its use and value in social research, we will first describe its basic nature. Then we will mention two conditions essential for its successful use.

Experimentation: Its basic nature. A researcher who decides to employ the experimental method in his or her work generally begins with a clear-cut goal: determining whether a given factor (variable) influences some specific form of social behavior. In order to study this question, the researcher follows two basic steps: (1) she varies the presence or strength of this factor in a systematic manner, and (2) seeks to determine whether these variations have any impact upon the behavior under study. The key idea behind these procedures is as follows: if the factor varied exerts such effects, individuals exposed to different levels or amounts should show different patterns of behavior. That is, exposure to a small amount of the factor should result in one level of behavior, exposure to a larger amount should result in another level, and so on.

Generally, the factor systematically varied by the experimenter is termed the *independent variable,* while the behavior studied is termed the *dependent variable.* In a typical experiment, then, subjects in several different groups (or conditions) are exposed to different levels of the independent variable (low, moderate, high). The behavior of these persons is then compared to determine whether it does in fact vary with different levels or amounts of the independent variable. If it does—and if two other conditions we shall mention shortly are met—it can be tentatively concluded that the independent variable does indeed affect the form of behavior being studied.

Since our discussion so far has been somewhat abstract, a concrete example may now prove useful. In this regard, let us consider an experiment designed to examine the *hypothesis* (an as yet untested suggestion) that pleasant scents such as perfume or cologne increase attraction between individuals meeting for the first time. The independent variable in such research would be the presence

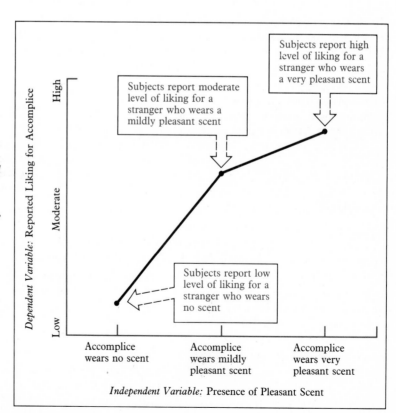

FIGURE 1.6   The experimental method: A concrete example.

In the study shown here, the independent variable *involved the presence of a pleasant scent. The* dependent variable *was some measure of liking or attraction. Results indicated that the independent variable did in fact affect this aspect of social behavior. Subjects reported a higher level of liking for the accomplice when this person wore a mildly pleasant scent than when he or she wore no scent. And they reported even greater attraction for the accomplice when this person wore a very pleasant scent.*

Subjects report high level of liking for a stranger who wears a very pleasant scent

Subjects report moderate level of liking for a stranger who wears a mildly pleasant scent

Subjects report low level of liking for a stranger who wears no scent

High

Moderate

Low

Dependent Variable: Reported Liking for Accomplice

Accomplice wears no scent

Accomplice wears mildly pleasant scent

Accomplice wears very pleasant scent

Independent Variable: Presence of Pleasant Scent

(and perhaps intensity) of a pleasant scent. Thus, we might expose three different groups of subjects to contrasting levels of this factor (no scent, presence of a mildly pleasant scent, presence of a highly pleasant scent). This could be accomplished quite readily by having subjects meet and interact briefly with another person who, unknown to them, is an accomplice of the researcher. This accomplice (often termed a *confederate* in social psychology) might wear no scent in one condition, a mildly pleasant scent in another, and a very pleasant scent in a third. The dependent variable would then be some measure of subjects' liking for this person, or their first impressions of him. If pleasant scents do actually affect attraction between strangers, we would expect that subjects exposed to a very pleasant aroma will express a higher degree of liking for the accomplice than those exposed to a mildly pleasant scent. And these persons, in turn, will express more liking for the accomplice than those not exposed to any pleasant scent. If such results were obtained (or if the three groups of subjects differed in some other way) we could conclude, at least tentatively, that pleasant scents do in fact affect this aspect of social behavior (see Figure 1.6)—a finding certain to please the giant perfume and cosmetics industry. (Actually, several experiments concerned with this topic have been performed [Baron, 1983c]. They are mentioned in Chapter 15.)

At this point we should note that the example just presented describes an extremely simple case—the simplest type of experiment one could conduct. In many instances, researchers wish to examine the impact of several independent variables at once. For example, in the study just described, mode of dress (neat or sloppy) and sex of the persons meeting might also be considered, along with the impact of pleasant scents. When several variables are included in an experiment, a larger amount of information about some aspect of social behavior can be obtained. And, even more importantly, potential **interactions** between two or more variables can be examined. That is, we can determine whether the impact of one independent variable is affected in some manner by one or more other variables. For example, in the project we have been describing, we might find that males respond more strongly than females to the presence of pleasant aromas. Or, we might learn that pleasant scents exert stronger effects upon attraction when individuals are dressed up than when they are not. Because social behavior is usually affected by many factors and conditions at once, knowledge of such interactions is important. Thus, we will have reason to discuss them at many points in the chapters that follow.

Experimentation: Two essential conditions. Earlier (on p. 16), we noted that before we can conclude that an independent variable has affected some form of behavior, two important conditions must be met. Because a basic understanding of these is essential for evaluating the usefulness of any experiment, we will now describe them for you.

The first involves what is generally termed **random assignment of subjects to experimental groups.** According to this principle, each person taking part in a study must have an equal chance of being exposed to each level of the independent variable. The reason for this rule is simple; if subjects are *not* randomly assigned to each group, it may prove impossible to determine whether differences in their later behavior stem from differences they brought with them to the study, or from the impact of the independent variable. For example, returning to the study just described, consider what would happen if, for some reason, all the subjects assigned to the very pleasant scent conditions came from a single housing unit, one in which there was an epidemic of terrible head colds. Further, imagine that subjects in the mildly pleasant and no scent groups came from other units, in which the epidemic of colds had not yet struck. Under these conditions, results might well reveal that subjects in the mildly pleasant scent condition report greater liking for the accomplice than those in the no scent condition, but that those in the very pleasant scent group do not react in a similar way. If the researcher conducting this investigation were not aware of the fact that participants in one of the groups all had colds, she might then be led to the following conclusion: mildly pleasant scents increase attraction toward a stranger, but very pleasant scents do not. As you can readily see, this conclusion might well be false. After all, persons in a key experimental group probably could not detect the perfume or cologne even if they tried! In order to avoid problems such as these, it is crucial that subjects taking part in an experiment be randomly assigned to its various groups. If they are not, interpretation of the results obtained can be quite problematic.

The second condition to which we referred earlier may be stated as follows: insofar as possible, all other factors that might also affect subjects' behavior, aside from the independent variable, must be held constant. To see why this is so, consider the following situation. In the study on pleasant scent we have been considering, the researcher pays little attention to the possible impact of other variables. Thus, as bad luck would have it, the accomplice varies her style of dress. Specifically, this person dresses in her nicest clothes when wearing the very pleasant scent, dresses neatly when wearing the pleasant scent, but dresses more casually when wearing no scent. (Assume that because of the lingering quality of the perfume used, it is necessary to conduct the no scent, mildly pleasant scent, and very pleasant scent conditions on different days.) Results are as follows: subjects report highest attraction toward the accomplice when she wears very pleasant scent, somewhat lower attraction when she wears pleasant scent, and lowest attraction when she wears no scent. What do these findings mean? Actually, we can't tell. There is no way of knowing whether these results stem from the presence of pleasant scents, or from the accomplice's style of dress. In short, these two variables (pleasant scent and mode of dress) are **confounded:** the potential effects of each cannot be separated or disentangled (see Figure 1.7).

In the case we have just described, such confounding between variables is easy to spot. In many instances, though, it can enter in more subtle and hidden ways. For this reason, researchers must always be on guard to prevent its occurrence. The general rule they must follow is simply this: insofar as possible, all factors other than the one under study (the independent variable) should be held constant. Only when this is the case can the results of an experiment be interpreted with confidence. (Before proceeding please read the **Focus on Research** insert on pp. 20 – 21. It describes the advantages and disadvantages of conducting experiments in two contrasting types of settings.)

[margin handwritten note: Controlled variables to avoid confounding]

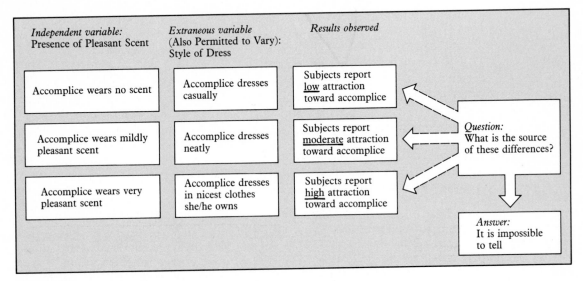

FIGURE 1.7 *Confounding of variables: A dangerous trap for unwary experimenters.*

When factors other than the independent variable are not held constant in an experiment, it may be impossible to interpret the results. In the example shown here, the independent variable involved the presence of pleasant scents. However, another factor—the accomplice's style of dress—was also allowed to vary. As a result, it is impossible to determine whether this factor (dress), the presence of pleasant scent, or both, produced the pattern of findings obtained.

The Correlational Method: Knowledge through Systematic Observation

Earlier, we noted that experimentation is generally viewed as one of the most powerful techniques for conducting research on social behavior. This is so for several reasons, but perhaps the most important relates to the establishment of cause-and-effect relationships. Briefly, if systematic variations in an independent variable produce systematic changes in some form of behavior (i.e., in some dependent variable), it is often reasonable to assume that a *cause-and-effect* link exists between these two factors. That is, changes in the independent variable can be viewed as having caused changes in the behavior under study. And since science is often concerned with establishing just this type of causality, experimentation offers an important "plus."

Unfortunately, it is frequently the case that for either practical or ethical reasons, the experimental method cannot be employed. With respect to practical limitations, it is sometimes true that systematic variation of the key independent factors lies beyond an experimenter's control. For example, consider the case of a social psychologist who suspects that height exerts a strong effect on the success of political candidates, with tall persons winning election more frequently than short ones. Clearly, he could not vary the stature of individuals running for public office in order to study this intriguing possibility through direct experimentation.

*Experimentation:
Laboratory or Field?*

For most of us, the terms "experiment" and "laboratory" seem closely linked. Indeed, when we hear about an experiment, whether in medicine, chemistry, or psychology, we tend to assume that it was conducted in a research laboratory. In general, this assumption is correct. The most common location for experiments in most areas of science *is* the formal laboratory. And this is no accident; there are compelling reasons for conducting experiments in such settings. First, it is usually easier to establish systematic control over the independent variables of interest in a formal laboratory than elsewhere. Second, laboratories offer important gains with respect to overall efficiency. Equipment can be quickly repaired or adjusted, and other aspects of the research can be rapidly altered after each session. And of course, research participants report directly to the laboratory for their appointments, an arrangement that saves much valuable time for experimenters.

Along with these major pluses, though, come certain drawbacks. Because they exist in special locations (e.g., on university campuses, in special research facilities), it is often difficult to induce persons from a wide range of backgrounds to visit laboratories; they simply find it inconvenient to do so. To the extent such diversity among subjects is lacking, generalizability of the obtained results may be reduced. (In many cases, this does not appear to be a serious problem, for the findings of laboratory studies are quite robust, and can be generalized to a considerable extent. In some instances, though, such generality is less certain, and a degree of caution seems justified.) Second, because research lab-

oratories are special and unfamiliar places, subjects may often behave quite differently in them than they do in other, more natural settings. In particular, they may try to guess the experimenter's hypothesis, and then behave either in ways that tend to confirm it, or in ways that serve to disprove it. Cues that reveal the hypothesis under study in an experiment are known as **demand characteristics,** and they are often present in laboratory settings. Needless to add, when subjects respond to such cues, the findings of the research project may be totally invalid. After all, they stem from participants' desire to "help" or "hurt" the experimenter by confirming or disconfirming his or her predictions—not from the impact of the independent variable. Fortunately, there are several techniques for countering the influence of demand characteristics (e.g., the person collecting the data may be kept in "the dark" about the major hypothesis under investigation). But such cues always remain a potential danger in experiments conducted in laboratory settings.

Partly because of these problems, many researchers in social psychology choose to conduct their experiments in the real world, outside the boundaries of formal laboratories. Thus, in recent years, busy shopping malls (DeJong, 1981), jogging tracks (Strube, Miles, & Finch, 1981), crowded beaches (Moriarty, 1975), bustling taverns (Pennebaker et al., 1979), and even prisons (Saulnier & Perlman, 1981) have served as the scene for carefully conducted research. The advantages offered by such settings are obvious. When they conduct their experiments in natural locations, social psy-

Turning to ethical restrictions, other serious problems often arise. It may, in principle, be possible to vary the independent factors of interest, but doing so would raise important ethical questions. For example, imagine that a researcher has reason to believe that certain events play a key role in triggering dangerous riots. Clearly, it would be unethical for her to stage such events in some

TABLE 1.1   Laboratory and field experiments: Some pluses and minuses. (Study Diagram)

As shown here, both field and laboratory experiments offer important advantages. At the same time, however, both suffer from certain drawbacks.

	Advantages	Disadvantages
Laboratory experiments	High degree of control over independent variables of interest High degree of efficiency (e.g., subjects report for appointments) Impact of extraneous (confounding) variables can be lessened Rights and safety of subjects can be protected through informed consent and debriefing	Artificiality Potential impact of demand characteristics Restricted subject populations; generality of results may be reduced in some cases
Field experiments	Realistic; social behavior can be studied under conditions and in settings where it normally occurs Wide range of subjects can be observed Potential impact of demand characteristics lessened	Lower degree of control over independent variables Greater possibility of impact of extraneous (confounding) variables Difficult to protect rights and safety of participants (e.g., informed consent and debriefing often impossible)

chologists can often observe the behavior of a highly diverse sample of subjects. Indeed, if they choose with care, they can investigate the actions of persons from virtually every walk of life. Second, by shifting their studies to the field, researchers gain the opportunity to observe various forms of social behavior under the conditions in which they normally occur. Clearly, then, field research offers important advantages. But it, too, suffers from certain problems. Most important of these is the fact that when working in field settings, researchers must often surrender some degree of control over extraneous variables—factors other than the independent variable that may also affect subjects' behavior. Because of this loss of experimental control, the findings of field experiments are often more open to conflicting interpretations than those of laboratory studies. Second, field experiments often raise important ethical issues. Is it appropriate to expose subjects to independent variables without informing them that this will occur, and without obtaining their prior consent to participate? These are complex questions, with no simple answers. (We will return to these and related issues later; see pp. 28–29.)

In sum, there is a definite trade-off involved in the choice between laboratory and field experimentation. Both offer key advantages, but both also suffer from specific drawbacks (see Table 1.1 for a summary of these). For this reason, there are no hard and fast rules for choosing between them. Rather, individual researchers must select the approach that seems best suited to the specific topics they wish to study. Both techniques are useful and, when employed with skill and care, can add substantially to our knowledge of human social behavior.

locations but not in others, in order to determine if collective violence is actually more frequent under the first set of conditions than under the second. Similarly, consider the dilemma faced by a social psychologist who suspects that one major reason why people fall out of love involves the discovery of important attitudinal differences between themselves and their mates. Again, it would be unethical for him or her to conduct an experiment in which some happy couples are led to believe that such differences exist while others are not, in order to compare the relative rates of divorce or separation in these contrasting groups.

In these and many less dramatic cases, use of the experimental method may not be feasible. Fortunately, when such conditions prevail, it is not necessary for researchers to give up in despair. An alternative approach, known as the **correlational method,** exists. In this technique, attempts are made to determine whether two or more variables are related by engaging in careful observation of both. If changes in one are found to be consistently associated with changes in the other, evidence for a link between them is obtained. Please note that in contrast to the experimental method, *no attempt is made to vary one of the factors in a systematic manner in order to observe its effects upon the other.* Rather, naturally occurring variations in both are observed to determine whether they tend to occur together in some fashion.

Perhaps a concrete example of the correlational method will help you to grasp its nature, and to see just how it differs from direct experimentation. Our strategy here will be to return to the topic described earlier — the impact of pleasant scent on attraction — to indicate how it might be studied through systematic observation.

In order to accomplish this task, we might proceed as follows. First, we would identify settings in which individuals meet and interact with strangers (e.g., dances, bars, job interviews, stores). Then, we would carefully (and discreetly!) observe a large number of social interactions in these settings. In conducting these observations, we would make systematic records of (1) the presence and strength of pleasant scents (i.e., do one or more of the participants wear perfume, cologne, etc.?) and (2) the apparent level of liking between the persons involved. (The latter could be assessed by a variety of different measures, ranging from mutual smiling and arrangements for future meetings, through formal ratings following a job interview.) If there is in fact a link between pleasant scents and attraction, we might find that individuals meeting for the first time *do* tend to show signs of greater liking for one another in the presence of such scents than in their absence.

As this example suggests, the correlational method of research can be used to investigate a wide range of interesting topics. Thus, in recent years, correlational studies have been performed to examine such diverse questions as "What factors account for the success of generals?" (Simonton, 1980), through "How can jealousy be used as a tactic in romantic relationships?" (White, 1980). Further, the correlational approach offers several key advantages. It can be readily employed to study behavior in many real-life settings, away from the restraints of the formal laboratory. It can be employed to study ongoing social behavior without disrupting or changing it. And, as we noted earlier, it can be applied to topics and issues that, because of practical or ethical constraints, cannot be studied through direct experimentation. We should also note, however, that this basic approach suffers from one major drawback: in contrast to experimentation, the findings it yields are often somewhat uncertain with respect to cause-and-effect relationships. Since this is an important point, with crucial implications, we will now comment upon it further.

FIGURE 1.8 *Why correlation does not necessarily imply causation.*

As this cartoon suggests, the fact that changes in one variable are accompanied by changes in another does not necessarily imply that there is a causal link between them. Despite Ms. Overberry's beliefs, it is quite unlikely that changes in climate or volcanic eruptions are actually caused by the election of Democrats. [GOOSEMYER by Parker and Wilder © 1980 Field Enterprises, Inc. Courtesy of Field Newspaper Syndicate.]

Correlation and causation: Why the first doesn't always imply the second. The central fact we wish to communicate is this: if two variables are found to be related in a correlational study, this tells us very little about the existence of a direct causal link between them. That is, the fact that changes in one variable are accompanied by changes in another does *not* necessarily mean that alterations in the first *caused* alterations in the second (see Figure 1.8 for an amusing illustration of this point). Perhaps, once again, the best means of clarifying this key concept is through a concrete example.

Imagine that in a carefully conducted study employing systematic observation a researcher finds evidence for a link between crowding and crime. That is, the more crowded the living conditions in a given area (e.g., the greater the number of people per square block), the higher the crime rate tends to be. One interpretation of this finding is straightforward: crowding somehow causes crime. (For example, it may be that living in close proximity to others multiplies temptations.) Another, and sharply contrasting interpretation, however, is as follows: actually, there is no direct link between crowding and crime. Rather, the apparent bond between these factors stems from the fact that both are the result of a third variable: poverty. Briefly, the poorer people are, the smaller the living quarters they can afford. And the poorer they are, the greater their sense of despair, and the weaker their restraints against engaging in illegal actions. But which of these two contrasting interpretations is correct? Does crowding in fact cause crime? Or do both of these conditions actually stem from a third, underlying variable? From simple correlational data, it is impossible to tell (see Figure 1.9 on p. 24).

We trust that by now, the moral of this discussion is clear. The existence of even a strong correlation between two factors should not be interpreted as a definite indication that they are causally linked. Such conclusions are justified only in the presence of additional, confirming evidence.

Primarily for the reasons we have just described, social psychologists have tended to prefer the experimental method, with its firmer conclusions regard-

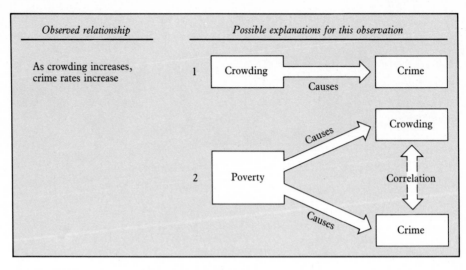

FIGURE 1.9   *Correlation versus causation: A subtle but crucial distinction.*

The fact that one variable increases as another increases (or decreases as another decreases) does not necessarily mean that the first causes the second. For example, the finding that crime rates rise with crowding does not necessarily indicate that crowding somehow causes crime. Instead, the apparent link between these two variables may derive from the fact that both stem from a third factor: poverty.

ing causality, to observational procedures of research. However, in recent years, sophisticated techniques for establishing cause-and-effect relationships on the basis of correlational data have been developed. Partly for this reason, and partly because of growing concern with complex topics best studied outside the laboratory, there has been a modest trend toward increased use of correlational methods of research in social psychology during the past few years. Whether this trend will continue or be reversed remains to be seen. Regardless of its future fate, however, two points are clear. First, both experimentation and systematic observation are useful methods and can contribute greatly to our knowledge of social behavior. Second, whichever approach they adopt, social psychologists will continue to improve and refine their research techniques in the decades ahead.

Theory: Essential Guide to Research

Over the years, students in our classes have often asked us the following questions: "How do social psychologists choose the topics of their research?" or "How do they plan all these studies anyway?" One answer is fairly simple: often, the ideas for research projects are suggested by observation of the social world around us. That is, researchers notice some aspect of social behavior that is puzzling or surprising, and then plan investigations to shed new light on such mysteries. But this is far from the only source of research ideas in our field. Another and far more important one can be stated in a single word: **theory.**

Briefly, theory represents attempts, by scientists, to answer the question "why?" In short, it involves efforts to understand precisely *why* certain events occur as they do, or *why* various processes unfold in a specific manner. Thus, theory goes beyond mere observation or description of various aspects of social behavior; it seeks to *explain* them. The attainment of comprehensive and accurate theories is a major goal of all science, and social psychology is certainly no exception to this basic rule. Thus, a great deal of research in our field is concerned with efforts to construct, refine, and test such frameworks. But what, precisely, are theories? And what is their value in social psychology? Perhaps the best means of answering such questions is through a concrete example.

Imagine that we observe the following: when people work together in a group, each member exerts less effort on the joint task than when they work alone. (This phenomenon is known as *social loafing* and will be discussed in detail in Chapter 11.) The observation just described is certainly useful in and of itself. After all, it allows us to predict what will happen when individuals work together, and it also suggests the possibility of intervening in some manner to prevent such negative outcomes. And these two accomplishments — *prediction and intervention* (control) — are major goals of science. Yet, the fact that social loafing occurs does not, by itself, explain *why* it takes place. It is at this point that theory enters the picture.

In older and more advanced fields such as physics or chemistry, theories often consist of mathematical equations (e.g., the famous $E = mc^2$). In social psychology, however, efforts to explain social behavior usually involve verbal statements. For example, a theory designed to account for social loafing might read as follows: When persons work together, they realize that their outputs will not be individually identifiable. Further, they realize that all participants will share in the responsibility for the final outcome. As a result, they conclude that they can get away with "taking it easy," and so exert less effort on the task. Note that in essence, this theory (like all others) consists of two essential parts: several basic concepts (e.g., the extent to which work can be individually identified; the degree to which responsibility for final outcomes is shared; individual effort), plus statements concerning the relationships between these concepts. Note also that the theory is assumed to be true when we begin. However, this is only the beginning, not the end, of the process. The next, and crucial step, is that of deriving predictions from the theory — predictions that can be tested in actual research. These predictions are known as **hypotheses** and are derived from the theory in accordance with basic principles of logic. On the basis of such logic, it is assumed that if the theory is correct, certain predictions follow. And then these predictions (hypotheses) are put to the test in actual research. For example, the theory of social loafing just outlined leads to the following hypothesis, among others: If individuals can be convinced that their work is in fact identifiable, social loafing will be reduced. It is important to note that theories are useful only to the extent that they generate testable predictions. Indeed, if they do not lead to such hypotheses, they cannot be viewed as scientific theories in the true sense of this term. For example, consider the following "theory": The reason why certain politicians are charismatic is that they have sold their souls to the devil, who is now intervening on their behalf. Obviously, the devil and his actions lie outside the realm of science. Thus, such a

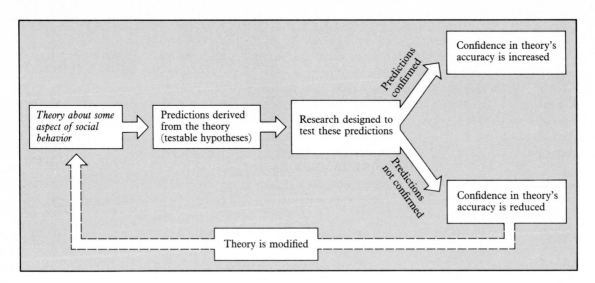

FIGURE 1.10   *Theory: Putting it to the test.*

When predictions derived from a theory are confirmed in actual research, confidence in its accuracy is increased. However, when such predictions (hypotheses) are disconfirmed, confidence in the theory's accuracy is reduced. In this latter case, the theory may be modified so as to generate other predictions, or rejected.

theory is not a theory at all; it does not generate predictions testable by scientific means (i.e., by the experimental or correlational methods of research described earlier).

If the predictions derived from a theory are supported by research findings, confidence in its accuracy is increased. If, in contrast, such predictions are not confirmed, confidence in the theory is weakened. But please note: theories are not "set in stone." If predictions derived from them are disconfirmed, the theories themselves may be altered, so as to generate new predictions. And then these, in turn, can be tested. (Please see Figure 1.10 for a summary of this process.)

In sum, theories serve as important guides to research in social psychology. As we noted earlier, they are certainly not the only source of hypotheses about social behavior — informal observation, conflicting results in past research, and even common sense can all lead to interesting and valuable work. But in a key sense, theories are the most important basis for research in our field. Indeed, they do not merely serve as guides to such work; in many cases, they provide firm foundations for it as well.

The Quest for Knowledge and the Rights of Individuals: In Search of an Appropriate Balance

In their use of experimentation and systematic observation, and in their reliance on comprehensive theories, social psychologists do not differ from researchers in many other fields. In fact, these same basic procedures are employed (with some modifications) by almost all scientists. There is one technique, however, that seems to be unique to research in social psychology: **deception.** Because it continues to be widely used by social psychologists (Gross & Fleming, 1982) and also because it raises complex ethical issues, it is well worthy of our attention here.

Deception: What it is and why it's used. Basically, the use of deception in social psychology involves attempts, by specific researchers, to conceal the true purpose of their studies from persons participating in them. This can be accomplished in many different ways. For example, it can involve the omission of key information about an experiment. Similarly, it can involve the provision of false or misleading information. And often it centers around the presence of **confederates** or *accomplices,* individuals who, while working with the researcher, pretend to be subjects. Such persons behave in predetermined ways, and their actions often serve a dual function. First they form the basis for manipulating the independent variables of interest. And second, they help to conceal the major purpose of the study from actual subjects.

Regardless of the precise form deception takes, its use is based on a straightforward belief: if the persons taking part in a social psychological study know the true purpose behind it, their behavior may be changed by such knowledge. And then it will be impossible to gather valid information about the specific aspects of social behavior being investigated. That this is a very reasonable idea is easily illustrated. For example, imagine that a researcher wishes to conduct an experiment concerned with reactions to being stared at by another person. Before beginning each session, he informs participants about this major purpose. That is, he tells them that he wishes to learn whether they will become angry when stared at by a stranger. Will this information affect subjects' behavior? Almost certainly it will; in fact, after learning about the true purpose of the investigation, participants may be more amused than irritated by the stares they now receive from an accomplice.

We could go on to present many other examples, but we're certain that the main point is obvious. In many cases, it may be necessary to conceal the true goals of a research project from the persons participating in it. If this is *not* done, their behavior may be strongly affected by this knowledge. And the chances of obtaining meaningful results will be slim indeed.

Deception: The problems it raises. While deception often seems to be a valuable tool for research in social psychology, it raises important issues. First, it is possible that individuals exposed to such procedures will resent having been led astray by the experimenter once they learn of this fact. As a result, they may adopt a negative and mistrustful attitude toward psychological research and psychology (Christensen, 1977). Second, the possibility exists that deception, no matter how temporary, may result in some type of harmful consequences for subjects (Kelman, 1967). For example, they may experience discomfort, stress, negative shifts in their self-esteem, or other negative outcomes. We should hasten to note, at this point, that in most cases, the type of deception employed by social psychologists in their research appears to have little chance of producing such effects. But it must also be admitted that in a few rare instances, some type of harmful outcome to research participants cannot be totally ruled out. For example, in some studies, subjects have been exposed to conditions specifically designed to cause them to experience anger, depression, or guilt (Alloy, Abramson, & Viscusi, 1981; Donnerstein & Berkowitz, 1981). Similarly, in other experiments, they have been exposed to stimuli they may find unpleasant, such as explicit forms of erotica, or scenes of human suffering (Zillmann, Bryant, & Carveth, 1981). And in still others, they have been induced to engage in behaviors they view as wrong or objectionable, such as planning an illegal burglary similar to the infamous Watergate incident (West, Gunn, & Chernicky, 1975), or inflicting what seem to be painful electric shocks on an innocent victim who has done nothing to deserve such treatment (Milgram, 1974). (Needless to add, no harm was actually present in such studies; participants were merely led to believe that it was part of the procedures.) We repeat: such cases have been rare. In a great majority of the studies conducted by social psychologists, deception has been far more trivial in nature, and seems to have had little chance of producing any harm. But the fact that it has usually been quite harmless in no way guarantees that this is always the case. Thus, the use of deception in social research poses a complex dilemma that cannot be ignored.

Continued use of deception: Some essential safeguards. How, then, do social psychologists resolve this complex issue? In short, how do they balance the need for deception against its potential costs? At present, opinion remains divided. Some of our colleagues have concluded that deception, no matter how useful in research, is inappropriate and must be avoided (Baumrind, 1979). In contrast, many others (seemingly a large majority) believe that temporary deception *is* acceptable, provided that certain safeguards are followed (Baron, 1981a). The most important of these are **informed consent,** thorough **debriefing,** and *confidentiality of results.*

Informed consent involves providing research participants with as full a description of the procedures to be followed as feasible, prior to their decision to take part in a given study. In short, when informed consent is employed, subjects participate in an experiment only after learning what it will involve. In contrast, debriefing follows rather than precedes each experimental session. It consists of providing participants with a full explanation of all major aspects of the study, including its major goals, the hypotheses being examined, and an explanation of the need for the temporary deceptions used (see Figure 1.11). Further, during debriefing all questions raised by subjects are answered, and any negative reactions on their part are discussed and eliminated. The basic guideline followed is this: participants should leave the session in *at least* as favorable and positive a state as when they arrived.

A third condition that must be met is strict *confidentiality.* Information gathered from subjects — or about them — must be held in strictest confidence. Preferably, data should be coded, so that it cannot be identified with participants' names. But in any case, the information collected in a study should be used *only* for research purposes, and must never be released to persons wishing to use it for other ends.

FIGURE 1.11   Debriefing: An essential safeguard in social research.

During debriefing, all aspects of an experiment, including the major hypothesis and the need for temporary deception, are fully explained.

That informed consent and thorough debriefing go a long way toward eliminating the potential costs associated with deception is suggested by the findings of several studies directly concerned with this issue. First, it has been found that an overwhelming majority of research participants view temporary deception as quite acceptable, and do not resent its use (Rogers, 1980b). Second, and even more impressive, there is some indication that, following thorough debriefing, subjects who have participated in studies involving deception actually report more positive feelings about the value of psychological research than do subjects who have taken part in investigations that do not include deception (Smith & Richardson, 1983). Of course, even in the light of such favorable reactions it is unwise to take the safety or appropriateness of deception for granted. Rather, the key phrase for all researchers who wish to use it in their studies must remain: "Danger: Sensitive human being. Proceed with utmost caution." (Before proceeding, please see the **On the Applied Side** section on pp. 30–31.)

Using This Book: A Displaced Preface

Before concluding, we would like to comment briefly on several features of this text. Usually, such information is included in the Preface, but since most people seem to skip such messages from authors these days, we feel that presenting some of our remarks here makes good sense.

First, we'd like to call your attention to the overall organization of our book. Basically, our plan has been to move from reactions and processes occurring largely within individuals to behaviors and processes involving inter-action between two or more persons. Thus, we will begin with such topics as

ON THE
APPLIED SIDE

*Social Psychology's Practical Benefits:
On the Costs of Being a "Secret Donor"*

During the spring of 1981, American social psychology suffered a major disaster. U.S. government funding for basic research in our field was slashed by more than 75 percent. (Professor Baron, who was then serving as Program Director for Social and Developmental Psychology at the National Science Foundation in Washington, D.C., witnessed these disturbing events at first hand.) Looking back, it is apparent that a number of different factors contributed to this serious setback. Among the most important of these, though, seems to be the following: many members of the Reagan administration (who had just taken office) were convinced that social psychology, along with other behavioral sciences, had little to offer in terms of practical benefits to society. In their view, it had received steady or growing federal support for several decades without yielding much in return. Thus they believed it was a prime candidate for major cuts at a time when many government programs were being scaled down or even eliminated.

Clearly, this was a serious charge, and one that was soon followed by drastic action. But is it justified? Has social psychology actually failed to deliver concrete, practical benefits to society? Our reply, as you can probably guess, is "No, no, a thousand times no!" On the contrary, it is our firm belief that basic research in social psychology has borne much sweet fruit—that it has provided much of practical benefit to society. Unfortunately, though—and here comes the ironic part—social psychology itself has rarely received credit for these contributions (Fisch & Daniel, 1982). The reason for this is simple: most social psychologists are concerned primarily with uncovering basic scientific knowledge about social behavior. Thus, after they attain such information, they usually leave it to others to put it to practical use. The general pattern, then, is something like this. Through basic (and often difficult)

research, social psychologists acquire new insights into human social relations. Then the members of some closely related field borrow this knowledge and put it to practical use. The result: these fields, *not* social psychology, receive credit for the payoffs that follow. A prime example of this process is provided by the contribution of social psychology to the field of *organizational behavior* (O.B.).

As its name implies, this field (which has shown explosive growth in recent years) is primarily concerned with understanding human behavior in organizational settings. Specifically, organizational behavior is highly practical in orientation, and seeks techniques for improving the efficiency and productivity of a wide range of organizations (e.g., large business, government agencies). In seeking to accomplish this goal, it has been greatly aided by social psychology. During recent decades, social psychologists have uncovered much valuable information about human behavior in group or organizational settings. For instance, they have clarified the factors that influence leader effectiveness, identified useful ways for groups to reach complex decisions, uncovered techniques for assisting individuals in the task of coping with psychological stress, and identified key sources of bias that may influence ratings of individual performance. Such knowledge is clearly applicable to improving organizational effectiveness, and practitioners in the field of O.B. have been quick both to recognize this fact, and to act upon it. Thus, by combining such social psychological knowledge with the results of their own research, they have been able to develop concrete programs for raising both the morale and efficiency of many organizations. Indeed, most recently, they have been concentrating on the task of devising steps to help U.S. and Canadian businesses cope with the strong challenge from their Japanese competitors. Needless to say, such work is of im-

FIGURE 1.12   Social psychology: A source of many practical benefits to society.

Knowledge and insights uncovered by social psychologists have made important contributions to all of the fields represented here, and to many others as well. Unfortunately, though, social psychology has often failed to receive credit for these benefits. [Source: Photos by Wide World Photos (top left); Abigail Heyman/Archive Pictures, Inc. (top right); Michal Heron, ©1981 (bottom).]

mense practical value. But—alas!—little if any of the credit for it has gone to social psychology.

In a similar manner, knowledge uncovered by social psychologists has been borrowed and applied in fields as diverse as education, law, architecture, marketing, and advertising (see Figure 1.12). The practical benefits deriving from such applications have ranged from more persuasive public service messages on the one hand, through increased fairness in the selection of juries on the other, and we will be referring to them at many points in this book (e.g., Bickman, 1981; Greenberg & Ruback, 1982). Again, the major role played by our field in the attainment of these benefits has gone largely unnoticed.

We trust that by now, you have been swayed by some of our arguments. Social psychology, we

firmly believe, *has* made many practical contributions to society and human welfare. Yet, because social psychologists tend to concentrate on the task of uncovering basic knowledge rather than on applying it to practical problems, these contributions have remained something of a well-kept secret. Unfortunately, recent events in the United States and elsewhere suggest that such modesty is no longer appropriate. Rather, it may now be time for social psychologists to lay claim to the practical payoffs deriving from their work. Failure to do so may leave our field in a highly vulnerable position, and will severely impair its ability to continue as a cornerstone or foundation for several key applied disciplines.

social perception and social cognition, and then turn to specific forms of social interaction such as aggression, social influence, and group processes.

Next, we wish to mention several specific features of our text that are designed to make it easier and more convenient for you to use. First, each chapter is preceded by an outline of the major topics covered. Second, all chapters are followed by a summary that reviews the crucial points made. Third, key terms or concepts are printed in **boldface type** and are defined in the glossary that follows each chapter. Fourth, all figures and graphs contain special labels designed to call your attention to the findings being presented. Fifth, a list of sources for further information follows each chapter. Most of these sources are fairly easy to read and all are as up to date as we could make them.

Finally, we should note that we have included two distinct types of special inserts throughout the text. The first of these is labeled *Focus on Research* (see the one on pp. 20–21 for an example). Inserts of this type contain either descriptions of special research procedures employed by social psychologists (e.g., techniques to measure cooperation or aggression) or discussions of recent studies in social psychology. Our main reason for including them is simple: to provide you with a feel for what is currently going on at the frontiers of social psychological research.

The second type of insert is titled *On the Applied Side* (see the one on pp. 8–9). These focus primarily on the practical implications of social psychology — ways in which the knowledge it yields can contribute to the solution of a wide range of practical problems. And occasionally they address somewhat broader issues relating to our field and its place in modern society (the insert on pp. 30–31 provides a good example of this second use). As we have already noted, we believe quite strongly that social psychology has much to offer from a practical as well as a "basic science" perspective. Our Applied Side inserts represent an attempt to emphasize this belief. (By the way, all inserts are mentioned in the text so you will know just when to read them and how they relate to the major topics being discussed.)

To conclude: it is our hope that these and other features of our text will assist us in communicating knowledge about social behavior in a manner you will find interesting — or at least tolerable! And we also hope that they will allow some of our own excitement about the field to come through in an undistorted way. To the extent we succeed in these basic tasks — and only to that extent — will we be satisfied that, as authors, teachers, and social psychologists, we have done our part.

Summary

Social psychology may be defined as the scientific field that seeks to comprehend the nature and causes of individual behavior in social situations. In short, social psychologists focus primarily on the task of comprehending how and why individuals behave, think, and feel as they do in situations involving the presence of other persons.

Speculation concerning the nature of social interaction has continued without interruption since ancient times. However, scientific study of this topic is quite recent. Thus, social psychology first emerged as an independent field of study only in the early decades of this century. Once established, it grew rapidly, and by the 1960s was already hard at work examining virtually every imaginable aspect of social behavior. During the 1970s, a number of key topics rose to prominence in social psychology. These include *attribution* (the process through which we seek to infer the causes of others' behavior), the study of *sex roles*, and the impact of the *physical environment* on social behavior. At present, two major trends characterize our field. First, there is growing interest in **social cognition** — the role of memory, attention, information processing, and other cognitive processes in key aspects of social behavior. Second, there is increasing concern with the *application* of social psychological knowledge to many applied fields or topics (e.g., the legal process, personal health, organizational behavior).

In conducting their research, social psychologists generally use one of two major approaches — the **experimental** or **correlational method.** The first involves procedures in which one or more factors are systematically varied, in order to examine the impact of such changes upon one or more aspects of social behavior. The second involves careful observation of existing relationships between two or more variables. Both approaches offer important advantages, but because the experimental method provides firmer evidence concerning cause-and-effect relationships, it has often been preferred by social psychologists.

Often, social psychologists employ **deception** in their research. This technique involves attempts to conceal the true purpose of an experiment from the persons participating in it. The use of deception stems from the view that if subjects know the true nature of a research project, their behavior will be altered by this knowledge, and results will be invalid. The use of deception raises important ethical issues, but most social psychologists believe that it is permissible, provided two basic safeguards — informed consent and thorough debriefing — are adopted.

Glossary

cognitive dissonance *An unpleasant state induced when individuals notice inconsistency between their own attitudes, or between their attitudes and their behavior. Individuals generally strive to eliminate dissonance whenever it occurs.*

confederates *Individuals who assist researchers by playing specific roles in a study (e.g., pretending to be other subjects in it). Such persons behave in prearranged ways, and their actions often serve as a means of manipulating the key independent variables of interest.*

confounding of variables *Refers to situations in which factors other than the independent variable under investigation in an experiment are permitted to vary. Confounding makes it impossible to determine whether the results of a study stem from* *the effects of the independent variable or from other factors.*

correlational method *A method of research based on careful observation of two or more variables. If changes in one are consistently associated with changes in another, evidence for a link between them is obtained.*

debriefing *Procedures conducted at the end of an experimental session, during which subjects are informed of the true purpose of the study and the major hypotheses under investigation.*

deception *A procedure in which the true purpose of an experiment is concealed from the persons participating in it. Use of deception stems from the view that if subjects know the actual purpose of a study, their behavior will be changed by such knowledge.*

demand characteristics *Any cues serving to communicate the hypothesis under investigation in an experiment to subjects. To the extent demand characteristics exist, the results of an experiment may be invalid.*

experimental method *A research approach in which one factor (the independent variable) is systematically changed or manipulated in order to determine whether such variations affect a second factor (the dependent variable).*

hypotheses *Propositions or assertions open to direct scientific test. Often hypotheses are derived, through logic, from theories. In other cases, though, they may be suggested by informal observation or previous research.*

informed consent *Procedures in which subjects are told, in advance, about the major tasks and activities they will perform during an experiment. They then participate in the study only if they are willing to engage in these activities.*

interaction between variables *Refers to situations in which the impact of one variable is affected by one or more other variables. In order to study such effects, social psychologists often include several independent variables in their experiments.*

random assignment of subjects to groups *A basic requirement of the experimental method. According to this principle, participants in a research project should have an equal chance of being exposed to each level of the independent variable under investigation. If such conditions are not met, it may be impossible to determine whether any differences between various groups in an experiment are due to the impact of the independent variable, or to differences between the subjects in each of these conditions.*

social cognition *Refers to all aspects of cognition and all cognitive processes (e.g., memory, attention, cognitive organization) that play a role in social behavior.*

social psychology *The scientific field that seeks to comprehend the nature and causes of individual behavior in social situations.*

theory *Refers to attempts, by scientists, to explain natural phenomena (e.g., some aspect of social behavior). Theories generally consist of two major parts: basic concepts, and assertions regarding the relationships between these concepts.*

For More Information

Baron, R. A. *Behavior in organizations: Understanding and managing the human side of work.* Boston: Allyn and Bacon, 1983.
This text provides a broad survey of the field of organizational behavior. By skimming through this book, you can get a clear idea of how knowledge gathered by social psychologists has helped contribute to the solution of many practical problems in business, industry, and organizations generally.

Gilmour, R., & Duck, S. (Eds.) *The development of social psychology.* New York: Academic Press, 1980.

In this book, a number of noted social psychologists present their views on the current state of their field, its past history, and how it may develop in the future. This is an excellent source if you wish to learn more about the way modern social psychology took shape.

Jung, J. *The experimenter's challenge: Methods and issues in psychological research.* New York: Macmillan, 1982.
This text explains many aspects of psychological research in a clear, straightforward manner. If you would like to find out more about how psychologists

actually conduct their research projects, this is a useful source to consult.

Reich, J. W. (Ed.) *Experimenting in society: Issues and examples in applied social psychology.* Glenview, Ill.: Scott, Foresman, 1982.
This book contains a number of interesting articles dealing with the application of social psychological theories and methods to applied topics. The papers included have been carefully chosen, and deal with such important issues as energy conservation, pollution, criminal justice, and individual health.

CHAPTER 2

Social Perception:
Knowing Others . . . and Ourselves

Nonverbal Communication:
"Reading" the Language of Expressions, Gazes, and Gestures

Unmasking the Face: Facial Expressions as Guides to the Moods and Emotions of Others / Gazes, Looks, and Stares: The Language of the Eyes / Body Language: Gestures, Movements, and Postures / Individual Differences in the Use of Nonverbal Cues: Expressiveness and Gender

Attribution: Understanding the Causes of Behavior

From Acts to Dispositions: Using Others' Behavior as a Guide to Their Stable Characteristics / Kelley's Theory of Causal Attribution: How We Answer the Question of "Why?" / Major Theories of Attribution: A Note on Their Interface / Attribution: Some Important Sources of Bias

Self-attribution: Knowing and Understanding Ourselves

Bem's Theory of Self-perception: When Behavior Serves as a Source of Self-knowledge / Schachter's Theory of Emotion: "You Can't Know What You Feel Until You Name It"

Special Inserts

FOCUS ON RESEARCH
   The Role of Facial Feedback: Do We Show What We Feel, Feel What We Show, . . . or Both?

ON THE APPLIED SIDE
   Bias in Causal Attribution: Some Negative Potential Effects

ON THE APPLIED SIDE
   Attribution as a Form of Therapy: When a New Causal Framework Can Help

The phone is ringing as you enter your apartment. "Oh no," you think to yourself, "I hope it's not another of those salespeople. They always seem to call just at dinner time when I'm really busy." But when you pick up the receiver, you find that it is actually your good friend Diane.

"Hello, Jodi, is that you?" she asks.

"Yeah, hello Diane. What's up? I just got home this minute and have to rush out in less than an hour, so I don't have a lot of time to talk right now."

"Hold on, this will only take a minute," she replies. "I just wanted to tell you the latest: Melanie Cooper has just taken off with that guy she met at Howard's party. She left a note for Marty saying it was all over and that she had found the true love of her life. He found it when he came back from Los Angeles."

"Wow!" you utter in surprise. "I can't believe it. What a rotten thing to do. Marty's such a nice guy. I always knew she was no good deep down inside . . . never did trust her."

"Yeah," Diane agrees, "It sure seems rotten. . . . But you know, Marty has been awful jealous lately. Diane told me just a couple of weeks ago that he was really beginning to get to her, asking for full reports on where she's been all day, stuff like that. That kind of thing can really drive you nuts."

"Sure it can," you agree, "but even so, how could she just dump him like that? I mean, after all those things he's done for her. Helped her to get that job, bought her that car. . . . Heck, if I had a man doing things like that for me, *I'd think twice before up and leaving him, just like that."*

"Me too," Melanie replies. "But that guy was awful charming. . . . And he claimed to have connections in Hollywood. I'll bet he promised to do something for her in that department."

"Well," you admit, "that might be tempting. She's always wanted a career in show business. But still, I can't approve of what she's done. Poor Marty will be crushed."

"I expect he will," Diane answers. "But you know, there's one more thing: Melanie's always been real true-blue to the other men in her life. Fact is, it was usually her who got the brush-off, so you really couldn't describe her as being fickle. . . . Oh well, unless she comes back, we'll never know the whole story. Anyway, I've got to run. Just wanted to let you know. See you tomorrow. . . ."

After you hang up the phone, you stand there thinking. How could Melanie do it? Marty really cared about her. And he seemed to treat her right. Only a bad person could hurt him like this. . . . Yet, it is *true that he's been terribly jealous lately, without any cause you know about. And a chance in Hollywood . . . that might be enough to turn almost any woman's head. . . . What would you do in the same situation, you wonder? So, is Melanie just an ungrateful wretch, or did she just come up against overwhelming temptation — the kind almost no one could resist? You are still pondering this question when your eyes fall on the clock: 6:45! You have less than half an hour left! Your rush to prepare dinner and change clothes soon pushes all thoughts of Melanie and her unexpected actions totally out of your mind.*

Admit it: other people are often something of a mystery. They say and do things we don't expect, have motives or intentions we don't understand, and seem to perceive the world in ways very different from ourselves. Yet, given their central importance in our lives, this is one mystery we cannot afford to leave unsolved. For this reason, we often engage in attempts to understand what makes them "tick"—to comprehend their major motives and traits. Like the characters in the story above, we seek to determine just *why* they have acted as they have. Is it because of internal factors, such as their own intentions, or external factors centering around the situations they face? Is it because of stable traits they carry with them from setting to setting, or temporary causes such as current moods and fleeting motives? These are only a few of the key questions we must address. And as will soon be evident, the answers we obtain often have important, practical effects. Social psychologists generally term the process through which we seek such knowledge about others **social perception,** and have long accorded it a central place in their field. The reasons for this are obvious. First, the specific ways in which we perceive and understand others strongly shape both our evaluations of, and relations with, these persons. Indeed, it is hard to imagine any aspect of social behavior that is *not* affected by such information. Second, knowledge about others is essential for accurate predictions of their future behavior—a key task of social relations. And as suggested by Figure 2.1, errors in this respect can be both embarrassing and costly. For these reasons, many social psychologists view social perception as a very central process, and we fully concur with this view.

FIGURE 2.1   *Social perception: A key task of daily life.*

When our efforts to understand the persons around us fail, the results can be embarrassing—or even worse! [Source: Drawing by Wm. Hamilton; © 1976 The New Yorker Magazine, Inc.]

"No, Charles, I don't have a cold. What you hear in my voice is contempt."

While our efforts to understand the people around us (and ourselves as well) focus on many different issues, two of these are most important. First, we seek to recognize the *temporary* causes of others' behavior—their current moods, feelings, and emotions. Second, we attempt to comprehend the more *lasting* causes of their actions—their stable traits, motives, and intentions. Information on the first of these tasks is often provided by **nonverbal cues,** such as facial expressions, eye contact, and body posture or movements (body language). Information relating to the second task, in contrast, is usually gained through a more complex process known as *attribution*. Here, we seem to act as "naive scientists," attempting to understand others through fairly systematic observations of their behavior (e.g., Harvey & Weary, 1981). Because **nonverbal communication** and *attribution* both represent important aspects of social perception, and also because they provide us with somewhat different kinds of information about others, we will consider each in detail here. A third aspect of social perception—*impression formation*—will be reserved for Chapter 3, mainly because it involves basic elements of social cognition (e.g., the encoding and memory of social information).

Nonverbal Communication: "Reading" the Language of Expressions, Gazes, and Gestures

Often, behavior is strongly affected by temporary factors or causes. Transient moods, fleeting emotions, fatigue, and even various drugs can all exert powerful effects on individual behavior. To mention just a few examples, most persons seem far more willing to do simple favors for strangers when in a good mood than when in a bad one (e.g., Cialdini, Kenrick, & Baumann, 1982). Similarly, most individuals are far more likely to lash out against others in some fashion when angry or irritable than when calm and happy (Geen & Donnerstein, 1983). And both the perceptions and behavior of many persons differ markedly under the influence of alcohol and in its absence. Because these temporary causes are both important and real, it is often useful to know something about them. But how, precisely, can we obtain such knowledge? How can we know whether another person is in a pleasant or irritable mood, whether she is experiencing anger, sorrow, or joy, and so on? One answer involves the use of direct *social communication:* we simply ask these persons about their current states, and they tell us. In a surprising number of cases, this procedure works; indeed, recent evidence suggests that verbal statements are the most important single source of information about others' current feelings (Krauss et al., 1981). In many instances, however, it fails. Other persons refrain from providing the information we seek. Or even worse, they actively seek to conceal it from us through some form of deception (Zuckerman et al., 1982). Fortunately, when these conditions prevail, it is *not* necessary for us to throw up our hands in despair. Instead, we can turn to another revealing source of knowledge about these temporary causes of behavior: *nonverbal cues.* In short, we can learn much about the current moods, feelings, and physical states of the persons around us by examining their facial expressions, eye contact with us, gestures, and body movements (Argyle, 1982). Moreover—and here is the surprising part—we can often accomplish this task *even in cases where they do not wish to reveal such information.* For this reason alone, this eloquent, but subtle, unspoken language is well worthy of our careful attention.

Unmasking the Face: Facial Expressions as Guides to the Moods and Emotions of Others

More than 2,000 years ago, the famous Roman orator Cicero remarked that "The face is the image of the soul." By this comment he meant that human feelings and emotions are often reflected on the face, and can be "read" there from various recognizable expressions. Modern research indicates that in this respect, Cicero and many other observers of human behavior were correct: often, it *is* possible to learn much about the current moods and emotions of others from careful observation of their facial expressions. But what emotions, precisely, are revealed in this fashion? At first, this seems to be a simple question. In reality, though, it has proven to be quite complex. Conflicting results and findings were reported for many years, and it is only recently that a fairly clear-cut answer has emerged.

Today, most experts agree that only six different emotions are represented by distinct facial expressions. These are happiness, sadness, surprise, fear, anger, and disgust (Buck, 1984; Izard, 1977). But please note: this does *not* mean that we are capable of showing only six different facial expressions—far from it. Emotions occur in many combinations (e.g., anger along with fear, surprise together with happiness). Further, each of these reactions can vary greatly in intensity. Thus, although there appear to be only six basic "themes" in facial expressions, the number of variations on them is truly tremendous.

Facial expressions: Are they universal? Suppose that you traveled to a remote corner of the globe, and visited an isolated group of people who had never before met an outsider. Further, imagine that you observed their behavior in a number of basic situations—ones very likely to make them happy, angry, sad, or disgusted. Would these individuals show facial expressions similar to your own in such cases? And would you be able to recognize these distinct expressions just as you can recognize them among members of your own culture? The answer to both questions appears to be "yes." For example, consider an intriguing series of studies conducted by Ekman and Friesen (1975). These scientists traveled to isolated areas of New Guinea and asked persons living there to imagine various emotion-provoking events (your friend has come to visit and you are happy; you find a dead animal that has been lying in the hot sun for several days). Then, these subjects were asked to show, by facial expressions, how they would feel in each case. As you can see from Figure 2.2, their expressions were very similar to ones you might show yourself in these situations. Thus, it appears that when experiencing the emotions just listed, human beings all over the world tend to show highly similar facial expressions.

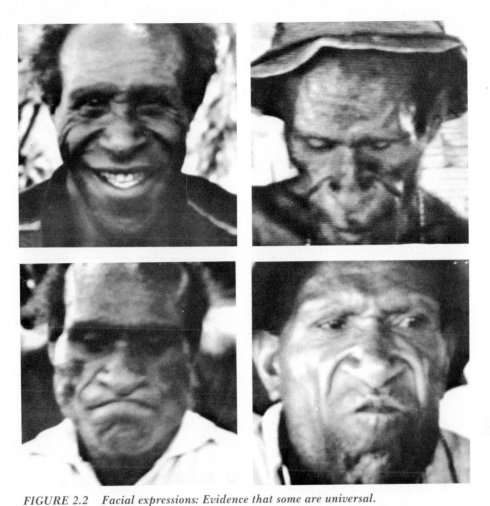

FIGURE 2.2   *Facial expressions: Evidence that some are universal.*

When asked to imagine various emotion-provoking events, members of isolated groups living in New Guinea demonstrated facial expressions such as the ones shown here. The fact that these are quite similar to the expressions shown by persons living in many other countries provides evidence for the view that some expressions, at least, are universal in occurrence. (The expressions shown here represent happiness, sadness, anger, and disgust.) [Source: From Ekman & Friesen, 1975, p. 27; by permission of the authors.]

But what about the meanings of such expressions; are these also universal? Again, the answer seems to be "yes." Some support for this conclusion is provided by Figure 2.2. We doubt that you had any trouble in recognizing the expressions shown by the person in these photos, despite the fact that he comes from an isolated region of New Guinea. And systematic research confirms this observation. When individuals living in widely separated countries are shown photos of strangers demonstrating anger, fear, happiness, sadness, surprise, and disgust, they are quite accurate in identifying these emotions (e.g., Ekman,

1973). Thus, it appears that a smile is interpreted as a sign of happiness, a frown as a sign of sorrow, and so on all over the globe.

In general, then, there seems to be considerable universality in facial expressions. Persons from different cultures tend to show distinct—but similar—facial expressions when experiencing anger, sorrow, joy, or other strong feelings. And they readily recognize such expressions as representing specific emotions when these are shown by others, even persons from outside their own group. Unfortunately, there is one major complication in this relatively neat picture that should not be overlooked. Social groups often differ sharply with respect to unstated rules concerning the display of various emotions. For example, in the United States it is considered bad manners to demonstrate facial expressions reflecting disgust or anger in many settings (e.g., few dinner guests will recoil in horror, even when served a dish they truly hate). In other cultures, in contrast, such expressions are not prohibited, or may even be encouraged as fully appropriate. Because of differences in such **display rules,** underlying similarity in facial expressions may sometimes be masked. That is, the persons involved may all possess tendencies to smile when happy, to grit their teeth when angry, and so on, but these are overridden by cultural rules and learning. In many cases, though, the impact of display rules is less pronounced; and then, the type of universality described above does tend to occur. Largely because it does, the language of the face—in contrast to that of spoken words—rarely requires an interpreter.

Facial expressions: When do they develop? Infants only a few weeks old often show facial expressions that, in adults, would readily be interpreted as indicative of specific emotions. According to common sense, however, these expressions are largely meaningless. Rather than revealing anger, happiness, fear, or surprise, they simply reflect internal physical events, such as gas bubbles or the like. Is this true? Actually, recent findings suggest that it is not. Growing evidence (Feldman, 1982; Izard, 1977) indicates that infants as young as only one or two months can demonstrate discrete facial expressions closely related to their emotional states. For example, in one series of studies, Izard and his co-workers (Izard et al., 1980) exposed infants one to nine months old to various emotion-provoking situations (e.g., separation from their mothers, medical inoculations). The facial expressions shown by the infants in these situations were then videotaped and studied in a systematic manner. In particular, they were analyzed by means of the *Facial Expression Scoring Manual,* a carefully developed guide that provides both verbal descriptions and cross-culturally standardized photos of the brow, eye, and mouth regions of the face during nine distinct facial patterns. Results pointed to the intriguing conclusion noted previously: infants as young as only one or two months can demonstrate discrete emotional expressions. When confronted with the emotion-provoking events just described, they often show facial expressions quite similar to those evidenced by adults in comparable circumstances (please see Figure 2.3).

The existence of such clear-cut facial expressions among young infants is important in at least two ways. First, since children in this age group cannot communicate verbally, facial expressions arm them with an alternative useful

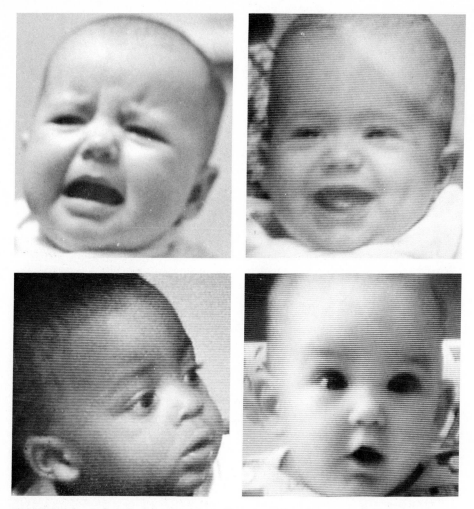

FIGURE 2.3   Infant facial expressions: More revealing than you might once have guessed.

These illustrations (taken from videotapes) suggest that even infants only a few months old are capable of showing discrete and easily recognized facial expressions. [Source: Photos courtesy Dr. Carroll Izard.]

means of transmitting important information to their caregivers. Second, such expressions may play a key role in the formation of strong affective bonds between infants and their parents. For example, mothers and fathers may experience positive reactions when their infants smile. And there may also be important emotional rewards in changing their youngsters' expressions from ones of distress to ones of contentment. In these and other ways, the very early appearance of discrete facial expressions may exert powerful effects upon later social development. (For a discussion of some surprising links between facial expressions and underlying emotional states, please see the **Focus on Research** section on pp. 46–47.)

*The Role of Facial Feedback:
Do We Show What We Feel, Feel What
We Show, . . . or Both?*

Suppose that a club or social group to which you belong decides to put on a play. Further, imagine that your part in it requires you to show great sorrow or grief. In order to prepare for this role, you practice making the appropriate facial expressions as you speak your lines. Soon, you become quite skilled at this task; the expressions you show closely resemble genuine ones. Will they then exert any impact upon your actual feelings? In short, will you tend to feel sadder when demonstrating these posed expressions than when not doing so? Surprisingly, you may. Growing evidence points to the conclusion that facial expressions do not simply reflect underlying emotions. In some cases, at least, they may also intensify or even generate such feelings. For example, consider an intriguing study conducted by Lanzetta, Cartwright-Smith, and Kleck (1976). These researchers asked subjects to either suppress or exaggerate their facial reactions during a series of painful electric shocks. Results indicated that those who exaggerated their expressions rated the shocks as more aversive—and also demonstrated higher levels of physiological arousal to them—than subjects who suppressed their expressions. In short, outward facial expressions actually influenced internal reactions to the shocks. Similar and perhaps even more revealing findings have been reported recently by Zuckerman and his colleagues (1981).

In this experiment, male and female subjects were shown either pleasant videotaped scenes (e.g., a monologue from the Carol Burnett show), neutral scenes (e.g., films of an apple harvest), or unpleasant scenes (e.g., a film about traffic fatalities).

Within each of these groups, one third of the participants were asked to *suppress* their facial reactions, one third were told to *exaggerate* them, and one third were not given any special instructions. Thus, their reactions were *spontaneous* ones. While watching the various scenes, subjects' physiological reactions were carefully recorded. And immediately after conclusion of the tapes, they rated their own emotional reactions to them. Results were quite revealing. Individuals told to exaggerate their facial expressions showed higher levels of arousal to both the pleasant and unpleasant scenes, and also reported stronger positive and negative reactions than subjects asked to suppress these outward expressions (see Figure 2.4).

Together, the findings reported by Lanzetta et al. (1976), Zuckerman et al. (1981), and other teams of researchers offer strong support for the **facial feedback hypothesis:** the view that facial expressions can strongly affect our emotional states. But why is this the case? How can such expressions influence our internal feelings or arousal? The answer seems to involve the process of *classical conditioning*. Throughout our lives, facial expressions are closely associated with emotion-provoking events. Moreover, since such expressions tend to occur quite quickly (almost instantaneously), they frequently precede internal, physiological reactions. As a result of such repeated pairing, facial expressions gradually become *conditioned stimuli* for internal emotional states. Thus, many emotion-provoking situations may proceed as follows: some external event occurs, and facial expressions quickly follow. Then these expressions serve as con-

*Gazes, Looks, and Stares:
The Language of the Eyes*

Have you ever had a conversation with someone wearing dark glasses? If so, you may recall that this was an uncomfortable situation. The reason for your

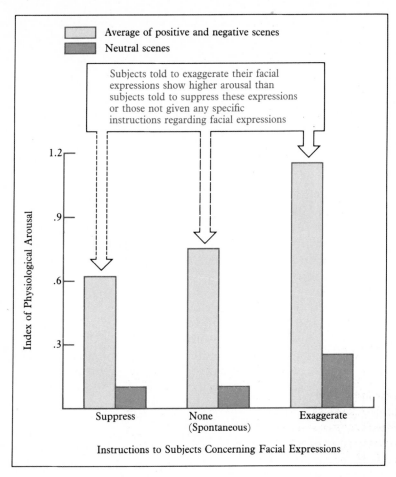

Average of positive and negative scenes

Neutral scenes

Subjects told to exaggerate their facial expressions show higher arousal than subjects told to suppress these expressions or those not given any specific instructions regarding facial expressions

Index of Physiological Arousal

1.2

.9

.6

.3

Suppress

None (Spontaneous)

Exaggerate

Instructions to Subjects Concerning Facial Expressions

FIGURE 2.4   The facial feedback hypothesis: Empirical support.

Individuals told to exaggerate their facial expressions showed higher levels of physiological arousal in response to pleasant and unpleasant scenes than persons asked to suppress these reactions. (Individuals not given any special instructions about their facial expressions were in between these two other groups in level of arousal.) These findings provide support for the facial feedback hypothesis. [Source: Based on data from Zuckerman et al., 1981.]

ditioned stimuli, either eliciting or intensifying internal arousal and the subjective experiences we usually label as emotions.

We should hasten to add that at present, little direct evidence for this process exists. Regardless of the precise mechanism involved, however, the fact that "we feel what we show" as well as "show what we feel" points to an important conclusion: in many cases, emotional reactions may be more susceptible to direct, voluntary control than has previously been suspected. If we actively suppress our facial reactions, we may also reduce the intensity of our emotional experiences, while if we exaggerate them, we may intensify such feelings. In short, the two-way link between facial expressions and our internal states may provide us with an effective technique for controlling the latter. Given the importance of regulating our emotions and feelings in many social contexts, this is a provocative possibility, truly worthy of further study.

negative reactions is simple: you could not see this person's eyes. As a result, you were denied access to important nonverbal cues concerning her or his feelings and reactions. Ancient poets frequently described the eyes as "windows to the soul" and in an important sense, they were correct. We *do* often learn a great deal about others' internal states from their eye contact with us. For example, we often interpret a high level of gazing from another as a sign of liking or friendliness (Kleinke, Meeker, & LaFong, 1974). In contrast, if others avoid eye contact with us, we usually conclude that they are unfriendly, don't like us, or simply wish to avoid social interaction. That the level and pattern of eye contact provided by another person can strongly affect our reactions to him or her is suggested by the results of a study conducted by Imada and Hakel (1977). These researchers arranged for accomplices playing the role of a job inter- viewee to show either high or low levels of eye contact with their interviewer. Results indicated that when they showed a high degree of visual contact, they received significantly more positive ratings as a future employee than when they demonstrated a low level of eye contact.

Staring: When gazing goes too far.   While a high level of eye contact from others is usually viewed as a sign of liking or positive feelings, there is one important exception to this general rule. If another person gazes at us in a continuous manner, and maintains such contact regardless of any actions on our part, he or she may be said to be **staring.** As you probably know from your own experience, this is a decidedly unpleasant experience — one that makes us feel nervous or tense (Strom & Buck, 1979). Thus, it is not surprising that when confronted with such treatment by a stranger, many individuals seek to withdraw from the situation in which such staring occurs (Greenbaum & Rosenfield, 1978). Even worse, some evidence suggests that stares are often interpreted as a sign of hostility or anger, both by people and animals (Ellsworth & Carlsmith, 1973).

Together, these findings seem to imply that staring always produces nega- tive effects. After all, people become upset when they are stared at, view such treatment as a sign of hostility, and may react to it with anger or attempts to escape. But additional evidence suggests that occasionally staring can yield more desirable outcomes. For example, such treatment has been found to increase offers of aid from passersby, at least in some situations (Ellsworth & Langer, 1976). You have probably experienced one form of this yourself. Recall how much harder it is to walk by persons collecting for charity without making a donation once they have stared at you and caught your eye. It is for this reason that we often try to look at the sidewalk (or elsewhere) when approaching such individuals. Findings such as these suggest that stares, while often quite unpleasant, are not always negative in their effects. Such cases, though, appear to be exceptions to the general rule. In most situations, staring is a potent and potentially dangerous nonverbal cue — one that should be used with great caution.

Body Language: Gestures, Movements, and Postures

Look at the photos in Figure 2.5. Can you tell anything about the feelings of the persons shown? We're sure that you can, even though all cues provided by their faces have been removed. The reason for this is simple: people often reveal much about their current moods or emotions through the movements, positions, and postures of their bodies. Together, nonverbal cues from such sources are often termed **body language,** and they provide us with several types of information.

FIGURE 2.5   *Body language: Silent . . . but eloquent.*

*Even though you cannot see the faces of the persons shown here, you can
probably guess what emotions they are experiencing. This is because cues
provided by the position and posture of their bodies are very informative in this
respect. [Source: Photo (left) by Linda Ferrer, © 1981/Woodfin Camp and
Associates; photo (right) courtesy of West Point Academy.]*

First, as we just noted, body language often reveals much about the current
emotional states of others. Large numbers of movements—especially ones in
which a particular part of the body does something to another—suggest
emotional arousal. The more individuals engage in such behavior, the higher
their level of arousal or nervousness seems to be (Knapp, 1978). For example, if
you notice that a stranger with whom you are conversing continuously fidgets,
licks her lips, and scratches her head, you will probably conclude that she is
nervous or ill at ease (Ekman, 1977).

More specific information about others' feelings is often provided by
gestures. These fall into several different categories, but perhaps the most
important are **emblems**—body movements carrying a highly specific meaning
within a given culture. For example, in the United States (and several other
countries) extending one's hand with a closed fist but the thumb pointing up
signifies a positive reaction. Similarly, moving the index finger in a circular
motion around one ear often means that some person being discussed is
confused, illogical—or worse! Emblems vary greatly from culture to culture.
And some are used much more frequently in certain parts of the world than in
others (Morris et al., 1979). But all human societies have at least some signals of
this type for greetings, departures, insults, and the description of physical states
(e.g., hunger, thirst, fatigue).

Together, cues provided by others' body movements, posture, and gestures often paint a vivid picture of their emotions and thoughts. But this is not
the entire story. Body language also tells us much more. Among these, perhaps
the most important is their reactions to *us.* While certain body movements or
postures indicate liking, others signal disliking or rejection (Mehrabian, 1968).
For example, research on this topic reveals that we usually interpret the

following actions by another person as signs of a positive reaction to us: sitting so as to face us directly, leaning in our direction, nodding in agreement to what we say. In contrast, we interpret the following body cues as signs of negative reactions: sitting so as to avoid facing us directly, leaning away, looking at the ceiling (or elsewhere) while we are speaking, and shaking their heads in disagreement to our verbal comments (Clore, Wiggins, & Itkin, 1975).

In sum, body movements and posture can often tell us much about other persons. They often reveal their emotions, communicate specific messages, and provide clues as to their feelings about us. Given the usefulness of such information, it is obvious that learning to read this unspoken physical language can often be well worth the effort.

Individual Differences in the Use of Nonverbal Cues: Expressiveness and Gender

Human beings differ greatly with respect to verbal skills. While some are both eloquent and persuasive, others find it difficult to express even the simplest of thoughts; and most, of course, are somewhere in between. If people vary in terms of their ability to employ spoken language, it seems only reasonable to expect that they will differ, too, in their capacity to make use of the unspoken, nonverbal one. And in fact, growing evidence suggests that this is the case. Some individuals seem to be much better at transmitting and interpreting nonverbal cues than others. But who, precisely, are these persons? In short, what characteristics produce — or at least are associated with — high and low nonverbal skills? Recent investigations indicate that two factors — differences in overall *level of expressiveness* and *gender* — are both important.

Expressiveness: A key dimension in nonverbal communication. Think back over the many persons you have known in recent years. Can you remember one who showed clear facial expressions, used gestures freely, and engaged in a large amount of body movement? In contrast, can you also recall someone who made little use of such nonverbal cues? We doubt that you experienced any problems in remembering persons of both types, for informal experience suggests that human beings differ sharply along the dimension of overall *expressiveness*. To the extent such differences exist, they may well play a key role in nonverbal skills. Specifically, we would predict that persons high in expressiveness will generally be more successful *senders* (transmitters) of nonverbal messages than persons low on this dimension. Systematic evidence on this and related issues has been reported by Friedman and his colleagues (Friedman et al., 1980).

These researchers constructed a brief questionnaire, the *Affective Communication Test* (ACT), designed to assess individual differences in expressiveness. (Sample items: "I like to remain unnoticed in a crowd," "I show that I like someone by hugging or touching that person.") Persons completing the ACT obtain a very wide range of scores, thus confirming the informal view that large differences on this dimension exist. And these differences in expressiveness, in turn, seem closely linked to important aspects of social behavior. For example in one study, Friedman et al. (1980) administered the ACT to 300 students. These

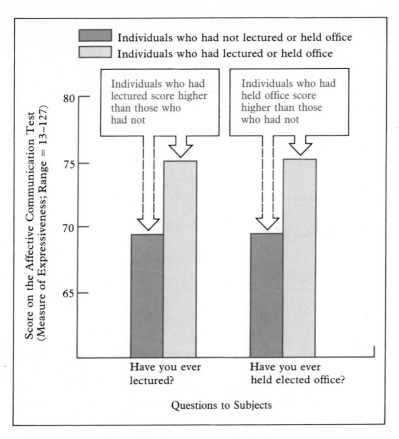

FIGURE 2.6   Individual differences in expressiveness: Evidence for their impact.

Expressiveness may affect a wide range of social behavior or social experience. For example, individuals who report having given a lecture or having held an elected office in some organization score higher on a test of this characteristic than persons who do not report such experiences. [Source: Based on data from Friedman et al., 1980.]

subjects also answered a number of questions about their personal lives, including ones concerned with whether they had ever given a lecture, been elected to an office in an organization, or held a major part in a play. It was predicted that the more expressive individuals were, the more likely they would be to have had such experiences; and as you can see from Figure 2.6, results confirmed this hypothesis. Individuals who had given a lecture or held elected office *did* score higher on the ACT than persons who had not engaged in these activities. In other studies, Friedman et al. obtained evidence suggesting that expressiveness is also related to success in various occupations. For example, physicians popular with their patients scored higher on the ACT than those who were less popular. And successful salespersons tended to score higher on expressiveness than unsuccessful ones.

Together, these findings point to the view that expressiveness is closely linked to success in nonverbal communication. Apparently persons high on this dimension provide others with clear nonverbal cues. As a result, they are more likely than less expressive individuals to get their message across. And in a key sense, of course, this is what social communication is all about!

The role of gender: Why—often—females have an edge. Have you ever heard the phrase "feminine intuition"? If so, you probably know that it refers to the belief that women possess a special "sixth sense" that allows them to understand and predict social events that seem totally mysterious to males. While such ideas lie largely outside the realm of science, we should note that in a limited sense, at least, they may have a basis in fact. A growing body of evidence points to the conclusion that in general, females are markedly superior to males in the use of nonverbal cues. Specifically, they can both read and transmit such unspoken messages more effectively (e.g., Mayo & Henley, 1981). As a result of this advantage, they may often notice a host of subtle reactions that are overlooked by males. Little wonder, then, that females sometimes seem—at least to puzzled males—to possess something akin to mystical social powers! But how, specifically, do these differences arise? Why are females so often superior to males in the use of nonverbal cues? The answer suggested by recent research is as follows.

In many cultures, traditional stereotypes of masculinity and femininity differ sharply. For example, in most Western nations, the traditional view holds that males are assertive, logical, and dominant. In contrast, the corresponding view of females suggests that they are expressive, supportive, and sensitive (please see our discussion of this topic in Chapter 5). These contrasting views of the supposed traits of males and females, in turn, may strongly affect child-rearing practices for the two sexes. In particular, parents may actively encourage females to pay attention to nonverbal cues, while failing to encourage such behavior among boys. To the extent this is the case, it is hardly surprising that females develop a considerable edge in this department.

Support for this general perspective is provided by the results of several different studies (e.g., Buck, 1977; LaFrance & Carmen, 1980). Perhaps the most convincing evidence for its accuracy, however, is contained in a series of investigations conducted recently by Zuckerman and his associates (Zuckerman, Amidon, Bishop, and Pomerantz, 1982). In this research, the scores obtained by subjects on standard measures of masculinity and femininity (as traditionally defined) were related to their success as encoders (transmitters) of nonverbal cues. Several studies were performed, employing different tasks (e.g., subjects described people they liked or disliked; they viewed pleasant or unpleasant scenes) and different measures of nonverbal accuracy. Regardless of these variations, however, results were much the same: the higher individuals scored in femininity, the better they were as senders of nonverbal signals. And the higher subjects scored in masculinity, the poorer they were in this respect. Further, this was true both for facial expressions and for nonverbal cues relating to the voice (e.g., its tone) (see Figure 2.7). Perhaps most important of all, these findings were largely independent of participants' biological sex. Individuals scoring high in femininity tended to be accurate transmitters of nonverbal cues *regardless of whether they happened to be females or males.* Similarly, individuals scoring high in masculinity tended to be relatively poor at this task, again, *regardless of whether they happened to be males or females.* As you can readily see, these findings suggest that current differences between men and women with respect to the transmission of nonverbal cues are probably *not* biological "givens"; on the contrary, they seem to stem from societal views about what is and what is not appropriate behavior for each sex, plus the contrasting child-

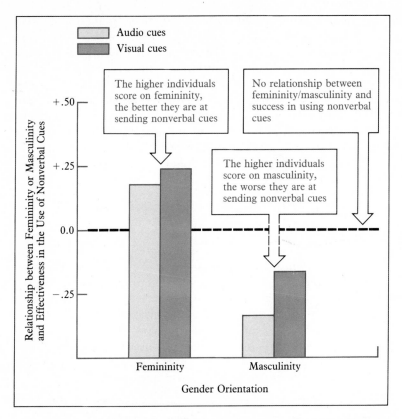

FIGURE 2.7 *Masculinity,*
femininity, and effectiveness in
the use of nonverbal cues.

*The higher individuals score on a
standard test of* **femininity**, *the
better they tend to be as senders of
nonverbal cues. In contrast, the
higher individuals score on a
measure of* **masculinity**, *the poorer
they are as transmitters of such
signals. Further, these differences
hold both for cues relating to the
voice (e.g., changes in its tone) and
cues relating to the face (e.g.,
various expressions). [Source: Based
on data from Zuckerman et al.,
1982.]*

rearing practices these encourage (Feldman, 1982). To the extent this is the case—and considerable evidence suggests that it is—the advantage in nonverbal communication suggested by the phrase "feminine intuition" certainly loses a large part of its apparent mystery.

Individual differences in nonverbal accuracy: Some practical effects. Whatever their specific source, large individual differences in the abilities to send and receive nonverbal cues clearly exist. This fact, in turn, raises an intriguing question: Do such differences matter? That is, do they have any practical effects? We believe that the answer is "yes." The ability to accurately communicate one's own feelings and to accurately assess the emotions of others can be useful in many different settings. For example, it seems likely that successful negotiators, charismatic leaders, and effective salespersons are all highly skilled at these tasks. That is, they can get their own messages across, and can accurately read the persons around them. In addition, growing evidence suggests that such accuracy in the use of nonverbal cues can also play a key role in long-term, intimate relationships such as marriage. For example, in one revealing experiment, Sabatelli, Buck, and Dryer (1983) found that the better wives' ability to read poorly encoded nonverbal messages from their husbands, the fewer the complaints about the relationship voiced by both partners. Similarly, the greater the accuracy of wives in transmitting their own nonverbal messages, the fewer the complaints voiced by their husbands. In short, nonverbal skills on the part of wives seemed to contribute to improved levels of marital satisfaction or adjustment. (Interestingly, the same pattern was not observed for males. Indeed, the greater the sending accuracy of husbands, the *greater* the frequency of marital complaints voiced by their wives. Perhaps this is due to the fact that a high level of emotional expressiveness is contrary to traditional views of masculinity and is, therefore, perceived as somewhat inappropriate.)

To conclude: existing evidence suggests that the abilities to transmit and "read" nonverbal cues can often yield important practical payoffs. Given this fact, these skills may be ones well worth developing.

Attribution: Understanding the Causes of Behavior

Accurate knowledge about others' current moods or feelings can be very useful. Indeed, in many situations, it is essential for interacting with them in an effective manner. Yet, despite this fact, it is only part of the picture. Knowing how someone feels right now may help explain his or her present behavior, but it may be of little use in predicting how this person will act tomorrow—or perhaps even an hour from now. Emotions and moods change so quickly that they do not provide a firm basis for understanding others' behavior across time and across situations. In our efforts to know the persons around us, therefore, we are often concerned with the more stable causes behind their actions. The process through which we seek to acquire such information is known as **attribution**, and involves our efforts to develop a causal analysis of the social world. In short, it centers on our attempts to comprehend *why* others (and we) act in certain ways (see Figure 2.8). But what is the basic nature of this process? How does it unfold? And how accurate are the results it yields? These and related questions have been addressed by major *attribution theories.* A number of these have been proposed during the past three decades (e.g., Heider, 1958). However, in this discussion, we will focus on two that have been especially

FIGURE 2.8   Attribution: A basic part of social life.

As suggested by this cartoon, we frequently attempt to understand the reasons behind others' behavior—to comprehend precisely why they have acted in a certain way. And like Lt. Fuzz, we make many errors in this complex task. [Source: © King Features Syndicate, Inc., 1979. World rights reserved.]

influential—theories initially proposed by Jones and Davis (1965) and Kelley (1972).

From Acts to Dispositions:
Using Others' Behavior as a Guide to Their
Stable Characteristics

In our attempts to know the persons around us, we draw on several sources of information. First, we pay close attention to their physical appearance, realizing that such factors as age, style of dress, and attractiveness all yield important clues about their major traits. Second, we sometimes seek to gain such knowledge directly by asking others to reveal their thoughts and motives to us. By far the most important source on which we draw, however, is other persons' behavior. That is, we observe their overt action and then use this information to infer their possession of certain traits, motives, or intentions.

At first glance, this might seem to be a simple task. After all, others' behavior provides us with a rich source on which to base such attributions. Unfortunately, though, the situation is complicated by two important factors. First, other persons often seek to mislead or deceive us about their underlying traits and motives. In such cases, of course, it is difficult to learn much about them from their overt actions. Indeed, if we are not careful, we may be led to seriously false conclusions. Second, and of even greater importance, others' actions often stem from external factors beyond their control, *not* from their lasting traits or dispositions. For example, imagine that you observe a politician kissing babies and shaking hands with potential voters (see Figure 2.9). Does this mean that she is an intrinsically kind and friendly person, well deserving of your vote? Not necessarily. It may simply reflect the fact she wants to win election, and knows that such actions—tiresome as she may personally find them—are necessary for attaining this goal. In cases such as this, using others' behavior as a guide to their lasting traits or motives may lead us seriously astray.

How, then, do we cope with these complications? How, in short, do we decide either that others' behavior reflects their "true" characteristics or, alternatively, that it stems from other, temporary factors? One answer is

FIGURE 2.9   *Inferring others' characteristics from their behavior: Often trickier than it seems.*

Can you infer the traits or characteristics of the person shown from his behavior? Probably you cannot. The actions he is performing may be ones required by a specific social role or other external forces. [Source: UPI photo.]

provided by the theory of **correspondent inference,** first proposed by Jones and Davis (1965) and later expanded by Jones and McGillis (1976). According to this theory, we accomplish this difficult task by focusing our attention on certain types of actions—those most likely to be informative in this regard. First, we consider only behaviors that seem to have been freely chosen; ones that, instead, were somehow forced on the person in question, tend to be ignored. Second, we pay careful attention to behaviors that produce unique or *noncommon effects*—effects that would *not* be produced by other, different actions. The advantage provided by such behaviors is readily illustrated. For example, imagine that one of your friends had just been married. Further, suppose that her spouse (1) is highly attractive, (2) has a very pleasant personality, and (3) has just inherited a vast fortune. Would this information tell you anything definite about your friend? Probably not. There are so many potential reasons for her having married this man (his good looks, charm, wealth) that it is impossible to determine which one was of primary importance to her. But now, in contrast, imagine that your friend has just married someone who (1) is highly unattractive, (2) is known to be a grouch, and (3) has just inherited vast wealth. Here, the situation is very different. There is only one obvious reason for her choice: her mate's great wealth. In this case, then, you might well conclude that your friend values money more than other things, such as personal happiness or a fulfilling sex life. Indeed, you might conclude that she is downright mercenary! By comparing these two situations, you should be able to see why we generally learn more about others from actions on their part that produce noncommon effects than from actions without any distinctive consequences.

According to Jones and Davis, there is a third basis for our success in forming correspondent inferences. In general, we seem to pay more attention to behaviors by others that are low in *social desirability* than behaviors that are high on this dimension. In short, we are usually more willing to draw conclusions about others from actions they perform that are not approved or encouraged by society (or required by specific social roles) than from actions that *are* approved in this manner. For example, consider the politician mentioned previously. If you see her kissing babies, shaking hands with voters, or attending church with her family on Sunday, you may be quite reluctant to develop any firm attributions about her stable traits; after all, all these actions are considered appropriate for persons running for public office. But imagine, instead, that you see her refusing to kiss babies, declining to shake hands offered to her, and sticking pins in voodoo dolls of her opponents. Here, you would probably be more willing to reach conclusions about her lasting characteristics, for these actions are both unusual and socially undesirable.

In sum, the theory proposed by Jones and Davis suggests that we are most likely to conclude that others' behavior reflects their stable traits (i.e., to reach *correspondent inferences* about them) when these actions (1) are perceived as occurring by choice, (2) yield distinctive, noncommon effects, and (3) they are seen as being socially undesirable. Actually, the overall process is a bit more complex than this. For example, we are generally willing to reach firm inferences about others when their actions have a direct impact upon us than when they do not—a tendency known as **hedonic relevance.** And we also tend to emphasize behaviors that seem to be intended to harm or benefit us—an effect known as **personalism.** Thus, returning to our politician, we would generally be more willing to draw firm conclusions about her underlying values from her vote for a bill that raises our taxes than her vote for a bill that fails to affect us in any manner (the role of hedonic relevance). And we would also be more likely to form correspondent inferences about her if the hand she refuses to shake (or baby she fails to kiss) is our own (personalism). In general, though, these factors do not alter the basic process. In most cases, we proceed like amateur detectives, trying to unravel the mystery of other persons by focusing on a specific set of clues: key aspects of their overt behavior.

Kelley's Theory of Causal Attribution: How We Answer the Question of "Why?"

At the start of this chapter, we described an incident in which a young woman took off for points unknown (perhaps Hollywood!) with a new lover. In discussing her behavior, two of her friends sought an explanation for this unexpected action. Was it something about *her* as a unique person (she's a no-good ingrate), something about her current life situation (her previous lover was insanely jealous), or a combination of both? In their efforts to deal with these questions, her acquaintances did not focus solely upon her current behavior. For example, they also took her actions on other occasions into account (they noted that she had been faithful to earlier lovers). Nor did they simply seek to determine whether her flight to "greener pastures" reflected a stable, internal trait. Their analysis of the situation was somewhat broader, and tried to take note of a wider range of potential causes.

In many life situations, the attributional tasks we face are similar to the ones in this story. We want to know *why* another person has behaved in some manner, not simply whether this action reflects his or her lasting dispositions. And often, we seek to reach such conclusions on the basis of repeated observations of this individual's behavior—not a single instance. But how do we proceed in such cases? How, in short, do we attempt to determine whether another's behavior has stemmed mainly from internal causes (some aspect of this individual), external causes (some aspect of the social or physical world), or a combination of the two? Intriguing answers to these and related questions are provided by a theory proposed by Harold Kelley (Kelley, 1972; Kelley & Michela, 1980).

According to Kelley, in our attempts to answer the question "why" about others' behavior, we focus on three major dimensions. First, we consider **consensus**—the extent to which other persons react in the same manner as this individual to a particular stimulus. Second, we consider **consistency**—the extent to which this person reacts to this stimulus in the same way on other occasions. And third, we consider **distinctiveness**—the extent to which this person reacts in the same manner to other, different stimuli. (Note: please don't confuse consistency and distinctiveness. Consistency refers to the extent to which an individual reacts in a similar manner to the *same* stimulus or situation on different occasions. In contrast, distinctiveness refers to the extent to which he or she reacts in a similar manner to *different* stimuli or situations. If an individual reacts in the same way to a wide range of stimuli, distinctiveness is *low*.)

Kelley's theory suggests that we are most likely to attribute another's behavior to *internal* causes under conditions of low consensus, high consistency, and low distinctiveness. In contrast, we are most likely to attribute another's behavior to *external* causes under conditions of high consensus, high consistency, and high distinctiveness. And we generally attribute it to a *combination* of these factors under conditions of low consensus, high consistency, and high distinctiveness. (Please see Figure 2.10 for a summary of these suggestions.) Perhaps a concrete example will help illustrate the reasonable nature of Kelley's proposals.

Imagine that you are dining in a restaurant with some friends, and one of them acts in the following manner: she takes one bite of her food and then shouts loudly for the waiter. When he appears, she demands that the dish be taken back to the kitchen and replaced. Is her behavior due to internal or external causes? In short, is your friend a fussy eater, almost impossible to please, or is the dish really so terrible that it deserves to be returned? According to Kelley's theory, your decision would depend on the three factors mentioned above. First, assume that the following conditions prevail: (1) no one else at your table complains (consensus is low); (2) you have seen your friend return this same food on other occasions (consistency high); (3) you have seen your friend complain loudly in a similar fashion in many other restaurants (distinctiveness is low). In this case, Kelley's theory suggests that you would attribute her behavior to internal causes. For example, you would conclude that your friend is very hard to please or just likes to complain.

Now, in contrast, assume that the following conditions exist: (1) several other diners at your table also complain about their food (consensus is high); (2) you have seen your friend return this same dish on other occasions (consistency is high); and (3) you have *not* seen her complain in this manner in other restaurants (distinctiveness is high). Under these conditions, you would attribute her behavior to external causes (perhaps the food is poorly prepared or ice-cold).

As we noted earlier, Kelley's theory is an eminently reasonable one, and this fact becomes clearly visible when it is applied to concrete situations such as the ones described above. Further, it has generally been confirmed by the findings of a large number of experiments (e.g., Ferguson & Wells, 1980; McArthur, 1972; Pruitt & Insko, 1980). When provided with information about consensus, consistency, and distinctiveness, individuals do generally attribute others' behavior to internal causes, external causes, or a combination of the two in accordance with the pattern Kelley predicts. We should note, though, that research on this framework also suggests the need for certain modifications. Several of these are described below.

Naive causal hypotheses: When we act as "cognitive misers." First, as you might well guess, the type of causal analysis outlined by Kelley is both effortful and time-consuming. For these reasons, individuals do not adopt it in many situations. Rather, they tend to jump to quick and easy conclusions about the causes

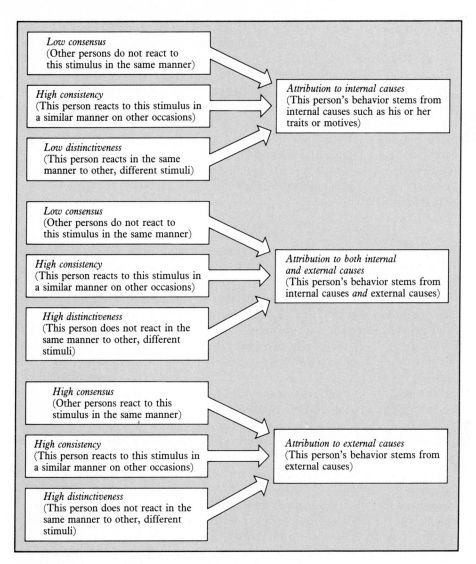

FIGURE 2.10　Deciding whether others' behavior stems from internal or external causes: Some key dimensions.

According to Kelley (1972) we take three different factors into account in deciding whether another person's behavior stems mainly from internal factors, external causes, or a combination of the two.

behind others' actions, without much attention to consensus, consistency, or distinctiveness (Hansen, 1980). The basis for such "naive causal hypotheses" is simple: we know from past experience that certain kinds of behavior generally stem from internal causes, while other types generally derive from external factors. Thus, when we observe such actions on the part of others, we don't feel that it is necessary to engage in a careful analysis of such questions as whether they acted in this way before, or whether other people show similar behavior.

Instead, we simply assume that internal or external factors were dominant. For example, suppose you see another person laugh in response to a joke or a funny movie. How would you explain this action? Probably, you would be much more likely to attribute it to the joke or movie itself than to some characteristic of the person (e.g., the fact that he has a great sense of humor and laughs at just about anything). In contrast, suppose that you saw a football player throw a perfect fifty-yard pass. Here, you would probably be much more likely to attribute his performance to skill or ability than to various external factors (e.g., the wind was blowing just right). In these and many other cases, we simply go along with past experience in assuming that certain types of behavior can reasonably be explained by internal or external factors. In short, we act as "cognitive misers," doing as little attributional work as we can get away with in a given situation (Fiske & Taylor, 1983).

The underutilization of consensus. A second modification of Kelley's theory is suggested by the following research finding: in general, individuals seem to make less use of information about consensus than the theory would predict. That is, when confronted with situations in which the causes of another's behavior are uncertain, they tend to rely more on information about consistency and distinctiveness (in forming their attributions) than upon equivalent information about consensus. Moreover, this tendency to neglect information about consensus seems to be stronger when making judgments about our peers (members of our own social group) than about nonpeers (persons belonging to other groups; Higgins & Bryant, 1982). One reason for our failure to utilize consensus information to the fullest may be as follows. We realize that individuals differ greatly in their opinions and perceptions of the social world. Thus, learning that others have acted in the same manner or differently from the persons whose behavior we wish to explain is informative *only* if these individuals closely resemble this target person. If they do not, information about consensus is not very revealing. This explanation makes intuitive sense and is supported by some research findings (Fiske & Taylor, 1983). Regardless of whether it is correct or not, though, one fact is certainly clear: in our efforts to comprehend the causes of others' behavior, we do not seem to view all sources of information as equal. (We will have more to say about the underutilization of information about consensus in Chapter 3.)

Discounting and augmenting: Attributions about single events. Kelley's theory, as we have described it, is primarily concerned with situations in which we have the opportunity to observe another's behavior in several situations and across time. Often, though, this is not the case. Rather, we must try to understand the causes of someone's behavior on the basis of a single incident. How do we proceed in such cases? Kelley offers several suggestions, and here we will focus on two. First, he notes that in such instances, we often follow the **discounting principle.** This suggests that we should downplay the importance of any potential cause of another person's behavior to the extent that other possible causes are also present. For example, consider the "flight to Hollywood" example mentioned earlier. Here, we might hesitate to attribute the young woman's desertion of her generous lover to internal factors (e.g., an ungrateful personality) because we also know about other potential causes behind her actions (e.g., the young man in her life has been mistreating her lately, acting in an insanely jealous fashion). Interestingly, it does not seem to be the number of alternative causes present that is crucial. Rather, the degree of discounting seems to depend, largely, on the valence or importance of these alternative explanations (Hull & West, 1982). Thus, if we observe another person behave in some manner and there is an obvious reason for this action, three additional but trivial potential causes for the same action will *not* result in much discounting. In contrast, a single alternative cause we judge to be important (e.g., one that is associated with large rewards) may produce considerable discounting. In any case, by encouraging a degree of caution in many situations, the discounting principle helps us to avoid jumping to unfounded—and perhaps false—conclusions about the causes behind others' behavior.

A second strategy we employ in situations where we must base our attributions upon a single event or observation is known as the **augmenting** principle. This applies to situations in which a factor that might *facilitate* a given form of

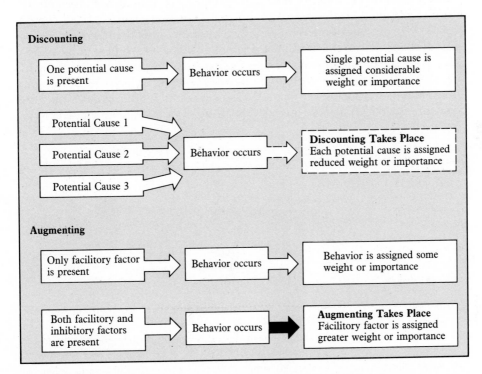

FIGURE 2.11 *Discounting and augmenting: Two basic principles of causal attribution.*

The discounting principle *(upper diagram) suggests that we attach less weight or importance to a given cause of some behavior when other potential causes of that behavior are also present. The* augmenting principle *(lower diagram) indicates that if a given behavior occurs in the presence of both facilitory and inhibitory factors, we assign added weight to the facilitory one.*

behavior and a factor that might *inhibit* it are both present. If the behavior in question occurs despite the inhibitory condition, we give enhanced weight to the facilitative one (we augment it). And this makes a good deal of sense; after all, it succeeded in producing the behavior in the face of important barriers. For example, returning to the preceding restaurant example, assume that the occasion for this meal is a day-long job interview: the young woman in question is being considered for a very desirable job. Here, concern over making a bad impression would certainly tend to inhibit the act of complaining loudly about her food. Thus, if she does this anyway, we would probably *augment* the facilitative causes; that is, we would conclude that the food must really have been pretty terrible (or that she really is a chronic complainer). Together, the discounting and augmenting principles help explain how we reach conclusions about the causes of others' behavior even when we cannot observe it across time or in several situations. Thus, both offer revealing clues about an important aspect of attribution. (Please see Figure 2.11 on p. 61 for a summary of discounting and augmenting.)

Causal attribution: The key dimensions. Finally, we should note that in our efforts to explain the behavior of other persons, we do not concentrate solely on the internal–external dimension described by Kelley and other theorists. While this is certainly one of the key dimensions involved, several others, too, seem to play a role. Intriguing information on this issue has been reported recently by Kelley himself. Together with a colleague (Wimer & Kelley, 1982), he conducted a study in which several hundred subjects read sentences describing the behavior of fictitious persons (e.g., Jack is afraid of women; Alice slipped on the

TABLE 2.1   *Key dimensions of causal attribution: A summary.*

Research findings suggest that we perceive the causes behind others' behavior as varying along several key dimensions. For example, we perceive such causes as ranging from temporary to fairly permanent, and as varying from simple to complex in nature. (Source: Based on findings reported by Wimer & Kelley, 1982.)

Dimension of causal attribution	Description / key causal questions
1. The person	To what extent does this cause involve something about the person involved?
2. Good vs. bad	To what extent does this cause produce good outcomes as opposed to bad ones?
3. Simple vs. complex	To what extent does this cause produce some event or behavior by itself, in a simple manner?; to what extent is it involved in a complex, interrelated network of causes?
4. Enduring vs. transient	To what extent does this cause persist over time as opposed to being temporary?
5. Motivation	To what extent does this cause involve conscious desires or motives?

glass and fell down; Stanley was successful at robbing the bank). For each sentence, subjects indicated what they felt to be the most likely cause of the behavior described. Then they rated this explanation on a number of different dimensions (e.g., to what extent is it something that happens rarely or often; to what extent did it involve something about the person in question). Analyses of these ratings revealed several key dimensions. These are shown in Table 2.1, and as you can see, the familiar internal–external distinction did appear. In addition, however, subjects also perceived the causes of others' behavior as falling along several other dimensions (simple–complex, good–bad). These findings suggest that even in our everyday attempts to explain others' actions we are quite sophisticated, and operate in a manner consistent with the complex task we face. As Wimer and Kelley (1982) note, such complexity must be taken carefully into account if we are ever to fully grasp individuals' efforts to understand the social world around them.

Major Theories of Attribution: A Note on Their Interface

The theories proposed by Jones and Davis (1965) and Kelley and his associates (e.g., Kelley & Michela, 1980) paint somewhat different pictures of attribution. Moreover, they focus on contrasting aspects of this overall process. Is one, then, better or more useful than the other? Actually, we believe that this is akin to posing the question: "Which is better, an apple or a pear?" These two perspectives are not opposed to each other in any manner. Rather, they have simply chosen to concentrate their attention on different — but related — questions and issues. For example, Jones and Davis are primarily concerned with the process through which we infer others' lasting dispositions from their overt actions. In contrast, Kelley and others have emphasized the tactics we use in attempting to determine whether others' behavior stems from internal causes, external causes, or both. Similarly, Jones and Davis focus primarily on how we perceive the causes of others' behavior; Kelley deals both with this topic and also with explanations for our own actions. In our opinion, then, a choice between these approaches is neither necessary nor constructive. Both are insightful and have added to our understanding of key social processes. In short, they are simply different — but complementary — conceptual frameworks useful in understanding our efforts to answer the question "Why?"

Attribution: Some Important Sources of Bias

Our discussion of causal attribution so far seems to suggest that it is a highly rational process. Whether we adopt the framework proposed by Jones and Davis or the alternative view offered by Kelley, the overall image is much the same: individuals seeking to unravel the causes of others' behavior focus on certain key factors and then follow a relatively orderly process en route to their conclusions. In general, this view is correct; attribution *is* quite logical in several respects. But we must also note that it is subject to important types of bias — ones that can lead us into serious error concerning the reasons behind others' (or even our own) behavior. We will examine several of these here, and also note some of their unsettling practical implications.

The fundamental attribution error: Overestimating the role of disposi-
tions. Imagine that while standing in a checkout line in a store, you observe the following scene: the clerk on duty shouts angrily at one of the customers and orders him to take his business elsewhere. How would you account for this rude behavior? Research findings point to an intriguing answer: the chances are quite good that you would conclude (however tentatively) that the clerk is an irritable and unpleasant person, best avoided. In fact, you might quickly move to another line yourself! This simple example illustrates what is perhaps the most common form of bias in attribution: a strong tendency to account for others' actions in terms of dispositional rather than situational causes. That is, we tend to perceive others as acting as they do largely because they are "that kind of person"; the many situational factors that may also affect their behavior tend to be ignored. Indeed, we even show this type of bias in situations where we know full well that others' actions were *not* under their own control. For example, many studies demonstrate the following effect: if we read essays written by other persons favoring a particular point of view, we tend to assume that they hold these views *even if it is made clear that they were ordered to support them* (e.g., Jones et al., 1971; Yandrell & Insko, 1977). This general bias in our attributions, known as the **fundamental attribution error,** seems to stem from an obvious cause. When we observe another person's behavior, we tend to focus on his or her actions; the context in which they take place often fades into the background. Thus, as several authors have noted, "behavior tends to engulf the field"; it captures our attention to such a degree that important situational factors are overlooked.

   In closing we should note that the tendency to overestimate the importance of dispositional factors in others' behavior is *not* universal. For example, recent evidence suggests that it can be reversed by encouraging individuals to focus on the situation rather than the person (Quattrone, 1982). Generally, though, we do seem to show a strong tendency to explain others' behavior in dispositional terms, even when such explanations are largely unwarranted. And this can be viewed as constituting an important type of bias in our causal attributions (Reeder, 1982).

The actor-observer effect: You may trip, but I was pushed. A second and closely related type of attributional bias can be readily illustrated. Imagine that, while walking along the street, you see another person stumble and fall. How would you explain this behavior? As suggested previously, the chances are good that you would attribute it to characteristics of this individual—for example, his clumsiness. But now suppose that at another time, the same thing happens to *you*. Would you explain your own behavior in the same terms? Probably not. Instead, you might well assume that *you* tripped because of situational causes— uneven paving, slippery heels on your shoes, and so on.
   This tendency to attribute our own behavior to external or situational causes but that of others to internal ones is generally termed the **actor-observer**

"I am a madcap! You are a nut!"

effect (Jones & Nisbett, 1971), and it has been demonstrated in many different experiments (e.g., Eisen, 1979; Monson & Snyder, 1977). It seems to stem, in part, from the fact that we are quite aware of the situational factors affecting our own behavior, but less aware of these factors when we turn our attention to the actions of others. Thus, we tend to perceive our actions as stemming largely from situational causes, but that of others as deriving more heavily from their dispositions (Taylor & Fiske, 1978) (see Figure 2.12).

While the actor-observer effect appears to be both frequent and general, it, too, can be eliminated or reversed under appropriate conditions. For example, if individuals can be induced to *empathize* with another person—to see the world as that person does—they tend to explain his or her actions in more situational terms (Gould & Sigall, 1977). And a recent study by Monson and Hesley (1982) suggests that when clear situational causes for some behavior are present, the attributions of actors and observers may become much more similar. Finally, the actor-observer effect can also be overcome by yet another type of attributional bias: our strong tendency to take credit for positive events or outcomes, while denying responsibility for negative ones. This important form of bias is discussed in the following section.

The self-serving bias: On the tendency to assume that we can do no wrong. Suppose that you take an important exam and obtain a very high score. How would you explain this outcome? The actor-observer bias seems to suggest that you would attribute it to situational factors (e.g., the test was easy, scoring was lenient). But would this be the case? We doubt it. Instead, the chances are good that you would explain your success by reference to internal causes—your high level of intelligence, the long hours of studying you did. Now, imagine that you take the same test but obtain a very low score. How would you explain *this* result? Here, the chances are good that you would perceive it as stemming from situational factors, such as the unfairness of the test, the poor instructor in the course, and so on. In short, the actor-observer bias might well be overturned by a different "slant" to the attribution process: our tendency to take credit for positive behaviors or outcomes, but to deny responsibility for bad or negative ones. This is generally termed the **self-serving bias** (Miller & Ross, 1975), and has been confirmed by the results of a large number of experiments (Arkin et al., 1976; Carver et al., 1980; Van Der Pligt & Eiser, 1983). Indeed, it has even been observed among the players and coaches of major sports teams (Lau & Russell, 1980). Such persons account for their wins largely in terms of internal causes (e.g., their team's high ability, its heroic efforts). In contrast, they are much more willing to attribute losses to external factors (e.g., a poor playing field, unexpected injuries to key players). Fortunately, it appears that our tendency to take credit for successes seems to be somewhat stronger than our tendency to shirk responsibility for losses (Riess, 1981). We say "fortunately," for if we habitually explained away all our failures by attributing them to external factors outside our control, there would be little chance of learning from our mistakes!

Two contrasting explanations for the self-serving bias have been offered. The first suggests that this tendency stems from a strong desire to protect our self-esteem. By taking credit for positive outcomes and denying responsibility for negative ones, we enhance our feelings about ourselves, and so accomplish an important personal task. In contrast, a second interpretation emphasizes the role of *self-presentation* (Weary & Arkin, 1981). According to this view, the self-serving bias merely reflects our desire to present a positive public image — to appear in a favorable light to others. Which of these views is correct? Actually, both *ego-defensive* and self-presentational forces may be at work in generating the self-serving bias. But a recent study by Greenberg, Pyszcynski, and Solomon (1982) seems to suggest that the former may sometimes dominate. In this study, male subjects were led to believe either that they had done quite well or done quite poorly on a standard test of intelligence. Within each of these conditions, half were told that the experimenter was simply evaluating the test and had no interest in their scores; indeed, they were told to keep their answer sheets and to put them out of sight. In contrast, the remainder were told that the experimenter *was* interested in their score, and they were instructed to write it down next to their name. Following these events, subjects in all groups rated the extent to which various factors (e.g., their ability or effort, the ease or difficulty of the test, luck) contributed to their performance. It was predicted that if the self-serving bias stems from ego-defensive needs, it would appear regardless of whether subjects' scores were private (known only to themselves) or public. If the self-serving bias stems mainly from the desire to present oneself in a favorable light, however, it should appear only under public conditions. As you can see from Figure 2.13, results confirmed the first of these views: the self-serving bias appeared under both private and public conditions. Apparently, then, this bias in our causal explanations does not stem entirely from social factors, such as our concern with making a good impression on others. In

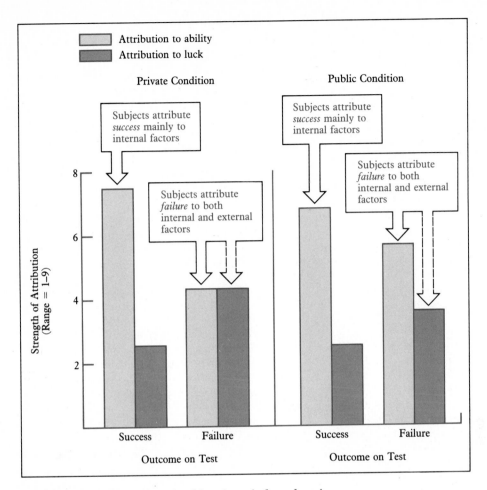

FIGURE 2.13   *The self-serving bias: A tactic for enhancing our self-esteem.*

As shown here, individuals led to believe that they had done quite well on a test attributed their outcome mainly to internal causes (i.e., their own ability). In contrast, those informed that they had done poorly attributed these results to both external and internal causes. Further, this pattern appeared under private as well as public conditions. These findings suggest that the self-serving bias often stems from our strong desire to protect or enhance our self-esteem. [Source: Based on data from Greenberg, Pyszcynski, & Solomon, 1982.]

some cases, at least, it reflects a strong desire to enhance or protect our self-image. (For a discussion of some of the problems that may arise from various errors or sources of bias in attribution, please see the **On the Applied Side** insert on pp. 68–69.)

The self-serving bias: Does it really work? The evidence reported by Greenberg et al. (1982) suggests that our tendency to attribute success to internal factors and failure to external ones often stems from the desire to protect our self-esteem. But additional findings indicate that, on some occasions, we adopt

68

 ON THE APPLIED SIDE

Bias in Causal Attribution: Some Negative Potential Effects

As we have just seen, our attributions concerning the causes of others' (and our own) behavior are subject to several sources of bias. They appear to be "slanted" in certain ways, so that we are much more likely to reach some conclusions about the causes behind various actions than others. Do these tendencies have any practical effects? Or are they merely interesting—but relatively unimportant—sidelights to an otherwise highly rational process? Unfortunately, it is our impression that the sources of bias we have considered are both all too practical—and all too negative—in their impact.

First, consider the fundamental attribution error described here. As you may recall, this refers to our tendency to perceive others' behavior as stemming primarily from stable, internal causes (e.g., their own traits or dispositions). Because of this form of bias, we often come to expect greater consistency in the behavior of other persons than is justified. Actually, of course, their actions—like our own—are strongly shaped by many temporary, situational causes. Thus, it may vary as these causal factors alter. Yet in many cases we tend to ignore this crucial fact. The result: we are quite surprised when the persons around us do not demonstrate the high levels of consistency or stability we have come—quite erroneously—to expect.

Next, let us return to the actor-observer effect. This form of bias expands upon the fundamental attribution error by noting that just as we overestimate the role of internal causes in others' behavior, we also overemphasize the impact of external ones upon *our* actions. Consider what this implies. Because of this form of bias, we may often overlook important consistencies in our own actions or feelings. And as a result, we may fail to obtain fuller comprehension of our traits or motives. For example, consider the case of a young man who gets into repeated arguments with his supervisors and so loses one job after another. Because of the actor-observer effect, he may perceive the causes of these incidents as entirely external: he blames bad luck or the built-in hostility of managers for his misfortunes. Actually, though, his run-ins with his bosses may stem from his own traits—stubbornness, unwillingness to compromise, or general abrasiveness. But because of the tendency to perceive his own actions as deriving largely from external sources, he may never realize this crucial fact.

Finally, consider the self-serving bias. This, too, can lead us into serious difficulties. Recall that it involves a strong tendency on our part to attribute positive outcomes or success to internal causes (e.g., our own sterling qualities), but failures or negative

this strategy as a means of enhancing our public image—in order to "look good" in the eyes of others (Weary & Arkin, 1981). This fact, in turn, raises an important question: Is the self-serving strategy really successful? That is, does it actually enhance the evaluations we receive from others? A recent study conducted by Carlston and Shovar (1983) offers a very mixed answer.

In this investigation, male and female subjects first learned that a stranger had either succeeded or failed on a test. They then received information suggesting that he or she had attributed this outcome either to internal causes (e.g., his or her own ability) or external causes. After learning about these attributions, subjects rated the stranger on several dimensions, including ability, honesty, and modesty. Results provided several insights into the potential

outcomes to external factors (e.g., bad luck, an extremely difficult or unfair task). Unfortunately, this form of bias can often be the cause of much interpersonal friction. In situations where two or more persons work together on some task, each may perceive success as stemming mainly from his or her contributions, but failure as deriving mainly from the shortcomings of his or her partners. The result: scenes like the one shown in Figure 2.14.

In sum, we believe that several sources of bias in causal attribution may have important practical consequences. <u>Because of these "slants" in the attribution process, we may often reach erroneous conclusions about the causes of others'—or our own—behavior. And these, in turn, may serve as the basis for misunderstandings or difficulties in our interpersonal relations.</u> The moral, then, is simple: in social perception—and especially in attempting to grasp the causes of others' behavior—beware of basic errors!

---

benefits—and costs—associated with use of a self-serving strategy. First, this tactic did in fact seem to enhance subjects' ratings of the stranger's ability. When this person succeeded, he received higher ratings if he attributed this success to internal factors rather than to external ones. When he failed, he received higher ratings when he attributed this negative outcome to external rather than internal factors. As shown in Table 2.2, however, these benefits were quite small in magnitude. And on several other dimensions, ratings of the stranger were actually *reduced* by his or her use of the self-serving strategy. For example, this person was rated as less modest and less honest when adopting the self-serving strategy than when not following it (refer to Table 2.2). In sum, it appears that attributing our successes to internal causes and our failures to

TABLE 2.2   *Benefits—and costs—of the self-serving strategy.*

Use of the self-serving strategy (attributing success to internal factors but failure to external ones) enhanced subjects' ratings of a stranger's ability. However, use of this strategy actually **reduced** *their ratings of this person's honesty and modesty. (Numbers shown indicate subjects' ratings of the stranger on each dimension. Those numbers printed in blue ink reflect use of the self-serving strategy. Compare these with numbers printed in black.) (Source: Based on data from Carlston & Shovar, 1983.)*

Attributions	Ratings of stranger along various dimensions		
	Ability	*Honesty*	*Modesty*
Successful Stranger			
Stranger attributes success to internal causes	7.60	6.34	4.85
Stranger attributes success to external causes	7.12	6.76	6.00
Unsuccessful Stranger			
Stranger attributes failure to internal causes	2.64	6.32	5.78
Stranger attributes failure to external causes	3.24	5.25	4.67

external ones may indeed cause others to view us as slightly higher in ability. At the same time, though, it may cause us to appear dishonest or immodest. In these respects, the self-serving bias may not be very "self-serving" at all!

Self-attribution:
Knowing and Understanding Ourselves

So far in our discussion of attribution, we have focused mainly on the manner in which we come to know and understand others. At this point, we will turn to a related question of equal importance: how do we come to know and understand *ourselves?* At first glance, you might assume that this is a simple task. After all, our own feelings, motives, and intentions are open to our direct inspection; thus, it should be easy to obtain information about them by turning our attention inward (Carver & Scheier, 1981). To a degree, this is certainly true. But think again: there are at least two important complications in this process. First, we are often unaware of at least some of the factors that affect our own behavior (Nisbett & Ross, 1980; Nisbett & Wilson, 1977). We may know that we acted in a given manner but are uncertain—or even wrong—about *why* we did so. Second, it is often difficult, if not impossible, to evaluate our own traits, abilities, or attitudes without reference to the persons around us. For example, how do you know whether you are attractive or unattractive, charming or dull, intelligent or unintelligent? To a surprising extent, only from information provided by others. As we will note again in Chapter 7, looking inward—or into a mirror—is simply not enough (see Figure 2.15). Thus, in our attempts to understand ourselves, we must often rely heavily on social information provided by others and additional sources of knowledge in the

FIGURE 2.15   *Understanding ourselves: Is looking inward enough?*

How do you know whether you are attractive or unattractive, competitive or easygoing, hard to tempt or easy to tempt? Often, looking inward is not enough. Only other persons, and our relations with them, can shed light on such questions. [Source: Photo by Ellen Sheffield, © 1980 / Woodfin Camp and Associates.]

external world around us. This basic fact was first called to the attention of social psychologists by two well-known researchers — Daryl Bem and Stanley Schachter. Because the theories they proposed have important implications, and also because they have stimulated a great deal of interesting research, we will consider them here.

Bem's Theory of Self-perception: When Behavior Serves as a Source of Self-knowledge

The central idea behind Bem's theory of **self-perception** can be stated simply: Often, we come to know our own attitudes or emotions partly by inferring them from observations of our own behavior (Bem, 1972). If we have acted in some manner, we seem to reason, then we must have an attitude or feeling consistent with such behavior. What we *do*, in short, serves as a useful guide to what is happening inside! We should quickly add that Bem assumes that this process is most likely to take place in situations where our own internal cues or feelings are weak or ambiguous. For example, if we violently dislike another person, we generally don't have to infer such feelings from the fact that we usually avoid his or her company. Similarly, Bem suggests that we will use our overt actions as a guide to our attitudes or emotions only in situations where this behavior was freely chosen. If, instead, it was somehow forced upon us, we will refrain from drawing such conclusions.

Surprising as it may seem, Bem's theory is supported both by informal observation and actual research findings. With respect to the former, can you recall incidents in your own life when you were surprised to find that your behavior was not consistent with what you thought were your own internal feelings? For example, have you ever found, once you started eating, that you were hungrier than you thought? Or have you ever been in a situation where, once you lost your temper, you found that you were far angrier than you

Bem's Theory of Self-perception [handwritten note in right margin]

believed? In such cases we discover that we really do not know our own internal states as well as we assumed. And in such cases, our overt actions often help us to gain a more accurate picture of these hidden processes.

With respect to actual research, Bem's theory has been supported by several different lines of work. For example, it has been found that when individuals perform some action consistent with an attitude, they may come to hold this view more strongly than they did before (e.g., Kiesler, Collins, & Miller, 1969). Perhaps the most intriguing investigations deriving from Bem's theory, however, have been ones concerned with **intrinsic motivation.**

Self-perception and intrinsic motivation: The "overjustification" effect. There are many activities individuals perform simply because they find them enjoyable. Behaviors ranging from amateur sports and hobbies through gourmet dining and lovemaking all fall under this general heading. Such activities may be described as stemming from *intrinsic motivation.* That is, the persons who perform them do so largely because of the pleasure they yield — *not* because of any hope of external rewards. But what would happen if such individuals were provided with extra payoffs for engaging in these behaviors? For example, what would happen if we actually paid someone for sipping vintage wines, or for pursuing a favorite hobby? Bem's theory offers an intriguing answer. Briefly, it predicts that under some conditions, at least, the persons involved would experience a reduction in intrinsic motivation. In short, they would no longer find these activities quite so appealing. The reason for this is as follows. Upon observing their own behavior, such "overrewarded" persons may conclude that they chose to engage in these activities partly to obtain the external rewards provided. As a result, they may then perceive their own intrinsic interest in them as lower than was previously the case. In sum, such persons may shift from explaining their behavior in terms of intrinsic motivation ("I engage in this activity because I enjoy it") to accounting for their actions in terms of external rewards ("I engage in this activity partly to obtain some external reward"). Phrased somewhat differently, such persons may have too many good reasons (justifications) for performing such behavior to view it as intrinsically motivated (please refer to Figure 2.16).

Support for this reasoning has been obtained in many different experiments (e.g., Deci, 1975; Lepper & Greene, 1978; Wilson, Hull, & Johnson, 1981). In these and other studies, subjects provided with extrinsic rewards for engaging in some task they initially enjoy later showed lower quality performance and reduced tendencies to select these behaviors over others than subjects not given such rewards. Thus, it appeared that their intrinsic interest in such tasks had in fact been reduced. Further, additional evidence suggests that such effects are most likely to occur under the conditions predicted by Bem's theory — when internal cues relating to the tasks at hand (e.g., attitudes toward them) are unclear or low in salience (Fazio, 1981).

But while it is clear that external rewards can sometimes undermine intrinsic motivation, it is equally apparent that this is not always the case. As you already know, sports heroes, rock musicians, and movie stars often receive gigantic payoffs for engaging in activities they enjoy. And their enthusiasm for football, music, or acting does not seem to be reduced by such rewards. The key

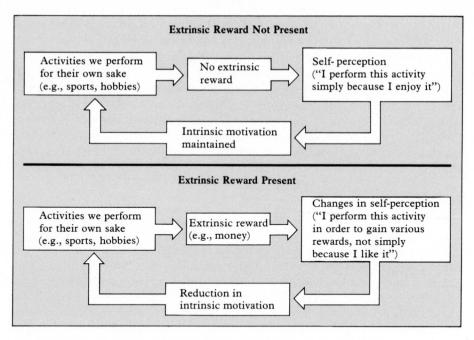

FIGURE 2.16   *Self-perception: Its role in intrinsic motivation.*

When individuals perform some activity they enjoy in the absence of extrinsic rewards, their intrinsic motivation *to engage in this behavior is maintained (upper panel). When they receive extrinsic rewards for performing this activity, however, their perceptions about why they do so may shift. As a result, their intrinsic motivation may be sharply reduced (lower panel).*

question, then, is "When, precisely, does the overjustification effect occur?" Recent studies offer some intriguing answers. First, it appears that external rewards do not reduce interest in enjoyable tasks if an individual's initial interest in it is made salient. Apparently, if we keep the built-in appeal of the activity uppermost in mind, intrinsic motivation can survive intact (Fazio, 1981). Second, if external rewards are offered as a sign of competence or effectiveness in performing some activity, they may not reduce our motivation to perform it; on the contrary, they may actually enhance intrinsic interest (Rosenfield, Folger, & Adelman, 1980). In contrast, if such rewards appear to represent an attempt to control our behavior, or increase our effort, motivation may well be reduced. For example, consider the case of an employee who loves her work and who does it so well that she receives a cash bonus from her company. If she perceives the bonus as a sign of appreciation and approval, her motivation may well be enhanced. If, instead, she perceives it as a calculated attempt to prevent her from moving to another firm, her motivation may be reduced. In short, the purpose behind the reward may be crucial. Third, it appears that substantial rewards maintain intrinsic motivation better than small or unsatisfying ones (Fiske & Taylor, 1983). And finally, whether external rewards reduce or enhance intrinsic motivation seems to depend on the initial orientation of individuals toward the tasks in question. If their orientation is largely expressive (they approach the task as valuable for its own sake), extrinsic rewards may well lower their intrinsic interest or motivation. In contrast, if their orientation is mainly instrumental (they approach the task as a means to various ends), the provision of extrinsic rewards may well *increase* intrinsic interest (Caldwell, O'Reilly, & Morris, 1983).

In sum, several factors seem to determine whether external payoffs will reduce, fail to affect, or even enhance intrinsic motivation. Given the frequency with which such rewards are used to encourage desired forms of behavior, careful attention to these conditions seems essential. After all, if they are overlooked, concrete rewards may backfire and actually *reduce* the likelihood of the actions they are designed to enhance.

Schachter's Theory of Emotion:
"You Can't Know What You Feel Until You Name It"

How do you know if you are angry or sad, happy or in love? The obvious answer is: you just know. By turning your attention inward and examining your internal states, you can determine which particular emotion you are experiencing at a given moment. Is this actually the case? Certain findings cast doubt on these assumptions. Most importantly, it has been found that the internal physiological reactions produced by a wide range of events—ones we would expect to elicit fear, anger, joy, or even sexual excitement—tend to be quite similar (Fehr & Stern, 1970). For this reason, the task of determining what emotion we are experiencing from inspection of such reactions may be more difficult than at first meets the eye. Partly on the basis of such facts, Stanley Schachter and his associates (Schachter & Singer, 1962; Schachter, 1964) proposed an alternative view of the process through which we come to know our own emotions. According to this theory, emotion-provoking events elicit internal arousal. Then, sensing this excitement, we look outward, into the external world around us, to discover the basis for its presence. The external cues we observe then lead us to select a label for our arousal. And this, in turn, determines the precise emotion we experience. For example, if we feel aroused following an insult, we label our reaction as "anger." If, in contrast, we experience arousal in the presence of an attractive member of the opposite sex, we label it as "sexual attraction." In short, we perceive ourselves as experiencing whatever emotion external cues suggest we should be experiencing (please refer to Figure 2.17).

In order to test this model of emotion, Schachter and Singer (1962) conducted an experiment in which subjects were given injections of a drug that produces heightened arousal (epinephrine). After receiving this drug, they were exposed to the actions of an accomplice who either behaved in a euphoric manner (e.g., he shot papers at a wastebasket) or demonstrated extreme anger while filling out a questionnaire. (His anger was understandable; the questionnaire contained items such as "With how many men other than your father has your mother had extramarital relationships?") Within each of these groups, some of the subjects were provided with accurate information about the effects of the drug (e.g., they were told it would raise their heart rate or cause facial flushing); others were not given such information. Schachter and Singer reasoned that because they had a ready explanation for their increased arousal,

[margin note:] Schachter's Theory of Emotion

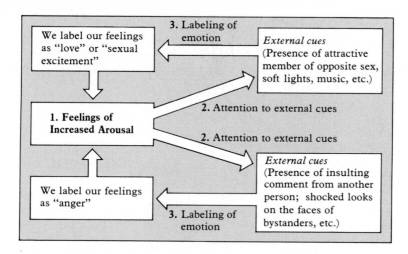

FIGURE 2.17 *Perceptions of our own emotions: The role of external cues.*

According to a theory proposed by Schachter, the emotions we experience are often affected by external cues. Briefly, the process is as follows: (1) we experience feelings of arousal; (2) we examine external cues to determine why we are experiencing such feelings; (3) we label our arousal in a manner consistent with these cues. Thus, feelings of arousal can be labeled —and interpreted—as "love" or "anger" depending on the context in which they occur.

subjects given accurate information about the impact of the drug would *not* be affected by the confederate's behavior. In contrast, those not provided with such information might use his actions as a basis for interpreting their own feelings. Results provided support for these predictions. Subjects *not* informed about the actual effects of the drug reported feeling happier when they saw the accomplice behave euphorically and angrier when they saw him demonstrate signs of irritation than subjects provided with such information.

These results, and those of several related studies, have been interpreted as offering support for Schachter's basic suggestion: feelings of arousal for which we have no ready explanation will often be interpreted in ways consistent with external cues. In all fairness, though, we should note that recent experiments raise important questions about the generality of this conclusion. For example, it appears that individuals generally interpret unexplained arousal negatively, as feelings of unease or nervousness. Thus, it may be quite difficult to induce them to interpret it in positive terms, even in the presence of appropriate external cues (e.g., Marshall & Zimbardo, 1979; Maslach, 1979). Does this mean, then, that Schachter's theory is incorrect—that we do *not* come to know our own emotions partly through external cues and the labels these suggest? This is a difficult question to answer, for existing evidence is mixed. However, taking several lines of research into account, it is our view that the following conclusion is reasonable. Schachter was at least partly correct, for in many situations, the arousal we experience in response to emotion-provoking events *is* ambiguous. In such cases, we do seem to search for clues to its meaning in the social world around us (e.g., Brodt & Zimbardo, 1981; Scheier, Carver, & Gibbons, 1979). In other cases, in contrast, our arousal is more clear-cut in nature, and here we are much less likely to interpret it largely in terms of external factors. Regardless of which situation prevails, though, it is certainly the case that, in determining how we feel, we *do* pay attention to information from external sources, as well as to feedback from within our own bodies. In this basic sense, Schachter's theory is indeed correct. (To see how knowledge about attribution and self-perception can be put to practical use, please see the **On the Applied Side** insert on pp. 76–77.)

ON THE
APPLIED SIDE

*Attribution as a Form of Therapy:
When a New Causal Framework Can Help*

Many persons suffering from emotional or behavioral problems seem to adopt an attributional perspective that intensifies their difficulties. Briefly, they assume that their fears, social anxieties, insomnia, or other symptoms stem largely from *internal* causes (e.g., defects in their own personalities, deep-seated neuroses, etc.). Once they reach such conclusions, of course, the situation may worsen; after all, they now spend many painful hours worrying about these seemingly "uncorrectable" causes (Storms & Nisbett, 1970). Can anything be done to break this unfortunate circle? Research findings suggest an encouraging answer. A number of studies indicate that major improvements can follow **attribution therapy**—i.e., when individuals are somehow induced to reattribute their problems to *external* rather than internal causes. For example, insomniacs may find it easier to get to sleep if they attribute their wakefulness to traffic noise instead of some lasting health problem. Similarly, persons suffering from intense social anxieties can sometimes function more effectively if they attribute their difficulties to the newness of their surroundings rather than to a basic inability to get along with others.

Unfortunately, however, there is a built-in problem connected with this approach. Many *external* causes of emotional problems are fairly permanent in nature. For example, traffic noise cannot be easily eliminated. And most persons cannot readily avoid situations in which they meet new people or enter new surroundings. Reattributing one's problems to external causes in such cases may not be very helpful, since these causes, too, are likely to persist. Happily, another tactic can be adopted in such situations. Individuals can be encouraged to perceive their difficulties as stemming mainly from *temporary* rather than stable causes. For example, insomniacs might be induced to believe that their

sleeplessness stems from some aspect of their diet rather than from some feature of their personality. To the extent individuals adopt such a perspective, they may become more hopeful about the possibility of future improvements. As a result, they may worry less and so actually experience substantial improvements (Weiner, 1980). Evidence for the occurrence of such beneficial effects has recently been reported by Wilson and Linville (1982).

These investigators began by identifying college freshmen who had done less well than they expected during their first semester and who were therefore quite concerned about their grades. Half of these individuals were then provided with information suggesting that their current difficulties stemmed largely from temporary causes. For example, they were informed that most students attain higher grades as they progress through college. And they watched taped interviews with juniors and seniors who reported that this had in fact been true for them. In contrast, subjects in a control condition received no information of this type. Results produced by this simple technique were quite dramatic. First, on an immediate index of performance administered at the time of the first session and again one week later (items from the Graduate Record Examination), subjects in the reattribution condition did significantly better. Second, over the next year, persons in this group showed a significant improvement in grades. In contrast, those in the control group actually showed a slight drop. And finally, while only 5 percent of those in the reattribution condition dropped out of school during the next year, fully 25 percent of those in the control group took this step (see Figure 2.18). In short, merely providing subjects with information indicating that their academic problems were the result of temporary factors produced important,

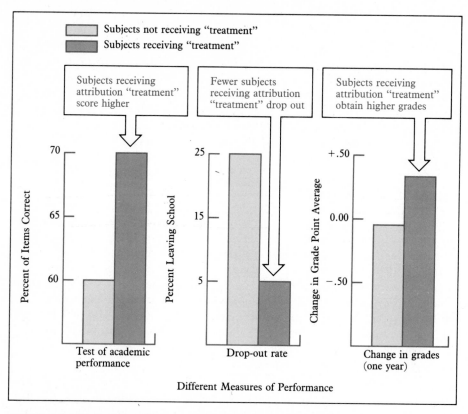

FIGURE 2.18 *Coping with one common personal problem: An attributional approach.*

When freshmen students worried about their college grades were led to believe that their current problems stemmed mainly from temporary factors, dramatic effects were produced. In contrast to other freshmen not given such "attribution therapy," such persons scored higher on a brief test of academic performance, attained higher grades during the next year, and showed a much lower rate of leaving school. Such findings suggest that techniques based on attribution can be highly effective in helping individuals cope with a wide range of personal problems. [Source: Based on data from Wilson & Linville, 1982.]

positive changes in their performance. When it is realized that these results stemmed from procedures requiring only a few minutes, they become especially impressive.

The results reported by Wilson and Linville (1982) and those obtained in related studies point to the conclusion that techniques based on attribu-

tion can often be useful in treating a wide range of personal problems. To the extent that this is in fact the case, the knowledge about this basic social process gathered by our colleagues in recent years may well turn out to be of major practical as well as scientific benefit.

Summary

In our attempts to understand the temporary causes of others' behavior — their current moods, feelings, and emotions — we often focus on **nonverbal cues.** That is, we use information provided by their facial expressions, eye contact with us, and body posture or movements as a basis for determining their current states. Such cues can be very informative, and reveal others' moods or feelings about us even in cases where they wish to conceal such knowledge. Large individual differences in the abilities to both send and "read" nonverbal cues exist. However, in general, females appear to be much better at these tasks than males.

Knowledge about the more lasting causes of others' behavior is obtained through the process of **attribution.** Here, we observe others' overt actions and from this, attempt to infer their traits, motives, and intentions. One key attributional task we face involves determining whether others' behavior stems mainly from internal or external causes. Research evidence suggests that in reaching such conclusions, we focus on information relating to three factors: *consensus, consistency,* and *distinctiveness.* In addition, we perceive the causes of others' behavior as varying along such dimensions as simple versus complex, enduring versus transient, and good versus bad. Attribution is far from a totally rational process. Indeed, it is often subject to a number of potential sources of bias. Among the most important of these are the *fundamental error,* the *actor-observer effect,* and the *self-serving bias.*

The task of understanding the causes of our own behavior is more difficult than at first meets the eye. A theory proposed by Bem suggests that often, we infer our attitudes or feelings from our overt actions. A related theory offered by Schachter argues that knowledge of our own emotions, too, is gained from external sources. Specifically, when we experience feelings of arousal we examine the world around us for possible causes of such reactions. The label suggested by external cues then determines the emotion we experience. Research findings offer support for both theories, but it appears that the processes they describe are most likely to occur in situations where our internal reactions are relatively weak or ambiguous.

Glossary

actor-observer effect   *Refers to our tendency to attribute our own behavior largely to external causes, but the behavior of others to internal causes.*

attribution   *The process through which we attempt to determine the causes of others' behavior and gain understanding of their stable traits and dispositions.*

attribution therapy   *Attempts to help individuals cope with personal problems by somehow inducing them to attribute these problems to external or temporary causes. Procedures based on this general approach have been effective in the treatment of such problems as insomnia, social anxieties, and poor grades.*

augmenting principle *Refers to our tendency to attach greater weight or importance to some causal factor if it produces an event (e.g., some type of behavior) in the presence of other, inhibitory factors.*

body language *Cues provided by the position, posture, and movement of another person's body.*

consensus *The extent to which actions shown by one person are also shown by others. Consensus is one of the factors we consider in deciding whether another person's behavior stems mainly from internal or external causes.*

consistency *The extent to which another person responds to a given stimulus in the same manner on various occasions.*

correspondent inferences *Inferences about the stable traits of others about which we have a high degree of confidence. Such inferences are often based on (1) actions producing noncommon effects, (2) behaviors others freely choose to perform, and (3) actions that are low in social desirability.*

discounting principle *Refers to our tendency to downplay the importance of a given potential cause of some behavior to the extent that other potential causes are also present.*

display rules *Rules in a given culture concerning the conditions under which it is appropriate to display various emotions. The existence of contrasting display rules in different cultures often tends to mask universality in facial expressions.*

distinctiveness *The extent to which a given person responds in a similar manner to different stimuli or in different situations. Distinctiveness is one of the key factors we consider in deciding whether another's behavior stems mainly from internal or external causes.*

emblems *Body movements that transmit a highly specific message within a given culture.*

facial feedback hypothesis *The view that our facial expressions can affect our internal physiological states, and also our subjective experiences of various emotions.*

fundamental attribution error *Refers to our tendency to overestimate the contribution of stable, internal causes to others' behavior.*

hedonic relevance *Refers to the fact that the greater the impact of another person's behavior upon us, the greater our tendency to perceive it as stemming from his or her lasting dispositions.*

intrinsic motivation *Refers to the motivation to perform various activities because they are enjoyable in themselves.*

nonverbal communication *Communication between individuals that does not involve the content of spoken language. Nonverbal communication can be based upon facial expressions, eye contact, tone of voice, and body position or movements.*

nonverbal cues *Cues provided by others' facial expressions, eye contact, body position or movement, and other sources. These can often reveal the current moods or emotions of other persons, and their liking or disliking for us.*

personalism *Refers to the fact that when we perceive another's behavior as intended to harm or benefit us, we are more likely to attribute it to stable dispositions than when we do not perceive it as seeking such goals.*

self-perception *Refers to the process through which we seek to know and understand our own feelings, traits, and motives. In short, self-perception involves our attempts to understand the causes of our own behavior.*

self-serving bias *Refers to our tendency to view positive outcomes as stemming from internal causes (e.g., our own traits), but negative outcomes as stemming largely from external ones.*

social perception *The process through which we seek to know and understand the persons around us. Social perception involves attribution, nonverbal communication, and impression formation (see Chapter 3).*

staring *Eye contact in which one person continues to gaze at another for an extended period of time, regardless of what the stared-at individual does.*

For More Information

Argyle, M., Furnham, A., & Graham, J. A. *Social situations.* Cambridge: Cambridge University Press, 1981.
   An intriguing discussion of the factors affecting behavior in social situations. The text considers many important topics, such as the informal (and often unstated) rules governing social interaction, what happens when these rules are broken, and the different goals individuals seek in various social settings. In addition, considerable attention is directed to the ways in which social situations are perceived and understood. All in all, a thoughtful and enlightening volume.

Buck, R. *Nonverbal behavior and the communication of affect.* New York: Guilford, 1984.
   A comprehensive discussion of many key aspects of

nonverbal communication. Among the topics covered are the evolution of emotion communication, the development of emotion and emotion communication, and accuracy in the use of nonverbal cues. An especially interesting chapter deals with the role of nonverbal communication in social interaction. This is a very informative and up-to-date source if you want to know more about nonverbal communication.

Druckman, D., Rozelle, R. M., & Baxter, J. C. *Nonverbal communication: Synthesis, theory, and research.* Beverly Hills, Calif.: Sage, 1982.
A briefer and less technical discussion of nonverbal communication than that contained in the text by Ross Buck. Several aspects of social perception in addition to nonverbal communication are considered (e.g., attribution, impression formation). One especially interesting topic covered is deception and how to recognize it.

Fiske, S. T., & Taylor, S. E. *Social cognition.* Reading, Mass.: Addison-Wesley, 1983.
An excellent discussion of many aspects of social perception and social cognition. The chapters on attribution are outstanding and should help you to understand the nature of this key process. The book is clearly (even charmingly) written, and presents very up-to-date coverage. We strongly recommend it.

Harvey, J. H., & Weary, G. *Perspectives on attributional processes.* Dubuque, Iowa: William C. Brown Co., 1981.
A brief and clearly written introduction to attribution. Major theories are reviewed, and important applications of attribution (e.g., to the treatment of personal problems) are described. This is an excellent source to examine if you would like to learn more about this important aspect of social perception.

CHAPTER 3

Social Cognition:
Thinking about (and Making Sense of)
the Social World

Schemata: Cognitive Frameworks for Understanding the Social World

Social Schemata: Their Nature, Origins, and Development/Social Schemata: Their Impact on Social Cognition

Social Cognition: Some Basic Processes

Attention: Beginning at the Beginning/Person Memory: Remembering Social Information/Social Inference: Reasoning about Others

Forming Impressions of Others: Social Cognition and the Integration of Social Information

Cognitive Algebra in Impression Formation: The Weighted-Average Model/ Impressions of Others: A Cognitive Perspective

Special Inserts

FOCUS ON RESEARCH
Studying Social Cognition: Methods for Measuring the Unseen

ON THE APPLIED SIDE
Errors in Social Inference: Some Unsettling, Practical Effects

FOCUS ON RESEARCH
Cognition and Affect: How Feelings Shape Thought, and Thought Shapes Feelings

The job market is very tight, so when your company advertised for a new lab technician, you were literally swamped with applications. For the past three days you and Lynn Goldsbury, the other person for whom the new employee will work, have been interviewing applicants and going over their records. You've finally managed to narrow the field to two, and right now you and Lynn are meeting to try to choose between them. Your discussions go something like this:

"Well, I really favor Ms. Chesnowski," Lynn remarks. "She has the experience we need. And from talking to her, I can see that she's very conscientious—someone we can really count on. I think she's the logical choice."

You respond with some heat. "Come on, Lynn, how can you describe her as reliable? Didn't you notice that she's had five different jobs during the past six years? You call that reliable? I don't."

Lynn looks a bit confused. "Hmmm . . . now that you mention it, I do remember that she's changed jobs a lot. But that can happen to anyone; you wouldn't want her to stay where she's unhappy, would you? Anyway, I like her and would enjoy working with her."

"Well, I've got my doubts," you reply. "Maybe you like her so much because you were in a real good mood when she interviewed. Wasn't that the day you and Hal made up?"

Lynn denies that her mood could have influenced her judgment, and your conversation continues. But after twenty minutes, it's clear that you are getting nowhere, so you agree to turn to the other candidate, William Dennings.

"Now here we've got a strong person," you begin. "Dennings really impressed me; I think he's sharp—a quick thinker if ever I saw one."

Lynn shows great surprise at this remark: "Hey, who did you *interview? Sharp? I thought he was dull, dull, dull! And his recommendations bear me out. Listen to this (she reads from one of his letters): 'While Mr. Dennings is a solid and satisfactory employee, one could never describe him as a quick study. . . .' Does that sound like someone who's bright?"*

Now it's your turn to look surprised. "Gosh, I don't remember seeing that comment. I must have missed it. . . . But anyway, he graduated from Fielding College. My first assistant was from there, and she was first-rate. I think we should keep that in mind."

"Aha!" Lynn exclaims. "A Fielding graduate! No wonder he wore that creepy tie. There's **another** *strike against him."*

At this, you both laugh. But more than an hour has passed, and it's apparent that you will not resolve matters today. With this fact in mind, you agree to study the complete files once more and to meet again tomorrow. Perhaps you'll be able to reach a decision then.

After Lynn leaves, you find yourself pondering your strange disagreement. You both interviewed the same people and worked from the same folders. Yet somehow you came up with very different impressions of the two job candidates. Why? Was it because of differences in your past experience that led you to focus on different aspects of their qualifications? Was it because you tended to remember contrasting—and nonoverlapping—facts about them? Did your mood on the days when they were interviewed really matter? These and related questions pass quickly through your mind. In fact, you are still considering them when your phone begins to ring noisily, thus signaling the resumption of your busy, hectic day.

S o far in your life you may never have had to hire a new employee. Yet even if this is so, you have certainly performed tasks similar to those faced by the two characters in our story. On many occasions you have thought about other persons in an effort to understand them and their behavior more completely. In short, you have thought about others in order to make better sense out of a confusing social world. But what, precisely, is the nature of such thought? How does it proceed? And what determines its final outcomes or conclusions? These are important questions, for **social cognition** is a key aspect of daily life. Indeed, it is hard to imagine any other activity that occurs with greater frequency than thinking about others (or ourselves; see Figure 3.1). Moreover, the outcomes of such thought have major practical effects. After all, it is through social cognition that we form judgments of others, reach decisions about them, and draw inferences about their future behavior (Higgins, Herman, & Zanna, 1981). In recent years, social psychologists have grown increasingly aware of these facts. As a result, they have turned growing attention to the topic of social thought. Indeed, at the present time, social cognition is one of the most active areas of study in our field.

As you can readily see, social cognition is closely related to social perception. After all, both topics relate to the basic processes underlying our comprehension of the social world. Yet they also differ in two key respects. First, social cognition is somewhat broader in scope. As you may recall from Chapter 2,

FIGURE 3.1 *Social cognition: A basic part of daily life.*

As suggested by this cartoon, thinking about other persons—and trying to understand them—is a very common activity. [Source: Drawing by Geo. Price; © 1982 The New Yorker Magazine, Inc.]

research on social perception focuses on a central theme: How do we come to understand the causes behind others' behavior? In contrast, research on social cognition addresses an even more basic issue: How do we think about other persons generally? In short, it seeks to determine how we notice, store, integrate, and remember social information.

Second, research on social cognition stems from somewhat different bases than research on social perception. As we saw in Chapter 2, social psychologists have long been interested in the question of how we perceive the persons around us. Thus, their work on this process is largely a "homegrown" product, closely intertwined with the history of our field. In contrast, recent interest in social cognition has been stimulated, in part, by developments outside social psychology. During the past decade, investigators studying human cognition (memory, attention, reasoning) have made extraordinary progress. Impressed with these gains, many social psychologists have sought to apply the principles, methods, and findings of such work to their own field. The results of doing so, we believe, have been both beneficial and productive (e.g., Higgins, Herman, & Zanna, 1981). But it is important to note that a number of the concepts and principles described in this chapter have, in fact, been "imported" into social psychology from other fields. For example, at several points, we will suggest that human beings often face a basic cognitive dilemma: they must deal with a vast array of complex social information, but possess only *limited capacity* for processing such input. Similarly, we will frequently refer to distinct *stages* in the overall process of social thought (e.g., the encoding, integration, and decoding of information). As you will soon see, these and other perspectives borrowed from cognitive science have proven extremely useful to social psychologists in their attempts to understand social cognition. But if you find them somewhat different in flavor from those presented in other portions of this text, don't be surprised. They are, after all, select and valuable imports! (For a discussion of several research methods developed by cognitive scientists, but ingeniously adapted by social psychologists for use in their own work, please see the **Focus on Research** section on pp. 86–87.)

As we noted earlier, research on social cognition has literally exploded in volume during the past few years. For this reason, we cannot possibly acquaint you with all of the intriguing lines of study now being actively pursued. What we *can* do, though, is offer a summary of current knowledge about several topics often viewed as being of key or central importance. Specifically, our discussion will proceed as follows. First, we will examine a basic element of social thought —the *schema*. **Schemata** are cognitive frameworks built up through experience, and as we will soon note, once developed, they often exert powerful effects upon the perception, processing, and recall of social information. Second, we will examine several basic processes within social cognition: **attention, person memory,** and **social inference.** For each, we will describe its essential nature and mention several factors that seem to affect its operation. Finally, we will turn to the manner in which information about others is combined into consistent *impressions* of them. This is a traditional topic in social psychology, but recent efforts to analyze the specific cognitive processes that underlie it have contributed greatly to our sophistication in this area.

*Studying Social Cognition:
Methods for Measuring the Unseen*

Cognitive events are internal: they occur within people's heads. How, then, can they be systematically studied? This is the basic dilemma confronting all scientists wishing to investigate the ways in which we think, remember, or decide. The most obvious solution to this puzzle is enticingly simple: why not merely ask individuals to report on their cognitive processes as these take place? The answer is equally straightforward: often, human beings are only dimly aware of such events at best (Nisbett & Ross, 1980). Thus, they can rarely describe them in useful or revealing ways. Does this mean that we must throw up our hands in despair, concluding that some aspects of human experience are forever beyond our reach? Far from it! Several other techniques for studying social thought exist, and these seem to offer a much firmer basis for comprehending this intriguing topic (Taylor & Fiske, 1981). Because such techniques are used in much of the research reported in this chapter, it is important for you to become familiar with them. Thus, we will describe several here.

Let us begin at the beginning with what is often viewed as the first step in social cognition—*attention*. How can we determine what aspects of social stimuli (e.g., their vividness, salience) cause them to become the focus of our attention? Two basic approaches exist. First, we can place individuals in a situation where they are exposed to several different stimuli at once, and permit them to focus on any of these that they choose. Under these conditions, the amount of time they spend looking at (or listening to) various materials can tell us much about the relative attention-eliciting value of these items. Second, we can provide subjects with some means of controlling the duration of their exposure to various stimuli (e.g., some type of switch; see Figure 3.2). Here, the greater the amount of time they devote to each, the greater its attention-evoking properties can be assumed to be. Unfortunately,

there is one major complication associated with these measures which you may have already noticed: all assume that people are in fact thinking about whatever they look at. If you have ever engaged in vivid daydreams while your eyes followed an instructor back and forth across the front of a room, you know that this idea can sometimes rest on very uncertain grounds. Nevertheless, in many cases, the amount of time spent by individuals in examining various stimuli does provide us with a good first guess as to the extent to which they are likely to serve as the focus of attention.

Second, consider retention or *memory*. How can we measure this key process? Again, two basic methods exist. First, we can expose individuals to social information and then, at some later time, ask them to remember as much of it as possible. This is known as *recall*. Second, we can expose subjects to social information and then, at some later time, ask them to recognize this material when it is presented together with other information they did not initially see. This is known as *recognition*. Recognition is usually easier to perform than recall, since it merely requires subjects to decide whether they have or have not seen certain items before. In contrast, recall involves both a search through memory for the required information and the decision that the items retrieved are indeed the ones desired. Both measures are useful and often help us determine the factors that affect this key aspect of social cognition.

Third, let us turn to *inference*, the process through which we combine information in order to reach some conclusion or decision. How can this complex task be rendered visible, or at least assessable in some manner? One answer involves *decision time*—the period required by individuals to draw a given inference or answer a specific question. The longer this interval, the more difficult or effortful the process is assumed to be. For example, imagine

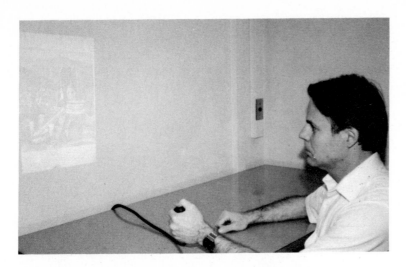

FIGURE 3.2 *Measuring attention: One technique.*

The attention-eliciting properties of various stimuli can be assessed by providing subjects with some means of controlling their duration. The longer a given stimulus is examined, the greater its attention-evoking value is assumed to be.

that subjects require more time to predict others' behavior from inconsistent information than from fully consistent information. This finding suggests that the inference process is somehow slowed by inconsistency. But decision time can often tell us much more about inference than its relative ease or difficulty. It can also provide information on the specific steps occurring within this process. For example, imagine that we have reason to assume that in inferring guilt or innocence from available evidence, individuals first add all the facts pointing toward innocence, then add all the facts pointing toward guilt, and then subtract one from the other. If this is so, providing them with information in which facts pointing toward guilt and facts pointing toward innocence have already been combined should speed their decision time. If this is actually the case, then our model of inferences in this type of situation is supported. If, instead, providing individuals with such integrated information makes no difference, our model may well be wrong. Through these and related procedures, decision times can tell us much about the nature of social inference.

Finally, we should note that additional methods, specifically designed to shed light on the *processes* involved in social cognition, also exist. One of these involves *computer simulation.* Here, a re-

searcher prepares a computer program which, he or she believes, reflects the manner in which human beings process some type of social information. Such information is fed into the program, and the inferences or judgments it yields are then compared with similar output from actual human subjects. If the computer-generated and people-generated outputs match quite closely, the researcher has some evidence for the accuracy of her or his model. If they do not, it is back to the drawing boards once again! Another technique for validating process models of social cognition involves the use of *structural equations.* Through this statistical technique researchers can determine how closely the data from their experiments conform to predictions from their models. Obviously, the closer the fit, the greater their confidence that they do in fact, understand certain aspects of human thought.

To conclude: because cognitive events and processes are hidden from direct view, the task of studying them is quite formidable. However, social psychologists have proven more than equal to this challenge, and have developed several procedures for investigating social cognition. In short, through ingenuity—and much hard work!—they have devised workable solutions to the task of rendering the unseen visible.

***FIGURE 3.3   Why is this
cartoon funny?***

*Because of prior experience (e.g.,
watching "Dallas"?) we expect
Texans to be tall. In other words,
our* **schema** *for members of this
group includes "tallness" as one of
their major attributes. It is the
violation of this expectation that
makes the scene shown here mildly
amusing. [Source: © 1983;
reprinted courtesy of Bill Hoest.]*

"No, I'm the one from Rhode Island . . . he's from Texas."

Schemata: Cognitive Frameworks
for Understanding the Social World

Look at the cartoon in Figure 3.3. Why, precisely, is it amusing? (If you are
from Texas or Rhode Island, please don't take offense; the cartoon is meant to
be humorous, nothing more!) The answer, we believe, lies in what this drawing
suggests about the nature of social thought. Briefly, it reminds us that often, our
perceptions of other persons (or our inferences about them) are strongly
affected by our past experience. In this particular case, direct contact with
Texans or watching television shows such as "Dallas" has taught us that Texans
are tall—or at least are supposed to be tall. Thus, when confronted with two
strangers, one large and the other small, we quickly jump to the conclusion that
the tall one is the representative of the Lone Star State.

Needless to add, such effects are by no means restricted to the task of
guessing others' home states (or provinces). On the contrary, they appear to be
quite general in scope (Fiske & Linville, 1980). In fact, growing evidence
suggests that we rarely receive social information in a totally passive manner.
Instead, such input is usually filtered, organized, and interpreted through
existing cognitive structures—ones that are already firmly in place when it
arrives. These structures—usually known as *schemata*—reflect our past experience with the social world. And once they are established, they tend to exert
profound effects upon key aspects of our social thought, as well as upon our
behavior (Fiske & Taylor, 1983; Hastie, 1981). We will consider some of these

important effects below. Before doing so, however, we will comment briefly on the nature and development of social schemata.

Social Schemata: Their Nature, Origins, and Development

In the most general sense, schemata can be viewed as something akin to *cognitive scaffolds within our minds.* That is, they are frameworks, built up through experience, that help provide order, structure, and organization for new incoming information. In more precise terms, then, social schemata can be defined as *richly interconnected networks of information relevant to various concepts,* (i.e., various aspects of the social world; Fiske & Linville, 1980). These networks, in turn, are abstracted from experience with specific instances of the concepts in question. Perhaps a concrete example will help clarify these comments (and help provide you with a schema for interpreting and understanding schemata!).

Throughout your life, you have met many elderly persons—individuals in their 60's, 70's, and 80's. Each of these individuals, of course, was unique, as are all human beings. Yet, if you were now asked to describe "the elderly," you would probably have little difficulty in doing so. Why? The answer seems to be that, on the basis of all your experience with older persons, you have abstracted a general notion of what it means to fall within this category—what it means to be elderly (Brewer, Dull, & Lui, 1981). Included in this knowledge structure might be a list of the *traits* you assume older persons possess (low energy, conservative political views), several *behaviors* you believe they often show (staying at home, puttering in the garden), and notions about their *physical appearance* (they have grey hair, wrinkled skin). Together, these interconnected ideas and pieces of information constitute a *schema*—your personal cognitive framework for understanding and thinking about the members of one important social group (see Figure 3.4). (At this point, we should mention that together, your ideas of the characteristics of the typical elderly person also constitute a **prototype.** Prototypes are cognitive structures quite similar in nature to schemata. However, while schemata specify general expectations about the features shown by typical category members, prototypes go a bit further: they specify the single best example of that category. For example, many persons, showing a wide range of traits, might fit within your schema for the elderly. However, your prototype for such persons—the clearest or best example you can imagine—might resemble the silver-haired, smiling grandmothers or grandfathers often shown in elementary school texts. While they do differ in these and other ways, prototypes and schemata are closely related, so these terms are often used interchangeably in the literature on social cognition. For this reason, we will not distinguish sharply between them here.)

In a similar manner, you might develop separate schemata for the members of various ethnic and racial groups, for persons in different occupations, and even for the two sexes. All of these knowledge structures would constitute what social psychologists term **role schemata**—frameworks for handling information about the members of broad social groups. As we will

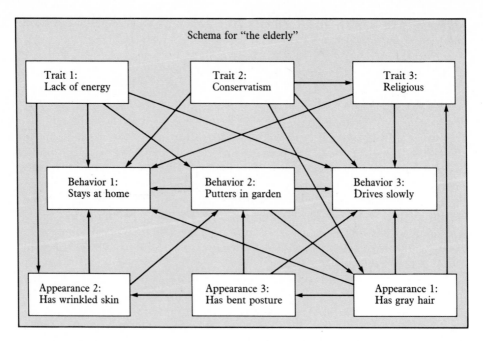

FIGURE 3.4   *One social schema.*

A particular person might have a schema *for "the elderly" similar to the one shown here. Such a schema would include several traits (e.g., conservatism, lack of energy), specific behaviors (e.g., staying at home, puttering in the garden), and notions about the physical appearance of such persons (e.g., they have wrinkles, grey hair). All of this information would be richly interconnected (as suggested by the many arrows).*

note in this chapter, and again in Chapter 5, schemata of this type are of major importance, for they relate closely to stereotypes and prejudice (Hamilton, 1981). But although they are important, they are far from the only type of schemata we possess; several others exist as well.

First, we also possess such cognitive frameworks for specific traits, and for goals or perspectives relating to various aspects of social behavior. For example, with respect to traits, most of us develop schemata for such important individual characteristics as friendliness, arrogance, ambition, and irritability. On the basis of experience with many persons, we come to know what such traits are like, how they can be recognized, and how they relate to one another. In a similar manner, we may develop schemata for certain goal orientations or outlooks on social life. Thus, most of us have a fairly clear conception of the "hard-driving, future-executive type," "the jock," and the "playboy/playgirl." When frameworks of this sort are applied to particular individuals (or are used to represent them), they are termed **person schemata.** They then refer to traits or other characteristics possessed by specific persons, regardless of their membership in various social groups.

Second, we often develop what have been termed **self-schemata.** As this term suggests, these are cognitive frameworks relating to our own traits or behavior (Markus & Sentis, 1982; Rogers, Kuiper, & Kirker, 1977). In order to understand their operation, simply ask yourself the following questions: Are you honest? Kind? Lazy? Sexy? Most of us have little difficulty in answering. This is because during our lives, we have many opportunities on which to observe our own behavior and feelings, and also because we receive a great deal of social input from others. On the basis of such experience we usually form a stable conception of our own personality along many different dimensions. The word "many" should not be read as "all," however. Because our life histories are unique, none of us have the opportunity to assess our characteristics on all potentially relevant dimensions. Thus, while our self-schema may be clear and well-developed with respect to certain traits, it may remain ambiguous or unclear in terms of others. In any case, once self-schemata take shape, they strongly affect the manner in which we perceive and process new information pertaining to ourselves.

Finally, we also possess **event schemata** or **scripts.** These are cognitive structures reflecting the normal or usual course of events in various familiar situations or are views of these situations themselves (e.g., Bower, Black, & Turner, 1979; Schank & Abelson, 1977). For example, on the basis of wide experience, most of us know what to expect in job interviews, at parties, or during visits to restaurants. We generally know how people will behave in such settings, and also how this behavior will unfold across time. Thus, when such expectations are violated, we often find the situation curiously disturbing. For example, imagine how you would react if, at a restaurant, a waiter asked for your order without showing you the menu. Similarly, consider your feelings if, at a party, a stranger asked you to come to his or her apartment without first talking to you for at least several minutes. In both cases you would probably be quite upset, and for good reason: the persons involved are clearly failing to play by the rules—that is, they are not behaving in accordance with your internal cognitive scripts for such situations.

By now we assume you are convinced of both the common occurrence and importance of social schemata. And if you need further proof in this regard, the next section, in which we consider the impact of these frameworks on social cognition, should provide it. For the moment, though, let us consider another issue. Granted that schemata are a basic fact of social thought, what, precisely do they buy us? In other words, what benefits do they confer? The answer to this question involves a basic fact about social cognition: *in our attempts to make sense out of social reality, we generally seem to seek simplicity.* That is, we often attempt to understand what is in fact a very complex world by simplifying it. To the extent this principle holds—and a great deal of evidence suggests that it does—schemata actually buy us quite a lot (Fiske & Linville, 1980). Briefly, they often save us a great deal of cognitive work or effort. Once they are developed, they spare us the task of having to make sense out of the same stimuli and events over and over again. To see why this is so, consider the following questions: What are blacks/whites/teenagers/social psychologists really like? What can we expect to happen on a first date? How can we recognize an honest person when we meet one? Schemata provide ready answers to these questions and to a host of others. So, in brief, they appear to offer substantial benefits from the perspective of enhanced cognitive efficiency: life (or at least social thought) is easier with them than without them. But please take note: efficiency is not the same thing as accuracy, and a quick answer is not always the best one. In their overall impact, then, schemata are actually something of a mixed bag. To understand why this is so, let us turn to a discussion of their specific effects on several aspects of social cognition.

Social Schemata: Their Impact on Social Cognition

How, precisely, do schemata affect social cognition? The answer is: in many different ways. Indeed, research findings suggest that it may be hard to find any aspect of social thought that is *not* strongly influenced by these lasting cognitive frameworks (e.g., Hastie et al., 1980; Hastie, 1983; Wyer & Gordon, 1982). Since space limitations prevent us from examining all of these effects, however, we will focus primarily on those that have usually been viewed as among the most general and important. Specifically, we will consider the impact of social schemata upon (1) perceptions of others' behavior, (2) selective attention to certain types of information, and (3) memory for the behavior and characteristics of others.

Schemata and perception: In examining the social world, do we "see" only what we expect? It is often said that people see the world through different eyes. What this statement implies, of course, is that our perceptions of the people and events around us are filtered—or sometimes distorted—by our own unique perspectives. Since these outlooks on the world, in turn, are shaped by our past experience, it seems reasonable to suggest that schemata may often play a role in such effects. That is, we may frequently interpret the social world in ways suggested by (and consistent with) these cognitive frameworks. For example, once we label another person as possessing some key trait, we may tend to perceive all of his or her actions as consistent with our schema for this characteristic. Similarly, after we develop a role schema for the members of some social group, we may perceive all of their actions as confirming this framework. Clear and unsettling evidence for the occurrence of just such effects has recently been reported by Sagar and Schofield (1980).

These investigators wished to examine the possibility that because the schemata for blacks and whites held by many individuals in the United States differ, the behavior of persons belonging to these two groups would also be perceived in different terms. Specifically, they predicted that because the schema for blacks contains more negative traits and information than the corresponding schema for whites, ambiguous actions by blacks might well be viewed as meaner or more threatening than identical behaviors by whites. In order to test this possibility, black and white boys in the sixth grade of various schools were given verbal descriptions and shown drawings of four different ambiguous actions (e.g., one student bumping into another in the hall; one student poking another in class). In half of the cases, the person performing these actions was black, while in the remainder he was white. After receiving these descriptions and information, subjects were asked to rate how well various

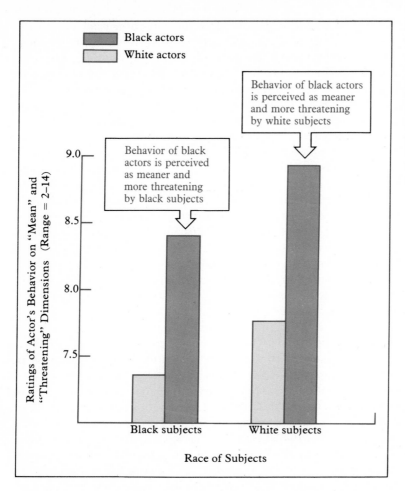

FIGURE 3.5 *Schemata: Their impact on perception.*

Both black and white children perceived ambiguous actions as being meaner and more threatening when performed by blacks than when performed by whites. These findings illustrate the powerful impact of schemata (in this case, ones relating to race) upon social perception. [Source: Based on data from Sagar & Schofield, 1980.]

Figure content labels: Black actors; White actors. Box: "Behavior of black actors is perceived as meaner and more threatening by white subjects". Box: "Behavior of black actors is perceived as meaner and more threatening by black subjects". Y-axis: Ratings of Actor's Behavior on "Mean" and "Threatening" Dimensions (Range = 2–14), with marks 9.0, 8.5, 8.0, 7.5. X-axis: Black subjects, White subjects; Race of Subjects.

adjectives described the actors' behavior (e.g., to what extent was it playful, friendly, mean, threatening). As you can see from Figure 3.5, a clear pattern of findings emerged. Both black and white children rated the ambiguous behaviors as considerably meaner and more threatening when performed by black than white actors.

When it is recalled that the behaviors observed by subjects were identical in all cases, these results take on added significance. Indeed, when combined with similar findings in several other studies, they point to the conclusion that often, our perceptions of others' behavior can be powerfully affected by existing schemata. And the process, unfortunately, does not always stop there. Once we perceive others as behaving in certain ways, or as possessing specific traits, we may adjust our own actions so as to take account of these "facts." This, in turn, may initiate an important type of self-fulfilling process. The result: we more or less induce the persons around us to behave in ways that confirm our expectations. For this and other reasons, the powerful impact of schemata upon our perceptions of the social world should not be overlooked.

Schemata and selective attention: On the search for confirming evidence. Schemata do not generally emerge overnight; rather, they are constructed on the
basis of repeated experiences with members of different groups, persons possessing certain traits, and a wide range of social situations. Further, as we noted
earlier, once they are developed, they save us a great deal of cognitive work.
Given these facts, it seems only reasonable to assume that <u>schemata will usually</u>
<u>be quite resistant to change.</u> And in fact, this is the case. Indeed, they tend to
alter slowly, if at all, even in the face of contradictory evidence (e.g., Anderson,
Lepper, & Ross, 1980). One reason for such perseverance involves our tendency to discount inconsistent information — to see it as unreliable or uncertain
(Lord, Ross, & Lepper, 1979). Another concerns selective attention. Often,
information relevant to our schemata (and, perhaps, especially our self-schema)
seems to serve as the center of our attention more readily than other information. Indeed, recent findings suggest that this may occur in an *automatic*
manner — without any conscious intent on our part to focus on such input
(Bargh, 1982). In addition, we seem to direct more of our attention to evidence
serving to confirm our schemata than to evidence tending to refute them. An
experiment conducted by Swann and Read (1981) clearly illustrates this fact.

These investigators reasoned that when given a choice between information that is consistent with their self-concept (i.e., their self-schema) and information that is inconsistent with this concept, individuals will tend to choose the
former. After all, by doing so, they can strengthen or bolster their internal
picture of their own traits and characteristics. In order to test this possibility,
Swann and Read first asked subjects to complete a brief questionnaire on which
they rated themselves on several traits. Two of these were crucial: assertiveness
and emotionality. On the basis of subjects' self-ratings, they were divided into
four groups: *self-assertives, self-unassertives, self-emotionals,* and *self-unemotionals.*
At this point, participants were informed that the study was concerned with
how people get acquainted, and it was further explained that their self-ratings
would now be shown to another subject who would answer a series of questions
about them. Subjects were then given two lists, supposedly containing the
questions this other person would answer, and were asked to choose the five
from each that they would most like to see. The questions on one list dealt with
assertiveness. Moreover, half of these items were stated in terms that would
yield feedback confirming the presence of this trait (e.g., "What makes you
think that this . . . person . . . will complain in a restaurant . . . ?"). The
remainder were stated in terms that would tend to confirm the absence of this
trait (e.g., "What leads this person not to complain when the neighbors are too
loud?"). Questions on the second list, in contrast, dealt with emotionality. And
again, half were stated so as to provide feedback confirming this trait (e.g.,
"What about this person makes you think that he or she would go to pieces if a
friend died?"), and half were stated in terms that would tend to confirm its
absence (e.g., "Why do you think that this person doesn't get angry, even when
provoked?"). It was predicted that in their choices participants would tend to
select questions whose answers would lend support to their own self-concepts.
Thus, assertive individuals would select items suggesting that they are in fact
assertive, while nonassertive persons would choose questions offering feedback

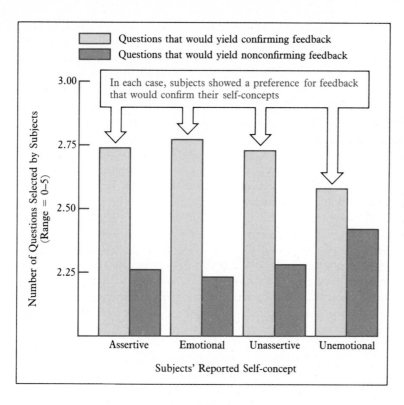

Questions that would yield confirming feedback

Questions that would yield nonconfirming feedback

In each case, subjects showed a preference for feedback that would confirm their self-concepts

Number of Questions Selected by Subjects (Range = 0–5)

3.00

2.75

2.50

2.25

Assertive   Emotional   Unassertive   Unemotional

Subjects' Reported Self-concept

FIGURE 3.6 *Self-schemata and the search for confirming feedback.*

When given a choice between feedback that would confirm or not confirm their self-concepts (their self-schemata), subjects showed a marked preference for the former. Thus, assertive and emotional persons chose feedback that would confirm these traits, while nonassertive and unemotional subjects chose feedback that would confirm these *self-concepts. [Source: Based on data from Swann & Read, 1981.]*

that they are indeed low on this trait. As you can see from Figure 3.6, evidence in favor of this hypothesis was obtained. In general, subjects did tend to express a preference for those questions most likely to confirm their self-schemata.

Needless to add, these findings have important implications. Briefly, they indicate that our self-schema, once established, becomes something of a tightly closed system. We tend to discount or reject information inconsistent with it and instead actively search for evidence that confirms its overall accuracy. Moreover, other findings (Swann & Read, 1981) suggest that we actually tend to view such self-confirming input as more informative than feedback that does not bolster our self-schema in this fashion. Given the importance of obtaining an accurate grasp of our own traits and abilities, it is clear that these tendencies can sometimes be costly ones. Indeed, in extreme cases, they totally prevent us from gaining valuable insights into our own uniqueness.

Schemata and memory: Remembering what we already "know." Suppose that you go to a party and, while there, have a brief conversation with an honest-to-goodness sea captain—the first you have ever met. Several days later, one of your friends asks what this person was really like. Your reply: "Salty, very salty." Assuming you are not simply trying to be funny, this statement—and other aspects of your description of the captain—might well illustrate another key fact about schemata: often they exert powerful effects upon our memory. Specifically, we usually seem to remember information that is relevant to these cognitive frameworks (either consistent or inconsistent) better than information that is unrelated to them (e.g., Cohen, 1982; Hastie & Kumar, 1979). Moreover, in some cases, we seem to "remember" such information even when it wasn't really present! Returning to the saga of the sea captain, you probably possess a well-developed schema for members of this profession, built up through countless Hollywood epics and sea stories. Thus, when asked to remember what an actual sea captain is like, your memory might well be strongly influenced by this framework. Such effects have actually been noted in several experiments (e.g., Rothbart, Evans, & Fulero, 1979). For example, in one such study (Cohen, 1981), male and female subjects watched brief video-tapes in which a husband and wife celebrated the wife's birthday. Before viewing the tape, half of the subjects were informed that the woman was a librarian, while the remainder were told that she was a waitress. Immediately after the tape ended, some subjects answered a number of questions designed to test their memory for information it contained. Other subjects, in contrast, did not answer these questions until four or seven days later. Results were clear: participants tended to remember more information consistent with their schemata for the woman's supposed occupation than information inconsistent with

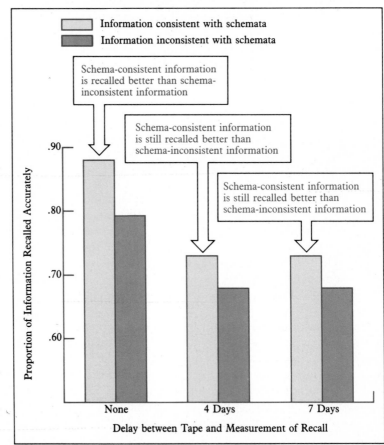

FIGURE 3.7   *Schemata: Their*
impact on social memory.

After viewing a brief videotape in which a woman interacted with her husband, subjects recalled more information consistent with their schemata of her supposed occupation (librarian or waitress) than information not consistent with these cognitive frameworks. Moreover, this was true regardless of whether they tried to recall this material immediately after the tape or several days later. [Source: Based on data from Cohen, 1981.]

these cognitive frameworks. Moreover, this was true regardless of when subjects answered the questions (see Figure 3.7). Since the content of the tape was carefully arranged so that the woman actually demonstrated an equal number of behaviors and traits typically attributed to librarians and waitresses, these results point to a powerful—and persistent—impact of schemata upon memory.

Social schemata: Summing up. To conclude: schemata seem to exert strong and pervasive effects upon social cognition. They influence our interpretation of events we observe, focus our attention on certain aspects of the social world, and influence our memory for the behavior and traits of other persons. In these and other ways, our past experience—and the lasting cognitive structures it yields—can often shape our current understanding of the persons around us, and of ourselves.

Social Cognition: Some Basic Processes

Cognition is anything but static. Indeed, it makes far more sense to view it as a rushing stream, filled with swirls, eddies, and cross-currents, than as a placid lake, in which little change occurs even over long periods of time. To fully understand social thought, in brief, we must grasp the ways in which it develops, grows, and changes. Recognition of this important fact has led social psychologists to detailed study of three processes that contribute greatly to the dynamic nature of social cognition: *attention, memory,* and *inference.*

Attention: *Beginning at the Beginning*

Before social information can be understood or processed, it must somehow be brought from the "outside" to the "inside." That is, it must be incorporated into our cognitive system or *encoded.* But before this can occur, another, even more basic, step must take place: the information must become the focus of our *attention;* we must notice it in some manner (Bargh, 1982). In a key sense, then, attention is truly the start of the entire process. But what aspects of social stimuli lead them to attract our attention? And what are the effects of such focus on other aspects of social thought? Answers to these and related questions have begun to emerge from ongoing research.

What do we tend to notice? The effects of salience and vividness. One day you go to the beach. Thousands of people are present, lying in the sun or paddling in the water, but you quickly focus on one: a young woman who, in contrast to every other female in sight, has decided to go topless. A few days later, you visit another beach and see the same young woman. In this case, though, almost every other female present is dressed in the same manner. Will you be as likely to notice her again? Probably not. This simple example illustrates a basic fact about attention. In general, we tend to notice stimuli that are *salient*—ones that somehow stand out from other persons or objects also present on the scene (McArthur, 1981). And several different factors seem to contribute to such

FIGURE 3.8   Salience: A basic principle of effective advertising.

Ads that are novel or unusual are the ones most likely to catch our attention. © 1982 Time Inc., courtesy Fortune.Reprinted by permission.

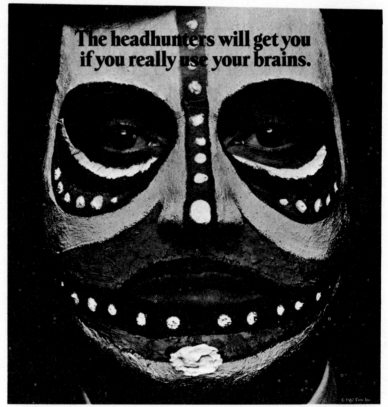

The headhunters will get you if you really use your brains.

Put all your smarts to work and pretty soon you'll be the one the executive searchers are searching for.

Encourage it. The more headhunters on your trail, the faster you'll get to the top.

The nice thing is, you don't have to hide your ambition under a bushel anymore.

Now you can be up-front about your drive for success. That's what the fast track is all about.

If you're a fast-tracker, your business reading undoubtedly starts with FORTUNE.

It's where you get the help you need to make the most out of your brains.

It's the authority. The horse's mouth. The last word. It's the source you rely on when you've *got* to be right.

In marketing, management, technology, the works—FORTUNE's where you get a vital couple of steps on the competition.

It's how to make it—and keep it.

And for advertising to the fast-track people, there's nothing else like FORTUNE.

Absolutely nothing!

FORTUNE
How to succeed.

salience. For example, we tend to notice stimuli that are somehow novel, extreme, colorful, and large to a greater extent than stimuli that are ordinary, moderate, dull, or small. These principles are well-known to advertisers, of course, who use them to good advantage to capture and hold our interest (please refer to Figure 3.8).

But salience is not the only factor that counts where attention is concerned. Some findings point to the view that *vividness, too, is important* (Nisbett & Ross, 1980). This generally refers to the emotion-provoking, imagery-inducing properties of a stimulus; and again, the greater the degree to which persons or objects possess such properties, the more likely they are to attract and hold our attention. Thus, for example, an ad depicting a horrible automobile crash, with injured victims strewn all over the ground, would generally be more likely to grip our attention than one simply presenting a graph illustrating a rise in the number of such events. Somewhat surprisingly, though, the impact of vividness seems to be weaker and less consistent than that of salience (Taylor & Thompson, 1982). And this factor also seems to exert weaker or more tenuous effects on later aspects of social cognition (e.g., Reyes, Thompson, & Bower, 1980). Perhaps this is due in part to the fact that vivid stimuli, by eliciting strong emotions, actually divert attention away from a portion of the information they contain. Whatever the cause, however, salience seems to be somewhat more important in attracting our attention than mere vividness.

At this point we should note that attention is not simply "pulled from without" by the characteristics of various stimuli (salience or vividness). While this is true in many cases, there also seems to be a conscious component to this process. That is, we can, in fact, consciously choose to direct our attention to certain aspects of the social world rather than others (Bargh, 1982). Thus, even in its initial step, social cognition is far from a passive process.

Attention: What are its effects? Since attention is a necessary first step in social cognition, it is only reasonable to assume that it will affect later stages of this process. Generally, this is the case. For example, salient stimuli do seem to affect our judgments of people or events to a greater degree than nonsalient stimuli (Harvey et al., 1980). And this makes good sense; after all, it is difficult to form an opinion of a person or event if we have not even noticed their presence. Similarly — but more surprisingly — attention exerts powerful effects upon our perceptions of causality. Briefly, when we search the social world for the factors behind some action or event, those stimuli that attract our attention tend to get the nod. For example, the people we notice most in a group are the ones we view as being most influential (Taylor & Fiske, 1978). And behavior that catches our attention is often perceived as being especially revealing about another's underlying dispositions (Fiske, Kenney, & Taylor, 1982). In short, we tend to "see" causality wherever we focus our attention.

Finally, stimuli to which we direct our attention (often ones high in salience) tend to elicit more extreme evaluations generally than stimuli to which we devote less attention (McArthur, 1981). This tendency, in turn, can exert important effects upon social perception. For example, one recent study suggests that if we expect another person to be highly susceptible to influence, focusing our attention upon him strengthens our impression that he is, indeed, a "pushover" (Strack, Erber, & Wicklund, 1982). As Taylor and Fiske (1983) have noted, then, the stimuli to which we direct our attention *do* seem to become "larger than life." In sum, attention plays an important role in social cognition, and recent experiments have begun to clarify the nature of these effects.

Self-focused attention: The effects of looking inward. Before concluding our discussion of attention, we should comment briefly on one additional fact: the external world is not the only focus of our interest. Often, we direct our attention *inward,* and concentrate upon ourselves. What are the effects of this process? Originally, researchers studying such self-focused attention assumed that it produced three major results. First, such attention (*objective self-awareness*) leads us to compare ourselves to our own internal ideals and standards. Second, since we generally fall short of these ideals, self-attention is usually aversive (Wicklund, 1975). Finally, since it is unpleasant, we generally seek to avoid it; if this cannot be accomplished, however, we may make strenuous efforts to live up to our ideals — to close the gap between what we are and what we feel we should be. Initial findings offered some support for the accuracy of this view (Gibbons & Wicklund, 1976). However, more recent experiments suggest the need for certain modifications in it.

Briefly, it now appears that when we focus our attention inward (perhaps because we see our image in a mirror, or because something another person says or does causes us to think about our own internal standards) we don't necessarily find ourselves lacking. Sometimes we *do* note a gap between our current behavior and our ideals. But on other occasions, we may find that we are actually doing quite well; indeed, we may even be *exceeding* these standards rather than falling short of them (Carver & Scheier, 1981). For this reason, we do not necessarily find self-attention aversive, nor always seek to avoid it. Instead, shifting our focus inward seems to stimulate a continuing *adjustment process*, in which we compare our behavior to our internal standards, adjust it in some manner, and then begin the process over again. Only if such adjustments are impossible — that is, if it is clear that we cannot gain closer approach to our

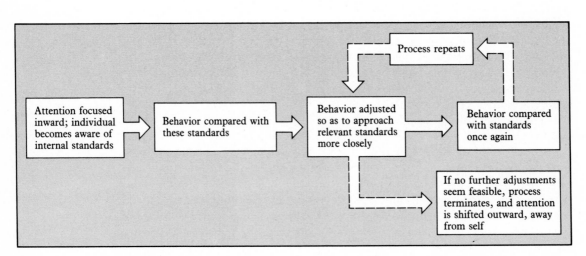

FIGURE 3.9   *Self-focused attention: Some basic effects.*

When individuals focus their attention inward, they become aware of their internal standards. They then enter an adjustment process in which they attempt to alter their behavior so as to bring it into closer alignment with these standards. Once such adjustments are made, they compare their behavior to the standards once again. The process continues until individuals are satisfied that their behavior and standards match, or they become convinced that no further adjustments in this direction are possible. [Source: Based on a model suggested by Carver & Scheier, 1981.]

internal standards—will we tend to withdraw from self-attention (please refer to Figure 3.9). A large body of research findings offer support for this general view (e.g., Scheier & Carver, 1982), and we will touch on such work in several later sections of this text. For the moment, though, we wish to note just one major implication it suggests: conditions that lead individuals to focus their attention inward may often increase the consistency between their attitudes and values on the one hand, and their overt behavior on the other. Since such consistency plays a key role in many aspects of social behavior, it is clear that self-attention has important and far-reaching effects. (We will return to the relationship between attitudes and behavior in Chapter 4.)

Person Memory: Remembering Social Information

Do you remember your first love? Your first teacher? Your first boss? In all probability, you met and interacted with these people years in the past. Yet, when you try to bring them to mind today, you probably experience little difficulty in doing so. With just a bit of effort, you can vividly recall their appearance, their traits, and several of their behaviors (especially ones directed toward you!). Clearly, then, we have an impressive capacity for remembering information about other persons. Indeed, such memories can persist largely unchanged for many years—even across an entire lifespan. From a practical point of view, our ability to retain such knowledge is very fortunate. On many occasions, we are asked to make decisions or judgments about other individuals, and at such times they are rarely present "in the flesh." For example, none of the candidates are present when we step into a voting booth. Similarly, job applicants are usually absent when we choose between them. And even potential lovers or lifetime mates may be far away when we weigh their proposals. In these and countless other instances, then, being able to recall information about others is of great practical significance. But how, specifically, do we accomplish this task? What kind of information do we actually store in person memory? And what factors enhance or interfere with its successful operation? These are only a few of the intriguing questions examined by social psychologists in recent years, and we will touch on all of them here.

What? *The contents of person memory.* Potentially, there is an almost limitless range of things we could remember about others. After all, human beings are extremely complex and vary along virtually every dimension one can imagine. In fact, though, person memory seems to consist mainly of information about others' *appearance, behavior,* and *traits.*

Interestingly, when asked to describe another person, most individuals begin with physical appearance, and only then move on to traits and behaviors (Fiske & Taylor, 1983). This suggests that despite many warnings to the contrary, we do pay much attention to the way others look. (In this regard, please see our discussion of the effects of physical beauty in Chapter 6.) Generally, our memory for others' appearance is quite good; after meeting someone, even briefly, we can often recognize them weeks or even months later. Yet, research on the accuracy of eyewitness testimony suggests that we do make important errors in this respect (Loftus, 1979). In particular, many people find it far more difficult to recognize persons from outside their own racial or ethnic group than persons from within it (Brigham et al., 1982). Thus, good as it may be, memory for others' appearance is far from perfect. (We will return to this topic in Chapter 5.)

Information about others' traits and behaviors is often organized into richly interconnected knowledge structures known as *schemata.* Since we have already described these and their effects in some detail, we will not return to them here. Suffice it to say that once these structures are developed, they play an important role in memory and may often aid us in recalling the traits or actions of specific persons.

In sum, person memory seems to consist primarily of knowledge about others' appearance, their observable behaviors, and their major traits. Moreover, the contents of such memory are not left to float about in a jumbled mass. Rather, they appear to be tightly structured around lasting cognitive frameworks (i.e., schemata).

Person memory: Some major factors. In general, our memory for other persons is quite impressive. Yet all of us have encountered acute embarrassment in situations where a total stranger steps up to us and says: "Hi, remember me? We met at . . . ." Such incidents call our attention to a crucial fact about person memory: good as it is, it is far from infallible. Indeed, sometimes it can let us down quite badly. This fact, in turn, raises our next question: what conditions influence its operation? In short, what variables either enhance or impair our ability to remember information about others? Research findings point to some intriguing answers.

Organized impressions, or isolated facts? The role of task instructions in person memory. Suppose that before meeting another person for the first time, you were specifically told either to form an overall impression of her, or to try to remember as many details as possible about what she said and did. In which case would you be able to recall more information about her? Surprisingly, the results of several experiments suggest that you would probably do much better under the first condition than under the second (e.g., Hamilton, Katz, & Leirer, 1980; Wyer & Gordon, 1982). For example, in the study conducted by Hamilton and his colleagues (1980), subjects read a series of sentences describing a stranger's behavior (e.g., this person read the evening newspaper; cleaned house before company came). In one condition, participants were told to try to form an overall impression of this individual from the descriptions. In another, they were asked to remember the exact wording of each sentence they read. Later, both groups attempted to recall as many of these brief descriptions as possible. As you can see from Figure 3.10, those given the impression-formation set did considerably better than those given the memory instructions. Moreover, this was true in two different experiments, conducted with separate groups of subjects.

At first glance, these results may seem puzzling. Why would individuals told to form an overall impression of a stranger actually recall more facts about this person than subjects told merely to memorize such information? The

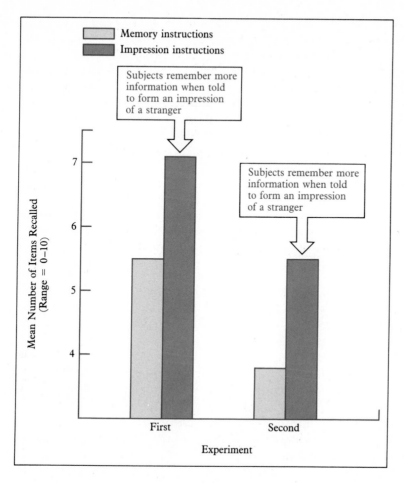

Memory instructions
Impression instructions

Subjects remember more information when told to form an impression of a stranger

Subjects remember more information when told to form an impression of a stranger

Mean Number of Items Recalled (Range = 0–10)

7

6

5

4

First   Second

Experiment

FIGURE 3.10   *The impact of task instructions on person memory.*

Subjects told to form an overall impression of a stranger were later able to remember more information about this person than subjects told to memorize the exact wording of sentences about him/her. Further, this was the case in two separate experiments, conducted with different groups of participants. [Source: Based on data from Hamilton, Katz, & Leirer, 1980.]

answer seems to lie in the beneficial impact of *organization* upon memory. In general, information that is organized into a coherent whole is easier to remember than information not structured in this manner (Smith, Adams, & Schorr, 1978). Applying this principle to the results just outlined, a clear explanation emerges. Since individuals in the impression-formation group sought to develop an integrated "picture" of the fictitious stranger, they could profit from the beneficial impact of organization. In contrast, those in the memory condition, who merely tried to remember isolated facts about the stranger, could not. In short, the difference in overall performance between the two groups can be understood in these terms.

The findings reported by Hamilton et al. (1980) and several other researchers point to an intriguing conclusion about our behavior in many real-life settings: often we do the right thing. That is, when we meet new persons for the first time, we generally concentrate on forming integrated impressions of them, *not* upon memorizing specific facts about their appearance, behavior, or traits. And as we have just seen, this may be an effective strategy for maximizing our later recall of information about them.

Priming: The effects of category accessibility on person memory. Suppose that right after watching the movie *E.T.*, you went to a party and met someone who had recently moved to your town from very far away (another state or even another country). Do you think you might be more likely to notice (and later remember) signs of homesickness on the part of this individual at that time than if you met him on some other occasion? A growing body of research evidence suggests that this might well be the case. Apparently, when we encounter other persons, the precise things we notice and remember about them can be strongly affected by the particular portions of our memory (i.e., *categories*) that are active or *accessible*. Thus, if our category for "homesickness" or "loneliness" is active, we are likely to remember information relating to these behaviors; if, instead, our categories for "hostility" or "passion" are active (perhaps because we have just seen another kind of movie) we are more likely to notice and remember *these* types of information. Such effects are often described as **priming.** Briefly, they refer to the fact that events or conditions that render a particular memory category accessible may affect our later recall of social information relating to that category.

Convincing evidence for the occurrence of such effects has been gathered in many studies (e.g., Higgins, King, & Mavin, 1982; Higgins, Rholes, & Jones, 1977). As an example of this research, let us consider a well-known investigation conducted by Srull and Wyer (1980).

In this study, male and female students first performed a sentence construction task designed to prime one of their memory categories—hostility. The task involved constructing simple sentences from four words, and a total of fifty items was included. In one case, fifteen of these were suggestive of hostility (e.g., leg break arm his), while the remainder were neutral in content (e.g., her found know I). In another condition, thirty-five of the fifty items were suggestive of hostility. Srull and Wyer predicted that the greater the number of priming items included, the stronger the effect of this variable on subjects' person memory. After completing the sentence task, participants in both groups read a paragraph describing the behavior of a stranger. The information it contained was quite neutral with respect to the trait previously primed (hostility). Finally, all subjects rated the imaginary stranger on a number of dimensions, several of which related to this trait (for example, they were asked to indicate how hostile, unfriendly, and unlikable he was). Another aspect of the study involved the amount of delay between the various activities just described. For half of the subjects, the interval between the priming task and receipt of information about the stranger was varied. One third experienced no delay, another third experienced a delay of twenty-four hours, and the final third a delay of fully a week. For the other half of the participants, the interval between receipt of information about the stranger and the rating task was varied. Again, one third experienced no delay, one third experienced a delay of twenty-four hours, and the final third experienced a delay of seven days.

Results confirmed Srull and Wyer's major predictions, but also offered some surprises. First, as expected, the greater the number of priming items in the sentence construction task, the greater subjects' tendency to perceive the stranger as being hostile. Second, and also as predicted, the greater the interval

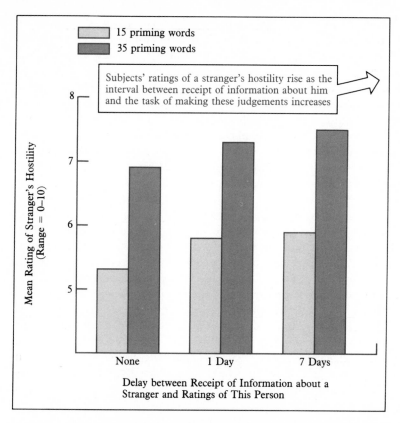

□ 15 priming words
■ 35 priming words

Subjects' ratings of a stranger's hostility rise as the interval between receipt of information about him and the task of making these judgements increases

Mean Rating of Stranger's Hostility (Range = 0–10)

8 —

7 —

6 —

5 —

None   1 Day   7 Days

Delay between Receipt of Information about a
Stranger and Ratings of This Person

FIGURE 3.11 *Priming: An important factor in person memory.*

The greater the number of priming words subjects had previously seen (i.e., words related to the concept of hostility), the greater their tendency to perceive a stranger as showing this trait. Further, subjects' ratings of this person's hostility rise as the interval between receipt of information about him and the task of making these judgements increases. [Source: Based on data from Srull & Wyer, 1980.]

between the priming task and receipt of information about the stranger, the smaller the priming effects observed. Finally, and more surprising, the greater the interval between receipt of information about the stranger and judgments about him, the *larger* the magnitude of the priming effects (please refer to Figure 3.11). This latter finding suggests that once a memory category has been primed, it may be strengthened in a fairly lasting way. As a result, it is more likely to be used on future occasions — even ones occurring days or weeks later. To the extent this is true, we might expect different individuals to vary greatly in terms of the accessibility of various memory categories. After all, their life experiences are unique, and these should be reflected in equally unique patterns of **category accessibility.** That this is in fact the case is suggested by the results of a study by Higgins, King, and Mavin (1982). These researchers found that individuals do indeed differ greatly with respect to the memory categories they find most and least accessible. Moreover, such differences are reflected in their recall of information about and impressions of other persons. The existence of such individual differences, in turn, points to an unsettling general conclusion: in many cases, different observers will tend to remember sharply contrasting sets of "facts" about a stranger. And such differences, in turn, may lead them to equally divergent impressions and judgments about this person. In short, differences in the internal structure of our memory systems may lead us to perceive the social world through very dissimilar eyes.

Visual imagery: One reason why some people are better than others at social memory. Individuals differ greatly with respect to social memory. While some seem capable of remembering a wealth of complex facts and information, others have great difficulty in merely recalling names or in recognizing faces. And given the importance of accurate person memory, such differences can often matter. (For example, consider the embarrassment that results when, during an introduction, one person forgets another's name!) But what, precisely, accounts for such variations in person memory? Why are some people so much better at this task than others? In all probability, several factors play a role. For example, some individuals possess more and better developed social schemata than others. As we noted earlier, this should give them a definite edge in remembering social information. Another factor, and one we have not yet considered, involves individual differences in *visual imagery.* Recent findings suggest that persons who are capable of forming vivid visual images of other persons or social events seem to have a major edge in person memory over those who are less accomplished at this task. Moreover, they seem to be better at recalling information about others' attitudes, background, and behavior, not simply their physical appearance (Swann & Miller, 1982). Such effects may stem from the fact that vivid images help us to organize incoming information, and so to store it more effectively. Alternatively, they may occur because visual images assist us in retrieving information from memory. Regardless of the precise mechanism involved, current evidence points to the following conclusion: forming vivid images of the social world may often be helpful from the perspective of recalling information about it.

Social Inference: Reasoning about Others

One basic way in which we seek to obtain knowledge about the social world is through *inference.* That is, we begin with a set of beliefs or propositions about others or some situation, and from these try to reach certain conclusions. In short, we attempt to make sense out of the social world by reasoning about it. But what is this reasoning like? Do we follow the same rules of logic in thinking about others that we do in thinking about other aspects of our experience? Research on this basic issue has yielded some surprising results (Hastie, 1983). First, it appears that in thinking about others we are far from totally logical. Indeed, we seem to demonstrate many important forms of bias in such inference. Second, in an attempt to simplify this complex task, we often make use of basic rules or principles (**heuristics**) designed to save us a great deal of cognitive work. Since both of these points are central to a grasp of social inference, we will now explore them further.

Biases in social inference: How, in thinking about others, we often go astray. Mr. Spock, a central character in the "Star Trek" television series, prided himself on being totally logical. Further, he spent considerable effort in trying to get the mere humans about him to think in a similar fashion (see Figure 3.12). If he were familiar with the findings of recent research on social inference,

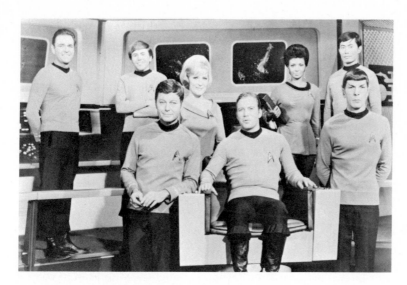

FIGURE 3.12   Social inference: Definitely not up to Mr. Spock's standards.

Mr. Spock (of the well-known television series "Star Trek") was often dismayed by the lack of logic displayed by human members of the crew of the Enterprise. *[Source: Paramount Pictures Corp.]*

however, he might well throw up his hands in despair, for these investigations indicate that such reasoning suffers from several sources of bias.

Overemphasizing extremity: Bias in the sampling of information.   One important way in which our reasoning about others departs from total logic involves a tendency to be unduly influenced by extreme examples. Often, it seems, we permit such instances to badly bias our conclusions. For example, consider a study by Rothbart et al. (1978). Here, subjects read fifty statements about imaginary strangers. Most of these were fairly neutral in nature, but ten described criminal actions. For half of the subjects, these crimes were relatively mild in nature (shoplifting, vandalism). For the remainder, though, they were very serious (murder, rape). After reading these descriptions, participants in both groups were asked to estimate the frequency of criminal acts among the strangers involved. Results can be simply stated: subjects who read about extreme crimes reported significantly higher estimates of crime frequency than subjects who read about more moderate ones. In short, the inclusion of a small number of extreme instances had strongly biased subjects' conclusions. Similar findings have been reported in a number of other studies (Taylor & Crocker, 1981). Thus, it seems clear that, in reasoning about others, we often allow extreme or unusual cases to unduly affect us.

Underutilizing baserates: Ignoring information about typicality.   In attempting to reach conclusions about another person from his or her behavior, or about a social group from one of its members, we should obviously pay close attention to a central issue: how *typical* is this behavior or this person? Only if the behavior is representative of the way in which someone usually acts, or if the individual we observe is representative of the larger social group, should we proceed with generalizations. Surprisingly, however, we do *not* seem to follow this rule. On the contrary, research evidence suggests that often we tend to ignore information about typicality altogether (Kahneman & Tversky, 1972; Kahneman, Slovic, & Tversky, 1982). (Note, by the way, that this type of bias is closely related to our tendency to ignore consensus information in forming causal attributions; refer to Chapter 2.) A dramatic illustration of our inclination to overlook typicality is provided by a study conducted by Hamill, Wilson, and Nisbett (1980).

In this experiment, subjects saw a videotape in which a person posing as a prison guard was interviewed by a psychologist. For half of the participants, the guard behaved in a very humane manner (e.g., he noted that the major task of prisons was that of helping prisoners get back on their feet). For the remainder, however, he behaved in a brutal manner (e.g., he noted that all prisoners were "losers" who should be kept away from society). Prior to watching one of these two tapes, one third of the subjects were told that the man shown in the interview was quite typical of prison guards in general. A second third was informed that he was very atypical (i.e., far more humane or inhumane than most other guards). The final third received no information about the representativeness of this particular guard. Following completion of the film, subjects answered a series of questions designed to assess their attitudes toward prison guards. Hamill and his colleagues reasoned that if individuals do pay attention to information about **baserates** (typicality), they should be affected by the guard's behavior only when he was described as being typical of other members of his group. As you can see from Figure 3.13, however, this was definitely *not* the case. Regardless of this person's supposed representativeness, subjects expressed more positive attitudes about guards when the particular one they had observed had behaved in a humane fashion than when he had acted in a brutal manner. Further, their ratings did not vary with the information on typicality: subjects seemed to totally ignore such input.

These and other findings suggest that in reaching conclusions about others, we often pay little attention to the question of whether their current behavior is indicative of their actions in general, or whether they are in fact a typical member of their social group. Needless to add, overlooking such information can often lead us to false generalizations and to other errors with serious social consequences.

Assessing covariation: Determining what aspects of the social world go together. Many informal observations about people or groups focus on **covariation.** They suggest that certain behaviors or traits go together—that the presence of one usually implies the presence of the other, or that changes in one are accompanied by alterations in the other. For example, it is often contended that "blondes have more fun" or that "still waters run deep." (The latter statement, of course, suggests that strong, silent types are often very different on the inside than their calm exterior suggests.) How do we go about assessing such views? If we were perfectly rational thinkers, we would go through a series of logical steps. For example, we would begin by deciding what data are needed to assess such covariation. Then, we would systematically sample appropriate cases and weigh all the evidence. In the context of our earlier comments about social inference, you will not be surprised to learn that we rarely follow such

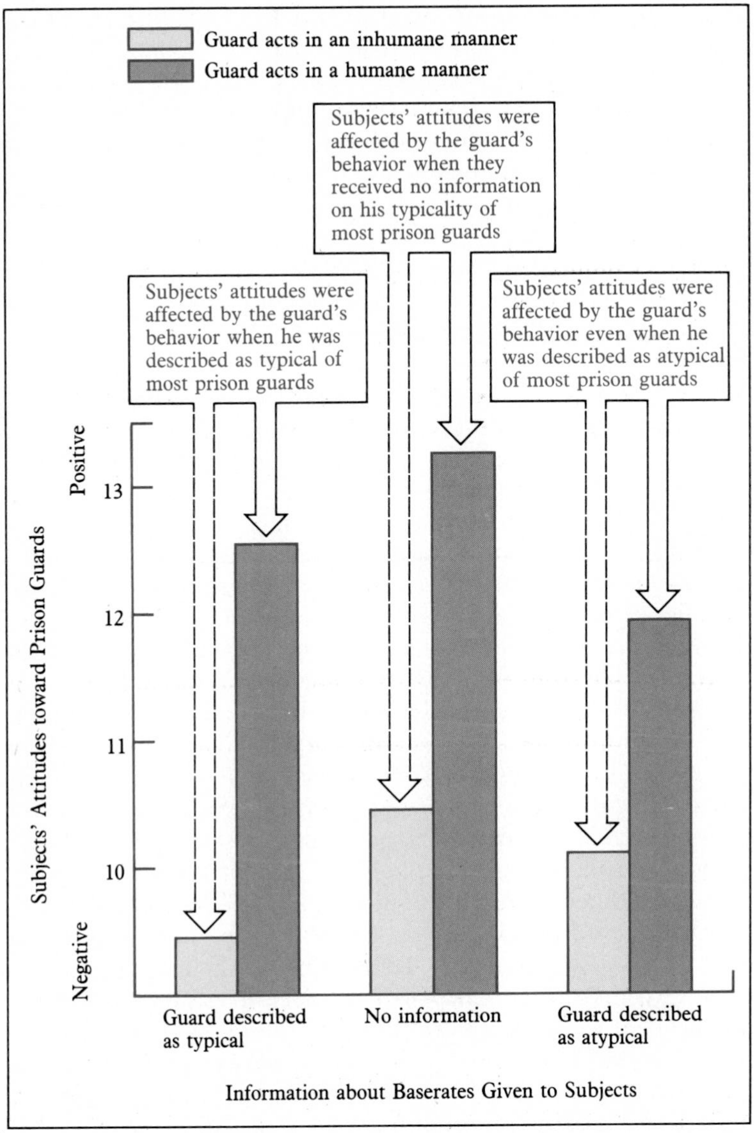

FIGURE 3.13 One form of bias in social inference: Ignoring information on baserates.

Subjects' attitudes toward prison guards were strongly affected by the behavior of one guard who acted in a humane or inhumane manner during an interview. Further, this was the case even when this person was described as being quite atypical of prison guards in general. These findings suggest that often, we do not pay sufficient attention to baserate information in drawing social inferences. [Source: Based on data from Hamill, Wilson, & Nisbett, 1980.]

procedures. Instead, we seem to allow our prior expectations to guide our judgments in this respect. If we do not expect two variables to be related, we may underestimate their actual degree of covariation (Nisbett & Ross, 1980). However, if we *do* anticipate such a link, we may inflate it beyond its true value. This latter effect is known as **illusory correlation,** and it can lead us into serious inferential errors. For example, if we become convinced that being blonde and having fun are in fact linked, we may conclude that blonde persons are a poor choice for responsible jobs: after all, they are too busy enjoying life to the hilt! More disturbing, illusory correlation can also contribute to the occurrence of prejudice and discrimination. On the basis of prior expectations (e.g., cultural stereotypes) many persons become convinced that membership in various racial, ethnic, or religious groups is linked with the possession of negative traits—despite much evidence to the contrary. And then, on the basis of such illusory correlation, they conclude that such persons are to be avoided, excluded—or worse. In these and many other cases, our seeming inability to assess covariation in an accurate manner can have important social consequences.

The use of simple heuristics: The "quick and easy route" to social inference. Several times in this chapter, we have noted that human beings are "cognitive misers": if they can avoid cognitive work, they tend to do so. Consistent with this fact, it has been found that in drawing inferences about the social world, we often rely on shortcuts—simple principles that permit us to reach such conclusions quickly and with relatively little effort. Several of these principles (or *heuristics*) exist, but here we will consider only two: availability and representativeness.

Availability: A quick method for estimating frequency or likelihood. One basic task we perform in social inference is that of estimating the frequency or likelihood of various events. For example, imagine that at some future time, you are asked to evaluate the performance of someone working under your direction. One question on the evaluation form is: "Does this employee show initiative?" In order to answer, you try to recall instances in which the person in question acted in this manner—situations in which he "took charge," and coped effectively with unexpected events. If a number of such occurrences come readily to mind, you may well decide to assign him a high rating. If, instead, you have difficulty in thinking of such events, you may conclude that he does not show much initiative and then assign him a lower rating. In either case, your final decision may be strongly affected by the sheer **availability** of relevant information. Research findings suggest that often we tend to follow this general principle (Kahneman & Tversky, 1973; Tversky & Kahneman, 1978). That is, the more quickly we can bring something to mind, or the greater the number of instances of it we can recall, the more frequent we judge it to be. But does this method work? Does it provide us with a rapid method for forming accurate estimates of frequency or likelihood? The answer seems to be: "sometimes." In many cases, the estimates provided by the availability heuristic *are* quite useful. After all, if we can think of many examples of something, this is often a good sign that it is frequent or common. On other occasions, though, following this simple rule can lead us far astray. For example, without knowing it, we may have only a restricted or biased sample of past events or behaviors at our disposal. To the extent this is so, we may well arrive at inaccurate conclusions. Similarly, the presence of a small number of dramatic instances that come readily to mind may lead us to greatly overestimate the frequency or likelihood of certain events. In sum, availability does indeed often provide a quick-and-easy route to important forms of social influence. But it can also lead us seriously astray, and should always be employed with considerable caution.

Representativeness: A quick method for estimating probability. Imagine that you have just met your next-door neighbor for the first time. On the basis of a brief conversation with him, you determine that he is exceptionally neat, somewhat shy, has a good vocabulary, and dresses quite conservatively. During your discussion, though, he never got around to mentioning his occupation, so now you are wondering about this. Is he an attorney, a business executive, a librarian, or a dancer? One quick way of answering this question would be to compare his apparent traits with those of the typical members of each of these fields. In other words, you might simply ask yourself how closely he resembles the "average" attorney, executive, librarian, or dancer. If you proceeded in this fashion (and concluded that he was probably a librarian), you would be using the **representativeness** *heuristic.* This is a general principle we employ to guide social inference when we wish to estimate some probability — for example, the likelihood that a specific person belongs to some group. The advantage it confers is obvious: by means of this heuristic, we can make rapid decisions about such matters. But it, too, can lead us into error. Thus, if our initial impression of our neighbor were somehow wrong (e.g., he is not really neat or conservative; he was dressed this way when we met because he was on his way to an important job interview), our inference, too, can be wrong. As is the case with almost all cognitive processes, then, there is a trade-off between speed and accuracy: we can be quick, but only at the cost of potential losses in accuracy. (For a discussion of some of the problems that can stem from common errors in social inference, please see the **On the Applied Side** insert on pp. 112–113.)

Forming Impressions of Others: Social Cognition and the Integration of Social Information

Imagine that it is the first day of a new semester, and you are attending one of your classes. The instructor enters, spends about ten minutes making some introductory remarks, and then dismisses the group. Later that day, one of your friends asks you what you thought of this person. Without much hesitation, you launch into a summary of your reactions; indeed, you even make firm predictions about how much you will like the course and how much you will learn from it. In short, on the basis of only a few minutes of a one-way interaction with this instructor (she spoke, you merely listened), you have already formed a clear first impression of her. Probably, you do not find this incident surprising: we take our ability to form such impressions very much for granted. In reality, though, it is quite impressive. After all, when we meet other persons for the first time, they present us with a vast array of new information. In order to form consistent overall impressions of them, therefore, we must somehow be able to combine this varied input in a quick and efficient manner. But how, precisely, do we accomplish this complex task? In their attempts to answer this question, social psychologists have generally adopted two different perspectives. The first and more traditional approach focuses on the precise manner in which we combine

Errors in Social Inference: Some Unsettling, Practical Effects

Early in our discussion of social inference, we noted that Mr. Spock (of "Star Trek" fame) would probably shudder in horror at the manner in which human beings perform this process. The implications of our shortcomings in this respect, however, are far more serious than negative reactions on the part of an imaginary character. Indeed, they are both broad and unsettling in scope. At this point, then, we would like to call some of these to your attention, and also suggest techniques for reducing their potential impact.

First, consider our tendency to be strongly influenced by extreme cases. Because of this bias, we may often conclude that certain events or behaviors are far more common than is actually the case. For example, after reading a scathing article about a member of Congress who added dozens of relatives to her staff, charged lavish parties to the taxpayers, and spent most of her time traveling to glamorous world capitals, we might conclude that such actions are commonplace among legislators, even if they are not. (In fact, the parties are usually smaller, and the travel less frequent.) And then, we may become quite cynical about the entire political process, and decide not to waste our time by voting in future elections. In this and many other cases, the tendency to draw firm inferences from a few extreme cases can have important, negative consequences.

Second, recall our tendency to ignore the typicality of some event or behavior (i.e., information about baserates). This tendency can often lead us to false impressions of others. Even obnoxious and hostile individuals can usually present a pleasant "front" for short periods of time. Thus, if we ignore information about the extent to which such actions are representative of their behavior in general, we may be led to sadly mistaken conclusions (see Figure 3.14).

Since we have already considered the role of illusory correlation in prejudice and discrimination, we will not repeat our comments here. Suffice it to say that our shortcomings in assessing covariation sometimes cause us to associate various traits with specific social groups, even in the absence of any firm evidence for such connections.

Finally, we should note that our heavy reliance on the availability heuristic may help account for the puzzling persistence of discredited beliefs (Ross et al., 1977). That is, even after we have received considerable evidence suggesting that some belief is false and have accordingly rejected it, it may remain high in availability. And this fact, in turn, may be sufficient to insure that it continues to affect our social thought. In short, consciously deciding that it is wrong is not enough; as long as it still comes easily to mind, its impact may persist.

As we're sure you will agree, all of these problems are potentially important ones. Indeed, there can be little doubt that errors in social inference often get us into serious trouble—both as individuals and as societies. Is there any means of reducing their impact? To date, relatively little research has focused on this issue. However, existing evidence points to the usefulness of two basic approaches. First, we can employ formal education to call these problems to people's attention, and to arm them with more effective strategies for conducting social inference. With a little effort, almost everyone can

information about others. For example, research within this framework has sought to determine whether, in carrying out this task, we basically *add* diverse input about others or *average* it in some manner. The second and somewhat newer approach attempts to link impression formation to basic aspects of social cognition. In short, it seeks to explain this process in terms of schemata, attention, and person memory. Both lines of investigation have added greatly to our knowledge, so we will touch on each in the present discussion.

FIGURE 3.14   The dangers of ignoring typicality: A convincing illustration.

*Even tyrants such as Stalin sometimes act in a kind or benevolent manner. For this reason, it is important to take the **typicality** of others' behavior into account in social inference. If we do not, we can often be led to dangerously false conclusions. [Source: Photo by R. Gates/Frederic Lewis Photographers.]*

grasp the importance of taking baserate information into account, the dangers of placing too much emphasis on extreme cases, and other common pitfalls of social thought. Being aware of these sources of error does not, of course, insure positive outcomes. But it is at least a step in the right direction (Nisbett & Ross, 1980). Second, we can try to insure that important social decisions are made in group settings. In some cases, at least, input from other persons can help individuals recognize their own inferential errors. Thus, collective efforts may be somewhat less subject to several of the problems we have discussed than decisions by individuals. As we will note in Chapter 11, however, decisions made in groups often suffer from another set of problems. Thus, such procedures may not always be effective. In any case, these and other efforts to avoid serious errors in social inference seem well worthwhile. After all, without them, our attempts to make sense out of the social world around us may sometimes leave us worse off than when we began!

Cognitive Algebra in Impression Formation: The Weighted-Average Model

In combining varied information about others, we might proceed in several distinct ways. First, we could simply *add* separate pieces of information together. If this were the case, the greater the amount of positive input we have about another person, the more favorable our final impression would be.

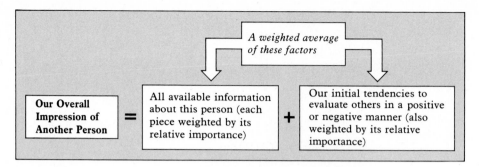

FIGURE 3.15   *Impressions of others: The weighted-average model.*

Considerable evidence suggests that our impressions of others are based upon a weighted average of (1) all available information about them, and (2) our own predisposition to evaluate others in a positive or negative manner.

Similarly, the more negative input we have about this individual, the more unfavorable our overall impression. Second, we might *average* such diverse information in a simple fashion. If we proceeded in this manner, our global impressions would represent simple averages of all the positive and negative input we received (Anderson, 1981). In fact, however, dozens of experiments suggest that we do not adopt either of these basic tactics. Instead, we seem to base our impressions on a special type of average—a *weighted average* that takes account of (1) all available information about others (with each item weighted by its relative importance) and (2) our own initial disposition to evaluate others in a positive or negative fashion (please refer to Figure 3.15). Since this weighted-average model of impression formation has stimulated a great deal of research, we will now examine it in more detail.

The weighted-average model: A closer look. When we say that information about others is weighted according to its importance, we simply mean the following: all inputs do *not* exert an equal impact on our final impressions. Rather, some exert greater and some a lesser influence. Several different factors seem to determine which information receives a relatively "heavy" weighting and which a relatively "light" one. First, we seem to pay more attention to information about others from highly credible sources than information from less reliable ones (Rosenbaum & Levin, 1969). Second, we seem to assign greater weight to information about others that we obtain first (Asch, 1946). Such *primacy effects,* as they are often termed, help explain why it is often so hard to alter impressions of others once they are formed. And they suggest that common sense is correct in offering the following advice: at all costs, make a good first impression! Third, we seem to assign greater weight to negative information about others than to positive information (Fiske, 1980; Hamilton & Zanna, 1972). In short, we evaluate others more in terms of their worst attributes or behavior than their best. Finally, we attach more weight or importance to information relating to extreme behavior by others (either very positive or very negative) than to information about more moderate actions

(Fiske, 1980). Given our tendency to rely on such "atypical" behaviors in identifying the major traits of others (see Chapter 2), this last fact is hardly surprising.

While information about others and the weight we assign to it exert strong effects upon our final impression, this is only part of the story. In addition, our impressions are influenced by our initial dispositions to evaluate others in a positive or negative manner (refer to Figure 3.15). These tendencies seem to exist prior to our receipt of any information about other persons. Thus, in a sense, they reflect dispositions we bring with us to a first meeting with them. And as you might well expect, they can run the entire range from strong tendencies to evaluate everyone favorably (e.g., the well-known "Pollyanna syndrome") through opposite tendencies to evaluate everyone negatively (e.g., the "Ebenezer Scrooge syndrome"). Whatever their specific nature, though, these dispositions often exert strong effects upon our overall impressions of others (Kaplan, 1976).

To conclude: existing evidence suggests that our overall impressions of others are not formed in a random or haphazard manner. Rather, they seem to stem from an orderly—if unconscious—process involving a special type of averaging.

Impressions of Others: A Cognitive Perspective

In one sense, the weighted-average model tells us much about **impression formation.** After all, it indicates how, in general terms, we combine varied information about others into unified impressions of them. Further, it calls attention to several factors that strongly influence our overall reactions to strangers. Despite these advantages, though, it suffers from one major drawback: it does not directly address the cognitive mechanisms underlying this basic process. For example, it fails to consider the potential role of schemata, attention, or person memory in the development of first impressions. In recent years, a growing number of our colleagues have noted this important fact (e.g., Carlston, 1980; Ostrom, Lingle, Pryor, & Geva, 1979). Further, they have undertaken systematic research designed to rectify this situation—to clarify the foundations of impression formation in social cognition. The research they have conducted has yielded varied and often complex findings. But two basic facts are increasingly clear. First, impressions of others do *not* develop in a cognitive vacuum; rather, they generally reflect the operation of basic aspects of social cognition we have already considered. And second, attempts to understand impression formation in this cognitive context can greatly enhance our sophistication about its basic nature. In order to acquaint you with the flavor and general nature of this recent work, we will now describe a cognitive model of this process outlined recently by Burnstein and Schul (1982).

Social judgments: An information-processing view. According to Burnstein and Schul (1982), impression formation can be divided into four distinct, but closely connected stages. The first is *initial encoding.* During this phase, information about another person is transformed into an internal representation. In

*Cognition and Affect:
How Feelings Shape Thought, and
Thought Shapes Feelings*

Cognition plays a major role in our lives. We think about other persons, ourselves, and many other topics—often far into the night! And these thoughts, by shaping major decisions and judgments, often exert powerful and far-ranging effects. As you already know, however, cognition is only part of the total picture. We do not merely think; usually we *feel* as well. Thus, a thorough understanding of human social behavior must, of necessity, include attention to moods and emotions, as well as to memory, inference, and thought. Social psychologists have always been aware of this fact, and in later portions of this text we will focus on several forms of behavior that are strongly shaped by feelings or emotions (e.g., aggression, helping, attraction). Since we have just spent many pages discussing cognition, though, it seems only reasonable to raise the following question: what is the link between these two basic processes? In short, what is the link between feelings and thought? One possibility, of course, is that they are quite independent: each goes its own way with little impact on the other (Zajonc, 1980). While this seems to be true in some cases (see Figure 3.16), growing evidence points to the conclusion that often there is a strong connection between them (Zajonc & Markus, 1983). That is, cognition shapes our feelings, and feelings, in turn, influence cognition (Abelson et al., 1982; Smith & Kleugel, 1982).

First, consider the impact of cognition on emotion (Clark & Fiske, 1982). We have already examined one aspect of this relationship in Chapter 2, when we discussed Schachter's theory of emotion and Bem's theory of self-perception. As you may recall, these theories suggest that often, we do not know our own feelings or attitudes directly. Rather, these internal reactions are somewhat ambiguous. As a result, we must look outward—at our own behavior or other aspects of the external world— for clues about their essential nature. In such cases, the emotions or feelings we experience are strongly determined by the interpretations or cognitive

FIGURE 3.16 *Feelings and thought: Sometimes they are independent.*

On some occasions (such as the one shown here), affect and cognition appear to be quite independent. Although the judge is clearly amused by the antics of the defendant and his attorney, his decision is not influenced by these feelings. In many other instances, though, affect and cognition are more closely linked. [Source: Drawing by Vietor; © 1982 The New Yorker Magazine, Inc.]

"Funny. Very funny. But guilty."

labels we select. A second way in which cognition can affect emotions is through the activation of schemata containing a strong affective component. For example, if we label an individual as belonging to some group, the schema for this social category may suggest what traits he or she possesses. In addition, it may also tell us how we *feel* about such persons. Such effects are most clearly visible with respect to strong racial, ethnic, or religious stereotypes. But they occur in other contexts as well.

While cognition often shapes affect, our emotions, in turn, frequently influence our cognitive processes. First, strong feelings often interrupt such activities. For example, recall how hard it is to work on tasks requiring concentration or thought when you are frightened, elated, or otherwise aroused. Such effects are both common and pro-

nounced. Second, many experiments suggest that moods or feelings can strongly influence our perceptions, memory, and overt behavior (Clark & Isen, 1982; Isen, 1984). Individuals who are in a pleasant mood tend to see the world—including other persons—in a positive, favorable light. In contrast, those who are depressed, angry, or unhappy often show the opposite pattern. And persons who are in a good mood, even because of an event as trivial as finding a dime in a phone booth, are often more willing to offer aid to strangers than persons who are not experiencing such positive affect (please refer to our discussion of this topic in Chapter 8). Finally, current emotions or moods can even affect memory. When feeling happy, individuals tend to recall other positive events or experiences, while when feeling unhappy, they tend to

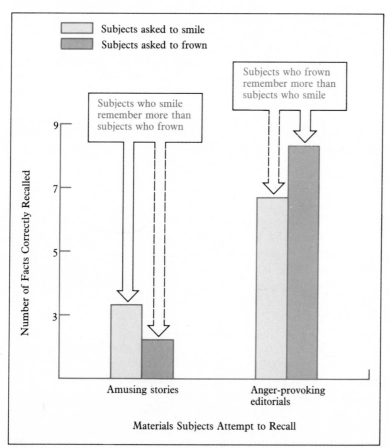

FIGURE 3.17   Mood and memory: Evidence for a link.

Subjects who tried to recall the contents of amusing stories were more successful at this task if they smiled than if they frowned. Similarly, subjects who tried to recall anger-provoking editorials were more successful in remembering such information if they frowned than if they smiled. These findings suggest that current mood can often exert powerful effects on memory. [Source: Based on data from Laird et al., 1982.]

remember more negative events (Clark & Isen, 1982). An intriguing illustration of such effects is provided by a recent study conducted by Laird et al. (1982).

In this experiment, subjects first read either humorous passages designed to make them feel happy (stories by Woody Allen) or editorials designed to make them angry (e.g., discussions of corruption in the U.S. government). In a second phase of the study, they attempted to recall as much as possible about the contents of these passages. While doing so, half were asked to smile while the remainder were asked to frown. (As we noted in Chapter 2, such posed facial expressions often seem to exert powerful effects upon our actual feelings.) Results pointed to a strong effect of mood upon recall. Specifically, subjects who attempted to remember the Woody Allen stories were more successful at this task if they smiled rather than frowned while performing it. Similarly, subjects who tried to recall the anger-inducing editorials did better if they frowned rather than smiled (see Figure 3.17). (We should note, incidentally, that such findings were obtained only among subjects whose moods were affected by their facial expressions. Individuals whose internal states were unaffected by smiles or frowns did not show a similar pattern.)

In sum, there seem to be close and important links between affect and cognition. The way we think is strongly influenced by the way we feel, and vice versa. But how, precisely, do these two behavioral systems influence one another? Where, specifically, are the points of contact between them? At the moment, little is known about this key issue. One possibility, suggested recently by Zajonc and Markus (1983) notes that both affect and cognition are represented in our *motor system*—the complex arrangement of muscles, receptors, and brain mechanisms that underlies all bodily movement. Given this basic fact, it seems possible that one important interface between affect and cognition occurs at this level. This proposal is consistent with a considerable body of past research. Until it is subjected to direct test, however, it should be viewed as mainly speculative in nature. At the least, though, it provides researchers with one starting point for their investigations of this complex issue. In any case, regardless of the precise manner in which affect and cognition influence one another, the following conclusion is evident: in order to fully understand human social behavior, we must devote careful attention to both. Neither the cold light of reason nor the warm glow of emotion is, by itself, sufficient to fully illuminate this intriguing topic.

short, information about various features of the social world are brought "inside" and become part of our cognitive system. The second stage involves *elaborative encoding*. At this point, social information is linked to prior knowledge. That is, it is attached to various social schemata that are already present and were developed on the basis of past experience. The third phase in the overall process involves *integration*. Here, the information we have gathered, and which is now part of our cognitive system, is "pulled together" into a consistent whole. This may involve combining portions of several schemata and is, in a sense, the most active step we have considered so far. Finally, in the fourth phase, *decision*, the now-integrated information is interpreted within the context of an evaluative schema (a schema for evaluating other persons or various portions of their behavior) and then translated into some sort of response—a rating on a scale, or smile, or some other outward sign of our final judgment. (Please see Figure 3.18 for a summary of these suggestions.) In sum, according to the framework proposed by Burnstein and Schul (1982), forming impressions of others is a complex cognitive process, involving the encoding, integration, and recall of social information.

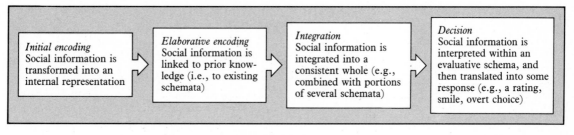

FIGURE 3.18   Impression formation: A cognitive approach.
According to a cognitive model proposed recently by Burnstein and Schul (1982), impression formation involves four distinct phases: (1) initial encoding, (2) elaborative encoding, (3) integration, and (4) decision. [Source: Based on a model proposed by Burnstein & Schul, 1982.]

Evidence for the accuracy of this model has been obtained in several studies. For example, in one investigation, Burnstein and Schul (1982) reasoned that because initial encoding involves dealing with separate pieces of social information, the speed of this process should drop as the number of traits describing another person increases. In contrast, since such information has already been combined by the time integration takes place, the number of traits presented should have little influence on the speed of *this* process. However, because integration does involve combining information into a consistent whole, it should be slowed by inconsistency between the traits presented. All of these predictions were confirmed in several related studies. The number of traits presented exerted stronger effects on encoding than integration, while the opposite was true with respect to the degree of consistency between these traits.

To conclude: the information-processing model outlined by Burnstein and Schul seems to offer a useful framework for understanding impression formation. Thus, in this case, as in many others we will note throughout this text, knowledge about social cognition offers a solid "entering wedge" for obtaining new insights about a key aspect of the social world. (Do our feelings influence our thoughts about others? And do our cognitions in turn, influence our feelings? For a discussion of these intriguing questions, please see the **Focus on Research** insert on pp. 116–118.)

Summary

Social cognition is concerned with the manner in which we think about other persons and ourselves. Research in this area has been stimulated by important advances in cognitive science, and has borrowed some of the principles and research methods of this closely related field.

Schemata consist of interconnected networks of information relating to various concepts. They are built up through experience and exert powerful effects upon our perceptions of the social world, where we direct our attention, and our memory for social information.

A number of basic processes play a role in social cognition. **Attention** determines what information enters our cognitive system. It is strongly affected by *salience* and to a lesser degree by *vividness*. Attention can be turned inward and focused on the self, as well as outward toward the external world. **Person memory** contains information about others' appearance, behavior, and traits. It is affected by whether we attempt to form an overall impression of another or simply try to recall isolated facts about them, and also by the accessibility of various categories within memory. Vivid visual imagery can enhance person memory. **Social inference** is the process through which we reason about others and the social world. It is characterized by several important biases or errors (e.g., overreliance on extreme cases, a lack of attention to information about the typicality of various events or behavior). In addition, it often relies on simple *heuristics*—quick and easy routes to social conclusions. Among the most important of these are availability and representativeness.

In forming **impressions of others,** we seem to combine diverse social information through a special type of *weighted averaging*. Recent studies of impression formation have attempted to examine the specific cognitive processes it involves (e.g., the encoding and integration of information). Such research has linked impressions of others to social cognition and added greatly to our sophistication about this social task. Affect and cognition appear to be closely linked. Thoughts shape feelings, and feelings, in turn, often affect cognitive processes.

Glossary

attention *The first step in social cognition. Only stimuli that are noticed (i.e., that become the focus of our attention) can be encoded and so enter our cognitive system.*

availability *A basic principle (heuristic) often adopted in social inference. According to availability, information we can remember or bring easily to consciousness is viewed as being frequent or important.*

baserates *Refers to the prevalence or frequency of occurrence of some behavior or trait. It is important to take careful account of baserates (i.e., the typicality of behavior or traits) when drawing social inferences.*

category accessibility *Refers to the extent to which various portions of our memory can be recalled or brought into conscious thought. Such accessibility can*

often be enhanced by *priming*—exposure to one or more instances of the categories in question.

covariation *The extent to which two traits, behaviors, or other characteristics seem to vary together (i.e., changes in one are accompanied by changes in the other). Often we make important errors in estimating such covariation.*

event schemata *Schemata reflecting the usual course of events in various familiar situations. For example, an event schema for a visit to a restaurant includes taking a seat, reading the menu, ordering, eating one's food, paying the bill, and leaving.*

heuristics *Basic principles or rules that allow us to draw social inferences in a rapid manner, and to change complex processes into simpler ones. Two basic heuristics are* availability *and* representativeness.

illusory correlation *The false perception that certain traits or behaviors covary when in fact they do not.*

impression formation *The process through which we form consistent impressions of others. Recent evidence suggests that this process involves four cognitive stages: initial encoding, elaborative encoding, integration, and decision.*

person memory *Refers to a lasting store of information about other persons. Person memory is affected by a number of different factors, such as priming and visual imagery.*

person schemata *Cognitive frameworks relating to the traits and characteristics possessed by specific persons.*

priming *Refers to increases in the accessibility of certain categories within memory produced by recent exposure to instances of these categories. For example, the category "homesickness" might be primed by seeing the movie E.T.*

prototypes *Cognitive structures similar to schemata. Prototypes consist of a "typical" instance of some concept with all major features specified. New instances are compared with the prototype to determine whether they do indeed fall within this category.*

representativeness *A basic principle (heuristic) often followed in social inference. Representativeness suggests that the more closely an individual, trait, or behavior resembles the "average" member of some category, the more likely it is to be an instance of that category.*

role schemata *Schemata referring to the members of broad social categories (for example, ethnic, racial, or age-related groups).*

schemata *Interconnected networks of information relevant to various concepts, built up through past experience. Schemata strongly affect the perception, recall, and processing of social information.*

scripts *See "event schemata."*

self-schemata *Schemata referring to an individual's own traits and behaviors.*

social cognition *Refers to a very active area of research within social psychology concerned with the manner in which we think about others and attempt to make sense out of the complex social world.*

social inference *Refers to the manner in which we reason about other persons or the social world. In social inference, we begin with a set of beliefs or propositions and then, through reasoning, attempt to draw conclusions from this information.*

For More Information

Fiske, S. T., & Taylor, S. E. *Social cognition.* Reading, Mass.: Addison-Wesley, 1983.
An up-to-date introduction to the field of social cognition. Many of the topics covered in the present chapter are discussed in detail, including social schemata, attention, person memory, and social inference. The examples presented are clear, the writing witty, and the conclusions offered both thoughtful and thought-provoking. All in all, an exceptionally valuable book.

Hastorf, A., & Isen, A. (Eds.). *Cognitive social psychology.* New York: Elsevier-North Holland, 1981.
The basic theme of this book is as follows: an important key to understanding the nature of complex social behavior lies in comprehending cognition. This insightful idea is emphasized in a number of excellent chapters by experts on many aspects of the cognitive approach in social psychology. A very useful source.

CHAPTER 4

Attitudes and Attitude Change: Reactions to the Social World

Attitude Formation:
The Role of Learning and Experience

Social Learning: Acquiring Attitudes from Others/The Role of Direct Experience: Attitudes from Contact with Attitude Objects

Attitude Measurement: Assessing the Unseen, Part 2

Self-report Measures: Attitude Scales or Questionnaires/The Bogus Pipeline and Unobtrusive Measures: Techniques for Improving the Accuracy of Attitude Measurement

Changing Attitudes: The Persuasion Approach

Characteristics of the Communicator: Why Some People Are More Persuasive than Others/Characteristics of the Communication: It's Not Just Who You Are; What You Say Counts Too/Characteristics of the Recipients: Why Some People Are Easier to Persuade than Others/The Effects of Repeated Exposure: Why, Often, Familiarity Breeds Content

Changing Attitudes: The Dissonance Approach

The Theory of Cognitive Dissonance: Inconsistency, Attitudes, and Attitude Change/ Dissonance and Attitude-Discrepant Behavior: The Effects of Forced Compliance/Dissonance and Effort: Why Suffering May Lead to Liking

Attitudes and Behavior: The Essential Link

Attitude Strength: Strong Attitudes Predict Behavior More Successfully than Weak Ones/Attitude Specificity: Specific Attitudes Predict Behavior Better than Global Ones/Attitude Relevance: Attitudes That Affect Outcomes Are Better Predictors of Behavior than Attitudes That Do Not

Special Inserts

FOCUS ON RESEARCH
Message Content and Persuasion: The Role of Recipients' Self-schemata

FOCUS ON RESEARCH
*The Physiology of Persuasion:
Patterns of Brain Activity during Pro- and Counterattitudinal Messages*

FOCUS ON RESEARCH
When Attitude Change Fails: Resistance to Persuasion

ON THE APPLIED SIDE
Dissonance, Arousal, and Social Drinking

It's 6:00 A.M. when suddenly your alarm begins to ring. Sleepily, you stretch out a hand to switch it off. "Oh, how I hate Mondays," you think as you crawl painfully out of bed. "Why do they have to open the office at 8:00 A.M. instead of 9:00 or even 9:30 like in New York or California? I guess they just want to make people suffer!" Thinking such thoughts, you head for the bathroom to begin preparations for another day. A few minutes later, you are in the kitchen concentrating on another matter: breakfast. One glance into the cabinet tells you that there is nothing to eat but a box of stale cornflakes. Shuddering at the thought of this drab and tasteless food, you decide to settle for a hot cup of coffee. As you sip it, you leaf through the morning paper and notice that your local team has just won an important game. "Good, very good," you think. "Now they have a real shot at the championship. At least there's one good thing on this rotten morning." After finishing your coffee, you grab your coat and head for the garage. As you do, your face begins to brighten: this is one of the best times of your entire day. You round a corner and there it is — your beautiful new sports car, gleaming quietly in all its understated, silver-grey elegance. "Ah," you muse, "what a machine. So what if I have to do without food and clothes . . . at least I've got this.*" Nestled behind the wheel, you listen with pleasure as the motor roars into life. Of course, you realize that driving your car to the office alone each day is wasteful — fuel is expensive. And it is directly contrary to your strong pro-environmental views. After all, good public transportation exists, and you could travel that way. But who cares — a person has to have some pleasures, right? Right! Unfortunately, the trip downtown is even worse than usual. One of the bridges you must cross is still under repair, despite the fact that crews have been working on it for six months. "Curse the Highway Commission," you think as you sit unmoving in bumper-to-bumper traffic. "If this were a private job, they'd have finished it months ago. What corruption!" To soothe your frazzled nerves, you slip a tape of your favorite music into the player. This helps, and by the time you reach the office, you are in better spirits. As you get out of your car, you see Jim Olson. He's one of your favorite people, so you shout to get his attention, and then walk with him to the building. When you finally arrive at your office, you find four messages already tacked to the door. One announces yet another staff meeting. "Oh, no," you groan, "not today when I have so much to do. . . . Won't they ever learn that these meetings are a total waste of time? . . ."*

Each of us leads a unique life, so your own mornings probably begin with a somewhat different set of events than the ones listed here. Yet, despite this fact, we are confident of one thing: you, too, start each day — and then continue through it — with a series of reactions to the social world around you. In short, like the person in our story, you are far from totally neutral to the many events, ideas, objects, and people you encounter. On the contrary, you

"Oh, good. Apparently Dr. Sturgeon and Dr. Winestaff have agreed to disagree."

probably have positive or negative feelings about many of these, hold various beliefs about them, and tend to behave in certain ways when you meet them. Further, such reactions are often quite stable over time. Thus, if you hate cornflakes today, you will probably also dislike them tomorrow. And if you love silver-grey sports cars now, but believe that they contribute to unnecessary driving, you will probably continue to hold these views in the future. Social psychologists generally term such reactions **attitudes.** Specifically, they define attitudes as *relatively lasting clusters of feelings, beliefs, and behavior tendencies directed toward specific persons, ideas, objects, or groups* (Eagly & Himmelfarb, 1978; Rajecki, 1982). As you can readily see, such reactions often have important effects. First, they may strongly shape our perceptions of the social world. That is, attitudes may determine how we interpret and react to various situations. Second, they often exert powerful effects upon our overt actions. In this manner, they may shape our relations with others and influence a wide range of important social behaviors (see Figure 4.1).

Because social psychologists have long been aware of such effects, they have devoted a great deal of attention to the systematic study of attitudes. Indeed, the investigation of such reactions has been central to our field for several decades. In the present chapter, therefore, we will attempt to acquaint you with some of the major findings uncovered in this extensive work. In order to do so, we will focus on four related topics. First, we will examine the manner in which attitudes are *formed*. As you will soon see, this process involves basic forms of social learning and also direct experience with various attitude objects. Second, we will briefly describe some of the ways in which these largely hidden reactions can be *measured*. Third, we will address a key question with important practical implications: how can attitudes be *altered* or *changed*? And finally, we will turn to the link between *attitudes* and *behavior*. When and how do they shape our overt actions? As we will soon note, the answers to such questions are more subtle and more complex than you might at first imagine.

In considering each of these topics, we will draw upon a wealth of what might be termed "traditional" findings and theories (Rajecki, 1982). In addition, however, we will also focus on a new, *information-processing* perspective concerning attitudes—one that seeks to link such reactions to several of the cognitive processes considered in Chapter 3 (Fazio et al., 1983; Petty & Cacioppo, 1981). This new approach has added much to our understanding of attitudes, so we will call attention to it at several appropriate points.

Attitude Formation: The Role of Learning and Experience

Heroines and heroes may be born, but liberals, bigots, conservatives, and "Moonies" are clearly made. Very few persons would suggest that children enter the world with political preferences, racial hatreds, or religious views already fully formed. Rather, it is generally agreed that such reactions must be acquired over an extended period of time. Indeed, this seems to be true for most, if not all, of our attitudes—everything from our reactions to social ideas or groups, through our reactions toward specific foods or styles of dress. But how, precisely, are such attitudes gained? What processes account for their rapid formation and development? Research findings suggest that the two play a crucial role: **social learning** and **direct experience.**

Social Learning: Acquiring Attitudes from Others

One major source of our social attitudes is obvious: other people. Briefly, we acquire our preferences and aversions, beliefs, and behavior tendencies from the persons around us. Such *social learning*, in turn, seems to take two major forms. The first is illustrated by situations in which parents actively praise their children for expressing views similar to their own, but criticize them for expressing views different from theirs. In such cases, of course, the youngsters quickly come to state—and hold—attitudes quite similar to those recommended by their mothers and fathers. Learning of this type is often known as **instrumental conditioning,** and it rests upon a basic principle of human behavior: in general, individuals learn to perform actions that yield positive outcomes and actions that help them to avoid or escape from negative results. With respect to attitudes, of course, positive outcomes can usually be gained by

FIGURE 4.2   *Social learning: One major source of attitudes.*

Parents, teachers, and other adults often take great pains to assure that children acquire attitudes similar to their own. [Source: Photo (left) © David Burnett 1981/Contact Press Images; photo (right) © Gaylord Herron/Archive Pictures, Inc.]

expressing the "right" views—ones similar to those held by persons who control important rewards. In the case of children, as we have just noted, these are usually parents, other relatives, or teachers. And such individuals often go out of their way to assure that youngsters adopt attitudes highly similar to their own (see Figure 4.2). Among adults, in contrast, the key persons may be employers, fellow workers, or members of high-status groups to which an individual would like to belong. In all such cases, the basic process remains very much the same: an individual acquires certain attitudes because it is instrumental to do so; holding these views yields desired, positive outcomes.

But this is not the only way in which we acquire attitudes from others. In addition, a second process—**modeling**—often plays a role. Here, individuals develop specific views simply by observing the words or behavior of others, even in the total absence of direct rewards for doing so. Such effects can frequently be seen in situations where parents do not actively attempt to instruct their children in given views, but *do* demonstrate these in their own actions. In such cases, youngsters seem to quickly "tune in" on the attitudes held by their mothers and fathers, and adopt them for their own use. In many other situations, in contrast, parents, teachers, and others purposely demonstrate certain actions and in this manner seek to encourage various attitudes among the children in their care. Regardless of the presence or absence of such intentions, however, modeling effects are quite powerful and can exert a long-lasting impact upon attitudes.

The Role of Direct Experience:
Attitudes from Contact with Attitude Objects

There's an old saying that goes something like this: "You can't know what you'll like until you try it." What this statement suggests, of course, is that try as we may, we can't always predict our reactions to various persons, situations, or objects. Only after we have had direct contact with them do our attitudes take shape. In fact, this suggestion seems to be correct. In many cases, our attitudes are formed through direct contact with attitude objects—not simply "borrowed" from other persons through some form of social learning. For example, imagine that you ask a friend to describe some new dish he has just tried. His comments may provide you with some idea of its ingredients and how it is cooked. But they probably will *not* reveal whether you will like it yourself. Only actual tasting will answer this question and permit you to formulate an attitude. Similarly, listening to or reading statements about another person may arm you with a great deal of information about her supposed characteristics. However, only a face-to-face meeting will allow you to decide whether you actually like or dislike her. In these and many other cases, our attitudes stem from direct experience with the persons, ideas, groups, or objects they involve.

That attitudes are formed through direct experience is hardly surprising. We have all formed (or even radically changed) our views in this manner. More unexpected, however, is the fact that attitudes developed through direct experience often seem to be stronger and easier to remember than ones acquired less directly (e.g., through observation of the words or actions of others). Evidence pointing to these conclusions has recently been obtained by Fazio and his colleagues (e.g., Fazio et al., 1983; Fazio & Zanna, 1981). As an example of this research, let us consider a well-designed investigation by Fazio et al. (1982).

In this experiment, male and female subjects either worked on samples of five types of puzzles (e.g., ones involving words, ones involving tracing a path through a maze) or merely watched a videotape in which a female worked on them. Immediately following this direct or indirect experience, half of the participants performed another task. Here, they were shown slides in which each type of puzzle was paired with a positive or negative adjective. As each slide was shown, they were to press a button marked "Yes" if the adjective described their attitude toward the puzzle or a button marked "No" if it did not. It was predicted that because their attitudes toward the puzzles would be more clearly formed, subjects who had actually worked them would respond more quickly than those who had not. The remaining participants did *not* perform the reaction time task immediately after direct or indirect experience with the puzzles. Instead, they first rated their interest in each type of puzzle and only then responded on the "Yes" and "No" buttons. It was expected that rating the puzzles would lead all subjects—both in the direct and the indirect experience conditions—to form clear attitudes toward them. However, Fazio and his colleagues still predicted that those who had actually worked on the puzzles would respond more quickly. This would be the case because they would find it easier to recall their attitudes than those who had merely watched the videotape. As you can see from Figure 4.3, results offered strong support for both predictions. Regardless of whether subjects performed the reaction time task

FIGURE 4.3 *Attitude formation: Direct experience helps.*

When asked to indicate whether various adjectives were or were not indicative of their attitudes toward certain puzzles, subjects who had previously had direct experience with these puzzles responded more quickly than those who had not had such experience. Moreover, this was the case regardless of whether they expressed their attitudes prior to the reaction-time task or did so only after its completion. These results suggest that attitudes formed through direct experience are often stronger than those formed in the absence of such experience. [Source: Based on data from Fazio et al., 1982.]

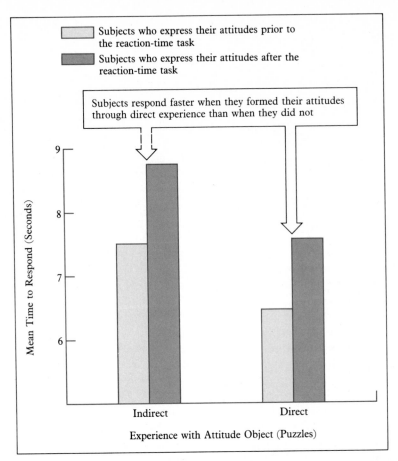

immediately after exposure to the puzzles, or only after expressing their attitudes toward them, those in the direct experience condition responded significantly faster than those in the indirect experience group (those who had merely watched the tape).

These and related findings lend support to the view that attitudes developed through direct contact with attitude objects are stronger and more readily accessed within memory than attitudes developed without such contact. And since only attitudes we can bring to mind can affect our actual behavior, these results point to another intriguing conclusion: attitudes formed through direct experience often exert stronger or more consistent effects upon overt actions than attitudes formed in the absence of such experience. We will return to this point in our discussion of the link between attitudes and behavior (see p. 159).

Attitude Measurement: Assessing the Unseen, Part 2

In Chapter 3 we noted that because they are internal events, cognitive processes cannot be directly observed. As a result, several techniques for making them — or their consequences — visible are necessary. The same problem exists with respect to attitudes. Few people go about announcing their views on important matters to every stranger. Rather, most prefer to keep their attitudes very much to themselves, and reveal them only to close friends and on special occasions. How, then, can we manage to assess these views? Many techniques for accomplishing this goal have been developed by social psychologists. However, most of these are based upon *self-reports* and involve the use of **attitude scales** or **questionnaires.**

Self-report Measures: Attitude Scales or Questionnaires

Have you ever asked a friend for his views on some issue? If so, you are already familiar with *self-report measures* of attitudes. The basic idea behind this approach is both sensible and straightforward: if we ask others for their views, they can usually state these in a relatively clear and accurate manner. In one sense, this is probably correct. Often, we *can* get a basic idea of others' attitudes from their verbal statements. But this informal procedure also suffers from several major drawbacks. For example, when asked to state their views, many persons begin to ramble and soon get far away from the issue at hand. Second, when individuals state their attitudes verbally, there is no ready means for assessing the strength or intensity of these views. Third, most persons, it appears, are quite reluctant to admit that they do not hold clearly formed attitudes about important issues. Thus, when asked for their views, they do not reply "No comment" or "I don't know." Rather, they tend to make them up on the spot. Obviously, such "instant attitudes" are of doubtful reliability and may offer a poor guide to future actions.

In order to avoid these and related problems, social psychologists usually seek to measure attitudes by more formal means, generally involving the use of scales or questionnaires. These *attitude scales* or *questionnaires* contain several carefully chosen or constructed items relating to the issue, object, or group of interest. Subjects' attitudes are then revealed by their responses to the questions included. A number of techniques for selecting or devising the final items exist, and several of these are quite sophisticated in scope. Moreover, the questions on an attitude scale can be presented to respondents in a wide range of formats. A detailed discussion of these matters is beyond the scope of this discussion and would lead us far afield. But we can at least briefly outline one basic technique of measuring attitudes that is used by many researchers — **Likert scaling.**

In this approach, the items on the attitude scale are chosen to be either highly favorable or highly unfavorable toward the attitude object — that is, the issue, group, or object of interest. Respondents are then asked to indicate the extent to which they agree or disagree with each of these statements. To the degree that they endorse statements favorable to the attitude object or reject statements unfavorable to it, they are assumed to hold a positive view. To the extent that they endorse statements unfavorable to the attitude object or reject statements favorable to it, in contrast, they are assumed to hold a negative view.

TABLE 4.1   *Likert scales: Three possible formats.*

In Likert attitude scales, *individuals indicate the extent to which they agree or disagree with statements relating to the attitude under study. Three different formats for making such judgments are shown here.*

Indicate the extent to which you agree or disagree with each of the following statements by circling one of the terms below it:

1. Given enough time, "Reaganomics" will probably succeed in pulling the U.S. economy out of its current, troubled state.

    strongly agree   agree   uncertain   disagree   strongly disagree

2. The economic policies adopted by the Reagan administration are unfair and should be reversed as soon as possible.

    strongly agree   agree   uncertain   disagree   strongly disagree

---

Indicate the extent to which you agree or disagree with each of the following statements by circling one of the numbers below it.

1. Given enough time, "Reaganomics" will probably succeed in pulling the U.S. economy out of its current, troubled state.

    -5 -4 -3 -2 -1 0 $+1$ $+2$ $+3$ $+4$ $+5$

2. The economic policies adopted by the Reagan administration are unfair and should be reversed as soon as possible.

    -5 -4 -3 -2 -1 0 $+1$ $+2$ $+3$ $+4$ $+5$

Indicate the extent to which you agree or disagree with each of the following statements by placing a check on the line below it.

1. Given enough time, "Reaganomics" will probably succeed in pulling the U.S. economy out of its current, troubled state.

    strongly disagree ———————————————————————— strongly agree

2. The economic policies adopted by the Reagan administration are unfair and should be reversed as soon as possible.

    strongly disagree ———————————————————————— strongly agree

---

In its original form, Likert scaling employed five possible responses: Strongly Agree; Agree; Uncertain; Disagree; Strongly Disagree. Individuals completing the questionnaire indicated their views by circling one of these choices, or by circling a number corresponding to each phrase (1 = Strongly Agree, 2 = Agree, and so on). In recent years, however, researchers studying attitudes have employed a wide range of different formats for this task. For example, respondents have been asked to place a check mark along a line labeled "Strongly Agree" at one end and "Strongly Disagree" at the other. And in other instances, they have been asked to circle a number between -10 and $+10$—again, to indicate their agreement or disagreement with various attitude statements. Several different formats for measuring attitudes are shown in Table 4.1. As you can see, these vary greatly. The basic task, though, remains the same: individuals simply indicate the extent to which they endorse or reject various statements relating to some person, issue, object, or group.

The Bogus Pipeline and Unobtrusive Measures: Techniques for Improving the Accuracy of Attitude Measurement

Self-report measures of the type just described often yield useful information about the attitudes held by individuals. Unfortunately, though, they suffer from one crucial flaw: on some occasions, individuals wish to conceal rather than reveal their true attitudes. This can be true for many reasons. For example, they may realize that their views are unpopular or extreme. Similarly, they may want to make a good impression on the experimenter by reporting the views they believe she or he wants to hear. Are there any means for overcoming such problems? In fact, there are. Two procedures that can prove helpful in this regard are the *bogus pipeline* and *unobtrusive measures.*

The *bogus pipeline* was devised more than a decade ago by Jones and Sigall (1971). Its major features can be summarized as follows. First, subjects are

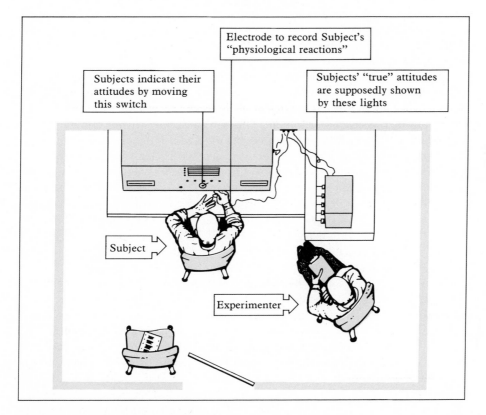

FIGURE 4.4   *The bogus pipeline.*

In procedures known as the bogus pipeline, subjects are told that the equipment shown here will, by measuring physiological reactions, reveal their true opinions. If subjects accept this description as accurate, there is no reason for them to "fake" their answers. Thus, useful information about their attitudes can be obtained. [Source: Drawing courtesy of Bem P. Allen.]

attached to a special machine and told that by measuring tiny electrical changes in their muscles, it can assess their true opinions (see Figure 4.4 on p. 133). To convince them that this is actually the case, they are then asked for their views on several issues. Since their attitudes on this topic were measured several weeks in the past, the experimenter can then "rig" the situation so that the machine seems to report these attitudes very accurately. On the basis of such experience, subjects are led to believe that the equipment can, in fact, determine their true, inner views. Once this belief is established, of course, there is no reason for them to attempt to conceal their attitudes: after all, the equipment will be able to "see through" such deception! Participants are then asked to express their views on a new set of issues not presented earlier. Presumably, their reports with respect to these issues are then more truthful than might otherwise be the case.

Evidence that this technique does yield more accurate measures of attitudes than standard questionnaires has been obtained in several studies (e.g., Allen, 1975; Gaes, Kalle, & Tedeschi, 1978). We should note, however, that not all findings have been positive (e.g., Cherry, Byrne, & Mitchell, 1976). Further, use of the bogus pipelines raises important practical problems (e.g., because of the equipment needed, data can be obtained from only one person at a time). Even when such problems are considered, though, it appears that this procedure represents an interesting and promising approach.

A second technique for overcoming the reluctance of many persons to reveal their attitudes — *unobtrusive measures* — is based on a simple fact: often, human behavior leaves lasting traces of its occurrence (e.g., written records, effects on the physical environment). These traces can provide valuable information about the attitudes of the persons involved. Further, such knowledge can usually be gained without affecting these individuals in any manner — hence the term "unobtrusive." Many different traces of behavior are useful in this respect. For example, voting records reveal much about current political views. Similarly, the sales of various products indicate preferences or changing tastes among consumers. And the number of tickets sold for concerts, plays, and movies can clarify the current popularity of various performers or types of entertainment. Even in the absence of such formal records, though, we can often learn much about attitudes by studying the physical traces left by human behavior. A clear example of the use of such measures is provided by an incident involving that master of observation, Sherlock Holmes. In one of his cases, the famous detective informs a client, a doctor, that he has a busier and more successful practice than his next-door neighbor, who is also a physician. When the client expresses surprise at Holmes's knowledge of this fact, the detective quickly explains the basis for his conclusion: the steps leading to the client's office are worn several inches lower than those leading to that of his neighbor! Of course, social psychologists rarely employ measures precisely like this one. They are often unavailable and can be affected by a wide range of factors other than attitudes (perhaps in this case, the two sets of steps were constructed of different materials, and so wore out at different rates). But behavioral scientists *do* often attempt to gain information about attitudes indirectly, through careful study of the lasting traces produced by human decisions and preferences (Webb et al., 1981).

Together, the bogus pipeline and techniques based upon the use of unobtrusive measures provide social psychologists with alternative means for assessing human attitudes. Needless to add, these methods—like all others employed in science—are far from perfect. Yet, when used with skill and care, they can play a helpful role, aiding in the attainment of information that might otherwise remain hidden from view.

Changing Attitudes: The Persuasion Approach

In the 1980s, the business of changing attitudes is definitely a big one. If you have any doubts on this score, simply switch on your TV or radio, or flip through the pages of any magazine. Almost at once, you will be flooded by attempts to alter your opinions. Commercials will urge you to buy various products; political candidates will plead for your vote; and public service organizations will caution you against smoking, drinking, speeding, or overeating. In short, you will encounter attempts to change your attitudes at every turn (see Figure 4.5).

Efforts to alter our attitudes take many forms, ranging from bribes on the one hand, through threats on the other. Perhaps the single most common technique, however, involves the use of **persuasive communications.** These are written, spoken, televised, or filmed messages seeking to change our attitudes through "logical" argument and convincing "facts." As our quotation marks suggest, the arguments presented are often far from logical, and the facts anything but accurate. Usually, though, these flaws are concealed, and the messages maintain at least an outward appearance of reason and authority.

As you probably know from your own experience, all persuasive appeals are *not* equally effective. Some advertisements greatly increase the sales of

FIGURE 4.5 *Attempts at persuasion: A common part of modern life.*

Attempts to change our attitudes (and behaviors relating to them) are an inescapable part of life in the late twentieth century. [Source: Photo by Frances M. Cox, © 1981/Omni-Photo Communications, Inc.]

specific products; others totally fail in this regard. Some political candidates win election after election; others lose, and soon drop from sight. And some charities manage to attract large public donations, while others collect much smaller amounts. What accounts for such differences? Part of the answer lies in the target attitudes. Some attitudes are strongly established and central to the persons who hold them. Thus, as you might expect, they are difficult, if not impossible, to change (Judd & Krosnick, 1982). Another reason for differences in the success of persuasive appeals, however, lies in these messages themselves. Because they possess certain features, some attempts at persuasion are much more likely to succeed than others. Research on this issue has continued for several decades, and has identified many factors that play a role in the impact of persuasive messages. The most important of these, though, seem to fall under three major headings: (1) *characteristics of the communicator* (who delivers the message?), (2) *characteristics of the communication* (what does it say and how?), and (3) *characteristics of the recipients* (who are the people who receive it?).

Characteristics of the Communicator: Why Some People Are More Persuasive than Others

Suppose that late one night, you tune in a television talk show. Two guests and a moderator are discussing an issue about which you do not have any strong views: the establishment of special trade barriers designed to protect the clothing industry in your country. One of the discussants is a grey-haired professor from a prestigious university. She holds several advanced degrees in economics, and is a well-known expert on world trade. Further, she has a very pleasant appearance, and speaks fluently and with great conviction. As the discussion continues, it becomes clear that she favors free trade. In fact, she repeatedly notes that trade barriers usually backfire, ultimately doing more harm than good to the countries that establish them. In sharp contrast, the other discussant is a businessman, who owns a factory in the threatened industry. He has a rough voice, unkempt appearance, and delivers his comments in a halting and uncertain manner. But his views are equally strong: he has seen many companies in his industry close because of foreign competition, and he argues as best as he can for some kind of government protection. Which of these individuals is more likely to have an impact upon your attitudes? The answer is obvious: the well-groomed, knowledgeable professor. Admittedly, this imaginary situation is extreme—it's really not much of a contest. But it serves to call attention to an important fact: where persuasion is concerned, all communicators are definitely *not* equal (see Figure 4.6). While some seem capable of swaying large numbers of persons to their views, others are quite ineffective in this respect. Why, precisely, is this the case? Research findings suggest that several factors—all of which are present in our example—play an important role.

Communicator attractiveness: Liking as a basis for persuasion. Common sense suggests that often we will be more willing to accept influence from persons we like than from persons we find less appealing. And in this case, informal

"Al, you've been chosen Businessman of the Year by the Junior Chamber of Commerce."

FIGURE 4.6   Communicator effectiveness: An extreme case.

As shown here, some communicators are far more effective than others in changing attitudes. [Source: Drawing by Stevenson; © 1971 The New Yorker Magazine, Inc.]

observation is correct. In general, communicators who are liked by their audiences *do* seem to be more successful changing attitudes than ones who are disliked (e.g., Kiesler & Kiesler, 1969). Further, this appears to be true regardless of whether communicator attractiveness derives from physical appearance, or from positive traits seemingly possessed by this person. We should note, though, that there seems to be one major exception to this rule. If the recommendations of a liked communicator are perceived as stemming from *internal* causes (his or her special interests or bias), while those of a disliked communicator are seen as deriving from *external* causes (important facts that should not be ignored), the typical pattern can be reversed. That is, under these conditions, a disliked communicator can actually exert more influence than a liked one. In short, as attribution theory would suggest, the reasons behind a communicator's statements may take precedence over our liking or disliking for this person in determining whether we will accept or reject his message (e.g., Wachtler & Counselman, 1981).

Incidentally, we should note that the task of eliciting a fairly high level of liking from an audience may often prove somewhat easier than one might guess.

Recent findings (Sears, 1983) indicate that most individuals have a strong *person-positivity bias.* That is, they tend to evaluate other persons (even total strangers) in a favorable manner—at least initially. Further, they also tend to evaluate human beings more favorably than other types of attitude objects (e.g., issues, physical objects, collectivities, or groups). For example, students generally assign higher ratings to their professors than to the courses they teach. Similarly, individuals evaluate specific politicians more favorably than they do the collectivity of "politicians in general" (Sears, 1983). Because of this general person-positivity bias, communicators probably often begin on the "plus" side of neutrality; and if they avoid engaging in words or actions that dissipate this initial good will, they can often turn it to their advantage.

Communicator style: Speed of speech and persuasion. In the example presented earlier, we noted that the professor offered her comments in a fluent and convincing manner. Her opponent, in contrast, delivered his remarks in a slow and halting style. Do such differences in the speed of presentation count? A growing body of evidence suggests that the answer is "yes." Individuals who speak rapidly while delivering a persuasive message are often perceived as more knowledgeable, truthful, and persuasive than those who speak more slowly (Apple, Streeter, & Krauss, 1979). Further, communicators who speak at a faster-than-average pace are actually more effective in changing their audience's attitudes than ones who speak at a relatively slow rate (Miller et al., 1976). At first glance, these results may seem surprising. After all, we are frequently warned that "fast talkers" are to be mistrusted. Why, then, do we permit such persons to persuade us? One possibility lies in our past experience and what it has taught us about the causes of a fast rate of speech. Briefly, many of us have learned that people who can deliver verbal statements quickly often know more about their subject matter than persons who must pause and search for every word. Similarly, we also realize that rapid speech is a sign of heightened arousal, and this in turn is suggestive of deep conviction or belief. Together, these impressions may lead us to greater acceptance of influence from fast talkers than from slow ones. Regardless of the precise mechanisms involved, however, there is little doubt that where persuasion is concerned, sheer speed can yield an important edge. Needless to add, this is a fact communicators should take carefully into account when planning their own persuasive appeals.

Communicator credibility: If you can't trust the experts, whom can you trust? When we are children, we tend to view all adults as valid sources of information. If they tell us something, we reason, it must be true. All too soon, however, these youthful illusions are shattered. Through many disappointing experiences, we come to realize that communicators actually differ greatly in terms of *credibility.* Some are to be believed and trusted (e.g., parents, certain teachers), while others are to be doubted and mistrusted (e.g., TV announcers, some of our friends). And once we acquire this basic concept, it strongly affects our willingness to accept persuasive communications from different sources. Messages or recommendations from persons high in credibility are far more likely to affect our attitudes than similar messages from sources low in credibility (Hovland, Janis, & Kelley, 1953). But on what cues, specifically, do we base our judgments of **communicator credibility?** We have already mentioned one in our discussion of the speed of speech. Two other factors, however, seem even more important: a communicator's *expertise* and his or her *intentions.*

[handwritten annotation: what do we base communicator credibility?]

The importance of apparent expertise has been demonstrated in a number of different experiments (e.g., Maddux & Rogers, 1980). For example, in one recent study (Hennigan, Cook, & Gruder, 1982), male and female subjects read an essay arguing for the establishment of special programs designed to help individuals use their leisure time more effectively. In one condition the essay was attributed to a distinguished professor at a prestigious university (a person similar to the character in the story at the start of this discussion). In another, it was attributed to a school dropout with no special qualifications in this area. As you might expect, subjects' attitudes about this topic were more strongly affected by the essay when they believed that it had been written by the high-expert source.

Important as it is, however, expertise is only part of the total story. Our judgments about communicator credibility are also strongly determined by others' apparent *motives* or *intentions* (recall our discussion of attribution in Chapter 2). Briefly, if a communicator has much to gain from changing our attitudes, we tend to view him as low in credibility. In contrast, if he has little to gain from altering our views—or actually seems to argue against his own best interests—we may perceive him as much higher on this dimension. For exam-

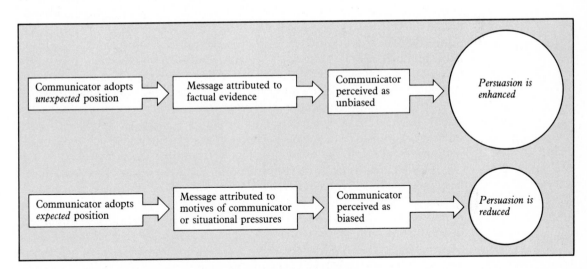

FIGURE 4.7 *Persuasion: The role of communicator motives.*

When communicators adopt unexpected positions—ones inconsistent with their background or personal interests—their messages are often attributed to factual evidence, and they are viewed as being relatively unbiased. This, in turn, enhances persuasion. When, in contrast, communicators adopt expected positions, they are seen as more biased, and persuasion is reduced. [Source: Based on suggestions by Wood & Eagly, 1981.]

ple, consider the incident described on page 136. The factory-owner on the TV talk show obviously had much to gain from government intervention in free trade; after all, his own business might be saved by such action. In contrast, the professor did not appear to have anything obvious to gain from a continuation of free trade (assuming she has not invested in foreign companies!). For this reason, as well as the worker's lower expertise, he might well be viewed as lower in credibility than his opponent.

Direct evidence for the impact of a communicator's apparent motives on both judgments of credibility and attitude change has been obtained in several studies (e.g., Eagly & Himmelfarb, 1978). For example, in an intriguing study, Wood and Eagly (1981) found that when a communicator adopts an unexpected position—one that seems inconsistent with her background or interests —we tend to attribute her message to actual evidence. This, in turn, leads us to perceive such a communicator as unbiased, a reaction that may greatly enhance her success at persuasion (see Figure 4.7 on p. 139). In sum, it appears that communicators whose appeals seem to stem from "good" motives or intentions have a much better chance of altering our attitudes than communicators whose appeals seem to stem from purely selfish ones.

Characteristics of the Communication: It's Not Just Who You Are; What You Say Counts Too

Imagine that you are part of a huge audience that has come to hear the words of a famous doctor—one of the world's greatest experts on good health and long life. As a distinguished scientist and winner of the Nobel prize, her honesty and expertise are beyond question. Further, as she is introduced you notice that she is an individual of impressive physical appearance. The room becomes quiet and she begins. At her first words—"Do you want to know the secret of good health and happiness?"—thousands of people lean forward and strain to catch the pearls of wisdom about to follow. "Well, my friends, I will tell you," she continues in a clear and resonant voice. "After long years of research, I am convinced that the secret of good health is . . . pickled rhubarb!" For a moment there is stunned silence. Then howls of laughter erupt all over the auditorium and soon the speaker is hooted from the stage.

This incident is certainly a bizarre one. But it serves to call attention to a key point: the success of a persuasive appeal depends on its _contents_ as well as on its source. In short, where attitude change is concerned, "what" is often just as important as "who." Since the specific content of any persuasive communication must vary with the particular issue it addresses, social psychologists quickly realized that it is probably not possible to formulate a list of words or arguments capable of enhancing _all_ such appeals. Instead, therefore, they have focused on questions relating to the general form and nature of persuasive messages (e.g., should these present both sides of an issue or only one?). Perhaps the most intriguing question addressed in such research has been the following: are communications that induce strong emotional reactions among an audience more successful in changing attitudes than communications lacking in such content? We will focus on this topic.

FIGURE 4.8   Fear appeals: Sometimes an effective technique of persuasion.

*Persuasive messages designed to induce strong emotional arousal among recipients (**fear appeals**) can be effective in changing attitudes. However, research findings suggest that this is true only under certain conditions. [Photo by Alan Carey/The Image Works.]*

Emotion-inducing appeals: Fear as a basis for persuasion. Can people be frightened into changing their attitudes? Over the centuries, many communicators seem to have assumed that they can. Rulers have often tried to gain support by outlining the dire effects that will follow if their rivals gain power. Similarly, clergy in all religions have threatened their followers with terrible suffering if they stray from the "straight and narrow." You have probably encountered many fear-inducing communications yourself. For example, in recent years, many health and safety organizations have placed ads such as the one shown in Figure 4.8, in the hopes of changing attitudes toward smoking, speeding, the use of contraceptives, and so on. Do such emotion-provoking appeals really work? Will people actually change their attitudes in response to strong fear-inducing messages? The answer offered by systematic research seems to be a cautious "Yes." Such effects *can* occur, but only under certain specific conditions.

Typically, studies designed to examine the effects of fear appeals have used the following strategy. One group of participants is exposed to a very frightening persuasive message. (For instance, they hear statements about the dangers of smoking while watching vivid films of an actual lung cancer operation.) In contrast, a second group is exposed to less frightening materials. (For example, these persons may receive an antismoking message while seeing simple charts illustrating the link between smoking and disease.) Finally, a third (control) group receives no communication at all. The results of many studies of this type suggest that under some conditions, at least, strong fear can indeed enhance attitude change (e.g., Higbee, 1969; Leventhal, 1970). For example, unsettling pictures of decayed teeth and diseased gums produce greater shifts in attitudes toward dental hygiene than less frightening communications based on plastic models of teeth (Dembroski, Lasater, & Ramirez, 1978). It is important to note, though, that such effects occur only under certain conditions. In particular, it appears that **fear appeals** are effective in shifting attitudes only when (1) such appeals are quite strong, (2) the persons who receive them believe that the dangers shown are likely to occur, and (3) these persons believe that the recommendations for avoiding such dangers presented in the message will actually work (Mewborn & Rogers, 1979; Rogers, 1975).

The fact that fear appeals are successful in changing attitudes only under the conditions just mentioned suggests that their impact does not stem simply

Message Content and Persuasion:
The Role of Recipients' Self-schemata

In our discussion of social cognition (see Chapter 3), we noted that as a result of experience, individuals develop *schemata*—cognitive frameworks that assist them in organizing, interpreting, and recalling social information. Further, we noted that information relevant to such schemata is often easier to notice and remember than information unrelated to these frameworks. This fact points to an intriguing possibility: perhaps the impact of persuasive messages can be enhanced by somehow matching them to recipients' schemata. In short, knowledge of an audience's schemata may be helpful in devising the specific content and arguments of a persuasive communication. Evidence in support of this reasoning has recently been reported by Cacioppo, Petty, and Sidera (1982).

These investigators conducted an experiment designed to examine the role of *self-schemata* upon reactions to a persuasive appeal. They reasoned that to the extent a message was relevant to such schemata, its influence might be enhanced. In order to examine this possibility, they first identified two groups of individuals: ones with a *religious orientation* (a religious self-schema) and ones with a *legalistic orientation* (a legalistic self-schema). Both groups were then exposed to a persuasive message supposedly prepared by a congressional representative. The message dealt either with a ban on government support for abortions, or the reinstatement of capital punishment; in both cases, the speaker adopted a position similar to that held by most subjects. A key aspect of the study involved the type of arguments contained in the messages. Some subjects received versions in which most of the arguments were relevant to their self-schemata, while others heard versions in which these arguments were not relevant to these cognitive frameworks. Specifically, half of the subjects with a religious self-schema heard a message based largely on religious arguments (e.g., "There is a sacramental quality to the nature of life that demands that we show the utmost reverence for it."), while half heard a message based mainly on legalistic arguments (e.g., "The right to life is one that is constitutionally safeguarded."). Similarly, half of the subjects with a legalistic self-schema heard a message incorporating religious arguments, and half heard one based mainly on legalistic arguments. Following exposure to the message, all participants rated its persuasiveness, and also wrote down everything they thought about during its presentation. Cacioppo et al. reasoned that subjects would find the messages more persuasive and would have more favorable thoughts about them when they were relevant to their own self-schema than when they were unrelated to these cognitive frameworks. Both predictions were confirmed (please refer to Figure 4.9).

These results suggest that the impact of a persuasive message can indeed be affected by its degree of relevance to recipients' self-schemata. When such relevance is present, recipients may find the

---

from the arousal (fear) they induce. Rather, it appears to derive from cognitive factors, such as subjects' beliefs about the effectiveness of the recommendations offered (Mewborn & Rogers, 1979). Whatever the precise basis for the effects of fear appeals, though, existing evidence seems to point to the following conclusion: under some conditions, at least, frightening one's audience may indeed be a useful first step toward persuasion. (For discussion of another aspect of persuasive communications that may strongly affect their success, please see the **Focus on Research** section above.)

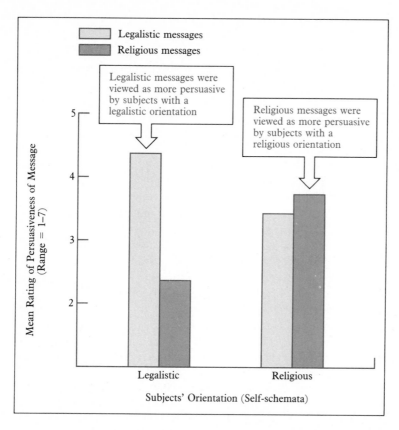

FIGURE 4.9 *Persuasion and self-schemata.*

When the arguments in persuasive messages were relevant to recipients' self-schemata, they viewed these appeals as more persuasive and had more favorable thoughts about them than was true when such messages were not *relevant to their self-schemata. These findings suggest that adjusting the content of persuasive communications so as to take account of the cognitive structures of their audience can often enhance their success. [Source: Based on data from Cacioppo, Petty, & Sidera, 1982.]*

message easy to understand and recall, and may also view it as quite convincing. In contrast, when such relevance is lacking, they may find it difficult to comprehend or remember, and may react to it in a more negative fashion. Of course, communicators can rarely hope to have the kind of systematic information obtained by Cacioppo et al. (1982) at their disposal. As a result, assessing the self-schemata of the members of a given audience will usually pose a difficult task. However, given information about the age, income, and social background of such persons, educated guesses along these lines can often be made. In any case, efforts to identify the schemata of at least some audience members may prove very worthwhile; when the arguments in a communicator's appeal are tailored so as to reflect these cognitive frameworks, handsome dividends in terms of increased persuasion may well be obtained.

Characteristics of the Recipients:
Why Some People Are Easier to Persuade than Others

A useful rule of thumb often adopted by psychologists is this: if you can think of a way in which individuals might differ, they probably do. And susceptibility to persuasion is no exception to this general rule. Human beings appear to vary greatly in this respect. Some are highly resistant to almost all forms of influence, others are swayed easily even by very weak appeals, and most fall somewhere in between. But what factors account for such differences? In the past, efforts to answer this question focused largely on personality variables. It was reasoned that people possessing certain traits or characteristics would probably be easier (or harder) to influence than others. And research findings offered some support for this view. For example, it was found that individuals high in the *need for social approval* (the desire to be liked by others) are often easier to influence than persons lower in this need (Skolnick & Heslin, 1971). Similarly, it was observed that under some conditions, persons low in *self-esteem* are more readily swayed by persuasive messages than those who are higher on this dimension (Zellner, 1970). More recently, however, the focus of such research has shifted to cognitive processes. Specifically, several investigators have suggested that the key to understanding individual differences in persuadability may lie in the cognitive processes stimulated by a communicator's appeal (e.g., Petty, Ostrom, & Brock, 1981). A study conducted by Wood (1982) provides an excellent example of research relating to this perspective.

In this experiment, Wood reasoned that susceptibility to persuasion may often be strongly affected by subjects' ability to remember information relevant to a communicator's message. The greater their ability to accomplish this task (i.e., to recall attitude-relevant facts and information), the greater their ability to formulate counterarguments against the communicator's position, and so the smaller their degree of attitude change. In order to test this possibility, Wood first had subjects express their attitudes on a timely topic — preservation of the environment. Then, she asked them to list all of the facts they believed to be true about this issue, and also to list specific instances in which they had engaged in actions relevant to this topic. It was assumed that subjects who listed a large number of beliefs and behaviors have greater access to attitude-relevant facts and information stored in their memories than those who listed a relatively small number.

In a second portion of the study, conducted one to two weeks later, participants read a persuasive message arguing against preservation of the environment. They then indicated their opinions about this issue once again. In addition, they also listed their thoughts about the message. Results were quite revealing. As predicted, individuals who could readily bring attitude-relevant beliefs or behaviors to mind (i.e., those who listed a large number of beliefs and behaviors about the environment during the first session) showed smaller amounts of attitude change than those who were less successful at such recall (see Figure 4.10). Further, as expected, individuals who could remember many behaviors pertaining to preservation of the environment also reported fewer favorable thoughts about the communicator's message and a greater number of counterarguments against it than those who could remember only a small number of such attitude-relevant behaviors.

These findings and those of other studies (e.g., Petty et al., 1981) point to two general conclusions. First, individuals do in fact differ greatly in their ability to bring attitude-relevant information to mind. And second, such differences strongly affect their reactions to persuasive messages. In response to the question "Why are some people easier to persuade than others?" therefore, a partial answer seems to be: because some have better (or more easily accessed) memo-

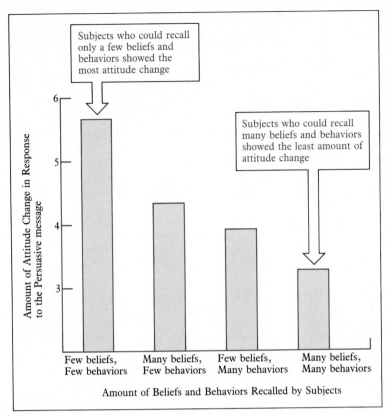

FIGURE 4.10   *Memory and persuasion.*

Individuals who could recall a relatively large number of beliefs or behaviors relevant to a persuasive message showed less attitude change in response to this appeal than individuals who could recall a smaller number of beliefs and behaviors. These findings suggest that the ability to access relevant beliefs and information from memory may play an important role in reactions to persuasion. [Source: Based on data from Wood, 1982.]

ries. (What kind of neural or physiological events occur within our brains during persuasion? For a discussion of this provocative question, please see the **Focus on Research** section on pp. 146–147.)

The Effects of Repeated Exposure: Why, Often, Familiarity Breeds Content

Before concluding our discussion of various factors that affect persuasion, we should consider one final topic: the effects of *repeated exposure* (often known, in social psychology, as the **mere-exposure effect**). As you already know, advertisers seem to place great faith in the view that repetition is an effective technique for changing attitudes. Indeed, they often show the same commercials over and over again, until most of us are totally sick of seeing them (please refer to Figure 4.12 on p. 148). Are such procedures effective? In short, does repeated exposure to the same stimulus tend to alter our attitudes toward it in a favorable direction? A large body of research suggests that this is indeed the case. Within certain limits, the more times we are exposed to a given stimulus, the more favorable our reactions to it become.

The first evidence pointing to this conclusion was obtained some years ago by Zajonc (1968). In several studies, he systematically varied the frequency with

The Physiology of Persuasion: Patterns of Brain Activity during Pro- and Counterattitudinal Messages

Are cognitive events mirrored in physiological processes? At present, most psychologists believe that they are. Specifically, a large majority believe that when we think, remember, form images, or engage in any other cognitive activity, corresponding neural and physiological events must be taking place within our brains. But what, precisely, are these events? Can they be studied? And can information about them help us to understand the nature of cognitive processes themselves? Research findings have begun to provide answers to all of these questions (Cacioppo & Petty, 1983). Investigations performed by scientists from several different fields have begun to uncover the neural bases of memory, emotion, and thought (Dunn, 1980). Progress in this respect has also been made by social psychologists, who have focused much attention on the physiological processes underlying attitude change and persuasion. As an example of this exciting new work, we will consider a study performed by Cacioppo, Petty, and Quintanar (1982).

These investigators based their research on growing evidence that the two hemispheres of the brain function in somewhat different ways (Corballis, 1980; Tucker, 1981). In particular, it appears that the left hemisphere—the part in which major centers governing speech and other verbal functions are located—is the primary site of abstract thought and related intellectual processes. In contrast, the right hemisphere seems to function in a more global and less analytical manner. Stimuli in the external world are represented in it in a more direct and less elaborate fashion. As a result, the right hemisphere often seems to be involved in stronger and more expansive emotional experiences. On the basis of these findings, Cacioppo and his colleagues reasoned that individuals who demonstrate different patterns of activation in the two hemispheres during persuasive communications might well also show contrasting reactions to these messages. Specifically, those with a relatively high level of activity in the right hemisphere might engage in cognitive processes reflecting their initial positive or negative reactions to the communication. As a result, their thoughts about it would tend to be quite polarized—largely favorable or unfavorable in nature. In contrast, those showing relatively high activity in the left hemisphere might engage in more complex and elaborate cognition about the message. Because of this fact, their thoughts about it would tend to be less polarized—more balanced between favorable and unfavorable reactions.

In order to test these intriguing predictions, Cacioppo et al. (1982) exposed subjects to four persuasive communications. These messages dealt with two different issues (e.g., should students be guaranteed season basketball tickets?) and for each, one message favored the views held by most participants, while the other was opposed to these opinions. Prior to each message, subjects received a forewarning, describing the topic with which it would deal and the position it would advocate. Then, after a 45-second pause, they heard a one-minute taped appeal. The electrical activity in their brains (their EEGs) was recorded throughout this period. After each pair of tapes was completed, subjects were asked to write down all their thoughts during these communications. And then, when all tapes were complete, they indicated whether each of their thoughts was favorable, unfavorable, or neutral/irrelevant with respect to the speaker's position. Results offered strong support for the predictions just outlined (see Figure 4.11). That is, subjects who demonstrated relatively high levels of activity in the right hemisphere showed greater polarization in their thoughts about the persuasive messages than those who demonstrated high levels of activity in the left cerebral hemisphere. In other words, those with high activity in the right hemisphere reported thinking mostly favorable thoughts about the proattitudinal message, and mostly unfavorable ones about the counterattitudinal message. In contrast, those with high activity in the left hemisphere reported a more mixed pattern of thoughts in both cases.

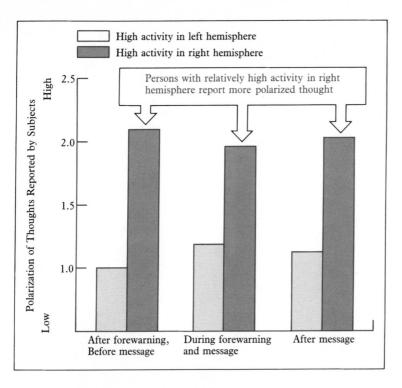

FIGURE 4.11   *Brain activity and polarized thought.*

Individuals who demonstrated relatively high levels of activity in their right *cerebral hemispheres prior to, during, and after persuasive messages later reported more polarized thoughts about these messages than persons who showed relatively high levels of activity in their* left *cerebral hemispheres. These differences provide important clues about the nature of the cognitive processes occurring during persuasion. [Source: Based on data from Cacioppo, Petty, & Quintanar, 1982.]*

In a related follow-up experiment, Cacioppo et al. reasoned that perhaps the earlier results stemmed from a simple fact: as individuals think about attitude issues or persuasive messages, their views become increasingly polarized. Hence, there is a gradual shift from activity in the left hemisphere (reflecting abstract, logical thought) to activity in the right hemisphere (reflecting less elaborate cognition). In order to test this possibility, they exposed subjects to eight attitude statements—four with which they agreed and four with which they disagreed (e.g., driving 55 mph to conserve energy; increasing the number and use of nuclear power plants). After reading each statement, participants were asked to close their eyes and to think about it (Tesser, 1978). Half were allowed 20 seconds for such activity, and half 90 seconds. As predicted, those given more time for such thought showed greater activity in their right hemispheres. Further, within the 90-second group, the longer subjects thought about each statement, the greater the activity in their right hemisphere.

Together, the results of these studies offer important insights into the basic processes underlying

persuasion. They suggest that at first, before we have made up our minds about a given appeal, we often engage in logical and quite elaborate thought about it. At this time, our left cerebral hemispheres are relatively active. Later, after we have reached a conclusion or formed an opinion, the need for such cognition decreases. Then, activity shifts to our right cerebral hemispheres. In addition, it appears that individual differences with respect to this process may exist and play an important role. For example, it is possible that persons with "closed minds" on some issue may show high activity in the right cerebral hemisphere from the start. In contrast, those who are more open-minded on a given issue may demonstrate more initial activity in the left hemisphere. At present, these suggestions are somewhat speculative in nature; further research is needed before they can be accepted with confidence. But one fact is already clear: by studying the neural activities occurring within our brains, we may gain important insights into the nature of persuasion and the basic cognitive processes that underlie it.

FIGURE 4.12   Repetition: Does it really work?

Advertisers often repeat the same commercial over and over again. Does such repetition actually enhance our attitudes toward the products in question? Research findings indicate that, up to a point, this may be so. [Source: Courtesy of Proctor and Gamble.]

which various stimuli (e.g., Chinese characters, photos of strangers) were shown to subjects, and then measured their liking for these materials. Regardless of the stimuli used, results were much the same: the more often they were viewed by subjects, the more favorably they were evaluated.

Impressed by Zajonc's findings, many other researchers turned their attention to the same topic. The studies they conducted soon extended his initial results in several ways. First, this work quickly revealed that frequency of exposure effects occur with respect to a very wide range of stimuli. For example, the favorability of subjects' reactions toward such diverse items as art prints, simple drawings, music, and even photos of their own faces was found to increase with rising frequency of exposure (Heingartner & Hall, 1974; Mita, Dermer, & Knight, 1977). Second, such effects seem to apply to negative as well as to positive stimuli. For example, they have been observed for photos of strangers described as being criminals as well as for photos of persons described as famous scientists (Zajonc et al., 1974). Third, and perhaps most surprising, frequency-of-exposure effects even seem to occur under conditions where individuals are unaware of the fact that they are more familiar with some stimuli than with others. This intriguing fact was first demonstrated in a study conducted by Wilson (1979).

In this investigation, subjects wore stereo headphones and received different stimuli in each ear. One side of the headphones presented a voice reading a literary passage. Subjects were asked to listen to the voice, repeat what it said aloud, and at the same time, check for errors in a written copy of the passage. As you can readily guess, these were difficult and attention-absorbing tasks. While they performed them, though, the other side of the headphones provided different input. Here, three distinctive tone sequences were played five times each, at five second intervals. When the passage ended, subjects were presented with six tone sequences, three of which they had previously heard, and three of which they had not. They were then asked to indicate whether each of these was "old" or "new"—whether they had heard it before or not. As expected, they performed this task at only chance level; after all, their attention had been fully absorbed by the passage and the proofreading task, and in many cases they were not even aware of the tones played to their other ear. Finally, subjects were asked to indicate their reactions to all six tones along a scale ranging from "dislike" to "like." As you can see from Figure 4.13, these ratings were higher for tones they had actually heard before. Further, this was true *regardless of whether they recognized them as familiar or not.* Apparently, then, our reactions to

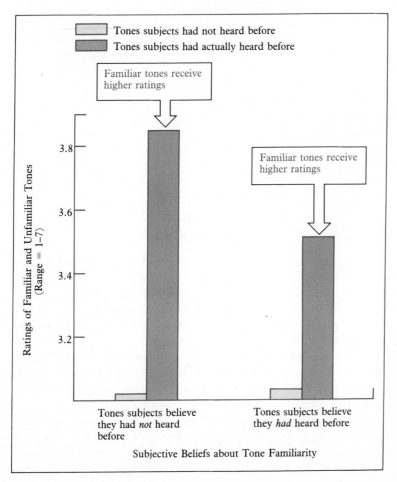

FIGURE 4.13   *The mere-exposure effect: Evidence that awareness is not required.*

Subjects assigned higher ratings to tone sequences they had previously heard than to tone sequences they had not previously encountered. Further, this was true regardless of whether they believed that they had heard them at an earlier time. These results suggest that repeated exposure can enhance reactions to various stimuli even under conditions where individuals are unaware of their degree of familiarity with them. [Source: Based on data from Wilson, 1979.]

various stimuli can be affected by prior exposure to them, even if we are quite unaware of such experiences.

Additional studies suggest that the frequency-of-exposure effect operates in many real-life situations as well as in laboratory settings. (Please see Chapter 6 for further discussion of this topic.) For example, in political elections, the winners are usually those candidates who are most familiar to voters (e.g., famous persons or incumbents). And in situations where none of the candidates are well known to start with, those who spend most on their campaigns—and so gain greatest "media exposure"—usually emerge victorious (Grush, 1980; Grush, McKeough, & Ahlering, 1978). In short, where politics is concerned, victory does not necessarily go to the persons who are most qualified. Rather, it may simply belong to those who are most familiar.

We should hasten to add that other findings point to some limitations on this relationship. For example, increasing frequency of exposure seems to result in positive reactions only in the case of relatively complex stimuli. Such effects do not occur with respect to simple materials (Smith & Dorfman, 1975). Similarly, as common sense suggests, liking for a given stimulus does *not* increase indefinitely with rising frequency of exposure. Beyond some point, continued exposure may actually result in lowered rather than enhanced evaluations (Zajonc et al., 1972). This may be why new songs rapidly gain popularity and then—just as quickly—fade from view. And it may also explain why, after watching a given TV commercial for what seems to be the thousandth time, we groan loudly at the mere hint of another appearance. Within very broad limits, though, increasing exposure to many aspects of the social world seems to enhance rather than reduce evaluative reactions. As suggested by the heading at the start of this section, then, familiarity may, in many cases, actually serve to breed content. (How effective, in general, are attempts at persuasion? For a discussion of this important issue please see the **Focus on Research** section on pp. 152–153.)

Changing Attitudes: The Dissonance Approach

Have you ever had the experience of saying something you didn't believe or of acting in a way contrary to your actual views? Probably you have. Often factors such as family ties, laws, or simple good sense leave us little choice in this respect. For example, we must often act in a friendly manner toward superiors on the job, even if we dislike them. Similarly, we must often say things we don't believe in order to please others or to avoid hurting their feelings.

In many cases we pass through such situations with our attitudes largely unchanged. We behave the way we must, and our beliefs remain unaltered. In others, though, the performance of such *attitude-discrepant behavior* seems to have a surprising effect. Once we have said or done something inconsistent with our true attitudes, our views may actually change. In short, we seem to alter our attitudes in order to bring them more in line with our overt actions. Such effects are far from rare, and you have probably experienced them yourself at one time or another. (For example, have you ever found that after telling another person something you didn't actually believe, it came to seem more reasonable than before?) The question of *why* such effects occur, however, is a puzzling one. Why does the performance of actions inconsistent with our attitudes sometimes lead to changes in these underlying cognitions? One compelling answer is provided by the theory of **cognitive dissonance,** a very influential view in social psychology (Festinger, 1957; Wicklund & Brehm, 1976).

The Theory of Cognitive Dissonance: Inconsistency, Attitudes, and Attitude Change

Dissonance theory begins with a very reasonable suggestion: human beings dislike inconsistency. Specifically, we do not like inconsistency among our various attitudes, on the one hand, or between our attitudes and our overt behavior on the other. When such conditions arise, we experience an unpleasant state known as *dissonance.* And as we shall soon note, it is our attempts to deal with—and reduce—these feelings that often lead to attitude change. In more formal terms, dissonance is said to occur whenever one cognitive element present in our thoughts implies the opposite of another cognitive element, also present. (A cognitive element is anything we know or hold to be true about ourselves, the world around us, or our own behavior.) To illustrate how this special type of inconsistency can lead to important shifts in our attitudes, let us return briefly to the story at the beginning of this chapter.

As you may recall, the person in that incident held strong proenvironmental views. That is, he was quite concerned about protecting the environment from pollution and other dangers. At the same time, though, he loved his powerful new sports car and drove it to work each day. To make matters worse, he drove to work alone and chose to do so despite the presence of good public transportation in his city. According to the theory of cognitive dissonance, this person is an excellent candidate for feelings of dissonance. Each time he thinks about this inconsistency between his attitudes and his behavior, he should experience an unpleasant state of dissonance. After all, there is a large and noticeable gap between what he believes and what he actually does (please refer to Figure 4.15 on p. 155).

Since dissonance is indeed often an unpleasant state (or, at least, is labeled as such; Fazio & Cooper, 1983), the young man in our story would probably seek to reduce it. But how could he accomplish this task? Actually, through several different means. First, he might attempt to *add consonant elements*—thoughts consistent with one or the other of those producing dissonance—to the situation. For example, he might recall that his new car gets far better gas mileage than his old one. Thus, driving it to work actually saves gasoline and cuts down on pollution, relative to his previous behavior. Second, he might seek to *reduce or minimize the importance of some of the cognitive elements involved.* Thus, he might think about the fact that several million people commute to work each day in his city. As a result, his decision to drive is of trivial importance. Third, and most crucial from the point of view of attitude change, he *may actually alter one or both of the cognitive elements producing the dissonance.* For example, he might reconsider and actually decide to take public transportation to work several

When Attitude Change Fails: Resistance to Persuasion

On any given day, we are exposed to a large number of persuasive messages. Commercials, political speeches, editorials—all are designed to alter our views in some manner. Given the frequency of such attempts, and the fact that they are often contradictory in nature, one point is clear: if we yielded to all of these appeals—or even to a small fraction of them—we would soon be in a pitiable state. Our attitudes would change from day to day, or even from hour to hour; and our behavior would probably show a strange pattern of shifts, reversals, and re-reversals! Obviously, this is not the case. Usually, our attitudes are quite stable, and do *not* change on a momentary basis. On the contrary, we generally show a great deal of stability in this respect. Thus, it is probably safe to conclude that far more attempts at persuasion fail than succeed. Why? What factors arm us with such impressive resistance to even powerful efforts to change our views? As you can probably guess, many play a role. Among the most important, however, seem to be **reactance, forewarning, and inoculation.**

Reactance: Protecting our personal freedom. Have you ever been in a situation where, because you felt that someone was trying to exert undue influence on you, you leaned over backwards to do the opposite of what he or she wanted? If so, you are already familiar with the operation of *reactance.* In social psychology, this term refers to the unpleasant, negative reactions we experience whenever we feel that someone is trying to limit our personal freedom. Research findings suggest that when we perceive that this is the case, we often tend to shift in a direction directly opposite to that being recommended—an effect known as *negative attitude change* (e.g., Sensenig & Brehm, 1968; Worchel & Brehm, 1971; Rhodewalt & Davison, 1983). Indeed, so strong does the desire to resist undue influence seem to be that in some cases, individuals shift away from a view being advocated even if it is one they might normally accept.

Two explanations for such behavior have been offered. Brehm's original view held that reactance—and negative attitude change—stems mainly from the desire of most persons to believe that they are the masters of their own fate. Consistent with this motive, we tend to reject pressure or persuasion from others. A second explanation is based upon the notion of *self-presentation.* According to this view, individuals are strongly concerned with "looking good" to others. Further, they realize that yielding to influence attempts may cause them to appear weak or indecisive. For this reason, they react to such attempts with efforts to reassert at least the *appearance* of freedom and autonomy. Since it is their public image that is of major concern, however, this is true only in situations where their resistance can be observed. In cases where it will not be visible to others, they may in fact yield to the communicator's influence (Baer et al., 1980). Regardless of the basis for reactance and negative attitude change, the existence of these processes suggests that "hard-sell" attempts at persuasion will often fail. When individuals perceive such appeals as direct threats to their personal freedom (or their public image) they may be strongly motivated to resist. And such resistance, in turn, may result in total failure for many would-be persuaders.

Prior knowledge of persuasive intent: Why (sometimes) to be "forewarned" is indeed to be "forearmed." On many occasions when we receive a persuasive message, we know full well that it is designed to change our views. Indeed, situations in which a communicator manages to catch us totally unprepared are probably quite rare. But does such advance knowledge of persuasive intent help? In short, does it aid us in resisting later persuasion? A growing body of research evidence suggests that it may (e.g., Cialdini & Petty, 1979; Petty & Cacioppo, 1981). When we know that a speech, taped message, or written appeal is designed to alter our views, we are often less likely to be affected by it than if we do

not possess such knowledge. Moreover, this seems to be especially true with respect to attitudes and issues that we consider important (Petty & Cacioppo, 1979). The basis for these beneficial effects seems to lie in the impact of forewarning upon key cognitive processes. When we receive a persuasive message, especially one that is contrary to our current views, we often formulate counterarguments against it. Knowing about the content of such a message in advance, then, provides us with extra time in which to prepare such defenses. Similarly, forewarning may also give us more time in which to recall relevant facts and information from memory—facts that may prove useful in refuting a persuasive message (Wood, 1982). For these and related reasons, to be forewarned is indeed to be forearmed, at least in cases where we care enough about the topics in question to make active use of this knowledge.

Inoculation: Protection against "bad ideas." A third factor that sometimes helps us to resist at-

tempts at persuasion was suggested by McGuire (1969) some years ago. Briefly, he proposed that exposing individuals to arguments against their views—but which are then strongly refuted—may serve to "inoculate" them against later persuasive appeals. That is, having heard various arguments against their attitudes demolished, individuals may be better equipped to withstand later attempts at persuasion.

In order to test these suggestions, McGuire and Papageorgis (1961) conducted a well-known study in which subjects in two groups were exposed to contrasting procedures. The first (a *supportive defense*) involved the presentation of several arguments supporting their views on various issues (e.g., the benefits of penicillin). The second (a *refutational defense*) involved the presentation of several weak arguments against the subjects' initial views, all of which were then strongly refuted. (Participants in a third condition did not receive either type of "immunization.") Several days later, subjects were exposed to strong attacks against their attitudes. Following these, their views were assessed once again. As McGuire and Papageorgis (1961) predicted, the refutational defense was quite effective in protecting participants against later attitude change. Indeed, it proved to be much more successful in this respect than the supportive defense. These and related findings point to an intriguing conclusion: previous exposure to "bad ideas" (views contrary to our own) in a weak or readily refuted form may indeed serve to immunize us against later attempts at persuasion.

To conclude: because of the operation of reactance, forewarning, and several other factors, our resistance to persuasion is great. Of course, attitude change *does* occur in some cases; to deny this fact would be to suggest that advertising, propaganda, and persuasive messages always fail. But the opposite conclusion—that we are helpless toys in the hands of powerful communicators—is equally false. Resisting persuasion is an ancient human art, and there is every reason to believe that it is just as effective today as it was in the past (please see Figure 4.14 on p. 153). Because of this fact, attitude change is often much easier to plan or imagine than it is to actually achieve.

---

times a week. Obviously, this would eliminate the gap between his attitudes and his behavior. Alternatively, he might change his views about protecting the environment, concluding that he really doesn't care about this issue as strongly as he once believed. In this latter case, of course, dissonance would lead to important shifts in his underlying views.

But given that an individual chooses to reduce dissonance through change in one or more cognitive elements, which of these are actually altered? The answer is: the element least resistant to change. In short, in overcoming dissonance, as in dealing with many other situations in life, we seem to opt for the path of least resistance. Thus, the young man in our example might well weaken his proenvironmental stance. After all, he has already bought the car, and deciding that he really isn't so concerned about the dangers of pollution may be far less painful than leaving his new vehicle in the garage each day. In any case, regardless of how dissonance is resolved in a given situation, one general point is clear. When such feelings are intense, something has to give, and usually this is the cognitive element that is least resistant to change.

Dissonance and Attitude-Discrepant Behavior: The Effects of Forced Compliance

Now that we have described some of the basic aspects of dissonance theory, we can return to the main point of this discussion: indicating how it both predicts and explains the effects of attitude-discrepant behavior. In outline form, the explanation is as follows. Whenever an individual says or does something inconsistent with his or her true beliefs, dissonance results. This reaction can be reduced in several ways, but the most important are these: (1) the person involved can change his or her attitudes so that they are consistent with the action performed, or (2) the person can alter his or her cognitions about this behavior. (The behavior itself can't be changed since it has already been completed.) In many cases, it is difficult to change one's cognitions about past actions. After all, behaviors often produce undeniable effects. Thus, in

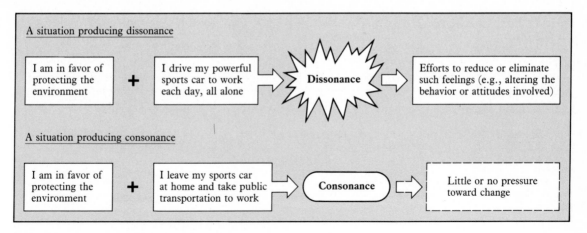

FIGURE 4.15   Dissonance: The price of inconsistency.

When our attitudes and our behavior are inconsistent, an unpleasant state of dissonance *is produced. This, in turn, leads to efforts to eliminate such feelings (e.g., by changing our attitudes or behavior or minimizing the importance of the elements involved in such inconsistency). In contrast, when our attitudes and our behavior are consistent, a state of* consonance *exists. Here, little pressure toward change is present.*

such instances, it is easier to alter the relevant attitudes. Attitude change, then, stems from this source. Perhaps a specific example will help to clarify this process and related matters.

Imagine that during a meeting, your boss voices support for a specific policy—one with which you personally disagree. Then, even worse, she turns to you and asks you to state your opinion in front of all the other members of your department. What will you do? It's hard to predict for sure, but let us assume that in this case you "waffle." That is, you murmur that you are undecided, but are leaning toward the boss's position. According to dissonance theory, you are then likely to experience considerable dissonance. After all, there is a noticeable gap between your words and your underlying views. But will this then lead to shifts in your attitudes about the key policy? The answer is: it depends. And what it depends upon, primarily, is your reasons for engaging in attitude-discrepant behavior (i.e., your reasons for saying something you don't really believe). If you have *many* good reasons for endorsing your boss's position (e.g., the last person to contradict her was fired!), dissonance will be low, and you will probably *not* alter your private views. In contrast, if you have very *few* reasons for going along with her position, dissonance will be high. And in this case, you may well experience considerable pressure to alter your attitudes toward the policy in question. In short, dissonance theory leads to the prediction that the less justification we have for engaging in attitude-discrepant behavior, the greater the dissonance produced by such actions, and the more attitude change we will tend to show.

This general principle, in turn, leads to an intriguing prediction: in situations where individuals are offered rewards for engaging in attitude-discrepant

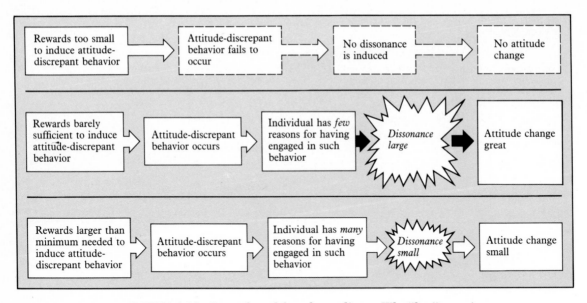

FIGURE 4.16   Rewards and forced compliance: Why "less" sometimes leads to "more."

When individuals are provided with rewards just barely sufficient to induce them to engage in attitude-discrepant behavior, dissonance is maximized, and considerable attitude change may result (middle panel). When the rewards provided are either too small to induce attitude-discrepant behavior (top panel) or are larger than the minimum needed to produce such actions (bottom panel), dissonance and attitude change will both be smaller.

behavior (i.e., in situations involving **forced compliance**) the dissonance produced — and therefore the amount of attitude change that follows — will be maximum when such rewards are just barely sufficient to induce the inconsistent actions. Any smaller, and attitude-discrepant behavior is unlikely to occur. Any larger, and the increased justification provided by large payoffs will serve to lessen the total amount of dissonance. In sum, dissonance leads to the somewhat startling prediction that often less may well produce more: small rewards may actually induce greater degrees of attitude change than large ones (please refer to Figure 4.16).

Surprising as this prediction may seem, it has actually been confirmed in a large number of studies (e.g., Riess & Schlenker, 1977). For example, in the first and perhaps most famous of these experiments (Festinger & Carlsmith, 1959), subjects were offered either a small reward ($1.00) or a large one ($20.00) for telling another person that some dull tasks they had just performed were really quite interesting. (One of the tasks consisted of placing spools on a tray, dumping them out, and repeating the process over and over again.) After engaging in this attitude-discrepant behavior, subjects were asked to indicate their own liking for the tasks. As predicted by the "less-leads-to-more" effect, they actually reported liking the dull tasks more when they had received the small reward for describing them favorably than when they had received a large reward.

While this and many other studies lend support to predictions based on dissonance theory, we should note that recent experiments indicate that the **less-leads-to-more effect** occurs only under certain conditions (Sogin & Pallak, 1976). First, as might be expected, such effects occur only in situations where individuals believe that they had a choice as to whether to perform the attitude-discrepant behavior. Second, small rewards lead to greater amounts of attitude change than large ones only when individuals feel that they were *personally responsible* both for the chosen course of action and any negative effects produced (e.g., Goethals, Cooper, & Naficy, 1979). And finally, the less-leads-to-more effect does *not* occur when individuals view the payment they receive as a bribe, rather than as well-deserved pay (Schlenker et al., 1980). These and related findings suggest that there are in fact important limits on the impact of forced compliance. Yet, we should note that in many situations the conditions just outlined *do* exist. Individuals often believe that they enjoy freedom of action, even when they do not. And they frequently accept responsibility for their own behavior even in cases where it produces negative consequences. As a result, the strategy of offering others just barely enough reward to induce them to say or do things they do not believe may often be an effective one. In many cases, it can lead to important—and lasting—shifts in existing attitudes.

Dissonance and Effort: Why Suffering May Lead to Liking

As we have just seen, dissonance theory has been employed to explain the often surprising effects of attitude-discrepant behavior. And its success in this regard is certainly impressive. However, this is far from the only context in which the implications of dissonance have been explored. Indeed, the theory has also been applied to a number of other topics, such as the effects of making decisions (e.g., Converse & Cooper, 1979; Younger, Walker, & Arrowood, 1977), and the interpretation of feelings of heightened arousal (Fazio & Cooper, 1983). One of the most intriguing questions it has addressed, however, is this: What are the effects of effort on the evaluation of various goals, tasks, or items? Here, once again, dissonance theory leads to some fascinating—and counter-intuitive—predictions.

Consider the various goals you have sought in your own life. Which of these did you value most highly once they were attained? Probably, your answer is something like this: "The ones for which I had to work hardest." In short, we usually tend to evaluate goals, tasks, or objects requiring the expenditure of a great amount of effort more favorably than ones requiring less effort (or cost). Why is this the case? One possibility is that goals for which we must work very hard are actually higher in intrinsic worth. Thus, it is only natural that we evaluate them more favorably. Another and sharply different explanation is offered by dissonance theory. Briefly, it suggests that we may come to evaluate goals or items requiring great effort very favorably largely because of this effort itself (**effort justification**). The reasoning behind this proposal is as follows. If

FIGURE 4.17   Disconfirmed expectancies: One major cause of dissonance.

When individuals work hard to attain some goal, but then find that it is not all that they expected, considerable dissonance may result. [Source: Drawing by Wm. Hamilton; © 1978 The New Yorker Magazine, Inc.]

"I got what I wanted, but it wasn't what I expected."

we expend a great deal of effort in attaining some goal, but then evaluate it negatively, dissonance is produced (see Figure 4.17). After all, the fact that we worked so hard to gain it is inconsistent with such negative reactions. One way of reducing these feelings, of course, is to somehow convince ourselves that we really didn't invest much effort in attaining this goal. Given that long years of study, hours of hard work, or great expense are difficult to ignore, though, this solution is often not a feasible one. In contrast, another means of eliminating such dissonance is far easier to employ: we can raise our evaluations of the goal or item in question. In short, we can perceive it in a more favorable light, and in this way, justify our past effort.

The occurrence of precisely such effects has been observed in several different experiments (e.g., Aronson & Mills, 1959; Gerard & Mathewson, 1966). For example, in one study with important practical implications (Cooper, 1980), persons who expressed great fear of snakes were asked to participate in one of two different kinds of "therapy." One group was asked to imagine a series of scenes involving increasing contact with snakes (e.g., finding one in their sleeping bag; jumping into a pit filled with snakes!). The second group merely performed a series of physical exercise. Because the first form of treatment was much more effortful than the second (at least from a psychological perspective), Cooper reasoned that subjects who had freely chosen to perform it would perceive it as more effective and would then actually approach a live snake more closely than subjects who merely exercised. Results offered strong support for this hypothesis. Subjects in the high-effort group were willing to stand more than two feet closer to a snake than those in the low-effort group. These and related findings suggest that the explanation for the impact of effort on attitudes offered by dissonance theory is correct: often, we come to perceive goals for which we have had to pay dearly in a favorable light because doing so allows us to justify these past costs or effort. (For an interesting look at how the use of alcohol may be linked to the need to reduce dissonance, see the **On the Applied Side** section on pp. 160–161.)

Attitudes and Behavior: The Essential Link

Do attitudes shape behavior? Your first answer is likely to be "Of course!" After all, you can readily recall many incidents in which your own actions were strongly determined by your current views about some person, issue, or group. Yet, if you give this matter a bit more thought, you will also be able to remember instances in which your overt actions did *not* reflect your attitudes. As we noted earlier, unless you have lived a totally charmed life, you have probably often found it necessary to say things you did not believe, to refrain from speaking your mind to others, and to act in ways that you knew to be inconsistent with your true opinions. At first glance, then, the link between attitudes and behavior appears to be complex. Sometimes attitudes predict overt actions, and sometimes they do not. Has such complexity been confirmed by research findings? In fact, it has. While early investigations seemed to suggest that attitudes are only weak predictors of human behavior (e.g., LaPiere, 1934), recent studies point to a more positive conclusion. Attitudes, it appears, *can* exert powerful effects upon overt actions. However, this is the case only when certain conditions prevail. The list of such factors seems to lengthen each year, but among the most important are these: (1) **attitude strength,** (2) **attitude specificity,** and (3) **attitude relevance.**

Attitude Strength: Strong Attitudes Predict Behavior More Successfully than Weak Ones

Suppose that two persons favor a freeze on further production of nuclear weapons. One has deep convictions about the need for such a ban; the other is only mildly in favor of this action. Which will be more likely to translate these views into overt behavior (e.g., into signing a petition)? The answer seems obvious: the individual with the strong opinions. Strong attitudes, in short, should be better predictors of behavior than weak ones. Is this actually the case? Several recent experiments indicate that it is (e.g., Fazio et al., 1982; Snyder & Kendzierski, 1982). For example, attitudes formed through direct experience with an attitude object are more closely linked to overt actions than ones formed in an indirect manner. As we noted earlier, such attitudes are also often stronger than views formed in the absence of such experience. Similarly, attitudes that are strengthened through repeated expressions are better predictors of later behavior than ones that are not enhanced in this manner. But why is this the case? Why do strong attitudes affect behavior to a greater degree than weak ones? The answer seems to involve a basic fact: only attitudes we can remember or bring to mind can guide overt actions. And strong attitudes

ON THE
APPLIED SIDE

*Dissonance, Arousal,
and Social Drinking*

Dissonance, we have noted at several points, is an unpleasant psychological state. Most persons feel uncomfortable when they discover that their attitudes, or their attitudes and their behavior, are inconsistent. Further, some evidence suggests that dissonance is also arousing—it increases the level of physiological activation among persons who experience it (e.g., Cooper & Croyle, 1982; Fazio & Cooper, 1983). The most direct means of reducing such arousal, of course, involves attempts to eliminate inconsistency. And as we have already seen, individuals often adopt this strategy when confronted with dissonance. But informal observation suggests that another tactic for dealing with such feelings may also exist. When people experience unpleasant arousal stemming from other sources (job-related stress, sexual frustration, failure) they often turn to various drugs as a means of handling such discomfort. For example, by taking a drink—or perhaps several—they find that they can reduce these unpleasant feelings. This fact points to an intriguing possibility: will such an approach also succeed in reducing dissonance-produced arousal? In short, can persons faced with inconsistency between their attitudes and their behavior lessen their psychological discomfort by means of alcohol or other drugs? A series of experiments conducted by Steele, Southwick, and Critchlow (1981) point to the conclusion that they can.

In these investigations, subjects first completed an attitude questionnaire that assessed, among other things, their views on a large tuition hike at their university. Then, in a second part of the study, they were asked either to write down arguments in favor of such an increase, or to list arguments against it. Needless to say, those who argued in favor of the increase in tuition were engaging in

counterattitudinal behavior. Thus, they experienced considerable dissonance. In a third portion of the research, subjects were asked to taste and rate several substances. For some, these were beer; for others, they were vodka-laced cocktails; and for still others, they were merely distilled water or coffee. Following these procedures, subjects' attitudes toward the tuition issue were measured once again. Steele and his colleagues reasoned that among subjects who wrote against the tuition hike, no dissonance would be generated. Thus, little attitude change would occur in this group regardless of the substances they swallowed. In contrast, those who wrote in favor of the tuition increase would experience dissonance. And among these subjects, it was suggested, alcohol might help to reduce the unpleasant feelings accompanying this state. To the extent it did, subjects would no longer experience any pressure to change their views in order to bring them into closer line with their overt actions. Neither coffee nor water were expected to yield such effects, however. Thus, subjects who drank these substances were expected to show the type of shifts in their attitudes usually produced by cognitive dissonance. As you can see from Figure 4.18, results offered support for all of these predictions. In short, drinking beer or cocktails *did* seem to eliminate subjects' need to alter their views; neither coffee nor water had such effects. (By the way, the amount of alcohol consumed by subjects was quite small—none were anywhere near being intoxicated.)

As you can readily see, these findings have important practical implications. Dissonance—alas!—is an all-too-common aspect of daily life. As we have already noted, good manners, family ties, and other factors often cause us to say things we

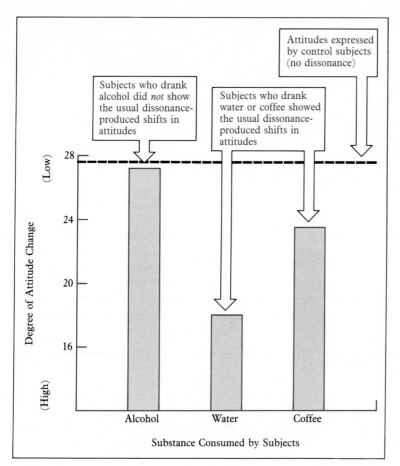

FIGURE 4.18   Alcohol: An alternative route to dissonance reduction?

*When individuals drank small quantities of beer or vodka after engaging in attitude-discrepant behavior, they failed to show the shifts in attitude usually produced by cognitive dissonance. In contrast, when they drank water or coffee, the usual dissonance-induced shifts **did** occur. These findings suggest that the unpleasant arousal associated with dissonance can sometimes be reduced by alcohol, as well as by changing one's views. [Source: Based on data from Steele, Southwick, & Critchlow, 1981.]*

don't mean, or to do things we would rather avoid. Further, dissonance also stems from many decisions—especially ones that are difficult or important. Given the frequency of dissonance in everyday life, it seems quite possible that some persons turn to alcohol or other drugs as a quick-and-easy means of reducing such feelings. In short, the desire to avoid cognitive dissonance may contribute, along with several other factors, to their dependency on such substances. To the extent this is actually the case, new forms of treatment for such dependency, based on providing individuals with more constructive means for handling dissonance, may prove useful. Perhaps such procedures will be developed in the years ahead. In the meantime, however, one fact already seems clear: knowledge about cognitive dissonance obtained by social psychologists has shed new light on a form of human behavior with important—and sometimes tragic—consequences.

appear to be more readily accessed from memory than weak ones (Snyder & Kendzierski, 1982). Regardless of the precise mechanisms involved, however, there seems little doubt that when attempting to predict specific behaviors from attitudes, the strength of these views should be taken carefully into account. The stronger the attitudes in question, the more likely they are to serve as useful predictors.

attitude
specificity

Attitude Specificity: Specific Attitudes Predict Behavior Better than Global Ones

It's election day, and you step into the voting booth and close the curtain. Your general political philosophy is conservative, so usually you vote for Republican candidates. This time, though, you face a dilemma: the candidate chosen by this party is someone you find obnoxious. While he *is* a conservative like yourself, you dislike his style, many of his statements, and even his face. In contrast, you find his opponent (a middle-of-the-road Democrat) much more pleasant. How would you vote? In a moment you have made your choice: for the first time in years you have given your support to a Democrat. Incidents such as this are far from rare, and they call our attention to an important fact: in many cases, our overt actions are more strongly affected by specific, focused attitudes than by general or global ones. Thus, as in this example, our attitudes toward particular candidates may outweigh our more general political philosophy in voting decisions. Similarly, in actual research, it has been found that intense annoyance over a lack of parking spots may overwhelm proenvironmental views, and lead individuals to support the construction of more parking garages (Borgida & Campbell, 1982). Finally, we should note that many studies indicate that highly accurate predictions of overt behavior can often be derived from individuals' *behavioral intentions* → specific intentions to act in certain ways (e.g., Fishbein & Azjen, 1975; Kantola, Syme, & Campbell, 1982). Such intentions can, in one sense, be viewed as highly specific attitudes. In any case, these and related findings (e.g., Heberlein & Black, 1976) point to the following conclusion: In attempting to predict overt behavior from attitudes, it is often more useful to focus on specific views than on general or global ones.

Attitude Relevance: Attitudes That Affect Outcomes Are Better Predictors of Behavior than Attitudes That Do Not

Imagine that you are a senior at a large university. During your last semester, the administration introduces a plan requiring all students to complete three years of foreign language study prior to graduation. It will take effect two years in the future and you, like almost all other students, are against it. One day, you are approached by a person who asks you to help in an active campaign to defeat the new plan. Will you agree? While we can't say for sure, the chances are good that you will refuse; after all, you will be long gone before the requirement takes effect, and it will have no impact upon you. But now imagine that you are a freshman, and that your college studies will be strongly affected by the plan. How will you react now? Here, the chances are probably much higher that you will agree to aid in the campaign. And the reason is obvious: you have much to lose by *not* acting on your attitudes. Situations such as this one point to an important fact: often the strength of the link between our attitudes and our behavior is affected by what has been termed *vested interest.* When the actions implied by such views can have strong effects upon our outcomes, the relationship is a close one. When such actions promise to have little impact upon our lives, attitude-behavior consistency may be much lower. Direct evidence for this conclusion is provided by the results of a study conducted by Sivacek and Crano (1982).

This investigation centered around a real-life issue that arose several years ago in the state of Michigan. A proposal to raise the minimum drinking age from 18 to 20 (Proposal D) had been offered and was on the ballot. Sivacek and Crano took advantage of this issue to examine the impact of vested interest on the attitude-behavior link. In order to do so, they first identified three groups of

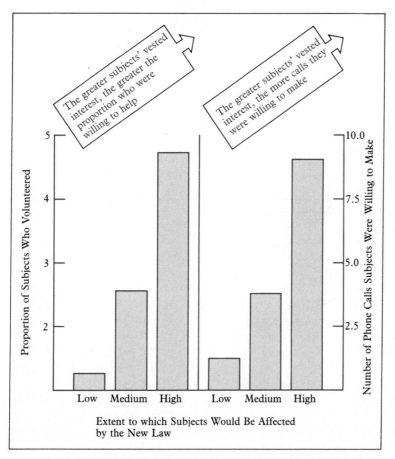

FIGURE 4.19 Vested interest: A strong determinant of the attitude-behavior link.

Subjects who would be strongly affected by a new law were more willing to campaign against it than individuals who would be affected to a lesser degree. In short, the greater their **vested** interest in defeating this proposal, the stronger their tendency to translate their negative attitude toward it into overt actions. [Source: Based on data from Sivacek & Crano, 1982.]

subjects: ones who would be 21 before the law took effect and so would not be affected by it; ones who would be affected by it for at least two years; and persons who were in between these two extremes. Subjects in each of these categories were then telephoned and asked to assist a group of students who were campaigning against the proposal. Specifically, they were asked to phone others and try to persuade them to vote against it. All subjects were against the new law, but consistent with the vested-interest hypothesis, Crano and Sivacek predicted that those who would be most strongly affected by it would be most likely to act on these attitudes: they would be most willing to help and would volunteer to call more persons than subjects in the other two conditions. As you can see from Figure 4.19 (on p. 163), results confirmed these predictions. The greater the impact of the proposal upon participants, the stronger their tendency to translate their views into overt actions.

In sum, existing evidence suggests that attitudes can, in fact, affect behavior. Whether this is the case, however, depends on a number of different factors. When attitudes are strong and readily accessible, when they are specific, and when the actions they imply promise to strongly affect our lives, the attitude-behavior link may be a firm one. When, in contrast, they are weak, unfocused, and lacking in relevance to our outcomes, this relationship may be more tenuous. The central question then, appears to be *"When* and *how* do attitudes affect behavior?"* not simply *"Do* they exert such effects?" And as we have tried to note, social psychologists have already begun to provide firm — and potentially useful — answers.

Summary

We are rarely completely neutral to the persons, groups, objects, or issues around us. Rather, we usually have beliefs about them, feelings toward them, and behavioral tendencies concerning them. When such reactions cluster around a particular object, person, or issue, and are relatively lasting, they may be viewed as forming an **attitude.**

Children are not born with the complex attitudes they will later hold as adults. Rather, these are formed through a gradual process of *social* learning or acquired through *direct experience* with attitude objects.

Attempts to alter attitudes often involve **persuasive communications.** Many factors influence the success of such appeals, but among the most important are: (1) *characteristics of the communicator* (e.g., his or her credibility), (2) *characteristics of the communication* (e.g., its use of emotional appeals), and (3) *characteristics of the recipients* (e.g., their self-esteem, ability to access various attitudes from memory). Recent findings also suggest that attitudes toward many stimuli are affected by *repeated exposure.* Within certain limits, the more often they are presented, the more they tend to be liked.

Attitudes can also often be changed by somehow inducing individuals to engage in *attitude-discrepant* behavior. The **dissonance** generated in such situations may lead such persons to alter their attitudes in order to make them more consistent with their overt actions. Dissonance also helps explain why goals for which we have worked very hard are usually evaluated more favorably than goals requiring less cost or effort. Recent evidence suggests that dissonance can sometimes be reduced by certain drugs (e.g., alcohol). This factor may contribute, along with several others, to alcohol dependence and related problems.

Research findings suggest that attitudes can, in fact, influence behavior. Whether this is the case or not, though, depends on a number of different factors, including attitude *strength*, attitude *specificity*, and attitude *relevance*.

Glossary

attitude relevance *Refers to the degree to which behaviors implied by a given attitude affect an individual's outcomes. The greater such relevance (also known as* **vested interest***), the stronger the link between attitudes and behavior.*

attitude scales (questionnaires) *Instruments for measuring attitudes. Persons completing such scales are asked to indicate their degree of agreement or disagreement with various statements about the attitude object.*

attitude specificity *Refers to the extent to which an attitude is focused on a specific attitude object. The greater such specificity, the stronger the link between attitudes and behavior.*

attitude strength *Refers to the strength of the association between an attitude object and the affective, cognitive, and behavioral tendencies relating to it. The stronger such bonds, the closer the link between attitudes and behavior.*

attitudes *Relatively enduring organizations of feelings, beliefs, and behavior tendencies directed toward specific persons, issues, objects, or groups.*

bogus pipeline *A method for measuring attitudes in which subjects are led to believe that their true reactions will be revealed by a device that measures their physiological responses. Since subjects assume that their attitudes will be revealed by the equipment, they may be less likely to attempt to conceal these views than would otherwise be the case.*

cognitive dissonance *An unpleasant state induced by recognition of inconsistency in one's attitudes, or between one's attitudes and overt behavior. Attempts to reduce dissonance often result in attitude change.*

communicator credibility *Refers to the extent to which a communicator is viewed as being reliable or trustworthy as a source of information.*

direct experience *Refers to situations in which attitudes are formed through direct contact with attitude objects. Attitudes formed in this manner appear to be stronger and more readily accessed from memory than attitudes formed in the absence of direct experience.*

effort justification *Refers to situations in which individuals have expended much effort to obtain some goal, only to discover that it is less valuable or desirable than they assumed. In order to reduce the dissonance produced in such cases, they may raise their evaluation of the goal, thereby seeking to justify the effort they expended.*

fear appeals *Persuasive communications containing fear-arousing materials. Research findings suggest that such appeals can be effective in changing attitudes, but only under certain conditions.*

forced compliance *Refers to situations in which individuals are induced (usually through rewards) to state views inconsistent with their true attitudes. Such behavior produces dissonance and may then result in attitude change.*

forewarning *Advance information about a communication's persuasive intent. Forewarning often helps individuals to resist persuasion by providing them with extra time in which to prepare counterarguments against the message.*

inoculation *A technique for increasing resistance to persuasion. In the most effective form of inoculation* (**refutational defense**), *weak arguments against an individual's attitudes are presented and then refuted. This seems to strengthen resistance to later attempts at persuasion.*

instrumental conditioning *A form of learning in which certain responses (but not others) are followed by reward. Research findings suggest that this process plays an important role in attitude formation.*

less-leads-to-more effect *Refers to the fact that in forced compliance situations, maximum attitude change results when individuals are provided with rewards just barely sufficient in size to induce them to perform the attitude-discrepant behavior.*

Likert scaling *A technique for measuring attitudes in which respondents are asked to indicate the extent to which they agree or disagree with attitude statements that are favorable or unfavorable toward the attitude object.*

mere-exposure effect *(also known as the* frequency-of-exposure effect*) Refers to the fact that the more frequently we are exposed to a given stimulus, the more favorable to it our reactions tend to become.*

modeling *Refers to the process in which one individual acquires behaviors shown by another simply as a result of observing these actions. Research findings suggest that modeling plays an important role in attitude formation.*

persuasive communications *Written, spoken, filmed,* or televised messages designed to alter the attitudes of the persons who receive them.*

reactance *An unpleasant state stemming from the perception that one's personal freedom is being threatened — usually by influence attempts from others. When reactance occurs, individuals often engage in actions designed to restore or maintain their personal freedom.*

social learning *Refers to several processes through which individuals acquire attitudes, behavior, or knowledge from the persons around them. Both modeling and instrumental conditioning appear to play a role in such learning.*

suffering-leads-to-liking effect *See "effort justification."*

unobtrusive measures *Indirect measures of behavior, often based on written records or the physical traces of human activities. Unobtrusive measures are often useful in attaining information about attitudes.*

For More Information

Petty, R. E., & Cacioppo, J. T. *Attitudes and persuasion: Classic and contemporary approaches.* Dubuque, Iowa: Wm. C. Brown, 1981.
This excellent text reviews current knowledge about attitude change and persuasion in a thorough and up-to-date manner. An important feature is coverage of the newer, information-processing view of persuasion. All in all, a valuable and informative source.

Rajecki, D. W. *Attitudes: Themes and advances.* Sunderland, Mass.: Sinauer Associates, 1982.
A very thorough survey of current knowledge concerning attitudes and their effects. Separate chapters examine such intriguing topics as methods of attitude research, the repeated-exposure effect, and persuasive communications. An excellent source to consult if you would like to know more about attitudes.

Wicklund, R. A., & Brehm, J. W. *Perspectives on cognitive dissonance.* Hillsdale, N.J.: Erlbaum, 1976.
A summary and critique of research on the theory of cognitive dissonance. Many of the topics examined in this chapter (for example, the effects of attitude-discrepant behavior) are considered in detail. This is a very useful source to read if you would like to know more about the fascinating effects of dissonance.

Zanna, M. P., Higgins, E. T., and Herman, C. P. (Eds.) *Consistency in social behavior: The Ontario Symposium* (Vol. 2). Hillsdale, N.J.: Erlbaum, 1983.
The chapters in this volume deal with various aspects of attitudes, social cognition, and the relationship between attitudes and behavior. They are written primarily for a scientific audience, so you may find several difficult to follow. The contributors are all noted experts in this area, however, so the effort is well worthwhile.

CHAPTER 5

Prejudice and Discrimination:
Why All Too Often (and with Little Reason)
Differences Count

**Prejudice and Discrimination:
What They Are and How They Are Measured**

*Prejudice: Social Identity as a Basis for Rejection / Discrimination: Prejudice in
Action / Prejudice: How It Is Measured*

Theoretical Explanations of Prejudice: The Origins of Hate

*Direct Intergroup Conflict: Competition as a Basis for Bigotry / "Us" versus "Them":
Social Categorization as a Basis for Prejudice / Authoritarianism: Personality as
a Basis for Prejudice / Early Experience as a Basis for Prejudice: The Role of
Social Learning*

Reducing Prejudice: Some Steps in the Right Directions

*Breaking the Chain of Bigotry: On Learning Not to Hate / Enhanced Intergroup
Contact: On the Positive Effects of Acquaintance*

Prejudice Based on Sex: A Special, Timely Case

*Prejudice against Women: Why It Sometimes (and in Some Places) Hurts to Be
Female / Discrimination against Females: Keeping Women in "Their Place"*

**Sex Roles and Sexual Identity:
Masculine, Feminine, or Androgynous?**

Sex Typing: Some Alternate Views / A Note on Androgyny: The Best of Both Worlds?

Special Inserts

FOCUS ON RESEARCH
   Stereotypes: An Unsettling Note on Their Self-confirming Nature

FOCUS ON RESEARCH
   The Illusion of Outgroup Homogeneity: A Cognitive Basis for Prejudice

ON THE APPLIED SIDE
   Failure of the Equal Rights Amendment: A Social Psychological Perspective

*It has often been said that "you can't go home again," and in a key sense, this is true. Usually, we **cannot** return to the simpler ideas and perspectives of our youth. But there is nothing to prevent us from going back for an occasional visit, and this is precisely what you are doing today, for you have returned to the small town of your birth to attend the tenth reunion of your high school class. You are enjoying the opportunity to see many of your childhood friends once again and, at the moment, are standing with several, describing your new life in a large Florida city. Suddenly, one member of the group — Michael Fleming — makes a disturbing remark:*

"Well, Florida sounds nice and all, but what about those Cubans? I'll bet they really ruin it, don't they?"

Mike's remark comes as a surprise, for you don't remember him as being especially prejudiced. Yet, his words clearly suggest that he holds a strong negative view of Cubans.

"Gee, Mike," you reply, "I don't know what you mean. There are plenty of Cubans around, all right, but they're no problem. Most are darn good people and I get along with them fine."

*"Oh come on, don't give me that," Mike answers with some heat. "We may be far off the beaten track out here, but we **do** get the news. I know what those people are like — a rotten bunch of animals. I wish they'd go back where they belong, with their good buddy Fidel."*

*Your response to these words is a strong protest. "You've got to be kidding. Don't you know that most of them left Cuba to get **away** from Castro? They don't like him any more than you do."*

*"Sure," says Mike, "that's what they'd **like** you to believe. But they don't fool me. Half are a bunch of commie spies, at least. And anyway, even if they're not, I know one thing for sure: they're about the saddest collection of human garbage ever seen. Prostitutes, thieves, and drunks — that's what came over on those boats. If we had any guts, we'd throw the whole bunch back into the sea!"*

You are really shaken now. How can Mike hold these views? Sure, there are criminals in the Cuban community, just as there are criminals in every large group. But most are decent, hard-working people. And their culture and food have really added a lot to your city. You are about to set Mike straight on these points, when Hazel Peters, another old friend, comes up and joins the group. At her approach, the conversation dissolves into warm greetings and hugs, so the matter is dropped and seemingly forgotten. But later, as you sit in your hotel room, your thoughts return to Mike's remarks once again. Where did he ever get these ideas about Cubans? As far as you can tell, there isn't a single one in the whole town, so Mike has probably never even met one. But this hasn't stopped him from forming a powerful hatred for them. And how can a rational person like Mike believe that most of these people are Communists, when many were imprisoned or even tortured by the Castro regime? "Gee," you think to yourself, "if a decent guy like Mike can think like this, it's no wonder we've got problems . . . "

Most people would agree that the phrase "Don't jump to conclusions" offers good advice well worth following. Yet somehow, where other persons are concerned, we often seem to lose sight of its existence. In many cases we *do* jump to conclusions about others. Even worse, these usually rest on the flimsiest type of foundation imaginable: their membership in some social group. Thus, we often form judgments about others solely on the basis of their ethnic, racial, religious, or even sexual identity. This tendency to jump to "social conclusions" about others lies at the heart of two key processes we will consider in this chapter: **prejudice** and **discrimination.**

As we're sure you already realize, these forces pose a serious, continuing threat to all of human society. Indeed, it is probably safe to state that over the centuries, they have been responsible for more needless human suffering than any other factors we might mention (see Figure 5.1). For this reason as well as others, prejudice and discrimination have long been of central interest to social psychologists. In their efforts to investigate these processes, our colleagues have focused on a wide range of issues and topics. Central among these, however, have been the following: (1) what is the basic nature of prejudice and discrimination? (2) how do these processes originate? and (3) what steps can be taken to reduce their occurrence? In the discussion that follows, we will examine current knowledge with respect to each of these questions. In addition, we will also focus on a specific form of prejudice that has recently been the subject of a great deal of interest: that based on sex.

Prejudice and Discrimination: What They Are and How They Are Measured

Are prejudice and discrimination the same? Common usage of these two words seems to suggest that they are. Reporters, civil rights leaders, and even some social scientists tend to use them as synonyms. Actually, though, they refer to two distinct, if closely linked, phenomena. *Prejudice* describes a special type of attitude — generally, a negative one toward the members of some distinct social group. In contrast, *discrimination* refers to specific negative actions directed against these individuals. We will now expand upon this distinction in more detail.

Prejudice: Social Identity as a Basis for Rejection

As we have just seen, social psychologists generally view prejudice as a special type of attitude. In particular, they usually define it in the following manner: *prejudice is an attitude toward the members of some specific group, leading the persons who hold it to evaluate others in a characteristic fashion (usually negative), solely on the basis of their membership in that group.* When we say that a given person is prejudiced against the members of some social group, we generally mean that he or she tends to evaluate its members negatively merely because they belong

FIGURE 5.1 *Prejudice and discrimination: Malignant forces in human history.*

Throughout recorded history, prejudice and discrimination have been responsible for a tremendous amount of needless human suffering. [Source: Photo (top) from the New York Public Library Picture Collection; photo (left) copyright Martha Stewart / The Picture Cube.]

to that group. Their individual behavior or characteristics play little role and rarely enter into the picture.

When prejudice is defined as a special type of attitude, two major implications follow. First, as we noted in Chapter 4, attitudes often operate as *schemata*—cognitive frameworks for organizing, interpreting, and recalling information (Fiske & Taylor, 1983). Thus, when individuals are prejudiced against the members of some specific group, they tend to notice, remember, and process only certain kinds of information about such persons. And as you can readily guess, this tends to be quite negative in nature.

Second, as an attitude, prejudice possesses the three major components of all attitudes mentioned in Chapter 4. That is, it involves cognitive, affective, and behavioral aspects. The *cognitive* component of prejudice centers around beliefs and expectations held by individuals about the members of a particular group. These are often termed **stereotypes,** and once they are formed, these preconceived notions about others tend to be quite persistent. Even worse, they often seem to operate in a self-fulfilling nature, leading the persons toward whom they are directed to behave in ways that confirm their accuracy. (We will return to such effects in more detail in the **Focus on Research** section on pp. 174–175.) In contrast, the *affective* component of prejudice involves the negative emotions or feelings prejudiced persons experience toward the members of specific social groups. As you probably know from your own experience, prejudice is far from a "cool" or purely cognitive reaction. Thus, full comprehension of its nature must involve attention to its emotional or affective side. Finally, the *behavioral* aspect of prejudice involves tendencies to act in negative ways toward the persons or groups who are the object of such attitudes. When these tendencies spill over into overt actions, they constitute *discrimination*—the next major topic we will consider. (Before turning to discrimination, however, please read the **Focus on Research** section on pp. 174–175.)

Discrimination: Prejudice in Action

As we noted in Chapter 4, <u>attitudes are not always reflected in overt actions</u>. Indeed, there is often a substantial gap between the views individuals hold and their actual behavior. Prejudice is no exception to this general rule. In many situations, persons holding negative attitudes toward the members of various groups find that they cannot express these hatreds directly. Laws, social pressure, and even the fear of retaliation all serve to prevent them from engaging in openly negative actions against the targets of their dislike. In many other cases, though, such restraining forces are absent. And here, the negative beliefs, feelings, and behavior tendencies that constitute prejudice may find expression in overt actions. These behaviors—generally known as *discrimination*—can take many different forms. At relatively mild levels, they may involve simple avoidance. At stronger levels, they can involve exclusion from jobs, education, or social organizations (see Figure 5.2). And in extreme cases, discrimination may appear as open physical assaults. Regardless of their precise form, however, the ultimate outcome is always the same: members of the target group are harmed in some fashion.

Subtle forms of discrimination: Striking with the unseen blow. Bigots, like other persons, much prefer to "have their cake and eat it too." In the context of prejudice, this suggests that they generally prefer to harm the targets of their dislike without any repercussions for doing so. In short, they prefer to discriminate against these persons without being caught in the act or punished for it in any manner. Can this goal be accomplished? Unfortunately, a growing body of evidence suggests that it can. Several hidden forms of discrimination exist and are used by prejudiced persons to conceal their negative views. Among the most common of these appear to be (1) the withholding of aid from persons who need it, (2) the performance of trivial, tokenistic actions, and (3) the tendency to perceive the members of disliked groups as being physically similar to one another.

Reluctance to help: "Let someone else do it." The first of these tactics—withholding aid from the members of disliked groups—is often used with consider-

**FIGURE 5.2   Social exclusion:
One common form of
discrimination.**

*Discrimination often involves
exclusion — the seemingly
irrational barring of certain
individuals from participation in
various social, educational, or
employment activities. [Source:
Drawing by Weber; ©1979 The
New Yorker Magazine, Inc.]*

"So long, Bill. This is my club. You can't come in."

able finesse. Contrary to what you might at first expect, prejudiced persons do *not* engage in blanket refusals to assist the objects of their bigotry. Rather, they usually act in this manner only under conditions where they can somehow "get away" with such actions — when there are other explanations for their failure to help aside from prejudice. Thus, such persons seem more likely to refrain from aiding the members of groups they dislike in situations where other potential helpers are present than in situations where they are absent (Gaertner & Dovidio, 1977). The reason for this is simple: when other potential helpers are present, bigoted persons can attribute their own failure to act to the belief that *these* individuals would take any necessary action. In this manner, then, they get neatly off the hook. Fortunately, some evidence suggests that the use of this particular subtle form of discrimination may be on the wane, at least in the United States. A recent study by Shaffer and Graziano (1980) found little

Stereotypes: An Unsettling Note on Their Self-confirming Nature

Suppose that most of the persons around you believe that you have a violent temper and are both moody and emotional. Further, imagine that the basis for these beliefs is simple: you possess red hair. Will these views, which can be seen as part of a widely held stereotype about redheads, exert any impact upon your behavior? The chances are good that they might. Because others perceive you as possessing certain traits, they may treat you in specific ways. For example, they may lean over backwards to avoid making you angry. And such treatment, in turn, may well shape your own behavior. After all, if others expect you to act like an emotional volcano, you may be strongly tempted to do so. That is, you may often "blow your stack" in response to even mild provocations. To the extent you come to behave in this fashion, of course, you will confirm the view that redheads really *are* emotional and moody.

If such effects were limited to stereotypes about hair color, they would be intriguing, but of little practical importance. Unfortunately, however, this is far from the case. Growing evidence suggests that similar self-fulfilling processes may be at work with respect to stereotypes of much greater importance —ones dealing with racial, religious, or sexual identity (Christensen & Rosenthal, 1982). An especially convincing demonstration of such effects has recently been reported by Skrypnek and Snyder (1982).

These researchers asked pairs of subjects (one male and one female) to perform a task supposedly related to the division of labor within organizations. The task itself was simple: the teams had to agree on how to divide each of twenty-four pairs of tasks between them. One third of the tasks were stereotypically masculine in nature (e.g., fix a light switch), one third were stereotypically feminine

(e.g., ice a cake), and one third were neutral with respect to gender (e.g., paint a chair). A crucial aspect of the study took place before the teams began to work on the division-of-labor task. At this time, the male member received information suggesting that his partner was a male, received information suggesting that this person was a female, or received no information on this matter. (Subjects could not see one another, so there was no reason for them to doubt this input.) It was expected that in the first two cases, stereotypes concerning the characteristics of males and females would be activated and would affect the male subjects' behavior toward their partner. This, in turn, would lead these individuals to behave in ways serving to confirm such stereotyped beliefs. Thus, if their male partner believed that they were a male too, the female subjects would tend to act in a manner consistent with this view; that is, they would tend to choose "masculine" tasks to perform. If, in contrast, he believed that they were female, they would tend to confirm *this* belief. Specifically, they would show a preference for "feminine" activities.

Results offered strong support for Skrypnek and Snyder's predictions. As expected, the female subjects chose masculine tasks when they had been described to their partner as a male, but more feminine ones when described to him as a female. Moreover, this was true in two distinct phases of the study—one in which the male could express his preferences first, and another in which the female target could take this initiative (see Figure 5.3). In short, it appeared that the female subjects did come to behave in ways that fulfilled the stereotypes held by their partners. But how, precisely, did this occur? Additional findings shed revealing light on the nature of this self-fulfilling process. First, the initial choices of the male subjects were strongly

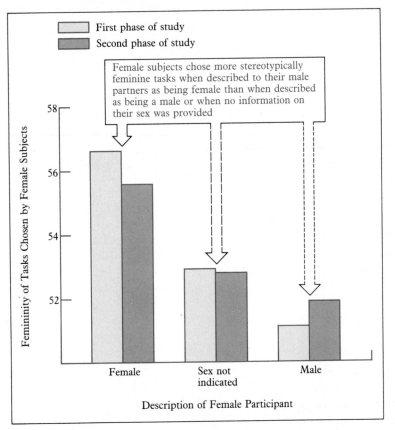

FIGURE 5.3 *Stereotypes: Evidence for their self-confirming nature.*

Female subjects participating in a division-of-labor task with a male partner tended to behave in ways that confirmed this person's sex role stereotypes. Thus, they chose tasks that were more feminine in nature when their partner believed that they were a female than when he believed that they were a male or had been given no information on their sex. Further, this was true in two separate phases of the experiment—one in which the male expressed his preferences first and another in which the female had this advantage. [Source: Based on data from Skrypnek & Snyder, 1982.]

affected by information about the sex of their partner. When they believed that this person was a female, they chose more masculine tasks to perform than when they believed her to be a male. Second, information on their partner's sex also affected their reactions to disagreement. When they believed that their partner was a female, they were much less willing to shift their choices and compromise than when they believed that she was a male.

While the findings obtained by Skrypnek and Snyder (1982) are concerned primarily with stereotypes relating to gender, other studies have reported similar results with respect to stereotypes dealing with race, ethnic identity, and even physical beauty (e.g., Work, Zanna, & Cooper, 1974;

Snyder, Tanke, & Berscheid, 1977). These results suggest that the type of self-fulfilling process outlined here is all too general in scope. In addition we should add that some evidence (Christensen & Rosenthal, 1982) points to the conclusion that *stigmatized groups*—ones who are the object of strong, irrational prejudice—often possess traits that may enhance their susceptibility to such effects (e.g., low self-esteem). To the extent this is true, it is hardly surprising that stereotypes are quite persistent and that in some cases, at least, they seem to contain a grain of truth. Indeed, given the especially vicious type of self-confirming circle they initiate, it could hardly be otherwise.

tendency on the part of either black or white subjects to offer more aid to members of their own race. We can only hope, of course, that the absence of differential helping in this study reflects a corresponding decline in racial bias during the past decade.

Tokenism: "Haven't I done enough already?" A second and perhaps more common form of subtle discrimination involves **tokenism.** The basic mechanism here is simple. Prejudiced individuals engage in trivial, positive actions toward the members of groups they dislike (e.g., they hire a single "show" black person; they eat lunch — once — with an Hispanic individual). And then, they use these actions as a rationale for refusing other, more important actions (e.g., adoption of truly fair hiring practices), or as a justification for later discrimination. "Don't bother me," such persons seem to say. "Haven't I done enough for blacks/Hispanics/women already?" Evidence for the use of such tactics has been reported in several studies (e.g., Dutton & Lake, 1973; Dutton & Lennox, 1974). In these experiments, white subjects who had performed a small favor for a black stranger were less willing to engage in a more effortful problack action at a later time than subjects who had not performed this small, tokenistic action. Such findings confirm the observation that often individuals use small, positive actions as justification for later discrimination. However, we should note that this is not always the case. Rather, such effects seem to occur only when the initial positive action serves to activate negative stereotypes about the minority group. This conclusion is supported by the findings of an ingenious study carried out by Rosenfield and his colleagues (Rosenfield et al., 1982).

In this experiment, white subjects were first exposed to information that threatened their belief that they were quite unprejudiced: they received false feedback suggesting that they had reacted negatively to scenes of friendly interracial interaction. Following this experience, they were approached by a black stranger who asked for a small favor. In one condition, he posed as a panhandler and requested money. In another, he posed as a graduate student and asked subjects to sign a petition favoring increased funds for research on sickle-cell anemia. In both cases, most subjects complied. Rosenfield and his co-workers predicted that only when the confederate acted as a panhandler would negative stereotypes about blacks be activated. Thus, only in this condition would subjects later demonstrate reduced willingness to engage in larger, prominority actions. To test this prediction, subjects were asked, several minutes later, to donate their time to effortful prominority activities (e.g., participation in an Interracial Brotherhood Week). As you can see from Figure 5.4, those who had previously been approached by the panhandler did show a much lower tendency to take part in such actions than those who had been asked to sign a petition. Thus, helping was reduced only by an experience likely to activate negative racial stereotypes. These findings suggest that small beneficial actions directed toward minority group members do not always serve as a basis for later discrimination. Only when they place such persons in an unfavorable light do they operate in this manner. Unfortunately, of course, there are many situations in which doing a small favor for minority persons *is* associated with negative stereotypes about them. And in such cases, it appears, trivial

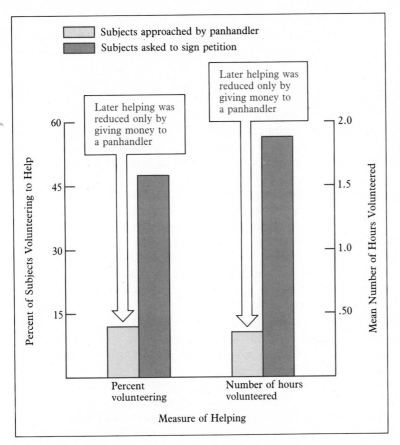

FIGURE 5.4 Tokenism: Some limiting conditions.

White subjects were less willing to engage in effortful problack activities after giving money to a black panhandler than after signing a petition presented by a black graduate student. These findings suggest that small, tokenistic actions serve as a basis for later discrimination only when they serve to activate negative stereotypes about minority persons. [Source: Based on data from Rosenfield et al., 1982.]

positive actions can play a tokenistic role and pave the way for later negative behavior.

Cross-group recognition: "They all look alike to me." Have you ever heard one of your friends or acquaintances remark: "They all look alike to me"? If so, you already know what this statement means—and perhaps what it implies as well. Basically, persons making such remarks wish to indicate that they have great difficulty in telling the members of some social group apart. To them, all Chinese, blacks, Hispanics, or whites look very much alike. At first glance, these words might seem to represent simple statements of fact—or even of perplexity. On closer inspection, though, they seem reflective of a negative attitude toward the group in question. When individuals say "They all look alike to me," they do not simply mean that they cannot distinguish between members of a given group. In many cases, they also wish to suggest that this task is not worth the effort. Since the entire group, taken as a whole, is not important or valuable, why bother about individuals within it? This tendency to lump all members of a specific social group together, then, can be reflective of strong prejudice. And even worse, it can often exert harmful effects upon the people in question. On a personal basis, individuals belonging to a minority group may find it annoying to learn that they are not recognized separately, even after repeated contact with prejudiced persons. And in legal proceedings, the tendency to lump all members of a given group together can have extremely serious consequences (e.g., Brigham, 1980). The tendency to perceive all members of a disliked group as physically similar, then, can be viewed as a third subtle form of discrimination.

But what about the actual occurrence of such effects; do individuals really find it harder to recognize members of groups other than their own? In fact, they do. A large body of research findings suggests that many persons have greater difficulty in recognizing people from outside their group than people from within it. For example, when black and white subjects are shown photos of strangers and then asked to recognize them among a much larger group of photos, they are usually more successful in this task when the strangers belong to their own race than when they belong to the other race (e.g., Barkowitz & Brigham, 1982; Brigham & Williams, 1979). That similar effects occur outside the laboratory in highly realistic settings is indicated by the results of an ingenious study carried out by Brigham and his colleagues (Brigham, Maass, Snyder, & Spaulding, 1982). In this investigation, the researchers arranged for two accomplices—one black and one white—to visit convenience stores in Florida. Each accomplice engaged in one or more unusual activities designed to enhance his distinctiveness (e.g., paying for a purchase entirely with pennies; asking for detailed directions to a local airport). Later, two hours after the second accomplice had left, a team of experimenters entered the store and explained that they were law interns. They then showed the clerk on duty two arrays of six photos (one containing blacks and the other whites), and asked if he or she had seen any of these persons within the past twenty-four hours. Photos of the accomplices were included, so it was possible to measure the accuracy with which clerks could now identify these persons.

Results were somewhat unsettling. First, overall accuracy was quite low, despite the accomplices' unusual behavior, and despite the fact that they had been present on the scene only two hours earlier. Indeed, they were correctly recognized only 48.6 percent of the time. These findings, of course, raise important questions about the accuracy and usefulness of eyewitness testimony. Second, cross-race differences in recognition occurred (although these were somewhat smaller in scope than in previous laboratory studies). As shown in Figure 5.5, both black and white clerks were more successful in identifying accomplices of their own race than in identifying accomplices of the other race. Thus, they did seem to find individuals from a group other than their own harder to tell apart than individuals from their own group.

Taken as a whole, the findings reported by Brigham et al. (1982) seem somewhat discouraging. They suggest that the tendency to view all members of groups other than one's own as physically similar exists in real-life settings where it can exert major harmful effects. Fortunately, though, one additional result of their study offers an important ray of hope: the greater the degree of interracial contact reported by the clerks, the greater their success in cross-race recognition. This fact suggests that increased contact with the members of

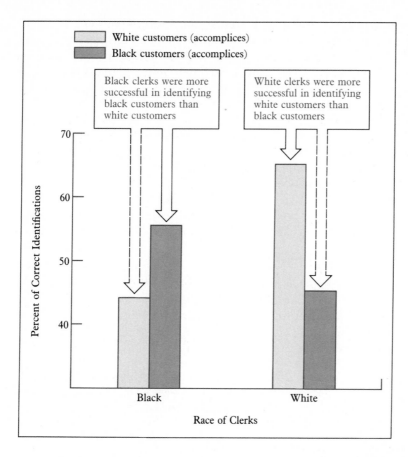

FIGURE 5.5 *Cross-race versus own-race recognition: Evidence that there is a difference.*

Both black and white clerks were somewhat more successful in recognizing persons of their own race who had recently visited their stores than persons of a different race. [Source: Based on data from Brigham et al., 1982.]

groups other than one's own can go a long way toward eliminating the "they-all-look-alike-to-me" effect. And since perceiving others as unique individuals physically may make it harder to view them as similar in terms of traits or behavior, this may represent a first, important step toward the shattering of a wide range of stereotypes.

Prejudice: How It Is Measured

Most of us have little difficulty in telling hate-filled bigots from persons deeply committed to fair treatment for all. Individuals falling at the extremes along this dimension reveal their attitudes in many ways (e.g., their verbal statements, their overt actions). But what about the large group falling somewhere in between? How can we measure the extent to which they may be viewed as relatively prejudiced or unprejudiced? One answer is suggested by our definition of prejudice as a special kind of attitude. This view suggests that attempts to assess prejudice should focus on its cognitive, affective, and behavioral components. As we will now see, this has actually been the approach adopted by many social psychologists.

The measurement of prejudiced beliefs: Stereotypes, past and present. Attempts to measure stereotypes generally employ a straightforward method. Individuals are presented with a list of traits and asked to indicate which are characteristic of some social group (e.g., blacks, whites, Japanese, Jews). Many studies using this approach have been conducted (e.g., Moe, Nacoste, & Insko, 1981; Smedley & Bayton, 1978). And discouragingly, they point to the conclusion that many stereotypes tend to persist. Thus, even in the 1980s, after several decades of rapid social change, large numbers of persons seem willing to assume that all members of various racial, ethnic, and religious groups possess specific traits or characteristics. For example, in the United States, many whites continue to believe that lower-class blacks, at least, are ignorant, dangerous, and rude. Similarly, many blacks perceive whites as sly, deceitful, and biased (Sagar & Schofield, 1980; Smedley & Bayton, 1978). Fortunately, such views seem to have faded somewhat (Moe et al., 1981). But at present, they are still very much with us.

The measurement of prejudiced feelings. While stereotypes play a key role in prejudice, they are, as we have noted, only part of the picture. Thus, social psychologists have also sought to assess the affective (emotional) component of this process. Generally, they have accomplished this task through the use of various kinds of *attitude scales.* Since we described these in detail in Chapter 4, we will not return to them here. We should note, though, that when used to investigate prejudice, attitude scales contain items specifically designed to assess the strength of individuals' positive or negative feelings toward various social groups.

The measurement of discriminatory tendencies. Attempts to measure the behavioral component of prejudice have often involved the use of **social distance scales.** These are scales specifically designed to assess the degree of closeness or intimacy to which individuals are willing to admit the members of various social groups. Such scales often list a number of relationships, and ask subjects to indicate whether they would or would not admit the members of some group to each of these degrees of intimacy. As you might guess, social distance scales often reveal unsettling gaps between individuals' verbal statements about minority groups, and descriptions of how they might actually behave toward them. Thus, persons claiming to be totally unprejudiced, and reporting positive feelings toward various minorities, often also report great reluctance to enter into close social contact with them. (For example, they state that they would not want to have such persons as neighbors or as relatives through marriage.) On an encouraging note, we should add that such tendencies toward exclusion also seem to be on the wane, at least within the United States. In a recent study on this issue, Moe, Nacoste, and Insko (1981) asked white school children to complete a social distance scale relating to blacks. Their responses were then compared with those of similar children who completed the same scale in 1966. As you can see in Figure 5.6, results pointed to a substantial drop in reported discriminatory tendencies during this period. That is, the youngsters in the more recent sample (who completed the scale in 1979) seemed much more

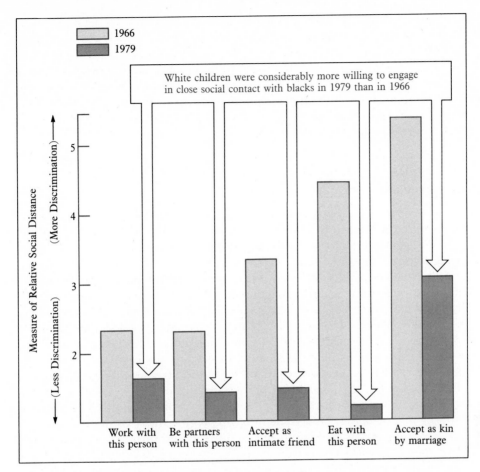

FIGURE 5.6   *Discrimination: Some evidence of a decline.*

White children who completed a social distance scale in 1979 reported being considerably more willing to engage in close social contact with blacks than children who completed a similar scale in 1966. These findings suggest that there may have been a drop in tendencies toward overt discrimination during this period, at least within the United States where the study was conducted. (Note: higher scores indicate greater tendencies toward discrimination.) [Source: Based on data from Moe, Nacoste, & Insko, 1981.]

willing to engage in close social contact with blacks than the youngsters in the earlier, 1966 sample. Whether these shifts in verbal reports will translate into actual reductions in discrimination, of course, remains to be seen. But the changes in this direction were substantial, and one can always hope!

Theoretical Explanations of Prejudice: The Origins of Hate

Where does prejudice come from? Why do individuals so often hold strong negative attitudes toward the members of groups other than their own? And why do they come to view such persons as somehow inferior to themselves? These are crucial questions with important implications, for understanding the origins of prejudice may help us to develop effective strategies for overcoming its impact. Unfortunately, prejudice is far too complex in scope to permit us the luxury of simple answers. Instead, it appears to stem from several different sources, none of which should be ignored. Among the most important of these seem to be (1) *direct intergroup conflict,* (2) *social categorization,* (3) *specific personality traits,* and (4) *early learning experiences.*

Direct Intergroup Conflict: Competition as a Basis for Bigotry

In recent years, a growing number of Cubans have moved to the United States. (We referred to this fact in the story at the start of this chapter.) Most have settled in South Florida, with the result that, at present, Miami is virtually a bilingual city. Since these people came seeking political freedom and since Cuba and Florida have traditionally enjoyed a great deal of mutual commerce, we might expect this migration to go quite smoothly. After all, there is an historical basis for mutual respect and acceptance. In fact, however, it has not. Many long-time residents of Miami have objected strongly to this sudden influx of "foreigners." And many—blacks and whites alike—have begun to voice negative views about Cubans in general. In short, prejudice has reared its ugly head in an area previously more famous for its palm trees, oranges, and tropical climate. Why has this been the case? According to one explanation for the occurrence of prejudice, the answer is simple. As the Cubans have arrived in growing numbers, they have come into competition with existing residents for jobs, housing, and schools. And this competition, in turn, has stimulated the development of anti-Cuban attitudes. In short, one major explanation of prejudice suggests that often, it stems from direct economic competition between distinct social groups (Sherif, 1966).

Support for this view is provided by a well-known series of field studies conducted some years ago by Sherif and his colleagues (Sherif, 1966; Sherif et al., 1961). In these studies, boys attending special summer camps were divided into two distinct groups which then lived and played together. As a result of these shared experiences, the boys soon developed strong feelings of attachment for their respective groups. Once they did, the two units were brought into direct competition (e.g., they competed in sports events and other contests). The effects of such competition were quickly apparent: the two groups soon came to view each other in highly negative ways. And these negative feelings, in turn, readily spilled over into overt actions (e.g., the groups engaged in open fights). In short, repeated competition did seem to induce strong negative feelings between the groups.

In a final stage of the experiment, attempts were made to reduce these hostile reactions. While a number of procedures were tried, only one proved effective: arranging conditions so that the groups had to work *together* to achieve various goals or overcome a common threat. (For example, they joined forces to compete against a group of outsiders.) Taken as a whole, the findings of Sherif's

research suggest that direct intergroup conflict can often serve as one important basis for the emergence of strong, intergroup prejudice.

"Us" versus "Them": Social Categorization as a Basis for Prejudice

A second major perspective on the origins of prejudice begins with a basic
fact: often individuals divide the social world around them into two distinct
categories—"us" and "them." In short, they view the persons they encounter
either as belonging to their own group (usually termed the **ingroup**) or to some
other recognizable group (an **outgroup**). If this process of **social categorization**
stopped there, it would have little bearing upon prejudice. Unfortunately,
though, this is not the case. Instead, sharply contrasting feelings and beliefs are
usually attached to members of the ingroup and members of various outgroups.
While persons in the former ("us") category are viewed in highly favorable
terms, those in the latter ("them") are frequently seen in a more negative light
(Wilder & Thompson, 1980). They are assumed to possess undesirable characteristics, and are strongly disliked. Moreover, such negative feelings and beliefs
are attributed to personal traits of the outgroup. In short, these—not unfounded—stereotypes are viewed as the cause of such prejudice (Hemstone &
Jaspars, 1982).

That such tendencies exist and operate in a wide range of settings is
indicated by the findings of a growing body of research (e.g., Locksley, Ortiz, &
Hepburn, 1980; Tajfel & Turner, 1979). In these studies, subjects generally
expressed more negative attitudes toward members of outgroups and treated
them in less favorable ways than members of their own ingroup. Further, this
was the case *even when these categories were established in an arbitrary fashion and had
no bearing upon social categories existing outside the experimental context.* Such
findings suggest that in some settings, at least, prejudice may well stem from our
tendency to divide the social world into "us" and "them."

But why, precisely, is this the case? Why does such categorization lead to
contrasting feelings and beliefs about the persons involved? One intriguing
answer has been suggested by Tajfel and his colleagues (e.g., Tajfel & Turner,
1979; Turner, 1978). Their reasoning is as follows: membership in a given
social group can serve to enhance an individual's self-esteem. However, this will
be true only to the extent that this group compares favorably with other social
entities. For this reason, individuals tend to perceive their ingroup as superior
to other groups with whom they have contact. Unfortunately, the members of
these groups have a similar tendency. They, too, wish to perceive their own
group as best. The ultimate outcome, then, is readily predictable: each group
seeks to view itself as superior to its rivals, and prejudice arises out of this clash
of perceptions. (Tajfel and his co-workers term this process *social competition* to
distinguish it from intergroup conflict over jobs, housing, etc. Please see Figure
5.7, p. 184, for a summary of these suggestions.)

Support for the accuracy of this interpretation has been obtained in several
recent studies (e.g., Skevington, 1981; Turner, 1978). Thus, social competition
does appear to play a role in the ingroup/outgroup effect we have been

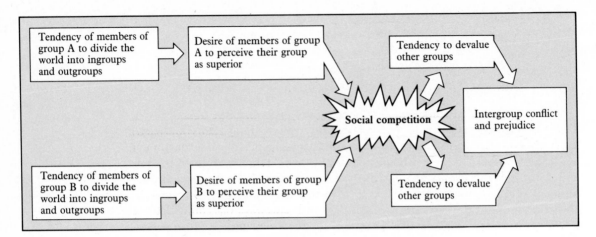

FIGURE 5.7   Social categorization: An important basis for prejudice.

According to Tajfel and his colleagues, individuals have a basic tendency to divide the social world into two distinct categories: their own ingroup ("us") and outgroups ("them"). Once such social categorization *has occurred, members of each group seek to perceive it as superior to other groups on important dimensions. The resulting* social competition *leads each group to devalue the others and this, in turn, may be an important source of both intergroup conflict and prejudice.*

discussing. Regardless of the precise mechanisms involved, though, one fact seems clear: the basic human tendency to divide the social world into "us" and "them" often plays a key role in the occurrence of racial, ethnic, and religious prejudice. (For a discussion of basic cognitive processes that may also underlie our tendency to enhance the qualities of our own group but disparage those of outgroups, please see the **Focus on Research** section on pp. 186–187.)

Authoritarianism: Personality as a Basis for Prejudice

The members of various "hate" groups obviously differ sharply with respect to the targets of their prejudice. Some despise blacks, others whites; some hate Catholics, and others Jews. Regardless of their particular brand of bigotry, though, most persons of this type seem to share certain traits. On close inspection, they often appear to be "uptight" and filled with as much fear as hatred. Further, most seem all too willing to subjugate themselves to the dictates of an all-powerful leader who promises to somehow save them from the objects of their fear and loathing. Observations of such similarity have led some scientists to seek the origins of prejudice in personality structure. That is, they have sought to identify the traits or characteristics that predispose individuals toward such negative, irrational reactions. Perhaps the best-known work of this type is that carried out by Adorno and her colleagues (Adorno et al., 1950).

These researchers reasoned that prejudice is often linked to a broad and complex cluster of traits they termed the **authoritarian personality.** Briefly, high authoritarian individuals are ones showing a pattern of submissive obedience to authority, and punitive rejection of groups other than their own. Further, such persons also tend to view the world in rigid black-and-white categories. Either you are a member of their own group and are for them, or you are a member of some other, rejected group and must be against them. According to Adorno et al., authoritarian individuals develop such traits partly as a result of the harsh, punitive child-rearing practices employed by their parents (e.g., Stephan & Rosenfield, 1978).

The view that prejudice stems from specific personality traits has been examined in many studies conducted over more than three decades. While the findings of such work have not always been consistent, most has confirmed the existence of a link between the traits mentioned above and various forms of prejudice (e.g., Cherry & Byrne, 1976). Thus, it does seem that in some cases, at least, strong negative reactions to groups other than one's own stem from largely internal causes: key aspects of one's own personality.

Early Experience as a Basis for Prejudice: The Role of Social Learning

A fourth explanation for the occurrence of prejudice rests upon the following assumption: such reactions are primarily learned. According to this view, children acquire negative attitudes toward various social groups because they are exposed to such views on the part of others (e.g., parents, friends) or because they are specifically trained in them (i.e., rewarded for expressing such reactions). In sum, prejudice is learned through the same processes and in the same manner as are other attitudes and forms of social behavior.

While parents, teachers, and friends seem to play a major role in this process, the mass media too, are important. For example, until quite recently, members of racial and ethnic minorities appeared only rarely in movies or on television. And when they did, they were usually shown in demeaning or at best comic roles (see Figure 5.9 on p. 188). Given repeated exposure to such materials, it is far from surprising that many children soon acquired the belief that the members of such groups must be unimportant or inferior. After all, why else would they always be shown in such a negative light?

Fortunately, this situation has changed somewhat in recent years in the United States and other countries. Members of various racial and ethnic minorities now appear more frequently and are represented in a more positive fashion than was true in the past (refer to Figure 5.9). Even today, though, they do not always receive fully equal treatment (Weigel, Loomis, & Soja, 1980). Thus, there appears to be considerable room for improvement. And until such change occurs, the potential of the mass media for reducing rather than encouraging intergroup prejudice will remain at least partly unrealized.

*The Illusion of Outgroup Homogeneity:
A Cognitive Basis for Prejudice*

Earlier in this chapter, we noted that many persons perceive the members of groups other than their own as looking very much alike. That is, they tend to view outgroup members as showing greater physical similarity than members of their own group. Unfortunately, this tendency to overestimate the degree of homogeneity among outgroup members is not restricted to physical appearance: it seems to extend to behavior as well. As suggested by such phrases as "They're all pretty much alike" or "You know what *they* are," many persons seem to assume that outgroup members behave, think, and feel very much alike. In short, they view these individuals as being far more homogeneous on key dimensions than members of their own group.

Systematic evidence for the occurrence of such effects has accumulated rapidly in recent years (e.g., Quattrone & Jones, 1980; Linville & Jones, 1980). In these studies, outgroup members were in fact perceived in simpler or more homogeneous terms than ingroup members. Such findings confirm the existence of this perceptual or cognitive bias, and suggest that it may play a key role in the persistence of many stereotypes. But when, precisely, do such effects occur? Are they general, appearing in many situations and with many different groups; or are they more restricted in scope? At first glance, we might expect that this illusion of outgroup homogeneity is most likely to take place under conditions in which various social groups have little contact with one another. After all, once such contact begins, the persons involved will soon be confronted by the individuality of outgroup members. And then they may find it increasingly difficult to assume that all such persons are very much alike. Despite the reasonable nature of this suggestion, however, it does not appear to be correct. Instead, growing evidence indicates that the assumption of outgroup homogeneity may exist—and *persist*—even in cases where the groups in question are in prolonged intimate contact (e.g., Linville, 1982). Clear evidence pointing to this conclusion is provided by a series of related studies conducted by Park and Rothbart (1982).

In the first of these investigations, male and female subjects were asked to examine fifty-four attitude statements, and indicate what percent of men or women would agree with each. The statements were chosen so as to be stereotypically feminine (e.g., "I would like to care for a small baby as a way to express my love"), stereotypically masculine (e.g., "I often seek out competitive challenges . . ."), or neutral (e.g., "Job interviews make me nervous"). It was predicted that both males and females would assume greater homogeneity among members of the other sex than among members of their own sex. Specifically, they would estimate that a higher proportion of outgroup than ingroup persons would endorse stereotypic statements. Correspondingly, they would also estimate that a higher proportion of ingroup than outgroup members would endorse *counter*stereotypic statements. All of these predictions were confirmed (please refer to Figure 5.8). Both males and females seemed to assume greater homogeneity on the part of members of the opposite sex than their own sex. It is important to note, by the way, that these differences emerged despite the high level of daily contact between males and females in American society. It appears, then, that even prolonged, daily contact between two groups may not be sufficient to eliminate the illusion of outgroup homogeneity.

Further support for the generality of this tendency was obtained by Park and Rothbart in a second study. Here, the members of three different sororities were asked to indicate how similar or dissimilar the members of each organization were to one another. As expected, the women in each sorority perceived greater similarity among the members of the other social groups than among the members of their own.

When the findings obtained by Park and Rothbart are combined with those reported by other investigators (e.g., Linville, 1982), a consistent pic-

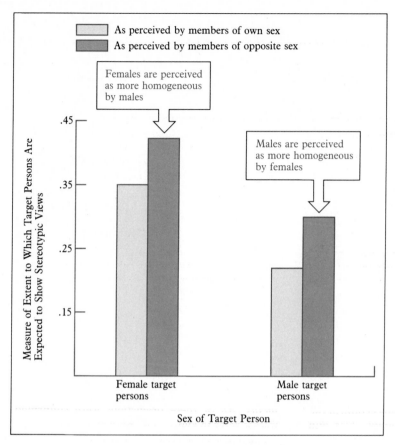

As perceived by members of own sex

As perceived by members of opposite sex

Females are perceived as more homogeneous by males

Males are perceived as more homogeneous by females

Measure of Extent to Which Target Persons Are Expected to Show Stereotypic Views

.45

.35

.25

.15

Female target persons

Male target persons

Sex of Target Person

FIGURE 5.8 *The tendency to view outgroups as more homogeneous than ingroups: Empirical evidence.*

As shown here, both males and females view members of the opposite sex as more homogeneous than members of their own sex with respect to the possession of stereotypic sex role attitudes. These findings offer support for the view that in general, we perceive the members of groups other than our own as more homogeneous than members of our own group in terms of attitudes, behavior, and traits. [Source: Based on data from Park & Rothbart, 1982.]

ture of some of the cognitive factors contributing to prejudice emerges. Many individuals, it seems, tend to process and recall social information about ingroup and outgroup members differently. First, as we have just seen, they perceive outgroup persons as more homogeneous—both physically and behaviorally—than ingroup persons. Second, they tend to recall less specific, differentiating information about outgroup members (Park & Rothbart, 1982). And third, they often have simpler cognitive representations of outgroup than ingroup members (Linville, 1982). We should add that these cognitive or perceptual biases appear to be quite general in scope, and are not readily overcome even by direct contact between the groups in question.

Given these facts, the persistence of many stereotypes is far from surprising. To an unsettling degree, such reactions seem to rest upon basic aspects of social cognition, as well as upon irrational hatreds or fears. Of course, this does not imply that these harmful forms of bias cannot be overcome. On the contrary, recent findings are somewhat encouraging in this respect (Linville, 1982). But to the extent prejudice and discrimination stem from basic cognitive processes, new techniques will probably be required for countering their impact. It is certainly our hope—and also our firm expectation—that these will be developed by social psychologists in the years ahead.

FIGURE 5.9   *Mass media treatment of minority groups: A look at the past.*

In the past, members of various minority groups were usually depicted in unfavorable or comic roles in movies and other forms of the mass media. Fortunately, some degree of change in this pattern has occurred in recent years.

Reducing Prejudice: Some Steps in the Right Directions

Prejudice and the discriminatory behavior it breeds create tremendous problems both for individuals and entire societies. For this reason alone (not to mention considerations of social justice) it is important to reduce its occurrence. But do techniques for accomplishing this crucial task exist? Our answer, we're afraid, must be somewhat hedged. Prejudice is a complex process, stemming from many different sources. Thus, it is unlikely that any single tactic can be totally effective in eliminating its presence. Instead, a wide range of procedures, each aimed at one source or aspect of prejudice and suitable for use under specific conditions, are required. Fortunately, a number of such strategies have been developed and tested by social psychologists. Among the most effective of these appear to be (1) efforts to block the formation of prejudice during early socialization and (2) the enhancement of constructive intergroup contact.

Breaking the Chain of Bigotry: On Learning Not to Hate

As we have noted repeatedly, parents play a key role in shaping their children's attitudes. And included among the many views that they transmit are various forms of prejudice. For this reason, one useful technique for reducing these negative reactions involves attempts to shatter this chain of bigotry — to somehow discourage parents from providing their offspring with direct training in prejudice and discrimination. As we're sure you can appreciate, this is a difficult task. Psychologists cannot, of course, intervene directly in parent-child relations. Doing so would be unethical, if not downright illegal. What they *can*

not to mention impractical

do, however, is call parents' attention to the prejudiced views they are transmitting, and to the important future costs attached to these attitudes. While some die-hard bigots may actually wish to turn their children into hate-filled copies of themselves, most parents genuinely wish to arm them with a more positive view of the social world. Thus, campaigns designed to enhance parents' awareness of this process, and to discourage them from demonstrating prejudice in their own behavior, may yield major positive results.

But there is no reason for attempts to "nip prejudice in the bud" to end there. Teachers, too, can play a positive role. One dramatic illustration of this fact is provided by a famous demonstration performed some years ago by Jane Elliot, an Iowa school teacher. In an attempt to help her all-white class of third graders understand the negative effects of prejudice, Ms. Elliot divided her students into two groups on the basis of eye color. On the first day of the demonstration, the brown-eyed group was assigned an inferior status in class. Brown-eyed children were ridiculed by the teacher and by the blue-eyed students. They were denied classroom privileges and, as a sign of their low status, were made to wear a special collar (see Figure 5.10). This treatment continued for several days and was then reversed, so that the blue-eyed students now became the victims of irrational prejudice.

FIGURE 5.10   Discrimination: Gaining first-hand experience with its negative effects.

In a well-known classroom demonstration, children were made the victims of discrimination on the basis of their eye color. First brown-eyed youngsters and later blue-eyed children were described by their teacher as being inferior, and were treated in unfavorable ways. As shown here, they found this experience to be painful and upsetting.

Not surprisingly, youngsters in both groups found the experience of serving as the victims of unfair discrimination quite upsetting. Indeed, it even lowered their performance on standard classroom tasks. The purpose of the demonstration, of course, was that of providing the children with firsthand experience with the evils of discrimination. It was hoped that in this way, their own tendency to engage in such behavior would be sharply reduced. (A vivid record of the entire demonstration is presented in the documentary film, *The Eye of the Storm.*)

Enhanced Intergroup Contact: On the Positive Effects of Acquaintance

A second major technique for counteracting prejudice involves direct contact between the groups involved. Basically, this approach suggests that increased interaction between the members of different social groups will contribute to a reduction in prejudice between them (e.g., Stephan, 1978). This may be the case for several different reasons. First, as they become better acquainted, the persons involved may come to realize that their attitudes and beliefs are more similar than they at first assumed. This growing recognition of similarity, in turn, may lead to increased attraction. Second, repeated contact between members of the two groups may lead to positive feelings or attitudes through the "mere-exposure" effect discussed in Chapter 4. Third, favorable contact between the groups may lead to a disconfirmation of negative, stereotyped beliefs held by each side. And fourth, such contact may help overcome the illusion of outgroup homogeneity discussed earlier. (Please see Figure 5.11 for a summary of these suggestions.) For these reasons, direct **intergroup contact** may sometimes be effective in reducing prejudice. Research findings suggest, though, that such positive effects occur only under specific conditions.

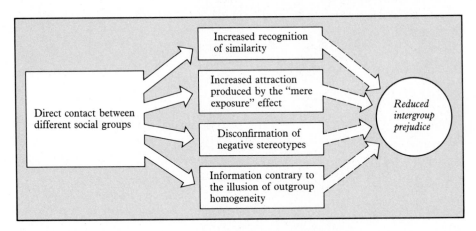

FIGURE 5.11   *Intergroup contact: How it exerts its effects.*

As shown here, increased contact between different social groups can serve to lessen prejudice in several ways.

Conditions for Direct Contact to be effective
equality

First, it is essential that such contact take place under conditions of equal social, economic, or task-related status (e.g., Riorden & Riggiero, 1980). If, instead, the members of the two groups differ in these respects, communication between them may be difficult, and prejudice can actually be increased. We should note that in this respect, steps designed to enhance the status of previously deprived groups by giving them an extra advantage at present (e.g., affirmative action programs) seem quite helpful. While many persons view such procedures as unfair, the improvements in status they confer on minority group members do seem to enhance the positive impact of intergroup contact (Norvell & Worchel, 1981). Second, it is crucial that the two groups engage in relatively informal contacts. Formal, restricted interactions do not seem helpful in countering stereotyped beliefs. Finally, it is important that the group meet under cooperative conditions. Contact under these circumstances seems quite effective in reducing intergroup hostility and in generating positive feelings (e.g., Blake & Mouton, 1979; Worchel, Andreoli, & Folger, 1977).

informal

cooperative

When these conditions are met, direct contact between the members of different racial or ethnic groups can lead to sharp reductions in prejudice (e.g., Clore et al., 1978). For example, in a series of interesting studies on this issue, Aronson and his colleagues employed cooperation as a means of reducing racial prejudice among school children (e.g., Aronson, Bridgeman, & Geffner, 1978). The basic procedure they used (termed the *jigsaw method*) was simple. Groups of six students worked together on a specific lesson. Each member of the group was required to master a single portion of the lesson and present it to the others. Successful group performance could be attained only if each person performed his or her task adequately. Thus, all members had to cooperate in order to attain a shared group goal. The results achieved with this simple procedure were impressive. Following exposure to the jigsaw method (and the cooperative intergroup contact it involved), students showed reduced racial stereotyping and increased liking for members of the other race. The fact that similar outcomes have been attained in several other studies (e.g., Wilder & Thompson, 1980) points to the following conclusion: under appropriate conditions, increased intergroup contact may well lead to major reductions in prejudice. In short, getting to know others better can often represent an effective step toward viewing them in more positive—and less rigid—terms.

Prejudice Based on Sex: A Special, Timely Case

Prejudice, we're afraid, is an all too common part of social life. It exists in virtually all human societies and can be based on a wide range of social characteristics. Thus, persons belonging to one group may reject those belonging to another solely on the basis of their race, ethnic background, religion, social class, age, or even political persuasion. Among the most unsettling—and in some ways surprising—bases for prejudice, though, is a very basic human distinction: sex. Throughout most of history and in most cultures, females have been treated very much like a minority group. They have been the object of pronounced negative stereotyping. They have been largely excluded from economic and political power. And they have often suffered overt discrimination (e.g., they have been barred from many jobs, social organizations, and certain types of training). Fortunately, overt practices such as these seem to be decreasing, at least in some places and to some degree. Further, the past decade has been marked by a shift toward more egalitarian sex role attitudes on the part of both men and women (although, surprisingly, this trend seems to have leveled off—or perhaps even to have been slightly reversed!—within the past two or three years; Helmreich, Spence, & Gibson, 1982). Despite such changes, though, there is little doubt that discrimination based on sex continues in many settings (Taylor & Ilgen, 1981; Terborg, 1977). Given the negative effects produced by such prejudice and the major social changes that have stemmed from efforts to overcome it, we believe that **sexism** is an important topic, fully deserving of our careful attention. Thus, we will focus upon this form of prejudice and the complex issues that surround it in the following discussion.

Prejudice against Women: Why It Sometimes (and in Some Places) Hurts to Be Female

As we noted earlier, females have often been the object of widespread stereotyping. To some degree, this has also been true of males. In fact, it is probably safe to say that stereotypes concerning the traits supposedly possessed by both sexes are present in all societies (see Figure 5.12). In most cases, though, the ones assigned to females are somewhat less desirable than the ones assigned to males. For example, in American culture, the stereotype for males includes such traits as assertiveness, ambition, self-confidence, logical thought, decisiveness, and dominance. In contrast, the corresponding stereotype for females includes such characteristics as submissiveness, dependence, gentleness, passivity, emotionality, lack of ambition, and lack of self-confidence (Frieze et al., 1979). Even worse, these contrasting stereotypes seem to color the evaluation of various activities, so that behaviors or tasks that are seen as basically masculine are valued more highly than ones that are seen as basically feminine. For

FIGURE 5.12   *Sex role stereotypes: Fading, but still with us.*

As shown here, stereotypes about the behavior and traits of both sexes seem to exist—and persist—in many societies. [Source: ©1981 King Features Syndicate Inc. World rights reserved.]

example, jobs or occupations usually performed by males tend to be evaluated more positively than ones typically performed by females (Touhey, 1974), although this is not uniformly the case (Suchner, 1979).

In sum, there can be little doubt that clear-cut stereotypes about the assumed characteristics of males and females exist in most cultures, and that these exert powerful and far-ranging effects. But how accurate are such beliefs? Do males and females actually differ in the ways suggested by cultural wisdom? Or, as is the case with most stereotypes, are these views largely inaccurate and misleading? Recent studies have provided intriguing answers to such questions.

Stereotypes about women and men: Myth or reality? At the present time, stereotypes about the supposed traits of females and males are the subject of a great deal of research attention (e.g., Eagly & Steffen, 1983). Thus, the total picture regarding their accuracy is as yet incomplete. Evidence gathered to date, however, seems to point to the following general conclusion: where differences between the sexes are concerned, such views tend to overstate the case. Males and females do indeed differ in several respects. But the number and size of such differences is not nearly as great as prevailing stereotypes suggest (Deaux, 1976; Lott, 1978). For example, consider a recent study by Steinberg and Shapiro (1982).

In this investigation, male and female business students completed several standard measures of personality—tests designed to assess a wide range of traits. If cultural stereotypes about the characteristics of men and women are accurate, we might expect to find males scoring higher on traits often linked to success as a top manager (e.g., assertiveness, decisiveness, leadership, self-assurance). If these stereotypes are inaccurate, however, few differences of this type should occur. As you can see from Figure 5.13 (p. 194), results offered strong support for the latter view. Few differences between the male and female students emerged. And, interestingly, when they did appear, it was usually the *females* who scored higher on dimensions linked to managerial success!

Similar results have also been obtained in other studies conducted with adults (e.g., Wexley & Pulakos, 1982). And investigations performed with children, too, point to the conclusion that stereotypes concerning the traits of males and females overstate the case. For example, in a careful study, Lott (1978) asked teachers and parents to indicate how often boys and girls might behave in various ways. Data from these questionnaires revealed that both groups believed that the sexes would differ sharply in many respects (e.g., they assumed that boys would disobey adults, show off with peers, and argue more than girls). When these beliefs were compared with observations of children's actual behavior, however, they were generally *not* confirmed. The behavior of boys and girls did differ in a few respects, but these contrasts were neither as large nor as numerous as predicted by widely held stereotypes.

To conclude: existing evidence suggests that stereotypes concerning differences between the sexes are only partly true at best. While the behavior of males and females does differ in some respects, these differences are smaller, both in degree and in number, than has often been assumed. In short, there appears to be somewhat more myth than reality in such cultural stereotypes.

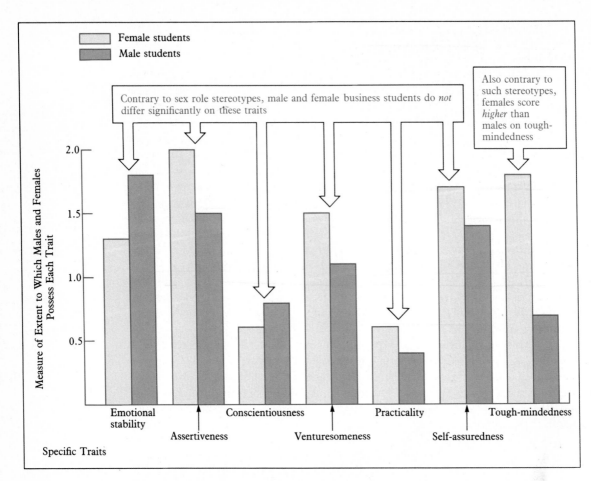

FIGURE 5.13   *Male and female executives: The stereotype that failed.*

In an informative study, Steinberg and Shapiro (1982) compared the personality traits of male and female business students. As shown here, few differences emerged. And in cases where females and males did differ, females often seemed to have the edge; they scored higher on traits associated with future success as a manager. [Source: Based on data from Steinberg & Shapiro, 1982.]

Discrimination against Females: Keeping Women in "Their Place"

Discrimination against females has been both general and widespread in many societies. They have been barred from equal participation or equal opportunities in many spheres of life, ranging from politics through education. Perhaps the most unsettling and persistent barriers of this type, however, have occurred with respect to employment. Thus, it is upon this topic that we will focus here.

In the early 1980s, women make up more than 40 percent of the total labor force in the United States. This figure is even higher in other nations, and the

FIGURE 5.14   Women in the 1980s: New jobs, new roles.

In recent years, women have entered many fields once considered to be the sole domain of men. [Source: Photo (left) ©1982 by Frances M. Cox/Omni-Photo Communications, Inc.; photo (right) ©John Lei/Omni-Photo Communications, Inc.]

trend toward growing female employment shows no sign of abating. As television, magazines, and movies suggest, women now find work in many fields once considered the sole domain of men (see Figure 5.14). Yet, despite these gains, one fact remains unaltered: females continue to be concentrated in relatively dull and dead-end jobs. As Steinberg and Shapiro (1982, p. 306) have noted: "Women populate corporations but they rarely run them." At one time, this state of affairs stemmed mainly from overt discriminatory practices. And even today, some businesses attempt to exclude women or at least keep them in low-status jobs. But recent laws and court rulings in several nations have tended to lessen such practices. Thus, at present, the unfavorable, second class status of females in the world of work seems to stem largely from other and more subtle factors. Key among these are strong tendencies by many persons to (1) attribute successful performance by females to luck or chance and (2) reject the competence or legitimacy of female leaders.

Devaluing female achievement: Luck, skill, or effort? When individuals perform some task, the success or failure they achieve can be attributed to several potential causes. Specifically, a given level of performance can be viewed as stemming mainly from internal factors such as ability and effort, or external factors such as luck or task difficulty. As you might well guess, in most cases,

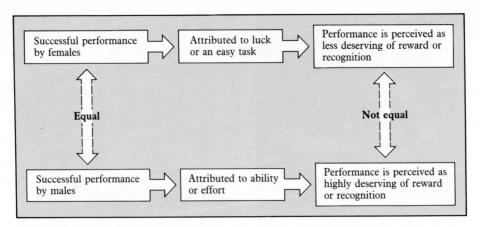

FIGURE 5.15   Explanations for successful performance:
Different for males and females.

Recent studies suggest that successful performance by females and males is often attributed to different causes. While good performance by males is usually perceived as deriving from high ability or effort, similar performance by females is often seen as stemming mainly from good luck or an easy task.

good performance stemming from ability or effort is viewed as more deserving of recognition than similar performance deriving from luck or an especially easy task (Weiner et al., 1972; Mitchell & Kalb, 1982). For this reason, raises, promotions, and other corporate rewards are frequently dispensed to persons viewed as having succeeded because of high ability or outstanding effort. In contrast, such payoffs are awarded far less frequently to persons seen as having succeeded because of luck or an easy job. All this probably strikes you as quite reasonable, and, to a degree, it is. But now consider the following fact: a number of recent studies suggest that many persons tend to attribute successful performance by males and females to different factors. In particular, success by males is often attributed to their ability or effort. In contrast, similar levels of performance by females are often viewed as stemming mainly from luck or an easy task (Stevens & DeNisi, 1980). In short, if a man succeeds, it is assumed that he worked very hard, or that he possesses a high level of ability. If a female attains the same level of performance, however, it is assumed that she merely "lucked out," or that the task she performed really wasn't very difficult (see Figure 5.15).

Needless to say, these tendencies operate against the advancement of women in business settings. After all, even when they attain the same output or performance as their male colleagues, this success is discounted or devalued (e.g., it is perceived as stemming from "lucky breaks"). A crucial task for the years ahead, then, is the elimination of this subtle but extremely damaging form of bias.

Questioning the competence or legitimacy of female leaders. As overt discriminatory practices against females in the world of work have begun to fade, increasing numbers of women have moved into managerial-level jobs. Indeed, some now occupy the very highest rungs on the proverbial corporate ladder. At first glance, then, it would appear that progress toward equality, at least in the realm of employment, has been both steady and substantial. Unfortunately, however, gaining appointment to positions of authority appears to be only part of the battle. Once they have attained managerial rank, women often discover that they face another difficult problem. In many cases, the members of both sexes tend to view them as less competent than their male counterparts. Further, this seems to be the case despite growing evidence that male and female managers show very similar, if not identical, patterns of behavior (e.g., Donnell & Hall, 1980; Wexley & Pulakos, 1982). A clear illustration of this second form of bias is provided by a study conducted by Sanders and Schmidt (1980).

In this experiment, male and female subjects worked on a difficult card-sorting task. Before beginning, they were told that a quota for their perform-ance had been set by an engineering student who would, in a sense, act like a

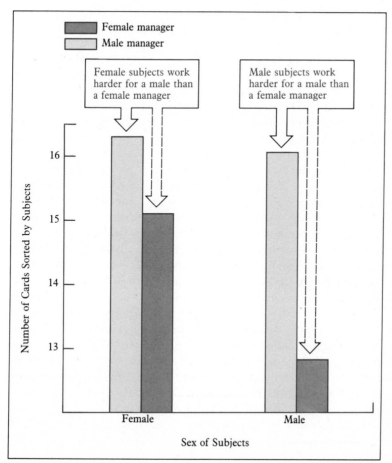

FIGURE 5.16   Female leaders: Often the victims of subtle bias.

Both male and female subjects worked harder to meet a quota set by a manager when they believed this person was male than when they believed that she was female. These findings suggest that female leaders may often enjoy lower levels of cooperation from their subordinates than male leaders—a factor that may interfere with their performance in this role. [Source: Based on data from Sanders & Schmidt, 1980.]

manager in an industrial setting. Half of the subjects then learned that this person was male, while the remainder learned that she was female. After receiving this information, participants actually worked on the task. As you can see from Figure 5.16 (p. 197), results offered clear evidence for the presence of a strong bias against female managers. Subjects actually sorted fewer cards when they believed that they were working under the direction of a female than when they thought they were working under the direction of a male. Further —and perhaps more surprisingly—this was the case for female as well as male participants in the study (although the difference was smaller for females).

These findings have important implications. Briefly, they suggest that female managers or leaders may often obtain lower levels of cooperation from their subordinates. This, in turn, may lead them to appear less successful or effective than their male counterparts. And the final result may then be the emergence of an especially vicious circle, in which female managers are assumed to be less competent, receive less cooperation because of this fact, and then are made to *appear* ineffective as a result of such sabotage by subordinates. Clearly, efforts to prevent or break this disconcerting pattern are essential.

Internal barriers to achievement: Do females fear success? The factors we have considered so far can be viewed as largely external in nature. That is, they stem from the perceptions and actions of individuals who must work with, hire, and promote women in the world of work. As we have seen, these often present formidable obstacles to female growth and achievement. Unfortunately, however, they may not represent the entire story. In addition, it has been contended, females must also overcome *internal* barriers as well (Terborg, 1977). Specifically, they must grapple with conflicts between traditional conceptions of appropriate feminine behavior, and the requirements of many high-level jobs or careers. Only if such conflicts are resolved, several authors believe, can women rise to levels and positions appropriate to their abilities. Perhaps the most controversial proposal along these lines is the suggestion that many females **fear success:** they are afraid that if they are *too* successful or competitive, they will lose part of their own essential femininity (Horner, 1970, 1972). Initial studies on this topic seemed to confirm the widespread existence of such concerns. However, more recent investigations indicate that fear of success is much less common among females than once assumed (Condry & Dyer, 1976). Further, such anxieties seem to occur among males as well. Thus, at present, there are no firm grounds for assuming that fear of success poses a general, major barrier to female achievement. As noted by Terborg (1977), though, other internal obstacles may exist. For example, many women may feel—often incorrectly—that they simply do not possess the traits required for careers in science, business, or the professions. To the extent they hold such views, of course, they may feel inhibited about entering these fields. At present, little direct evidence on the impact of this and other potential internal barriers to female achievement exists. However, should future research indicate that these are in fact important, concrete steps to overcome their influence will be required.

Sex Roles and Sexual Identity:
Masculine, Feminine, or Androgynous?

In many cases, the first words spoken about newborn infants refer to their sex. And from the moment that parents hear a nurse or physician state "It's a girl" or "It's a boy," they begin to think about and behave toward their children in contrasting ways. Given this fact, it is not surprising that within a few short years, toddlers acquire a clear sexual identity (e.g., Constantinople, 1979). Indeed, many three-year-olds will even insist that they be treated appropriately —in the "right" manner for a boy or a girl. The process through which children gain such identity and knowledge of the behaviors and traits assumed by their culture to constitute femininity or masculinity is known as **sex role development** or simply **sex typing.** Several explanations for its rapid occurrence have been suggested, but here we will focus on three: the **social learning view, gender schema theory,** and **self-schema theory.**

Sex Typing: Some Alternate Views

As its name implies, the *social learning view* assumes that sexual identity and sex roles are learned. Basically, it contends that two kinds of learning are involved. The first is *modeling* (or observational learning). Youngsters tend to imitate the persons around them, especially their parents. Further, they tend to imitate the actions of similar models more than those of dissimilar models (Perry & Bussey, 1979). As a result, they gradually come to demonstrate many of the behaviors shown by their same-sex parent.

While learning of this type is occurring, a second process—*learning through reinforcement* (instrumental conditioning)—also takes place. Parents often provide praise and other forms of reward to their children for imitating the "right" models—others of their own sex. And often, they criticize or punish their offspring for imitating the "wrong" models—members of the opposite sex. Through a combination of modeling and direct reinforcement, then, children come to behave more and more like their same-sex parent (see Figure 5.17 on p. 200). And out of this similarity, presumably, comes the child's growing awareness of his or her sexual identity. In short, as the process continues, children gradually come to realize that they are a "girl like mommy" or a "boy like daddy."

A second and sharply contrasting view of sex typing has recently been proposed by Bem (1981). This approach—known as *gender schema theory*— focuses primarily on the basic cognitive mechanisms underlying sex role development. It begins with the suggestion that sex typing rests, in part, on the development of a clear-cut *gender schema*. As you may recall from our discussion of schemata in Chapter 3, these are cognitive frameworks acquired through experience that both guide and organize an individual's processing of new information. Thus, once schemata are formed, they affect the manner in which all relevant, incoming information is interpreted, processed, and remembered.

FIGURE 5.17   Imitation: An important process in sex typing.

The social learning view of sex typing suggests that children acquire sexual identity and sex roles through imitation of their same-sex parent and other social models. [Source: Photo (left) ©Michal Heron 1978/Woodfin Camp and Associates; photo (right) ©Joan Liftin/Archive Pictures, Inc.]

According to Bem, many children quickly acquire a *gender schema*—a cognitive framework reflecting their society's beliefs about the attributes of males and females and the differences between them. Once this schema takes shape, it influences their processing of a wide range of social information. For example, persons with a firmly established gender schema tend to categorize the behavior of others as either masculine or feminine. Similarly, they may process and recall behaviors consistent with the gender schema more easily than ones not consistent with this framework. In short, for such sex-typed persons, gender is a key concept or dimension—one they often use in their attempts to make sense out of the social world.

Going further, Bem notes that a key step in sex typing occurs when the individual's self-concept is assimilated to the gender schema. As this takes place, children come to perceive traits or characteristics specified by the schema as closely linked (if not central) to their self-identity. Thus, they begin to evaluate their own adequacy or worth in terms of the gender schema. Specifically, they view their own preferences, attitudes, and behaviors as acceptable only to the extent that these are consistent with those specified by the schema. As Bem herself puts it (1981, p. 355): "The gender schema becomes . . . a standard or guide . . . and self-esteem becomes its hostage."

Evidence consistent with gender schema theory has been obtained in several studies. For example, as the theory suggests, sex-typed persons do tend to categorize others' behavior as being either masculine or feminine (Bem, 1981). Despite these positive findings, though, gender schema theory has recently been criticized by Crane and Markus (1982) on the following grounds:

it ignores important differences between persons with masculine and feminine identities. Specifically, Crane and Markus note that many individuals possess distinct self-schemas for masculinity and femininity, not just a single schema for gender. Among persons who are clearly sex-typed along traditional lines, one of these schemas—the one relevant to their own gender identity—is usually stronger than the other. Thus, masculine persons possess a more fully developed schema for masculinity than for femininity. For feminine individuals, in contrast, this pattern is reversed. Among individuals who are not clearly sex-typed, however, the situation is somewhat different. Some persons (usually described as *androgynous*) seem to possess well-developed schemata for both masculinity and femininity. (We will consider such persons later.) In contrast, others seem to have only weak schemata in both cases. Crane and Markus suggest that depending on their own sexual identity (and the corresponding self-schemata), different individuals will process contrasting types of information with varying degrees of ease. For example, ones with a masculine sexual identity will process information relevant to this self-schema more efficiently than information pertaining to femininity. And again, this pattern will be reversed for persons with a feminine sexual identity. In contrast, androgynous and undifferentiated individuals may fail to show such differences.

Support for these predictions (and **self-schema theory**) has been reported by Markus and her colleagues (Markus et al., 1982). In this investigation, male and female students were asked to indicate whether various adjectives were or were not characteristic of themselves. They performed this task by pushing buttons labeled "me" or "not me" each time a word was shown on a cathode tube display. Twenty of the adjectives were stereotypically feminine in nature (e.g., emotional), twenty were stereotypically masculine (e.g., aggressive), and twenty were neutral with respect to gender (e.g., industrious). Prior to responding to the adjectives, subjects completed a questionnaire that permitted Markus and her co-workers to divide them into three groups: those with a masculine sex-role orientation, those with a feminine sex role orientation, and those who were not clearly sex-typed in this manner. Consistent with self-schema theory, Markus et al. predicted that because persons with traditional sex role orientations possess well-established schemas, they would respond differentially to the three groups of adjectives. Specifically, masculine persons would respond more quickly to the masculine than feminine words, while the opposite would be true for feminine persons. Individuals lacking a traditional sex role orientation, in contrast, would respond equally quickly to all groups of adjectives. As you can see from Figure 5.18 (p. 202), results offered clear support for these expectations.

The evidence obtained by Bem, Markus et al., and others offers strong support for the view that basic cognitive mechanisms play a key role in sex typing. However, we should note that considerable support for the role of social learning, too, exists (e.g., Sears, Lau, & Alpert, 1965). Thus, at present, it is not possible to make a clear choice between these views. And in fact, such a choice may actually be unnecessary. Learning, cognitive processes, and several other factors may all contribute to the overall occurrence of sex role development. Thus, none should be overlooked. Regardless of the relative contribution of these factors, though, one general conclusion is clear: by the time they are three

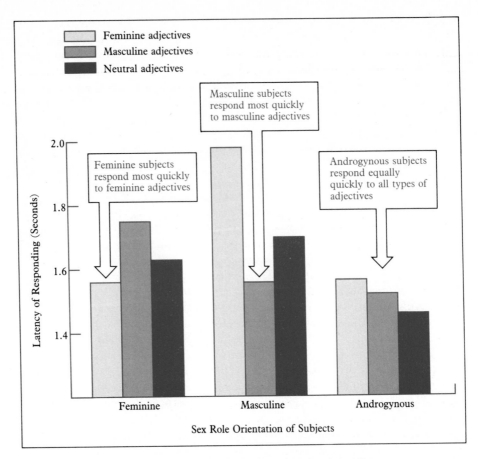

FIGURE 5.18   *Schemata relating to gender: Evidence for their effects.*

Individuals with a feminine sex role orientation responded more quickly to feminine than to masculine or neutral adjectives. Similarly, individuals with a masculine sex role orientation responded more quickly to masculine than to feminine or neutral adjectives. In contrast, persons who were not clearly sex typed (those who were androgynous) responded equally quickly to masculine, feminine, and neutral adjectives. These findings point to the important role of schemata relating to gender in the processing of a wide range of social information. [Source: Based on data from Markus et al., 1982.]

or four, most children have gained a firm sexual identity, and begun to show behaviors consistent with the male or female sex roles specified by their society.

A Note on Androgyny: The Best of Both Worlds?

On the basis of our discussion so far, you might conclude that however it unfolds, the process of sex typing produces predictable results: males possessing "masculine" traits and a traditionally masculine sex role orientation and females possessing "feminine" traits and a traditionally feminine sex role perspective. To a degree, this is true. Many persons do acquire such orientations early in life and maintain them ever afterwards. But it is important to note that this is not the only — or perhaps the best — outcome of sex typing. In contrast to these patterns, some individuals, usually described as showing **androgyny,** develop a broader and more varied sex role identity. Such persons often view themselves as possessing a mixture of both masculine and feminine traits (Bem, 1974, 1979). For example, an androgynous male might perceive that he is warm, tender, and cheerful as well as assertive, competitive, and confident. Similarly, an androgynous female might perceive that she is dominant, logical, and decisive, as well as sensitive, emotional, and kind. Alternatively, androgynous individuals can be viewed as ones who are high on *both* masculinity and femininity (Spence & Helmreich, 1979). Regardless of their specific mixture of traits, however, androgynous persons seem to possess well-developed schemata for both genders. That is, they have clear cognitive frameworks representing both masculine and feminine behaviors and traits. And in their own lives, they seem capable of drawing freely upon both.

That many persons show at least a degree of androgyny is suggested by the findings of a growing body of research (e.g., Antill & Cunningham, 1982; Wiggins & Holzmuller, 1983). Indeed, such individuals may now outnumber men and women demonstrating wholly traditional masculine or feminine patterns, at least in some countries and among younger age groups. Given recent shifts toward a blurring of previously sharp sex role distinctions, this fact is hardly surprising. But what of the impact of these changes; have they been as beneficial as some of their advocates suggest? In fact, existing evidence on this issue is mixed. At first, several studies seemed to suggest that androgyny does indeed confer important advantages on those who possess it. For example, it appeared that such individuals are happier and better adjusted than rigidly sex-typed persons (e.g., Basow, 1981). Similarly, some findings indicated that androgynous individuals are more flexible than sex-typed ones, and so are better able to cope with stressful life events such as the death of a close relative or loss of their jobs (Shaw, 1982). However, a recent review of all relevant research conducted to date (Taylor & Hall, 1982) found little overall support for the view that androgynous persons are higher in psychological well-being than their sex-typed peers. Specifically, there seemed to be little indication that androgynous persons are higher in self-esteem, better adjusted, or higher in ego development. In view of these mixed findings, it seems premature to conclude that androgyny is an important aid to personal adjustment or satisfaction. However, even if it fails to yield such benefits, it may contribute to society in another crucial way. To the extent individuals either possess or comprehend the traits traditionally associated with both genders, they may well find it difficult to maintain stereotyped conceptions about one or the other of these groups. In short, androgyny may help to eliminate the type of gender-based prejudice discussed earlier. If this is indeed the case — and existing evidence suggests that it is — androgyny may well yield major dividends for society as a whole. (Why did the Equal Rights Amendment to the U.S. Constitution fail? For a discussion of some possible answers, see the **On the Applied Side** section on pp. 204–205.)

Failure of the Equal Rights Amendment: A Social Psychological Perspective

Equality of rights under the law shall not be denied or abridged by the United States or by any state on account of sex.

These twenty-four words form the heart of the Equal Rights Amendment—a proposed amendment to the Constitution of the United States submitted to Congress in March 1972. When it was first offered, the ERA seemed to enjoy general, widespread support. Indeed, within a few short years, fully thirty-five states had ratified its passage; only three more were needed for it to become the law of the land. But then—quite suddenly—the situation altered. Several states that had initially voted in favor of the amendment rescinded their approval. And others adamantly refused to grant their endorsement. By June 1982, time had run out: the amendment had failed to gain passage and could no longer be considered (at least, not until it was reintroduced, and the entire process started over once again).

Considering the eminently reasonable nature of the ERA and the widespread support it initially enjoyed, this outcome is both unsettling and puzzling. Why, precisely, did the amendment fail? Supporters of the ERA point an accusing finger at their opponents, and suggest that their efforts were foiled by a strong coalition of conservative forces. To a degree, this is certainly true. The ERA *was* opposed by many political, social, and religious groups, and these became better organized with the passage of time. Further, it is also the case that starting in the late 1970s, the United States experienced a general shift toward conservatism. But careful analysis of the struggle suggests that other factors, too, were at work. In particular, it seems possible that supporters of the amendment themselves took actions and stands serving to unleash forces harmful to the goal they were seeking. Several of these are suggested by findings and principles we have considered in earlier chapters, and we would like to call them to your attention here.

First, it should be noted that many supporters of the amendment were quite passionate in their convictions. As a result of their powerful feelings about the cause of equal rights, they often made statements of a somewhat extreme nature. For example, they suggested that the ERA was desperately needed because of the unbearable mistreatment of females in modern U.S. society. As you can probably guess, many persons found such statements puzzling. After all, their own experience told them that while women did have legitimate complaints and had in fact been the objects of discrimination, the situation was not quite *that* bad. Consistent with principles of attitude change we discussed in Chapter 4 then, such persons may have totally rejected these views. And this rejection, in turn, may have led them to question their initial support for the ERA. In sum, the relatively extreme statements made by some ERA supporters may have backfired badly and served to undermine rather than strengthen support for its acceptance.

A second factor that may have played a role in the failure of the ERA is suggested by *balance theory*. Briefly, this theory (which we will consider in Chapter 6) suggests that individuals find situations in which persons whom they like share their views about the social world more psychologically "comfortable" than situations in which this is not the case (Heider, 1958; Newcomb, 1981). Thus, for example, we are pleased to discover that a good friend agrees with us about some issue or person, but disturbed to learn that he or she holds very different views from our own on these matters. Applying this basic principle to the political struggle over the ERA, an intriguing possibility emerges. Often, it appears, highly vocal supporters of this amendment were persons found to be quite unappealing by many "average citizens." The result, then, was something like this: many persons found themselves confronting a situation in which people they disliked (certain supporters of the ERA) stated views with which they initially agreed. Balance theory suggests that in such cases, something has to "give"

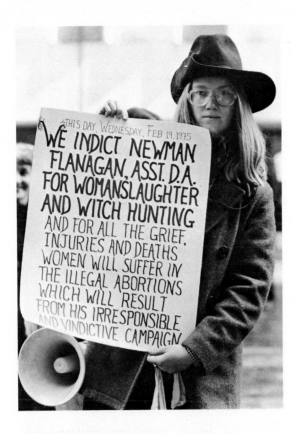

FIGURE 5.19 *Reactance: A possible role in the defeat of the ERA?*

Supporters of the ERA sometimes stated that they would boycott the products of certain states or wage campaigns to defeat specific politicians unless these entities and persons came out in favor of this amendment. Did such tactics backfire by eliciting reactance? *Research findings suggest that this is a distinct possibility. [Source: Photo ©Ellen Shub/The Picture Cube.]*

—there will be considerable pressure toward some change that restores psychological balance. And in many cases, we're afraid, what "gave" was initial, mild support for the ERA. "If he/she is for it," many citizens seemed to reason, "then it can't be all that good." The impact of such shifts in attitude upon the ultimate fate of the ERA is too obvious to require further comment.

Finally, consider this point. In their attempts to gain support for the ERA, some of its strongest advocates issued many threats. For example, they stated that they would launch campaigns to defeat specific politicians if they did not immediately endorse the ERA, or that they would call boycotts of specific states or cities if they failed to vote in favor of this measure (see Figure 5.19). Such tactics, we believe, may well have served to stimulate *reactance*. That is, the persons or organizations in question may have been angered by these remarks, and chosen to oppose the ERA simply to demonstrate that they could not be intimidated or pushed

around. (Please refer to our discussion of reactance in Chapter 4.) To the extent this was the case, the ERA may have lost important ground among persons or groups who might otherwise have favored its adoption.

We believe that together, these and other social psychological forces may have served to weaken support for the ERA and to undermine its chances for passage. But please note: we are certainly *not* suggesting that these were the only factors—or even the most important ones—responsible for this disturbing outcome. On the contrary, we realize that many other factors, too, played a role (the organized opposition and political shifts mentioned previously). We do feel, though, that a social psychological perspective on this situation is useful and sheds important light on an otherwise puzzling chain of events. And perhaps most important of all, we feel that attention to such forces may aid supporters of enhanced social justice to avoid similar pitfalls in the years ahead.

Summary

Prejudice may be viewed as a negative attitude toward the members of some social group. In contrast, **discrimination** involves specific harmful actions directed toward the objects of prejudice. Discrimination is sometimes overt, but in many cases it takes more subtle forms such as tokenism, reluctance to help, or viewing all members of the disliked group as being physically and behaviorally similar.

Several different explanations for the existence of prejudice have been proposed. One suggests that it stems from direct intergroup conflict. A second indicates that it derives from social categorization (the tendency to divide the social world into "us" and "them") and resulting social competition. Prejudice may also be linked to specific personality factors, and to early learning experiences during socialization. Efforts to reduce prejudice have often centered around changes in child-rearing practices and increased contact between different groups. This latter strategy seems to be effective, but only when intergroup contact occurs under conditions of equal status and in a cooperative context.

Women constitute a majority in terms of numbers in many societies. Yet, their exclusion from political and economic power suggests that they have often been treated in a manner similar to minority groups. Females have often been the objects of negative stereotypes. Further, they have also been the victims of actual discrimination, especially in employment settings.

Individuals gain sexual identity and basic knowledge of the sex roles prescribed by their society early in life. Such sex typing seems to involve learning and the development of *gender schemas*—cognitive frameworks concerning the attributes of males and females and the differences between them. While many individuals acquire an exclusively masculine or feminine sex role orientation, others are *androgynous*. Such persons perceive themselves as possessing characteristics traditionally associated with both sexes.

Glossary

androgyny *One possible outcome of the process of sex role development. Androgynous individuals perceive that they possess traits that are usually associated with both males and females.*

authoritarian personality *Refers to a cluster of traits, including submissive obedience to authority and rigid black-white thinking. Together, these seem to predispose individuals toward a high degree of prejudice.*

discrimination *Negative behaviors directed toward the members of some disliked group. Discrimination may be viewed as the overt expression of prejudice.*

fear of success *The supposed anxiety on the part of females that a high degree of success will bring about a loss in femininity. Recent evidence suggests such fears may be less common than was once believed.*

gender schema theory *A theory of sex role development suggesting that this process involves the formation of a schema relating to gender, and* *assimilation of an individual's self-concept to this schema.*

ingroups *Refers to the group to which an individual belongs.* Research findings suggest that, in general, the members of a given social group tend to perceive it as superior to other groups along many key dimensions.

intergroup contact *A technique for the reduction of prejudice based on increased contact between the members of different social groups.* Experiences of this type do seem effective in reducing prejudice, but only when they take place under cooperative conditions.

outgroups *Refers to groups other than the one to which an individual belongs.* Members of outgroups are often derogated and perceived as homogeneous in traits, behavior, and physical appearance.

prejudice *A negative attitude toward the members of some specific social group.*

self-schema theory *With respect to sex typing, the view that individuals generally possess separate schemas for masculinity and femininity.* The schema pertaining to their own gender is better developed and becomes part of the individual's self-image or identity.

sex role development (sex typing) *The process through which children acquire a clear sexual identity and knowledge of the behaviors considered appropriate for their own gender.*

sexism *Refers to negative attitudes toward females (or males).* Sexism involves stereotyped beliefs about the members of one sex, negative feelings toward them, and tendencies to discriminate against them.

social categorization *Refers to our basic tendency to divide the social world into two discrete categories: the group to which we belong ("us") and groups to which we do not belong ("them").*

social distance scales *Questionnaires designed to measure tendencies to discriminate against the members of some social group.* Social distance scales generally ask the persons completing them to indicate the degree of intimacy to which they would be willing to admit members of various racial, ethnic, or religious groups.

social learning view (of sex typing) *The view that children acquire sexual identity and knowledge of sex roles through imitation and direct reinforcement.*

stereotypes *Beliefs and expectations individuals hold about the members of some social group.* Stereotypes lead the persons holding them to assume that all members of a given social group possess much the same traits.

tokenism *Refers to instances in which individuals perform trivial, positive actions for members of a minority group and then use this as a basis for avoiding more meaningful beneficial actions.*

For More Information

Basow, S.A. *Sex role stereotypes: Traditions and alternatives.* Monterey, Calif.: Brooks/Cole, 1981.
A clear (but relatively brief) discussion of the nature and transmission of sex role stereotypes. Attention is also directed to androgyny, the flexible integration (within a single person) of both masculine and feminine traits.

Katz, P.A. (Ed.). *Toward the elimination of racism.* Elmsford, N.Y.: Pergamon, 1976.
A collection of articles by leading experts on prejudice. Together, these papers provide a useful overview of psychological knowledge about racism, and means for reducing its impact.

Patchen, M. *Black-white contact: Its social and academic effects.* W. Lafayette, Ind.: Purdue University Press, 1982.
This well-written book reports the results and implications of a major study focused on the effects of school desegregation within the United States. The investigation described focused on interracial behaviors as well as interracial attitudes and uncovered some important facts about the impact of desegregation on the academic performance of blacks and whites. Given the importance of the issues involved, it is timely and informative reading.

Chapter 6

Attraction, Friendship, and Love

Reacting to Strangers:
Proximity, Feelings, and Affiliative Needs

Propinquity: Exposure Leads to Familiarity/Feelings: Conditioned Emotional Reactions/Need for Affiliation: Individual Differences in the Desire for Relationships

Evaluating Acquaintances:
Attractiveness, Similarity, and Reciprocity

Physical Attractiveness: We Do Judge Books by Their Covers/Similarity: Seeking Ourselves in Others/Reciprocity: Maintaining Social Relationships with Mutually Positive Evaluations

Falling in (and out of) Love

Passionate Love and Companionate Love/Breaking Up: When Love Grows Cold

Special Inserts

FOCUS ON RESEARCH
   What Is Physical Attractiveness?

FOCUS ON RESEARCH
   Similarity as a Threat: The Need to Be Unique

ON THE APPLIED SIDE
   Rejection: When Love Is a One-Way Street

Dave and Judy first became aware of one another in their biology class. They had been assigned to the same laboratory table. Right away he noticed her long blonde hair and decided he was very lucky to get such a good-looking lab partner. She also liked his looks, and his jokes made her laugh. Since they walked in the same direction after class, they soon found themselves walking together and talking briefly about the class, an upcoming exam, and similar topics. After a couple of weeks, Dave asked her if she wanted to have a coke at the student union while they tried to figure out a homework assignment. She did.

It was a few weeks after that before they had what could be called an actual date. Dave had been feeling lonely since he and a long-time girl friend broke up during the summer, but he didn't know anything about Judy's personal life. He wanted to ask her to come with him to see a well-known comedian who would be performing on campus, but what if she said "no"? She might already be involved with someone else, or she might not like this comedian, or she just might not want to go out with him. If she rejected him, biology class would be painful for the rest of the semester.

As it turned out, she did want to go and had been wondering why he was so shy. They both laughed a lot at the TV star's routines. Afterward, they had a couple of bottles of beer at a nearby hangout and laughed again about some of the jokes and then talked about their biology instructor and some of the odd things he did. Suddenly, there was a lull in the conversation and Dave felt a sense of panic. "What will we talk about now? I don't even know this girl. I don't know anything about her. What do we have in common besides one college course and tonight's show?"

Judy was sitting quietly, reading the label on her beer bottle. She said, "You know, this reminds me of having breakfast when I was little and reading everything that was written on the cereal box." He laughed: "You did that, too?" They quickly began comparing notes on their childhood likes and dislikes. Over the next two hours they also began talking about their current attitudes and values.

At the end of the evening, as she was going back to her dormitory, Judy said, "That was fun. It's strange, but we're an awful lot alike." Dave smiled. "I had fun, too. You won't believe it, but I was afraid that we might not have anything to talk about."

A large portion of our time is spent interacting with those we encounter in our everyday lives. Sometimes, we instantly decide whether we like or dislike a stranger, and sometimes such reactions develop slowly over time. The process frequently begins, as with Dave and Judy, simply because we find ourselves in close physical proximity in a classroom, at work, or elsewhere. Once two people begin to interact, they tend to express their ideas and to compare them in the attempt to discover areas of similarity and agreement.

Under the appropriate circumstances, the attraction toward the other person may be intense, and they can perceive themselves as being in love.

From the earliest days of social psychology, there has been an interest in understanding the details of this sort of interpersonal behavior. The general question has been, "What are the determinants of interpersonal evaluations?" That is, why does a given individual like one person, dislike another, and feel indifferent about a third? We tend to react to one another in terms of degrees of positive versus negative attitudes, and these interpersonal responses indicate our **attraction** to one another (Berscheid, 1976). Thus, attraction is simply *the evaluation of another person along a positive–negative dimension.* This dimension is illustrated in Figure 6.1.

In addition to examining the determinants of attraction, social psychologists have become increasingly interested in studying the development of

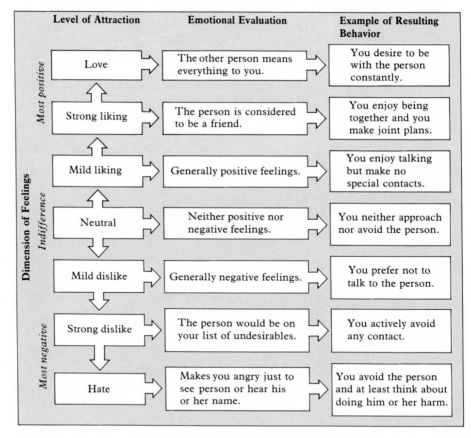

FIGURE 6.1   *Attraction: Interpersonal attitudes.*

Interperson attraction *refers to an attitudinal dimension involving the evaluation of others in relatively positive or negative terms. Such evaluations reflect how we feel emotionally about other individuals and determine how we tend to behave toward them. Attraction ranges from the negative extreme of* hate *to the positive extreme of* love.

relationships from first impressions to the formation of acquaintanceships and friendships (Duck & Gilmour, 1981; Hinde, 1981; McCarthy, 1981). Further, they are concerned with the way in which we form intimate relationships and in the factors that make them successful and long-lasting versus unsuccessful and relatively brief (Burgess, 1981; Hatfield & Traupmann, 1981; Huston & Levinger, 1978). We will touch on each of these major problems in the following pages.

In this chapter, we will first examine the process of becoming acquainted by looking at the variables involved in *reacting to strangers* — proximity, emotions, and affiliative needs. Then the factors that affect the process of *evaluating acquaintances* will be discussed — physical attractiveness, similarity, and reciprocal judgments of one another. In the final section of the chapter, we will take a close look at what is involved in *falling in love* and at why relationships break up. We will also cover three special topics: the meaning of *physical attractiveness,* the need to be *unique,* and the painful effects of interpersonal *rejection.*

Reacting to Strangers: Proximity, Feelings, and Affiliative Needs

Before we can even begin to get to know someone, it is necessary to become aware of that person as an individual. One selects only a relatively few people to know out of the thousands that are encountered over the years. Why some and not others? It is usually assumed that a given person is liked or disliked because of certain qualities he or she possesses or lacks. In part, that is true, as will be discussed in the next section. There are some factors, however, that have nothing to do with the other person — factors that set the stage for acquaintanceships to form. Potential friends emerge from the mass of strangers if you are brought together by physical proximity or **propinquity,** if you are experiencing positive rather than negative **emotions,** and if your **need for affiliation** is sufficiently strong.

Propinquity: Exposure Leads to Familiarity

The first step in becoming acquainted with a stranger is often a series of accidental contacts. If you see someone in an adjoining classroom seat day after day or stand near someone at the bus stop each morning as you go to work, that individual gradually becomes familiar to you, and you feel friendlier toward such a person. With infants, too, the more frequently they are exposed to a stranger, the more positively they respond to that person (Levitt, 1980), as in Figure 6.2 (on p. 214). Other instances of the effects of repeated exposure were described in Chapter 4.

Initial responses to a stranger: Propinquity helps. It has been known for several decades now that any characteristic of the environment that increases the *propinquity* (physical proximity) of two individuals in their everyday lives increases the probability of their getting to know and like one another (Festinger et al., 1950). Thus you are more likely to become acquainted with the

FIGURE 6.2   Becoming familiar with a stranger's face.

Infants quickly learn to discriminate among faces, and they react negatively to the presence of a stranger. When such a person returns again and again, the infant's response grows increasingly positive. Repeated contacts establish familiarity and, therefore, a comfortable interpersonal atmosphere. [Source: Photo by Elihu Blotnick/Omni-Photo Communications.]

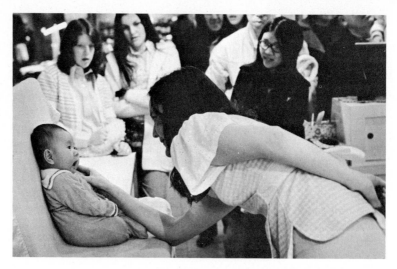

person sitting next to you in class or the person assigned to the dorm room next to yours than with anyone sitting or living farther away from you. This is true regardless of such things as whether you share similar academic majors, religious backgrounds, or interests (Caplow & Forman, 1950). In married student housing areas, propinquity is so important that couples given apartments within 22 feet of one another are very likely to become friends; with apartments 88 feet or more apart, friendships almost never form (Festinger et al., 1950).

In addition to simple measures of distance ("physical proximity"), friendships are also influenced by factors that increase the ease of interaction ("functional proximity"). An example would be side-by-side seats in a classroom versus equally close seats in different rows. Most students placed side-by-side get to know one another by the end of the semester while those with more distant seats (even those sitting face-to-back in adjoining rows) usually remain strangers (Byrne, 1961). Sometimes seats are assigned alphabetically by the instructor. In such situations, it is interesting to find that friendships are most likely to form between those whose last names begin with the same letter or an adjoining letter of the alphabet (Segal, 1974). Many of your own college friendships and perhaps even a romance or two will very likely begin through the effects of classroom seat arrangements or dormitory room assignments.

These effects are by no means confined to a college campus. In a big city housing project for the elderly, most friendships develop between people living on the same floor (Nahemow & Lawton, 1975), precisely the same pattern that is true for college dormitories (Evans & Wilson, 1949). A similar trend holds in apartment complexes and even determines the closeness of the friendships. The closer two people live, the more likely they are to become "best friends" as opposed to simply good friends (Ebbesen et al., 1976).

Why? Propinquity equals repeated exposure. Propinquity apparently leads to liking because it brings about **repeated exposure** among those who are interacting. That is, *because* of the placement of a seat in a lecture hall or of an

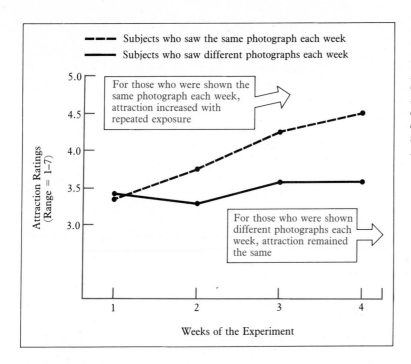

- - - Subjects who saw the same photograph each week
— Subjects who saw different photographs each week

For those who were shown the same photograph each week, attraction increased with repeated exposure

For those who were shown different photographs each week, attraction remained the same

Attraction Ratings (Range = 1–7)

Weeks of the Experiment

FIGURE 6.3 *Attraction increases with repeated exposure.*

Repeated exposure to another person, even in a photograph, leads to increased attraction over time. Presumably, propinquity leads to acquaintanceship because it brings about repeated exposure for pairs of individuals. [Source: Adapted from Moreland & Zajonc, 1982.]

apartment doorway, some individuals (initially strangers) see each other time after time. As was discussed in Chapter 4, Zajonc and his colleagues have consistently shown that repeated exposure to various stimuli results in increasingly favorable attitudes toward that stimulus (Moreland & Zajonc, 1979; Zajonc, 1968).

In one experiment, subjects were shown the photograph of a male college student once a week for four weeks to test the effect of repeated exposure on attraction (Moreland & Zajonc, 1982). Half of the subjects saw the same photograph each week (as in a situation where propinquity brings about repeated exposure) and half saw a different photograph each week. At the end of each session, all subjects were asked to make several ratings, including liking, of the person or persons they had been exposed to. As shown in Figure 6.3, the more often the stranger had been seen, the better he was liked.

It should be noted, however, that repeated exposure doesn't *always* have a positive effect. Attraction seems to develop only if the initial reaction to the other person is neutral or mildly positive. If the very first impression is negative, increased familiarity may only make things worse (Brockner & Swap, 1976; Grush, 1976). The nature of the interaction also matters. Repeated exposure to someone who insults you each time is unlikely to lead to friendship. This fact is clearly illustrated in an experiment conducted by Swap (1977). Female undergraduates interacted with one another in a series of tasks on either eight, four, two, or one occasions, or they didn't interact at all. The stranger gave the subject either rewards or punishments when they interacted. Repeated exposure to a rewarding stranger led to increased attraction while repeated exposure to a punishing stranger led to *decreased* attraction.

Feelings: Conditioned Emotional Reactions

Do feelings influence our behavior? One interesting example of this has been provided by anthropologist James Schaefer who visited more than 100 bars in Minnesota and Montana observing the relationship between the songs being played on the jukebox and the amount of drinking by the customers (Littlel, 1981). Sad songs such as "I'm So Lonesome I Could Cry" by Hank Williams or "Don't It Make Your Brown Eyes Blue" by Crystal Gayle led to an increase in alcohol consumption. It was concluded that "the songs have a self-pitying mood that is associated with heavier drinking." At the opposite extreme was the fast and loud music at disco bars where there was so little drinking that a cover charge was generally necessary. If the emotions aroused by music affect the consumption of alcohol, do they also affect interpersonal behavior? In other words, could an emotion-arousing stimulus such as music cause people to react in a positive or negative way to one another?

Emotions and attraction. Music is pervasive in our society and not just in bars. We are exposed to music we like on our radios and stereos and sometimes to music we dislike when others make the selection. To determine the effect of this type of stimulation on attraction, May and Hamilton (1980) first found the most and least liked music of female college students: rock and avant-garde classical. Then other females took part in an experiment in which they rated the photographs of male strangers. While they did this, there was either silence or one of the two types of music playing in the background. As you can see in Figure 6.4, attraction toward the person in the photograph was least positive if

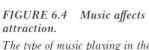

FIGURE 6.4   Music affects attraction.

The type of music playing in the background was found to affect attraction toward a stranger depicted in a photograph. Compared to students who made the ratings in a silent room, those who were exposed to music they enjoyed (rock) liked the stranger slightly better while those who heard music that was unpleasant to them (avant-garde) liked the stranger considerably less. [Source: Based on data from May & Hamilton, 1980.]

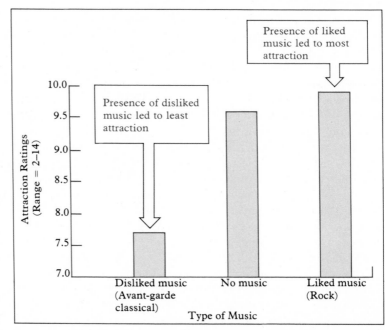

FIGURE 6.5   Good news and bad news: Both affect attraction.

Any events that influence one's emotional state tend to influence interpersonal attraction. When the emotions are negative (as might be elicited by this news announcement), we like others less than when the emotions aroused are positive. [Source: Saturday Review. *Cartoon by Peter Steiner, reprinted with permission.]*

"Good evening, ladies and gentlemen. This is a news capsule. All hell is breaking loose. I'm John Davis. This has been a news capsule. Good evening."

the avant-garde music was playing and most positive if there was a rock selection.

Other studies consistently show that various events that bring about positive feelings increase attraction while those that elicit negative feelings decrease attraction. Examples range from hot, uncomfortably humid rooms (Griffitt, 1970) to happy versus sad movies (Gouaux, 1971). In a similar fashion, depressed individuals make us feel depressed, and this leads to their being liked less (Coyne, 1976; Winer et al., 1981).

An interesting influence on our everyday feelings is the sort of news provided by newspapers, radio, and television. Though the evening news is seldom as bad as that suggested in Figure 6.5, reports of war, riots, murder, terrorists, economic problems, natural disasters, and so forth can be depressing. CBS reporter Charles Kuralt (1972) once suggested that Americans would be happier if they occasionally turned off their radios and TVs and refused to read their newspapers for several days at a time. In an experimental test of the effect of such news on emotions and on attraction, Veitch and Griffitt (1976) arranged for subjects to hear a news broadcast just before the study began. The "radio" they listened to was actually a cassette recording containing a series of either good or bad news stories. The good news brought about a positive emotional reaction, and subjects who heard it expressed greater liking toward a stranger. Bad news had the opposite effect—negative feelings and decreased attraction.

Why? Conditioned emotional responses. According to one of the theories developed to explain interpersonal attraction, all of our likes and dislikes are based on emotional responses (Byrne, 1971; Clore & Byrne, 1974). At its simplest

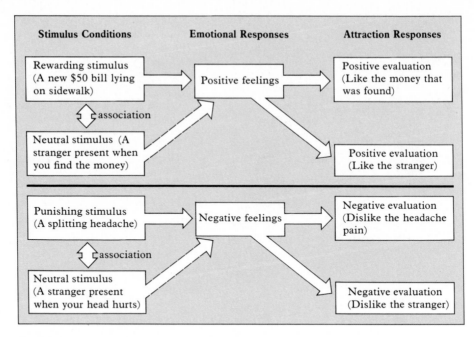

**FIGURE 6.6   *The reinforcement-affect model:*
*Responding to feelings and conditioned feelings.***

*According to the reinforcement-affect model of attraction, our likes and
dislikes are based on feelings that are aroused by rewarding and punishing
stimulus events. Rewarding stimuli elicit positive feelings and are liked;
punishments elicit negative feelings and are disliked. When a neutral stimulus
(such as a stranger) is present when those feelings are aroused, that stranger
becomes associated with the reward or the punishment. At that point, the
feelings become* conditioned *to that new stimulus. As a result, a person to
whom we might have responded neutrally now is evaluated in a positive or
negative way.*

level, this means that when anyone makes us feel good, we respond with liking;
we dislike whomever makes us feel bad. Any variable (such as propinquity and
repeated exposure) that leads to attraction does so because positive feelings are
aroused.

   This formulation, known as the **reinforcement-affect model** of attraction,
has an additional element, as shown in Figure 6.6. We not only respond to the
feelings another person *arouses* in us, but also to anyone who is simply *associated
with* such feelings. This conditioning of emotional responses explains why
attraction is influenced by music, heat, movies, radio news, and so forth. Such
things can arouse our positive or negative feelings; these feelings become
associated with anyone who happens to be present, and we tend to like or dislike that person accordingly. Once such an association between emotions
and another person is made, that person acquires the power to arouse those
same feelings. This process is known as **second-order classical conditioning**
(Moran, 1981).

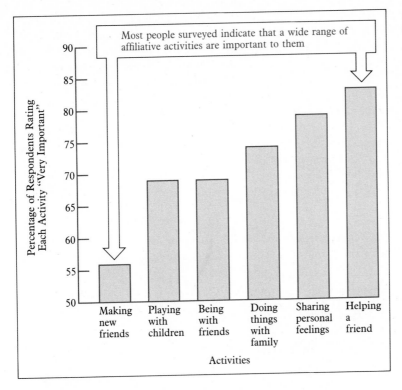

FIGURE 6.7   Very important affiliative activities.

Affiliative activities seem to be highly valued by most individuals. In a large-scale survey, the majority of participants rated a variety of interpersonal interactions as "very important." [Source: Based on data from Research and Forecasts, Inc., 1981.]

Need for Affiliation:
Individual Differences in the Desire for Relationships

Human beings, as well as representatives of many other species, spend a good deal of time interacting with one another (Deni et al., 1980). A recent survey of Americans by a life insurance company indicated that several aspects of interpersonal relationships were evaluated as "very important" by most of the respondents (Research and Forecasts, Inc., 1981). A summary of some of their evaluations is shown in Figure 6.7.

It is also true that individuals differ a great deal in their affiliative tendencies. Some of us are loners, while others are extremely sociable. Even the same person may feel differently on different days, sometimes desiring company and sometimes preferring to be alone. Presumably, such differences among people (and within the same people over time) help to determine whether the effects of propinquity and positive emotions actually lead two strangers to interact.

Need for affiliation as a trait. Beginning with the work of Murray (1938/1962), several measures of the *need for affiliation* have been developed. Research with such instruments has revealed, for example, that males high in affiliation need are self-confident, and they tend to talk more to attractive females than do males whose affiliation need is low (Crouse & Mehrabian, 1977).

When a relationship actually forms, each of the individuals involved responds not only to the affiliative aspects but to other needs as well, sometimes causing conflict. For example, when two people are intensely involved, each person's affiliation need may be satisfied, but the need for independence may be frustrated. In a study of university freshmen, it was found that those high in need for affiliation were increasingly satisfied as their relationships progressed over the first semester of college (Eidelson, 1980). In contrast, those with low affiliative needs tended to feel less satisfied with their associations over time, especially if the person also had a high need for independence. You can see how two individuals with somewhat different patterns of needs could be puzzled by one another as their friendship developed. One could be very pleased by the tightening bonds of a close relationship while the other could begin to feel trapped.

Need for affiliation as a situational response. You are sitting in your room reading your social psychology textbook when suddenly you hear what sounds

FIGURE 6.8   Stressful situations can increase affiliative needs.

Whenever an event creates anxiety or fear, there is a tendency for affiliative behavior to increase. People seek out others to communicate, compare perceptions, and reduce their anxiety. [Source: Photo by Laurence Nelson, Copyright © 1980 by Laurence Nelson.]

like an explosion not far away. It is so loud and so close that you are a little frightened. What do you do? Most people react by seeking out others, even strangers, to discuss the situation, to compare perceptions, and to decide what is going on and what to do about it (see Figure 6.8).

In a series of now-classic experiments, Schachter (1959) was able to show that anxiety and fear lead to an increased desire to affiliate with others—at least for individuals who are first-born or only children. When experimental subjects expected to receive painful electric shocks, they preferred waiting with other subjects rather than being alone. When no painful shock was involved, they preferred being by themselves or had no preference. Though it has been shown repeatedly that frightened individuals respond in this way, other kinds of arousal have different effects. For example, those about to take part in an *embarrassing* experiment preferred to wait without the company of others (Fish et al., 1978).

The explanation for the effect of fear on affiliation seems to be that this emotion arouses the desire to communicate with others about what is happening. When such *social comparison* occurs, it reduces anxiety. That is, talking to others who share our fears tends to make us less afraid. This process was shown in an experiment with college students who were supposedly waiting for an electric shock experiment. Compared to controls, they actually did interact more and spent more time discussing the upcoming experience (Morris et al., 1976).

Evaluating Acquaintances: Attractiveness, Similarity, and Reciprocity

Once two individuals are brought together by such variables as propinquity, if their emotional state is positive and if they each have sufficiently strong affiliative needs, they might be expected to interact. At this point, however, other variables become important. Whether friendship (or even acquaintanceship) develops now depends on *attractiveness*, the *similarity* of the two people, and on the *reciprocity* of their responses to one another. Such variables determine whether two people ignore one another, become casual acquaintances, or develop a close friendship.

Physical Attractiveness: We Do Judge Books by Their Covers

First impressions rest in large part on appearances. When we see someone for the first time, we notice such things as race, age, height, weight, clothing, facial features, hair color, and so forth. We also notice what they do, how they respond to others, and anything unusual about them. The process that occurs when we evaluate a stranger seems to rest on two basic responses—positive versus negative emotional reaction and high versus low concern about their well being. When subjects were given cues about the appearance and behavior of strangers, emotion and concern were found to predict attraction toward the strangers (Kelley, 1982a). If the appearance and behavior of the other person

TABLE 6.1   Reacting to a stranger: Feelings and concern.

When college students were given bits of information about a stranger's appearance and/or behavior, their reactions tended to reflect positive versus negative feelings and high versus low concern. Attraction based on such first impressions was greatest when the stranger evoked positive feelings and high concern. (Source: Based on data from Kelley, 1982a.)

Greatest Attraction (Positive Feelings and High Concern)
   A male with a friendly smile who listened attentively to an experimenter's instructions.
   A very attractive female wearing stylish clothes who behaved gracefully.

Less Attraction (Negative Feelings and High Concern)
   A nervous male or female with a badly scarred, discolored face.

Still Less Attraction (Positive Feelings and Low Concern)
   A female with a photograph of a nude male in her coat pocket.
   A clumsy male who stumbled and dropped an armful of textbooks and notebooks.

Least Attraction (Negative Feelings and Low Concern)
   A female with a photograph of a nude female in her coat pocket.
   A male who arrived thirty minutes early for an experiment, read dull magazines and silly comic books for an hour, and then discovered he was scheduled for the next day.

aroused positive feelings and a high sense of concern and involvement, attraction was greatest. Negative feelings and lack of concern led to the least attraction. Table 6.1 indicates how those responses combine to determine attraction toward someone you see for the first time. Possibly this is one of the reasons that most people tend to avoid social interaction with those who are handicapped or otherwise different from the norm (Belgrave & Mills, 1981). They may be concerned, but their emotional response is negative.

There is also an evaluation of strangers along a dimension of **physical attractiveness,** and that turns out to be a major factor in determining whether one thinks a friendship or acquaintanceship is desirable or possible (Dion, 1980). Attempts to specify what precisely is meant by attractiveness are discussed in the **Focus on Research** section on pages 224–225.

The effects of attractiveness. In various studies of male-female interactions, the attractiveness of the other person is found to be crucial to both genders (Curran & Lippold, 1975; Folkes, 1982; Walster et al., 1966). Nevertheless, not everyone responds to physical attractiveness in the same fashion. For example, traditionally sex-typed males and females are more responsive to physically attractive strangers than are androgynous individuals (Andersen & Bem, 1981).

It is generally assumed, though, that attractive people have various positive qualities. Thus, females judge attractive males to be brighter, more moral, and better adjusted than unattractive males (May & Hamilton, 1980). For both sexes, attractiveness is perceived as indicating that the person is poised, interesting, sociable, independent, exciting, and sexually warm (Brigham, 1980). Less attractive individuals are believed to be deviant in a variety of ways including psychopathology, political radicalism, and homosexuality (Jones et al., 1978; Unger et al., 1982). College students who are low in attractiveness believe they are likely to become mentally ill in the future (O'Grady, 1982). Physically attractive males are judged to be more masculine and attractive females to be more feminine than those who are relatively unattractive (Gillen, 1981).

Being with attractive people even "rubs off" on others; the friends of an attractive same-sex peer are rated more positively than the friends of someone who is unattractive (Kernis & Wheeler, 1981). Judgments of attractiveness are not simply influenced by physical appearance — even one's name can affect this perception. In one study, equally attractive female photos were labeled with desirable first names (Kathy, Jennifer, and Christine) or with less desirable names (Ethel, Harriet, and Gertrude). Those females who were thought to have the "better" names were judged to be more beautiful (Garwood et al., 1980).

Most of these beliefs about physically attractive and unattractive individuals are thought to be based on stereotypes and therefore unrelated to the actual qualities of those being judged. There are *some* behavioral differences related to appearance, however. As you might expect, attractive males and females interact well with their opposite sex counterparts and have more dates (Reis et al., 1980). There are some sex differences in the effects of attractiveness. Attractive males have more social interactions with the opposite sex (and fewer interactions with other males), are more assertive, and have less fear of

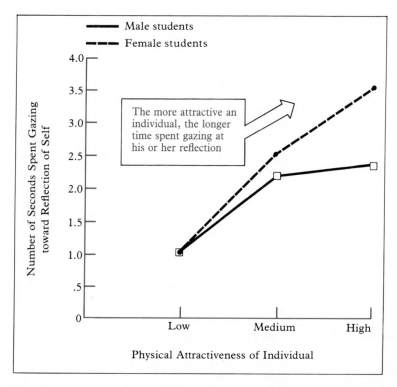

FIGURE 6.9 Mirror, mirror— Gazing at one's attractiveness.

People seem to respond positively to their own physical attractiveness as well as to that of others. When students were observed passing a mirrored wall, the more attractive they were judged to be, the greater the amount of time they spent gazing at themselves. [Source: Based on data from McDonald & Eilenfield, 1980.]

What Is Physical Attractiveness?

When *Playgirl* magazine asks readers for their nominations of the world's sexiest men, there is agreement that such individuals as Senator Gary Hart, newsman Tom Brokaw, and singer Willie Nelson belong in the top ten. A California group called Man Watchers, Inc., comes up with such "most watchable men" as scientist Carl Sagan, singer Wayne Newton, and football star Vince Ferragamo. The favorite leading men in American movies in recent years have been John Travolta, Christopher Reeve, and Burt Reynolds (*Parade*, March 22, 1981, p. 9). These and similar lists by males identifying the most beautiful women are somewhat puzzling in that it is difficult to perceive any commonality among these seemingly most attractive men or most attractive women. Though the exact meaning of male or female beauty may not yet be generally understood, we spend a great deal of money on books and products that promise to make us one of the desirable few (Howard, 1980).

Psychologists have approached the question of defining attraction in a variety of ways. When female preferences in male physiques are examined, it is found that they like thin legs, a thin waist, broad shoulders, and small buttocks (Beck et al., 1976; Horvath, 1981; Lavrakas, 1975). That is, men should be shaped more or less like Robert Redford. With respect to height, it is usually assumed that the taller a man is, the better, whether in business (Korda, 1975), politics (Feldman, 1971), or as a romantic partner (Gillis & Avis, 1980). In a study of interpersonal attraction, however, it was found that female college students prefer males of medium height to those who are very short or very tall (Graziano et al., 1978). Nevertheless, there is a social norm that within couples the male should be the taller of the two, as in Figure 6.10, even if a little

FIGURE 6.10 *A powerful social rule: The norm that a male should be taller than his female partner.*

It is the social norm for the male to be taller than his female partner. If he is not, both individuals often try to make it so by wearing heels of appropriate lengths or even, as Tom does here, by exaggerating the truth. [Source: © 1978 Universal Press Syndicate. Reprinted with permission. All rights reserved.]

225

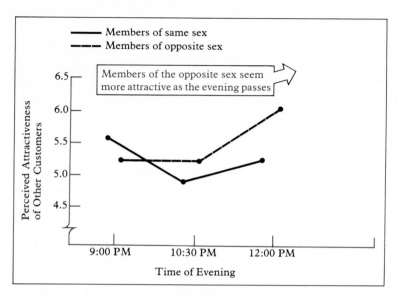

FIGURE 6.11 Potential partners seem to get "prettier" at closing time.

Perceptions of physical attractiveness depend in part on the situation. In a series of bars, it was found that, as closing time approached, customers rated the opposite sex as increasingly attractive. This effect did not hold for ratings of same-sex customers, so it was apparently not the effect of alcohol. [Source: Based on data from Pennebaker et al., 1979.]

exaggeration is necessary. In terms of preferences, undergraduate females say that they want a partner six inches taller than themselves while males want a partner four and a half inches shorter than they are (Gillis & Avis, 1980).

Studies of male judgments suggest that they are attracted to females with medium-sized breasts (Kleinke & Staneski, 1980) and medium-sized legs and buttocks (Wiggins et al., 1968). Males seem to respond most positively to narrow hips and an absence of too many curves (Horvath, 1979, 1981). For both sexes, obesity is perceived as unattractive (Harris et al., 1982).

It has been more difficult to specify cues to facial attractiveness. There is evidence that certain infant characteristics (large eyes and head, small nose and chin, rounded features, soft skin) elicit positive responses from adults (Hildebrandt & Fitzgerald, 1977; Sternglanz et al., 1972). Interestingly enough, males find these same characteristics attractive in adult females (M. R. Cunningham, 1981). Sociobiologists explain these preferences on the basis of males seeking young females who are most likely to be able to reproduce. In a similar vein, females are believed to be seeking such biologically valuable survival characteristics as power,

rank, and dominance that are identified by a jutting chin, beard, grey hair, baldness, or height (M. R. Cunningham, 1981; Freedman, 1979; Guthrie, 1976). While most social psychologists would find it hard to agree, these theorists are suggesting that what we perceive as attractiveness is a matter of cues that help males find a partner to bear offspring and help females find a powerful provider.

Beyond these various anatomical details, perceptions of attractiveness are also influenced by the situation. There is a *contrast effect* in that an individual is rated as more attractive if he or she is in the presence of someone who is unattractive (Kernis & Wheeler, 1981). In the opposite direction, males were found to rate a female lower in attractiveness if they had just been watching the glamorous "Charlie's Angels" on television (Kenrick & Gutierres, 1980). A person's needs also affect such judgments. As in the Mickey Gilley song, the girls (and boys) in a bar actually do get "prettier at closing time." When bar patrons were asked to rate others at various times during the night, ratings of the attractiveness of opposite-sex fellow customers increased as the evening progressed, while ratings of same-sex customers were unaffected (Pennebaker et al., 1979). See Figure 6.11.

rejection. Attractive and unattractive females have an equal number of social interactions, while those who are attractive are less assertive and less trusting of the opposite sex (Reis et al., 1982). Attractive people expect to succeed in social situations (Abbott & Sebastian, 1981). When they walk past a mirrored wall in a public setting, relatively attractive individuals are observed to spend more time gazing at themselves than do those who are less attractive (Lipson et al., 1983; McDonald & Eilenfield, 1980), as shown in Figure 6.9 (on p. 223). There is at least one disadvantage to being physically attractive. Such individuals are seen as being "typical," and it is actually more difficult to remember having seen them before (Light et al., 1981).

Two-by-two: Finding an equally attractive partner. Since most people seem to think physical attractiveness is very desirable and since not everyone resembles a movie star, how are interpersonal choices made? One answer is provided by the **matching hypothesis**—the proposal that each of us chooses a partner who is similar to ourselves in physical attractiveness (Berscheid et al., 1971). In effect, people may ideally *prefer* the best-looking of all possible partners, but they realistically *choose* someone they feel they can get. Such matching is not simply a feature of campus romances. The same tendency influences casual dates, engagements, and marriages (Murstein, 1972). Married couples, regardless of age or length of marriage, are similar in attractiveness (Price & Vandenberg, 1979). Even more surprising perhaps is the fact that same-sex friends also tend to resemble each other in attractiveness, and this is true for both males and females (Cash & Derlega, 1978).

What happens when a pair is mismatched with respect to attractiveness? Among dating couples, if one of the partners is relatively more attractive than the other, he or she tends to have more friends of the opposite sex and to worry less about the possible unfaithfulness of the less attractive partner (White, 1980a). When the male is more attractive than the female, he is more likely to desire involvement with other women. The powerful influence of this variable is shown clearly in the fact that, over a nine-month period, couples mismatched for attractiveness are more likely to break up than well-matched couples.

Similarity: Seeking Ourselves in Others

When two strangers actually begin to interact, to talk to one another, what do they say? You might think about your first conversation with someone sitting next to you in class or what you talked about on a first date. For one thing, strangers tend to ask one another more questions than do those who are already acquainted (Kent et al., 1981). What seems to go on is that people want to know one another's values, beliefs, and attitudes. Each indicates his or her likes and dislikes and expects the other person to do the same. Since the days of Aristotle, it has been observed that people like those who agree with them and dislike those who disagree. This tendency is sufficiently well known that most people are aware that it is the social norm (Jellison & Oliver, 1983). The goal seems to be to find others who are as much like ourselves as possible. The well-established fact that **attitude similarity** leads to attraction is simply one aspect of a general tendency to respond positively to those who most closely resemble ourselves.

Attitude similarity and attraction. In the first half of this century, many studies were conducted that compared the attitudes of pairs of friends, engaged couples, and spouses. It was consistently found that such pairs were more similar in their attitudes than were randomly matched pairs of individuals (e.g., Schuster & Elderton, 1906; Winslow, 1937). Beginning in the 1950s, these correlational studies were replaced by laboratory experiments in which attitude similarity was manipulated to determine its effect on attraction (e.g., Schachter, 1951). Here, the positive effect of similar attitudes on liking was even more clear. The effect is so regular that it is possible to predict how much one person will like another on the basis of the *proportion* of attitudinal issues on which they agree. This relationship is illustrated in Figure 6.12.

The similarity-attraction effect operates not only in an experimental laboratory but also among couples paired in a computer dating setting (Byrne et al., 1970) and among same-sex strangers spending ten days together in a fallout shelter (Griffitt & Veitch, 1974). Similarity not only leads to greater attraction but to actual behavioral differences such as returning to a laboratory to work with an attitudinally similar stranger (Gormly & Gormly, 1981). The relation-

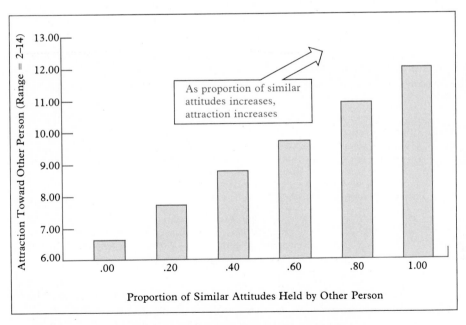

FIGURE 6.12 *A linear relationship: Proportion of similar attitudes and attraction.*

Attraction toward a stranger increases in a straight line as the proportion of similar attitudes expressed by that person increases. The more someone shares our views, the more we like him or her. [Source: Based on data from Byrne & Nelson, 1965.]

ship also operates in the opposite way. If a person likes someone on the basis of physical attractiveness (Marks & Miller, 1982; Marks et al., 1981) or political charisma (Granberg & King, 1980), that individual is perceived as holding similar attitudes. It seems that our positive responses to the superficial characteristics of an individual lead us to assume (often mistakenly) that we hold the same basic attitudes and values. It is not difficult to find unhappy examples of this process in unwise choices involving either mates or political leaders.

Explaining the similarity effect. Most theorists agree that attitude similarity is positive because it confirms one's judgments about the world. Thus, there is a *social comparison* process (Sanders, 1982) in which we find out whether some other person can help establish the "validity" of what we have already decided about politics, nuclear war, economics, religion, rock music, or whatever. If someone believes what you believe, he or she is saying in effect that you are correct, and this makes you feel good. Then, you like that person. Disagreement has the opposite effect. It should be noted that we do not *always* reject dissimilar others. Besides seeking to validate what we believe, there is also the need to seek information in order to try to find out the truth. Under some circumstances, we like the company of a dissimilar stranger to help reduce our confusion (Russ et al., 1980) or to talk about our opposing views (Gormly, 1979). In the **Focus on Research** section on pages 230–231 is an examination of the special circumstances in which similarity can actually be threatening.

Assuming that similarity is generally positive, one explanation of the way it operates is provided by **balance theory.** It is proposed that human beings have a natural inclination to organize their likes and dislikes in a symmetrical fashion that results in **balance** (Cacioppo & Petty, 1981; Newcomb, 1981; Rodrigues & Newcomb, 1980). An example is when two people like one another and agree about whatever they are discussing. When two people like one another and disagree, there is **imbalance,** and this unpleasant state motivates the individuals to do something to restore balance. When two people do not like one another, there is **nonbalance,** and both agreement and disagreement are a matter of indifference.

Personality and behavioral similarity. There is little or no disagreement about the fact that attitude similarity leads to attraction under almost all circumstances. With respect to similarity of personality and behavior, however, there is some controversy. Put in its simplest form, do birds of a feather flock together or do opposites attract? Convincing arguments can be—and have been— made for each possibility.

In the first place, there are some personality characteristics that are liked by almost everyone, *regardless* of degree of similarity. For example, relatively dominant individuals are preferred to relatively submissive ones by both dominant and submissive others (Palmer & Byrne, 1970). Also, heterosexual males are fairly negative toward homosexual ones, regardless of how much their attitudes on other topics are in agreement (Krulewitz & Nash, 1980), presumably because sexual preference is judged to be more important than similarity of general attitudes.

For many characteristics, though, we tend to choose friends who are similar to ourselves. This response to similarity has been shown in many studies of everyday life relationships. For example, college women were found to prefer roommates who were similar to themselves in social characteristics and various values (Hill & Stull, 1981). Friends are found to be similar to one another in their ability to understand facial cues to emotion (Brauer & DePaulo, 1980). Among high school best friends, there is greater than chance similarity with respect to age, sex, religion, and race (Kandel, 1978). After age seven or eight, there is an increasing tendency for children to seek companions close to their own age (Ellis, Rogoff, & Cramer, 1981; Z. Rubin, 1980).

We also like those who behave as we do. With college students paired in a series of games, subjects indicated that they liked partners whose game behavior resembled their own (Knight, 1980). We even like those who imitate our behavior and make the same choices and decisions that we do (Roberts et al., 1981; Thelen et al., 1981). On various personality characteristics (such as androgyny versus traditional sex roles), similarity is liked better than dissimilarity (Pursell & Banikiotes, 1978). On those personality characteristics (such as locus of control) on which friends are actually no more similar than random strangers, they *believe* themselves to be similar (Feinberg, Miller, & Ross, 1981). Liking is also greater between two people if they are similar in assessing other people (Neimeyer & Neimeyer, 1981).

The greatest amount of disagreement about the effect of personality variables has been concerning *needs*. It has been proposed that **need compatibility** (or similar needs) is a positive factor in a relationship. It has also been proposed that **need complementarity** (opposite and compatible needs) leads to friendship because both individuals find it reinforcing. For example, a person who has a strong need to be nurturant should like one who has a strong need to be cared for, and vice versa. As reasonable as this idea seems, research suggests that once again similarity is the key to attraction. In one study, Meyer and Pepper (1977) found that husbands and wives who were well-adjusted in their marriage were more similar in their needs than couples who were having problems. Need compatibility seems to be more important to a relationship than complementarity.

Self-disclosing behavior and attraction. One of the indications that a friendship is developing beyond mere acquaintanceship is the extent to which two people engage in self-disclosure. That is, they begin to reveal intimate, private aspects of their past life and of their present feelings (Davis & Perkowitz, 1979; Sharabany et al., 1981). Two individuals are likely to become more intimate in their disclosures than are groups of three or more people (Taylor et al., 1979). At the beginning of a relationship, disclosure is greater if the other person is physically attractive (Brundage et al., 1977; Kleinke & Kahn, 1980) or otherwise appears to be desirable as a potential friend (Gelman & McGinley, 1978).

Since people differ in their general willingness to make disclosures about themselves, perhaps it is not surprising to find that *similarity* in this behavior leads to attraction (Daher & Banikiotes, 1976). In general, pairs of female friends engage in more intimate self-disclosure than do pairs of male friends

FOCUS
ON RESEARCH

Similarity as a Threat: The Need to Be Unique

The finding that similarity leads to attraction is such a consistent one that several investigators have been motivated to search for exceptions to the general rule. One direction this search has taken involves the identification of individual differences in the response to similar others. For example, individuals who are high in **sensation seeking** (those who like excitement, thrills, and unpredictability) are more positive toward dissimilar others and less positive toward similar others, when compared to low sensation seekers (Williams et al., 1982). Personality factors also influence some aspects of male-female attraction: self-accepting males tend to be attracted to females who adopt nontraditional roles, while males low in self-acceptance prefer traditional females (Grube et al., 1982). Still other research suggests that attraction is greatest toward other people who are similar to our ideals rather than similar to ourselves as we actually are (Wetzel & Insko, 1982).

One line of research that seeks exceptions to the similarity-attraction effect stems from **uniqueness theory**—the proposition that each of us wishes to be a unique human being (Snyder & Fromkin, 1980). This desire can presumably be threatened by similarity (see Figure 6.13.) There is a great deal of anecdotal evidence that people desire *both* to be like others (see Chapter 7) and to stand out from the crowd. In the musical play, *The Fantasticks*, one of the characters prays, "Dear God, please don't let me be normal." What actually seems to happen is that we vary between two extremes, depending on the situation (Sobel, 1980). If you are in a group in which you are *very* different from others, you may try to conform and blend into the mass. If you are in a group in which you are *very* similar to everyone else, you may try to do something to stress your differentness and individuality.

In one experimental test of uniqueness theory, Snyder and Endelman (1979) gave undergraduates a measure of attitudes, personality attributes, interests, and background. The subjects later were shown what were described as the responses of another student (actually responses made up by the experimenters), and this "stranger" was either 5, 50, or 95 percent similar to the subject. When subjects were brought into the next room, they could sit as close to or as far from the other person's chair as they wished (he or she was supposedly out of the room for a few minutes). The prediction was

FIGURE 6.13 Uniqueness theory: Can there be too much similarity?

The major proposition of uniqueness theory is that each of us is motivated to be recognized as different from others—as one of a kind. If that is true, high levels of similarity would be somewhat aversive. Would you like to be in a group of people in which everyone had exactly the same opinions, interests, and skills and even dressed and looked alike? [Source: Culver Pictures, Inc.]

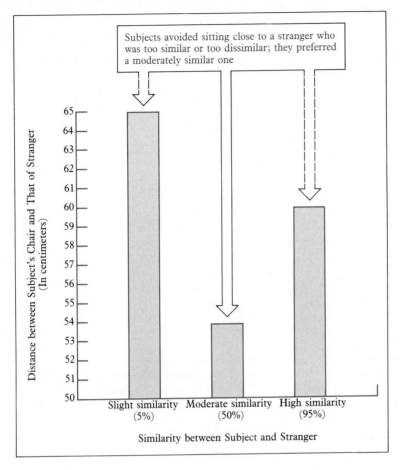

FIGURE 6.14 *Seeking moderate similarity: Avoiding the extremes.*

Uniqueness theory predicts that both extreme dissimilarity and extreme similarity are aversive. When subjects had the opportunity to place their chairs near where a stranger was sitting, they positioned themselves closer to a moderately similar individual than to either a very similar or very dissimilar one. [Source: Based on data from Snyder & Endelman, 1979.]

Within the figure:

Subjects avoided sitting close to a stranger who was too similar or too dissimilar; they preferred a moderately similar one

y-axis: Distance between Subject's Chair and That of Stranger (In centimeters)

x-axis: Similarity between Subject and Stranger
Slight similarity (5%) — Moderate similarity (50%) — High similarity (95%)

that subjects would like a moderately similar stranger best and hence sit closer to such a person than to a very similar or very dissimilar one. As can be seen in Figure 6.14, that is precisely what happened. Even in this study, however, it should be noted that verbal measures of attraction showed only a similarity effect: the greater the similarity, the greater the liking. The authors interpreted this to mean that subjects say what they believe they *should* be feeling but that their behavior reflects what they *actually* do feel.

One final aspect of the uniqueness formulation is that there are individual differences in the motive to be unique. The Need for Uniqueness Scale (Snyder & Fromkin, 1980) asks subjects to indicate how much they agree with statements such as:

I do not always need to live by the rules and standards of society.
I always try to follow rules.
I would rather be just like everyone else than be called a "freak."

As you might expect, those who score high on this scale are perceived by their friends as unique, perceive themselves in the same way, and are threatened by information indicating their similarity to others.

Altogether, it appears that there is a motive to be more or less like others *and* to be somewhat different from others. Perhaps the ideal friendships are those in which we can fit in with the group while, at the same time, we can experience a sense of uniqueness.

FIGURE 6.15   Response to the self-disclosures of males and females.

In general, males who disclose very much about themselves to relative strangers are evaluated negatively. Highly disclosing females in an experiment received positive evaluations if the topic involved a family suicide or their sexual preferences. Neither males nor females were evaluated positively when the topic was competitiveness and the desire to succeed. [Source: Based on data from Kleinke & Kahn, 1980.]

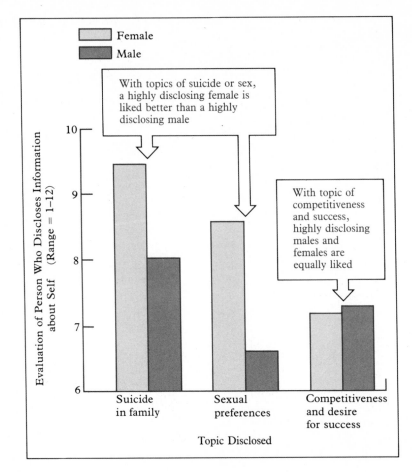

(Cohn & Strassberg, 1983; Rubin & Shenker, 1978). For females, it appears to be positive to be singled out by another female who wants to disclose things about herself (Petty & Mirels, 1981; Taylor et al., 1981).

Despite the fact that males appear to have become more open and disclosing over the past ten years (J. D. Cunningham, 1981), males who disclose a lot tend to be evaluated negatively. With females, it depends on what they disclose. To investigate the effect of the content of disclosures, Kleinke and Kahn (1980) had male and female confederates pretend to reveal extremely intimate details of their past or of their desires to strangers. As shown in Figure 6.15, highly disclosing females who talked about a parent's suicide or about their sexual preferences were liked more than males who discussed such topics. In disclosing feelings of competitiveness and desire for success, neither males nor females were liked very much. Presumably, it is perceived to be unfeminine to want to compete and succeed. No topic has yet been reported, by the way, about which a male can disclose intimate details to relative strangers without being evaluated negatively.

Reciprocity: Maintaining Social Relationships with Mutually Positive Evaluations

One of the most powerful variables influencing your attraction toward another person is the way that person feels about you. Friendships are strengthened by signs of mutual respect, interest, and attraction. A one-way relationship involving lack of reciprocal attraction is not likely to continue. Everyone likes a positive response from others and dislikes indications of negative feelings. An individual tends to be pleased about a positive evaluation even if it is inaccurate and the flatterer is someone who has a reason to seek that person's good will (Drachman et al., 1978).

Research has repeatedly shown that people like almost anyone who evaluates them positively and dislike those who evaluate them negatively (Byrne, 1971). Even those who say positive things about *someone else* are liked better than those who have only negative things to say (Folkes & Sears, 1980). It is important in any relationship from friendship to marriage that the participants show their positive feelings about one another from time to time.

Because many people have difficulty in expressing their interpersonal evaluations in words, often we must rely on behavioral cues. For example, when two people talk to one another and ignore you, you react badly and assume that they don't like you very much (Geller et al., 1974). If the people who behaved in that way were your friends, your reaction might be even stronger. That is, our *expectancy* is that our friends like us, evaluate us positively, and will do nice things for us. For those we dislike, the expectancies are the opposite. What happens when such expected reciprocity is *not* fulfilled?

In one experiment, attraction (and expectancies about reciprocal attraction) was manipulated by presenting female subjects with evidence that another female student was similar or dissimilar in attitudes (Riordan et al., 1982). Then the subject had a time-consuming task of alphabetizing decks of index cards while the other person had something much easier to do. The experimenter suggested that the subject request help from that person (actually, a confederate) when she was done. For half the subjects, the request was granted, and the confederate said, "Oh, sure. Why don't you give me half of what you have left?" For the other subjects, the request was refused, and the confederate said, "No, I'm going to leave." Changes in attraction measured before and after this interaction showed the effect of expectancies that were or were not met. As you will note in Figure 6.16 (on p. 234), the greatest change was in liking for a similar person who said "no" to the request. Attraction toward such a person dropped sharply. On the other hand, if the subject expected something negative (from a dissimilar stranger), a willingness to help led to *increased* attraction. It appears that we expect the words and deeds of others to match our feelings about them. A relationship lasts only as long as attraction is reciprocal.

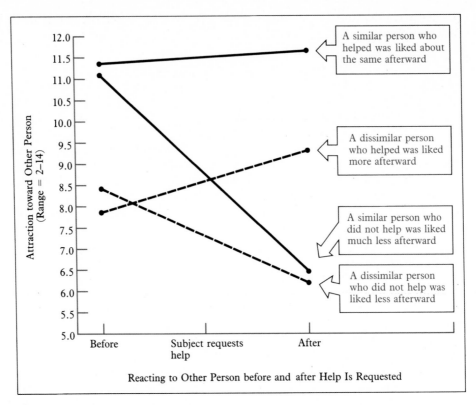

FIGURE 6.16 *Changes in attraction: Behavioral cues to reciprocity.*

One index of how another person feels about you is his or her willingness to provide help when you request it. Since there is a general tendency to like similar others and dislike dissimilar ones, we expect them to feel the same way about us. When their helping behavior doesn't match what is expected, there is a dramatic decrease in liking for a similar person who does not help and an increase in liking for a dissimilar person who does. When helping behavior matches expectations, a similar person who helps is still liked while a dissimilar person who does not is liked even less afterward. [Source: Based on data in Riordan et al., 1982.]

Falling in (and out of) Love

Whenever two people perceive one another as potential sexual partners, a relationship can move beyond acquaintanceship and friendship. There is the possibility of **love.** Only in recent years has love become the focus of research interest. What have social psychologists discovered about this emotional state?

Passionate Love and Companionate Love

A question that arises in most of our lives is whether or not we are in love. In this section, we will examine two kinds of love, and you will discover that they differ considerably.

Passionate love: Falling head over heels. Most of the recent theoretical and research interest has been centered on **passionate love.** This refers to an intense, sometimes overwhelming emotional state in which an individual thinks about his or her lover constantly, wants to spend as much time as possible with that person, and is very often unrealistic in judging the loved one (Murstein, 1980). A measure of passionate love (Hatfield, 1983b) includes items that indicate the intense feelings that are involved. Examples are: "Since I've been with ———, my emotions have been on a roller coaster. Sometimes I can't control my thoughts; they are obsessively on ———." Our language has terms such as "falling in love" that suggest some sort of accidental process analogous to slipping on a banana peel (Solomon, 1981). That may be partially true.

A widely held current theory of passionate love indicates that three major conditions are necessary (Berscheid & Walster, 1974; Hatfield & Walster, 1981). The first condition is that one must be raised in a culture that believes in the concept and teaches it to its young people. The idea of love arose in the Middle Ages in Europe, and it was thought to be a pure and holy emotion unrelated to sexual desire. It was not until the end of the seventeenth century in England that it became common to consider an ideal marriage as one based on love (Stone, 1977). In present day India, romantic love is just now replacing family or community arrangements as the basis for marriage among the middle class, and popular Indian movies are now depicting couples whose love leads them to defy their parents (Kaufman, 1980). In Western nations, love is stressed in stories beginning in childhood (see Figure 6.17) and continues throughout life. By adolescence, a great many individuals are ready to experience the glories of love for themselves (Dion & Dion, 1975). It has even been found that the more a person thinks about love, the more likely he or she is to have the experience (Tesser & Paulhus, 1976).

FIGURE 6.17   Learning about love.

Love appears to be a learned response, and this emotion is experienced only in cultures that expose their citizens to the appropriate models. In Europe and the Western Hemisphere, for example, even the stories of childhood often stress the idea of a couple falling in love, getting married, and living happily ever after. [Source: Culver Pictures © Walt Disney Productions. World Rights Reserved.]

The second condition for passionate love to occur is the presence of an appropriate love object. For most people, that means a physically attractive member of the opposite sex. If one believes strongly that love can occur at any moment, it is possible to undergo love "at first sight." Approximately 50 percent of the adults in one study reported having this happen to them at least once (Averill & Boothroyd, 1977).

The third condition is probably crucial to intense infatuation — emotional arousal that is *interpreted* as love. In Chapter 2, we described the way in which our labels for our own emotions can depend on external cues, and in Chapter 9 we will describe how one kind of emotional excitement can transfer to another. Even if subjects only *believe* they are aroused by being falsely informed of a heart rate increase, their judgments of the opposite sex are affected (Kerber & Coles, 1978). Various kinds of actual arousal have been found to influence romantic feelings, attraction, and sexual interest in experiments involving fear (Dutton & Aron, 1974), erotic excitement (Istvan & Griffitt, 1978a), and embarrassment (Byrne et al., 1981). Even anger at parents' attempts to break up an affair leads to increased feelings of love (Driscoll et al., 1972). Once the emotional state is defined as love, there is an increase in a brain chemical (phenylethylamine) that maintains the emotional "high" (Leonard, 1980). That same chemical, by the way, is contained in chocolate, the most popular gift on Valentine's Day. There is, incidentally, some dispute about the role of mislabeled arousal as the foundation of love (Kenrick et al., 1979; Kenrick & Johnson, 1979). When negatively arousing situations lead to attraction, it is suggested that an opposite-sex stranger provides reinforcement. For example, when subjects are expecting to receive an electric shock, the presence of a confederate reduces their fear and increases attraction toward the confederate (Riordan & Tedes-

FIGURE 6.18 *An unromantic explanation of passionate love.*

According to the three-factor theory of passionate love, an individual is likely to fall in love and experience an intense emotional response if three conditions are present. (1) The person's cultural background must have provided information about the existence of love and provided real or fictional models of loving couples. (2) The person must encounter someone who is perceived as an appropriate and desirable love object. (3) There must be an emotionally arousing state that is interpreted by the person as love and so labeled. Passionate love thus is believed to represent the blending of aspects of the present situation with past learning accompanied by a mislabeled state of arousal.

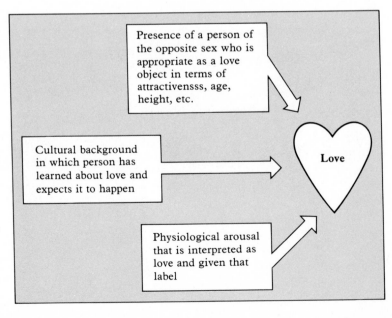

chi, 1983). Whatever the ultimate explanation, this remains an active research area, and the three-factor theory of passionate love is summarized in Figure 6.18. You may be surprised to learn that men are found to fall in love more easily than women and that women fall out of love more easily than men (Rubin et al., 1981). Nevertheless, Hatfield's (1983a) review of the literature suggests that men and women are very similar in what they hope to obtain from a relationship. Both sexes want love *and* sex, and both want intimacy *and* the power to control what goes on. It sometimes happens, of course, that one person falls in love but is not loved in return; see the **Applied Side** section on pages 238–239.

Companionate love: A close, caring friendship. Despite the somewhat flimsy and often unrealistic basis of a passionate love affair, it is possible for a relationship to begin in that way and yet mature into **companionate love.** This term refers to a deep and lasting friendship involving the kinds of factors discussed earlier in the chapter such as positive emotions, similarity, and reciprocal liking and respect. In addition, love involves *caring* to a greater extent than does simple friendship relations (Steck et al., 1982). It is difficult to write a catchy song or an exciting movie about companionate love, but this seems to be how couples are able to reach that elusive interpersonal goal of a lasting relationship.

   With companionate love, two people discover their similarities and their common interests. One difficulty with the dating process and with passionate love is that the participants often ignore some of the friendship-relevant variables and concentrate instead on appearance and sexual desirability. As a consequence, friends are found to be more similar in interests and in personality than are dating partners, whereas those who date are similar primarily in sex role attitudes (Peraino, 1982) and physical attractiveness. For a mature, lasting relationship to develop, two individuals must learn to enjoy one another as close *friends.* Each places a great value on the other, and both individuals are concerned about the other's happiness and welfare (Rubin, 1974). As the late Goodman Ace (1980) wrote: "Like is always understanding. Love is often too demanding."

Breaking Up: When Love Grows Cold

   For most people, the expectation is that love will lead two people to marry, live together, and have a sexual relationship, though not necessarily in that order. Unfortunately, as is generally known, marriages are about as likely to end in divorce as to last (see Figure 6.20 on p. 240). Further, staying married does not necessarily indicate happiness. A few years ago, advice columnist Ann Landers (1977) asked her readers, "If you had it to do over again, would you marry the person to whom you are now married?" She received 50,000 pieces of mail in the first ten days, and the replies split fairly evenly with 55 percent saying "yes" and 45 percent saying "no." Even if that is a somewhat biased sample, such data plus the high divorce rate suggest that love and a close relationship may be only temporary (Cimbalo et al., 1976). What goes wrong?

*Rejection — When Love Is a
One-Way Street*

When I was a young man I vowed never to marry until I found the ideal woman. Well, I found her — but, alas, she was waiting for the ideal man.

Composer Robert Schumann

In movies, a common theme is the love affair that begins in a one-sided way. For example, a man may fall wildly in love with a woman, but she can't stand the sight of him. She rejects him, insults him, and demands that he leave her alone. Nevertheless, the audience and the hero know that deep down she really is attracted to him and not to her boring fiance. After much persistence, the hero wins her over, she realizes her true feelings, and love wins out. Sometimes, as in *The Graduate*, the heroine is not convinced until literally the last minute (see Figure 6.19).

In real life, rejection is a somewhat different matter. In the first place, rejections are very common. One survey of undergraduates revealed that 72 percent of the males and 45 percent of the females had been rejected by a member of the opposite sex (Folkes, 1982). The rejection involved the other person refusing an invitation to a date, having a meal together, etc. The fact that males are more likely to take the initiative means they are more likely to be rejected. This is probably why they have a higher level of dating anxiety than females (Machlowitz, 1981). Those who do the re-

jecting often do not tell the truth as to why. The reasons most often given by the rejector are usually socially acceptable such as "I have to study for finals," "I want to go to the movies instead," or "I am seriously involved with someone else." The actual reasons for rejection are often more personal and unpleasant, such as not finding the other person attractive, thinking he or she is too old, resenting being asked at the last minute, or not agreeing with the person's religious beliefs (Folkes, 1982).

When an individual is rejected, he or she tends to want to accept the polite excuse and to believe it. The possibility that you are rejected because someone doesn't like your looks or your personality is extremely threatening. In that case, it is really *you* being rejected, and that is terrible information to receive. Repeated rejections can be devastating. The rejected person feels unhappy and uncomfortable, and there is a tendency to evaluate oneself negatively (Nadler et al., 1980). For those reasons, we attempt to avoid this situation by evaluating ourselves and assessing the possible reactions of others *before* an invitation is extended. We gauge the likelihood of being turned down, and try to prevent it from happening (Shanteau & Nagy, 1979). Anyone who has an inaccurate perception of his or her attributes or who is unable to read the cues provided by potential partners is eventually going to experience a lot of interpersonal pain. An extreme example is John Hinckley, who mistakenly

---

Jealousy: Fear of real and imagined rivals. One of the more common threats to a relationship is **jealousy**. This reaction involves the thoughts, feelings, and behaviors that follow the threat to self-esteem and to the relationship posed by a rival (White, 1981a). The rival may be real or imaginary, and the romantic attraction between the rival and one's partner may take place in the present, in the past, or even as a potential future event. Those individuals who are most jealous tend to feel inadequate, dependent, and concerned about sexual exclusivity (White, 1981b). The more that a husband and wife express such feelings, the more their offspring tend to react in the same way when they grow up

FIGURE 6.19   Rejection—It's less discouraging in the movies.

It is a familiar movie theme that rejection does not really interfere with love—it only postpones the moment when the two lovers are united. In real life, rejection is more likely to be painful and to end the relationship even before it starts. [Source: The Cinemabilia Shop.]

believed that Jody Foster would stop rejecting him if he engaged in the "heroic" act of shooting President Reagan.

Finally, does real life resemble the movies? Does the rejected person try harder and eventually convince the other person that this is true love? As you might guess, being rejected by a potential partner leads the one who is rejected to give up on that person (Walster et al., 1973). Most of us are not motivated to continue making approaches to someone who repeatedly turns us down or even someone

we think is playing "hard to get." To sum up, rejection occurs with surprising frequency, is usually polite, painful, and generally taken as a final answer. If you are really attracted to another person who approaches you, and it is really impossible to get together on that occasion, it would be wise to let your feelings be known as clearly as possible. Otherwise, that person is not likely to keep on pursuing you. Don't count on the movies as a reliable guide to what will happen next.

◆

(Bringle & Williams, 1979). Interestingly enough, those who plan to become involved in extramarital affairs are less likely to feel jealous themselves (Buunk, 1982).

Some people deliberately attempt to make their partners jealous by their actions (White, 1980). Students report that they have done this by talking about their attraction toward someone else, openly flirting, actually dating someone else, talking about former lovers, and sometimes by telling a lie about such things. Among college students, these tactics were reported by 31 percent of the females and 17 percent of the males. Those who engaged in this behavior

FIGURE 6.20   The painful ending of close relationships.

Despite the intensity of a love affair and the glowing expectations of newlyweds, many relationships fail. Positive feelings change to indifference or even hate, lovers break up, and marriages end in divorce. Social psychological research is just beginning to seek the reasons for the deterioration of relationships. [Source: Photo © Joel Gordon 1983.]

did so in order to test the relationship, persuade the other person to spend more time together, to get revenge or otherwise punish the partner, or to raise their own self-esteem. It might be added that inducing jealousy is a dangerous game that can quickly lead to more serious difficulties in the relationship.

The deterioration and ending of a relationship. Levinger (1980) conceptualizes relationships as consisting of five phases: initial attraction, building a relationship, continuation, deterioration, and ending. He suggests that deterioration starts when one or both partners begin to view conditions as worse than they were before. Both college students and those who are older respond to unhappiness in a relationship in either an active or a passive way (Rusbult & Zembrodt, 1983). Active responses include ending the relationship or trying to improve it. Passively, one can simply wait for improvement to occur or just allow deterioration to take place. Research indicates that commitment to a relationship is greater, and the couple is less likely to break up, if three factors are present: high satisfaction, an absence of suitable alternatives, and a lot of time or effort already invested by the two partners (Rusbult, 1980; Rusbult et al., 1982). Sometimes, individuals *expect* a relationship to fail because they have observed it happen to others. One or both members of the pair may experience a change of values or needs that make a new life seem preferable (Levinger, 1980). Breaking up is not usually a rational process in which people sit down and calculate the pluses and minuses of remaining together. Instead, it is an emotional, at times irrational, decision based on many internal and external pressures (Duck, 1982).

Why do couples *believe* they split up? A study of over 200 college students who were in love discovered that about half the couples had broken up after two years passed (Hill et al., 1976). Both males and females said the relationships failed because they were bored and because they discovered they had different interests or backgrounds, dissimilar sexual attitudes, conflicting ideas about marriage, or were not equally intelligent. In other words, love died when the individuals found out that some of the basic elements of a close friendship were absent. Genuine friendship seems to be one of the secrets of a love affair that lasts.

Summary

Attraction is the evaluation of another person along a dimension ranging from love to hate.

Acquaintanceship with a stranger often begins when two people are brought together by environmental factors; **propinquity** leads to repeated exposure which leads to a positive interpersonal response. It has been proposed that the basis of all attraction is one's emotional state. Feelings can be aroused either by the other person or by totally unrelated events, but in either case they become *conditioned* to that person, forming the basis of liking or disliking. Initial contact between strangers is most probable if the **need for affiliation** is sufficiently strong, either in terms of a trait or a situationally determined response.

Once two individuals interact, other variables assume importance. **Physical attractiveness** plays a very important role, especially when a romantic relationship is a possibility. There is also a consistently positive effect for various types of **similarity,** ranging from attitudes to personality characteristics. There is also a need for **uniqueness,** so too much similarity can lead an individual to seek ways to express his or her differentness. In an ongoing relationship, **reciprocity** becomes vital in that each person wants and expects the other to express a positive evaluation in words and deeds from time to time.

The ultimate attraction response is **love.** Most familiar is **passionate love,** an intense emotional state that occurs when one is raised in a culture that stresses love, when an appropriate love object is present, and when some type of physiological arousal is attributed to love. **Companionate love** is a more stable and more lasting basis for a relationship in that it involves a deep and caring friendship. Relationships break up frequently, and the reasons include **jealousy,** expectations of failure, lack of commitment, changes in one or both of the partners, and the presence of more desirable alternatives.

Glossary

attitude similarity *The degree to which two individuals share the same attitudes.*

attraction *The evaluation of another person along a positive-negative dimension ranging from love to hate.*

balance *In Newcomb's theory, the pleasant state that exists when two people like each other and agree about some topic.*

balance theory *A cognitive theory of interpersonal attraction. Attraction is assumed to be based on the relationships among cognitions about another person and various objects or topics of communication.*

companionate love *Love that rests on a firm base of friendship, common interests, mutual respect, and concern for the other's happiness and welfare.*

emotion *A physiological state of arousal associated with specific cognitive labels and appropriate behavior.*

imbalance *In Newcomb's theory, the unpleasant state that exists when two people like one another but disagree about some topic. Each is motivated to change some aspect of the interaction in order to achieve balance or nonbalance.*

jealousy *The thoughts, feelings, and actions that are instigated by a real or imagined rival's threat to one's self-esteem and to one's relationship with a lover.*

love *An emotional state involving attraction, sexual desire, and concern about the other person. It represents the most positive level of attraction.*

matching hypothesis *The proposal that males and females of approximately equal social assets such as physical attractiveness will select one another as partners.*

need for affiliation *The motive to seek interpersonal relationships and to form friendships.*

need compatibility *The proposal that, for at least some sets of needs, similarity should have a positive influence on attraction. For example, a highly sexed person would be expected to get along well with a highly sexed spouse, whereas an individual with low sex needs would prefer a spouse whose needs are equally low.*

need complementarity *The proposal that, for at least some sets of needs, dissimilarity should have a positive influence on attraction. For example, a dominant person would be expected to get along well with a submissive spouse.*

nonbalance *In Newcomb's theory, the indifferent state that exists when two people dislike one another and don't care whether they agree or disagree on various topics.*

passionate love *An intense and often unrealistic emotional response to another person. It is interpreted by the individuals involved as "love."*

physical attractiveness *The combination of facial features, bodily shape, and grooming that is accepted in a given culture at a given time as being that which is most desirable.*

propinquity *Physical proximity. As propinquity between two individuals increases (as a function of their physical surroundings), the probability of their interacting and becoming acquainted increases.*

reinforcement-affect model *A theory proposing that all evaluations are based on positive and negative emotions. These evaluations are directed at whatever stimulus object is responsible for the emotion and at any other previously neutral stimulus that happens to be associated with the emotional arousal.*

repeated exposure *The theory that repeated contact with any stimulus results in a decreased negative response and an increased positive response to it.*

second-order classical conditioning *When a response to an unconditioned stimulus has been associated with a previously neutral stimulus (the conditioned stimulus), that second stimulus can be paired with a new neutral stimulus. The pairing of a conditioned stimulus with this new neutral stimulus is known as second-order classical conditioning.*

self-disclosure *The tendency to reveal intimate details about oneself to another person.*

sensation seeking *The tendency to enjoy exciting, thrilling, and unpredictable activities and situations.*

uniqueness theory *The theory that (along with a need for conformity) there is a motive to be different from everyone else, to stand out from the crowd.*

For More Information

Duck, S., & Gilmour, R. *Personal relationships.* London: Academic Press, 1981–1982.
This is a series of four volumes, each consisting of chapters by various experts in the field. Together, they provide an extensive review of research on the way in which interpersonal relationships develop and sometimes deteriorate. The four volumes cover the general topics: Studying personal relationships *(1981),* Developing personal relationships *(1981),* Personal relationships in disorder *(1981), and* Dissolving personal relationships *(1982).*

Hatfield, E., & Walster, G. W. *A new look at love.* Reading, Mass.: Addison-Wesley, 1981.
A well-written and comprehensive summary of current research and theory dealing with love. Both passionate and companionate love are described and discussed.

Pope, K. S. *On love and loving: Psychological perspectives on the nature and experience of romantic love.* San Francisco: Jossey-Bass, 1980.
This is a collection of chapters that cover many aspects of the topic of love. Sections deal with love and human development, theories of love, cultural determinants, love in a therapeutic relationship, and the role of love as part of one's identity.

Rubin, Z. *Children's friendships.* Cambridge, Mass.: Harvard University Press, 1980.
This book on friendship in childhood won a National Media Award for its excellence in communicating psychological research to the general public. It covers interpersonal attachments in infancy and the preschool years as well as the later development of same- and opposite-sex relationships. A great deal of information is provided, and it is a delight to read.

Snyder, C. R., & Fromkin, H. L. *Uniqueness: The human pursuit of difference.* New York: Plenum, 1980.
The theory of uniqueness as a human need is presented along with historical, literary, and research demonstrations of its importance. The way in which people vary in this need is shown, and the contradictory demands of conforming to the group and standing out from the group are described.

CHAPTER 7

Social Influence:
Changing the Behavior of Others

Conformity: To Get Along, Often We Must "Go Along"

Conformity in the Laboratory: The Subject's Dilemma/Factors Affecting Conformity: Attraction, Group Size, Social Support, and Sex/The Bases of Conformity: Why We Often Choose to "Go Along"/Minority Influence: Why the Majority Doesn't Always Rule

Compliance: To Ask—Sometimes—Is to Receive

Ingratiation: Liking as a Basis for Social Influence/Multiple Requests: Using the Old "One-Two Punch" to Induce Compliance

Obedience: Social Influence by Demand

Destructive Obedience: Some Laboratory Demonstrations/Destructive Obedience: Why Does It Occur?/Destructive Obedience: Can It Be Reduced?

Special Inserts

FOCUS ON RESEARCH
   Conformity and Private Attitudes: Why Social Support Sometimes Backfires

FOCUS ON RESEARCH
   *"Low-balling": Changing the Rules in Midgame—
   and Getting Away with It!*

ON THE APPLIED SIDE
   Modeling: Social Influence and the Enhancement of Human Welfare

You've only been with the advertising firm of Pitch, Fitch, and Goad for ten months, but already your career has shifted into high gear. You've just been promoted from Trainee to Special Assistant. And more important, you've begun to acquire the reputation of a young man on the move. Your relations with Jill Harkins, Head of your department, are excellent, and you look forward to a bright future with the company. Right now, though, you don't have much time to dwell on your past accomplishments, for it's time for the weekly staff meeting. You and your associates file into the conference room and Jill, with her usual efficiency, calls the meeting quickly to order.

"Well," she begins, "our main job today is reaching a final decision on that campaign for Plasti-Chem Foods. I've given it a lot of thought, and I can summarize my own reactions in three words: I love it. If this doesn't sell cakes and pies, I don't know what will. But what are your *reactions?"*

The first to reply is Bill McGregor, a senior copy-writer and consultant. "I fully agree, Jill," he states. "I think it's first-rate. I mean, that cherubic little symbol—what's she called, 'Mother Fletcher'?—is just great. Yeah, I'm definitely for it."

Next to reply is Cheryl Jones, another senior copy-writer. "I'm for it, too," she says with enthusiasm. "I agree with Bill—that symbol is superb. People will recognize it, remember it, and look for it. I don't see how we can miss."

You listen with growing horror as one member of the staff after another agrees. How can this be, you wonder? You yourself hate it. In fact, you are fully convinced that it will be a disaster; it is far too corny and obvious for today's sophisticated consumers. But all your colleagues seem to see it differently. What's wrong? Did you miss something? Did you even examine the correct drawings and plans? You don't have long to sort through these possibilities, for suddenly Jill turns to you and asks: "Well, Hal, we haven't heard from you yet. What does the bright junior member of our team think?" Sheer panic grips you. What should you do? Should you go along with the others? Or would it be best to say what you really think—that the whole campaign is a disaster? After a long pause, you hear yourself mutter "Oh, I guess it's O.K. I'll go along with the group." Jill takes this weak statement as a sign of endorsement, and smiling, calls for a vote. The outcome is predictable: the ad campaign for Mother Fletcher's Cakes and Pies is adopted unanimously and enthusiastically.

Later, in the quiet of your own office, you ponder your behavior during the meeting. You are fully convinced that the campaign is wrong and will fail. So why did you knuckle under and agree with the others? The pressure was great, but you could have resisted if you really wanted to do so. Oh well, it's too late now. But as you gather up your belongings and head for home, you vow to be better prepared the next time around.

At one time or another, most of us have had the following fantasy: somehow we gain a special power that permits us to control the behavior of other persons. Through this power, we can induce them to behave in any way we wish. This is a tantalizing daydream—and for good reason. Other people play a crucial role in our lives. Thus, the ability to shape their behavior to our wishes would provide us with a ready means of satisfying most of our needs, goals, and desires. Unfortunately, though, no magic formula for attaining such control exists. People have minds of their own, and are willing to yield to our wishes only on some occasions and under some conditions. Thus, the fantasy of exerting total control over them must remain just that—an enticing but largely unattainable illusion.

While *total* control over others remains beyond our grasp, however, there are many tactics we can use to at least move in this direction. In short, there are many strategies and procedures we can employ to exert *influence* over others— to alter their behavior, attitudes, or feelings in ways we desire. The investigation of such techniques and the processes that underlie their success have long been topics of major interest in social psychology. Thus, we will focus on these issues in the present chapter. As you probably know from your own experience, attempts at exerting such **social influence** take many different forms (see Figure 7.1 for an illustration of this fact). Among the most important of these, however, are *conformity, compliance,* and *obedience.*

Conformity occurs in situations where individuals change their behavior in order to adhere to widely accepted standards or beliefs (often termed *social norms*). A clear example of such effects was provided by the story at the beginning of this chapter. In the incident it described, a young man chose to contradict his own beliefs rather than disagree with the views of several other persons. As we will soon see, such pressures toward conformity are very common and can affect our behavior (as well as our private attitudes) in many situations. In contrast, **compliance** represents a somewhat more direct form of social influence. Specifically, it occurs in situations where individuals alter their behavior in response to *direct requests* from others. Many techniques for enhanc-

FIGURE 7.1   *Social influence: The range of specific tactics is great.*

As shown here, there are many tactics for influencing the behavior of other persons. [Source: © Field Enterprises, Inc., 1981.]

ing compliance exist, and, when used with skill and care, these can be very effective indeed. Finally, obedience occurs in situations where persons change their behavior in response to direct commands from others. Usually, the persons issuing such orders possess the means for enforcing them. But as we shall soon see, they are often successful in inducing considerable amounts of submission even in cases where this is not so.

In the remainder of this chapter, we will examine each of the major types of social influence just described. In addition, we will call your attention to some of the factors that influence the effectiveness of these various tactics.

Conformity: To Get Along, Often We Must "Go Along"

Have you ever found yourself in a situation where you felt that you stuck out like the proverbial-sore thumb? If so, you are already familiar with pressures toward conformity. In such situations, you probably felt a strong desire to "get back into line"—to fit in with the other people around you. Such pressures toward conformity seem to stem from the fact that in many situations there are both spoken and unspoken rules indicating how we should or ought to behave. These are known as **social norms,** and in some cases they are quite explicit. For example, governments often function through constitutions and written codes of law. Athletic contests are usually regulated by written rules. And signs along highways describe expected behaviors in foot-high letters.

In contrast, other norms are unspoken and implicit (e.g., Cary, 1978). For example, most of us obey such unwritten rules as "Don't wink (or stare) at strangers on the street," and "Don't come to parties or other social gatherings exactly on time." And we are often strongly influenced by current—and ever-changing—standards of dress, speech, and style (see Figure 7.2 on p. 250).

Regardless of whether social norms are explicit or implicit, however, most are obeyed by most persons much of the time. For example, few people visit restaurants without leaving some sort of tip for their waitress or waiter. Few drivers back up or attempt U-turns on the interstate highway system. And perhaps even fewer boo and hiss during a ballet. At first glance, you might view this strong tendency toward conformity—toward adherence with society's expectations about how we should behave—as objectionable. After all, it does prevent us from "doing our own thing" on many occasions. Actually, though, there is a strong, rational reason for the existence of so much conformity: without it we would quickly find ourselves in the midst of social chaos! For example, imagine what would happen outside movie theaters, in supermarkets' checkout lines, and even at the doors of departing planes if the people present did not follow the simple rule: "Form a line and wait your turn." Similarly, consider the intense danger to both drivers and pedestrians if there were no clear-cut (and widely followed) traffic regulations. In many cases, then, conformity seems to serve a useful function. But this does not imply that it is *always* helpful. At times, norms governing individual behavior appear to have no obvious purpose—they simply exist (e.g., why must men wear ties and women

FIGURE 7.2   Social norms: Often, they are hard to disobey.

Our behavior is strongly affected by social norms. Thus, when unspoken rules dictate that we should wear short hair and dress neatly, we tend to behave in this manner. And when they dictate that we should wear longer hair and dress informally, we tend to adopt this *appearance. (From left to right, the three photos shown reflect styles of the 1950s, 1970s, and 1980s.) [Source: Photos (left and center) by Harold M. Lambert/Frederic Lewis Photographs; photo (right) © Ulrike Welsch.]*

dresses on certain occasions? and why must dinner guests hang back and show a degree of reluctance when first called to the table?). It is precisely in cases such as these — where norms exist without conferring any obvious practical benefits — that many persons object to the strong pressure to obey them.

The wide occurrence of conformity was recognized both within social psychology and outside it for many decades. Yet, surprisingly, it was not until the 1950s that this key topic was subjected to systematic study. At that time, Solomon Asch (1951) conducted a series of revealing experiments that added much to our knowledge of this basic form of social influence. Because Asch's research paved the way for much additional research on conformity, we will examine it briefly before turning to a review of more recent investigations.

Conformity in the Laboratory: The Subject's Dilemma

In a sense, we have already outlined the basic situation studied by Asch. As you may recall, the story at the beginning of this chapter described an incident in which a young man holding one opinion learned that several of his co-workers held sharply contrasting views. Then he was asked to state his own position. As you can readily see, he faced a painful dilemma: should he remain independent and report his opinions accurately? Or should he yield to social pressure and go along with the group? Such situations are all too common in life, and, as Asch recognized, they present an excellent context in which to study the impact of pressures toward conformity.

In order to capture the essence of such dilemmas in the laboratory, Asch asked subjects to respond to a series of simple perceptual problems such as the one in Figure 7.3. On each problem, they indicated which of three comparison lines matched a standard line in length. Several other persons were also present during the session (usually six to eight), but, unknown to the actual subject, they were all confederates of the experimenter. On various prearranged occasions (twelve out of eighteen problems) these persons offered answers that were clearly false (e.g., they unanimously stated that line B matched the standard line in Figure 7.3). On such trials, subjects faced the same dilemma as the character in our story: should they go along with the group, or stick to their guns and provide what they felt were correct answers? You may be surprised to learn that, like our fictitious character, subjects were strongly tempted to conform. Indeed, fully 75 percent of those tested by Asch in several studies went along with the group's false answers at least once. (Please note: most persons resisted this temptation on most occasions. But a large majority did conform one or more times.) These results, and those obtained in many later studies (e.g., Allen & Wilder, 1980) point to an unsettling conclusion: many persons find it less upsetting to contradict the evidence of their own eyes than to disagree openly with the unanimous judgments of several others.

At this point, we should note that the social influence exerted by groups upon their members can involve two distinct components (Deutsch & Gerard, 1955). The first of these, known as **normative social influence,** involves our tendency to conform to the positive expectations of others. When yielding to this type of influence, we conform because we wish to behave as others expect us to behave—perhaps as a means of gaining their acceptance or approval. The second, known as **informational social influence,** stems from our tendency to employ other persons as a source of information. Here, we conform because we use the actions of others as guides to understanding the world around us— guides that can help us act in an appropriate and effective manner. Asch did not design his research to separate these two components, and in retrospect it seems likely that both contributed to the high levels of conformity he observed. In many life situations, though, one or the other may predominate. For example, if we like or admire others and wish to win their approval, their impact on us may stem mainly from normative social influence. In contrast, if we view others as

[handwritten marginal notes: "Conforming to expectations"; "Conforming to information from others."; "We use significant others a frame of reference"]

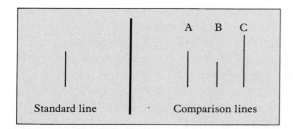

FIGURE 7.3 *Asch's line-judging task: An example.*

An example of the problems used by Asch in his early studies of conformity. Subjects' task was that of indicating which of the three comparison lines (A, B, or C) matched the standard line in length. They gave their answers only after hearing the responses of several other persons, all of whom were confederates of the experimenter.

possessing some special knowledge or expertise in a given situation, their influence over us may derive primarily from informational sources. Keep an eye peeled for both of these components in your own life; you will probably find that in different situations, they are present—and functioning—to different degrees.

A problem of efficiency—and an answer: The Crutchfield apparatus. Asch's research clearly yielded important insights into the nature of conformity. But as you may already have noticed, it suffered from one major drawback: the procedure it employed is quite inefficient. In order to study the reactions of a single subject, the presence of six, seven, or even eight confederates is required. This problem of efficiency was soon remedied by Richard Crutchfield (1955), who devised a new technique for obtaining data from several subjects at once—and without the need for even a single accomplice. The approach he devised is known, appropriately, as the **Crutchfield technique,** and proceeds as follows.

When subjects arrive in the laboratory, they are seated in individual booths. On the front of each is a panel of lights and a series of switches (see Figure 7.4). They are then told that they will all be responding to a series of problems, and that the answers given by each person will be shown to the others by means of the lights. Supposedly, the answers of the first person will appear in the first row, those of the second in the next row, and so on. In reality, all subjects are instructed to respond last (or in some cases, next to last). Further, all of the lights are actually controlled by the experimenter. Under these conditions, it is possible to study the willingness of each participant to go along with false group answers. This is so for a simple reason: on any trial, the lights in all booths can be lit in a pattern suggesting that each of other persons present has chosen the same, incorrect answer. (Remember: all the lights are really under the experimenter's control.) If subjects give the same response, they may be viewed as having yielded to the implicit group pressure. If they do not, then they may be viewed as having remained independent. (Please refer to Figure 7.4.) As you can see, the Crutchfield procedure is highly efficient. It is not surprising, therefore, that with only minor changes it has been used in much subsequent research on the nature of conformity.

Factors Affecting Conformity: Attraction, Group Size, Social Support, and Sex

While conformity appears to be an all-too-common aspect of human behavior, even a moment's reflection suggests that it does not occur to the same degree in all settings, or among all groups of persons. This basic observation, in turn, raises an interesting question: What factors determine the extent to which individuals yield to conformity pressure? Several decades of research on this issue have generated a long list of variables that play a role in this regard—factors that mediate the impact of conformity pressure upon individuals. Here, we will focus upon four that seem to be among the most important: (1) *attraction* to the influencing group, (2) the *size* of this group, (3) the presence or absence of *social support*, and (4) the *sex* of the persons exposed to social pressure.

 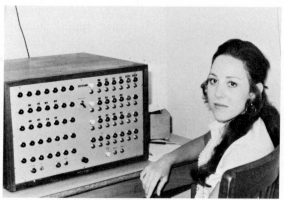

FIGURE 7.4 *The Crutchfield device: A more efficient technique for the study of conformity.*

The equipment shown here (known as the **Crutchfield device**) *is often used to study conformity under controlled laboratory conditions. Each subject is seated before a panel such as the one shown in the left photo, and told that the responses of the other participants will be represented by the lights it contains. In reality, these are controlled by the experimenter, through the larger panel shown in the photo on the right. By means of this equipment, subjects can be led to believe that all of the other persons present have given some specific answer. Then their tendency to yield to such implicit group pressure can be observed. (When subjects give their own answers, these are shown on the experimenter's control panel in the right photo.)*

Attraction and conformity: One basic reason why some groups are more influential than others. Suppose that a noted astronomer learned that most attorneys subscribe to a particular magazine. Would she feel any pressure to order this periodical herself? Probably not. Similarly, imagine that a computer technician learned that most stockbrokers prefer a specific brand of clothing. Would this lead him to change his own buying habits? Again, the answer is probably "no." In both cases, conformity pressure would be minimal. But why? The answer should be obvious: we do not conform to the standards or behavior of just *any* group. Rather, conformity tends to be directed toward groups we like and with whom we wish to compare ourselves. Social psychologists term such groups **reference groups,** and generally, they consist of persons to whom we are similar in some key respects, or of persons to whom we would like to be similar (Forsyth, 1983; Newcomb et al., 1967). As you can readily see, there is no obvious reason why attorneys should serve as a reference group for an astronomer, or why stockbrokers should serve as one for a computer technician. Thus, these latter groups would probably exert little impact upon the persons in question. The key point to keep in mind, then, is this: only if we adopt others as a reference group will we experience pressure to conform to their norms or standards. Conformity, in short, is often highly selective in nature.

Conformity and group size: Why (with respect to social influence) "more" isn't always "better." A second factor that exerts important effects upon our tendency to conform is the size of the influencing group. Common sense suggests that the greater the number of persons around us who behave in some manner or who voice some opinion, the greater our tendency to do likewise. Up to a point this seems to be true. As the number of group members exerting social influence rises up to about three to five persons, conformity, too, increases (Gerard, Wilhelmy, & Conolley, 1968). Beyond this level, however, further growth in group size does not appear to enhance our willingness to "go along."

At first glance, this seems puzzling. Why shouldn't social pressure—and our tendency to yield to it—increase as group size rises? One possible answer has been suggested by Wilder (1977). He proposes that conformity may fail to increase as group size rises because beyond some point, individuals exposed to social pressure begin to suspect *collusion.* That is, they begin to suspect that the group members are all working together to influence them and are *not* expressing their individual views or preferences.

If this suggestion is correct, an interesting prediction follows: social influence from several small groups may be more effective in changing individuals' behavior or attitudes than social influence from a single, large group. This would be the case because in the former condition, there would be no grounds for suspecting collusion among the separate groups. In the latter case, however, individuals might assume that all group members were simply cooperating to exert influence upon them. This prediction has been confirmed in an interesting study carried out by Wilder (1977). In this investigation, subjects exposed to social influence from two groups consisting of two persons each did show greater shifts in their views than subjects exposed to influence from a single group of four. (Needless to say, the views expressed by group members were identical regardless of whether two or four members were involved.)

In view of these findings and those of other investigations, it seems reasonable to offer the following tentative conclusion. Our tendency to conform may indeed increase as the number of persons or groups exerting social pressure upon us rises. However, it is the number of *independent* sources of influence —not simply the actual number of persons involved—that is crucial (see Figure 7.5).

The effects of social support: Does having an ally help? In Asch's initial research (and also in many later studies of conformity) subjects were exposed to social pressure from a unanimous group. That is, all of the other persons present seemed to hold views different from their own. Under such conditions, it is hardly surprising that many individuals give up and yield to social pressure. But what would happen if persons facing such pressure discovered that they had an *ally*—another member of the group who shared their views, or at least failed to endorse the same position as the majority? It seems reasonable to expect that under such circumstances conformity might be reduced. And the results of many different experiments suggest that this is actually the case (e.g., Allen & Levine, 1971; Morris & Miller, 1975). In these studies, subjects provided with an ally or partner showed much less conformity than subjects not supplied with social support.

Perhaps the effectiveness of such support in counteracting pressures toward conformity is best suggested by two additional findings. First, conform-

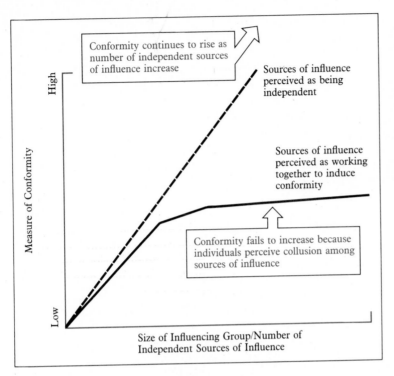

High

Measure of Conformity

Low

Conformity continues to rise as
number of independent sources
of influence increase

Sources of influence
perceived as being
independent

Sources of influence
perceived as working
together to induce
conformity

Conformity fails to increase because
individuals perceive collusion among
sources of influence

Size of Influencing Group/Number of
Independent Sources of Influence

**FIGURE 7.5   *Conformity and
group size: A summary of recent
findings.***

*Recent evidence suggests that
conformity rises with the number of
persons exerting social pressure—
but only up to a point. Beyond some
level, individuals begin to suspect
collusion among group members
and fail to show further increases in
conformity. However, conformity
may continue to rise if the sources of
influence involved are perceived as
being independent.*

ity is reduced even when the partner or ally is an individual not competent to perform the group task. (For example, in one study involving visual judgments, conformity was reduced even by a partner who wore Coke-bottle-thick glasses and who could not see the relevant stimuli [Allen & Levine, 1971].) And second, it is not even crucial that the ally share subjects' views. Conformity is reduced even if he or she merely differs from the other group members without accepting the subjects' position. In short, simply breaking the unanimity of the group may sometimes be sufficient to reduce pressures toward conformity (Allen & Levine, 1971).

These and other findings suggest that almost any form of social support can be helpful in terms of resisting social pressure. In short, in most cases, some support is better than none. But as you might also guess, certain types are more effective than others. For example, it appears that support that is received early in the game—before pressures toward conformity have had a chance to mount—is more helpful than support that is received somewhat later (Morris, Miller, & Spangenberg, 1977). Apparently, learning that someone else shares their views can help to strengthen individuals' confidence in their own judgments, and so enhance their ability to resist group pressure as it comes into play. This fact has important practical implications that should not be overlooked. If you ever find yourself in a situation in which pressures toward conformity are rising, and you feel that they should be resisted, try to speak out as quickly as possible. The earlier you do, the greater the chances of rallying others to your cause. (For a discussion of some unexpected costs associated with social support, see the **Focus on Research** section on pp. 256–257.)

Conformity and Private Attitudes: Why Social Support Sometimes Backfires

Our comments about social support so far seem to suggest that it exerts only beneficial effects. Briefly, the presence of an ally helps individuals resist pressures toward conformity in a wide range of situations—something that is certainly a plus. Closer examination of such situations, however, reveals that in some cases social support may actually backfire. That is, it may *enhance* rather than reduce the overall impact of group pressure. To see why this is so, we must first consider the fact that in such cases there is often a gap between what individuals say—their public statements—and their underlying attitudes. That is, after exposure to conformity pressure, individuals may state perceptions or views they really don't believe. As you may recall from Chapter 4, such conditions often lead to the arousal of an unpleasant state of dissonance. And such dissonance, in turn, produces powerful pressures toward its reduction. One way this can be accomplished in conformity situations, of course, is for the persons involved to change their underlying attitudes—to modify these so that they are now more in line with their verbal statements. In short, after saying something they don't really believe, such persons may experience strong pressure to alter their private views and then actually do so.

But now consider the role of social support in this context. If an individual hears another person state a view similar to his or her own and then, on the basis of such support, refuses to comply, neither dissonance nor attitude change will occur. In contrast, consider what happens if, after receiving so-cial support, an individual still yields to group pressure. Here, dissonance may actually be intensified. After all, the person in question has now stated a view he or she doesn't believe *despite the presence of support for refusing to do so.* This intense dissonance, in turn, may then exert strong pressure in the direction of shifts in the individual's underlying views. In sum, dissonance theory suggests that if persons yield to social pressure despite the presence of social support, they may then show larger shifts in their private attitudes than would be the case in the absence of such support (see Figure 7.6 for a summary of these suggestions). Truly, this would represent a case in which social support backfires—and with a vengeance!

That such effects actually occur is suggested by a series of studies conducted by Stroebe and Diehl (1981). For example, in one of these investigations, male students at a German university were asked to write essays in favor of making all grants to students repayable at the end of their studies—a view they strongly rejected. After agreeing to write this essay, half of the subjects heard another person (actually, an accomplice of the experimenter) refuse to do likewise; the remainder heard this person agree to prepare the essay. Another aspect of the study involved the apparent consequences of the counterattitudinal behavior. Half of the participants learned that these would be low (their essays would simply be used to construct an attitude scale). The other half learned that they would be severe (their essays would be used to persuade other individuals). This

---

Sex differences in conformity: Illusory or real? Many early experiments designed to study conformity yielded an intriguing and sometimes unexpected finding: females seemed to be far more conforming than males (e.g., Crutchfield, 1955). This result, in turn, was often interpreted as reflecting a key difference between the sexes. Indeed, for more than two decades, basic texts in social psychology tended to report this finding as if it were an established and unquestioned fact. During the past six or eight years, however, this situation has altered greatly. Recent evidence suggests that there are strong grounds for

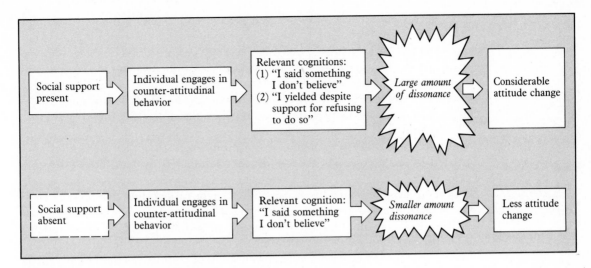

FIGURE 7.6 *Social support: How it can sometimes backfire.*

Dissonance theory predicts that if individuals yield to social pressure and engage in counterattitudinal behavior despite the presence of social support (upper panel) they may actually show larger shifts in underlying attitudes than would be the case in the absence of such support (lower panel).

variable was included in the experiment because past research indicated that dissonance would occur only in the context of severe consequences (please refer to our discussion of this point in Chapter 4).

On the basis of the reasoning noted above, Stroebe and Diehl predicted that under high consequences, subjects exposed to a noncomplying accomplice would actually show *more* change in their views than those exposed to a complying confederate. However, under low consequences where dissonance would not occur, the opposite would be true. Both of these predictions were strongly confirmed.

These findings and those obtained in other studies conducted by Stroebe and Diehl suggest that the presence of an ally is not always beneficial in conformity situations. While such persons can often aid individuals in resisting group pressure, their impact on underlying attitudes may be quite different. In fact, if the persons involved *do* yield to such pressure, the presence of a noncomplying ally can serve to increase rather than to reduce the magnitude of shifts in their private views. In such cases, of course, the availability of active social support can be viewed as anything *but* an unmixed blessing.

rejecting the view that females are always—or even usually—more conforming than males. Several distinct lines of evidence point to this conclusion.

First, it appears that the type of materials used in early research on conformity may have contributed to the sex differences observed. Specifically, in several experiments reporting greater conformity among females, the materials employed seem to have been more familiar to men than to women. Since it is well-known that individuals are usually more willing to yield to social pressure when uncertain about their behavior than when more confident in this respect, it seems possible that females showed greater conformity in many studies for this reason. The findings of a recent review suggest that this type of bias was not present in all, or even most, past research (Eagly & Carli, 1981). Yet, convincing evidence for its impact does exist. Indeed, at least one well-known experiment has demonstrated that when items less familiar to males than to females are used, the usual sex difference is reversed. Under these conditions, males actually show *greater* conformity than females (Sistrunk & McDavid, 1971).

Second, and perhaps more surprising, it has been found that sex differences in conformity favoring men are more likely to appear in studies conducted by male researchers than in ones conducted by female investigators (Eagly & Carli, 1981). This somewhat unsettling fact suggests that subtle sources of bias may often have contributed to the observation that females yield more readily than males to social pressure. For example, it may be the case that male researchers unintentionally designed the settings of their studies in such a way that males felt more comfortable or confident while participating in them. As a result, they may have shown lower levels of conformity than their female counterparts for this reason. Please take note: we are certainly *not* suggesting that male researchers, being chauvinists at heart (!) set out to demonstrate greater conformity among females, and designed their studies accordingly; far from it. Rather, they may simply have fallen prey to unconscious sources of bias that "loaded the dice" in favor of reduced conformity among male participants.

Finally, we should note that growing evidence suggests that females are definitely *not* more conforming than males in all settings. Rather, it appears that if any differences of this type exist, they are most likely to emerge under special conditions. Specifically, differences between males and females seem most common in situations where individuals are exposed to social pressure and then their reactions to it can be observed by others—that is, under conditions of *direct surveillance* (Cooper, 1979). When, in contrast, such surveillance is absent, males and females tend to show equal levels of conformity (Eagly, Wood, & Fishbaugh, 1981).

In sum, there appears to be little firm support for the view that females are more susceptible to social influence than males. Why, then, does this stereotype persist? One possibility has been outlined by Eagly and Wood (1982). These researchers suggest that the key to this puzzle may lie in widespread inferences or assumptions about the relative status of males and females. Many persons, it seems, tend to assume that females occupy lower status positions in society than males. Further, they also assume that the lower an individual's status, the more likely this person is to accept social influence from others. Together, these beliefs lead to the perception that females are more conforming than males— even though this is not actually the case. Support for these suggestions has actually been obtained by Eagly and Wood (1982) in an integrated series of studies. For example, in one of these investigations, males and females seated in a coffee shop were approached and asked to read a brief story in which one employee of a business attempted to influence the views of another employee of the opposite sex. In half of the cases, the communicator was male and the recipient female; in the remainder, the reverse was true. In addition, half of the stories included job titles (e.g., bank vice president, bank teller), thus informing

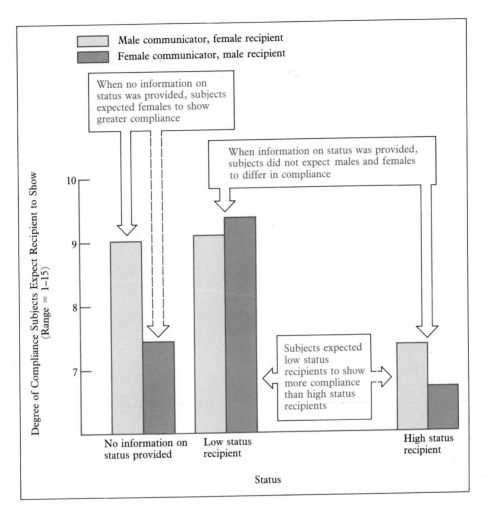

Male communicator, female recipient

Female communicator, male recipient

When no information on status was provided, subjects expected females to show greater compliance

When information on status was provided, subjects did not expect males and females to differ in compliance

Subjects expected low status recipients to show more compliance than high status recipients

Degree of Compliance Subjects Expect Recipient to Show
(Range = 1–15)

10

9

8

7

No information on status provided

Low status recipient

High status recipient

Status

FIGURE 7.7   *Susceptibility to social influence: Status or sex?.*

When no information on the status of the persons involved was provided, male and female subjects predicted that a female employee would be more susceptible to influence from a male employee than vice versa. However, when information on status was present, this factor — not sex — played a key role in determining subjects' predictions. Specifically, they expected that low status persons would be more susceptible to influence than high status ones. [Source: Based on data from Eagly & Wood, 1982.]

subjects of the status of the persons involved. In the remaining instances, information of this type was omitted. After reading the story, subjects were asked to indicate the extent to which the recipient would be influenced by the communicator. Eagly and Wood predicted that when no information on status was provided, subjects would tend to assume that females are lower in this regard than males. Thus, they would expect greater compliance by female recipients than by male recipients. In contrast, when information on status was provided, this factor, rather than sex, would affect their judgments. Specifically, low status recipients would be perceived as complying to a greater extent than high status ones, regardless of their sex. As you can see from Figure 7.7 (on p. 259), results offered strong support for these predictions. These findings and evidence gathered by other investigators (e.g., Instone, Major, & Bunker, 1983) suggests that widespread—but often false—assumptions about the relative status of males and females may lie at the root of many gender stereotypes. In short, these views may account for our tendency to perceive important differences in the behavior of the two sexes even when they don't really exist.

To conclude: do the sexes differ in terms of their overall levels of conformity? On the basis of existing evidence, our answer is: almost certainly not. While women and men may show contrasting levels of conformity in specific situations, there is little support for the existence of any general or large-scale differences between them. In sum, it appears that this particular sex difference—like several others we considered in Chapter 5—has been exaggerated and is probably far more illusory than real.

The Bases of Conformity: Why We Often Choose to "Go Along"

As we have just seen, many factors influence the occurrence and extent of conformity. Despite this fact, though, one central point is apparent: such behavior is very common. To repeat a phrase we used once before, "most people conform to most norms or expectations most of the time." Before concluding, therefore, we must address one final question: Why, precisely, is this the case? Why, in short, do we usually choose to "go along" with the norms or rules established by society, or by the groups to which we belong? As we're sure you can guess, there are no simple or clear-cut answers to this question. Many forces contribute to our strong tendency to conform. Two of the most important, though, involve our *past reinforcement for conforming* and the process of *social comparison.*

With respect to reinforcement, it is apparent that in one sense much of our early experience can be viewed as training for conformity. Youngsters are often rewarded with praise or approval for expressing the "right" views—those favored by their parents, teachers, and other adults. And they are generally also rewarded for behaving like the persons around them, but punished for behaving in ways that are viewed as somehow different. This process continues without pause throughout childhood and adolescence. Thus, by the time we are adults, we have generally learned that being similar to others is a good basis for attaining their approval and acceptance, while being different places us in danger of their censure or rejection. Little wonder, then, that we find agreeing with the persons around us, or being similar to them, pleasant (see Figure 7.8) but find disagreeing with them or being different upsetting.

A second important basis for conformity is suggested by the theory of social comparison (Festinger, 1954; Suls & Miller, 1977). Briefly, this theory suggests that human beings have a strong drive to evaluate their own opinions or abilities—to find out where they stand on various key dimensions. Unfortu-

"Good, we're all agreed. I like it when we're all agreed."

nately, there is no way to accomplish this task in a purely objective manner. In contrast to physical properties or quantities such as height, weight, and temperature, no measuring devices exist for assessing the accuracy of our opinions, our level of attractiveness to members of the opposite sex, or a whole host of similar matters. Instead, we must rely on other persons as a basis for such knowledge. Specifically, we can evaluate our attitudes or traits only by comparing ourselves with the persons around us—by engaging in social comparison. But whom do we select for such comparisons? In general, the answer seems to be: individuals who are moderately similar to ourselves. Comparisons with such persons seem to yield more information than equivalent ones with persons who are either very different from or very similar to ourselves (e.g., Fazio, 1979; Goethals & Darley, 1977). Regardless of the specific others we select for social comparison, though, there can be little doubt that our tendency to engage in this process often paves the way for a high degree of conformity. After all, if we employ others as a basis for attaining self-knowledge and establishing social reality, we may find it quite disturbing to learn that they hold views or perceptions divergent from our own. Indeed, faced with such discrepancies, we may experience strong pressure to change at least the public aspect of our views. In sum, our reliance on others as a basic source of information about our traits, attitudes, and abilities all but assures that we will conform in many spheres of life.

Together, reinforcement for behaving and thinking like others and our drive for social comparison set the stage for a high level of conformity. Indeed, given the powerful and pervasive impact of these processes, it is far from surprising that conformity is our typical mode of behavior in a wide range of settings. In a basic sense, it could hardly be otherwise.

Minority Influence: Why the Majority Doesn't Always Rule

So far in this discussion we have treated conformity as something of a one-way street: the majority exerts its influence and the minority helplessly knuckles under (at least to some degree). In many cases, this is indeed the pattern, for, as we noted earlier, conformity is a widespread and pervasive occurrence. At the same time, though, we should note that history is filled with events in which small but resolute minorities have turned the tables on larger majorities and *exerted* rather than *yielded to* social influence. For example, individuals such as Freud, Pasteur, and Galileo confronted large and virtually unanimous majorities among their peers. Yet, over time, they won large numbers of these persons over to their side. Similarly, in recent years, small but resolute groups of reformers (e.g., ones seeking full racial or sexual equality) have often succeeded in swaying public opinion in the directions they desire. Such events suggest that minorities are not always powerless in the face of large majorities. On the contrary, they can sometimes exert strong effects upon their peers. But how, precisely, can this be accomplished? How can minorities change the views of many other persons? Research findings point to two specific strategies.

One, proposed by Hollander (1964), involves two distinct phases. In the first, persons holding dissenting views conform; they go along with the majority and its views. By adopting this posture, Hollander suggests, such persons gain the esteem and approval of other group members—something he terms *idiosyncrasy credits.* Later, at an appropriate, crucial point, dissenters can "cash in" these credits, using them to exert influence on their peers. If they have acquired a high enough level of esteem or approval (enough idiosyncrasy credits), they may well succeed in gaining acceptance for their views. A second and contrasting approach has been suggested by Moscovici and his colleagues (e.g., Moscovici & Faucheux, 1972; Moscovici & Personnaz, 1980). Here, individuals wishing to exert minority influence adopt a strategy of consistent dissent. That is, they state their opposition to the majority right from the start and continue to do so in a consistent and forceful manner. According to Moscovici, such actions may shake the complacency or confidence of the majority and induce such persons to reexamine their views. The result may then be important shifts in their attitudes.

Evidence gathered to date offers support for the success of both of these approaches (e.g., Hollander, 1960; Moscovici & Faucheux, 1972). But a key question remains: is one more effective than the other? Information on this important issue has recently been provided by Bray, Johnson, and Chilstrom (1982). These researchers arranged for groups of six persons (four subjects and two confederates) to meet and discuss a series of problems. The problems were quite diverse, involving such issues as a proposed increase in student tuition, and a plan to charge students for athletic tickets that had previously been free. After considering each problem, subjects recorded their individual views on eleven-point scales, ranging from "strongly disagree" to "strongly agree." Since subjects' views on each issue were known in advance (virtually all were opposed to the tuition increase), these ratings could be used to assess the extent to which the confederates (the dissenting minority) exerted social influence. During the discussion of each problem, the two accomplices followed either the strategy recommended by Hollander or the one proposed by Moscovici and his associates. Specifically, in one condition, they agreed with the real subjects on the first two opinion items but then, on the final issue (charges for athletic tickets), they adopted a dissenting position (they came out in favor of such charges). In contrast, in the second condition they followed Moscovici's proposals, disagreeing with the group consistently and confidently on each issue.

[margin annotations: (One view Hollander) ; (another view Moscovici)]

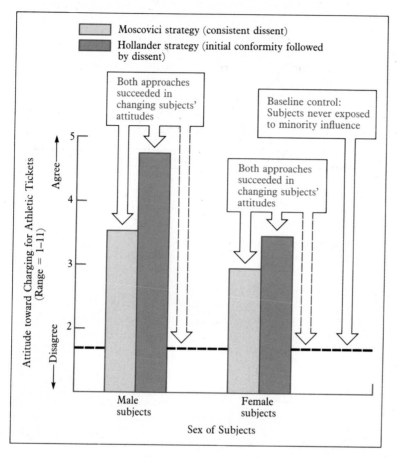

FIGURE 7.9   *Minority influence: Two effective strategies.*

Both the strategy recommended by Hollander (initial conformity followed by dissent) and the strategy suggested by Moscovici (consistent dissent) were effective in exerting minority influence. Subjects exposed to either of these tactics reported being more favorable toward a charge for athletic tickets than subjects in a control group who were never exposed to such influence. Note that in general, males were influenced to a greater extent than females by both strategies. [Source: Based on data from Bray, Johnson, & Chilstrom, 1982.]

The results of the study yielded much valuable information. First, as you can see from Figure 7.9, both techniques for exerting minority influence worked: subjects exposed to either of these approaches reported being more in favor of ticket charges than subjects in a control group who had never been exposed to minority influence (please refer to Figure 7.9). In addition, interesting differences between the Hollander and Moscovici approaches emerged. Among males, the strategy recommended by Hollander (conformity first, then dissent) seemed to be more effective. However, among females, the two approaches did not differ. Finally, in an additional and closely related study employing only one rather than two confederates (Bray et al., 1982), the Hollander tactic seemed to be more successful. At the moment, there are no simple or clear explanations for these findings; further research is necessary to determine why the two procedures differ in these respects. But the findings reported by Bray and his colleagues and those obtained in related studies (e.g., Wolf & Latané, 1983) do point to the following basic conclusion: <u>minorities are definitely *not* powerless pawns in the hands of large majorities. On the contrary, if they adopt appropriate strategies, they can turn the tables and *exert* rather than passively *submit to* social influence.</u>

Compliance:
To Ask — Sometimes — Is to Receive

Requests from others are a basic part of life. Friends and acquaintances ask for favors. Representatives of charities—and even panhandlers—plead for our funds. Lovers, spouses, or roommates ask us to alter some aspect of our behavior. Strangers request the time of day, directions, or change. We could go on and on, for the list is almost endless. By now, though, you have probably grasped the main point: attempts to gain compliance through direct requests represent one of the most common, if not *the* most common, form of social influence.

At first glance, this general approach to changing others' behavior may strike you as quite straightforward. And in its most basic form it is: persons seeking compliance simply voice their wishes, and then hope for the best. In many cases, though, attempts to employ this form of influence are far more subtle and complex. Briefly, individuals wishing to alter others' behavior through direct requests do not present their petitions cold. Rather, they engage in preliminary steps designed to tip the balance in their favor and enhance their chances for success. Many different techniques can be used for this purpose, and a number of these are quite ingenious. In this discussion, though, we will focus our attention upon two major types: *ingratiation* and the use of *multiple requests.*

Ingratiation: Liking as a Basis for Social Influence

One extremely common tactic for inducing compliance from others rests on the following assumption: if other persons like us, they will be more willing to yield to our wishes than if they don't like us. On the basis of this eminently reasonable suggestion, we often engage in a technique known as **ingratiation.** Basically, this involves attempts to influence others by first increasing their liking for us and then, after this is accomplished, exposing them to various requests (Jones, 1964). Several procedures can be employed to enhance our appeal to others. For example, we can seek to convince them that we share their opinions or are similar to them in other respects. As we noted in Chapter 6, a large body of research evidence indicates that perceived similarity is often an important basis for interpersonal attraction (e.g., Byrne, 1971). Similarly, we can concentrate on demonstrating excellent task performance. In general, persons who perform at high levels are evaluated more favorably than those who perform less adequately. And such positive reactions seem to generalize, spreading from task performance to a wide range of personal characteristics (Wall & Adams, 1974). By far the most common tactic of ingratiation, however, involves the communication of high personal regard to the target persons. This technique—often termed *other-enhancement*—frequently takes the form of *flattery:* exaggerated and undeserved praise of others. And often it succeeds: praising the persons around us *does* enhance their liking for us. But as you may know from your own experience, tactics of this type must be applied with care. If the recipients of flattery perceive that we are using it as a tool of social influence, they often react with anger rather than increased liking. For this reason, less direct techniques for communicating positive evaluations to others, such as hanging on their every word, or encouraging them to tell us about themselves, are often more successful (Wortman & Linsenmeier, 1977). In any case, regardless of the precise tactics used, if ingratiation is carried out with skill and care, it can serve as an effective strategy for increasing compliance.

Multiple Requests: Using the Old "One-Two Punch" to Induce Compliance

Often, when individuals seek compliance with their wishes, they do not restrict their efforts to a single request. Rather, they employ a kind of "one-two punch" with respect to social influence. The basic idea behind this strategy is simple: one request can serve as a kind of set-up for another. That is, an initial request can help to increase the probability that a second—and perhaps more important one—will gain acceptance. Two basic strategies are used most frequently in this manner: the *foot-in-the-door* and the *door-in-the-face*.

The foot-in-the-door: *Small request first, large request second*. There is an old saying that goes: "Give them an inch and they'll take a mile." What it refers to is the fact that often, individuals seeking compliance with their wishes begin with a small or trivial request. And then, once this has been granted, they escalate to larger or more important ones. The use of this technique—which is often known as the **foot-in-the-door** approach—can be observed in many different settings. For example, panhandlers often begin their appeals not with an open request for money, but rather with smaller appeals such as a request for the time of day. Similarly, door-to-door salespersons often start their pitches by asking potential customers to accept a free sample or even merely a brochure describing their products. In these and many other instances the basic strategy is much the same: somehow induce another person to comply with a small initial request and thereby increase the chances that he or she will agree to a much larger one. That the foot-in-the-door technique is often quite successful is shown by the findings of many separate experiments.

For example, in the first and perhaps most famous study concerned with this topic (Freedman & Fraser, 1966) a number of homemakers were called on the phone by a male experimenter who identified himself as a member of a consumers' group. At this time, he asked subjects to answer a few simple questions about the kinds of soaps they used at home. A few days later, the same individual called again and made a much larger request. This time, he asked if his organization could send a five- or six-man crew to the subject's home to conduct a thorough inventory of all the products he or she had on hand. It was explained that this survey would take about two hours. Further, the men would require complete freedom to search through the house—including all closets, cabinets, and drawers. As you can see, this was a truly gigantic request. Yet, despite this fact, fully 52.8 percent of the persons called twice agreed! In contrast, only 22.2 percent of those in a control group who were called only once and presented with the large request "cold" consented. These findings suggest that the strategy of starting with a small request and then moving to a large one can be highly effective.

Similar findings have been obtained in many other studies (e.g., DeJong, 1979, 1981; Seligman, Bush, & Kirsch, 1976). Further, the results of these experiments suggest that the foot-in-the-door effect may be quite general in scope. For example, it seems to occur when requests are made in person as well as on the phone (Rittle, 1981). It has also been found to increase compliance with a wide variety of requests, ranging from signing a petition (Baron, 1973a) or participating in an experiment (Wagener & Laird, 1980) through contributing to charity (Pliner et al., 1974) and placing a giant sign on one's front lawn (Freedman & Fraser, 1966).

Additional evidence points to two possible explanations for the success of this technique. First, it may be the case that once individuals agree to a small initial request from a stranger, they undergo subtle shifts in their self-perceptions. Specifically, they come to see themselves as the kind of person who does that sort of thing—who offers help to people who request it. Thus, when contacted again and presented with a much larger request, they agree in order to be consistent with their changed (and enhanced) self-image (Snyder & Cunningham, 1975). Indirect support for this view has been obtained in several studies indicating that the foot-in-the-door effect is stronger or more consistent under conditions where strong external reasons for complying with the initial request are absent than under conditions where they are present (e.g., DeJong & Musilli, 1982; Uranowitz, 1975). This finding is consistent with the self-perception explanation for the following reasons. When strong external justifications for compliance exist, individuals may attribute their helpfulness to these factors and fail to experience shifts in self-perception. In contrast, when such external justifications are absent, they may attribute their initial compliance to internal causes (e.g., their own traits), and so experience shifts in self-perception (see Figure 7.10).

FIGURE 7.10 Compliance and self-perception: The mediating role of external factors.

When individuals have strong external reasons for complying with a request from another person, they may attribute their compliance to these factors (upper panel). Thus, they will fail to experience shifts in self-perception as a result of compliance. In contrast, when external reasons for complying are absent (lower panel), compliance will be attributed to internal causes. As a result, shifts in self-perception may follow such behavior.

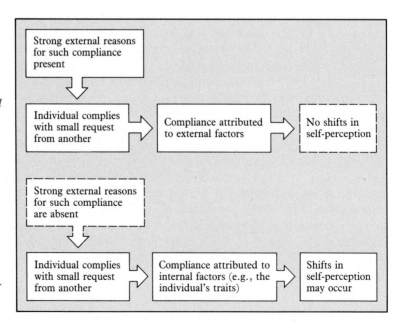

Second, it seems possible that after agreeing to a small request, individuals come to hold a more positive view of helping situations generally. That is, they may come to see such situations as less threatening or potentially unpleasant than was originally the case. And these shifts in situational perceptions, in turn, may enhance their later willingness to comply with even large requests. Evidence for this view is provided by a recent study conducted by Rittle (1981). In this investigation, male and female students in a two-request (foot-in-the-door) condition were first approached by an eight-year-old child, who asked them to help him operate a vending machine. A few minutes later, they took part in a study in which, as part of a larger questionnaire, they rated their own willingness to help others, and their perceptions of the unpleasantness of helping situations generally. Finally, at the conclusion of this study, they were exposed to a second, large request: would they volunteer their time to another research project, for which they would receive no credit or pay? Subjects in a control (one-request) condition were simply presented with this large request "cold": they were never asked for help by the child.

Results were quite revealing. First, as expected, the foot-in-the-door effect occurred: subjects in the two-request group agreed to donate more of their time

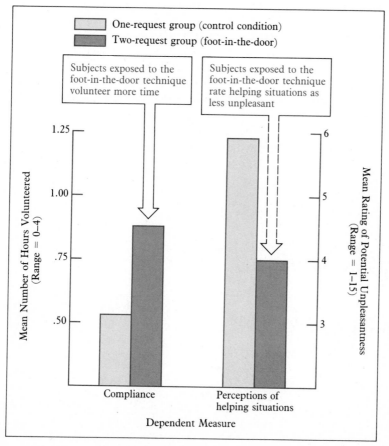

FIGURE 7.11 *The foot-in-the-door and shifts in situational perceptions.*

Individuals exposed to two requests (the foot-in-the-door group) agreed to donate more of their time to a study than those exposed to a single large request. In addition, those in the two-request condition reported perceiving helping situations as less unpleasant generally than those in the one-request control group. These findings support the view that the foot-in-the-door effect stems, at least in part, from shifts in situational perceptions. [Source: Based on data from Rittle, 1981.]

to the volunteer study than those in the one-request group (see Figure 7.11). Further, consistent with the view that the success of this technique stems, at least in part, from shifts in perceptions about helping situations generally, subjects in the two-request condition reported perceiving such situations as less unpleasant than those in the one-request control group (refer to Figure 7.11 on p. 267). Interestingly, only weak support for the self-perception view discussed above was obtained; subjects in the two-request condition reported perceiving themselves as only slightly more willing to help others than those in the control group.

At the present time, it is not possible to choose definitively between these two explanations for the existence of the foot-in-the-door effect. And in fact, such a choice may be unnecessary. Shifts in both self-perceptions and situational perceptions may contribute to the occurrence of this effect. One point that *is* clear, however, is the following: in many cases, the foot-in-the-door technique, can serve as a useful strategy for increasing compliance by others. It does not succeed under all conditions; for example, it may fail when the large request involves behaviors that are very costly or unpleasant (Foss & Dempsey, 1979). But in many settings, and with respect to a wide range of target actions, the tactic of beginning with a small request and then shifting to a somewhat larger one can be highly effective.

The door-in-the-face: Large request first, small request second. While the technique of beginning with a small request and then moving to a larger one seems quite useful, an opposite strategy, too, can often succeed. Here, we start by asking for a very large favor—one other persons are almost certain to refuse. And then, when they do, we shift to a smaller request—the favor we really wanted all along. (Please see Figure 7.12 for an example of this strategy.) This approach—often termed the **door-in-the-face** tactic—has been investigated by social psychologists in recent years and seems to be quite effective.

FIGURE 7.12   *The door-in-the-face: Another technique for gaining compliance.*

One effective technique for obtaining compliance—the door-in-the-face *approach—is illustrated in this cartoon. The basic idea behind this strategy is straightforward: Begin with a very large request and then, when this is rejected, back down to a much smaller one—the one desired all along.*
[Source: © King Features Syndicate, Inc., 1972. World rights reserved.]

For example, in an initial study on this tactic, Cialdini and his colleagues (Cialdini et al., 1975) stopped college students on the street and presented them with a gigantic request: would they agree to serving as nonpaid counselors for juvenile delinquents two hours a week for a two-year period? As you might expect, none agreed to this proposal. When the experimenters then scaled down their request to a much smaller one—taking a group of delinquents on a two-hour trip to the zoo—however, 50 percent agreed. In contrast to this figure, only 16.7 percent of a second group of students agreed to this small request when it was presented alone, without the first, giant request. Similar results obtained in other studies suggest that the door-in-the-face approach may often be a useful one for exerting social influence (e.g., Cann, Sherman, & Elkes, 1975; Cialdini & Ascani, 1976). But again, why does it succeed? Two explanations have been suggested.   *2 reasons*

The first is based on the notion of *reciprocal concessions*. When an individual who starts with a very large request backs down to a smaller one, this may be viewed by the persons receiving these requests as a concession. And then, they may feel required to make a similar concession themselves. After all, the requester has retreated in order to meet them halfway; how can they refuse to do likewise? For this reason, they may become more willing to comply with the second, smaller request.

Another possibility involves concern over what social psychologists term *self-presentation.* In most situations, we wish to make a good impression on others—to present ourselves in a favorable light. And this may well be true in cases where we are presented with requests from a stranger. In incidents of this type, we may be reluctant to refuse a second, small request after refusing an initial large one, because it will result in negative self-presentation. That is, it may lead to our appearing as unhelpful and inconsiderate persons. Support for this suggestion has been obtained in a study conducted by Pendleton and Batson (1979). Briefly, these researchers found that subjects felt that others would indeed view them as unfriendly or unconcerned if they refused modest requests for help.

At present, conclusive evidence concerning the basis for the door-in-the-face effect is lacking. It seems likely, though, that both explanations outlined above play a role in its occurrence. That is, we may often be inclined to say "yes" to a moderate request after refusing a large one because we feel compelled to match the requester's concessions and because we wish to present ourselves to others in a positive, flattering light.

The foot-in-the-door and the door-in-the-face: How can both succeed? Before concluding this discussion of the impact of multiple requests, we must address one final question about which you may have already begun to wonder: How can both the foot-in-the-door and the door-in-the-face tactics succeed? In short, how can starting with a small request and moving to a larger one, as well as starting with a large request and then retreating to a smaller one, both yield enhanced compliance? Actually, the answer is straightforward: both techniques work because they stem from different processes. But because they do, they may well tend to operate under different conditions.

First, it appears that in order to succeed, the door-in-the-face approach must involve two requests by the same person. If, instead, the requests are presented by different individuals, the effect may fail to occur (Cann, Sherman, & Elkes, 1975). In a key sense, this is not surprising. After all, if an individual has refused a large request from one person, there is no reason why he or she should experience pressure to make a concession to another stranger. (Recall that the door-in-the-face may stem from pressures toward reciprocal concessions.)

In contrast, the foot-in-the-door technique seems to work quite well even in cases where different persons make the first and second requests. Again, this is as we might expect. If an individual has experienced a shift in self-perceptions or come to see helping situations as less unpleasant as a result of agreeing to an initial small request posed by one person, these changes may well transfer to a new situation involving a larger request by another stranger.

Still another difference between the foot-in-the-door and the door-in-the-face techniques involves the time interval between the two requests. For the door-in-the-face approach to work, this interval must be relatively short. Only if this is the case can pressures toward mutual concessions operate and induce increased compliance with the second request. In contrast, the foot-in-the-door technique may succeed even if the first and second requests are separated by several days (e.g., Seligman, Bush, & Kirsch, 1976). As we might expect, shifts in self or situation perceptions seem to persist, once produced.

In sum, both the foot-in-the-door and the door-in-the-face techniques seem to represent effective means for gaining compliance from others. As we have just suggested, though, each may work best under somewhat different conditions. (For discussion of still another tactic for inducing compliance, see the **Focus on Research** section on pp. 272–273.)

TABLE 7.1   The foot-in-the-door, door-in-the-face, and low-ball techniques: A summary.

Although the three techniques summarized here differ greatly in basic nature, all appear to be effective means for gaining enhanced compliance.

Technique	First request	Second request	Effect
Foot-in-the-door technique	Small; one with which target persons are almost certain to comply	Larger; the request desired all along	Compliance with second request is enhanced
Door-in-the-face technique	Large; one target persons are almost certain to reject	Smaller; the request desired all along	Compliance with second request is enhanced
Low-ball technique	Low in cost or high in benefits	Higher in cost or lower in benefits	Individuals comply despite a change in costs or benefits

The foot-in-the-door, the door-in-the-face, and low-balling: Summing up. We realize that by now, we have covered a lot of ground, and that you may find it difficult to keep the basic nature of the three tactics we have considered firmly in mind. In order to help you do so—and also to assist you in grasping the key differences between them—we have prepared the summary in Table 7.1. Please examine it carefully; it should help you to comprehend the nature and operation of these three techniques for gaining compliance from others.

Obedience: Social Influence by Demand

In a key sense, the most direct technique that one person can use to modify the behavior of another is that of simply ordering him or her to obey. This approach is less common than either conformity or compliance, but it is certainly far from rare (see Figure 7.13). Military officers shout commands that they expect to be followed at once. Business executives issue orders to their subordinates on a regular basis. And coaches, umpires, and referees often order athletes to perform certain actions or stop performing others. Obedience to the commands of such authority figures is far from surprising. After all, such persons usually possess the ability to inflict punishment on those who fail to carry out their orders. More surprising, though, is the fact that even persons lacking in such power can sometimes induce high levels of submission from others. Indeed, it appears that under some conditions even relatively powerless sources of authority can coerce many persons into engaging in harmful, de-

FIGURE 7.13   Obedience: The most direct form of social influence.

Authority figures such as the person shown here can often command a high level of obedience from large numbers of subordinates. [Source: Photo © Thomas Hopker 1978/ Woodfin Camp & Associates.]

"Low-balling": Changing the Rules in Midgame — and Getting Away with It!

If you should ever shop for a new car and be unlucky enough to fall into the hands of a dishonest dealer, you might encounter the following chain of events. First, the salesperson with whom you interact will make an extremely attractive offer—one much lower than other prices you have been quoted. Indeed, this offer may be so good that you accept it at once. As soon as you do, however, the next step in the process will occur. The salesperson may suddenly indicate that an expensive option you thought was included is *not* part of the offer. Or he or she may go to see the manager for approval of the deal and then return, stating sadly that it has been rejected. And then, in the key, final step, the salesperson will offer you another arrangement, less attractive than the one you eagerly accepted.

Common sense suggests that under these conditions you will change your mind and refuse to buy the car. But auto dealers know from past experience that this is not the case. Even though the deal now offered is less favorable than the first one, you may stick to your initial decision and go ahead with the purchase. This technique is known as **"low-balling"** or "throwing the low-ball," and you should be on your guard against it: unfortunately, it is all too common in the world of business.

At this point, we should hasten to note that the low-ball technique is by no means restricted to purchasing a car. Rather, it is a strategy that can be used for obtaining compliance in many different settings. In general terms, it operates as follows. First, an individual is induced to make an active decision concerning some target behavior (e.g., making a purchase, doing a favor for the requester). And then, the situation is changed so that the behavior in question becomes less attractive or more costly. The low-ball succeeds if the persons involved go ahead and perform the desired target action anyway, despite these changes.

Evidence for the effectiveness of the low-ball procedure has been reported in several studies conducted by Cialdini and his co-workers (Cialdini et al., 1978). For example, in one investigation, the experimenters approached graduate students in their own dorm rooms and asked them to display posters in support of the local United Way fund drive. In one condition (a control group) subjects were told that they would have to go down to the front desk of the dorm to get the posters *before* they made their decision about helping. In another (the low-ball condition), they were told about this required effort only *after* agreeing to display the posters. Results offered strong support for the impact of the low-ball technique. While only 20 percent of the subjects in the control group actually went to the desk to get the posters, fully 60 percent of those in the low-ball condition performed this behavior.

These and other results suggest that the low-ball strategy can be a useful one for inducing compliance with various requests. But why, precisely, does it work? One possibility has been suggested by Cialdini and his colleagues. Briefly, they propose that individuals stick to their initial decisions even after the reasons for these have been changed because of a strong sense of commitment to performing the actions in question. That is, they are cognitively committed to buying the car, doing the requested favor, and so on, and find it difficult to alter this decision. While this is a reasonable explanation, another possibility has been proposed—and tested—by Burger and Petty (1981). These researchers suggest that the success of the low-ball procedure stems from the creation of an unfulfilled obligation to the initial *requester*. Briefly, they argue that once we agree to perform some action urged on us by another person, we feel obliged to honor this commitment, to do what we have promised to do for this individual. If this is indeed the case, then we would expect that the identity of the person making the second request is crucial. Only if the same individual comes back with the changed con-

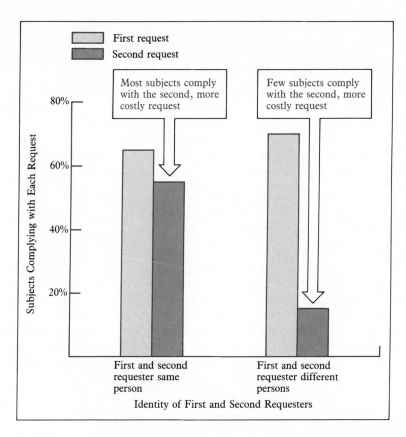

FIGURE 7.14 *The low-ball technique: Evidence concerning its basis.*

As shown here, individuals who had agreed to take part in an experiment for extra credit maintained this commitment when asked to participate without such credit by the original requester. In contrast, they showed much lower compliance when this more costly request was made by another, different person. These findings suggest that the success of the low-ball technique stems from a commitment or unfulfilled obligation to the original requester. [Source: Based on data from Burger & Petty, 1981.]

ditions (and the less favorable request) will compliance be enhanced. If a different individual makes this request, the low-ball technique may fail.

In order to test this prediction, Burger and Petty (1981) conducted an experiment in which subjects were first told that they could earn extra credit by serving in an experiment. A few minutes later, they were informed either by the same person or by another individual, that this credit could not be awarded. Yet, at this time, they were still asked to donate their time. As predicted, only when the request came from the same person did the low-ball effect occur. That is, only here did subjects "stick to their guns" and agree to donate their time, even though this behavior was now more costly (i.e., they would earn no credit for it). When, instead, the second request was presented by a different person, the low-ball effect failed to occur. Here, subjects

generally refused to help and showed the same low level of compliance as that demonstrated by subjects in a control group who had never been promised any extra credit (see Figure 7.14).

These findings, and those obtained in other studies conducted by Burger and Petty (1981) suggest that the success of the low-ball technique may well stem from felt obligations toward the initial requester. Regardless of the specific mechanisms involved, however, the powerful impact of this tactic points to the following conclusions. First, always be wary of deals that sound too good to be true; they may well be set-ups for what follows. And second, try to avoid making hasty, initial commitments. Once you do, it may be difficult to reverse these initial decisions, even when the reasons behind them alter greatly.

structive acts simply by ordering them to do so (e.g., Shanab & Yahya, 1977). Perhaps the clearest evidence for the occurrence of such effects has been reported by <u>Stanley Milgram</u> and his colleagues in a series of famous and controversial experiments (Milgram, 1964, 1974).

Destructive Obedience:
Some Laboratory Demonstrations

In these studies, Milgram wished to determine whether individuals would follow commands from an experimenter that they inflict considerable pain and suffering on another person—a totally innocent victim. In order to test this hypothesis, he informed subjects that they were taking part in a study of the effects of punishment on learning. Their task was then described as that of delivering electric shocks to another person (actually an accomplice of the researcher) each time he made an error in a simple learning task. These shocks were to be delivered by means of thirty numbered switches on the equipment shown in Figure 7-15. Further, subjects were told to move to the next higher switch each time the learner made an error. Since the first switch supposedly delivered a shock of 15 volts, it was clear that if the learner made many errors he would soon be receiving powerful jolts. Indeed, according to the labels on the equipment, the final shock would consist of 450 volts! In reality, of course, the accomplice (i.e., the learner) never received any shocks during the experiment.

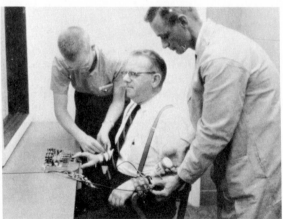

FIGURE 7.15   *Studying destructive obedience: The Milgram technique.*

The photo on the left shows the apparatus used by Milgram in his famous experiments on obedience. The photo on the right shows the experimenter (wearing a lab coat) and a subject (standing at the back) attaching electrodes to the learner's wrists. Please note: this person was an accomplice of the researcher and never received any shocks during the study. [Source: From the film Obedience, *distributed by the New York University Film Library. Copyright 1965 by Stanley Milgram. Reprinted by permission of the copyright holder.]*

The only real shock ever used was a mild pulse given to subjects from button 3 to convince them that the equipment was real (refer to Figure 7.15).

During the session, the learner (following instructions) made many errors. Thus, subjects soon found themselves facing a dilemma. Should they continue punishing this person with what seemed to be painful and dangerous shocks? Or should they refuse to participate? The experimenter pressured them to choose the former path, for whenever they hesitated or protested, he made one of a series of graded remarks. These began with a simple "Please go on," escalated to "It is absolutely essential that you continue," and finally shifted to "You have no other choice: you *must* go on." In the face of these comments, subjects could end the session only by openly defying the stern and imposing experimenter.

Since subjects were all volunteers and were paid for their participation in advance, you might predict that they would be quite resistant to these orders. Yet, in reality, fully *65 percent showed total obedience.* That is, they proceeded through the entire shock series to the final 450-volt level (see Figure 7.16). In

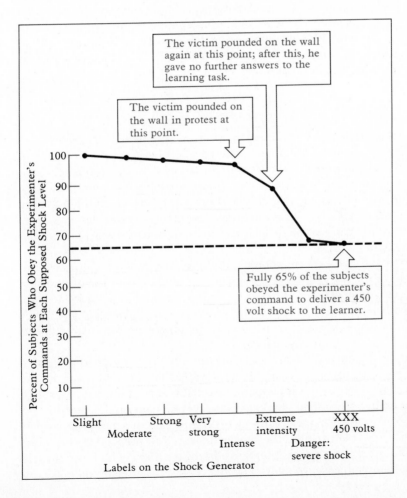

The victim pounded on the wall again at this point; after this, he gave no further answers to the learning task.

The victim pounded on the wall in protest at this point.

Fully 65% of the subjects obeyed the experimenter's command to deliver a 450 volt shock to the learner.

Percent of Subjects Who Obey the Experimenter's Commands at Each Supposed Shock Level

Slight
Moderate
Strong
Very strong
Intense
Extreme intensity
Danger: severe shock
XXX 450 volts

Labels on the Shock Generator

FIGURE 7.16   Obedience in the laboratory: An unsettling demonstration.

As shown here, a surprisingly high proportion of the subjects in Milgram's research obeyed the experimenter's commands that they deliver electric shocks of increasing strength to an innocent victim. Indeed, fully 65 percent continued to obey throughout the entire series (up to the 450-volt shock). [Source: Based on data from Milgram, 1963.]

contrast, subjects in a control group who were not exposed to such orders generally used only very mild shocks during the session. Of course, as you might expect, individuals subjected to the experimenter's commands often protested and asked that the session be ended. When ordered to proceed, however, a majority knuckled under to this pressure and continued to obey. (Indeed, as shown in Figure 7.16, they stuck to this course of action despite the fact that the victim pounded on the wall as if in intense pain on two separate occasions.)

In further experiments, Milgram (1965a, 1974) found that similar results could be obtained even under conditions that might be expected to reduce such obedience. For example, when the study was moved from its original location on the campus of Yale University to a rundown office building in a nearby city, subjects' level of obedience was virtually unchanged. Similarly, a large proportion of the participants (62.5 percent) continued to obey even when the accomplice complained about the painfulness of the shocks and begged to be released. And most surprising of all, many (about 30 percent) continued to obey even when doing so required that they grasp the victim's hand and force it down upon the shock plate! That these unsettling results were not due to special conditions prevailing in Milgram's laboratory is indicated by the fact that similar findings were soon reported in studies conducted in several different countries (e.g., Jordan, W. Germany, Australia), and with children as well as adults (e.g., Kilham & Mann, 1974; Shanab & Yahya, 1977). Thus, they actually seem to be alarmingly general in scope.

Destructive Obedience: Why Does It Occur?

To say that the results obtained by Milgram and other researchers are disturbing is a gross understatement. The parallels between the behavior of subjects in these studies of obedience and atrocities directed against civilians during time of war are too clear to require further comment. But why, precisely, did such effects occur? Why, in short, were subjects in these experiments so willing to yield to the commands of a relatively powerless source of authority? Careful examination of such research points to the role of a number of different factors.

First, although the experimenters in these studies were quite powerless to reward subjects for obeying their commands or punish them for disobeying, they possessed a high degree of apparent status. Dressed in a white lab coat, associated with a prestigious institution, and addressed by the title "Dr.," they were quite impressive. Given this fact, it is hardly surprising that many subjects were willing to follow their commands.

Second, at the start of the session, the experimenter explained to participants that he—not they—would be responsible for the well-being of the learner (i.e., the victim). This information probably served to counter at least some of the inhibitions subjects had against inflicting pain on this person.

Third, the gradual nature of the procedures used in such research may have played a key role. At first, the shocks delivered to the victim were quite mild, and almost all participants agreed to administer them. This is not surprising; indeed, many subjects probably expected that the learner would make few errors, and that they would never have to proceed very far into the shock series. But then, quickly, these expectations were violated: the victim made many errors, and the intensity of the shocks mounted rapidly. Consider the dilemma now faced by subjects: they had already consented to deliver the mild shocks. How could they now refuse to administer the stronger ones? In a sense, the situation they confronted resembled the foot-in-the-door approach. Having already complied with small requests from the experimenter (e.g., that they deliver very mild shocks), there was much social pressure to comply with his larger ones. In short, they were trapped into obeying by their own previous behavior and the nature of the situation (Gilbert, 1981).

Fourth, and related to the above, the gradual nature of the shock series may also have operated to produce obedience in another manner. Because each shock was only slightly stronger than the previous one, there was no natural point at which subjects could draw the line and disobey. This factor, too, may have contributed to the strong tendency to obey (Gilbert, 1981).

Together, these conditions seem to have set the stage for the high levels of obedience observed in the research by Milgram and others (see Figure 7.17 for a summary). And disturbingly similar conditions seem to exist in many life situations outside the laboratory. For example, military or police officers who order attacks on civilians usually possess many trappings of high status. Thus, even when their commands go against directives from higher sources of authority, these badges of power make it difficult for subordinates to disobey. Similarly, such commands often follow a gradual course, parallel to that present in research on obedience. At first, subordinates may simply be commanded to arrest, evacuate, or threaten potential victims. Soon, though, these commands are escalated into instructions to beat, torture, or even kill them. Finally, as is the case in laboratory research, no clear-cut point for shifting to disobedience is usually present. When should subordinates draw the line and refuse to follow

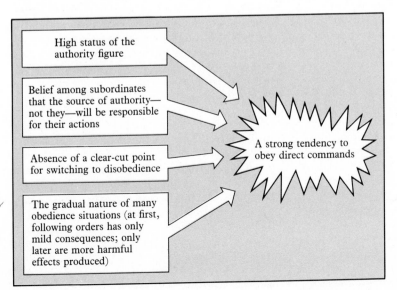

FIGURE 7.17   *The tendency to obey: Some key contributing factors.*

Several different factors seem to contribute to the high levels of obedience observed in laboratory studies and in many important life situations.

A Modeling: Social Influence and the Enhancement of Human Welfare

Consider the following incidents or events:

(1) Thousands of adoring fans mimic the mannerisms, hairstyle, and dress of a famous movie idol.

(2) After witnessing countless murders and gunfights on TV, a child responds to provocation from a playmate with overt violence.

(3) A married couple attends a torrid X-rated movie, where they witness several techniques of lovemaking they have never previously seen. That night, they use some of these in their own sexual relations.

(4) One member of an audience at a play begins to boo; soon many other persons jump to their feet and voice their disapproval in a similar manner.

In all of these incidents, the persons involved were strongly affected by exposure to the actions of others, either directly or indirectly. In short, their behavior, attitudes, or feelings were altered by observing the persons around them. In general, psychologists refer to such effects as **modeling,** and as you can readily see, they constitute yet another form of social influence (Bandura, 1977). Often, of course, the impact exerted through this process is unintended. For example, the movie idol may have adopted his hairstyle and mode of dress simply because they please him, *not* because of any desire to influence his fans. Similarly, the actors in the X-rated movie probably had no intention of influencing the persons who watch their performance. But even when such effects are unintended they still occur and can be both strong and general in nature.

Actually, exposure to the actions of others can affect social behavior in many different ways. Thus, we will have reason to return to such effects in several later chapters. For example, we will consider the impact of *helping models* upon prosocial behavior in Chapter 8. And we will examine the influence of *televised violence* on overt aggression in Chapter 9. For the moment, though, we wish to focus mainly on a slightly different topic: the use of modeling as a technique for enhancing human welfare.

At first glance, you may find the notion of using this form of social influence to produce beneficial effects somewhat puzzling. How, after all, can exposure to the actions of others contribute to personal well-being? The answer is quite straightforward. Growing evidence suggests that when persons suffering from many behavioral problems are exposed to appropriate *social models*—individuals who cope more effectively with these problems —they may experience rapid and major improvements. Thus, techniques based on modeling have been used to treat such varied problems as intense fears or phobias (e.g., Kornhaber & Schroeder, 1975), anxieties relating to sexual relations (e.g., Nemetz, Craig, & Reith, 1978), the inability to control one's temper (e.g., Sarason & Ganzer, 1971), and even addiction to alcohol and other drugs (Gotestam & Melin, 1974). As a concrete illustration of this highly beneficial work, we will consider the application of modeling techniques to the treatment of *social isolation.*

Sad to relate, almost all classrooms and neighborhoods contain youngsters who show little tendency to interact with their peers. Instead, these pathetic children play, work, and study in virtual isolation. Given the important role of early social experience and adequate social skills in later personal adjustment, such isolation represents a potentially serious problem. But can it be eliminated through modeling procedures? The results of a growing body of evidence suggest that it can (Conger & Keane, 1981). For example, consider a study conducted by Jakibchuk and Smeriglio (1976). In this investigation, preschool youngsters who were socially isolated were first identified by their teachers. Then these children were divided into several groups and exposed to contrasting types of treatment. In two groups, the children

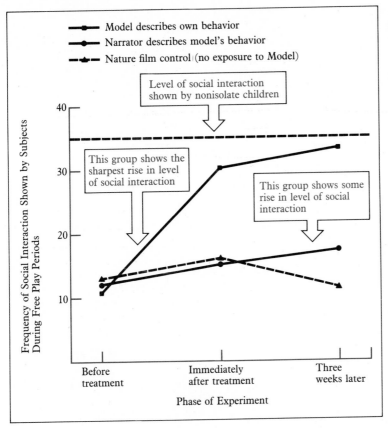

Model describes own behavior
Narrator describes model's behavior
Nature film control (no exposure to Model)

Level of social interaction shown by nonisolate children

This group shows the sharpest rise in level of social interaction

This group shows some rise in level of social interaction

Frequency of Social Interaction Shown by Subjects During Free Play Periods

40

30

20

10

Before treatment

Immediately after treatment

Three weeks later

Phase of Experiment

FIGURE 7.18 *Modeling and the elimination of childhood social isolation.*

After witnessing brief films in which a child of their own age overcame social isolation, children suffering from the same problem demonstrated concrete improvements. Specifically, they became much more willing to approach and interact with other youngsters. Interestingly, these effects were strongest when subjects heard the child models they observed verbally describe the changes in their behavior as they occurred. [Source: Based on data from Jakibchuk & Smeriglio, 1976.]

watched four brief films (five minutes each in length) showing a child of their own age who overcame initial isolation and gradually shifted to pleasant social interaction. In one of these conditions, the child model described his or her own behavior as it took place. In the second, a narrator described the child's behavior. Subjects assigned to a third, control group merely witnessed four brief nature films, equal in length to those seen by subjects in the two modeling conditions. The results of the experiment were quite dramatic. As you can see from Figure 7.18, children exposed to the modeling procedures showed increases in their rate of interaction with their peers, both immediately after watching the film, and also three weeks later. In contrast, children exposed to the control (nature) films did not show similar improvements. Further, the beneficial effects we have just described were much stronger when the child model described his or her own behavior than when this function was per-

formed by a narrator. These findings and similar results in other studies (e.g., Furman, Rahe, & Hartup, 1979) point to the following conclusion: even relatively brief exposure to appropriate social models can greatly assist children in overcoming this serious behavioral problem.

In concluding, we simply wish to call your attention to a key fact about social influence that is frequently overlooked. In and of itself, this basic process is quite neutral in nature. Like any other powerful force in the world around us, it can be used for beneficial or harmful purposes. On the one hand, it can be employed for purely selfish goals, such as inducing slavish conformity or destructive obedience. On the other, it can be used to teach individuals new skills, help them overcome serious personal problems, or to encourage positive forms of social behavior. The choice, in a very real sense, lies mainly in the hands of those who seek to wield it.

orders? This is largely a matter of judgment and conscience and must be determined by each individual in the absence of external guidelines.

In sum, many factors seem to contribute to the high levels of obedience observed in laboratory settings and in numerous life situations. Together, these factors merge into a powerful and compelling force—one most persons find difficult to resist. And the consequences, unfortunately, can often be devastating for large numbers of innocent, defenseless victims.

Destructive Obedience: Can It Be Reduced?

Admittedly, examining the many factors that contribute to obedience is somewhat disheartening. Yet this task also offers a positive side: understanding the conditions that facilitate such behavior can be of assistance in developing means for countering its occurrence. And in fact, several distinct steps for accomplishing this goal—for reducing the tendency toward obedience— apparently exist.

First, individuals exposed to commands from a source of authority may be reminded that they—not this individual—will be held responsible for any harm produced. Under these conditions, we might expect sharp reductions in the tendency to obey destructive commands. And the results of several studies suggest that this is actually the case (e.g., Hamilton, 1978; Kilham & Mann, 1974; Tilker, 1970). In these investigations, subjects informed that they would be held personally and directly responsible for the victim's safety showed much lower levels of obedience than those not armed with such information. Taken together, such findings suggest that often the impact of authority figures can be greatly reduced by a single, straightforward step: shifting the responsibility for the consequences of obedience onto the shoulders of those who obey.

Second, active steps may be taken to disrupt the gradual nature of many obedience situations. If the persons exposed to destructive commands are provided with a clear sign that beyond some point, obedience is inappropriate, their ability to resist may be greatly enhanced. That this is actually the case is suggested by the findings of several experiments (e.g., Milgram, 1965b; Powers & Geen, 1972). In these studies, individuals participating in the Milgram procedures were exposed to disobedient actions by one or more others—accomplices who simply refused to continue with the shocks. As you might expect, subjects' own willingness to obey was sharply reduced by these conditions. And, consistent with the view that the confederates' actions provided participants with an indication of just where to draw the line, their own refusals generally took place soon after witnessing these acts of rebellion.

A third approach that might also succeed in countering the tendency to obey involves efforts to define the exact limits of the power possessed by sources of authority. In many situations, individuals seem to assume that these are even broader than they really are. Thus, steps designed to deflate this seeming image of omnipotence might go a long way toward lessening the impact of commands from such persons.

To conclude: the power of authority figures to command obedience is certainly great. But, it seems, it *can* be countered or reduced under certain conditions. Overcoming this particular form of social influence, though, is far from easy. Thus, we must constantly be on guard to protect ourselves and others from its potentially dangerous and destructive impact. (For a discussion of a far more beneficial type of social influence, see the **On the Applied Side** section on pp. 278–279.)

Summary

Social influence occurs whenever one or more persons attempt to alter the attitudes, behavior, or feelings of one or more others. Such efforts take many different forms, but among the most important are *conformity, compliance*, and *obedience.*

Conformity occurs in situations where individuals change their behavior in order to adhere to widely accepted standards or beliefs (*social norms*). It is affected by many factors, including attraction to the influencing group, size of this group, and the presence of social support. Many early studies of conformity seemed to suggest that females are more susceptible to such influence than males. However, more recent evidence indicates that this is not the case and that there are no overall differences between the sexes with respect to conformity.

Compliance occurs when one or more persons alter their behavior in response to direct requests from others. It can sometimes be increased by flattery or other tactics of *ingratiation.* And it is often enhanced through the use of *multiple requests.* In one such technique, the *foot-in-the-door*, individuals are first exposed to a small request. Then, once they agree to this, a larger request is presented. In a second technique, the *door-in-the-face*, target persons first receive a very large request—one they are almost certain to reject. Then they are exposed to a second, smaller request. Both tactics seem capable of enhancing compliance, but under somewhat different conditions. In still another approach, *low-balling*, individuals are induced to agree to some request. And then the advantages of doing so are reduced. Despite these changes, many persons stick to their initial commitment and comply.

Obedience occurs in situations where one individual simply orders others to behave in some manner. Research findings suggest that many persons have strong tendencies toward such behavior. Thus they will often yield to commands from authority figures even when these require harmful acts. A number of factors seem to contribute to these tendencies, but fortunately several techniques for reducing their impact exist.

Often simply being exposed to the actions of others can exert strong effects upon our own behavior, feelings, or thought. Such effects are known as **modeling** and frequently are quite unintended in nature (i.e., the persons who act as social models and exert them have no overt desire to do so). Techniques based on modeling have been used to treat a wide range of serious behavioral problems (e.g., phobias, social isolation). Thus, it can be viewed as a potentially beneficial form of social influence.

Glossary

compliance *A form of social influence based on direct requests. Many techniques for maximizing compliance exist, including ingratiation and the use of multiple requests.*

conformity *A type of social influence based on pressure to adhere to social norms. When individuals conform, they usually do so in order to get into line with the accepted standards of groups to which they belong.*

Crutchfield technique *A procedure for studying conformity under controlled laboratory conditions. In this technique, subjects are led to believe that they will learn about others' responses to questions or problems by lights on a special panel. In reality, however, the experimenter controls these lights and uses them to exert social pressure upon subjects.*

door-in-the-face *A technique for enhancing compliance based on the strategy of beginning with a very large request and then, when this is rejected, backing down to a smaller request (the one desired all along).*

foot-in-the-door *A technique for gaining increased compliance based on the strategy of beginning with a small request and then, when this is granted, moving to a much larger request.*

informational social influence *Social influence based on our desire to understand ourselves and the social world around us.*

ingratiation *A technique for obtaining compliance in which a requester first attempts to increase his or her attractiveness to the target person. Once this is attained, attempts at social influence follow.*

low-ball technique (or low-balling) *A procedure for enhancing compliance based on the following strategy. First, an individual is asked to perform some target behavior under favorable conditions. Then the costs of this behavior are increased, or the benefits to be derived from it are reduced. If the technique is successful, however, individuals will stick to their original decision and perform the target behavior despite these changes.*

modeling *Refers to changes in the behavior, feelings, or thoughts of one or more individuals produced through their exposure to the behavior of one or more others. Techniques based on modeling have recently been used to treat a wide range of behavioral problems.*

normative social influence *Social influence based on our desire to be like other individuals, or to gain their acceptance and approval.*

obedience *A form of social influence based on direct commands or orders.*

reference group *Any group to which an individual belongs or would like to belong, and which he or she uses as a source of norms or behavioral standards.*

social comparison *Refers to the process by which we compare our attitudes, traits, values, and beliefs with those of the persons around us. We engage in such comparisons in order to assess our traits and evaluate the accuracy of our attitudes and beliefs.*

social influence *Refers to attempts on the part of one or more persons to change the behavior, feeling, or thought of one or more others.*

social norms *Rules indicating how individuals should or ought to behave. Such norms can be either formal and explicit (e.g., traffic regulations) or informal and implicit (e.g., unspoken rules about how close we should stand to other persons during conversations with them).*

For More Information

Forsyth, D. R. *An introduction to group dynamics.* Monterey, Calif.: Brooks/Cole, 1983.
  An excellent overview of the complex but fascinating processes that occur within groups. The discussions of conformity, obedience, and other forms of social influence are especially interesting, and expand upon coverage of these topics in the present chapter. All in all, an interesting, readable text.

Krupat, E. (Ed.). *Psychology is social: Readings and conversations in social psychology.* Glenview, Ill.: Scott, Foresman, 1982.
  The chapter on conformity and social influence in this book contains several thought-provoking articles. In addition, it offers an intriguing conversation between the editor and Herbert Kelman (an expert on social influence and its impact on society).

Milgram, S. *Obedience to authority.* New York: Harper, 1974.
This book presents a clear summary of Milgram's research on obedience. In addition, provocative discussions of the implications of this work for modern society are presented.

Wheeler, L., Deci, E. L., Reis, H., and Zuckerman, M. *Interpersonal influence* (2nd ed.). Boston: Allyn and Bacon, 1978.
A relatively brief discussion of many aspects of social influence. Several of the topics considered in this chapter are discussed.

CHAPTER 8

Prosocial Behavior:
Helping, Intervening, and Resisting

**Responding to an Unexpected Emergency:
Helping a Stranger in Distress**

*The Bystander Effect: When More Equals Less/The Rewards and Punishments of
Helping/Those Who Help: Characteristics Affecting Altruism/Those Who Are
Helped and Their Reactions to Aid*

Intervening to Stop a Wrongdoer As a Prosocial Act

*Once Again, the Bystander Effect/Responsibility and Commitment: The Ultimate
Motivation to Act*

Resisting Temptation: The Ability to Sacrifice Immediate Gains

The Lure of Nonviolent Crime/Cheating in School: The Students' Temptation

Special Inserts

FOCUS ON RESEARCH
Emotions and Attributions As Determinants of Altruism

ON THE APPLIED SIDE
What to Do about Shoplifters

ON THE APPLIED SIDE
How Can Cheating Be Stopped?

Several students sat at the table in the student union, sipping soft drinks and talking. It was the middle of the afternoon and most of them were finished with classes for the day.

*Jim leaned toward Tammy and asked, "Are you ready for the geology test next Friday?" "You know me," she replied. He **did** know how she was always prepared for tests. She read the book early, underlined all of the important points, and never missed a lecture. She had been getting straight **A**s since he first met her during their freshman year. Jim had something else in mind. He wasn't at all prepared for this exam. Band practice caused him to miss several lectures, and he was far behind in the reading assignments. He felt there was no way he could even do as well as he had the last time, and his parents were pretty upset about that low **C**. He didn't really want to cheat, but he didn't see any other way out of his dilemma. "Tam, would you let me sit next to you during the exam? I won't get you in any trouble—I promise." She looked at him with a puzzled expression. She liked Jim a lot, but he was asking her to participate in something she considered very wrong.*

Across the table, Joan was slipping the salt and pepper shakers and a pile of sugar packets into her purse. When she saw that Hal was watching her, she blushed slightly. "Our apartment is low on supplies, and I'm trying to do my share by bringing in a few things from time to time. This place will never miss them, and my roommates and I are flat broke this week." Hal felt extremely uncomfortable. On the one hand, he had recently written a feature story in the campus newspaper about how the cost of petty thefts and random vandalism were passed along to all the students in the form of higher prices and tuition increases. Why should he or anyone else have to pay for Joan's groceries? On the other hand, he did not know if he could muster the courage to tell her to put the stuff back where it belonged. Of course, he could just slip the word to the union manager that this individual had stolen a few things, but that seemed even harder to do.

Just then, there was a commotion across the aisle. A student at another table apparently had collapsed on the floor, and he was just lying there next to his chair. The two students nearest the fallen individual stared at him and then looked at each other. "What do you think is wrong with him?" "Maybe he had some kind of a seizure." "Maybe he's drunk." "Shouldn't somebody do something?" Several minutes went by before anyone was able to decide what to do.

These students found themselves involved in a series of interactions in which they had to deal with questions of ethics and social responsibility. Social psychological research concerned with such situations attempts to discover the determinants of **prosocial behavior.** That term refers to acts that have no obvious benefits for the individual who carries them out and may even involve risk or some degree of sacrifice; these acts do, however, benefit others, and they are based on ethical standards of behavior. In Chapter 10 we will discuss a related variety of helpful behaviors, including *cooperation,* consisting of instances in which people work together to reach a common goal.

Three quite different situations involving prosocial behavior have been the focus of research interest, and each will be covered in this chapter. We will first examine what is involved when an individual is suddenly confronted with the possibility of *helping a stranger in distress.* We will describe the variables that determine when bystanders do and do not behave as Good Samaritans by making an *altruistic* response. Next, we will turn to a somewhat more difficult situation in which another person is committing an illegal act. Here the individual must decide whether to take steps that involve *deterring a wrongdoer.* The third situation is one in which there is an incentive to engage in an unethical or illegal act. Prosocial behavior in this instance consists of *resisting temptation.* In addition, there is special coverage of the relationship between *emotions* and *helping,* the way in which store customers can be encouraged to *report a shoplifter,* and the methods used to *stop cheating.*

Responding to an Unexpected Emergency: Helping a Stranger in Distress

On an icy winter day in 1982, an airplane attempted to take off from Washington, D. C., but instead crashed into the Potomac River. One of the passengers who escaped from the plane found herself unable to swim to safety through the freezing water. She was close to drowning when a stranger, Lenny

FIGURE 8.1   The extremes of prosocial behavior: Risking one's life to save a stranger.

The opportunity to perform (or fail to perform) a prosocial act generally arises without warning when we are confronted with an emergency. A stranger is in trouble, and any bystander is faced with making a decision to provide help or not. Few of us meet a situation as dangerous as the bystander who plunged into the icy Potomac River to save a drowning survivor of an airplane crash. [Source: UPI photo.]

Skutnik, spotted her and plunged into the river to save her life. For this altruistic, prosocial act, Mr. Skutnik was rightly acclaimed to be a hero (see Figure 8.1). For most of us, the emergencies we encounter are far less serious, and our prosocial acts are not heroic ones. Unfortunately, there are also numerous examples of the opposite reaction when no help is provided. This sort of bystander apathy appeared in a newspaper account of an elderly lady who slipped on a sidewalk in a Midwestern town, broke her leg, and lay in the snow for two hours as passersby ignored her. While it is tempting to explain these stories in terms of compassionate versus indifferent bystanders, social psychological research indicates that several kinds of variables are operating. For example, response to the needs of a charity is greater when the request is made by middle-aged, well-dressed females than by casually dressed females of college age (Jackson & Latané, 1981), and individuals maintain a greater distance from a handicapped person seeking donations than from someone not handicapped (Pancer et al., 1979). Environmental variables also influence such behavior: students living in single-story dormitories are more helpful than those in four-story living quarters (Nadler et al., 1982). The investigators suggested that the greater density in the taller buildings accounted for the difference. By far the most powerful factor determining helping behavior is the presence of other people. An individual who is alone is much more likely to behave in a prosocial fashion than is that same person surrounded by other bystanders. We will examine the way in which this **bystander effect** operates.

The Bystander Effect: When More Equals Less

Accounts of actual incidents in which groups of people failed to provide help to a stranger in need led Darley and Latané (1968) to propose that helping behavior is less likely to occur as group size increases. This hypothesis was first tested in an experiment in which each subject was led to believe that there was only one other person participating in a discussion through an intercom system, or two other subjects, or five others. Actually, there was only the real subject and the appropriate number of tape recordings. After the discussion began, the stranger on one of the recordings gasped and seemed to be undergoing a seizure. How did the subjects respond? As predicted, the more fellow by-standers believed to be present, the less likely the subject was to try to provide help. Even when help *was* offered, the perceived presence of others led to a delay. Those who were alone responded in less than a minute. When there were supposed to be five bystanders, the subjects hesitated for three minutes before responding. This same effect has since been demonstrated repeatedly in labora-tory experiments and everyday life field settings (Latané & Darley, 1970).

The presence of others clearly inhibits prosocial behavior, but *why* does this occur? One way of conceptualizing such situations is in terms of a series of steps through which an individual must progress in order to arrive at a decision to help. As shown in Figure 8.2 on p. 290, Latané and Darley constructed this sort of model. The progression of steps suggests the possibility that different variables operate to influence prosocial behavior at various stages of the pro-cess. We will examine three such variables that have been studied extensively.

FIGURE 8.2   *Responding to a stranger in need: A cognitive model.*

In the cognitive model proposed by Latané and Darley, the individual who is confronted by an emergency situation such as a stranger in distress must go through a series of steps making several decisions. Each time, one decision leads to not behaving altruistically while the opposite decision takes the person one step closer to providing help. Aid is provided for the victim only if there is a "yes" decision at each of the five steps. [Source: Adapted from Byrne & Kelley, 1981.]

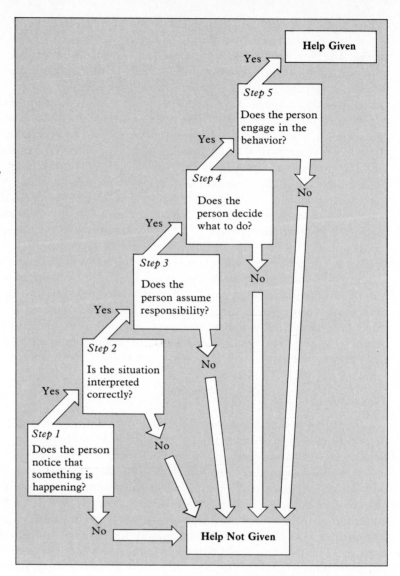

Who's in charge? The assumption of responsibility. In order to take any action to help a stranger, someone has to assume responsibility for providing aid. With a number of bystanders present, each is presumably able to help, and as a result there is a **diffusion of responsibility** (see Figure 8.3). Under those conditions, it takes something extra to goad one of the group into action. For example, if there is a recognized leader present to organize what is to be done, a group can suddenly be galvanized into action (Firestone et al., 1975). Even without the presence of a designated leader, just one helpful individual is likely to serve as a

"We've reached a decision, your honor . . . We'd rather not become involved!"

FIGURE 8.3 *Diffusion of responsibility: No one gets involved.*

When several people are confronted by a situation that requires action, there can be a diffusion of responsibility. *As a result, there may be no response by anyone. In this cartoon, the inaction of a group is depicted at its ridiculous extreme. [Source:* Grin and Bear It *by George Lichty © 1982 Field Enterprises, Inc. Courtesy of Field Newspaper Syndicate.]*

model for other bystanders to follow (Morgan, 1978). Similarly, when the group norm is social responsibility, the presence of others serves as a reminder and actually increases the probability of prosocial acts (Yinon et al., 1982). It is interesting to note that those who help after being exposed to very helpful models do not perceive themselves to be as altruistic as those who help in the absence of models (Thomas et al., 1981). It seems that the helpfulness can be attributed either to the presence of the model or to one's own altruistic tendencies.

One of the reasons that some people might fail to help is that they simply do not feel competent to assume responsibility in that particular situation; they do not know what to do or how to do it. That could explain why the presence of a leader to instruct or a model to demonstrate is quite important. It also follows that when an individual has learned how to deal with a given problem, this new-found competence should result in an increase in prosocial acts. Pantin and Carver (1982) provided such competence by exposing female undergraduates to three films that illustrated how to deal with emergencies by demonstrating several first-aid procedures. Three weeks later these individuals took part in a seemingly unrelated experiment, as did a group of control subjects who had not seen the movies. As in earlier bystander research, there was a discussion task in which each subject thought she was interacting with one or five other subjects. After the discussion had gotten underway, one of the strangers began choking and struggling for breath. As shown in Figure 8.4 on p. 292, among those who had not seen the movies, there was the familiar bystander effect, with aid being provided more slowly when there were others supposedly present. Among subjects who had seen the first-aid movies, there was no inhibition of their responses. Thus, the competence induced by the films appeared to result in the necessary assumption of responsibility. An additional finding was that the effect of the films on helping behavior was negligible if the emergency arose six weeks after viewing them. Perhaps it is necessary to be exposed to repeated reminders of what to do when such problems arise.

FIGURE 8.4   Eliminating the bystander effect: Competence leads to assuming responsibility.

In an experiment in which a stranger seemed to be choking, helping behavior was inhibited by the presence of others among subjects in the control group. The bystander effect was eliminated in the experimental group in which subjects had viewed first-aid films demonstrating what to do in such emergencies. Presumably, the movies induced competence, and this led the subjects to assume responsibility even when other bystanders were present. [Source: Based on data from Pantin & Carver, 1982.]

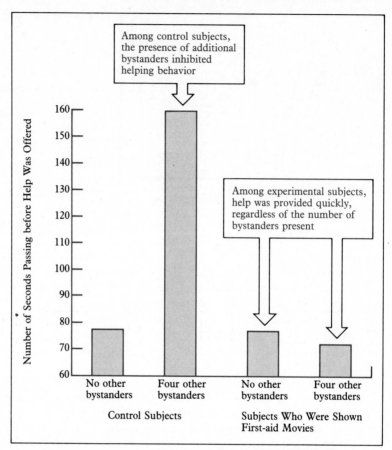

Among control subjects, the presence of additional bystanders inhibited helping behavior

Among experimental subjects, help was provided quickly, regardless of the number of bystanders present

Number of Seconds Passing before Help Was Offered

No other bystanders   Four other bystanders   No other bystanders   Four other bystanders

Control Subjects   Subjects Who Were Shown First-aid Movies

Avoiding potential ridicule.   Another reason that groups inhibit prosocial acts is the **fear of social blunders.** In any emergency, in order to respond, a person must stop whatever he or she is doing and then engage in some unusual, unexpected, out-of-the-ordinary behavior. In the experiments just described, a helpful subject had to decide that something was wrong, remove the earphones, and go to another room to find the victim or the experimenter. When alone, most people decide to do all of this without much hesitation. If several strangers are present, the tendency is to hold back rather than make a mistake. What if you misunderstood the situation? What if the noises are only someone's idea of a joke? Generally, people feel that it is better to "keep your cool" and avoid being a naive, blundering Charlie Brown who gets laughed at. The result of this social caution is that the victim is likely not to be helped or to be helped less quickly.

In part, strangers are inhibiting because the subject does not know them well enough to communicate and thus reach consensus about the problem and how best to solve it. When the other bystanders know one another, there is much less inhibition on prosocial responses than is true of strangers (Latané &

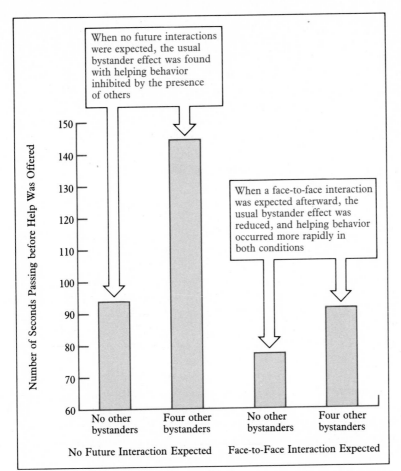

When no future interactions were expected, the usual bystander effect was found with helping behavior inhibited by the presence of others

When a face-to-face interaction was expected afterward, the usual bystander effect was reduced, and helping behavior occurred more rapidly in both conditions

Number of Seconds Passing before Help Was Offered

No other bystanders | Four other bystanders

No Future Interaction Expected

No other bystanders | Four other bystanders

Face-to-Face Interaction Expected

FIGURE 8.5 *Increasing the speed of prosocial responses: Expecting future contacts with fellow bystanders.*

The inhibitory effect of additional bystanders is decreased if the subject expects to interact with these strangers afterwards. It would seem that such interactions permit the individual to explain away any blunders and provide an incentive to avoid blame for failing to act. [Source: Based on data from Gottlieb & Carver, 1980.]

Rodin, 1969; Rutkowski et al., 1983). Even with strangers, it seems to matter whether there is the expectation of ever seeing them again (Yinon et al., 1982). When you see these individuals in the future, you will have the opportunity to explain your actions if you do make a fool of yourself. These variables were explored among female undergraduates by Gottlieb and Carver (1980), using the intercom discussion task once more. When the choking fit occurred, some believed they were alone as a bystander, and others believed that four additional strangers were present. Half the subjects believed that they would never meet their fellow participants, and half expected to interact afterward in a face-to-face session. Helping was faster in the two-person groups (the subject and the victim) than in the six-person groups (the subject, the victim, and four other bystanders), and the expectation of a future interaction increased the speed with which help was offered (see Figure 8.5). It seems that the bystander effect operates most strongly when the individuals involved are anonymous strangers who never expect to see one another again.

The Rewards and Punishments of Helping

It has been assumed by many theorists that people engage in altruistic behavior because such acts are rewarding. Essentially, prosocial acts make you feel good about yourself. Why should that be? There are several explanations for such a phenomenon. One possibility is that altruism is a built-in response tendency that has proven survival value (Cunningham, 1981). Thus, investigations reveal helping behavior in other species including zebras (Cunningham, 1981), birds (Brown et al., 1982), fish (Daniels, 1979), and even insects (Trivers & Hare, 1976). It is argued that cooperative behavior among related members of a species increases the odds of survival for the individual and for others representing a common gene pool (Axelrod & Hamilton, 1981). This line of reasoning leads to the conclusion that altruism is an integral part of human nature (Hoffman, 1981).

Even without a biological basis, it can be argued that prosocial behavior can lead to various kinds of rewards and hence can easily be learned (Grusec & Redler, 1980). Sometimes such acts result in punishment, and so individuals can learn to *avoid* helping others. Those alternate outcomes are depicted in Figure 8.6. Research designed to test this **reinforcement theory of prosocial behavior** has shown that the probability of helpful acts is affected by rewarding versus punishing outcomes to previous acts of altruism (McGovern et al., 1975; Moss & Page, 1972). Some altruistic acts (such as donating blood) can be very unpleasant and even anxiety-evoking for the person performing them. The greater the relief experienced by the individual after such an act, the more likely that person is to repeat it in the future. As a result, some individuals become "addicted" to particular types of altruism (Piliavin et al., 1982). In addition, if one is made uncomfortable by the distress of others, it can be a very positive experience to do something to relieve that distress. For example, when subjects are exposed to someone who appears to be receiving painful electric shocks, it is reinforcing to press a lever that seemingly shuts off the electricity (Weiss et al., 1971). As with other reinforced behaviors, the lever pressing

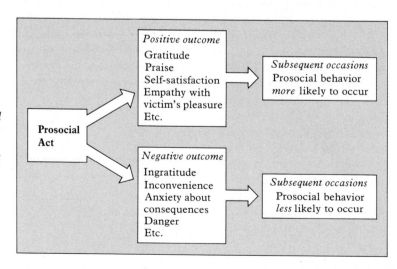

FIGURE 8.6   *Reinforcement theory:* When prosocial acts are rewarded or punished.

Reinforcement theory proposes that if prosocial behavior is rewarded, it will be more likely to occur in later situations. If it is not rewarded, and especially if it is punished, a prosocial act will be less likely to occur in later situations. Depending on the person's reinforcement history, he or she has learned to expect either positive or negative outcomes for acting in a prosocial way and hence will tend to engage in this kind of behavior or to avoid doing so.

Prosocial Act

Positive outcome
Gratitude
Praise
Self-satisfaction
Empathy with victim's pleasure
Etc.

Subsequent occasions
Prosocial behavior *more* likely to occur

Negative outcome
Ingratitude
Inconvenience
Anxiety about consequences
Danger
Etc.

Subsequent occasions
Prosocial behavior *less* likely to occur

becomes more and more rapid over a series of trials — except when the victim is someone who is disliked (Kelley & Byrne, 1976). It seems to be reinforcing only to help strangers or those we like (Pearce, 1980). We described in Chapter 6 the way in which liking is influenced by emotions. Since liking affects helping, it follows that one's emotional state would also affect helping. As will be seen in the **Focus on Research** box on pages 296–297, that is the case, but the relationship is more complex than you might expect.

The function of rewards becomes more complex when we consider cognitive activity. Human beings respond not only to simple external pleasures and pains but also to a set of beliefs, values, and expectancies about the consequences of what we do (Darley & Batson, 1973) or fail to do (Clark, 1976). Piliavin et al. (1981) suggest that the bystander who encounters an emergency must quickly weigh the positive and negative aspects of responding by using a kind of **bystander calculus.** If the costs (punishments) of providing help are greater than the benefits (rewards) of such behavior, the bystander is likely to pass the responsibility on to others, escape from the unpleasant situation, or misperceive what is going on, as in Figure 8.7. In a test of this cost–benefit

FIGURE 8.7   *Calculating the costs of altruism.*

When an individual encounters a stranger who is in need of help, there is a rapid calculation of the probable rewards and punishments associated with providing aid or failing to do so. The costs can be associated with the victim (for example, the person could be drunk or covered with blood) or with other demands on the bystander (for example, an appointment to keep or the desire to eat lunch). If the costs are too high, the bystander is likely to escape from the scene, let someone else take the responsibility, or decide that nothing is really wrong. On the other hand, if the victim is female and pretty, a man might decide that the rewards of helping outweigh the costs. [Source: Photo (left) © Joel Gordon 1974; photo (right) © Joel Gordon 1979.]

*Emotions and Attributions As
Determinants of Altruism*

It would seem to be obvious that an individual would be most motivated to engage in prosocial acts when he or she was in a positive mood (Cunningham et al., 1980). Similarly, negative feelings should lead to an unwillingness to help others. In fact, the research designed to test these propositions indicates that the process is more complicated than it appears.

Among the first such studies were investigations of generosity. When either children or adults succeed on a task, they give more money to a charitable cause afterward than when they have failed (Isen, 1970; Isen et al., 1973). Positive feelings also are found to increase the tendency to help a stranger in need (Yinon & Bizman, 1980). Isen and Levin (1972) manipulated subjects' mood in shopping malls by leaving dimes in the coin return slot in public telephones. The altruistic behavior of those who had just found money was compared with that of others who had not had such an experience. A female confederate waited near the phone booth and "accidentally" dropped a folder of papers as the caller emerged. Less than 5 percent of the shoppers who had not found money stopped to help the stranger. Among those who were happy about coming across a dime, almost 90 percent stopped and helped. These emotional effects are short-lived, sometimes lasting only a few minutes (Isen et al., 1976). Mood is also found to be affected by climate, and nice weather elicits a positive mood. Cunningham (1979) found that, as the amount of sunshine increased, helping behavior increased.

People even leave larger tips in restaurants on a sunny day than on a cloudy, rainy one.

As straightforward as such findings seem, other research indicates that positive feelings can sometimes lead to *less* helping behavior (Forest et al., 1980; Rosenhan et al., 1981). Some investigators suggest that a positive emotional state can result in perceiving oneself as having increased personal power: "I feel so good that nothing can stop me now." With that attitude, the individual may feel free to refuse to provide help to a stranger, especially if there are unpleasant aspects to helping. Thus, a positive mood can decrease the likelihood of engaging in embarrassing or dangerous prosocial acts.

The effects of negative feelings on helping have proven even more varied. Baumann et al. (1981) argue that sadness can increase helping because such behavior is gratifying and makes the helper feel less depressed. Various investigations indicate that a negative mood can inhibit altruism, facilitate it, or have no effect (Barden et al., 1981; Shelton & Rogers, 1981). The crucial factor seems to be whether the emotional state leads the person to focus on his or her own needs and concerns or on someone else's problems (Thompson et al., 1980). This difference in attentional focus was shown in an experiment in which subjects were told to imagine that a close friend was ill and dying. Some were instructed to think about their own reactions and others to think about how the friend must feel. The two groups were equally sad, but those who focused

model, the costs of helping were manipulated by Batson et al. (1978) for male subjects who had to go from one campus building to another to take part in an experiment. On the way, each subject encountered a young man slumped down in a doorway. The subjects could stop to help the stranger or continue on to keep the appointment. Costs were varied by means of instructions indicating that they had to hurry to make the deadline or that there was plenty of time, and

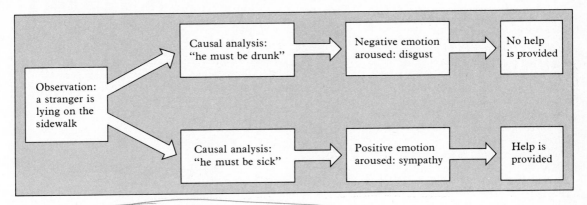

FIGURE 8.8   A causal analysis of emotions and helping.

Weiner (1980) has proposed that when we observe another person in need of help, we try to determine the cause of the problem. If we decide that the cause is internal and under that person's control, we react with negative emotions and thus reject the idea of helping. If we decide that the cause is beyond that person's control, we react positively and try to provide help.

on the friend's feelings were more helpful to a stranger afterward. In a similar way, self-focused attention (brought about by hearing a tape recording of one's own voice) interfered with prosocial behavior (Gibbons & Wicklund, 1982). It follows, therefore, that negative emotions can increase one's feelings of empathy for the plight of others (Thompson & Hoffman, 1980) *or* can create self-concern and disinterest in the needs of others. In addition, when an individual feels *personally responsible* for his or her negative mood, there is a greater willingness to help others (Rogers et al., 1982).

Still another factor influences emotions and helping. The potential helper must decide *why* another person needs help. Weiner (1980) suggests that a sequence of thoughts and emotions such as that shown in Figure 8.8 takes place. We observe a person in need, make an attribution as to the cause of the problem, experience either a positive or negative emotion based on our causal attribution, and then provide help or not as a function of the emotion. If someone seems to be in trouble because of internal, controllable causes, such as taking drugs, we are likely to react with disgust and let someone else handle the problem. When the difficulty is caused by events beyond the victim's control, such as a mugging, we feel sympathetic and try to help (Meyer & Mulherin, 1980).

It may be concluded, then, that the effect of emotional state on helping behavior is strongly influenced by the accompanying cognitions that include perceptions of personal power, whether attention is focused on self or on the victim, and on one's perception of the victim's difficulty and its causes.

by informing them of the high or low importance of their participation. As can be seen in Figure 8.9 on p. 298, as costs increased, the subjects were less and less inclined to stop and help the stranger. When the costs were lowest, eight out of ten students behaved altruistically, while only one in ten did so when costs were highest. It seems, then, that as costs vary, a person's willingness to help is strongly affected.

FIGURE 8.9 *As costs increase, altruism decreases.*

As the cost of helping goes up, altruism becomes less probable as a response. Subjects who passed a fellow student slumped down in a doorway were less likely to stop and help as the costs increased. Costs in this study involved the necessity to hurry to an experimental appointment and the stated importance of their participation. [Source: Data from Batson et al., 1978.]

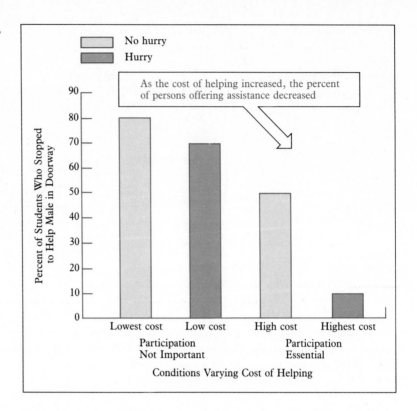

Those Who Help: Characteristics Affecting Altruism

Though we have described the powerful effects of the external situation on altruism, there are also some individual differences related to who will and will not provide help. The traditional focus has been on aspects of the individual's **character** such as conscience or **superego** (Freud, 1933) and the person's stage of moral development (Kohlberg, 1981; Piaget, 1932).

Kohlberg describes moral judgment as a series of stages that begin with the *preconventional level* in which a young child tries to do the right thing simply to avoid punishment and, later, to obtain rewards. By middle childhood, the *conventional level* is reached, and the individual tries to be a "good" boy or girl by rigidly adopting the rules of behavior provided by parents and others. In adolescence or adulthood, the *postconventional level* may be attained, and the individual is able to respond to abstract moral values and to adopt a set of ethical principles. Although age differences are associated with the various levels, specific individuals may never progress beyond the lower stages because of the absence of appropriate adult models or other factors that interfere. Moral growth is also most likely to occur if the individual actually faces moral dilemmas that involve cognitive dissonance. Presumably, dissonance reduction helps the person move toward higher levels of moral reasoning (Rholes et al., 1982). Though there is not much support for the generalized effects of a strong versus a weak superego on altruism, there is some evidence that differences in one's level of moral development are related to whether or not helping behavior occurs (Erkut et al., 1981). Most of the research interest, however, has been directed toward more limited aspects of individual differences.

Gender differences appear to depend on the nature of the situation and the kind of behavior required to provide help. Among children in the fifth and sixth grades, girls are perceived as more altruistic than boys, and these differences are reflected somewhat less strongly in their actual behavior (Shigetomi et al., 1981). Among adults, when someone drops a handful of coins or pencils in an elevator, help is more likely to be offered by male strangers to a female victim, especially in the southern portion of the United States (Latané & Dabbs, 1975). With a stalled car on the highway, the vast majority of those who stop to help are males, especially if the stranded motorist is a female (Pomazal & Clore, 1973; West et al., 1975). That same gender pattern is shown in response to hitchhikers: males stop to pick them up, especially to pick up a female (Pomazal & Clore, 1973; Snyder et al., 1974). In such situations, it seems possible that altruistic behavior may be serving romantic motives as well as prosocial ones.

Since one explanation of the failure to help is the fear of social blunders, McGovern (1976) predicted that those who score high on a "fear of embarrassment" test would be less likely to help a stranger in distress than those low in this fear. That prediction was confirmed, and once again it appears that altruistic responses can be inhibited by one's desire not to appear foolish in the eyes of others. Political ideology is found to influence the attributions made about why help is needed. Poverty, for example, is perceived by those on the political right as the result of either fate or the individual's own failings. On the political left, poverty is attributed to government policies and the acts of certain economic powers (Pandey et al., 1982). The former attributions lead to the conclusion that nothing can be done, while the latter attributions suggest actions to relieve the situation.

The strong desire to win praise and acceptance from others is known as the **need for approval.** Generally, prosocial behavior tends to elicit approving responses from others. With respect to a charity request, subjects gave more money when others were watching than when alone, and those high in need for approval gave more than those low in this need only when there were witnesses (Satow, 1975). Such findings suggest that, for some of us, prosocial acts provide a way to win praise. In contrast, those who hold strong religious values based on intrinsic motives tend to be helpful to others even when help is not requested. (Batson & Gray, 1981).

A great deal of the research on individual differences in providing help has dealt with **dispositional empathy** — the tendency to respond to the world from the perspective of others. The role of empathy in helping (Archer et al., 1981; Coke et al., 1978) is outlined in Figure 8.10 on p. 300. Archer et al. (1981) exposed subjects to a broadcast that indicated a person's need for help. Those subjects who were high in dispositional empathy and who in the presence of an experimenter received false feedback indicating they were aroused during the broadcast volunteered the greatest amount of their time to help the victim. Empathic emotional arousal is less likely to occur among **sociopathic** individ-

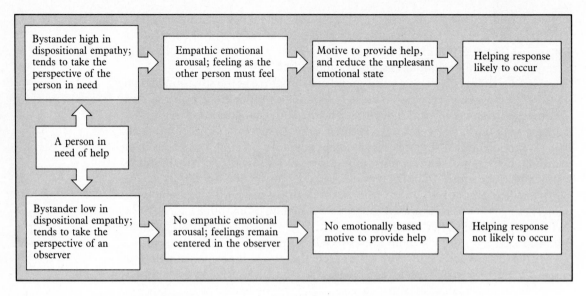

FIGURE 8.10   *Empathy and empathic arousal as motivators of helping behavior.*

It has been proposed that empathy plays an important role in influencing helping behavior. Dispositional empathy leads one to see the world from the victim's perspective, thus facilitating empathic emotional arousal. Such arousal is unpleasant and hence motivates the individual to provide help. Helping tends to reduce the uncomfortable arousal.

uals—those with antisocial tendencies whose feelings are self-centered (Marks et al., 1982). Some of these variables affecting helping behavior are summarized in Table 8.1.

Empathic tendencies can be manipulated by instructions to observe the victim versus instructions to try to imagine how the victim is feeling. The latter set leads to a high rate of helping behavior (Toi & Batson, 1982). In addition, empathy toward a victim is increased by information indicating similarities between victim and observer; this manipulation also leads to an increase in helping behavior (Batson et al., 1981).

Empathy is a sufficiently important component of prosocial behavior that considerable attention has been directed at determining how it develops or fails to develop in childhood (see Figure 8.11). Since identical twins are more similar in empathic concern than are fraternal twins, it appears that this tendency is at least partly hereditary (Matthews et al., 1981). Even newborn infants cry in response to the sound of another infant crying, but they show no such response to the sounds of their own crying, a chimpanzee, or an eleven-month-old child (Martin & Clark, 1981). It also seems well established that the motive to help increases with age throughout childhood (Bar-Tal et al., 1980; Berndt, 1981) and that adults value altruism more than do children (Suls et al., 1981). In part, older children behave more altruistically because they feel more competent and more responsible (Peterson, 1983). Of greatest concern are investigations showing that empathy depends in part on the child's early experiences. For one

TABLE 8.1   *Identifying those who help: Individual differences in prosocial behavior.*

Some of the research on helping behavior has identified particular characteristics that are associated with the likelihood of a bystander coming to the aid of a stranger in need.

Sex Differences

Among children, girls are somewhat more altruistic than boys.

Among adults, help is more likely to be offered by a male stranger to a female victim.

Personality Differences

Those high in fear of embarrassment are less likely to help.

Those high in sociopathic tendencies are less likely to help.

Those high in need for approval are more likely to help (if there are witnesses to their good deeds).

Those with strong religious values based on intrinsic motives are more likely to help.

Those high in empathy are more likely to help.

thing, empathy is found to be very low among abused children (Straker & Jacobson, 1981) and among those who are spanked a great deal by their fathers (Roe, 1980). Empathic females report more affection from their parents and more discussions of feelings with their mothers than do females low in empathy (Barnett et al., 1980). Finally, it is found that prosocial behavior is influenced by the kind of games children play. Kindergarten pupils who were in a cooperative games program for eighteen weeks showed more altruistic behavior afterward than did those who played a comparable number of traditional competitive

FIGURE 8.11   *Empathic concern is expressed early in life.*

The tendency to be empathic and to experience discomfort when others are distressed is apparently developed in early childhood. There is also some evidence of a genetic component to this trait. [Source: Photo © Joel Gordon 1976.]

games (Orlick, 1981). In summary, the determinants of empathy and altruism range from heredity to child-rearing practices to culturally sanctioned socialization activities.

Those Who Are Helped and Their Reactions to Aid

Though much of the research on altruism has concentrated on helpers and potential helpers, the victim also plays a role in this type of interaction. For example, similarity seems to be important. When females asked strangers for a dime to make a telephone call, their clothing influenced the probability of receiving the money. When well-dressed, they were more likely to receive a dime from well-dressed strangers (in an airport); when poorly dressed, the request was more successful with poorly dressed strangers (in a bus terminal) (Hensley, 1981). Further, someone who is potentially able to be a future provider of help receives more aid than someone who is not perceived as being able to reciprocate (Yinon et al., 1981).

Interestingly, people are more willing to ask for help from someone who is physically unattractive than from an attractive stranger (Nadler, 1980); the one exception is that females seek help from an attractive male more than from an unattractive one (Nadler et al., 1982). It is also found that those who are most willing to ask for help are individuals who are relatively insensitive to covert emotional cues present in potential helpers. That is, they accept the polite overt signs of helpfulness and ignore nonverbal cues indicating that the helper feels annoyed and inconvenienced (DePaulo & Fisher, 1981).

Though it might seem that someone who *needs* help would very much desire to be helped and would be extremely grateful for any aid received, the situation is more complex than that. Actually, most people do not like to ask for help (Broll et al., 1974) and feel that they will be viewed as less competent if they accept it (DePaulo & Fisher, 1980). In a sort of reverse bystander effect, as the number of potential helpers increases, help seeking is inhibited (Williams & Williams, 1983). Feelings of embarrassment and incompetence probably explain why help is more likely to be sought when the problem has an external source ("It's not my fault.") than when it is internally attributed (La Morto-Corse & Carver, 1980). Even the receipt of a gift can lead to discomfort, unless it is possible to reciprocate (Gergen et al., 1975). This need to "pay back" is also found with respect to helping behavior: those who are helped feel obligated to help someone else (Wilke & Lanzetta, 1982), as Priscilla assumes in Figure 8.12.

In receiving aid, most people prefer that it come from a friend or a similar stranger than from an enemy or a dissimilar stranger (Clark et al., 1974; Nadler et al., 1976). Nevertheless, help from a friend or similar stranger is more threatening to one's self-esteem (DePaulo et al., 1981; Fisher et al., 1978), especially if the task requires important skills such as intelligence or creativity (Nadler et al., 1983). In turn, the self-esteem of the one who provides aid tends to go up, especially if the victim badly needs help (Fisher et al., 1981). The importance of threats to self-esteem has been explored in some detail by Fisher et al. (1982), and they have come to a somewhat surprising conclusion. When self-esteem is threatened by aid, the victim responds with negative feelings and dislikes the helper as well as the aid, *but* there is a strong motive to help oneself

FIGURE 8.12 *Reciprocity: A basic rule of helping.*

A gift or a helpful action often implies that the recipient will reciprocate. For that reason, those who receive aid can feel uncomfortable unless there is an opportunity to pay back the one who provides help. [Source: © 1974 NEA, Inc. Reprinted by permission.]

in the future. When self-esteem is not threatened, the victim has positive feelings and likes the helper and the aid, but future self-help behavior becomes very unlikely. This series of reactions is summarized in the model in Figure 8.13.

One implication of such findings is that those who provide aid in the form of assistance to other nations, welfare for those in need, etc., must face a curious choice. They might consider whether they want the recipient to feel happy and express gratitude though becoming dependent, or to feel unhappy, ungrateful,

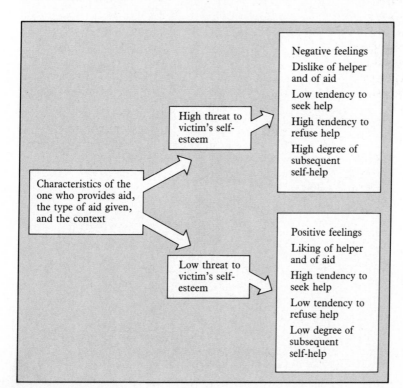

FIGURE 8.13 *Reactions to aid: Threat, affect, and self-help.*

A model showing how relative threat to the victim's self-esteem can result in quite different reactions was developed by Fisher et al. (1982). High threat leads to negative responses except for the fact that the victim tends to engage in self-help afterward. Low threat leads to positive responses but little self-help behavior afterward.

and motivated to take personal responsibility. Consistent with these research findings is some ancient Hindu advice to those who need help: "The mind of the men who receive gifts is acted on by the mind of the giver, so the receiver is likely to become degenerate. Receiving gifts is prone to destroy the independence of mind and encourage slavishness. Therefore accept no gifts" (quoted in Nadler & Fisher, 1982).

Intervening to Stop a Wrongdoer As a Prosocial Act

When we shift attention from altruistic behavior that helps someone in need to deterrent behavior that interferes with the misdeeds of a wrongdoer, the consequences of behaving in a prosocial fashion become somewhat more complicated (see Figure 8.14). In such a situation, any action or failure to act

FIGURE 8.14   *Deciding to intervene in a crime: The most difficult prosocial choice.*

The witness to an illegal act must make difficult decisions with respect to whether to take any action. He or she can (1) ignore the wrongdoing, (2) report the situation to the police or others who can take responsibility, or (3) interfere personally to stop the crime. The first choice helps the wrongdoer and does harm to the victim. The other two choices help the victim, bring harm to the wrongdoer, and involve the risk of retaliation. [Source: Photo © Arthur Tress 1981 / Woodfin Camp and Associates.]

either helps the wrongdoer and hurts the victim or the reverse. In addition, the prosocial individual who directly interferes or reports the illegal act to those in authority becomes open to the risk of retaliation. It is not difficult to find examples of instances in the daily papers that describe both failures to act and courageous interventions.

> In New York City on a bright November morning, a 25-year-old obstetrics nurse ran along a busy street screaming for help as her attacker chased her. One witness saw part of the chase out of her apartment window but went back to her chores when the young woman and her pursuer were out of sight. A deliveryman had to swerve to miss her as she ran in front of his truck. At one point, the nurse ran up to a man in his parked car and begged for help. She was pulled away by the attacker, and the man drove away. Shortly afterward, she was shot to death and her body set on fire in an abandoned building (condensed from an article in the *New York Times,* February 27, 1980).
>
> In Nashville, Tennessee, a thief reached into the car of a supermarket cashier, grabbed a sack containing over a thousand dollars, and ran off. Several other motorists saw the incident and began chasing the thief with their cars, trying to run him down. One of them was driven by a fiercely determined elderly woman. Then, a large man with a gun ordered the frightened robber to lie down on the pavement. Seeing a policeman nearby, the thief called out for help, "Save me! They're trying to kill me!" (condensed from an article in the *Albany Times-Union,* May 31, 1981).
>
> In New Bedford, Massachusetts, a woman was forced onto a pool table in Big Dan's Tavern and repeatedly raped by four men. The other patrons of the bar did nothing to stop the attack and did not even bother to call the police to come to the woman's rescue. Still more chilling, two of the bystanders shouted encouragement to the rapists and actually helped them hold down their victim (condensed from an article in *Newsweek,* March 28, 1983).

We will examine some of the variables that determine how those who witness a wrongdoing are likely to respond.

Once Again, the Bystander Effect

Just as in other emergency situations involving a stranger in need, the responses of witnesses to a crime have been found to be inhibited by the presence of other bystanders. Latané and Darley (1970) placed male under-graduates in a situation in which they believed they were simply waiting to be interviewed when a confederate quietly stole $40 from the receptionist's desk. The subject was either the only witness to the theft or one of two bystanders. In both conditions, the majority of the students neither said anything to the thief nor reported the incident to the receptionist. There was, however, more reporting of the crime when the subject was the sole witness. Despite the obviousness of the crime, the reluctant witnesses later said that they didn't notice it, thought the thief was only making change, or believed the money somehow got into his pocket by accident. In this and other studies of wrongdoing (Howard & Crana, 1974), the bystander effect is found in operation, and bystanders find it easy to remain passive, nonresponsive witnesses. There is, of course, a certain amount of ambiguity in these unexpected experiences; witnesses are more likely to do something if the victim makes it clear that a theft has occurred (DeJong et al., 1980).

Surprisingly, a helpful response to an incidence of violence is greater than response to a simple theft. Schwartz and Gottlieb (1980) arranged an experimental situation in which subjects believed they were participating in a study of ESP. They watched a TV screen depicting a confederate who was supposed to be sending pictures via ESP to another subject. Afterward, a questionnaire had to be filled out, and the subject was free to leave. The experimenter went away during the session, but a telephone number indicated where she could be reached. After several minutes of observation, the subject's TV monitor revealed a large, roughly dressed stranger enter the confederate's room, talk for a few minutes, and then start to leave after stealing an expensive pocket calculator. A violent argument followed, and the stranger attacked the confederate. He threw him against the wall, punched him repeatedly in the stomach, knocked him to the floor, and left him doubled up in apparent pain after kicking him several times. Half of the subjects believed that the ESP recipient could also see the attack, and half believed themselves to be the sole witness. Concealed cameras made it obvious that almost all of the subjects reacted to the emergency with concern. A total of 89 percent of the subjects responded to the emergency, and the type of help given was unrelated to the presence of another bystander or to the subject's gender. As the attacker was leaving, 33 percent went to aid the victim, 31 percent called the experimenter, and 25 percent rushed to try to confront the attacker. The bystander effect was shown in one respect, however; subjects responded more quickly when they were alone than when they believed themselves to be one of two bystanders.

Intervention in actual dangerous situations such as muggings, armed robbery, and bank holdups was studied by Huston et al. (1981). Individuals who had intervened in such crimes were interviewed and compared with a matched group of individuals who had failed to intervene in crimes. The major difference between the two groups appeared to be that interveners were more competent to deal with such situations. As shown in Figure 8.15, those who had intervened to stop a crime were much more likely to have had some form of training that involved dealing with emergencies. In addition, those who responded to crimes were taller and heavier and more likely to describe themselves as strong, aggressive, emotional, and principled. Thus, response to a violent crime is more probable if the individual is physically able to handle the wrongdoer, emotionally predisposed to action, and has had the appropriate training.

Judgments as to the morality of reporting and failing to report a crime are affected by how serious the crime is (Himmelfarb, 1980). The more serious the crime (for example, rape and homicide), the more morally right it is judged to be to report it. Those who report nonserious crimes (for example, vagrancy and receiving stolen goods) are perceived as moral, but they are not well liked. It appears that many individuals view these responses in the way that children react to the messages of "tattle tales." As is described in the **Applied Side**

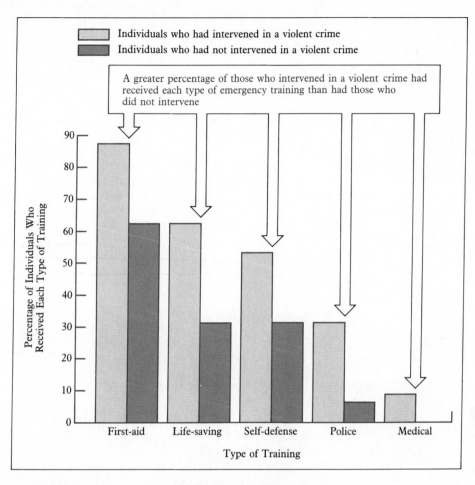

FIGURE 8.15   *Competence and response to a violent crime.*

A comparison of individuals who had intervened in actual instances of violent crime with individuals who failed to intervene revealed considerable differences in emergency training. Besides being well-trained to deal with various situations, those who intervened were found to be taller and heavier than noninterveners. Thus, those best able to deal with a criminal physically and best prepared to provide aid to a victim were the ones who took action. [Source: Based on data from Huston et al., 1981.]

section on pages 308–310, shoplifters are often viewed as having committed a nonserious offense and hence tend not to be informed on. It should be added that, in general, intentional transgressions are judged more negatively than accidental ones (Manstead & Semin, 1981).

Responsibility and Commitment: The Ultimate Motivation to Act

In various ways we have seen that people are most likely to respond in a prosocial way if they feel *responsible* for taking action. That is, those most likely

ON THE
APPLIED SIDE

What to Do about Shoplifters

All of us are victims of the crime of shoplifting. The cost of the stolen goods is simply passed on to the honest customers in the form of higher prices. In 1981, retailers estimated losses of 20 billion dollars to crime, with about half of that amount associated with shoplifting (Associated Press, September 13, 1981). Stealing merchandise from stores has reached epidemic proportions, and FBI statistics indicate that it has tripled in frequency in the United States over the past ten years (Klentz & Beaman, 1981). The odd thing is that most people

who see someone commit this kind of theft respond by doing nothing about it. In one study, there were forty instances of observed shoplifting in a supermarket, but only eight of these were reported (M. Harris, 1980). Interestingly, shabbily dressed thieves were reported more often than well-dressed ones (see Figure 8.16). It is as though people decide that if someone looks prosperous enough, it is all right for them to steal food. It is also found that this crime is more likely to be reported by individuals raised in small towns or rural areas than by those

FIGURE 8.16 *Shoplifters are seldom reported, especially if they are well-dressed.*

Though shoplifting ordinarily goes unreported in the majority of instances, one investigation found that shabbily dressed female shoplifters (right) were turned in more often than well-dressed ones (left). Overall, only 20 percent of the incidents were reported by other customers (Harris, 1980). [Source: Photo (left) © Bohdan Hrynewych / Southern Light; photo (right) © Frank Siteman 1983.]

raised in cities of 100,000 or more (Gelfand et al., 1973). It appears that, in small communities, the citizens are more dependent on one another to provide help when emergencies arise. The problem for retailers (and for each of us) is how to induce more people to respond like those raised in sparsely populated areas.

In attempting to increase the incidence of reporting this crime and thus to cut down on or eliminate shoplifting, merchants and experimenters have undertaken various approaches. One seemingly obvious solution is to set up reflecting mirrors and surveillance cameras that scan various sections of a store, and to use merchandise tags that set off an alarm if they are carried past a detection device at the door. The problem with this technological approach is that it makes the average customer feel uncomfortable, irritated, and powerless. Further, these devices can actually lead to an *increase* in shoplifting according to research conducted by Mills (1981). "Some people see the devices as a challenge. Their resentment toward the security program may, in some cases, be redirected at the stores in the form of deviant, illegal acts—shoplifting, price altering, vandalism, damaging merchandise, consumer fraud and the like" (Mills, p. E–14).

As with many types of crime, the most effective law enforcement procedure is a cooperative public. Since most of us are honest and since there are more ordinary citizens than there are security guards and police, it is our deterrent actions that provide the surest way to crime prevention and law enforcement. Field experiments have shown that the majority of shoppers will inform the management of a thief's activities if a fellow shopper (an experimental confederate) just reminds them of the right thing to do. Simple statements from a stranger such as "We should report it. It's our responsibility" were sufficient to persuade people to take action (Bickman & Rosenbaum, 1977). Even the victim of a crime is more likely to call the police if a bystander suggests that this be done (Ruback et al., 1979). Since it is not practical to station experimental confederates in every store in the land, how else might people be reminded of the right thing to do?

Over the past decade, many programs have been instituted in an attempt to increase the num-

ber of people actively involved in crime reporting. You may have read about such plans as Neighborhood Crime Watch or viewed Officer Friendly spots on television. With respect to shoplifting, campaigns using posters as reminders or mass media messages about the importance of informing on these criminals have been found to affect *attitudes* about shoplifting and *attitudes* about the act of reporting; nevertheless, there is no change in actual behavior (Bickman, 1975; Bickman & Green, 1977). In an expanded approach, Klentz and Beaman (1981) compared the effects of messages about how and why to report a shoplifter with messages about the social-psychological factors that inhibit an individual from reporting (such as diffusion of responsibility). In their experiment, the conditions consisted of information about reporting, information about inhibiting factors, a combination of the two kinds of information, and a control message about obesity and emotions. These investigators also compared the effectiveness of presenting such information in a lecture versus the use of written material. Approximately two weeks later, each subject was exposed to a staged shoplifting by a female confederate at the university bookstore. The behavior of interest was whether each subject did something about the crime or ignored it. Action could include telling the shoplifter to put the item back or reporting the incident to someone in authority. Of those who responded to the crime, 40 percent talked to the thief and 60 percent reported the crime to someone else. Altogether, only about one student in five acted to stop the crime, but the probability of taking action was strongly influenced by the experimental procedures, as summarized in Figure 8.17 on p. 310. The most effective method to increase the number of responsive customers was the presentation of a lecture about how and why to report this crime *and* the reasons that bystanders are usually inhibited about taking action. It was also found that males and females did not differ in responding to shoplifters.

Clearly, it is possible to bring about behavioral changes by exposing the public to appropriate information. Such exposure is followed by increases in the percentage of incidents that are halted by a bystander's actions. It will also be interesting to see if future research can find even more successful ways to induce citizens to report crimes. For exam-

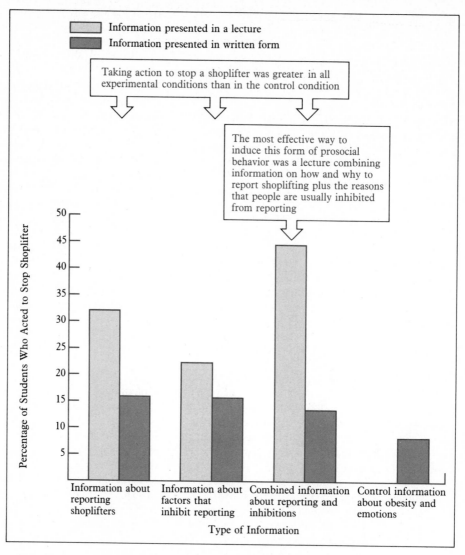

FIGURE 8.17   *Inducing customers to report a shoplifter.*

The incidence of responding to a shoplifter can be greatly increased by the presentation of information about how and why to respond and / or about why bystanders tend not to report such crimes. The most effective procedure was found to be a lecture that combined both types of information. [Source: Based on data from Klentz & Beaman, 1981.]

ple, if dramatic television spots depicted the observation of a shoplifter and the way in which observers felt inhibited but took appropriate action even so, perhaps a larger percentage of individuals would be induced to act. It is also quite possible that since you have now read about this research, you yourself might be more likely to do something the next time you notice someone engaging in the act of shoplifting.

to act are those who are in the position of being the only observer of an incident, those who are most competent to take action, those who have been reminded of their responsibilities, and so forth. What if this feeling of responsibility is manipulated directly?

Moriarty (1975) proposed that a **prior commitment** to take responsibility should greatly increase the probability of responding. On a crowded beach near New York City a confederate selected individuals who were sitting alone to serve as subjects. He placed his own blanket near that of the subject and turned his portable radio to a local rock station. A few minutes later, he spoke to the subject and either asked for a match or said, "Excuse me, I'm going to the boardwalk for a few minutes. Would you watch my things?" All of the subjects agreed to perform that favor, thus committing themselves in advance as responsible bystanders. In both conditions, the confederate then walked away, and a second experimenter approached. This person picked up the radio and hurriedly walked away with it. Would the subject respond to this blatant theft? The results of prior commitment were astonishing. Of those subjects who had simply been asked for a match, only 20 percent did anything about the stolen radio. Among those who had agreed to be responsible, 95 percent took action! They stood up, ran after the thief, accosted him, and some even grabbed him in order to rescue the radio. It seems that when people agree beforehand to take charge, they do so with a vengeance.

The effect of prior commitment has been demonstrated in several other settings ranging from watching a stranger's suitcase in an automat (Moriarty, 1975) to watching a fellow student's belongings in a library (Shaffer et al., 1975) or in a classroom (Austin, 1979). The idea that most of us are indifferent to the suffering of others or apathetic about the victims of crime does not appear to be true. All we need is a nudge toward assuming responsibility in order to behave prosocially. At that point, most of us find that we are indeed responsible citizens.

Resisting Temptation: The Ability to Sacrifice Immediate Gains

In everyday life we are constantly faced with choices that involve doing the right thing versus taking the easy way out by cheating, lying, stealing, or otherwise gaining some immediate reward in an unethical or illegal manner. The temptation to do the wrong thing can be very strong. In a large-scale survey involving over 24,000 respondents, surprisingly large percentages indicated that they had engaged in such behavior (Hassett, 1981). Some of the unethical and illegal acts they reported are shown in Figure 8.18 on p. 312. The same subjects also indicated that, if the opportunity arose, they would also do such things as driving away without telling the owner they had damaged his or her car (44 percent), keep an extra $10 change if a supermarket clerk made an error (26 percent), or buy a TV set they knew to be stolen (22 percent). These findings are disturbing but not at all isolated. For example, a study of nurses revealed that an average of twenty-five minutes a week is stolen by employees

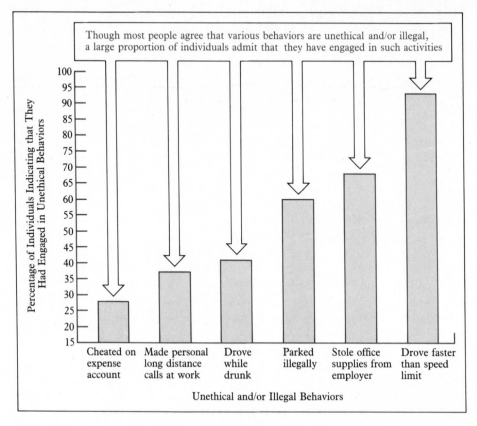

FIGURE 8.18   *Unethical behavior: A common occurrence.*

In a large-scale survey, a surprisingly large proportion of the respondents admitted engaging in a variety of activities that they knew to be wrong. [Source: Based on data from Hassett, 1981.]

taking longer work breaks than were authorized (Jones, 1981). What do we know about the conditions under which temptation is or is not resisted?

The Lure of Nonviolent Crime

Studying those who engage in major crimes such as murder or drug offenses suggests that personality characteristics are correlated with this kind of behavior (Laufer et al., 1981). With nonviolent crimes, the situation seems to play a major role with individuals deciding whether to act on the basis of the benefits to be gained, the probability of getting caught, and the costs involved if one's misdeeds are in fact discovered.

In an examination of data on actual nonviolent crimes, Lockard et al. (1980) found that fraud (an illegal act involving deceit such as lying about a product or property one is selling) seems to be popular. There is a low risk of indictment, a low penalty, and a high potential gain. This crime is practiced both in large cities and in rural areas. With respect to stolen property, the possible benefits are far exceeded by the high risks involved in getting caught, convicted, and punished. Those who steal property are primarily young males, but fraud is practiced by both men and women from about age twenty to sixty. In other words, as one matures, the assessment of costs and benefits leads to less risky crimes as the most tempting.

Tax evasion by means of lying or withholding information is a very common illegal act. In the Hassett (1981) survey mentioned earlier, 38 percent of the respondents admitted to having cheated on their tax returns. Among U.S. taxpayers who are audited by the Internal Revenue Service (IRS), 69 percent are found to owe the government additional money. In a laboratory simulation procedure in which tax returns were submitted, Friedland (1982) found that most subjects were willing to cheat but that such behavior decreased when the probability of being audited increased. Though the magnitude of the fines also affected this behavior, the greatest deterrent was the probability of getting caught. It is interesting to note that many tax evaders experience guilt at what they feel was the wrong thing to have done. The U.S. Treasury maintains a fund that consists of money sent in (usually anonymously) by tax cheats who want to make up for their past misdeeds. To date, over four million dollars have been sent in by those who wish to repay the government (Shribman, 1981). Those who write notes indicate feelings of guilt, the power of new-found religious faith, and the inability to sleep. One anonymous person sent in $50 with the message, "We hope you are more honest about this money than we were." The note was written on a commercial greeting card that read:

A cheerful reminder to let you know
I think of you often.

Cheating in School: The Students' Temptation

Have you ever copied someone else's answers on an exam or passed off someone else's term paper as your own original work? Sadly enough, if your reply is "no," you are in the minority. Hassett's (1981) survey found that 67 percent admitted cheating in school, and a 1978 Gallup youth survey yielded a similar figure (62 percent). Cheating is done more by males than females. Those with average grades or below cheat more than those who have above-average grades, but intelligence is unrelated to cheating (Johnson & Gormly, 1972). Besides the unethical aspects of cheating, those who steal grades in this manner are not only totally wasting their time in school but are unfairly lowering the grades of honest students. When you allow others to cheat without reporting their behavior, your response is no different than the situation in which you stand idly by as a thief gets away with his or her crime. It is worth considering one other aspect of cheating. You may one day find yourself driving across a bridge designed by an individual who cheated on his engineering school exams, or you may have a cavity filled by a dentist who was only able to pass dental school by copying the answers of a friend. Under such circumstances, would you be better off if someone had stopped their cheating and exposed their incompetence? In any event, you might be interested in learning who is most likely to cheat, under what conditions this behavior is most likely to occur, and (in the **Applied Side** section on pp. 314–315) what can be done to decrease such behavior (see Figure 8.20 on p. 316).

ON THE APPLIED SIDE *How Can Cheating Be Stopped?*

There are two major approaches that have been shown to be effective in reducing classroom cheating. First, there are attempts to alter the situation in a way that increases the perceived probability of getting caught. That is, perceived risk can be manipulated. As with many other unethical acts, the probability of being apprehended is relatively low, so cheaters are not strongly deterred by this fear. Of those who admit to having cheated, only 20 percent have ever been caught (Gallup, 1978). Interestingly enough, another survey indicated that only 20 percent of those who cheat ever fear getting caught (Norman & Harris, 1982). With low risk and little fear, high rates of cheating seem likely to continue. Heisler (1974) was able to increase the perceived risk and the resultant fear dramatically in a college class by staging a scene in which a confederate in the class cheated and then was "caught" by the instructor. This incident was followed by a decrease in cheating. Perhaps additional ways could be devised to convince students that cheating is risky and that severe penalties will actually be applied.

A second approach involves attempts to change the individuals who are tempted to cheat by raising their feelings of guilt. It has been found that 42 percent of those who cheat feel guilty afterward and another 11 percent feel guilty if the test or paper is an important one (Norman & Harris, 1982). Such findings suggest that attempts to impart increased ethical awareness might be effective in altering classroom cheating. As a consequence, many schools are offering ethics courses in an attempt to influence the present and future behavior of students (Britell, 1981; Hechinger, 1980).

In a series of experiments designed to test this general approach, Dienstbier et al. (1980) administered a vocabulary test to students, followed by reading materials dealing with moral theories. Some read about moral behavior as a response to fear of external punishment, while others read that such behavior is a response to internally generated guilt. Those in the externally oriented condition read that:

> After being scolded or punished a number of times by parents or others, the child begins to experience emotional tension when considering the possibility of being found violating the moral rules about things such as lying, cheating, or stealing . . . the individual will resist temptation to avoid the emotional tension which is tied to the risk of being found out . . . as we mature, the pleasure which we anticipate from others knowing that we have acted morally correct remains a strong motivating force in helping us to be strong in the face of temptation . . . research has demonstrated that often very strong feelings of emotional tension result when other people who are important to us discover and confront us over violations of moral values.

In contrast, those in the internally oriented condition read that:

> Even if the child has never been scolded or punished by parents, the child may begin to experience emotional tension when considering the violation of moral rules about things such as lying, cheating, or stealing . . . the individual will resist temptation to avoid the emotional tension even though no one else may ever know of the transgression . . . as we mature, the pleasure which we anticipate from knowing that we have acted morally correct remains a strong motivating force in helping us to be strong in the face of temptation . . . . Research has demonstrated that often very strong feelings

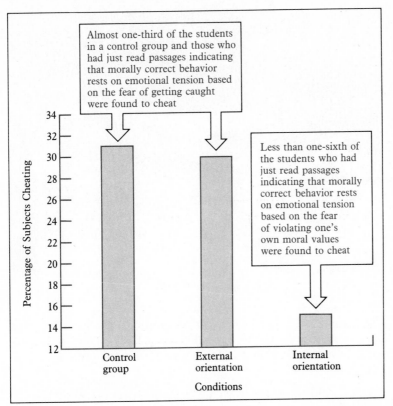

Almost one-third of the students in a control group and those who had just read passages indicating that morally correct behavior rests on emotional tension based on the fear of getting caught were found to cheat

Less than one-sixth of the students who had just read passages indicating that morally correct behavior rests on emotional tension based on the fear of violating one's own moral values were found to cheat

Percentage of Subjects Cheating

Control group External orientation Internal orientation

Conditions

FIGURE 8.19 *The reduction of cheating behavior: Guilt versus fear of being apprehended.*

Students in two experimental groups read passages that described morally correct behavior either as an externally oriented matter (fear of getting caught) or as an internally oriented matter (fear of violating one's own standards). Compared to a control group, cheating behavior decreased only among subjects exposed to the message stressing an internal orientation. [Source: Based on data from Dienstbier et al., 1980.]

of emotional tension result from individuals violating their own moral values, even though other people important to them do not know of those violations (Dienstbier et al., 1980, p. 210).

At this point, the students had the opportunity to cheat. They were given the correct answers and warned not to change any of their responses. During the next minute and a half, the experimenter was supposedly busy with a telephone call, making it relatively easy to cheat, apparently without being detected. Actually, there was a sheet of pressure-sensitive paper hidden in the test booklet so that any changed answers could be readily identified.

As shown in Figure 8.19, among students in the internally oriented guilt condition, cheating after

reading the material was half that in the condition involving externally oriented fear of detection. The latter group did not differ from the control group in amount of cheating. These investigators suggest that their procedure was effective because most of the students already possessed the appropriate moral schemas; they only needed a slight reminder to activate them.

It would be hoped that a variety of ways can be found to remind people that they desire to think of themselves as honest, ethical, and moral individuals. Perhaps it is easier to resist temptation if one realizes that the unethical behavior indicates a very different self-conception than the one they desire to have.

FIGURE 8.20 *The temptation to cheat: Immaturity, pressure, absence of guilt.*

The majority of American teenagers report having cheated in school. The ability to resist this temptation is in part a matter of personality characteristics, in part a matter of the situation, and in part a matter of whether ethical behavior is made salient. [Source: Photo © Marcia Weinstein 1981.]

Who cheats? When asked why they cheat, teenagers tend to say that others are doing it so "you have to protect yourself" (Gallup, 1978). There's also the admission that it's easier than studying and that it saves time (Norman & Harris, 1982). One high school student said:

> Cheating on tests and reports leaves hardly any guilt on my conscious (sic). There is always the pressure to excel to make high grades, and even if I'm prepared for an exam, I may cheat anyway. . . . Students cheat openly and obviously and many teachers do little or nothing about it. In short, I do it because I can get away with it.

In fact, however, not everyone cheats. Those who do so are found to be different along several personality dimensions from those who do not. For example, cheaters have been shown to be low in the ability to delay gratification (Yates & Mischel, 1979), high in sociopathic tendencies (Lueger, 1980), high in need for approval (Millham, 1974), low in interpersonal trust (Rotter, 1980), and high in chronic self-destructive tendencies (Kelley et al., 1983). Altogether, those who cheat tend to be emotionally and morally immature and unable to sacrifice short-term pleasures in order to obtain future rewards. When college students are placed in a situation in which a high level of effort is rewarded, they are more likely to work hard and less likely to cheat when performing later tasks) (Eisenberger & Masterson, 1983). Such findings suggest that when hard work is reinforced, generalization to other situations results in greater persistence and increased honesty.

In view of the personality characteristics associated with cheating, it is perhaps not surprising that those students who cheat on exams are also more likely to violate the law in ways varying from traffic offenses to burglary and rape (Heisler, 1974). There are some other findings that do not fit this pattern very well. In a Navy ROTC class, cheaters were found to be more socially active, to belong to more clubs, to hold more leadership positions, and to plan to become career officers to a greater extent than noncheaters (Johnson & Gormly, 1971). It is possible that cheating in a military setting does not rest on the same determinants as cheating elsewhere.

Cheating and arousal. The external situation has been found to play a role in cheating. When there is relatively low risk of detection, the chance to break the rules can be exciting. What risk there is simply "adds a thrill no different from a rock climber's thrill when he exposes himself to physical danger equally remote" (Scitovsky, 1980, p. 13). In addition, Lueger (1980) has proposed that any sort of arousal leads us to become distracted and less able to regulate our behavior. He presented adolescent boys with the opportunity to cheat on an intelligence test. Just before the test, they viewed either a relaxation film or an arousing one dealing with the effects of cigarette smoking. In the relaxed control condition, 43 percent cheated, while in the aroused group 70 percent cheated.

The effect of arousal could explain why cheating was found to *increase* in response to a pretest announcement concerning the severe punishment for those caught cheating — suspension from college (Heisler, 1974). The pressure for grades, competition with fellow students, and fear of academic failure might also add to students' arousal level and hence to increased cheating.

Summary

Prosocial behavior refers to acts that have no obvious benefits for the individual who carries them out and may even involve risk or some degree of sacrifice. Such acts benefit others, and they are based on ethical standards of behavior.

When emergencies arise that involve a stranger in need of help, aid is less likely to be provided (or to be provided less quickly) as the number of potential helpers increases. This phenomenon is known as the **bystander effect.** Among the explanations of the inaction of multiple bystanders is **diffusion of responsibility.** Responsibility is likely to be assumed by a designated leader, by those who observe a responsible model, and by those who feel competent to act in a specific situation. Another element in the bystander effect is the **fear of social blunders.** Altruistic behavior also varies as a function of rewards and punishments. Helping others can be intrinsically rewarding; external rewards and punishments for helping have an effect on the probability of subsequent helping; and in complex situations individuals seem to weigh the potential costs and benefits of helping versus failing to help. Though there is a general tendency for positive feelings to increase altruism and negative feelings to decrease such acts, cognitive factors are extremely important and can reverse these effects. Gender differences in helping depend on the specifics of the setting, and several personality variables are found to be associated with altruism, with **empathy** receiving the most research attention. Those in need of help are most likely to receive it if they are similar to the one who helps and if they are perceived as being able to reciprocate. Receiving aid can be very uncomfortable and threatening to self-esteem, but the result is future efforts at self-help. Aid that is nonthreatening tends to lead to a comfortable state of dependency.

When someone observes another person engaging in wrongdoing, a prosocial response not only helps the victim but also brings harm to the wrongdoer and raises the risk of retaliation. As in other emergency situations, inaction becomes more likely as the number of bystanders increases. Help is most likely to be provided by those who are competent to deal with the wrongdoer physically and/or to provide aid to the victim. The usual response to shoplifting is to ignore it and not inform on this type of thief. Such wrongdoing is reported most by those who were raised in small towns or rural areas and by those who are reminded about the right thing to do or informed about the inhibition to responding. When an individual makes a **prior commitment** to be responsible, the likelihood of taking action against a wrongdoer is extremely high.

It has been found that a large proportion of the general population admit to having been unable to resist temptation and have engaged in a wide variety of unethical or illegal behaviors. Nonviolent crimes such as fraud or tax evasion increase to the extent that there is a low risk of getting caught, the punishment is mild, and the potential gains are large. For students, cheating is one of the greatest temptations, and the majority of those surveyed report that they have cheated. Cheating is associated with personality characteristics involving emotional and moral immaturity and the inability to make present sacrifices to gain future rewards. In addition, situational factors that increase arousal also increase the incidence of cheating. In order to decrease cheating, it is necessary to convince potential cheaters that there is a high probability of detection and punishment or to remind them of their own values involving honesty, ethical behavior, and morality.

Glossary

bystander calculus *A description of the process that occurs when a bystander to an emergency weighs the perceived costs and benefits of providing help compared to the perceived costs and benefits of not helping.*

bystander effect *The finding that effective responses to an emergency become less likely or less rapid as the number of bystanders increases.*

character *Those aspects of an individual's values, beliefs, and personality that combine to constitute his or her ethical or moral quality.*

diffusion of responsibility *The proposition that when there are multiple observers of an emergency, the responsibility for taking action is shared by the*

group. As a result, each individual feels less responsible than if he or she were alone.

dispositional empathy *A personality trait characterized by the tendency to take the perspective of anyone in need. This trait leads to empathic emotional arousal (the tendency to feel as the other person must feel) when confronted by someone in need of help.*

fear of social blunders *The fear that people have of acting inappropriately or making a foolish mistake that will cause them to become an object of ridicule. This fear inhibits effective responses in an emergency.*

need for approval *A personality trait involving the desire to be accepted and liked by others.*

prior commitment *An individual's agreement ahead of time to assume responsibility if problems arise. An example is committing oneself to guard the property of another person against theft.*

prosocial behavior *Acts that have no obvious benefits for the individual who carries them out and may even involve risk or some degree of sacrifice. Such acts benefit others, and they are based on ethical standards of behavior.*

reinforcement theory of prosocial behavior *The theoretical model that emphasizes the importance of rewards and punishments on prosocial behavior.*

Altruism is assumed to vary as a function of its intrinsic reinforcement value, the occurrence of external rewards and punishments, and the individual's perception of expected rewarding or punishing consequences of particular behavior.

sociopathy *Behavior that involves antisocial acts, self-centered motives, and the tendency to be unconcerned about the feelings of others.*

superego *In Freud's theory, the internal mechanism that acts as a conscience and guides the person with respect to right and wrong behavior.*

For More Information

Boorman, S. A., & Levitt, P. R. *The genetics of altruism.* New York: Academic Press, 1980.
This book approaches prosocial behavior from the perspective of sociobiology. The authors suggest how genetic principles may have operated to encourage altruism in evolutionary development. They present a mathematical model to account for a trait of cooperation and apply it to both animal and human behavior.

Derlega, V. J., & Grzelak, J. (Eds.). *Cooperation and helping behavior: Theories and research.* New York: Academic Press, 1981.
This collection of original chapters by various experts in the field covers both cooperative behavior (see Chapter 10 in the present text) and helping behavior. The topics include altruism, the justice motive, responsive bystanders, the process of seeking help, and the motivation underlying prosocial behavior.

Eisenberg, N. (Ed.). *The development of prosocial behavior.* New York: Academic Press, 1982.
A series of investigators present theories and empirical findings relating to the development of prosocial behavior. The topics include social learning theory, the socialization process, altruism in children, cognitive and affective variables, and the way in which personality variables play a role in the acquisition of altruistic tendencies.

Piliavin, J. A., Dovidio, J. F., Gaertner, S. L., & Clark, R. D., III. *Emergency intervention.* New York: Academic Press, 1981.
These authors cover the psychological research and theory dealing with the process whereby bystanders get involved in the crises and emergencies of others. There is an emphasis on the responsive bystander and the variables that affect his or her behavior. The cost-benefit model is explained along with such variables as vicarious emotional arousal, the bystander effect, relevant personality traits, and cognitive factors.

Rosen, H. *The development of sociomoral knowledge: A cognitive-structural approach.* Irvington, N.Y.: Columbia University Press, 1980.
The author provides comprehensive coverage of the work of Piaget and Kohlberg on the developmental stages involving moral reasoning. This book consists of an in-depth look at this approach to character development.

Rushton, J. P., & Sorrentino, R. M. (Eds.). *Altruism and helping behavior.* Hillsdale, N.J.: Erlbaum, 1981.
This volume consists of a series of chapters by contributors who are actively involved in research on prosocial behavior. The topics include socialization processes, the effects of television, the role of education, empathy, emotional variables, the consequences of group size, and the reactions of those who receive help.

CHAPTER 9

Aggression:
Its Nature, Causes, and Control

Aggression: A Social Definition

**Theoretical Perspectives on Aggression:
In Search of the Roots of Violence**

*Aggression As Innate Behavior: Freud, Lorenz, and Sociobiology/Aggression As an
Elicited Drive: Motivation to Harm or Injure/Aggression As Learned Social
Behavior: Training for Violence*

**Social and Situational Determinants of Aggression:
External Causes of Violence**

*Frustration: Thwarting As a Potential Cause of Aggression/Direct Provocation: Why,
Often, Aggression Breeds Aggression/Social Models and Aggression: The Effects
of Viewing Violence/Heightened Arousal and Aggression: Can Violence Be
"Energized"?/Sexual Arousal and Aggression: Is There a Link?/Other Factors
Affecting Aggression: Aggressive Cues, Crowding, Heat, and Pain*

**Individual Determinants of Aggression:
Personality, Genes, and Sex**

*Sex Differences in Aggression: Myth or Reality?/Heredity and Aggression:
The XYY Syndrome*

Aggression: Its Prevention and Control

*Punishment: An Effective Deterrent to Aggression?/Catharsis: Does Getting It Out of
Your System Really Help?/Additional Techniques for the Reduction of
Aggression: Nonaggressive Models, Training in Social Skills, Cognitive
Interventions, and Incompatible Responses*

Special Inserts

FOCUS ON RESEARCH
Measuring Human Aggression: Hurt without Harm

FOCUS ON RESEARCH
Violent Pornography: A Special, Dangerous Case

ON THE APPLIED SIDE
Incompatible Responses: Some Potential, Practical Uses

It's a quiet Sunday afternoon, and you and several of your friends are sitting around reading the local paper. At one point, Michelle breaks the silence that has lasted for the past few minutes. "Listen to this," she says. And then she reads an unsettling article about a band of teenagers who have found a new and frightening outlet for their youthful energies: terrorizing elderly persons in their neighborhood. The gang's approach is simple. They wait outside local stores until they see an elderly man or woman leave. Then they follow this person home and force entry into his or her apartment. Once inside, they beat their helpless victim, and usually destroy his or her few possessions as well. The attacks are very brutal. Indeed, in one recent case, the gang left an eighty-four-year-old woman so badly injured that she was unable to get to the phone to summon help. As a result, she died a slow and painful death. And there seem to be no economic motives behind these repellent actions. In most cases, the teenagers do not even bother to hunt for the small amount of funds hidden away by their victims. As one of the members remarked during a confidential interview with a daring reporter, they do it "just for kicks."

When Michelle finishes reading the article, Jack shakes his head. "What animals!" he proclaims. "They ought to be publicly whipped. Preying on helpless old people . . . how low can you get?" But Elaine, his girlfriend, sees things differently. "I agree that it's terrible," she replies, "but can you really blame the kids? Just think about the kind of lives they've led. Growing up in the ghetto and coming from broken homes . . . with no jobs and no hope. I really don't think you can hold them responsible." "And don't forget drugs," adds Todd. "They're probably important too. Why I'll bet these kids are too stoned to know what they're doing most of the time." Jack, who has been listening to these remarks with growing irritation, breaks in at this point. "Yeah, yeah . . . and you might as well add all that TV violence while you're at it. Anyway, I don't care what *the causes are. I just think they should be punished. At least, let's get them off the streets so the old people will be safe." After this, the conversation continues for several minutes. Then it gradually peters out, and silence returns. As everyone goes back to reading the paper, though, you continue thinking about these upsetting incidents. What factors lie behind the callous and seemingly purposeless actions of these teenagers? The frustration of their impoverished, helpless lives? Drugs? The heat of the current summer? The pressure to be tough that exists in their neighborhood? All that TV violence? As you ponder this question, a frightening conclusion begins to take shape in your mind. Maybe* all *of these factors—plus several others too—play a role. In short, perhaps dangerous acts of human violence and cruelty actually stem from many different causes.*

As we're sure you already realize, aggression is an all too common aspect of human behavior. Evidence for its frequent occurrence is all around us. Just pick up any popular magazine, leaf through any newspaper, or tune in the evening news and you are almost certain to be confronted with reports of shocking atrocities and violence. War, terrorism, murder, child abuse, rape, torture—the list of human cruelty goes on and on. Given the frightening effects of aggression and its alarming frequency, it is far from surprising that social psychologists have focused a great deal of attention on this topic. Indeed, research on such behavior has continued without pause for several decades and has yielded many important insights. In the present chapter, we will summarize a portion of this work, focusing primarily on issues and findings we view as central to a thorough understanding of human violence. Briefly, our discussion will proceed as follows.

First, we will consider a very basic question: what, precisely, *is* aggression? As will soon be apparent, actions that inflict harm on others can take a wide range of forms (see Figure 9.1). Thus, the task of devising a useful definition of human aggression turns out to be quite complex. Second, we will examine several different *theoretical perspectives* on aggression—contrasting views concerning the origins and nature of such behavior. Third, we will focus on some of the major causes of aggression. As suggested by the preceding story, a very large number of these have been identified. However, most seem to fall into two major categories, often described as *situational* or *personal* in nature. Situational causes of **aggression** involve factors or conditions in the world around us that stimulate such behavior. Several of these, including frustration, direct provocation, exposure to televised violence, and heightened arousal (including sexual arousal) will be considered. In contrast, personal or individual determinants of aggression center around characteristics possessed by specific individuals. These include various personality traits (or clusters of traits), gender, and even physical characteristics. Together, such factors help account for the fact that

FIGURE 9.1   *Human aggression: One of its many different forms.*

As suggested by this scene, aggression takes many different forms. [Source: John Darling *by Armstrong & Batiuk © Field Enterprises, Inc. Courtesy of Field Newspaper Syndicate.]*

individuals often show sharply contrasting levels of aggression, even in the same or similar situations. Finally, we will turn to a key question with important practical implications: How can aggression be *prevented* or *controlled?* A number of different techniques for accomplishing these goals have been proposed (e.g., punishment, catharsis, the induction of responses incompatible with anger or aggression), but as we shall soon see, some seem more effective in this respect than others.

Aggression: A Social Definition

While many definitions of aggression have been offered, none has as yet been universally adopted by social psychologists. One definition of aggression that would probably be acceptable to many experts, though, is as follows: *Aggression is any form of behavior directed toward the goal of harming or injuring another living being who is motivated to avoid such treatment.* At first glance, this definition seems both simple and reasonable. In many respects, it is close to what we mean when we speak about "aggression" informally. However, closer examination reveals that it actually involves several features requiring careful attention.

definition of aggression

Aggression is behavior. First, our definition suggests that aggression is a form of behavior, not an emotion, need, or motive. Thus, it is important to distinguish it clearly from emotions that may or may not accompany it (e.g., anger), motives that may or may not underlie it (e.g., the desire to inflict pain on another), and from negative attitudes that sometimes enhance its occurrence (e.g., racial or ethnic hatred).

① *aggression is overt behavior*

Aggression and intention. Second, our definition of aggression limits application of this term to acts in which an aggressor intends to harm her or his victim. As you can readily see, including the notion of *intent* raises several difficulties. After all, intentions are hidden, private events. As such, they must be inferred from the events that both precede and follow alleged acts of aggression. And, as anyone who has watched courtroom dramas knows, there is much room for uncertainty and error in this complex process. Yet, despite such problems, there are strong reasons for retaining reference to such intentions in our definition of aggression (Mummendey, Bornewasser, Loschper, & Linneweber, 1982). First, if all mention of intent were eliminated, it would be necessary to view instances in which one person accidentally harms another as aggression. As you can readily see, this makes little sense. Second, if the notion of intent were excluded, it would be necessary to view the actions of surgeons, dentists, and even parents when they spank their children to correct their behavior as aggression. Since the actions performed by such persons are designed to help rather than harm the recipients, it seems unreasonable to describe them as aggressive in nature. Finally, if the notion of intent were excluded, instances in which attempts to harm or injure others are made — but fail — would not be labelled as aggression. This too makes little sense. If an individual fires a gun or throws a knife at another but misses, such behavior clearly represents aggres-

② *aggression depends upon intention*

sion. But without reference to the intentions behind these actions, we would be unable to label it in this manner; after all, no visible harm was produced. For all these reasons, it is essential to define aggression not simply as behavior that inflicts harm or injury on others, but rather as any action directed toward the goal of producing such effects.

Aggression is directed toward a live recipient. Suppose that, after being provoked in some manner, an individual returns home and punches his pillow as hard as possible. Is this aggression? According to our definition, it is not; only assaults against living beings qualify as such behavior, and hitting one's pillow —however hard—is unlikely to cause harm to the source of one's anger (or anyone else). Such behavior, then, is better viewed as purely *emotional* or *expressive* in nature. This does not imply, however, that assaults against inanimate objects *never* involve aggression. In fact, there are many instances in which behavior of this type is designed to inflict harm on another person in an indirect manner. For example, imagine that the man in our example decided to react to provocation somewhat differently. Instead of punching his pillow he pours gasoline over his tormentor's new sports car and then sets it on fire. Is this aggression? Obviously, it is. And the reason should be plain: in this case, an assault against an inanimate object (the car) is designed to inflict pain and suffering on another person—its owner. In short, it is the ultimate goal of such actions that is crucial. If assaults against inanimate objects are largely expressive in nature and are not designed to harm another living being (e.g., throwing rocks against a wall, kicking a tin can down the street), then they should not be viewed as acts of aggression. But if, instead, they seek to injure a live victim in some manner, it is appropriate to view them as overt (if indirect) acts of aggression.

Aggression involves an avoidance-motivated victim. Finally, our definition notes that aggression occurs only when the victim is motivated to avoid such treatment by the aggressor. In most cases, this is true, but there are a few exceptions. For example, some persons seem to enjoy being hurt by their lovers and may invite rather than shun such treatment. Similarly, persons who commit suicide actively seek the self-destruction they experience. According to our definition, such actions should not be viewed as aggression, for there is no apparent motive on the part of the victims to avoid the harm they experience.

Theoretical Perspectives on Aggression: In Search of the Roots of Violence

Aggression has always been one of the central mysteries of human behavior. From the story of Cain and Abel through current concerns over the very real danger of total nuclear destruction, thoughtful persons have pondered the paradox of human violence. How, they have wondered, can creatures capable of love, kindness, loyalty, and gratitude, also be capable of so much cruelty and harshness? Why, in short, do human beings so often turn on their fellow men

FIGURE 9.2 *Human aggression: A continuing, disturbing puzzle.*

That human beings exhibit a high level of aggression is obvious. The reasons behind such behavior, however, are far more difficult to discern. [Source: Culver Pictures, Inc.]

and women with a savagery unmatched by even the fiercest of predators (see Figure 9.2)? In a sense, we will be addressing these questions throughout the present chapter, as we consider various factors that contribute to the occurrence—and reduction—of overt aggression. Here, though, we will examine several large-scale answers to them—theoretical perspectives that seek to explain the roots of such behavior in a sweeping, general sense. As you can readily guess, many different perspectives of this type have been proposed. Most of these, though, seem to fall into three major categories. These attribute aggressive actions to (1) innate urges or tendencies, (2) externally elicited drives, or (3) existing social conditions coupled with previous social learning. Because these contrasting explanations for the origins of human violence have both stimulated and guided much research, we will examine each in turn.

Aggression As Innate Behavior: Freud, Lorenz, and Sociobiology

The oldest and probably best-known explanation for the occurrence of human aggression, **instinct theory,** suggests that human beings are somehow "programmed" for such behavior. The most famous early supporter of this view was Sigmund Freud, who held that aggression stems mainly from a powerful *death instinct* possessed by all human beings. According to Freud, this instinct is initially directed toward self-destruction. However, in most persons, it is soon redirected outward, and serves as a source of hostile impulses toward others. Freud believed that such impulses build up with the passage of time. Thus, if they are not released periodically in safe ways, they soon reach dangerous levels capable of producing strong acts of violence.

Another explanation of human aggression that focuses largely on innate tendencies has been proposed by the Nobel prize winning ethologist Konrad Lorenz. According to Lorenz (1966, 1974), aggression springs mainly from a built-in *fighting instinct* that humans share with many other species. Presumably, this instinct developed during the course of evolution because it yielded many benefits. For example, fighting serves to disperse populations over a wide area, thus ensuring maximum use of available resources. And since it is often closely related to mating, such behavior often helps to strengthen the genetic makeup of a species by assuring that only the strongest and most vigorous individuals manage to reproduce.

In the past decade, a third view holding that aggression is innate or genetically programmed has received growing attention. This approach, known as **sociobiology,** suggests that social behavior, like physical structure, is affected by evolution (Barash, 1977). That is, patterns of social behavior that aid individuals to survive and reproduce become increasingly common in the species. According to sociobiologists, then, the fact that human beings are quite aggressive points to a straightforward conclusion: at one time, such behavior was quite adaptive. Whether it continues to play such a role today, of course, is open to very serious question.

The theories proposed by Freud, Lorenz, and sociobiologists differ in many ways. Yet all are similar in one basic respect: they are somewhat pessimistic with respect to the possibility of preventing or controlling human aggression. This is because they all view such behavior as stemming mainly from innate drives or urges. And since these tendencies are assumed to be "built in," they cannot be readily eliminated. While Freud, Lorenz, and others did hold out some hope of channeling or controlling these aggressive urges, they did not feel that such motives could ever be totally eliminated. According to instinct theories, then, aggression—in one form or another—must always be with us.

Aggression As an Elicited Drive: Motivation to Harm or Injure

The instinct theories of aggression just described have attained widespread acceptance among the general public. In contrast, however, they have usually been rejected by social psychologists. The main reason for this rejection lies in the fact that, to a surprising degree, such theories are *circular* in nature. They begin by noting that aggression is a common form of human behavior. Then they explain such actions by proposing the existence of one or more aggressive instincts. Finally, they use the high incidence of overt aggression as support for the presence of such instincts. As you can see, this is indeed questionable logic! And while some means for breaking this logical circle exist, none are very convincing. For this reason, and also because they object to the pessimism implied by instinct theories, many social psychologists have tended to favor an

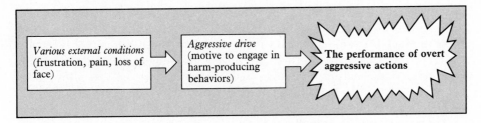

FIGURE 9.3 *Drive theories of aggression.*

According to drive theories *of aggression, various external conditions (frustration, physical pain, loss of face) elicit a drive to engage in harm-producing behaviors. Such* aggressive drive, *in turn, leads to the performance of overt attacks against others.*

alternate view based on the suggestion that aggression stems mainly from an externally elicited drive to harm or injure others. This approach is reflected in several different **drive theories** of aggression (e.g., Berkowitz, 1978; Berkowitz, Cochran, & Embree, 1981). Basically, such theories suggest that various external conditions (frustration, physical pain, loss of face) serve to arouse a strong motive to engage in harm-producing behaviors. And such aggressive drive, in turn, then leads to the performance of overt assaults against others (see Figure 9.3). By far the most famous of these theories is the well-known *frustration-aggression hypothesis*. According to this view (which we will examine in detail later), frustration (the blocking of ongoing goal-directed behavior) leads to the arousal of a drive whose primary goal is that of harming some person or object. And this drive, in turn, leads to attacks against various targets—especially the source of the frustration.

Because they suggest that external conditions rather than innate tendencies are crucial, drive theories of aggression seem to be somewhat more optimistic with respect to the prevention or control of such behavior than are instinct theories. Briefly, they seem to imply that the removal of all sources of frustration, pain, and similar experiences would go a long way toward eliminating overt acts of aggression. Unfortunately, though, such events are extremely common in everyday life. Thus, their total elimination from the world around us does not seem feasible. For this reason, drive theories, too, seem to leave human beings facing continuous—and largely unavoidable—sources of aggressive impulses. As a result, they are less encouraging with respect to the control of aggression than at first meets the eye.

Aggression As Learned Social Behavior: Training for Violence

In recent years, a third theoretical perspective on the nature of human aggression—the **social learning view**—has gained increasing acceptance. Supporters of this view (Bandura, 1973; Baron, 1977; Zillmann, 1979) emphasize the fact that aggression, dangerous and unsettling as it is, should be viewed primarily as a learned form of social behavior. In contrast to the central assumption of instinct theories, they argue that human beings are *not* born with a large array of aggressive responses at their disposal. Rather, they must learn these in much the same way that they learn other complex forms of behavior. Going further, supporters of this modern view also suggest that if we are to fully comprehend the nature of human aggression we must possess information about three basic issues: (1) the manner in which such behavior is acquired, (2) the rewards and punishments associated with its performance, and (3) the social and environmental factors that influence its occurrence. In contrast to other theories we have considered, then, the social learning view does *not* attribute aggression to one or a small number of causes. Rather, it suggests that the roots of such behavior are quite varied in scope, involving aggressors' past experience and learning, as well as many external, **situational** factors.

As you can readily see, the social learning view is somewhat more complex in scope than the other perspectives on aggression we have considered. In our view, though, it is also more sophisticated. Moreover, it offers another key advantage that should not be overlooked: it is quite optimistic concerning the possibility of preventing or controlling overt aggression. After all, if aggression is a learned form of behavior, it should be open to direct modification and change. For both of these reasons — its sophistication and basic optimism — the social learning view has gained increasing popularity in recent years. Indeed, it is probably fair to state that at present it is the most widely accepted theoretical perspective on aggression in social psychology.

Social and Situational Determinants of Aggression: External Causes of Violence

Contrary to what news accounts often suggest, aggression does *not* generally take place in a social or situational vacuum. Rather, it is generally triggered by the words and deeds of others, or by conditions existing in the environment surrounding potential aggressors. In short, it usually springs from specific factors that pave the way for its occurrence.

As you can probably guess, a very large number of conditions play a role in this regard — everything from frustration and direct provocation on the one hand, through drugs, sexual arousal, and even uncomfortable heat on the other. We will consider several of these factors here. Before turning to this task, however, we must pause briefly to consider a question that may already have crossed your mind: How can human aggression — and especially physical aggression — be studied under safe yet systematic conditions? (For a discussion of this central issue, please see the **Focus on Research** section on pp. 332–333.)

Frustration: Thwarting As a Potential Cause of Aggression

Suppose that you stopped one hundred people on the street at random and asked them the following question: What is the most important single cause of aggression? How would they reply? In all probability, most would answer with a single word: *frustration.* In other words, they would indicate that the most potent means of inducing human beings to aggress is thwarting their goals— somehow preventing them from getting what they want. Widespread acceptance of this view stems mainly from the well-known **frustration-aggression hypothesis** that we mentioned earlier. In its original form, this hypothesis suggested that (1) frustration always leads to some form of aggression, and (2) aggression always stems from frustration (Dollard et al., 1939). In short, it held that frustrated persons always engage in some type of aggression and that all acts of aggression result from some form of frustration.

As you can readily see, these assertions are highly appealing. After all, if they are accepted as true, a highly complex form of behavior (human aggression) is explained in one daring stroke. But are these proposals accurate? Does frustration really play the all-important role with respect to aggression that they suggest? The answer is almost certainly "no." Both portions of the frustration-aggression hypothesis seem to be far too sweeping in scope.

First, it is now clear that frustrated individuals do *not* always respond to thwarting with aggressive thoughts, words, or deeds. Rather, they may actually show a wide variety of reactions, ranging from resignation and despair on the one hand to attempts to overcome the source of their frustration on the other.

FIGURE 9.4   Aggression: Not always the result of frustration.

Public executioners, hired assassins, and professional soldiers often inflict harm or even death on others simply because they are paid to do so. Such actions suggest that contrary to the frustration-aggression hypothesis, aggression actually stems from many different factors. [Source: Frederic Lewis Photographs.]

FOCUS
ON RESEARCH

Measuring Human Aggression: Hurt without Harm

Researchers wishing to study human aggression under careful laboratory conditions face a puzzling dilemma. On the one hand, they wish to study a dangerous and potentially harmful form of behavior. On the other, they cannot possibly permit the individuals participating in their research to suffer any harm. How can this dilemma be solved? The answer currently accepted by most social psychologists involves the use of *temporary deception*. Briefly, subjects must be led to believe that they can harm another person in some manner—either physically or psychologically—when in fact they cannot. Under these conditions, their intentions to inflict negative outcomes on others can be studied without any risk of actual harm to these supposed victims. This basic approach is used to study both physical aggression and nonphysical (verbal) aggression. Since the specific procedures used with respect to these contrasting forms of aggression differ, though, we will describe them separately.

Turning first to the measurement of *physical aggression*, the basic approach is as follows. Subjects are seated in front of a special apparatus and told that by means of this equipment, they can deliver painful stimuli to another person (see Figure 9.4). In some studies these stimuli are electric shocks; in others they are loud noises; and in still others, they involve intense heat or extreme cold (e.g., Geen & Donnerstein, 1983). Regardless of their precise nature, though, it is also explained to participants that, through the apparatus, they can control the strength of these painful events. Thus, they can deliver anything from very mild through quite intense pain to the recipient. In reality, of course, this person is an accomplice of the experimenter and never receives any unpleasant stimuli during the study. But subjects are led to believe that this is the case, and everything possible is done to convince them that the victim's fate is actually in their hands. (For example, subjects are often given one or two

FIGURE 9.5 *Measuring physical aggression: One common technique.*

Left photo: Apparatus for the study of physical aggression (often known as "the aggression machine"). Subjects are told that by pushing various buttons on this device, they can deliver painful stimuli of varying strength (electric shocks, loud noises) to another person. Right photo: An experimenter recording subjects' behavior in this setting. Two measures of aggression are usually obtained: the strength and duration of the painful stimuli individuals choose to deliver to their supposed victim.

sample shocks or noise blasts solely to convince them that the apparatus is in fact real.) The intensity and the duration of the painful stimuli subjects choose to employ then serve as measures of their aggression (measures of their willingness to harm the supposed victim). The precise context for the delivery of these events also varies. For example, in a basic procedure devised by Buss (1961), subjects are told that the research is concerned with the impact of punishment on learning, and are asked to deliver shocks to the victim each time he or she errs on a simple learning task. In another approach, they are told that the study is concerned with the impact of unpleasant stimuli on physiological reactions, and are asked to deliver shocks, noises, or other aversive events to the supposed victim so that his or her physiological responses can be examined (e.g., Baron, 1980). Regardless of the specific stimuli and context used, however, the basic situation remains the same: subjects are led to believe that they can deliver painful stimuli of varying strength to another person, when in fact this is not actually the case.

Procedures for the measurement of nonphysical aggression differ in detail from those we have just discussed, but are much the same in concept. Here, subjects are led to believe that they can engage in actions that will harm another person in some manner not involving physical pain or injury. For example, in one technique devised by Zillmann and his colleagues (e.g., Ramirez, Bryant, & Zillmann, 1982) subjects rate the performance of an experimenter on the scales shown in Table 9.1. They are informed that their ratings of this person will be examined by a departmental committee, and will partly determine whether he or she receives continued financial support for graduate study. Needless to state, the more negative the ratings assigned to the experimenter by subjects, the higher their level of aggression is judged to be.

These basic procedures have been employed in many studies of human aggression. In fact, much of the information we will present in remaining sections of this chapter was obtained through their use. Before turning to the results of such research, therefore, we should consider one additional question: do these methods really work? That is, do they actually provide us with valid means for studying human aggression under safe, laboratory condi-

TABLE 9.1 Measuring verbal aggression: Hurting through words or ratings.

Rating scales used to measure verbal (nonphysical) aggression. In experiments using such scales, subjects are told that their ratings of another person in response to these questions will affect this individual in some manner (e.g., they will determine whether he or she is reappointed as a research assistant).

(1) How well did the above mentioned person perform his/her role as an experimenter? (Circle one number)

   1   2   3   4   5   6   7

(2) How would you rate his/her manner of interacting with others?

   Unpleasant and   Pleasant and
   discourteous   courteous
   1   2   3   4   5   6   7

(3) In your opinion, should this student be reappointed as a research assistant?

   Definitely not   Definitely yes
   1   2   3   4   5   6   7

tions? Several critics have expressed strong doubts in this regard, noting that the conditions existing in laboratory studies of aggression are so different from those of actual life that the findings obtained are of questionable value. In response to such comments, several researchers (e.g., Berkowitz & Donnerstein, 1982) have called attention to a key fact: in order for laboratory studies of aggression to yield valid information about this behavior, it is *not* crucial that the situations employed or the responses made by subjects closely resemble those outside the laboratory. Rather, what *is* crucial is that subjects perceive that they can harm the supposed victim in some manner. Since participants in laboratory studies of aggression generally believe that this is the case, the findings of such research can be viewed as valid.

In addition, we should note that there is direct empirical evidence for the usefulness of the laboratory techniques we have described. For example, with respect to physical aggression, several studies indicate that persons with a prior history of violent actions tend to inflict stronger levels of shock, noise, or heat on victims than persons without such a history (e.g., Gully & Dengerink, 1983; Shemberg, Leventhal, & Allman, 1968; Wolfe & Baron, 1971). Second, with respect to verbal aggression, it has been repeatedly found that subjects who are angered by an accomplice generally assign lower ratings to this person than subjects not similarly provoked (e.g., Zillmann, Baron, & Tamborini, 1981).

Together, these findings support the view that the techniques discussed earlier provide valid means for the study of human aggression under safe, laboratory conditions. Of course, as even researchers who use these methods will freely admit, they are far from perfect. For example, growing public awareness of such procedures makes it harder and harder to convince subjects that they can in fact harm the victim. Taken as a whole, though, existing evidence suggests that these procedures do seem to yield at least a rough index of the central concept we wish to measure: the overall willingness of individuals to inflict harm—physical or otherwise—on another human being.

───────────────────────────◆───────────────────────────

And in many cases, it appears the most likely reaction to powerful frustration is depression—*not* overt acts of aggression (Bandura, 1973).

Second, it is also apparent that all aggression does *not* result from frustration. People aggress for many different reasons and in response to many different factors. For example, boxers hit and sometimes injure their opponents because it is part of their job to do so, not because they are frustrated. Soldiers often attack and kill others out of a sense of patriotism or simply because it is their duty. And public executioners, as well as hired assassins, regularly kill individuals they do not know simply because they are being paid to carry out these actions (see Figure 9.4, p. 331). There can be little doubt, then, that aggression often stems from many factors aside from frustration. To suggest that it is always the result of thwarting can be quite misleading.

In view of these considerations, few researchers currently hold that frustration always leads to aggression, or that all aggression stems from such treatment. Instead, many have adopted a more moderate view proposing that frustration is simply one of many different causes of aggression (e.g., Berkowitz, 1978). At first glance, this position appears much easier to defend on logical grounds than the sweeping proposals just mentioned. Yet evidence regarding even *its* accuracy has been quite mixed. On the one hand, several experiments have reported that frustration often fails to enhance aggression (Buss, 1963, 1966; Taylor & Pisano, 1971). Indeed, a few studies have even reported that sometimes frustration may actually tend to *reduce* the level of aggression shown by thwarted persons, perhaps because they are depressed by such treatment (Gentry, 1970). In sharp contrast, other studies have found that frustration may indeed facilitate aggression, at least under some circumstances (e.g., Geen, 1968; Turner, Layton, & Simons, 1975). Moreover, some evidence suggests that frustration may increase attention to aggressive acts by others, and so enhance later violence in this manner (Parker & Rogers, 1981; please see our discussion of the impact of aggressive models, pp. 337–341). Clearly, then, the issue is far from resolved. However, careful examination of existing evidence points to the conclusion that whether frustration increases or fails to enhance aggression may depend largely on two important factors.

First, it appears that frustration increases aggression only when it is quite intense. When, in contrast, it is of only low or moderate strength, aggression may fail to be enhanced (Harris, 1974). Second, growing evidence suggests that frustration is more likely to facilitate aggression when it is perceived as arbitrary or illegitimate than when it is viewed as deserved or legitimate (e.g., Kulik & Brown, 1979; Worchel, 1974).

In sum, frustration appears to be only one of many different factors contributing to the occurrence of human aggression. Further, it is probably neither the most important nor the strongest of these variables. While it *can* stimulate aggression under some conditions, it may fail to exert such effects under other circumstances. Thus, it does not seem to play the very central role in such behavior it was once assigned.

Direct Provocation:
Why, Often, Aggression Breeds Aggression

As we have just seen, existing evidence suggests that frustration must be quite intense before it can elicit increments in overt aggression. In contrast, another factor — *direct verbal or physical provocation* — seems capable of producing such effects even when quite mild. Informal observation suggests that often, individuals react very strongly to mild taunts or glancing blows. Moreover, when they do, they may begin a process of escalation in which stronger and stronger provocations are quickly exchanged (Goldstein, Davis, & Herman, 1975). The results may then be disastrous for both sides.

Direct evidence for the strong impact of physical provocation on aggression has been obtained in many laboratory studies (e.g., Dengerink, Schnedler, & Covey, 1978; White & Gruber, 1982). In these experiments, individuals exposed to mounting provocation from a stranger (usually, in the form of ever-stronger electric shocks) have been found to respond to their tormentor in kind. That is, as provocation rises in intensity, so does their retaliation. And — alas! — at no point do they seem to "turn the other cheek" and ignore the harsh treatment they are receiving. Similar results have also been obtained with respect to verbal provocation. Here, too, individuals seem all too willing to respond aggressively to real or imagined slurs from others (e.g., Geen, 1968).

Together, these findings suggest that direct provocation from others — either physical or verbal — often plays a powerful role in eliciting overt aggression. Indeed, it may often play a much stronger role in this regard than frustration. The practical message contained in this research is clear: if you provoke the persons around you, you do so at your own — and often considerable — risk!

Attribution as a mediator of the impact of provocation: Accident or intention? Imagine the following situation. Another person pours hot coffee onto your lap, causing you considerable pain. Immediately after doing so, however, she apologizes profusely and gives every indication of regret and embarrassment. Would you grow angry and seek to retaliate against this person? In all likelihood you would not. But now, imagine the same situation with the following change: immediately after pouring the coffee onto your lap, the person in question laughs sadistically. Further, she makes no attempt to apologize for her obnoxious behavior. How would you react under these conditions? Probably, you would be much more likely to grow angry and seek revenge. Your contrasting reactions in these two situations call attention to a crucial fact. When confronted with provocative actions by others, we usually attempt to understand the basis for their occurrence. In short, we attempt to determine *why* these persons acted in this manner. And our attributions in this regard then play a crucial role in shaping our reactions to them. If, as in the first incident, we attribute others' behavior to external (e.g., accidental) causes, we are unlikely to respond with anger and aggression. But if, as in the second incident, we attribute it to internal causes (e.g, their motives or intentions), we are much more likely to respond in an aggressive manner (see Figure 9.6). In short, our reactions to provocation from others are strongly mediated by our attributions concerning this behavior.

Evidence for this mediating role of attributions in the relationship between provocation and aggression has been provided by several experiments (e.g., Albert, 1981; Dyck & Rule, 1978). In these studies, subjects responded much more strongly to a specific level of provocation when it appeared to be intended and purposeful than when it seemed to be unintended or accidental. These and related findings (e.g., Harvey & Enzle, 1978; Taylor, Shuntich, & Greenberg, 1979) point to the following conclusion. The impact of physical or verbal provocation upon aggression is often strongly affected by attributions about the

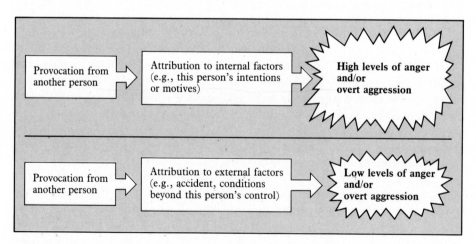

FIGURE 9.6   *Reactions to provocation: The mediating role of attributions.*

Often, our reactions to provocation from others are affected by our attributions concerning the causes of their behavior. If, as in the upper panel, we attribute others' actions to internal factors (e.g., a desire to annoy us), we are likely to respond with anger and aggression. But if, as in the lower panel, we attribute provocation to external factors (e.g., accident, factors beyond others' control), we are far less likely to respond aggressively.

causes of such actions. Only when we view the annoying words or deeds of others as stemming from internal causes are we likely to respond to such treatment with strong, overt aggression.

Social Models and Aggression: The Effects of Viewing Violence

In Chapter 7, we noted that exposure to the actions of other persons can strongly affect our attitudes, emotions, and behavior. The existence of such powerful *modeling effects*, in turn, raises an intriguing question closely related to our present discussion: Can aggression, too, be affected in this manner? That is, can exposure to **aggressive models**—others who behave in a violent manner—stimulate similar behavior among observers? The answer, as provided by a large body of research findings, seems to be "yes."

While some research on this topic has examined the impact of *live* aggressive models—other persons present "in the flesh" who behave in an aggressive manner (Baron & Bell, 1975; Donnerstein & Donnerstein, 1976)—most has focused on another basic question: can exposure to violence in the mass media (films, television) increase aggression by viewers? (See Figure 9.7.) Research concerned with this important issue can be viewed as having moved through three distinct phases, and we will now describe the methods and findings of each.

In the first and earliest phase—often known as the *"Bobo doll" studies*—nursery school children were exposed to short films in which an adult model aggressed against a large inflated toy clown (a Bobo doll) in unusual ways. For example, the model sat on the doll, punched it repeatedly on the nose, and so on

FIGURE 9.7 Exposure to media violence: Can it stimulate overt aggression?

Does exposure to media violence, such as the scene shown here, enhance aggression by TV viewers or moviegoers? A growing body of research suggests that under some conditions, this may actually be the case. [Source: The Cinemabilia Shop.]

(Bandura, 1965; Bandura, Ross, & Ross, 1963a, 1963b). Following exposure to these materials, or to a film in which the model behaved in a quiet and nonaggressive manner, the children were allowed to play freely in a room containing many toys, including several used by the model. Careful observation of their behavior in this setting revealed that the youngsters exposed to the aggressive model showed strong tendencies to imitate his or her behavior. Thus, they engaged in actions like those shown by the model much more frequently than subjects who had not watched this person assault the plastic doll. These findings indicate that even young children can acquire new ways of aggressing against others through exposure to filmed or televised violence. And this fact, in turn, led some investigators to suggest that perhaps exposure to such materials might stimulate later aggression by viewers. After all, they reasoned, if children learn new ways of harming others from TV or movies, won't they soon be tempted to put these behaviors to actual use? Such conclusions, and the studies on which they were based, were quickly subjected to strong criticism. For example, it was noted that subjects in this research simply hit an inflated plastic toy. Since no living target was harmed, critics argued, these actions should not be viewed as aggression (Klapper, 1968). Similarly, it was noted that the films seen by subjects differed from regular TV shows in several ways (e.g., they had no plot and provided no information about the basis for the model's strange behavior).

In order to deal with these and other criticisms, a second group of studies concerned with the impact of televised violence adopted sharply different procedures. In these experiments (which can be described as *laboratory studies of hurting*), children or adults in different conditions were first exposed either to violent TV programs and films, or to nonviolent shows and films. Then they were provided with an opportunity to aggress against another person — not a plastic toy — in some manner (e.g., Geen, 1978). In general, such investigations found that subjects exposed to filmed or televised violence directed stronger aggression against their supposed victim than subjects exposed to nonviolent materials. For example, in one such study (Liebert & Baron, 1972), children who watched an excerpt from a highly violent television show ("The Untouchables") later demonstrated greater willingness to inflict pain upon another child than youngsters who watched an equally exciting but nonviolent track race. (Needless to say, the victim was imaginary; thus, no one was ever harmed during the experiment.) Taken as a whole, this second wave of research on the impact of televised violence seemed to suggest that exposure to such materials can indeed sometimes facilitate similar aggressive behavior among viewers.

The third and most recent group of studies we will consider can be described as involving *long-term field research*. Such investigations have sought to determine whether prolonged exposure to media violence encourages overt aggression among viewers in settings outside the laboratory. Several studies concerned with this central issue have taken the form of experiments in which different groups of subjects are systematically exposed to contrasting amounts of media violence (e.g., Leyens et al., 1975; Parke et al., 1977). For example, in one study of this type (Leyens et al., 1975), two groups of boys attending a private school in Belgium were exposed to contrasting sets of films. One group saw five violent movies, one each day, while the other group saw five nonviolent films presented in the same manner. The boys' behavior was then observed as they went about their normal activities. Results were clear: subjects exposed to the highly aggressive films did indeed show an increase in several forms of aggression against others. In contrast, those exposed to the nonviolent films failed to show similar changes in behavior.

A related line of research, also concerned with the effects of prolonged exposure to televised violence, has followed somewhat different procedures (e.g., Eron, 1982; Huesmann, 1983). In these studies, which are primarily observational in nature, large groups of children are first tested to obtain information on two key factors: their exposure to televised violence and their current level of aggression. Information on the first of these factors is based on subjects' reports about the shows they watch plus violence ratings of these programs. Information about the second is gained from ratings of their behavior provided by classmates. But the research does not stop there. Instead, the same youngsters are tested again on later occasions, usually stretching over a period of several years. For example, in one such study by Eron and Huesmann

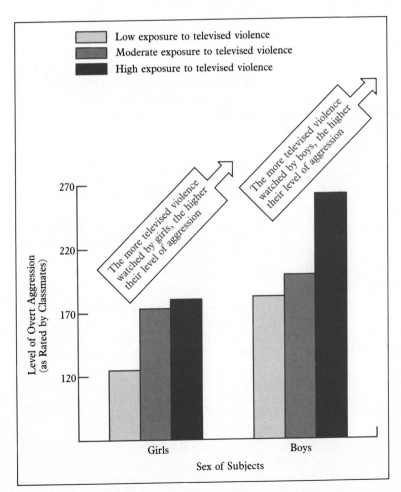

FIGURE 9.8 Televised violence: Evidence for its dangerous impact.

The greater the amount of televised violence watched by children, the higher their level of overt aggression toward others. Further, while boys are somewhat more aggressive than girls, both sexes seem to be affected by televised violence in a similar manner. [Source: Based on data reported by Eron, 1982.]

(Eron, 1982), 748 children (half in the first grade, half in the third grade) were first interviewed in 1977. Then as many of the same youngsters as possible were tested again in both 1978 and 1979. Results on all three occasions indicated that there is indeed a strong link between exposure to televised violence and aggression. As shown in Figure 9.8, the greater the amount of violence watched by subjects, the higher their rated levels of aggression. Moreover, as observed in earlier studies (e.g., Eron et al., 1972), the strength of this relationship seemed to increase over time, a result suggesting that the impact of televised violence upon viewers may be cumulative in nature. We should add that similar findings have been obtained with children in several different countries (e.g., Finland, Poland, Australia) (Eron, 1982). And they have also been observed across even longer periods of time — up to ten years or more (Eron et al., 1972). Together, such evidence, plus the field experiments described earlier, points to the following unsettling conclusion: long-term exposure to televised violence is in fact capable of encouraging overt aggression by children in a wide range of everyday settings.

The impact of televised violence: Why does it occur? Looking back over the three groups of studies we have described, it is clear that the results have been quite consistent. Regardless of the procedures used, the type of films or programs shown, and the measures of aggression gathered, most findings point to the following conclusion: exposure to filmed or televised violence can sometimes elicit similar actions on the part of viewers. Not all findings have been consistent with this view (e.g., Feshbach & Singer, 1971), but in general, the weight of available evidence favors the existence of an aggression-stimulating effect of observed violence. Clearly, this is an important finding, with practical implications. Before turning to these, however, we wish to address another basic question: Why, precisely, do such effects occur? How, in short, does exposure to media violence stimulate similar behavior on the part of the persons who watch it? Research findings point to the role of three related processes (Liebert et al., 1982).

First, exposure to media violence seems to weaken the *inhibitions* of viewers against engaging in similar behavior. After watching many persons — including the heroes and heroines of their favorite shows — perform aggressive actions, viewers seem to feel less restrained about performing such behaviors themselves. "After all," they seem to reason, "if *they* can act that way, why can't I?"

Second, as we noted earlier, exposure to media violence may arm viewers with new aggressive actions not previously at their disposal. And once these are acquired, it is only a fairly small step to being tempted to put them into use when appropriate conditions arise (e.g., when confronted with strong provocation from others).

Finally, and perhaps in some ways most disturbing, continued exposure to media violence reduces emotional sensitivity to violence and its harmful consequences. After watching countless murders, assaults, and fights, many persons seem to become somewhat *desensitized* to such materials. That is, they react to them calmly or even with boredom, rather than with shock and arousal (Geen, 1981; Thomas et al., 1977; Thomas, 1982). As you can readily see, such reduced emotionality in the face of violence may, in turn, make it easier for

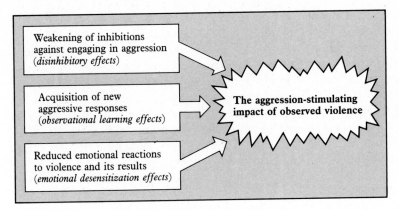

FIGURE 9.9   *Media violence: Mechanisms underlying its effects.*

As shown here, the impact of televised and filmed violence upon the behavior of viewers stems from three major sources: (1) a weakening of inhibitions against such behavior, (2) the acquisition of new aggressive responses, and (3) emotional desensitization to violence and its effects.

individuals to contemplate overt aggression, or actually engage in its performance.

In sum, the impact of televised or filmed violence upon the behavior of viewers seems to stem from several distinct sources (see Figure 9.9). In view of this fact, it is hardly surprising that such effects seem to be quite general in scope.

The impact of media violence: A concluding word. As we have already noted, many different studies indicate that exposure to media violence can facilitate aggression by at least some viewers. Further, recent surveys reveal that current TV offerings contain a large dose of such materials (e.g., Williams, Zabrack, & Joy, 1982). Together, these considerations point to a straightforward conclusion: the current high level of mayhem occurring on TV and theater screens may actually be exerting negative effects upon the social fabric of many societies. And certainly there is little indication that exposure to such materials can have beneficial aggression-reducing (i.e., cathartic) effects. But please take note: it is probably as unwise to overemphasize the potentially harmful results of media violence as it is to ignore them. The effects uncovered in much of the research we have described have been quite modest in scope and often temporary in duration. Thus, there is certainly no reason to assume that after watching their favorite aggression-packed show, individuals are likely to rush out and attack anyone unfortunate enough to get in their way. Rather, the impact of media violence seems to be much more subtle in nature, affecting the behavior of only some persons, on some occasions, and in some situations.

In sum, exposure to such violence *does* affect viewers and should certainly not be ignored. But we should always recall that it is only one of many different factors contributing to the occurrence of human aggression in social situations.

Heightened Arousal and Aggression: Can Violence Be "Energized"?

Suppose that a few minutes after a very frightening ride on a roller coaster, another person insulted you in a nasty manner. Would you be more likely to aggress against this individual at this time than if he or she insulted you when you were not physically aroused or excited? Interestingly, the results of many experiments suggest that this might be the case. It appears that sometimes heightened arousal, whatever its source, may serve to facilitate overt aggressive actions. Indeed, arousal stemming from such diverse sources as competitive games (Christy, Gelfand, & Hartmann, 1971), vigorous exercise (Zillmann, 1982), and even certain forms of music (Rogers & Ketcher, 1979) can all facilitate aggression under some conditions. But why, precisely, do such effects occur? The answer seems to involve a process known as **excitation transfer,** and several other factors as well (Zillmann, 1982). Briefly, excitation transfer refers to the fact that often, physiological arousal dissipates slowly over time. As a result, some portion of such arousal may persist as an individual moves from one situation to another. This residual excitement, in turn, can then transfer to the new context, and intensify any emotional experiences occurring in it. Perhaps returning to our roller coaster example will help clarify how such effects can influence overt aggression.

Immediately after the frightening ride is over, the person involved experiences a high level of arousal. As time passes, this arousal tends to dissipate. Yet a portion may still remain when he or she is insulted some moments later. This

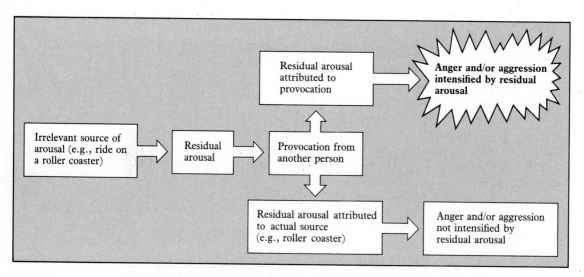

FIGURE 9.10   *Heightened arousal and aggression:*
The role of excitation transfer.

According to excitation transfer theory, *physiological arousal induced in one situation may persist and intensify emotional reactions in other, later situations. For example, if an individual experiences increased arousal unrelated to anger or aggression and is later provoked, residual arousal from the first situation may transfer to this second one and intensify feelings of anger. As a result, overt aggression, too, may be enhanced. But such effects only seem to occur when individuals attribute their residual arousal to provocation (upper pathway). If, instead, they correctly attribute it to its actual source, neither anger nor aggression is enhanced (lower pathway).*

residual arousal may then magnify or intensify any feelings of anger experienced by this person. And, in this manner, it may also enhance the strength or likelihood of overt aggressive reactions (see Figure 9.10). A large body of research findings suggest that such effects are quite common (e.g., Zillmann, Katcher, & Milavsky, 1972; Ramirez, Bryant, & Zillmann, 1982). However, we should hasten to add that they do not occur under all conditions. In order for residual excitation to enhance later aggression, the persons involved must interpret this arousal as stemming from the provocation they have endured. If, instead, they correctly attribute such feelings to their actual source (some previous irrelevant event such as a ride on a roller coaster), aggression will *not* be enhanced. Of course, as you probably know from your own experience, it is often difficult to determine the sources of current feelings of arousal. Indeed, when such reactions are intense, we usually pay little attention to the task of identifying their origins! For this reason, excitation transfer may well take place in many situations, and play a key role in facilitating overt aggressive actions.

Sexual Arousal and Aggression: Is There a Link?

If arousal stemming from such diverse sources as competition, physical exercise, frightening experiences, and even music can sometimes enhance aggressive behavior, it seems reasonable to pose a related question: Can sexual arousal, too, have such effects? Actually, it has often been proposed that there is a close and important link between sex and aggression. For example, Freud (1933) contended that desires to hurt or be hurt by one's lover are a normal part of sexual relations. Similarly, in a best-selling volume, Eric Berne (1964) suggested that the arousal of aggressive feelings often serves to heighten sexual pleasure for both men and women. These and related comments seem to imply that sexual arousal may indeed exert an important effect upon overt aggression. But is this really the case? Does this specific type of arousal actually affect our tendencies to aggress against others?

Initial studies designed to investigate this issue yielded a very confusing pattern of results. On the one hand, several investigations reported that exposure to erotic materials (and the increased sexual arousal so produced) enhanced overt aggression (e.g., Jaffe et al., 1974; Zillmann, 1971). On the other hand, though, several other experiments reported that exposure to erotica actually *reduced* later aggression (Baron, 1974a; Baron & Bell, 1973). Fortunately, this puzzling situation did not persist for long. Further research soon revealed that the effects of sexual arousal upon aggression depended very strongly on the type of erotic materials employed to induce such arousal. When these materials are quite mild in nature (e.g., nudes from *Playboy* or *Playgirl*, pictures of young men and women in bathing suits), aggression is reduced. When, instead, they are quite explicit (e.g., films of couples engaged in various acts of lovemaking), aggression is enhanced (Baron & Bell, 1977; Baron, 1979; Ramirez, Bryant, & Zillmann, 1982). In short, the relationship between sexual arousal and physical aggression seems to take the form shown in Figure 9.11.

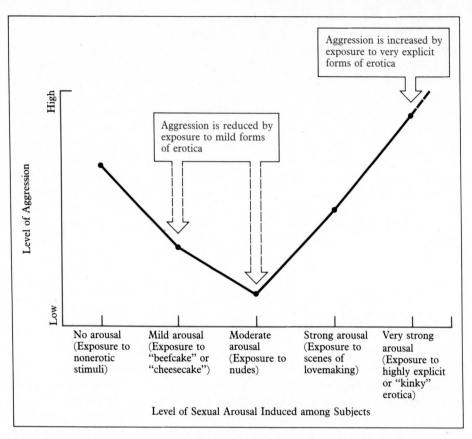

FIGURE 9.11   *Sexual arousal and aggression: The basic relationship.*

Recent studies suggest that the relationship between sexual arousal and aggression takes the form shown here. Mild or moderate levels of arousal (induced through exposure to mild forms of erotica) seem to reduce overt aggression. In contrast, high levels of arousal (induced through exposure to more explicit forms of erotica) tend to increase such behavior.

But what accounts for the shape of this function? Why do mildly erotic materials reduce aggression while more explicit ones enhance such behavior? One explanation is as follows. Exposure to erotica actually induces two distinct effects. First, such materials lead to *increased sexual arousal.* Second, they induce *positive and negative feelings* among the persons who view them. Whether aggression will then be increased or reduced depends largely on the pattern of such reactions. For example, consider mild erotic materials. Such stimuli tend to evoke low levels of arousal and mainly positive feelings. (Most people find them pleasant and like them.) Since positive emotional reactions may be incompatible with feelings of anger and overt aggression (Baron, 1977; Zillmann & Bryant, 1983), it is not surprising that such materials often reduce aggressive behavior. In contrast, consider explicit forms of erotica. These stimuli are usually quite arousing. And often, individuals exposed to them also experience negative reactions (e.g., they find them too explicit for their liking or even revolting in some manner). Together, such heightened arousal and feelings of annoyance may well facilitate overt aggression. Results offering support for this two-factor explanation have been obtained in several experiments (e.g., Zillmann et al., 1981). For example, White (1979) found that erotic materials inducing positive feelings among subjects reduced their level of aggression, while erotica inducing strong arousal plus negative feelings enhanced such behavior. Thus, it appears that the impact of sexual stimuli upon aggression varies with two key factors: the level of arousal they induce, and the positive or negative feelings they generate among the persons who view them.

In answer to the question at the start of this section, then, we can respond as follows: there is in fact an important link between sexual arousal and aggression. However, as is often the case with respect to key forms of human social behavior, the nature of this relationship has turned out to be far more complex than was at first suspected (Zillmann, in press). (For a discussion of the effects of exposure to an especially disturbing type of pornography, please see the **Focus on Research** section on pp. 346–347.)

Other Factors Affecting Aggression: Aggressive Cues, Crowding, Heat, and Pain

While frustration, direct provocation, and the other factors we have examined so far have received the greatest amount of attention from researchers, many other conditions also play a role in the occurrence of human aggression. For example, a series of studies by Leonard Berkowitz and his colleagues suggests that aggression can often be elicited by the presence of **aggressive cues**—stimuli associated with past anger or aggressive actions (Berkowitz, 1974). Thus, weapons can sometimes enhance overt aggression by their mere presence on the scene, even if they are not actually used in the assaults that take place. As Berkowitz has put it, "the trigger can pull the finger," as well as the reverse. Similarly, other research suggests that several *environmental factors* such as heat, crowding, noise, air pollution, and even negative air ions can facilitate overt aggression (Baron, Russell, & Arms, 1983). And still other studies conducted quite recently point to the important aggression-eliciting impact of *physical pain* (Berkowitz, Cochran, & Embree, 1981). We could go on to list many other factors as well, but by now the main point we wish to make should be clear: contrary to some of the theoretical views described earlier in this chapter, human aggression seems to stem from a multitude of different factors.

Individual Determinants of Aggression: Personality, Genes, and Sex

Think back over the many persons you have known during your life. Can you remember any who, because of a very low "boiling point" became involved in more than their share of aggressive incidents? Similarly, can you recall others

Violent Pornography:
A Special, Dangerous Case

As we have just seen, high levels of sexual arousal, especially when accompanied by feelings of annoyance or repulsion, seem capable of enhancing overt aggressive actions. Thus, it appears that some types of erotic materials, at least, can have potentially dangerous consequences. Unfortunately, however, the story does not end there. In recent years, the range of erotica available in magazines, X-rated films, and elsewhere has moved far beyond mere explicitness. Specifically, such materials have shown an alarming trend toward the inclusion of high levels of *sexual violence*—most of it directed toward women (Malamuth & Spinner, 1980). Such **violent pornography** includes scenes of rape, sadomasochism, and the use of sexual coercion. And often, it depicts female victims as inviting or actually enjoying these assaults. Do such materials exert any negative behavioral effects over and above those we have already described? Unfortunately, growing evidence suggests that they do (Malamuth & Donnerstein, 1982).

First, with respect to overt aggression, several studies suggest that exposure to violent pornography may serve to increase aggression by males against females (Donnerstein, 1980; Malamuth & Donnerstein, 1983). For example, in one study on this topic, Donnerstein and Berkowitz (1981) exposed male subjects to one of three different films: a noerotic movie showing a talk show, a purely erotic film in which a young couple made love, or an aggressive erotic film in which a woman is both physically and sexually assaulted by two men. Two versions of this final film existed. In one, the victim was shown as suffering during her mistreatment (the *negative outcome* condition), while in the other, she was shown as becoming a willing participant in the sexual activity (the *positive outcome* condition).

After viewing one of these films, subjects were angered or not angered by a female accomplice. Then, they obtained an opportunity to aggress against her by means of electric shock. Results were both clear and unsettling. While the purely erotic film failed to enhance aggression against the female victim, the aggressive erotic film did produce such effects. And in the case of subjects who had been angered by the victim, this was true even when she was shown as suffering during the assault. (Among subjects who had not been provoked, aggression was enhanced by the aggressive erotic film only when the victim was shown as "enjoying" her mistreatment; see Figure 9.12.)

But violent pornography seems to exert other negative effects as well. For example, exposure to such films seems to enhance the acceptance of false beliefs about rape—myths that seem to trivialize this repugnant crime (e.g., the view that many women have an unconscious wish to be raped). Similarly, exposure to such materials seems to increase the acceptance of interpersonal violence against women (Malamuth & Check, 1981). (We should note, by the way, that other evidence suggests that even *nonviolent* pornography can produce such effects if it is viewed on a regular basis [Zillmann & Bryant, 1983].)

Together, present findings indicate that the growing availability and popularity of violent pornography may represent a dangerous trend in society. Such materials seem to weaken restraints against violence toward women, to increase sexually calloused attitudes, and to trivialize rape. Does this mean, then, that they should be restricted or controlled in some manner? As we hope you realize, this is a social or political decision, largely outside the scope of science. Moreover censorship—even

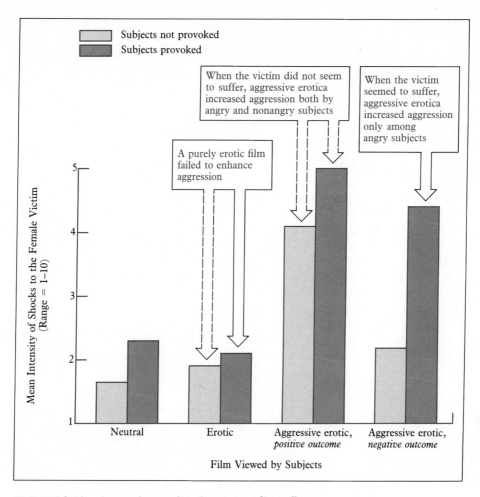

FIGURE 9.12   *Aggressive erotica: Some unsettling effects.*

Exposure to an aggressive erotic film in which the female victim did not appear to suffer enhanced later aggression against a female accomplice by both angry and nonangry subjects. In contrast, exposure to an aggressive erotic film in which the victim seemed to suffer as a result of an attack by two males enhanced later aggression only by angry individuals. Note that an erotic film with no violent content failed to increase later aggression. [Source: Based on data from Donnerstein & Berkowitz, 1981.]

in such a seemingly clear-cut case as this—is a dangerous step in any free society, and should be approached only with utmost caution. What we *can*

state, though, is this: In the light of current evidence, it is indeed difficult to find any redeeming social value in such materials.

who, because of an apparent lack of temper, almost never engaged in aggressive behavior? In all probability, you can. Bringing such persons to mind is more than a simple exercise in memory. It serves to underscore a very important point: individuals differ greatly in ways that dispose them either toward or away from aggression. Some possess traits and characteristics that lead them to aggress often and with high intensity. In contrast, others possess traits that orient them in the opposite direction—away from aggression and violence.

Psychologists have long been aware of such **individual determinants of aggression,** and have devoted much attention to their study. As you might guess, their research in this respect indicates that many factors play a role in determining a given person's level of aggression—everything from differences in the threshold for anger (Toch, 1980) through a large number of specific personality traits (e.g., Carver & Glass, 1978; Ohbuchi, 1982; see Figure 9.13). In this discussion, however, we will focus on two topics that have been of major interest to researchers and that seem to have important practical implications: (1) differences between the sexes in the tendency to aggress and (2) the possible role of genetic factors in aggression (the controversial XYY syndrome).

Sex Differences in Aggression: Myth or Reality?

Are males more aggressive than females? It has often been assumed that they are. Indeed, it has sometimes been proposed that females are truly the

FIGURE 9.13   Personality and aggression.

As this cartoon suggests, some individuals seem to become involved in far more than their share of aggressive incidents. [Source: © 1976 NEA, Inc. Reprinted by permission.]

"gentle sex," relatively free from aggressive urges—except when provoked by males! The basis for such beliefs is readily apparent. First, traditional sex roles tend to emphasize toughness and assertiveness for males, but gentleness and passivity for females. And crime statistics suggest that men are almost ten times as likely as women to be arrested for violent acts (Wilson, 1981). But what does systematic research on this issue reveal? Are these beliefs about the greater aggressiveness of males really justified? The answer, we believe, is "probably not."

Actually, initial studies concerned with this matter seemed to uncover findings consistent with the view stated above. That is, males were found to be more aggressive than females, and females generally received weaker assaults (at least from male aggressors) than did males (e.g., Buss, 1963). More recent investigations, however, have failed to confirm these results. Instead, they have generally reported the absence of any consistent differences between males and females with respect to overt aggression (Baron & Ball, 1974; Frodi, Macaulay, & Thome, 1977). What accounts for this sharp difference? Why were males found to be more aggressive in early laboratory studies but not in more recent ones? Two key possibilities exist.

First, as you already know, recent years have brought major shifts in prevailing sex roles. Many people no longer accept the view that males must be tough, ambitious, and assertive, while females must be kind, passive, and submissive. Rather, they feel that none of these traits are the sole property of one sex or the other. These and related changes may well constitute one factor serving to reduce any differences between males and females with respect to aggression. Second, close examination of the two groups of studies just mentioned reveals that in the first, strong provocation was generally absent. In the second, such annoyance *was* present. This fact points to the possibility that difference between the sexes in terms of aggression may occur only in the absence of direct provocation. When such conditions exist, in contrast, these differences may totally vanish.

Support for this suggestion is provided by the findings of several recent studies (Richardson et al., 1979; Richardson et al., 1983). For example, in the study by Richardson and her colleagues (Richardson et al., 1983) male and female subjects took part in a competitive reaction time task in which they tried to respond more quickly on each of a series of trials than an opponent. It was explained to subjects that on each occasion, the slower of the two players would receive a shock supposedly set for him or her by the other individual. In reality, however, the strength of these shocks was determined by the experimenter. During the study, subjects were made to "lose" on 50 percent of the trials. And on these occasions, they actually received a shock from the opponent. The strength of these jolts was gradually raised by the experimenter (remember *she*, not the other player, actually controlled the shocks). Thus, from subjects' point of view, it appeared that their opponent was behaving in an increasingly aggressive manner over time.

Within this general context, male and female subjects competed either against a member of their own or the opposite sex. Thus, sex differences in the tendency to aggress could be readily observed. Results were quite revealing. On

FIGURE 9.14   *Sex differences in aggression: The crucial role of provocation.*

In the absence of strong provocation, males often behave more aggressively than females. However, in the presence of such treatment, differences between the sexes frequently seem to disappear. [Source: Based on data from Richardson, Vandenberg, & Humphries, 1983.]

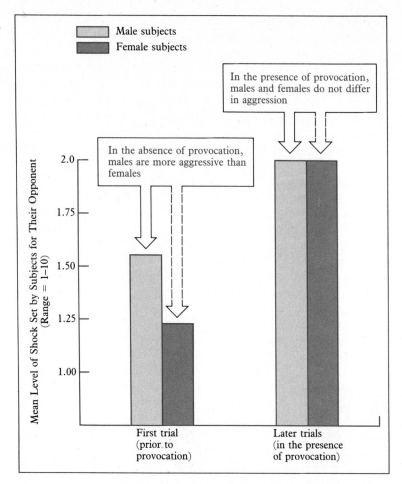

the first trial during the session—before any provocation from the opponent had occurred—clear sex differences existed. Males directed stronger shocks to their opponent than females, and female victims received weaker shocks than did males (see Figure 9.14). But on later trials, after provocation occurred, these differences generally vanished. In fact, there was some indication that female subjects actually raised the strength of their own shocks to the opponent faster than did the males.

In sum, it appears that differences between the sexes with respect to aggression are a "sometime thing." Under some conditions—the absence of strong provocation, or when aggression seems unjustified or inappropriate— females do seem to be less aggressive than males. But under others—in the face of strong provocation or when aggression seems appropriate—they may seek to inflict just as much harm upon the persons who annoy them as do their male counterparts.

Heredity and Aggression: The XYY Syndrome

Normally, the cells of the human body possess forty-six chromosomes. Two of these—X and Y—play a crucial role in the determination of sex. Men possess one X and one Y (*XY*) while women possess two X's (*XX*). On rare occasions, however, men possessing an extra Y chromosome (**XYY**) are encountered. For many years, this unusual pattern was viewed as being quite unimportant. In the mid-1960s, however, an interesting fact came to light. Men possessing an extra Y chromosome are far more common among prisoners than they are in the general population as a whole (Jacobs, Brunton, & Melville, 1965). While only one newborn baby boy in a thousand is an XYY, fully fifteen out of each 1,000 prisoners fall into this category (Jarvik, Klodin, & Matsuyama, 1973).

On the basis of this finding, and the fact that a few persons guilty of horrifying crimes of violence were found to be XYY individuals, some scientists suggested a startling possibility. Perhaps the extra Y chromosome possessed by such men caused them to be highly aggressive and so to end up in prison. In short, it was suggested that XYY individuals are "supermales," genetically programmed for violence. While this is a fascinating suggestion, it has not been supported by recent research (Bandura, 1973). Perhaps the most convincing evidence against this view has been obtained in a large-scale study conducted in Denmark by Witkin and his colleagues (Witkin et al., 1976).

In this investigation, a very large group of Danish men (4,591 in all) were tested for chromosome type. Out of this original group 4,139 were XYs, 12 were XYYs, and 16 were XXYs (another rare chromosome type). Information regarding the height, intelligence, and past criminal activities of all these persons were then gathered from public records. (These are very complete in Denmark). This information was then used to test several possibilities about the behavior of XYY individuals.

The first and most important was the suggestion that such persons are more aggressive than XYs. If this is the case, we would expect to find that XYY criminals are involved in acts of violence much more frequently than criminals showing the normal XY pattern. No evidence for this idea was obtained. Careful study of past records showed that XYYs were *not* more likely than XYs to commit such crimes as murder or assault.

A second possibility was that XYYs are not as bright as XYs and so are much more likely to be caught and convicted when they engage in criminal activities. Clear support for this suggestion was obtained. XYY individuals did score lower than XY persons on standard tests of intelligence. Further, records of their crimes suggested that this factor played a role in their being brought to justice. (Often, their crimes were so poorly planned and executed that they were almost certain to be caught and to be convicted.)

Taken as a whole, the findings of the research conducted by Witkin et al. (1976) point to the following conclusions. XYYs are *not* more likely than XYs to become involved in either violent or nonviolent crimes. When they engage in such activities, however, their lower level of intelligence may lead them to blunder in ways that increase the chances of their being caught and placed behind bars. Thus, it is this factor—*not* increased tendencies toward aggression—that accounts for the frequent presence of XYY individuals in prisons.

Aggression: Its Prevention and Control

Aggression, as we have already seen, stems from many different sources. Because of this fact, it is probably unreasonable to assume that such behavior can be prevented or reduced by any single technique. Rather, a number of different tactics, each most appropriate for use in a specific set of circumstances, are probably needed (Baron, 1983a). In this final section, we will examine several of these techniques, noting for each its basic nature and the major conditions that either foster or impair its success.

Punishment: An Effective Deterrent to Aggression?

Common sense suggests that either punishing aggressors for their violent behavior or simply threatening to do so may be an effective means of deterring such actions. On the basis of this belief, most societies have established severe penalties for aggressive crimes such as murder, rape, and assault (see Figure 9.15). In contrast to this general view, psychologists have been less certain about the ability of punishment to affect aggression and other forms of human behavior. Indeed, at one time, many experts on this process felt that punishment is quite ineffective and can produce only temporary effects at best. More recently, however, the pendulum of scientific opinion has swung the other way. Thus, a growing number of researchers now believe that if it is used with care,

FIGURE 9.15   Severe punishment: The price of violent crime in most societies.

In most societies, the penalties for aggressive crimes are severe.
[Source: Photo by Paul Conklin.]

punishment can exert both a powerful and permanent impact upon behavior (Bower & Hilgard, 1981). In order for it to operate successfully, however, several conditions must be met. First, punishment must follow the objectionable behavior immediately, or at least very quickly. Second, it must be of sufficient magnitude to be aversive to the recipient. And third, there must be a clear contingency between the individual's behavior and punishment. That is, it must be apparent that certain types of behavior will be followed by punishment with a very high probability, and such behavior must never be followed by approval or other forms of reward. Research findings suggest that when these conditions are met, punishment can be quite effective in altering the behavior of human beings and many other organisms.

Unfortunately, though, these principles seem to be largely ignored in cases where punishment is used to deter human violence. In most societies, the delivery of punishment for aggressive acts does *not* take place in accordance with these key conditions. The interval between the performance of a violent crime and punishment for it is often very long; indeed, it can be months or even years. The magnitude of punishment delivered can vary greatly, being harsh in some places at some times, but quite lenient or mild in other locations at other times. And finally, the contingency between aggressive acts and punishment is far from certain (e.g., most criminals realize that the likelihood of being caught and convicted is very slight). In view of such conditions, it is hardly surprising that punishment has often been quite ineffective as a means of deterring human violence. Indeed, it would be far more surprising if it *did* succeed in this respect. But again, this does not imply that such treatment itself is incapable of reducing aggression. On the contrary, research evidence suggests that it *can* exert such beneficial effects if appropriate conditions exist (e.g., Baron, 1973; Rogers, 1980a).

But the absence of several essential conditions is not the only reason why punishment often fails as a deterrent to human aggression. In addition, there are important complications stemming from the psychological impact of punishment itself. First, the recipients of such treatment may often view it as an unjustified attack against them — especially if they observe many other persons avoiding punishment for similar actions. To the extent they perceive it in this fashion, punishment is more likely to instill strong desires for revenge among such persons rather than lasting restraints against violence. Second, the individuals who deliver punishment may often serve as *aggressive models* for those who receive it. In this way, too, they may actually tend to stimulate rather than discourage similar actions by the recipients.

Are we to conclude, then, that punishment is largely useless as a means of deterring human aggression? We do not believe that this is so. As noted earlier, research findings suggest that if this procedure is used appropriately, it *can* succeed in deterring such actions. And, of course, when punishment involves the restraint of violent persons or their simple removal from society, it can prevent additional violence quite effectively. In order for punishment to succeed, however, it must be used with great skill and care. If it is, punishment can be of considerable use in the deterrence of human violence; if it is not, it will probably fail to exert such beneficial effects. And then, as its critics suggest, it may be viewed as a largely useless exercise in cruelty or retribution.

Catharsis: Does Getting It out of Your System Really Help?

Suppose that one day, you are strongly angered by your boss: she criticizes you harshly for something that was not your fault. After she leaves, you pick up the morning newspaper and tear it into small irregular shreds. Would this behavior make you feel better? And would it reduce your desire to "get even" with your boss in some manner? According to the famous **catharsis hypothesis,** the answer to both questions is "yes." Briefly, this view suggests that providing angry individuals with the opportunity to "blow off steam" through vigorous but nonharmful actions will (1) reduce their level of arousal and (2) lower their tendencies to engage in overt acts of aggression (see Figure 9.16). Both of these

FIGURE 9.16   *Catharsis: An effective means for preventing aggression?*

According to the catharsis hypothesis, *participation in vigorous but nonharmful activities can reduce the level of arousal experienced by angry persons, and also lower their tendencies to aggress against others. Presumably, then, the boy shown here would be less likely to assault another person after attacking the snowman. Unfortunately, though, evidence concerning the effectiveness of catharsis as a deterrent to overt aggression is quite mixed. [Source: Drawing by Lorenz; © 1972 The New Yorker Magazine, Inc.]*

suggestions have enjoyed widespread acceptance for a number of years. At present, though, neither is strongly supported by available research evidence.

First, with respect to the view that tension can often be reduced through participation in safe, nonharmful activities, results have been mixed. On the one hand, it appears that the arousal stemming from strong provocation *can* sometimes be reduced through participation in physically exhausting activities (Zillmann, 1979). Thus, tension reduction through the performance of cathartic activities seems possible. On the other hand, it also appears that the best means of reducing such arousal is through the performance of acts that directly harm the source of one's anger (Hokanson & Burgess, 1962; Hokanson, Burgess, & Cohen, 1963). That is, after being angered, individuals provided with an opportunity to physically harm the person who annoyed them often show larger and faster reductions in arousal than persons permitted to engage in other kinds of activity (Hokanson, 1970). At present, then, evidence concerning the tension-reducing impact of catharsis is far from compelling.

Turning to the suggestion that the performance of "safe" aggressive actions reduces the likelihood of more harmful forms of aggression, the picture is perhaps even more discouraging. Research on this topic indicates that overt aggression is *not* reduced by (1) watching scenes of filmed or televised violence (Geen, 1978), (2) attacks against inanimate objects (Mallick & McCandless, 1966), and (3) verbal assaults against others. Indeed, there is some evidence that aggression may actually be increased by each of these conditions.

As you can see, these findings cast serious doubt upon the widespread occurrence of catharsis. It might still be suggested, though, that such effects take place under one special set of conditions: when we can either inflict or observe direct harm to the persons who have annoyed us. That is, having evened the score, we may be less likely to attack such persons on later occasions. While this suggestion seems quite reasonable, evidence regarding it, too, has been mixed. Several experiments suggest that opportunities to harm the objects of our anger, or to see them harmed by someone else, do indeed reduce our tendencies to aggress against them on later occasions (Fromkin, Goldstein, & Brock, 1977; Konečni & Ebbesen, 1976). But several other studies indicate that such actions either fail to reduce later aggression or even tend to increase its occurrence (e.g., Geen, Stonner, & Shope, 1975). At present, there is no simple or obvious explanation for these conflicting findings. One possibility, though, is as follows. Contrary to popular belief, catharsis occurs only under highly specific conditions. Thus, its presence in some studies but not in others may stem from the fact that these conditions were met in some instances but not in others. Regardless of whether this explanation is accurate, existing evidence on the occurrence of catharsis seems to point to three tentative conclusions.

First, as just suggested, catharsis is not as widespread or general as once believed. Second, while the opportunity to even the score with persons who have annoyed us sometimes reduces our tendency to aggress against them on later occasions, this is not always so. Finally, while participation in cathartic activities may sometimes succeed in reducing aggression, the potential benefits of such procedures have probably been overstated in the past.

Additional Techniques for the Reduction of Aggression:
Nonaggressive Models, Training in Social Skills,
Cognitive Interventions, and Incompatible Responses

In a sense, our discussion up to this point may be viewed as somewhat discouraging. So far, we have indicated that neither punishment nor catharsis is quite as useful in controlling aggression as we might wish to believe. At this point, therefore, we will strike a much more positive note. In recent years, several new techniques for reducing human aggression have been devised (e.g., Baron, 1983a; Goldstein et al., 1981; Kremer & Stephens, 1983). And, encouragingly, initial results suggest that several of these procedures may be quite successful. Among the most promising of these are: (1) exposure to nonaggressive models, (2) training in social skills, (3) cognitive interventions, and (4) the induction of incompatible responses.

Exposure to nonaggressive models: The contagion of restraint. If exposure to aggressive models in films or on TV can induce heightened aggression among viewers, it seems only reasonable to expect that parallel exposure to nonaggressive models might produce opposite effects. That is, witnessing the actions of persons who demonstrate or urge restraint even in the face of strong provocation might serve to reduce the level of aggression shown by observers. That this is indeed the case is suggested by the findings of several experiments (e.g., Baron, 1972; Donnerstein & Donnerstein, 1976). In these studies, individuals exposed to the actions of nonaggressive models later demonstrated lower levels of aggression than persons not exposed to such models. And this was the case even when they had been strongly provoked prior to their opportunity to aggress (Baron & Kepner, 1970). Such findings suggest that it may be useful to plant nonaggressive models in tense and threatening situations; their presence on the scene may well serve to tip the balance away from violence. And at the very least, they may remind individuals that there are other ways of responding to provocation than through retaliation.

Training in social skills: Communication in place of violence. One major reason why many persons become involved in aggressive exchanges is disturbingly simple: they are severely lacking in essential social skills. For example, such individuals are unable to communicate their wishes to others, have an unfortunate style of self-expression, and are insensitive to cues that reveal the emotional states of other persons. As a result, they experience severe and repeated frustration, often misinterpret the actions or feelings of others, and blunder in ways that enrage the persons around them. Further, growing evidence suggests that persons lacking in such skills account for a high proportion of the violence occurring in any given society (Toch, 1969, 1980). To the extent this is true, one effective means of reducing the overall level of aggression might involve equipping such individuals with the skills they so sorely lack. In recent years, systematic programs for accomplishing this task have been developed (Goldstein et al., 1981). And preliminary findings suggest that they can be quite effective. After undergoing such training, individuals are much less likely to serve as either the source or target of violence. Indeed, their relations with many other persons, ranging from spouses to total strangers, seem to improve dramatically. In view of such results, this basic approach seems to be a very promising one, worthy of additional, careful study.

Cognitive interventions: The role of mitigating circumstances. Earlier, we noted that attribution often plays a major role in determining reactions to provocation. To review: if we decide that provocation from another person stems mainly from internal causes (e.g., his or her motives and intentions) we are much more likely to grow angry and respond aggressively than if we conclude that these actions stem largely from external factors beyond his or her control. This fact, in turn, points to an intriguing possibility: perhaps aggression can be reduced in many situations by conditions encouraging individuals to make such external attributions. In short, if persons exposed to provocation can be induced to interpret provocative actions by others as stemming mainly from external causes, later aggression may be greatly reduced. But how, precisely, can such shifts in attributions be produced? One possible answer is suggested by research on the impact of *mitigating circumstances* (e.g., Zillmann & Cantor,

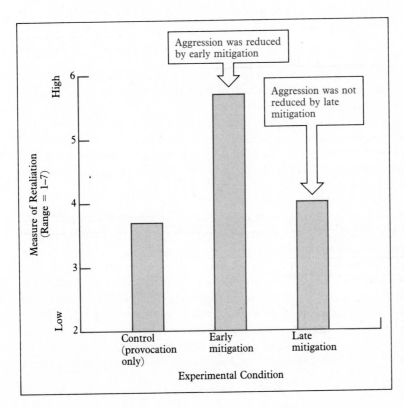

FIGURE 9.17   *Information about mitigating circumstances: Timing is crucial.*

*When individuals received information about mitigating circumstances immediately after being provoked (**early mitigation group**), their level of aggression was sharply reduced. However, when they did not receive such information until several minutes after being annoyed (**late mitigation group**), aggression remained quite high. These findings suggest that the timing of information about mitigating circumstances is crucial. [Source: Based on data from Kremer & Stephens, 1983.]*

1976). In such studies, individuals who have been annoyed by another either receive or do not receive information suggesting that the provocation they endured stemmed mainly from external causes. Then, they are provided with an opportunity to retaliate against the annoyer. The results of such research have been quite encouraging; indeed, they suggest that exposure to appropriate information concerning mitigating circumstances can often be highly effective in reducing both anger and overt aggression. For example, consider a recent study by Kremer and Stephens (1983). In this experiment, male subjects were first provoked by an experimenter who accused them, unjustly, of ruining recordings of their physiological responses by moving about. In one condition (*early mitigation*), subjects were then immediately informed (by another person) that the rude individual was very worried about a midterm exam. In another condition (*late mitigation*), subjects received the same information, but only several minutes after being angered. Finally, in a third (*control*) group, no information about mitigating circumstances was provided. Subjects' tendencies to retaliate against the rude experimenter were then measured by having them evaluate him on a questionnaire. Presumably, their ratings would determine whether he would continue to receive financial aid in the future. As you can see from Figure 9.17, p. 357, results were both clear and heartening. Specifically, subjects in the early mitigation group directed significantly lower retaliation against the experimenter than those in the control condition. In contrast, however, subjects in the late mitigation group did not demonstrate similar reductions in overt aggression. Apparently, information about mitigating circumstances must be presented soon after provocation in order to be effective; delay, in this respect, can prove quite costly!

At this point, we should insert a brief note of caution: in many situations, provocations *are* fully intended and do stem from internal causes. Under these circumstances, information about mitigating circumstances is not appropriate and will probably fail to deter retaliation. In many other instances, though, seemingly provocative actions are actually *not* intended. Thus, calling individuals' attention to this key fact may help to avert unnecessary retaliation and the reciprocal, escalating process that often characterizes human aggression (Goldstein, Davis, & Herman, 1975).

Incompatible responses: Empathy, humor, and mild sexual arousal. A final approach to the control of aggression rests upon the following basic principle. All organisms (including human beings) are incapable of engaging in two **incompatible responses** at once. For example, it is impossible both to daydream and balance your checkbook. Similarly, it is difficult (if not impossible) to feel depressed and elated at once. Extending this principle to the control of aggression, it seems possible that such harmful behavior can be reduced through the induction (among potential aggressors) of responses incompatible either with overt aggression itself or with the emotion of anger. And in fact, a growing body of research evidence suggests that this is the case. When angry

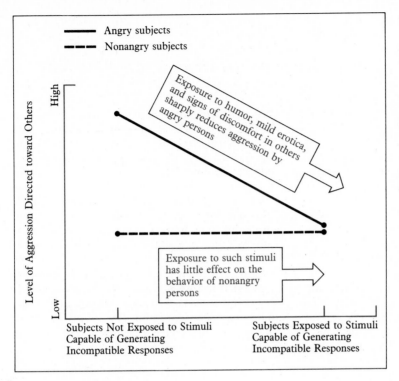

FIGURE 9.18 *The induction of incompatible responses: A summary of current research findings.*

Angry individuals who are exposed to stimuli such as mild erotica, amusing cartoons, or signs of discomfort on the part of others often show much lower levels of aggression than angry persons not exposed to such materials. These findings offer support for the view that the induction of responses incompatible with anger or overt violence may be an effective technique for reducing human aggression. (In contrast, exposure to such materials appears to have little effect upon the behavior of persons who have not been provoked.)

individuals are induced to experience emotional states incompatible with anger or overt aggression, such as *empathy, mild sexual arousal,* or *humor,* they do show reduced levels of aggression. Specifically, in such research, subjects were first angered or not angered, and then exposed either to stimuli such as mild forms of erotica and humorous cartoons, or more neutral materials (pictures of scenery and abstract art). When later given an opportunity to aggress against the person who annoyed them, angry participants showed much lower levels of attack if they had viewed the incompatible-response-generating stimuli than if they had seen the neutral materials (e.g., Baron, 1983b; Mueller & Donnerstein, 1976; see Figure 9.18). In contrast, the behavior of nonangry subjects was not affected by exposure to these stimuli. (This is not surprising: the level of aggression shown by such persons is generally so low that there is no room for further reductions.) These and other findings suggest that getting angry individuals "off the aggressive track," so to speak, may often be an effective means for preventing overt violence. (For a discussion of how the incompatible response strategy may be put to practical use, please see the **On the Applied Side** section on pp. 360–361.)

360

ON THE
APPLIED SIDE

*Incompatible Responses:
Some Potential, Practical Uses*

By now, two major points should be clear: (1) many different techniques for reducing human aggression exist, and (2) none of these—alas!—are perfect. This second point does not imply, however, that better strategies for accomplishing this crucial goal are forever beyond our grasp. On the contrary, we firmly believe that with continued refinement, such strategies *can* be developed. And in this regard, we are especially hopeful about the prospects of an approach based on the induction of incompatible responses. Three major reasons lie behind our optimism in this respect.

First, as noted earlier, growing research evidence supports the view that incompatible responses can be highly effective in reducing aggression by even extremely angry persons (Ramirez, Bryant, & Zillmann, 1982). Second, the incompatible response strategy avoids several drawbacks associated with other techniques for reducing aggression (e.g., it avoids the ethical issues raised by punishment, and the potential dangers associated with certain forms of catharsis). Finally, this strategy rests on a basic principle about behavior—one

that has been confirmed many times and that has already been put to major practical use (e.g., persons suffering from intense fears often overcome these reactions when trained to experience *relaxation,* an incompatible behavior, in situations that evoke such anxieties; Bellack, Hersen, & Kazdin, 1982). For all these reasons, we believe that the incompatible response strategy is an especially promising one. But how, precisely, can it be put to use? Basically, we feel that it may be helpful in three distinct contexts.

First, the induction of incompatible responses may often be effective in face-to-face interactions between individuals. Briefly, it can readily be applied in situations where one or more persons grows angry and so becomes ready to aggress (Baron, 1983). Humor seems especially useful in this regard, for tense and threatening situations can often be converted into friendlier ones by a well-chosen humorous remark. But other incompatible reactions, too, may prove effective. In sum, this basic strategy may be useful for heading off trouble in a wide range of ongoing social situations.

360

Summary

360

Aggression may be defined as any form of behavior directed toward the goal of harming another living being who is motivated to avoid such treatment. Many theoretical explanations for its occurrence exist, but most fall into one of three distinct categories. These attribute aggression to innate urges or tendencies, externally elicited drives, or present social conditions coupled with past social learning.

Many factors contribute to the occurrence of human aggression. Among these are *frustration, direct provocation* from others, exposure to *aggressive models* (e.g., televised violence), and *heightened arousal* (including the sexual arousal induced by several forms of erotica or pornography). Additional factors, such as crowding, heat, noise, pain, and aggressive cues may also play an important role in eliciting such behavior.

Second, the incompatible response strategy may be of considerable aid to persons who have difficulty controlling their own tempers. As you probably know, such persons frequently experience serious problems in their lives as a result of their "short fuses." If these individuals can learn to conjure up images that induce emotional states incompatible with anger, however, their ability to control their own behavior may be greatly enhanced.

Finally, it seems possible that incompatible responses can be used as one strategy for preventing an especially repellent type of violence—rape. Reports by women who have successfully fended off such attacks suggest that often they engaged in behaviors serving to induce incompatible reactions among their assailants. For example, they told these persons that they might soon be physically ill, or that they suffered from an ailment that caused them to lose control of their bodily functions during sex. And in even more surprising cases, potential victims have succeeded in averting assaults by turning to their assailants and asking them for help or protection—a tactic that may have induced feelings of empathy in the would-be rapists. Consider the following incident (Groth, 1979).

For example, one offender who had raped six women reported being deterred on one occasion: he spotted his potential victim while riding on a subway and decided that if she got

off alone . . . , he would rape her. She did exit alone in a rather remote area of town, but as the offender followed her, she turned to him and explained that because it was so late at night she didn't feel safe walking home alone and asked him if he would be kind enough to accompany her until she reached her house. He did so and never touched her, puzzled that his wish to rape her had suddenly disappeared. (p. 31)

Of course, we should hasten to add that such evidence, suggestive as it may be, is far from conclusive in nature. Thus, we certainly do not recommend that women rely on this approach as a basic means of self-defense. The fact that such informal reports are consistent with the findings of laboratory research, however, points to the possibility that the incompatible response strategy may ultimately find valuable application in this crucial area.

To conclude: both laboratory research and informal evidence suggest that the induction of incompatible responses among potential aggressors can often be highly effective in preventing violent outbursts. Additional evidence is certainly needed to confirm this possibility, as well as to reveal precisely *how* incompatible responses can best be used in potentially dangerous situations. It is our hope, though, that as such information becomes available, this strategy will shift from being merely promising to being of direct, practical value.

◆

Aggression is also affected by many traits or characteristics possessed by individuals. For example, it appears that under some conditions (e.g., in the absence of strong provocation) males may be more aggressive than females. Under other circumstances, however, the two sexes do not seem to differ in this respect. At one time, it was suggested that individuals possessing an extra Y chromosome (XYYs) were genetically programmed for violence. However, recent evidence fails to support this view.

A number of techniques for the reduction or control of human aggression have been developed. These include *punishment, catharsis, exposure to nonaggressive models,* and training in basic *social skills*. An additional strategy based upon the induction among aggressors of responses incompatible with anger or overt violence seems quite promising and may be effective in a wide range of settings.

Glossary

aggression *Any form of behavior directed toward the goal of harming or injuring another living being who is motivated to avoid such treatment.*

aggressive cues *Any stimuli associated with aggression, witnessed violence, or anger arousal. The presence of such cues can enhance overt aggression in a wide range of settings.*

aggressive models *Individuals who behave in an aggressive manner and, through such actions, influence others to act in a similar fashion. Such models are very common in films and television shows.*

catharsis hypothesis *The suggestion that providing angry persons with an opportunity to behave in a vigorous but nonharmful manner will (1) reduce their level of emotional arousal and (2) lower their tendency to aggress against others.*

drive theories of aggression *Theories that view aggression as stemming from particular external conditions serving to arouse the motive to harm or injure others. The most famous of these is the frustration-aggression hypothesis.*

excitation transfer *Refers to the fact that often physiological arousal induced in one situation may persist and transfer to other situations. Such residual arousal may then intensify any emotional experiences occurring in the later situation. In this way, arousal stemming from sources unrelated to aggression may serve to facilitate such behavior.*

frustration-aggression hypothesis *The view that frustration is a powerful elicitor of aggression. In its original form, the frustration-aggression hypothesis suggested that frustration always leads to aggression, and that aggression always stems from such thwarting.*

incompatible response strategy *A technique for the reduction of overt aggression based upon the induction, among potential aggressors, of emotional states or reactions incompatible with anger and overt violence.*

individual determinants of aggression *Refers to characteristics of individuals (e.g., personality traits, genetic background, sex) that play a role in the occurrence of aggression.*

instinct theory of aggression *The view that aggression stems from innate tendencies or urges. Among the most famous supporters of this perspective have been Sigmund Freud and Konrad Lorenz. Recently, it has also been adopted by several sociobiologists.*

situational determinants of aggression *Refers to external factors (e.g., the behavior of other persons, aspects of the physical environment) that influence the occurrence or strength of aggression.*

social learning theory of aggression *The view that aggression is a learned form of social behavior, acquired and maintained in much the same manner as other forms of social activity.*

sociobiology *The view that social behavior, like physical structure, is subject to evolution. According to this theory, members of any given species tend to show patterns of social behavior that help that species to survive and reproduce.*

violent pornography *Explicit forms of erotica in which one or more of the persons shown engage in acts of violence against one or more others. Often the victims of aggression in such materials are females.*

XYY syndrome *Refers to the suggestion that males possessing an extra Y chromosome are particularly prone to outbursts of violence. Although early evidence seemed consistent with this view, more recent findings have cast serious doubt upon its accuracy.*

For More Information

Baron, R. A. *Human aggression.* New York: Plenum, 1977.
This is a relatively nontechnical overview of research on human aggression. Separate chapters focus on social, environmental, and individual determinants of aggression. In addition, a discussion of techniques for the prevention and control of such behavior is included.

Geen, R. G., and Donnerstein, E. (Eds.). *Aggression: Theoretical and empirical reviews.* New York: Academic Press, 1983.

A collection of chapters dealing with many aspects of aggression, each prepared by an expert on this form of behavior. Many of the topics covered here (e.g., the effects of televised violence, catharsis, incompatible responses, the impact of sexual arousal on aggression) are examined in detail.

Liebert, R. M., Sprafkin, J. N., & Davidson, E. S. *The early window: Effects of television on children and youth* (2nd ed.) New York: Pergamon Press, 1982.
A timely review of the vast body of research

conducted to determine the behavioral effects of television. The sections dealing with the impact of televised violence expand upon coverage presented in this chapter. In addition, fascinating evidence concerning the impact of television advertising on children, and the impact of television on stereotypes of minorities and women is presented. All in all, an excellent, informative volume.

Malamuth, N. M., & Donnerstein, E. (Eds.). *Pornography and sexual aggression.* New York: Academic Press, 1983.
This book examines the impact of explicit erotica upon various aspects of aggression. Special attention is directed to the influence of such materials upon aggression toward females, and upon attitudes toward rape and other forms of sexual violence.

Zillmann, D. *Connections between sex and aggression.* Hillsdale, N.J.: Erlbaum, in press.
A thorough examination of one of the most intriguing relationships ever studied by psychologists: that between sexual arousal and aggression. Potential bases for this link in neurophysiology, motivation, emotion, and even cognitive processes are examined, and a wealth of scientific findings considered. An excellent source to consult if you would like to know more about this fascinating topic.

CHAPTER 10

Social Exchange:
Coming to Terms with Others

Cooperation and Competition: Working with — or against — Others

The Prisoner's Dilemma: One Technique for Studying Cooperative Behavior/ Situational Determinants of Cooperation: Tipping the Balance/Individual Determinants of Cooperation: Personal Factors in Social Exchange

Bargaining and Negotiation: Resolving Interpersonal Conflict

Extremity of Initial Offer: Why It Sometimes Pays to Be Unreasonable/Alternatives and Bargaining: The Benefits of Having an "Out"/Communication: Does It Really Help?/When Bargaining Fails: Alternative Strategies for Resolving Interpersonal Conflict

Perceived Fairness in Social Exchange: In Search of Social Justice

Judgments of Fairness in Social Exchange: Equity and Inequity/Equity or Equality? Justice, Impression Management, and Enhancing Our Own Self-image/Reactions to Unfairness: Tactics for Overcoming Injustice/A Note on Relative Deprivation: When Being a "Have-not" Generates Resentment

Special Inserts

FOCUS ON RESEARCH
   Love, Money, or . . . ? The "What" and "When" of Social Exchange

FOCUS ON RESEARCH
   Personality and Success in Social Exchange: Beware the High Mach!

ON THE APPLIED SIDE
   Social Exchange: Some Steps in the Right Direction

The tenants in your apartment complex — Tacky Acres Estates — are up in arms. During the past six months, service in the complex has slipped badly. Leaky faucets, clogged drains, and broken refrigerators remain unrepaired for days or even weeks. Maintenance of the grounds and pest control, too, have all but vanished. And heat has been barely adequate. Indeed, many residents thought they would literally freeze during a recent cold snap, when temperatures in most apartments plunged to the mid 40s Fahrenheit. To rub salt in the wounds, the rent has just been raised by more than 15 percent. Taking everything into account, the situation simply seems unfair: after all, why should residents pay more to receive less? Faced with this dilemma, tenants have taken direct action: they have organized a Residents' Association and chosen you and Chris Helson to present your grievances to the owners. Together, you and Chris have worked out an orderly plan for proceeding. You will begin by listing the tenants' complaints, and demanding that they all be rectified. Then, you will use some of the less important ones as "bargaining chips," trading these away in order to obtain the most important concessions you desire. If this approach doesn't work, however, you have two fall-back positions. First, you will suggest mediation by an impartial outside person. Spot checks of nearby apartments indicate that conditions at Tacky Acres are in fact the worst, so you are confident that if mediation takes place, residents will get most of what they want. Second, you will mention the possibility of legal action. Most tenants have indicated their willingness to contribute to a fund for hiring an attorney, and you intend to make this clear to the owners of the complex if they prove unreasonable. Armed with these plans, you have made an appointment to see the Resident Manager. You've heard that she's a smooth operator and a tough bargainer to boot. But as you approach her office, you and Chris are hopeful that an agreement satisfactory to both sides can be worked out . . .

While you may never have been involved in a situation precisely like this one, we have little doubt that you have had direct experience with several of its major elements. For example, like the tenants mentioned above, you have probably *cooperated* with others in order to gain some common goal. Similarly, you have probably *bargained* or *negotiated* with other persons over a wide range of issues. And finally, we are certain that, like the residents of Tacky Acres, you have been involved in many relationships in which you felt that you were being cheated or shortchanged in countless situations involving **social exchange** — ones in which you exchanged or traded something with others. Of course the "something" traded in such contexts (usually known as *resources*) varies greatly. In economic relationships such as

Love, Money, or . . . ? The "What" and "When" of Social Exchange

Earlier, we noted that many human relationships involve an element of exchange. That is, they involve at least some trading of resources between the participants. This basic fact, in turn, leads to an intriguing question: What resources, specifically, are exchanged in this manner? At first glance, you might reply "an infinite variety," and in a key sense, this is certainly correct. The specific items, behaviors, or services traded between individuals *are* tremendously varied. However, careful analysis of exchange relationships conducted by Foa and his colleagues (e.g., Donnenwerth & Foa, 1974; Foa, 1976) suggests that in fact, virtually everything traded in this fashion falls into just six basic categories. These are: *love* — any expression of affection, warmth, or comfort; *status* — judgments conveying high or low esteem; *information* — advice, opinions, instructions; *money*; *goods* — products or objects; and *services* — activities that benefit the recipient in some manner. Further, it appears that all these types of resources can be viewed as varying along two key dimensions. First, they differ with respect to what Foa terms *particularism* — whether, and to what degree, the value of the resources in question are influenced by the particular persons involved. For example, love is high on this dimension: who delivers it is very important. Information, in contrast, is somewhat lower. Second, the six resources also vary with respect to *concreteness* — the degree to which they take a specific form. Goods and services are high on this dimension, while information is

lower. Finally, growing evidence (e.g., Beach & Carter, 1976) suggests that human beings do not exchange various resources in a random or haphazard manner. On the contrary, in most cases, they tend to return resources similar to the ones they receive. Convincing evidence for this fact has recently been reported by Brinberg and Castell (1982).

These researchers presented male and female subjects with sentences indicating that another, imaginary person had performed behaviors that provided them with certain resources (e.g., this person had given them some goods; had told them about a lecture). In each case, subjects were then asked to indicate how likely they would be to perform certain behaviors in turn — ones that would provide the imaginary person with various resources. As you can see from Figure 10.1, results offered a clear-cut pattern: in general, subjects reported being much more likely to act in ways that would return the same type of resource to the imaginary person than in ways that would offer this individual other, different resources.

These results and those obtained in related studies (e.g., Foa, 1976; Foa & Foa, 1974) point to two basic conclusions. First, although social exchange can involve an almost infinite range of items or behaviors, this variety is captured, to a surprising degree, by the six basic categories listed above. Second, there is a strong element of reciprocity in such relationships. While individuals often return

those between buyers and sellers or employees and employers, it centers around concrete outcomes such as wages or products. In lasting social relationships such as marriage or friendship, in contrast, it often involves less tangible factors such as loyalty, status, or love. Regardless of the precise nature of the items or actions traded, however, there can be little doubt that an element of exchange is present in a wide range of human relationships. Indeed, in one sense, such exchange may be seen as playing a role in virtually every kind of social interaction (Kelley, 1979; Kelley & Thibaut, 1978). (Please see the **Focus on**

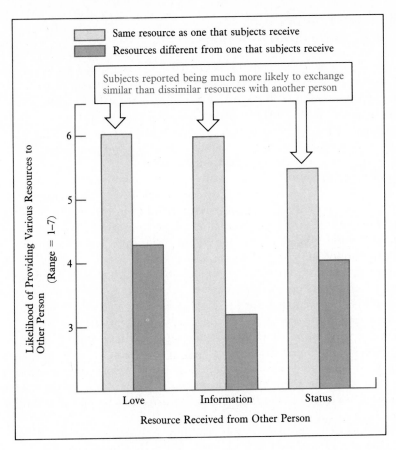

FIGURE 10.1 *Trading of similar resources: A basic fact of social exchange.*

In the study represented here, subjects were asked to indicate how likely they would be to provide different types of resources (love, information, status) to another person who had provided various resources to them. Results indicated that in general, subjects were more likely to return the same resource they had received than other resources. For example, if the other person provided them with information, they were more likely to offer this resource in return than either love or status. These findings suggest that social exchange usually involves the trading of similar rather than dissimilar resources between the persons involved. [Source: Based on data from Brinberg & Castell, 1982.]

less (or occasionally more) of a given resource than they receive, they do not generally seek to substitute one for another. Thus, they do not generally offer money in return for love, or services in return for information. In sum, social exchange generally centers around a limited number of resources, and proceeds within—rather than across—these specific domains. Given the frequency of social exchange, and its presence in a wide range of settings, knowledge of these basic facts promises to shed important new light on the nature of many human relationships.

Research section, above, for a discussion of the many kinds of resources regularly exchanged by human beings.)

Because of its importance in human relations, social exchange has long been a major topic in social psychology. While many aspects of this process have been studied, three have received the greatest amount of attention. These are **cooperation–competition, bargaining,** and perceived fairness or **equity.** Consistent with this emphasis in past research, we will focus most of our attention upon these topics.

Cooperation and Competition: Working with — or against — Others

As we noted in our discussion of prosocial behavior (see Chapter 8), individuals sometimes offer aid to others without expecting anything in return. While such one-way assistance does occur in many settings, however, it is probably less common than another type of behavior in which two or more persons work together or coordinate their actions so that the outcomes of each are enhanced. Such mutual, two-way assistance is generally known as *cooperation* and represents an important form of social exchange.

As you probably know from your own experience, individuals work together to gain a wide variety of goals (please see Figure 10.2). Thus, cooperation is a common form of social behavior. And given the obvious benefits it usually confers, you might at first expect that it will occur any time two or more persons seek the same goal. Unfortunately, though, there is an important reason why this cannot be so: *often the goals sought simply can't be shared.* To mention just a few examples, it is usually impossible for athletes or teams to share first prize, for several persons seeking the same promotion all to attain it, or for two would-be lovers to gain the affection of the same individual (at least, not at the same time!). In these and many other cases, cooperation is impossible, and an alternative form of behavior known as *competition* may develop. Here, each person strives to maximize his or her own outcomes, often at the expense of others. Because many attractive goals are sought by far more persons than can actually hope to attain them, competition too is a very common form of social interaction. And as you already know, it can often reach fierce and unsettling levels.

As we have just seen, there are some situations in which individuals have little choice but to compete with one another. Similarly, there are others in which anything but cooperation seems foolish (e.g., situations in which failure to cooperate will result in serious injury or even death for all concerned). In

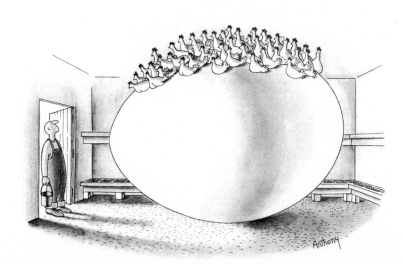

FIGURE 10.2   Cooperation: A surprising example.

When individuals cooperate, they can often attain goals none could reach alone. [Source: Drawing by Anthony; ©1976 The New Yorker Magazine, Inc.]

many settings, though, the persons involved have a choice: they can work either with or against one another. This basic fact, in turn, leads to an intriguing question: What factors tip the balance one way or the other in such cases? In short, what conditions lead individuals to choose cooperation over competition, or vice versa? We will examine several of these factors here. Before turning to this topic, however, we must pause briefly to consider another and perhaps even more basic question: How can tendencies toward cooperation or competition be studied in a systematic manner? One answer, accepted by many active researchers in this area, is outlined in the following section. Please read this discussion carefully, for the method it describes is used in much of the research we will soon consider.

The Prisoner's Dilemma: One Technique for Studying Cooperative Behavior

Imagine the following situation: two persons have been arrested on suspicion of a serious crime (e.g., armed robbery). Although it appears that they are guilty, firm evidence against them is lacking. In order to raise the odds of conviction, the district attorney (D.A.) places the suspects in separate rooms and offers each the following deal. If the prisoner will turn state's evidence and confess, then the D.A. will see to it that this person receives a very light sentence (only three months). The partner, however, will receive the maximum term (ten years in jail). The D.A. also explains to each prisoner that if neither confesses he will have to book them on a minor charge, and each will receive a fairly light punishment (one year in jail). However, he also warns that if both confess, he will charge each suspect with the more serious crime. In that case,

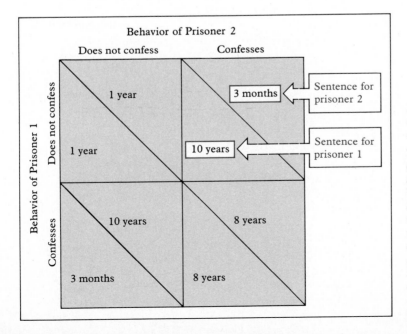

FIGURE 10.3 The prisoner's dilemma: A summary of possible outcomes.

The behavior of each prisoner (confess or not confess) is shown along the edges of the matrix. Within each of the four boxes, the outcomes for Prisoner 1 are indicated below the diagonal line, while those for Prisoner 2 are shown above this line. For example, if Prisoner 1 does not confess while Prisoner 2 does, Prisoner 1 receives a ten-year sentence, while Prisoner 2 receives only three months (upper right-hand box).

both will receive stiff sentences, but not the maximum one (each will get eight years). All possible outcomes in this situation are represented in Figure 10.3, shown on page 371. In this diagram, the behavior of each suspect (*confess* or *not confess*) is shown along the edges of the matrix. Within each of the four boxes, the outcomes for Prisoner 1 are indicated below the diagonal line, and those for Prisoner 2 above it. For example, if Prisoner 2 confesses but Prisoner 1 sticks to his story, Prisoner 2 will receive a sentence of only three months, while Prisoner 1 will receive the full ten-year punishment.

What will the prisoners do? As you can readily see, they face a difficult dilemma (hence the term **prisoner's dilemma**). On the one hand, it is to their mutual advantage to cooperate and refrain from confessing. In that way, each will receive a light sentence of only one year in jail. Thus, pressures toward trust and cooperation are strong. On the other hand, each is also tempted to betray his or her partner by turning state's evidence. By doing so, the person who confesses will gain an even shorter sentence (only three months). And, of course, there is the real danger of not confessing, while one is "sold out" by one's partner. Thus, pressures toward mutual betrayal and suspicion are also strong.

Because it involves the arousal of conflicting tendencies toward cooperation and competition, this situation seems to provide a fascinating context for the study of factors serving to tip the balance toward one or the other of these two forms of behavior. And in fact, social psychologists have adopted it for just this purpose. In research employing the prisoner's dilemma, the numbers in the matrix are changed from ones representing months and years in jail to ones representing money or arbitrary points (see Figure 10.4). And then subjects are presented with this matrix and asked to choose between the two available

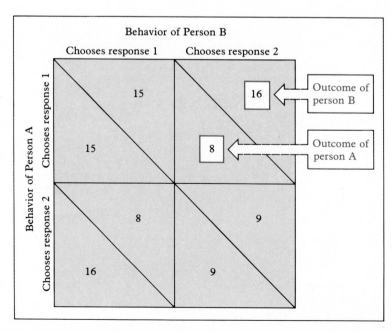

FIGURE 10.4   *The prisoner's dilemma: Its use in actual research.*

In research employing the prisoner's dilemma, subjects are often presented with an outcome matrix such as the one shown here. On each of several occasions, they choose between the two responses available (Response 1 and Response 2). The outcomes of both persons are then determined by their joint response. For example, if Person A chooses Response 1 while Person B chooses Response 2, Person A wins 8 points and Person B wins 16 points (upper right-hand box). Often, points can be converted to money or other prizes at the end of the session.

responses on a number of occasions. Since one of these responses (in this case, Response 1) represents cooperation while the other represents competition, participants' tendencies to engage in these two forms of behavior can readily be observed. Further, by varying conditions believed to tip the balance toward either cooperation or competition, the impact of such factors can be readily examined.

Given these advantages, it is not surprising that procedures based on the prisoner's dilemma have often been used by social psychologists to study cooperation and competition. Indeed, much of the research we will soon examine is based on such techniques. Before turning to this material, therefore, we should address one additional question: Do these procedures really work? Do they yield valid measures of human tendencies toward cooperation or competition? At present, this question is far from resolved. On the one hand, some critics (e.g., Gergen, 1978; Nemeth, 1972) argue that the tasks performed by subjects in such research are so artificial and so brief in duration that the findings obtained tell us little about real cooperation or competition. On the other hand, however, several lines of evidence offer support for the usefulness and validity of these methods. For example, individuals participating in the prisoner's dilemma often become highly involved in this task. As a result, they seem to experience tendencies toward cooperation and competition quite similar to those occurring in many life situations (e.g., Brickman, Becker, & Castle, 1979). Second, studies employing the prisoner's dilemma or related techniques often yield expected differences between persons from contrasting cultural backgrounds. Thus, individuals from highly competitive groups typically show higher levels of competition than those from cultures with a more cooperative orientation (e.g., Bond, Leung, & Wan, 1983; McClintock, 1974). Together, such evidence points to the conclusion that the prisoner's dilemma, while far from perfect, does provide a useful means for studying cooperation and competition under controlled laboratory conditions. In short, there seem to be some grounds for assuming that subjects' behavior in such games can often tell us much about the nature of social exchange in other, more realistic settings.

Situational Determinants of Cooperation: Tipping the Balance

Now that we have examined the major technique used by social psychologists to study cooperation and competition, we can return to the key question raised earlier: What factors tip the balance in favor of one or the other of these contrasting forms of behavior? A large number of studies have examined this issue, and their findings suggest that many conditions play a role in this respect. Among the most important of these, however, are the following: (1) the *behavior of other persons*—do *they* cooperate or compete? (2) our *attributions* about others—why, precisely, do they cooperate or compete? and (3) *group size*—how many people (or separate collections of people) are attempting to coordinate their behavior?

Reactions to cooperation from others: Do we reciprocate or exploit? Throughout our lives, we are urged to follow the "golden rule": Do unto others as we
would have others do unto us. Despite such recommendations, however, many
of our interactions with other persons seem, instead, to be governed by the
principle of **reciprocity.** In short, we often behave toward others as they have
acted toward us, *not* as we ourselves would prefer to be treated. And this
tendency toward reciprocity seems quite general in scope. Indeed, as we have
seen in previous chapters, it applies to behaviors as varied in nature as helping
on the one hand and aggression on the other (please refer to Chapters 8 and 9).
Given this high degree of generality, it seems reasonable to expect that reciprocity applies to social exchange as well. And research findings indicate that
usually it does. Very high levels of competition are generally met with similar
mistrust and confrontation (e.g., Rosenbaum, 1980); intermediate levels of
cooperation usually elicit corresponding guarded behavior from recipients
(e.g., Black & Higbee, 1973). And very high levels of cooperation can sometimes stimulate a high degree of trust and coordination in return (Kuhlman &
Marshello, 1975). The word "sometimes" should be emphasized, however, for

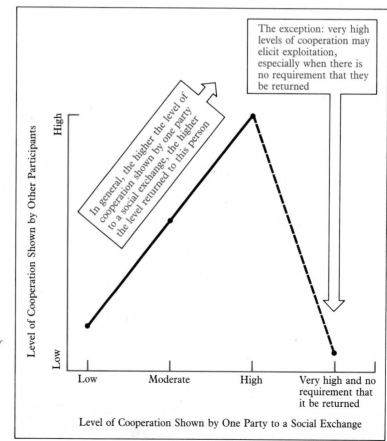

**FIGURE 10.5   *Cooperation:
Reciprocal—but only up to a
point.***

*Cooperation, like many other forms
of social behavior, is usually
governed by the principle of*
reciprocity. *Thus, the higher the
level of cooperation shown by one
party to a social exchange, the
higher the level returned by the other
participants. There seems to be one
major exception to this rule,
however: very high levels of
cooperation offered with no
requirement that they be returned
often elicit* exploitation *rather
than reciprocal trust.*

it appears that this will be the case only under certain conditions. Specifically, if one individual offers a high level of trust or cooperation to another, but makes it clear that such behavior will continue only if it is returned, cooperation may be enhanced. In contrast, if total trust or cooperation is offered without any requirement that it be reciprocated, a sharply different pattern may emerge. Here, many persons may be strongly tempted to take unfair advantage of their opponent and to respond to this individual's trust with exploitation (see Figure 10.5). That such temptation can be difficult to resist is suggested by the fact that in one well-known study (Shure, Meeker, & Hansford, 1965), fully 129 out of 143 participants responded to total cooperation from an opponent with strong exploitation. In sum, it appears that a high level of trust and cooperation will serve to induce similar behavior from recipients only when it is accompanied by an implicit message indicating that it will be quickly withdrawn if not matched.

To conclude: cooperation, like many other forms of social behavior, seems to be strongly influenced by the principle of reciprocity. In order for it to operate effectively, however, concrete steps designed to counter powerful temptations toward exploitation may be required.

Attribution and social exchange: Reacting to the apparent motives of others. Suppose that at some point in the future, you work for a large company. One of your fellow employees is a direct rival, and you have often competed with her for promotions, raises, and other benefits. One day, she appears in your office and makes a startling proposal: you should stop competing, and join forces. How would you react to this suggestion? Probably with a great deal of caution. Before deciding how to proceed, you would want to analyze carefully the motives behind her behavior. Is she sincere? Or is she merely "setting you up for the kill" in some fashion? Until you were confident that you knew the answer, you would be quite reluctant to proceed.

This situation, and many others like it, calls attention to a key fact about cooperation and competition: in choosing between these contrasting forms of behavior, we are strongly affected by more than others' overt actions. Often, we also pay careful attention to their motives and intentions. Thus, a second factor exerting powerful effects upon our tendencies to cooperate or compete with others concerns our *attributions* about the causes of their behavior.

Many studies provide direct evidence for the powerful impact of attributions on both cooperation and competition (e.g., Brickman, Becker, & Castle, 1979; Enzle, Hansen, & Lowe, 1975). Briefly, the findings of these experiments suggest that if we view another's behavior as stemming from a genuine desire to cooperate with us and so attain mutual benefits, we may well choose to cooperate with *them*. However, if we interpret their actions as stemming from a desire to manipulate or exploit us, we may spurn any overtures toward cooperation, and react competitively instead. And please note: in reaching such decisions, our attributions about the motives behind others' actions often seem to be crucial; their actual behavior appears to be of less importance

In a sense, the finding that our interpretations of others' behavior play a key role in our decision to cooperate or compete with them is far from surprising. As we have noted throughout this book, attributions frequently shape our interactions with other persons (see Chapters 2 and 9). Somewhat more surprising, however, is the fact that on some occasions this relationship can be reversed. That is, *our* tendencies to cooperate or compete with others can influence our attributions about them. Growing evidence suggests, for example, that if we behave cooperatively toward another person, we may come to view him or her as cooperative and expect such behavior in return. Similarly, if we behave competitively toward another, we may view that person as competitive, and expect him or her to act in this fashion. In short, our own tendencies to cooperate or compete may influence our perceptions of other persons and our expectations concerning their behavior (Dawes, McTavish, & Shaklee, 1977). Perhaps the clearest evidence for such effects has been reported in a study by Messé and Sivacek (1979).

In this experiment, female students played a one-trial prisoner's dilemma game against a partner. In addition to making their own choice in the game, subjects were also asked to predict how the other person would respond— whether she would choose to cooperate or compete. Messé and Sivacek predicted that in many cases participants would expect their opponent to behave as they themselves had. That is, they would expect her to cooperate if they had chosen this form of behavior but to compete if they had selected this option. As you can see from Figure 10.6, results offered strong support for this hypothesis. A high proportion of subjects did expect their partner to behave as they had.

FIGURE 10.6 *Predicting others' behavior in social exchange: A case of assumed similarity.*

As shown here, most persons participating in a prisoner's dilemma game expect their partner to behave as they do. If they cooperate, they expect this person to cooperate, while if they compete, they anticipate similar behavior from their opponent. [Source: Based on data from Messé & Sivacek, 1979.]

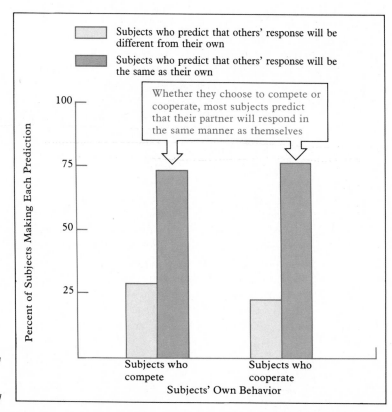

One factor that may account for our tendency to expect others to behave much as we do involves what has been termed the *false consensus effect.* This refers to the fact that often we view our own behavior as typical—as similar to that of most other persons. This belief, of course, can lead us to expect that others will behave very much as we do in a wide range of situations, including ones involving cooperation and competition. Regardless of the precise basis for the impact of our own behavior upon our perceptions of others, though, one fact is clear: attributions often exert powerful effects upon situations involving social exchange. In deciding whether to cooperate or compete with another individual, we do not simply respond to his or her overt actions. Rather, we often pay careful attention to the motives and intentions that lie behind these behaviors. For this reason, the occurrence of both cooperation and competition often involves far more than at first meets the eye.

Group size and cooperation: Another case in which "bigger" is definitely not "better." Cooperation between two individuals is often difficult to attain. Each person may have doubts or reservations about the true motives of the other and, as a result, may approach their dealings in a cautious manner. And since cooperation is usually reciprocated, this guarded strategy may slow or even prevent the development of mutual coordination. But what about larger numbers of persons; is cooperation even harder to establish when three, four, or more individuals are involved? Unfortunately, the findings of several studies suggest that it is (e.g., Fox & Guyer, 1978). As the number of persons participating in a social exchange rises, the level of cooperation often seems to drop. Several factors probably contribute to this disturbing pattern. First, the greater the number of persons present, the greater the likelihood that at least one will act in an exploitative, selfish manner. And then such behavior may spread throughout the group. Second, as the number of participants rises, *diffusion of responsibility* may develop (refer to Chapter 8). That is, each participant may come to feel that he or she will not be held responsible for any failure to achieve coordination. As a result, each may be tempted to compete.

One obvious step that can be taken to counter such effects, of course, is that of dividing the group into smaller units. Presumably, doing so will lessen the probability of selfish behavior within each of these units and will also reduce the occurrence of diffusion of responsibility. It is partly for this reason that large groups are often broken up into committees or even subcommittees. But this strategy, reasonable as it seems, may often have one negative side effect that can counter its potential benefits. Specifically, when a group is divided into sub-units, each of these may come to perceive the others as "out-groups," relative to their own "in-group." Thus, while coordination *within* each unit may be enhanced, cooperation between these units—the ultimate goal—may actually decrease. Evidence for the occurrence of precisely such effects has recently been reported by Komorita and Lapworth (1982).

These researchers conducted a study in which male undergraduates played a prisoner's dilemma game adapted for use with more than two people. Two key factors were varied in the experiment: the number of decision units (groups) present during each session (two, three, or six), and the size of these units (they consisted of one, two, or three persons). On each trial, subjects were shown a prisoner's dilemma-type matrix, and asked to choose one of the alternative responses. Individuals made their decisions alone, while groups of two or three persons were asked to reach unanimous agreement on their choice in each case. Regardless of group or unit size, all subjects were informed that by accumulating a large number of points in the game, they could win attractive prizes (e.g., ballpoint pens).

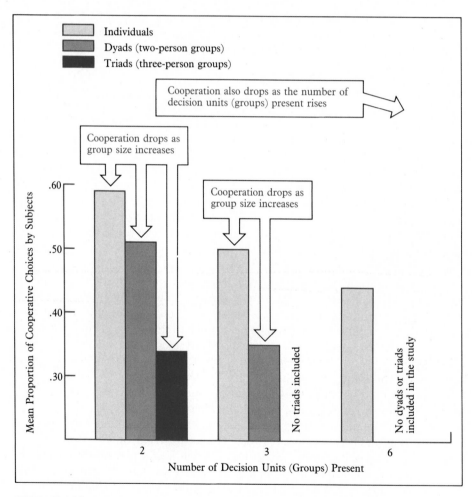

FIGURE 10.7   Group size and cooperation: Some discouraging results.

As shown here, cooperation decreased as the number of decision units (groups) rose, and also decreased as the size of these units increased. These findings suggest that cooperation may often be harder to attain in large groups than small ones. Further, they indicate that simply dividing large groups into several smaller ones may not, by itself, be effective in overcoming such effects. [Source: Based on data from Komorita & Lapworth, 1982.]

The results of the study were somewhat discouraging. Cooperation decreased as the number of decision units present during each session rose; and it also decreased as these units grew in size (see Figure 10.7). In short, cooperation became harder to attain as increasing numbers of persons became involved in the game; and it also became more elusive as the size of each subunit present rose. Together, these findings have two important implications. First, they suggest that, as reported in earlier research, cooperation does tend to drop as the number of participants in a social exchange increases. And second, they suggest that simply dividing large groups into smaller units may not be an effective technique, in and of itself, for countering such effects.

As you can readily see, this latter finding is especially unsettling. After all, in many real-life settings, it is crucial that cooperation be established among large numbers of persons. If dividing such groups into subunits will not turn the trick, what will? Komorita and Lapworth (1982) offer some intriguing suggestions in this respect. Briefly, they argue that despite the problems noted above, large groups should be divided into smaller units; after all, doing so will help to counter tendencies toward defection and diffusion of responsibility. When they are divided in this fashion, however, careful thought should be given to overcoming the potential problem of in-group/out-group divisions. Fortunately, several steps may prove useful in this respect. For example, subunits might be reminded, in clear terms, that they are not competing against each other; on the contrary, they are all working toward the same goal. The establishment of such *superordinate goals* often serves to reduce the intensity of in-group/out-group feelings (refer to Chapter 5). Similarly, subunits should be established in a manner that serves to minimize divisions between them (e.g., each should contain persons of varied status, background, or sex). If such steps are taken, Komorita and Lapworth suggest, dividing large groups into smaller subunits may in fact help to foster cooperation. At the very least, they will help to insure that "bigger" — while not necessarily "better" — is also not necessarily worse.

Individual Determinants of Cooperation: Personal Factors in Social Exchange

While situational factors exert a powerful impact upon the tendency to cooperate, they are only part of the total story. In addition, various traits or characteristics possessed by individuals play a crucial role in this respect. A large number of these factors exist, but here we will focus on two which seem of major importance: individual differences in *overall orientation toward social exchange,* and the *Type A behavior pattern.*

Cooperators, competitors, and individualists: Contrasting orientations toward social exchange. Think back over the many persons you have known. Can you remember several who are highly competitive — persons who view every interaction as one in which they must defeat others? Similarly, can you recall individuals who are almost always cooperative — persons who try to avoid competition whenever they can? Probably, you have little difficulty in bringing examples of both types to mind, for our informal experience tells us that there are large individual differences in the tendencies to both cooperate and compete. Not surprisingly, the existence of such differences has also been confirmed by systematic research (Blascovich, Nash, & Ginsburg, 1978; Van Egeren, 1979). Specifically, it appears that with respect to overall orientation toward social exchange, most individuals fall into one of three major categories.

First, there are **competitors.** These are persons whose primary motive is that of maximizing their own gains relative to others. In other words, they are mainly concerned with doing better than the persons around them. For this reason, they will often settle for negative results, as long as these exceed those of their opponents. Second, there are **cooperators.** Such individuals are primarily concerned with maximizing both their own gains and those of others. They want all parties to a social exchange to obtain positive outcomes, and are unhappy unless this is the case. Finally, there are **individualists.** These are persons whose major motive is that of maximizing their own gains. Generally, they have little interest in the outcomes of others, and do not care whether these persons do better or worse than they do. All that really interests them is the size of their own rewards. (Please see Figure 10.8 for a summary of the differences between competitors, cooperators, and individualists.

As you might expect, persons showing these contrasting orientations often behave differently in situations involving social exchange. For example, in the prisoner's dilemma, competitors usually try to exploit their opponent. In contrast, cooperators usually seek to work together with them. And individualists adopt whatever strategy serves to maximize their own rewards. In short,

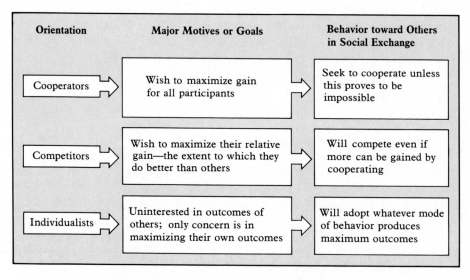

Orientation	Major Motives or Goals	Behavior toward Others in Social Exchange
Cooperators	Wish to maximize gain for all participants	Seek to cooperate unless this proves to be impossible
Competitors	Wish to maximize their relative gain—the extent to which they do better than others	Will compete even if more can be gained by cooperating
Individualists	Uninterested in outcomes of others; only concern is in maximizing their own outcomes	Will adopt whatever mode of behavior produces maximum outcomes

FIGURE 10.8   *Contrasting orientations toward social exchange.*
Cooperators, competitors, and individualists differ sharply with respect to their major motives in the context of social exchange. As a result, they often adopt markedly different patterns of behavior in such situations.

these basic differences in approach to social exchange are often readily visible in contexts where a choice between cooperation and competition exists.

The Type A behavior pattern and cooperation: Does being "hypercompetitive" really pay? In recent years, a great deal of attention has been focused on a cluster of traits known as the *Type A behavior pattern* (please see Chapter 14 for further discussion of this cluster). One reason for the high level of interest in this pattern is simple: *persons showing such traits (Type A's) are more than twice as likely as those not showing such traits (Type B's) to suffer serious heart attacks!* Included in the Type A behavior pattern are such characteristics as time urgency (always being in a hurry), a tendency to push oneself to the limit in almost all situations, and — most relevant to our current discussion — a high degree of competitiveness. Research findings suggest that Type A persons tend to perceive a wide range of situations and relationships as competitive in nature. And, moreover, they respond to such situations with higher levels of arousal than Type B's (Van Egeren, 1979). In short, they tend to view the world as a highly competitive place, in which they are constantly being pitted against formidable opponents.

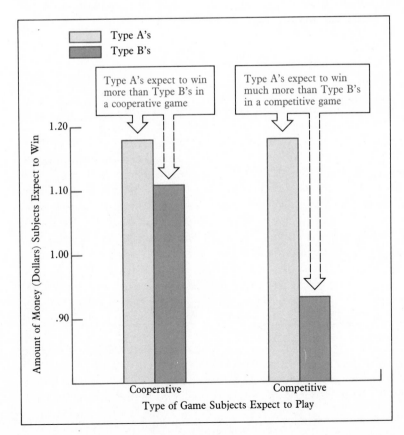

FIGURE 10.9   Type A's: Persons who expect to win.

Type A individuals expect to win more than Type Bs when playing a game with another person. Further, this difference is more pronounced when they expect the game to be competitive rather than cooperative in nature. [Source: Based on data from Gotay, 1981.]

But does this high level of competitiveness pay? Does it yield positive outcomes to Type A persons? Recent evidence suggests that in one sense, at least, it may. For example, consider a study by Gotay (1981). Here, individuals known to be Type A or Type B were told that they would soon play a game with another person. In one condition, the game was described as being cooperative in nature: they would work with their partner to "beat the bank." In another, it was described as being competitive: they would try to outwit their opponent. Before actually playing the game, subjects were then asked to predict how much they would win (this could range from nothing to $2.00). As expected, Type A's predicted that they would win more than Type B's. Further, Type A's were especially confident of defeating their opponent when the game was to be a competitive one (see Figure 10.9, p. 381). We might add that the findings of other studies suggest that these predictions are reasonable ones: Type A individuals *do* often attain better outcomes than Type B's in competitive situations (Van Egeren, 1979).

In sum, it appears that the high level of competitiveness shown by Type A's does sometimes pay: it increases their rewards in many situations involving social exchange. As we noted earlier, though, such persons seem to incur a high cost for this success. Indeed, their health — both physical and psychological — may suffer greatly. When these negative outcomes are added into the equation, we believe, the value of being a hypercompetitive Type A becomes questionable indeed.

Bargaining and Negotiation: Resolving Interpersonal Conflict

Regrettably, conflict is an all too common part of social life. Individuals, groups, and even nations often find themselves at odds over opposing interests and goals. And once it begins, conflict frequently takes on a self-perpetuating or entrapping nature, as each side seeks gains to justify the costs it has already endured (Brockner, Rubin, & Lang, 1981). One possible solution to conflict, of course, lies in the use of force. Each side can simply seek to overpower the other and so gain its goals. Since force or aggression often breeds counterforce, however, actions of this type may well be self-defeating in nature. In this regard, recall the recent struggle over the Falkland Islands. Argentina used military force to seize the island. Britain responded with force to recapture them, and a bitter, prolonged conflict quickly developed (see Figure 10.10).

Another and seemingly better solution to interpersonal conflict is offered by the process of **bargaining.** In this form of social exchange, individuals (or their representatives) engage in a mutual trading of offers and perhaps concessions. If the process is successful, an agreement acceptable to both sides may be obtained, and further conflict avoided. If it fails, however, discussion may be abandoned, and other, less desirable approaches adopted.

Bargaining is a complex process, involving many of the forms of behavior we have already considered (e.g., persuasion, social influence, nonverbal com-

FIGURE 10.10   Force: An ineffective tactic for resolving conflicts.

Force is rarely an effective technique for settling interpersonal—or international—disputes. Aggression generally breeds counteraggression. And even if one side succeeds in overpowering the other, the seeds for further conflict may be sown. [Source: UPI photo.]

munication). Despite this fact, however, much progress toward the goal of understanding its basic nature has been made. In this discussion, we will examine several of the factors that have been found to exert a major impact upon the course and outcome of bargaining, as well as various techniques that may prove useful in enhancing its likelihood of success.

Extremity of Initial Offer: Why It Sometimes Pays to Be Unreasonable

Suppose that one day you found yourself in the position of having to bargain with another person over the price of some item (e.g., a used car, a house, a camera). How should you begin? Should your first offer be a moderate one close to the point at which you think agreement is possible? Or should you start with a more extreme offer—one that is almost certain to be rejected by your opponent? Informal observation suggests that in many cases, bargainers seem to follow the second of these strategies. For example, auto dealers usually advertise the cars on their lots at prices far above their actual market value. And real estate brokers usually offer houses at prices much higher than the ones they hope to obtain. Is this strategy effective? The results of several studies suggest that it really is (e.g., Benton, 1971; Yukl, 1974). In these experiments, persons beginning with extreme initial offers have generally done better, in terms of final outcome, than persons using more moderate initial offers. Thus, when acting as a seller they obtain *more* for the product they offer for sale, and when acting as a buyer, they pay *less* for this item. So, beginning with a relatively

FIGURE 10.11   *Extreme initial offers: Effective, but sometimes risky.*

Beginning with an extreme initial offer can be a useful tactic in bargaining. If an offer is **too** extreme, however, it may anger the persons who receive it and cause them to terminate all negotiations. [Source: Drawing by Stevenson; © 1981 The New Yorker Magazine, Inc.]

"That's odd. I thought I made an offer they could live with."

extreme initial offer seems to be an effective procedure in many bargaining situations.

One reason this is so involves the effects of such offers on an opponent's aspirations. After receiving an extreme offer, many persons seem to lower their expectations considerably. That is, they no longer hope to do as well in the exchange as they had originally planned (Yukl, 1974). This reduction in ambitions, in turn, leads them to make larger concessions than might otherwise be the case. The end result, then, is that the "tough" bargainer—the one who begins with the extreme offer—emerges with a highly favorable settlement. In sum, one reason why taking an extreme initial position is so helpful is as follows: this strategy serves to discourage or demoralize the persons who receive it.

Before concluding, we should insert one note of caution. Beginning with an extreme offer runs a substantial risk of angering one's opponent. To the extent this is so, he or she may adopt an extreme position in return. Or, in some cases, this person may simply break off the negotiations in disgust (please see Figure 10.11). For this reason, extreme initial offers may sometimes boomerang and result in negative rather than positive outcomes for their users. Effective bargainers, then, must walk a thin line. They must begin with offers that are tough enough to throw their opponents off balance. But they must also avoid beginning with ones that are so extreme that they induce anger or overt withdrawal.

Alternatives and Bargaining:
The Benefits of Having an "Out"

Imagine once again that you were bargaining with another person over some issue or item. Suppose that during your negotiations, this person indicated that she had an alternative to making a deal with you. That is, if she failed to strike a bargain with you, she could turn elsewhere. Would this have any effect upon the outcome of your negotiations? Common sense suggests that it would. If you knew that your opponent had an alternative, it might well place pressure on you to meet her more than halfway—to make more concessions than would otherwise be the case. And if the tables were reversed (if *you* had an alternative but your opponent did not), this would have the opposite effect: you might tend to be tougher and less likely to make concessions than if you had no alternative. Evidence for just such effects has been obtained in several experiments (e.g., Komorita & Kravitz, 1979).

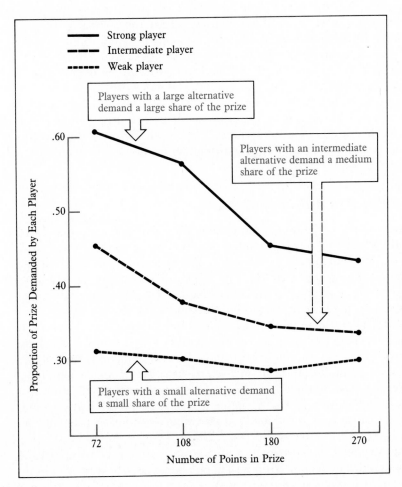

FIGURE 10.12   *Having an alternative: An important plus in bargaining.*

In the study shown here, subjects bargained about the division of various prizes consisting of arbitrary points. Each bargainer also had an "out": if no agreement was reached, all participants would receive some points anyway. However, the size of these alternatives varied, being large for one player, intermediate for another, and small for the third. Results indicated that the larger the alternative available, the greater the proportion of the prize demanded by subjects. [Source: Based on data from Komorita, Lapworth, & Tumonis, 1981.]

For example, in a recent investigation by Komorita, Lapworth, and Tumonis (1981), male students were asked to bargain, in three-person groups, over the division of various prizes. These prizes consisted of arbitrary points, and ranged from 72 to 270 units. It was explained that at the end of the session, participants would receive actual prizes worth up to $2.00, depending on the number of points they accumulated. In addition, subjects were also informed that if they failed to reach agreement about the division of each prize, they might obtain an alternative number of points. Thus, in a sense, all participants had an "out": even if they failed to reach agreement, they might obtain some points. (We should note that as in many real-life situations, it was not certain that this other "deal" would come through. In fact, the probability of obtaining the alternative could range from 25 percent through 100 percent.) The size of the alternatives available to the participants also varied. For one person (the *weak player*) it was small. For another (the *middle player*) it was intermediate in size. And for a third (the *strong player*) it was quite large. Komorita and his colleagues predicted that the larger this alternative, the greater the proportion of the prize each participant would demand, and as you can see from Figure 10.12, they were correct. Regardless of prize value, the strong player demanded a higher proportion than the weak participant. These findings, and those of other, related studies, point to two interesting — and practical — conclusions. First, one way to gain an important advantage in bargaining is to have a back-up deal available. And second, the more advantageous this alternative, the larger the edge it confers. For these reasons, it may often be useful to convince your opponents in bargaining situations that you have a choice — some option aside from reaching agreement with them. To the extent you succeed in this ploy, you may well put considerable pressure on others to meet you more than halfway.

Communication: Does It Really Help?

In a basic sense, bargaining cannot take place without some degree of communication between opponents. Unless they can exchange offers and counteroffers, the whole process may fail to get off the ground. But in many cases, bargainers enjoy more than this "bare bones" level of contact. Indeed, they may have the opportunity to discuss the issues facing them in a direct and open manner. At first glance, it is tempting to assume that such communication will exert uniformly positive effects upon the bargaining process. After all, it allows participants to get a clear picture of each other's positions, and may help them to locate an acceptable middle ground. Yet, close examination of the potential role of communication in such contexts suggests that it may have negative effects as well. For example, bargainers may use communication as a means of exerting pressure on their opponent, or even to deceive this person. To the extent that they do, the chances of reaching a solution may actually be reduced.

Research evidence concerning the impact of communication upon bargaining supports this mixed picture. On the one hand, several studies indicate that free and open communication *can* enhance agreement, especially when it is perceived as representing honest attempts to reach a solution (Kelley & Thibaut, 1978). On the other hand, however, additional studies reveal that under different conditions, communication can *hinder* rather than facilitate the bargaining process. In particular, three factors seem to set the stage for such outcomes.

First, communication may well interfere with progress toward an agreement when it takes the form of **threats** (Deutsh & Krauss, 1960; Shomer, Davis, & Kelley, 1966). Individuals who are threatened by their opponents—either implicitly or explicitly—usually react with anger rather than submission. And this is hardly surprising: backing down in response to such messages may result in a serious *loss of face.* And since this is an outcome most individuals strongly wish to avoid (Garland & Brown, 1972), they may respond to threats by stiffening their resistance or even by shifting to more extreme positions. For these reasons, communications containing threats can often exert negative effects upon the bargaining process.

Second, growing evidence suggests that direct face-to-face contact between opponents can sometimes reduce the likelihood of their reaching an agreement. For example, in one study conducted by Carnevale, Pruitt, and Seilheimer (1981), subjects participating in a bargaining game either could or could not see one another during the session. Surprisingly, results indicated that mutual outcomes were *reduced* by direct visual contact. Apparently, this stemmed from the fact that when the players could see one another, they tended to engage in attempts to intimidate or dominate each other through nonverbal cues (such as harsh facial expressions, prolonged and icy stares). Such strategies induced negative reactions among both participants, and so created an atmosphere in which compromise was difficult to attain. The implication of these results is clear: in some cases, at least, it may be easier for bargainers to reach an agreement when they communicate indirectly (e.g., over the telephone) than when they are in face-to-face contact.

Finally, it appears that the *timing* of communication, too, is crucial. In general, contact occurring *late* in a bargaining session seems more likely to yield positive effects than communication occurring *early.* The reason for this difference centers around the fact that communication between opponents is often used for contrasting purposes at these two times. Contact occurring early in a bargaining session is frequently employed for purposes of deception or intimidation. That is, it represents attempts by one or both opponents to lead the other astray. In contrast, contact later in bargaining is more likely to represent honest attempts to attain coordination, and may serve to focus bargainers' attention on the importance of reaching an agreement (Kelley & Thibaut, 1978). Direct evidence for the superiority of late over early communication in bargaining is provided by a study carried out by Stech and McClintock (1981). In this experiment, pairs of male subjects played the role of competing sellers, and attempted to underbid one another in order to make a deal with potential buyers. Conditions were arranged so that the low bidder on each trial received profits, while the high bidder experienced losses. However, if the two sellers offered their profits at identical prices, both could make a deal and the profit would be split between them. Clearly, then, the best strategy for them to follow was one in which they coordinated their prices. Within this general context, the availability of communication between the players was varied. In one condition, they could communicate throughout the session (CC). In another, they could communicate only during the first half (CN). In a third, the opposite was true: verbal communication was possible only during the second half of the session (NC). Finally, in a control group, no communication was possible at any time (NN). Findings offered strong support for the advantage of late over early communication during bargaining. Players obtained the worst outcomes of all in the CN condition—the one in which communication could take place early

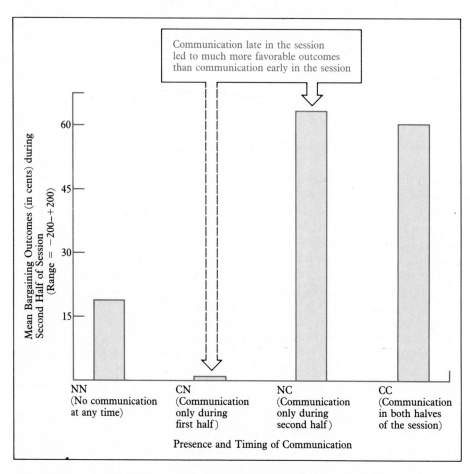

FIGURE 10.13   *Communication during bargaining: Timing is crucial.*

Individuals who could communicate with one another only during the second half of a bargaining session (the NC group) attained much higher outcomes in this situation than individuals who could communicate with each other only during the first half of the session (the CN group). In fact, subjects who could communicate only late in the session did slightly better than those who could communicate throughout the study (the CC group). [Source: Based on data from Stech & McClintock, 1981.]

in the session, but was then impossible. In contrast, they obtained much better results in the NC group—the one in which communication was available only late in the session. Indeed, subjects in this condition did just as well as those who had communication available at all times (the CC condition; see Figure 10.13).

To conclude: existing research evidence suggests that communication between opponents can indeed enhance bargaining outcomes under some conditions, especially when such contact is perceived as representing honest attempts to find a solution. But it can actually interfere with mutual coordination when it takes the form of threats, when it occurs early in the bargaining session, or when it involves direct face-to-face contact between participants. Thus, communication—like several other aspects of bargaining—must be used with great care. Only then will it yield the beneficial effects for which it is intended.

When Bargaining Fails: Alternative Strategies for Resolving Interpersonal Conflict

When bargaining succeeds, it yields highly beneficial outcomes. A settlement acceptable to both sides may be obtained and conflict—if not totally eliminated—is at least softened or reduced. Unfortunately, though, attempts at negotiation often fail. Despite their best efforts, the two sides may deadlock and prove unable to develop an appropriate compromise. As a result, bitter strikes, wars, and painful marital disputes continue unabated, often with devastating consequences for the persons involved. But given that attempts at bargaining have failed, what alternative strategies remain? In short, what additional tactics can be used to resolve interpersonal conflicts in cases where negotiation has proved fruitless? Fortunately, a number of such alternatives exist and offer considerable promise. In this discussion, we will focus on three: (1) the *GRIT approach,* (2) adoption of a *problem-solving orientation,* and (3) *third party intervention.*

The GRIT approach: Resolving conflict through reciprocity. One approach to the reduction of conflict has a long title, but is relatively straightforward in operation. This is the **graduated and reciprocated initiative in tension reduction** approach (**GRIT** for short; Osgood, 1979). This strategy starts when one party to a dispute announces (and then performs) a small unilateral concession that does not require any guarantee of similar action by the opponent. This move, of course, puts subtle pressure on the other side to make a corresponding move. If it does, the party that acted first can reciprocate. And then, through a series of small, unilateral steps, tension and conflict can be greatly reduced.

Evidence for the success of this approach has been obtained in several laboratory studies, in which the announcement of cooperative intentions by one participant has been found to facilitate conflict resolution (e.g., Lindskold & Aronoff, 1980). Further, it has been observed to operate effectively in a number of important, real-life events. For example, the GRIT strategy was used by President Kennedy when he announced, in 1963, that the United States would unilaterally cease testing nuclear weapons. Nikita Khrushchev (then premier of the Soviet Union) applauded his action and responded by calling a halt to the production of strategic bombers. Additional small steps by each side soon led to a reduction in tension between them, and ultimately to the signing of a formal test ban treaty. Events of this type closely match the GRIT approach as outlined in a wide range of contexts.

Adoption of a problem-solving strategy. A second major technique for resolving interpersonal conflict has been suggested by Pruitt and his associates (e.g., Pruitt, 1981; Pruitt & Lewis, 1977). According to this approach, conflict can be greatly reduced if the parties to a social exchange adopt a *problem-solving orientation* to their relations. In such an orientation, both sides view the exchange as a solvable problem—one in which their major task is that of finding an agreement acceptable to all. This contrasts sharply with the typical approach to such situations, in which each participant perceives his or her major task as that of defeating the opponent. According to Pruitt, adoption of a problem-solving orientation, in turn, often facilitates open and honest exchange of information among participants. And it also leads to a negotiating process in which each side frequently adjusts its offers in order to avoid becoming frozen into a single position.

Evidence for the success of this general approach has been obtained in many studies. In these investigations, bargainers were found to obtain better outcomes when they approached their negotiations as involving solvable problems than when they simply sought to maximize their own gains (e.g., Pruitt, 1981). Further, under a problem-solving approach, they showed more concern for their opponent's welfare, transmitted more accurate information to this person, and engaged in fewer pressure tactics. These findings suggest that the adoption of this type of orientation can often be highly effective in reducing interpersonal conflict.

Mediation: Third-party intervention as a tactic for resolving conflict. A third major technique for resolving persistent conflicts involves intervention by a neutral party. This can take the form of **mediation,** in which the third party merely suggests an agreement or concessions. Or, it can operate as **arbitration,** in which this person actually dictates the terms of an agreement. As you probably know, both mediation and arbitration are widely used to settle lasting disputes. And a considerable body of research suggests that in general, faith in this approach is justified: *third-party intervention* does often succeed in breaking deadlocks and reducing conflict (e.g., Rubin, 1980). As you might also expect, however, it is more effective under some conditions than others.

First, mediation tends to be more successful under conditions where mediators have some control over the future outcomes of the disputants than when they lack such influence (Hamilton, Swap, & Rubin, 1981). The reason for this seems obvious: when mediators can "sweeten the pot" by offering disputants something concrete for accepting their recommendations, their influence is likely to be greater than when they cannot offer such inducements.

FIGURE 10.14 **Mediation: Often it succeeds.**

President Carter acted as a mediator during the Camp David negotiations between Israel and Egypt. The fact that he possessed considerable ability to grant future benefits to both sides may have enhanced his effectiveness in this role. [Source: UPI photo.]

This factor may well have played an important role in the Camp David negotiations, which resulted in an historic agreement between Egypt and Israel. As you may recall, President Carter acted as a mediator in these discussions (see Figure 10.14). And clearly, he possessed considerable ability to grant future benefits to both sides (e.g., increased military or economic aid). Thus, it seems possible that the success of these negotiations stemmed, at least in part, from the conditions under which mediation took place.

Second, mediation seems more likely to yield positive outcomes when the conflict between the opposing sides is large than when it is relatively small (Hiltrop & Rubin, 1982). The reason for this is as follows. When the conflict between opponents is intense, mediation may be of great assistance in helping these persons to make concessions without losing *face*—without appearing weak or foolish in the eyes of onlookers. Thus, it may be highly beneficial in such instances. In contrast, when the conflict between opponents is small, they may feel that mediation is unnecessary; indeed, they may perceive it as unwarranted interference. To the extent this is true, mediation is unlikely to yield positive results.

In sum, third-party intervention can succeed. In order to be most effective, however, it must take careful account of the size of the existing conflict, the ability of the mediator to affect the future outcome of the parties involved, and several other factors. When these are given appropriate attention, such intervention can be of major aid in resolving interpersonal conflict. (Some people are far more successful than others in bargaining and other forms of social exchange. For a discussion of one key factor that may underlie such differences, see the **Focus on Research** section on pp. 392–393.)

FOCUS ON RESEARCH

Personality and Success in Social Exchange: Beware the High Mach!

Before proceeding further, please indicate your reactions to each of the statements in Table 10.1. (Do so by circling one number for each.)

When you are done, you will have completed a short form of a psychological test designed to measure the following belief: other persons can be read-ily swayed or manipulated for our own purposes. In a key sense, this belief underlies a set of suggestions for obtaining and holding power which was offered several centuries ago by the Italian philosopher Niccolo Machiavelli. Because of this fact, the re-searchers who devised this test (Christie & Geis,

---

TABLE 10.1   The Mach scale: A short form.

Please indicate your reactions to each of these statements by circling one number. If you agree strongly with a given statement, circle 5. If you agree, but to a lesser extent, circle 4, and so on. After you are finished, read the rest of this discussion to learn more about the relationship of these statements and the characteristics they measure to social exchange. [Source: Courtesy of Dr. R. Christie.]

	Disagree			Agree	
	a lot	a little	neutral	a little	a lot
(1) The best way to handle people is to tell them what they want to hear.	1	②	3	4	5
(2) When you ask someone to do something for you, it is best to give the real reasons for wanting it rather than giving reasons which might carry more weight.	1	2	3	④	5
(3) Anyone who completely trusts anyone else is asking for trouble.	①	2	3	4	5
(4) It is hard to get ahead without cutting corners here and there.	①	2	3	4	5
(5) It is safest to assume that all people have a vicious streak and it will come out when they are given a chance.	①	2	3	4	5
(6) One should take action only when sure it is morally right.	1	2	3	4	⑤
(7) Most people are basically good and kind.	1	2	3	4	⑤
(8) There is no excuse for lying to someone else.	1	2	3	④	5
(9) Most men forget more easily the death of their father than the loss of their property.	①	2	3	4	5
(10) Generally speaking, men won't work hard unless they're forced to do so.	1	②	3	4	5

1970a) named it the *Mach scale.* And the **Machiavellian** orientation it measures has considerable bearing on social exchange.

It seems reasonable to suggest that in many cases, persons who believe that others can readily be manipulated will act on this view. That is, they will seek to influence the persons around them to get them to act in ways that benefit *them.* As a result of the practice they gain in this respect, they soon become masters of the fine points of interpersonal manipulation. And this, in turn, may help them to be highly successful in situations involving social exchange.

That high scorers on the Mach scale do indeed often do better in social exchange than those scoring lower has been shown in several experiments. For example, in one study (Christie & Geis, 1970b), ten $1 bills were placed on a table in front of groups of three subjects. These persons were informed

that the money would belong to any two of them who could agree on how to divide it. One of the three persons was a high scorer on the Mach scale, one was a medium scorer, and one a low scorer. Not surprisingly, results indicated that the high Mach persons tended to do best in this situation. Indeed, they actually won several times as much money as did the low Mach players. Similar results have been obtained in a number of other studies (e.g., Christie, Gergen, & Marlowe, 1970). Thus, it appears that high Machs are often more successful in social exchange than low Machs. But why is this the case? Additional evidence points to the importance of three factors.

First, high Machs tend to show a pattern of cool detachment in situations involving social exchange. In contrast to other persons, they do not become emotionally involved with their opponents, nor even with their own actions. Rather, they operate in

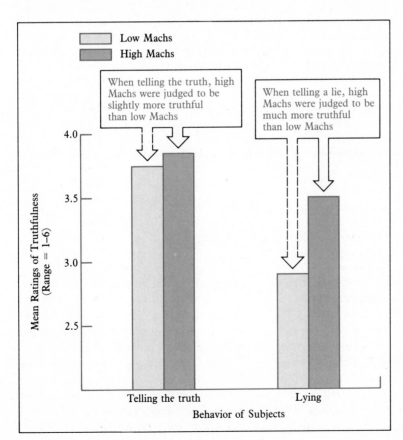

FIGURE 10.15   High Machs: Skilled deceivers.

When both groups were induced to tell a lie, high Mach individuals were perceived as being much more truthful than low Mach individuals. These findings support the view that high Machs are more effective liars than low Machs. [Source: Based on data from Geis & Moon, 1981.]

a pragmatic fashion directed toward the goal of maximizing their own outcomes. Second, high Machs appear to be both highly resistant to social influence and also quite skilled at its use. Thus, they are not easily swayed by opponents; on the contrary, it is *they* who usually manage to do most of the influencing. Third, high Machs are simply much better at deception than other persons. Direct evidence pointing to this conclusion has recently been reported by Geis and Moon (1981).

These researchers arranged for high Mach and low Mach persons to either witness or not witness a theft. (The theft involved an action in which their partner in a game took some money actually belonging to another, opposing team.) In both conditions, subjects were later asked by a member of the other team whether they knew anything about the supposed disappearance of the money. (In one case it really *had* disappeared; in the other, of course, it had not.) As subjects responded to these questions, their faces were videotaped. These tapes were then shown to another group of subjects, whose task was simply that of rating the truthfulness of the first group of individuals. It was predicted that high Machs would be more convincing liars than low Machs. That is, they would be judged as being more truthful by the second group of subjects — the ones who examined the videotapes — when they actually lied. As you can see from Figure 10.15, results offered strong support for this hypothesis. When they had witnessed the theft but denied all knowledge of it, high Mach subjects were in fact rated as far more truthful than low Mach subjects. In addition, high Machs appeared to be more persuasive overall: they were perceived as being more truthful than low Machs even when both groups of persons told the truth (i.e., when they had *not* seen the theft). Given that being an effective liar is often of great value in situations involving social exchange (this skill can help individuals to successfully bluff their opponents), it is clear that high Machs have an important edge over other persons in this respect, too.

Now that we have considered the meaning of Machiavellianism and its connection to social exchange, you may wish to go back and compute your own score on the Mach scale. For questions 1, 3, 4, 5, 9, and 10, simply add the numbers you have circled. For questions 2, 6, 7, and 8, reverse the scoring so that 5 becomes 1, 4 becomes 2, and so on. Then add the values for these two sets of questions together. An average score on this form of the Mach scale is 25, so if you scored well above this value, you are a high Mach. If you scored well below 25, though, you are a low Mach.

Perceived Fairness in Social Exchange: In Search of Social Justice

Have you ever taken part in a social exchange that you felt was unfair? Probably, your answer is "yes." Experiences of this type are too common in our relations with others for it to be otherwise. In most cases, such feelings of unfairness center around the belief that we have somehow been shortchanged — that we have received less than we deserve. But in others, they may stem primarily from the belief that we have received more than we should — that we have taken unfair advantage of others. Regardless of which of these reactions is involved, it is the perception on our part that a social exchange has been unfair that is of central importance. But what factors lead us to reach such conclusions? How do we determine whether a given exchange has been fair or unfair? Several decades of research on this topic suggest that our task in this respect is actually quite complex (e.g., Greenberg & Cohen, 1982). The basic process, though, is as follows. First, we examine the outcomes of all persons in an exchange. Then, we compare these to one of several abstract rules or standards. The closer the match between the actual outcomes we observe and the pattern suggested by our rule, the more likely we are to view the situation as fair. Actually, a number of different rules for evaluating social exchanges in this manner exist. Perhaps the most important of these, however, is one that takes careful account of the *relative* contributions and outcomes of all the persons involved.

Judgments of Fairness in Social Exchange: Equity and Inequity

The rule to which we have just referred is generally known as **distributive justice** or **equity.** It may be summarized as follows. Fairness exists in any social relationship when individuals who have made large contributions receive relatively large outcomes, those who have made small contributions receive small outcomes, and so on. In short, fairness is seen to exist when the outcomes and contributions of each person involved in the exchange "balance" in a special manner. (The term "outcomes" refers to all benefits an individual obtains from a social exchange; the term "contributions" refers to everything he or she contributes to it.) This type of balance can be represented by several different equations (e.g., R. J. Harris, 1980; Walster, Walster, & Berscheid, 1978). One of these, suggested by Adams (1965), is shown here.

Equity exists when:

$$\frac{\text{Outcomes of Person A}}{\text{Contributions of Person A}} = \frac{\text{Outcomes of Person B}}{\text{Contributions of Person B}}$$

What this equation implies is that fairness or equity will exist when the ratio between Person A's outcomes and contributions approximates the ratio for Person B. Equity, in short, is a relative judgment. In order for it to exist, it is *not* crucial that all persons involved in a social exchange receive the same outcomes or make the same contributions. What *is* crucial is that the ratios of these factors match. Thus, as noted earlier, equity will be seen to exist when persons making large contributions receive large outcomes and persons making small contributions receive small ones. It will *not* be judged to be present, however, in situations where persons making small contributions receive large rewards or where persons making large contributions receive small ones.

An impressive body of research findings supports the accuracy of these suggestions. In many cases, individuals *do* tend to perceive social relationships as fair when the kind of balance between contributions and outcomes we have described exists (Greenberg & Cohen, 1982; Leventhal, 1979). We should add, however, that such judgments are often influenced by an important form of bias: a strong tendency toward *egocentrism.*

Personal bias in judgments of fairness: Egocentrism strikes again. We have already encountered the tendency toward egocentrism in our discussion of attribution (please refer to Chapter 2). As you may recall, in that context, it

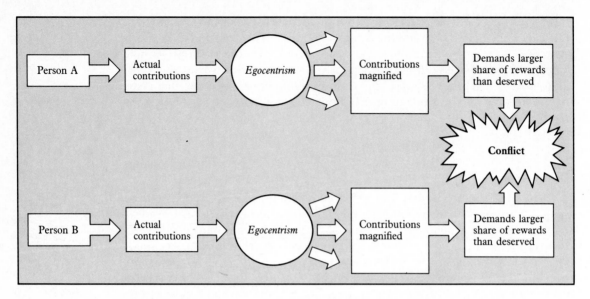

FIGURE 10.16 *Egocentrism: A common source of conflict in social exchange.*

Because of egocentrism, each participant to a social exchange tends to assume that his or her contributions to it have been greater than is actually the case. As a result, each may demand a larger share of available rewards or outcomes than is deserved. The overall result: considerable interpersonal conflict.

refers to our tendency to perceive good or successful behavior as stemming from internal causes (i.e., our own traits), but bad or unsuccessful behavior as stemming from external factors (i.e., ones beyond our control). With respect to judgments of fairness, *egocentrism* takes a slightly different form. Here it leads us to favor ourselves in terms of what we perceive to be a fair division of available rewards. In other words, egocentrism leads us to conclude that we deserve more than is actually the case in many situations (e.g., Messick & Sentis, 1979). For example, imagine that you and another person both work on a joint task (e.g., a project for one of your courses). Egocentrism would lead you to conclude that (1) your contributions to it are greater than is actually the case, and that (2) you therefore deserve a larger share of the credit or rewards than your partner. At the same time, however, he or she would probably have very similar reactions (refer to Figure 10.16). Clearly, then, egocentrism can often be the cause of considerable interpersonal friction in situations involving social exchange.

But this is not the only way in which egocentrism operates. Its influence can also be seen in our tendency to react far more negatively to situations in which we receive *less* than we feel we deserve than to situations in which we receive *more* than we believe is fair. In short, we appear to be far more sensitive to inequity when it works to our disadvantage than when it works to our benefit. Similarly, we also seem to be more upset by inequity when it involves us directly than when it involves only other, unrelated persons (e.g., Leventhal, 1979).

To conclude: the tendency toward egocentrism in judgments of fairness may often influence our behavior in situations involving social exchange. In general, we subscribe to the principle that all individuals should be treated fairly. That is, we believe that they should receive rewards closely matched to their relative contributions. In actual practice, however, we often seem willing to tolerate some degree of inequity — especially when it operates to our advantage.

Alternative approaches to fairness: Rules based on equality and relative needs. While the equity rule just described often plays an important role in our judgments of fairness, other standards, too, enter into this process. One of these is based upon the simple principle that all participants should receive equal outcomes. This approach — known as the **equality rule** — is somewhat *equality rule* less common than the one based on equity. However, it *is* followed under some conditions. First, it is often adopted when individuals believe that their outcomes on a task have been determined by chance or other factors beyond their control (e.g., Greenberg, 1980). This makes intuitive sense; after all, if outcomes are unrelated to effort or ability, the fairest distribution of rewards may be an equal division. Second, as we will see in more detail later, it is often followed in situations where individuals wish to maintain friendly relations with others, or make a good impression on them (Austin, 1980; Reis, 1981). Finally, it is more common in some cultures than in others. For example, it seems to be much more prevalent among Chinese than Americans (Bond, Leung, & Wan, 1982).

A third rule we sometimes employ in our judgments concerning fairness is *relative needs* based upon the *relative needs* of the persons taking part in a social exchange. According to this standard, individuals with strong needs should receive more than those with weaker ones. Thus, according to this rule, a social exchange is viewed as fair only to the extent that the needs of all participants are fulfilled. Evidence for the operation of this rule is provided by the results of several laboratory studies (Greenberg & Cohen, 1982). In addition, it can be recognized in many life situations. For example, in times of accident or disaster, help is usually provided first to those who are most in need of assistance. The fact that most persons view this as both fair and proper suggests that sometimes we *do* base our judgments of fairness on a standard of relative needs.

In sum it appears that our judgments concerning the fairness of any social exchange may rest on several different standards. Thus, the same pattern of outcomes may be perceived as fair or unfair, depending on which of these rules we apply. But how, precisely, do we choose between them? In particular, why do we adhere to the principle of equity or distributive justice in some situations, but to the principle of equality in others? It is to this question that we next turn.

Equity or Equality? Justice, Impression Management, and Enhancing Our Own Self-image

At first glance, it might seem that our task in choosing between the rules of equity and equality is a fairly easy one. Equity is appropriate in some contexts, equality in others, and we simply select the one that seems to fit best in a given situation. While this is certainly true to a degree, growing research evidence suggests that in many cases, our choice between contrasting rules may also stem from another source: our desire to attain various goals. And the nature of these goals, in turn, may differ sharply in the case of equality and the case of equity.

Turning to equality first, we often seem to select this rule because it helps us to make a positive impression on others (Reis, 1981). That is, dividing available rewards equally between all participants in a social exchange may help us to gain favor in the eyes of other persons, especially those who might otherwise have attained a smaller outcome. Thus, adherence to the rule of equality often serves as a technique of *impression management.* Through its use, we seek to induce positive feelings toward us on the part of others — feelings we hope to convert into concrete benefits at some future time. In contrast, adherence to the rule of equity permits us to attain other goals. Specifically, adoption of this rule may assist us in attaining or enhancing our own *self-image* (e.g., Gibbons & Wicklund, 1982; Reis & Burns, 1982). The reason for this is straightforward: most persons (at least in Western cultures) accept the view that there should be a close link between one's contributions or performance and one's outcomes. Thus, adopting the equity rule permits them to adhere to this valued internal standard. And considerable research suggests that, to the extent we live up to such ideals or standards, our self-image may benefit (e.g., Carver & Scheier, 1981a).

As you can readily see, these two goals may sometimes conflict. Adopting equality as a means of inducing positive reactions in others may be inconsistent with adhering to equity as a technique for enhancing our self-image. What do individuals do in such situations? Evidence gathered recently by Greenberg (1983) is quite revealing.

In this study, male and female students were asked to evaluate the performance of two temporary workers, and then to divide a set amount of pay ($10.00) between them. The two workers differed sharply in their performance, so that one was clearly superior to the other. Before dividing the available funds between the workers, half of the subjects were told that they would later meet the low-performing person to discuss his output with him. The other half were not led to anticipate such a meeting. Greenberg reasoned that under conditions where subjects anticipated meeting this person, they would be motivated to adopt the rule of equality; after all, by dividing the $10.00 equally, they would induce positive reactions on the part of the person they would later meet. A second major aspect of the study involved variations in subjects' level of self-awareness. While deciding how to divide the available pay, half of the participants saw their own reflection in a mirror; the remainder did not. It was expected that the presence of the mirror would increase subjects' self-awareness, and so would strengthen their motivation to adhere to the rule of equity.

The results of the study (which are summarized in Figure 10.17) were consistent with all of these expectations. Under conditions where subjects anticipated meeting the low-performing worker and were not exposed to their reflection in a mirror, they did seem to adhere to the rule of equality. Specifically, they tended to divide the $10.00 quite equally between the two workers.

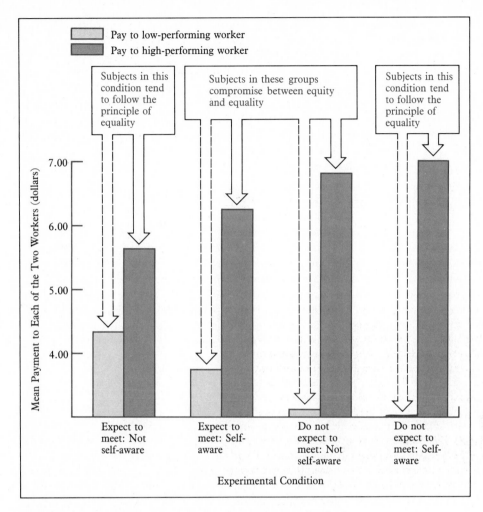

FIGURE 10.17 *Equity or equality: Factors affecting the choice.*

In the experiment represented here, subjects were asked to divide $10.00 between two workers, one of whom performed much better than the other. When they expected to meet the low performing person later, participants tended to divide the money in accordance with the rule of equality. In contrast, when they did not expect to meet this person and also saw their own reflection in a mirror, they divided it in accordance with the principle of equity. [Source: Based on data from Greenberg, 1983.]

In contrast, under conditions where they did not expect to meet this person, and were made self-aware by means of the mirror, they followed the rule of equity. That is, they gave much more of the rewards to the high-performing than to the low-performing worker. And in the two intermediate conditions, where the motives to engage in impression management and to enhance their own self-image were in conflict, they seemed to compromise, adopting neither equality nor equity.

These findings, and those obtained in related research (e.g., Gibbons & Wicklund, 1982) suggest that our decision to adopt either the rule of equity or the rule of equality in situations involving social exchange is quite complex. On the one hand, this choice is affected by situational constraints suggesting that one or the other of these rules is most appropriate in a given context. And on the other, it is also influenced by our desire to produce favorable impressions on others and to enhance our own self-image. Little wonder, then, that judgments concerning the fairness of our dealings with others are among the most difficult and effortful we are called upon to make.

Reactions to Unfairness: Tactics for Overcoming Injustice

Despite the complexities involved in deciding whether a given social exchange has been fair or unfair, we often do succeed in making such judgments. And then these judgments, in turn, exert strong effects upon our behavior and our relations with others. If, taking the rules and motives outlined above into account, we conclude that the situation is fair, few problems arise. We can continue interacting with the other parties to the exchange in a friendly and cordial manner. But if we decide that it has somehow been unfair, two major effects generally follow: (1) we experience strong negative reactions, and (2) we seek to reduce such feelings by eliminating the existence of injustice. Our attempts to accomplish these goals take many different forms.

First, we may try to eliminate feelings of inequity or unfairness by *altering our contributions to the social exchange*. Thus, if we feel that we have received less than we deserve, we may reduce our contributions. In contrast, if we feel that we have received more than is fair, we may actually increase such inputs (e.g., Reis & Burns, 1983). An example of the first strategy is provided by the actions of a worker who, concluding that her wages and other benefits are too low given the demands of her job, reduces productivity. An instance of the second type of reaction—increasing one's contributions to an exchange—might be seen in the behavior of an individual who receives a big promotion and then works harder or longer hours to justify this reward. Evidence that individuals often attempt to eliminate feelings of unfairness through adjustments in their contribution has been obtained in many experiments (e.g., Gibbons & Wicklund, 1982; Pritchard, Dunnette, & Jorgenson, 1972). In these studies subjects led to believe that they were receiving less than they deserved often reduced their effort or productivity on various tasks. In contrast, those led to believe that they were receiving *more* than they deserved often acted in an opposite manner: they raised their effort or performance (especially when they were made self-aware; Gibbons & Wicklund, 1982). Such findings suggest that under some conditions, at least, individuals attempt to eliminate feelings of unfairness by changing the nature of their contributions to a social exchange (Greenberg & Ornstein, 1983).

A second major strategy for eliminating feelings of unfairness is *altering our outcomes* in an exchange relationship. If we feel underrewarded, we may attempt to gain a larger share of available rewards, while if we feel overrewarded, we may actually seek to lower our share of the benefits. Instances of the first type are extremely common. For example, workers who feel underpaid often seek to increase their wages or other benefits through strikes. And friends, relatives, or lovers who feel that they are not receiving what they deserve in an intimate relationship may complain or take other actions to correct the situation (for example, they may demand more affection, sexual favors, and so on; Walster, Walster, & Traupmann, 1978). As you can probably guess, instances in which individuals attempt to eliminate feelings of unfairness by *reducing* the size of their outcomes are far less common. As we noted previously, most persons seem somewhat less sensitive to unfairness when it operates in their favor than when it operates to their disadvantage. However, the occurrence of this type of reaction, too, has been observed in laboratory studies (e.g., Leventhal, Weiss, & Long, 1969).

Interestingly, the tactic of restoring feelings of fairness through adjustments in the magnitude of one's outcomes may involve several social relationships rather than simply one. That is, an individual who feels cheated or exploited in one relationship may attempt to make up for such treatment by taking more than he or she deserves in another. Similarly, a person who feels that he or she has received more than is deserved in one case may actually take less than a fair share in another (Austin & Walster, 1975). In short, feelings of equity or fairness can be restored by adjusting one's outcomes across several different relationships, as well as by changes within one.

A third strategy we can adopt in response to unfairness is that of withdrawing from the relationship altogether. For example, if we feel cheated in our business dealings, we may avoid further transactions with the business or persons involved. Similarly, if we feel that we are being exploited in a marriage or romantic relationship, we may seek separation or divorce as an effective, if drastic, means of ending such treatment (see Figure 10.18). Once again, laboratory studies have confirmed the use of this strategy. Indeed, some

FIGURE 10.18 Withdrawal: One tactic for dealing with inequity.

One technique for eliminating feelings of inequity is simple: persons experiencing such reactions can withdraw from relationships in which they feel that they are being mistreated. [Source: The Cinemabilia Shop.]

Social Exchange: Some Steps in the Right Direction

Social exchange is a basic part of human life. Yet, unhappily, it is often far less positive than could be the case. Cooperation fails to develop in many situations where it would be of major benefit; conflict is all too common and frequently persists long past the point where it can do either side any good; and social relations are often unfair to one or more of the participants. In short, social exchange, which could be a source of much good, tends instead to yield negative outcomes. Can anything be done about this disconcerting state of affairs? Do the findings of social psychological research point to concrete steps that might be taken to improve both the nature and outcomes of such exchange? We believe that they do. While no perfect formula for ensuring mutually beneficial exchange relationships exists, the steps outlined here should at least help to maximize positive outcomes and minimize unnecessary conflict.

(1) *Build on reciprocity.* Cooperation, as we noted earlier, is usually reciprocal in nature. Thus, once it begins, it may continue almost of its own accord. A key point on which to focus, then, is getting such behavior started. This may require open calls for coordination, or actually taking the first step in this direction. In both cases, the effort may be well rewarded, for once begun, cooperation may quickly become the standard form of behavior in a given situation or relationship.

(2) *Avoid causing your opponents to lose face.* Most persons strongly dislike being made to appear weak or foolish in the eyes of others. Indeed, once they experience such outcomes, they may become far more concerned with revenge than with cooperation or honest negotiation. A basic rule of social exchange, therefore, should be: avoid inflicting such outcomes on your opponents. Always leave them room for

findings suggest that many persons prefer smaller rewards in fair relationships to larger ones in unfair exchanges (Schmitt & Marwell, 1972).

A final technique for reducing feelings of unfairness involves *changes in our perceptions* of an exchange relationship. When we experience feelings of unfairness, we may simply alter our perceptions of the relationship in question, so that the illusion of justice—if not justice itself—is restored. Such distortions in perception can take many forms. For example, persons who find themselves receiving the "short end of the stick" may rationalize this unpleasant state of affairs by concluding that because of some talent, noble birth, or special ability, the person exploiting them actually *deserves* an extra share of the rewards (e.g., Walster, Walster, & Berscheid, 1978). Or, in an even more bizarre manner, they may conclude that they are actually benefiting from the unfair treatment they receive. After all, a little suffering is good for the soul! Perhaps the most unsettling type of distortion that occurs in such situations, however, involves the tendency of persons receiving more than they deserve to derogate or devalue the persons they exploit—a phenomenon known as **victim derogation.** Such individuals often conclude that the victims of their unfair tactics

maneuver. And if you do defeat them, be sure to allow them to surrender gracefully. Above all, resist the temptation to gloat. While such actions may yield momentary pleasure, they are likely to prove very costly in the long run.

(3) *Attain the aid of mediators.* As we noted earlier, third-party intervention can often be an effective means for resolving interpersonal conflict. Thus, if your relations with another person seem in danger of slipping into deadlock, seek the advice of an impartial observer. Such a person does *not* have to be a professional or an expert; a friend or acquaintance will do, as long as he or she has no "ax to grind" in the particular situation. And try to follow the mediator's advice once it is obtained; the benefits of doing so may be substantial.

(4) *Use communication wisely.* When negotiating with another person, whether over economic or personal matters, try to be honest in your communications. Research findings suggest that communication used for deception or manipulation often backfires by inducing anger or resentment among recipients. And be sure to avoid attempts at intimidation and threats. These tactics may seem to work when first used, but are likely to sow the seeds for later serious conflict.

(5) *Beware of egocentrism.* It is all too easy, in our dealings with others, to fall prey to egocentrism—to assume that our contributions to an exchange have been greater than they are, or that we deserve more of the available rewards than is really fair. Such self-serving bias, in turn, can lead to considerable conflict with other persons. For this reason, it is important to keep the tendency toward egocentrism firmly in mind, and to call it to the attention of others when *they* show its influence. Doing so can help prevent many disagreements, and can assist in reducing feelings of inequity that actually have no basis in fact.

(6) *Proclaim—don't conceal—any feelings of unfairness.* Often, individuals who believe that they are being treated unfairly seek to hide such reactions from others. As you can readily see, this may be a counterproductive strategy. Indeed, it may totally eliminate any chance of correcting the situation before it gets out of hand. So, if you experience such feelings, try to get them out into the open as soon as possible. If you don't, the persons around you will probably assume that you are perfectly content. And then things are likely to get worse rather than better.

---

actually deserve the treatment they are receiving because, for example, they aren't very nice or very bright.

The occurrence of such effects has been demonstrated in several experiments (e.g., Leventhal, 1976; Stein, 1973). In this research, individuals who witness another person receiving unfair treatment (e.g., painful electric shocks while they receive no such shocks) have been found to lower their evaluation of or liking for this person. In short, they seem to convince themselves that the unfortunate victim is somewhat deserving of this treatment; after all, he or she really isn't very nice!

These are only some of the ways in which individuals seek to eliminate feelings of unfairness or inequity; others exist as well (e.g., Greenberg & Cohen, 1982). Regardless of the specific tactics employed, however, two facts are clear. Most persons strongly object to unfairness in their relationships or dealings with others. And when it occurs, they usually take active, forceful steps to counter its occurrence. (How can the negative effects of inequity be avoided? How can social exchange generally be improved? For some concrete suggestions, please see the **On the Applied Side** section above.)

A Note on Relative Deprivation:
When Being a "Have-not" Generates Resentment

When being a have not generates resentment rising expectations

Before concluding our discussion of fairness in social relationships, we should comment briefly on a closely related topic: *relative deprivation.* According to Crosby, a researcher who has devoted much attention to this topic (Crosby, 1982; Crosby & Gonzalez-Intal, 1983), individuals who discover that they do not possess certain benefits held by others do *not* necessarily experience feelings of resentment. Rather, they do so only under certain conditions—ones suggesting that they are deprived *relative* to those others or to what they deserve and might attain under other circumstances. Briefly, the conditions leading to such feelings are as follows: the persons in question (1) desire the benefits they do not now have, (2) perceive that other persons possess them, (3) feel entitled to them, (4) think it is feasible to attain them, and (5) do not see their current failure to do so as their own fault. In short, feelings of relative deprivation are most likely to develop when individuals realize that they do not possess benefits held by others, but conclude that under other conditions they could. Evidence offering support for these suggestions has recently been reported by Folger, Rosenfield, Rheaum, and Martin (1983).

These investigators conducted a study in which subjects worked on two distinct tasks. Instructions indicated that their performance on the first task would determine whether they would receive two units of credit for their time or only one. Half of the subjects then received feedback indicating that they were close to meeting the criterion for the larger payoff (the *high likelihood* group), while half learned that they were far below this point (the *low likelihood* group). The second task performed was used to vary the subjects' *referent states*—their beliefs about the possibility of attaining the larger reward under other conditions. Performance on this task, it was indicated, would have no impact on whether they themselves earned two units of credit or only one. However, for other persons, such performance would supposedly determine which of these payoffs was received. Half of the subjects then learned that this task was relatively easy and that, therefore, they would have had a good chance of gaining the large reward if this were the task that "counted" for them (the *high referent condition*). The remainder, in contrast, learned that it was relatively difficult, and that they would have had little opportunity of gaining the large reward even if this were the task that determined their payoffs (the *low referent condition*). After performing the second task, subjects completed a questionnaire on which they rated their feelings on several dimensions (e.g., how angry and upset they were). Folger and his colleagues predicted that when subjects did not expect to receive two credits for their work (the low likelihood group) they would be more upset when they felt that they might have earned this reward under other conditions (the high referent group) than if they did not believe this was the case (the low referent group). (Such beliefs about what might have occurred under other conditions were *not* expected to affect subjects' reactions in this manner when they anticipated receiving two credits for their work—

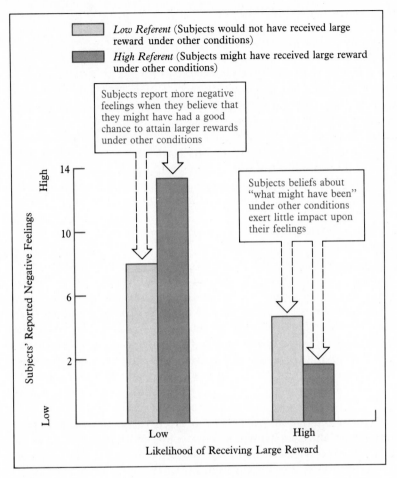

Low Referent (Subjects would not have received large reward under other conditions)

High Referent (Subjects might have received large reward under other conditions)

Subjects report more negative feelings when they believe that they might have had a good chance to attain larger rewards under other conditions

Subjects beliefs about "what might have been" under other conditions exert little impact upon their feelings

Subjects' Reported Negative Feelings

High

Low

14

10

6

2

Low   High

Likelihood of Receiving Large Reward

FIGURE 10.19   *Relative deprivation: Regrets about "what might have been."*

When subjects felt that they had little chance of attaining a large reward (low likelihood condition) they were more upset when it appeared that, under other conditions, they might *have had a good chance of gaining this payoff (the high referent group) than when it appeared that they would probably not have attained this reward in any case (the low referent group). In contrast, when subjects believed that they had a good chance of attaining a large reward (the high likelihood condition), beliefs about "what might have been" had little effect upon their feelings. [Source: Based on data from Folger et al., 1983.]*

that is, in the high likelihood group.) Analysis of responses to the questionnaire offered clear support for these predictions (see Figure 10.19).

As you can readily see, feelings of relative deprivation have important practical implications. For example, such reactions often arise in situations where individuals compare the benefits attained by their own social group with those obtained by other, different groups (Guimond & Dubé-Simard, 1983). In such cases, persons occupying disadvantaged positions in a given society (e.g., racial or ethnic minorities; females) may conclude that they have as much right to "the good things in life" as more privileged groups. These feelings, in turn, can then exert negative effects upon their relations with such persons, and so exert an unstabilizing influence on society as a whole. For these reasons, feelings of relative deprivation are important and should be taken into careful account whenever the question of justice or fairness in social relationships arises.

Summary

When individuals trade or exchange something (anything from love or affection through goods and services) they may be viewed as engaging in **social exchange.** One important form of such exchange is *cooperation,* behavior in which two or more persons work together or coordinate their actions to enhance the outcomes received by each. Another is *competition,* behavior in which each person attempts to maximize his or her own outcomes, often at the expense of others. Much research has focused on factors that tip the balance in social exchange toward one or the other of these two contrasting forms of behavior. Among the variables found to play an important role in this regard are (1) the behavior shown by others (do *they* cooperate or compete?), (2) attributions concerning the motives behind others' actions, and (3) group size. In addition, individual differences in overall orientation toward social exchange and specific personality traits (e.g., the Type A behavior pattern) influence the decision to cooperate or compete.

A second major form of social exchange is *bargaining*—a process in which individuals engage in a mutual trading of offers and counteroffers. Research on bargaining suggests that individuals can enhance their outcomes in negotiations by means of such tactics as taking an *extreme initial position,* convincing their opponents that they have an "out" (an alternative deal at their disposal), and certain forms of *communication.* When bargaining deadlocks, several strategies may prove useful in resolving the dispute. Among these are the *GRIT approach* (a tactic in which each side offers small, unilateral concessions), the adoption of a *problem-solving orientation* to the exchange, and intervention by a *third party* (e.g., a mediator).

Individuals seem to judge the fairness of social exchange by comparing the outcomes attained by all participants to those suggested by various rules or standards. One of these—the principle of **equity**—suggests that rewards should be assigned on the basis of each person's relative contributions. A second rule—*equality*—holds that all participants should receive equal outcomes. The choice between these and other rules for judging fairness is affected by many factors, including the motive to make a favorable impression on others, and the motive to adhere to one's own internal standards. When individuals conclude that an exchange has been unfair, they commonly take active steps to reduce such injustice. Among the tactics often used for this purpose are (1) altering the size of their contributions to or their benefits from the exchange, (2) withdrawing from the exchange, or (3) altering their perceptions of it.

Feelings of *relative deprivation* arise when individuals desire benefits they do not now enjoy, perceive that others possess them, and feel that they are entitled to them. Such reactions can exert negative effects upon relations between advantaged and disadvantaged persons and may also threaten the stability of society as a whole.

Glossary

arbitration *A form of third-party intervention in bargaining in which the recommendations of the person intervening are binding upon the parties involved. (That is, these recommendations must be accepted and followed.)*

bargaining *A form of social exchange in which individuals trade offers and counteroffers in an attempt to reach agreement about some issue of mutual concern.*

competition *A form of social exchange in which individuals attempt to maximize their own outcomes, often at the expense of others. Competition often develops in situations where several persons seek a single goal that cannot be shared among them.*

competitors *Individuals who have a highly competitive orientation toward social exchange. Their main goal is that of doing better than their opponents.*

cooperation *A form of social exchange in which two or more individuals work together or coordinate their behavior in order to attain a common goal.*

cooperators *Individuals who possess a cooperative orientation toward social exchange. Such persons seek to maximize others' outcomes as well as their own.*

distributive justice *See* equity.

equality rule *A rule governing the distribution of rewards among the participants to a social exchange. According to this rule, all participants should receive equal outcomes.*

equity *A rule or standard for judging fairness in any social exchange. According to equity (or* distributive justice*), fairness exists when the outcomes received by each participant are proportional to their relative contributions.*

graduated and reciprocated initiative in tension reduction (GRIT) *A strategy for resolving interpersonal conflict in which each side engages in a series of small, unilateral concessions.*

individualists *Persons whose major goal in social exchange is that of maximizing their own outcomes. The outcomes obtained by others are of little or no interest to them.*

Machiavellianism *Refers to a personality trait centering around the view that others can be readily manipulated or influenced. Persons high in Machiavellianism are often more successful in social exchange than those low in Machiavellianism, in part because they are better at various forms of deception.*

mediation *A form of third-party intervention in bargaining in which a presumably neutral person recommends a compromise solution.*

prisoner's dilemma *A class of situations involving strong pressures toward both cooperation and competition. Games based on the logical structure of the prisoner's dilemma are often used in the systematic study of cooperation and competition.*

reciprocity *A basic principle of social interaction suggesting that we should behave toward others as they have behaved toward us.*

social exchange *A basic form of interaction in which individuals trade or exchange something. What they exchange can range from goods or services on the one hand, to love, affection, and loyalty on the other.*

threats *A form of communication in which one individual warns another that negative actions or sanctions will follow if the recipient of the threat does (or does not) behave in some specified manner.*

victim derogation *Refers to the fact that often individuals who witness exploitation tend to derogate the victims of such treatment. By doing so, they convince themselves that the victims somehow deserve their unhappy fate.*

For More Information

Christie, R., & Geis, F. L. (Eds.). *Studies in Machiavellianism.* New York: Academic Press, 1970.
After more than a decade, this intriguing book is still the most comprehensive and definitive one in existence dealing with Machiavellianism. The effects of this manipulative orientation on social exchange are considered, and a number of ingenious experiments described. Chapter 1, which describes the nature of Machiavellianism, may be of special interest to you.

Greenberg, J., & Cohen, R. L. (Eds.). *Equity and justice in social behavior.* New York: Academic Press, 1982.
This book contains a number of chapters (each prepared by a noted expert) dealing with various aspects of equity and perceived justice. Recent research is reviewed, and the impact of equity and inequity on various aspects of social interaction are considered.

Paulus, P. B. (Ed.). *The psychology of group influence.* Hillsdale, N.J.: Erlbaum, 1980.
A collection of discussions (again, prepared by noted experts in the field) dealing with several of the topics examined in this chapter (cooperation and competition). This is a good source to consult if you would like to know more about various aspects of social exchange.

Pruitt, D. G. *Negotiation behavior.* New York: Academic Press, 1981.
A comprehensive discussion of the process of bargaining, prepared by one of the leading authorities on this topic in social psychology. Many interesting studies are summarized, and concrete steps for facilitating successful negotiation are described.

CHAPTER 11

Groups and Individual Behavior:
The Consequences of Belonging

Social Facilitation: When the Presence of Others Counts

The Drive Theory of Social Facilitation: Other Persons as a Source of Arousal/Social Facilitation: Mere Physical Presence, Concern over Evaluation, or . . . ?/The Distraction-Conflict Model: A Possible Resolution?

Deindividuation:
Groups, Self-awareness, and the Shattering of Restraint

Deindividuation: Its Causes, Nature, and Effects/Deindividuation: Some Relevant —and Unsettling—Evidence

Decision Making in Groups: How (Process) and What (Outcome)

How Groups Arrive at Decisions: Social Decision Schemes and Social Transition Schemes/What Groups Decide: Moderation or Polarization?

Leaders and Followers: Patterns of Influence within Groups

Are Leaders Born or Made? Charisma versus Technical Skill/Leadership As a Two-Way Street: The Modern, Transactional View/Leader Effectiveness: A Contingency Approach

Special Inserts

FOCUS ON RESEARCH
  Social Loafing and Social Impact: Why Groups Are Often Inefficient

ON THE APPLIED SIDE
  Countering Deindividuation: Some Potentially Useful Steps

FOCUS ON RESEARCH
  The Great Man/Great Woman Theory Revisited: Personality and Leadership

It's drizzling steadily, and a cold north wind is moaning through bare trees. Yet none of this deters the pickets gathered outside the Office of Domestic Affairs. They continue marching up and down, waving their signs and chanting their grievances. All are members of the International Order of Bureaucrats, and are here in support of a two-day-old strike called by their leaders. As a member of the union's Steering Committee, you were present when this fateful decision was reached, and as you march with the others, your thoughts go back to that emotion-charged day. When the meeting began, most of the members were clearly in favor of taking some kind of action; continued talks with the government representatives were clearly getting nowhere. But what action, precisely, should be adopted? Strikes by government employees are illegal in your country, and everyone remembered the fate of another union, whose members had taken this action a few years earlier: all were fired and most were still out of work. Yet, as the discussion proceeded, a gradual but steady shift toward more extreme views took place. Perhaps the turning point in this process occurred when Larry Shields took the floor and made an impassioned plea for strong action. Larry is not known for eloquence—far from it. Yet, somehow, he rose to new heights while addressing the group. After his remarks, the outcome seemed certain: a strike it would be. Looking back on this decision, you are somewhat puzzled. How could so many cautious people select the most radical course of action? Why did the committee shift steadily in this direction? Your thoughts along these lines are suddenly interrupted: a large group of police have arrived on the scene, and are demanding that the strikers leave. When they do not, the director of your agency suddenly emerges from a large limousine and orders you all back to work. His words are greeted with anger and derision. Then, suddenly, Bill Walker—a member of your own department known for his soft-spoken ways—hurls an egg at the director. It strikes him squarely on the shoulder, and it is as if Bill's action serves as some sort of signal. All at once, other strikers begin tossing tomatoes, rocks, and bottles at the police and the director. Others try to overturn his car. And still others attempt to storm the doors. You are shocked: most of these people are mild-mannered bureaucrats like yourself. Why are they acting in such a violent manner? You don't have much time to find out for at this very moment you are seized by three burly police and dragged away. The last scene you observe before the wagon door slams shut is an especially disturbing one. Fran Halving, a ninety-pound wisp of a girl, is hitting a police officer with the heavy end of her sign, while shouting obscenities that might well make a sailor blush . . .

During the course of our lives, most of us belong to many different social groups. First, we are part of a family. Then, we usually affiliate with a neighborhood "gang" or play group. Later, we join various clubs such as the Girl Scouts and Boy Scouts, or fraternities and sororities. And as adults, we enter various political groups, professional societies, or work-related associa-

FIGURE 11.1   *Groups:*
A major force in our lives.

Over the years, we become members
of many different groups. [Source:
Photo (top left) © Allen Ruid;
photos (top right and bottom) by Bill
Owens/Archive Pictures Inc.]

tions (see Figure 11.1). In most cases, we join such groups voluntarily: indeed, we are often willing to undergo prolonged and costly initiations in order to become members of them. The reason for this is clear: belonging to certain groups provides us with substantial benefits. At the least, it allows us to associate with people who share our values, attitudes, and interests. And in some cases, it can even help us to achieve important life goals, such as meeting an appropriate mate or furthering our career. Little wonder, then, that we often choose to associate with others in social groups.

But being part of a group is not a totally unmixed blessing. While such membership confers many benefits, it also exacts certain costs. And foremost among these is this: *groups often exert an impressive degree of influence upon their members*. In short, they often induce them to change their attitudes and behavior from what they would be under other circumstances, if they were *not* members of the group. In this context, consider the decision of the union Steering Committee in the incident just described. While most members of this group began with conservative and cautious views, they were soon influenced to adopt more extreme (and risky) ones during the group discussion. Similarly, recall the actions of the strikers in the same example. Would each of these persons have acted in the violent manner described if they were alone rather than part of a large crowd? It seems unlikely. Instead, we would predict that if alone, most would have obeyed the director's order to return to work. Thus, being part of a group strongly altered their reactions.

In these and many other contexts, groups exert powerful effects upon their members. Because such effects have many practical consequences, and also because they have been of major interest to social psychologists for decades, we will focus upon them here. Our discussion of group influence—the consequences of belonging—will proceed as follows. First, we will consider what is in some ways the simplest kind of group effect: changes in the performance of various tasks stemming from the presence of—or potential evaluation by—others. Such effects are often termed **social facilitation** but as we will soon see, they can involve impairments as well as improvements in performance. Second, we will examine the ability of groups to weaken the restraints of their members against engaging in wild, impulsive behavior—a process known as **deindividuation.** Third, we will focus on *decision making* in groups. Here, we will consider the process through which such decisions are made, and the question of whether, once reached, they are more or less extreme than similar decisions by individuals. Finally, because groups often exert their strongest influence through the actions of leaders, we will turn to the nature of **leadership.** In this regard, we will address two related questions: (1) why do some individuals but not others rise to positions of authority? and (2) what factors determine their success or effectiveness in this role?

Social Facilitation: When the Presence of Others Counts

Imagine that, as part of your job, you must deliver a speech to a large audience. You have several weeks to prepare, so you write the speech and then practice it at home in the quiet of your own room. Time passes, and finally, the moment of truth arrives: you hear your name announced by the moderator. How will you perform now that you are faced with a live audience? Will you stumble over your words and do worse than when you practiced alone? Or will the audience spur you on to greater effort and new heights of eloquence, as was

**FIGURE 11.2   *The presence of
others: A plus or a minus?***

*Does the presence of others enhance
or impair our performance on
various tasks? Research findings
suggest that, in fact, there is no
simple answer. [Source: Frederic
Lewis Photographs.]*

the case for the person in the chapter opening story? In short, what impact, if any, will the presence of others have on your behavior (see Figure 11.2)?

Interest in this basic question has a long history in social psychology. In fact, several of the earliest experiments in our field were conducted to examine the impact of an audience upon performance (Triplett, 1898). Unfortunately, the results of these studies were quite confusing. On the one hand, many suggested that performance on various tasks could be improved by the presence of others, either as passive spectators or as *coactors* (persons working on the same task). On the other hand, an equally large number of experiments pointed to the opposite conclusion: performance on many tasks could actually be impaired by the presence of other persons (Zajonc, 1966). In response to these confusing and contradictory findings, several early researchers literally threw up their hands in despair and turned their attention to other topics. And there, surprisingly, the matter rested for several decades. Indeed, it was not until the mid-1960s that an apparent solution to this puzzle emerged. At that time Robert Zajonc (1965) proposed a simple but elegant theory that seemed to account, in one stroke, for all of the previous inconsistent results. While recent evidence suggests that this view may not explain all effects stemming from the presence of an audience or coactors, it has stimulated a great deal of research and proven highly influential. Thus, it is worth considering in some detail.

The Drive Theory of Social Facilitation: Other Persons as a Source of Arousal

Before turning to Zajonc's view, we should pause briefly to clarify one key point: the term *social facilitation,* as currently used by our colleagues, refers to *any* effects on performance stemming from the presence of others. Thus, it includes decrements as well as improvements in task-related behavior. Please keep this fact in mind as you proceed. Now, back to Zajonc's influential theory.

The central idea behind his **drive theory of social facilitation** is quite straightforward: the presence of others leads to increments in our level of motivation or arousal. As you can readily see, this idea agrees quite closely with our own informal experience. Often, the presence of other persons — especially in the form of an audience that watches our behavior — does cause us to experience signs of heightened arousal (e.g., feelings of tension or excitement). But how can such increments in arousal, in turn, account for the finding that the presence of others sometimes enhances and sometimes impairs performance on various tasks? According to Zajonc, the answer involves two basic facts.

First, it is a well-known principle in psychology that increments in motivation or arousal enhance the performance of *dominant responses* — those an individual is most likely to perform in a given situation. (Two examples of dominant responses: your tendency to smile when someone smiles at you; your tendency to take a bite too soon and burn your mouth when confronted with a delicious, hot pizza). Thus, when motivation increases, our tendency to perform the strongest or most dominant responses at our disposal increases too. Second, such dominant responses can either be correct or incorrect for any task we are currently performing.

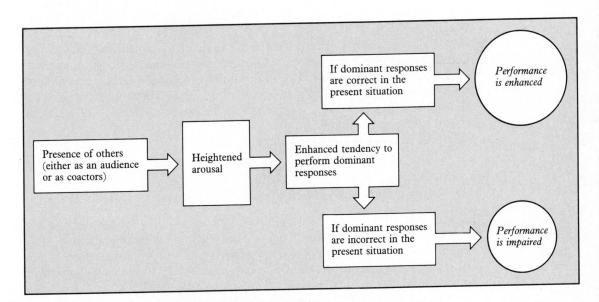

FIGURE 11.3   *The drive theory of social facilitation: A summary.*

*According to the **drive theory** of social facilitation, the presence of others increases our motivation or arousal. This heightened arousal, in turn, enhances the performance of dominant responses (our strongest responses in a given situation). If these are correct, performance is enhanced. If, in contrast, they are incorrect, performance is impaired.*

When these facts are combined with the suggestion that the presence of others is arousing, two intriguing predictions follow. First, the presence of others will facilitate performance when an individual's dominant responses in a given context are correct ones. Second, the presence of others may actually impair performance when his or her dominant responses in the situation are incorrect. (Please see Figure 11.3, p. 415, for a summary of these predictions.) Phrased another way, the presence of others will facilitate the performance of strong, well-learned responses, but may interfere with the performance of new and yet to be mastered forms of behavior.

Zajonc's theory was greeted with considerable enthusiasm among social psychologists. And this was hardly surprising: in one clean stroke it seemed to resolve a puzzle about social behavior that had persisted for sixty years. Further, when it was tested in actual experiments, it was strongly confirmed. A number of studies reported that, as predicted by the drive theory of social facilitation, the presence of an audience or coactors did tend to enhance the performance of dominant responses (e.g., Matlin & Zajonc, 1968; Zajonc & Sales, 1966). That is, individuals were in fact more likely to emit dominant responses when in the presence of others than when alone. And second, other research seemed to confirm the suggestion that the presence of other persons is arousing or motivating (e.g., Martens, 1969). Specifically, subjects were found to show higher levels of physiological arousal when they performed various tasks in front of an audience than when they performed the same tasks alone. In sum, within a few short years, a considerable body of evidence offered support for the essential accuracy of Zajonc's proposals (e.g., Cottrell, 1972; Geen & Gange, 1977).

While this early work on the drive theory of social facilitation was both valuable and informative, though, it did not address one basic question about which you may already have begun to wonder: Do such effects stem from the mere presence of others—their simple presence on the scene? Or are additional factors (e.g., our concern about their evaluations of us) also involved? It is to this important issue that we turn next.

Social Facilitation:
Mere Physical Presence, Concern over Evaluation,
or . . . ?

Imagine that you were working on some complex and difficult task (e.g., attempting to find the errors in a computer program, preparing your income tax return). Which of the following types of audience would exert a stronger effect upon your performance: several persons who watch your actions closely or an equal number who are present, but sound asleep? Common sense points to a simple answer: your performance would probably be more strongly affected by the awake than by the sleeping persons. After all, only the former individuals can observe and evaluate your behavior. Such considerations soon led several researchers to question Zajonc's assumption that social facilitation stems directly from the mere physical presence of others. Instead, they proposed that such effects may actually derive from **evaluation apprehension**—our concern over being evaluated by others. Specifically, it was proposed that the presence of others is arousing and produces social facilitation only when it serves as a cue for later positive or negative outcomes (Cottrell, 1972). And this, in turn, is most likely to occur when these persons seem to be evaluating our performance in some manner.

Support for this view (often termed the *learned drive* theory of social facilitation) was soon obtained in several studies (e.g., Innes & Young, 1975). For example, in one of these experiments, Cottrell and his colleagues (1968) had subjects perform a task involving the emission of previously learned responses under three different conditions: (1) alone in the room, (2) in the presence of two other persons who wore blindfolds, and (3) in the presence of two other persons who expressed interest in watching their behavior and who actually did so. Results indicated that social facilitation (an increase in subjects' tendencies to emit dominant responses) occurred only under the last condition —when members of the audience could observe and perhaps evaluate subjects' performance.

These and related findings (e.g., Bray & Sugarman, 1980; Markus, 1981) seem to build a convincing case for the view that social facilitation stems from evaluation apprehension rather than mere physical presence of others. At the very least, they suggest that the magnitude of social facilitation may be greater when individuals believe that their performance is being evaluated by an audience than when they feel that it is being largely ignored. We must note, however, that this reasonable conclusion has been called into question by other, contradictory findings. First, several studies conducted with human subjects (e.g., Hunt & Hillery, 1973; Markus, 1978) suggest that sometimes social facilitation can occur even in the absence of evaluation apprehension or any anticipation of positive or negative outcomes linked to the presence of others. Second, several experiments performed with animals indicate that the members of many different species are affected in much the same manner as we are by the presence of coactors or an audience (e.g., Rajecki, Kidd, & Ivins, 1976; Zajonc, 1980a). For example, in one intriguing study, Zajonc, Heingartner, and Herman (1969) found that the performance of an unusual group of subjects—roaches!—was strongly affected by the presence of an audience of four members of their own species. When the roaches' dominant response (running straight ahead) was correct, an audience facilitated their performance. (It decreased the amount of time they needed to reach a dark bottle and so escape from a bright light.) In contrast, when their dominant response was *incorrect* (a right turn was necessary to escape from the light and enter the bottle), the presence of an audience actually interfered with performance.

As you can readily see, these findings raise serious problems for the view that social facilitation stems mainly from evaluation apprehension. After all, it makes little sense to attribute concern about "looking good" in front of others to roaches, chickens, or other animals. Thus, evaluation apprehension does not seem to be a necessary condition for the occurrence of social facilitation in all cases. Yet, as we noted earlier, other studies seem to suggest that sometimes, at least, mere physical presence by itself is not enough. Rather, social facilitation occurs only when an audience or coactors can observe and perhaps pass judgment on our performance.

Taken as a whole, the evidence we have considered so far seems to leave us facing something of a dilemma. Does social facilitation stem from mere physical presence, from evaluation apprehension, or from some other factor? At present, no firm or final answer is available. However, one new approach, developed by Sanders, Baron, and Moore (1978) seems quite promising with respect to resolving this puzzle. Thus, it is to this perspective — known as the **distraction-conflict theory** of social facilitation — that we will turn next.

The Distraction-Conflict Model: A Possible Resolution?

Like the other explanations of social facilitation we have already considered, the distraction-conflict theory assumes that the impact of audiences and coactors on task performance stems from heightened arousal. In contrast to these other theories, however, it does not view such arousal as stemming either from the mere presence of others or evaluation apprehension. Rather, the distraction-conflict approach suggests that such heightened arousal derives from a special type of conflict. Briefly, the theory proposes that organisms performing various tasks in the presence of members of their own species are often pulled in two different directions at once. First, they have a strong tendency to orient toward and pay attention to the task at hand. Second, they have competing tendencies to orient toward and pay attention to the audience or coactors. (One reason for this latter tendency may be a desire to engage in *social comparison* — to compare their abilities and performance with that of others; Sanders, Baron, & Moore, 1978; Seta, 1982). The conflict produced by these two competing tendencies then leads to increments in motivation or arousal. And these, in turn, enhance the tendency to perform dominant responses (please refer to Figure 11.4).

As evidence for the accuracy of these proposals, Sanders, Baron, and Moore point to several major findings. First, they note that various sources of distraction — even nonsocial ones such as flashing lights — produce increments in arousal and so influence task performance in the way they predict. Thus, it appears that distraction does serve as a source of heightened motivation when it occurs during task performance (Sanders, 1981). Second, they note that subjects do actually report experiencing greater degrees of distraction when they perform various tasks in front of an audience than when they perform the same tasks alone (Baron, Moore, & Sanders, 1978). And third, they report that when subjects have little reason to orient toward or pay attention to other persons present on the scene (e.g., when these individuals are performing a different task than themselves), social facilitation fails to occur. In contrast, when subjects have strong grounds for directing attention to these others (e.g., when they are performing the same task or when subjects are made curious about their performance), such effects do appear.

Together, these findings seem to provide strong support for the basic assumptions of the distraction-conflict theory. And there can be little doubt that

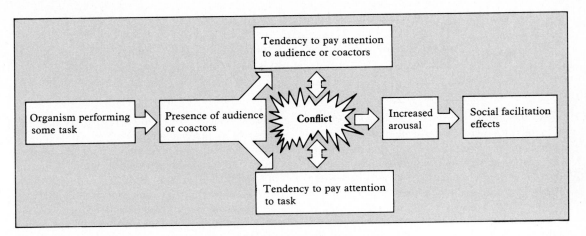

FIGURE 11.4 *The distraction-conflict theory of social facilitation.*

According to a theory proposed by Sanders, Baron, and Moore, the presence of others leads to competing tendencies to (1) pay attention to these persons, and (2) pay attention to the task at hand. The conflict generated by these competing tendencies results in heightened arousal. And this, in turn, produces social facilitation.

the theory itself offers important advantages. For example, since animals as well as human beings may be subject to the type of conflict described by Sanders and his colleagues, this theory helps explain why social facilitation occurs with many different species—even the roaches mentioned earlier. At the same time, though, we should add that certain "loose ends" remain (Geen, 1981). For example, it appears that, while the distracting effects of others tend to dissipate over time, those deriving from their mere physical presence do not (Zajonc, 1980). Further, growing evidence suggests that the presence of an audience or coactors may do more than merely increase arousal or produce shifts in attention. Such conditions may also cause individuals to turn their attention inward (Carver & Scheier, 1981a), and may lead them to inhibit overt practice of the task at hand (Berger et al., 1982). These effects are not considered by distraction-conflict theory, and their existence suggests the need for expansion of this approach. Until these and other issues are resolved, the theory offered by Sanders, Baron, and Moore should be viewed as an intriguing but as yet not fully verified framework for understanding social facilitation. We should note, though, that it has already provided several new insights into this process and stimulated a great deal of valuable research. Thus, while it may not offer a final or conclusive answer to the puzzle of social facilitation, distraction-conflict theory is certainly promising in scope and well worthy of further, careful attention. (Does working on a joint task with others affect our behavior in the same way as the presence of an audience? For a discussion of interesting research relating to this question, please see the **Focus on Research** section on pp. 420–421.)

*Social Loafing and Social Impact:
Why Groups Are Often Inefficient*

More than fifty years ago, a German psychologist named Ringelmann performed an interesting experiment. He asked workers to pull as hard as they could on a rope attached to a meter that measured the strength of their tugs. Results were quite surprising. While the total amount of force on the rope increased as group size rose, the amount of effort contributed by each person actually seemed to drop. Thus, while one subject pulling alone exerted an average of 63 kilograms of force on the meter, this dropped to only about 53 kilograms in groups of three, and was further reduced to only about 31 kilograms in groups of eight. In short, the greater the number of persons working on the task, the less effort each one seemed to show.

At first glance, the effect obtained by Ringelmann—often known as **social loafing**—seems quite puzzling. After all, as we have just seen in our discussion of social facilitation, the presence of other persons (coactors) often leads to increments in motivation. Why, then, does working on a task with several others seem to reduce individual effort? One possible answer is provided by the theory of **social impact,** proposed recently by Latané and his colleagues (e.g., Latané & Wolf, 1981).

According to social impact theory, the effect of any social force directed toward a group from an outside source is divided among its members. Thus, the greater the number of persons in the group (and also the greater their power or status, and proximity to one another), the less the impact of such force upon each one (Latané & Wolf, 1981). In short, it is as if the impact of social forces from outside the group is *diffused* in much the same way that responsibility for helping others is diffused among all the witnesses to an emergency (please refer to Chapter 8).

Social impact theory explains the findings reported by Ringelmann in the following manner. In Ringelmann's experiment, as well as in many other settings in which individuals work together on a task, there is external pressure to work as hard as

possible. Social impact theory suggests that this pressure is divided among all group members. Thus, as group size increases, each member experiences less pressure to comply. The result: the amount of effort expended by each individual drops and social loafing develops (see Figure 11.5).

Evidence for precisely this kind of effect has been reported by Latané and his colleagues in a fascinating series of experiments. For example, in one of the first of these (Latané, Williams, & Harkins, 1979), groups of male students were asked to clap or cheer as loudly as they could at specific times, so that, supposedly, the experimenters could determine how much noise people make in social settings. Subjects engaged in clapping and cheering either alone or in groups of two, four, or six persons. The strength of the sounds they made was recorded, and findings were clear: the amount of noise generated by each person decreased sharply as group size rose. Indeed, individuals produced less than half as much noise when members of groups of six as when they worked alone.

Follow-up research has replicated these results several times, and also indicated that they are quite general in scope (e.g., they occur among females as well as males, in several cultures, and under a wide range of work conditions; Harkins, Latané, & Williams, 1980; Weiner, Latané, & Pandey, 1981). Needless to add, such findings are somewhat discouraging. In essence, they suggest that many persons will "goof off" when working with others. And since groups perform many key tasks in modern society, this tendency has important practical implications. But is social loafing an unavoidable aspect of group performance? Or can something be done to lessen its occurrence? Fortunately, growing evidence points to the latter conclusion. In particular, it appears that the occurrence of social loafing can be sharply reduced by one simple step: arranging conditions so that the output or effort of individuals is uniquely identifiable. Direct evidence for the beneficial impact of such steps is provided by a

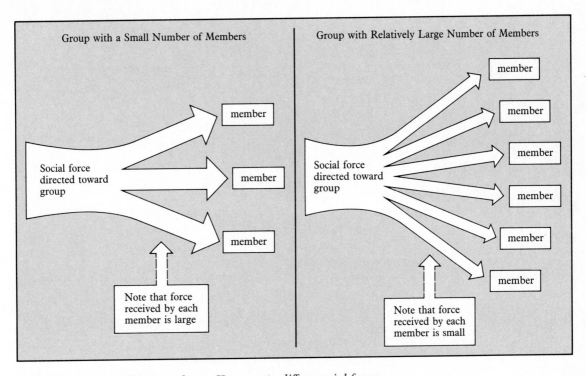

FIGURE 11.5 *Social impact theory: How groups diffuse social forces.*

According to social impact theory, *any social force directed toward a group is divided among all of its members. Thus, the greater the number of persons in a group, the less force or pressure each experiences. [Source: Based on suggestions by Latané & Wolf, 1981.]*

study conducted by Williams, Harkins, and Latané (1981).

In this experiment, male students were asked to shout as loudly as they could on a number of occasions. During the first stage of the study, subjects were led to believe that they would be shouting alone, with one other person (groups of two), or with five other persons (groups of six). In reality, however, they always shouted alone, so that the level of noise they produced under each of these conditions could be accurately measured. (Subjects wore earphones, so they could not know whether others were actually shouting.) As you can see from Figure 11.6 (p. 422), social loafing definitely occurred: subjects exerted less effort when they believed that they were shouting with one or five partners than when they believed that they were shout-

ing alone. In a second phase of the study, conditions were altered in a crucial way. Subjects were equipped with individual microphones, and told that from this point on, the experimenter would be able to measure their *individual* efforts even when they shouted in groups. The effect of this alteration was dramatic. When subjects believed that their individual performance could be identified, the tendency toward social loafing virtually disappeared. They worked almost as hard when they thought they were shouting with one or five partners as they did when they believed that they were shouting alone (refer to Figure 11.6, p. 422).

The results obtained by Williams and his colleagues, as well as those reported in other studies (e.g., Harkins & Petty, 1983), suggest that social loafing *can* be overcome. Thus, it is not an inescap-

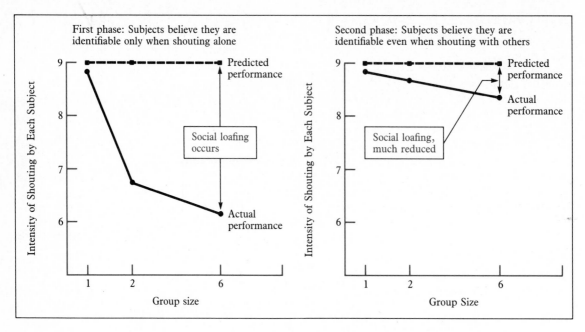

FIGURE 11.6   Social loafing: Overcoming its effects.

When subjects thought they were shouting together with one or five other persons, social loafing *occurred: they exerted less effort on this task than when they thought they were shouting alone (left panel). However, when subjects were informed that their individual efforts could be measured even when they shouted in groups, social loafing virtually disappeared (right panel). [Source: Based on data from Williams, Harkins, & Latané, 1981.]*

able side-effect of task performance by groups. When individual performance is made identifiable, the temptation to "take it easy" and conceal mediocre work within a larger group product may be sharply reduced. Unfortunately, the task of assessing the contributions of individual group members is often complex. Thus, social loafing may often prove quite difficult to eliminate. Further, recent findings suggest that other factors, too, may contribute to reduced motivation in group settings (e.g., Kerr & Bruun, 1983). For example, as group size increases, individuals may become more and more convinced that their own efforts are not essential. This growing belief that they are quite dispensable, in turn, may lead to lowered motivation. And, disturbingly, such results—often known as *free-rider effects*—can occur even when the contributions of individual members are readily identifi-

able (Kerr & Bruun, 1983). Reductions in motivation in group settings may also stem from the belief among individuals that one or more other members are engaging in such free-riding, and so playing them for a sucker (Kerr, 1983a).

In sum, several different forces operating within groups may tend to reduce the effort and motivation of individual members. Given the wide range of important tasks that are carried out in group settings, these effects may have unfortunate practical implications. For example, they may contribute to reduced productivity in many businesses, and to bad decisions by policy-setting groups. A major task facing researchers in this general area, then, is that of devising specific tactics for reducing the human tendency to "take it easy" while part of a task-performing group.

Deindividuation: Groups, Self-awareness, and the Shattering of Restraint

Have you ever attended a football, baseball, or soccer match at which members of the crowd shouted obscenities, threw things at the referees, or otherwise interfered with play? And have you ever gone to a party where, after things "warmed up," many persons present began acting in unusual or bizarre ways (e.g., saying ridiculous things, throwing food at one another, making passionate love in full view of onlookers)? If so, you are already acquainted with a basic fact about social behavior. Often, the presence of many other persons seems to weaken our restraints against engaging in wild, impulsive actions (see Figure 11.7). The process through which such effects occur is usually termed **deindividuation,** and it is upon this unsettling type of group influence that we will now focus.

If the reductions in restraints to which we just referred were limited to sports events or parties, they would be of only minor importance. Unfortunately, though, this is definitely *not* the case. Instead, it appears that under certain conditions, the presence of many other persons, or being part of a large crowd or group, can weaken restraints against much more serious forms of activity, such as vandalism, large-scale looting, or even interracial violence (Rogers & Prentice-Dunn, 1981). That such actions are attributable, at least in part, to the restraint-reducing impact of groups is suggested by the following fact: most of the persons taking part in such behaviors would never consider performing them while alone. Further, they are often genuinely embarrassed or upset by their actions when they have a chance to consider them in detail at a later, calmer time. Thus, there seem to be strong grounds for assuming that often, groups can induce their members to participate in activities they would never choose as individuals. But why, precisely, is this the case? How can the

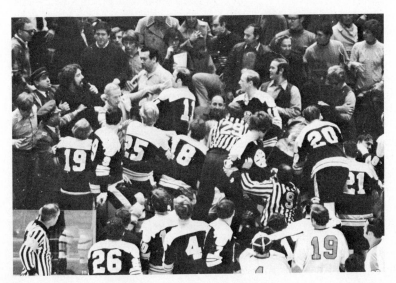

FIGURE 11.7   *Deindividuation: The "releasing" effects of groups.*

Being part of a large group often seems to weaken our restraints against impulsive or unusual forms of behavior. [Source: UPI photo.]

presence of many other persons weaken restraints against a wide range of impulsive and potentially dangerous behaviors? One intriguing answer has been suggested by Edward Diener (1980), a researcher who has spent more than a dozen years investigating the causes and nature of deindividuation.

Deindividuation:
Its Causes, Nature, and Effects

According to the theory proposed by Diener (which is based, in part, on earlier views offered by Zimbardo [1970] and others), the key to understanding deindividuation lies in its relation to *self-awareness.* In order to regulate our own behavior, adhere to social or personal standards, and make long-term plans, Diener suggests, we must be self-aware—aware of our own feelings, attitudes, and behavior (Buss, 1980; Carver & Scheier, 1981b). Deindividuation occurs when, because of certain environmental conditions, such self-awareness is blocked. Among the conditions producing such effects are anonymity (the belief that we are not identifiable as individuals), a high level of arousal, feelings of close group unity, and a focus on external events and goals. When such conditions exist, Diener suggests, two effects follow. First, self-awareness is sharply reduced. Second, individuals undergo important shifts in their perceptions or experience (they feel different, become caught up in the present, and experience distortions in their sense of time). Together, these shifts constitute a *deindividuated state.* And this state, in turn, produces many important effects. First, of course, it leads to weakened restraints against impulsive, and ordinarily prohibited, forms of behavior. Second, it reduces the ability of individuals to monitor or regulate their own actions. Third, it interferes with the ability to engage in rational thought or long-range planning. And finally, this state reduces individuals' concern with how others evaluate their behavior. (Please see Figure 11.8 for a review of these suggestions.)

To summarize: according to Diener, deindividuation develops when certain external conditions discourage individuals from focusing their attention inward and becoming self-aware. They then undergo related shifts in perception or experience and these, in turn, exert profound effects upon a wide range of cognitive processes and overt behavior. As we shall soon see, much research evidence is consistent with these suggestions. However, we should also note that Diener's theory has recently been modified in several useful ways by Prentice-Dunn and Rogers (1983).

Briefly, these researchers call attention to the fact that there are actually two distinct types of self-awareness (Buss, 1980; Carver & Scheier, 1981b). The first, *private self-awareness,* refers to attention to our own thoughts and feelings. The second, *public self-awareness,* refers to attention to ourselves as social objects—for example, concern about our appearance, or the kind of impression we are making on others. Prentice-Dunn and Rogers (1983) suggest that only reductions in private self-awareness are related to deindividuation. Specifically, they argue that reductions in such awareness, produced by certain external conditions (e.g., a high level of arousal, high group cohesiveness), make it difficult for individuals to regulate their own behavior in accordance

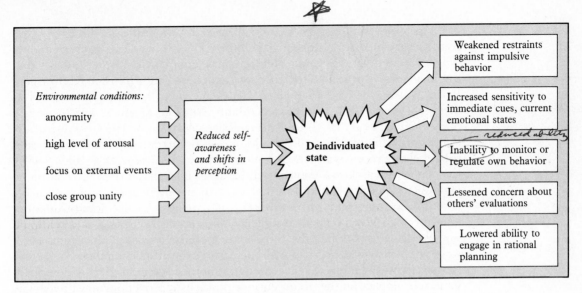

FIGURE 11.8   *Deindividuation: One theoretical perspective.*

According to a theory proposed by Diener (1980), certain environmental conditions (e.g., anonymity) lead to reduced self-awareness and accompanying shifts in perceptions and feelings. Together, these constitute a **deindividuated state.** *Deindividuation, in turn, produces several important effects (reduced restraints against impulsive behavior, lessened concern with the evaluations of others, etc.).*

with internal standards or existing social norms. Further, reductions in private self-awareness are accompanied by alterations in perceptual and emotional processes. Together, these changes constitute the subjective state of deindividuation, and serve to enhance impulsive, unrestrained behavior. Prentice-Dunn and Rogers note that reductions in public self-awareness, too, can lead to such behavior. However, in such cases, they contend, the intervening process is *not* deindividuation. Rather, it is individuals' conscious realization that they will not be held accountable for their actions. In short, Prentice-Dunn and Rogers (1983) suggest that it is reductions in *private* self-awareness that are central to the occurrence of deindividuation. By clarifying this important point, they have made a major contribution to our understanding of this unsettling group phenomenon.

Deindividuation: Some Relevant—and Unsettling—Evidence

Any process that can affect the occurrence of behaviors ranging from clowning and public lovemaking on the one hand through violence and destructive vandalism on the other is clearly worthy of careful study. Social psychologists have taken full account of this fact, and during the past two decades, have conducted many studies concerned with the causes and nature of deindividuation. Together, the findings of this research point to two general conclusions.

First, they suggest that deindividuation is a common occurrence—too common, we might add, for much comfort. Thus, it has been observed among individuals as diverse as young children, male and female college students, and the members of primitive societies (e.g., Diener, 1980; Johnson & Downing, 1979; Watson, 1973). Further, it has been found to occur in settings as divergent as research laboratories (Mann, Newton, & Innes, 1982), private homes (Diener et al., 1976), and even public streets (Mann, 1981). An especially interesting demonstration of this widespread occurrence of deindividuation is provided by a recent study carried out by Maruyama, Fraser, and Miller (1982).

These researchers reasoned that because children out trick-or-treating on Halloween experience high levels of arousal, are anonymous, and are usually accompanied by groups of friends, they may well experience deindividuation. And the high levels of petty vandalism and pranks occurring on Halloween suggest that this is in fact the case. In their study, however, Maruyama et al. were not primarily concerned with the occurrence of such impulsive behavior. Rather, they were interested in examining another potential effect of deindividuation: its impact on the occurrence of positive, approved forms of behavior. Specifically, they reasoned that deindividuation, by reducing self-awareness and concern with the evaluation of one's behavior, may well reduce prosocial actions. To test this possibility, experimenters stationed at six different houses greeted trick-or-treaters with a mild surprise. Instead of offering them small treats, as is customary in the United States, they asked these youngsters to donate part of *their* candy to children who had been hospitalized, and so could not be out trick-or-treating. In one condition, this was all that happened: the experimenter asked the children to donate some candy by placing it in a box; then, she left the room. In a second condition, she appointed one of the children as the "leader" of his or her group, and indicated that this person's name would be placed on the bag of candy collected. Finally, in a third condition, she indicated that each child was responsible for helping, and that their individual names would appear on any donations made. It was predicted that deindividuation would be countered by making the children responsible for helping. Thus, the smallest amount of candy would be donated when no mention of responsibility was made, more would be given when one child was made responsible, and the most would be donated when every child was individually responsible. Results indicated that this was indeed true, but only for small groups of youngsters (three or fewer). Among larger groups (four or more) donations did *not* increase with growing responsibility (see Figure 11.9). The implications of these results are, unfortunately, all too clear: when individuals can diffuse responsibility or remain anonymous in a large group, countering deindividuation may be quite a chore. Its persistence in many real-life situations, then, is not surprising.

These findings, and those obtained in many other studies suggest that deindividuation is far from rare. On the contrary, it may develop in a very wide range of settings if appropriate circumstances prevail. And when it does, the outcome for at least some of the persons involved may be dangerous indeed.

A second major conclusion suggested by research on deindividuation is as

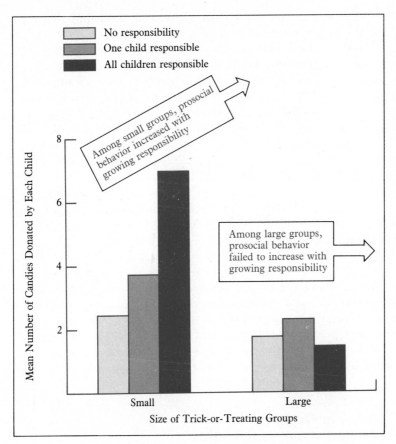

FIGURE 11.9 *Responsibility as a tactic for countering deindividuation: Some limiting conditions.*

Assigning direct responsibility to small groups of trick-or-treaters successfully countered deindividuation and enhanced prosocial behavior (donating candy to other children). In contrast, such tactics failed with larger groups of youngsters who could readily diffuse responsibility or remain anonymous. [Source: Based on data from Maruyama, Fraser, & Miller, 1982.]

follows: In general, it seems to develop and operate in the manner suggested by Diener (1980) and Prentice-Dunn and Rogers (1983). Thus, it is encouraged by certain external conditions (e.g., a high level of arousal, high group cohesiveness). It appears to involve reductions in private self-awareness and related shifts in experience or perception. And when it develops, it strongly enhances the performance of impulsive and often prohibited forms of behavior (Diener, 1979; Mann, Newton, & Innes, 1982; Prentice-Dunn & Rogers, 1980). For example, consider a recent study by Prentice-Dunn and Rogers (1982).

In this experiment, subjects were provided with an opportunity to aggress against a stranger (actually, an accomplice) by means of electric shock. Prior to these procedures, they were exposed to conditions designed either to enhance or reduce their private self-awareness and their public self-awareness. In order to enhance *private* self-awareness, the experimenter instructed subjects to focus their attention on their own thoughts and feelings while performing the experimental tasks. To reduce such awareness, in contrast, he asked them to focus their attention outward, not on themselves. To enhance *public* self-awareness, subjects were told that they would later meet the victim (i.e., the accomplice) to discuss their shocks with him. Further, they were informed that their shock levels were of major interest and would be recorded. To lower public self-awareness, participants were informed that they would never meet the victim, and that their shock levels would not be recorded. Both before and after delivering shocks to the accomplice, subjects completed a questionnaire designed to assess the subjective state of deindividuation. Inclusion of this questionnaire permitted the researchers to determine whether shifts in self-awareness produce deindividuation and whether, in turn, this state facilitates overt aggression. Results offered strong support for the theories proposed by Diener and Prentice-Dunn and Rogers. First, as expected, aggression against the victim was enhanced both by reduced private and public self-awareness. However, as suggested by Prentice-Dunn and Rogers (1983), a subjective state of deindividuation was produced *only* by reduced private self-awareness. Finally, and also consistent with the theories outlined earlier, aggression was indeed enhanced by the subjective state of deindividuation.

These findings and those obtained in other studies (e.g., Rogers & Prentice-Dunn, 1981) suggest that the framework proposed by Diener and later modified by Prentice-Dunn and Rogers is indeed a useful one for understanding deindividuation. And since comprehension of this complex process is a necessary first step toward countering its impact, Diener's theory, and recent research related to it, appears to have practical as well as purely scientific value. (For some thoughts on how our knowledge about deindividuation can be put to actual use, please see the **On the Applied Side** section on pp. 430–431.)

Decision Making in Groups:
How (Process) and What (Outcome)

Many key decisions are made by groups. Governments function largely through committees, subcommittees, and sub-subcommittees. Large corporations are controlled by boards of directors who meet regularly to shape company policy. And juries are often called upon to render verdicts that are, quite literally, matters of life and death for defendants. In sum, there is a strong tendency to entrust crucial decisions to the deliberations of groups. Several factors seem to contribute to this state of affairs. For example, it is generally believed that groups, by pooling the expertise of several persons, can often bring greater skill or knowledge to bear upon various problems than can individuals. Similarly, groups are viewed as being more conservative and less likely to "go off the deep end" in their decisions than are single persons.

Regardless of the specific factors behind this trust in groups, there can be little doubt that reaching decisions is one of the key tasks they are called upon to perform. For this reason, decision making by groups has long been of interest to social psychologists. In their efforts to clarify this central aspect of group functioning, our colleagues have generally focused on two major questions: (1) how, precisely, do groups move toward agreement — in short, what is the process of group decision making actually like? and (2) once they are made, what are group decisions like — specifically, do they differ in any manner from similar decisions by individuals? Recent, sophisticated research has shed considerable light on both of these issues (e.g., Davis, 1980; Kerr, 1981; Myers, 1983).

How Groups Arrive at Decisions: Social Decision Schemes and Social Transition Schemes

When groups first begin to discuss some issue, their members rarely agree. Rather, they usually hold a wide range of opinions, and offer several competing views on how to proceed. After some period of discussion, however, a decision is usually reached. Of course, this is not always the case; juries do become "hung" and other decision-making groups, too, may deadlock. But in most cases, *some* decision is ultimately reached. Is there any way of predicting this final outcome? In short, can we predict the decision a group is likely to reach from information about the views initially expressed by its members? Studies conducted by several different researchers suggest that in fact, we can (e.g., Davis, 1980; Laughlin, 1980).

Specifically, it appears that the final decision reached by a group can often be predicted by means of a small number of simple rules known as **social decision schemes.** These rules seek to relate the initial distribution of member views or preferences to the group's final decision, and are quite straightforward in nature. For example, one — the *majority-wins scheme* — suggests that in many cases, the group will opt for whatever position is initially supported by a majority of its members. According to this rule, then, group discussion serves mainly to confirm or strengthen the most popular view at the start of deliberations (see Figure 11.10). In contrast, another decision scheme — the *truth-wins*

"So it's nine great big votes yes and one teeny-weeny little vote no."

FIGURE 11.10   The power of majorities: Usually, hard to overcome.

As shown here, resisting pressure from a large majority is no easy task. Thus, it is far from surprising that group decisions can often be predicted by means of the simple majority-wins rule. [Source: Drawing by Vietor; © 1981 The New Yorker Magazine, Inc.]

 ON THE
APPLIED SIDE

Countering Deindividuation:
Some Potentially Useful Steps

Deindividuation, as we have seen, is a potentially dangerous affair. At best, it may encourage behaviors that are merely silly or annoying. At worst, it can lead to mob violence, destructive vandalism, and the like. Further, this process is far from rare. Conditions encouraging its development (such as anonymity) exist in many contexts and occur on many occasions. Given these alarming facts, one conclusion seems clear: techniques for countering deindividuation would be extremely useful. But can such strategies be developed? We believe that they can. In fact, it is our view that knowledge about deindividuation derived from social psychological research already points to a number of tactics that may prove helpful in stemming this dangerous process. Several of these are outlined here.

Countering anonymity. In many Hollywood westerns, sheriffs are shown defusing angry mobs by a simple tactic: they call individual members of the crowd by name (see Figure 11.11). Once identified in this manner, such persons seem to quickly surrender their plans to lynch the sheriff's prisoner. Research on deindividuation suggests that there may actually be a considerable grain of truth in such scenes. As we have noted, anonymity often plays a key role in the occurrence of deindividuation. Thus, somehow convincing the members of large crowds that they will *not* be submerged or hidden in the group may go a long way toward blocking this process. In most cases, of course, police and other law-enforcement officials will be unable to name the members of large crowds. But they *can* take other steps to strip away the anonymity usually enjoyed by such persons. For example, they can flourish large cameras and inform the persons present that they are being photographed or videotaped for later identification. It seems possible that when confronted with such conditions, crowds may choose to melt away rather than engage in large-scale violence.

Enhancing self-awareness. A key aspect of deindividuation involves reductions in self-awareness. When individuals discover that they are part of a large crowd, they often shift their attention outward, and pay little heed to their own values, standards, or attitudes. If such shifts can be prevented, deindividuation, too, may be blocked. But how can this be accomplished? Once again, research findings provide a clue. A large number of experiments suggest that when individuals are exposed to their own image, either in a mirror or on tape, self-awareness is enhanced (e.g., Carver & Scheier, 1981a; Greenberg, 1983). Consistent with such findings, it might prove feasible to enhance such awareness among large crowds by somehow exposing them to their own image. This, in turn, might be accomplished through the use of closed-circuit TV, or even the presence of shiny surfaces that cast reflections (e.g., glass shields or partitions). In any case, to the extent the persons present notice and pay attention to these stimuli, their self-awareness will increase, and deindividuation may thus be blocked.

---

rule—suggests that the correct solution or decision will ultimately predominate. And yet another scheme — the *first-shift rule*— predicts that the group will ultimately adopt a position consistent with the direction of the first shift in opinion shown by any of its members.

Surprising as it may seem, the results of recent research focused on these rules suggests that often they can predict final group decisions with a high

FIGURE 11.11   Countering anonymity: One possible tactic for blocking deindividuation.

In many Hollywood Westerns, sheriffs or marshals attempt to calm angry crowds through a simple tactic: they call various members by name. Once identified in this manner, these persons seem incapable of participating in mob violence. [Source: Culver Pictures, Inc.]

Strengthening internal restraints. In order for wild, impulsive behavior to take place, the internal restraints that usually hold such actions in check must be weakened. And deindividuation, of course, produces exactly this effect. One strategy for blocking its occurrence, then, might involve efforts to restore or strengthen these internal checks. Several steps may prove useful in this respect. For example, the persons involved can be reminded of the punishments that will follow impulsive, illegal actions. Threats of this type are often quite effective in deterring antisocial actions (Baron, 1973). Similarly, crowd members can be exposed to the actions of social models who both urge and demonstrate restraint. As we noted in Chapter 9, exposure to such persons can often strengthen internal checks against aggression and similar actions. Together, these and other tactics may succeed in restoring the inhibitions weakened by deindividuation. To the extent they do, the likelihood of wild, impulsive behavior may be lessened.

In short, deindividuation—like other behavioral processes—*can* be controlled. To achieve this outcome, though, specific, positive steps must be taken. Several of these are suggested by research findings, but their refinement and practical use will require much additional work. Given the potential savings in life, limb, and property that may result, however, there can be little doubt that accomplishing this task will be well worth the effort.

◆

degree of accuracy. Indeed, in several recent studies, group decisions involving complex matters (e.g., ambiguous criminal cases) have been accurately predicted up to 80 percent of the time by simple social decision schemes (e.g., Kerr, 1981). Of course, as you might suspect, different rules seem to be more successful under some conditions than others. Thus, the majority-wins scheme seems best in situations involving *judgmental tasks*—ones that are largely a matter of opinion, and for which no objectively correct decision exists. In contrast, the truth-wins rule seems best at predicting group decisions in cases where a correct answer or decision *is* available. In choosing among competing social decisions schemes, then, it is important to take basic aspects of the situation into account.

But given that the final decisions reached by groups can often be predicted, another and perhaps even more basic question remains: How, precisely, are such outcomes reached? How, in short, do groups actually move toward final agreement? This is a complex question, with no ready or simple answers. Yet, recent investigations have begun to shed considerable light on this matter, too (e.g., Foss, 1981). One basic strategy in such research has been to focus on **social transition schemes** — rules or models indicating how groups move through different patterns of member views or positions until a final decision is reached (e.g., Penrod & Hastie, 1980). As an example of such research — and of the intriguing results it has yielded — let us consider a study conducted by Kerr (1981).

In this experiment, groups of six male or six female students acted as jurors and deliberated over nine separate cases involving armed robbery. During the discussion of each case, subjects could indicate their personal verdict (guilty or not guilty) by pushing one of two buttons on a panel in front of them. They were free to change their view at any time and as often as they wished. Since these shifts (as well as subjects' initial and final decisions) were all recorded by the researcher, the group's route toward agreement could be precisely and continuously monitored. Subjects were also told that as in real trials, they were to attempt to reach a unanimous verdict. (If a group could not attain unanimous agreement within a period of time specified by the experimenter — for example, thirty minutes — it was considered to be hopelessly deadlocked.)

Results were both complex and revealing. First, as noted in earlier studies, the presence of a majority exerted powerful effects upon the final group decision. Group members were much more likely to shift toward a majority than to defect from one after it existed. Second, a special kind of momentum effect appeared. Once a group had begun to move in a given direction (i.e., toward a guilty or a nonguilty verdict), this movement tended to persist. Reversals of direction were quite rare. Third, the speed with which the groups reached a decision seemed to increase with growing experience. Thus, they tended to attain agreement on later cases more quickly than was true for the ones they discussed first (see Figure 11.12). Fourth, no differences between male and female groups were noted. Consistent with our comments in Chapter 7, then, there was no indication that females are more readily influenced by others than are males. Finally, it was found that the ultimate group decision could be predicted with a high degree of accuracy by the simple first-shift rule. In short, the final verdict was usually the one toward which the first shift in member opinions occurred. This last finding is especially interesting and suggests one practical strategy for influencing group decisions. Basically, it implies that an individual wishing to affect a group decision should start by voicing support for a view other than the one he or she actually favors. Then,

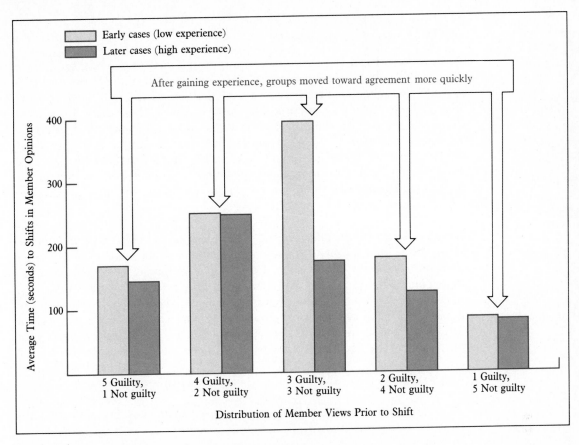

FIGURE 11.12 *Experience and movement toward agreement:*
Evidence for positive effects.

As groups gained increasing experience (as they examined more and more
cases), their speed in reaching decisions rose. Thus, they were considerably faster
in moving toward agreement on the last five cases they considered than on the
first four. [Source: Based on data from Kerr, 1981.]

quickly, this person should shift to this position. Doing so may put the first-shift
rule into effect and strongly shape the final outcome.

To conclude: research on social transition schemes and related topics
suggests that the movement of groups toward agreement is complex. Final
group decisions are affected by where the group has been (i.e., its previous
patterns of member views), how long it has been deliberating, and many other
factors. Yet, the process is far from random or haphazard; on the contrary, it
appears to be both orderly and predictable. Thus, there is every reason to
expect that with the completion of additional research, we will gradually gain
increased understanding of the process through which groups chart their route
to agreement.

What Groups Decide:
Moderation or Polarization?

Earlier, we called attention to an interesting fact. In general, groups are assumed to be more conservative than individuals. Specifically, they are perceived as being far less likely to adopt risky options or to "go off the deep end" than persons making decisions alone. At first glance, these suggestions seem quite reasonable. After all, the give-and-take of group discussion should help members to recognize the risks or flaws associated with various courses of action, and so aid them in avoiding these pitfalls. But is this really the case? Are groups really better at making decisions—or at least more conservative in this regard—than individuals? Research conducted during the past two decades provides some surprising answers.

Group versus individual decisions: A shift toward risk or a shift toward polarization? More than twenty years ago, a graduate student named James Stoner decided to base his master's thesis on these questions. That is, he set out to determine whether groups really *are* more conservative than individuals. To obtain evidence on this issue, he asked college students to play the role of advisers to imaginary persons supposedly facing choices between risky but attractive courses of action, and conservative but less attractive ones. For example, in one of these situations, a fictitious character faced the task of choosing between a secure but low-paying job, and a less secure but higher-paying one. (Please see Table 11.1 for additional examples of these *choice-dilemma questions.*)

During the first phase of the study, subjects made their recommendations regarding these situations alone. Then they met in small groups and discussed each problem until a unanimous agreement was reached. On the basis of common sense, Stoner expected that the decisions recommended by groups would be more conservative than those offered by their individual members. Surprisingly, however, just the opposite occurred. Time and time again, groups recommended riskier decisions than those adopted by individual members.

While the size of this difference was small, it quickly captured the attention of many social psychologists. The reason for this is simple: if groups do indeed make riskier decisions than individuals, important implications follow. For example, this suggests that juries, military councils, and government committees may be biased to adopt risky or even dangerous courses of action—*not* the safe or conservative ones common sense suggests. Impressed by such implications, many researchers focused their attention on this effect, which soon came to be known as the **risky shift** (e.g., Burnstein, 1983; Lamm & Myers, 1978). Many of the experiments they conducted seemed to confirm the initial findings reported by Stoner. That is, they too noted a shift toward increased risk following group discussions. In contrast, though, other studies failed to confirm such changes. And in a few cases, group discussion actually seemed to produce shifts toward *caution* rather than shifts toward risk (e.g., Knox & Safford, 1976). How could this be? How could group discussion produce both shifts toward caution and shifts toward risk? Gradually, a clear explanation emerged. What

TABLE 11.1   *Choice-dilemma items.*

These items are similar to the ones used by Stoner (and many other researchers) to compare individual and group decisions. Subjects are asked to answer each item twice—once alone, and then again after engaging in group discussion. Often their recommendations are riskier on the second occasion. (Source: Adapted from Kogan & Wallach, 1964).

---

1. Ms. F is currently a college senior who is very eager to pursue graduate study in chemistry leading to the Doctor of Philosophy degree. She has been accepted by both University X and University Y. University X has a world-wide reputation for excellence in chemistry. While a degree from University X would signify outstanding training in this field, the standards are so very rigorous that only a fraction of the degree candidates actually receive the degree. University Y, on the other hand, has much less of a reputation in chemistry, but almost everyone admitted is awarded the Doctor of Philosophy degree, though the degree has much less prestige than the degree from University X.

Imagine that you are advising Ms. F. Listed below are several probabilities or odds that Ms. F would be awarded a degree at University X, with the greater prestige.

Please check the *lowest* probability that you would consider acceptable to make it worthwhile for Ms. F to enroll in University X rather than University Y.

——— Place a check here if you think Ms. F should *not* enroll in University X, no matter what the probabilities.
——— The chances are 9 in 10 that Ms. F would receive a degree from University X.
——— The chances are 7 in 10 that Ms. F would receive a degree from University X.
——— The chances are 5 in 10 that Ms. F would receive a degree from University X.
——— The chances are 3 in 10 that Ms. F would receive a degree from University X.
——— The chances are 1 in 10 that Ms. F would receive a degree from University X.

2. Mr. A, an electrical engineer, who is married and has one child, has been working for a large electronics corporation since graduating from college five years ago. He is assured of a lifetime job with a modest, though adequate, salary, and liberal pension benefits upon retirement. On the other hand, it is very unlikely that his salary will increase much before he retires. While attending a convention, Mr. A is offered a job with a small, newly founded company that has a highly uncertain future. The new job would pay more to start and would offer the possibility of a share in the ownership if the company survived the competition of the larger firms.

Imagine that you are advising Mr. A. Listed below are several probabilities or odds of the new company's proving financially sound.

Please check the *lowest* probability that you would consider acceptable to make it worthwhile for Mr. A to take the new job.

——— The chances are 1 in 10 that the company will prove financially sound.
——— The chances are 3 in 10 that the company will prove financially sound.
——— The chances are 5 in 10 that the company will prove financially sound.
——— The chances are 7 in 10 that the company will prove financially sound.
——— The chances are 9 in 10 that the company will prove financially sound.
——— Place a check here if you think Mr. A should *not* take the new job no matter what the probabilities.

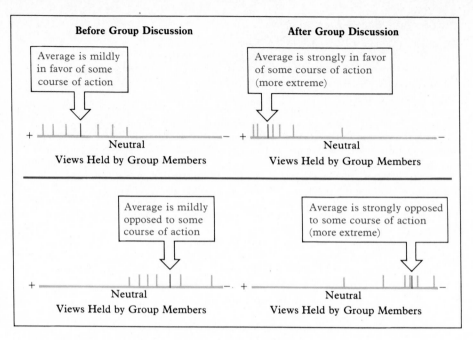

FIGURE 11.13   *Group polarization: Its basic nature.*

*After taking part in a group discussion, group members often shift toward
views that are more extreme (in the same general direction) than the ones they
held initially. Such shifts are known as* **group polarization** *effects.*

had at first seemed to be a shift toward risk was actually a more general
phenomenon — a *shift toward polarization.* In short, group discussion led individual members to become more extreme — *not* to move toward either risk or
caution. For example, if they were mildly in favor of a particular course of
action prior to the group discussion, they came to favor it even more strongly
after this procedure. And if they were mildly opposed to some action prior to
the group discussion, they came to be even more firmly against it after these
deliberations. Thus, the shifts induced by group discussion are more general in
scope than simple movements toward or away from risk. In essence, they
represent shifts in the direction of greater extremity or **group polarization.**
(Please refer to Figure 11.13 for a summary of these suggestions.)

As you can probably see, changes of this type have even broader implications than the so-called risky shift. Thus, it is not surprising that they have been
the subject of considerable interest among social psychologists. In the remainder of this discussion, however, we will focus on a key question relating to
such group-induced movements: Why do they take place?

Group polarization: Why does it occur? Several different explanations for the
occurrence of group polarization have been proposed (cf. Myers, 1983). However, two of these — the *social comparison* and *persuasive arguments* views — have
received most attention.

The social comparison approach starts with two reasonable assertions: (1) most individuals wish to maintain a positive self-image, and (2) one effective way of accomplishing this goal is comparing oneself favorably with others. Because of these tendencies, most persons seem to assume that they are better than average on at least some dimensions. That is, they assume that they compare favorably with others in at least some ways. Now, consider the impact of such beliefs within the context of group discussion. When such deliberations first begin, most group members assume that their views are probably more extreme than those held by the other participants — *in appropriate, valued directions.* In short, they assume that they hold views which are better or more enlightened than those of the other persons present. As you can readily see, it is impossible for everyone to be above average in this respect. Thus, a rude awakening soon arrives for many persons: they discover that their views are not nearly as extreme (in positive valued directions) as they at first believed. This discovery, in turn, puts pressure on them to shift to more extreme positions. The overall result, then, is that the group as a whole moves in this direction (e.g., Goethals & Zanna, 1979; Sanders & Baron, 1977). In sum, the social comparison view suggests that group polarization stems from (1) the desire of most persons to feel that they are better than average and (2) their tendency to shift to more extreme views when they learn, during group discussion, that this is not the case.

This explanation of group polarization is supported by several interesting findings. For example, individuals do tend to perceive themselves as being more extreme — in the "right" directions — than others (e.g., Wallach & Wing, 1968). Similarly, shifts toward extremity seem to occur in the total absence of group discussion, when individuals simply learn that their views are not as far above average as they assumed (Myers et al., 1980). Finally, as the social comparison view would predict, subjects tend to perceive others who have adopted extreme views in a more favorable light than others who have taken more moderate positions (Jellison & Davis, 1973). Together, these and other findings seem to provide firm support for the social comparison view. However, we should add that not all existing evidence is consistent with this theory. For example, individuals sometimes seem to recommend more extreme or risky decisions for strangers than for themselves (Laughlin & Earley, 1982). Clearly, this is inconsistent with the notion that most persons wish to appear above average in boldness or related characteristics. At present, therefore, it does not seem reasonable to view social comparison theory as a fully accurate account of group-induced shifts. And this fact, in turn, has led some researchers to offer a second, competing view.

This approach — generally known as *persuasive arguments theory* — rests on two basic assumptions. First, it contends that most of the arguments presented by group members during discussion support their own initial views. Second, it suggests that at least some of these arguments will be ones not previously considered by some members. When these two suggestions are combined, they point to a straightforward prediction: the group will shift toward the point of view that is supported by the largest number of convincing arguments. This will be the case because the greater the number (and quality) of the arguments favoring a given position, the greater the likelihood that some group members will be influenced by them and shift in its direction.

Support for this explanation of group-induced shifts derives from several different sources. First, it has been found that the greater the proportion of arguments favoring a particular point of view during group discussion, the greater the shift in its direction (Ebbesen & Bowers, 1974). Second, most of the persuasive arguments presented during group discussions support the initial positions held by a majority of group members (Vinokur & Burnstein, 1974). Given this fact, it is not at all surprising that groups shift toward greater extremity. In a sense, it is as if their members simply convince one another that the views with which they began are indeed the best or more accurate ones. These and other findings indicate that it is the exchange of persuasive arguments, not social comparison, that accounts for group polarization (Burnstein, 1983). However, here, too, some puzzling questions exist. Most importantly, it appears that such shifts occur even in situations involving simple perceptual judgments—cases where arguments and persuasion can play little if any role (Baron & Roper, 1976).

Taking all existing evidence into account, therefore, a clear choice between these two theories does not seem possible. And, in fact, such a choice may be unnecessary. It may actually be the case that *both* social comparison and the exchange of information play a role in the occurrence of group polarization. In short, individuals taking part in group discussions may shift toward more extreme views because (1) they wish to demonstrate that they hold "better than average views," and (2) they become convinced by the arguments they hear that certain views (ones similar to their own but even more extreme) are in fact the best or most accurate. Regardless of the precise basis for group polarization, however, the existence of this process has important implications. Briefly, its occurrence in many situations suggests that if they are not cautious, decision-making groups may gradually drift into positions that are more and more extreme—and more and more dangerous. In this regard, it is interesting to speculate about the potential role of such shifts in disastrous decisions by political or military groups who should, by all existing standards, know better (e.g., the decision by President Lyndon Johnson and his advisers to escalate the Viet Nam war; the decision by Argentinian President Galtieri and his associates to invade the Falkland Islands; see Figure 11.14). Did group polarization play a role in these events? At the moment, it is impossible to say. But if it did, it is clearly a force worth considering with care.

Leaders and Followers: Patterns of Influence within Groups

At different times during your life you have belonged to many groups. Think back over some of these now. With respect to each, can you recall one member who was more influential than the others? Probably you can. In almost every group one person wields more influence than all the rest. In short, one (or

FIGURE 11.14　Group polarization: A contributing factor in disastrous decisions?

Did group polarization contribute to the decision of President Johnson to escalate the Viet Nam war, or the decision of President Galtieri of Argentina to invade the Falkland Islands? The possibility certainly exists. [Source: UPI photo.]

sometimes several) acts as a *leader,* directing and shaping the actions of other group members.

Sometimes leaders are appointed from outside the group. For example, a new manager may be placed in charge of a department in a large corporation by the "top brass." In many cases, though, leaders are chosen by groups themselves, through a complex and often gradual process (e.g., Insko et al., 1980). Regardless of the manner in which they come to power, though, leaders clearly play a crucial role in group functioning. And given their powerful impact, our discussion of groups and their influence upon individual behavior would be sadly incomplete without attention to this topic. In this final section, therefore, we will focus on the nature and impact of leadership. Specifically, we will summarize current knowledge concerning two intriguing questions: (1) who becomes a leader—why do some persons but not others rise to positions of power and authority? and (2) what factors determine a leader's success once he or she has assumed this role?

Are Leaders Born or Made?
Charisma versus Technical Skill

Are some persons born to lead? According to one view of leadership—the **great man/great woman theory**—this is so. Briefly, this approach suggests that certain persons rise to positions of power and authority largely because they possess key traits—ones that set them apart from ordinary men and women and suit them for "life at the top." At first glance, these ideas are quite compelling. When we consider famous leaders, they *do* seem to differ from their followers in several respects. For example, all appear to possess boundless energy, a will of iron, and driving ambition. Yet, early attempts to construct a list of key traits predictive of great leadership failed. Try as they might,

FIGURE 11.15   *Leaders: Do they really share special traits?*

Do famous leaders share key traits that set them apart from ordinary persons? Attempts to test this possibility have generally yielded negative results. In most cases, it seems, it is difficult to distinguish leaders from followers without a "scorecard"! [Source: Drawing by Ziegler; © 1978 The New Yorker Magazine, Inc.]

(Official Government Photo)

Nov. 28 (UPI)—At his office in the capital city, the world's most powerful dictator greets the world's funniest standup comic.

researchers could not identify specific characteristics that set leaders apart from followers (see Figure 11.15). Indeed, after several decades of work on this topic, there seemed to be almost as many different lists as there were separate investigators! Faced with this discouraging state of affairs, most psychologists soon surrendered the search for a brief list of leader-producing traits and turned, instead, to a sharply different approach. (But please see the **Focus on Research** section on pp. 442–443 for a discussion of recent evidence indicating that leaders may actually differ from other persons in *some* respects.)

This newer perspective for understanding leadership—known as the **situational theory**—emphasized the importance of situational rather than personal factors. Specifically, it suggested that the person most likely to become a leader in any given setting is not necessarily the awe-inspiring great woman or man, whose charisma and charm hypnotize others into blind submission. Rather, it is usually the individual whose skills and competence happen to be the ones most useful to the group in a given context. According to this view, then, different persons may well rise to positions of leadership under different conditions. For example, consider the case of a skilled architect who possesses thorough knowledge of her field. She may well take charge during the construction of a major building. But when her company competes with others in a yearly athletic contest, she may readily surrender this authority and move to the sidelines. In short, the situational theory argues that the question "Who becomes a leader?" is best answered by reference to the task faced by the group and the general situation within which it must operate rather than in terms of a few crucial traits possessed by specific members (Hollander & Julian, 1970, 1978).

Leadership As a Two-Way Street: The Modern, Transactional View

The situational approach to leadership described earlier was valuable in many respects. For example, it called attention to the importance of several factors overlooked by the person-oriented great man/great woman approach. Yet it, too, was open to major criticism. Most important, it tended to view leadership as a kind of one-way affair, in which leaders influence their groups but are not, in turn, affected by their followers. Actually, this is far from the case. A large body of evidence suggests that leaders' behavior is often strongly shaped by the actions, demands, and perceptions of other group members (e.g., Beckhouse et al., 1975; Fodor, 1978). Thus, a full understanding of leadership seems to require that this aspect of the process, too, be taken into account.

As recognition of this key fact has grown in recent years, the situational approach to leadership has gradually merged into a new and more sophisticated view known as the **transactional perspective.** In essence, this theory argues that leadership should be viewed as a complex *social relationship* — not simply as the exercise of authority by one person over several others. Consistent with this broad framework, it recognizes the fact that leaders are influenced by, as well as exert influence over, their followers (e.g., Stein et al., 1980). Similarly, the transactional approach calls attention to the key role played by the perceptions of both leaders and followers concerning the link between them. For example, it predicts that group members will be more willing to accept influence from a leader when they view this person's position as legitimate than when they view it as illegitimate. Similarly, the transactional view predicts that followers will be more likely to accept influence from a leader when they perceive this person as possessing greater skill or competence than themselves (Price & Garland, 1981). Finally, it also takes note of the fact that the relations between a leader and each member of his or her group may vary greatly. Thus, the transactional perspective suggests that attention should be directed to these individual relations (often termed **vertical dyad linkages**), as well as to the overall exchange between leaders and the group (e.g., Liden & Graen, 1980; Vecchio, 1982).

To conclude: because it emphasizes the social nature of leadership, considers both personal and situational factors, and also takes account of leader and member perceptions, the transactional view is quite complex (see Figure 11.17 on page 444). Indeed, there can be little doubt that it is far more complex in some respects than the earlier perspectives it has replaced. Yet, growing evidence suggests that such complexity is justified; without it, we will probably be unable to attain full comprehension of leadership and leadership processes. The choice, in short, appears to be one between simpler but less adequate views, and a complex but more accurate one. We're sure you will agree that to the extent this is the case, accuracy — not simplicity — must get the nod.

The Great Man / Great Woman Theory Revisited: Personality and Leadership

In our discussion of the great man/great woman theory, we noted that initial evidence on this view was quite disappointing. Try as they might, researchers could not uncover a short list of traits serving to distinguish great leaders from other human beings. While these findings are certainly discouraging, they do not necessarily imply the total absence of *any* link between personality on the one hand, and leadership on the other. All great leaders may not share a single set of characteristics, but personality and leadership ability may still be related under some conditions and in some respects. Evidence that this is in fact the case has been provided by several recent studies (e.g., Costantini & Craik, 1980; Fodor & Smith, 1982).

For example, consider the study by Costantini and Craik (1980). These researchers sought to determine whether political leaders differ from the general public with respect to various traits. In order to assess this possibility, they obtained the cooperation of more than two thousand male and female political leaders, who agreed to complete a standard measure of personality (the Gough Adjective Checklist). These subjects were all delegates or alternates to their party's U.S. presidential conventions and were all highly active in political affairs. Since only persons of proven influence are chosen for this role by their local party organizations, Costantini and Craik assumed that all could reasonably be viewed as leaders.

The results of the study were quite revealing. As expected, political leaders *did* differ from other persons on several traits. First, they were found to be significantly higher in *self-confidence, need for achievement,* and *dominance.* Second, they scored significantly lower than other persons on *succorance* (the tendency to elicit sympathy or emotional support), *abasement* (the tendency to express feelings of inferiority through self-criticism or guilt), and *deference* (the tendency to seek subordinate roles in relations with others). In short, political leaders turned out to be the kind of confident, achievement-oriented, dominant persons that informal observation suggests they often are (see Figure 11.16). (We should note, by the way, that this pattern of results was identical for male and female leaders. Thus, where political leadership is concerned, gender appears to make little difference).

The findings obtained by Costantini and Craik and those reported by other researchers suggest that leaders do in fact differ from other persons in several respects. Alarmingly, though, additional evidence indicates that the traits serving to equip such persons for a swift rise to the top may not be ones promotive of effective group functioning. For example, in one recent study, Fodor and Smith (1982) compared the functioning of small groups headed by leaders known to be either very high or relatively low in the *need for power.* The groups met to discuss a business problem (whether a company should produce and market a new microwave oven), and the quality of their decision was carefully assessed. Results offered a highly consistent picture: groups headed by power-oriented leaders performed at a lower level than those headed by leaders less concerned with personal power. Specifically, they exchanged less information, considered fewer alternative courses of action, and reached poorer final decisions. In short, it appeared that a trait or motive often associated with the attainment of positions of authority was actually *harmful* to successful group functioning.

To conclude: evidence obtained in recent years suggests that as proposed by the great man/great woman theory, leaders may indeed differ from other persons in several ways. Thus, there may well

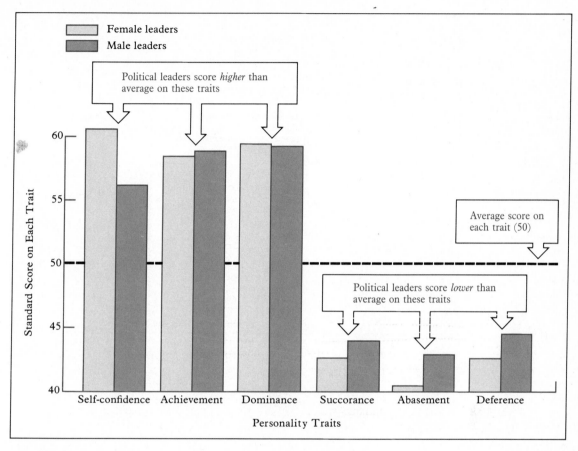

FIGURE 11.16   Leaders versus nonleaders: Some interesting contrasts.

*Political leaders seem to differ from other persons with respect to several traits.
As shown here, they are higher in self-confidence, dominance, and need for
achievement, but lower in succorance, abasement, and deference. Note that there
are no sex differences in this respect: male and female leaders show virtually
identical patterns. [Source: Based on data from Costantini & Craik, 1980.]*

be a grain of truth in this early view after all. But
please note: the fact that personality has *some* bearing upon leadership in no way implies that all great
leaders share a single set of characteristics. As we
have already seen, different groups confront radically different conditions and settings. Thus, it is
only reasonable to expect that they will often require leaders with contrasting personal traits. From
a social psychological perspective, then, the appropriate question to ask is *not* "What traits make a
person a great leader?" Rather, it is "What traits
are needed for effective leadership in a specific
group, facing specific tasks, at a specific time?"

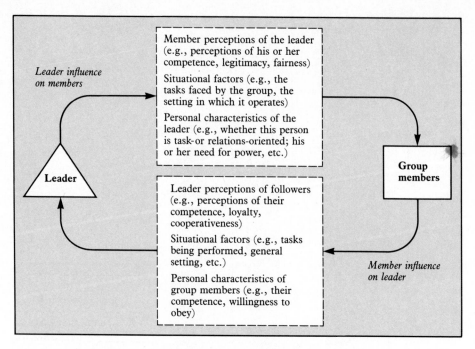

FIGURE 11.17   Leadership: A modern perspective.

At present, **leadership** *is viewed by most experts as a complex social relationship in which leaders both influence and are influenced by their followers. Further, it is realized that leader and member perceptions, as well as a host of situational and personal factors, all play a role in this overall process.*

Leader Effectiveness: A Contingency Approach

Before leaving the topic of leadership, we will examine one final question: What factors determine a leader's degree of success? In short, what conditions influence the extent to which he or she contributes to effective group performance? Because of its practical implications, this issue has been the focus of a great deal of research (e.g., Schriesheim & DeNisi, 1981). And much of this work has focused on a theory of leader effectiveness proposed by Fiedler and his colleagues (e.g., Fiedler, 1978).

According to this framework—known as the **contingency model of leader effectiveness**—a leader's success in directing his or her group depends on several different factors. The most important of these, though, involve: (1) the leader's overall orientation (reflecting his or her personal characteristics) and (2) certain features of the situation. Thus, consistent with the modern, transactional approach, Fiedler's theory assumes that both leader characteristics and situational factors play an important role in the process.

With respect to leader orientation, Fiedler notes that often such persons adopt one of two distinct approaches. Some leaders, he has found, are primarily concerned with *task performance*. Their major goal is that of completing the work at hand, and this receives the bulk of their attention. Such leaders are often described as showing a *task-oriented* perspective. In contrast, other leaders seem primarily concerned with maintaining good, friendly relations with their subordinates. Pleasant social interaction, in short, seems more important to them than a high degree of efficiency. Such leaders are often described as demonstrating a *relations-oriented* approach. As you can readily guess, task-oriented and relations-oriented leaders often differ in personal style. The former are frequently (but not always) directive and somewhat authoritarian, while the latter are often (but again, not always) friendlier and more informal. But given these contrasting orientations and styles, is one better than the other? Fiedler's answer is: *it all depends.* The relative success of these two styles of leadership, he suggests, depends on key aspects of the situation. Specifically, he argues that task-oriented leaders are often more effective when situational conditions are either very favorable or unfavorable to the leader, while relations-oriented leaders are often more effective under conditions that are moderately favorable or unfavorable. The reasoning behind these predictions is as follows. When conditions are moderately favorable, a friendly, nondirective leadership style can help smooth over differences of opinion within the group, and improve cooperation. Thus, relations-oriented leaders tend to "shine" in such cases. When conditions are highly unfavorable, in contrast, a directive style may be needed. Without it—and without the accompanying emphasis on production—the group may literally fall apart. Finally, when conditions are extremely favorable, a task-oriented approach may again be best. Here, group members are quite confident of attaining their goals, and morale tends to be high. Thus, an emphasis on interpersonal relations (as shown by relations-oriented leaders) is unnecessary; indeed, it may prove irritating and get in the way of good performance.

But what conditions, in turn, determine the extent to which a given situation is favorable or unfavorable to the leader? Here, Fiedler suggests that three are of key importance: (1) the leader's personal relations with other group members, (2) the extent to which group tasks are clearly structured, and (3) the power of the leader over other group members. The most favorable situation possible, then, is one in which the leader enjoys good relations with other members, the task is clearly structured, and she or he can exert considerable power over the group. In contrast, the most unfavorable situation is one in which the leader's relations with group members are poor, the task is unstructured, and the leader's power is limited. To repeat: Fiedler predicts that relations-oriented leaders will be more effective than task-oriented ones when conditions are moderately favorable or unfavorable. However, task-oriented leaders will be more effective than relations-oriented ones when such conditions are either highly favorable or highly unfavorable (see Figure 11.18, page 446).

As you can see, Fiedler's theory is fully consistent with the transactional perspective described earlier. It takes account of the social nature of leadership, and considers the impact of both personal characteristics of the leader and important situational constraints. But how has it fared when put to the test? In general, quite well. In fact, a recent review of more than 170 studies undertaken to test various aspects of the theory indicates that positive results were

FIGURE 11.18   The contingency model of leader effectiveness: Major predictions.

According to a theory proposed by Fiedler, relations-oriented leaders are more effective than task-oriented ones under moderately favorable or unfavorable situational conditions. However, the opposite is true when situational conditions are either highly favorable or highly unfavorable.

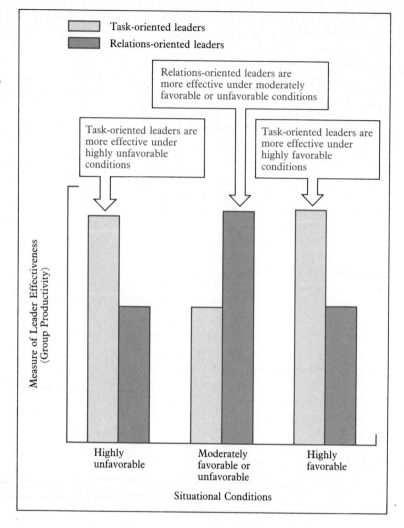

obtained in a large majority (Strube & Garcia, 1981). This does not mean, of course, that *all* relevant findings offer support for Fiedler's views: far from it. Further, the theory has been criticized on the grounds that it is somewhat ambiguous with respect to the classification of situations as relatively favorable or unfavorable to the leader. Obviously, to the extent such ambiguity exists, it is impossible to make clear-cut predictions regarding the effectiveness of task-oriented or relations-oriented leaders.

Despite these problems, though, it is clear that Fiedler's theory—and the general transactional approach it represents—have contributed much to our understanding of this important topic. The view that leader behavior and leader effectiveness stem from a complex interplay between situational factors, leader's orientation, social perceptions, and a host of other factors is certainly less dramatic than the earlier, great man/great woman theory. However, there is currently general agreement among experts in this area that it is also probably much closer to the truth.

Summary

Groups often exert powerful effects upon the attitudes and behavior of their members. Perhaps the simplest effect of this type is **social facilitation.** This term refers to effects on performance stemming from the presence of other persons (audiences or coactors). Research findings suggest that the presence of others is arousing and enhances the tendency to perform dominant responses. If these are correct, performance may be enhanced. If they are incorrect, performance may be impaired.

When individuals are part of a large group, they often seem willing to perform actions they would never perform while alone (e.g., mob violence, vandalism). This is due, in part, to the occurrence of **deindividuation**—a psychological state in which restraints against wild, impulsive behavior are weakened. Deindividuation, in turn, seems to stem from external conditions (e.g., anonymity) that reduce or block self-awareness.

Groups make many key decisions. Often, these can be predicted by *social decision schemes*—simple rules relating the initial distribution of members' views to the final group outcome. One such scheme suggests that the majority opinion usually prevails. Another predicts that the most accurate view is the one generally accepted. Recent studies have focused on the precise manner in which groups move toward agreement. Findings here suggest that once groups begin to shift toward a specific decision, they tend to continue in this direction (a kind of momentum effect). In the past, it was widely assumed that groups tend to make more conservative or cautious decisions than do individuals. Now, however, it is known that during discussion, groups tend to move toward *polarization.* That is, their members tend to adopt views more extreme than their initial ones, but in the same general direction.

The most influential member of a given group is often perceived as being its *leader.* One early view of leadership, the *great man/great woman theory,* held that leaders are born; they rise to positions of authority because they possess special traits. Little support for this view was obtained. A contrasting approach, the *situational view,* emphasized the importance of situational factors (e.g., the task facing the group). An even more sophisticated perspective—the *transactional theory*—views leadership as a complex social relationship, in which leaders both influence and are influenced by their followers. Many factors affect the success of leaders in facilitating group performance. According to the *contingency model* proposed by Fiedler, the most important of these involve the leader's overall orientation (whether this person is task-oriented or relations-oriented), and the favorability of the situation to the leader. In short, this view proposes that leader effectiveness stems from a complex interplay between situational factors, social factors, and the leader's characteristics.

Glossary

contingency theory (model) of leader effectiveness   *A theory suggesting that leader effectiveness is determined both by characteristics of leaders and certain characteristics of the situation they confront.*

deindividuation   *Refers to a psychological state characterized by lessened self-awareness and major shifts in perception and/or experience. Deindividuation is encouraged by certain external conditions (e.g., anonymity), and once it develops, it enhances the occurrence of wild, impulsive behavior.*

distraction-conflict theory   *An explanation for the occurrence of social facilitation effects. According to this view, the presence of others induces conflict between two tendencies: (1) paying attention to these persons and (2) paying attention to the task at hand. This conflict, in turn, is arousing, and enhances the tendency to perform dominant responses.*

drive theory of social facilitation   *The view that the mere presence of others increases arousal. Such heightened arousal, in turn, enhances the tendency to perform dominant responses. If these are correct, performance is improved. If they are incorrect, performance is impaired.*

evaluation apprehension   *Refers to concern over evaluations from others. Such concern or apprehension may often play a key role in the occurrence of social facilitation effects.*

great man/great woman theory   *A theory of leadership based on the view that all great leaders share certain traits that set them apart from ordinary persons and suit them for power or authority.*

group polarization   *Refers to the tendency of group members to shift toward more extreme positions than those they initially held, following group discussion. Several contrasting explanations for such shifts have been offered.*

leadership   *Refers primarily to a special type of influence—that exerted by one member of a group over several others. It is currently recognized, however, that leadership is a complex social relationship in which leaders are affected by followers as well as exert influence on these persons.*

risky shift   *Refers to the fact that following group discussion, individuals often recommend riskier or more daring decisions than they did prior to such discussion. Recent findings indicate that such shifts are actually part of a more general phenomenon: group polarization (see group polarization).*

situational theory of leadership   *Refers to the view that the persons most likely to become leaders in various groups are those who can best help their groups to attain major goals. In short, various aspects of the situation, rather than characteristics of potential leaders, are emphasized.*

social decision schemes   *Simple rules relating the initial distribution of member views to final group decisions. One social decision scheme suggests that the majority will usually prevail; another holds that the most correct or accurate position will usually predominate.*

social facilitation   *Refers to any effects upon performance stemming from the presence of others.*

social impact theory   *A view suggesting that the impact of an external social force upon a group is divided or diffused among the members. Thus, the larger the group, the smaller the impact of the force on each individual.*

social loafing   *Refers to the tendency of individuals performing a task to exert less effort on it when they work together with others than when they work alone.*

social transition schemes   *Rules or models that attempt to describe the manner in which groups move through different patterns of member views until a final decision is reached. In short, social transition schemes attempt to map the group's path to agreement.*

transactional perspective   *A modern approach to leadership emphasizing the fact that leadership is a complex social relationship between leaders and their followers. Thus, both leader and member perceptions, as well as personal and situational factors, must be taken into account.*

vertical dyad linkage approach   *A perspective on leadership emphasizing the fact that relations between leaders and each member of their group may vary substantially. Thus, it is important to consider these individual relations, as well as those between the leader and the group as a whole.*

For More Information

Diener, E. Deindividuation: The absence of self-awareness and self-regulation in group members. In P. B. Paulus (Ed.), *The psychology of group influence.* Hillsdale, N.J.: Erlbaum, 1980.
A well-written discussion of the nature of deindividuation. Factors that produce this state, the internal changes that accompany it, and the behavioral effects it produces are all considered.

Fiedler, F. E. Contingency model and the leadership process. In L. Berkowitz (Ed.), *Advances in experimental social psychology* (Vol. 11). New York: Academic Press, 1978.
An excellent summary of Fiedler's theory and research relating to it. In addition, practical techniques for improving leader effectiveness based on contingency theory are described.

Forsyth, D. R. *An introduction to group dynamics.* Monterey, Calif.: Brooks/Cole, 1983.
This excellent text examines many aspects of group functioning. You may find the discussions of leadership, deindividuation, group performance, and conformity/deviance especially interesting.

Myers, D. G. Polarizing effects of social interaction. In H. Brandstatter, J. H. Davis, & G. Stocker-Kreichgauer (Eds.), *Group decision processes.* London: Academic Press, 1983.
A fairly technical, but clearly written discussion of the nature and effects of group polarization. If you wish to learn more about this important aspect of group process, this is an excellent source to consult. (Incidentally, the chapters by J. H. Davis and N. L. Kerr contained in the same volume are also excellent; they deal with other aspects of group decisions.)

Paulus, P. B. (Ed.). *The psychology of group influence.* Hillsdale, N.J.: Erlbaum, 1980.
While this book is written primarily for professional social psychologists, several of the chapters it contains deal with topics we have considered, and are excellent sources of further information about them. In particular, you may wish to consult the units on deindividuation (mentioned previously), the impact of audiences (by R. L. Borden), and the mere presence of others (by R. B. Zajonc).

CHAPTER 12

Environment and Behavior:
Social Impact of the Physical World

The Interpersonal Environment: Responding to the Physical Presence of Others

Personal Space: The Determinants of Acceptable Distance/Violations of Personal Space: Being Invaded and Deciding Whether to Invade/Territorial Behavior: "Owning" Parts of the Environment/People in One's Immediate Environment: Being in a Crowd and Feeling Crowded

Negative Aspects of the Physical Environment: When Conditions Are Stressful

The Effects of Noise/The Effects of Heat/The Effects of Air Pollution

Positive Aspects of the Physical Environment: Excitement and Pleasure in a City

Affective Responses to the Environment/Creating a Desirable Urban Environment

Special Inserts

FOCUS ON RESEARCH
   Jump! Jump! Environmental Influences on Response to a Suicide Threat

ON THE APPLIED SIDE
   Where Would You Like to Live? Choosing the Ideal Environment

ON THE APPLIED SIDE
   Overpopulation: An Environmental Time Bomb

Imagine for a moment that you are living in a large urban center, several decades in the future. Further imagine that nothing has been done to correct any current trends toward a worsening of the environment. How might your day begin?

You and your spouse awake in the small cubicle that serves as your bedroom. It is part of a dormitory-apartment unit that you share with five other couples and their fifteen children. You have postponed parenthood for yourselves so far, hoping to move up the waiting list for one of the scarce two-family apartments. Still, it would be nice to have a little one of your own, maybe two. As usual, it is a hassle fighting for your turn in the bathroom. After you dress, you find the communal kitchen crowded and noisy, and the two of you quickly gulp down some imitation orange juice and coffee substitute before you leave for your respective jobs. At least, the juice and coffee taste better than the greenish tap water that is provided by the city.

You have to push your way into the packed elevator, and the air is thick with cigarette smoke. It is difficult to breathe because of the tobacco fumes and the press of bodies in the confined space. There are three elevators in your building, but the other two are temporarily shut down to conserve electricity.

Once you reach the street, you find that the outside air is brown and acrid, and there is talk of another smog alert. All of this unpleasantness is made worse by the oppressive heat, and you feel yourself perspiring heavily in the humid atmosphere.

The wealthier individuals still drive automobiles in the busy streets, but, like many others, the two of you share a motorcycle in your trip to the downtown office building where you work. The traffic is bumper to bumper and slow. The noise level from traffic, beeping horns, and construction is high, but you try to drown it out with music from portable radios blasting through your headphones.

As you park in the eighty-story garage and enter your place of work, you look at your spouse and wonder, "What kind of a life are we living? Is it worth it?"

We all hope very sincerely that our future lives are not at all like the ones in this pessimistic tale. It seems very probable that each of us would respond very badly to the crowded conditions, the noise, the polluted air, and all the rest. Such problems do not spring into being over night, and it is easy to ignore them in their early stages, to find good reasons to justify them as they become more serious, and to dismiss anyone who does become concerned for "overreacting" (see Figure 12.1, p. 454, for an example of such responses).

Most of us are aware that our surroundings can make us miserable when either the physical or interpersonal environment is undesirable in any way, and this reaction affects both psychological and physical functioning. In contrast, our surroundings can be a major source of pleasure when they make life seem exciting and well worth living. In recent years social psychologists have been

FIGURE 12.1   *Environmental problems: Concern versus justification.*

*As illustrated in these scenes from the land of Id, the reactions to environmental
deterioration include concern and alarm, attempts to justify present conditions,
and a negative response to those who point out the seriousness of the problem.
[Source: By permission of Johnny Hart and Field Enterprises Inc.]*

involved in determining just how we react to the positive and negative aspects
of the environment and how our behavior can bring about good and bad
changes in that environment.

Environmental psychology is a relatively new field that deals with the
interaction between the physical world and human behavior. Research has
shown clearly that our feelings, our actions, and even our state of health are
influenced by the world around us; it is equally clear that our behavior has both
short-term and long-term effects on that world (Evans, 1981). The way in which
humans affect the environment and efforts designed to influence such behavior
are discussed in Chapter 13.

Since environmental psychology deals with some of the most serious
problems facing society now and in the foreseeable future (for example, crowding, pollution, and the quality of life), we expect this field to play an increasingly
important role in our lives. It is promising to find that these interests are
international in scope (Canter & Craik, 1981) and that they involve the cooperative efforts of social psychologists, architects, urban planners, and many others
(Sommer, 1980). The goal is to understand the way in which the physical and
social environment affects behavior and to bring about environmental improvement.

In the following section, we will examine *the interpersonal environment* and
the way in which people respond to the presence of others as a function of how
many there are, how far away they are, and who they are. We will then turn to
the *negative aspects of the physical environment* of the kind described in our
introductory story, and examine the effects of such factors as noise, heat, and
polluted air. Next, we will discuss *positive aspects of the physical environment* and
learn how some external conditions bring about such pleasant reactions as

excitement, joy, and a sense of comfort. Attention will also be focused on three special topics: the way in which environmental factors influence *attempted suicides,* the kinds of variables involved in selecting an *ideal environment* for oneself, and the world-threatening problem of an increasingly *overpopulated environment.*

The Interpersonal Environment: Responding to the Physical Presence of Others

The world around us consists partly of other people, and we respond in various ways to their presence. For example, as the number of students in a classroom increases, the more each individual is likely to cough, especially if the subject being presented is not very interesting (Pennebaker, 1980). The effect of others can also be seen in situations such as a religious crusade. These events tend to reach a climax when members of the audience come forward "to make a decision for Christ": the larger the crowd, the greater the proportion of those who come forward in response to Billy Graham and other ministers (Newton & Mann, 1980). In the context of such interpersonal effects, psychologists have been particularly interested in the way in which people deal with *personal space* and the effects of interpersonal distance, *territorial behavior* and the identification of one's "ownership" of parts of the environment, and interpersonal *density* which under specific circumstances can be experienced as *crowding.*

Personal Space: The Determinants of Acceptable Distance

We tend to treat the area immediately surrounding our bodies as though it were an integral part of ourselves. This region is defined for each individual as his or her **personal space.** A few selected people are allowed to enter this space, but everyone else is expected to remain outside of it (see Figure 12.2 on page 456 for an example of typical interpersonal spacing among strangers or acquaintances).

Learning how to use personal space. It has long been observed that residents of different parts of the world vary widely in what are considered appropriate interpersonal distances. For example, very close interactions are common in Latin America, France, Greece, and the Middle East, while more distant interpersonal spacing is preferred in Great Britain, Sweden, Switzerland, and the United States (Hall, 1966; Sommer, 1969). These cross-cultural differences suggest that such behavior is learned, at least in part. It appears that our basic tendency is for close contact, as you might guess from watching puppies or kittens crawl over one another as they play. Children may also be observed to interact in that fashion before they gradually learn to space themselves at greater distances in the course of socialization experiences (Aiello & Aiello, 1974; Price & Dabbs, 1974; Shea, 1981). It is found, for example, that both males and females in the first three grades of school maintain closer spacing with respect to their playmates at recess than do fourth to sixth graders, and

FIGURE 12.2   Personal space: Maintaining a polite distance.

We act to maintain an "appropriate" distance between ourselves and those around us. This **personal space** *acts as a buffer zone that is ordinarily not violated by others. Among strangers or acquaintances, there tends to be a fairly constant distance that is close enough to permit communication but far enough away to avoid touching. [Source: Harold M. Lambert / Frederic Lewis Photographs.]*

they also touch one another about five times as frequently (J. W. Burgess, 1981).

Beyond these developmental trends, there are a number of characteristics that influence spacing. For example, pairs of same-gender strangers or acquaintances interact more closely than mixed-gender pairs (Severy et al., 1979); those from lower socioeconomic groups interact more closely than middle class representatives (Scherer, 1974); and mentally retarded children maintain much less interpersonal distance than children of normal intelligence (J. W. Burgess, 1981).

[handwritten margin notes: same gender / socioeconomic status / mentally deficient]

An interesting difference in personal space preferences has been discovered between violent and nonviolent individuals (Kinzel, 1970). Violent prisoners are found to require nearly three times as much area surrounding them in order to feel comfortable, compared to nonviolent prisoners. Walkey and Gilmour (1979) devised a technique using videotapes to assess prisoner reactions to viewing various approach distances. In subsequent research, Gilmour and Walkey (1981) found a clear difference between violent and nonviolent offenders in their tolerance for interpersonal closeness. Even ordinarily nonviolent undergraduates who have been angered by an insulting experimenter reveal expanded personal space needs and increased discomfort at close approach distances (O'Neal et al., 1980). It appears that what most of us perceive as a comfortable and reasonable distance can cause discomfort and hence elicit hostility in those who are violence-prone or who happen to be in an angry state. It seems likely that some acts of violence have been unwittingly triggered by interference with spatial preferences of this kind.

Personal space varies with the situation. As we find ourselves in different situations involving different kinds of relationships, our personal space needs change accordingly. Some years ago, Hall (1963, 1966) observed that Americans interact at one of four distances, depending on who the other people were and what behavior was taking place. The study of such behavior (known as **proxemics**) indicates that from 0 to 1½ feet is an **intimate distance** appropriate for such acts as lovemaking or fighting, while 1½ to 4 feet is a **personal distance** used by friends in conversation. For more formal interactions, 4 to 12 feet is the **social distance** we maintain in conducting impersonal business transactions, and over 12 feet is the **public distance** used between a speaker and his or her audience. Though it is probably helpful to consider these four broad categories, keep in mind that distance is really a continuous variable (Knowles, 1980). Closeness varies along a continuum, and our reactions to different degrees of closeness probably do so as well.

Most people seem to be aware of these unwritten rules of interpersonal distance. When students watch a videotape of people interacting, they indicate that intermediate spacing is preferable to either very close or very distant interactions (Thompson et al., 1979). The nature of the relationship matters, of course, and physical closeness is measurably more characteristic of friends than of strangers, especially if they are both females (Heshka & Nelson, 1972). Male friends in Western cultures seem to resist close interactions unless engaging in some kind of friendly aggression such as playful punches or arm wrestling. With opposite gender pairs, males and females both clearly differentiate friends

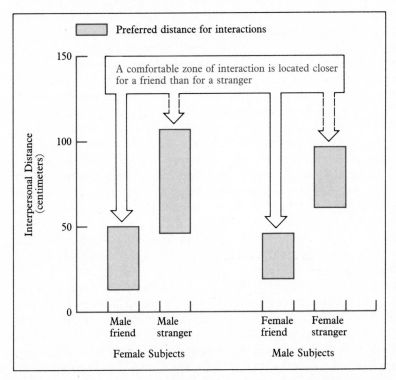

FIGURE 12.3 *Zones of personal comfort: Friends versus strangers.*

For both friends and strangers, there is a comfortable zone of interaction—any closer is too close and any farther away is too distant. Both males and females are more comfortable when an opposite-sex person standing relatively close is a friend rather than a stranger. [Source: Based on data in Ashton et al., 1980.]

and strangers with respect to what distances are appropriate. Ashton et al. (1980) asked pairs of friends and pairs of strangers to stand at various distances and report their reactions. As shown in Figure 12.3 on the preceding page, the preferred distance for a friend is notably closer than the preferred distance for a stranger.

Perhaps the broadest view of personal space is that when it is occupied by another person, there is a strong emotional reaction (Ashton & Shaw, 1980). In general, then, very close distances tend to magnify emotional responses, and both positive and negative feelings become more intense when distance decreases (Schiffenbauer & Schiavo, 1976).

Violations of Personal Space: Being Invaded and Deciding Whether to Invade

As has been suggested, people frequently report feelings of distress and discomfort when someone approaches them too closely. We will now examine in more detail the responses that are made to such invasions and also the behavior of those in a position to carry out an invasion.

Responding to an invasion of personal space. You may have had the experience of standing quietly by yourself on a street corner waiting for the light to change, when a stranger walked up and stood next to you. How did you feel? What did you do? Some years ago, the effects of such an invasion were investigated by Felipe and Sommer (1966). On the grounds of a mental hospital, a confederate walked up to within six inches of a patient and simply stood there. Compared to noninvaded patient controls, the targets of the close encounters quickly left the vicinity. The fact that these subjects were mental patients had nothing to do with the results. The same thing happens among normal people when a same-sex stranger stands close to them on the sidewalk when they are waiting to cross the street (Konečni et al., 1975). The closer a confederate stands in relation to the subject, the faster that person crosses the street. To find out how such an invader is perceived, Smith and Knowles (1979) repeated the sidewalk study, but had an experimenter on the other side of the street ready to interview each subject after he or she crossed over. As you might expect, the invader was described as unpleasant, rude, hostile, and aggressive. In addition to such perceptions, there is also a physiological response to an invasion, indicating that it is stressful to have a stranger inside of one's personal space. In a men's room, confederates used a urinal that was next to one used by a subject or two urinals away (Middlemist et al., 1976). The closer the confederate, the more time was required by the subject to begin urinating and the faster the act was completed (two physiological indicators of stress).

Besides a physical invasion of space in which another person stands or sits too close, there is another kind of invasion when a stranger points a camera at us. Guile et al. (1980) stationed a confederate with a camera by a flight of stairs at a university. When a student walked up the steps alone, the confederate either stood there with the camera hanging around his neck or pointed it toward the approaching individual. Only 9 percent showed any reaction to the confederate in the first condition, but 60 percent responded to the pointing camera with some sort of submissive behavior such as running away or embarrassment. Celebrities frequently engage in legal (and sometimes physical) battles with photographers who are accused of similar invasions of privacy.

As we noted earlier in describing intimate distance, closeness is not necessarily bad. The physical closeness of a good friend, a lover, or even an attractive stranger of the opposite sex may be a very positive experience (Knowles, 1978). The crucial variable seems to be how the invader is perceived. An "invasion" evokes a positive response, for example, when the invader is friendly and complimentary (Storms & Thomas, 1977), when adults are providing help to children (Cowen et al., 1982), and if one adult is requesting a favor of another (Baron, 1978; Willis & Hamm, 1980).

The fact that an invasion can be either positive or negative can best be understood in terms of the processes outlined in Figure 12.4. It appears that the presence of another human being in one's personal space leads to physiological arousal. Depending on how this arousal is labeled, the invaded person may feel angry, fearful, or pleased. As we have seen in other chapters dealing with a variety of emotions from love to hate, responses seem to depend in large part on the cognitive labeling that an individual applies to his or her aroused state.

To invade or not to invade: That is the decision. In most experiments dealing with the effects of spatial invasions, the invader is an experimental confederate who has been instructed to walk up to or sit beside a subject. In real life, any invasions are carried out by someone who must decide whether to approach, how close to approach, and so forth. It may surprise you, but invading can be as

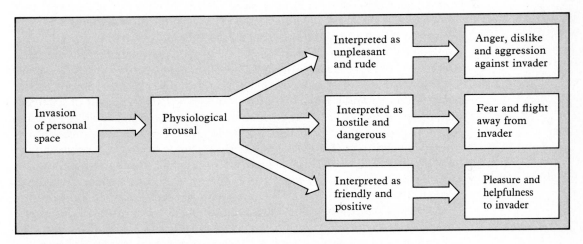

FIGURE 12.4 *Reactions to invasion depend on one's cognitions.*

When another individual enters your personal space, the initial response seems to be an increase in your physiological arousal. Depending on your interpretation of the situation, you apply quite different labels to your aroused state. As a function of what label is applied, your actual response to an invasion can be as varied as aggression, escape, and helpfulness.

FIGURE 12.5   When strangers are interacting, we are more likely to go around them than to invade their shared space.

Would you go around this interacting pair or walk right between them? We tend to avoid invading the personal space of others. When two people are conversing, a stranger is likely to go around them rather than in between. We treat such interactions as an extended zone of personal space shared by the two individuals. [Source: © LEA / Omni-Photo Communications, Inc.]

unpleasant as being invaded. Very often, the potential invader decides to avoid encroaching on a stranger's personal space, but just whose space is being invaded exerts considerable influence on this behavior.

One such setting for possible invasions is a drinking fountain. It has been found that the presence of a confederate sitting one foot away from the fountain leads passersby to avoid getting a drink, compared to situations where the confederate is five or ten feet distance (Barefoot et al., 1972). The presence of a stranger close to the fountain has no effect, however, if it is located in a densely packed hallway (Thalhofer, 1980). Possibly, the large number of people present can cause individuals to suspend the rules as to spatial invasions. Also, drinking is inhibited by the closeness of a male confederate but not of a female, presumably because sexist attitudes result in females being viewed as having lower status and hence posing less of a threat than males (Riess & Salzer, 1981).

Another common situation occurs when you encounter a pair of strangers talking in a hallway—do you go around them or between them? (See Figure 12.5.) There is a general tendency to walk around rather than through two interacting strangers (Efran & Cheyne, 1973), but who they are can be important. For example, a passerby is more willing to walk through an interacting male-female pair than between two people of the same gender (Walker & Borden, 1976). An invasion of a low status pair is more likely than if at least one of the two individuals is of relatively high status such as a professor, priest, or businessman (Bouska & Beatty, 1978). The racial composition of the pair also matters. In a shopping mall, Brown (1981) arranged for two confederates to stand conversing about 6 feet apart, and the pair consisted of either two whites, two blacks, or a racially mixed dyad. As you can see in Figure 12.6, male and female shoppers (who were primarily white) were more likely to walk through a pair of black strangers than through a pair of white strangers or a black-white pair. In addition, when going around a racially mixed pair, there was a

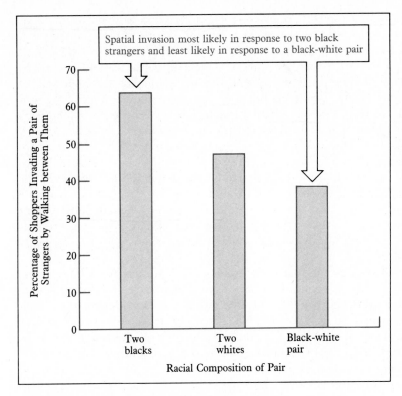

FIGURE 12.6 Spatial invasions: Race makes a difference.

In a shopping mall, pairs of confederates stood talking, and several hundred shoppers were observed as to whether they walked through or around the two individuals. Invasion (walking between the pair) was most frequent if they were both black and least frequent if one was black and one white. [Source: Based on data from Brown, 1981.]

significant tendency to pass behind the white stranger rather than behind the black one. The author interpreted these findings as a relative lack of consideration for the personal space of blacks. Across various studies, then, it appears that any perception of relatively lower status (on the basis of gender, clothing, or race) leads to a greater likelihood of an invasion of personal space.

We now turn to another aspect of spatial behavior—territoriality—in which portions of the environment are perceived as off limits to invaders.

Territorial Behavior: "Owning" Parts of the Environment

A **territory** is an area that an individual or a group occupies exclusively and defends against anyone who tries to intrude. Such behavior is characteristic of many species; even ants defend the space around their nests against fellow ants who happen to live in different colonies (Hölldobler & Lumsden, 1980). When any organism stakes out and defends a territory, that behavior is known as **territoriality.**

According to Altman (1975), there are three types of human territory. A **primary territory** is actually owned permanently or temporarily and is used regularly for an extended period of time—such as a house or apartment. A **secondary territory** is used regularly, but others share the space—such as an assigned seat in your three o'clock class. A **public territory** is temporarily possessed by whoever gets there first—such as a portion of a beach where you lie down. In a game arcade, players establish temporary possession of a given machine by touching it when a potential intruder approaches (Werner et al., 1981). People report feeling the greatest degree of safety and control in primary territories and the least in public territories (Taylor & Stough, 1978).

Within the home, family members tend to agree on the territorial attributes of various rooms (Sebba & Churchman, 1983). Some areas belong to an individual, such as a child's bedroom or the father or mother's study. An area may also be shared by two or more people—the parents' bedroom or the bedroom assigned to more than one child. Areas used by the whole family may be truly public and open to all, as is true of the living room, bathroom, and hallways. Still other areas are used by each family member, but one person is perceived as having jurisdiction over it (for example, the kitchen with the mother or father in charge). These divisions of living space seem to be useful in preventing misunderstandings about where each person is able to exert legitimate control.

You may have observed various animals use urination to mark off territory and identify it as their own, but humans have somewhat less offensive ways to indicate that a particular place belongs to them. Thus, your doormat may have your last name on it, your coat can be placed over the back of your chair in class, or your towel may be spread out on a certain spot on the beach (Edney & Jorden-Edney, 1974). The function of such markers is to inform others that this spot is off-limits to intruders; in this way large numbers of strangers can deal peacefully with one another without trespassing and without having to discuss it (Edgerton, 1979). If someone tries to break these informal rules, they are told to move along and return the space to the "owner" (Taylor & Brooks, 1980).

Privacy as the goal of territoriality. Altman (1975) suggested that people identify territories in order to obtain privacy. Interestingly, privacy seems to be sought most often in primary or public territories—by oneself at home or lost in a crowd of strangers (Taylor & Ferguson, 1980). In the new and populous environment a student encounters in leaving home and going away to college, the ways in which he or she is able to obtain privacy are a matter of some concern. In a dormitory, a variety of mechanisms can be used to regulate privacy. Of greater importance is the finding that a higher proportion of college freshmen who remain in school use these mechanisms than is true of freshmen who drop out (Vinsel et al., 1980). In addition, those who remain in school also are more likely than dropouts to seek contact with fellow students *when they desire companionship.* In other words, the successful students are best at controlling their interpersonal interactions (see Table 12.1 for a listing of the privacy regulating mechanisms used). This is one instance where differential use of territorial behavior is found to be related to extremely important consequences for the individual.

In that same dormitory investigation, the use of territorial markers (room decorations) by dropouts and remaining students was compared. Those who stayed in school were found to decorate their rooms with more diverse items than was true for dropouts, to have more maps and photos of the university and

TABLE 12.1 *Regulating one's territory for privacy or companionship.*

College freshmen who stayed in school were found to be more successful in developing mechanisms to obtain privacy and to obtain companionship than were freshmen who dropped out of school. This aspect of territorial behavior seems to be of considerable importance with respect to being able to adjust to a new environment such as a college dormitory. [Source: Based on data from Vinsel et al., 1980.]

	Percentage using each mechanism	
Obtaining privacy: *Mechanisms used to* *avoid interpersonal contacts*	*Freshmen staying in school*	*Freshmen dropping out of school*
Shut dormitory room door	94	84
Found a quiet place	69	42
Tuned out noise and slept	61	53
Tuned out noise and studied	54	47
Went walking alone	54	37
Prepared for bed in quiet place	22	0
Arranged for privacy in room	19	11
Used bathroom at quiet time	17	0
Obtaining companionship: *Mechanisms used to* *seek interpersonal contacts*		
Phoned someone	76	68
Visited someone's room	74	63
Opened dormitory room door	70	47
Invited people to their room	67	58
Studied in a busy place	33	21
Went to the student union	26	11
Played music to attract others	22	16
Used bathroom at a busy time	11	5

the surrounding region, and to have fewer decorations relating to home (e.g., photos of high school friends, parents, and siblings). Other research has shown individual differences in the extent to which *any* territoriality is shown. Among homeowners, those who erect signs, fences, hedges, or who have their initials on their doormats in order to mark their property respond to their doorbells more quickly than those without markers (Edney, 1972). Presumably, the territorial people are more concerned about having their privacy invaded and want to see who is at the door. The use of markers also leads to a feeling of safety and actually reduces the fear of becoming a crime victim (Patterson, 1978b). It has also been determined that homeowners tend to personalize their residences with markers to a greater extent than renters (Greenbaum & Greenbaum, 1981).

The prior residence effect: It's better to be the home team. Though Snuffy Smith has his own definition of "home-field advantage" (see Figure 12.7, p. 464),

**FIGURE 12.7   *The prior
residence effect: Playing on one's
home field.***

*In species ranging from fish to
human beings, it is found that an
individual on his or her home
territory is likely to have an
advantage over any intruder. This*
prior residence effect *leads to
more dominant behavior and the
tendency to control interactions. It
appears that Snuffy Smith has some
additional ideas about what
"home-field advantage" means.
[Source: © 1981 King Features
Syndicate, Inc. World rights
reserved.]*

members of various species seem to benefit from being on their home territory
as opposed to being elsewhere. For example, a chicken is more likely to peck a
strange bird when in its home cage than in the stranger's cage (Rajecki et al.,
1979). Even fish in a familiar aquarium assume dominance over any intruder
(Figler & Evensen, 1979). This territorial advantage is known as the **prior
residence effect.**

Studies of human beings reveal the same phenomenon, and not only with
respect to playing at home on one's own basketball court or football field. For
example, Edney (1975) had pairs of undergraduates work on a task in the
dormitory room of one of the two individuals. Those in their own room felt
more relaxed and more in control of the situation than the visitors. Residents
also are found to be more successful at performing such tasks (Martindale,
1971) and more likely to dominate a conversation (Conroy & Sundstrom, 1977)
than someone visiting the room. Even when three people are involved in a
discussion, the one whose room is the site of the interaction tends to have the
greatest influence on the outcome, and this is equally true of individuals who
ordinarily are high or low in dominance (Taylor & Lanni, 1981). Altogether,
the evidence is consistent that individuals have an advantage when they compete with others within their own private territory.

We will next turn to research that deals with the effects of crowds of people
on the behavior of individuals. As indicated in the **Focus on Research** panel on

pages 466–467, individuals surrounded by others do not necessarily behave as they do when alone.

People in One's Immediate Environment: Being in a Crowd and Feeling Crowded

We will now focus on the most obvious aspects of the interpersonal environment — the sheer number of people who are present in one's residence, on the job, or in the surrounding community. What are the effects of increasing numbers of fellow human beings? Some now classic animal studies that were first conducted with rats over two decades ago provided evidence of extremely negative consequences (Calhoun, 1962, 1971). Even though the animals were well fed and had plenty of water, rats in a densely packed environment reacted in a variety of negative ways ranging from aggression to cannibalism to physical illness. Later studies indicated physical changes such as a delay in the age of puberty (Massey & Vandenbergh, 1980).

With human beings, the research strategy is ordinarily to compare existing settings of low and high density and to look for corresponding differences in behavior. For example, it has been found that, as density increases in a preschool, there is more aggression and verbal abuse (Loo, 1979). Prison represents an extreme example of continuing high density living. As the number of prisoners in an institution increases, inmates have more disciplinary problems, report more illnesses, and are more likely to commit suicide (McCain et al., 1980). Even considering larger areas, population matters. For example, voting behavior is affected: as population per square mile increases, the proportion of voters casting ballots declines (Preuss, 1981). The sheer number of people living in a community is related to much more destructive forms of behavior as well. In a recent study of 175 cities in the United States, Kelley (1982) found that population was positively related to a variety of crimes. The number of murders, rapes, robberies, and car thefts per person increased as community size increased (see Figure 12.10, page 468). Strangely enough, the opposite trend was shown for the ratio of divorces to marriages; marriage breakups were more frequent in the smaller communities than in the larger ones. It should be noted that similar findings have sometimes been attributed to socioeconomic status. That is, densely populated areas often contain a higher proportion of low income individuals (Freedman et al., 1975). This does not seem to be the explanation for the relationship between crime and community size, however, because Kelley (1982) found the same relationship regardless of the income level of the various localities.

In general, then, this sort of research could be taken to mean that, for both rats and human beings, increased population brings only problems. As we shall see shortly, other variables are involved so that the relationships are more complex than they first appear (Taylor, 1980).

Density versus crowding. Because human behavior is greatly affected by our perceptions, it is necessary to make a distinction between the objective physical state of **density** and the subject's psychological state of **crowding** (Gillis, 1979;

Jump! Jump! Environmental Influences on Response to a Suicide Threat

A Puerto Rican handyman perched on a 10th floor ledge for an hour yesterday morning as many persons in a crowd of 500 on upper Broadway shouted at him in Spanish and English to jump. Even as cries of "Jump!" and "Brinca!" rang out, policemen pulled the man to safety. . . .

New York Times

An all too familiar story in our newspapers and at times on the televised news is the seemingly callous and cruel reactions of spectators to an individual poised on the ledge of a building, threatening to end his or her life (see Figure 12.8). Mann (1981) has collected accounts of such situations in several countries and found 166 incidents between 1964 and 1979 involving crowds witnessing actual and threatened suicides. Groups of people gathered at this kind of scene vary greatly in what they do. Some show curiosity and will wait as long as eleven hours for the final plunge to take place. Others impatiently urge the person to jump and get it over with. In the worst examples, people scream obscenities and throw rocks at those working to save the victim. Still others cheer a successful rescue as when Muhammad Ali talked a man out of jumping from a Los Angeles building.

From the earliest days of social psychology, there has been interest in crowd behavior, and it seems reasonable to suggest that lone bystanders would react differently than groups of people. For one thing, there is **contagion** in a group, so that if one person engages in a particular act (such as applauding or laughing), others copy this behavior

FIGURE 12.8 *Reacting to a potential suicide victim: Sympathy, curiosity, or ridicule?*

A recurring scene in urban settings is the individual who threatens suicide by jumping from a tall building. The reactions of bystanders to such an event vary widely, and several environmental variables are found to influence these reactions. [Source: Wide World Photos.]

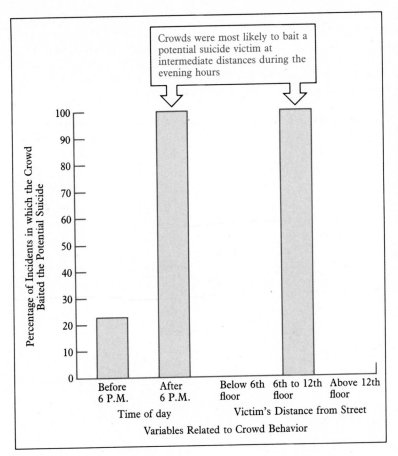

Crowds were most likely to bait a potential suicide victim at intermediate distances during the evening hours

Percentage of Incidents in which the Crowd Baited the Potential Suicide

100
90
80
70
60
50
40
30
20
10
0

Before 6 P.M.   After 6 P.M.   Below 6th floor   6th to 12th floor   Above 12th floor

Time of day   Victim's Distance from Street

Variables Related to Crowd Behavior

FIGURE 12.9   Baiting the victim: Anonymity and dehumanization.

Examination of crowd behavior in response to potential suicides threatening to leap from buildings identified two environmental variables that are related to baiting (yelling at the victim to jump, etc.). Such callous actions were most likely to occur in the evening and if the victim was on a floor located an intermediate distance from the street and sidewalk. This kind of irresponsible cruelty seems to occur when there is anonymity (darkness) and when the victim is far enough away to make dehumanization possible but close enough to hear the taunts. [Source: data from Mann, 1981.]

and it ripples through the crowd (Freedman et al., 1980; Freedman & Perlick, 1979). It is quite possible that additional factors operate to determine the behavior of the group.

To examine such factors, Mann (1981) selected newspaper stories of potential suicides who threatened to jump from a building. He examined those that contained any mention of crowd behavior and divided them into those in which there was and was not baiting of the victim. There was a trend for there to be more baiting if the crowd contained more than 300 people and if the incident occurred during the summer months. Two variables, however, were strongly related to baiting behavior. As shown in Figure 12.9, the baiting of a threatened

suicide was more likely to occur in the evening than during the day and if the victim was between the sixth and twelfth floors of the building. Why would time of day and distance of the victim from the street influence bystander cruelty?

One possible answer is that people are more likely to behave in an irresponsible and vicious manner if they are anonymous, and one's identity is somewhat hidden under cover of darkness. We have described this concept in terms of *deindividuation* earlier in the book (see Chapter 11). One aspect of deindividuation is the dehumanization of the victim. Surprisingly, an intermediate distance between victim and crowd increased the probability of baiting behavior. It was suggested that if victims were relatively close, they could be recognized as individuals (and not dehumanized), while very distant victims were too far away to hear the taunts.

Thus, response to a potential suicide is in part a matter of environmental variables. Callous cruelty seems to be precipitated by darkness and distance (and perhaps by density and heat). The explanation does not lie in some automatic effect of such variables but in their tendency to make people feel anonymous and less responsible for their actions, to cause them to perceive the victim as less human, and to affect their emotional state.

———————————◆———————————

Paulus, 1980; Stokols, 1972). For example, you might be in a large crowd at a football game and enjoy it, or in a large crowd on a subway and hate it. Density may be equally high in the two settings, but you only feel crowded in the second one. When an individual does feel crowded, there is an increase in blood pressure, in self-reported negative emotions, and in observed tenseness and annoyance (Epstein et al., 1981; Walden & Forsyth, 1981).

A distinction is sometimes made between **social density** (increased numbers of people in the same physical space) and **spatial density** (same number of

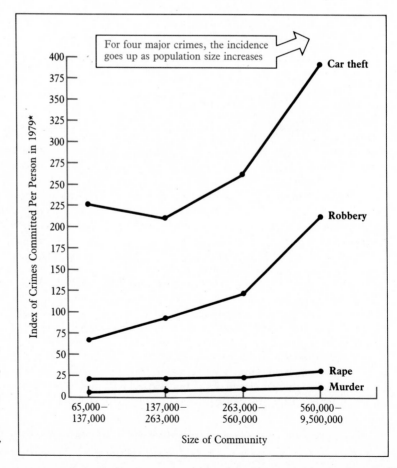

FIGURE 12.10   Population effects: Crime and community size.

As the size of a community increases, the incidence of various types of crime increases, as shown by a study of 175 cities in the United States. Thus, the larger the community, the greater number of murders, rapes, robberies, and car thefts per person. [Source: Based on data from Kelley, 1982.]

people in a smaller physical space). In either case, the negative effects of crowding are most likely to occur if the person is with strangers as opposed to friends (McClelland, 1976), if the individual is studying as opposed to partying (Cozby, 1973), and, in general, if the presence of others interferes with the ability to reach a goal (McCallum et al., 1979). Senior citizens seem to respond well to high density housing conditions because they welcome the social interaction (Patterson, 1978a). In a similar way, when you have nothing to do, crowds of people can be fun, but when you are trying to accomplish something, they may get in your way. Consistent with this proposal, perceived crowding was greater at a street fair when the participants were trying to do something such as making a purchase than when they were simply seeking entertainment such as people-watching (Morasch et al., 1979). It is also found that extraneous sources of stress (such as not being able to sign up for a desired course during a crowded registration period) lead an individual to feel more crowded (Gochman & Keating, 1980). As you might expect, there is a general tendency for task performance to suffer as density increases (Langer & Saegert, 1977; Paulus et al., 1976).

Density seems to be of greatest importance if it is a factor in one's day to day existence. As would be predicted on the basis of how negative emotions influence attraction (see Chapter 6), crowded conditions lead to decreased liking of those who are there (R. M. Baron et al., 1976; Griffitt & Veitch, 1971). In a densely packed dormitory, roommates are not as well liked as in less crowded dorms (Zuckerman et al., 1977). This negative reaction among high density residents generalizes to strangers, too (Baum & Valins, 1973; Valins & Baum, 1973). Even the difference between two-person and three-person rooms is significant with those in groups of three experiencing more social tension and negative emotions (Aiello et al., 1981) and obtaining lower grades (Karlin et al., 1979). One problem with groups of three is that two of the roommates tend to form a close relationship (a **coalition**), leaving the third person isolated. When this happens, the isolate reports a greater feeling of being crowded, has more somatic complaints, and is more dissatisfied with the room and the roommates than is true for the other two people (Reddy et al., 1981).

Personality variables can affect reactions in these situations. Individuals high in **affiliative tendency** (a person who seeks friendships, likes to be with people, etc.) report less stress in a densely packed dorm than do those low in affiliative tendency (Miller et al., 1981). In addition, some people ("screeners") are better than others ("nonscreeners") at dealing with excessive amounts of stimulus information. Screeners reduce the stress of too much input by setting up priorities as to what they attend to and what they ignore. College students who score high in screening are more successful than nonscreeners in adapting to a high-density dormitory setting (Baum et al., 1982). There are also a number of studies that report a sex difference. Males usually experience more stress than females as density increases (e.g., Aiello et al., 1979; Leventhal & Levitt, 1979), but in the dormitory setting the opposite is true, possibly because females spend more time in their rooms than males do (Aiello et al., 1981).

Crowding: What can be done about it? Though the relationship between density and stress may be interesting, you are probably wondering what can be done about it. One theoretical explanation as to why we might react negatively and feel crowded is that there is a loss of control and a feeling of helplessness in an environment of high density (Baum et al., 1978; Epstein, 1981). To counteract this, it is possible to inform individuals beforehand as to the situation and what to expect; the presence of such information leads to much less stress (Baum et al., 1981; Fisher & Baum, 1980; Paulus & Mathews, 1980). The importance of perceived control was shown in an interesting field experiment. In a densely packed elevator, subjects who were standing by the control panel felt less crowded and actually thought the elevator was larger than those standing away from the panel (Rodin et al., 1979).

A different sort of solution lies in attempts to change the environment in order to reduce the stress of overcrowding. It is found that the arrangement of tents at a campsite is important; the absolute number of campers in a given location is not as important as whether it is possible to obtain privacy (Womble & Studebaker, 1981). For example, campers felt less crowded with tents on the edge of the site or deep in the woods than elsewhere. In a dormitory room there is more discontent when there are twin beds rather than bunk beds (Rohner, 1974). The bunk bed arrangement provides more room to move about, and it insures that the other person is out of sight at night. In the busy lobby of a federal prison, visitors reported a lower level of perceived crowding when signs were installed indicating correct procedures and locations. The signs also led to reduced discomfort, anger, and confusion as well as to a shorter amount of time spent in the registration process (Wener & Kaminoff, 1983). The most ambitious example of environmental change was carried out by Baum and Davis (1980). When a long dormitory hallway (used by forty students) was divided into two shorter hallways (used by twenty students each), feelings of being crowded decreased and there were fewer social problems. With that structural change, there were fewer people to interact with each day, an increase in privacy, and much less stress.

Negative Aspects of the Physical Environment: When Conditions Are Stressful

Many people first became interested in environmental questions with respect to negative events such as air pollution. When we are faced with environmental events that threaten our well-being, the initial response is one of **stress** (Baum et al., 1981). As we will describe in Chapter 13, stress occurs in any situation which an individual perceives himself or herself as being unable to control. An individual experiences fear, anxiety, and anger in the process of perceiving the threat, trying to cope with it, and eventually adapting to it. Three general classes of stressful events have been identified by Lazarus and Cohen (1977): general **cataclysmic phenomena** (e.g., natural disasters, war, the oil shortage), more **limited powerful events** (e.g., illness, death of a loved one, loss of one's job), and **daily hassles** (e.g., overcrowding, noisy neighbors, smog). Zimring (1981) would add aspects of the "built environment" to this third group in that our houses, sidewalks, cities, and so forth are often designed in

FIGURE 12.11 *Environmental stress: Coping with daily hassles.*

The environment can be a major source of stress when it threatens our well-being. Many of the stressors consist of daily hassles *that include such things as crowded highways, dirty air, excessive heat, and noise. Our responses to these events can range from nervousness and irritability to illness, serious behavioral disruptions, and even death. [Source: Photo © Joel Gordon 1978.]*

ways that do not fit our needs and so cause us stress (see Figure 12.11). It is the daily hassles and their effects which are of greatest interest to environmental psychologists because such events are most likely to be controllable. Reactions to stress range from minor to serious and include nervous movements (e.g., clasping hands, tapping your knee), smoking, interpersonal difficulties, a breakdown of defenses, illness, and death (Baum et al., 1981; LeCompte, 1981). We will examine the stressors of *noise, heat,* and *air pollution* to determine how they affect behavior.

The Effects of Noise

The definition of **noise** is partly subjective. If you don't like a particular sound and don't want to hear it, it is noise to you. Technically, noise is a sound composed of many frequencies that are not in harmonious relation to one another. Legally, noise pollution is defined in terms of loudness and the length of time it continues. Research has shown that noise is especially unpleasant if it is *unpredictable* and *uncontrollable.* The power to control noise by being able to shut it off reduces the feeling of helplessness and the negative emotional responses; this makes it possible to perform in a more or less normal manner (Glass et al., 1969; Sherrod et al., 1977).

Noise and health. In the typical residential or work setting, we are often unable to control the noise that intrudes on us, and the results can be disastrous. Exposure to sustained noise causes blood pressure to rise (Cohen et al., 1981; Peterson et al., 1981), hearing to become impaired (Glass et al., 1969), and general health to decline (Cohen & Weinstein, 1981). One very familiar type of unpredictable and uncontrollable loud noise is that of airplanes landing and

**FIGURE 12.12   Noise:
A serious health risk.**

The worst effects of noise occur when loud, unpredictable sounds occur in circumstances over which an individual has no control. Anyone who lives or works near an airplane terminal is subjected to noise that has all three of these characteristics. The effects of such exposure include a greater than average probability of requiring treatment in a mental hospital, delivering babies with birth defects, and dying of a stroke. [Source: Frederic Lewis Photographs.]

taking off (see Figure 12.12); what are the effects on those who live or work in the vicinity of a busy airport? People who live in such neighborhoods have a higher rate of admissions to mental hospitals than matched controls who live elsewhere (Meecham & Smith, 1977). Children born to parents residing near the Los Angeles International Airport have a higher proportion than average of birth defects such as harelips and cleft palates (Timnick, 1978). That kind of noise can also kill. The death rate from strokes is 15 percent higher among those residing near an airport than in other locations (Dellinger, 1979).

Noise and behavior. When a school is located close to an active airport, the children's ability to perform is impaired (Cohen et al., 1980). In one school, there was a flight overhead an average of once every two and one-half minutes. When compared to children in quiet schools, those subjected to periodic noise were found to be more likely to give up trying to solve a puzzle before their time was up. Thus, the noise seemed to engender feelings of helplessness, and thus led to a higher rate of failure. It was also found that adaptation does *not* seem to occur; after a year of exposure to the planes, the same effects were observed (Cohen et al., 1981). Controlled laboratory experiments also show that performance on cognitive tasks such as mental arithmetic can be affected by noise level (Frankenhaeuser & Lundberg, 1977; Loeb et al., 1982).

If you have ever tried to carry on a conversation in a noisy setting, you already are aware that one effect of noise is annoyance or anger, in part because social interaction is disrupted (Jones et al., 1981). These negative feelings can extend to various sorts of interpersonal behavior ranging from a decreased tendency to provide a stranger with assistance (Mathews & Cannon, 1975) to an increase in aggressive behavior (Donnerstein & Wilson, 1976; Konečni, 1975). Such findings make it appear quite possible that noise pollution is an important variable that contributes to the level of violence in large population centers.

The Effects of Heat

Many of us complain about the temperature when we perceive it to be too hot or too cold. Research on this environmental factor has concentrated almost entirely on the effects of heat. Is our behavior affected by high temperatures?

Performance declines as temperature rises. One effect of heat is to reduce the efficiency with which we can perform tasks (Bell, 1981). In one experiment, both noise level and temperature were varied in the room where subjects were performing two tasks simultaneously (Bell, 1978). Both variables influenced how well the subjects did, and the number of errors increased as noise level rose *and* as temperature rose (see Figure 12.13).

A curvilinear relationship with aggression. Heat, like noise, causes people to feel annoyed and to express more dislike toward other people (Griffitt, 1970).

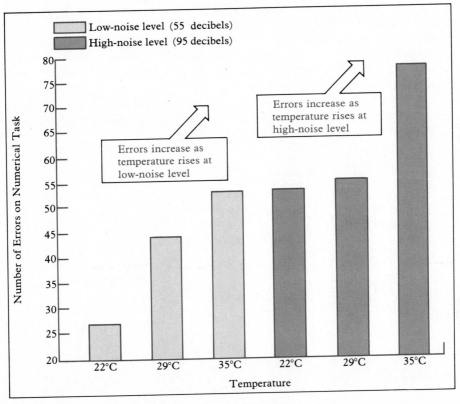

FIGURE 12.13 *Errors increase as temperature and noise level rise.*

Both room temperature and noise level were found to interfere with task performance. Subjects who had to carry out a motor task with one hand while indicating the answers to a numerical task with the other hand made more errors as the temperature increased and *as the noise level rose. [Source: Adapted from Bell, 1978.]*

When such investigations were extended to aggression, however, there was a surprising finding. A series of experiments established that aggression increases with a moderate increase in temperature, but that very high temperatures actually reverse the trend and *reduce* aggression (Baron, 1972; Baron & Bell, 1975, 1976; Bell & Baron, 1976). This relationship between temperature and aggression is hypothesized to occur because moderately hot conditions cause annoyance, anger, and so forth, while extremely hot conditions are so unpleasant that the individual is motivated to escape and seek comfort rather than aggress against others. The result is a *curvilinear* relationship between temperature and aggression.

Such laboratory findings led Baron and Ransberger (1978) to question the common belief that riots are most likely to break out on the hottest days of summer. They examined weather bureau records to obtain the prevailing temperatures of those locations where 102 riots took place in the United States between 1967 and 1971. As can be seen in Figure 12.14, the curvilinear relationship that was discovered in the laboratory was found to hold true with respect to actual violence in the streets. The most dangerous outbreaks of aggressive crowd behavior occurred when temperatures were in the mid-eighties, but riots dropped off sharply when it was hotter than that. Other investigators have suggested different conclusions (Carlsmith & Anderson, 1979), but, taken as a whole, laboratory and field data seem to indicate that group violence is less likely during a long hot summer than during a long moderately hot summer.

When we turn from aggressive group activity to violent crime, the curvilinear relationship seems to disappear. Instead, recent studies of assault (includ-

FIGURE 12.14 *Riots reach a peak when it is* **moderately** *hot.*

Contrary to the common belief that riots and other acts of violence are increasingly likely to occur as the temperature rises, one study found the relationship to be a curvilinear one. Riots are most frequent when it is only moderately hot. At either cooler or hotter temperatures, aggression decreases. [Source: Adapted from Baron & Ransberger, 1978.]

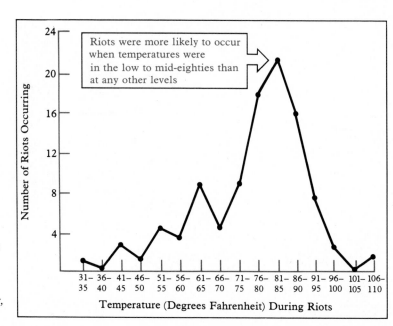

Riots were more likely to occur when temperatures were in the low to mid-eighties than at any other levels

ing homicide, rape, battery, and armed robbery) indicate that such crimes increase as temperature increases (Anderson & Anderson, 1983; Harries & Stadler, 1983). As a separate issue, it might be noted that assaults are most frequent on weekends.

The Effects of Air Pollution

Air pollution gradually has become a matter of widespread concern, and political battles arise regularly between those who want to clean up the emissions of cars, factories, and coal-burning furnaces and those who feel that the costs of such environmental purity are too great (Smith, 1981). Over half of the total U.S. population lives in cities in which the quality of the air is low (President's Council on Environmental Quality, 1978), and the situation is even worse in other countries. We all know that dirty air can be ugly, that it can smell bad, and that it can make us cough, sneeze, and cry (see Figure 12.15). Are there any negative effects that are even more serious?

The physical dangers of polluted air. With respect to health, the evidence is growing that some of the substances in the air we breathe can be exceedingly dangerous and can even kill us. For example, in areas that have petroleum refineries, there are airborne chemicals such as hydrocarbons. Those who live nearby have a significantly higher rate of cancer of the lungs, nasal cavities, sinuses, and skin than those who live elsewhere (Blot et al., 1977). Not only is there danger to those who are directly exposed to substances such as chemical fumes or paint, but their offspring are in danger, too. In one study, children who developed a brain tumor before the age of ten were much more likely than controls to have parents whose occupations exposed them to fumes, paints,

FIGURE 12.15   Polluted air: More than an ugly annoyance.

The concern over air pollution began with the simple reaction that dirty air is ugly, unpleasant, and the cause of minor respiratory problems. Continuing research has shown, however, that pollution affects our emotions and our health. Even more critical, polluted air can be fatal. [Source: Photo by Roswell Angier / Archive Pictures, Inc.]

chemical solvents, and similar substances (Peters et al., 1981). It is not clear precisely how this effect operates, but the best guess is that the pollution affects sperm cells, the fetus during pregnancy, the mother's milk, and, even more directly, the home atmosphere when soiled clothes are brought home from work.

Cars and trucks create problems for health, too. A medical researcher at Yale, Leon Robertson, has found that, as the number of motor vehicles in a given area increase, the number of deaths due to cancer shows a corresponding increase (*Los Angeles Times,* September 20, 1981). It should be noted that all of these studies are *correlational* and cannot show a definite cause-and-effect relationship between pollution and cancer (see Chapter 1). Nevertheless, the evidence is sufficiently consistent that many investigators are convinced of its validity.

It is also possible to create your own personal pollution by smoking cigarettes, and this activity is clearly related to increased risk of lung cancer and emphysema. A large-scale Japanese study found that passive smoking (which occurs when a nonsmoker must breathe the tobacco fumes of others) is also dangerous (*Time,* July 6, 1981, p. 43). For example, nonsmoking wives of heavy smokers had a much higher rate of lung cancer than the nonsmoking wives of nonsmokers. In addition to health problems, nonsmokers are found to react with depression, anxiety, and hostility when around those who smoke, and they dislike such individuals (Bleda & Sandman, 1977).

Negative effects on behavior. The general effects of air pollution on human behavior have received only limited research attention (Evans & Jacobs, 1981). Among the findings: as air pollution increases, people tend to avoid outdoor recreational activities (Chapko & Solomon, 1976) and to feel less happy and more likely to rate both people and objects negatively (Rotton et al., 1978). With respect to aggression, the effects are like those of heat; moderately bad-smelling air leads to increased aggression, but with an extremely unpleasant odor, aggression decreases (Rotton et al., 1979). When the pollution is sufficiently bad, people are motivated to escape the situation and find clean air to breathe.

One response to negative environmental conditions is to move — to seek a new environmental setting for one's life. Some of the variables entering into such a decision are examined in the **Applied Side** panel on pages 478–479.

Positive Aspects of the Physical Environment: Excitement and Pleasure in a City

When we discuss such variables as crowding, noise, and air pollution, it is easy to assume that all aspects of urban living are negative. People *feel* safer in suburban neighborhoods than in an urban environment (Lavrakas, 1982). At the time the Declaration of Independence was signed, 90 out of every 100 Americans lived in the countryside on farms; today, only 5 out of every 100 do so (Bell, 1975). In fact, over 56 million people in the United States live in cities of 100,000 or more (Krupat, 1980). Similar population shifts have occurred around the world. What effect does this shift in environmental settings have on human behavior? What are the sources of annoyance? (See Lévy-Leboyer, 1982.) Such questions have led to an increasing interest in evaluating the environment (Canter & Kenny, 1982).

Affective Responses to the Environment

On a trip, or just after a move to a new city, how do you react? One obvious response is aesthetic: how attractive is the environment? (See Bernard & Gottesdiener, 1982.) In confronting a scene such as the one shown in Figure 12.16, you may also experience a variety of emotions. In a complex urban environment, especially for a newcomer, there is too much to comprehend all at once — an information overload (Milgram, 1970). Nevertheless, research indicates that our emotional responses to our surroundings fall along two dimensions: the degree to which the environment seems exciting or dull and the degree to which we find it pleasant or unpleasant (Russell et al., 1981). The

FIGURE 12.16 *Emotional responses to the environment: How does it make you feel?*

When we are confronted by the complexity of a new environment, our emotional reactions are mixed. Nevertheless, people are found to respond primarily on the basis of how arousing or unarousing the setting seems to be and the extent to which it is pleasing or displeasing. [Source: Photo © Frank Siteman, 1980.]

ON THE
APPLIED SIDE

Where Would You Like to Live?
Choosing the Ideal Environment

Some people tend to assume that their birthplace is where they should spend the remainder of their lives. Most of the people on earth, in fact, never stray far beyond the neighborhood where they grew up. For one thing, when we find ourselves facing a new and different environment, it can be an unpleasant experience. Even tourists vacationing on tropical islands find themselves depressed and uncomfortable by the third day (Pearce, 1981). We consider the United States to be a very mobile society, and 40 million people move within the nation each year (Bowman et al., 1981). Nevertheless, according to the 1980 census, 63.8 percent of all U.S. citizens live in the state where they were born. Regardless of the shortcomings of a given locale, a person can more or less adapt to heat, cold, dampness, dryness, recurring natural disasters, dirt and litter, overcrowding, crime, polluted air, or whatever else comes along.

For a variety of reasons, other people seek new environments as they move elsewhere in search of economic opportunity, land, freedom, or the general possibility of finding a better life. If there were no constraints, and you could pick the ideal environment for yourself, what would it be like? Among U.S. citizens, the states that attract the most outsiders to relocate there are Alaska, Arizona, Florida, Nevada, and Wyoming while the states that attract the fewest are Alabama, Kentucky, Mississippi, Pennsylvania, and West Virginia. The major difference between the two groups may be simply job availability rather than environmental desirability. It is found that people don't always move where they say they would prefer to live (Fredrickson et al., 1980). An examination of where million-

aires reside would seem to bypass the employment problem. According to a U.S. Treasury study of income tax returns, the states with the highest proportion of millionaires are Delaware, Nevada, New York, Texas, and Connecticut.

Perhaps it is more reasonable to examine cities rather than states with respect to variables that determine desirability. It is obvious that there are many variables to consider—population, climate, cost of living, and crime rate, for example. Further, people differ as to their preferences (some dislike cold, snowy winters and some dislike hot, humid summers) and in the relative importance they place on different variables (some prefer an exciting city with a greater risk of crime and some prefer a peaceful rural area with little or no criminal activity). For example, in a 1981 interview in *Playboy* magazine, Mayor Ed Koch of New York City stated that he could not imagine living in the suburbs, much less in the rural hinterlands of the state. Recent trends in this country show that not everyone agrees with the mayor. In the 1970s, the smallest towns (under 2,500 population) grew almost twice as fast as the total population (Trippett, 1980).

When you begin to compare cities, variable by variable, you need to think about your own preferences and values. Table 12.2 shows two such variables and lists the ten most populous urban areas in the United States, according to the 1980 census, and the ten cities with the lowest rates of nonviolent crime. With just these two variables in mind, if you wanted to live in a large city with a low crime rate, Philadelphia might be the place for you.

A quite different approach to discovering what environments people prefer is to show them photo-

various combinations of the two dimensions are found to include most of the affective reactions that people have in response to the environment, as shown in Figure 12.17 on page 480.

There has also been some attempt to identify the specific aspects of urban environments that give rise to positive and excited responses. As you might expect, people are most positive about settings that include some natural

TABLE 12.2   Comparing cities: Size and crime rate.

In selecting a place to live, size is one variable, but there are many other factors including climate, cultural offerings, beauty, cost of living, and crime rate. An individual could consider all of the variables of greatest importance in his or her life, compare different locations with respect to those variables, and then make a decision about an ideal place to live. [Source: Data from Bowman et al., 1981, and 1980 U.S. Census.]

Size of City		Incidence of nonviolent crimes	
Ten largest urban areas	*Population*	*Ten cities with lowest crime rate*	*Property crimes per 100,000 residents*
New York City	15,588,985	Pittsburgh, Pennsylvania	2,919
Los Angeles–Long Beach	9,477,926	Burlington, Vermont	3,013
Chicago	6,711,391	Albany, New York	3,694
Philadelphia	4,114,354	Charleston, West Virginia	3,718
Detroit	3,808,676	Fargo, North Dakota	3,911
San Francisco–Oakland	3,191,913	Philadelphia, Pennsylvania	4,110
Washington, D.C.	2,762,423	Buffalo, New York	4,187
Boston	2,678,473	Nashville, Tennessee	4,360
Dallas–Fort Worth	2,451,555	Cleveland, Ohio	4,508
St. Louis	1,848,363	Sioux Falls, South Dakota	4,604

graphs of different settings and then assess their reactions. When subjects were shown a series of color slides depicting either scenes of nature or of urban settings, there were consistent differences in ratings of pleasantness and in physiological reactions (Ulrich, 1981). On all of the dependent variables, the scenes of nature elicited more positive reactions. Not only does natural beauty have the most beneficial psychological and physiological effects, but some natural environments are preferred over others. With subjects ranging in age from third graders to senior citizens, Balling and Falk (1982) found that children prefer scenes of savannas (flat grassy plains with a scattering of trees), while those who are older come to like more familiar natural settings such as forests just as well. The authors concluded that there may be an inborn preference among human beings for particular settings because of our long evolutionary history originating on the savannas of East Africa. With age, however, we can learn to like other settings to an equal degree. You may or may not accept this sociobiological interpretation, but it is interesting to contemplate why it is that many people go to a great deal of trouble to surround their houses with small grassy plains containing a scattering of trees or to create city parks that resemble the scenes experienced by our early ancestors.

In any event, the question of an ideal environment is obviously a very complex one. The answer for each of us seems to depend on our experiences, our individual preferences and values, and perhaps on our biological heritage.

features (trees, grass, water, and so forth) and architecture that stands out as unusual and identifiable. The most negative reactions are elicited by old and cluttered settings such as alleys and factories (Herzog et al., 1982).

A city's excitement and degree of pleasantness can affect behavior beyond simply one's emotions. City dwellers actually walk faster than those in small towns (Bornstein & Bornstein, 1976). The high proportion of strangers leads to

FIGURE 12.17   Four kinds of environmental settings.

Emotional reactions to one's environment combine to reveal four major clusters of response. You can probably think of settings you have experienced that fit each of these descriptions. [Source: Based on data from Russell et al., 1981.]

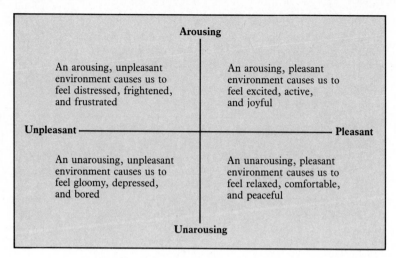

An arousing, unpleasant environment causes us to feel distressed, frightened, and frustrated

An arousing, pleasant environment causes us to feel excited, active, and joyful

Unpleasant ——————————— Pleasant

An unarousing, unpleasant environment causes us to feel gloomy, depressed, and bored

An unarousing, pleasant environment causes us to feel relaxed, comfortable, and peaceful

Arousing

Unarousing

distrust, and city dwellers tend to avoid eye contact (Newman & McCauley, 1977) and to be wary of shaking an outstretched hand (Milgram, 1977). Though it is hard to form friendships as a newcomer in such an environment, once friends *are* made, the relationships resemble those in small towns (Franck, 1980). When the environment is pleasing, people respond well to others, including a persuasive speaker who is attempting to influence attitudes (Biggers & Pryor, 1982).

Creating a Desirable Urban Environment

The effect of architecture on many aspects of our feelings, attitudes, and behavior is gradually becoming clear. For example, studies in Germany have revealed that Nazi architecture, built during Hitler's reign, is perceived as brutal, intimidating, and heavy (Espe, 1981). It should also be noted that we are not just passive bystanders, but that we actually use these settings and share the space with others in ways that help us reach our goals or that interfere with our striving (Canter & Rees, 1982; Ellis, 1982).

Growing awareness of such effects has led to some remarkable changes in our cities by master planners such as James Rouse, who has been responsible for the exciting innovations at Harborplace in Baltimore, Boston's Faneuil Hall Marketplace, and California's Santa Monica Place (Demarest, 1981). As can be seen in Figure 12.18, the goal is deliberately to create environments that are arousing and pleasing so that people will feel good about their surroundings and, as a consequence, good about themselves. Rouse would like each inner city to be "a warm and human place, with diversity of choice, full of festival and delight" (Demarest, 1981, p. 42). In addition, we need to feel comfortable with our surroundings (Pineau, 1982).

There is a nationwide group known as Partners for Livable Places that consists of about 300 organizations dedicated to making cities more enjoyable places to live (Von Eckardt, 1981). Their interests range from restoration of

FIGURE 12.18   Creating urban environments with people in mind.

When attention is paid to the human factor, environments can be designed to maximize positive feelings, and they can be a source of joy. This is true both of restorations of older settings such as Harborplace in Baltimore and Faneuil Hall Marketplace in Boston and in totally new structures such as Santa Monica Place. [Source: Photo (top left) by Peter Southwick / Stock, Boston; photo (top right) from the Baltimore Office of Promotion and Tourism © 1982 Bob Willis; photo (bottom) courtesy of the Santa Monica Place Merchants Association.]

run-down areas in towns such as Paterson, New Jersey, and Savannah, Georgia, to turning old railroad stations into shopping centers. Not all attempts at improvement have to be on a grand scale. In Seattle, manhole covers are being redesigned as maps to aid pedestrians. The goal in each instance is to improve the environment so that it fits the residents' style of life and even enhances it (Singer, 1982).

Though population centers can be exciting, it does not follow that unlimited growth is desirable. Some of the problems of overpopulation are discussed in the **Applied Side** panel on pages 482–483.

ON THE
APPLIED SIDE *Overpopulation:*
An Environmental Time Bomb

Overpopulation will exacerbate problems to the breaking point. Figures tell us there are already more people on earth than we need to move even the heaviest piano. If we do not call a halt to breeding, by the year 2000 there will be no room to serve dinner unless one is willing to set the table on the heads of strangers. Then they must not move for an hour while we eat. Of course energy will be in short supply and each car owner will be allowed only enough gasoline to back up a few inches.

Woody Allen, 1980

Though he presents the problem in a humorous way, Woody Allen is pointing out the most serious of all environmental problems—overpopulation (Toney et al., 1981). The basic dilemma is the result of two simple facts. (1) Our planet contains only a fixed amount of such human necessities as land, water, air, and fossil fuels. The quantities are finite, and no more are being created. (2) Human beings are reproducing in such a way that their numbers steadily increase. Our rate of growth is nearly three times as great as that of any other mammal. The problem, then, is that more and more people each year must compete for the same amount of resources (Jensen, 1978). The result is an overpopulated planet on which the residents face shortages of food, water, and energy, and a declining quality of life. (See Figure 12.19.) This observation, by the way, was first made by Aristotle and others in ancient Greece (Feen, 1981).

Though the United States is not one of the fastest growing nations and is a "success story" with respect to family planning, it records six births a minute, or 8,600 since this time yesterday. If you also consider immigration, the U.S. population grows by about 4,900 people a day (subtracting deaths and those who leave the country from births and those who move here). These figures do not include illegal immigration, by the way, which has

FIGURE 12.19 Overpopulation as an environmental disaster.

The consequences of an ever-increasing number of human beings on this planet are an inevitable competition for fundamental necessities and a steady decline in the quality of life. [Source: Photo © Thomas Hopker 1981/Woodfin Camp and Associates.]

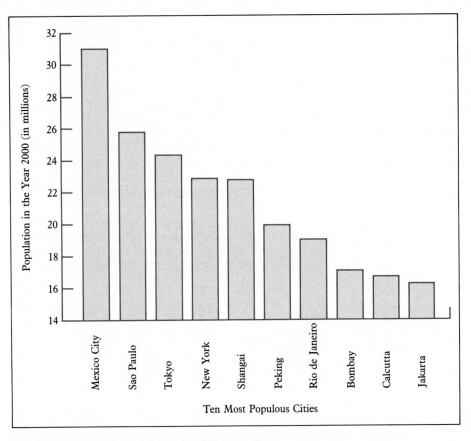

FIGURE 12.20 *The urban world of the near future.*

Population growth will make the ten largest cities in the world in the year 2000 much larger than those of today. One way to put these figures in perspective is to remember that the total population of the United States when it was founded was only about four million. [Source: Based on data in Nossiter, 1980.]

been estimated to involve about 800,000 additional individuals each year (*ZPG National Reporter*, September 1977). Perhaps the first problem to be noted is that, the more individuals produced in a given generation, the greater the competition for schools, jobs, and income. Easterlin (1980) has shown that those born in the baby boom of the 1950s and early 1960s have faced just such difficulties and will continue to do so. In the next forty years, the U.S. population is expected to reach at least 252,000,000 and will perhaps go as high as 373,000,000 (Alan Guttmacher Institute, June 9,

1978). In contrast to these projections, Nobel prize-winner Linus Pauling has proposed that the present population of this country needs to be *reduced* to about 150 million (Associated Press, February 7, 1976).

As bad as such considerations may appear, the picture becomes considerably darker when we turn to the total world population (Byrne, 1983). Each day, the earth gains about 200,000 people. One picture of the future is provided by a look at a projection of city populations in the year 2000 (Nossiter, 1980), as shown in Figure 12.20. Part of this anticipated growth is through additional births and part is through migration from the rural areas to the city. It required from the dawn of our species until about 1800 for humankind to grow to a total of one billion. One way to visualize a billion people is to realize that it represents 308 cities the size of present-day Chicago; and these people must have a place to live, food to eat, water to drink, and some source of energy. A decent life also requires that they have transportation, education, medical care, useful jobs, entertainment, and intellectual stimulation. Every time an additional billion people are added to the world's total, it means another 308 Chicagos. By 1976, the total world population was four billion. We *double* the number every 35 years. So, by the year 2011 there will be eight billion, in 2046 there will be sixteen billion, and on and on.

Actually, this process *cannot* go on and on. It is very unlikely that it will continue for 350 years, producing a population of 4,000,000,000,000 human beings (Coale, 1974). It is literally impossible for it to go on for 6,700 years, by which time all the matter in the known universe will consist of human flesh (Asimov, 1975). So, what will happen?

There are four major possibilities, and you might want to think very carefully about these alternatives. It is your world and your life that are involved.

(1) We can go on as we now are and simply *wait* until the problem solves itself by means of starvation, disease, or nuclear war (Heilbroner, 1974).

(2) We can take steps to *force* people to limit family size and require that those couples who have had two offspring then be sterilized. At one point, "voluntary sterilization" in India was transformed into just such a totalitarian endeavor (Kramer, 1979).

(3) We can *encourage* people to limit family size with rewards for not having children and government bonuses or tax breaks for avoiding parenthood.

(4) We can *educate* people about the problem and hope that they spontaneously decide to avoid the overproduction of offspring. With an affluent and well-educated population such as in Sweden, the population growth is so small that it will be 1,386 years before a doubling takes place (Ibrahim, 1980).

The choices, then, are straightforward. We can wait for disaster, adopt one of two forms of coercion (force versus enticement), or we can work hard to educate people so that they can decide for themselves to avert catastrophe. Which alternative do you prefer, and which do you think is likely to occur?

Summary

Environmental psychology deals with the relationship between the physical world and human behavior. Among the major concerns of this field are the *interpersonal environment* and its influences, the *negative aspects of the physical environment*, and the *positive aspects of the physical environment*.

Each of us treats the area surrounding our bodies as a zone of **personal space,** and any invasion of this zone elicits an emotional reaction, including fear, anger, and attraction. The size of one's personal space and one's response to appropriate distances, invasions, or invading the space of others varies with culture, socioeconomic group, gender, race, and the relationship between the individuals involved. **Territoriality** refers to behavior involving the identification and defense of a particular space. Among human beings, this includes various acts to personalize our living quarters to attain privacy. It is interesting to note that both lower animals and humans are more dominant and more effective on their home territory than on that of others. One additional aspect of the interpersonal environment is the number of people we are with, and a distinction is made between the physical **density** of this group and the subjective perception that there is **crowding.** The sheer number of people can have either positive or negative effects, but perceived crowdedness is a negative experience in which the person feels blocked and unable to control events. Attempts to reduce crowding have been successful in restoring a positive psychological state.

Various events in the physical environment are a cause of **stress,** and research has documented the negative effects. For example, repeated exposure to *noise* can have serious physical and psychological consequences; behavioral effects include a decreased ability to work, unwillingness to assist others, and increased aggression. *Heat* has a negative effect on performance, but its effect on aggression is curvilinear. *Air pollution* can cause serious health problems and is also found to influence interpersonal behavior in a negative fashion.

Despite all of the undesirable effects of the physical environment, it is also possible for our surroundings to be *exciting* and *pleasing*. Cities can be designed or restored in such a way as to add beauty and joy to the lives of those who live in them. Ultimately, the most threatening feature of the environment is the growing number of people on our planet; *overpopulation* must be controlled in order to prevent truly disastrous consequences.

Glossary

affiliative tendency *Behavior characterized by its orientation toward friendship formation, social interests, and the desire to interact with others.*

cataclysmic phenomena *Stressful events such as a war or natural disaster that are widely shared within a society.*

coalition *Within a larger body of people, a subgroup that is held together by friendship or common goals.*

contagion *The rapid spread of an emotion (such as fear) or a behavior (such as coughing) through a group.*

crowding *The perception that too many people are occupying a given space. This subjective evaluation of one's surroundings is stressful.*

daily hassles *Stressful events such as crowded living conditions or noisy work conditions that are cumulative in their effects.*

density *An objective physical condition that is defined by the number of people occupying a particular space of a given size.*

environmental psychology *The field that deals with the interaction between the physical world and human behavior.*

intimate distance *In Hall's system, the appropriate interpersonal distance (zero to one and one-half feet) for affectionate interactions, contact sports, and aggression.*

limited powerful events *Stressful events such as illness or loss of one's job that affect a small number of individuals.*

noise *Technically, a sound composed of many nonharmonious frequencies. Subjectively, an unpleasant sound—especially if it is loud, unpredictable, and uncontrollable.*

personal distance *In Hall's system, the appropriate distance (one and one-half to four feet) for close contacts between friends and acquaintances.*

personal space *The zone around each individual into which most other people are not supposed to trespass.*

primary territory *In Altman's system, space that is used regularly on a long-term basis as an essential part of a person's everyday activities (for example, one's home).*

prior residence effect *The advantage that both human beings and lower animals have when they are on their home territory. It involves both* dominance and general effectiveness in interacting with others.

proxemics *The study of the distance people place between and among themselves in various kinds of interactions.*

public distance *In Hall's system, the appropriate interpersonal distance (more than twelve feet) for formal contacts between a speaker and an audience.*

public territory *In Altman's system, a space that is occupied only temporarily and is available to whoever gets there first (for example, a picnic table in a park).*

secondary territory *In Altman's system, a space that is used regularly by specific people on a limited basis (for example, one's classroom).*

social density *The number of individuals who occupy a space of a given size.*

social distance *In Hall's system, the appropriate interpersonal distance (four to twelve feet) for impersonal and businesslike contacts.*

spatial density *The size of the space occupied by a given number of individuals.*

stress *A response to an external threat that involves fear, anxiety, and anger.*

territorial behavior (or **territoriality**) *A variety of actions people engage in to stake out and defend portions of the environment against intrusion.*

territory *An area that an individual or a group occupies exclusively and defends against any intruders.*

For More Information

Baum, A., & Singer, J. E. (Eds.). *Advances in environmental psychology.* Vol. 4. *Environment and health.* Hillsdale, N.J.: Erlbaum, 1982.
A series of contributors present recent data outlining the ways in which environmental factors influence physical and mental health. Topics include the effects of residential quality, medical setting, and the importance of control, plus an examination of air pollution, crowding, and noise.

Fisher, J. D., Bell, P. A., & Baum, A. *Environmental psychology* (2nd ed.). New York: Holt, Rinehart, and Winston, 1984.
An excellent coverage of the field of environmental psychology by three individuals who are active contributors to research in this area.

Harvey, J. (Ed.). *Cognition, social behavior, and the environment.* New York: Academic Press, 1981.
A variety of investigators from different fields bring together work on cognitive and environmental variables to show how social behavior is affected by
their interaction. The focus is on the way in which cognitive factors influence an individual's response to the environment.

Isaacs, S. L. *Population law and policy: Source materials and issues.* New York: Human Sciences Press, 1981.
This is the first book to deal with the effects of local, national, and international laws on matters that affect population growth. Examples include laws concerning abortion, sterilization, and family planning as well as legal matters that involve incentives designed to control family size.

Lévy-Leboyer, C. *Psychology and environment.* Beverly Hills, Calif.: Sage, 1982.
This translated volume by a French investigator provides an overview of environmental psychology. An attempt is made to integrate research and theory dealing with perception of the environment, environmental stress, the use of space, and the design of environments to fit human needs.

CHAPTER 13

Applying Social Psychology

The Legal System: Social Psychology in the Courtroom

Eyewitness Testimony: Accurate or Inaccurate?/The Attorneys and the Judge/ Defendants and Jurors: The Role of Interpersonal Variables

Behavioral Medicine: Health Care and Social Psychology

Preventive Medicine: Worth a Pound of Cure/Life Stresses: Losing Control over Events/Medical Specialists and Institutions: Reducing the Threat

The Work Place: Behavior in Organizations

Work and the Worker/Achieving Job Satisfaction and Assessing Its Effects/ Appraising Job Performance: Attribution Processes in an Organizational Setting

Special Inserts

ON THE APPLIED SIDE
   Crime in the Neighborhood: Evaluating a Community Project

FOCUS ON RESEARCH
   Initiating Environmental Improvement

ON THE APPLIED SIDE
   Time, Schedules, and Circadian Principles

Jeff Haley was trying to be a brave eight-year-old, but his mother was obviously upset when the pediatrician announced that her son would have to be hospitalized in order to remove his badly infected tonsils. Mrs. Haley was not worried so much by the operation itself as by the experience her little boy would have to go through. Her own childhood terror was still vivid in her mind as she remembered being treated for a serious respiratory infection when she was about Jeff's age. She had never even spent the night away from her parents before that, and all those strangers seemed to be constantly poking her or sticking a thermometer in her mouth and giving her injections. The three days in the hospital stood out as a horrible time in her early years, and she hadn't faced an operation like poor Jeff. She tried not to show her alarm as she asked the doctor about the arrangements.

"I'll try to schedule the operation for Friday morning, and they'll want you to bring Jeff in the night before. Prior to that, I would like for you and your husband to bring Jeff by the children's ward to see a little movie. I hope you can do that this evening if possible."

Mrs. Haley was puzzled as to the purpose of seeing a movie, and Jeff was in a wide-eyed daze. He didn't feel very good anyway and now something awful was apparently about to happen to him.

That night at the hospital, a middle-aged volunteer greeted Jeff and his parents and led them down a corridor to a small room furnished with a few comfortable chairs facing a television set that was attached to a video cassette recorder. "Just have a seat, and I'll start a tape that I think you'll find interesting. It lasts about twenty minutes, and I'll come back then to answer any questions you might have."

The tape was a locally produced one with the title, "Matthew Has an Operation." It had been filmed at the hospital and began with Matthew's father driving to the admissions entrance where the patient and his mother were greeted by a nurse's aide who helped them with the paperwork while his father parked the car in the nearby lot. The narrator, in a friendly voice, described each step they went through. Jeff thought that Matthew looked funny in his hospital gown, and he watched intently each thing that was done, right up to the anesthetic that made Matthew "so sleepy that the next thing he knew he was waking up several hours after his operation was over." The movie ended with the family leaving the hospital as a happy-looking Matthew rode out to his car in a wheel chair. The volunteer came back to the room, and they talked briefly about the film. She added that with Jeff's operation there was a special treat. He could have all the ice cream he wanted afterward.

Driving home, Jeff felt much more relaxed about what was going to happen. His vague fears were gone. He now knew something about the hospital and what would take place there. Even his parents seemed to be calmer than they were on the way over. Besides, he could hardly wait for the ice cream that woman promised.

The use of such videotapes (as well as audio and slide presentations) to prepare both children and adults for forthcoming medical procedures is just one of the ways that psychological principles and findings are being utilized in applied settings. The application of psychology tends to be perceived in one of two ways. Some view psychological research as essentially isolated from the real world and irrelevant to it. Others believe that all psychologists are engaged in psychotherapy with emotionally disturbed patients. As we hope you have learned so far in this textbook, social psychology fits neither of these descriptions, and basic research in our field tends to lead rather naturally to application. The wide array of behaviors of applied research interest ranges from labor-management negotiations to love affairs and from diffusing an aggressive confrontation to eliminating classroom cheating. Increasingly, social psychological research involves a scientific concern with building theories and establishing relationships between variables and also a technological concern with using such theories and data to bring about beneficial changes in the world around us.

Though the applied interests of social psychologists have been evident since the 1930s (Reich, 1981), many investigators have become increasingly sensitive to the importance of the applied implications of their research. There is also a trend among many social psychologists to spend their time exclusively in solving problems encountered in society (Saxe & Fine, 1980). Salazar (1981) argues that in third world countries application should be the primary activity of social psychologists. He provides examples of this approach in applied research on nationalism and patriotism in Venezuela. It has been predicted that future social psychologists will be spending a portion or all of their careers in nonacademic settings working on applied problems (Bickman, 1981). In fact, over the past few years the percentage of new Ph.D.s in social psychology who accepted jobs in universities has dropped from about one-half of the group to just over one-third (Stapp & Fulcher, 1982). The remainder are employed in hospitals, government agencies, business organizations, and other nontraditional places of work. Thus, **applied social psychology** is defined as social-psychological research and practice in real-world settings directed toward the understanding of human social behavior and the attempted solution of social problems (Fisher, 1982).

The scope of this application is sufficiently broad and the growth of applied social activity is sufficiently rapid that only a portion of the field can be described in any detail. Examples of some recent applications are presented in Table 13.1. Despite the importance of these and many other applied efforts, we are forced to limit our coverage here to a small number of very active problem areas.

We will first examine the importance of *social psychology in the courtroom* and show how psychological research is relevant to every aspect of the legal process. We will then turn to the growing area of *behavioral medicine* and describe some of the ways in which psychology can contribute to health care. The role of social psychology in the work place will be outlined with an emphasis on *behavior in organizations*. In addition, there will be discussions of applications involving an

TABLE 13.1   *Applying social psychology: From national defense to baseball.*

The application of psychological principles and techniques to varied problem areas is increasingly characteristic of our field.

Recent applications	Source
Utilizing attribution theory to explain and defuse popular conceptions of international conflicts	Rabin, 1982
Using polling techniques to determine public opinion on national issues	Kinsley, 1981
Training combat troops with the use of video discs combined with computers	McNett, 1982
Determining the various irrelevant variables that affect teacher ratings	Morgan & Ogden, 1981
Simulating spacecraft living conditions to establish the long-term effects on astronauts of existence in an isolated and confined environment	Foltz, 1981
Investigating how well consumers comprehend the cost of products	Capon & Kuhn, 1979
Evaluating the effectiveness of public service announcements on radio and television	McAbee & Cafferty, 1982
Discovering the variables that affect attendance at major league baseball games	Becker & Suls, 1983

evaluation of a community project to fight *neighborhood crime,* the initiation of behavior leading to *environmental improvement,* and adjustment to time changes that violate *circadian principles.*

The Legal System: Social Psychology in the Courtroom

Our legal system is based on procedures that are designed to yield objective and fair decisions. For example, only some types of information are relevant to a given trial, and everything else must be excluded from the proceedings or disregarded by the jurors should it be presented. As Figure 13.1, p. 492, suggests, the reactions of human beings may not necessarily conform to such idealistic rules. In earlier chapters, we have described numerous examples of the way in which perceptions, judgments, and actions are affected by social psychological processes. Recall for a moment the research on attributions and nonverbal communication (Chapter 2), social cognition and impression formation (Chapter 3), attitudes and persuasion (Chapter 4), prejudice (Chapter 5), interpersonal attraction (Chapter 6), social influence (Chapter 7), the determinants of aggression (Chapter 9), and the many effects of environmental factors (Chapter 12). It should not be difficult to imagine how these same variables operate within the legal system. For example, psychological research has clearly demonstrated that witnesses do not always remember events accurately, that

FIGURE 13.1   *Ideal legal procedures versus psychological realities.*

Society rests on its system of laws. One of the hallmarks of an advancing civilization is its efforts to ensure the impartial functioning of its legal apparatus in ways that are objective and fair to all of its citizens. No matter how much we embrace these values and applaud the efforts made to live up to them, psychologists have long stressed the fact that each participant in the system (witnesses, attorneys, judges, defendants, jurors) is a human being whose memories, biases, and judgments are affected by many factors unrelated to the goals of objectivity and fairness. The judge in this cartoon is giving a proper legal instruction to the jury, but you might guess that it is an impossible one for human beings to obey. [Source: Saturday Review; © Barbara Falk.]

"The jury is instructed to ignore the witness's last outburst!"

the behavior of attorneys and judges can bias trial outcome, and that numerous characteristics of defendants and jurors interact to determine the decisions that are reached (Ellison & Buckhout, 1981; Loh, 1981).

The courtroom is not a new research interest for psychologists. Some of the earliest studies beyond the laboratory dealt with applied legal research (Münsterberg, 1907). The impact of this research has been shown in an impressive line of legal decisions including the use of IQ tests to assign children to special classes, the definition of insanity, and the determination of a defendant's competency to stand trial (McGlynn & Dreilinger, 1981; Roesch, 1979), and Supreme Court rulings on the effects of racial segregation (Loftus & Monahan, 1980). The relationship between psychological research and the legal system has led to a growing number of law-related courses in graduate psychology programs (Grisso et al., 1982), programs that offer specialized training in **forensic psychology** (Poythress, 1979), and a new Psychology and Law division of the American Psychological Association (Greenberg, 1981). We will now examine a sample of the applied research that deals with psychological variables in the legal system.

Eyewitness Testimony: Accurate or Inaccurate?

The testimony of an eyewitness to a crime is considered to be of crucial importance in a trial. The problem is that those who testify are often inaccurate, and what they say is often distorted and downright wrong (Rodgers, 1982; Yarmey, 1979). Though these conclusions are based in part on the poor performance of witnesses in experimental studies, such witnesses are in fact more accurate than witnesses to real-life crimes (Maass & Brigham, 1982; Murray & Wells, 1982). How accurate are witnesses in identifying the person they observed committing a crime? Buckhout (1980) filmed a mock crime that consisted of a mugging in which a woman's purse was stolen. This film was broadcast as part of a television news show. Just afterward, a lineup was shown with six suspects, one of whom had been the "criminal" in the film. Of 2,000 viewers who watched the mugging on TV, over 1,800 of them identified the wrong man as the criminal or incorrectly decided that none of the six committed the crime. The white mugger was perceived as being black or Hispanic by 33 percent of the witnesses, and a few reported having personally been mugged by one of the experimenters. As shown in Figure 13.2, there was only chance accuracy in identifying the culprit correctly. In a laboratory study in which subjects viewed a slide presentation depicting assault and rape, identification of the criminal among a group of nine photographs was also at the chance level (Yarmey & Jones, 1983). Even without the emotional arousal involved in witnessing a crime, memories are faulty. In Chapter 5, a study was described in which drug store clerks were asked to identify two customers who had been in

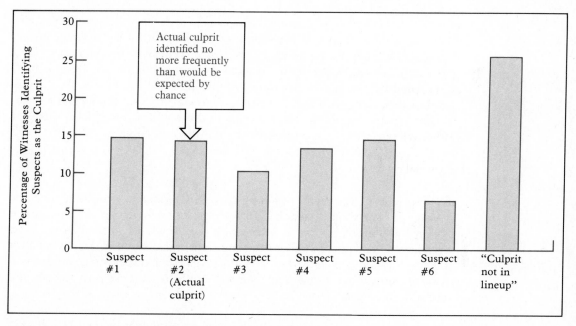

FIGURE 13.2   *Eyewitness Identification: No better than chance.*

After seeing a film of a mock crime on television, viewers were shown a lineup and asked to identify the "criminal." The overwhelming majority picked the wrong man or incorrectly decided that the culprit was not in the lineup. Only 14.1 percent made a correct identification — about the number one would expect by chance. [Source: Based on data from Buckhout, 1980.]

their store in the past two hours; accurate identifications were made only about a third of the time (Brigham et al., 1982). Given such findings, perhaps it is not surprising that in a real trial in Florida, an eyewitness identified an innocent bystander in the courtroom as the criminal. The judge declared the bystander guilty though he was later released (*Playboy*, May 1981, p. 66).

Are there any remedies to correct the inaccuracy of eyewitnesses? Some have argued that children should be permitted to testify in trials because they actually make fewer inaccurate statements than adults (Goodman & Michelli, 1981). It is found that accuracy is increased if witnesses are encouraged to avoid guesses and to say "I don't know" when they are unsure (Warnick & Sanders, 1980b). Further, when there are multiple eyewitnesses, accuracy is very high when unanimous agreement is reached or when a large portion of the group agrees on a given point (Sanders & Warnick, 1982). In addition, group discussions among the witnesses before testifying lead to greater accuracy than the independent testimony of individuals (Warnick & Sanders, 1980a).

When witnesses testify, judges and jurors must make decisions about the credibility of the individual. Among other things, it has been found that belief in the witness is influenced by that individual's gender, race, socioeconomic status, appearance, and behavior on the witness stand (Whobrey et al., 1981). Once a key witness has been discredited, for whatever reason, does that person's testimony have any effect on the judgments of members of the jury? A series of studies has yielded quite confusing results. For example, when the one eyewitness to a crime was shown to need eyeglasses but to have been without them when the crime occurred, that nearsighted person's testimony nevertheless led to a decision that the defendant was guilty (Loftus, 1974). Other studies indicate that jurors can ignore discredited testimony (Weinberg & Baron, 1982) or even overcompensate by deciding that the opposite must be true (Hatvany & Strack, 1980). It appears that the effects of a discredited witness depend on such variables as the reason for discrediting and the way in which this is done, but additional research is required to clarify this phenomenon.

The Attorneys and the Judge

The roles played by the opposing attorneys and by the presiding judge are critical in a courtroom trial (see Figure 13.3). The attorneys make decisions as to who will present testimony, what questions are asked, and how the case is summarized. The judge decides what questions and answers are legally relevant and how the case is explained to the jury as well as making posttrial decisions as to sentencing. What do we know about the effects of these activities on jury verdicts?

Attorney strategy and behavior. In the opening statement by the two sides in a trial, each attorney provides the jury with a broad description of the case—a preview of what is to come. Each side has to decide whether to present an extensive overview of the evidence and arguments or simply to give a brief introduction. In a recreation of an actual trial that involved crossing state lines with a stolen vehicle, the length of the opening statement by the prosecution

FIGURE 13.3 *Directing the action in a trial: The judge and the opposing attorneys.*

The judge and the opposing attorneys play critical roles in a trial, and their actions are found to influence the decisions made by members of the jury. [Source: Photo © Julie Houck 1983.]

and the defense was found to affect the final verdict (Pyszczynski & Wrightsman, 1981). Specifically, when there was a brief opening statement by the prosecution and an extensive statement by the defense, only 21 percent of the jurors found the defendant guilty; when the reverse was true, 67 percent decided on a guilty verdict. Another element in the opening statement is the promise to present evidence later on that will be overwhelmingly convincing. For example, Pyszczynski et al. (1981) had the defense attorney claim:

> Finally, we will provide evidence that will show conclusively that Ron could not possibly have stolen the car. Specifically, we will present testimony proving that he was seen at the Sundown Motel in Murray at the very time the crime was taking place . . . there is certainly no way he could have stolen the car. (p. 437)

Even though no such evidence was presented later in the trial, this statement led to fewer guilty verdicts than were given in a control condition in which the statement did not appear. This effect was nullified, however, when the prosecutor in his summary reminded the jury that the promised evidence never materialized.

The evidence presented by the attorneys and the specific words they use also affect how jurors respond. The use of photographic evidence was investigated in a study involving a suit by the parents of a ten-year-old boy who was injured in an abandoned building (Whalen & Blanchard, 1982). The monetary damages were greatest when the boy had been badly injured and the injuries were displayed in a color photograph. Presumably, the color pictures were more emotionally arousing than either black and white photographs or verbal descriptions and hence led the jury to side with the injured party. Emotion can also be manipulated by the words attorneys use. When subjects watched a film of two cars colliding, some were asked about their "bumping" into one another while others were asked about the cars "smashing." Those asked about *smashing* cars testified incorrectly about seeing broken glass while those asked about *bumping* saw no glass (Loftus, 1980). See Figure 13.4, p. 496.

FIGURE 13.4   *Did the cars bump or smash? The question influences the answer.*

The words used by attorneys in questioning witnesses can influence the responses obtained. When subjects viewed a film of two cars colliding, those asked about their "smashing" reported seeing broken glass in the accident. Those asked about their "bumping" did not report this incorrect detail (Loftus, 1980). [Source: Photo © Jerry Howard 1983 / Positive Images.]

It seems to be a common assumption that justice is best served by having an adversary arrangement in which lawyers act as advocates of their respective clients (or of the state and of the defendant). In a nonadversary system, the lawyer's role is to seek the truth rather than to win the case. Sheppard and Vidmar (1980) compared these two approaches by presenting witnesses with a tape recording and photographs of a bar fight. The plaintiff pushed the defendant to the floor, and the downed man then retaliated and struck the one who pushed him with a wine bottle. Witnesses were afterwards interviewed by an advocate of one of the two men or by a nonadversary lawyer. In the latter instance, they gave accurate accounts of what happened in the bar. With adversary lawyers, the testimony was biased in the direction of whichever side had asked them the questions. Some members of the legal profession are beginning to raise questions about the fairness of the present system (Frankel, 1975), and defendants are perceived as *least* satisfied when they take part in an adversarial procedure and lose (Austin et al., 1981). Some observers suggest that having an attorney totally on your side who loses the battle is more frustrating than not having such a supporter during the trial.

The effect of the judge.   Two elements of judicial behavior have been explored by psychologists: instructions to disregard certain testimony or evidence and the final instructions given to the jury.

When there is a decision that portions of what has been said by an attorney, a witness, or the defendant is irrelevant, the jury may be told to disregard that material. The problem is that such statements cannot simply be forgotten on demand (Kassin & Wrightsman, 1980). In a simulated trial, Thompson et al. (1981) included inadmissible evidence in a robbery-murder case in which an alibi was or was not supported. In both cases, the judge had to rule the evidence inadmissible because it was obtained in an illegal wiretap. The judge's closing comments to the jury instructed them to ignore that testimony. When the testimony <u>favored the defendant, the jurors were less likely to convict him even though they were supposed to ignore the crucial evidence</u>. Testimony against the defendant led to no higher conviction rate than in a condition in which the evidence was totally absent. <u>The nature of the evidence also matters</u>. Jurors could respond to instructions to ignore a confession obtained under threat but not when the confession was obtained by a promise of leniency — even though both are equally inadmissible (Kassin & Wrightsman, 1981).

In presenting the final charge to the jury, the judge has the last word as to the meaning of the evidence. Do these comments influence jury decisions? Cavoukian and Doob (1980) presented subjects with the details of a robbery trial. The evidence in the case was either clear-cut or uncertain. At the end of the trial the judge either gave neutral remarks or attacked the believability of the defense witnesses. The negative remarks were found to increase the ratings of "guilty" regardless of the quality of the evidence, as shown in Figure 13.5. These personal comments by a judge can also have the opposite effect. In a transcript of an actual rape case, subjects who were exposed to damaging inadmissible evidence against the defendant (and to the judge's biased closing statements against the defendant) were *less* likely to find him guilty than when the judge was neutral or biased against the victim (Lenehan & O'Neill, 1981). In contrast, when the damaging evidence and judge's bias were against the victim, the subjects tended to go along with the judge's opinion. It is clear, then, that

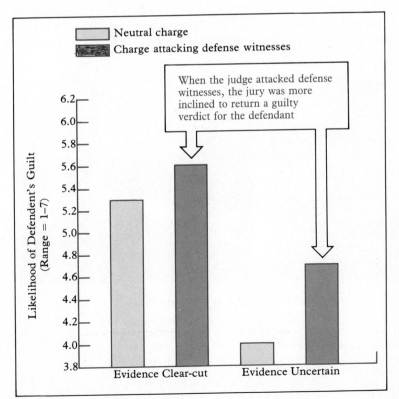

FIGURE 13.5 *The effects of biased remarks made by the judge.*

The judge's charge to the jury can affect decisions about a defendant's guilt. In both a clear-cut case and one that was more uncertain, judgments of guilt were greater when the judge attacked the credibility of the defense witnesses while summarizing the evidence for the jury. [Source: Based on data from Cavoukian & Doob, 1980.]

biased remarks from the bench can affect the decisions of jurors. The direction of such influence is complex, however, and depends on such factors as whether the bias is against a witness, the victim, or the defendant.

Defendants and Jurors: The Role of Interpersonal Variables

Presumably, the members of a jury listen to the evidence presented on both sides, and then render a verdict based on that evidence. As you might guess from what you have learned in this book about interpersonal relationships, other variables act to influence the reactions of jurors. Most of those other variables are totally irrelevant to the merits of the case; instead, they represent responses based on prejudice, attraction, attributions, and personality traits (see Figure 13.6). How do these variables operate?

The behavior, appearance, and attitudes of defendants. Both judges and jurors make attributions (see Chapter 2) about the *reasons* for the defendant's actions. In actual criminal cases, Harrel (1981) discovered that jurors take alcohol use into account in responding to a defendant. Minor crimes committed while drinking drew less severe sentences than the same crimes committed while sober, but the reverse was true for more serious crimes. It appears that minor offenses at least can be excused if the blame is placed on alcohol rather than on the one who committed the offense. Also, a defendant who indicated feelings of remorse was judged less severely than one who indicated a lack of concern about the crime. Jurors are inclined to assume that a defendant who invokes the

FIGURE 13.6   Physical appearance as a factor in the courtroom.

Social-psychological research indicates that variables known to influence liking (such as physical attractiveness) also tend to influence judgments made in the courtroom. In general, liked defendants (including those who make a nice appearance) are dealt with more leniently than those who are disliked. With the defendant shown here, do you think you would be more favorably disposed to him if he came into court as in Photo A or Photo B? [Source: Photos © Julie Houck 1983.]

Fifth Amendment of the U.S. Constitution is guilty even though it is one's legal right to avoid self-incrimination (Shaffer & Case, 1982).

Physically attractive defendants tend to be treated more leniently in a courtroom than unattractive ones. Though research subjects indicate that appearance should obviously be irrelevant in decisions of guilt or innocence (Efran, 1974), many experiments have shown that punitiveness decreases as the attractiveness of a defendant increases (Michelini & Snodgrass, 1980). The type of crime can affect this relationship. Thus, an attractive burglar is at an advantage in the courtroom but an attractive swindler is actually at a disadvantage (Sigall & Ostrove, 1975). Since most such findings were obtained in laboratory studies, you might think that jurors in real trials would not be foolish enough to be influenced by a defendant's looks. In real criminal cases, Stewart (1980) found a clear relationship between sentencing and attractiveness. As shown in Figure 13.7, unattractive defendants were much more likely to receive a prison sentence than attractive ones. These findings are disturbing, but it has also been found that the attractiveness effect can be reduced by increasing the amount of factual information provided to jurors (Baumeister & Darley, 1982) and by instructions from the judge reminding them of the criteria for reaching a guilty verdict (Weiten, 1980).

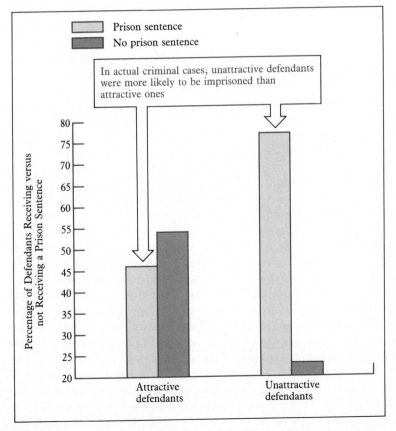

Prison sentence
No prison sentence

In actual criminal cases, unattractive defendants were more likely to be imprisoned than attractive ones

Percentage of Defendants Receiving versus not Receiving a Prison Sentence

80
75
70
65
60
55
50
45
40
35
30
25
20

Attractive defendants   Unattractive defendants

FIGURE 13.7   Sentencing: It can depend on the defendant's attractiveness.

In actual criminal trials as well as in simulated jury experiments, attractive defendants receive more lenient treatment than unattractive ones. In a study of 67 defendants, the majority of those who were attractive received no prison sentence. For the unattractive ones, almost four out of five received sentences. [Source: Based on data from Stewart, 1980.]

The race of the defendant also plays a role (Stokes & Prestholdt, 1972). For example, in a rape trial, a white defendant is most likely to be believed by a white juror and a black defendant by a black juror (Ugwuegbu, 1979). Again, data from actual trials are consistent with laboratory findings. In Stewart's (1980) investigation of the outcome of criminal trials, 63 percent of the white defendants were convicted, while 81 percent of the nonwhites were found guilty. With respect to imprisonment, these racial differences were even greater: 43 percent of the whites were incarcerated and 75 percent of the nonwhites.

Many of these findings can be conceptualized as stemming from interpersonal likes and dislikes (see Chapter 6). The more a juror is attracted to a defendant, the more lenient the response. Thus, favorability of jury decisions are found to be influenced by the degree of defendant-juror attitude similarity (Shepherd & Sloan, 1979) and by the positiveness of the defendant's personality characteristics (Izzett & Leginski, 1974).

It should also be noted that interpersonal attraction toward the victim of a crime can influence how a juror responds. The more a juror can identify with the victim of a crime, the more guilty the defendant is judged to be (Kaplan & Miller, 1979). In a similar way, the more physically or psychologically attractive the victim, the more severe the punishment of the defendant whether the victim had a car stolen (Kerr, 1978a), was raped (Thornton, 1977), or was accidentally killed (Landy & Aronson, 1969). The reaction seems to be that an attractive victim has more to lose, so the defendant should receive more punishment.

The ladies and gentlemen of the jury.   The characteristics of judges, attorneys, defendants, witnesses, and victims tend to be important to the extent that they affect how members of the jury respond. It is the jurors who must decide guilt and innocence and at times make recommendations as to punishment. Keep in mind the discussion of how groups arrive at decisions in Chapter 11. Given all of the biases that have been discovered in psychological research, it is clear why jury selection is important for the opposing attorneys. Each side hopes to end up with a panel biased toward its case, or at least not biased the other way. On the basis of psychological research, the lawyer's chances of making the correct decisions in the selection process can be improved (Horowitz, 1980). In fact, several jury research firms have been created to help lawyers select the right jury and to present their arguments in the most effective way (Lewin, 1982).

Personality traits are associated with the decisions made by jurors. For example, males high in empathy are more likely to reach a verdict of not guilty, and the same is true for both males and females who feel independent and autonomous (Mills & Bohannon, 1980). A personality trait frequently studied in this context is **authoritarianism** (see Chapter 14). Those who are authoritarian tend to submit to authority, conform to conventional norms, and express hostility toward those who deviate from the norms. The opposite extreme of this dimension, **egalitarianism,** consists of those who respect authority less, are less tied to conventional norms, and are more tolerant of those who deviate. Given this description, it is perhaps not surprising to find that authoritarian jurors are more punitive toward a disliked defendant, while egalitarians respond fairly and equally to those they like and to those they dislike (Mitchell &

**FIGURE 13.8   *Unfair punishment: Juror personality and
status of defendant.***

*The personality of a juror can affect his or her judgment in various ways and
such variables can interact with characteristics of the defendant. For example,*
authoritarian *jurors are more punitive toward a disliked defendant if that
person is an ordinary citizen, but with a police officer on trial it is the*
egalitarian *juror who responds in that same biased fashion (Mitchell, 1979).*
[Source: Photos by Cary S. Wolinsky/Stock, Boston.]

Byrne, 1982). More surprisingly, these roles are found to reverse when the
defendant is a police officer rather than an ordinary citizen (Mitchell, 1979). In
this instance, the egalitarians are biased against a disliked defendant, and the
authoritarians are fair (see Figure 13.8). In a related finding, jurors scoring low
on a measure of dogmatic (close-minded) attitudes were more punitive toward a
heterosexual defendant than toward a homosexual one (Shaffer & Case, 1982).
It seems that egalitarianism and low dogmatism can be associated with unfair
jury decisions in response to certain defendants.

Some specific attitudes also affect jurors' decisions. Those who favor
capital punishment are likely to vote for conviction (Jurow, 1971), and those
stressing law and order tend to favor severe sentences (Legant, 1973). It has also
been found that males who lean toward convicting the defendant have more
children and lower incomes than lenient males (Moran & Comfort, 1983).
Though the perceived seriousness of crimes is related to the judgments as to
how severe the punishment should be (Gescheider et al., 1982), jurors are less
likely to vote for conviction as the punishment becomes more severe (Kerr,
1978b). There are also problems with serving on more than one jury in a row.
There is a contrast effect in that serving in a trial in which the prosecution
makes a strong case leads to greater leniency in a subsequent trial (Kerr et al.,
1982).

Finally, the crime itself and a juror's attitudes about it partially determine
what verdict is reached. With an unpopular law such as Prohibition in the 1920s

ON THE APPLIED SIDE

Crime in the Neighborhood: Evaluating a Community Project

Psychological involvement in the concerns of the law is not limited to the courtroom. A wide array of problems has captured the attention of psychologists, including negotiating with terrorists who are holding hostages (Bracey, 1980), the close bond between captives and their captors—the **Stockholm syndrome** (Strentz, 1980), and the assessment of hostages after their release (Schaar, 1981). In addition, research has dealt with the selection and evaluation of police (Spielberger, 1979), the attempt to identify the characteristics of an unknown murderer (McNett, 1982), and the relationship between law enforcement officers and the citizens of their community (Tyler & Folger, 1980).

In many such undertakings, the applied psychologist designs and conducts **evaluation research.** This refers to the way in which any new program is assessed—its costs, benefits, and its impact on individuals. A crime control experiment and its evaluation has been described by Fowler (1981). The setting was an urban residential neighborhood in Hartford, Connecticut. The goal was to reduce the number of burglaries and robberies in that neighborhood (see Figure 13.9).

The focus was on two specific crimes because burglaries and robberies were occurring with disturbing frequency. These crimes are almost always committed by someone the victim does not know, and they arouse a great deal of fear. The Hartford project was based on three integrated approaches to crime reduction. First, a police team was assigned

permanently to the neighborhood so that relationships could develop between officers and citizens and so that the police would gain familiarity with the area and its crime problems. Second, resident organizations were formed to work with police and to strengthen the sense of identification with the community. Third, aspects of the neighborhood environment were redesigned by closing some streets, introducing some one-way streets, and generally attempting to enhance identification of the area as "ours" to be defended against outsiders coming in to commit crime.

In order to evaluate the effectiveness of these innovations, data were gathered over a one-year period, including police statistics on crime, repeated surveys of community residents and of the police working there, and observation of the way environmental changes affected traffic and pedestrian use. What was the impact of this crime prevention program?

One success was a decline in the rate of burglaries based on comparisons with an earlier period and with the remaining sections of Hartford. In addition, the residents were found to *feel* that they were less likely to be burglary victims. This crime was now viewed as a less important problem after a year of the program. In other words, both this crime and the fear of this crime had been reduced.

The evidence for robbery and other street crimes showed the same trends, but the major change here was a relocation of the activity. Crimi-

---

or today's marijuana statutes, there is a tendency to favor the defendant (Kaplan, 1971). In contrast, rape has been perceived as more and more serious over the past decade, and therefore a rapist is increasingly likely to be judged harshly (Nagao & Davis, 1980). Even with this type of crime, attitudes and beliefs can determine outcome. Those individuals who accept various myths about rape (for example, "When women go around braless or wearing short skirts and tight tops, they are just asking for trouble") are less likely to define various incidents as constituting rape and hence less likely to convict the offender (Burt & Albin, 1981). The number of offenses with which the defend-

FIGURE 13.9 *Evaluating programs designed to prevent crime.*

When an effort is made to reduce crimes such as burglary or robbery, the effectiveness of these procedures can be assessed by means of **evaluation research.** *This involves (1) a comparison of crime statistics before and after the new program goes into effect, (2) a weighing of the relative costs and benefits of what was done, (3) a determination of how people perceive the project, and (4) a series of recommendations concerning future innovations. [Source: Photo © Michal Heron 1982/Woodfin Camp and Associates.]*

nals began to avoid the residential side streets and concentrated on the commercial areas.

Changing the environment led to a considerable reduction in traffic on the residential streets, though pedestrian patterns did not change much. Nevertheless, residents reported that they used the streets more, were better able to recognize strangers, and were more likely to keep an eye on their neighbors' houses on a routine basis. This kind of informal social control is believed to be the most important element in reducing crime.

Despite the partial success of these efforts to reduce crime, many residents were not convinced that the program did any good. Some felt it had not worked, and others felt that the changes could have occurred even without such things as alterations in the streets. When there are innovative programs of any kind, it is necessary to consider whether specified goals have been met *and* whether the community accepts what has taken place (Severy et al., 1981). Evaluation research permits us to determine both aspects of the effects of new programs.

ant is charged also influences the jury. With multiple offenses combined in a single trial ("joining" of the charges), there is a higher rate of conviction. In such instances, jurors become confused about the evidence, rate it as more incriminating, and attribute the defendant's behavior to a criminal disposition (Tanford & Penrod, 1982).

Once again, psychological variables are found to be a major influence in the way a legal proceeding concludes. In the **Applied Side** section above, we show how legal psychology has gone beyond the courtroom to deal directly with crime and its prevention.

FIGURE 13.10   Psychological reactions as an integral part of health care.

Psychological variables enter into health matters at every step ranging from one's life-style to the relationship between physician and patient. One would guess that the physical condition of the patient in this cartoon is not helped by his psychological reaction to the apparent lack of expertise among his physicians. [Source: © 1981; reprinted courtesy of Bill Hoest.]

"Then we're all agreed: That skinny red thing is the appendix."

Behavioral Medicine: Health Care and Social Psychology

Consider for a moment the following bits of information. Among American males aged fifty-five to sixty-four, the suicide rate is three times greater for whites than for nonwhites (Shearer, 1982). A photograph of goldenrod plants can induce sneezing, and the sight of a plastic rose is able to set off an asthma attack (Anderson, 1982). When the need for power is frustrated, the body's immune system against infection is weakened so that various diseases increase in frequency and severity (McClelland, 1982). It appears that psychological variables operate to influence self-destruction, allergic reactions, and susceptibility to infections. If so, it is logical to suppose that the appropriate alterations in psychological determinants can result in dramatic improvements in psychological and physical health. (See Figure 13.10 for a cartoonist's view of the potential importance of psychological factors, such as faith in the physicians' ability, in affecting health care.)

It was once widely believed that illness was a purely physical problem for which it was important to seek physical means of prevention and cure. We now know that there are physical reactions to psychological stress, learned habits that benefit or harm one's body, a relationship between personality traits and the development of specific illnesses, and the necessity to cope with illness, with the behavior of medical practitioners, and with health-related institutions (Baum & Singer, 1980; Matarazzo, 1980). The growing involvement of psychologists in the prevention and treatment of physical illness has evolved into the field of **behavioral medicine** (Gentry, 1982; Hamburg, 1982). One of the major trends in social psychology has been research on issues related to health and the development of graduate training programs with this emphasis (Evans, 1982).

In addition to the relevance of psychological variables to medical problems, there is a practical reason to seek nonmedical approaches to health care. The increased demand for treatment over the past thirty years cannot continue at the same rate for another thirty years, or one-half of the population will have to obtain M.D. degrees to be able to treat the other half (Rachman & Philips, 1980). In the following pages, we will examine some of the important ways that behavioral science is being applied to such concerns.

Preventive Medicine: Worth a Pound of Cure

There is little disagreement as to the value of acting to prevent health-related problems. One approach is to teach children some basic facts about health care as early as possible — emphasizing exercise, good nutrition, and the avoidance of cigarettes (Edwards et al., 1982). The greatest stumbling block, however, is not lack of knowledge but in motivating people to act in their own best interests.

Personality variables and effective preventive behavior. Most programs deal with adults and must contend with individual differences in following sound advice (Wurtele et al., 1982). Personality variables are frequently found to predict who does and does not comply with a program of prevention. For example, most of us know that regular physical exercise is beneficial to health but only some of us are able to stick to such a program. Dishman et al. (1980) found that the best predictor was a measure of self-motivation. A test composed of such items as "I have a lot of will power" correctly classified 80 percent of all subjects as to whether they continued to engage in regular physical exercise.

Dieting to reduce excess weight is another painful health-related procedure. Saltzer (1980) found that successful weight-loss behavior is best predicted by a measure of subjects' perceived expectations of their close friends. Their knowledge of the negative consequences of obesity was unrelated to what they did about losing weight. Engaging in effective oral hygiene practices (regular brushing and flossing) was found to be related to a measure of perceived self-effectiveness (Beck & Lund, 1981). In such research, as well as in studies of alcohol use (DiTecco & Schlegel, 1982) and drug dependence (Gossop, 1982), simple knowledge of good health practices and a realization of the consequences is not enough. Instead, there seem to be very specific personality traits and self-perceptions that lead to appropriate versus inappropriate behavior (see Figure 13.11, page 506).

Preventing cigarette smoking before it starts. Most medical scientists agree that the connection between cigarette smoking and diseases such as lung cancer is well established. It has been suggested by a former cabinet member that "people who smoke are committing slow-motion suicide." People realize there are severe negative consequences to health and even to social acceptability, but there are also perceived positive consequences such as tension reduction, peer acceptance, and weight reduction (Chassin et al., 1981; Fishbein, 1982). Also, while one might decide to quit smoking, it is very difficult to give up any

FIGURE 13.11   Health-enhancing behavior: Information is not enough.

The greatest challenge to preventive medicine is not in identifying good health practices but in motivating individuals to follow them. A number of personality characteristics have been found to predict who will and will not maintain programs of physical exercise, dieting, dental hygiene, and so forth. It is clear that knowledge of what to do and awareness of the consequences are not sufficient to bring about the necessary behavior changes. [Source: Photo by Donna Ferrato / Contact Press Images.]

substance to which a person has become addicted or dependent upon (Evans, 1980; Shipley, 1981). So, as important as it is to help smokers quit, it is even more important to prevent such behavior from ever starting.

To accomplish this, several programs have been designed to convince children and teenagers to avoid becoming nicotine addicts. This age group is especially important because there has actually been an increase in the amount of smoking among young females (Evans et al., 1980; Reinhold, 1981). For middle adolescents, smoking is viewed as a social asset that attracts the opposite sex (Barton et al., 1982; Chassin et al., 1981). By the time they reach the seventh grade, most children are convinced that smoking is dangerous—at least eventually. A common belief is that you can smoke when you are young because only old people die from lung cancer, emphysema, and heart attacks. Nathan Maccoby has suggested that "Most kids of 12 think of themselves as immortal" (Reinhold, 1981). In addition, adolescent smokers (compared to nonsmokers) assume that smoking behavior is much more common than is actually the case (Sherman et al., 1983). They thus believe that it couldn't be so bad if most people are doing it. Given these considerations, can this behavior be prevented?

Since the junior high years seem to be the most vulnerable to yielding to pressure to smoke, Evans (1982, 1983) designed a prevention program to help young people in resisting various social influences, including pressure from parents and peers (Krosnick & Judd, 1982). Several techniques were employed. Brief videotapes presented the basic information and featured youngsters the same age as the target population. The actors also portrayed situations in which there is resistance to smoking temptations—refusing a cigarette offered by a friend, for example. There were subsequent tapes dealing with parents who

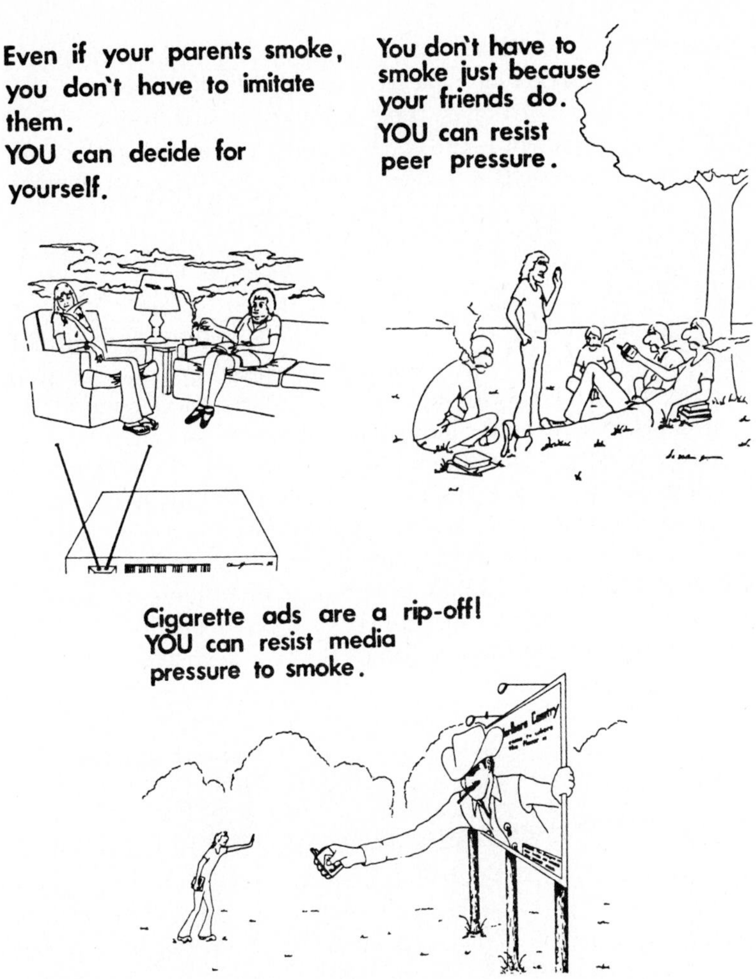

Even if your parents smoke, you don't have to imitate them.
YOU can decide for yourself.

You don't have to smoke just because your friends do.
YOU can resist peer pressure.

Cigarette ads are a rip-off!
YOU can resist media pressure to smoke.

FIGURE 13.12   *Encouraging youngsters to resist pressures to smoke.*

In a program designed to prevent smoking among seventh graders, videotapes and posters were used to warn these young teenagers about the various pressures they face to induce them to smoke and to encourage them to resist. (Source: Social Psychology and Behavioral Medicine, *J. Richard Eiser (Ed.). Copyright © 1982 by John Wiley & Sons, Ltd. Reprinted by permission of John Wiley & Sons, Ltd.]*

smoke and with cigarette advertising. In addition, classroom posters were displayed as reminders (see Figure 13.12), and group discussions reinforced all of these messages.

Compared to control subjects, those in the experimental program were much less likely to begin smoking during the first quarter of the seventh grade. Long-term follow-up data are beginning to be available, and the program seems to have a positive impact on behavior in subsequent years. Such programs, along with antismoking television and radio ads, may be in part responsible for the declining percentage of smokers among high school seniors. Smoking decreased by 25 percent in this group from 1977 to 1980. Only 21 percent now report smoking cigarettes daily, though the percentage is slightly higher for females than for males (Peterson, 1981). Through a combination of approaches, it seems to be possible to change health-related behavior for the better.

Life Stresses: Losing Control over Events

We don't ordinarily think of economic issues such as inflation, interest rates, or unemployment in terms of psychological processes or health-related outcomes (see Figure 13.13). In testimony before a Congressional committee, data presented by M. Harvey Brenner indicated a very real association among such variables (Pines, 1982). When unemployment rises by 1 percent, 1.9 percent more people die from heart disease, cirrhosis of the liver, and other stress-related diseases over the next six years. Unemployed workers show an increase in such symptoms as dizziness, inability to sleep, and high blood pressure (Bluestone & Harrison, 1982). The U.S. economic slump of 1970 (a 1.4 percent rise in unemployment) was linked to 51,570 deaths by 1975. Research in Israel and the United States found that the perceived threat of

FIGURE 13.13   *Economic disruption leads to stress, disease, and even death.*

Economic problems such as unemployment or inflation are found to create psychological distress and to result in increases in behavioral and physical disorders, as well as increases in death rates from various diseases. The basic problem seems to be the individual's loss of perceived control *over the events in his or her life. [Source: Photo by Earl Dotter / Archive Pictures, Inc.]*

inflation influences not only buying practices but the amount of distress experienced by each country's citizens (Epstein & Babad, 1982). In recent years, several investigators have attempted to document and explain such reactions to the stresses of everyday life.

Perceived control and the effects of stressful life events. It has been proposed that a basic human need is the experience of **perceived control** over the events in our lives (Rodin et al., 1982). Both psychological well-being and physical health benefit from the perception of control, and both suffer when control is lost. Those who are chronically depressed report little sense of control, but perceived control increases when a positive mood is induced (Alloy et al., 1981). Even in relatively brief laboratory experiments, the sense of being able to control aversive stimuli reduces the stressfulness of shock, loud noises, and so forth while increasing one's ability to endure them (Gatchel & Proctor, 1976; Staub et al., 1971). Exposure to uncontrollable situations is followed by an increase in physiological symptoms (Pennebaker et al., 1977). Animal studies also indicate that physical symptoms occur when control is lost (Davis et al., 1977). Thus, whenever individuals are encouraged to assume control, they feel better both emotionally and physically, and they are often able to institute useful changes in the world around them.

In most of our day to day lives, it is easy to assume that things are progressing smoothly and routinely because of what we do. We may work hard, treat others politely, save our money, take vitamins, brush after every meal, or whatever, and the world rolls along predictably as a consequence. The truth, of course, is that we have little or no control over many of the major events of life. When stressful occurrences arise, as they inevitably do, they act as powerful reminders of our lack of control, we experience distress, and our physical health can suffer accordingly. While it has been proposed that *any* life changes (for example, divorce, marriage, parenthood) result in an increase in physical illness, recent research suggests that this effect is true only for undesirable events (Vinokur & Selzer, 1975), especially if they are uncontrollable (Suls & Mullen, 1981). Control is not necessarily good if it implies that you brought disaster on yourself. Hammen and Mayol (1982) classified various life events in terms of their relative desirability and the extent to which the individual is responsible for their occurrence, as shown in Table 13.2, p. 510. Feelings of depression were associated only with undesirable events for which the person feels responsible, and these events were the most upsetting. Stress-induced illness seems to be avoided by some individuals—those who are most attentive to and aware of their internal bodily states (Mullen & Suls, 1982). It is possible that these individuals quickly become aware of their reactions to stress and then do something about it. It also appears that stress-resistant people tend to share a particular set of attitudes toward life ("psychological hardiness"), including an openness to change, a sense of involvement and commitment, and a feeling of control over their lives (Pines, 1980). Thus, stress not only injures our health by way of psychological reactions but other psychological reactions can prevent these effects. The disorienting aspects of major life changes can also have a

TABLE 13.2   *The effect of life events: Desirability and responsibility.*

The effect of stressful life events on depression and physical symptoms seems to depend on whether they are positive or negative events and whether the individual is responsible for their occurrence. The most upsetting events and those causing the most depression are undesirable ones for which the individual is responsible. [Source: Adapted from Hammen & Mayol, 1982.]

Desirable life events	Undesirable life events	
(These cause the least distress)	*Individual responsible* (These cause the most distress)	*Individual not responsible* (These cause some distress)
Graduation	Getting fired	Relative sent to prison
Engagement	Divorce	Miscarriage
Planned pregnancy	Dropping out of school	Death of close friend

positive aspect. Adapting to major life changes sometimes requires emotional changes that result in a new and more mature perception of one's environment (Stewart et al., 1982).

Reducing the effects of stress. Besides the fact that some individuals are stress-resistant, are there other factors that can reduce the negative consequences? It is found that old age, retirement, and geographical relocation are not stressful so long as the person maintains control by means of retirement planning, living in a structured environment, and having economic security (Hendrick et al., 1982). Also, when a person has social support, the physical effects of stress are decreased (Holahan & Moos, 1981). Helpful support can be provided by family members, fellow workers, employers and supervisors, and friends. It has also been found that when individuals face a stressful crisis such as the diagnosis of cancer, loss of a spouse, or the death of an infant, they believe that their extreme distress is somehow inappropriate and so they fail to seek the support and help of others (Silver & Wortman, 1980; Wortman & Dunkel-Schetter, 1979). It can be of great benefit to learn that one's feelings are perfectly legitimate.

In contrast to the various effects just described, some kinds of stress are actually beneficial. Greenberger et al. (1981) investigated several hundred tenth and eleventh graders, comparing those who were holding their first part-time job (a potential source of new stress) with those who had never worked. Six kinds of work stressors were identified: environmental conditions, work tasks, conflict between work and other demands, work supervisors, work organization, and wages. Those adolescents who held jobs reported fewer physical symptoms than those who did not. Further, for boys, those who experienced the most work stress reported the fewest symptoms. The only negative effect of exposure to job stress, for both sexes, was an increase in the use of alcohol and marijuana. Perhaps the sense of control, the challenge, and the economic rewards of an adolescent job are useful in instilling feelings of self-reliance, and good health is one of the side effects.

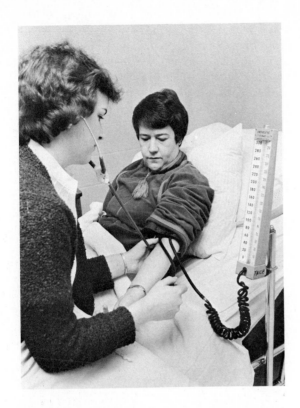

Medical Specialists and Institutions: Reducing the Threat

One of the effects of an illness or an accident is the sudden loss of perceived control and the necessity of becoming at least temporarily dependent on others (see Figure 13.14). The resulting fear, anger, and helplessness may interfere with peace of mind and delay recovery (Evans, 1980; Gottesman & Lewis, 1982). Psychological research has begun to identify the aspects of medical interactions and medical settings that increase or decrease the maladaptive responses of patients (Blascovich, 1982). For example, when children are told what a dentist is doing and what to expect, they report less anxiety and physical discomfort (Siegel & Peterson, 1980), and adults respond the same way (K. Klein, 1982). Also, patients feel better if the physician does something—even a diagnostic test that yields negative results (Sox, 1982).

Interacting with a medical specialist. The decision to see a doctor in the first place depends on what friends advise rather than simply the seriousness of the physical problem (Sanders, 1981). Once there, interpersonal variables continue to be important. The factors influencing the relationship between a patient and the individual providing health care are much the same as those involved in forming a friendship. It is helpful if the practitioner *likes* the patient, but as you might expect on the basis of the attraction research in Chapter 6, physicians react negatively to patients dissimilar from themselves (Klein, 1982). Rodin and

Janis (1979) suggest that physicians, dentists, nurses, and others must *establish the similarities* between self and patient and indicate a *positive evaluation* of that person. Medical practitioners need to learn effective nonverbal communication such as touch, facial expressiveness, and tone of voice to gain the patient's trust (Friedman, 1979). At that point, the relationship becomes helpful because the health specialist can use his or her power to motivate the patient to engage in necessary activities (Rodin & Janis, 1979). Even such variables as a nurse's uniform can cause problems. Sterling (1980) found that both male and female patients are less likely to interact with a nurse dressed in a standard white uniform than with a nurse in street clothes. Nurses, by the way, like patients who have a clear-cut diagnosis better than patients with an ambiguous one (Gillmore & Hill, 1981). They seem to feel that uncertainty as to diagnosis means that the patient is not really in pain.

One of the duties of a physician is to provide factual information to the patient, and most patients do not receive as much as they desire (Ley, 1982). In video recordings of actual doctor-patient interactions, Pendleton (1982) found that physicians provided the least information to working class patients who are the ones most in need of it. It might be assumed that such behavior is based on past experience in which such patients were unable to understand or remember what they had been told. In fact, as Figure 13.15 indicates, the reverse is true. The lower the socioeconomic class of the patient, the higher the proportion of information remembered. Possibly, these individuals possessed the least amount of relevant information so they paid greater attention to the physician's

FIGURE 13.15   Socioeconomic status differences in remembering what the doctor says.

When physicians provided information during office visits, patients were found to remember a high proportion of that material afterward. Despite the fact that these physicians were least likely to provide information to patients of lower socioeconomic status, such individuals were found to remember the greatest percentage of what they had been told. [Source: Based on data from Pendleton, 1982.]

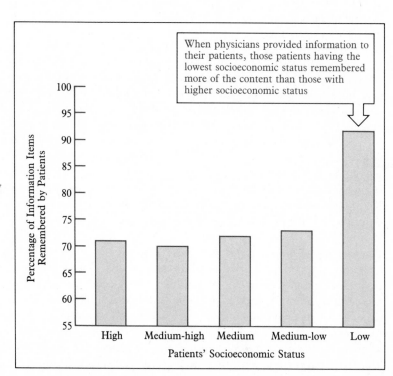

When physicians provided information to their patients, those patients having the lowest socioeconomic status remembered more of the content than those with higher socioeconomic status

comments. There are, of course, individual differences in the desire to receive information and to use it in self-help procedures (Krantz et al., 1980).

Institutional environments: Hospitals and nursing homes. In the United States alone, about 37 million patients are admitted to hospitals annually (Taylor, 1979). If illness lowers one's perceived control, being institutionalized is even a greater blow (Taylor, 1982). Discomfort and pain seem to be much more bearable when the patient knows what is happening and thus can view the hospital world as predictable (Corah & Boffa, 1970; Ray, 1982). One way to accomplish that goal is the use of the kind of *modeling techniques* discussed briefly in Chapter 7. For children about to undergo surgery, the chance to watch a movie about a seven-year-old boy going to the hospital for an operation was very helpful (Melamed & Siegel, 1975). Compared to a control group, the patients who saw the operation film were less anxious before and after the operation and even showed better adjustment when they went home. Adults respond well to similar presentations, and the result is less fear, less pain, and a better response to treatment (Langer et al., 1975).

The behavior of hospital personnel is also crucial. Nurses can be taught to stop reinforcing certain psychosomatic symptoms by ignoring them, and the symptoms extinguish (Redd, 1980). Appropriate psychological intervention can also reduce anxiety, hostility, and depression among cancer patients (Gordon et al., 1980). There are also physical problems in a hospital in that one out of twenty patients acquires a new infection *after* hospitalization (Raven & Haley, 1980). These infections can be cut in half if hospital personnel can be persuaded to improve such behaviors as wearing masks in an isolation room and washing their hands after handling a contaminated dressing (Raven & Haley, 1982). The use of social influence procedures and reinforcement are effective ways to bring about these behavioral changes (Haley et al., 1980).

Simply growing old is, in our culture, a negative event associated with lowered self-esteem and decreased feelings of control (Rodin & Langer, 1980). An institutional setting can add to the problems. A nursing home for the elderly, even under the best of conditions, is likely to make a formerly independent individual suddenly helpless and powerless in an environment controlled by others (Wack & Rodin, 1978). Kind, supportive, helpful staff members often manage to reinforce dependent behavior among the residents (Barton et al., 1980; Blum & Minkler, 1980). Common reactions are apathy, depression, and hopelessness (Ziegler & Reid, 1979). When such a setting is changed to foster self-reliance (for example, having each resident take care of a potted plant), there is a dramatic increase in activity, interest in the surroundings, sociability, and an even more dramatic decrease in the death rate (Langer & Rodin, 1976; Rodin & Langer, 1977). Anything that reintroduces the feeling of control is apparently important. For example, when cognitive activity is encouraged and rewarded, memory loss is reversed (Langer et al., 1979).

There are other findings suggesting that control may play a more complex role than we have thought. In a study of elderly nursing home residents, Janoff-Bulman and Marshall (1982) found that psychological well-being was highest among those who perceived themselves to be high in control and healthy and whose life was not greatly changed by being in the institution. The surprising finding was that, 30 months later, those highest in feelings of well-being were *most* likely to have died. It appears that those individuals who feel they had more control before being institutionalized are the most unhappy with their new environment; but they are also most likely to survive there.

In summary, the recipients of medical care want to be liked and to be informed. Factors that increase a sense of responsibility, control, and self-reliance tend to have significant effects on feelings and behavior. It also seems to be true that surprisingly minor changes in the behavior of medical practitioners and in the structure of medical institutions can affect these responses.

In the previous chapter, we discussed the many ways in which environmental factors can have negative effects on one's emotional state, health, and behavior. In the **Focus on Research** section on pages 516–518 we examine some of the ways in which people can be encouraged to bring about positive environmental changes.

The Work Place: Behavior in Organizations

A major way in which social psychology is applied involves the study of behavior within organizational settings, as you might expect on the basis of earlier descriptions of topics such as bargaining (Chapter 10) and leadership (Chapter 11). For most men and about half of the women in the United States, much of their time is spent working at a job outside of the home. Work-related activities consume the largest segment of our waking hours (Robinson, 1977). This activity takes place primarily within organizations, and the study of **organizational behavior** has broad consequences for both employers and employees (Baron, 1983). Specifically, organizational behavior is defined as the field that seeks to understand and predict human behavior in organizational settings by means of the scientific study of individuals, groups, and the structure and function of organizations. Such application almost always raises questions of values, and the organizational psychologist sometimes is in conflict between the needs of the workers and the needs of their employers (Shimmin, 1981), as well as in potential conflicts involving political ideology (Dobrzyński, 1981).

Work and the Worker

Historically, the armed forces constituted one of the first major organizations in which a large number of "workers" functioned under the direction of a small number of "managers." Essentially, the traditional conception of how to motivate soldiers to perform the best possible job grew out of the relationship between those with total power and those with none. That is, the job of the upper class officers was to design the most efficient tactics using the best available weapons, and the lower class enlisted men were forced to do exactly as they were ordered or face the consequences of rebukes, floggings, and even execution (Middlekauff, 1982). With the industrial revolution, managers of

FIGURE 13.16   *Scientific management: Money as the motivator.*

With the industrial revolution, managers of complex manufacturing operations faced the task of motivating large numbers of employees to work efficiently and effectively. The concept of scientific management *indicated that with standardized tools, appropriate selection of personnel, and monetary incentives, maximum productivity could be obtained. [Source: Merrimac Valley Textile Museum.]*

industrial firms were faced with the problem of running an efficient, productive organization without resorting to slave labor or military discipline. In the early days of this century, an approach known as **scientific management** was described by Taylor (1911). This concept involved both attention to the job itself (standardized tools and carefully selected personnel) and an attempt to motivate the workers (see Figure 13.16). Motivation was assumed to be a matter of desire for gain, and thus money was used as the primary incentive for good performance. This combination of an efficient job performed by a worker seeking financial rewards often led to increased productivity, but something had been omitted. Other aspects of human motivation were ignored—that is, employees also need respect, security, and a feeling of worth. Research that identified these missing ingredients in management theory led to the **human relations** approach in which it was recognized that employees are human beings who need more than a paycheck to work their best. In fact, people are found to set higher standards for personal satisfaction than for financial satisfaction (Levin et al., 1980).

From a somewhat different historical background (the Protestant Reformation) came another concept: the work ethic. This is the belief that a man or woman becomes a better person by the act of working (Rice et al., 1980). Many of us seem to have accepted that view, and surveys show that over two-thirds of American workers say they would continue on their jobs even if they had all the money they needed (U.S. Department of Commerce, 1977). Marxist writers, on the other hand, simply assume that the work ethic is a clever capitalist ploy to make the exploited workers feel that they are doing something worthwhile (Hunt, 1976). Whatever the reason, people report deriving much of their satisfaction in life from the work they do (Katzell & Yankelovich, 1975).

R *Initiating Environmental Improvement*

In the discussion of environmental psychology in Chapter 12, it may have seemed as though human beings are only passive targets when behavior is affected by crowding, noise, urban surroundings, and so forth. In recent years, there has been an increasing awareness of our ability to take charge and actively to apply our knowledge to bring about environmental improvement. It is possible for each of us to behave in such a way as to live in cleaner surroundings, conserve energy, and modify the world around us (Cook & Berrenberg, 1981). Further, according to a nationwide poll, most Americans indicate a willingness to make economic sacrifices in order to protect and improve the environment (Shabecoff, 1981), and these concerns are greatest among those who are young and better educated (Strand, 1981). Unfortunately, our behavior does not always match our ideals. One active area of applied social psychology deals with efforts to encourage behavior that has a positive impact on the environment.

Though no one advocates dirty air or garbage-filled sidewalks, many people continue to pollute and litter. As we found in the study of prosocial behavior (Chapter 8), individuals need to assume responsibility and to be reminded of the right thing to do. In Spokane, Washington, there was a campaign to stop the open burning of leaves because of its effect on air pollution. Research indicated that leaf burning was given up among those residents who had become aware of the consequences and who felt they shared in the responsibility for clean versus polluted air (Van Liere & Dunlap, 1978).

Littering is another familiar problem, one that costs U.S. taxpayers a half billion dollars annually to pick up 6.9 million tons of discarded trash. It would, of course, be simpler (and cheaper) if everyone refrained from littering in the first place. Solutions range from providing rewards to those who collect litter (Clark et al., 1972) to making sure that bags and cans are available for depositing trash

(Geller et al., 1976). Would reminders in the form of signs help? Reiter and Samuel (1980) investigated the effects of two kinds of signs on littering in a multistory downtown public parking garage. On different levels, there were either no signs posted or one of two types of signs—a gentle reminder ("Pitch In") or a stern warning ("Littering is Unlawful and Subject to a $10 fine"). Since it has been found that littering increases in response to the presence of litter (Krauss et al., 1978), another variable was included: the area was clean or littered. To provide each driver with potential litter, paper announcements thanking them for supporting the downtown area were placed on each windshield. As shown in Figure 13.17, littering was less frequent when no previous litter was present, and much less when either kind of reminder sign was present. It should be added that a repeat of the experiment a week later in the same garage indicated a negative reaction to the signs (and increased littering), possibly because the users of the garage resisted being told what to do. In any event, the presence of containers and various types of reminders have led to dramatic decreases in the amount of littering in such cities as Indianapolis, San Bernardino, and Charlotte (*Time*, May 19, 1980, p. 51).

With respect to energy conservation, most people are convinced of the seriousness of the problem (Olsen, 1981), but generally lack awareness as to how much energy is being consumed by their appliances, thermostat settings, and so forth (Weber & Price, 1980). With regular information provided as to amount of electricity being used, consumption drops by 10 percent (Seligman et al., 1980). Another successful approach in an apartment complex was an energy conservation contest. The program produced a drop of 6.6 percent in the use of natural gas over a three-month period (McClelland & Cook, 1980). It is also found that a general appeal by the President to readjust thermostats has little effect on behavior (Luyben, 1982). The most important step

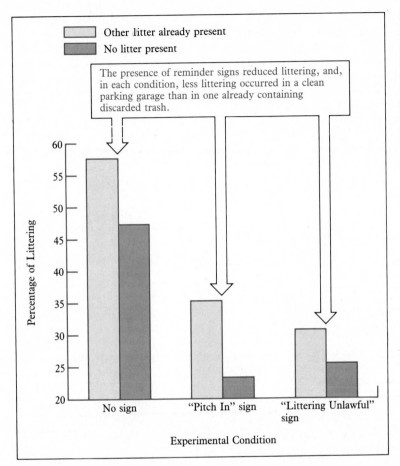

FIGURE 13.17 *Littering: Modeling and reminding.*

In a downtown parking garage, the littering behavior of its patrons was affected both by the presence of existing litter and by signs either asking or telling them not to litter. People litter less when the setting is relatively clean and when signs remind them not to do so. [Source: Based on data from Reiter & Samuel, 1980.]

The presence of reminder signs reduced littering, and, in each condition, less littering occurred in a clean parking garage than in one already containing discarded trash.

Other litter already present

No litter present

Percentage of Littering

No sign

"Pitch In" sign

"Littering Unlawful" sign

Experimental Condition

seems to be that of persuading an individual to engage in an energy conserving act for the first time. Once the behavior has actually been carried out, it is likely to be continued afterward (Macy & Brown, 1983).

In a study of ride-sharing programs to conserve gasoline, it was concluded that the use of computers to match commuters on the basis of schedules and other variables results in successful carpools (Owens, 1981). In other words, finding compatible fellow commuters can be compared to finding a desirable computer date. In general, people will respond positively to energy-conserving measures if they are convinced that the benefits outweigh the costs, if the changed behavior is consistent with

their values and life-style, if they are dissatisfied with the current situation, and if change does not require undue effort (Becker et al., 1981; Darley & Beniger, 1981).

Though we sometimes overlook the fact, we need not feel bound to accept unpleasant or inconvenient surroundings with passive resignation. Even third-grade students can learn to redesign their classrooms to create a more livable environment for themselves (van Wagenberg et al., 1981). In a hospital setting, Becker and Poe (1980) asked employees, patients, and visitors for suggestions about design changes for one of the wings. Alterations were then made, following the suggestions: a fresh coat of paint, the addition of murals and wall hangings, improved lighting, carpeting for the nurses' station, and better furniture for visitors. These changes resulted in improved morale for patients and staff; a generally more positive mood prevailed. In addition, the health care was viewed as being of higher quality, and the public areas were used more during the evening hours. Thus, with a little prompting, the users of the environment were able to suggest changes that resulted in a much more pleasant and livable environmental setting.

To sum up, it has repeatedly been found that, with increased awareness and with encouragement to assume responsibility, individuals are able to take significant steps toward environmental improvement.

Presumably, whether an individual is happy on the job should be related both to productivity and to general contentment in life (Rice et al., 1980). In the **Applied Side** section on pages 520–521, a specific cause of problems (time schedules) and possible solutions will be explored. First, we will look at the general issues involved in **job satisfaction.**

Achieving Job Satisfaction and Assessing Its Effects

Presumably, workers who are most satisfied with their jobs lead happier lives and perform better for their employers. Research indicates a gradual decline in job satisfaction among American workers in recent years (Smith et al., 1977). Most members of the job force, especially blue-collar workers, feel that they would be happier working at a different job (Kahn, 1972).

What factors enter into job satisfaction? There is no one simple answer (Frances & Lebras, 1982), but satisfaction increases with good working conditions and wages (Berger & Cummings, 1978), freedom to make decisions about one's activities and work schedules (Locke, 1976; Walton, 1972), and an absence of close and sometimes arbitrary supervision (Ilgen et al., 1975). Flexible time schedules (or **flexitime**) are found to reduce absenteeism but not necessarily to increase job satisfaction (Narayanan & Nath, 1982). Such flexible schedules are nevertheless especially important for families in which both husband and wife work, single-parent families, and those who only want to work part-time (Stetson, 1981).

Job enlargement appears to help—designing jobs so as to increase the number and variety of tasks performed (Aldag & Brief, 1979). Such enrichment at Sweden's Volvo plant was well received by both labor and management, and it led to an improvement in quality, though a lower rate of productivity (Gyllenhammar, 1977). Whether with respect to money and other benefits or simply the way an individual is treated, the absolute conditions are not as crucial as *fairness* (T. R. Mitchell, 1979). People expect to receive equitable treatment.

It has also been found that satisfaction differs in public- and private-sector occupations (Smith & Nock, 1980). Blue-collar workers find the greatest job satisfaction in the public sector while white-collar workers are more satisfied in the private sector. It seems that there is a feeling of security and respect in

FIGURE 13.18   *Job commitment: Identifying with the organization.*

Since job commitment is one component of job satisfaction, any organizational activity that increases such commitment benefits both the employees and the employer. Many Japanese firms have led the world in this respect by providing job security, identification with the company, and a general sensitivity to employees' deepest needs and concerns. [Source: Photo © Fred Mayer 1980/Woodfin Camp and Associates.]

blue-collar government jobs, but those in white-collar positions feel frustrated in that setting. A Canadian study found that a large proportion of white-collar workers expressed a desire for more feedback, the opportunity for growth and development, and the chance to participate in decisions affecting their work (Srinivas, 1981).

An essential element in job satisfaction is **job commitment** (Coombs, 1979). A worker is committed to an occupation to the extent that he or she feels involved, loyal, and able to identify with the company. Commitment increases when workers have a high need to achieve and are given some degree of responsibility in the firm. Commitment is also enhanced by the company's success and by symbols and activities that involve identification. Japanese firms have traditionally done an excellent job in creating such commitment (see Figure 13.18), and some American companies have borrowed their techniques. For example, Tupperware dealers are brought together weekly for rallies at which they sing, receive awards, learn about new products, and play games (Kupferberg, 1980). The effects of job characteristics on involvement are very similar across cultures as different as India and the United States (Sekaran & Mowday, 1981).

Commitment and job satisfaction can pay off, not only in human terms, but in efficiency and profits as well. Satisfied employees are absent from work less frequently, and worker turnover is lower. A study of a large bank indicated that even a small increase in worker satisfaction led to a savings of $20,000 to $30,000 each year (Mirvis & Lawler, 1977). There is not, however, the general relationship between satisfaction and productivity in all situations that one might expect (Locke, 1976). For a variety of reasons, nevertheless, most of us would prefer to see job satisfaction maximized (Lawler, 1982).

ON THE
APPLIED SIDE

Time, Schedules, and Circadian Principles

Though it is difficult to believe, as recently as one hundred years ago most people were not ruled by clocks, watches, and schedules (Bell, 1975). Instead, lives were ordered by the sun, the cock crowing, and the passing seasons. The coming of the railroad created a need for precise time, and the factory created a need for schedules and time clocks that applied to worker and manager alike. In 1876, the wind-up clock was invented in Connecticut, and life was never the same again. Once time became a precious commodity, organized workers eventually struck to reduce work to an eight-hour day (1886) and a forty-hour week (1940).

While most of us have more or less adjusted to the demands of working approximately eight hours a day, five days a week, the need for many industries and emergency services is for around-the-clock operations. A little over one-fourth of the U.S. work force is exposed to some rescheduling of time as a consequence (Czeisler et al., 1982). The possible solutions to that demand are to have some workers on the job in the daytime and others at night (though not very many want the night shift) or to rotate shifts. The difficulty with rotation is that human beings have a biological system governing their hours of sleeping and waking known as the **circadian principle**. This simply means that our bodies have evolved to function in twenty-four-hour cycles, the length of the earth's daily rotation. Within this daily rhythm, many bodily functions such as temperature and kidney output are regu-

lated (Perry, 1982). When workers are placed on rotating shifts, circadian principles tend to be violated, and the result is dissatisfaction, health problems, increased turnover, and lowered productivity. Shifting of schedules can be carried out without major disruption if the shifts are delayed as long as possible. This allows the body to reset its "clock" gradually. Thus, when workers who change shifts every week were compared with workers who shifted every twenty-one days, the second group reported much greater job satisfaction and their health record was superior. In addition, the turnover rate was lower and productivity higher.

There are even more serious possible problems with disrupted circadian cycles (Perry, 1982). Since the body normally hits its low ebb between 3 and 5 A.M., a newly shifted night worker is relatively inefficient during these hours until his or her body has adjusted. It is noteworthy that the accident at the Three Mile Island nuclear plant occurred at 4 A.M. with a crew that had just recently rotated to the night shift. Similarly, it is found that when police officers rotate weekly, their judgmental errors increase, and it is more difficult for them to reason in emergencies.

If rotating shifts create problems in the work force, consider for a moment the problem encountered in the jet age with airline personnel. The rapid change in time zones has effects as negative as the rapid changes in work shifts. When a person travels at jet speed toward the west, it becomes

Appraising Job Performance:
Attribution Processes in an Organizational Setting

In the discussion of attribution theory in Chapter 2, we pointed out that each of us tends to explain the behavior of others in terms of internal and external causes. In a job situation, exactly the same processes operate when one individual must evaluate the performance of another (see Figure 13.19 on page

TABLE 13.3   Jet lag: Countering circadian disruption.

The disruption of circadian processes *caused by rapid air travel can be minimized by the anti-jet-lag diet, developed by Dr. Charles Ehret at the Argonne National Laboratory. It is used by airline personnel, those who must fly for business, and the Army's rapid-deployment forces. [Source: Adapted from Perry, 1982.]*

Recommendations for jet travelers crossing time zones

(1)   Eat lightly the day before a long flight. Stick to a low-calorie, low-carbohydrate diet such as eggs, cottage cheese, fish, salad, consommé, and fruit.

(2)   When you board the plane, set your watch for the time zone to which you are flying and behave according to that time. Thus, eat and sleep when it is appropriate for the time zone indicated on your watch.

(3)   On the plane and at your destination, stick to a high-protein breakfast and lunch and a high-carbohydrate dinner for the first day or two.

(4)   Go to bed early in your new time zone.

earlier in the day than is true for his or her bodily clock. Travel toward the east has the opposite effect; it becomes later relative to bodily rhythms. Adaptation to this jet lag is more rapid after westbound travel than after eastbound travel (Czeisler et al., 1982). It is speculated that a circadian problem might lead to plane crashes, such as one in Mexico City in 1979 at an early morning hour. The crew was warned to avoid a particular runway that was closed for repairs, but the pilot tried to land there anyway (Perry, 1982). Less dramatic, but of equal potential seriousness, are the countless instances in which judgment and efficiency are impaired among those passengers who must fly as part of their occupations—individuals in business, government, sports, and entertainment. There are remedies that can help with this problem, as outlined in Table 13.3. These procedures were developed at the Argonne National Laboratory and have proven useful to numerous business travelers as well as vacationers. A special group for which these recommendations are a must are the members of the U.S. Army's rapid-deployment forces. The success of the delayed rotation of shift workers and of the anti-jet-lag diet indicate that, though it may not be nice to fool Mother Nature, sometimes it is necessary.

522). It is not simply a matter of how well or how badly the worker carried out a given task; there is also the evaluator's perception of the *reasons* for such a performance. Suppose, for example, that one employee is a hard worker who puts in long hours selling a store's products, while a relatively lazy co-worker happens to wait on a wealthy customer who makes an extremely large purchase. At the end of the day, the two salespeople have taken in about the same amount of money for the store. Which one would you prefer to have as an employee?

FIGURE 13.19   Evaluating performance: Attributing causes to internal versus external factors.

When the performance of others is evaluated, attribution processes tend to operate. In general, greater value is placed on behavior resulting from internal factors such as ability or effort. Further, effort has more impact on evaluation than ability. [Source: Photo © Joan Liftin 1980 / Archive Pictures Inc.]

Which one would be in line for a larger raise? Most of us would lean toward the hardworking individual despite the fact that both brought in a good daily profit.

In general, someone's performance is evaluated more favorably if it can be attributed to internal factors such as ability or effort rather than to external factors such as luck or the ease of the task. When performance is bad, the same factors enter into the appraisal of the person's failure. There is less negative evaluation attached to a poor performance that rests on bad luck or a difficult task than when the same performance is attributed to lack of talent or inadequate effort.

Because we are generally more likely to assign internal causes to the behavior of others, supervisors tend to give more credit than is due to a good performance and assign more blame than is fair to a poor performance. This bias can be overcome by making sure that supervisors gain experience in carrying out the task in question. Once they discover firsthand that situational factors can affect performance, they are less likely to explain everything in terms of internal causes (Mitchell & Kalb, 1982).

There is a further distinction that is made in evaluating job performance. With respect to internal causes, evaluators are more impressed by effort than by ability. Such differentiation has been shown in research in which subjects observed the performance of confederates who were good, average, or poor at their work (Knowlton & Mitchell, 1980). Information was provided as to the ability of the "workers" and the amount of effort they put into the task. It was found that the performance evaluations were more influenced by effort than by ability. That is, a good performance attributed to effort is rated higher than the same performance attributed to ability. Similarly, a poor performance resting on lack of effort is judged more negatively than one caused by lack of ability. You might keep in mind that those who evaluate you are likely to be impressed more by what you actually do on the job than by whatever talent you bring with you.

It should be clear that the application of social psychological principles to organizational problems is useful in providing better understanding of human behavior in that context and in suggesting ways to overcome ineffective or biased decisions.

Summary

Applied social psychology is social-psychological research and practice in real-world settings directed toward the understanding of human social behavior and the attempted solution of social problems.

Interest in the psychological aspects of the legal system has a long history and has resulted in the development of training programs in **forensic psychology.** A great deal of research has established the inaccuracy of eyewitness testimony regarding a crime, but some alterations in procedure (for example, group discussion among eyewitnesses) can greatly improve the usefulness of such testimony. Attorneys' influence on jury decisions begins with their opening statements (varying in such respects as length and claims of evidence to come), includes the specific words they use in questioning witnesses, and is especially powerful in an adversarial trial setting. The judge decides on the relevance of testimony and other evidence (though any instructions to disregard material may not be effective), and the final charge to the jury can affect the verdict. Decisions about a defendant are influenced by his or her behavior on the stand, drinking history, invocation of Fifth Amendment rights, physical attractiveness, race, and whether the jury likes the individual. In addition, juror decisions are influenced by their personality characteristics such as **authoritarianism,** general attitudes about law and order, and attitudes about the crime in question. Beyond the courtroom, evaluation research has been applied in such areas as determining the effectiveness of programs to fight neighborhood crime.

Behavioral medicine refers to a wide array of psychological applications related to physical health. In the field of preventive medicine, there are studies of individual differences associated with good health practices, including adherence to exercise programs, diets, and dental hygiene practices. A great deal of effort has been expended in successful programs designed to persuade teenagers not to begin smoking cigarettes. Health can be impaired by various stresses that occur in everyday life, especially those that are unpleasant and represent a loss of **perceived control** over events plus undesirable events for which the individual feels responsible. Some individuals are more stress-resistant than others, and social support can be extremely helpful. The relationship between a patient and a medical practitioner is enhanced by the same variables that lead to interpersonal attraction. Patients want to be liked and to be provided with factual information. Institutions such as hospitals can be less threatening if information about procedures, etc., is provided beforehand through the use of filmed models, for example. Institutionalization for the elderly can be devastating, but not if there is encouragement of self-reliance, responsibility, and control. Individuals need not be passive recipients of environmental influences, and our behavior can have beneficial effects on the environment.

Organizational behavior refers to the study of what people do in organizational settings. The early emphasis in this field was **scientific management** that concentrated on standardized tools, personnel selection, efficient performance, and monetary incentives for workers. It gradually became clear that people have additional needs, and the **human relations** approach emphasizes the importance of respect, security, autonomy, and a feeling that one's job is meaningful. Though **job satisfaction** is not a perfect predictor of productivity, it is a goal that tends to benefit both employer and employees. Besides good working conditions and suitable wages, satisfaction is increased by providing flexible schedules, freedom to make decisions, more divergent tasks per job, equitable treatment, and any other features that promote **job commitment.** It is also found that the evaluation of job performance is strongly affected by the attributions made as to the internal and external causes of success and failure. Around-the-clock schedules in many organizations are necessary, but the rotation of workers from shift to shift causes serious problems by disrupting their **circadian processes.** These problems can be overcome by such procedures as making shifts every twenty-one days rather than weekly and by altering one's diet and activity pattern.

Glossary

applied social psychology *Social-psychological research and practice in real-world settings directed toward the understanding of human social behavior and the attempted solution of social problems.*

authoritarianism *The personality dimension that ranges from the authoritarian personality to the egalitarian personality. Authoritarians are characterized by adherence to conventional values, submission to a strong leader, aggression toward those who deviate, and a concern with power.*

behavioral medicine *The study and practice involving the psychological aspects of the prevention and treatment of physical illness.*

circadian principle *The twenty-four-hour bodily cycle that consists of regular variations in sleeping, wakefulness, body temperature, and kidney production.*

egalitarianism *The opposite personality extreme from authoritarianism. It is characterized by a democratic approach to the role of leaders, tolerance for deviant ideas and appearance, disinterest in power, and a concern for the free expression of ideas and feelings.*

evaluation research *Research designed to determine the effects of any program involving social intervention with respect to its costs, benefits, and impact on individuals.*

flexitime *The policy that permits employees to arrange their work schedules at hours convenient to them while maintaining the same total number of working hours.*

forensic psychology *The study of the relationship between psychology and the law. This includes eyewitness reliability, and factors involving* *attorneys, judges, defendants, victims, and jurors.*

human relations *An approach to management and organizational behavior that recognizes the importance of a variety of human needs in the work setting.*

job commitment *The extent to which an individual feels loyal to the organization for which he or she works and feels identified and involved with it.*

job enlargement *The practice of expanding the content of a job so as to include more different and varied tasks for each worker.*

job satisfaction *The extent to which a worker is content with his or her position in an organization, the work conditions, compensation, and general treatment relative to others in the organization.*

organizational behavior *Refers to the field that studies human behavior in organizational settings. It includes attention to individual processes, group processes, and organizational structure and function.*

perceived control *The extent to which an individual believes that he or she is able to influence the course of events.*

scientific management *An early approach to management and organizational behavior that emphasized the importance of designing jobs and tasks efficiently and of using monetary incentives to motivate workers.*

Stockholm syndrome *The tendency of hostages to identify with their captors and to express negative attitudes toward their rescuers. The name is based on an incident in Sweden involving the reactions of the captives in a bank robbery.*

For More Information

Baron, R. A. *Behavior in organizations.* Boston: Allyn and Bacon, 1983.
A comprehensive and up-to-date introduction to the field of organizational behavior. It describes how basic psychological principles such as learning, personality, perception, attitudes, and motivation are relevant to behavior in the organizational setting. Also covered are the work-related aspects of stress, communication, decision making, group behavior, leadership, and various aspects of organizational structure and functioning.

Eiser, J. R. (Ed.). *Social psychology and behavioral medicine.* New York: Wiley, 1982.
The broad scope of the field of behavioral medicine is encompassed by this collection of original chapters by experts in the field. Included are sections dealing with theory and research involving the psychological aspects of coronary-prone behavior, accidents, cancer, smoking, alcohol abuse, drug dependence, providing medical information to patients, and reactions to illness, surgery, aging, and death.

Ellison, K. W., & Buckhout, R. *Psychology and criminal justice.* New York: Harper & Row, 1981.
This textbook deals with the wide range of psychological applications in the legal system. Among the many topics covered are jury selection, eyewitness testimony, crime victims, the training of police, expert witnesses, and capital punishment.

Saxe, L., & Fine, M. *Social experiments: Methods for design and evaluation.* Beverly Hills, Calif.: Sage, 1981.
This is an excellent description of the way in which research methodology is applied to the evaluation of social programs. Included are illustrations of such research in areas including education, health care, and criminal justice.

CHAPTER 14

Personality and Social Behavior:
The Role of Individual Differences

Personality Traits: Stable Characteristics across Situations

Personality and Behavior: The Ups and Downs of a Concept/Identifying and Measuring Personality Variables/Predicting Behavior with Personality Variables

Loneliness: Those Who Feel Left out of Social Interactions

Measuring Loneliness and Describing Lonely Individuals/All the Lonely People: Where Do They All Come From?/The Effect of Loneliness on Behavior

The Type A-Type B Personality Dimension: Who Succeeds and Who Survives?

The Type A Behavior Pattern and Its Development/Contrasting Responses of Type A and Type B Individuals

Locus of Control: Assigning Responsibility for Life's Outcomes

Generalized Expectancies about Obtaining Rewards and Avoiding Punishments/ Internality versus Externality: A Pervasive Influence on Behavior

Special Inserts

FOCUS ON RESEARCH
Personality and Auto Accidents: Characteristics of DWI Offenders

ON THE APPLIED SIDE
Overcoming Shyness and Increasing Sociability

ON THE APPLIED SIDE
Reducing Coronary Heart Disease by Altering Personality Patterns

Dave and Wendy were planning to get married after a whirlwind romance. They had been attracted to one another from the very beginning, and both individuals soon felt certain that they were in love. He had just joined a large business firm and seemed to have a bright future. She was completing a graduate degree in chemistry and had equally promising prospects. They went out a lot, enjoyed the same movies, and felt a very strong and mutual physical attraction. After knowing each other only two months, they decided to set a wedding date.

Shortly before the big day, they visited Dave's parents who lived in a rambling suburban house. Dave opened the front door without knocking, and a noisy, confusing scene greeted them. His parents were busy carrying food and drinks into the family room. Two couples from the neighborhood were playing an electronic game on the television set. One of Dave's younger sisters periodically ran in and out of the back door with a friend. After introductions were made, Dave and Wendy filled their plates, buffet style, and sat on pillows while still more friends, neighbors, and family members wandered in casually to join the gathering. There were even three people in the corner whom no one seemed to know.

In this growing hubbub, Dave was obviously having the time of his life. His eyes glowed with pleasure at this scene of friendly social interaction. He liked being with people, and the informal atmosphere felt just right to him. She tried to hide it, but Wendy was miserable. She liked being isolated with someone she cared for such as Dave or even the two of them with a couple of close friends, but this crowded scene was an unpleasant disaster in her view. In fact, she much preferred being alone in her apartment with a good book and her stereo than trying to make small talk with this hoard of strangers.

Dave said, "Isn't this fun? I hope our home can be this friendly and full of joy." Wendy didn't know what to say. Her dreams of the two of them living quietly in some secluded spot no longer seemed very realistic. She began to think the unthinkable: "Maybe we should wait a while on the wedding and get to know one another a little better." Dave could see that she was unhappy, and he, too, began to have doubts.

What these two individuals were discovering is the fact that different people can react in very different ways to the same social situation. We differ from one another in genetic makeup, in our childhood experiences, and in many variations in culture, social class, race, religion, and other factors that have helped determine who we are. The end result is that each of us possesses relatively lasting dispositions that are known as personality characteristics or **traits.** Despite the power of the situational factors to which we all respond, variations in our behavior are often found to be associated with relevant traits.

TABLE 14.1   *Personality variables: An integral component of social behavior.*

Throughout this text, the effect of individual differences on social behavior has been pointed out. The examples presented here should serve as reminders of how often social psychologists find it useful to concentrate on both *situational variables and personality characteristics.*

Social behavior	Relevant personality variables	Relationship discussed in chapter no.
Nonverbal communication	Expressiveness and masculinity-femininity	2
Persuasibility	Need for social approval and self-esteem	4
Bigotry	Racial prejudice and authoritarianism	5
Interpersonal interactions	Need for affiliation	6
Helping others	Fear of embarrassment, need for approval, and dispositional empathy	8
Cheating	Ability to delay gratification, sociopathy, interpersonal trust, and chronic self-destructiveness	8
Competitiveness in games	Type A personality pattern	10
Social exchange and effectiveness as liar	Machiavellianism	10
Leadership	Need for power	11
Jury decisions	Authoritarianism	13

Throughout this book, we have noted the ways in which certain traits can be used to predict individual differences in response to particular situations. On the basis of earlier chapters, you might remember how various social behaviors were found to be influenced not only by situational variables but *also* by personality characteristics. Look at Table 14.1 for a brief summary of some of these social-personality relationships. It can be seen that responses to stimulus events are often *mediated* by personality factors. As a result, behavior can best be predicted by combining what we know about the effects of the situation with what we know about the specific individual.

In the present chapter, we will take a closer look at a representative sample of such personality variables and the ways in which they affect social behavior. Specifically, attention will be focused on *loneliness* and the accompanying reactions to the difficulties of forming friendships; *coronary-prone behavior* and its effect on performance, interpersonal behavior, and health; and *locus of control* as a fundamental set of assumptions as to whether one's fate rests on internal or external factors. In addition, we will examine the personality characteristics of those guilty of *driving while intoxicated,* ways to overcome *shyness* and increase *sociability,* and procedures to reduce the risk of *coronary heart disease* through *personality change.*

Personality Traits:
Stable Characteristics across Situations

As was explained in Chapter 1, *social psychology* is defined as the scientific field that seeks to comprehend the nature and causes of individual behavior in social situations. Traditionally, this meant studying the ways in which specific classes of stimulus events affect human behavior. A closely related field, *personality psychology*, concentrates its interest on the ways in which people differ in their responses to a given stimulus. More specifically, **personality** is defined as the relatively enduring characteristics of an individual that are expressed in a variety of situations. Personality variables represent what the individual brings to the situation, while social variables are represented in the situation itself. These two fields of psychology are not in conflict; they both strive to predict human behavior, and they simply represent different approaches to the same goal.

Before we describe the ways in which personality variables are identified, measured, and used in research, we will discuss a long-standing controversy involving their usefulness in predicting human behavior.

Personality and Behavior:
The Ups and Downs of a Concept

Historically, personality psychologists (and many others) assumed that human behavior was largely a function of stable internal characteristics (Sampson, 1977). For this reason, people could be expected to behave consistently from situation to situation and from year to year. A woman who was sociable at the office was assumed to be equally sociable wherever she went. A hostile boy was assumed to grow into a hostile man. William James (1950) suggested that, by the age of thirty, a person's characteristics were "set like plaster," never to soften again.

This view of behavior led to the development of numerous personality tests in the first half of this century. These *global measures* were designed to detect as much as possible about an individual's basic personality, and this knowledge would presumably be useful in predicting how he or she would behave in response to quite varied stimulus conditions. Such measures ranged from *projective tests* using ambiguous materials including ink blots (Rorschach, 1921) and drawings (Morgan & Murray, 1938) to *objective tests* asking for true-false responses to a long list of statements (Hathaway & McKinley, 1940). The general concept was an appealing one: personality assessment seemingly would be able to provide a way to predict what individuals would do under a variety of quite different conditions.

Doubts about personality traits: Situational factors as determinants of behavior. Personality tests gained wide popularity in applied settings ranging from mental hospitals to industrial organizations, and they were the object of intensive research. Disappointing results gradually led many critics to express doubts about the utility of this entire approach. One of the most influential was Julian Rotter (1954, p. 334) who reviewed the work done with personality measures

FIGURE 14.1   The situation as the crucial determinant of human behavior.

An emphasis on the importance of situational variables points to the power of external factors in influencing our feelings and our actions. The gentleman shown here obviously behaves one way in his office during the work day and quite differently at home in the evening. [Source: Drawing by M. Stevens; ©1982 The New Yorker Magazine, Inc.]

and concluded, "The very best techniques we have are of doubtful validity for predicting the specific behavior of any person in a particular situation."

One response to such a devastating conclusion was an attempt to build better tests. A more revolutionary decision was reached by one of Rotter's former students, Walter Mischel. In a series of publications, he argued that any theory of human behavior based on the concept of traits is inadequate because behavior is simply not consistent across situations (Mischel, 1968, 1977). As with the man depicted in Figure 14.1, how we feel and how we act are determined more by external variables than by internal ones. The possibility was raised that a belief in the consistency of behavior was only an illusion (Schweder, 1975). For example, studies of people over a twenty-year span reveal little behavioral consistency from one time period to another. A counter-argument is that consistency is greater over a shorter period of time (Schaie & Parham, 1976), if larger samples of behavior are observed on each occasion (Epstein, 1979), and if multiple situations are included (Moskowitz, 1982).

One implication of the "situational revolution" in the field of personality was the possibility that the traditional approach of social psychology had been correct all along. Perhaps behavior *could* best be predicted by focusing attention on social situations. An ironic difficulty with that view was that social psychologists were becoming increasingly interested in the role of personality traits in influencing social behavior (Blass, 1977). In fact, it appears that the situation *alone* is no more powerful in predicting behavior than are traits alone (Funder & Ozer, 1983). How might these discrepancies be resolved?

Integrating social and personality psychology. Probably the most accurate assessment of the debate about personality versus situation is to conclude that both approaches are valuable and that both are improved by a greater attention to the *specific* situations in which *specific* personality traits operate (Pervin, 1976). We know that traits play a role in determining social behavior. The question is: how do we decide what traits might be important in which situations? A good deal of recent research provides some useful guidelines in this respect.

(1) *The more narrow and limited the trait, the better it is likely to be in predicting behavior.* Instead of relying on very broad characteristics, much of the current interest in traits is directed at very circumscribed aspects of individual behavior. Thus, investigators may find it difficult to relate general, abstract variables such as extraversion to actual behavior in a given situation. With a narrow trait such as energetic behavior, however, there is much greater success. Individuals who engage actively in exercising, swimming, running, and other sports are perceived as *energetic* by their friends, by experimental observers, and by themselves (McGowan & Gormly, 1976). With such specification, consistency across situations clearly occurs.

(2) *Some people are consistent on certain traits; other people are consistent on others.* Rather than seeking universal consistency, Kenrick and Stringfield (1980) propose that personality consistency can be found if we realize that not everyone is equally consistent-inconsistent on the same characteristics. To test this hypothesis, they asked subjects to select those traits on which they were most and least consistent across situations. For example, how consistent are *you* with respect to being emotional, friendly, shy, suspicious, or self-assured? It was found that only on dimensions identified as high in consistency for a particular person was there close agreement among parents, friends, and self about the individual's behavior. In addition, across traits, some people are simply more consistent than others, and hence their behavior can more easily be predicted by the use of personality measures (Bem & Allen, 1974).

(3) *The less powerful the situational pressures, the greater the influence of personality traits.* Monson et al. (1982) have suggested a simple yet important rule for deciding when traits can and cannot be used to predict behavior. When an external factor has a strong effect on most people (e.g., attitude similarity and liking, Chapter 6), it is difficult to find any traits that affect this response. On the other hand, with weak or conflicting external pressures (e.g., classroom cheating, Chapter 8), several specific traits are related to what individuals do.

Altogether, the debates about personality versus the situation seem to have led to an improved conception of the way in which the two classes of variables operate and how they can be integrated as predictors of behavior. With this integration of personality and social psychology in mind, let us now turn to the question of how personality variables are measured and how they are used in correlational and experimental research.

Identifying and Measuring Personality Variables

You might wonder how psychologists have identified the traits or dimensions along which people differ (Hogan et al., 1977). Most trait names originated in informal observations that influenced our language long before there was a science of behavior. In a classic study back in 1936, Allport and Odbert went through the dictionary and discovered close to 20,000 English words that describe differences among people. Since many of these words overlap in meaning, they were able to reduce the list to 171 *different* terms. To date, no one

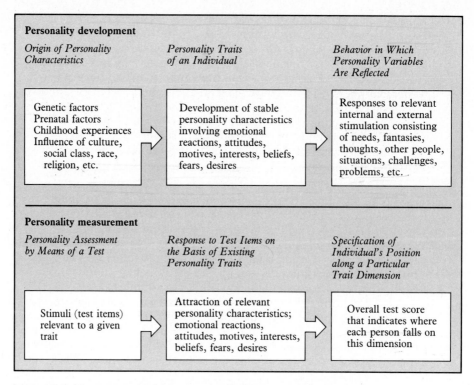

FIGURE 14.2   *The development and assessment of personality traits.*

Individual differences in personality characteristics are presumably brought about by a variety of background factors ranging from genetic determinants to cultural influences. In order to utilize these differences in predicting behavior, it is necessary to develop personality tests. Test scores are assumed to reflect relatively stable dispositions, and these scores can be used to assist in the prediction of responses to particular situations.

has attempted to measure all of these dimensions. Instead, the typical pattern has been to identify a single trait that is of theoretical or applied interest and then to construct a test that assesses this characteristic. The general way in which traits develop and the rationale behind their measurement are outlined in Figure 14.2.

There are a number of ways in which to approach the measurement of a trait, but one example should provide the general idea. In the 1930s and 1940s, fascist ideology was gaining in popularity in many parts of the world, as represented by Mussolini in Italy, Franco in Spain, Hitler in Germany, and numerous military dictatorships from Latin America to Japan. Among the results of this political movement were World War II, genocide, and oppressive totalitarian governments. After the war, a group of psychologists decided that there must be a basic personality trait that leads an individual to accept such a belief system and way of life (see Figure 14.3). Essentially, the measurement procedure consisted of trying to express as test items the kinds of attitudes and values that are held by fascists (Adorno et al., 1950). Without going into detail,

FIGURE 14.3 *Understanding the Nazi movement by means of a personality trait.*

When large numbers of people reveal attitudes, beliefs, or actions that differentiate them from others, a personality trait is often sought to explain this behavior and to predict its occurrence in the future. The Nazi movement in Germany in the 1930s and 1940s led psychologists to propose that the trait of authoritarianism *could be a meaningful approach to understanding the phenomenon, and the* F Scale *was constructed to measure this aspect of personality. [Source: Charles Harbutt/Archive Pictures, Inc.]*

the authoritarianism scale was built by first giving these preliminary items to large numbers of people. Then, each item was evaluated as to whether it correlated with the other items and hence could serve as one unit on the trait measure. Items that did not show this pattern were either rewritten for a second try or eliminated as unrelated to the trait (Byrne & Kelley, 1981). Several such **item analyses** resulted in a widely used personality measure that assesses the trait of **authoritarianism;** the test is known as the **F Scale,** with F standing for fascism. Among the successful test items that make up the final scale are such statements as:

> What the youth need most is strict discipline, rugged determination, and the will to work and fight for family and country.
> Obedience and respect for authority are the most important virtues children should learn.

Once such a measure has been constructed, there are two primary ways in which it is evaluated. A useful test is one that has acceptable **reliability** and **validity.** Reliability refers to the *consistency* with which any instrument measures a variable. Thus, a test is reliable if the various items measure the same construct (that is, if responses on each item are highly correlated with responses on all the other items) and if test responses are stable over time (that is, an individual receives the same score when tested on different occasions). Many studies have established that the F Scale is a reliable measuring device. Validity refers to whether the test measures what it is supposed to. Most personality tests are evaluated with respect to **construct validity.** This term refers to the series of relationships that are established between test scores and other theoretically relevant responses. There is no single criterion that could be used as *the* index of authoritarianism, so construct validity is based on whether the test is related to a great many things that make theoretical sense. For example, individuals who obtain high scores on the F Scale are found to be raised in traditional, restrictive families (Kagitcibasi, 1970), to be politically conservative (Byrne & Przybyla, 1980), to believe what authority figures tell them (Levy, 1979), to aggress against low-status victims (Epstein, 1965), and to be negative about sex and the violation of sexual norms (Garcia & Griffitt, 1977). In other words, these and other studies provide good evidence for the construct validity of the test in that F Scale scores are related to various kinds of behavior in a way that is consistent with the theory of authoritarianism.

For some traits, it has been found that further statistical analysis is useful to subdivide the trait into a series of related traits. For example, you might consider differences in how people interact with other people. It might seem, offhand, that individuals are relatively friendly or relatively distant and that an interpersonal trait of friendliness might be a meaningful construct. Research by Wiggins (1978) has shown, however, that interpersonal behavior is best considered as involving a series of eight personality traits that consist of such characteristics as gregariousness, dominance, arrogance, coldness, aloofness, laziness, unassumingness, and warmth. In this instance, eight different tests were constructed to assess these different aspects of how people interact with others (see Figure 14.4).

As a final word about identifying and measuring traits, you should know that not every proposal about traits is successful. Sometimes what seems to be a perfectly reasonable observation about the existence of a trait turns out to be incorrect. Suppose, for example, that a psychologist decides that people differ in their response to round objects and that it would be useful to construct a measure of *roundism*. He then makes up a large number of test items having to do with attitudes about baseballs, ball bearings, green peas, tires, pebbles, cantaloupes, and the moon. Do you think it is probable that he will end up with a reliable, valid measure of a new trait?

FIGURE 14.4   *Interpersonal behavior: Multiple traits underlie individual differences.*

In some situations, a series of related traits must be considered simultaneously. For example, Wiggins (1978) found that interpersonal behavior differs along eight dimensions: gregariousness, dominance, arrogance, coldness, aloofness, laziness, unassumingness, and warmth. [Source: Bill Burke/Archive Pictures, Inc.]

Predicting Behavior with Personality Variables

Once a trait has been identified and a test has been constructed to measure it, this variable can be used in research. In some instances, the research involves an examination of the *correlation* between test scores and some other behavior. For example, if anxiety is found to be negatively correlated with grades in school, this means that those individuals who score *highest* on this personality dimension tend to receive the *lowest* grades (and vice versa). Such research is sometimes referred to as the study of *response-response relationships* because test responses are correlated with some other behavioral response. In the **Focus on Research** panel on pages 538–539, one such investigation is described in greater detail.

In social psychology, much of the research is *experimental* in design in that a stimulus variable is manipulated, and its effect on a response variable is determined. This type of investigation yields *stimulus-response relationships.* When these two approaches are combined and integrated, behavior is almost always predicted more accurately than when attention is directed *only* at traits or *only* at stimulus variables (Cronbach, 1957). As we suggested earlier, this integrated research is conducted with increasing frequency (Sarason et al., 1981), and its design is shown graphically in Figure 14.5. The personality variable in this sort of experiment is often described as *moderating* or *mediating* the effect of the stimulus on the response.

As an example of this approach, consider one of the relationships discussed in Chapter 6. Many propinquity studies have indicated that the distance be-

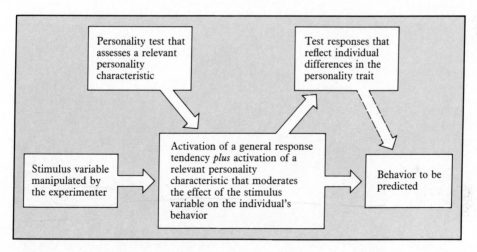

FIGURE 14.5 *Integrative research using both social and personality variables.*

*To an increasing extent, research is designed to combine the traditional social psychological emphasis on the effect of situational (or stimulus) variables on behavior and the traditional personality psychological emphasis on the relationship between test scores and behavior. The result is experimentation in which behavior is predicted more accurately because **both** situational and personality factors are considered simultaneously.*

FOCUS
ON RESEARCH

Personality and Auto Accidents: Characteristics of DWI Offenders

There is growing concern about the problem of automobiles being driven by those who are drunk. The usual solution to attempt to reduce the incidence of driving while intoxicated (DWI) is to pass laws that punish those who are caught by means of larger fines, longer jail sentences, and stiffer restrictions on the person's right to drive. Drunk drivers pose a serious threat to themselves and to innocent bystanders, and many of those arrested on DWI charges are later diagnosed as alcoholics (O'Leary et al., 1976). Rather than simply punishing these individuals after an accident has brought them to the attention of the police (see Figure 14.6), the possibility of prevention has been explored by seeking common personality characteristics shared by those who drive while drunk. It has been found that those arrested for DWI have distinctive drinking problems in that they drink more frequently and

more heavily, experience more negative effects from drinking, and are more likely to use alcohol to reduce tension than is true of others who consume alcohol (Donovan, 1980). Thus, they might be expected to be similar on various personality traits. Research was undertaken to identify the relevant variables.

A large number of males who had been arrested on DWI charges were studied by Donovan and Marlatt (1982). Each subject was given a series of questionnaires designed to assess the kinds of factors hypothesized to be related to problem drinking behavior. The items dealt with each man's general background, behavior related to drinking itself, attitudes about driving, and a number of personality scales. Statistical analysis of their responses revealed that the group could actually be divided into five subgroups, based on their test responses. These

FIGURE 14.6 The menace of DWI: Using personality tests to identify those who pose a risk.

Intoxicated drivers account for the majority of serious automobile accidents. An individual who is arrested for driving while intoxicated can obviously be punished, but this ordinarily occurs after an accident has taken place. It would be preferable to identify such individuals before their drinking and driving actions threaten anyone's safety. The use of personality measures provides a possible way to approach the problem by spotting such drivers before they can cause accidents, injuries, and deaths. [Source: Ed Carlin/Frederic Lewis Photographers.]

**TABLE 14.2 Personality research:
Characteristics of high-risk drunken drivers.**

*Personality variables were found to differentiate males arrested for DWI, and
five subgroups were identified on the basis of their test scores. It may be seen
that these personality subgroups are associated with different levels of driving
while intoxicated and also with different accident records. The eventual goal of
this type of research is to identify the individuals posing the greatest risk by
administering personality tests as screening devices. Then efforts would be made
to modify their drinking behavior and the personality characteristics that
accompany it. [Source: Based on data from Donovan & Marlatt, 1982.]*

Risk level based on driving accidents and convictions	Days per month that they drive while intoxicated	Driving related accidents per year	Personality characteristics
High	11.7	.28	Aggressiveness while driving; competitive about speed; reckless when upset; high in sensation seeking, assaultiveness, hostility, and irritability; moderately depressed; emotionally unstable; low sense of control
Moderate	9.4	.13	High in depression and resentment; unassertive; low in emotional adjustment, sense of control, and sense of responsibility
Moderate	8.8	.14	Drives for tension reduction; low in depression, resentment, and sense of control
Low	7.0	.09	Assertive, high in emotional adjustment; low in depression
Low	5.8	.08	Assertive; high in emotional adjustment; low in depression

subgroups contained different kinds of individuals, and they differed in the risk they pose to themselves and others.

Though all of the subjects had been arrested on the same charge, two of the personality subgroups did not appear to contain particularly maladjusted individuals. In contrast, the other three groups revealed more disturbing characteristics. Police records confirmed that the personality differences were in fact related to the number of annual automobile accidents in which the drivers were involved. These five groups are described in Table 14.2, along with some of their related characteristics. Though the three highest risk groups are each dangerous on the road, it can be seen that they differ from one another with respect to personality traits. Even more unlike the others are the two lowest risk subgroups whose members are very similar in being assertive, emotionally adjusted, and free of depression.

The aim of this research is to make it possible to identify the drivers who are the greatest danger and then to attempt to alter their behavior. Thus, there are efforts to teach individuals how to control their drinking behavior (Brown, 1980) and to improve related personality problems such as depression, resentment, lack of assertiveness, and the perception that one's life is externally controlled (e.g., Lewinsohn et al., 1978; Novaco, 1975). Presumably, this approach to the DWI offender holds more promise of success than simply increasing the level of punishment for those who get caught.

tween seats in a classroom (stimulus variable) affects friendship formation (response variable). That is, the closer two people sit to one another, the more likely they are to get to know and like one another. The relationship is not a perfect one; for example, some individuals can sit side by side all semester and never even learn one another's name. This kind of exception to the general rule suggests the possibility that a personality variable is moderating the effect of propinquity on attraction. An obvious candidate would be *need for affiliation,* and we could test this possibility by administering a test to determine where each class member scores with respect to the desire to form friendships, to be with people, etc. If the hypothesis were correct, we could then say that friendship formation in such a setting is influenced by both propinquity and each individual's affiliation need.

Loneliness:
Those Who Feel Left out of Social Interactions

Long before psychologists came on the scene, observers of American behavior such as Alexis de Tocqueville noticed that **loneliness** was a common characteristic, with people "locked in the solitude of their own hearts" (quoted in Bernikow, 1982, p. 25). In recent studies of loneliness as a personality variable, the term refers primarily to the subjective experience of lacking close interpersonal relationships (Peplau & Perlman, 1982). Thus, a person can feel lonely and yet be surrounded by other people at work, in his or her living arrangements, and even in social settings. Interest in this characteristic has led to attempts to measure the feeling of loneliness, describe those who are lonely, determine how this state affects individuals at different stages of their lives, and examine the way in which loneliness has an influence on interpersonal behavior.

Measuring Loneliness
and Describing Lonely Individuals

The **UCLA Loneliness Scale** was developed by Russell et al. (1980) to assess individual differences in this trait, and some of the test items are shown in Table 14.3. As is often the case in constructing a test, the first step was to gather an initial sample of items that appeared to deal with the experience of loneliness. When these items were administered to various groups, statistical analyses indicated which statements were related to one another and which ones should be discarded as irrelevant (Russell, 1982). The final test is made up of twenty statements of the type presented in the table, and some that are worded in the reverse way (for example, "I have a lot in common with the people around me."). It was determined that the test is reliable in that it is internally consistent and relatively stable over time.

Some of the first investigations of its construct validity dealt with the relationship between scores on the Loneliness Scale and other personality characteristics (Russell, 1982). For example, college students attending a clinic group that dealt with loneliness scored much higher than a more general sample

TABLE 14.3   *Measuring loneliness: When a person feels isolated.*

These are sample items from the UCLA Loneliness Scale. *For each statement,*
subjects indicate how often they experience the particular feeling. The higher
the score an individual obtains, the stronger and more general is the person's
perceived loneliness. [Source: Adapted from Russell et al., 1980.]

	Never	*Rarely*	*Sometimes*	*Often*
(1) There is no one I can turn to.	1	2	3	4
(2) I feel left out.	1	2	3	4
(3) No one really knows me well.	1	2	3	4
(4) My social relationships are superficial.	1	2	3	4

of students enrolled in psychology courses. In addition, individuals who score high in loneliness also tend to report feeling depressed, anxious, dissatisfied, unhappy, and shy. Jones et al. (1981) found that loneliness is also associated with feeling self-conscious in public, social anxiety, low self-esteem, and a low level of altruism. Such findings, by the way, extend beyond the college population and also hold true for senior citizens (Perlman et al., 1978).

Test scores are correlated in the expected way with a number of specific behaviors such as the amount of time spent alone each day, the number of times an individual has dinner without a companion, and the number of weekends spent by oneself. In addition, those who score high in loneliness engage in fewer social activities, have fewer close friends, and are likely not to be dating (Russell et al., 1980).

Altogether, it appears that the UCLA Loneliness Scale is a reliable and valid measure of this personality characteristic. The next principal question deals with the origins of loneliness. Why are some people more lonely than others?

All the Lonely People:
Where Do They All Come From?

There is not yet much solid evidence as to the way in which particular childhood experiences bring about a lonely adulthood. Most human beings probably experience some degree of loneliness during their early years for reasons ranging from family relocation in new settings to an accident or illness that causes a period of enforced solitude. There are, however, some childhood experiences that seem especially likely to be linked to later interpersonal problems (see Figure 14.7, page 542).

When a child is lacking in social skills, loneliness is not likely to be merely a temporary problem (Rubin, 1982). There are several elements involved in making and keeping friendships, and children must learn how to join in a group's ongoing activities, how to provide some level of reinforcement for others during an interaction, how to deal with disagreements when they arise, and how to be sufficiently sensitive to the feelings of others (Putallaz & Gottman, 1981; Rubin, 1980). It has been proposed that nursery school is where

FIGURE 14.7   Childhood loneliness: Knowing how to make friends.

Children can experience loneliness for many reasons, as when a family moves and the child is suddenly "the new kid in town." In time, such situations tend to take care of themselves in that friendships form and strangers turn into familiar playmates. When the cause is lack of social skills, however, the isolation is likely to continue over the years. [Source: Photo ©Michael Hardy 1978/Woodfin Camp and Associates.]

such skills are developed and practiced because appropriate social behavior with peers is not likely to be acquired from one's parents or even one's siblings (Rubin, 1982). Thus, through trial and error, success and failure, each of us can learn what works in social settings. When the right skills are not learned, the result may be withdrawal and loneliness or an aggressive, bullying pattern of behavior. We described in Chapter 7 how such behavior leads to general aggressiveness. In either instance, the major hope for changing the inappropriate style is through intervention by professionals who can provide the necessary learning experiences (Asher & Renfrew, 1981). Such procedures are described in the **Applied Side** panel on pages 544–545.

It should be emphasized again that "loneliness" refers to an unpleasant subjective state and is not synonymous with being alone. A child, for example, may be quite able to make friends and deal with them well and yet prefer to spend a good deal of time alone. There is no reason why an individual should not enjoy solitude to pursue a hobby, read, listen to music, or think. Spending time by oneself does not necessarily indicate that there is an emotional problem in need of treatment (Suedfeld, 1982).

Though childhood makes a great many demands on our social abilities, it is probably in adolescence that the greatest amount of loneliness occurs (Brennan, 1982). This is the period during which we begin the separation from our parents, initiate the search for an intimate love relationship, and come to realize that our decisions are a matter of personal responsibility. The result is that many of us face periods of loneliness, as shown in a study by Brennan and Auslander (1979). As can be seen in Figure 14.8, a great many teenagers report a feeling of isolation with respect to parents, teachers, and peers. In that same investigation, it was found that more girls than boys indicate that they feel lonely. Individuals who are most lonely are likely to be shy, have low self-esteem, feel powerless, possess poor social skills, and lack interest in other people (Brennan, 1982).

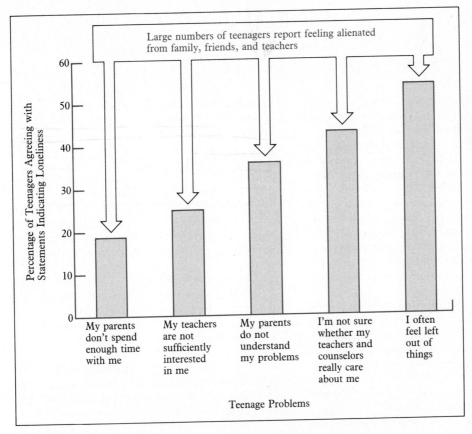

FIGURE 14.8   *Adolescent loneliness: Feeling isolated from everyone.*

In a survey of teenagers, sizeable proportions reported feelings of isolation and loneliness with respect to their parents, teachers, and peers. [Source: Based on data from Brennan & Auslander, 1979.]

These same characteristics appear in studies of college students who feel chronically lonely (Cutrona, 1982). Even those who have never known this feeling may experience it in college. As one student said after seven months on campus:

> Coming to a large university such as this was a big change for me. After being voted in junior high and senior high school "Best Personality" and "Most Popular," I had to start over. Walking a long distance, seeing nothing but strangers was rather difficult at first, but I find myself getting used to it. (p. 291)

The Effect of Loneliness on Behavior

Much of the research on the effects of loneliness suggests that certain kinds of social behavior are influenced by feelings of loneliness and that they also contribute to the person's inability to form close relationships. For example,

Overcoming Shyness and Increasing Sociability

In the discussion of loneliness, it was suggested that this behavior tends not to change unless others intervene to bring about behavioral change. One aspect of being lonely is a feeling of **shyness** (Zimbardo, 1977), and outside help is often required to overcome this problem also. The shy person feels that he or she cannot deal well with others, especially members of the opposite sex. There are fears of having nothing to say or of saying things that will appear foolish and embarrassing. When faced with situations requiring interaction, the heart beats faster and the pulse rate goes up. Is there a way to reduce such feelings and to make interpersonal situations more comfortable?

An intriguing experimental solution to the problem of shyness was devised by Brodt and Zimbardo (1981). These investigators provided shy female subjects with a new explanation for their pounding heart and fast pulse, one based on external factors. Each subject interacted with an attractive male confederate in what was described as a study of responses to noise pollution. The experimental group was told that the noise increased the pulse rate and heart rate, while the control group was told that the effects were a dry mouth and a slight tremor. In other words, some of the shy individuals were given a reason for their physiological reactions that was unrelated to shyness or to being in a social interaction. After the noise bombardment stopped, the subject and the confederate were left alone to interact for five minutes. As predicted, those subjects in the experimental group behaved as if they were not shy when talking to their partner; they were verbally fluent and assertive in the interaction. Simply by changing the attribution about their physical symptoms from shyness to noise pollution, there was a dramatic change in how they dealt with a social challenge.

Such findings suggest that behaviors related to shyness and loneliness rest in large part on cognitive factors. That is, failure to interact with others stems from what an individual believes about himself or herself, how social situations are interpreted, and

the assumptions that are made about the reactions of others. With respect to several kinds of behavior problems, cognitive therapy has been found to be of great value (Beck, 1976). The general idea is that internal reality (the way a person *perceives* himself or herself and the external world) plays a major role in determining how that person feels and acts. For example, someone who decides that he is unattractive (even if it is untrue) will be unhappy, expect rejection, avoid the opposite sex, and so forth. Behavioral change in such instances requires cognitive change.

To apply this approach to loneliness, Young (1982) begins by assessing in detail each person's patterns of friendships: who the friends are, how often they interact, how much caring and disclosure are involved, and the degree of physical intimacy. Among other things, it is determined whether the major problem is in starting a relationship in the first place or in moving from a superficial to a deep relationship. The most important thing the therapist can do is to make the client's thoughts, actions, and emotions explicit and to induce changes in the cognitions that will break up the maladaptive pattern and induce a positive chain reaction. Some typical patterns are shown in Table 14.4, and they provide some insight into how loneliness operates. In each instance, the therapist's task is to guide the client into examining his or her patterns of loneliness and to question some of the beliefs and assumptions that have led to unhappiness.

As was mentioned in the description of loneliness in childhood, another approach is to deal directly with the behavior itself. Thus, it is possible to teach social skills, to persuade the individual to engage in rewarding social events, and to provide information about enjoyable activities that can be undertaken alone (Rook & Peplau, 1982). The most extensive work has been directed at **social skills training** in which clients observe successful models, practice such behavior themselves and view videotapes of their performances, and carry out "homework" assignments (Curran, 1977). Those

TABLE 14.4 *The cognitive basis of loneliness:*
Thoughts and assumptions.

For the cognitive therapist, the approach to relieving loneliness is to identify the
patterns of thoughts and assumptions that lead to unhappy emotions and
maladaptive social behavior. Once these cognitive elements are identified and
altered, the emotions and the resulting behavior also undergo change. [Source:
Adapted from Young, 1982.]

Loneliness patterns	Accompanying thoughts	Maladaptive assumptions	Associated emotions	Resulting behavior
Discontent about being alone	I can't stand being alone.	There must be something wrong with me if I'm alone.	Boredom, sadness	Spends time alone and in-active
Low self-concept	I'm dull and boring.	It's essential to be lively and witty to have any friends.	Hopeless	Avoids other people
Social anxiety	I'll make a fool of myself.	Other people are judging me all the time.	Shyness	Avoids talking to others
Mistrust	I don't like most people.	People will take advantage of you if they can.	Bitter	Avoids friend-ships
Sexual anxiety	I'm not a good lover.	Sex is a perform-ance that the other person is evaluating.	Frustrated, ashamed	Avoids sexual relationships
Anxiety about emotional commitment	I'll lose myself if I get too close.	I should be able to meet my partner's emotional ex-pectations of me always.	Trapped	Avoids close relationships

with social problems also receive instructions in very specific activities such as how to begin a conversation, speak comfortably on the telephone, give compliments and receive them, deal with silence, and even how to enhance their physical attractiveness. Such training is usually provided for groups of clients, and the entire process is completed in a little over two months. In a similar way, those who are shy can learn social skills along with a change in the general way they react to interpersonal situations (Pilkonis & Zimbardo, 1979).

Finally, it should be added that many lonely individuals seek to bring about their own behavioral change with some success (e.g., by trying harder to be friendly, joining a club, dieting, learning to dance), and that sometimes it is the situation that requires change rather than the individual (Rook & Peplau, 1982). Altogether, it appears that there are a variety of effective ways to relieve loneliness. As with most personality characteristics, even relatively stable and long-lasting patterns of behavior can undergo remarkable changes for the better.

when students who receive high scores on the loneliness scale are compared with those scoring low, the lonely individuals are found to deal less well with a stranger in a brief interaction (Jones et al., 1982). Specifically, lonely individuals refer to the other person less, are less inclined to continue talking about topics the other person brings up, ask fewer questions, and generally pay less attention to the partner. These conversational differences suggest a lack of interest that often leads to rejection. Those who are lonely expect others to rate them negatively even when this is not accurate (Jones et al., 1981). Not only do individuals find out less about others, they also disclose less about themselves both in the laboratory setting and in real life (Berg & Peplau, 1982; Solano et al., 1982). In addition, they differ from nonlonely individuals in initiating self-disclosures to same-sex partners with a highly intimate topic and to opposite-sex partners with a topic of low intimacy. Altogether, those who are lonely seem to have developed inadequate interpersonal skills. Thus, they manage to "turn off" potential friends by showing disinterest, expressing negative expectancies, and engaging in inappropriate levels of self-disclosure.

Among the most widespread effects of loneliness are the tendency to be cynical about other people, to feel pessimistic, and to believe that external events control one's life (Jones, 1982). With respect to the opposite sex, those who are lonely are less likely to believe that people marry for love and more likely to feel that divorce will probably end their own marriages (Jones et al., 1980).

The condition of loneliness tends to persist without outside intervention, because the coping strategies of lonely individuals serve to maintain the problem and even to make it worse. For example, the more lonely someone is, the more he or she believes the condition to be permanent while turning to wish-fulfilling fantasy as a solution (Revenson, 1981). Unhappiness with this condition leads to isolated activities such as reading and working hard and to self-destructive behavior such as drinking too much alcohol and taking drugs (Paloutzian & Ellison, 1979). It can be concluded, then, that loneliness is a pervasive and persistent characteristic that affects a great deal of one's interpersonal behavior.

The Type A-Type B Personality Dimension: Who Succeeds and Who Survives?

There is general agreement among medical scientists that the risk of cardiovascular disorders increases as a function of various physical factors: age, the level of serum cholesterol, blood pressure, and cigarette smoking. Nevertheless, the combination of such variables does not permit very accurate prediction of who will and will not develop coronary heart disease (Jenkins, 1976; Keys, 1970). What else might be responsible for the development of this disease? The possibility that personality variables may play a major role has been recognized for at least 2,000 years, since Celsus proposed that fear, anger, and other states of the mind are apt to excite the pulse. In the centuries since then, many physicians have suggested that emotional arousal has an effect on the

FIGURE 14.9 *Type A personality:*
Working hard to develop a coronary.

The Type A *coronary-prone behavior pattern is characterized by an aggressive,*
competitive, rushed approach to most situations. Even a quiet afternoon of
fishing can become a stressful and arousing challenge to the Type A person.
[Source: © 1981 King Features Syndicate, Inc. World rights reserved.]

heart, and in 1868 a German physician observed that those who are coronary-prone tend to speak in a loud voice and to become what we today label as workaholics (Dembroski & MacDougall, 1982). Systematic investigation of the psychological aspects of heart disease did not get underway until the 1950s when Friedman and Rosenman (1959) described the **Type A** coronary-prone behavior pattern. They were able to show that individuals who are hardworking, aggressive, always in a hurry, etc., were more likely to develop coronary heart disease than were those with opposite characteristics—the relaxed, easy-going, and sociable **Type B** individuals (Friedman, 1977). Though much of the initial research concentrated on males, the same relationship seems to hold true for females (Haynes et al., 1980). The possibility of changing this personality style as a way to prevent heart attacks is explored in the **Applied Side** panel on pages 548–549. As suggested in the cartoon in Figure 14.9, these behavioral differences are reflected in whatever an individual undertakes to do. In addition, recent psychological research has provided evidence that this personality characteristic is related to behavior in many interpersonal situations. Some of this research will now be described.

The Type A Behavior Pattern and Its Development

It is now well-established that the typical Type A person responds to various kinds of tasks as competitive challenges. It is important to achieve success, but the Type A feels that there is never enough time to get things done. Other people can interfere with work, take up time, and otherwise cause the Type A individual to become impatient and irritable (Rosenman & Friedman, 1974). The high need for success leads to a preference for working alone when under pressure (Dembroski & MacDougall, 1978) and to becoming angry when

548

THE
APPLIED SIDE *Reducing Coronary Heart Disease by Altering Personality Patterns*

Despite the professional and probable financial benefits that Type A behavior brings about, we have seen that this personality pattern results in various emotional problems, interpersonal difficulties, and—most seriously—with life-threatening heart attacks. It has been proposed that if individuals could be taught to relax, avoid pressure, and slow down, such behavioral changes would conceivably lead to a more contented and longer life. In Table 14.5 are some suggestions for behavioral change provided by Brody (1980b).

In order to reach as many people as possible, large-scale campaigns have been undertaken in newspapers and on television (Meyer et al., 1980). Some investigators have raised questions as to whether this approach is really effective (Leventhal et al., 1980). These psychologists concluded that simple exposure to information in the media led to no reduction in cardiovascular risk despite the fact that knowledge increased. It seemed to be necessary to include face-to-face interactions along with other approaches.

An intensive attempt to bring about behavioral change has been undertaken at Stanford University by a team of investigators (*APA Monitor,* February, 1980). About 600 individuals who have already had at least one heart attack are taking part in the study. They meet in small groups to discuss their lives, their problems, and their typical behavior. They practice dealing with various situations in a Type B fashion, and they give one another advice. There are also control group patients who simply receive health care from a cardiologist or their personal physicians. In the experimental groups, high-risk Type A individuals are taught, for example, to avoid situations that evoke their characteristic be-

havior. One man won a contest in which he and his wife were supposed to run through a warehouse touching as many items as they could in sixty seconds; each such item would be given to the couple as a prize. After discussing this with the group, the man realized how upset he would be in that situation, and he arranged to get the prizes without the pressure of hurrying around the warehouse. In addition to the importance of avoiding time pressure, angry and hostile responses must be controlled because they show the closest relationship to the incidence of heart attacks.

This attempt to change lifestyles does not always work, of course. One accountant would not accept the group's advice to set a reasonable limit on the number of tax returns he agreed to complete for clients. Instead, he overbooked himself, worked fourteen to sixteen hours a day, seven days a week, for several months. In other words, he continued the lifestyle of an extreme Type A pattern. The results were fatal. He had a heart attack and was buried shortly before the April 15 tax deadline (Brody, 1980a). Nevertheless, this approach appears to be largely a successful one in that the expected number of heart attacks among Type A's in the program has been cut in half, according to preliminary reports.

Other therapy programs that emphasize self-control, relaxation training, and group support also seem to be successful. After six treatment sessions, male executives scored lower on the Jenkins Activity Survey, reacted with less anger and impatience, and revealed an improved physiological response to stress (Levenkron et al., 1983).

In the general enthusiasm about changing Type A behavior, a note of caution about going too far

anything or anyone gets in the way (Carver & Glass, 1978). Type A individuals do not believe in avoiding problems or responsibilities, and they want to do things perfectly (Smith & Brehm, 1981). These various pressures lead to problems with sleeping (Hicks et al., 1980). Time is all important (Strube, 1982), and Type A's tend to arrive early for appointments and to feel irritated

TABLE 14.5   Self-help for the Type A person.

On the basis of what is known about Type A behavior and coronary heart disease, it has been proposed that some relatively simple changes in one's lifestyle could make a profound difference in health risks. There is not yet any evaluation of the effectiveness of this self-help approach, but such suggestions seem very sensible. [Source: Adapted from Brody, 1980b.]

Tips for the Type A individual	Questions to ask yourself
(1) Evaluate yourself.	What are your goals in life? How are you spending your time? What is really important in your life?
(2) Don't turn your life into a numbers game.	Is my value only a matter of quantity? How important is it to count my accomplishments? Are there obligations, clubs, committees, or other duties that I can give up?
(3) Forget about being a superperson.	Do I have to be the best at *everything?* Do I have to control all aspects of my life? Does it have to be perfect, or can I let someone else do the job?
(4) Spend some time alone.	Do I have to be busy every minute?
(5) Take time for cultural relaxation.	Can't I find time each week to see a play, read a book, visit a museum, or even walk through a park?
(6) Forget about constantly hurrying.	Can I leave early and have plenty of time to get there? Is this appointment necessary or can I break it? Do I have to look at my watch all the time? Can I just stop, take a break, and relax?
(7) Overcome your feelings of hostility.	Is this incident really important enough to get mad about? Should I really expect others to be perfect? Can I spend more time around Type B's?

might be wise. Though it is generally assumed that the Type A pattern is maladaptive, keep in mind the finding that the most successful individuals in at least one profession were found to be those who fall in this category. There is another recent finding that suggests that, while Type B's may have a low risk of heart attacks, they face other sorts of problems. Compared to Type A's, those who are Type B tend to be careless and self-destructive with respect to drinking alcohol, overeating, getting medical care, and driving a car (Kelley et al., 1983). Thus, the busy, overcontrolled, perfectionist Type A person seems to be doing the right things in many aspects of his or her life.

when others are late (Gastorf, 1980). Those who are Type A's work more quickly than Type B's, get more done, and perceive that time is passing by more quickly (Yarnold & Grimm, 1982). In social situations, Type A's feel uncomfortable and have a sense of insecurity (Jenkins et al., 1977). At the opposite behavioral extreme is the Type B individual who does not strive for success, is

TABLE 14.6   *Common behavioral characteristics of Type A individuals.*

Even without a personality test, the extreme Type A person is relatively easy to identify on the basis of his or her behavior. The calm, unhurried, friendly Type B individual is characterized by the absence of these indicators. [Source: Adapted from Brody, 1980a.]

Typical Type A characteristics

Doing more than one thing at the same time

Scheduling an increasing number of activities and having less time for each

Ignoring one's surroundings (not "stopping to smell the roses")

Urging others to hurry up and finish what they are saying

Becoming irritated at slow cars blocking traffic or at having to wait in line

Believing that it's better to do it yourself if you want it done right

Using a lot of hand gestures when talking

Nervously tapping fingers or jiggling legs

Using a lot of obscenities and other explosive speech patterns

Having to be on time always

Finding it difficult to sit with nothing to do

Playing to win every game, even with children

Measuring success quantitatively (income, number of clients, number of publications, etc.)

When speaking, engaging in head nodding, fist-clenching, table pounding

Becoming impatient when watching others carry out a task

Rapid eye-blinking or eyebrow-lifting

careless about time, and gets along well with other people (Glass, 1977). Some of the basic habits of the Type A individual are summarized in Table 14.6.

Though such behavior can be identified on the basis of everyday observations, a more precise measure is provided by a personality test, the **Jenkins Activity Survey** (Jenkins et al., 1979). This is a self-report test in which subjects describe their own behavior with respect to eating rapidly, losing their temper, overworking, and so forth. Most studies of this personality variable have used this instrument to assess individual differences in Type A behavior.

Surprisingly, only a modest amount of research effort has been directed at determining the *origins* of Type A versus Type B behavior. It is important to learn why people are different in this respect. For one thing, it appears that Type A individuals were raised in families in which high, though ambiguous, standards were set with the mother pushing her child to do well and then to do better (Matthews, 1977; Matthews et al., 1977). The child's reaction is to work hard, strive for success, and try to reach as many goals as possible in order to maintain parental approval. On the basis of such findings, Strube and Ota (1982) went a step further and proposed that such parent-child interactions were more likely to occur for firstborn children than for those who are later-born. For one thing, expectations are often greatest and more unrealistic for the first child in the family than for subsequent ones. In addition, as more children are born, there is simply less time for the parents to push them toward achievement. In any event, this is precisely what was found. Among college students, those who were firstborn obtained higher Type A scores than did the later-born. Further, for both males and females, the larger the family, the stronger the relationship between birth order and Type A behavior.

Other investigators have identified such pressures as Little League and programs for gifted children. That is, sports activities can be focused on the importance of winning rather than simply on having a good time. Children identified as gifted may be pushed harder and harder to achieve rather than simply to develop their potential. Parents sometimes assume that a child must be Number One in whatever he or she undertakes (Brody, 1980a). In general, the research suggests that such pressure-oriented parent-child interactions contribute to individual differences in this personality characteristic. Clearly, we need to know more about the details of how parents accidentally influence their offsprings' Type A and Type B patterns of behavior.

It is also possible that some aspects of Type A behavior are attributable to the situation. For example, you might expect Type A characteristics to increase in intensity in demanding occupations that put a premium on speed, competition, quantifiable output, and deadlines. On the basis of this sort of reasoning, Morell and Katkin (1982) compared the scores of female professionals with the scores of homemakers and found that the former group was much higher in Type A characteristics. It seems also that the higher the job status, the greater the incidence of Type A behavior. The authors speculated that as women have more opportunities to pursue high-level goals in education and in their careers, they will also catch up to men in the development of coronary heart disease. It is possible, of course, that those women with Type A characteristics find themselves motivated to enter professions and to work toward higher and higher status. If so, personality characteristics can be seen to lead the individual to certain situations rather than developing *because* of the situation.

Contrasting Responses
of Type A and Type B Individuals

Most of the research dealing with this personality variable has concentrated on expanding what is known about how Type A and Type B individuals differ in their response to a variety of situations. Primarily, there has been interest in achievement-related behavior and in interpersonal behavior.

Responding to achievement-related challenges. It has been found that deadlines hold different meaning for those differing along this personality dimension. Type A's work hard no matter what (even though deadlines make them feel pressured), but Type B's respond with extra effort only if someone sets a time limit on getting the work done (Burnam et al., 1975). In contrast, when there are positive incentives to perform well, Type A's are more responsive than Type B's (Blumenthal et al., 1980). The Type A person tends to focus attention on the task at hand and to ignore any distractions that could interfere with getting the job done (Matthews & Brunson, 1979). Type A's complain less than Type B's about hard work (Weidner & Matthews, 1978).

It is not unusual in various occupations to find one's regular work interrupted by phone calls, visitors, or additional tasks that must be attended to. It would be expected that the Type A person works as hard as is necessary to get the main task done, even when the demands and interruptions increase. Fazio et al. (1981) tested this hypothesis by presenting Type A and Type B students with a proofreading assignment. Half of the subjects simply proofread a manuscript, but the other half had a more distracting job in which they proofread, counted the number of times the word "object" appeared in the material they read, and were interrupted at unpredictable times by a signal to go to a different room and solve anagrams and then return to the proofreading. As shown in Figure 14.10, the requirement of having three jobs to do at once interfered with the performance of Type B individuals. For those who were Type A, however, the opposite effect occurred. They actually got more done under the more difficult work conditions.

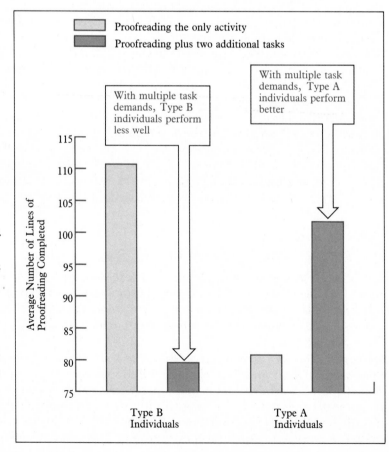

FIGURE 14.10 *Performance under demanding conditions: Type A's do better than Type B's.*

Type A and Type B students were compared in their performance on a straightforward proofreading task and on the same task made more demanding by additional requirements (having to do a word count) and being interrupted periodically to carry out a third task. Type B individuals performed the primary task less well under the more demanding conditions, but Type A individuals did a better job when the stress was greatest. [Source: Based on data from Fazio et al., 1981.]

One reason for such findings, perhaps, is that Type A's more than Type B's tend to focus their attention on important tasks while ignoring trivial ones (Stern et al., 1981). This cognitive difference extends to the way in which information is processed. In a concept-formation task, Type A's to a greater extent than Type B's pay attention to central material and ignore that which is peripheral (Humphries et al., 1983). Though Type A's respond well to a challenge, the price they pay is an accompanying increase in cardiovascular activity (Goldband, 1980; Jorgensen & Houston, 1981; Pittner et al., 1983). Also, coronary-prone individuals react to the stress of multiple tasks with a greater increase in blood pressure and higher levels of substances in the blood associated with cardiovascular problems (Glass et al., 1980).

There is a general tendency for the Type A person to want to maintain control of whatever is going on (Rhodewalt & Davison, 1983). When faced with an uncontrollable task, they respond with frustration and anger (Levine & Moore, 1979). In addition, the Type A person sets high goals for himself or herself, even in childhood (Matthews & Siegel, 1983), so that even after doing well there is a greater feeling of failure than is true for those who are Type B (Snow, 1978). Because Type A's also fear failure more than is true for Type B's (Gastorf & Teevan, 1980), they tend to suppress complaints such as experiencing a negative emotional response or feeling tired (Carver et al., 1976; Pittner & Houston, 1980). When presented with a series of unsolvable problems on which they necessarily fail, the problem-solving ability of Type A subjects begins to decline rapidly, and they angrily blame themselves and the situation for their inability to succeed (Brunson & Matthews, 1981). In the same situation, Type B's continue using effective strategies and placed the blame on the task, the experimenter, and chance. It appears that lack of success is much harder for a Type A than a Type B person.

You might wonder how these various findings dealing with responses to work challenges, distractions, and so forth are related to behavior in real life. That is, do Type A individuals tend to work hard and to succeed? In one investigation of social psychologists, it was found that superior scientific achievement is related to Type A behavior (Matthews et al., 1980). It seems possible that in some other fields, the hardworking tendencies of the coronary-prone individuals would also lead to success.

Interpersonal behavior of Type A's and Type B's. The original description of the Type A personality suggested that such individuals would have various difficulties in dealing with other people, especially in working with them. Type A's need to control the situation and to do better than opponents. The result is a belief that they know a great deal about other people and that they can predict what others will do (Smith & Brehm, 1981). In a task on which people could either cooperate or compete, Type A's predicted that they would win more money than Type B's predicted for themselves, especially when competition was involved (Gotay, 1981).

It also seems that a Type A orientation is associated with masculinity among both males and females (DeGregorio & Carver, 1980), as is depicted in Figure 14.11, p. 544. Presumably, this relationship is based in part on the fact

FIGURE 14.11   *Masculinity:* *A characteristic of Type A's of both sexes.*

There is a general tendency for the Type A behavior pattern to be associated with masculinity. The greatest adjustment problems are faced by Type A's who are low *in masculinity. This combination is found to be associated with low self-esteem among both males and females and with depression and social anxiety for females. [Source: Based on data from DeGregorio & Carver, 1980.]*

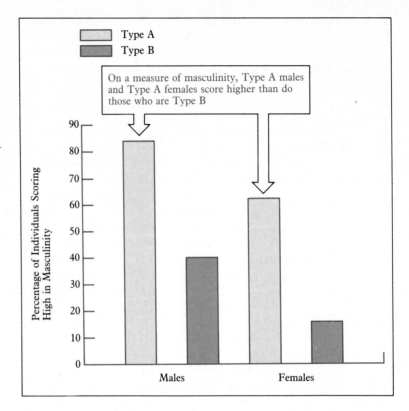

that the aggressive, achieving aspects of coronary-prone behavior have traditionally been characterized as masculine behaviors. With respect to adjustment, the most difficult problems were experienced by those Type A males and females who, unlike the usual pattern, were *low* in masculinity. Such a combination seems to cause difficulties in interpersonal relationships. Females high in Type A characteristics and low in masculinity were depressed and socially anxious. Both males and females with that pattern were low in self-esteem.

A very special interpersonal setting is a marriage. Here, husbands and wives express their personality attributes in their interactions with one another and in their social activities. In what ways might Type A and Type B patterns of behavior affect marital behavior? Becker and Byrne (1983) attempted to answer this question by asking a number of couples to respond to questionnaires dealing with their daily activities. Compared with Type B males, those who were Type A reported less communication with their wives, more time spent in work-related activities at home, and a lower frequency and briefer duration of marital sex. Type A females relax less frequently and for shorter periods of time than their Type B counterparts. For Type A's of both sexes, there is little pleasure in purely social activities. It appears that the hard-driving, work-oriented style that characterizes the Type A pattern in the outside world strongly carries over into the homelife of such individuals.

Locus of Control:
Assigning Responsibility for Life's Outcomes

> One doesn't get where [Senator John] Glenn has got by waiting around for lightning to strike, something he is frank enough to admit. "My view," he says, "is that to sit back and let fate play its hand out and never try to influence it at all is not the way man was meant to operate."
>
> In the military, influencing fate is called "sniveling." (Kramer, 1983, p. 20)

In psychology, trying to influence one's fate is called **internal locus of control.** The opposite assumption about life, that each of us is a helpless pawn controlled by luck, fate, and other uncontrollable outside forces, is known as **external locus of control.** These contrasting belief systems constitute the two poles of a personality dimension proposed by Julian Rotter (Rotter & Hochreich, 1975). We will first discuss the theoretical background of this trait and its measurement and then describe some of the research involving individual differences in **locus of control.**

Generalized Expectancies about Obtaining Rewards and Avoiding Punishments

In Rotter's personality theory, a given behavior is conceptualized as depending on an individual's *expectancy* that the behavior will lead to a reinforcement and the *value* he or she places on that reinforcement. As with many theories of behavior, people are described as acting so as to maximize rewards and minimize punishments.

In addition to what is expected and valued in a particular situation, each of us also acquires a more general set of beliefs about life and how reinforcements operate. Presumably on the basis of early experiences, an individual comes to believe and to expect that reinforcements can be controlled by his or her own actions *or* only by uncontrollable outside forces (Phares, 1978). At the internal extreme of this belief system is the assumption that skill, hard work, foresight, and taking responsibility will pay off. At the external extreme, events are assumed to depend on chance, luck, and powerful outside forces (see Figure 14.12, page 556).

To measure these generalized expectancies, almost a dozen different locus of control measures have been constructed (Lefcourt, 1982), including tests for young children. The instrument that Rotter (1966) devised is known as the **I-E Scale.** Anyone taking the test is asked to choose between two alternatives for each item. In the following examples, the internal versus the external meaning of each choice should be clear: Select the alternative you believe to be more true.

(1) ____ a. Many of the unhappy things in people's lives are partly due to bad luck.
b. People's misfortunes result from the mistakes they make.

FIGURE 14.12   *Locus of control: Outcomes based on luck or skill.*

The locus of control belief system is defined by the extent to which individuals assume that their rewards and punishments are under internal or external control. For some, life is a game of chance, and they wait helplessly and hopefully for the right number to come up. For others, life is a challenging contest, and they utilize skills and effort in the attempt to master it. [Source: Photo (left) ©Eric Roth 1978/The Picture Cube; photo (right) © Jerry Howard 1983/Positive Images.]

(2) ___ a. In the case of the well-prepared student there is rarely if ever such a thing as an unfair test.
   b. Many times exam questions tend to be so unrelated to course work that studying is really useless.

There has been a great deal of research interest in how internals and externals respond in a variety of social situations, and we will now summarize some of these important findings.

Internality versus Externality: A Pervasive Influence on Behavior

Interest in this trait has focused not only on how internal and external adults behave but also on the *reason* for these individual differences. Why do we develop a particular set of expectancies about our ability to control fate?

Developing locus of control expectancies. A good deal of early research on this variable suggests that those with an internal orientation were raised by mothers who expected them to behave independently at an early age and who were not concerned with trying to control every aspect of their behavior (Chance, 1965). Other studies find that the parents of internals tend to baby them and to be protective, affectionate, and approving (Katkovsky et al., 1967). In general, parents of internals expect a lot of their offspring and also offer a great deal of affectionate involvement. Externals are likely to have experienced more rejection, hostile control, and criticism (Davis & Phares, 1969). Long after infancy and childhood, college students who are relatively external recall their parents as being restrictive (Johnson & Kilmann, 1975). It seems that an external orientation develops in response to overcontrolling, critical parental behavior. Parents of internals are warm and accepting, but they also expect a lot. It should be stressed that those who are internal were not simply spoiled and overindulged. To become internally oriented, the child must learn that reinforcements depend on his or her behavior (Crandall, 1973). *Reinforcement contingencies* are thus crucial.

Differences in locus of control are found to be related to differences in responding in many social situations. For example, when a task involves competition, internals outperform externals, though the two groups do equally well on a cooperative task (Nowicki, 1982). As might be expected, externals are more likely to conform than internals (Crowne & Liverant, 1963). In several studies, internals are found to resist the influence of experimenters, and they tend to behave in a way opposite to what is intended (Lefcourt, 1982). In general, internal individuals seem to be less inclined to submit in an unquestioning way to the group or to an authority figure than is true for externals.

It is theorized, by the way, that maladjustment should be associated with either extreme of this trait. That is, a well-adjusted individual would not be expected to feel helpless and unable to take responsibility for anything *nor* to believe that he or she could totally control events (Lefcourt, 1982). To date, however, research has generally shown that internality is a more positive asset than externality. For example, external school children are found to be undersocialized (neurotic and impulsive) and to be hyperactive (Linn & Hodge, 1982; Raine et al., 1982).

Locus of control as a factor in achievement. If you think for a moment of the demands made in school or on the job, it should be obvious that a person with internal expectations would be more apt to succeed than an externally oriented individual. What do the data indicate?

The majority of investigations in this area report that internality is related to higher grades in school and to achievement (Bar-Tal & Bar-Zohar, 1977; Findley & Cooper, 1983). Significantly, the academic difficulties faced by racial minorities and others who are disadvantaged are compounded by locus of control factors. In the United States, externality is common among nonwhites, and this orientation leads to a perception of school as a hopeless exercise in futility (Lefcourt, 1982; Pettigrew, 1967). The effects of locus of control continue through the school years, and even beyond the B.A. degree. Over a five-year period, graduate students who are internals are more likely to complete their requirements and be granted a Ph.D. degree than are externals (Otten, 1977).

In a work situation, it might appear obvious that as one's pay increases there would be a tendency to work harder and to be more satisfied with one's job. Actually, the relationship between salary and effort or salary and satisfaction is more complex than that, and one of the complicating factors is locus of control. Earn (1982) placed college students in a situation requiring them to solve a series of simple puzzles. Some were paid nothing for the task, some received $2.50, and a third group was given $5.00. When asked afterward to rate how much they liked the work, internals and externals responded quite

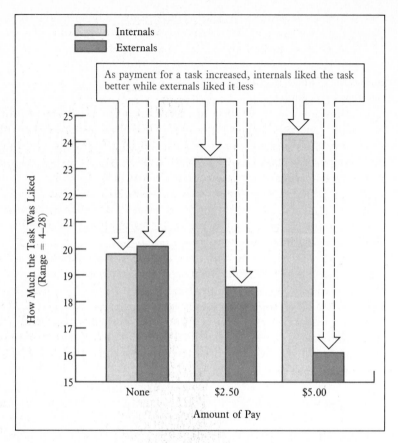

differently, as shown in Figure 14.13. The higher the pay, the more positive the internally oriented students were about the task, but the reverse was true for those with an external orientation. In addition, the amount of time spent working when the experimenter was absent increased with pay level for internals and decreased with pay level for externals. The author suggested that internals interpret the rewards as an indication of how competent they are. Externals in contrast perceive themselves as less skillful at the task even though objectively the two groups did equally well. For them, the amount of the rewards seemed irrelevant except perhaps to suggest that the task must be unpleasant if the experimenter was willing to pay them to do it. If these same reactions and perceptions hold true in actual work settings, it can be predicted that internals would work harder and be more satisfied than would externals.

Changing locus of control. Like other personality traits, locus of control is a generally stable attribute of individuals (Wolfle & Robertshaw, 1982). Nevertheless, change is possible. Some changes occur as the result of everyday life events. The most general one is aging: internality increases as children grow older (Penk, 1969). Presumably, as we age we find ourselves more and more able to exert some control over our outcomes. Adults in administrative jobs similarly show increases in internality as the time spent in such positions increases (Harvey, 1971). When a very disrupting life event occurs, there is a shift toward external locus of control. For example, women who are physically abused by their husbands are more external than non-battered women (Cheney & Bleker, 1982). The longer a woman remains in such an abusive situation, the higher she scores in externality. In addition, women who go through the trauma of divorce show a sharp rise in externality, but this later drops back to the pre-divorce level (Doherty, 1983).

Since internal locus of control is generally agreed to be advantageous, several procedures have been developed to try to increase internality. In a school, for example, teachers were instructed to encourage children to develop internal control expectancies through the use of reinforcement principles. Before-and-after measures revealed an increase in internality (Reimanis, 1971). The same investigator was also successful in bringing about such changes in college students by means of specially designed counseling sessions. Not only did the students become more internal, they also reported such behavior changes as renting a new apartment, changing their majors, and seeking out their instructors to obtain feedback.

These studies, as well as others, provide hope that adults and children can be taught to perceive themselves in a different, more active, and more hopeful way. To a degree, we can each exert control over our lives. The more individuals there are who accept that idea, the fewer there will be who view themselves as helpless objects at the mercy of uncontrollable events.

Summary

Relatively stable individual differences in behavior are known as personality **traits**. Personality is defined as the combination of relatively enduring characteristics of an individual that are expressed in a variety of situations. The traditional assumption of most personality psychologists was that behavior depended primarily on the operation of stable internal characteristics. Disappointment with the predictive power of tests led many psychologists to emphasize the importance of situational variables. Currently, there is a trend toward integrating the trait and situational approaches and an attempt to specify when traits are and are not useful.

Most of the traits of interest to psychologists were first observed long before there was a science of behavior. Many personality tests are composed of items that were initially based on theory but then were evaluated by means of **item analysis** procedures. The final version of a personality test must have acceptable **reliability** (consistency of measurement) and convincing **construct validity** (relationships between test scores and relevant behaviors). Such tests are used to predict behavior in *correlational studies* and, along with situational variables, in *experimental investigations*. In the latter instance, personality variables are said to *moderate* or *mediate* the effect of a stimulus on a response.

The trait of **loneliness** refers to an individual's subjective perception that he or she lacks close interpersonal relationships. The *UCLA loneliness scale* is used to measure this characteristic. High scorers tend to report feeling depressed and anxious, self-conscious in public, and shy. For some, loneliness begins in childhood when an individual fails to learn appropriate social skills, and it can intensify in adolescence if there is difficulty in establishing a close, loving relationship. The ineffectiveness of the lonely person in dealing with others leads to a cynical and pessimistic outlook. The most successful attempts to reduce loneliness consist of **cognitive therapy** and **social skills training.**

The hardworking, aggressive individual who is always in a hurry is identified as having a **Type A** coronary-prone behavior pattern. This trait is assessed by the *Jenkins Activity Survey.* Those who score high on the Type A end of this dimension tend to be raised in families with high, though ambiguous standards, tend to be the firstborn child in the family, and tend to be in demanding occupations that involve speed, competition, and deadlines. In many different sorts of achievement-related tasks, Type A's perform differently from the more relaxed Type B individuals; they are able to handle demanding situations and ignore distractions, and they complain less. Both in the laboratory and in everyday life, those who are Type A are likely to succeed. Interpersonally, the Type A pattern leads to difficulties in that such individuals become impatient and irritated with others. Attempts to alter Type A behavior and hence reduce the risk of heart attacks have concentrated on trying to persuade such individuals to relax, slow down, and avoid the situations that elicit their usual behavior.

In Rotter's personality theory, it is proposed that individuals develop a generalized expectancy involving **internal** versus **external locus of control.** The learning of such expectancies appears to begin early in one's life in response to parental affection, restrictiveness, criticism, and independence training. Those who are internally oriented do well in competitive situations, resist conformity pressures and social influence, and succeed in achievement situations. One's locus of control can be changed by factors such as the type of job one holds and by training procedures designed to alter expectancies.

Glossary

authoritarianism *The personality dimension that ranges from the authoritarian personality to the egalitarian personality. Authoritarians are characterized by adherence to conventional values, submission to a strong leader, aggression toward those who deviate, and a concern with power.*

cognitive therapy *Psychotherapy in which the emphasis is on altering the client's maladaptive thought processes.*

construct validity *The series of relationships established between scores on a personality test and other theoretically relevant responses.*

external locus of control *The generalized belief that reinforcements are controlled by external factors over which the individual has no influence.*

F Scale *The Fascist Scale, a personality test that was constructed to measure the trait of authoritarianism.*

I-E Scale *A personality test that measures locus of control and identifies where individuals fall along the internal-external dimension.*

internal locus of control *The generalized belief that reinforcements are controlled by oneself through the power of such factors as ability and effort.*

item analysis *In test construction, this is a procedure in which each item is evaluated with respect to its relation to a criterion. Often the criterion is the individual's performance on the total test.*

Jenkins Activity Survey *A personality test that measures coronary-prone behavior (Type A) and its opposite (Type B).*

locus of control *The generalized expectancy as to where the control for one's reinforcements lie—either in uncontrollable outside forces or within oneself.*

loneliness *The personality dimension that deals with the subjective experience of isolation in which the individual feels unhappy and cut off from close personal relationships.*

personality *The combination of the relatively enduring characteristics of an individual that are expressed in a variety of situations.*

reliability *The consistency with which a measuring instrument assesses a variable.*

shyness *The characteristic state that involves the feeling that one cannot interact in a satisfactory way with other people, especially members of the op-posite sex. The shy person feels that he or she does not know what to say and is likely to say something foolish.*

social skills training *A therapeutic intervention technique that concentrates on teaching individuals what to do and what to say in interpersonal interactions.*

trait *A behavioral dimension or personality characteristic involving differences among individuals.*

Type A *Those individuals at the extreme of a personality dimension involving coronary-prone behavior characterized by a hardworking, aggressive, time-pressured lifestyle.*

Type B *Those individuals at the low-risk extreme of the coronary-prone dimension. Their behavior is easygoing and relaxed; they are unconcerned about time pressures and unlikely to develop cardiovascular disease.*

UCLA loneliness scale *The personality test that assesses the extent to which an individual is experiencing loneliness.*

validity *The extent to which a test is related to or able to predict relevant behavior.*

For More Information

Byrne, D., & Kelley, K. *An introduction to personality.* Englewood Cliffs, N.J.: Prentice-Hall, 1981. *An undergraduate text that is a basic introduction to the field of personality. Both the individual differences emphasis of the field of personality psychology and the situational emphasis of the field of social psychology are represented. The integration of these approaches is stressed.*

Dembroski, T. M., Weiss, S. M., Shields, J. L., Haynes, S. G., & Feinleib, M. (Eds.). *Coronary-prone behavior.* New York: Springer-Verlag, 1978. *A thorough coverage of the theoretical background and the research findings related to the Type A coronary-prone behavior pattern. The topics include the assessment of this personality variable, the cultural and child-rearing antecedents of the behavior, and a description of techniques used to alter Type A behavior and its accompanying risk of cardiovascular disease.*

Lefcourt, H. M. *Locus of control: Current theory and research* (2nd ed.). Hillsdale, N.J.: Erlbaum, 1982. *An up-to-date review of the theory underlying the concept of locus of control and of the several decades of research involving internality and externality. Specific topics include the measurement of this construct, developmental studies, the correlates of the internal-external dimension, and the way in which one's orientation can undergo change.*

Peplau, L. A., & Perlman, D. *Loneliness: A sourcebook of current theory, research, and therapy.* New York: Wiley, 1982. *A large group of contributors have combined to provide an extensive examination of the personality variable of loneliness. Topics range from its origins in childhood to intervention techniques that are designed to change it. A unique feature is a comprehensive bibliography of all the loneliness research conducted between 1932 and 1981.*

CHAPTER 15

*Sexuality: The Most Intimate
Social Behavior*

Changes in Sexuality: Society, Attitudes, and Behavior

Differences among and within Societies/Increasingly Permissive Attitudes about Sexual Practices/Behavioral Changes: Greater Frequency and Variety

Sexual Attraction

Sexual Attraction in Other Species/The Role of Smell and Appearance in Human Sexual Attraction/Sexual Attraction Based on Psychological Cues

The Effects of Erotic Images on Motivation, Fantasy, and Behavior

Imagination as an Aphrodisiac/External Images as Triggers for Fantasy and Arousal/Behavioral Effects of Erotica

Erotophobia-Erotophilia: Attitudes about Sexuality

Measuring Sexual Attitudes and Their Development/Erotophobia as a Predictor of Sexual Behavior/The Influence of Erotophobia on Other Sex-Related Behaviors

Special Inserts

FOCUS ON RESEARCH
> *Negative Consequences of the Sexual Revolution: Pressure, Parenthood, and Pestilence*

FOCUS ON RESEARCH
> *Sexual Attraction to One's Own Gender: The Determinants of Homosexual Behavior*

ON THE APPLIED SIDE
> *Repeated Exposure to Erotica: Less Arousal but More Callous Attitudes*

Mrs. Harrison enjoyed having her young nephews stay with her over the weekend, but sometimes she felt that taking care of an eight- and a ten-year-old was more responsibility than she cared to assume. Both Carl and Tommy had seemed to have a good time at the park that afternoon, but this evening there would be a little quiet time in front of the television to end the day. After dinner her husband said he wanted to watch a movie on the cable about Halloween or something. That sounded entertaining for the boys.

By 7:30, they were gathered in the family room, ready for the show to begin. Mr. Harrison was already beginning to nod off in his easy chair. In the first scene of the movie, a young woman stood in front of a mirror in her bedroom and began to undress. "Oh no," thought Mrs. Harrison, "it's going to be one of those sex shows. I can't let these children watch that." The scene continued as the actress slowly removed all of her clothing, though only her back was visible on the screen. "I'll just pretend that something is wrong with the TV set and try to interest them in a game of Monopoly." She stood up and began walking toward the set. In the movie, a man's feet could now be seen moving silently through the dark woods and up to the window of the woman's room. "I'd better act quickly, or they're going to be carrying on with Lord knows what perversion right here in front of these impressionable babies."

Just then, the camera pulled back to reveal that the man outside the window was carrying a meat cleaver, already dripping with blood. His demented face was twisted into a fiendish grin as he climbed up to the open window. His fangs dripped foam as he mouthed the word "kill" over and over. Mrs. Harrison sat back down with a sigh of relief. "Thank goodness. It's only an old fashioned horror film and not some filth. They're so cute sitting there wide-eyed and scared to death."

For a great many people, sexual words and pictures are perceived as quite a bit more offensive and dangerous than anything having to do with violence or aggression. Especially where children are concerned, it is felt that murder is preferable to intercourse as a suitable topic for fiction or even the six o'clock news. These attitudes and beliefs represent only one of the ways in which **sexuality** affects our lives. There are few aspects of human behavior that cause us more difficulty—and result in more pleasure—than the control and expression of our sexual needs. The most intimate portion of a loving relationship consists of sexual interactions, and yet sexual motives can also cause pain and suffering. The negative side of sex includes guilt and frustration, unwanted pregnancies, sexually transmitted diseases, and criminal behavior in which an unwilling victim is forced to submit to someone's degrading erotic whims.

Psychological research in this area has increased at a rapid rate since the 1970s, and in this chapter we will present some of the most recent highlights of this work. We will first outline the dramatic *changes in sexuality* (in society, attitudes, and behavior) that have characterized the past several decades. Then, we will see how research on interpersonal attraction has been extended to include *sexual attraction* as well as the more general determinants of human and animal mate selection. The role of fantasy in human sexuality will then be described as we examine the *effects of erotic images on motivation, fantasy, and behavior.* In addition, there will be special coverage of the *negative consequences of the sexual revolution,* the *determinants of homosexual behavior,* and the effects of *repeated exposure to erotica.*

Changes in Sexuality: Society, Attitudes, and Behavior

As almost everyone is aware, there have been notable changes during the twentieth century in people's attitudes about sex and in their patterns of sexual behavior. As is suggested in Figure 15.1, such changes are most obvious across generations. Though it is impossible to state with certainty the underlying reasons, it is clear that much of Western Civilization has truly undergone a **sexual revolution.** We will examine the extent of some of these changes in the present section.

Perhaps the most striking aspect of human sexual behavior is the fact that it varies dramatically across cultures and across generations. In effect, the expression of this biological need is strongly influenced by the prevailing attitudes and beliefs of a given time and place. What people do, how frequently they do it, with whom, at what age, as well as what they communicate about sex are thus determined much more by psychological factors than biological ones. We will

FIGURE 15.1   *Changes in sexual attitudes: When generations collide.*

Perhaps the most obvious feature of the sexual revolution is the way in which members of different generations think, talk, and act with respect to sexual matters. Though the gap between parents and their offspring is exaggerated in this cartoon, the trend toward generational differences in knowledge, permissiveness, and experience is well-documented in survey research. [Source: Reprinted courtesy Penthouse Magazine © 1983.]

"My parents still think oral sex is what guys talk about after intercourse."

now examine some of these variations as they have taken place during recent years.

Differences among and within Societies

Cross-cultural studies of differences in sexual practices often focus on primitive societies that seem to have little in common with our own experiences. In recent years, however, interest has been directed at contemporary behavior in the industrialized nations. It appears that the most dramatic changes toward greater sexual permissiveness and experimentation have centered primarily in Western Europe (with Scandinavia in the forefront), North America, and Japan (Christensen, 1969; Perlman et al., 1978; Sigusch & Schmidt, 1973). In other contemporary societies such as Russia (Orionova, 1981) and the People's Republic of China (Butterfield, 1980), the response to nudity, erotic books and movies, premarital sex, etc. are much more repressive and seemingly "old fashioned."

It is instructive to examine the most permissive societies to try to comprehend the extent of the revolution in sexual standards. Not too long ago, a street scene such as that in Figure 15.2 would have been unlawful. Anyone viewing

FIGURE 15.2 Societal change: The decline of legal regulation of sexuality.

Laws regulating sexual censorship have been a familiar part of Western Civilization since the early 1700s. In the present century, however, they have rapidly weakened and even disappeared in many parts of Europe, North America, and Japan. [Source: Photo © Jim Anderson 1980 / Woodfin Camp and Associates.]

these public displays in the 1980s might find it hard to believe that a novel such as *Ulysses* (with only a small amount of sexual content) was the center of censorship battles in U.S. courts from 1914 to 1933. By the 1960s, legal objections were no longer raised to the publication of sexual words or descriptions of sexual activities.

Pictures have always caused more problems than printed words, presumably because even small children can grasp their meaning. Apparently, extraterrestrials must also be protected. NASA was forced by public pressure to remove drawings of an unclothed human couple from the Voyager spacecraft in order to avoid spending tax dollars "on sending smut to outer space" (Wade, 1977). It was not until 1953 that *Playboy* magazine began its existence with a not-very-revealing nude photograph of Marilyn Monroe. The progression since then has been a slow but steady increase in the explicitness of what is shown, the depiction of male nudity in *Playgirl* and *Cosmopolitan* magazines, and the display of interacting nudes of the same and opposite sex in those publications plus *Penthouse, Oui, Hustler,* and many others. The only barriers still separating these mass circulation magazines from hard-core *pornography* in the United States are the pictorial taboos of erection, penetration, and ejaculation. Such pornography is legal now, but there are restrictions about its public display and its sale to minors.

Like magazines, movies pose the problem of being immediately understandable to anyone who views them. Strict censorship in the United States

FIGURE 15.3   *The production code: Chastity in the movies.*

Movie censorship in American movies in the 1930s and 1940s was governed by a production code that specified what could and could not be shown on the screen. Most of the regulations dealt with sex and prevented even the suggestion that married couples might occupy the same bed. [Source: Culver Pictures.]

began in 1934, shortly after the advent of sound films. A production code was drawn up to specify what could and could not be shown. The duration of a kiss was clearly limited. Two people could not occupy the same bed even to converse unless there was at least one foot firmly planted on the floor. Movies of that period made it appear that all married couples slept chastely in twin beds, as in Figure 15.3. By 1968, the old rules seemed increasingly unrealistic, and a rating system was introduced to restrict audiences by age rather than place any restrictions on movie content. The proportion of G-rated movies (all ages admitted) dropped from 41 percent in 1968 to 3 percent in 1980 (Yagoda, 1980). Audiences shun "family" movies, so moviemakers add a little extra violence or the word "damn" to movies like *Star Wars* or *The Black Hole* to earn at least a PG rating. In an X-rated film, every possible sexual act can be shown, but one has to be eighteen years of age or older in order to be admitted. For home viewers, the sale and rental of prerecorded videotapes have been substantially supported by the popularity of X-rated films. In fact, the absence of such material on video discs has been pinpointed by some as the reason for their apparent commercial failure. Beyond books, magazines, and movies, a similar increase in permissiveness can be traced in the theater and on television, though generally neither medium approaches the explicitness of movies.

Though no one can say with any degree of assurance which came first, it is clear that the changes just described are paralleled by equally striking changes in sexual attitudes and behavior. We will now turn to these more personal manifestations of the sexual revolution.

Increasingly Permissive Attitudes about Sexual Practices

Between the pioneering studies of Alfred Kinsey and his colleagues (Kinsey et al., 1948, 1953) and the more recent survey research of Morton Hunt (1974), there were a great many shifts in American attitudes about sex. These changes have consistently been in the direction of a greater willingness to tolerate the sexual practices of others. People are much more likely now than in previous decades to feel that their neighbors' private acts are not a matter for public concern. An amusing version of this permissive tone was first stated in the 1890s by a lady testifying at the trial of Oscar Wilde. She said, "I have no objection to anyone's sex life so long as they don't practice it in the street and frighten the horses."

One way to show the changes in attitude from generation to generation is to compare the attitudes of different age groups concerning various topics. In addition, there is evidence that amount of education, especially at the college level, is positively associated with permissive attitudes. Glenn and Weaver (1979) examined data from nationwide surveys involving several thousand subjects. Among the questions were items dealing with premarital sexual relations. The results are shown in Figure 15.4, p. 570. At each age level, permissiveness increases as educational level increases. The greatest change, however, is across generations. Between the oldest and youngest subjects in the study, acceptance of premarital intercourse more than doubled.

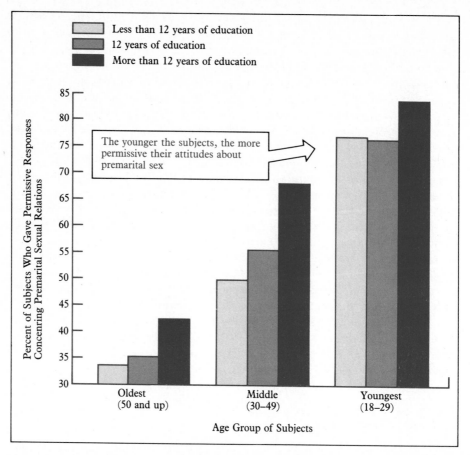

**FIGURE 15.4   *Acceptance of premarital sex:
Generational and educational effects.***

*Surveys in the United States indicate that permissive attitudes about such
activities as premarital sexual relationships increase to some extent as
educational level increases. The greatest change is across generations, with
younger subjects responding much more permissively than older ones. [Source:
Based on data from Glenn & Weaver, 1979.]*

Behavioral Changes:
Greater Frequency and Variety

The increased permissiveness in attitudes has been accompanied by similar
changes in sexual behavior. One result is that males and females are becoming
much more alike in their sexual activity than was true in the past. Though males
were historically more likely to engage in premarital sex than females, in recent
years the practices of the two groups have become essentially the same (Curran,
1975). The data shown in Figure 15.5 indicate that in this century each age
group of Americans has been more likely to engage in premarital sex than the
previous one, with the greatest change occurring among females. It should be

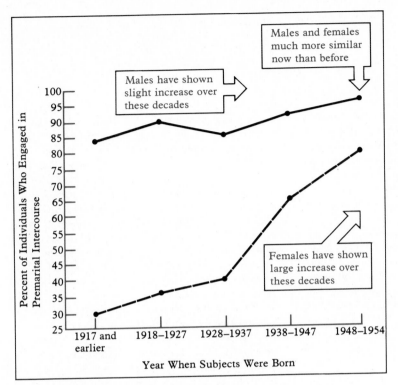

FIGURE 15.5 *Premarital intercourse: Males and females converge.*

Along with sexual attitudes, the sexual behavior of males and females in the United States has become more permissive as well. Each decade there has been a large increase in the percentage of females who engage in premarital intercourse. Thus, males and females are now quite similar in this aspect of sexual behavior. [Source: Based on data from Hunt, 1974.]

noted, however, that the transition from virginal to nonvirginal status in adolescence is not necessarily a totally positive experience. College women, for example, frequently report guilt and anxiety about having had intercourse for the first time and often feel that they were exploited by their male partners (Weis, 1983). Further, both males and females who have intercourse at the earliest ages tend to be independent, to place a low value on academic achievement, to be less religious, to feel less close to parents, and to be more involved in the use of alcohol, marijuana, and various illicit drugs (Jessor et al., 1983). Also, those who become sexually active before age fifteen are less likely to perceive sex and love as closely related (Rosen et al., 1982).

Such generational changes pervade almost every aspect of sexual behavior. It is found, for example, that younger subjects are more likely to report engaging in sex more frequently, including acts of intercourse, masturbation, and oral sex (Downey, 1980). There is little or no change in the incidence of homosexuality, and the only reported *decline* in sexual frequency involves male visits to prostitutes and acts of sex between humans and animals.

If the sexual revolution can be defined in terms of more explicit sexual depictions in society, a greater tolerance for the sexual practices of others, and an increasingly frequent and varied heterosexual pattern of behavior, it clearly has taken place. Whether one evaluates these changes as good or bad is another matter, as is discussed in the **Focus on Research** section on pages 572–573.

Negative Consequences of the Sexual Revolution: Pressure, Parenthood, and Pestilence

Usually, discussions of sexuality are heavily loaded with value judgments. Among those upset about the changes, many individuals feel that the increased permissiveness characteristic of the sexual revolution is totally wrong and constitutes the abandonment of morality and the decline of civilized society. For example, in the newsletter of the Pro-Family Forum, Lottie Beth Hobbs of Fort Worth writes, "Have you worried about your children being negative and depressed? Have you grieved over the lack of respect for authority? Have you wondered why society takes violence and death so lightly?" (Nocera, 1982). The answer, she believes, lies in the books found in public schools, and the solution lies in censorship and the banning of certain volumes from the libraries. On the opposite side, many individuals (including most sex researchers) feel that the liberalization of recent decades is a victory for enlightened thinking and the beginning of less repressive and healthier lives for us all (Schmidt, 1982).

Frankly, there is no way that research can provide an answer as to the goodness or badness of modern sexuality. It *is* possible, however, to document some of the consequences of the sexual changes. Perhaps because the data are easier to obtain, there is more hard evidence on the negative side than on the positive. We will briefly discuss three problem areas.

First, a number of studies report that data such as that presented in the present chapter can lead some individuals to feel pressured to change their own attitudes and behavior. For example, if most people now approve of and engage in premarital intercourse, those who do not do so indicate that they often feel odd or even in the wrong because of their virginal status. Obviously, survey data about what others believe or how they behave should *not* be a guide for oneself, but there are perceived pressures to conform to the current norm. A similar pressure is felt by females who read about such phenomena as multiple orgasms and then find themselves not having even one. In the *Redbook* survey of about 20,000 women, failure to reach orgasm resulted in negative feelings ranging from slightly frustrated to angry for 47 percent of those who responded (Sarrel & Sarrel, 1980). In a previous era, when female orgasm was either unknown, ignored, or believed to be a sign of moral weakness, these frustrated reactions would not have been very likely.

Second, the increase in premarital intercourse has not been accompanied by a similar increase in the use of contraception. Sexual activity begins at a very early age for many individuals, and the younger a person is at first intercourse, the less likely he or she is to practice any form of birth control (Cvetkovitch & Grote, 1983). Once a pattern of sexual activity is begun, it is not unusual for it to continue a year or more without contraceptive protection (Allgeier, Przybyla, & Thompson, 1981). The result is approximately one million unwanted teenage pregnancies in the United States each year, including 30,000 girls who are fourteen years old or younger (Alan Guttmacher Institute, 1976). Though the number of abortions is increasing and the rate of miscarriage is high among these young mothers, over 600,000 teenage girls give birth each year. Compared to older groups, the babies of teenagers are more likely to have a low birth weight and are more likely to die before reaching the age of one. The mothers themselves are more likely to develop anemia, and their death rate during pregnancy and birth is much higher than among mothers in their twenties. The very young mothers tend to drop out of school, to be

TABLE 15.1   The herpes diseases.

Genital herpes (or herpes simplex 2) is one of a family of viruses that can have mild to serious effects on human beings. As with herpes simplex 1, its worst symptoms for adults are likely to be itching and blisters, but it can be deadly if contracted by a newborn infant. So far, there is no known prevention or cure for this disease, and it is now the second most common sexually transmitted disease. [Source: Based on data in Miller, 1976; Wallis, 1982.]

Disease	Immediate effects	Long-term effects
Herpes simplex 1	Cold sores, fever blisters, usually on the mouth. Blisters burst after a few days and form hard, crusted sores that last a week or two.	Can recur at unpredictable intervals. Can be fatal to infants. Though rare, can lead to encephalitis or damaged vision.
Herpes simplex 2	Painful blisters on the penis, vagina, cervix, thighs, buttocks, and any other area of sexual contact. After about three weeks, the blisters dry up and vanish. There is also itching, fever, and headaches.	Can recur at unpredictable intervals. When newborn infants are infected by their mothers, up to 60 percent die, and half of the survivors suffer blindness or brain damage. Though rare, can lead to a mild form of meningitis.

unemployed, and, if they marry, to be divorced within six years. Altogether, this aspect of the sexual revolution is one of the saddest for those who conceive, those who are conceived, and for society.

Third, the increase in sexual activity, including sex with a variety of partners, has been accompanied by a startling increase in the incidence of venereal disease, or **sexually transmitted disease.** Both gonorrhea and syphilis are at record highs, but there is also an as-yet-incurable disease that has struck about 20,000,000 Americans—**genital herpes** (Felman et al., 1983). This sexually transmitted disease, also known as herpes simplex 2, is one of a family of five viruses that include cold sores, chicken pox, and mononucleosis. The effects of genital herpes and its closest relative (herpes simplex 1) are summarized in Table 15.1. Though there is as yet no safe and effective prevention or cure, it can only be contracted by direct contact with someone in the active stage (that is, with blis-

ters present). The use of a condom for intercourse is a useful precaution. The symptoms for adults who contract herpes 2 are likely to be mild, but it can kill or seriously impair a newborn infant. The only way to protect the child from its infected mother is to perform a caesarean section.

Though the symptoms of herpes disappear after about three weeks, the disease remains in the body with the potential to break out again and again at unpredictable times. Much more serious is the recent outbreak of Acquired Immunity Disease Syndrome (AIDS), primarily among gay males. This disease is also incurable as yet, and most of the victims die. Whatever your moral evaluation of the sexual changes of the twentieth century, almost everyone agrees that it is of crucial importance to avoid the negative effects of sexually transmitted disease, unwanted pregnancies, and pressures to conform.

Sexual Attraction

In Chapter 6, we discussed the factors that influence attraction, friendship, and the development of love. Is there any difference between being strongly attracted to someone of the opposite sex and being *sexually attracted* to that person? Can a male and a female become close friends without necessarily having any desire for an intimate sexual relationship? Such questions are frequently raised in our everyday lives, but they have not been the object of very much direct research attention. As a first step toward finding the answers, we will examine some of the relevant evidence that deals with the determinants of **sexual attraction.**

Sexual Attraction in Other Species

Unlike human beings and a small number of other species, most animals engage in sexual activity only during a brief breeding season (Manning, 1981). For example, the only time that male and female red deer interact sexually at all is during a six-week period each autumn. There is a worm in the Pacific Ocean (the palolo) that engages in reproductive activity just once a year, at dawn one week after the November full moon. A great many female mammals such as cats and dogs go through regular estrus cycles throughout the year, and sexual intercourse occurs only when the female is at the point in her cycle when an egg is available for fertilization. Each species must be responsive to cues that sexual activity can take place, and at that point there is often some selectivity as to the choice of a mate, as in Figure 15.6.

Cues to sexual readiness. There are various kinds of sexual cues to which different species respond. By far the most common is the female secretion of a substance, known as a **sexual pheromone,** that attracts the male and arouses him sexually. Such species-specific attractants have been studied in ants (Höll-

FIGURE 15.6   *Sexual attraction in animals.*

Since few species are continuously active sexually in the way that human beings are, they respond to cues that indicate reproductive readiness. The most common such cues are olfactory, in the form of **sexual pheromones** *secreted by the female that attract and arouse males of the same species. Beyond that, in many higher species at least, there is an element of selectivity as choices are made among potential mates. [Source: Photo by Leo Vals / Frederic Lewis Photographs.]*

dobler & Haskins, 1977), beetles (Byers & Wood, 1981), snakes (Garstka & Crews, 1981), mice (Cooper, 1978), hamsters (Singer et al., 1976), dogs (Goodwin et al., 1979), and monkeys (Michael et al., 1971). When a very small amount of an artificial sex pheromone is applied to spayed female dogs, any nearby male becomes sexually aroused and attempts to engage in intercourse (Goodwin et al., 1979).

Interestingly enough, there are also cues that act as signals for avoiding sex. When male rats have copulated to the point of exhaustion, they make ultrasonic vocalizations which seem to be messages to the female indicating that he is in a socially withdrawn state (Anisko et al., 1978).

Mate selection. As Darwin, among others, observed, once males are attracted by such cues as pheromones, females engage in some sort of selection process. Female seals, for example, encourage fighting among the bulls who lust after them. Presumably, the strongest and most aggressive one wins the right to mate and thus provides the best opportunity for conceiving strong offspring who will survive (Lamar, 1976).

The general criterion for such selection behavior is *fitness*. The more fit the mate, the more likely is copulation to take place. Males are found to be much less selective, and in most species they mate with multiple partners if the opportunity arises. For the discriminating female, the cues to fitness are most likely to be such variables as size, ability to dominate the female and any rivals, and the attractiveness of the male (as in birds that display their feathers) or of the nest he builds to entice a mate (Manning, 1981).

When a species is monogomous (as humans more or less are), the problem is a little different. These permanent pairings are characteristic of several kinds of birds and of a few mammals. Both the male and the female have to make a careful selection, because they will be paired for life. These mates tend to be fairly similar in size and appearance. A common pattern is for the male to stake out a territory (often after fighting other males to get it), and this area tends to be a good breeding site with an ample supply of food. He then sings or otherwise advertises his assets until the "right" female comes along. The male is likely to attack whoever invades his territory, male or female, and an attractive female seems to be one who submits to his aggressiveness rather than retreating (Manning, 1981).

We can now ask whether the study of sexual attraction in animals has any relevance to such behavior in human beings. To what extent do we react to smell, fitness, dominance, territorial displays, and so forth? As will be discussed next, there are at least rough analogues to some of these phenomena in human sexual interactions.

The Role of Smell and Appearance in Human Sexual Attraction

Though it is tempting to assume that animal behavior provides detailed guidelines as to how humans might be expected to react, that conceptual leap is not as reasonable as it may appear. Among the problems are the diversity of animal behaviors from which to choose (Zillmann, 1983) and the pervasive effects of cultural influences on what humans do (Manning, 1981). The role of smell provides a good example.

Sniffing out a sexual partner. It is a popular belief that sexual attraction is something automatic and mysterious, something that occurs when two people have the right sexual "chemistry" (Zehner, 1981). To judge by the amount of money spent each year on perfume, cologne, after-shave lotion, deodorant, scented soap, and all the rest (Winter, 1978), it appears that most people believe that sexual attractiveness is a matter of achieving just the right smell. Figure 15.7 depicts a small sample of the many products that are designed to provide each of us with an alluring aroma. Recently, some manufacturers have moved directly toward sexual attractants by adding the pheromones of boars to perfumes and other products (D. White, 1981)!

The well-established effect of sexual pheromones in other species would logically appear to be of equal importance in human behavior. Investigators have isolated substances in human vaginal secretions that are chemically similar to the pheromones of other primates (Sokolov et al., 1976), and these substances vary appropriately during the menstrual cycle so that they peak during ovulation when conception is possible (Michael et al., 1971). The difficulty is that research on responses to the smell of these secretions does not indicate that they are particularly attractive to either males or females (Doty et al., 1975). When a synthetic human pheromone is applied to a female's skin, she and her husband are no more likely to have intercourse than when a placebo is applied (Morris & Udry, 1978). Among the difficulties in finding human pheromonal

FIGURE 15.7   *Odor as a sexual attractant.*

It seems to be generally accepted that various smells make human beings sexually attractive. The advertisements for numerous products for males and females encourage and support the belief that the right odor will entice multitudes of potential partners. The various products may provide each of us with a pleasant aroma, but the effects on sexual attraction are not nearly as clear-cut as the advertisements imply. [Source: Photo by Antonio Mendoza, Picture Cube.]

effects are the influence of other variables on attraction and arousal, the masking of such smells by all of the other fragrances we apply to our bodies, and the fact that primates (including rhesus monkeys) are able to respond sexually even when they are deprived of a sense of smell (Goldfoot et al., 1978).

There are only limited amounts of research evidence as to the social effects of odor. It has been reported that subjects of both genders who were exposed to pheromones (without their knowledge) rated photographs of women as more sexually attractive than when pheromones were absent. In a dentist's waiting room, a seat sprayed with a human pheromone attracted women and repelled men (D. White, 1981), which seems to be the opposite of what would be expected. In an experiment closer to our everyday experiences, Baron (1981b) exposed undergraduate males to a female confederate who was or was not wearing perfume (Jungle Gardenia). Her clothing was also varied. Her attire was either informal (sweatshirt and jeans) or neat (blouse, skirt, and hose). Afterward, the males were asked to indicate the attractiveness of the confederate. As can be seen in Figure 15.8, the presence of the perfume affected the ratings, but clothing style determined whether it was a positive or negative effect. The perfumed confederate was perceived as more attractive when dressed informally and as *less* attractive when dressed neatly. In addition, a

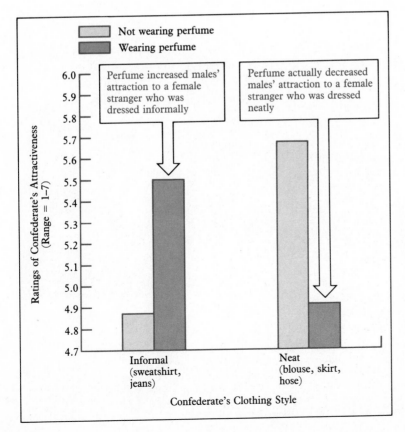

FIGURE 15.8   *Perfume and attractiveness: It depends on what you're wearing.*

In an experiment designed to test the effect of odor on perceptions of attractiveness, male subjects responded to an informally or neatly dressed female confederate who was or was not wearing perfume. The perfume led to more positive ratings when she was dressed informally and to more negative ratings when she was dressed neatly. It appears that human responses to odor are relatively complex and are influenced by a variety of factors. [Source: Based on data from Baron, 1981.]

female wearing perfume and informal clothes was rated as warm and romantic while the combination of perfume and neat clothes yielded ratings of colder and less romantic. In related research on job applicants, male interviewers rated those who wore perfume or cologne more negatively while female interviewers responded in the opposite way to odors (Baron, 1983a). Similarly, male interviewers responded most negatively to a female applicant who wore perfume *and* engaged in positive nonverbal behaviors such as smiling, making eye contact, and leaning toward the interviewer (Baron, 1983b). It appears that human responses to smell are considerably more complex than those of lower animals; other factors can eliminate or even reverse the effect of smell as a sexual attractant.

Seeing a sexual partner. As you might assume from the discussion of physical attractiveness in Chapter 6, sexual attraction in human beings is based in large part on visual cues. Research has repeatedly shown that both males and females equate attractiveness with such characteristics as being sexually warm (Dion et al., 1972), with being acceptable as a date and as a spouse (Byrne et al., 1970), and having physical appeal (Janda et al., 1981). Though there is not a gender difference in this respect, the physical attractiveness of females seems to be the crucial determinant of whether they are perceived as sexually desirable (Dion,

FIGURE 15.9 *Sexually attractive females: Different eras, different standards.*

The generally accepted standards of sexual attractiveness in females clearly varies over time and across cultures. Consider the differences among these representatives of 1882 (pale, narrow waisted), 1952 (full-figured with an emphasis on large breasts), and 1982 (tan, athletic, assertive). [Source: Photo (left) from the Sophia Smith Collection, Smith College; photo (center) © "The News"; photo (right) © by Ulrike Welsch.]

1981). For males as sex objects, pure attractiveness can be supplemented or even replaced by such variables as skill, strength, courage, and assertiveness.

If female appearance is all-important to sexual attraction, what are the essential features? Curry (1972) suggests that since medieval times in England, the ideal beauty was described as being blond and blue eyed with red lips, even white teeth, small waist, and soft skin. For at least 4,000 years, the ideal of large breasts has led women to wear special devices to make their bosoms appear bigger than they actually are (Lowman, 1980). More recently, the ideal American beauty has been described as athletic, physically assured, and strong (Corliss, 1982). Figure 15.9 presents samples of three versions of sexually attractive females. It would appear that cultural factors play a considerable part in shaping the perceptions that are dominant at a given time and place.

Comparatively little research has been directed at examining the physical details that elicit sexual attraction. In one such study, females with medium-sized breasts were liked better and judged as more appealing than those with either very small or very large breasts. Large-breasted females were judged to be relatively unintelligent, incompetent, immoral, and immodest (Kleinke & Staneski, 1980). It seems probable that the definition of sexual attraction purely in terms of appearance is only part of the story. To what else do we respond?

Sexual Attraction Based on Psychological Cues

When we turn to psychological variables as the basis of sexual attraction, there is a surprising amount of evidence to indicate the importance of non-physical attributes. For example, Tesser and Reardon (1981) point out the many ways in which sexual attraction is based on cognitive processes—beliefs, thoughts, and fantasies. We may wonder what *he* can possibly see in *her,* or vice versa, but each person is responding in large part to their conception of what the other individual is like. More specifically, sexual attraction is found to be influenced by such diverse variables as social skills (Cook, 1981), social background, and even attitude similarity (Fisher & Byrne, 1981). In the **Focus on Research** panel on pages 580–581, attraction to one's own gender is discussed.

Some aspects of attraction are tied to what is believed to be appropriate behavior for interacting males and females. When couples converse for the first time, males tend to dominate the conversation, select the topics, and push toward a more intimate level of interaction than the female might desire (Davis, 1978). When a female acts friendly in such an encounter, males are likely to interpret her behavior as being flirtatious and seductive and even as indicating promiscuity (Abbey, 1982). The traditional male role is to take the lead in initiating contact, making dates, and engaging in sexual intercourse. Shortly before the birth of Christ, Ovid observed the same phenomenon, but proposed that "Could men agree to ask no woman first, the asker's role perforce would be reversed" (1971, p. 14). Even in the 1980s, men say that this role reversal would be a positive development, but, when females take the initiative in dating, the resulting relationship tends not to last (Kelley et al., 1981).

*Sexual Attraction to One's Own Gender:
The Determinants of Homosexual Behavior*

Throughout recorded history, the tendency of some males to engage in sexual acts with other males and of some females to engage in sexual acts with other females has been observed. Depending on the time and place, such behavior has been treated with tolerance and with hatred, accepted as a normal aspect of human activity and condemned as a sin or a crime, and such behavior has resulted in imprisonment, medical treatment, and execution. Since 1974, those who engage in homosexual acts are no longer classified by the American Psychiatric Association as being emotionally disturbed and requiring treatment.

The general heterosexual public seems to regard those who practice homosexuality with somewhat restrained acceptance and with amusement based in part on anxiety and fear. There is a good deal of evidence that **homophobia** (the fear that homosexuals might inflict their preferences on others) is widespread. Since one of the bases of this phobia is the belief that a seemingly "straight" person might have unconscious gay tendencies, there has been considerable interest in discovering the way in which such behavioral tendencies develop.

Since the earliest Kinsey surveys (Kinsey et al., 1948), it has been generally known that people cannot simply be divided into two groups: heterosexuals and homosexuals. Though many individuals are exclusively involved with members of the opposite sex and many are exclusively involved with members of the same sex, many others (bisexuals) enjoy sexual activities with both genders. To further complicate matters, there are definitional problems with respect to those who change their sexual orientation from same- to opposite-gender partners or vice versa and those who have one or two experiences different from their usual pattern. Leaving these questions aside, let us look at the evidence involving the determinants of more or less

exclusively homosexual behavior versus more or less exclusively heterosexual behavior.

All of the theories and the associated research can be divided into two broad explanations. It has been proposed that sexual interest in one's own gender is based on biological factors *or* on learning experiences. On the biological side, there has been interest in seeking specific genes that bring about homosexuality (e.g., Pritchard, 1962; Slater, 1962) and in specific hormone variations that rested on malfunctions occurring before or after birth (Feldman & MacCulloch, 1971; Margolese, 1970). Some researchers, such as Bell et al. (1981), failing to identify common family factors in the histories of homosexuals, have simply assumed that unknown biological differences must somehow provide the explanation. To date, there is simply no consistent evidence that sexual preferences are associated with either genetic or hormonal variables.

Theories based on learning experiences have been more numerous. Gallup and Suarez (1982) suggest that when people have difficulty in obtaining or achieving satisfaction with a heterosexual partner, frustration leads them to seek someone of the same gender. Others propose that a given culture at a given time simply creates a subgroup, and role demands determine how those with a homosexual label are supposed to behave (e.g., Hoffman, 1968; McIntosh, 1968). Parental behavior has been proposed as the "cause" of the offspring's homosexual preferences. Thus, Green (1974) hypothesized that some parents consciously or unconsciously reinforce behavior that is inappropriate for the child's gender. In support of this proposition, gay males report more types of cross-gender behavior in childhood than do heterosexual males (Harry, 1983). Certain family constellations, such as (for males) a weak father and a strong mother or (for females) a father who is too intimate, have been

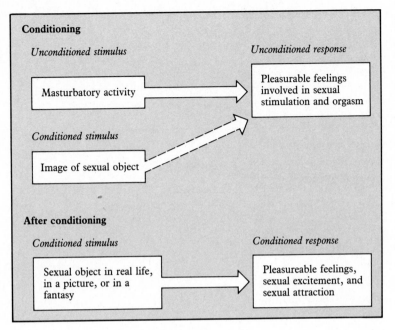

FIGURE 15.10 *Storms's conditioning model: Learning a sexual preference.*

According to the conditioning model of Storms (1981), homosexual preferences are learned just as any other sexual preferences are learned. The image of a person of the same sex (or opposite sex or both sexes) is associated during early masturbatory activity with the pleasures of sexual stimulation and orgasm. Subsequently, those images serve to evoke excitement and sexual attraction. In such youthful "conditioning trials," people learn to respond to particular classes of stimuli as sexually arousing.

described as characterizing the childhood of those who later become homosexual (Bieber, 1962; Kaye, 1972). As with the biological explanations, no consistent evidence is available to support any of the psychological theories either.

The most recent conceptualization of homosexual development (Storms, 1981) is also based on a learning model, but it is specific to the experience of each individual. The theory rests on conditioning as the underlying reason for a person's sexual attraction to the same sex, opposite sex, or both. It is hypothesized that masturbatory activity serves as the unconditioned stimulus for sexual pleasure. When this experience occurs in association with the image of someone (most likely in the form of a picture or a fantasy), that image becomes conditioned to the positive emotions of sexual stimulation and to the powerful reinforcement of orgasm (see Figure 15.10). This same model would also explain how some people learn to respond sexually to particular kinds of clothing, to pain, to animals, or whatever it's simply a matter of associating arousal and pleasure with a given stimulus.

The major evidence supporting this conditioning model is somewhat indirect. For example, in Western cultures, boys and girls are likely to be separated when they are young, so early sexual activity is likely to occur in the context of same-gender images. Thus, those who mature at the earliest age are more likely to associate same-gender images with sexuality. Interestingly enough, a homosexual orientation is more characteristic of early maturing individuals (e.g., Goode & Haber, 1977), including male athletes (Garner & Smith, 1977), than of late maturing ones. In a similar way, the theory explains why male and female homosexuals are more likely to develop when all of the offspring in the family are of the same gender (Gundlach, 1977; Schubert et al., 1976).

Though investigators are far from reaching agreement as to the determinants of homosexuality, the concept of sexual preference as a learned, rather than a built-in, response is appealing to many psychologists.

TABLE 15.2   *Shared fantasies as a basis of attraction.*

Those with unusual sexual preferences also report erotic fantasies that differ from the fantasies of controls. Sexual attraction is likely to be high toward a potential partner who accepts and shares the unusual practices and who is also excited by similar fantasies. [Source: Based on data in Gosselin, 1981.]

Erotic fantasies reported by transvestites, fetishists, and sadomasochists more frequently than by control group

(1) Being forced to do something
(2) Wearing clothes of the opposite sex
(3) Being whipped or spanked
(4) Being tied up
(5) Being hurt by a partner
(6) Being excited by material or clothing
(7) Whipping or spanking someone
(8) Tying someone up
(9) Using objects for stimulation
(10) Forcing someone to do something

Perhaps the most obvious and least investigated basis for sexual attraction involves an individual's sexual behavior. That is, it seems reasonable to suggest that a person's sexual preferences would be very positive or very negative factors in attracting a sexual partner. Istvan and Griffitt (1980) provided college students with information about the sexual experience of an opposite-sex stranger and also assessed the experience of each subject. Afterward, the subjects evaluated the stranger on several dimensions, including his or her desirability as a date and as a spouse. Surprisingly, the only effect was that a highly experienced stranger was rated as undesirable by some of the subjects. Inexperienced males were negative about a highly experienced female, and both inexperienced and moderately experienced females were negative in response to a highly experienced male.

Beyond such variations in sexual experience, Gosselin (1981) points out that individuals with unusual sexual interests have difficulties in identifying like-minded partners. He examined the preferences of four groups of males: those whose sexual pleasure is enhanced by wearing female clothing (transvestites), wearing rubber garments (rubber fetishists), wearing leather garments (leather fetishists), and giving or receiving pain (sadomasochists). These individuals belonged to organizations composed of others with similar sexual interests. It was found that they differed from a control group not only in their sexual practices but also in their erotic fantasies. As shown in Table 15.2, these four groups were significantly more likely than the controls to report a variety of specific erotic fantasies. A partner who can share such fantasies and practices is of course highly prized. These males describe the ideal female partner as beautiful, distant, peaceful, authoritarian, theatrical, cruel, and enthusiastically uninhibited about sex. Further, the women with whom they had sex (wives, girl friends, female sadomasochists, specialized prostitutes) fit the ideal surprisingly well.

The Effects of Erotic Images on Motivation, Fantasy, and Behavior

In the previous section, we discussed sexual attraction and arousal in response to such external stimuli as odor, appearance, and the behavior of potential sex objects. Such effects emphasize the connections between the behavior of lower animals and ourselves. For human beings, however, there are some apparently unique factors that exert an even more powerful effect on sexual responsivity. We are affected by both internal and external erotic images in the form of pictures and words, and these images influence sexual arousal, thought processes, and overt sexual activity.

Imagination as an Aphrodisiac

Throughout history, people have sought to identify certain foods, spices, or exotic chemicals that would arouse them (or their partner) to new heights of sexual passion. Psychological research suggests that the most powerful such aphrodisiac is less expensive, safer, and more easily available than anyone knew: it lies in our ability to create erotic mental images. For example, when married couples were asked just to think about a series of erotic scenes, they reported a much higher level of sexual excitement than other couples who viewed analogous photographs or read parallel erotic stories (Byrne & Lamberth, 1971). Response to self-created fantasies is so strong that it has been suggested that individual differences in *sex drive* may rest primarily on whether a person learns to think about sex a great deal rather than on some biological factor such as hormones. When college students were simply asked to write as many sexual fantasies as they could during a 20-minute period, they engaged in significantly more sexual behavior the following week than did students who were not asked to create fantasies (Eisenman, 1982). Women who ordinarily create sexual fantasies while engaging in sexual acts are found to be more physiologically responsive to fantasy and to an erotic stimulus than nonfantasizing women (Stock & Geer, 1982). In fact, dysfunctional patients often must be *taught* to engage in erotic fantasy (Wagner & Green, 1981).

When we dream, involuntary sexual fantasies frequently occur, and the result is physiological arousal and even orgasm at times. When we are awake, such fantasies occur voluntarily. They range from idle daydreams to deliberate efforts to become aroused (Campagna, 1976). When people masturbate or engage in sex with a partner, they frequently combine such activity with fantasy sex in order to enhance their pleasure (Sue, 1979) and to control the timing of orgasm (Przybyla et al., 1983).

A person's fantasies may consist of memories of past experiences, stories borrowed from books or movies, or original creations. Examples of each type

TABLE 15.3   *Private sexual fantasies:*
Remembered, borrowed, created.

When college students were asked, under conditions of anonymity, to describe a favorite sexual fantasy, they reported scenes that were based on memories, stories they had seen or read, and original ideas. Such thoughts seem to occur periodically throughout the day, though some individuals spend more time thinking about erotic matters than others.

Male sexual fantasies

Imagination based on memory of past events:
I would like to think "way back when" when I lost my virginity to one of the most voluptuous young ladies I ever met. I met her on a beach, I was only seventeen years old and when she told me to take her home, I had no idea what was in store for me. Looking back on it, I was literally *raped.* She taught me everything . . . oral sex, anal sex, etc. I feel everyone should go thru an experience like that.

Imagination based on films and magazines:
To have more than one woman in bed. To just literally be attacked by two big-busted beautiful females that just do anything and everything to me the entire night. Oh thank heaven.

Imagination based on original ideas:
I am walking down the street and a whole bunch of great looking girls start chasing after me and finally catch me and force me to have sex with each one of them.

Female sexual fantasies

Imagination based on memory of past events:
I go to the home of a very close friend—walk in the door and he is upset, crying. I lead him to a couch and sit there quietly, holding him, sharing thoughts. We kiss and begin to get more and more excited. We undress each other, touching until we have intercourse and then lie in each other's arms. It's quiet, secure, enjoyable.

Imagination based on films and books:
I've fantasized two males having sex with me at the same time. It seems exciting at the time I'm fantasizing it but I don't think I could ever do it. It's with one male having intercourse with me and the other stimulating other parts of my body and eventually both have intercourse simultaneously.

Imagination based on original ideas:
It's hard for me to describe. It's like I'm in another world that's mostly males. Females are very submissive. Males buy and trade females. I'm always trying to escape to be with my boyfriend. Sex is usually the punishment for disobeying. But with my boyfriend, sex is kind of like the goal of my escaping.

are presented in Table 15.3. These stories were written anonymously by male and female college students who were asked to reveal one of their favorite fantasies. According to the subjects, these imaginative acts took place when they were in class, during a study break, during sexual arousal, when they were going to sleep or waking up, and when they encountered an attractive member of the opposite sex. In other words, thinking about sex plays a pervasive role in the lives of many individuals.

External Images as Triggers for Fantasy and Arousal

Even though internal sex fantasies are a common occurrence, much more research interest has been generated by the role of external sex fantasies in the form of magazines, books, pictures, and so forth (Yaffé & Nelson, 1982). As was pointed out earlier in this chapter, the content of such material now runs the gamut from mildly erotic depictions of partial nudity to the most hard-core pornography. The effects of this sort of stimulation were almost entirely a matter of speculation leading to wildly divergent opinions until behavioral scientists began conducting relevant experiments in the late 1960s. What has been learned about the effects of erotica?

Effects on physiological arousal. In the detailed laboratory study of Masters and Johnson (1966), bodily changes that occur during a sexual episode (the **sexual response cycle**) have been generally accepted as consisting of four phases: excitement, plateau, orgasm, and resolution. That is, arousal builds rapidly as stimulation begins, levels off at a high state as stimulation continues, reaches a peak or climax, and then slowly fades back to a nonaroused state. When subjects are exposed to an erotic stimulus such as a sensual story or a sexually explicit movie, they go through an identical cycle except that the orgasm phase ordinarily does not occur.

Specifically, individuals who listen to or view erotic stimuli are found to experience an increased blood supply in the genital region that leads to swelling and reddening of the tissue, accompanied by an increase in temperature. In addition, fluids that lubricate the sexual organs tend to be secreted. These reactions take place and increase in magnitude as the erotic material is presented until a relatively high level is reached. At the conclusion of the presentation, these physical aspects of arousal begin to recede.

Much of the research on such bodily reactions has used physiological measures as well as self-reports of arousal (Kelley & Byrne, 1983). The male response has been assessed with a **penile plethysmograph** that attaches to the penis and detects changes in volume or circumference. For female measurement, there is the **vaginal photoplethysmograph** that involves the insertion of a light source into the vagina and the measurement of the amount of light reflected from the surrounding walls (Geer, 1975). A still newer measurement technique is the **thermograph** that measures temperature changes in the genitals during the various phases of the sexual response cycle (Seeley et al., 1980). Though such physical indications of arousal are generally accompanied by self-reports of excitement, Hatch (1979) proposes that a combination of verbal and physiological measures is best.

How does an external fantasy lead to arousal? Though it may not seem to be a problem until you stop and think about it, why should images of other people's sexual acts cause anyone to become sexually aroused? The characters in a movie, for example, may be engaging in foreplay or intercourse, but the audience is simply sitting in a theater and eating popcorn. In the case of an erotic photograph or drawing, any response is usually to nameless characters whose background, relationship, and emotions are unknown. Nevertheless, the viewer reacts physiologically just as if he or she were interacting with an enthusiastic mate.

The process whereby such external images lead to arousal seems to involve cognitive activity in that the external stimuli are translated into internal images in which the viewer is an active participant. The arousal that occurs is in response to one's own personal fantasy version of the external presentation. This theoretical description of the effects of erotica is difficult to test directly because the primary activity takes place internally. To manipulate these unseen cognitions, Geer and Fuhr (1976) devised an ingenious procedure. They asked male subjects to listen to an erotic story and *at the same time* to engage in nonsexual cognitive tasks that would interfere with any internal fantasizing. This was accomplished through a procedure known as *dichotic listening* in which earphones delivered a stimulus to one ear (an erotic story) and a different stimulus (random numbers) to the other ear. It was found that the more complex the task required with the numbers, the less sexually aroused the men were in response to the story. Just listening to the numbers did not interfere with arousal, adding each pair of numbers interfered some, and classifying each pair as odd or even and above or below 50 interfered a great deal. In each instance, the subjects *heard* the story and knew what it was about, but they were presumably too busy to process it and turn it into a personal fantasy.

Since most people report having visual rather than auditory fantasies, Przybyla and Byrne (1983) proposed that it would be more difficult to interfere with visual erotica than with auditory material. The reason is that pictorial material can be utilized as it is in one's private imagery, while auditory material must be translated into pictures before it becomes a personal fantasy. If so, the cognitive interference brought about by the various tasks with the numbers should have much less effect on arousal when the erotica consists of a movie than when it consists of an oral presentation of the same story. Male and female college students either watched a videotape of an explicit sex film or listened to an auditory tape containing a description of the activities shown in the movie. The interference was created in the same way as in the previous study with numbers to be listened to, added, or classified. The results, shown in Figure 15.11, were just as predicted for the males: complex cognitive activity interfered with arousal in response to the auditory material but not in response to pictorial erotica. For females, cognition decreased arousal in response to both kinds of sexual stimuli. It appears that males and females may differ in how they deal with visual erotic images.

There is an additional variable of interest in determining the way in which people respond to erotic images — anxiety or fear. Strangely enough, there is anecdotal and clinical evidence suggesting that these negative emotions should prevent sexual responsiveness and, alternatively, that they should *enhance* sexual responsiveness. Many sex therapists suggest, for example, that perform-

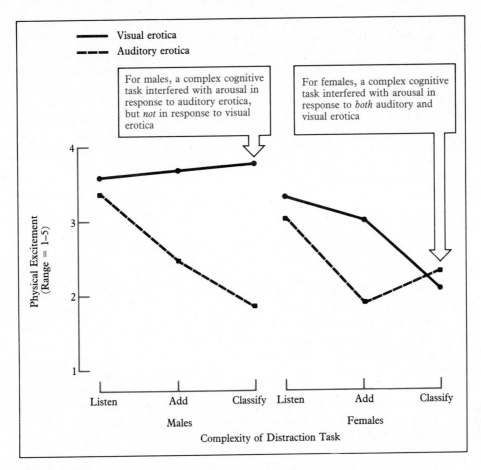

FIGURE 15.11 *Processing auditory and visual erotica:*
Sexual excitement versus cognitive activity.

The role of internal cognitive processing in responding to external erotic
material is investigated by exposing subjects to erotica, requiring cognitive
activity of varying complexity, and determining the resulting level of sexual
arousal. Both males and females are less aroused by auditory erotica as they
engage in increasingly complex cognitive tasks. With visual erotica, females are
equally distracted by cognitive activity, but males are not. It is possible that
males and females process sexual visual images differently. [Source: Based on
data from Przybyla & Byrne, 1983.]

ance fears and anxiety about sexual matters prevent normal sexual responding,
thus bringing about dysfunctions. In contrast, there is the belief that sexual
excitement is greatest when there is danger such as the fear of getting caught. In
laboratory studies of response to erotic films, there is consistent support for the
proposition that anxiety increases arousal. In the first experimental tests of this
phenomenon, it was found that when females (Hoon et al., 1977) or males
(Wolchik et al., 1980) are shown an anxiety-producing film such as the depiction of auto accidents, their arousal to an erotic film shown afterward is greater

than if they first saw a neutral film. Since such effects could be the result of feeling relieved at the conclusion of the unpleasant movie, Barlow et al. (1982) examined what happens when anxiety is created *during* exposure to an erotic movie. Males were shown explicit films under neutral conditions and under conditions in which a light signal indicated that they would receive an electric shock. Just as in the previous studies, sexual arousal (as measured by a penile plethysmograph) was greater in the anxiety condition than in the neutral condition. It appears that anxiety (at least at the moderate levels produced in a laboratory) serves to increase sexual excitement in response to erotic images. Zillmann's theory of excitation transfer (see Chapter 9) provides one explanation of such findings.

Behavioral Effects of Erotica

The various censorship laws mentioned at the beginning of this chapter were not enacted in response to expressed fears of erotic material affecting private fantasies or causing sexual arousal, though **pornography** has often been defined as material that does just that. The assumption was that when erotica brought about sexual thoughts and physiological excitement, it would then lead to undesirable behavior. Whether such stimulation does, in fact, bring about behavioral changes is the crucial question in any public policy about censorship of sexual images (Wills, 1977). While we are waiting for the necessary research to be conducted and the results to be transformed into public policy, it should be noted that sexual content is a common element in everyday television programs even though this imagery is very different from hard-core pornography (Diamond, 1980). Some samples from one day's television programming are shown in Table 15.4. Little is yet known about the effects of these daily messages on the attitudes, beliefs, and behavior of those who view it.

The censorship issue is not ancient history, by the way. Though the Catholic church recently closed down its office that reviewed movie content in the United States (Ostling, 1980), other institutions still perform this function. The state of Maryland runs a censorship board that decides what movies may be shown and what scenes must be omitted to make a film acceptable (Carlinsky, 1978). There is currently a resurgence of the drive to censor books (Arons, 1981) and even to burn them (Ramirez, 1981). Four out of ten Americans want more restrictions on what can be legally published (Gordon, 1980). Some women's organizations are attacking pornography as the cause for the increase in the incidence of rape (Lederer, 1980). The major difficulty is that the desire for increased censorship as well as the desire for total freedom from it tend to be based on opinions rather than on facts. Those opinions, in turn, are highly correlated with one's political orientation as liberal or conservative (Brown et al., 1978). The question to be answered by psychological research is whether exposure to erotica has any influence on interpersonal behavior, on the nature and frequency of subsequent sexual acts, and—most importantly—on the occurrence of sex crimes.

TABLE 15.4   *TV sex: From the tube into the living room.*

Though television programs are quite different from explicit erotica and hard-core pornography, they contain a great deal of soft-core sexual material and innuendo. The effects of such content on viewers is virtually unknown. [Source: Based on material in Diamond, 1980.]

Time	TV source	Content
8:35 A.M.	Commercial	Nude couple in a Japanese bath.
9:00 A.M.	Talk show	Author promoting book about a "love child."
11:30 A.M.	Game show	Question: What are cold showers good for?
12:30 P.M.	Soap opera	Woman commits suicide because her husband is having an affair.
1:00 P.M.	Soap opera	Female has pregnancy symptoms and tells male he is the father.
1:00 P.M.	Soap opera	Female hired by male to prove that rival can be seduced by a pretty woman.
2:00 P.M.	Soap opera	Male tries to force female into prostitution.
3:00 P.M.	Soap opera	Female kisses male who decides to file for divorce from his wife.
4:00 P.M.	Situation comedy	Male makes pass at female seeking to rent an apartment.
5:00 P.M.	Game show	Host to female panelist: "After I just gave you a kiss and a little tongue!"
8:00 P.M.	Situation comedy	Attractive female is photographed in the nude.
9:30 P.M.	Situation comedy	Dialogue: "Do you like sex?" "If something's too easy, men don't appreciate it."
11:00 P.M.	News	A prostitute talks about being trapped into the profession by the money.

Interpersonal effects of erotica. When individuals are sexually aroused, their evaluations of the opposite sex and their interpersonal behavior are altered in ways that are not too surprising. For example, males who are aroused by sexual stimuli perceive females as more physically attractive and sexually responsive than do unaroused males (Stephan et al., 1971). In fact, both positive *and* negative responses to relevant cues are affected by arousal. Exposure to erotica leads both males and females to perceive a good-looking stranger as attractive and desirable as a date; when the opposite sex stranger is unattractive, however, he or she is perceived as *less* attractive by aroused subjects (Istvan & Griffitt, 1983). This intensifying effect of arousal is depicted in Figure 15.12, p. 590. In a similar way, sexual arousal leads males to associate feelings of love with their female partners (Dermer & Pyszczynski, 1978).

In addition to affecting perceptions, arousal by erotica also influences overt behavior. Individuals who are aroused by sexual pictures (and who feel posi-

FIGURE 15.12   *Erotica and perception: An intensifying effect.*

Sexual arousal seems to intensify an individual's responses to members of the opposite sex. For both males and females, exposure to erotica leads to more positive ratings of an attractive stranger and more negative ratings of an unattractive one. [Source: Based on data from Istvan & Griffitt, 1983.]

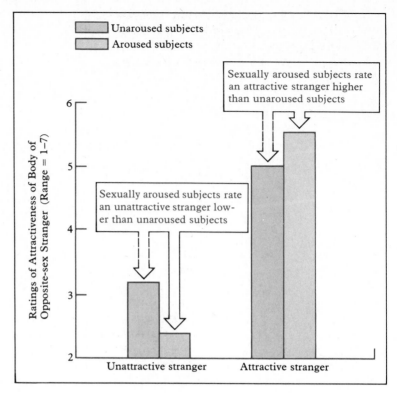

tively about being aroused) spend more time looking at an opposite-sex stranger and sit closer to such an individual. Those to whom arousal is a negative experience tend to avoid looking at or sitting near someone of the opposite sex (Griffitt et al., 1974).

Erotica: Motivating and modeling effects.   We have described how erotic stimuli induce sexual excitement, and it seems reasonable to suppose that those who are excited would be motivated to seek sexual satisfaction. In addition, it has been found that those who view filmed models engaging in various kinds of behavior are likely to imitate these models (see Chapter 9). With respect to sexual behavior, we might also expect the viewers to imitate the behavior of filmed models. Thus, there is good reason to believe that exposure to explicit erotic stories and pictures would increase the probability of *some* type of sexual activity afterward and also increase the probability of the specific acts that were depicted.

The motivating effects of sexual stimuli have been consistently verified in experimental research. Individuals who are shown erotic slides or films are more likely to engage in a sexual act during the next few hours than individuals exposed to nonsexual material. For example, unmarried students show an increase in masturbation (Amoroso et al., 1971), and married couples are more likely to engage in intercourse after exposure to erotica (Cattell et al., 1972). The latter study also found that the more aroused an individual was in response to sexual slides, the greater the probability of intercourse afterward. Such effects are relatively weak and do not tend to be long-lasting. An analogy might be exposure to a very tempting food commercial on TV. The sight of delicious food can arouse your appetite and send you to the kitchen for a snack, but long-term effects on the amount of food you consume seem unlikely.

Modeling in response to erotica has been more difficult to demonstrate. Subjects in much of the research simply seem to do *something* sexual, not necessarily what they watched others do. As with the food analogy, a commercial might show a chocolate cake, but you could satisfy your hunger with a cookie if that were what was easily available. In addition to availability, another consideration is the possible presence of anxiety that is attached to certain sexual acts. For those with particular inhibitions, it might be necessary for the anxiety to be reduced before the behavior could occur. Finally, experiments in which there is a single exposure to erotica followed by an assessment of that night's sexual activity does not take into account the fact that humans often think about various kinds of behavior for a period of time before they actually carry it out. To study modeling effects, then, experimenters must take into account anxiety reduction, planning of future activity, and availability of a willing partner.

The effect of erotica on anxiety and on future plans was shown by Wishnoff (1978). His subjects were undergraduate females who had never engaged in intercourse and who reported high levels of anxiety. These fully informed, volunteer subjects were shown one of three 15-minute videotapes: explicit sex (including nudity and various positions of intercourse), nonexplicit sex (kissing, light petting while clothed), and nonsex (no sexual content). After viewing the tapes, sexual anxiety was lowest among subjects who had viewed the explicit sex tape and highest among those who saw the nonsex material (see Figure 15.13, page 592). These undergraduate females were also asked about their plans to engage in sex in the near future, and their expectations are shown in the same figure. Out of twelve sexual activities (ranging from breast fondling while clothed to oral sex and intercourse), those who saw the explicit sex film expected to engage in about eleven of them. The figures for intercourse are quite startling. *All* of those who viewed the explicit sex film expected to have coital activity, while only 15 percent of those in the other two groups had such plans. Whether such expectancies were fulfilled was not investigated, and the availability of a suitable partner is obviously one of the prerequisites.

Other research has controlled for the availability factor by studying the effects of a masturbation film on the subsequent masturbatory activity of those who watched it. Heiby and Becker (1980) found that female subjects engaged in autosexual activity more frequently after viewing a filmed model engage in that behavior. In summary, then, filmed models shown taking part in explicit acts are found to affect viewers by reducing sexual anxiety, inducing plans to copy the model's actions, and (when availability is taken into account) increasing the frequency of the behavior shown in the erotic material.

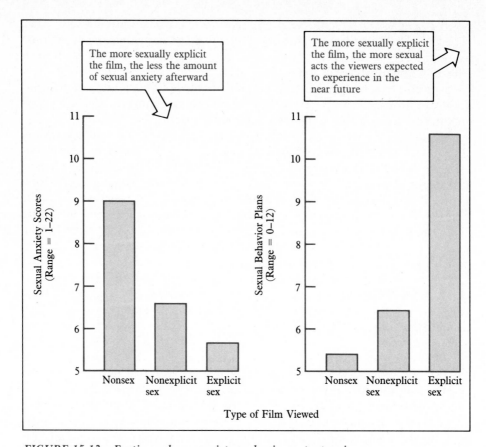

FIGURE 15.13   Erotica reduces anxiety and raises expectancies.

Undergraduate females were shown a 15-minute videotaped film whose content was either nonsexual, nonexplicit sex, or explicit sex. The more explicit the sex in the film, the less the sexual anxiety afterward and the more sexual acts the viewers planned to engage in. The effects of erotica on these intermediate responses (anxiety and expectations) are believed to occur before there are observable effects on overt behavior that imitates the filmed models. [Source: Based on data from Wishnoff, 1978.]

Sex crimes: The ultimate danger of erotica. Given what is known about the effects of erotica on arousal and subsequent behavior, is it possible that some people who are exposed to sexual stimuli attempt to satisfy their needs afterward by peeping into windows, revealing their bodies to strangers, or committing violent crimes such as rape? It might be noted that the vast majority of such offenses are committed by males, and that males are more likely to seek out erotic magazines, books, and movies than are females. In any event, it is not easy to determine the causes of complex human behavior, but three types of data are relevant.

First, males convicted of sex crimes have been compared with other kinds of criminals and with noncriminals. Strangely enough, sex offenders are found to have had *less* contact with erotica during their adolescence than is true of

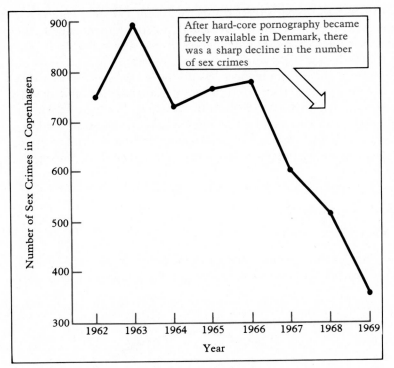

FIGURE 15.14 illustration with embedded text:

"After hard-core pornography became freely available in Denmark, there was a sharp decline in the number of sex crimes"

y-axis: Number of Sex Crimes in Copenhagen (300–900)
x-axis: Year (1962–1969)

FIGURE 15.14 Availability of pornography: A deterrent to sex crime?

Beginning in 1965, pornography became legally available to the general public in Danish shops, in vending machines, and through the mail. Though many had expected this deluge of erotica to increase sex crimes, Copenhagen police statistics revealed the opposite effect. There was a sharp decline in the frequency of sexual offenses, and this decline continued over the next several years. [Source: Based on data from Ben-Veniste, 1971.]

nonoffenders (Goldstein et al., 1974). Those who carry out sex crimes report childhood experiences involving sexual repression and sexually restrictive parents. By the time they reach adulthood, offenders have heard, seen, read, and talked less about sex than those who do not commit sexual crimes.

Second, societies that do not have censorship can be examined for the incidence of sex crimes that occur there. Denmark provided a convenient test of the effects of pornography on crime, because that country threw out all censorship laws in the 1960s and permitted all forms of explicit sexual material to be produced, displayed, and sold. If such stimuli evoke criminal behavior, one would expect a large rise in the number of sex crimes following the change in the law. Instead, there was a marked decrease in sex crimes, as shown in Figure 15.14, and the decline continued over the succeeding years. All classes of sex crimes dropped in frequency, including rape and homosexual offenses (Commission on Obscenity and Pornography, 1970). As one example, cases of child molestation dropped from 220 per year to 87 (Kutchinsky, 1973). Such evidence suggests the possibility that erotica does not lead to crime and that its availability might even help prevent these acts. There is, however, another type of evidence that casts doubt on this conclusion.

The third sort of relevant data were described in Chapter 9. Investigators have begun to look at the content of erotica with respect to its behavioral effects. When sexual content is combined with violence, there are a number of quite negative effects, including male aggression toward females. On the basis of several types of research evidence, Malamuth and Donnerstein (1983b) conclude that themes of sexual violence affect inhibitory anxiety (aggression becomes more acceptable), beliefs about sexual violence (myths about rape appear more reasonable), thoughts and fantasies (aggression and sex are more likely to be blended), and behavior (aggression, especially against females, increases). While this chain of influences has not been tied specifically to the commission of sexual crimes, they are sufficiently disturbing in themselves to constitute a warning signal about erotica. At the very least, it can be concluded that violent content in the context of sexual interactions has undesirable effects. In addition, some of the findings noted in the **Applied Side** section, on pages 596–597, indicate that even nonaggressive erotica may affect those who view it in unacceptable ways.

Erotophobia-Erotophilia: Attitudes about Sexuality

When we first begin learning about the mysteries of sexual behavior, strong emotional responses very often accompany the learning process. As a

FIGURE 15.15   Learning about sex: Positive or negative emotional associations.

Socialization experiences involving sexual learning vary from person to person in their emotional content. When negative emotions are evoked, the result seems to be long-lasting negative attitudes about many aspects of sexuality (erotophobia). When positive emotions are evoked, the result is long-lasting positive attitudes about sexuality (erotophilia). It seems that the males in the imaginary society depicted here might learn more erotophilic attitudes than the females. [Source: Grin and Bear It *by George Lichty. © 1983 Field Enterprises, Inc. Courtesy of Field Newspaper Syndicate.]*

"We'll have to talk soon, son . . . about the birds and the bees and clubs."

result of different socialization experiences, some individuals are apt to associate sexual cues with anxiety, fear, guilt, and unpleasantness. Others, with different learning experiences, are more likely to associate sexual cues with interest, curiosity, joy, and pleasure, as in the cartoon shown in Figure 15.15. The lasting result of these differential learning experiences consists of personality differences along a dimension that ranges from extremely negative attitudes about sex (**erotophobia**) to extremely positive attitudes (**erotophilia**). We will examine the implications of these differences for various aspects of behavior.

Measuring Sexual Attitudes and Their Development

The two major tests that have been constructed to assess this personality dimension are the **Sex Guilt Scale** (Mosher, 1968) and the **Sexual Opinion Survey** (Fisher et al., 1983). Both instruments present subjects with a series of statements about various aspects of sexuality ranging from pornography to premarital sex, and response choices vary in terms of the expression of positive and negative attitudes. In the interest of simplicity, we will combine studies that have used these tests and speak of relatively erotophobic (those high in sex guilt) and relatively erotophilic (those low in sex guilt) individuals. The basic difference between these two extremes is that, for erotophobics, sexual stimuli are emotionally negative, act as punishers, and elicit avoidance behavior. For erotophilics, such stimuli are emotionally positive, act as reinforcers, and elicit approach behavior (Griffitt & Kaiser, 1978; O'Grady, 1982a).

On the basis of several investigations, it can be concluded that erotophobia is most likely to develop in a family background that encompasses conservative values and involves a religious affiliation that includes frequent church attendance; in such homes, sex tends to be avoided as a topic of conversation (Fisher & Byrne, 1978; Gerrard, 1980).

The effect of broader cultural influences on sexual attitudes has been shown by Abramson and Imai-Marquez (1982) in a comparison of Japanese-Americans who were first-, second-, or third-generation residents of the United States. It was assumed that the American culture is more permissive than the Japanese in defining what is sexually appropriate and pleasurable and in setting sexual standards. If society can be assumed to shape its members sexually (Abramson, 1982), it would follow that as a family's exposure to this permissive culture increased, erotophobia would decrease. The first-generation Japanese-Americans (*Issei*) immigrated to the United States between 1890 and 1924; their offspring (*Nisei*) constituted the second generation and were born between 1910 and 1940. The third-generation (*Sansei*) individuals were born after World War II. From the *Issei* to the *Sansei*, there is a steady increase in "Americanization" or acculturation. As can be seen in Figure 15.17 on page 598, these generational changes are associated with a dramatic decrease in erotophobia. Such findings may simply reflect differences across age groups that are found in most segments of our society. The fact that males give more erotophilic responses than females within each generation group is consistent with other investigations of differences between the genders in sexual attitudes.

*Repeated Exposure to Erotica:
Less Arousal but More Callous Attitudes*

One difference between the laboratory study of the effects of erotica and what goes on in everyday life is that usually an experimenter provides only a relatively brief erotic stimulus. Most studies engage subjects for an hour or less of their time, show them one set of slides or one film, and then attempt to find out how they have been affected by the experience. In real life, by contrast, people spend many hours in front of their television sets, at the movies, and so forth, and this behavior is repeated day after day, year after year (see Figure 15.16). Might our findings and our conclusions about the behavioral

effects of erotica be altered if an extended time span were the focus of our studies?

There are two types of evidence that appear to be relevant to what might be occurring outside of the laboratory. First, the strong arousal effects that appear in the single-exposure investigations show a rapid decline when the erotic material is presented repeatedly over a series of days for males (Howard et al., 1971) and for married couples (Mann et al., 1974). This *habituation effect* is not limited to sexual stimuli, of course, and you know that you quickly become habituated and unresponsive to other

FIGURE 15.16   Extended exposure to erotica: What are the effects?

Though laboratory studies of the effects of erotica are generally limited in their time span, real-life exposure to sexual content consists of countless hours spent watching television, reading books and magazines, and viewing movies. It appears quite possible that this kind of extended exposure influences behavior in ways that do not show up in brief experimental investigations. [Source: Photo © Frank Siteman 1983.]

arousing stimuli; consider having the same food each day or watching a horror film over and over. With erotica, when the same 11-minute sexually explicit movie was viewed by male and female undergraduates every 24 hours for four consecutive days, arousal not only decreased each day, but there was an accompanying sharp increase in negative feelings (Kelley, 1982b). These students found the experience to be an increasingly unpleasant one. It seems that when explicit erotica is readily available and experienced, it loses much of its appeal. Such findings seem somewhat inconsistent with the repeated exposure effects described in Chapter 6. The precise conditions under which familiarity leads to positive (liking) versus negative (boredom) responses have not yet been isolated. We do know, however, that with sexual material the introduction of a totally new erotic stimulus tends to be exciting and pleasant (Howard et al., 1971; Kelley, 1982b). Nevertheless, the fact that pornography quickly becomes unarousing and boring suggests that most people would not choose to spend much of their time viewing erotica unless there was considerably more novel content than appears to be presently available or even possible.

Such findings could lead to the conclusion that society would benefit from providing as much erotica as possible so that it will lose its novelty and its possible ability to excite some people to antisocial acts. The implications are not really that clear, however. As Zillmann and Bryant (1983) point out, the boredom and the negative emotions caused by massive exposure to erotica could have negative effects on attitudes and fantasies involving interpersonal relationships. This brings us to the second type of evidence about real life pornography effects.

To test the proposed effects of overexposure to sexual themes, Zillmann and Bryant (1983) looked at various consequences of repeated exposure to sexual films. Male and female undergraduates were shown six films at a time each week for six weeks. For some, the thirty-six movies had nothing to do with sex, for some half of the movies were erotic and half were nonsexual, and for one group all thirty-six films dealt explicitly with activities such as intercourse and oral sex. After this massive exposure experience, the subjects were given various tests and questionnaires each week for the next three weeks. Did the movies have any effect on their responses?

After the six-week marathon, both physiological and self-report measures indicated that the more exposure an individual had had to erotica, the less aroused he or she was when shown new (but similar) sexual scenes. Exposure to large amounts of erotica also had the effect of decreasing any feelings of repulsion in response to unusual new material showing sadomasochism and sex with animals. In other words, it was as though the extended exposure to relatively familiar sexual images had made even quite deviant sexual depictions seem less shocking and more acceptable.

The exposure experience also had effects on various beliefs and attitudes that were apparent three weeks after the erotic showings had stopped. Those who underwent the extended exposure to erotica were afterward more likely to overestimate the amount of deviant sexuality in society, recommend shorter prison sentences for rapists, and accept the showing of explicit films to minors. Perhaps even more surprisingly, seeing the thirty-six sex films led males to express more callousness toward females and induced both sexes to express less support for women's liberation.

What are the implications of these findings? It would be tempting to condemn all erotica and to suggest that its presence is a danger to society in that it evokes negative, callous attitudes in which women are viewed as mere objects and a crime such as rape is viewed as trivial. These are matters of some consequence, and we might want to protect ourselves from the promotion of such unacceptable views. There is also another possibility that should be considered. If much of present-day erotica elicits these reactions, should all sexual stimuli be condemned or should the content of such offerings be examined more closely? It should be possible to create explicit erotica that promotes the importance of affection and love within a relationship and that presents males and females as equally valued participants. Such erotica might elicit very different responses than traditional sex films do. Affectional, egalitarian sex might also become boring and unarousing over time, but exposure to it would not be expected to engender negative attitudes and values.

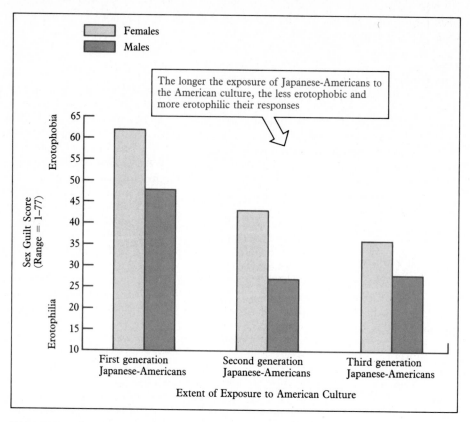

FIGURE 15.17   *The decline of erotophobia across generations.*

A comparison of sex guilt *scores of Japanese-Americans across three generations indicates that as exposure to a more permissive culture increases, erotophobic responses decrease. It should also be noted that males are more erotophilic than females in each generational group. [Source: Based on data from Abramson & Imai-Marquez, 1982.]*

Erotophobia as a Predictor of Sexual Behavior

As might be expected, individual differences in erotophobia-erotophilia are related to differences in a number of sex-related activities. For example, given a choice of magazines to read, erotophiles select *Playboy* or *Penthouse* while erotophobes choose *Outdoor Life* or *Newsweek* (Schill & Chapin, 1972). Erotophobic subjects are less responsive to sexual films than are those who are erotophilic. After viewing such a movie, those with negative sexual attitudes are more likely to report feelings of disgust, anxiety, and fear (Mosher & O'Grady, 1979). Sexual attitudes also influence one's fantasy behavior. Moreault and Follingstad (1978) gave undergraduate females examples of erotic fantasies and then asked them to write their own. Erotophobic subjects produced briefer fantasies, mentioned sexual organs less frequently, included a smaller range of sexual acts, wrote less vivid fantasies, and reported greater embarrassment in response to the task. In a similar way, when erotophobes and erotophiles are asked to draw pictures of nudes, the former individuals produce much less sexually explicit figures than do the latter (Przybyla & Byrne, 1982). Still other research indicates that erotophobia is associated with negative feelings about discussing sexual matters (Fisher et al., 1980). It seems likely, on the basis of such findings, that those with negative sexual attitudes tend to avoid talking about and thinking about sexual matters in their everyday lives as well as in the laboratory.

It also follows that this personality dimension would be related to overt sexual behavior. As erotophobia increases, the probability of engaging in premarital sex decreases (Gerrard, 1980; Gerrard & Gibbons, 1982; Mosher & Cross, 1971). The relationship is sufficiently strong that it is possible to predict the probability of a female college student's current sexual activity on the basis of scores on the Sex Guilt Scale. Comparing samples in two different years, Gerrard (1982) found that, as erotophobia increases, a student was more likely to report being sexually inactive, as shown in Figure 15.18. In this investigation, a sexually active student was defined as one who engaged in intercourse at least once a month. It can also be seen that the same relationship held true in each of the years sampled (1973 and 1978), despite the fact that those who were

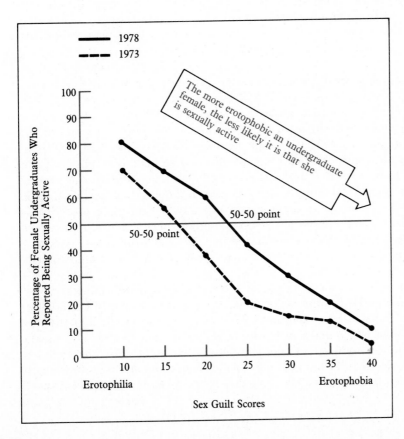

FIGURE 15.18 *As sex guilt increases, sexual activity decreases.*

Survey research among university females indicates a strong relationship between erotophobia and the likelihood of being sexually active. The higher the sex guilt score, the lower the probability of engaging in intercourse. The same trend held in 1973 and 1978, but a larger proportion of the 1978 sample reported engaging in sexual activity. An interesting finding was that a sex guilt score of 14 constituted the 50 percent probability point for sexual activity in 1973, but a score of 23 indicated that point in 1978. It is as though a higher level of sex guilt was required to prevent sexual behavior in 1978 than in 1973. [Source: Based on data in Gerrard, 1982.]

sexually active increased from 35 to 51 percent of the population. The threshold for sexual activity was defined as the guilt score that divided the group 50–50 into the active and the inactive. It was concluded that a coed had to be at a higher level of guilt in 1978 (score of 23) to remain inactive than in 1973 (score of 14).

In addition to predicting whether or not college students engage in intercourse, erotophobia is also related to how often the behavior occurs, the extent to which fantasy is utilized during those acts, and how much the behavior is enjoyed (Byrne et al., 1982). Somewhat surprisingly, it is the erotophilic students who report the greater number of problems with their sexual functioning—difficulties such as orgasm occurring too rapidly or too slowly. A possible explanation of this finding is that someone with positive attitudes about sex is more likely to have high (and perhaps unrealistic) expectations about the quality of his or her performance. It has also been found that erotophobia is higher among heterosexual males than among those identifying themselves as homosexual (Clayton & Fisher, 1983).

The Influence of Erotophobia on Other Sex-Related Behaviors

Because emotional responses to sexual topics are quite intense, they tend to generalize widely across a variety of activities that are related to sex. It would be expected that erotophobia-erotophilia would consistently predict the tendency to approach or to avoid any sex-related situation.

Educational and medical settings. An undergraduate course on human sexuality tends to attract students who are more erotophilic than average. Nevertheless, a wide range of sexual attitudes is represented among those who enroll. If erotophobic attitudes lead to negative emotional responses to many of the topics that are discussed in lectures, presented in films, or described in the text, it would be expected that learning would be hindered. In support of this hypothesis, Fisher (1980) found that erotophilic students outperformed erotophobic ones on examinations in such a class even though their performance in nonsex courses was equal. In other words, when sex was the topic, erotophobia interfered with comprehension, retention, and/or performance. In a related investigation, erotophobics remembered less material from a twenty-minute lecture on sterilization and abortion than did erotophilics when tested immediately after the lecture (Schwartz, 1973).

Most of us feel somewhat reluctant about visiting a doctor's office and even about obtaining various kinds of checkups. If, in addition, the problem involves any portion of one's sexual anatomy or functioning, it would be hypothesized that erotophobia would make an avoidance response much more likely. A study involving several hundred women confirmed this expectation. Erotophobic females reported that they obtained gynecological examinations less frequently than did erotophilic females; the same differences held true for breast self-examinations (Fisher et al., 1983). It appears that negative attitudes about sex can interfere with important health care procedures.

Contraceptive behavior. One of the more consistent findings of the past several years is that the majority of sexually active teenagers in the United States either use no method of contraception or use contraception inconsistently (Alan Guttmacher Institute, 1981). The result is now about one million teenage pregnancies annually among those who are unmarried. These unwanted conceptions end in abortion (46 percent), out-of-wedlock births (26 percent), and hasty marriages prior to the baby's birth (12 percent). The remaining 16 percent end in miscarriages. Why would a teenage couple risk unwanted parenthood by not using contraceptive devices? The most frequent explanation is that those involved did not have adequate knowledge. Though this is undoubtedly important in many instances (Allgeier, 1983), research on erotophobia suggests a different explanation. Those individuals who have the most negative attitudes about sexuality would be expected to avoid every aspect of the necessary contraceptive process—from acknowledging their sexual intentions to themselves to obtaining the necessary services and devices (Byrne, 1983).

In studies of the sexual behavior of noncollege teenagers, the avoidance of contraceptives or the use of noneffective methods can quite reasonably be attributed to misinformation about the details of fertility, the relative effectiveness of different procedures, and/or about how and where to obtain appropriate contraception (Zelnick & Kantner, 1980). With college student populations, however, the very same sort of behavior occurs among late adolescents and young adults who are bright and knowledgable and who have easy access to contraceptives. In a series of studies of both male and female undergraduates, it is consistently found that, as erotophobia increases, individuals are less likely to utilize the contraceptive services of a student health center (Fisher et al., 1979), less likely to use contraceptives (Fisher, 1978), less likely to use effective forms of contraception (Gerrard, 1982), and more likely to conceive (Gerrard, 1977).

On the basis of such research, it would appear that the maladaptive behavior of sexually active noncontraceptors could be altered by procedures designed to change their negative reactions to sexual cues. A program designed by Gerrard et al. (1982) tested the effectiveness of changing the behavior of sexually active college women through the use of two different methods. All subjects were unmarried and using either ineffective contraceptive techniques or no contraception. The investigators compared an approach involving *information only* with a procedure combining information with *cognitive restructuring* in which various assumptions and erroneous ideas about contraception were examined. There was also a control group that received no treatment.

The factual information given to both treatment groups was the same, but the cognitive restructuring subjects also were induced to deal with their negative attitudes and beliefs. Both treatment groups met a week later for discussions; one focused on information and the other on feelings and misconceptions (for example, many individuals believe incorrectly that pregnancy is impossible

FIGURE 15.19   *Changing contraceptive behavior.*

Unmarried, sexually active undergraduate females who used no contraception or an inadequate method took part in this investigation. They either received no treatment, information about contraceptives, or information plus cognitive restructuring procedures designed to change their attitudes. Comparing the students' behavior before the study began and four months afterward, the experimenters found impressive increases in effective contraception for both treatment groups. The greatest change occurred in the information plus attitude change condition in which three-quarters of the participants switched to an effective method of contraception. [Source: Based on data from Gerrard et al., 1982.]

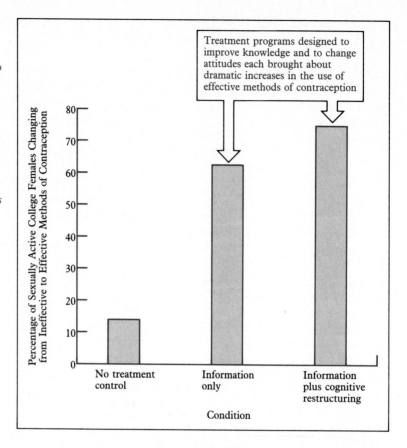

Treatment programs designed to improve knowledge and to change attitudes each brought about dramatic increases in the use of effective methods of contraception

with infrequent sex, that the health risks of birth control pills are greater than the health risks of pregnancy and childbirth, or that contraceptive planning indicates lust rather than love).

The three groups of students were compared with respect to their contraceptive usage before the study began and three months afterward. Figure 15.19 shows how effective the procedures were. The subjects who received information and those who also underwent cognitive restructuring reported impressive behavioral change, but the greatest change was in the latter group. It seems accurate to conclude that this type of intervention program is very effective and that the combination approach is better than facts alone.

Summary

Sexuality pervades our lives in both pleasant and unpleasant ways. There have been dramatic *changes* in this behavior in recent decades, and current research focuses on such topics as *sexual attraction* and the *effects of erotic images* on behavior.

Twentieth century changes in sexual attitudes and practices have been described as a **sexual revolution.** The most rapid changes have taken place in Western Europe, North America, and Japan. The changes include increased legal tolerance for sexual content in books, magazines, and movies. Such societal changes have been paralleled by more permissive attitudes and striking increases in the frequency and variety of sexual activity. It was noted that these changes include several negative features such as the *pressure* some individuals feel to participate in the new sexual norms and to "perform" well, the high incidence of unplanned and unwanted *pregnancies* among teenagers, and the increase in sexually transmitted *diseases.*

In most species, **sexual attraction** is based on internal and external cues that are related to the female's ability to conceive. Her readiness is often communicated by the secretion of a **sexual pheromone** whose odor attracts and excites males of her species. The general criterion for mate selection is *fitness* so that variables such as size and dominance influence which males are able to mate. For human beings, the role of odor is not at all clear-cut, and variables such as appearance, actions, and sexual interests seem to be of greater importance. Sexual attraction toward one's own gender varies along a continuum from exclusive homosexual preference to exclusive heterosexual preference. Though no explanation for these behavioral differences is totally accepted as yet, theories stressing either biological or learning determinants have been proposed.

For humans, *imagination* and *fantasy* are found to be of great importance with respect to sexual expression. Self-created fantasies can elicit high levels of *physiological arousal.* External images have the same effect, apparently by instigating personal internal fantasies that are processed cognitively. Though concerns about **pornography** have a long history, research on the behavioral effects of erotica has only been conducted in recent years. It has been found that exposure to erotica affects *interpersonal responses* to heterosexual cues, increases the *probability* of sexual activity, and can lead to *modeling behavior* under the appropriate conditions. There is no direct evidence that erotica leads to *sex crimes,* but themes of *sexual violence* are found to have undesirable effects on aggressive beliefs, fantasies, and behavior. Such findings, plus additional evidence on the negative consequences of *repeated exposure* to erotic stimuli, raise questions as to the appropriate place for such material in society.

Attitudes about sexuality vary along a positive-negative dimension that ranges from **erotophilia** to **erotophobia.** This trait is measured by the *sex guilt scale* and the *sexual opinion survey.* Negative attitudes seem to develop in families that are conservative and religious and in which sex is discussed infrequently. Sexually restrictive or permissive cultural influences also play an important role in developing attitudes about sexual matters. The more erotophobic an individual, the more he or she is likely to avoid sexual cues ranging from erotic magazines to premarital intercourse. In addition, negative sexual attitudes interfere with acquiring knowledge about sex-related matters, obtaining necessary medical examinations, and utilizing effective methods of contraception. The latter behavior can be changed by means of intervention procedures that provide both information and attempts to bring about attitude change.

Glossary

erotophilia *Attitudes about a variety of sexual topics that are relatively positive and permissive.*

erotophobia *Attitudes about a variety of sexual topics that are relatively negative and restrictive.*

genital herpes *A sexually transmitted disease that is caused by a virus and for which no cure is yet available. It is closely related to cold sores, chicken pox, and mononucleosis.*

homophobia *The fear of homosexuality experienced by some heterosexuals. It ranges from the belief that homosexuals will try to inflict their preferences on others to anxieties about one's own sexual orientation.*

penile plethysmograph *An instrument that measures male sexual arousal by detecting changes in the circumference or volume of the penis.*

pornography *Originally, pornography meant writing by or about prostitutes. The word came to mean any material whose primary function was to arouse sexual thoughts and cause sexual excitement. Now, it is interpreted to mean any sexual material that violates the standards of a particular community. Operationally, in the United States it is often defined by the pictorial representation of erection, penetration, and/or ejaculation.*

Sex Guilt Scale *The personality test that assesses the tendency to punish oneself with anxiety whenever sexual standards are violated in either thought or deed. High sex guilt is associated with a pattern of negative attitudes about various sexual topics.*

sexual attraction *The response to various kinds of cues (including odor, appearance, and behavior) that leads one individual to perceive another as a desirable sexual partner.*

Sexual Opinion Survey *The personality test that assesses positive and negative attitudes about various sexual topics and places individuals along an erotophobia-erotophilia dimension.*

sexual pheromone *A secretion whose odor serves as a sexual attractant to members of the opposite gender.*

sexual response cycle *Masters and Johnson described the physiological responses of sexuality as falling into four phases: excitement, plateau, orgasm, and resolution.*

sexual revolution *The changes of the twentieth century in many societies toward greater sexual permissiveness and tolerance accompanied by increases in the frequency and variety of sexual activities.*

sexuality *All aspects of sexual functioning ranging from physiological processes and anatomical structures to the fantasies, attitudes, beliefs, emotions, and activities involving procreational and recreational sex.*

sexually transmitted disease *Diseases such as gonorrhea, syphilis, AIDS, and genital herpes that are transmitted from person to person primarily by sexual interactions including genital, oral, and anal contact.*

thermograph *An instrument that measures male and female sexual arousal by detecting changes in skin temperature.*

vaginal photoplethysmograph *An instrument that measures female sexual arousal by detecting changes in the amount of blood in the vaginal walls as indicated by the amount of light that passes through.*

For More Information

Byrne, D., & Fisher, W. A. (Eds.). *Adolescents, sex, and contraception*. Hillsdale, N.J.: Erlbaum, 1983.
A collection of chapters by investigators active in the fields of psychology, sociology, and health education. The problems of teenage pregnancy are described, and the various barriers to effective contraception are outlined. Several possible solutions are offered, ranging from the successful activities of a university health service to proposed changes in sex education.

Cook, M. (Ed.). *The bases of human sexual attraction*. London: Academic Press, 1981.
Original chapters by a series of authors who deal with many aspects of sexual attraction, ranging from animal studies to cross-cultural research to laboratory experimentation. Among the variables examined are physical attractiveness, social skills, and the influence of special sexual desires.

Malamuth, N. M., & Donnerstein, E. (Eds.). *Pornography and sexual aggression*. New York: Academic Press, 1983.
A series of invited chapters that concentrate on the problem of pornography as an instigator of sexual aggression. Included are studies of the mass media as well as laboratory research. This book provides the most recent information now available about how erotic material can influence fantasies, attitudes, emotions, beliefs, and overt behavior.

Offir, C. W. *Human sexuality*. New York: Harcourt Brace Jovanovich, 1982.
An interesting and comprehensive overview of human sexuality. The topics include a history of sexual laws and customs, the scientific study of sex, anatomy and physiology, love, sexual behavior, homosexuality, deviant and dysfunctional behavior, diseases, the developmental process, and reproduction and birth control. This is an introductory text written for undergraduates.

Zelnik, M., Kantner, J. F., & Ford, K. *Sex and pregnancy in adolescence*. Beverly Hills, Calif.: Sage, 1981.
This book describes the results of two large-scale national surveys dealing with the sexual behavior of females between the ages of fifteen and nineteen. Among the topics included are sexual activity, changes in sexual behavior over time, contraceptive use and nonuse, pregnancy, abortion, and unwed motherhood.

Zillmann, D. *Connections between sex and aggression*. Hillsdale, N.J.: Erlbaum, 1983.
A very scholarly examination of the proposed association between sexual and aggressive impulses and behaviors. Ranging from historical accounts to descriptions of research involving animals, neuroanatomy, and physiological processes, the chapters lead up to a description of emotion transfer theory and human behavioral studies.

Bibliography

Abbey, A. Sex differences in attributions for friendly behavior: Do males misperceive females' friendliness? *Journal of Personality and Social Psychology,* 1982, *42,* 830–838.

Abbott, A. R., & Sebastian, R. J. Physical attractiveness and expectations of success. *Personality and Social Psychology Bulletin,* 1981, *7,* 481–486.

Abelson, R. P., Kinder, D. R., Peters, M. D., & Fiske, S. T. Affective and semantic components in political person perception. *Journal of Personality and Social Psychology,* 1982, *42,* 619–630.

Abramson, P.R. *The sexual system: A theory of human sexual behavior.* San Francisco: Academic Press, 1982.

Abramson, P. R., & Imai-Marquez, J. The Japanese-American: A cross-cultural, cross-sectional study of sex guilt. *Journal of Research in Personality,* 1982, *16,* 227–237.

Ace, G. Humor through adversity. *Saturday Review,* 1980, *7* (10), 14.

Adams, J. S. Inequity in social exchange. In L. Berkowitz (Ed.), *Advances in experimental social psychology* (Vol. 2). New York: Academic Press, 1965.

Adorno, T. W., Frenkel-Brunswick, E., Levinson, D. J., & Sanford, R. N. *The authoritarian personality.* New York: Harper & Row, 1950.

Aiello, J. R., & Aiello, T. DeC. The development of personal space: Proxemic behavior of children 6 through 16. *Human Ecology,* 1974, *2,* 177–189.

Aiello, J. R., Baum, A., & Gormley, F. P. Social determinants of residential crowding stress. *Personality and Social Psychology Bulletin,* 1981, *7,* 643–649.

Aiello, J. R., Nicosia, G., & Thompson, D. E. Physiological, social, and behavioral consequences of crowding on children and adolescents. *Child Development,* 1979, *50,* 195–202.

Alan Guttmacher Institute. *Eleven million teenagers.* New York: Alan Guttmacher Institute, 1976.

Alan Guttmacher Institute. *Teenage pregnancy: The problem that hasn't gone away.* New York: Alan Guttmacher Institute, 1981.

Albert, R. D. Effects of a victim's attributions on retaliation and transmission of aggression.

Unpublished manuscript, University of Illinois, 1981.

Aldag, R. J., & Brief, A. P. *Task design and employee motivation.* Glenview, Ill.: Scott, Foresman, 1979.

Allen, B. P. Social distance and admiration reactions of "unprejudiced" whites. *Journal of Personality,* 1975, *43,* 709–726.

Allen, V. L., & Levine, J. M. Social support and conformity: The role of independent assessment of reality. *Journal of Experimental Social Psychology,* 1971, *4,* 48–58.

Allen, V. L., & Wilder, D. A. Impact of group consensus and social support on stimulus meaning: Mediation of conformity by cognitive restructuring. *Journal of Personality and Social Psychology,* 1980, *39,* 1116–1124.

Allen, W. My speech to the graduates. *New York Teacher,* 1980, *21* (40), 10.

Allgeier, A. R. Informational barriers to contraception. In D. Byrne and W. A. Fisher (Eds.), *Adolescents, sex, and contraception.* Hillsdale, N.J.: Erlbaum, 1983.

Allgeier, E. R., Przybyla, D. P. J., & Thompson, M. E. Planned sin: The influence of sex guilt on premarital sexual and contraceptive behavior. Unpublished manuscript, Bowling Green State University, 1981.

Alloy, L. B., Abramson, L. Y., and Viscusi, D. Induced mood and the illusion of control. *Journal of Personality and Social Psychology,* 1981, *41,* 1129–1140.

Allport, F. H. *Social psychology.* Boston: Houghton Mifflin, 1924.

Allport, G. W., & Odbert, H. S. Trait-names: A psycholexical study. *Psychological Monographs,* 1936, *47* (211).

Altman, I. *The environment and social behavior.* Monterey, Calif.: Brooks/Cole, 1975.

Amoroso, D. M., Brown, M., Pruesse, M., Ware, E. E., & Pilkey, D. W. An investigation of behavioral, psychological, and physiological reactions to pornographic stimuli. In *Technical report of the Commission on Obscenity and Pornography* (Vol. 8). Washington, D.C.: U.S. Government Printing Office, 1971.

Andersen, S. M., & Bem, S. L. Sex typing and androgyny in dyadic interaction: Individual differences in responsiveness to physical attractiveness. *Journal of Personality and Social Psychology*, 1981, *41*, 74–86.

Anderson, A. How the mind heals. *Psychology Today*, 1982, 16, (12), 51–56.

Anderson, C. A., & Anderson, D. C. Ambient temperature and violent crime: Tests of the linear and curvilinear hypotheses. *Journal of Personality and Social Psychology*, 1983, in press.

Anderson, C. A., Lepper, M. R., & Ross, L. Perseverance of social theories: The role of explanation in the persistence of discredited information. *Journal of Personality and Social Psychology*, 1980, *39*, 1037–1049.

Anderson, N. H. *Foundations of information integration theory*. New York: Academic Press, 1981.

Anisko, J. J., Suer, S. F., McClintock, M. K., & Adler, N. T. The relationship between 22 kHz ultrasonic signals and sociosexual behavior in the rat. *Journal of Comparative and Physiological Psychology*, 1978, *92*.

Antill, J. D., & Cunningham, J. D. Sex differences in performance on ability tests as a function of masculinity, femininity, and androgyny. *Journal of Personality and Social Psychology*, 1982, *42*, 718–728.

Apple, W., Streeter, L. A., & Krauss, R. B. Effects of pitch and speech rate on personal attributions. *Journal of Personality and Social Psychology*, 1979, *37*, 715–727.

Archer, R. L., Diaz-Loving, R., Gollwitzer, P. M., Davis, M. H., & Foushee, H. C. The role of dispositional empathy and social evaluation in the empathic mediation of helping. *Journal of Personality and Social Psychology*, 1981, *40*, 786–796.

Argyle, M. The social skills of intercultural interaction. In S. Bochner (Ed.), *Cross-cultural interaction*. Oxford: Pergamon, 1982.

Arkin, R. M., Gleason, J. M., & Johnston, S. Effects of perceived choice, expected outcome, and observed outcome of an action on the causal attributions of actors. *Journal of Experimental Social Psychology*, 1976, *12*, 151–158.

Arons, S. The crusade to ban books. *Saturday Review*, June 1981, pp. 17–19.

Aronson, E., Bridgeman, D. L., & Geffner, R. Interdependent interactions and prosocial behavior. *Journal of Research and Development in Education*, 1978, *12*, 16–27.

Aronson, E., & Mills, J. The effect of severity of initiation on liking for a group. *Journal of Abnormal and Social Psychology*, 1959, *59*, 177–181.

Asch, S. E. Forming impressions of personality.

Journal of Abnormal and Social Psychology, 1946, *41*, 258–290.

Asch, S. E. Effects of group pressure upon the modification and distortion of judgment. In H. Guetzkow (Ed.), *Groups, leadership, and men*. Pittsburgh: Carnegie, 1951.

Asher, S. R., & Renfrew, P. D. Children without friends: Social knowledge and social skill training. In S. R. Asher and J. M. Gottman (Eds.), *The development of children's friendships*. New York: Cambridge University Press, 1981.

Ashton, N. L., & Shaw, M. E. Empirical investigations of a reconceptualized personal space. *Bulletin of the Psychonomic Society*, 1980, *15*, 309–312.

Ashton, N. L., Shaw, M. E., & Worsham, A. P. Affective reactions to interpersonal distances by friends and strangers. *Bulletin of the Psychonomic Society*, 1980, *15*, 306–308.

Asimov, I. Colonizing the heavens. *Saturday Review*, 1975, *2* (20), 12–13, 15–17.

Austin, W. Sex differences in bystander intervention in a theft. *Journal of Personality and Social Psychology*, 1979, *37*, 2110–2120.

Austin, W. Friendship and fairness: Effects of type of relationship and task performance on choice of distribution rules. *Personality and Social Psychology Bulletin*, 1980, *6*, 402–408.

Austin, W., and Walster, E. Equity with the world: The trans-relational effects of equity and inequity. *Sociometry*, 1975, *38*, 474–496.

Austin, W., Williams, T. A., III, Worchel, S., Wentzel, A. A., & Siegel, D. Effect of mode of adjudication, presence of defense counsel, and favorability of verdict on observers' evaluation of a criminal trial. *Journal of Applied Social Psychology*, 1981, *11*, 281–300.

Averill, J. R., & Boothroyd, P. On falling in love in conformance with the romantic ideal. *Motivation and Emotion*, 1977, *1*, 235–247.

Axelrod, R., & Hamilton, W. D. The evolution of cooperation. *Science*, 1981, *211*, 1390–1396.

Baer, R., Hinkle, S., Smith, K., & Fenton, M. Reactance as a function of actual versus projected autonomy. *Journal of Personality and Social Psychology*, 1980, *38*, 416–422.

Balling, J. D., & Falk, J. H. Development of visual preference for natural environments. *Environment and Behavior*, 1982, *14*, 5–28.

Bandura, A. Influence of models' reinforcement contingencies on the acquisition of imitative responses. *Journal of Personality and Social Psychology*, 1965, *1*, 589–595.

Bandura, A. *Aggression: A social learning analysis*. Englewood Cliffs, N.J.: Prentice-Hall, 1973.

Bandura, A. *Social learning theory.* Englewood Cliffs, N.J.: Prentice-Hall, 1977.

Bandura, A., Ross, D., & Ross, S. Imitation of film-mediated aggressive models. *Journal of Abnormal and Social Psychology,* 1963, *66,* 3–11. (a)

Bandura, A., Ross, D., & Ross, S. Vicarious reinforcement and imitative learning. *Journal of Abnormal and Social Psychology,* 1963, *67,* 601–607. (b)

Barash, D. P. *Sociobiology and behavior.* New York: Elsevier, 1977.

Barden, R. C., Garber, J., Duncan, S. W., & Masters, J. C. Cumulative effects of induced affective states in children: Accentuation, inoculation, and remediation. *Journal of Personality and Social Psychology,* 1981, *40,* 750–760.

Barefoot, J. C., Hoople, H., & McClay, D. Avoidance of an act which would violate personal space. *Psychonomic Science,* 1972, *28,* 205–206.

Bargh, J. A. Attention and automaticity in the processing of self-relevent information. *Journal of Personality and Social Psychology,* 1982, *43,* 425–436.

Barkowitz, P., & Brigham, J. C. Recognition of faces: Own-race bias, incentive, and time delay. *Journal of Applied Social Psychology,* 1982, *12,* 255–268.

Barlow, D. H., Sakheim, D. K., & Beck, J. G. Anxiety increases sexual arousal. Unpublished manuscript, SUNY at Albany, 1982.

Barnett, M. A., Howard, J. A., King, L. M., & Dino, G. A. Antecedents of empathy: Retrospective accounts of early socialization. *Personality and Social Psychology Bulletin,* 1980, *6,* 361–365.

Baron, R. A. Aggression as a function of ambient temperature and prior anger arousal. *Journal of Personality and Social Psychology,* 1972, *21,* 183–189. (a)

Baron, R. A. Reducing the influence of an aggressive model: The restraining effects of peer censure. *Journal of Experimental Social Psychology,* 1972, *8,* 266–275. (b)

Baron, R. A. The "foot-in-the-door" phenomenon: Mediating effects of size of first request and sex of requester. *Bulletin of the Psychonomic Society,* 1973, *2,* 113–114. (a)

Baron, R. A. Threatened retaliation from the victim as an inhibitor of physical aggression. *Journal of Research in Personality,* 1973, *7,* 103–115. (b)

Baron, R. A. Aggression as a function of victim's pain cues, level of prior anger arousal, and exposure to an aggressive model. *Journal of Personality and Social Psychology,* 1974, *29,* 117–124. (a)

Baron, R. A. The aggression-inhibiting influence of heightened sexual arousal. *Journal of Personality and Social Psychology,* 1974, *30,* 318–322. (b)

Baron, R. A. *Human aggression.* New York: Plenum, 1977.

Baron, R. A. Invasions of personal space and helping: Mediating effects of invader's apparent need. *Journal of Experimental Social Psychology,* 1978, *14,* 304–312.

Baron, R. A. Heightened sexual arousal and physical aggression: An extension to females. *Journal of Applied Social Psychology,* 1979, *9,* 103–114.

Baron, R. A. Olfaction and human social behavior: Effects of pleasant scents on physical aggression. *Basic and Applied Social Psychology,* 1980, *1,* 163–172.

Baron, R. A. The "costs of deception" revisited: An openly optimistic rejoinder. *IRB: A Review of Human Subjects Research,* 1981, *3,* 8–10. (a)

Baron, R. A. Olfaction and human social behavior: Effects of a pleasant scent on attraction and social perception. *Personality and Social Psychology Bulletin,* 1981, *7,* 611–616. (b)

Baron, R. A. *Behavior in organizations.* Boston: Allyn and Bacon, 1983. (a)

Baron, R. A. The reduction of human aggression: An incompatible response strategy. In R. G. Geen and E. Donnerstein (Eds.), *Aggression: Theoretical and empirical reviews.* New York: Academic Press, 1983. (b)

Baron, R. A. The control of human aggression: An optimistic perspective. *Journal of Social and Clinical Psychology,* 1983, in press. (c)

Baron, R. A. The "sweet smell of success"? The impact of pleasant artificial scents (perfume or cologne) on evaluations of job applicants. *Journal of Applied Psychology,* 1983, in press. (d)

Baron, R. A. Too much of a good thing? The effects of positive nonverbal cues and the use of artificial scent (perfume) on evaluations of job candidates. Unpublished manuscript, Purdue University, 1983. (e)

Baron, R. A. Reducing organizational conflict: An incompatible response approach. Manuscript submitted for publication, Purdue University, 1983.

Baron, R. A., & Ball, R. L. The aggression-inhibiting influence of nonhostile humor. *Journal of Experimental Social Psychology,* 1974, *10,* 23–33.

Baron, R. A., & Bell, P. A. Effects of heightened sexual arousal on physical aggression. *Proceedings of the 81st Annual Convention of the American Psychological Association*, 1973, 171–172.

Baron, R. A., & Bell, P. A. Aggression and heat: Mediating effects of prior provocation and exposure to an aggressive model. *Journal of Personality and Social Psychology*, 1975, *31*, 825–832.

Baron, R. A., & Bell, P. A. Aggression and heat: The influence of ambient temperature, negative affect, and a cooling drink on physical aggression. *Journal of Personality and Social Psychology*, 1976, *33*, 245–255.

Baron, R. A., & Bell, P. A. Sexual arousal and aggression by males: Effects of type of erotic stimuli and prior provocation. *Journal of Personality and Social Psychology*, 1977, *35*, 79–87.

Baron, R. A., & Kepner, C. R. Model's behavior and attraction toward the model as determinants of adult aggressive behavior. *Journal of Personality and Social Psychology*, 1970, *14*, 335–344.

Baron, R. A., & Ransberger, V. M. Ambient temperature and the occurrence of collective violence: The "long, hot summer" revisited. *Journal of Personality and Social Psychology*, 1978, *36*, 351–360.

Baron, R. A., Russell, G. W., & Arms, R. L. Negative ions and behavior. *Journal of Personality and Social Psychology*, 1984, in press.

Baron, R. M., Mandel, D. R., Adams, C. A., & Griffen, L. M. Effects of social density in university residential environments. *Journal of Personality and Social Psychology*, 1976, *34*, 434–446.

Baron, R. S., Moore, D., & Sanders, G. S. Distraction as a source of drive in social facilitation research. *Journal of Personality and Social Psychology*, 1978, *36*, 816–824.

Baron, R. S., & Roper, G. Reaffirmation of social comparison views of choice shifts: Averaging and extremity effects in an autokinetic situation. *Journal of Personality and Social Psychology*, 1976, *33*, 521–530.

Bar-Tal, D., & Bar-Zohar, Y. The relationship between perception of locus of control and academic achievement. *Contemporary Educational Psychology*, 1977, *2*, 181–199.

Bar-Tal, D., Raviv, A., & Leiser, T. The development of altruistic behavior: Empirical evidence. *Developmental Psychology*, 1980, *16*, 516–524.

Barton, E. M., Baltes, M. M., & Orzech, M. J. Etiology of dependence in older nursing home residents during morning care: The role of staff behavior. *Journal of Personality and Social Psychology*, 1980, *38*, 423–431.

Barton, J., Chassin, L., Presson, C. C., & Sherman, S. J. Social image factors as motivators of smoking initiation in early and middle adolescence. *Child Development*, 1982, *53*, 1499–1511.

Basow, S. A. *Sex role stereotypes: Traditions and alternatives.* Monterey, Calif.: Brooks/Cole, 1981.

Batson, C. D., Cochran, P. J., Biederman, M. F., Blosser, J. L., Ryan, M. J., & Vogt, B. Failure to help when in a hurry: Callousness or conflict? *Personality and Social Psychology Bulletin*, 1978, *4*, 97–101.

Batson, C. D., Duncan, B. D., Ackerman, P., Buckley, T., & Birch, K. Is empathic emotion a source of altruistic motivation? *Journal of Personality and Social Psychology*, 1981, *40*, 290–302.

Batson, C. D., & Gray, R. A. Religious orientation and helping behavior: Responding to one's own or to the victim's needs? *Journal of Personality and Social Psychology*, 1981, *40*, 511–520.

Baum, A., Aiello, J. R., & Calesnick, L. E. Crowding and personal control: Social density and the development of learned helplessness. *Journal of Personality and Social Psychology*, 1978, *36*, 1000–1011.

Baum, A., Calesnick, L. E., Davis, G. E., & Gatchel, R. J. Individual differences in coping with crowding: Stimulus screening and social overload. *Journal of Personality and Social Psychology*, 1982, *43*, 821–830.

Baum, A., & Davis, G. E. Reducing the stress of high-density living: An architectural intervention. *Journal of Personality and Social Psychology*, 1980, *38*, 471–481.

Baum, A., Fisher, J. D., & Solomon, S. K. Type of information, familiarity, and the reduction of crowding stress. *Journal of Personality and Social Psychology*, 1981, *40*, 11–23.

Baum, A., & Singer, J. E. (Eds.). *Advances in environmental psychology.* Vol. 2. *Applications of personal control.* Hillsdale, N.J.: Erlbaum, 1980.

Baum, A., Singer, J. E., & Baum, C. S. Stress and the environment. *Journal of Social Issues*, 1981, *37* (1), 4–35.

Baum, A., & Valins, S. Residential environments, group size, and crowding. *Proceedings of the 81st Annual Convention of the American Psychological Association*, 1973, 211–212.

Baumann, D. J., Cialdini, R. B., & Kenrick, D. T.

Altruism as hedonism: Helping and self-gratification as equivalent responses. *Journal of Personality and Social Psychology*, 1981, *40*, 1039–1046.

Baumeister, R. F., & Darley, J. M. Reducing the biasing effect of perpetrator attractiveness in jury simulation. *Personality and Social Psychology Bulletin*, 1982, *8*, 286–292.

Baumrind, D. The costs of deception. *IRB: A Review of Human Subjects Research*, 1979, *6*, 1–4.

Beach, L. R., & Carter, W. B. Appropriate and equitable repayment of social debts. *Organizational Behavior and Human Performance*, 1976, *16*, 280–293.

Beck, A. T. *Cognitive therapy and the emotional disorders.* New York: International Universities Press, 1976.

Beck, K. H., & Lund, A. K. The effects of health threat seriousness and personal efficacy upon intentions and behavior. *Journal of Applied Social Psychology*, 1981, *11*, 401–415.

Beck, S. B., Ward-Hull, C. I., & McLear, P. M. Variables related to women's somatic preferences of the male and female body. *Journal of Personality and Social Psychology*, 1976, *34*, 1200–1210.

Becker, F. D., & Poe, D. B., Jr. The effects of user-generated design modifications in a general hospital. *Journal of Nonverbal Behavior*, 1980, *4*, 195–218.

Becker, L. J., Seligman, C., Fazio, R. H., & Darley, J. McC. Relating attitudes to residential energy use. *Environment and Behavior*, 1981, *13*, 590–609.

Becker, M. A., & Byrne, D. Type A behavior and daily marital activities. Unpublished manuscript, SUNY at Albany, 1983.

Becker, M. A., & Suls, J. Take me out to the ballgame: The effects of objective, social and temporal performance information on attendance at major league baseball games. Unpublished manuscript, SUNY at Albany, 1983.

Beckhouse, L., Tanur, J., Weiler, J., & Weinstein, E. And some men have leadership thrust upon them. *Journal of Personality and Social Psychology*, 1975, *31*, 557–566.

Belgrave, F. Z., & Mills, J. Effect upon desire for social interaction with a physically disabled person of mentioning the disability in different contexts. *Journal of Applied Social Psychology*, 1981, *11*, 44–57.

Bell, A. P., Weinberg, M. S., & Hammersmith, S. K. *Sexual preference: Its development in men and women.* Bloomington, Ind.: Indiana University Press, 1981.

Bell, D. The clockwatchers: Americans at work. *Time*, 1975, *106* (10), 55–57.

Bell, P. A. Effects of noise and heat stress on primary and subsidiary task performance. *Human Factors*, 1978, *20*, 749–752.

Bell, P. A. Physiological, comfort, performance, and social effects of heat stress. *Journal of Social Issues*, 1981, *37* (1), 71–94.

Bell, P. A., & Baron, R. A. Aggression and heat: The mediating role of negative affect. *Journal of Applied Social Psychology*, 1976, *6*, 18–30.

Bellack, A. S., Hersen, M., & Kazdin, A. E. *International handbook of behavior modification and therapy.* New York: Plenum, 1982.

Bem, D. J. Self-perception theory. In L. Berkowitz (Ed.), *Advances in experimental social psychology* (Vol. 6). New York: Academic Press, 1972.

Bem, D. J., & Allen, A. On predicting some of the people some of the time: The search for cross-situational consistencies in behavior. *Psychological Review*, 1974, *81*, 506–520.

Bem, S. L. The measurement of psychological androgyny. *Journal of Consulting and Clinical Psychology*, 1974, *42*, 155–162.

Bem, S. L. Theory and measurement of androgyny: A reply to the Pedhazur-Tetenbaum and Locksley-Colten critiques. *Journal of Personality and Social Psychology*, 1979, *37*, 1947–1954.

Bem, S. L. Beyond androgyny: Some presumptuous prescriptions for a liberated sexual identity. In J. Sherman & F. Denmark (Eds.), *The future of woman: Issues in psychology.* New York: Psychological Dimensions, 1980.

Bem, S. L. Gender schema theory: A cognitive account of sex typing. *Psychological Review*, 1981, *88*, 354–364.

Bem, S. L. Gender schema theory and self-schema theory compared: A comment on Markus, Crane, Bernstein, and Siladi's "Self-schemas and gender." *Journal of Personality and Social Psychology*, 1982, *43*, 1192–1194.

Benson, P. L., Karabenick, S. A., & Lerner, R. M. Pretty pleases: The effects of physical attractiveness, race, and sex on receiving help. *Journal of Experimental Social Psychology*, 1976, *12*, 409–415.

Benton, A. A. Some unexpected consequences of jeopardy. *Proceedings of the 79th Annual Convention of the American Psychological Association*, 1971, *6*, 223–224.

Ben-Veniste, R. Pornography and sex crime: The Danish experience. In *Technical report of the Commission on Obscenity and Pornography* (Vol. 7). Washington, D.C.: U.S. Government Printing Office, 1971.

Berg, J. H., & Peplau, L. A. Loneliness: The

relationship of self-disclosure and androgyny. *Personality and Social Psychology Bulletin*, 1982, *8*, 624–630.

Berger, C. J., & Cummings, L. L. Organizational structure, attitudes and behaviors. In B. Shaw (Ed.), *Research in organizational behavior* (Vol. 1). Greenwich, Conn.: JAI, 1978.

Berger, S. M., Carli, L. C., Garcia, R., & Brady, J. J., Jr. Audience effects in anticipatory learning: A comparison of drive and practice-inhibition analyses. *Journal of Personality and Social Psychology*, 1982, *42*, 378–386.

Berkowitz, L. Some determinants of impulsive aggression: Role of mediated associations with reinforcements for aggression. *Psychological Review*, 1974, *81*, 165–176.

Berkowitz, L. Whatever happened to the frustration-aggression hypothesis? *American Behavioral Scientist*, 1978, *21*, 691–708.

Berkowitz, L., Cochran, S. T., & Embree, M. C. Physical pain and the goal of aversively stimulated aggression. *Journal of Personality and Social Psychology*, 1981, *40*, 687–700.

Berkowitz, L., & Donnerstein, E. External validity is more than skin deep: Some answers to criticisms of laboratory experiments. *American Psychologist*, 1982, *37*, 245–257.

Bernard, Y., & Gottesdiener, A. Rôle de la dimension esthétique dans l'évaluation spontanée d'un habitat. *International Review of Applied Psychology*, 1982, *31*, 169–183.

Berndt, T. J. Age changes and changes over time in prosocial intentions and behavior between friends. *Developmental Psychology*, 1981, *17*, 408–416.

Berne, E. *Games people play.* New York: Grove Press, 1964.

Bernikow, L. Alone. Yearning for companionship in America. *New York Times Magazine*, August 15, 1982, pp. 24–29, 32, 34.

Bernstein, M., & Crosby, F. An empirical examination of relative deprivation theory. *Journal of Experimental Social Psychology*, 1980, *16*, 442–456.

Berscheid, E. Theories of interpersonal attraction. In B. B. Wolman & L. R. Pomeroy (Eds.), *International encyclopedia of neurology, psychiatry, psychoanalysis, and psychology.* New York: Van Nostrand Reinhold, 1976.

Berscheid, E., Dion, K., Walster, E., & Walster, G. W. Physical attractiveness and dating choice: A test of the matching hypothesis. *Journal of Experimental Social Psychology*, 1971, *7*, 173–189.

Berscheid, E., & Walster, E. A little bit about love. In T. L. Huston (Ed.), *Foundations of interpersonal attraction.* New York: Academic Press, 1974.

Bickman, L. Bystander intervention in a crime: The effect of a mass-media campaign. *Journal of Applied Social Psychology*, 1975, *5*, 296–302.

Bickman, L. (Ed.). *Applied social psychology annual 2.* Beverly Hills, Calif.: Sage, 1981.

Bickman, L., & Green, S. K. Situational cues and crime reporting: Do signs make a difference? *Journal of Applied Social Psychology*, 1977, *7*, 1–18.

Bickman, L., & Rosenbaum, D. P. Crime reporting as a function of bystander encouragement, surveillance, and credibility. *Journal of Personality and Social Psychology*, 1977, *35*, 577–586.

Bieber, I. *Homosexuality: A psychoanalytic study.* New York: Basic Books, 1962.

Biggers, T., & Pryor, B. Attitude change: A function of emotion-eliciting qualities of environment. *Personality and Social Psychology Bulletin*, 1982, *8*, 94–99.

Black, T. E., & Higbee, K. L. Effects of power, threat, and sex on exploitation. *Journal of Personality and Social Psychology*, 1973, *27*, 382–388.

Blake, R., & Mouton, J. Intergroup problem solving in organizations: From theory to practice. In W. Austin & S. Worchel (Eds.), *The social psychology of intergroup relations.* Monterey, Calif.: Brooks/Cole, 1979.

Blascovich, J. Social psychology in family medicine. In L. Bickman (Ed.), *Applied social psychology annual 3.* Beverly Hills, Calif.: Sage, 1982.

Blascovich, J., Nash, R. F., & Ginsburg, G. P. Heart rate and competitive decision making. *Personality and Social Psychology Bulletin*, 1978, *4*, 115–118.

Blass, T. On personality variables, situations, and social behavior. In T. Blass (Ed.), *Personality variables in social behavior.* Hillsdale, N.J.: Erlbaum, 1977.

Bleda, P. R., & Sandman, P. H. In smoke's way: Socio-emotional reactions to another's smoking. *Journal of Applied Psychology*, 1977, *62*, 452–458.

Blot, W. J., Brinton, L. A., Fraumeni, J. F., Jr., & Stone, B. J. Cancer mortality in U.S. counties with petroleum industries. *Science*, 1977, *198*, 51–53.

Bluestone, B., & Harrison, B. *The deindustrialization of America: Plant closings, community abandonment, and the dismantling of basic industries.* New York: Basic Books, 1982.

Blum, S. R., & Minkler, M. Toward a continuum of caring alternatives: Community based care for the elderly. *Journal of Social Issues*, 1980, *36* (2), 133–152.

Blumenthal, J. A., McKee, D. C., Haney, T., & Williams, R. B. Task incentives, Type A behavior pattern, and verbal problem solving performance. *Journal of Applied Social Psychology*, 1980, *10*, 101–114.

Bond, M. H., Leung, K., and Wan, K. C. The impact of task and maintenance contributions on reward distribution: How does cultural collectivism operate? Unpublished manuscript, Chinese University of Hong Kong, 1983.

Borgida, E., & Campbell, B. Belief relevance and attitude-behavior consistency: The moderating role of personal experience. *Journal of Personality and Social Psychology*, 1982, *42*, 239–247.

Bornstein, M. H., & Bornstein, H. G. Cities fast paced. *Rocky Mountain News*, February 19, 1976.

Bouska, M. L., & Beatty, P. A. Clothing as a symbol of status: Its effect on control of interaction territory. *Bulletin of the Psychonomic Society*, 1978, *11*, 235–238.

Bower, G. H., Black, J. B., & Turner, T. J. Scripts in memory for text. *Cognitive Psychology*, 1979, *11*, 177–220.

Bower, G. H., & Hilgard, E. R. *Theories of learning* (5th ed.). Englewood Cliffs, N.J.: Prentice-Hall, 1981.

Bowman, T. F., Giuliani, G. A., & Minge, M. R. *Finding your best place to live in America*. New York: Red Lion, 1981.

Bracey, D. H. Forensic psychology and hostage negotiation: Introductory remarks. In F. Wright, C. Bahn, & R. W. Rieber (Eds.), *Forensic psychology and psychiatry*. New York: New York Academy of Sciences, 1980.

Brauer, D. V., & DePaulo, B. M. Similarities between friends in their understanding of nonverbal cues. *Journal of Nonverbal Behavior*, 1980, *5*, 64–68.

Bray, R. M., Johnson, D., & Chilstrom, J. T., Jr. Social influence by group members with minority opinions: A comparison of Hollander and Moscovici. *Journal of Personality and Social Psychology*, 1982, *43*, 78–88.

Bray, R. M., & Sugarman, R. Social facilitation among interaction groups: Evidence for the evaluation-apprehension hypothesis. *Personality and Social Psychology Bulletin*, 1980, *6*, 137–142.

Brennan, T. Loneliness at adolescence. In L. A. Peplau & D. Perlman, *Loneliness: A sourcebook of current theory, research, and therapy*. New York: Wiley, 1982.

Brennan, T., & Auslander, N. *Adolescent loneliness: An exploratory study of social and psychological pre-dispositions and theory* (Vol. 1). Prepared for the National Institute of Mental Health, Juvenile Problems Division, Grant No. R01-MH 289 12-01, Behavioral Research Institute, 1979.

Brewer, M. B., Dull, V., & Lui, L. Perceptions of the elderly: Stereotypes as prototypes. *Journal of Personality and Social Psychology*, 1981, *41*, 656–670.

Brickman, P., Becker, L. J., & Castle, S. Making trust easier and harder through two forms of sequential interaction. *Journal of Personality and Social Psychology*, 1979, *37*, 515–521.

Brickman, P., & D'Amato, B. Exposure effects in a free-choice situation. *Journal of Personality and Social Psychology*, 1975, *32*, 415–420.

Brigham, J. C. Limiting conditions of the "physical attractiveness stereotype": Attributions about divorce. *Journal of Research in Personality*, 1980, *14*, 365–375. (a)

Brigham, J. C. Perspectives on the impact of lineup compositions, race, and witness confidence on identification accuracy. *Law and Human Behavior*, 1980, *4*, 315–322. (b)

Brigham, J. C., Maas, A., Snyder, L. D., & Spaulding, K. Accuracy of eyewitness identifications in a field setting. *Journal of Personality and Social Psychology*, 1982, *42*, 673–681.

Brigham, J. C., & Richardson, C. B. Race, sex, and helping in the marketplace. *Journal of Applied Social Psychology*, 1979, *9*, 314–322.

Brigham, J. C., & Williamson, N. L. Cross-racial recognition and age: When you're over 60, do they still "all look alike"? *Personality and Social Psychology Bulletin*, 1979, *5*, 218–222.

Brinberg, D., & Castell, P. A resource exchange theory approach to interpersonal interactions: A test of Foa's theory. *Journal of Personality and Social Psychology*, 1982, *43*, 260–269.

Bringle, R. G., & Williams, L. J. Parental-offspring similarity on jealousy and related personality dimensions. *Motivation and Emotion*, 1979, *3*, 265–286.

Britell, J. K. Ethics courses are making slow inroads. *New York Times*, April 26, 1981, Education Section 12, p. 44.

Brockner, J., Rubin, J. Z., & Lang, E. Face-saving and entrapment. *Journal of Experimental Social Psychology*, 1981, *17*, 68–79.

Brockner, J., & Swap, W. C. Effects of repeated exposure and attitudinal similarity on self-disclosure and interpersonal attraction.

Journal of Personality and Social Psychology, 1976, *33,* 531–540.

Brodt, S. E., & Zimbardo, P. G. Modifying shyness-related social behavior through symptom misattribution. *Journal of Personality and Social Psychology,* 1981, *41,* 437–449.

Brody, J. E. Study suggests changing behavior may prevent heart attack. *New York Times,* September 16, 1980, pp. C-1, C-3. (a)

Brody, J. E. Rushing your life away with "Type A" behavior. *New York Times,* October 22, 1980, pp. C-1, C-12. (b)

Broll, L., Gross, A. E., & Piliavin, I. Effects of offered and requested help on help seeking and reactions to being helped. *Journal of Applied Social Psychology,* 1974, *4,* 244-258.

Brown, C., Anderson, J., Burggraf, L., & Thompson, N. Community standards, conservatism, and judgments of pornography. *Journal of Sex Research,* 1978, *14,* 81–95.

Brown, C. E. Shared space invasion and race. *Personality and Social Psychology Bulletin,* 1981, *7,* 103–108.

Brown, J. L., Brown, E. R., Brown, S. D., & Dow, D. D. Helpers: Effects of experimental removal on reproductive success. *Science,* 1982, *215,* 421–422.

Brown, R. A. Conventional education and controlled drinking education courses with convicted drunken drivers. *Behavior Therapy,* 1980, *11,* 632–642.

Brundage, L. E., Derlega, V. J., & Cash, T. F. The effects of physical attractiveness and need for approval on self-disclosure. *Personality and Social Psychology Bulletin,* 1977, *3,* 63–66.

Brunson, B. I., & Matthews, K. A. The Type A coronary-prone behavior pattern and reactions to uncontrollable stress: An analysis of performance strategies, affect, and attributions during failure. *Journal of Personality and Social Psychology,* 1981, *40,* 906–918.

Buck, R. Nonverbal communication of affect in preschool children: Relationships with personality and skin conductance. *Journal of Personality and Social Psychology,* 1977, *35,* 225–236.

Buck, R. *Nonverbal behavior and the communication of affect.* New York: Guilford Press, 1984.

Buckhout, R. Nearly 2,000 witnesses can be wrong. *Bulletin of the Psychonomic Society,* 1980, *16,* 307–310.

Burger, J. M., & Petty, R. E. The low-ball compliance technique: Task or person commitment? *Journal of Personality and Social Psychology,* 1981, *40,* 492–500.

Burgess, J. W. Development of social spacing in normal and mentally retarded children. *Journal of Nonverbal Behavior,* 1981, *6,* 89–95.

Burgess, K. L. Relationships in marriage and the family. In S. Duck & R. Gilmour (Eds.), *Personal relationships. 1: Studying personal relationships.* London: Academic Press, 1981.

Burnam, M. A., Pennebaker, J. W., & Glass, D. C. Time consciousness, achievement striving, and the Type A coronary-prone behavior pattern. *Journal of Abnormal Psychology,* 1975, *84,* 76–79.

Burnstein, E. Persuasion as argument processing. In M. Brandstatter, J. H. Davis, & G. Stocker-Kreichgauer (Eds.), *Group decision processes.* London: Academic Press, 1983.

Burnstein, E., & Schul, Y. The informational basis of social judgments: Operations in forming an impression of another person. *Journal of Experimental Social Psychology,* 1982, *18,* 217–234.

Burt, M. R., & Albin, R. S. Rape myths, rape definitions, and probability of conviction. *Journal of Applied Social Psychology,* 1981, *11,* 212–230.

Buss, A. H. *The psychology of aggression.* New York: Wiley, 1961.

Buss, A. H. Physical aggression in relation to different frustrations. *Journal of Abnormal and Social Psychology,* 1963, *67,* 1–7.

Buss, A. H. Instrumentality of aggression, feedback, and frustration as determinants of physical aggression. *Journal of Personality and Social Psychology,* 1966, *3,* 153–162.

Buss, A. H. *Self-consciousness and social anxiety.* San Francisco: W. H. Freeman, 1980.

Butterfield, F. Love and sex in China. *New York Times Magazine,* January 13, 1980, pp. 15–17, 43–44, 46–49.

Buunk, B. Anticipated sexual jealousy: Its relationship to self-esteem, dependency, and reciprocity. *Personality and Social Psychology Bulletin,* 1982, *8,* 310–316.

Byers, J. A., & Wood, D. L. Antibiotic-induced inhibition of pheromone synthesis in a bark beetle. *Science,* 1981, *213,* 763–764.

Byrne, D. The influence of propinquity and opportunities for interaction on classroom relationships. *Human Relations,* 1961, *14,* 63–69.

Byrne, D. *The attraction paradigm.* New York: Academic Press, 1971.

Byrne, D. Sex without contraception. In D. Byrne & W. A. Fisher (Eds.), *Adolescents, sex, and contraception.* Hillsdale, N.J.: Erlbaum, 1983.

Byrne, D., Ervin, C. R., & Lamberth, J. Continuity between the experimental study of attraction and real life computer dating. *Journal of Personality and Social Psychology,* 1970, *16,* 157–165.

Byrne, D., & Kelley, K. *An introduction to personality.* Englewood Cliffs, N.J.: Prentice-Hall, 1981.

Byrne, D., & Lamberth, J. The effect of erotic stimuli on sex arousal, evaluative responses, and subsequent behavior. In *Technical report of the Commission on Obscenity and Pornography* (Vol. 8). Washington, D.C.: U.S. Government Printing Office, 1971.

Byrne, D., & Nelson, D. Attraction as a linear function of proportion of positive reinforcements. *Journal of Personality and Social Psychology,* 1965, *1,* 659–663.

Byrne, D., & Przybyla, D. P. J. Authoritarianism and political preferences in 1980. *Bulletin of the Psychonomic Society,* 1980, *16,* 471–472.

Byrne, D., Przybyla, D. P. J., & Grasley, D. Sexual dysfunctions among undergraduates as correlates of sexual attitudes. Paper presented at the meeting of the Eastern Psychological Association, Baltimore, April 1982.

Byrne, D., Przybyla, D. P. J., & Infantino, A. The influence of social threat on subsequent romantic attraction. Paper presented at the meeting of the Eastern Psychological Association, New York City, April 1981.

Cacioppo, J. T., & Petty, R. E. Effects of extent of thought on the pleasantness ratings of P-O-X triads: Evidence for three judgmental tendencies in evaluating social situations. *Journal of Personality and Social Psychology,* 1981, *40,* 1000–1009.

Cacioppo, J. T., & Petty, R. E. (Eds.), *Social psychophysiology: A sourcebook.* New York: Guilford Press, 1983.

Cacioppo, J. T., Petty, R. E., & Quintanar, L. R. Individual differences in relative hemispheric alpha abundance and cognitive responses to persuasive communications. *Journal of Personality and Social Psychology,* 1982, *43,* 623–636.

Cacioppo, J. T., Petty, R. E., & Sidera, J. A. The effects of a salient self-schema on the evaluation of proattitudinal editorials: Top-down versus bottom-up message processing. *Journal of Experimental Social Psychology,* 1982, *18,* 324–338.

Caldwell, D. F., O'Reilly, C. A., III, & Morris, J. H. Responses to an organizational reward: A field test of the sufficiency of justification hypothesis. *Journal of Personality and Social Psychology,* 1983, *44,* 506–514.

Calhoun, J. B. Population density and social pathology. *Scientific American,* 1962, *206* (3), 139–148.

Calhoun, J. B. Space and the strategy of life. In A. H. Esser (Ed.), *Environment and behavior: The use of space by animals and men.* New York: Plenum, 1971.

Campagna, A. G. The function of men's erotic fantasies during masturbation. *Dissertation Abstracts International,* 1976, *36,* 6373-B.

Cann, A., Sherman, S. J., & Elkes, R. Effects of initial request size and timing of a second request on compliance: The foot-in-the-door and the door-in-the-face. *Journal of Personality and Social Psychology,* 1975, *32,* 774–782.

Canter, D., & Craik, K. H. Environmental psychology. *Journal of Environmental Psychology,* 1981, *1,* 1–11.

Canter, D., & Kenny, C. Approaches to environmental evaluation: An introduction. *International Review of Applied Psychology,* 1982, *31,* 145–151.

Canter, D., & Rees, K. A multivariate model of housing satisfaction. *International Review of Applied Psychology,* 1982, *31,* 185–208.

Cantor, N., & Mischel, W. Traits as prototypes: Effects on recognition memory. *Journal of Personality and Social Psychology,* 1977, *35,* 38–48.

Cantor, N., Mischel, W., & Schwartz, J. C. A prototype analysis of psychological situations. *Cognitive Psychology,* 1982, *14,* 45–77.

Caplow, T., & Forman, R. Neighborhood interaction in a homogeneous community. *American Sociological Review,* 1950, *15,* 357–366.

Capon, N., & Kuhn, D. Logical reasoning in the supermarket: Adult females' use of a proportional reasoning strategy in an everyday context. *Developmental Psychology,* 1979, *15,* 450–452.

Carlinsky, D. People. *Playboy,* December 1978, p. 48.

Carlsmith, J. M., & Anderson, C. A. Ambient temperature and the occurrence of collective violence: A new analysis. *Journal of Personality and Social Psychology,* 1979, *37,* 337–344.

Carlston, D. E. The recall and use of traits and events in social inference processes. *Journal of Experimental Social Psychology,* 1980, *16,* 303–328.

Carlston, D. E., & Shovar, N. Effects of performance attributions on others' perceptions of the attributor. *Journal of Personality and Social Psychology,* 1983, *44,* 515–525.

Carnevale, P. J. D., Pruitt, D. G., & Seilheimer, S. D. Looking and competing: Accountability and visual access in integrative bargaining. *Journal of Personality and Social Psychology,* 1981, *40,* 111–120.

Carver, C. S., Coleman, A. E., & Glass, D. C. The coronary-prone behavior pattern and the suppression of fatigue on a treadmill test. *Journal of Personality and Social Psychology,* 1976, *33,* 460–466.

Carver, C. S., DeGregorio, E., & Gillis, R. Ego-defensive bias in attribution among two categories of observers. *Personality and Social Psychology Bulletin,* 1980, *6,* 44–50.

Carver, C. S., & Glass, D. C. Coronary-prone behavior pattern and interpersonal aggression. *Journal of Personality and Social Psychology,* 1978, *36,* 361–366.

Carver, C. S., & Scheier, M. F. *Attention and self-regulation: A control-theory approach to human behavior.* New York: Springer Verlag, 1981. (a)

Carver, C. S., & Scheier, M. F. The self-attention-induced feedback loop and social facilitation. *Journal of Experimental Social Psychology,* 1981, *17,* 545–568. (b)

Cary, M. S. Does civil inattention exist in pedestrian passing? *Journal of Personality and Social Psychology,* 1978, *36,* 1185–1193.

Cash, T. F., & Derlega, V. J. The matching hypothesis: Physical attractiveness among same-sexed friends. *Personality and Social Psychology Bulletin,* 1978, *4,* 240–243.

Cattell, R. B., Kawash, G. F., & De Young, G. E. Validation of objective measures of ergic tension: Response of the sex erg to visual stimulation. *Journal of Experimental Research in Personality,* 1972, *6,* 76–83.

Cavoukian, A., & Doob, A. N. The effects of a judge's charge and subsequent recharge on judgments of guilt. *Basic and Applied Social Psychology,* 1980, *1,* 103–114.

Chance, J. E. Internal control of reinforcements and the school learning process. Paper presented at the meeting of the Society for Research in Child Development, Minneapolis, 1965.

Chapko, M. K., & Solomon, H. Air pollution and recreational behavior. *Journal of Social Psychology,* 1976, *100,* 149–150.

Chassin, L., Presson, C. C., Sherman, S. J., Corty, E., & Olshavsky, R. W. Self-images and cigarette smoking in adolescence. *Personality and Social Psychology Bulletin,* 1981, *7,* 670–676.

Cheney, A. B., & Bleker, E. G. Internal-external locus of control and repression-sensitization in battered women. Paper presented at the meeting of the American Psychological Association, Washington, D. C., August 1982.

Cherry, F., & Byrne, D. Authoritarianism. In T. Blass (Ed.), *Personality variables in social behavior.* Hillsdale, N.J.: Erlbaum, 1976.

Cherry, F., Byrne, D., & Mitchell, H. E. Clogs in the bogus pipeline: Demand characteristics and social desirability. *Journal of Research in Personality,* 1976, *10,* 69–75.

Christensen, D., & Rosenthal, R. Gender and nonverbal decoding skill as determinants of interpersonal expectancy effects. *Journal of Personality and Social Psychology,* 1982, *42,* 75–87.

Christensen, H. T. Normative theory derived from cross-cultural family research. *Journal of Marriage and the Family,* 1969, *31,* 209–222.

Christie, R., & Geis, F. L. (Eds.). *Studies in Machiavellianism.* New York: Academic Press, 1970. (a)

Christie, R., & Geis, F. L. The ten dollar game. In R. Christie & F. L. Geis (Eds.), *Studies in Machiavellianism.* New York: Academic Press, 1970. (b)

Christie, R., Gergen, K. J., & Marlowe, D. The penny-dollar caper. In R. Christie & F. L. Geis (Eds.), *Studies in Machiavellianism.* New York: Academic Press, 1970.

Christy, P. R., Gelfand, D. M., & Hartmann, D. P. Effects of competition-induced frustration on two classes of modeled behavior. *Developmental Psychology,* 1971, *5,* 104–111.

Cialdini, R. B., & Ascani, K. Test of a concession procedure for inducing verbal, behavioral, and further compliance with a request to give blood. *Journal of Applied Psychology,* 1976, *61,* 295–300.

Cialdini, R. B., Cacioppo, J. T., Bassett, R., & Miller, J. A. Low-ball procedure for producing compliance: Commitment then cost. *Journal of Personality and Social Psychology,* 1978, *36,* 463–476.

Cialdini, R. B., Kenrick, D. T., & Baumann, D. J. Effects of mood on prosocial behavior in children and adults. In N. Eisenberg-Berg (Ed.), *The development of prosocial behavior.* New York: Academic Press, 1982.

Cialdini, R. B., & Petty, R. Anticipatory opinion effects. In R. Petty, T. Ostrom, & T. Brock (Eds.), *Cognitive responses in persuasion.* Hillsdale, N.J.: Erlbaum, 1979.

Cialdini, R. B., Petty, R. E., & Cacioppo, J. T. Attitude and attitude change. *Annual Review of Psychology,* 1981, *32,* 357–404.

Cialdini, R. B., Vincent, J. E., Lewis, S. K., Catalan, J., Wheeler, D., & Darby, B. L.

Reciprocal concessions procedure for inducing compliance: The door-in-the-face technique. *Journal of Personality and Social Psychology,* 1975, *31,* 206–215.

Cimbalo, R. S., Faling, V., & Mousaw, P. The course of love: A cross-sectional design. *Psychological Reports,* 1976, *38,* 1292–1294.

Clark, M., & Isen, A. M. Toward understanding the relationship between feeling states and social behavior. In A. Hastorf & A. Isen (Eds.), *Cognitive social psychology.* New York: Elsevier North-Holland, 1982.

Clark, M.S., & Fiske, S. T. *Affect and cognition: The 17th Annual Carnegie Symposium.* Hillsdale, N.J.: Erlbaum, 1972.

Clark, M. S., Gotay, C. C., & Mills, J. Acceptance of help as a function of similarity of the potential helper and opportunity to repay. *Journal of Applied Social Psychology,* 1974, *4,* 224–229.

Clark, R. D., III. On the Piliavin & Piliavin model of helping behavior: Costs are in the eye of the beholder. *Journal of Applied Social Psychology,* 1976, *6,* 322–328.

Clark, R. N., Hendee, J. C., & Burgess, R. L. The experimental control of littering. *Journal of Environmental Education,* 1972, *4,* 22–28.

Clayton, J. P., & Fisher, W. A. Affective responses to erotic stimuli: A comparison of homosexual and heterosexual men. Paper presented at the meeting of the Midwestern Psychological Association, Chicago, May 1983.

Clore, G. L., Bray, R. M., Itkin, S. M., & Murphy, P. Interracial attitudes and behavior at a summer camp. *Journal of Personality and Social Psychology,* 1978, *36,* 107–116.

Clore, G. L., & Byrne, D. A reinforcement-affect model of attraction. In T. L. Huston (Ed.), *Foundations of interpersonal attraction.* New York: Academic Press, 1974.

Clore, G. L., Wiggins, N. H., & Itkin, S. Gain and loss in attraction. Attributions from nonverbal behavior. *Journal of Personality and Social Psychology,* 1975, *31,* 706–712.

Coale, A. J. The history of human population. *Scientific American,* 1974, *231* (3), 40–51.

Cohen, C. E. Person categories and social perception: Testing some boundaries of the processing effects of prior knowledge. *Journal of Personality and Social Psychology,* 1981, *40,* 441–452.

Cohen, C. E. Goals and schemata in person perception: Making sense from the stream of behavior. In N. Cantor & J. F. Kihlstrom (Eds.), *Cognition, social interaction, and personality.* Hillsdale, N.J.: Erlbaum, 1982.

Cohen, S., Evans, G. W., Krantz, D. S., & Stokols, D. Physiological, motivational, and cognitive effects of aircraft noise on children. *American Psychologist,* 1980, *35,* 231–243.

Cohen, S., Evans, G. W., Krantz, D. S., Stokols, D., & Kelly, S. Aircraft noise and children: Longitudinal and cross-sectional evidence on adaptation to noise and the effectiveness of noise abatement. *Journal of Personality and Social Psychology,* 1981, *40,* 331–345.

Cohen, S., & Weinstein, N. Nonauditory effects of noise on behavior and health. *Journal of Social Issues,* 1981, *37* (1), 36–70.

Cohn, N. B., & Strassberg, D. S. Self-disclosure reciprocity among preadolescents. *Personality and Social Psychology Bulletin,* 1983, *9,* 97–102.

Coke, J. S., Batson, C. D., & McDavis, K. Empathic mediation of helping: A two-stage model. *Journal of Personality and Social Psychology,* 1978, *36,* 752–766.

Commission on Obscenity and Pornography. *The report of the Commission on Obscenity and Pornography.* Washington, D.C.: U.S. Government Printing Office, 1970.

Comstock, G., Chaffee, S., Katsman, N., McCombs, M., & Roberts, D. *Television and human behavior.* New York: Columbia University Press, 1979.

Condry, J., & Dyer, S. Fear of success: Attribution of cause for the victim. In D. N. Ruble, I. H. Frieze, & J. E. Parsons (Eds.), Sex roles: Persistence and change. *Journal of Social Issues,* 1976, *32,* 63–83.

Conger, J. C., & Keane, S. P. Social skills intervention in the treatment of isolated or withdrawn children. *Psychological Bulletin,* 1981, *90,* 478–495.

Conroy, J., III, & Sundstrom, E. Territorial dominance in a dyadic conversation as a function of similarity of opinion. *Journal of Personality and Social Psychology,* 1977, *35,* 570–576.

Constantinople, A. Sex-role acquisition: In search of the elephant. *Sex Roles,* 1979, *5,* 121–133.

Converse, J., Jr., & Cooper, J. The importance of decisions and free-choice attitude change: A curvilinear finding. *Journal of Experimental Social Psychology,* 1979, *15,* 48–61.

Cook, M. Social skill and human sexual attraction. In M. Cook (Ed.), *The bases of human sexual attraction.* London: Academic Press, 1981.

Cook, S. W., & Berrenberg, J. L. Approaches to encouraging conservation behavior: A review and conceptual framework. *Journal of Social Issues,* 1981, *37,* 73–107.

Coombs, L. C. The measurement of commitment

to work. *Journal of Population*, 1979, *2*, 203–223.

Cooper, A. J. Neonatal olfactory bulb lesions: Influences on subsequent sexual behavior of male mice. *Bulletin of the Psychonomic Society*, 1978, *11*, 53–56.

Cooper, H. M. Statistically combining independent studies: Meta-analysis of sex differences in conformity research. *Journal of Personality and Social Psychology*, 1979, *37*, 131–146.

Cooper, J. Reducing fears and increasing assertiveness: The role of dissonance reduction. *Journal of Experimental Social Psychology*, 1980, *16*, 199–213.

Cooper, J., & Croyle, R. Cognitive dissonance: Evidence for physiological arousal. Unpublished manuscript, Princeton University, 1982.

Corah, N. L., & Boffa, J. Perceived control, self-observation, and response to aversive behavior. *Journal of Personality and Social Psychology*, 1970, *16*, 1–4.

Corballis, M. C. Laterality and myth. *American Psychologist*, 1980, *35*, 284–295.

Corliss, R. The new ideal of beauty. *Time*, 1982, *120* (9), 72–77.

Costantini, E., & Craik, K. H. Personality and politicians: California party leaders, 1960-1976. *Journal of Personality and Social Psychology*, 1980, *38*, 641–661.

Cottrell, N. B. Social facilitation. In C. G. McClintock (Ed.), *Experimental social psychology*. New York: Holt, Rinehart and Winston, 1972.

Cottrell, N. B., Wack, D. L., Sekerak, G. J., & Rittle, R. H. Social facilitation of dominant responses by the presence of an audience and the mere presence of others. *Journal of Personality and Social Psychology*, 1968, *9*, 245–250.

Cowen, E. L., Weissberg, R. P., & Lotyczewski, B. S. Physical contact in helping interactions with young children. *Journal of Consulting and Clinical Psychology*, 1982, *50*, 219–225.

Coyne, J. C. Depression and the response of others. *Journal of Abnormal Psychology*, 1976, *85*, 186–193.

Cozby, P. Effects of density, activity, and personality on environmental preferences. *Journal of Research in Personality*, 1973, *7*, 45–60.

Crandall, V. C. Differences in parental antecedents of internal-external control in children and in young adulthood. Paper presented at the meeting of the American Psychological Association, Montreal, 1973.

Crane, M., & Markus, H. Gender identity: The

benefits of a self-schema approach. *Journal of Personality and Social Psychology*, 1982, *43*, 1195–1197.

Cronbach, L. J. Beyond the two disciplines of scientific psychology. *American Psychologist*, 1957, *30*, 116–127.

Crosby, F. J. *Relative deprivation and working women*. London: Oxford University Press, 1982.

Crosby, F. J., & Gonzalez-Intal, A. M. Relative deprivation and equity theories: A comparative analysis of approaches to felt injustice. In R. Folger (Ed.), *The sense of injustice: Social psychological perspectives*. New York: Plenum, 1981.

Crosby, F., & Gonzalez-Intal, A. M. Relative deprivation and equity theory: Felt injustice and the undeserved benefits of others. In R. Folger (Ed.), *The sense of injustice: Social psychological perspectives*. New York: Plenum, 1983.

Crouse, B. B., & Mehrabian, A. Affiliation of opposite-sexed strangers. *Journal of Research in Personality*, 1977, *11*, 38–47.

Crowne, D. P., & Liverant, S. Conformity under varying conditions of personal commitment. *Journal of Abnormal and Social Psychology*, 1963, *66*, 547–555.

Crutchfield, R. A. Conformity and character. *American Psychologist*, 1955, *10*, 191–198.

Cunningham, J. D. Self-disclosure intimacy: Sex, sex-of-target, cross-national, and "generational" differences. *Personality and Social Psychology Bulletin*, 1981, *7*, 314–319.

Cunningham, M. R. Weather, mood, and helping behavior: Quasi experiments with the sunshine Samaritan. *Journal of Personality and Social Psychology*, 1979, *37*, 1947–1956.

Cunningham, M. R. Sociobiology as a supplementary paradigm for social psychological research. In L. Wheeler (Ed.), *Review of personality and social psychology* (Vol. 2). Beverly Hills, Calif.: Sage, 1981.

Cunningham, M. R., Steinberg, J., & Grev, R. Wanting to and having to help: Separate motivations for positive mood and guilt induced helping. *Journal of Personality and Social Psychology*, 1980, *38*, 181–192.

Curran, J. P. Convergence toward a single sexual standard? *Social Behavior and Personality*, 1975, *3*, 189–195.

Curran, J. P. Skills training as an approach to the treatment of heterosexual-social anxiety: A review. *Psychological Bulletin*, 1977, *84*, 140–157.

Curran, J. P., & Lippold, S. The effects of physical

attractiveness and attitude similarity on attraction in dating dyads. *Journal of Personality,* 1975, *43,* 528–539.

Curry, W. *The Middle English ideal of personal beauty.* New York: A.M.S. Press, 1972.

Cutrona, C. E. Transition to college: Loneliness and the process of social adjustment. In L. A. Peplau and D. Perlman, *Loneliness: A sourcebook of current theory, research, and therapy.* New York: Wiley, 1982.

Cvetkovich, G., & Grote, B. Adolescent development and teenage fertility. In D. Byrne & W. A. Fisher (Eds.), *Adolescents, sex, and contraception.* Hillsdale, N.J.: Erlbaum, 1983.

Czeisler, C. A., Moore-Ede, M. C., & Coleman, R. M. Rotating shift work schedules that disrupt sleep are improved by applying circadian principles. *Science,* 1982, *217,* 460–463.

Daher, D. M., & Banikiotes, P. G. Interpersonal attraction and rewarding aspects of disclosure content and level. *Journal of Personality and Social Psychology,* 1976, *33,* 492–496.

Daniels, R. A. *Science,* 1979, *205,* 831.

Darley, J. M., & Batson, C. D. "From Jerusalem to Jericho": A study of situational and dispositional variables in helping behavior. *Journal of Personality and Social Psychology,* 1973, *27,* 100–108.

Darley, J. M., & Beniger, J. R. Diffusion of energy-conserving innovations. *Journal of Social Issues,* 1981, *37* (2), 150–171.

Darley, J. M., & Latané, B. Bystander intervention in emergencies: Diffusion of responsibility. *Journal of Personality and Social Psychology,* 1968, *8,* 377–383.

Davis, D., & Perkowitz, W. T. Consequences of responsiveness in dyadic interaction: Effects of probability of response and proportion of content-related responses on interpersonal attraction. *Journal of Personality and Social Psychology,* 1979, *37,* 534–550.

Davis, H., Porter, J. W., Livingston, J., Hermann, T., MacFadden, L., & Levine, S. Pituitary-adrenal activity and leverpress shock escape behavior. *Physiological Psychology,* 1977, *5,* 280–284.

Davis, J. D. When boy meets girl: Sex roles and the negotiation of intimacy in an acquaintance exercise. *Journal of Personality and Social Psychology,* 1978, *36,* 684–692.

Davis, J. H. Group decision and procedural justice. In M. Fishbein (Ed.), *Progress in social psychology.* Hillsdale, N.J.: Erlbaum, 1980.

Davis, W. L., & Phares, E. J. Parental antecedents of internal-external control of reinforcement. *Psychological Reports,* 1969, *24,* 427–436.

Dawes, D. M., McTavish, J., & Shaklee, H. Behavior, communication, and assumptions about other people's behavior in a commons dilemma situation. *Journal of Personality and Social Psychology,* 1977, *35,* 1–11.

Deaux, K. *The behavior of women and men.* Belmont, Calif.: Brooks/Cole, 1976.

Deci, E. L. *Intrinsic motivation.* New York: Plenum, 1975.

DeGregorio, E., & Carver, C. S. Type A behavior pattern, sex role orientation, and psychological adjustment. *Journal of Personality and Social Psychology,* 1980, *39,* 286–293.

DeJong, W. An examination of self-perception mediation of the foot-in-the-door effect. *Journal of Personality and Social Psychology,* 1979, *37,* 2221–2239.

DeJong, W. Consensus information and the foot-in-the-door effect. *Personality and Social Psychology Bulletin,* 1981, *7,* 423–430.

DeJong, W., Marber, S., & Shaver, R. Crime intervention: The role of a victim's behavior in reducing situational ambiguity. *Personality and Social Psychology Bulletin,* 1980, *6,* 113–118.

DeJong, W., & Musilli, L. External pressure to comply: Handicapped versus nonhandicapped requesters and the foot-in-the-door phenomenon. *Personality and Social Psychology Bulletin,* 1982, *8,* 522–527.

Dellinger, R. W. Jet roar: Health problems take off near airports. *Human Behavior,* 1979, *8* (5), 50–51.

Demarest, M. He digs downtown. *Time,* 1981, *118* (8), 42–48, 53.

Dembroski, T. M., Lasater, T. M., & Ramirez, A. Communicator similarity, fear-arousing communications, and compliance with health care recommendations. *Journal of Applied Social Psychology,* 1978, *8,* 254–269.

Dembroski, T. M., & MacDougall, J. M. Stress effects on affiliation preferences among subjects possessing the Type A coronary-prone behavior pattern. *Journal of Personality and Social Psychology,* 1978, *36,* 23–33.

Dembroski, T. M., & MacDougall, J. M. Coronary-prone behavior, social psychophysiology, and coronary heart disease. In J. R. Eiser (Ed.), *Social psychology and behavioral medicine.* New York: Wiley, 1982.

Dengerink, H. A., Schnedler, R. W., & Covey, M. K. Role of avoidance in aggressive responses to attack and no attack. *Journal of*

Personality and Social Psychology, 1978, *36,* 1044–1053.

Deni, R., Vacino, J., & Epstein, M. Effects of kinship, age, and sex on social preferences in rats measured in an operant response situation. *Bulletin of the Psychonomic Society,* 1980, *16,* 31–33.

DePaulo, B. M., Brown, P. L., Ishii, S., & Fisher, J. D. Help that works: The effects of aid on subsequent task performance. *Journal of Personality and Social Psychology,* 1981, *41,* 478–487.

DePaulo, B. M., & Fisher, J. D. The costs of asking for help. *Basic and Applied Social Psychology,* 1980, *1,* 23–35.

DePaulo, B. M., & Fisher, J. D. Too tuned-out to take: The role of nonverbal sensitivity in help-seeking. *Personality and Social Psychology Bulletin,* 1981, 7, 201–205.

Dermer, M., & Pyszczynski, T. A. Effects of erotica upon men's loving and liking responses for women they love. *Journal of Personality and Social Psychology,* 1978, *36,* 1302–1309.

Deutsch, M., & Gerard, H. B. A study of normative and informational social influence upon individual judgment. *Journal of Abnormal and Social Psychology,* 1955, *51,* 629–636.

Deutsch, M., & Krauss, R. M. The effect of threat upon interpersonal bargaining. *Journal of Abnormal and Social Psychology,* 1960, *61,* 181–189.

Diamond, E. Thy neighbor's television. *American Film,* 1980, *5* (10), 19–22.

Diener, E. Deindividuation, self-awareness, and disinhibition. *Journal of Personality and Social Psychology,* 1979, *37,* 1160–1171.

Diener, E. Deindividuation: The absence of self-awareness and self-regulation in group members. In P. B. Paulus (Ed.), *The psychology of group influence.* Hillsdale, N.J.: Erlbaum, 1980.

Diener, E., Fraser, S. C., Beaman, A. L., & Kelem, R. Effects of deindividuation variables on stealing among Halloween trick-or-treaters. *Journal of Personality and Social Psychology,* 1976, *33,* 178–183.

Dienstbier, R. A., Kahle, L. R., Willis, K. A., & Tunnell, G. B. The impact of moral theories on cheating: Studies of emotion attribution and schema activation. *Motivation and Emotion,* 1980, *4,* 193–216.

Dion, K. K. Physical attractiveness, sex roles, and heterosexual attraction. In M. Cook (Ed.), *The bases of human sexual attraction.* London: Academic Press, 1981.

Dion, K. K., Berscheid, E., & Walster, E. What is beautiful is good. *Journal of Personality and Social Psychology,* 1972, *24,* 285–290.

Dion, K. K., & Dion, K. L. Self-esteem and romantic love. *Journal of Personality,* 1975, *43,* 39–57.

Dishman, R. K., Ickes, W., & Morgan, W. P. Self-motivation and adherence to habitual physical activity. *Journal of Applied Social Psychology,* 1980, *10,* 115–132.

DiTecco, D., & Schlegel, R. P. Alcohol use among young adult males: An application of problem-behavior theory. In J. R. Eiser (Ed.), *Social psychology and behavioral medicine.* New York: Wiley, 1982.

Dobrzynski, M. Applying psychology in organizations, seen from the point of view of an East European country. *International Review of Applied Psychology,* 1981, *30,* 387–391.

Doherty, W. J. Impact of divorce on locus of control orientation in adult women: A longitudinal study. *Journal of Personality and Social Psychology,* 1983, *44,* 834–840.

Dollard, J., Doob, L., Miller, N., Mowrer, O. H., & Sears, R. R. *Frustration and aggression.* New Haven: Yale University Press, 1939.

Donnell, S. M., & Hall, J. Men and women as managers: A significant case of no significant difference. *Organizational Dynamics,* 1980, 60–77.

Donnenwerth, G. V., & Foa, U. G. Effects of resource class on retaliation to injustice in interpersonal exchange. *Journal of Personality and Social Psychology,* 1974, *29,* 785–793.

Donnerstein, E. Aggressive erotica and violence against women. *Journal of Personality and Social Psychology,* 1980, *39,* 269–277.

Donnerstein, E., & Berkowitz, L. Victim reactions in aggressive erotic films as a factor in violence against women. *Journal of Personality and Social Psychology,* 1981, *41,* 710–724.

Donnerstein, E., & Donnerstein, M. Research in the control of interracial aggression. In R. G. Geen & E. C. O'Neal (Eds.), *Perspectives on aggression.* New York: Academic Press, 1976.

Donnerstein, E., & Wilson, D. W. The effects of noise and perceived control upon ongoing and subsequent aggressive behavior. *Journal of Personality and Social Psychology,* 1976, *34,* 774–781.

Donovan, D. M. *Drinking behavior, personality factors, and high-risk driving.* Unpublished doctoral dissertation, University of Washington, 1980.

Donovan, D. M., & Marlatt, G. A. Personality subtypes among driving-while-intoxicated offenders: Relationship to drinking behavior and driving risk. *Journal of Consulting and Clinical Psychology*, 1982, *50*, 241–249.

Doty, R. L., Ford, M., Preti, G., & Huggins, G. R. Changes in the intensity and pleasantness of human vaginal odors during the menstrual cycle. *Science*, 1975, *190*, 1316–1318.

Downey, L. Intergenerational change in sex behavior: A belated look at Kinsey's males. *Archives of Sexual Behavior*, 1980, *9*, 267–317.

Drachman, D., de Carufel, A., & Insko, C. A. The extra credit effect in interpersonal attraction. *Journal of Experimental Social Psychology*, 1978, *14*, 458–465.

Driscoll, R., Davis, K. E., & Lipetz, M. E. Parental interference and romantic love: The Romeo and Juliet effect. *Journal of Personality and Social Psychology*, 1972, *24*, 1–10.

Duck, S. A topography of relationship disengagement and dissolution. In S. Duck (Ed.), *Personal relationships. 4: Dissolving personal relationships.* London: Academic Press, 1982.

Duck, S., & Gilmour, R. (Eds.). *Personal relationships. 1: Studying personal relationships.* London: Academic Press, 1981.

Dunn, A. J. Neurochemistry of learning and memory: An evaluation of recent data. *Annual Review of Psychology*, 1980, *31*, 343–390.

Dutton, D. G., & Aron, A. P. Some evidence for heightened sexual attraction under conditions of high anxiety. *Journal of Personality and Social Psychology*, 1974, *30*, 510–517.

Dutton, D. G., & Lake, R. A. Threat of own prejudice and reverse discrimination in interracial situations. *Journal of Personality and Social Psychology*, 1973, *28*, 94–100.

Dutton, D. G., & Lennox, V. L. Effect of prior "token" compliance on subsequent interracial behavior. *Journal of Personality and Social Psychology*, 1974, *29*, 69–71.

Dyck, R., & Rule, B. G. The effect of causal attributions concerning attack on retaliation. *Journal of Personality and Social Psychology*, 1978, *36*, 521–529.

Eagly, A. H., & Carli, L. Sex of researchers and sex-typed communications as determinants of sex differences in influenceability: A meta-analysis of social influence studies. *Psychological Bulletin*, 1981, *90*, 1–20.

Eagly, A. H., & Himmelfarb, S. Attitudes and opinions. In M. R. Rosenzweig & L. W. Porter (Eds.), *Annual Review of Psychology* (Vol. 29). Palo Alto, Calif.: Annual Reviews, 1978.

Eagly, A. H., & Steffen, V. Gender stereotypes are a product of inferences about social roles.

Journal of Personality and Social Psychology, 1983, in press.

Eagly, A. H., & Wood, W. Inferred sex differences in status as a determinant of gender stereotypes about social influence. *Journal of Personality and Social Psychology*, 1982, *43*, 915–928.

Eagly, A. H., Wood, W., & Fishbaugh, L. Sex differences in conformity: Surveillance by the group as a determinant of male nonconformity. *Journal of Personality and Social Psychology*, 1981, *40*, 384–394.

Earn, B. M. Intrinsic motivation as a function of extrinsic financial rewards and subjects' locus of control. *Journal of Personality*, 1982, *50*, 360–373.

Easterlin, R. A. *Birth and fortune: The impact of numbers on personal welfare.* New York: Basic Books, 1980.

Ebbesen, E. B., & Bowers, R. J. Proportion of risky to conservative arguments in a group discussion and choice shift. *Journal of Personality and Social Psychology*, 1974, *29*, 316–327.

Ebbesen, E. B., Kjos, G. L., & Konečni, V. J. Spatial ecology: Its effects on the choice of friends and enemies. *Journal of Experimental Social Psychology*, 1976, *12*, 505–518.

Edgerton, R. B. *Alone together: Social order on an urban beach.* Berkeley: University of California Press, 1979.

Editors. What other women think. *Parade*, March 22, 1981, p. 9.

Edney, J. J. Property, possession, and permanence: A field study in human territoriality. *Journal of Applied Social Psychology*, 1972, *2*, 275–282.

Edney, J. J. Territoriality and control: A field experiment. *Journal of Personality and Social Psychology*, 1975, *31*, 1108–1115.

Edney, J. J., & Jordan-Edney, N. L. Territorial spacing on a beach. *Sociometry*, 1974, *37*, 92–104.

Edwards, J. D., Hotch, D. F., & Bickman, L. Measuring children's health-related attitudes and knowledge. In L. Bickman (Ed.), *Applied social psychology annual 3.* Beverly Hills, Calif.: Sage, 1982.

Efran, M. G. The effect of physical appearance on the judgement of guilt, interpersonal attraction, and severity of recommended punishment in a simulated jury task. *Journal of Research in Personality*, 1974, *8*, 45–54.

Efran, M. G., & Cheyne, J. A. Shared space: The cooperative control of spatial areas by two interacting individuals. *Canadian Journal of Behavioral Science*, 1973, *5*, 201–210.

Eidelson, R. J. Interpersonal satisfaction and level

of involvement: A curvilinear relationship. *Journal of Personality and Social Psychology,* 1980, *39,* 460–470.

Eisen, S. V. Actor-observer differences in information inferences and causal attribution. *Journal of Personality and Social Psychology,* 1979, *37,* 261–272.

Eisenberger, R., & Masterson, F. A. Required high effort increases subsequent persistence and reduces cheating. *Journal of Personality and Social Psychology,* 1983, *44,* 593–599.

Eisenman, R. Sexual behavior as related to sex fantasies and experimental manipulation of authoritarianism and creativity. *Journal of Personality and Social Psychology,* 1982, *43,* 853–860.

Ekman, P. Cross cultural studies of facial expression. In P. Ekman (Ed.), *Darwin and facial expression.* New York: Academic Press, 1973.

Ekman, P. Biological and cultural contributions to body and facial movement. In J. Blacking (Ed.), A.S.A. Monograph 15, *The anthropology of the body.* London: Academic Press, 1977.

Ekman, P., & Friesen, W. V. *Unmasking the face.* Englewood Cliffs, N.J.: Prentice-Hall, 1975.

Ellis, P. Shared outdoor space and shared meaning. *International Review of Applied Psychology,* 1982, *31,* 209–222.

Ellis, S., Rogoff, B., & Cramer, C. C. Age segregation in children's social interactions. *Developmental Psychology,* 1981, *17,* 399–407.

Ellison, K. W., & Buckhout, R. *Psychology and criminal justice.* New York: Harper & Row, 1981.

Ellsworth, P. C., & Carlsmith, J. M. Eye contact and gaze aversion in an aggressive encounter. *Journal of Personality and Social Psychology,* 1973, *28,* 280–292.

Ellsworth, P. C., & Langer, E. J. Staring and approach: An interpretation of the stare as a nonspecific activator. *Journal of Personality and Social Psychology,* 1976, *33,* 117–122.

Enzle, M. E., Hansen, R. D., & Lowe, C. A. Causal attribution in the mixed-motive game: Effects of facilitory and inhibitory environmental forces. *Journal of Personality and Social Psychology,* 1975, *31,* 50–54.

Epstein, R. Authoritarianism, displaced aggression, and social status of the target. *Journal of Personality and Social Psychology,* 1965, *2,* 585–589.

Epstein, S. The stability of behavior: I. On predicting most of the people much of the time. *Journal of Personality and Social Psychology,* 1979, *37,* 1097–1126.

Epstein, Y. M. Crowding stress and human behavior. *Journal of Social Issues,* 1981, *37* (1), 126–144.

Epstein, Y. M., & Babad, E. Y. Economic stress: Notes on the psychology of inflation. *Journal of Applied Social Psychology,* 1982, *12,* 85–99.

Epstein, Y. M., Woolfolk, R. L., & Lehrer, P. M. Physiological, cognitive, and nonverbal responses to repeated exposure to crowding. *Journal of Applied Social Psychology,* 1981, *11,* 1–13.

Erkut, S., Jaquette, D. S., & Staub, E. Moral judgment-situation interaction as a basis for predicting prosocial behavior. *Journal of Personality,* 1981, *49,* 1–14.

Eron, L. D. Parent-child interaction, television violence, and aggression of children. *American Psychologist,* 1982, *37,* 197–211.

Eron, L. D., Huesmann, L. R., Lefkowitz, M. M., & Walder, L. O. Does television violence cause aggression? *American Psychologist,* 1972, *27,* 253–263.

Espe, H. Differences in the perception of National Socialist and classicist architecture. *Journal of Environmental Psychology,* 1981, *1,* 33–42.

Evans, G. W. Introduction. *Journal of Social Issues,* 1981, *37* (1), 1–3.

Evans, G. W., & Jacobs, S. V. Air pollution and human behavior. *Journal of Social Issues,* 1981, *37* (1), 95–125.

Evans, M. C., & Wilson, M. Friendship choices of university women students. *Educational and Psychological Measurement,* 1949, *9,* 307–312.

Evans, R. I. A new applied challenge to social psychologists: Behavioral medicine. In L. Bickman (Ed.), *Applied social psychology annual 1.* Beverly Hills, Calif.: Sage, 1980.

Evans, R. I. Training social psychologists in behavioral medicine research. In J. R. Eiser (Ed.), *Social psychology and behavioral medicine.* New York: Wiley, 1982.

Evans, R. I. Deterring smoking in adolescents: Evolution of a research program in applied social psychology. *International Review of Applied Psychology,* 1983, *32,* 71–83.

Evans, R. I., Henderson, A. H., Hill, P. C., & Raines, B. E. Current psychological, social, and educational programs in control and prevention of smoking: A critical methodological review. In A. M. Gotto & R. Paoletti (Eds.), *Atherosclerosis reviews* (Vol. 6). New York: Raven, 1979.

Evans, R. I., Rozelle, R. M., Maxwell, S. E., Raines, B. E., Dill, C. A., Guthrie, T. J., Henderson, A. H., & Hill, P. C. The Houston Project: Focus on target-based filmed interventions. Paper presented at the meeting of the American Psychological Association, Montreal, September 1980.

Fazio, R. H. Motives for social comparison: The construction-validation distinction. *Journal of Personality and Social Psychology,* 1979, *37,* 1683–1698.

Fazio, R. H. On the self-perception explanation of the over-justification effect. *Journal of Experimental Social Psychology,* 1981, *17,* 417–426.

Fazio, R. H., & Cooper, J. Arousal in the dissonance process. In J. T. Cacioppo & R. E. Petty (Eds.), *Social psychophysiology.* New York: Guilford Press, 1983.

Fazio, R. H., Cooper, M., Dayson, K., & Johnson, M. Control and the coronary-prone behavior pattern: Responses to multiple situational demands. *Personality and Social Psychology Bulletin,* 1981, *7,* 97–102.

Fazio, R. H., Jeaw-mei, C., McDonel, E. C., & Sherman, S. J. Attitude accessibility, attitude-behavior consistency, and the strength of the object-evaluation association. *Journal of Experimental Social Psychology,* 1982, *18,* 339–357.

Fazio, R. H., Powell, M. C., & Herr, P. M. Toward a process model of the attitude-behavior relation: Accessing one's attitude upon mere observation of the attitude object. *Journal of Personality and Social Psychology,* 1983, in press.

Fazio, R. H., & Zanna, M. P. Direct experience and attitude-behavior consistency. In L. Berkowitz (Ed.), *Advances in experimental social psychology* (Vol. 14). New York: Academic Press, 1981.

Feen, R. H. Classical roots of the Z.P.G. movement. *ZPG Reporter,* August/September, 1981, 3.

Fehr, R. S., & Stern, J. A. Peripheral physiological variables and emotion: The James-Lange theory revisited. *Psychological Bulletin,* 1970, *74,* 411–424.

Feinberg, R. A., Miller, F. G., & Ross, G. A. Perceived and actual locus of control similarity among friends. *Personality and Social Psychology Bulletin,* 1981, *7,* 85–89.

Feldman, M. P., & MacCulloch, M. J. *Homosexual behavior: Therapy and assessment.* Oxford: Pergamon, 1971.

Feldman, R. S. (Ed.). *Development of nonverbal behavior in children.* Seacaucus, N.J.: Springer-Verlag, 1982.

Feldman, S. The presentation of shortness in everyday life—height and heightism in American society: Toward a sociology of stature. Paper presented at the meeting of the American Sociological Association, Chicago, 1971.

Felipe, N. J., & Sommer, R. Invasions of personal space. *Social Problems,* 1966, *14,* 206–214.

Felman, Y. M., Young, A. W., Siegal, F. P., & Scham, M. Sex and herpes. *Medical Aspects of Human Sexuality,* 1983, *17* (1), 24L, 24N, 24Q-24R, 24W, 24Z, 24BB, 24DD, 24HH.

Ferguson, T. J., & Wells, G. L. Priming of mediators in causal attribution. *Journal of Personality and Social Psychology,* 1980, *39,* 461–470.

Feshbach, S., & Singer, R. D. *Television and aggression.* San Francisco: Jossey-Bass, 1971.

Festinger, L. *A theory of cognitive dissonance.* Evanston, Ill.: Row, Peterson, 1957.

Festinger, L. A. A theory of social comparison processes. *Human Relations,* 1954, *7,* 117–140.

Festinger, L., & Carlsmith, L. M. Cognitive consequences of forced compliance. *Journal of Abnormal and Social Psychology,* 1959, *58,* 203–210.

Festinger, L., Schachter, S., & Back, K. *Social pressures in informal groups: A study of a housing community.* New York: Harper, 1950.

Fiedler, F. E. Contingency model and the leadership process. In L. Berkowitz (Ed.), *Advances in experimental social psychology* (Vol. 11). New York: Academic Press, 1978.

Figler, M. H., & Evensen, J. Experimentally produced prior residence effect in male convict cichlids: The role of initial proximity to territorial markers. *Bulletin of the Psychonomic Society,* 1979, *13,* 130–132.

Findley, M. J., & Cooper, H. M. Locus of control and academic achievement: A literature review. *Journal of Personality and Social Psychology,* 1983, *44,* 419–427.

Firestone, I. J., Lichtman, C. M., & Colamosca, J. V. Leader effectiveness and leadership conferral as determinants of helping in a medical emergency. *Journal of Personality and Social Psychology,* 1975, *31,* 343–348.

Fisch, R., & Daniel, H. D. Research publication trends in experimental social psychology: 1971–1980—A thematic analysis of the Journal of Experimental Social Psychology, the European Journal of Social Psychology, and the Zeitschrift fur Sozialpsychologie. *European Journal of Social Psychology,* 1982, *12,* 395–412.

Fish, B., Karabenick, S., & Heath, M. The effects of observation on emotional arousal and affiliation. *Journal of Experimental and Social Psychology*, 1978, *14*, 256–265.

Fishbein, M. Social psychological analysis of smoking behavior. In J. R. Eiser (Ed.), *Social psychology and behavioral medicine.* New York: Wiley, 1982.

Fishbein, M., & Azjen, I. *Belief, attitude, intention, and behavior: An introduction to theory and research.* Reading, Mass.: Addison-Wesley, 1975.

Fisher, J. D., & Baum, A. Situational and arousal-based messages and the reduction of crowding stress. *Journal of Applied Social Psychology*, 1980, *10*, 191–201.

Fisher, J. D., DePaulo, B. M., & Nadler, A. Extending altruism beyond the altruistic act: The mixed effects of aid on the help recipient. In J. P. Rushton & R. M. Sorrentino (Eds.), *Altrusism and helping behavior.* Hillsdale, N.J.: Erlbaum. 1981.

Fisher, J. D., Harrison, C. L., & Nadler, A. Exploring the generalizability of donor-recipient similarity effects. *Personality and Social Psychology Bulletin*, 1978, *4*, 627–630.

Fisher, J. D., Nadler, A., & Whitcher-Alagna, S. Recipient reactions to aid. *Psychological Bulletin*, 1982, *91*, 27–54.

Fisher, R. J. The professional practice of applied social psychology: Identity, training, and certification. In L. Bickman (Ed.), *Applied social psychology annual 3.* Beverly Hills, Calif.: Sage, 1982.

Fisher, W. A. *Affective, attitudinal, and normative determinants of contraceptive behavior among university men.* Unpublished doctoral dissertation, Purdue University, 1978.

Fisher, W. A. Erotophobia-erotophilia and performance in a human sexuality course. Unpublished manuscript, University of Western Ontario, 1980.

Fisher, W. A., & Byrne, D. Individual differences in affective, evaluative, and behavioral responses to an erotic film. *Journal of Applied Social Psychology*, 1978, *8*, 355–365.

Fisher, W. A., & Byrne, D. Social background, attitudes, and sexual attraction. In M. Cook (Ed.), *The bases of human sexual attraction.* London: Academic Press, 1981.

Fisher, W. A., Byrne, D., Edmunds, M., Miller, C. T., Kelley, K., & White, L. A. Psychological and situation-specific correlates of contraceptive behavior among university women. *Journal of Sex Research*, 1979, *15*, 38–55.

Fisher, W. A., Byrne, D., & White, L. A. Emotional barriers to contraception. In D.

Byrne & W. A. Fisher (Eds.), *Adolescents, sex, and contraception.* Hillsdale, N.J.: Erlbaum, 1983.

Fisher, W. A., Miller, C. T., Byrne, D., & White, L. A. Talking dirty: Responses to communicating a sexual message as a function of situational and personality factors. *Basic and Applied Social Psychology*, 1980, *1*, 115–126.

Fiske, S. T. Attention and weight in person perception: The impact of negative and extreme behavior. *Journal of Personality and Social Psychology*, 1980, *38*, 889–906.

Fiske, S. T., Kenney, D. A., & Taylor, S. E. Structural models for the mediation of salience effects on attribution. *Journal of Experimental Social Psychology*, 1982, *18*, 105–127.

Fiske, S. T., & Linville, P. W. What does the schema concept buy us? *Personality and Social Psychology Bulletin*, 1980, *6*, 543–557.

Fiske, S. T., & Taylor, S. E. *Social cognition.* Reading, Mass.: Addison-Wesley, 1983.

Foa, U. G. Resource theory of social exchanges. In J. S. Thibaut, J. Spence, & R. Carson (Eds.), *Contemporary topics in social psychology.* Morristown, N.J.: General Learning Press, 1976.

Foa, U. G., & Foa, E. B. *Societal structures of the mind.* Springfield, Ill.: Charles C Thomas, 1974.

Fodor, E. M. Simulated work climate as an influence on choice of leadership style. *Personality and Social Psychology Bulletin*, 1978, *4*, 111–114.

Fodor, E. M., & Smith, T. The power motive as an influence on group decision making. *Journal of Personality and Social Psychology*, 1982, *42*, 178–185.

Folger, R., Rosenfield, D., Rheaume, K., & Martin, C. Relative deprivation and referent cognitions. *Journal of Experimental Social Psychology*, 1983, *19*, 172–184.

Folkes, V. S. Communicating the reasons for social rejection. *Journal of Experimental Social Psychology*, 1982, *18*, 235–252.

Folkes, V. S. Forming relationships and the matching hypothesis. *Personality and Social Psychology Bulletin*, 1982, *8*, 631–636.

Folkes, V. S., & Sears, D. O. Does everybody like a liker? Unpublished manuscript, University of California at Los Angeles, 1980.

Foltz, D. Behavioral science has clearly played the understudy compared to hard science and engineering in the first two decades of America's race in space. Not quite so in the Soviet Union, say the experts. *APA Monitor*, 1981, *12* (8 & 9), 8–9, 71.

Forest, D., Clark, M. S., Mills, J., & Isen, A. M. Helping as a function of feeling state and nature of the helping behavior. *Motivation and Emotion*, 1980.

Forsyth, D. R. *An introduction to group dynamics.* Monterey, Calif.: Brooks/Cole, 1983.

Foss, R. D. Structural effects in simulated jury decision making. *Journal of Personality and Social Psychology*, 1981, *40*, 1055–1062.

Foss, R. D., & Dempsey, C. B. Blood donation and the foot-in-the-door technique: A limiting case. *Journal of Personality and Social Psychology*, 1979, *37*, 580–590.

Fowler, F. J., Jr. Evaluating a complex crime control experiment. In L. Bickman (Ed.), *Applied social psychology annual 2.* Beverly Hills, Calif.: Sage, 1981.

Fox, J., & Guyer, M. Public choice and cooperation in N-person prisoner's dilemma. *Journal of Conflict Resolution*, 1978, *22*, 468–481.

Frances, R., & Lebras, C. The prediction of job satisfaction. *International Review of Applied Psychology*, 1982, *31*, 391–410.

Franck, K. A. Friends and strangers: The social experience of living in urban and non-urban settings. *Journal of Social Issues*, 1980, *36* (3), 52–71.

Frankel, M. The search for truth: An umpireal view. *University of Pennsylvania Law Review*, 1975, *123*, 1031–1059.

Frankenhaeuser, M., & Lundberg, U. The influence of cognitive set on performance and arousal under different noise loads. *Motivation and Emotion*, 1977, *1*, 139–149.

Fredrickson, C., Heaton, T. B., Fuguitt, G. V., & Zuiches, J. J. Residential preferences in a model of migration intentions. *Population and Environment*, 1980, *3*, 280–297.

Freedman, D. G. *Human sociobiology: A holistic approach.* New York: Free Press, 1979.

Freedman, J. L., Birsky, J., & Cavoukian, A. Environmental determinants of behavioral contagion: Density and number. *Basic and Applied Social Psychology*, 1980, *1*, 155–161.

Freedman, J. L., & Fraser, S. C. Compliance without pressure: The foot-in-the-door technique. *Journal of Personality and Social Psychology*, 1966, *4*, 195–202.

Freedman, J. L., Heshka, S., & Levy, A. Population density and pathology: Is there a relationship? *Journal of Experimental Social Psychology*, 1975, *11*, 539–552.

Freedman, J. L., & Perlick, D. Crowding, contagion, and laughter. *Journal of Experimental Social Psychology*, 1979, *15*, 295–303.

Freud, S. *New introductory lectures on psycho-analysis.* New York: Norton, 1933.

Friedland, N. A note on tax evasion as a function of the quality of information about the magnitude and credibility of threatened fines: Some preliminary research. *Journal of Applied Social Psychology*, 1982, *12*, 54–59.

Friedman, H. S. Nonverbal communication between patients and medical practitioners. *Journal of Social Issues*, 1979, *35* (1), 82–99.

Friedman, H. S., Prince, L. M., Riggio, R. E., & DiMatteo, M. R. Understanding and assessing nonverbal expressiveness: The affective communication test. *Journal of Personality and Social Psychology*, 1980, *39*, 333–351.

Friedman, M. Type A behavior pattern: Some of its pathophysiological components. *Bulletin of the New York Academy of Medicine*, 1977, *53*, 593–604.

Friedman, M., & Rosenman, R. H. Association of a specific overt behavior pattern with increases in blood cholesterol, blood clotting time, incidence of arcus senilis and clinical coronary heart disease. *Journal of the American Medical Association*, 1959, *169*, 1286–1296.

Frieze, I. H., Parsons, J. E., Johnson, P. B., Ruble, D. N., & Zellman, G. L. *Women and sex roles: A social psychological perspective.* New York: Norton, 1979.

Frodi, A., Macaulay, J., & Thome, P. R. Are women always less aggressive than men? A review of the experimental literature. *Psychological Bulletin*, 1977, *84*, 634–660.

Fromkin, H. L., Goldstein, J. H., & Brock, T. C. The role of "irrelevant" derogation in vicarious aggression catharsis: A field experiment. *Journal of Experimental Social Psychology*, 1977, *13*, 239–252.

Funder, D. C., & Ozer, D. J. Behavior as a function of the situation. *Journal of Personality and Social Psychology*, 1983, *44*, 107–112.

Furman, W., Rahe, D., & Hartup, W. Rehabilitation of socially withdrawn preschool children through mixed-age and same-age socialization. *Child Development*, 1979, *50*, 915–922.

Gaertner, S. L., & Dovidio, J. F. The subtlety of white racism, arousal, and helping behavior. *Journal of Personality and Social Psychology*, 1977, *35*, 691–707.

Gaes, G. G., Kalle, R. J., & Tedeschi, J. T. Impression management in the forced compliance situation: Two studies using the bogus pipeline. *Journal of Experimental Social Psychology*, 1978, *14*, 493–510.

Gallup, G. Gallup youth survey. *Indianapolis Star,* October 18, 1978.

Gallup, G. G., Jr., & Suarez, S. D. Homosexuality as a byproduct of selection for optimal heterosexual strategies. Unpublished manuscript, State University of New York at Albany, 1982.

Garcia, L., & Griffitt, W. Authoritarianism-situation interactions in the determination of punitiveness: Engaging authoritarian ideology. Unpublished manuscript, Kansas State University, 1977.

Garland, H., & Brown, B. R. Face-saving as affected by subjects' sex, audiences' sex, and audience expertise. *Sociometry,* 1972, *35,* 380–389.

Garner, B., & Smith, R. W. Are there really any gay male athletes? An empirical survey. *Journal of Sex Research,* 1977, *13,* 22–34.

Garstka, W. R., & Crews, D. Female sex pheromone in the skin and circulation of a garter snake. *Science,* 1981, *214,* 681–683.

Garwood, S. G., Cox, L., Kaplan, V., Wasserman, N., & Sulzer, J. L. Beauty is only "name" deep: The effect of first-name in ratings of physical attraction. *Journal of Applied Social Psychology,* 1980, *10,* 431–435.

Gastorf, J. W. Time urgency of the Type A behavior pattern. *Journal of Consulting and Clinical Psychology,* 1980, *48,* 299.

Gastorf, J. W., & Teevan, R. C. Type A coronary-prone behavior pattern and fear of failure. *Motivation and Emotion,* 1980, *4,* 71–76.

Gatchel, R. J., & Proctor, J. D. Physiological correlates of learned helplessness in man. *Journal of Abnormal Psychology,* 1976, *85,* 27–34.

Geen, R. G. Effects of frustration, attack, and prior training in aggressiveness upon aggressive behavior. *Journal of Personality and Social Psychology,* 1968, *9,* 316–321.

Geen, R. G. Some effects of observing violence upon the behavior of the observer. In B. A. Maher (Ed.), *Progress in experimental personality research* (Vol, 8). New York: Academic Press, 1978.

Geen, R. G. Behavioral and physiological reactions to observed violence: Effects of prior exposure to aggressive stimuli. *Journal of Personality and Social Psychology,* 1981, *40,* 868–875. (a)

Geen, R. G. Evaluation apprehension and social facilitation: A reply to Sanders. *Journal of Experimental Social Psychology,* 1981, *17,* 252–256. (b)

Geen, R. G., & Donnerstein, E. (Eds.). *Aggression:*

Theoretical and empirical reviews. New York: Academic Press, 1983.

Geen, R. G., & Gange, J. J. Drive theory of social facilitation: Twelve years of theory and research. *Psychological Bulletin,* 1977, *84,* 1267–1288.

Geen, R. G., Stonner, D., & Shope, G. L. The facilitation of aggression by aggression: Evidence against the catharsis hypothesis. *Journal of Personality and Social Psychology,* 1975, *31,* 721–726.

Geer, J. H. Direct measurement of genital responding. *American Psychologist,* 1975, *30,* 415–418.

Geer, J. H., & Fuhr, R. Cognitive factors in sexual arousal: The role of distraction. *Journal of Consulting and Clinical Psychology,* 1976, *44,* 238–243.

Geis, F. L., & Moon, T. H. Machiavellianism and deception. *Journal of Personality and Social Psychology,* 1981, *41,* 766–775.

Gelfand, D. M., Hartmann, D. P., Walder, P., & Page, B. Who reports shoplifters? A field-experimental study. *Journal of Personality and Social Psychology,* 1973, *25,* 276–285.

Geller, D. M., Goodstein, L., Silver, M., & Sternberg, W. C. On being ignored: The effects of the violation of implicit rules of social interaction. *Sociometry,* 1974, *37,* 541–556.

Geller, E. S., Witmer, J. F., & Orebaugh, A. L. Instructions as a determinant of paper-disposal behaviors. *Environment and Behavior,* 1976, *8,* 417–439.

Gelman, R., & McGinley, H. Interpersonal liking and self-disclosure. *Journal of Consulting and Clinical Psychology,* 1978, *46,* 1549–1551.

Gentry, W. D. Effects of frustration, attack, and prior aggressive training on overt aggression and vascular processes. *Journal of Personality and Social Psychology,* 1970, *16,* 718–725.

Gentry, W. D. What is behavioral medicine? In J. R. Eiser (Ed.), *Social psychology and behavioral medicine.* New York: Wiley, 1982.

Gerard, H. B., & Mathewson, G. C. The effects of severity of initiation on liking for a group: A replication. *Journal of Experimental Social Psychology,* 1966, *2,* 278–287.

Gerard, H. B., Wilhelmy, R. A., & Conolley, E. S. Conformity and group size. *Journal of Personality and Social Psychology,* 1968, *8,* 79–82.

Gergen, K. J. Experimentation in social psychology: A reappraisal. *European Journal of Social Psychology,* 1978, *8,* 507–527.

Gergen, K. J., Ellsworth, P., Maslach, C., & Seipel, M. Obligation, donor resources, and reactions to aid in three cultures. *Journal of Personality and Social Psychology,* 1975, *31,* 390–400.

Gerrard, M. Sex guilt in abortion patients. *Journal of Consulting and Clinical Psychology,* 1977, *45,* 708.

Gerrard, M. Sex guilt and attitudes toward sex in sexually active and inactive female college students. *Journal of Personality Assessment,* 1980, *44,* 258–261.

Gerrard, M. Sex, sex guilt, and contraceptive use. *Journal of Personality and Social Psychology,* 1982, *42,* 153–158.

Gerrard, M., & Gibbons, F. X. Sexual experience, sex guilt, and sexual moral reasoning. *Journal of Personality,* 1982, *50,* 345–359.

Gerrard, M., McCann, L., & Geis, B. The antecedents and prevention of unwanted pregnancy. In A. Rickel, M. Gerrard, and I. Iscoe (Eds.), *Social and psychological problems of women: Prevention and crisis intervention.* New York: McGraw-Hill, 1982.

Gescheider, G. A., Catlin, E. C., & Fontana, A. M. Psychophysical measurement of the judged seriousness of crimes and severity of punishments. *Bulletin of the Psychonomic Society,* 1982, *19,* 275–278.

Gibbons, F. X., & Wicklund, R. A. Selective exposure to self. *Journal of Research in Personality,* 1976, *10,* 98–106.

Gibbons, F. X., & Wicklund, R. A. Self-focused attention and helping behavior. *Journal of Personality and Social Psychology,* 1982, *43,* 462–474.

Gilbert, S. J. Another look at the Milgram obedience studies: The role of the gradated series of shocks. *Personality and Social Psychology Bulletin,* 1981, *7,* 690–695.

Gillen, B. Physical attractiveness: A determinant of two types of goodness. *Personality and Social Psychology Bulletin,* 1981, *7,* 277–281.

Gillis, A. R. Household density and human crowding: Unravelling a nonlinear relationship. *Journal of Population,* 1979, *2,* 104–117.

Gillis, J. S., & Avis, W. E. The male-taller norm in mate selection. *Personality and Social Psychology Bulletin,* 1980, *6,* 396–401.

Gillmore, M. R., & Hill, C. T. Reactions to patients who complain of pain: Effects of ambiguous diagnosis. *Journal of Applied Social Psychology,* 1981, *11,* 14–22.

Gilmour, D. R., & Walkey, F. H. Identifying violent offenders using a video measure of interpersonal distance. *Journal of Consulting and Clinical Psychology,* 1981, *49,* 287–291.

Glass, D. C. *Behavior patterns, stress, and coronary disease.* Hillsdale, N.J.: Erlbaum, 1977.

Glass, D. C., Krakoff, L. R., Finkelman, J., Snow, B., Contrada, R., Kehoe, K., Mannucci, E. G., Isecke, W., Collins, C., Hilton, W. F., & Elting, E. Effect of task overload upon cardiovascular and plasma catecholamine responses in Type A and B individuals. *Basic and Applied Social Psychology,* 1980, *1,* 199–218.

Glass, D. C., Singer, J. E., & Friedman, L. N. Psychic cost of adaptation to an environmental stressor. *Journal of Personality and Social Psychology,* 1969, *12,* 200–210.

Glenn, N. D., & Weaver, C. N. Attitudes toward premarital, extramarital, and homosexual relations in the U.S. in the 1970s. *Journal of Sex Research,* 1979, *15,* 108–118.

Gochman, I. R., & Keating, J. P. Misattributions to crowding: Blaming crowding for nondensity-caused events. *Journal of Nonverbal Behavior,* 1980, *4,* 157–175.

Goethals, G. R., Cooper, J., & Naficy, A. Role of foreseen, foreseeable, and unforeseeable behavioral consequences in the arousal of cognitive dissonance. *Journal of Personality and Social Psychology,* 1979, *37,* 1179–1185.

Goethals, G. R., & Darley, J. M. Social comparison theory: An attributional approach. In J. M. Suls & R. L. Miller (Eds.), *Social comparison processes: Theoretical and empirical perspectives.* Washington, D.C.: Hemisphere, 1977.

Goethals, G. R., & Zanna, M. P. The role of social comparison in choice shifts. *Journal of Personality and Social Psychology,* 1979, *37,* 1469–1476.

Goldband, S. Stimulus specificity of physiological response to stress and the Type A coronary-prone behavior pattern. *Journal of Personality and Social Psychology,* 1980, *39,* 670–679.

Goldfoot, D. A., Essock-Vitale, S. M., Asa, C. S., Thornton, J. E., & Leshner, A. I. Anosmia in male rhesus monkeys does not alter copulatory activity with cycling females. *Science,* 1978, *199,* 1095–1096.

Goldstein, A. P., Carr, E. G., Davidson, W. S., & Wehr, P. *In response to aggression.* New York: Pergamon Press, 1981.

Goldstein, J. H., Davis, R. W., & Herman, D. Escalation of aggression: Experimental studies. *Journal of Personality and Social Psychology,* 1975, *31,* 162–170.

Goldstein, M. J., Kant, H. S., & Hartman, J. J. *Pornography and sexual deviance.* Berkeley: University of California Press, 1974.

Goode, E., & Haber, L. Sexual correlates of

homosexual experience: An exploratory study of college women. *Journal of Sex Research,* 1977, *13,* 12–21.

Goodman, G. S., & Michelli, J. A. Would you believe a child witness? *Psychology Today,* November 1981, pp. 82–84, 86, 90, 93, 95.

Goodwin, M., Gooding, K. M., & Regnier, F. Sex pheromone in the dog. *Science,* 1979, *203,* 559–561.

Gordon, S. Sexual politics and the far right. *Impact '80,* 1980, *1* (3), 1–2.

Gordon, W. A., Freidenbergs, I., Diller, L., Hibbard, M., Wolf, C., Levine, L., Lipkins, R., Ezrachi, O., & Lucido, D. Efficacy of psychosocial intervention with cancer patients. *Journal of Consulting and Clinical Psychology,* 1980, *48,* 743–759.

Gormly, A. V. Behavioral effects of receiving agreement or disagreement from a peer. *Personality and Social Psychology Bulletin,* 1979, *5,* 405–408.

Gormly, J. B., & Gormly, A. V. Approach-avoidance: Potency in psychological research. *Bulletin of the Psychonomic Society,* 1981, *17,* 221–223.

Gosselin, C. The influence of special sexual desires. In M. Cook (Ed.), *The bases of human sexual attraction.* London: Academic Press, 1981.

Gossop, M. Drug-dependence: The mechanics of treatment evaluation and the failure of theory. In J. R. Eiser (Ed.), *Social psychology and behavioral medicine.* New York: Wiley, 1982.

Gotay, C. C. Cooperation and competition as a function of Type A behavior. *Personality and Social Psychology Bulletin,* 1981, *7,* 386–392.

Gotestam, K. G., & Melin, L. Covert extinction of amphetamine addiction. *Behavior Therapy,* 1974, *5,* 90–92.

Gottesman, D., & Lewis, M. S. Differences in crisis reactions among cancer and surgery patients. *Journal of Consulting and Clinical Psychology,* 1982, *50,* 381–388.

Gottlieb, J., & Carver, C. S. Anticipation of future interaction and the bystander effect. *Journal of Experimental Social Psychology,* 1980, *16,* 253–260.

Gouaux, C. Induced affective states and interpersonal attraction. *Journal of Personality and Social Psychology,* 1971, *20,* 37–43.

Gould, R., & Sigall, H. The effects of empathy and outcome on attribution: An examination of the divergent-perspectives hypothesis. *Journal of Experimental Social Psychology,* 1977, *13,* 480–491.

Graen, G. B., Ottis, J. B., & Alvares, K. M. The contingency model of leadership effectiveness: Some experimental results. *Journal of Applied Psychology,* 1971, *55,* 205–210.

Granberg, D., & King, M. Cross-lagged panel analysis of the relation between attraction and perceived similarity. *Journal of Experimental Social Psychology,* 1980, *16,* 573–581.

Graziano, W., Brothen, T., & Berscheid, E. Height and attraction: Do men and women see eye-to-eye? *Journal of Personality,* 1978, *46,* 128–145.

Green, R. *Sexual identity conflict in children.* New York: Basic Books, 1974.

Greenbaum, P., & Rosenfield, H. W. Patterns of avoidance in response to interpersonal staring and proximity: Effects of bystanders on drivers at a traffic intersection. *Journal of Personality and Social Psychology,* 1978, *36,* 575–587.

Greenbaum, P. E., & Greenbaum, S. D. Territorial personalization: Group identity and social interaction in a Slavic-American neighborhood. *Environment and Behavior,* 1981, *13,* 574–589.

Greenberg, J. Attention focus and locus of performance causality as determinants of equity behavior. *Journal of Personality and Social Psychology,* 1980, *38,* 579–585.

Greenberg, J. Self-image vs. impression management in adherence to distributive justice standards: The influence of self-awareness and self-consciousness. *Journal of Personality and Social Psychology,* 1983, *44,* 5–19.

Greenberg, J., & Cohen, R. L. (Eds.). *Equity and justice in social behavior.* New York: Academic Press, 1982.

Greenberg, J., & Ornstein, S. High status job title as compensation for under-payment: A test of equity theory. *Journal of Applied Psychology,* 1983, *68,* 285–297.

Greenberg, J., Pyszczynski, T., & Solomon, S. The self-serving attributional bias: Beyond self-presentation. *Journal of Experimental Social Psychology,* 1982, *18,* 56–67.

Greenberg, M. S. Examining the criminal justice system. *Contemporary Psychology,* 1981, *26,* 913–914.

Greenberg, M. S., & Ruback, R. B. *Social psychology of the criminal justice system.* Monterey, Calif.: Brooks/Cole, 1982.

Greenberger, E., Steinberg, L. D., & Vaux, A. *Developmental Psychology,* 1981, *17,* 691–703.

Griffitt, W. Environmental effects on interpersonal affective behavior: Ambient effective temperature and attraction. *Journal of Personality and Social Psychology*, 1970, *15*, 240–244.

Griffitt, W., & Kaiser, D. L. Affect, sex guilt, gender, and the rewarding-punishing effects of erotic stimuli. *Journal of Personality and Social Psychology*, 1978, *36*, 850–858.

Griffitt, W., May, J., & Veitch, R. Sexual stimulation and interpersonal behavior: Heterosexual evaluative responses, visual behavior, and physical proximity. *Journal of Personality and Social Psychology*, 1974, *30*, 367–377.

Griffitt, W., & Veitch, R. Hot and crowded: Influence of population density and temperature on interpersonal affective behavior. *Journal of Personality and Social Psychology*, 1971, *17*, 92–98.

Griffitt, W., & Veitch, R. Preacquaintance attitude similarity and attraction revisited: Ten days in a fall-out shelter. *Sociometry*, 1974, *37*, 163–173.

Grisso, T., Sales, B. D., & Bayless, S. Law-related courses and programs in graduate psychology departments. *American Psychologist*, 1982, *37*, 267–278.

Gross, A. E., & Fleming, I. Twenty years of deception in social psychology. *Personality and Social Psychology Bulletin*, 1982, *8*, 402–408.

Groth, A. N. *Men who rape: The psychology of the offender.* New York: Plenum, 1979.

Grube, J. W., Kleinhesselink, R. R., & Kearney, K. A. Male self-acceptance and attraction toward women. *Personality and Social Psychology Bulletin*, 1982, *8*, 107–112.

Grusec, J. E., & Redler, E. Attribution, reinforcement, and altruism: A developmental analysis. *Developmental Psychology*, 1980, *16*, 525–534.

Grush, J. E. Attitude formation and mere exposure phenomena: A nonartifactual explanation of empirical findings. *Journal of Personality and Social Psychology*, 1976, *33*, 281–290.

Grush, J. E. The impact of candidate expenditures, regionality, and prior outcomes on the 1976 Democratic presidential primaries. *Journal of Personality and Social Psychology*, 1980, *38*, 337–347.

Grush, J. E., McKeough, K. L., & Ahlering, R. F. Extrapolating laboratory exposure research to actual political elections. *Journal of Personality and Social Psychology*, 1978, *36*, 257–270.

Guile, M. N., Shapiro, N. R., & Boice, R.

Reactivity to being photographed: An invasion of personal space. *Bulletin of the Psychonomic Society*, 1980, *16*, 113–114.

Guimond, S., & Dubé-Simard, L. Relative deprivation theory and the Quebec nationalist movement: The cognition-emotion distinction and the personal-group deprivation issue. *Journal of Personality and Social Psychology*, 1983, *44*, 526–535.

Gully, K. J., & Dengerink, H. A. The dyadic interaction of persons with violent and nonviolent histories. *Aggressive Behavior*, 1983, *9*, 13–20.

Gundlach, R. H. Sibship size, sibsex, and homosexuality among females. *Transnational Mental Health Research Newsletter*, 1977, *19*, 3–7.

Guthrie, R. D. *Body hotspots.* New York: Van Nostrand Reinhold, 1976.

Gyllenhammar, P. G. How Volvo adapts work to people. *Harvard Business Review*, July–August 1977, 102–113.

Haley, R. W., Quade, D., Freeman, H. E., Bennett, J. V., & the CEC SENIC Planning Committee. The study of the efficacy of nosocomial infection control (SENIC Project): Summary of study design. *American Journal of Epidemiology*, 1980, *111*, 472–485.

Hall, E. T. A system for the notation of proxemic behavior. *American Anthropologist*, 1963, *65*, 1003–1026.

Hall, E. T. *The hidden dimension.* New York: Doubleday, 1966.

Hamburg, D. A. Health and behavior. *Science*, 1982, *217*, 399.

Hamill, R., Wilson, T. D., & Nisbett, R. E. Insensitivity to sample bias: Generalizing from atypical cases. *Journal of Personality and Social Psychology*, 1980, *39*, 578–589.

Hamilton, D. L. *Cognitive processes in stereotyping and intergroup behavior.* Hillsdale, N.J.: Erlbaum, 1981.

Hamilton, D. L., Katz, L. B., & Leirer, V. O. Cognitive representation of personality impressions: Organizational processes in first impression formation. *Journal of Personality and Social Psychology*, 1980, *39*, 1050–1063.

Hamilton, D. L., & Zanna, M. P. Differential weighting of favorable and unfavorable attributes in impressions of personality. *Journal of Experimental Research in Personality*, 1972, *6*, 204–212.

Hamilton, T. P., Swap, W. C., & Rubin, J. Z. Predicting the effects of anticipated third party intervention: A template-matching approach. *Journal of Personality and Social Psychology,* 1981, *41,* 1141–1152.

Hamilton, V. L. Obedience and responsibility: A jury simulation. *Journal of Personality and Social Psychology,* 1978, *36,* 126–146.

Hammen, C., & Mayol, A. Depression and cognitive characteristics of stressful life-event types. *Journal of Abnormal Psychology,* 1982, *91,* 165–174.

Hansen, R. D. Commonsense attribution. *Journal of Personality and Social Psychology,* 1980, *39,* 996–1009.

Harkins, S. G., Latané, B., & Williams, K. Social loafing: Allocating effort or taking it easy? *Journal of Experimental Social Psychology,* 1980, *16,* 457–465.

Harkins, S. G., & Petty, R. E. The role of intrinsic motivation in eliminating social loafing. *Journal of Personality and Social Psychology,* 1983, in press.

Harrel, W. A. The effects of alcohol use and offender remorsefulness on sentencing decisions. *Journal of Applied Social Psychology,* 1981, *11,* 83–91.

Harries, K. D., & Stadler, S. J. Determinism revisited: Assault and heat stress in Dallas, 1980. *Environment and Behavior,* 1983, *15,* 235–256.

Harris, M. Dressing for success. *Money,* December 1980, p. 8.

Harris, M. B. Mediators between frustration and aggression in a field experiment. *Journal of Experimental Social Psychology,* 1974, 561–571.

Harris, M. B., Harris, R. J., & Bochner, S. Fat, four-eyed, and female: Stereotypes of obesity, glasses, and gender. *Journal of Applied Social Psychology,* 1982, *12,* 503–516.

Harris, R. J. Equity judgments in hypothetical, four-person partnerships. *Journal of Experimental Social Psychology,* 1980, *16,* 96–115.

Harry, J. Defeminization and adult psychological well-being among male homosexuals. *Archives of Sexual Behavior,* 1983, *12,* 1–19.

Harvey, J. H., & Weary, G. *Perspectives on attributional processes.* Dubuque, Iowa: William Brown, 1981.

Harvey, J. M. Locus of control shift in administrators. *Perceptual and Motor Skills,* 1971, *33,* 980–982.

Harvey, J. M., Yarkin, K. L., Lightner, J., & Town, J. P. Unsolicited interpretation and recall of interpersonal events. *Journal of Personality and Social Psychology,* 1980, *38,* 551–568.

Harvey, M. D., & Enzle, M. E. Effects of retaliation latency and provocation level on judged blame-worthiness for retaliatory aggression. *Personality and Social Psychology Bulletin,* 1978, *4,* 579–582.

Hassett, J. But that would be wrong . . . *Psychology Today,* November 1981, pp. 34–35, 37–38, 41, 44, 46, 49–50.

Hastie, R. Schematic principles in human memory. In E. T. Higgins, C. P. Herman, & M. P. Zanna (Eds.), *Social cognition: The Ontario Symposium* (Vol. 1). Hillsdale, N.J.: Erlbaum, 1981.

Hastie, R. Social inference. In *Annual Review of Psychology* (Vol. 34). Palo Alto, Calif.: Annual Reviews, Inc., 1983.

Hastie, R., & Kumar, P. A. Person memory: Personality traits as organizing principles in memory for behaviors. *Journal of Personality and Social Psychology,* 1979, *37,* 25–38.

Hastie, R., Ostrom, T. M., Ebbesen, E. B., Wyer, R. S., Hamilton, D. L., Carlston, D. E. (Eds.). *Person memory: The cognitive basis of social perception.* Hillsdale, N.J.: Erlbaum, 1980.

Hatch, J. P. Vaginal photoplethysmography: Methodological considerations. *Archives of Sexual Behavior,* 1979, *8,* 357–374.

Hatfield, E. Passionate love scale. Personal communication, 1983. (a)

Hatfield, E. What do women and men want from love and sex? In E. R. Allgeier & N. B. McCormick (Eds.), *Changing boundaries: Gender roles and sexual behavior.* Palo Alto, Calif.: Mayfield, 1983. (b)

Hatfield, E., & Traupmann, J. Intimate relationships: A perspective from equity theory. In S. Duck & R. Gilmour (Eds.), *Personal relationships. 1 : Studying personal relationships.* London: Academic Press, 1981.

Hatfield, E., & Walster, G. W. *A new look at love.* Reading, Mass.: Addison-Wesley, 1981.

Hathaway, S. R., & McKinley, J. C. A multiphasic personality schedule (Minnesota): 1. Construction of the schedule. *Journal of Psychology,* 1940, *10,* 249–254.

Hatvany, N., & Strack, F. The impact of a discredited key witness. *Journal of Applied Social Psychology,* 1980, *10,* 490–509.

Haynes, S., Feinleib, M., & Kannel, W. The relationship of psychosocial factors to coronary heart disease in the Framingham Study: Eight-year incidence of coronary heart disease. *American Journal of Epidemiology,* 1980, *111,* 37–58.

Heberlein, T. A., & Black, J. S. Attitudinal specificity and the prediction of behavior in a field setting. *Journal of Personality and Social Psychology*, 1976, *33*, 474–479.

Hechinger, F. M. Studies examine the issue of ethics. *New York Times*, December 30, 1980, pp. C1, C3.

Heiby, E., & Becker, J. D. Effect of filmed modeling on the self-reported frequency of masturbation. *Archives of Sexual Behavior*, 1980, *9*, 115–121.

Heider, F. *The psychology of interpersonal relations*. New York: Wiley, 1958.

Heilbroner, R. *An inquiry into the human prospect*. New York: Norton, 1974.

Heingartner, A., & Hall, J. V. Affective consequences in adults and children of repeated exposure to auditory stimuli. *Journal of Personality and Social Psychology*, 1974, *29*, 719–723.

Heisler, G. Ways to deter law violators: Effects of levels of threat and vicarious punishment on cheating. *Journal of Consulting and Clinical Psychology*, 1974, *42*, 577–582.

Helmreich, R. L., Spence, J. T., & Gibson, R. H. Sex-role attitudes: 1972–1980. *Personality and Social Psychology Bulletin*, 1980, *8*, 656–663.

Hemstone, M., & Jaspars, J. Explanations for racial discrimination: The effects of group decision on intergroup attributions. *European Journal of Social Psychology*, 1982, *12*, 1–16.

Hendrick, C., Wells, K. S., & Faletti, M. V. Social and emotional effects of geographical relocation on elderly retirees. *Journal of Personality and Social Psychology*, 1982, *42*, 951–962.

Hennigan, K. M., Cook, T. D., & Gruder, C. L. Cognitive tuning set, source credibility, and the temporal persistence of attitude change. *Journal of Personality and Social Psychology*, 1982, *42*, 412–425.

Hensley, W. E. The effects of attire, location, and sex on aiding behavior: A similarity explanation. *Journal of Nonverbal Behavior*, 1981, *6*, 3–11.

Herzog, T. R., Kaplan, S., & Kaplan, R. The prediction of preference for unfamiliar urban places. *Population and Environment*, 1982, *5*, 43–58.

Heshka, S., & Nelson, Y. Interpersonal speaking distance as a function of age, sex, and relationship. *Sociometry*, 1972, *35*, 491–498.

Hicks, R. A., Allen, J. G., Armogida, R. E., Gilliland, M. A., & Pellegrini, R. J. Reduction in sleep duration and Type A behavior. *Bulletin of the Psychonomic Society*, 1980, *16*, 109–110.

Higbee, K. L. Fifteen years of fear arousal: Research on threat appeals, 1953–1968. *Psychological Bulletin*, 1969, *72*, 426–444.

Higgins, E. T., & Bryant, S. L. Consensus information and the fundamental attribution error: The role of development and in-group versus out-group knowledge. *Journal of Personality and Social Psychology*, 1982, *43*, 889–900.

Higgins, E. T., Herman, C. P., & Zanna, M. P. (Eds.). *Social cognition: The Ontario symposium on personality and social psychology*. Hillsdale, N.J.: Erlbaum, 1980.

Higgins, E. T., Herman, C. P., & Zanna, M. P. (Eds.). *Social cognition: The Ontario Symposium* (Vol. 1). Hillsdale, N.J.: Erlbaum, 1981.

Higgins, E. T., King, G. A., & Mavin, G. H. Individual construct accessibility and subjective impressions and recall. *Journal of Personality and Social Psychology*, 1982, *43*, 35–47.

Higgins, E. T., Rholes, W. S., & Jones, C. R. Category accessibility and impression formation. *Journal of Experimental Social Psychology*, 1977, *13*, 141–154.

Hildebrandt, K. A., & Fitzgerald, H. E. Facial feature determinants of perceived infant cuteness. Paper presented at the meeting of the Midwestern Psychological Association, Chicago, May 1977.

Hill, C. T., Rubin, Z., & Peplau, L. A. Breakups before marriage: The end of 103 affairs. *Journal of Social Issues*, 1976, *32*, 147–168.

Hill, C. T., & Stull, D. E. Sex differences in effects of social and value similarity in same-sex friendship. *Journal of Personality and Social Psychology*, 1981, *41*, 488–502.

Hiltrop, J. M., & Rubin, J. Z. Effects of intervention mode and conflict of interest on dispute resolution. *Journal of Personality and Social Psychology*, 1982, *42*, 665–672.

Himmelfarb, S. Reporting and nonreporting of observed crimes: Moral judgments of the act and actor. *Journal of Applied Social Psychology*, 1980, *10*, 56–70.

Hinde, R. A. The bases of a science of interpersonal relationships. In S. Duck & R. Gilmour (Eds.), *Personal relationships. 1: Studying personal relationships*. London: Academic Press, 1981.

Hoffman, M. *The gay world*. New York: Basic Books, 1968.

Hoffman, M. L. Is altruism part of human nature? *Journal of Personality and Social Psychology*, 1981, *40*, 121–137.

Hogan, R., DeSoto, C., & Solano, C. Traits, tests, and personality research. *American Psychologist*, 1977, *32*, 255–264.

Hokanson, J. E. Psychophysiological evaluation of the catharsis hypothesis. In E. I. Megargee & J. E. Hokanson (Eds.), *The dynamics of aggression.* New York: Harper, 1970.

Hokanson, J. E., & Burgess, M. The effects of three types of aggression on vascular processes. *Journal of Abnormal and Social Psychology,* 1962, *64,* 446–449.

Hokanson, J. E., Burgess, M., & Cohen, M. E. Effects of displaced aggression on systolic blood pressure. *Journal of Abnormal and Social Psychology,* 1963, *67,* 214–218.

Holahan, C. J., & Moos, R. H. Social support and psychological distress: A longitudinal analysis. *Journal of Abnormal Psychology,* 1981, *90,* 365–370.

Hollander, E. P. Competence and conformity in the acceptance of influence. *Journal of Abnormal and Social Psychology,* 1960, *61,* 365–369.

Hollander, E. P. *Leaders, groups, and influence.* New York: Oxford University Press, 1964.

Hollander, E. P., & Julian, J. W. Studies in leader legitimacy, influence, and innovation. In L. Berkowitz (Ed.), *Advances in experimental social psychology* (Vol. 5). New York: Academic Press, 1970.

Hollander, E. P., & Julian, J. W. A further look at leader legitimacy, influence, and innovation. In L. Berkowitz (Ed.), *Group processes.* New York: Academic Press, 1978.

Hölldobler, B., & Haskins, C. P. Sexual calling behavior in primitive ants. *Science,* 1977, *195,* 793–794.

Hölldobler, B., & Lumsden, C. J. Territorial strategies in ants. *Science,* 1980, *210,* 732–739.

Hoon, P., Wincze, H., & Hoon, E. A test of reciprocal inhibition: Are anxiety and sexual arousal in women mutually inhibitory? *Journal of Abnormal Psychology,* 1977, *86,* 65–74.

Horner, M. Femininity and successful achievement: A basic inconsistency. In J. M. Bardwick et al. (Eds.), *Feminine personality and conflict.* Belmont, Calif.: Wadsworth, 1970.

Horner, M. Toward an understanding of achievement-related conflicts in women. *Journal of Social Issues,* 1972, *28,* 157–176.

Horowitz, I. A., Bordens, K. S., & Feldman, M. S. A comparison of verdicts obtained in severed and joined criminal trials. *Journal of Applied Social Psychology,* 1980, *10,* 444–456.

Horvath, T. Correlates of physical beauty in men and women. *Social Behavior and Personality,* 1979, *7,* 145–151.

Horvath, T. Physical attractiveness: The influence of selected torso parameters. *Archives of Sexual Behavior,* 1981, *10,* 21–24.

Hovland, C. I., Janis, I. L., & Kelley, H. H. *Communication and persuasion.* New Haven, Conn.: Yale University Press, 1953.

Howard, J. L., Reifler, C. B., & Liptzin, M. B. Effects of exposure to pornography. In *Technical Report of the Commission on Obscenity and Pornography* (Vol. 8). Washington, D.C.: U.S. Government Printing Office, 1971.

Howard, M. The vanity industry. *New Republic,* 1980, *183* (10 & 11), 25–28, 30.

Howard, W., & Crana, W. D. Effects of sex, conversation, location, and size of observer group on bystander intervention in a high risk situation. *Sociometry,* 1974, *37,* 491–507.

Huesmann, L. R. Television violence and aggressive behavior. In D. Pearl & L. Bouthilet (Eds.), *Television and behavior: Ten years of scientific progress and implications for the 80's.* Washington, D.C.: U.S. Government Printing Office, 1983.

Hull, J. G., & West, S. G. The discounting principle in attribution. *Personality and Social Psychology Bulletin,* 1982, *8,* 208–213.

Humphries, C., Carver, C. S., & Neumann, P. G. Cognitive characteristics of the Type A coronary-prone behavior pattern. *Journal of Personality and Social Psychology,* 1983, *44,* 177–187.

Hunt, M. *Sexual behavior in the 1970s.* Chicago: Playboy, 1974.

Hunt, P. J., & Hillery, J. M. Social facilitation in a coaction setting: An examination of the effects over learning trials. *Journal of Experimental Social Psychology,* 1973, *9,* 563–571.

Hunt, R. G. *Interpersonal strategies for system management.* Monterey, Calif.: Brooks/Cole, 1976.

Huston, T. L., & Levinger, G. Interpersonal attraction and relationships. In M. R. Rosenzweig & L. W. Porter (Eds.), *Annual Review of Psychology* (Vol. 29). Palo Alto, Calif.: Annual Reviews Inc., 1978.

Huston, T. L., Ruggiero, M., Conner, R., & Geis, G. Bystander intervention into crime: A study based on naturally-occurring episodes. *Social Psychology Quarterly,* 1981, *44,* 14–23.

Ibrahim, Y. M. World fertility in rapid decline, according to vast new study. *New York Times,* July 15, 1980, p. C–1.

Ilgen, D. R., Campbell, D. J., Peters, L. H., & Fisher, C. D. Work role perceptions: Their affective and behavioral consequences. Unpublished manuscript, Purdue University, 1975.

Imada, A. S., & Hakel, M. D. Influence of nonverbal communication and rater proximity on impressions and decisions in simulated employment interviews. *Journal of Applied Psychology*, 1977, *62*, 295–300.

Innes, J. M., & Young, R. F. The effect of presence of an audience, evaluation apprehension and objective self-awareness on learning. *Journal of Experimental Social Psychology*, 1975, *11*, 35–42.

Insko, C. A., Thibaut, J. W., Moehle, D., Wilson, M., Diamond, W. D., Gilmore, R., Solomon, M. R., & Lipsitz, A. Social evolution and the emergence of leadership. *Journal of Personality and Social Psychology*, 1980, *39*, 431–448.

Instone, D., Major, B., & Bunker, B. B. Gender, self confidence, and social influence strategies: An organizational simulation. *Journal of Personality and Social Psychology*, 1983, *44*, 322–333.

Isen, A. M. Success, failure, attention, and reaction to others: The warm glow of success. *Journal of Personality and Social Psychology*, 1970, *15*, 294–301.

Isen, A. M., Clark, M., & Schwartz, M. F. Duration of the effect of good mood on helping: "Footprints on the sands of time." *Journal of Personality and Social Psychology*, 1976, *34*, 385–393.

Isen, A. M., Horn, N., & Rosenhan, D. L. Effects of success and failure on children's generosity. *Journal of Personality and Social Psychology*, 1973, *27*, 239–247.

Isen, A. M., & Levin, P. F. The effect of feeling good on helping: Cookies and kindness. *Journal of Personality and Social Psychology*, 1972, *21*, 384–388.

Istvan, J., & Griffitt, W. Emotional arousal and sexual attraction. Unpublished manuscript, Kansas State University, 1978.

Istvan, J., & Griffitt, W. Effects of sexual experience on dating desirability and marriage desirability: An experimental study. *Journal of Marriage and the Family*, 1980, *42*, 377–385.

Izard, C. *Human emotions*. New York: Plenum Press, 1977.

Izard, C., Huebner, R. R., Risser, D., McGinnes, G. C., & Dougherty, L. M. The young infant's ability to produce discrete emotion expressions. *Developmental Psychology*, 1980, *16*, 132–140.

Izzett, R. R., & Leginski, W. Group discussion and the influence of defendant characteristics in a simulated jury setting. *Journal of Social Psychology*, 1974, *93*, 271–279.

Jackson, J. M., & Latané, B. Strength and number of solicitors and the urge toward altruism. *Personality and Social Psychology Bulletin*, 1981, *7*, 415–422.

Jacobs, P. A., Brunton, M., & Melville, M. M. Aggressive behavior, mental subnormality, and the XYY male. *Nature*, 1965, *208*, 1351–1352.

Jaffe, Y., Malamuth, N., Feingold, J., & Feshbach, S. Sexual arousal and behavioral aggression. *Journal of Personality and Social Psychology*, 1974, *30*, 759–764.

Jakibchuk, Z., & Smeriglio, V. L. The influence of symbolic modeling on the social behavior of preschool children with low levels of social responsiveness. *Child Development*, 1976, *47*, 838–841.

James, W. *The principles of psychology*. New York: Dover, 1950.

Janda, L. H., O'Grady, K. E., & Barnhart, S. A. Effects of sexual attitudes and physical attractiveness on person perception of men and women. *Sex Roles*, 1981, *7*, 189–199.

Janoff-Bulman, R., & Marshall, G. Mortality, well-being, and control: A study of a population of institutionalized aged. *Personality and Social Psychology Bulletin*, 1982, *8*, 691–698.

Jarvik, L. F., Klodin, V., & Matsuyama, S. S. Human aggression and the extra Y chromosome: Fact or fantasy? *American Psychologist*, 1973, *28*, 674–682.

Jellison, J. M., & Davis, D. Relationships between perceived ability and attitude extremity. *Journal of Personality and Social Psychology*, 1973, *27*, 430–436.

Jellison, J. M., & Oliver, D. F. Attitude similarity and attraction: An impression management approach. *Personality and Social Psychology Bulletin*, 1983, *9*, 111–115.

Jenkins, C. D. Recent evidence supporting psychologic and social risk factors for coronary disease. *New England Journal of Medicine*, 1976, *294*, 987–994, 1033–1038.

Jenkins, C. D., Zyzanski, S. J., & Rosenman, R. H. *Jenkins Activity Survey*. New York: Psychological Corporation, 1979.

Jenkins, C. D., Zyzanski, S. J., Ryan, T. J., Flessas, A., & Tannenbaum, S. I. Social insecurity and coronary-prone Type A responses as identifiers of severe atherosclerosis. *Journal of Consulting and Clinical Psychology*, 1977, *45*, 1060–1067.

Jensen, N. F. Limits to growth in world food production. *Science*, 1978, *201*, 317–320.

Jessor, R., Costa, F., Jessor, L., & Donovan, J. E. Time of first intercourse: A prospective study. *Journal of Personality and Social Psychology*, 1983, *44*, 608–626.

Johnson, B. L., & Kilmann, P. R. The relationship between recalled parental attitudes and internal-external control. *Journal of Clinical Psychology*, 1975, *31*, 40–42.

Johnson, C. D., & Gormly, J. Achievement, sociability, and task importance in relation to academic cheating. *Psychological Reports*, 1971, *28*, 302.

Johnson, C. D., & Gormly, J. Academic cheating: The contribution of sex, personality, and situational variables. *Developmental Psychology*, 1972, *6*, 320–325.

Johnson, R. D., & Downing, L. L. Deindividuation and valence of cues: Effects on prosocial and antisocial behavior. *Journal of Personality and Social Psychology*, 1979, *37*, 1532–1538.

Jones, D. M., Chapman, A. J., & Auburn, T. C. Noise in the environment: A social perspective. *Journal of Environmental Psychology*, 1981, *1*, 43–59.

Jones, E. E. *Ingratiation: A social psychological analysis.* New York: Appleton-Century-Crofts, 1964.

Jones, E. E., & Davis, K. E. From acts to dispositions: The attribution process in person perception. In L. Berkowitz (Ed.), *Advances in Experimental Social Psychology* (Vol. 2). New York: Academic Press, 1965.

Jones, E. E., & McGillis, D. Correspondent inferences and the attribution cube: A comparative reappraisal. In J. H. Harvey, W. J. Ickes, & R. F. Kidd (Eds.), *New directions in attribution research* (Vol. 1). Hillsdale, N.J.: Erlbaum, 1976.

Jones, E. E., & Nisbett, R. E. *The actor and the observer: Divergent perceptions of the causes of behavior.* Morristown, N.J.: General Learning Press, 1971.

Jones, E. E., & Sigall, H. The bogus pipeline: A new paradigm for measuring affect and attitude. *Psychological Bulletin*, 1971, *76*, 349–364.

Jones, E. E., Worchel, S., Goethals, G. T., & Grumet, J. F. Prior expectancy and behavioral extremity as determinants of attitude attribution. *Journal of Experimental Social Psychology*, 1971, *7*, 59–80.

Jones, J. W. Dishonesty, burnout, and unauthorized work break extensions.

Personality and Social Psychology Bulletin, 1981, *7*, 406–409.

Jones, W. H. Loneliness and social behavior. In L. A. Peplau & D. Perlman, *Loneliness: A sourcebook of current theory, research, and therapy.* New York: Wiley, 1982.

Jones, W. H., Freeman, J. A., & Goswick, R. A. The persistence of loneliness: Self and other determinants. *Journal of Personality*, 1981, *49*, 27–48.

Jones, W. H., Hannson, R. C., & Phillips, A. L. Physical attractiveness and judgments of psychotherapy. *Journal of Social Psychology*, 1978, *105*, 79–84.

Jones, W. H., Hansson, R. O., & Smith, T. G. Loneliness and love: Implications for psychological and interpersonal functioning. Unpublished manuscript, University of Tulsa, 1980.

Jones, W. H., Hobbs, S. A., & Hockenbury, D. Loneliness and social skill deficits. *Journal of Personality and Social Psychology*, 1982, *42*, 682–689.

Jorgensen, R. S., & Houston, B. K. The Type A behavior pattern, sex differences, and cardiovascular response to and recovery from stress. *Motivation and Emotion*, 1981, *5*, 201–214.

Judd, C. M., & Krosnick, J. A. Attitude centrality, organization, and measurement. *Journal of Personality and Social Psychology*, 1982, *42*, 437–447.

Jurow, G. L. New data on the effect of a "death-qualified" jury on the guilt determination process. *Harvard Law Review*, 1971, *84*, 567–611.

Kagitcibasi, C. Social norms and authoritarianism: A Turkish-American comparison. *Journal of Personality and Social Psychology*, 1970, *16*, 444–451.

Kahn, R. L. The meaning of work: Interpretations and proposals for measurement. In A. A. Campbell & P. E. Converse (Eds.), *The human meaning of social change.* New York: Basic Books, 1972.

Kahneman, D., Slovic, P., & Tversky, A. (Eds.). *Judgment under uncertainty: Heuristics and biases.* Cambridge: Cambridge University Press, 1982.

Kahneman, D., & Tversky, A. Subjective probability: A judgment of representativeness. *Cognitive Psychology*, 1972, *3*, 430–454.

Kahneman, D., & Tversky, A. On the psychology

of prediction. *Psychological Review,* 1973, *80,* 237–251.

Kandel, D. B. Similarity in real-life adolescent friendship pairs. *Journal of Personality and Social Psychology,* 1978, *36,* 306–312.

Kantola, S. J., Syme, G. J., & Campbell, N. A. The role of individual differences and external variables in a test of the sufficiency of Fishbein's model to explain behavioral intentions to conserve water. *Journal of Applied Social Psychology,* 1982, *12,* 70–83.

Kaplan, J. *Marijuana—The new prohibition.* New York: World, 1971.

Kaplan, M. F. Measurement and generality of response dispositions in person perception. *Journal of Personality,* 1976, *44,* 179–194.

Kaplan, M. F., & Miller, L. E. Effects of juror's identification with the victim depend on likelihood of victimization. *Law and Human Behavior,* 1979.

Karlin, R. A., Rosen, L. S., & Epstein, Y. M. Three into two doesn't go: A follow-up on the effects of overcrowded dormitory rooms. *Personality and Social Psychology Bulletin,* 1979, *5,* 391–395.

Kassin, S. M., & Wrightsman, L. S. Prior confessions and mock juror verdicts. *Journal of Applied Social Psychology,* 1980, *10,* 133–146.

Kassin, S. M., & Wrightsman, L. S. Coerced confessions, judicial instructions, and mock juror verdicts. *Journal of Applied Social Psychology,* 1981, *11,* 489–506.

Katkovsky, W., Crandall, V. C., & Good, S. Parental antecedents of children's beliefs in internal-external control of reinforcement in intellectual achievement situations. *Child Development,* 1967, *28,* 765–776.

Katzell, R. A., & Yankelovich, D. *Work, productivity, and job satisfaction.* New York: Psychological Corporation, 1975.

Kaufman, M. T. Love upsetting Bombay's view of path to altar. *New York Times,* November 16, 1980, p. 12.

Kaye, H. E. Lesbian relationships. *Sexual Behavior,* April 1972.

Kelley, H. H. Attribution in social interaction. In E. E. Jones et al. (Eds.), *Attribution: Perceiving the causes of behavior.* Morristown, N.J.: General Learning Press, 1972.

Kelley, H. H. *Personal relationships: Their structures and processes.* Hillsdale, N.J.: Erlbaum, 1979.

Kelley, H. H., & Michela, J. L. Attribution theory and research. *Annual Review of Psychology,* 1980, *31,* 457–501.

Kelley, H. H., & Thibaut, J. *Interpersonal relations:* *A theory of interdependence.* New York: Wiley, 1978.

Kelley, K. Predicting attraction to the novel stimulus person: Affect and concern. *Journal of Research in Personality,* 1982, *16,* 32–40. (a)

Kelley, K. Variety is the spice of erotica: Repeated exposure, novelty, and sexual attitudes. Paper presented at the meeting of the Eastern Psychological Association, Baltimore, April 1982. (b)

Kelley, K. Population size or density inflects eight social indices: Unpublished manuscript, State University of New York at Albany, 1982. (c)

Kelley, K., & Byrne, D. Attraction and altruism: With a little help from my friends. *Journal of Research in Personality,* 1976, *10,* 59–68.

Kelley, K., & Byrne, D. Assessment of sexual responding: Arousal, affect, and behavior. In J. Cacioppo & R. Petty (Eds.), *Social psychophysiology.* New York: Guilford Press, 1983.

Kelley, K., Byrne, D., Przybyla, D. P. J., Eberly, C. C., Eberly, B. W., Greendlinger, V., Wan, C. K., & Gorsky, J. Chronic self-destructiveness: Conceptualization, measurement, and construct validation. Unpublished manuscript, SUNY-Albany, 1983.

Kelley, K., Pilchowicz, E., & Byrne, D. Response of males to female-initiated dates. *Bulletin of the Psychonomic Society,* 1981, *17,* 195–196.

Kelly, E. L. Consistency of the adult personality. *American Psychologist,* 1955, *10,* 659–681.

Kenrick, D. T., Cialdini, R. B., & Linder, D. E. Misattribution under fear-producing circumstances: Four failures to replicate. *Personality and Social Psychology Bulletin,* 1979, *5,* 329–334.

Kenrick, D. T., & Gutierres, S. E. Contrast effects and judgments of physical attractiveness: When beauty becomes a social problem. *Journal of Personality and Social Psychology,* 1980, *38,* 131–140.

Kenrick, D. T., & Johnson, G. A. Interpersonal attraction in aversive environments: A problem for the classical conditioning paradigm? *Journal of Personality and Social Psychology,* 1979, *37,* 572–579.

Kenrick, D. T., & Stringfield, D. O. Personality traits and the eye of the beholder: Crossing some traditional philosophical boundaries in the search for consistency in all the people. *Psychological Review,* 1980, *87,* 88–104.

Kent, G. G., Davis, J. D., & Shapiro, D. A. Effect of mutual acquaintance on the construction of conversation. *Journal of Experimental Social Psychology,* 1981, *17,* 197–209.

Kerber, K. W., & Coles, M. G. H. The role of perceived physiological activity in affective judgments. *Journal of Experimental Social Psychology,* 1978, *14,* 419–433.

Kernis, M. H., & Wheeler, L. Beautiful friends and ugly strangers: Radiation and contrast effects in perceptions of same-sex pairs. *Personality and Social Psychology Bulletin,* 1981, *7,* 617–620.

Kerr, N. L. Beautiful and blameless: Effects of victim attractiveness and responsibility on mock jurors' verdicts. *Personality and Social Psychology Bulletin,* 1978, *4,* 479–482. (a)

Kerr, N. L. Severity of prescribed penalty and mock jurors' verdicts. *Journal of Personality and Social Psychology,* 1978, *36,* 1431–1442. (b)

Kerr, N. L. Social transition schemes: Charting the group's road to agreement. *Journal of Personality and Social Psychology,* 1981, *41,* 684–702.

Kerr, N. L. Motivation losses in small groups: A social dilemma analysis. Unpublished manuscript, Michigan State University, 1983. (a)

Kerr, N. L. Social transition schemes: Model, method, and applications. In J. H. Davis & H. Brandstatter (Eds.), *Group decision making processes.* New York: Academic Press, 1983. (b)

Kerr, N. L., & Bruun, S. E. The dispensability of member effort and group motivation losses: Free-rider effects. *Journal of Personality and Social Psychology,* 1983, *44,* 78–94.

Kerr, N. L., Harmon, D. L., & Graves, J. K. Independence of multiple verdicts by jurors and juries. *Journal of Applied Social Psychology,* 1982, *12,* 12–29.

Keys, A. Coronary heart disease in seven countries: XIII multiple variables. *Circulation,* 1970, *41,* 138–144.

Kiesler, C. A., Collins, B. E., & Miller, N. *Attitude change: A critical analysis of theoretical approaches.* New York: John Wiley & Sons, 1969.

Kiesler, C. A., & Kiesler, S. B. *Conformity.* Reading, Mass.: Addison-Wesley, 1969.

Kilham, W., & Mann, L. Level of destructive obedience as a function of transmitter and executant roles in the Milgram obedience paradigm. *Journal of Personality and Social Psychology,* 1974, *29,* 696–702.

Kinsey, A., Pomeroy, W. B., & Martin, C. E. *Sexual behavior in the human male.* Philadelphia: Saunders, 1948.

Kinsey, A., Pomeroy, W. B., Martin, C. E., &

Gebhard, P. H. *Sexual behavior in the human female.* Philadelphia: Saunders, 1953.

Kinsley, M. The art of polling. *The New Republic,* June 20, 1981, pp. 16–19.

Kinzel, A. S. Body-buffer zone in violent prisoners. *American Journal of Psychiatry,* 1970, *127,* 59–64.

Klapper, J. T. The impact of viewing "aggression": Studies and problems of extrapolation. In O. N. Larsen (Ed.), *Violence and the mass media.* New York: Harper & Row, 1968.

Klein, D. Doctors react negatively to patients with differing behavior, report says. Associated Press, March 11, 1982.

Klein, K. Disconfirmed expectancies and imagined distress in a role-play of a visit to the dentist. *Motivation and Emotion,* 1982, *6,* 181–192.

Kleinke, C. L., & Kahn, M. L. Perceptions of self-disclosers: Effects of sex and physical attractiveness. *Journal of Personality,* 1980, *48,* 190–205.

Kleinke, C. L., Meeker, F. B., & LaFong, C. Effects of gaze, touch, and use of name on evaluation of "engaged" couples. *Journal of Research in Personality,* 1974, *7,* 368–373.

Kleinke, C. L., & Staneski, R. A. First impressions of female bust size. *Journal of Social Psychology,* 1980, *110,* 123–134.

Klentz, B., & Beaman, A. L. The effects of type of information and method of dissemination on the reporting of a shoplifter. *Journal of Applied Psychology,* 1981, *11,* 64–82.

Knapp, M. L. *Nonverbal communication in human interaction* (2nd ed.). New York: Holt, Rinehart and Winston, 1978.

Knight, G. P. Behavioral similarity, confederate strategy, and sex composition of dyad as determinants of interpersonal judgments and behavior in the prisoner's dilemma game. *Journal of Research in Personality,* 1980, *14,* 91–103.

Knowles, E. S. Personal space. In P. B. Paulus (Ed.), *Group influence.* Hillsdale, N.J.: Erlbaum, 1978.

Knowles, E. S. Convergent validity of personal space measures: Consistent results with low intercorrelations. *Journal of Nonverbal Behavior,* 1980, *4,* 240–248.

Knowlton, W. A., Jr., & Mitchell, T. R. Effects of causal attributions on a supervisor's evaluation of subordinate performance. *Journal of Applied Psychology,* 1980, *65,* 459–466.

Knox, R. E., & Safford, R. K. Group caution at the race track. *Journal of Experimental Social Psychology,* 1976, *12,* 317–324.

Kohlberg, L. *The philosophy of moral development.* New York: Harper & Row, 1981.

Komorita, S. S., & Kravitz, D. A. The effects of alternatives in bargaining. *Journal of Experimental Social Psychology,* 1979, *15,* 147–157.

Komorita, S. S., & Lapworth, C. W. Cooperative choice among individuals versus groups in an N-person dilemma situation. *Journal of Personality and Social Psychology,* 1982, *42,* 487–496.

Komorita, S. S., Lapworth, C. W., & Tumonis, T. M. The effects of certain vs. risky alternatives in bargaining. *Journal of Experimental Social Psychology,* 1981, *17,* 525–544.

Konečni, V. J. Annoyance, type and duration of post-annoyance activity, and aggression: The "cathartic" effect. *Journal of Experimental Psychology: General,* 1975, *104,* 76–102.

Konečni, V. J., & Ebbesen, E. G. Disinhibition versus the cathartic effect: Artifact and substance. *Journal of Personality and Social Psychology,* 1976, *34,* 352–365.

Konečni, V. J., Libuser, L., Morton, H., & Ebbesen, E. B. Effects of a violation of personal space on escape and helping responses. *Journal of Experimental Social Psychology,* 1975, *11,* 288–299.

Korda, M. *Power: How to get it, how to fight it!* New York: Random House, 1975.

Kornhaber, R. C., & Schroeder, H. E. Importance of model similarity on extinction of avoidance behavior in children. *Journal of Consulting and Clinical Psychology,* 1975, *43,* 601–607.

Kramer, B. China, in big effort to slow population growth, is likely to impose harsh economic punishment. *Wall Street Journal,* October 3, 1979, p. 40.

Kramer, M. John Glenn: The right stuff? *New York,* 1983, *16* (5), 18–25.

Krantz, D. S., Baum, A., & Wideman, M. V. Assessment of preferences for self-treatment and information in medical care. *Journal of Personality and Social Psychology,* 1980, *39,* 987–990.

Krauss, R. M., Apple, W., Morency, N., Wenzel, C., & Winton, W. Verbal, vocal, and visible factors in judgments of another's affect. *Journal of Personality and Social Psychology,* 1981, *40,* 312–320.

Krauss, R. M., Freedman, J. F., & Whitcup, M. Field and laboratory studies of littering. *Journal of Experimental Social Psychology,* 1978, *14,* 109–122.

Kremer, J. F., & Stephens, L. Attributions and arousal as mediators of mitigation's effect on retaliation. *Journal of Personality and Social Psychology,* 1983, *45,* 335–343.

Krosnick, J. A., & Judd, C. M. Transitions in social influence at adolescence: Who induces cigarette smoking? *Developmental Psychology,* 1982, *18,* 359–368.

Krulewitz, J. E., & Nash, J. E. Effects of sex role attitudes and similarity on men's rejection of male homosexuals. *Journal of Personality and Social Psychology,* 1980, *38,* 67–74.

Krupat, E. Social psychology and urban behavior. *Journal of Social Issues,* 1980, *36,* (3), 1–8.

Kuhlman, D. M., & Marshello, A. F. J. Individual differences in game motivation as moderators of preprogrammed strategy effects in prisoner's dilemma. *Journal of Personality and Social Psychology,* 1975, *32,* 922–931.

Kulik, J. A., & Brown, R. Frustration, attribution of blame, and aggression. *Journal of Experimental Social Psychology,* 1979, *15,* 183–194.

Kupferberg, S. The party line: Tupperware and capitalism. *The New Republic,* 1980, *183* (24), 10–13.

Kuralt, C. Reporting the "little people." *Columbia Journalism Review,* 1972, *10,* 17–22.

LaFrance, M., & Carmen, B. The nonverbal display of psychological androgyny. *Journal of Personality and Social Psychology,* 1980, *38,* 36–49.

Laird, J. D., Wagener, J. J., Halal, M., & Szegda, M. Remembering what you feel: Effects of emotion on memory. *Journal of Personality and Social Psychology,* 1982, *42,* 646–657.

Lamar, R. Female animals have a lot to say about choice of mate. *The Stanford Observer,* March 1976, p. 2.

Lamm, H., & Myers, D. G. Group-induced polarization of attitudes and behavior. In L. Berkowitz (Ed.), *Advances in experimental social psychology.* New York: Academic Press, 1978.

La Morto-Corse, A. M., & Carver, C. S. Recipient reactions to aid: Effects of locus of initiation, attributions, and individual differences. *Bulletin of the Psychonomic Society,* 1980, *16,* 265–268.

Landers, A. "Like spouse?" Poll startles. *Field Enterprises,* March 28, 1977.

Landy, D., & Aronson, E. The influence of the character of the criminal and his victim on the decisions of simulated jurors. *Journal of Experimental Social Psychology,* 1969, *5,* 141–152.

Langer, E. J., Janis, I. L., & Wolfer, J. A. Reduction of psychological stress in surgical patients. *Journal of Experimental Social Psychology*, 1975, *11*, 155–165.

Langer, E. J., & Rodin, J. The effects of choice and enhanced personal responsibility for the aged: A field experiment in an institutional setting. *Journal of Personality and Social Psychology*, 1976, *34*, 191–198.

Langer, E. J., Rodin, J., Beck, P., Weinman, C., & Spitzer, L. Environmental determinants of memory improvement in late adulthood. *Journal of Personality and Social Psychology*, 1979, *37*, 2003–2013.

Langer, E. J., & Saegert, S. Crowding and cognitive control. *Journal of Personality and Social Psychology*, 1977, *35*, 175–182.

Lanzetta, J. T., Cartwright-Smith, J., & Kleck, R. E. Effects of nonverbal dissimulations on emotional experience and autonomic arousal. *Journal of Personality and Social Psychology*, 1976, *33*, 354–370.

LaPiere, R. T. Attitudes and actions. *Social Forces*, 1934, *13*, 230–237.

Latané, B. Psychology of social impact. *American Psychologist*, 1981, *36*, 343–356.

Latané, B., & Dabbs, J. M., Jr. Sex, group size, and helping in three cities. *Sociometry*, 1975, *38*, 180–194.

Latané, B., & Darley, J. M. *The unresponsive bystander: Why doesn't he help?* New York: Appleton-Century-Crofts, 1970.

Latané, B., & Rodin, J. A lady in distress: Inhibiting effects of friends and strangers on bystander intervention. *Journal of Experimental Social Psychology*, 1969, *5*, 189–202.

Latané, B., Williams, K., & Harkins, S. Many hands make light the work: The causes and consequences of social loafing. *Journal of Personality and Social Psychology*, 1979, *37*, 822–832.

Latané, B., & Wolf, S. The social impact of majorities and minorities. *Psychological Review*, 1981, *88*, 438–453.

Lau, R. R., & Russell, D. Attributions in the sports pages. *Journal of Personality and Social Psychology*, 1980, *39*, 29–38.

Laufer, W. S., Johnson, J. A., & Hogan, R. Ego control and criminal behavior. *Journal of Personality and Social Psychology*, 1981, *41*, 179–184.

Laughlin, P. R. Social combination processes of cooperative problem-solving groups on verbal intellective tasks. In M. Fishbein (Ed.), *Progress in social psychology*. Hillsdale, N.J.: Erlbaum, 1980.

Laughlin, P. R., & Earley, P. R. Social combination models, persuasive arguments theory, social

comparison theory, and choice shift. *Journal of Personality and Social Psychology*, 1982, *42*, 273–280.

Lavrakas, P. J. Female preferences for male physiques. *Journal of Research in Personality*, 1975, *9*, 324–334.

Lavrakas, P. J. Fear of crime and behavioral restrictions in urban and suburban neighborhoods. *Population and Environment*, 1982, *5*, 242–264.

Lawler, E. E., III. Strategies for improving the quality of work life. *American Psychologist*, 1982, *37*, 486–493.

Lazarus, R. S., & Cohen, J. B. Environmental stress. In I. Altman and J. F. Wohlwill (Eds.), *Human behavior and environment* (Vol. 1). New York: Plenum, 1977.

LeCompte, W. A. The ecology of anxiety: Situational stress and rate of self-stimulation in Turkey. *Journal of Personality and Social Psychology*, 1981, *40*, 712–721.

Lederer, L. *Take back the night.* New York: William Morrow, 1980.

Lefcourt, H. M. *Locus of control: Current trends in theory and research.* Hillsdale, N.J.: Erlbaum, 1982.

Legant, P. The deserving victim: Effects of length of pretrial detention, crime severity, and juror attitudes on simulated jury decisions. Unpublished doctoral dissertation, Yale University, 1973.

Lenehan, G. E., & O'Neill, P. Reactance and conflict as determinants of judgment in a mock jury experiment. *Journal of Applied Social Psychology*, 1981, *11*, 231–239.

Leonard, J. Private lives. *New York Times*, February 13, 1980, p. C16.

Lepper, M., & Greene, D. (Eds.). *The hidden costs of reward.* Hillsdale, N.J.: Erlbaum, 1978.

Levenkron, J. C., Cohen, J. D., Mueller, H. S., & Fisher, E. B., Jr. Modifying the Type A coronary-prone behavior pattern. *Journal of Consulting and Clinical Psychology*, 1983, *51*, 192–204.

Leventhal, G., & Levitt, L. Physical, social, and personal factors in the perception of crowding. *Journal of Nonverbal Behavior*, 1979, *4*, 40–55.

Leventhal, G. S. The distribution of rewards and resources in groups and organizations. In L. Berkowitz & E. Walster (Eds.), *Advances in experimental social psychology* (Vol. 9). New York: Academic Press, 1976.

Leventhal, G.S. What should be done with equity theory? New approaches to the study of fairness in social relationships. In K.J. Gergen

& M. S. Greenberg (Eds.), *Social exchange theory.* New York: Wiley, 1979.

Leventhal, G. S., Weiss, T., & Long, G. Equity, reciprocity, and reallocating rewards in the dyad. *Journal of Personality and Social Psychology,* 1969, *13*, 300–305.

Leventhal, H. Findings and theory in the study of fear communications. In L. Berkowitz (Ed.), *Advances in experimental social psychology* (Vol. 5). New York: Academic Press, 1970.

Leventhal, H., Safer, M. A., Cleary, P. D., & Gutmann, M. Cardiovascular risk modification by community-based programs for life-style change: Comments on the Stanford study. *Journal of Consulting and Clinical Psychology,* 1980, *48*, 150–158.

Levin, I. P., Faraone, S. V., & Herring, R. D. Measuring personal satisfaction under varying economic conditions. *Bulletin of the Psychonomic Society,* 1980, *16*, 356–358.

Levine, M. P., & Moore, B. S. Trans-situational effects of lack of control and coronary-prone behavior. Paper presented at the meeting of the American Psychological Association, New York, September 1979.

Levinger, G. Toward the analysis of close relationships. *Journal of Experimental Social Psychology,* 1980, *16*, 510–544.

Levitt, M. J. Contingent feedback, familiarization, and infant affect: How a stranger becomes a friend. *Developmental Psychology,* 1980, *16*, 425–432.

Levy, S. Authoritarianism and information processing. *Bulletin of the Psychonomic Society,* 1979, *13*, 240–242.

Lévy-Leboyer, C. L'évaluation subjective des nuisances: Quelle mesures pour quel objectifs? *International Review of Applied Psychology,* 1982, *31*, 253–269.

Lewin, K., Lippitt, R., & White, R. K. Patterns of aggressive behavior in experimentally created "social climates." *Journal of Social Psychology,* 1939, *10*, 271–299.

Lewin, T. Jury research: Ethics argued. *New York Times,* March 9, 1982, p. D2.

Lewinsohn, P. M., Munoz, R. F., Youngren, M. A., & Zeiss, A. M. *Control your depression,* Englewood Cliffs, N.J.: Prentice-Hall, 1978.

Ley, P. Giving information to patients. In J. R. Eiser (Ed.), *Social psychology and behavioral medicine.* New York: Wiley, 1982.

Leyens, J. P., Camino, L., Parke, R. D., & Berkowitz, L. Effects of movie violence on aggression in a field setting as a function of group dominance and cohesion. *Journal of Personality and Social Psychology,* 1975, *32*, 346–360.

Leyens, J. P., Herman, G., & Dunand, M. The influence of an audience upon reactions to filmed violence. *European Journal of Social Psychology,* 1982, *12*, 131–142.

Liden, R. C., & Graen, G. Generalizability of the vertical dyad linkage model of leadership. *Academy of Management Journal,* 1980, *23*, 451–465.

Liebert, R. M., & Baron, R. A. Some immediate effects of televised violence on children's behavior. *Developmental Psychology,* 1972, *6*, 469–475.

Liebert, R. M., Sprafkin, J. N., & Davidson, E. S. *The early window: Effects of television on children and youth* (2nd ed.). New York: Pergamon, 1982.

Light, L., Hollander, S., & Kayra-Stuart, F. Why attractive people are harder to remember. *Personality and Social Psychology Bulletin,* 1981, *7*, 269–276.

Lindskold, S., & Aronoff, J. R. Conciliatory strategies and relative power. *Journal of Experimental Social Psychology,* 1980, *16*, 187–198.

Linn, R. T., & Hodge, G. K. Locus of control in childhood hyperactivity. *Journal of Consulting and Clinical Psychology,* 1982, *50*, 592–593.

Linville, P. W. The complexity-extremity effect and age-based stereotyping. *Journal of Personality and Social Psychology,* 1982, *42*, 183–211.

Linville, P. W., & Jones, E. E. Polarized appraisals of out-group members. *Journal of Personality and Social Psychology,* 1980, *38*, 689–703.

Lipson, A. L., Przybyla, D. P. J., & Byrne, D. Physical attractiveness, self-awareness, and mirror-gazing behavior. *Bulletin of the Psychonomic Society,* 1983, *21*, 115–116.

Littlel, L. Sad country tunes may turn your brown eyes red. *Albany Times-Union,* August 17, 1981, p. 1.

Lockard, J. S., Kirkevold, B. C., & Kalk, D. F. Cost-benefit indexes of deception in nonviolent crime. *Bulletin of the Psychonomic Society,* 1980, *16*, 303–306.

Locke, E. A. The nature and causes of job satisfaction. In M. D. Dunnette (Ed.), *Handbook of industrial and organizational psychology.* Chicago: Rand McNally, 1976.

Locksley, A., Ortiz, V., & Hepburn, C. Social categorization and discriminatory behavior: Extinguishing the minimal intergroup discrimination effect. *Journal of Personality and Social Psychology,* 1980, *39*, 773–783.

Loeb, M., Holding, D. H., & Baker, M. A. Noise stress and circadian arousal in self-paced computation. *Motivation and Emotion,* 1982, *6,* 43–48.

Loftus, E. The incredible eyewitness. *Psychology Today,* 1974, *8* (7), 116–119.

Loftus, E. *Eyewitness testimony.* Cambridge, Mass.: Harvard University Press, 1979.

Loftus, E., & Monahan, J. Trial by data: Psychological research as legal evidence. *American Psychologist,* 1980, *35,* 270–283.

Loh, W. D. Perspectives on psychology and law. *Journal of Applied Social Psychology,* 1981, *11,* 314–355.

Loo, C. M. A factor analytic approach to the study of spatial density effects on preschoolers. *Journal of Population,* 1979, *2,* 47–68.

Lord, C. G., Ross, L., & Lepper, M. R. Biased assimilation and attitude polarization: The effects of prior theories on subsequently considered evidence. *Journal of Personality and Social Psychology,* 1979, *37,* 2098–2109.

Lorenz, K. *On aggression.* New York: Harcourt, Brace, & World, 1966.

Lorenz, K. *Civilized man's eight deadly sins.* New York: Harcourt Brace Jovanovich, 1974.

Lott, B. Behavioral concordance with sex role ideology related to play areas. *Journal of Personality and Social Psychology,* 1978, *36,* 1087–1100.

Lowman, J. History of bras. *Albany Times-Union,* April 3, 1980, p. 33.

Lueger, R. J. Person and situation factors influencing transgression in behavior-problem adolescents. *Journal of Abnormal Psychology,* 1980, *89,* 453–458.

Luyben, P. E. Prompting thermostat setting behavior: Public response to a presidential appeal for conservation. *Environment and Behavior,* 1982, *14,* 113–128.

Maass, A., & Brigham, J. C. Eyewitness identifications: The role of attention and encoding specificity. *Personality and Social Psychology Bulletin,* 1982, *8,* 54–59.

Machlowitz, M. In dating, men remain the more troubled sex. *New York Times,* April 28, 1981, pp. C1, C5.

Macy, S. M., & Brown, M. A. Residential energy conservation: The role of past experience in repetitive household behavior. *Environment and Behavior,* 1983, *15,* 123–141.

Maddux, J. E., & Rogers, R. W. Effects of source expertness, physical attractiveness, and supporting arguments on persuasion: A case

of brains over beauty. *Journal of Personality and Social Psychology,* 1980, *39,* 235–244.

Malamuth, N. M., & Check, J. V. P. The effects of mass media exposure on acceptance of violence against women: A field experiment. *Journal of Research in Personality,* 1981, *15,* 436–446.

Malamuth, N. M., & Donnerstein, E. The effects of aggressive-erotic stimuli. In L. Berkowitz (Ed.), *Advances in experimental social psychology* (Vol. 15). New York: Academic Press, 1983. (a)

Malamuth, N. M., & Donnerstein, E. (Eds.). *Pornography and sexual aggression.* New York: Academic Press, 1983. (b)

Malamuth, N.M., & Spinner, B. A longitudinal content analysis of sexual violence in the best-selling erotic magazines. *The Journal of Sex Research,* 1980, *16,* 226–237.

Mallick, S. K., & McCandless, B. R. A study of catharsis of aggression. *Journal of Personality and Social Psychology,* 1966, *4,* 591–596.

Mann, J., Berkowitz, L., Sidman, J., Starr, S., & West, S. Satiation of the transient stimulating effect of erotic films. *Journal of Personality and Social Psychology,* 1974, *30,* 729–735.

Mann, L. The baiting crowd in episodes of threatened suicide. *Journal of Personality and Social Psychology,* 1981, *41,* 703–709.

Mann, L., Newton, J. W., & Innes, J. M. A test between deindividuation and emergent norm theories of crowd aggression. *Journal of Personality and Social Psychology,* 1982, *43,* 260–272.

Manning, A. Sexual attraction in animals. In M. Cook (Ed.), *The bases of human sexual attraction.* London: Academic Press, 1981.

Manstead, A. S. R., & Semin, G. R. Social transgressions, social perspectives, and social emotionality. *Motivation and Emotion,* 1981, *5,* 249–261.

Margolese, M. S. Homosexuality: A new endocrine correlate. *Hormones and Behavior,* 1970, *1,* 151–155.

Marks, E. L., Penner, L. A., & Stone, A. V. W. Helping as a function of empathic responses and sociopathy. *Journal of Research in Personality,* 1982, *16,* 1–20.

Marks, G., & Miller, N. Target attractiveness as a mediator of assumed attitude similarity. *Personality and Social Psychology Bulletin,* 1982, *8,* 728–735.

Marks, G., Miller, N., & Maruyama, G. Effect of targets' physical attractiveness on assumptions of similarity. *Journal of Personality and Social Psychology,* 1981, *41,* 198–206.

Markus, H. Self-schemata and the processing of

information about the self. *Journal of Personality and Social Psychology,* 1977, *35,* 63–78.

Markus, H. The effect of mere presence on social facilitation: An unobtrusive test. *Journal of Experimental Social Psychology,* 1978, *14,* 389–397.

Markus, H. The drive for integration: Some comments. *Journal of Experimental Social Psychology,* 1981, *17,* 257–261.

Markus, H., Crane, M., Bernstein, S., & Siladi, M. Self-schemas and gender. *Journal of Personality and Social Psychology,* 1982, *42,* 38–50.

Markus, H., & Sentis, K. The self in social information processing. In J. Suls (Ed.), *Social psychological perspectives on the self.* Hillsdale, N.J.: Erlbaum, 1982.

Marshall, G. D., & Zimbardo, P. G. Affective consequences of inadequately explained physiological arousal. *Journal of Personality and Social Psychology,* 1979, *37,* 970–988.

Martens, R. Palmar sweating and the presence of an audience. *Journal of Experimental Social Psychology,* 1969, *5,* 371–374.

Martin, G., & Clark, R. Infants and empathy: Is empathy an innate or a learned response? *Parents,* December 1981, p. 8.

Martindale, D. A. Territorial dominance behavior in dyadic verbal interaction. *Proceedings of the 79th Annual Convention of the American Psychological Association,* 1971, *6,* 305–306.

Maruyama, G., Fraser, S. C., & Miller, N. Personal responsibility and altruism in children. *Journal of Personality and Social Psychology,* 1982, *42,* 658–664.

Maslach, C. Negative emotional biasing of unexplained arousal. *Journal of Personality and Social Psychology,* 1979, *37,* 953–969.

Massey, A., & Vandenbergh, J. G. Puberty delay by a urinary cue from female house mice in feral populations. *Science,* 1980, *209,* 821–822.

Masters, W. H., & Johnson, V. E. *Human sexual response.* Boston: Little, Brown, 1966.

Matarazzo, J. D. Behavioral health and behavioral medicine: Frontiers for a new health psychology. *American Psychologist,* 1980, *35,* 807–817.

Mathews, K. E., & Cannon, L. K. Environmental noise level as a determinant of helping behavior. *Journal of Personality and Social Psychology,* 1975, *32,* 571–577.

Matlin, M. W., & Zajonc, R. B. Social facilitation of word associations. *Journal of Personality and Social Psychology,* 1968, *10,* 455–460.

Matthews, K. A. Caregiver-child interactions and the Type A coronary-prone behavior pattern. *Child Development,* 1977, *48,* 1752–1756.

Matthews, K. A., Batson, C. D., Horn, J., & Rosenman, R. H. "Principles in his nature which interest him in the fortune of others . . . ": The heritability of empathic concern for others. *Journal of Personality,* 1981, *49,* 237–247.

Matthews, K. A., & Brunson, B. I. Allocation of attention and the Type A coronary-prone behavior pattern. *Journal of Personality and Social Psychology,* 1979, *37,* 2081–2090.

Matthews, K. A., Glass, D. C., & Richins, M. The mother-son observation study. In D. C. Glass, *Behavior patterns, stress, and coronary disease.* Hillsdale, N.J.: Erlbaum, 1977.

Matthews, K. A., Helmreich, R. L., Beane, W. E., & Lucker, G. W. Pattern A, achievement striving, and scientific merit: Does pattern A help or hinder? *Journal of Personality and Social Psychology,* 1980, *39,* 962–967.

Matthews, K. A., & Siegel, J. M. Type A behaviors by children, social comparison, and standards for self-evaluation. *Developmental Psychology,* 1983, *19,* 135–140.

May, J. L., & Hamilton, P. A. Effects of musically evoked affect on women's interpersonal attraction toward and perceptual judgments of physical attractiveness of men. *Motivation and Emotion,* 1980, *4,* 217–228.

Mayo, C., & Henley, N. M. (Eds.). *Gender and nonverbal behavior.* Seacaucus, N.J.: Springer-Verlag, 1981.

McAbee, T. A., & Cafferty, T. P. An assessment of the effectiveness of televised public service announcements as a linking mechanism between human service agencies and potential clients. Unpublished manuscript, University of South Carolina, 1982.

McArthur, L. A. The how and what of why: Some determinants and consequences of causal attribution. *Journal of Personality and Social Psychology,* 1972, *22,* 171–193.

McArthur, L. Z. Illusory causation and illusory correlation: Two epistemological accounts. *Personality and Social Psychology Bulletin,* 1980, *6,* 507–519.

McArthur, L. Z. What grabs you? The role of attention in impression formation and causal attribution. In E. T. Higgins, C. P. Herman, & M. P. Zanna (Eds.), *Social cognition: The Ontario Symposium.* Hillsdale, N.J.: Erlbaum, 1981.

McCain, G., Cox, V. C., & Paulus, P. B. The effect of prison crowding on inmate behavior. Unpublished manuscript, University of Texas, Arlington, 1980.

McCallum, R., Rusbult, C. E., Hong, G. K., Walden, T. A., & Schopler, J. Effects of resource availability and importance of behavior on the experience of crowding. *Journal of Personality and Social Psychology,* 1979, *37,* 1304–1313.

McCarthy, B. Studying personal relationships. In S. Duck & R. Gilmour (Eds.), *Personal relationships. 1: Studying personal relationships.* London: Academic Press, 1981.

McClelland, D. C. The need for power, sympathetic activation, and illness. *Motivation and Emotion,* 1982, *6,* 31–41.

McClelland, L. Interaction level and acquaintance as mediators of density effects. *Personality and Social Psychology Bulletin,* 1976, *2,* 175–178.

McClelland, L., & Cook, S. W. Promoting energy conservation in master-metered apartments through group financial incentives. *Journal of Applied Social Psychology,* 1980, *10,* 20–31.

McClintock, C. G. Development of social motives in Anglo-Americans and Mexican-American children. *Journal of Personality and Social Psychology,* 1974, *29,* 348–354.

McDonald, P. J., & Eilenfield, V. C. Physical attractiveness and the approach/avoidance of self-awareness. *Personality and Social Psychology Bulletin,* 1980, *6,* 391–395.

McDougall, W. *Introduction to social psychology.* London: Methuen, 1908.

McGlynn, R. P., & Dreilinger, E. A. Mock juror judgment and the insanity plea: Effects of incrimination and sanity information. *Journal of Applied Social Psychology,* 1981, *11,* 166–180.

McGovern, L. P. Dispositional social anxiety and helping behavior under three conditions of threat. *Journal of Personality,* 1976, *44,* 84–97.

McGovern, L. P., Ditzian, J. L., & Taylor, S. P. The effect of one positive reinforcement on helping with cost. *Bulletin of the Psychonomic Society,* 1975, *5,* 421–423.

McGowan, J., & Gormly, J. Validation of personality traits: A multicriteria approach. *Journal of Personality and Social Psychology,* 1976, *34,* 791–795.

McGuire, W. J. The nature of attitudes and attitude change. In G. Lindzey & E. Aronson (Eds.), *Handbook of social psychology* (Vol. 3). Reading, Mass.: Addison-Wesley, 1969.

McGuire, W. J., & Papageorgis, D. The relative efficacy of various types of prior belief-defense in producing immunity against persuasion. *Journal of Abnormal and Social Psychology,* 1961, *62,* 327–337.

McIntosh, M. The homosexual role. *Social Problems,* 1968, *16* (2), 182–192.

McNett, I. Military psychologists: Their mission is to shape better soldiers. *APA Monitor,* 1982, *13* (4), 27. (a)

McNett, I. Tracking the mind of a killer. *APA Monitor,* 1982, *13* (1), 8–9. (b)

Meecham, W. C., & Smith, H. G. *British Journal of Audiology.* Quoted in N. Napp, Noise drives you crazy—jets and mental hospitals. *Psychology Today,* June 1977, p. 33.

Mehrabian, A. Relationship of attitude to seated posture, orientation, and distance. *Journal of Personality and Social Psychology,* 1968, *10,* 26–30.

Melamed, B. G., & Siegel, L. J. Reduction of anxiety in children facing hospitalization and surgery by use of filmed modeling. *Journal of Consulting and Clinical Psychology,* 1975, *43,* 511–521.

Messé, L. A., & Sivacek, J. M. Predictions of others' responses in a mixed-motive game: Self-justification or false consensus? *Journal of Personality and Social Psychology,* 1979, *37,* 602–607.

Messick, D. M., & Sentis, K. P. Fairness and preference. *Journal of Experimental Social Psychology,* 1979, *15,* 418–434.

Mewborn, C. R., & Rogers, R. W. Effects of threatening and reassuring components of fear appeals on physiological and verbal measures of emotion and attitudes. *Journal of Experimental Social Psychology,* 1979, *15,* 242–253.

Meyer, A. J., Nash, J. D., McAlister, A. L., Maccoby, N., & Farquhar, J. W. Skills training in a cardiovascular health education campaign. *Journal of Consulting and Clinical Psychology,* 1980, *48,* 129–142.

Meyer, J. P., & Mulherin, A. From attribution to helping: An analysis of the mediating effects of affect and expectancy. *Journal of Personality and Social Psychology,* 1980, *39,* 201–210.

Meyer, J. P., & Pepper, S. Need compatibility and marital adjustment in young married couples. *Journal of Personality and Social Psychology,* 1977, *35,* 331–342.

Michael, R. P., Keverne, E. B., & Bonsall, R. W. Pheromones: Isolation of male sex attractants from a female primate. *Science,* 1971, *172,* 964–966.

Michelini, R. L., & Snodgrass, S. R. Defendant characteristics and juridic decisions. *Journal of Research in Personality,* 1980, *14,* 340–350.

Middlekauff, R. *The glorious cause.* New York: Oxford University Press, 1982.

Middlemist, R. D., Knowles, E. S., & Matter, C. F. Personal space invasions in the lavatory: Suggestive evidence for arousal. *Journal of Personality and Social Psychology,* 1976, *33,* 541–546.

Milgram, S. Behavioral study of obedience.

Journal of Abnormal and Social Psychology, 1963, *67,* 371–378.

Milgram, S. Liberating effects of group pressure. *Journal of Personality and Social Psychology,* 1965, *1,* 127–134. (a)

Milgram, S. Some conditions of obedience and disobedience to authority. *Human Relations,* 1965, *18,* 57–76. (b)

Milgram, S. The experience of living in cities. *Science,* 1970, *167,* 1461–1468.

Milgram, S. *Obedience to authority.* New York: Harper, 1974.

Milgram, S. *The individual in a social world.* Reading, Mass.: Addison-Wesley, 1977.

Miller, D. T., & Ross, M. Self-serving biases in the attribution of causality: Fact or fiction? *Psychological Bulletin,* 1975, *82,* 213–225.

Miller, N., Maruyama, G., Beaber, R. J., & Valone, K. Speed of speech and persuasion. *Journal of Personality and Social Psychology,* 1976, *34,* 615–624.

Miller, S., Rossbach, J., & Munson, R. Social density and affiliative tendency as determinants of dormitory residential outcomes. *Journal of Applied Social Psychology,* 1981, *11,* 356–365.

Miller, S. S. *Symptoms.* New York: Crowell, 1976.

Millham, J. Two components of need for approval score and their relationship to cheating following success and failure. *Journal of Research in Personality,* 1974, *8,* 378–392.

Mills, C. J., & Bohannon, W. E. Character structure and jury behavior: Conceptual and applied implications. *Journal of Personality and Social Psychology,* 1980, *38,* 662–667.

Mills, M. All that security may increase shoplifting. *Associated Press,* September 13, 1981.

Mirvis, P. H., & Lawler, E. E., III. Measuring the financial impact of employee attitudes. *Journal of Applied Psychology,* 1977, *62,* 1–8.

Mischel, W. *Personality and assessment.* New York: Wiley, 1968.

Mischel, W. On the future of personality measurement. *American Psychologist,* 1977, *32,* 246–254.

Mita, T. H., Dermer, M., & Knight, J. Reversed facial images and the mere-exposure hypothesis. *Journal of Personality and Social Psychology,* 1977, *35,* 597–601.

Mitchell, H. E. Informational and affective determinants of juror decision making. Unpublished doctoral dissertation, Purdue University, 1979.

Mitchell, H. E., & Byrne, D. Minimizing the influence of irrelevant factors in the courtroom: The defendant's character, judge's instructions, and authoritarianism. In K. M. White & J. C. Speisman, *Research*

approaches to personality. Monterey, Calif.: Brooks/Cole, 1982.

Mitchell, T. R. Organizational behavior. In M. R. Rosenzweig & L. W. Porter (Eds.), *Annual review of psychology* (Vol. 30). Palo Alto, Calif.: Annual Reviews, 1979.

Mitchell, T. R., & Kalb, L. S. Effects of job experience on supervisor attributions for a subordinate's poor performance. *Journal of Applied Psychology,* 1982, *67,* 181–188.

Moe, J. L., Nacoste, R. W., & Insko, C. A. Belief versus race as determinants of discrimination: A study of Southern adolescents in 1966 and 1979. *Journal of Personality and Social Psychology,* 1981, *41,* 1031–1050.

Monson, T. C., & Hesley, J. W. Causal attributions for behaviors consistent or inconsistent with an actor's personality traits: Differences between those offered by actors and observers. *Journal of Experimental Social Psychology,* 1982, *18,* 416–432.

Monson, T. C., Hesley, J. W., & Chernick, L. Specifying when personality traits can and cannot predict behavior: An alternative to abandoning the attempt to predict single-act criteria. *Journal of Personality and Social Psychology,* 1982, *43,* 385–399.

Monson, T. C., & Snyder, M. Actors, observers, and the attribution process. *Journal of Experimental Social Psychology,* 1977, *13,* 89–111.

Moran, G. Second-order classical conditioning of meaning in the Staats format. *Bulletin of the Psychonomic Society,* 1981, *18,* 299–300.

Moran, G., & Comfort, J. C. Scientific juror selection: Sex as a moderator of demographic and personality predictors of impaneled felony juror behavior. *Journal of Personality and Social Psychology,* 1982, *43,* 1052–1063.

Morasch, B., Groner, N., & Keating, J. P. Type of activity and failure as mediators of perceived crowding. *Personality and Social Psychology Bulletin,* 1979, *5,* 223–226.

Moreault, D., & Follingstad, D. R. Sexual fantasies of females as a function of sex guilt and experimental response cues. *Journal of Consulting and Clinical Psychology,* 1978, 46, 1385–1393.

Moreland, R. L., & Zajonc, R. B. Exposure effects may not depend on stimulus recognition. *Journal of Personality and Social Psychology,* 1979, *37,* 1085–1089.

Moreland, R. L., & Zajonc, R. B. Exposure effects in person perception: Familiarity, similarity, and attraction. *Journal of Experimental Social Psychology,* 1982, *18.*

Morell, M. A., & Katkin, E. S. Jenkins Activity

Survey scores among women of different occupations. *Journal of Consulting and Clinical Psychology,* 1982, *50,* 588–589.

Morgan, B. B., Jr., & Ogden, G. D. Non-instructional correlates of student ratings: A brief review. *International Review of Applied Psychology,* 1981, *30,* 409–427.

Morgan, C. D., & Murray, H. A. Thematic Apperception Test. In H. A. Murray, *Explorations in personality.* (1938). New York: Science Editions, 1962.

Morgan, C. J. Bystander intervention: Experimental test of a formal model. *Journal of Personality and Social Psychology,* 1978, *36,* 43–55.

Moriarty, T. Crime, commitment, and the responsive bystander: Two field experiments. *Journal of Personality and Social Psychology,* 1975, *31,* 370–376.

Morris, D., Collett, P., Marsh, P., & O'Shaughnessy, M. *Gestures: Their origins and distribution.* London: Cape, 1979.

Morris, N. M., & Udry, J. R. Pheromonal influences on human sexual behaviour: An experimental search. *Journal of Biosocial Science,* 1978, *10,* 147–157.

Morris, W. N., & Miller, R. S. The effects of consensus-breaking and consensus-preempting partners on reduction of conformity. *Journal of Experimental Social Psychology,* 1975, *11,* 215–223.

Morris, W. N., Miller, R. S., & Spangenberg, S. The effects of dissenter position and task difficulty on conformity and response to conflict. *Journal of Personality,* 1977, *45,* 251–266.

Morris, W. N., Worchel, S., Bois, J. L., Pearson, J. A., Rountree, C. A., Samaha, G. M., Wachtler, J., & Wright, S. L. Collective coping with stress: Group reactions to fear, anxiety, and ambiguity. *Journal of Personality and Social Psychology,* 1976, *33,* 674–679.

Moscovici, S., & Faucheux, C. Social influence, conformity bias, and the study of active minorities. In L. Berkowitz (Ed.), *Advances in experimental social psychology* (Vol. 6). New York: Academic Press, 1972.

Moscovici, S., & Personnaz, B. Studies in social influence. V. Minority influence and conversion behavior in a perceptual task. *Journal of Experimental Social Psychology,* 1980, *16,* 270–282.

Mosher, D. L. Measurement of guilt in females by self-report inventories. *Journal of Consulting and Clinical Psychology,* 1968, *32,* 690–695.

Mosher, D. L., & Cross, H. J. Sex guilt and premarital sexual experiences of college students. *Journal of Consulting and Clinical Psychology,* 1971, *36,* 27–32.

Mosher, D. L., & O'Grady, K. E. Sex guilt, trait anxiety, and females' subjective sexual arousal to erotica. *Motivation and Emotion,* 1979, *3,* 235–249.

Moskowitz, D. S. Coherence and cross-situational generality in personality: A new analysis of old problems. *Journal of Personality and Social Psychology,* 1982, *43,* 754–768.

Moss, M. K., & Page, R. A. Reinforcement and helping behavior. *Journal of Applied Social Psychology,* 1972, *2,* 360–371.

Mueller, C., & Donnerstein, E. The effects of humor-induced arousal upon aggressive behavior. *Journal of Research in Personality,* 1976, *11,* 73–82.

Mullen, B., & Suls, J. "Know thyself": Stressful life changes and the ameliorative effect of private self-consciousness. *Journal of Experimental Social Psychology,* 1982, *18,* 43–55.

Mummendey, A., Bornewasser, M., Loschper, G., & Linneweber, V. Defining interactions as aggressive in specific social contexts. *Aggressive Behavior,* 1982, *8,* 224–228.

Münsterberg, J. *On the witness stand.* New York: McClure, 1907.

Murray, D. M., & Wells, G. L. Does knowledge that a crime was staged affect eyewitness performance? *Journal of Applied Social Psychology,* 1982, *12,* 42–53.

Murray, H. A. *Explorations in personality.* New York: Science Editions, 1962. (Originally published, 1938.)

Murstein, B. I. Love at first sight: A myth. *Medical Aspects of Human Sexuality,* 1980, *14* (9), 34, 39–41.

Murstein, B. I. Physical attractiveness and marital choice. *Journal of Personality and Social Psychology,* 1972, *22,* 8–12.

Myers, D. G. Polarizing effects of social interaction. In H. Brandstatter, J. H. Davis, & G. Stocker-Kreichgauer (Eds.), *Group decision processes.* London: Academic Press, 1983.

Myers, D. G., Bruggink, J. B., Kersting, R. C., & Schlosser, B. S. Does learning others' opinions change one's opinions? *Personality and Social Psychology Bulletin,* 1980, *6,* 253–260.

Nadler, A. "Good looks do not help": Effects of helper's physical attractiveness and expectations for future interaction on help-seeking behavior. *Personality and Social Psychology Bulletin,* 1980, *6,* 378–383.

Nadler, A., Bar-Tal, D., & Drukman, O. Density

does not help: Help-giving, help-seeking, and help-reciprocating of residents of high and low student dormitories. *Population and Environment,* 1982, *5,* 26–42.

Nadler, A., & Fisher, J. D. Recipient reactions to aid: Research and theory validation. In L. Berkowitz (Ed.), *Advances in experimental social psychology,* 1983.

Nadler, A., Fisher, J. D., & Itzhak, S. B. With a little help from my friend: Effect of a single or multiple act aid as a function of donor and task characteristics. *Journal of Personality and Social Psychology,* 1983, *44,* 310–321.

Nadler, A., Fisher, J. D., & Streufert, S. When helping hurts: Effects of donor-recipient similarity and recipient self-esteem on recipient reactions to aid. *Journal of Personality,* 1976, *44,* 392–409.

Nadler, A., Jazwinski, C., Lau, S., & Miller, A. The cold glow of success: Responses to social rejection as affected by attitude similarity between the rejected and chosen individuals. *European Journal of Social Psychology,* 1980, *10,* 279–289.

Nadler, A., Shapiro, R., & Ben-Itzhak, S. Good looks may help: Effects of helper's physical attractiveness and sex of helper on males' and females' help-seeking behavior. *Journal of Personality and Social Psychology,* 1982, *42,* 90–99.

Nagao, D. H., & Davis, J. H. Some implications of temporal drift in social parameters. *Journal of Experimental Social Psychology,* 1980, *16,* 479–496.

Nahemow, L., & Lawton, M. P. Similarity and propinquity in friendship formation. *Journal of Personality and Social Psychology,* 1975, *32,* 205–213.

Narayanan, V. K., & Nath, R. A field test of some attitudinal and behavioral consequences of flexitime. *Journal of Applied Psychology,* 1982, *67,* 214–218.

Neimeyer, G. J., & Neimeyer, R. A. Functional similarity and interpersonal attraction. *Journal of Research in Personality,* 1981, *15,* 427–435.

Nemeth, C. A critical analysis of research utilizing the prisoner's dilemma paradigm for the study of bargaining. In L. Berkowitz (Ed.), *Advances in experimental social psychology* (Vol. 6). New York: Academic Press, 1972.

Nemetz, G. H., Craig, K. D., & Reith, G. Treatment of female sexual dysfunction through symbolic modeling. *Journal of Consulting and Clinical Psychology,* 1978, *46,* 72–73.

Newcomb, T. M. Dyadic balance as a source of

clues about interpersonal attraction. In B. I. Murstein (Ed.), *Theories of attraction and love.* New York: Springer, 1971.

Newcomb, T. M. Heiderian balance as a group phenomenon. *Journal of Personality and Social Psychology,* 1981, *40,* 862–867.

Newcomb, T. M., Koenig, K., Flacks, R., & Warwick, D. *Persistence and change: Bennington College and its students after 25 years.* New York: Wiley, 1967.

Newman, J., & McCauley, C. Eye contact with strangers in city, suburb, and small town. *Environment and Behavior,* 1977, *9,* 547–558.

Newton, J. W., & Mann, L. Crowd size as a factor in the persuasion process: A study of religious crusade meetings. *Journal of Personality and Social Psychology,* 1980, *39,* 874–883.

Nisbett, R. E., & Ross, L. *Human inference: Strategies and shortcomings of social judgment.* Englewood Cliffs, N.J.: Prentice-Hall, 1980.

Nisbett, R. E., & Wilson, T. D. Telling more than we can know: Verbal reports on mental processes. *Psychological Review,* 1977, *84,* 231–259.

Nocera, J. The big book-banning brawl. *The New Republic,* 1982, *187* (11), 20, 22–25.

Norman, J., & Harris, M. Students talk about their education. *Albany Times-Union,* January 13, 1982, p. 11.

Norvell, N., & Worchel, S. A reexamination of the relation between equal status contact and intergroup attraction. *Journal of Personality and Social Psychology,* 1981, *41,* 902–908.

Nossiter, B. D. World population explosion is slowing, U.N. finds. *New York Times,* June 15, 1980, p. 10.

Novaco, R. W. *Anger control: The development and evaluation of an experimental treatment.* Lexington, Mass.: D. C. Heath, 1975.

Nowicki, S., Jr. Competition-cooperation as a mediator of locus of control and achievement. *Journal of Research in Personality,* 1982, *16,* 157–164.

O'Grady, K. E. "Affect, sex guilt, gender, and the reward-punishing effects of erotic stimuli": A reanalysis and reinterpretation. *Journal of Personality and Social Psychology,* 1982, *43,* 618–622. (a)

O'Grady, K. E. Sex, physical attractiveness, and perceived risk for mental illness. *Journal of Personality and Social Psychology,* 1982, *43,* 1064–1071. (b)

Ohbuchi, K. Negativity bias: Its effects in attribution, hostility, and attack-instigated aggression. *Personality and Social Psychology Bulletin*, 1982, *8*, 49–53.

O'Leary, D. E., O'Leary, M. R., & Donovan, D. M. Social skills acquisition and psychosocial development of alcoholics: A review. *Addictive Behaviors*, 1976, *1*, 111–120.

Olsen, M. E. Consumers' attitudes toward energy conservation. *Journal of Social Issues*, 1981, *37*, 108–131.

O'Neal, E. C., Brunault, M. A., Carifio, M. S., Troutwine, R., & Epstein, J. Effect of insult upon personal space preferences. *Journal of Nonverbal Behavior*, 1980, *5*, 56–62.

Orionova, G. A woman's-eye view of Russia. *Cosmopolitan*, November 1981, pp. 194, 196.

Orlick, T. D. Positive socialization via cooperative games. *Developmental Psychology*, 1981, *17*, 426–429.

Osgood, C. E. GRIT for MBFR: A proposal for unfreezing force-level postures in Europe. *Peace Research Reviews*, 1979, *8*, 77–92.

Ostling, R. N. A scrupulous monitor closes shop. *Time*, October 6, 1980, pp. 70–71.

Ostrom, T. M., Lingle, J. H., Pryor, J. B., & Geva, N. Cognitive organization of person perception. In R. Hastie et al. (Eds.), *Person memory: The cognitive basis of social perception*. Hillsdale, N.J.: Erlbaum, 1979.

Otten, M. W. Inventory and expressive measures of locus of control and academic performance: A five-year outcome study. *Journal of Personality Assessment*, 1977, *41*, 644–649.

Ovid. *The art of love*. Translated by B. P. Moore. Avon, Conn.: Heritage, 1971.

Owens, D. D., Jr. Ridesharing programs: Governmental response to urban transportation problems. *Environment and Behavior*, 1981, *13*, 311–330.

Palmer, J., & Byrne, D. Attraction toward dominant and submissive strangers: Similarity versus complementarity. *Journal of Experimental Research in Personality*, 1970, *4*, 108–115.

Paloutzian, R. F., & Ellison, C. W. Emotional, behavioral, and physical correlates of loneliness. Paper presented at the UCLA Research Conference on Loneliness, Los Angeles, May 1979.

Pancer, S. M., McMullen, L. M., Kabatoff, R. A., Johnson, K. G., & Pond, C. A. Conflict and avoidance in the helping situation. *Journal of Personality and Social Psychology*, 1979, *37*, 1406–1411.

Pandy, J., Sinha, Y., Prakash, A., & Tripathi, R. C. Right-left political ideologies and attribution of the causes of poverty. *European Journal of Social Psychology*, 1982, *12*, 327–331.

Pantin, H. M., & Carver, C. S. Induced competence and the bystander effect. *Journal of Applied Social Psychology*, 1982, *12*, 100–111.

Park, B., & Rothbart, M. Perception of out-group homogeneity and levels of social categorization: Memory for the subordinate attributes of in-group and out-group members. *Journal of Personality and Social Psychology*, 1982, *42*, 1051–1068.

Parke, R. D., Berkowitz, L., Leyens, J. P., West, S. G., & Sebastian, R. J. Some effects of violent and nonviolent movies on the behavior of juvenile delinquents. In L. Berkowitz (Ed.), *Advances in experimental social psychology* (Vol. 10). New York: Academic Press, 1977.

Parker, D. R., & Rogers, R. W. Observation and performance of aggression: Effects of multiple models and frustration. *Personality and Social Psychology Bulletin*, 1981, *7*, 302–308.

Patterson, A. H. Housing density and various quality-of-life measures among elderly urban dwellers: Some preliminary concepts. *Journal of Population*, 1978, *1*, 203–215. (a)

Patterson, A. H. Territorial behavior and fear of crime in the elderly. *Environmental Psychology and Nonverbal Behavior*, 1978, *2*, 131–144. (b)

Paulus, P. B. Crowding. In P. B. Paulus (Ed.), *Psychology of group influence*. Hillsdale, N.J.: Erlbaum, 1980. (a)

Paulus, P. B. (Ed.). *Psychology of group influence*. Hillsdale, N.J.: Erlbaum, 1980. (b)

Paulus, P. B., Aunis, A. B., Seta, J. J., Schkade, J. K., & Matthews, R. W. Crowding does affect task performance. *Journal of Personality and Social Psychology*, 1976, *34*, 248–253.

Paulus, P. B., & Matthews, R. W. Crowding, attribution, and task performance. *Basic and Applied Social Psychology*, 1980, *1*, 3–13.

Pearce, P. L. Strangers, travelers, and Greyhound terminals: A study of small-scale helping behaviors. *Journal of Personality and Social Psychology*, 1980, *38*, 935–940.

Pearce, P. L. "Environment shock": A study of tourists' reactions to two tropical islands. *Journal of Applied Social Psychology*, 1981, *11*, 268–280.

Pendleton, D. The communication of medical information: What is given and what is remembered? Unpublished manuscript, University of Oxford, 1982.

Pendleton, M. G., & Batson, C. D. Self-presentation and the door-in-the-face technique for inducing compliance. *Personality and Social Psychology Bulletin*, 1979, *5*, 77–81.

Penk, W. Age changes and correlates of internal-external locus of control scales. *Psychological Reports*, 1969, *25*, 856.

Pennebaker, J. W. Perceptual and environmental determinants of coughing. *Basic and Applied Social Psychology,* 1980, *1,* 83–91.

Pennebaker, J. W., Burnam, M. A., Schaeffer, M. A., & Harper, D. C. Lack of control as a determinant of perceived physical symptoms. *Journal of Personality and Social Psychology,* 1977, *35,* 167–174.

Pennebaker, J. W., Dyer, M. A., Caulkins, R. S., Litowitz, D. L., Ackerman, P. L., Anderson, D. B., & McGraw, K. M. Don't the girls get prettier at closing time: A country and western application to psychology. *Personality and Social Psychology Bulletin,* 1979, *5,* 122–125.

Penrod, S., & Hastie, R. A computer simulation of jury decision making. *Psychological Review,* 1980, *87,* 133–159.

Peplau, L. A., & Perlman, D. Perspectives on loneliness. In L. A. Peplau & D. Perlman (Eds.), *Loneliness: A sourcebook of current theory, research, and therapy.* New York: Wiley, 1982.

Peraino, J. M. Personality similarity in friendships and romantic relationships. Paper presented at the meeting of the American Psychological Association, Washington, D.C., August 1982.

Perlman, D., Gerson, A. C., & Spinner, B. Loneliness among senior citizens: An empirical report. *Essence,* 1978, *2* (4), 239–248.

Perlman, D., Josephson, W., Hwang, W. T., Begum, H., & Thomas, T. L. Cross-cultural analysis of students' sexual standards. *Archives of Sexual Behavior,* 1978, *7,* 545–558.

Perry, D. G., & Bussey, K. The social learning theory of sex differences: Imitation is alive and well. *Journal of Personality and Social Psychology,* 1979, *37,* 1699–1712.

Perry, N. J. Industrial time clocks—often at odds with those inside a worker's body. *New York Times,* November 28, 1982, pp. F8–F9.

Pervin, L. A. A free-response description approach to the analysis of person-situation interaction. *Journal of Personality and Social Psychology,* 1976, *34,* 465–474.

Peters, J. M., Preston-Martin, S., & Yu, M. C. Brain tumors in children and occupational exposure of parents. *Science,* 1981, *213,* 235–237.

Peterson, E. A., Augenstein, J. S., Tanis, D. C., & Augenstein, D. G. Noise raises blood pressure without impairing auditory sensitivity. *Science,* 1981, *211,* 1450–1452.

Peterson, I. Sharp decline in daily smoking by high school seniors is found. *New York Times,* January 15, 1981, p. A20.

Peterson, L. Influence of age, task competence, and responsibility focus on children's altruism. *Developmental Psychology,* 1983, *19,* 141–148.

Pettigrew, T. F. Social evaluation theory: Convergences and applications. In D. Levine (Ed.), *Nebraska symposium on motivation.* Lincoln: University of Nebraska Press, 1967.

Petty, R. E., & Cacioppo, J. T. Effects of forewarning of persuasive intent and involvement on cognitive responses and persuasion. *Personality and Social Psychology Bulletin,* 1979, *5,* 173–176.

Petty, R. E., & Cacioppo, J. T. *Attitudes and persuasion: Classic and contemporary approaches.* Dubuque, Iowa: Wm. C. Brown, 1981.

Petty, R. E., & Mirels, H. L. Intimacy and scarcity of self-disclosure: Effects on interpersonal attraction for males and females. *Personality and Social Psychology Bulletin,* 1981, *7,* 493–503.

Petty, R. E., Ostrom, T. M., & Brock, T. C. (Eds.). *Cognitive responses in persuasion.* Hillsdale, N.J.: Erlbaum, 1981.

Phares, E. J. Locus of control. In H. London & J. E. Exner, Jr. (Eds.), *Dimensions of personality.* New York: Wiley, 1978.

Piaget, J. *The moral judgment of the child.* Glencoe, Ill.: Free Press, 1948. (Originally published, 1932.)

Piliavin, J. A., Callero, P. L., & Evans, D. E. Addiction to altruism? Opponent-process theory and habitual blood donation. *Journal of Personality and Social Psychology,* 1982, *43,* 1200–1213.

Piliavin, J. A., Dovidio, J. F., Gaertner, S. L., & Clark, R. D., III. *Emergency intervention.* New York: Academic Press, 1981.

Pilkonis, P. A., & Zimbardo, P. G. The personal and social dynamics of shyness. In C. E. Izard (Ed.), *Emotions in personality and psychotherapy.* New York: Plenum, 1979.

Pineau, C. The psychological meaning of comfort. *International Review of Applied Psychology,* 1982, *31,* 271–283.

Pines, M. Psychological hardiness: The role of challenge in health. *Psychology Today,* 1980, *14* (7), 34–36, 39–40, 43–44, 98.

Pines, M. Recession is linked to far-reaching psychological harm. *New York Times,* April 6, 1982, pp. C1–C2.

Pittner, M. S., & Houston, B. K. Response to stress, cognitive coping strategies, and the Type A behavior pattern. *Journal of Personality and Social Psychology,* 1980, *39,* 147–157.

Pittner, M. S., Houston, B. K., & Spiridigliozzi, G. Control over stress, Type A behavior pattern, and response to stress. *Journal of Personality and Social Psychology,* 1983, *44,* 627–637.

Pliner, P., Hart, H., Kohl, J., & Saari, D. Compliance without pressure: Some further data on the foot-in-the-door technique.

Journal of Experimental Social Psychology, 1974, *10,* 17–22.

Pomazal, R. J., & Clore, G. L. Helping on the highway: The effects of dependency and sex. *Journal of Applied Social Psychology,* 1973, *3,* 150–164.

Powers, P. C., & Geen, R. G. Effects of the behavior and the perceived arousal of a model on instrumental aggression. *Journal of Personality and Social Psychology,* 1972, *23,* 175–184.

Poythress, N. G., Jr. A proposal for training in forensic psychology. *American Psychologist,* 1979, *34,* 612–621.

Prentice-Dunn, S., & Rogers, R. W. Effects of deindividuating situational cues and aggressive models on subjective deindividuation and aggression. *Journal of Personality and Social Psychology,* 1980, *39,* 104–113.

Prentice-Dunn, S., & Rogers, R. W. Effects of public and private self-awareness on deindividuation and aggression. *Journal of Personality and Social Psychology,* 1982, *43,* 503–513.

Prentice-Dunn, S., & Rogers, R. W. Deindividuation in aggression. In R. Geen & E. Donnerstein (Eds.), *Aggression: Theoretical and empirical reviews.* New York: Academic Press, 1983.

President's Council on Environmental Quality, Environmental Protection Agency. Washington, D.C.: U. S. Government Printing Office, 1978.

Preuss, G. G. The effects of density and urban residence on voter turnout. *Population and Environment,* 1981, *4,* 246–265.

Price, G. H., & Dabbs, J. M. Sex, setting and personal space: Changes as children grow older. *Personality and Social Psychology Bulletin,* 1974, *1,* 362–363.

Price, K. H., & Garland, H. Compliance with a leader's suggestions as a function of perceived leader/member competence and potential reciprocity. *Journal of Applied Psychology,* 1981, *66,* 329–336.

Price, R. A., & Vandenberg, S. G. Matching for physical attractiveness in married couples. *Personality and Social Psychology Bulletin,* 1979, *5,* 398–400.

Pritchard, M. Homosexuality and genetic sex. *Journal of Mental Science,* 1962, *108,* 616–623.

Pritchard, R. D., Dunnette, H. D., & Jorgenson, D. O. Effects of perceptions of equity and inequity on worker performance and satisfaction. *Journal of Applied Psychology,* 1972, *56,* 75–94.

Pruitt, D. G. *Negotiation behavior.* New York: Academic Press, 1981.

Pruitt, D. G., & Lewis, S. A. The psychology of integrative bargaining. In D. Druckman (Ed.), *Negotiations: A social-psychological perspective.* New York: Halsted, 1977.

Pruitt, D. J., & Insko, C. A. Extension of the Kelley attribution model: The role of comparison-object consensus, target-object consensus, distinctiveness, and consistency. *Journal of Personality and Social Psychology,* 1980, *39,* 39–58.

Przybyla, D. P. J., & Byrne, D. Expressive behavior as a function of erotophobia-erotophilia. Unpublished manuscript, State University of New York at Albany, 1982.

Przybyla, D. P. J., & Byrne, D. The mediating role of cognitive processes in self-reported sexual arousal. *Journal of Research in Personality,* 1983, in press.

Przybyla, D. P. J., Byrne, D., & Kelley, K. The role of imagery in sexual behavior. In A. A. Sheikh (Ed.), *Imagery: Current theory, research, and application.* New York: Wiley, 1983.

Pursell, S. A., & Banikiotes, P. G. Androgyny and initial interpersonal attraction. *Personality and Social Psychology Bulletin,* 1978, *4,* 235–243.

Putallaz, M., & Gottman, J. Social skills and group acceptance. In S. R. Asher & J. M. Gottman (Eds.), *The development of children's friendships.* New York: Cambridge University Press, 1981.

Pyszcznski, T., Greenberg, J., Mack, D., & Wrightsman, L. S. Opening statements in a jury trial: The effect of promising more than the evidence can show. *Journal of Applied Social Psychology,* 1981, *11,* 434–444.

Pyszczynski, T. A., & Wrightsman, L. S. The effects of opening statements on mock jurors' verdicts in a simulated criminal trial. *Journal of Applied Social Psychology,* 1981, *11,* 301–313.

Quattrone, G. A. Overattribution and unit formation: When behavior engulfs the person. *Journal of Personality and Social Psychology,* 1982, *42,* 593–607.

Quattrone, G. A., & Jones, E. E. The perception of variability within in-groups and out-groups: Implications for the law of small numbers. *Journal of Personality and Social Psychology,* 1980, *38,* 141–152.

Rabin, R. International conflicts usually shades of gray. *APA Monitor,* 1982, *13* (1), 14.

Rachman, S. J., & Philips, C. *Psychology and behavioral medicine.* Cambridge: Cambridge University Press, 1980.

Raine, A., Roger, D. B., & Venables, P. H. Locus of control and socialization. *Journal of Research in Personality,* 1982, *16,* 147–156.

Rajecki, D. S. *Attitudes: Themes and advances.* Sunderland, Mass.: Sinauer Associates, 1982.

Rajecki, D. W., Kidd, R. F., & Ivins, B. Social facilitation in chickens: A different level of analysis. *Journal of Experimental Social Psychology,* 1976, *12,* 233–246.

Rajecki, D. W., Nerenz, D. R., Freedenberg, T. G., & McCarthy, P. J. Components of aggression in chickens and conceptualizations of aggression in general. *Journal of Personality and Social Psychology,* 1979, *37,* 1902–1914.

Ramirez, A. Academic freedom 1981. *New York Teacher,* March 29, 1981, pp. 9–12.

Ramirez, J., Bryant, J., & Zillmann, D. Effects of erotica on retaliatory behavior as a function of level of prior provocation. *Journal of Personality and Social Psychology,* 1983, *43,* 971–978.

Raven, B. H., & Haley, R. W. Social influence in a medical context. In L. Bickman (Ed.), *Applied social psychology annual 1.* Beverly Hills, Calif.: Sage, 1980.

Raven, B. H., & Haley, R. W. Social influence and compliance of hospital nurses with infection control policies. In J. R. Eiser (Ed.), *Social psychology and behavioral medicine.* New York: Wiley, 1982.

Ray, C. The surgical patient: Psychological stress and coping resources. In J. R. Eiser (Ed.), *Social psychology and behavioral medicine.* New York: Wiley, 1982.

Redd, W. H. Stimulus control and extinction of psychosomatic symptoms in cancer patients in protective isolation. *Journal of Consulting and Clinical Psychology,* 1980, *48,* 448–455.

Reddy, D. M., Baum, A., Fleming, R., & Aiello, J. R. Mediation of social density by coalition formation. *Journal of Applied Social Psychology,* 1981, *11,* 529–537.

Reeder, G. D. Let's give the fundamental attribution error another chance. *Journal of Personality and Social Psychology,* 1982, *43,* 341–344.

Reich, J. W. An historical analysis of the field. In L. Bickman (Ed.), *Applied social psychology annual 2.* Beverly Hills, Calif.: Sage, 1981.

Reimanis, G. Effects of experimental IE modification techniques and home environment variables on IE. Paper presented at the meeting of the American Psychological Association, Washington, D.C., 1971.

Reinhold, R. Of smoking, children and a deep belief in immortality. *New York Times,* May 10, 1981, p. 20E.

Reis, H. T. Self-presentation and distributive justice. In J. T. Tedeschi (Ed.), *Impression management theory and social psychological research.* New York: Academic Press, 1981.

Reis, H. T., & Burns, L. B. The salience of the self in responses to inequity. *Journal of Experimental Social Psychology,* 1982, *18,* 464–475.

Reis, H. T., Nezlek, J., & Wheeler, L. Physical attractiveness in social interaction. *Journal of Personality and Social Psychology,* 1980, *38,* 604–617.

Reis, H. T., Wheeler, L., Spiegel, N., Kernis, M. H., Nezlek, J., & Perri, M. Physical attractiveness in social interaction: II. Why does appearance affect social experience? *Journal of Personality and Social Psychology,* 1982, *43,* 979–996.

Reiter, S. M., & Samuel, W. Littering as a function of prior litter and the presence or absence of prohibitive signs. *Journal of Applied Social Psychology,* 1980, *10,* 45–55.

Research and Forecasts, Inc. *The Connecticut Mutual Life report on American values in the '80s: The impact of belief.* Hartford: Connecticut Mutual Life Insurance Co., 1981.

Revenson, T. A. Coping with loneliness: The impact of causal attributions. *Personality and Social Psychology Bulletin,* 1981, *7,* 565–571.

Reyes, R. M., Thompson, W. C., & Bower, G. H. Judgmental biases resulting from differing availabilities of arguments. *Journal of Personality and Social Psychology,* 1980, *39,* 2–12.

Rhodewalt, F., & Davison, J., Jr. Reactance and the coronary-prone behavior pattern: The role of self-attribution in responses to reduced behavioral freedom. *Journal of Personality and Social Psychology,* 1983, *44,* 220–228.

Rholes, W. S., Bailey, S., & McMillan, L. Experiences that motivate moral development: The role of cognitive dissonance. *Journal of Experimental Social Psychology,* 1982, *18,* 524–536.

Rice, R. W., Near, J. P., & Hunt, R. G. The job-satisfaction/life-satisfaction relationship: A review of empirical research. *Basic and Applied Social Psychology,* 1980, *1,* 37–64.

Richardson, D. C., Bernstein, S., & Taylor, S. P. The effect of situational contingencies on female retaliative behavior. *Journal of Personality and Social Psychology,* 1979, *37,* 2044–2048.

Richardson, D. C., Vandenberg, R. J., & Humphries, S. A. Gender versus power: A new approach to the study of sex differences in retaliative aggression. *Journal of Personality,* 1983, in press.

Riess, M., & Salzer, S. Individuals avoid invading the space of males but not females. Paper presented at the meeting of the American Psychological Association, Los Angeles, August 1981.

Riess, M., & Schlenker, B. R. Attitude change and responsibility avoidance as modes of dilemma resolution in forced-compliance situations. *Journal of Personality and Social Psychology,* 1977, *35,* 21–30.

Riordan, C., & Riggiero, J. Producing equal-status interracial interaction: A replication. *Social Psychology Quarterly,* 1980, *43,* 131–136.

Riordan, C. A., Quigley-Fernandez, B., & Tedeschi, J. T. Some variables affecting changes in interpersonal attraction. *Journal of Experimental Social Psychology,* 1982, *18,* 358–374.

Riordan, C. A., & Tedeschi, J. T. Attraction in aversive environments: Some evidence for classical conditioning and negative reinforcement. *Journal of Personality and Social Psychology,* 1983, *44,* 683–692.

Rittle, R. H. Changes in helping behavior: Self- versus situational perceptions as mediators of the foot-in-the-door effect. *Personality and Social Psychology Bulletin,* 1981, *7,* 431–437.

Roberts, M. C., Wurtele, S. K., Boone, R., Metts, V., & Smith, V. Toward a reconceptualization of the reciprocal imitation phenomenon: Two experiments. *Journal of Research in Personality,* 1981, *15,* 447–459.

Robinson, J. P. *How Americans use time: A social-psychological analysis of everyday behavior.* New York: Praeger, 1977.

Rodgers, J. E. The malleable memory of eyewitnesses. *Science 82,* 1982, *3* (5), 32–35.

Rodin, J., Bohm, L. C., & Wack, J. T. Control, coping, and aging: Models for research and intervention. In L. Bickman (Ed.), *Applied social psychology annual 3.* Beverly Hills, Calif.: Sage, 1982.

Rodin, J., & Janis, I. L. The social power of health-care practitioners as agents of change. *Journal of Social Issues,* 1979, *35,* 60–81.

Rodin, J., & Langer, E. J. Long-term effects of a control-relevant intervention with the institutionalized aged. *Journal of Personality and Social Psychology,* 1977, *35,* 897–902.

Rodin, J., & Langer, E. Aging labels: The decline of control and the fall of self-esteem. *Journal of Social Issues,* 1980, *36* (2), 12–29.

Rodin, J., Solomon, S. K., & Metcalf, J. Role of control in mediating perceptions of density. *Journal of Personality and Social Psychology,* 1979, *36,* 988–999.

Rodrigues, A., & Newcomb, T. M. The balance principle: Its current state and its integrative function in social psychology. *Interamerican Journal of Psychology,* 1980, *14,* 85–136.

Roe, K. V. Toward a contingency hypothesis of empathy development. *Journal of Personality and Social Psychology,* 1980, *39,* 991–994.

Roesch, R. Determining competency to stand trial: An examination of evaluation procedures in an institutional setting. *Journal of Consulting and Clinical Psychology,* 1979, *47,* 542–550.

Rogers, M., Miller, N., Mayer, F. S., & Duvall, S. Personal responsibility and salience of the request for help: Determinants of the relation between negative affect and helping behavior. *Journal of Personality and Social Psychology,* 1982, *43,* 956–970.

Rogers, R. W. A protection motivation theory of fear appeals and attitude change. *Journal of Psychology,* 1975, *91,* 93–114.

Rogers, R. W. Aggression-inhibiting effects of anonymity to authority and threatened retaliations. *Personality and Social Psychology Bulletin,* 1980, *6,* 315–320. (a)

Rogers, R. W. Subjects' reactions to experimental deception. Unpublished manuscript, University of Alabama, 1980. (b)

Rogers, R. W., & Ketcher, C. M. Effects of anonymity and arousal on aggression. *Journal of Psychology,* 1979, *102,* 13–19.

Rogers, R. W., & Prentice-Dunn, S. Deindividuation and anger-mediated interracial aggression: Unmasking regressive racism. *Journal of Personality and Social Psychology,* 1981, *41,* 63–73.

Rogers, T. B., Kuiper, N. A., & Kirker, W. S. Self-reference and the encoding of personal information. *Journal of Personality and Social Psychology,* 1977, *35,* 677–688.

Rohner, R. P. Proxemics and stress: An empirical study of the relationship between living space and roommate turnover. *Human Relations,* 1974, *27,* 697–702.

Rook, K. S., & Peplau, L. A. Perspectives on helping the lonely. In L. A. Peplau & D. Perlman, *Loneliness: A sourcebook of current theory, research, and therapy.* New York: Wiley, 1982.

Rorschach, H. *Psychodiagnostics.* Berne: Hans Huber, 1921.

Rosen, R. H., Herskovitz, L., & Stack, J. M. Timing of the transition to nonvirginity among unmarried adolescent women. *Population Research and Policy Review,* 1982, *1,* 153–170.

Rosenbaum, M. E. Cooperation and competition. In P. B. Paulus (Ed.), *The psychology of group influence.* Hillsdale, N.J.: Erlbaum, 1980.

Rosenbaum, M. E., & Levin, I. P. Impression formation as a function of source credibility and the polarity of information. *Journal of*

Personality and Social Psychology, 1969, *12,* 34–37.

Rosenberg, S., & Gara, M. An empirically based analysis of the modern history of personality and social psychology. Unpublished manuscript, Rutgers University, 1981.

Rosenfield, D., Folger, R., & Adelman, H. F. When rewards reflect competence: A qualification of the overjustification effect. *Journal of Personality and Social Psychology,* 1980, *39,* 368–376.

Rosenfield, D., Greenberg, J., Folger, R., & Borys, R. Effect of an encounter with a black panhandler on subsequent helping for blacks: Tokenism or conforming a negative stereotype? *Personality and Social Psychology Bulletin,* 1982, *8,* 664–671.

Rosenhan, D. L., Salovey, P., & Hargis, K. The joys of helping: Focus of attention mediates the impact of positive affect on altruism. *Journal of Personality and Social Psychology,* 1981, *40,* 899–905.

Rosenman, R. H., & Friedman, M. Neurogenic factors in pathogenesis of coronary heart disease. *Medical Clinics of North America,* 1974, *58,* 269–279.

Ross, L., Lepper, M. R., Strack, F., & Steinmetz, J. Social explanation and social expectation: Effects of real and hypothetical explanations on subjective likelihood. *Journal of Personality and Social Psychology,* 1977, *35,* 817–829.

Rothbart, M., Evans, M., & Fulero, S. Recall for confirming events: Memory processes and the maintenance of social stereotypes. *Journal of Experimental Social Psychology,* 1979, *15,* 343–355.

Rothbart, M., Fulero, S., Jensen, C., Howard, J., & Birrell, P. From individual to group impressions: Availability heuristics in stereotype formation. *Journal of Experimental Social Psychology,* 1978, *14,* 237–255.

Rotter, J. B. *Social learning and clinical psychology.* Englewood Cliffs, N.J.: Prentice-Hall, 1954.

Rotter, J. B. Generalized expectancies for internal versus external control of reinforcement. *Psychological Monographs,* 1966, *80* (Whole No. 609).

Rotter, J. B. Trust and gullibility. *Psychology Today,* 1980, *14* (5), 35–38, 40, 42, 102.

Rotter, J. B., & Hochreich, D. J. *Personality.* Glenview, Ill.: Scott, Foresman, 1975.

Rotton, J., Barry, T., Frey, J., & Soler, E. Air pollution and interpersonal attraction. *Journal of Applied Social Psychology,* 1978, *8,* 57–71.

Rotton, J., Frey, J., Barry, T., Milligan, M., & Fitzpatrick, M. The air pollution experience and physical aggression. *Journal of Applied Social Psychology,* 1979, *9,* 397–412.

Ruback, R. B., Greenberg, M. S., & Wilson, C. E. Theft victims' decision to call the police: Some parameters of bystander influence. Paper presented at the meeting of the American Psychological Association, New York City, September 1979.

Rubin, J. Z. Experimental research on third-party intervention in conflict: Toward some generalizations. *Psychological Bulletin,* 1980, *87,* 379–391.

Rubin, Z. From liking to loving: Patterns of attraction in dating relationships. In T. L. Huston (Ed.), *Foundations of interpersonal attraction.* New York: Academic Press, 1974.

Rubin, Z. Breaking the age barrier to friendship. *Psychology Today,* March 1980, pp. 96, 98, 101. (a)

Rubin, Z. *Children's friendships.* Cambridge, Mass.: Harvard University Press, 1980. (b)

Rubin, Z. Children without friends. In L. A. Peplau & D. Perlman, *Loneliness: A sourcebook of current theory, research, and therapy.* New York: Wiley, 1982.

Rubin, Z., Peplau, L. A., & Hill, C. T. Loving and leaving: Sex differences in romantic attachments. *Sex Roles,* 1981, *7,* 821–835.

Rubin, Z., & Shenker, S. Friendship, proximity, and self-disclosure. *Journal of Personality,* 1978, *46,* 1–22.

Rusbult, C. E. Commitment and satisfaction in romantic associations: A test of the investment model. *Journal of Experimental Social Psychology,* 1980, *16,* 172–186.

Rusbult, C. E., & Zembrodt, I. M. Responses to dissatisfaction in romantic involvements: A multi-dimensional scaling analysis. *Journal of Experimental Social Psychology,* 1983, *19,* 274–293.

Rusbult, C. E., Zembrodt, I. M., & Gunn, L. K. Exit, voice, loyalty, and neglect: Responses to dissatisfaction in romantic involvements. *Journal of Personality and Social Psychology,* 1982, *43,* 1230–1242.

Russ, R. C., Gold, J. A., & Stone, W. F. Opportunity for thought as a mediator of attraction to a dissimilar stranger: A further test of an information seeking interpretation. *Journal of Experimental Social Psychology,* 1980, *16,* 562–572.

Russell, D. The measurement of loneliness. In L. A. Peplau & D. Perlman, *Loneliness: A sourcebook of current theory, research, and therapy.* New York: Wiley, 1982.

Russell, D., Peplau, L. A., & Cutrona, C. E. The

revised UCLA Loneliness Scale: Concurrent and discriminant validity evidence. *Journal of Personality and Social Psychology,* 1980, *39,* 472–480.

Russell, J. A., Ward, L. M., & Pratt, G. Affective quality attributed to environments: A factor analytic study. *Environment and Behavior,* 1981, *13,* 259–288.

Rutkowski, G. K., Gruder, C. L., & Romer, D. Group cohesiveness, social norms, and bystander intervention. *Journal of Personality and Social Psychology,* 1983, *44,* 545–552.

Sabatelli, R. M., Buck, R., & Dreyer, A. Nonverbal communication accuracy in married couples: Relationship with marital complaints. *Journal of Personality and Social Psychology,* 1982, *43,* 1088–1097.

Sagar, H. A., & Schofield, J. W. Racial and behavioral cues in black and white children's perceptions of ambiguously aggressive acts. *Journal of Personality and Social Psychology,* 1980, *39,* 590–598.

Salazar, J. M. Research on applied social psychology in Venezuela: An illustrative case. Paper presented at the meeting of the XVIII Congreso Interamericano de Psicologia. Santo Domingo, June 1981.

Saltzer, E. B. Social determinants of successful weight loss: An analysis of behavioral intentions and actual behavior. *Basic and Applied Social Psychology,* 1980, *1,* 329–341.

Sampson, E. E. Psychology and the American ideal. *Journal of Personality and Social Psychology,* 1977, *35,* 767–782.

Sanders, G. S. Driven by distraction: An integrative review of social facilitation theory and research. *Journal of Experimental Social Psychology,* 1981, *17,* 227–25l. (a)

Sanders, G. S. The interactive effect of social comparison and objective information on the decision to see a doctor. *Journal of Applied Social Psychology,* 1981, *11,* 390–400. (b)

Sanders, G. S. Social comparison as a basis for evaluating others. *Journal of Research in Personality,* 1982, *16,* 21–31.

Sanders, G. S., & Baron, R. S. Is social comparison irrelevant for producing choice shifts? *Journal of Experimental Social Psychology,* 1977, *13,* 303–314.

Sanders, G. S., Baron, R. S., & Moore, D. L. Distraction and social comparison as mediators of social facilitation effects. *Journal of Experimental Social Psychology,* 1978, *14,* 291–303.

Sanders, G. S., & Schmidt, T. Behavioral discrimination against women. *Personality and Social Psychology Bulletin,* 1980, *6,* 484–488.

Sanders, G. S., & Warnick, D. H. Evaluating identification evidence from multiple eyewitnesses. *Journal of Applied Social Psychology,* 1982, *12,* 182–192.

Sarason, I. G., & Ganzer, V. J. Modeling: An approach to the rehabilitation of juvenile offenders. Final report to the Social and Rehabilitation Service of the Department of Health, Education, and Welfare. Washington, D.C., June, 1971.

Sarason, I. G., Smith, R. E., & Diener, E. Personality research: Components of variance attributable to the person and the situation. *Journal of Personality and Social Psychology,* 1981.

Sarrel, P., & Sarrel, L. The Redbook report on sexual relationships. *Redbook,* October 1980, pp. 74–80.

Satow, K. L. Social approval and helping. *Journal of Experimental Social Psychology,* 1975, *11,* 501–509.

Saulnier, K., & Perlman, D. The actor-observer bias is alive and well in prison: A sequel to Wells. *Personality and Social Psychology Bulletin,* 1981, *7,* 559–564.

Saxe, L., & Fine, M. Reorienting social psychology toward application: A methodological analysis. In L. Bickman (Ed.), *Applied social psychology annual 1.* Beverly Hills, Calif.: Sage, 1980.

Schaar, K. Hostage crisis in review: Psychology's continuing role. *APA Monitor,* 1981, *12* (3), 1, 8, 13.

Schachter, S. Deviation, rejection, and communication. *Journal of Abnormal and Social Psychology,* 1951, *46,* 190–207.

Schachter, S. *The psychology of affiliation.* Stanford, Calif.: Stanford University Press, 1959.

Schachter, S. The interaction of cognitive and physiological determinants of emotional state. In L. Berkowitz (Ed.), *Advances in experimental social psychology* (Vol. 1). New York: Academic Press, 1964.

Schachter, S., & Singer, J. E. Cognitive, social, and physiological determinants of emotional states. *Psychological Review,* 1962, *69,* 379–399.

Schaie, K. W., & Parham, I. A. Social responsibility in adulthood: Ontogenetic and sociocultural change. *Journal of Personality and Social Psychology,* 1974, *30,* 483–492.

Schaie, K. W., & Parham, I. A. Stability of adult personality traits: Fact or fable? *Journal of Personality and Social Psychology,* 1976, *34,* 146–158.

Schank, R., & Abelson, R. *Scripts, plans, goals, and*

understanding: An inquiry into human knowledge structures. Hillsdale, N.J.: Erlbaum, 1977.

Scheier, M. F., & Carver, C. S. Cognition, affect, and self-regulation. In M. S. Clark & S. T. Fiske (Eds.), *Affect and cognition: The 17th annual Carnegie symposium on cognition.* Hillsdale, N.J.: Erlbaum, 1982.

Scheier, M. F., Carver, C. S., & Gibbons, F. X. Self-directed attention, awareness of bodily states, and suggestibility. *Journal of Personality and Social Psychology,* 1979, *37,* 1576–1588.

Scherer, S. E. Proxemic behavior of primary school children as a function of their socioeconomic class and subculture. *Journal of Personality and Social Psychology,* 1974, *29,* 800–805.

Schiffenbauer, A., & Schiavo, R. S. Physical distance and attraction: An intensification effect. *Journal of Experimental Social Psychology,* 1976, *12,* 274–282.

Schill, T., & Chapin, J. Sex guilt and males' preference for reading erotic magazines. *Journal of Consulting and Clinical Psychology,* 1972, *39,* 516.

Schlenker, B. R., Forsyth, D. R., Leary, M. R., & Miller, R. W. A self-presentational analysis of the effects of incentives and attitude change following counterattitudinal behavior. *Journal of Personality and Social Psychology,* 1980, *39,* 553–557.

Schmidt, G. Sex and society in the eighties. *Archives of Sexual Behavior,* 1982, *11,* 91–97.

Schmitt, D. R., & Marwell, G. Withdrawal and reward reallocation as responses to inequity. *Journal of Experimental Social Psychology,* 1972, *8,* 207–221.

Schriesheim, C. A., & DeNisi, A. S. Task dimensions as moderators of the effects of instrumental leadership: A two-sample replicated test of Path-Goal leadership theory. *Journal of Applied Psychology,* 1981, *66,* 589–597.

Schubert, H. J., Wagner, M. E., & Reiss, B. F. Sibship size, sibsex, and homosexuality among male outpatients. *Transnational Mental Health Research Newsletter,* 1976, *18,* 3–8.

Schuster, E., & Elderton, E. M. The inheritance of psychical characters. *Biometrika,* 1906, *5,* 460–469.

Schwartz, S. Effects of sex guilt and sexual arousal on the retention of birth control information. *Journal of Consulting and Clinical Psychology,* 1973, *41,* 61–64.

Schwartz, S. H., & Gottlieb, A. Bystander anonymity and reactions to emergencies.

Journal of Personality and Social Psychology, 1980, *39,* 418–430.

Schweder, R. A. How relevant is an individual difference theory of personality? *Journal of Personality,* 1975, *43,* 455–484.

Scitovsky, T. Why do we seek more and more excitement? *Stanford Observer,* October 1980, p. 13.

Sears, D. O. The person-positivity bias. *Journal of Personality and Social Psychology,* 1983, *44,* 233–250.

Sears, R. R., Lau, L., & Alpert, R. *Identification and child rearing.* Stanford, Calif.: Stanford University Press, 1965.

Sebba, R., & Churchman, A. Territories and territoriality in the home. *Environment and Behavior,* 1983, *15,* 191–210.

Seeley, T. T., Abramson, P. R., Perry, L. B., Rothblatt, A. B., & Seeley, D. M. Thermographic measurement of sexual arousal: A methodological note. *Archives of Sexual Behavior,* 1980, *9,* 77–85.

Segal, M. W. Alphabet and attraction: An unobtrusive measure of the effect of propinquity in a field setting. *Journal of Personality and Social Psychology,* 1974, *30,* 654–657.

Sekaran, U., & Mowday, R. T. A cross-cultural analysis of the influence of individual and job characteristics on job involvement. *International Review of Applied Psychology,* 1981, *30,* 51–64.

Seligman, C., Becker, L. J., & Darley, J. M. Encouraging residential energy conservation through feedback. In A. Baum & J. E. Singer (Eds.), *Advances in environmental psychology* (Vol. 3). Hillsdale, N.J.: Erlbaum, 1980.

Seligman, C., Bush, M., & Kirsch, K. Relationship between compliance in the foot-in-the-door paradigm and size of first request. *Journal of Personality and Social Psychology,* 1976, *33,* 517–520.

Sensenig, J., & Brehm, J. W. Attitude change from implied threat to attitudinal freedom. *Journal of Personality and Social Psychology,* 1968, *8,* 324–330.

Seta, J. J. The impact of comparison processes on coactors' task performance. *Journal of Personality and Social Psychology,* 1982, *42,* 281–291.

Severy, L. J., Forsyth, D. R., & Wagner, P. J. A multimethod assessment of personal space development in female and male, black and white children. *Journal of Nonverbal Behavior,* 1979, *4,* 68–86.

Severy, L. J., Houlden, P., & Wilmoth, G. H.

Community acceptance of innovative programs. In L. Bickman (Ed.), *Applied social psychology annual 2.* Beverly Hills, Calif.: Sage, 1981.

Shabecoff, P. Poll finds strong support for environmental code. *New York Times,* October 4, 1981, p. 30.

Shaffer, D. R., & Case, T. On the decision to testify in one's own behalf: Effects of withheld evidence, defendant's sexual preferences, and juror dogmatism on juridic decisions. *Journal of Personality and Social Psychology,* 1982, *42,* 335–346.

Shaffer, D. R., & Graziano, W. G. Effect of victims' race and organizational affiliation on receiving help from blacks and whites. *Personality and Social Psychology Bulletin,* 1980, *6,* 366–372.

Shaffer, O. R., Rogel, M., & Hendrick, C. Intervention in the library: The effect of increased responsibility on bystanders' willingness to prevent a theft. *Journal of Applied Social Psychology,* 1975, *5,* 303–319.

Shanab, M. E., & Yahya, K. A. A behavioral study of obedience in children. *Journal of Personality and Social Psychology,* 1977, *35,* 530–536.

Shanteau, J., & Nagy, G. F. Probability of acceptance in dating choice. *Journal of Personality and Social Psychology,* 1979, *37,* 522–533.

Sharabany, R., Gershoni, R., & Hofman, J. E. Girlfriend, boyfriend: Age and sex differences in intimate friendships. *Developmental Psychology,* 1981, *17,* 800–808.

Shaw, J. S. Psychological androgyny and stressful life events. *Journal of Personality and Social Psychology,* 1982, *43,* 145–153.

Shea, J. D. C. Changes in interpersonal distances and categories of play behavior in the early weeks of preschool. *Developmental Psychology,* 1981, *17,* 417–425.

Shearer, L. How to cope. *Parade,* November 21, 1982, p. 9.

Shelton, M. L., & Rogers, R. W. Fear-arousing and empathy-arousing appeals to help: The pathos of persuasion. *Journal of Applied Social Psychology,* 1981, *11,* 366–378.

Shemberg, K. M., Leventhal, D. B., & Allman, L. Aggression machine performance and rated aggression. *Journal of Experimental Research in Personality,* 1968, *3,* 117–119.

Shepherd, D. H., & Sloan, L. R. Similarity of legal attitudes, defendant social class, and crime intentionality as determinants of legal decisions. *Personality and Social Psychology Bulletin,* 1979, *5,* 245–248.

Sheppard, B. H., & Vidmar, N. Adversary pretrial procedures and testimonial evidence: Effects of lawyer's role and Machiavellianism. *Journal of Personality and Social Psychology,* 1980, *39,* 320–332.

Sherif, M. A study of some social factors in perception. *Archives of Psychology,* 1935 (no. 187).

Sherif, M. *In common predicament: Social psychology of intergroup conflict and cooperation.* Boston: Houghton Mifflin, 1966.

Sherif, M., Harvey, O. J., White, B. J., Hood, W. E., & Sherif, C. W. *Intergroup conflict and cooperation: The Robber's Cave experiment.* Norman: University of Oklahoma Book Exchange, 1961.

Sherman, S. J., Presson, C. C., Chassin, L., Corty, E., & Olshavsky, R. The false consensus effect in estimates of smoking prevalence: Underlying mechanisms. *Personality and Social Psychology Bulletin,* 1983, *9,* 197–207.

Sherrod, D. R., Hage, J. N., Halpern, P. L., & Moore, B. S. Effects of personal causation and perceived control on responses to an aversive environment: The more control, the better. *Journal of Experimental Social Psychology,* 1977, *13,* 14–27.

Shigetomi, C. C., Hartmann, D. P., & Gelfand, D. M. Sex differences in children's altruistic behavior and reputations for helpfulness. *Developmental Psychology,* 1981, *17,* 434–437.

Shimmin, S. Applying psychology in organizations. *International Review of Applied Psychology,* 1981, *30,* 377–386.

Shipley, R. H. Maintenance of smoking cessation: Effect of follow-up letters, smoking motivation, muscle tension, and health locus of control. *Journal of Consulting and Clinical Psychology,* 1981, *49,* 982–984.

Shomer, R. W., Davis, A., & Kelley, H. H. Threats and development of coordination: Further studies of the Deutsch and Krauss trucking game. *Journal of Personality and Social Psychology,* 1966, *4,* 119–126.

Shribman, D. Taxpayers make peace with U.S. *New York Times,* September 22, 1981, p. A28.

Shure, G. H., Meeker, R. J., & Hansford, E. A. The effectiveness of pacifist strategies in bargaining games. *Journal of Conflict Resolution,* 1965, *9,* 106–117.

Siegel, L. J., & Peterson, L. Stress reduction in young dental patients through coping skills and sensory information. *Journal of Consulting and Clinical Psychology,* 1980, *48,* 785–787.

Sigall, H., & Ostrove, N. Beautiful but dangerous:

Effects of offender attractiveness and nature of the crime on juridic judgment. *Journal of Personality and Social Psychology*, 1975, *31*, 410–414.

Sigusch, V., & Schmidt, G. Teenage boys and girls in West Germany. *Journal of Sex Research*, 1973, *9*, 107–123.

Silver, R. L., & Wortman, C. B. Coping with undesirable life events. In J. Garber & M. E. P. Seligman (Eds.), *Human helplessness*. New York: Academic Press, 1980.

Simonton, D. K. Land battles, generals, and armies: Individual and situational determinants of victory and casualties. *Journal of Personality and Social Psychology*, 1980, *38*, 110–119.

Singer, A. G., Agosta, W. C., O'Connell, R. J., Pfaffmann, C., Bowen, D. V., & Field, F. H. Dimethyl disulfide: An attractant pheromone in hamster vaginal secretion. *Science*, 1976, *191*, 948–950.

Singer, J. E. The need to measure life style. *International Review of Applied Psychology*, 1982, *31*, 303–315.

Sistrunk, F., & McDavid, J. W. Sex variable in conforming behavior. *Journal of Personality and Social Psychology*, 1971, *17*, 200–207.

Sivacek, J., & Crano, W. D. Vested interest as a moderator of attitude-behavior consistency. *Journal of Personality and Social Psychology*, 1982, *43*, 210–221.

Skevington, S. M. Intergroup relations and nursing. *European Journal of Social Psychology*, 1981, *11*, 43–59.

Skolnick, P., & Heslin, R. Approval dependence and reactions to bad arguments and low credibility sources. *Journal of Experimental Research in Personality*, 1971, *5*, 199–207.

Skrypnek, B. J., & Snyder, M. On the self-perpetuating nature of stereotypes about women and men. *Journal of Experimental Social Psychology*, 1982, *18*, 277–291.

Slater, E. Birth order and maternal age of homosexuals. *Lancet*, 1962, *1*, 69–71.

Smedley, J. W., & Bayton, J. A. Evaluative race-class stereotypes by race and perceived class of subjects. *Journal of Personality and Social Psychology*, 1978, *36*, 530–535.

Smith, E. E., Adams, N., & Schorr, D. Fact retrieval and the paradox of interference. *Cognitive Psychology*, 1978, *10*, 438–464.

Smith, E. R., & Kluegel, J. R. Cognitive and social bases of emotional experience: Outcome, attribution, and affect. *Journal of Personality and Social Psychology*, 1982.

Smith, F. J., Scott, K. D., & Hulin, C. L. Trends in job related attitudes of managerial and professional employees. *Academic Management Journal*, 1977, *20*, 454–460.

Smith, G. F., & Dorfman, D. D. The effect of stimulus uncertainty on the relationship between frequency of exposure and liking. *Journal of Personality and Social Psychology*, 1975, *31*, 150–155.

Smith, M. P., & Nock, S. L. Social class and the quality of work life in public and private organizations. *Journal of Social Issues*, 1980, *36* (4), 59–75.

Smith, R. J. The fight over clean air begins. *Science*, 1981, *211*, 1328–1330.

Smith, R. J., & Knowles, E. S. Affective and cognitive mediators of reactions to spatial invasions. *Journal of Experimental Social Psychology*, 1979, *15*, 437–452.

Smith, S., & Richardson, D. Amelioration of deception and harm in psychological research: The important role of debriefing. *Journal of Personality and Social Psychology*, 1983, *44*, 1075–1082.

Smith, T. W., & Brehm, S. S. Cognitive correlates of the Type A coronary-prone behavior pattern. *Motivation and Emotion*, 1981, *5*, 215–223. (a)

Smith, T. W., & Brehm, S. S. Person perception and the Type A coronary-prone behavior pattern. *Journal of Personality and Social Psychology*, 1981, *40*, 1137–1149. (b)

Snow, B. Level of aspiration in coronary-prone and noncoronary-prone adults. *Personality and Social Psychology Bulletin*, 1978, *4*, 416–419.

Snyder, C. R., & Endelman, J. R. Effects of degree of interpersonal similarity on physical distance and self-reported attraction: A comparison of uniqueness and reinforcement theory predictions. *Journal of Personality*, 1979, *47*, 492–505.

Snyder, C. R., & Fromkin, H. L. *Uniqueness: The human pursuit of difference*. New York: Plenum, 1980.

Snyder, M., & Cunningham, M. R. To comply or not to comply: Testing the self-perception explanation of the "foot-in-the-door" phenomenon. *Journal of Personality and Social Psychology*, 1975, *31*, 64–67.

Snyder, M., Grether, J., & Keller, K. Staring and compliance: A field experiment on hitch-hiking. *Journal of Applied Social Psychology*, 1974, *4*, 165–170.

Snyder, M., & Kendzierski, D. Acting on one's attitudes: Procedures for linking attitude and behavior. *Journal of Experimental Social Psychology*, 1982, *18*, 165–183.

Snyder, M., Tanke, E. D., & Berscheid, E. Social

perception and interpersonal behavior: On the self-fulfilling nature of social stereotypes. *Journal of Personality and Social Psychology,* 1977, *35,* 656–666.

Sobel, D. Desire to be unique—a universal goal. *New York Times,* December 1, 1980, p. B16.

Sogin, S. R., & Pallak, M. S. Bad decisions, responsibility, and attitude change: Effects of volition, foreseeability, and locus of causality of negative consequences. *Journal of Personality and Social Psychology,* 1976, *33,* 300–306.

Sokolov, J. J., Harris, R. T., & Hecker, M. R. Isolation of substances from human vaginal secretions previously shown to be sex attractant pheromones in higher primates. *Archives of Sexual Behavior,* 1976, *5,* 269–274.

Solano, C. H., Batten, P. G., & Parish, E. A. Loneliness and patterns of self-disclosure. *Journal of Personality and Social Psychology,* 1982, *43,* 524–531.

Solomon, R. C. The love lost in clichés. *Psychology Today,* October 1981, pp. 83–85, 87–88.

Sommer, R. *Personal space.* Englewood Cliffs, N.J.: Prentice-Hall, 1969.

Sommer, R. Environmental psychology—a blueprint for the future. *APA Monitor,* 1980, *11* (8 & 9), 3, 47.

Sox, H. *Annals of Internal Medicine,* 1982, *95.*

Spence, J. R., & Helmreich, R. L. The many faces of androgyny: A reply to Locksley and Colten. *Journal of Personality and Social Psychology,* 1979, *37,* 1032–1046.

Spielberger, C. D. (Ed.). *Police selection and evaluation: Issues and techniques.* New York: Praeger, 1979.

Srinivas, K. M. Psychology, labour and worklife: New challenges. *International Review of Applied Psychology,* 1981, *30,* 261–275.

Srull, T. K., & Wyer, R. S., Jr. Category accessibility and social perception: Some implications for the study of person memory and interpersonal judgments. *Journal of Personality and Social Psychology,* 1980, *38,* 841–856.

Stang, D. J., & Crandall, R. Familiarity and liking. In T. M. Steinfatt (Ed.), *Readings in human communication.* Indianapolis: Bobbs-Merrill, 1977.

Stapp, J., & Fulcher, R. The employment of 1979 and 1980 doctorate recipients in psychology. *American Psychologist,* 1982, *37,* 1159–1185.

Staub, E., Tursky, B., & Schwartz, G. Self-control and predictability: Their effects on reactions to aversive stimulation. *Journal of Personality and Social Psychology,* 1971, *18,* 157–162.

Stech, F., & McClintock, C. G. Effects of communication timing on duopoly bargaining

outcomes. *Journal of Personality and Social Psychology,* 1981, *40,* 664–674.

Steck, L., Levitan, D., McLane, D., & Kelley, H. H. Care, need, and conceptions of love. *Journal of Personality and Social Psychology,* 1982, *43,* 481–491.

Steele, C. M., Southwick, L. L., & Critchlow, B. Dissonance and alcohol: Drinking your troubles away. *Journal of Personality and Social Psychology,* 1981, *41,* 831–846.

Stein, G. M. Children's reactions to innocent victims. *Child Development,* 1973, *44,* 805–810.

Stein, R. T., Hoffman, L. R., Cooley, S. J., & Pearse, R. W. Leadership valence: Modeling and measuring the process of emergent leadership. In J. G. Hunt & L. L. Larson (Eds.), *Crosscurrents in leadership.* Carbondale: Southern Illinois University Press, 1980.

Steinberg, R., & Shapiro, S. Sex differences in personality traits of female and male master of business administration students. *Journal of Applied Psychology,* 1982, *67,* 306–310.

Stephan, W., Berscheid, E., & Walster, E. Sexual arousal and heterosexual perception. *Journal of Personality and Social Psychology,* 1971, *20,* 93–101.

Stephan, W. G. School desegregation: An evaluation of predictions made in Brown v. Board of Education. *Psychological Bulletin,* 1978, *85,* 217–238.

Stephan, W. G., & Rosenfield, D. Effects of desegregation on racial attitudes. *Journal of Personality and Social Psychology,* 1978, *36,* 795–804.

Sterling, F. E. Net positive social approaches of young psychiatric inpatients as influenced by nurses' attire. *Journal of Consulting and Clinical Psychology,* 1980, *48,* 58–62.

Stern, G. S., Harris, J. R., & Elverum, J. Attention to important versus trivial tasks and salience of fatigue-related symptoms for coronary-prone individuals. *Journal of Research in Personality,* 1981, *15,* 467–474.

Sternglanz, S. H., Graz, J. L., & Murakami, M. Adult preferences for infantile facial features: An ethological approach. *Animal Behavior,* 1972, *25,* 108–115.

Stetson, D. Work innovations improving morale. *New York Times,* September 30, 1981, p. 53.

Stevens, G. E., & DeNisi, A. S. Women as managers: Attitudes and attributions for performance by men and women. *Academy of Management Journal,* 1980, *23,* 355–361.

Stewart, A. J., Sokol, M., Healy, J. M., Jr., Chester, N. L., & Weinstock-Savoy, D. Adaptation to life changes in children and adults: Cross-sectional studies. *Journal of Personality and Social Psychology*, 1982, *43*, 1270–1281.

Stewart, J. E., II. Defendant's attractiveness as a factor in the outcome of criminal trials: An observational study. *Journal of Applied Social Psychology*, 1980, *10*, 348–361.

Stock, W. E., & Geer, J. H. A study of fantasy-based sexual arousal in women. *Archives of Sexual Behavior*, 1982, *11*, 33–47.

Stokes, L. D., & Prestholdt, P. Race and person perception: Evaluations and decisions by simulated jurors. Paper presented at the meeting of the Southeastern Psychological Association, Atlanta, April 1972.

Stokols, D. On the distinction between density and crowding: Some implications for future research. *Psychological Review*, 1972, *79*, 275–278.

Stokols, D. Environmental psychology. In M. R. Rosenzweig & L. W. Porter (Eds.), *Annual review of psychology* (Vol. 30). Palo Alto, Calif.: Annual Reviews, 1978.

Stone, L. *The family, sex and marriage in England: 1500–1800.* New York: Harper, 1977.

Stoner, J. A. F. A comparison of individual and group decisions involving risk. Unpublished master's thesis, School of Industrial Management, MIT, 1961.

Storms, M., & Nisbett, R. E. Insomnia and the attribution process. *Journal of Personality and Social Psychology*, 1970, *16*, 319–328.

Storms, M. D. A theory of erotic orientation development. *Psychological Review*, 1981, *88*, 340–353.

Storms, M. D., & Thomas, G. C. Reactions to physical closeness. *Journal of Personality and Social Psychology*, 1977, *35*, 412–418.

Strack, F., Erber, R., & Wicklund, R. A. Effects of salience and time pressure on attribution of causality and non-causality. *Journal of Experimental Social Psychology*, 1982, *18*, 581–594.

Straker, G., & Jacobson, R. S. Aggression, emotional maladjustment, and empathy in the abused child. *Developmental Psychology*, 1981, *17*, 762–765.

Strand, P. J. The energy issue: Partisan characteristics. *Environment and Behavior*, 1981, *13*, 509–519.

Strentz, T. The Stockholm Syndrome: Law enforcement policy and ego defenses of the hostage. In F. Wright, C. Bahn, & R. W. Rieber (Eds.), *Forensic psychology and psychiatry.* New York: New York Academy of Sciences, 1980.

Stroebe, W., & Diehl, M. Conformity and counterattitudinal behavior: The effects of social support on attitude change. *Journal of Personality and Social Psychology*, 1981, *41*, 876–889.

Strom, J. C., & Buck, R. W. Staring and participants' sex: Physiological and subjective reactions. *Personality and Social Psychology Bulletin*, 1979, *5*, 114–117.

Strube, M. J. Time urgency and Type A behavior: A methodological note. *Personality and Social Psychology Bulletin*, 1982, *8*, 563–565.

Strube, M. J., & Garcia, J. E. A meta-analytic investigation of Fiedler's contingency model of leadership effectiveness. *Psychological Bulletin*, 1981, *90*, 307–321.

Strube, M. J., Miles, M. E., & Finch, W. H. The social facilitation of a simple task: Field tests of alternative explanations. *Personality and Social Psychology Bulletin*, 1981, *7*, 701–707.

Strube, M. J., & Ota, S. Type A coronary-prone behavior pattern: Relationship to birth order and family size. *Personality and Social Psychology Bulletin*, 1982, *8*, 317–323.

Suchner, R. W. Sex ratios and occupational prestige: Three failures to replicate a sexist bias. *Personality and Social Psychology Bulletin*, 1979, *5*, 236–239.

Sue, D. Erotic fantasies of college students during coitus. *Journal of Sex Research*, 1979, *15*, 299–305.

Suedfeld, P. Aloneness as a healing experience. In L. A. Peplau & D. Perlman, *Loneliness: A sourcebook of current theory, research, and therapy.* New York: Wiley, 1982.

Suls, J., & Mullen, B. Life change and psychological distress: The role of perceived control and desirability. *Journal of Applied Social Psychology*, 1981, *11*, 379–389.

Suls, J., Witenberg, S., & Gutkin, D. Evaluating reciprocal and nonreciprocal prosocial behavior: Developmental changes. *Personality and Social Psychology Bulletin*, 1981, *7*, 25–31.

Suls, J. M., & Miller, R. C. (Eds.). *Social comparison processes: Theoretical and empirical perspectives.* Washington, D.C.: Halsted-Wiley, 1977.

Swann, W. B., & Miller, L. C. Why never forgetting a face matters: Visual imagery and social memory. *Journal of Personality and Social Psychology*, 1982, *43*, 475–480.

Swann, W. B., Jr., & Read, S. J. Acquiring self-knowledge: The search for feedback that fits. *Journal of Personality and Social Psychology*, 1981, *41*, 1119–1128.

Swap, W. C. Interpersonal attraction and repeated exposure to rewarders and punishers. *Personality and Social Psychology Bulletin*, 1977, *3*, 248–251.

Tajfel, H. (Ed.). Differentiation between social groups: Studies in the social psychology of intergroup relations. *European Monographs in Social Psychology, No. 14.* London: Academic Press, 1978.

Tajfel, H., & Turner, J. An integrative theory of intergroup conflict. In W. G. Austin & S. Worchel (Eds.), *The social psychology of intergroup relations.* Monterey, Calif.: Brooks/Cole, 1979.

Tanford, S., & Penrod, S. Biases in trials involving defendants charged with multiple offenses. *Journal of Applied Social Psychology,* 1982, *12,* 453–480.

Taylor, D. A., Gould, R. J., & Brownstein, P. J. Effects of personalistic self-disclosure. *Personality and Social Psychology Bulletin,* 1981, *7,* 487–492.

Taylor, F. W. *The principles of scientific management.* New York: Harper & Brothers, 1911.

Taylor, M. C., & Hall, J. A. Psychological androgyny: Theories, methods, and conclusions. *Psychological Bulletin,* 1982, *92,* 347–366.

Taylor, R. B. Conceptual dimensions of crowding reconsidered. *Population and Environment,* 1980, *3,* 298–308.

Taylor, R. B., & Brooks, D. K. Temporary territories?: Responses to intrusions in a public setting. *Population and Environment,* 1980, *3,* 135–144.

Taylor, R. B., De Soto, C. B., & Lieb, R. Sharing secrets: Disclosure and discretion in dyads and triads. *Journal of Personality and Social Psychology,* 1979, *37,* 1196–1203.

Taylor, R. B., & Ferguson, G. Solitude and intimacy: Linking territoriality and privacy experiences. *Journal of Nonverbal Behavior,* 1980, *4,* 227–239.

Taylor, R. B., & Lanni, J. C. Territorial dominance: The influence of the resident advantage in triadic decision making. *Journal of Personality and Social Psychology,* 1981, *41,* 909–915.

Taylor, R. B., & Stough, R. R. Territorial cognition: Assessing Altman's typology. *Journal of Personality and Social Psychology,* 1978, *36,* 418–423.

Taylor, S., & Fiske, S. T. Salience, attention, and attribution: Top of the head phenomena. In L. Berkowitz (Ed.), *Advances in experimental social psychology* (Vol. 11). New York: Academic Press, 1978.

Taylor, S. E. Hospital patient behavior: Reactance, helplessness, or control? *Journal of Social Issues,* 1979, *35* (1), 156–184.

Taylor, S. E. Social cognition and health.

Personality and Social Psychology Bulletin, 1982, *8,* 549–562.

Taylor, S. E., & Crocker, J. Schematic bases of social information processing. In E. T. Higgins, C. A. Herman, & M. P. Zanna (Eds.), *Social cognition: The Ontario Symposium.* Hillsdale, N.J.: Erlbaum, 1981.

Taylor, S. E., & Fiske, S. E. Getting inside the head: Methodologies for process analysis. In J. Harvey, W. Ickes, & R. Kidd (Eds.), *New directions in attribution research* (Vol. 3). Hillsdale, N.J.: Erlbaum, 1981.

Taylor, S. E., & Thompson, S. C. Stalking the elusive "vividness" effect. *Psychological Review,* 1982, *89,* 155–181.

Taylor, S. M., & Ilgen, D. R. Sex discrimination against women in initial placement decisions: A laboratory investigation. *Academy of Management Journal,* 1981, *4,* 859–865.

Taylor, S. P., & Pisano, R. Physical aggression as a function of frustration and physical attack. *Journal of Social Psychology,* 1971, *84,* 261–267.

Taylor, S. P., Shuntich, R. J., & Greenberg, A. The effects of repeated aggressive encounters on subsequent aggressive behavior. *Journal of Social Psychology,* 1979, *197,* 199–208.

Terborg, J. R. Women in management: A research review. *Journal of Applied Psychology,* 1977, *62,* 647–664.

Tesser, A. Self-generated attitude change. In L. Berkowitz (Ed.), *Advances in experimental social psychology* (Vol. 11). New York: Academic Press, 1978.

Tesser, A., & Paulhus, D. L. Toward a causal model of love. *Journal of Personality and Social Psychology,* 1976, *34,* 1095–1105.

Tesser, A., & Reardon, R. Perceptual and cognitive mechanisms in human sexual attraction. In M. Cook (Ed.), *The bases of human sexual attraction.* London: Academic Press, 1981.

Thalhofer, N. N. Violation of a spacing norm in high social density. *Journal of Applied Social Psychology,* 1980, *10,* 175–183.

Thelen, M. H., Frautschi, N. M., Roberts, M. C., Kirkland, K. D., & Dollinger, S. J. Being imitated, conformity, and social influence: An integrative review. *Journal of Research in Personality,* 1981, *15,* 403–426.

Thomas, G. C., Batson, C. D., & Coke, J. S. Do good Samaritans discourage helpfulness? Self-perceived altruism after exposure to highly helpful others. *Journal of Personality and Social Psychology,* 1981, *40,* 194–200.

Thomas, M. H. Physiological arousal, exposure to a relatively lengthy aggressive film, and aggressive behavior. *Journal of Research in Personality*, 1982, *16*, 72–81.

Thomas, M. H., Horton, R. W., Lippincott, E. C., & Drabman, R. S. Desensitization to portrayals of real-life aggression as a function of exposure to television violence. *Journal of Personality and Social Psychology*, 1977, *35*, 450–458.

Thompson, D. E., Aiello, J. R., & Epstein, Y. M. Interpersonal distance preferences. *Journal of Nonverbal Behavior*, 1979, *4*, 113–118.

Thompson, R. A., & Hoffman, M. L. Empathy and the development of guilt in children. *Developmental Psychology*, 1980, *16*, 155–156.

Thompson, W. C., Cowan, C. L., & Rosenhan, D. L. Focus of attention mediates the impact of negative affect on altruism. *Journal of Personality and Social Psychology*, 1980, *38*, 291–300.

Thompson, W. C., Fong, G. T., & Rosenhan, D. L. Inadmissible evidence and juror verdicts. *Journal of Personality and Social Psychology*, 1981, *40*, 453–463.

Thornton, B. Effect of rape victim's attractiveness in a jury simulation. *Personality and Social Psychology Bulletin*, 1977, *3*, 666–669.

Tilker, H. A. Socially responsible behavior as a function of observer responsibility and victim feedback. *Journal of Personality and Social Psychology*, 1970, *14*, 95–100.

Timnick, L. Birth defects linked to noise from jets? *Indianapolis Star*, February 26, 1978.

Toch, H. *Violent men.* Chicago: Aldine, 1969.

Toch, H. *Violent men* (rev. ed.). Cambridge, Mass.: Schenkman, 1980.

Toi, M., & Batson, C. D. More evidence that empathy is a source of altruistic motivation. *Journal of Personality and Social Psychology*, 1982, *43*, 281–292.

Toney, M. B., Stinner, W. F., & Kim, Y. The population debate: A survey of opinions of a professional organization's membership. *Population and Environment*, 1981, *4*, 156–173.

Touhey, J. C. Effects of additional women professionals on ratings of occupational prestige and desirability. *Journal of Personality and Social Psychology*, 1974, *29*, 86–89.

Triplett, N. The dynamogenic factors in pacemaking and competition. *American Journal of Psychology*, 1898, *9*, 507–533.

Trippett, F. Small town, U.S.A.: Growing and groaning. *Time*, 1980, *116* (9), 73–74.

Trivers, R. L., & Hare, H. Haplodiploidy and the evolution of the social insects. *Science*, 1976, *191*, 249–263.

Tucker, D. M. Lateral brain function, emotion, and conceptualization. *Psychological Bulletin*, 1981, *89*, 19–46.

Turner, C. W., Layton, J. F., & Simons, L. S. Naturalistic studies of aggressive behavior: Aggressive stimuli, victim visibility, and horn honking. *Journal of Personality and Social Psychology*, 1975, *31*, 1098–1107.

Turner, J. Social categorization and social discrimination in the minimal group paradigm. In H. Tajfel (Ed.), *European Monographs in Social Psychology, No. 14.* London: Academic Press, 1978.

Tversky, A., & Kahneman, D. Causal schemata in judgments under uncertainty. In M. Fishbein (Ed.), *Progress in social psychology.* Hillsdale, N.J.: Erlbaum, 1977.

Tyler, T. R., & Folger, R. Distributional and procedural aspects of satisfaction with citizen-police encounters. *Basic and Applied Social Psychology*, 1980, *1*, 281–292.

Ugwuegbu, D. C. E. Racial and evidential factors in juror attribution of legal responsibility. *Journal of Experimental Social Psychology*, 1979, *15*, 133–146.

Ulrich, R. S. Natural versus urban scenes: Some psychophysiological effects. *Environment and Behavior*, 1981, *13*, 523–556.

Unger, R. K., Hilderbrand, M., & Madar, T. Physical attractiveness and assumptions about social deviance: Some sex-by-sex comparisons. *Personality and Social Psychology Bulletin*, 1982, *8*, 293–301.

U.S. Department of Commerce. *Social indicators, 1976: Selected data on social conditions and trends in the United States.* Washington, D.C.: U.S. Government Printing Office, 1977.

Uranowitz, S. W. Helping and self attributions: A field experiment. *Journal of Personality and Social Psychology*, 1975, *31*, 852–854.

Valins, S., & Baum, A. Residential group size, social interaction, and crowding. *Environment and Behavior*, 1973, *5*, 421–440.

Vanbeselaere, N. Mere repeated exposure and experimental stress as determiners of stimulus evaluations. *Motivation and Emotion*, 1980, *4*, 61–69.

Van Der Pligt, J., & Eiser, J. R. Actors' and observers' attributions, self-serving bias, and positivity bias. *European Journal of Social Psychology*, 1983, *13*, 95–104.

Van Egeren, L. E. Social interactions, communications, and the coronary-prone behavior pattern: A psychophysiological study. *Psychosomatic Medicine,* 1979, *41,* 2–18.

Van Liere, K. D., & Dunlap, R. E. Moral norms and environmental behavior: An application of Schwartz's norm-activation model to yard burning. *Journal of Applied Social Psychology,* 1978, *8,* 174–188.

van Wagenberg, D., Krasner, M., & Krasner, L. Children planning an ideal classroom: Environmental design in an elementary school. *Environment and Behavior,* 1981, *13,* 349–359.

Vecchio, R. P. A further test of leadership effects due to between-group variation and within-group variation. *Journal of Applied Psychology,* 1982, *67,* 200–208.

Veitch, R., & Griffitt, W. Good news, bad news: Affective and interpersonal effects. *Journal of Applied Social Psychology,* 1976, *6,* 69–75.

Vinokur, A., & Burnstein, E. Effects of partially shared persuasive arguments on group-induced shifts: A group problem-solving approach. *Journal of Personality and Social Psychology,* 1974, *29,* 305–315.

Vinokur, A., & Selzer, M. L. Desirable vs. undesirable life events: Their relationship to stress and mental disease. *Journal of Personality and Social Psychology,* 1975, *32,* 329–337.

Vinsel, A., Brown, B. B., Altman, I., & Foss, C. Privacy regulation, territorial displays, and effectiveness of individual functioning. *Journal of Personality and Social Psychology,* 1980, *39,* 1104–1115.

Von Eckardt, W. Toward more livable cities. *Time,* 1981, *118* (18), 108, 110.

Wachtler, J., & Counselman, E. When increasing liking for a communicator decreases opinion change: An attribution analysis of attractiveness. *Journal of Experimental Social Psychology,* 1981, *17,* 386–395.

Wack, J., & Rodin, J. Nursing homes for the aged: The human consequences of legislation-shaped environments. *Journal of Social Issues,* 1978, *34* (4), 6–21.

Wade, N. NASA bans sex from outer space. *Science,* 1977, *197,* 1163–1165.

Wagener, J. J., & Laird, J. D. The experimenter's foot-in-the-door: Self perception, body weight, and volunteering. *Personality and Social Psychology Bulletin,* 1980, *6,* 441–446.

Wagner, G., & Green, R. *Impotence: Physiological, psychological, and surgical diagnosis and treatment.* New York: Plenum, 1981.

Walden, T. A., & Forsyth, D. R. Close encounters of the stressful kind: Affective, physiological, and behavioral reactions to the experience of crowding. *Journal of Nonverbal Behavior,* 1981, *6,* 46–64.

Walker, J. W., & Borden, R. J. Sex, status, and the invasion of shared space. *Representative Research in Social Psychology,* 1976, *7,* 28–34.

Walkey, F. H., & Gilmour, D. R. Comparative evaluation of a videotaped measure of interpersonal distance. *Journal of Consulting and Clinical Psychology,* 1979, *47,* 575–580.

Wall, J. A., & Adams, J. S. Some variables affecting a constituent's evaluations of and behavior toward a boundary role occupant. *Organizational Behavior and Human Performance,* 1974, *11,* 290–308.

Wallach, M. A., & Wing, C. W. Is risk a value? *Journal of Personality and Social Psychology,* 1968, *9,* 101–106.

Wallis, C. Battling an elusive invader. *Time,* 1982, *120* (5), 68–69.

Walster (Hatfield), E., Aronson, V., Abrahams, D., & Rottman, L. Importance of physical attractiveness in dating behavior. *Journal of Personality and Social Psychology,* 1966, *4,* 508–516.

Walster (Hatfield), E., Walster, G. W., & Berscheid, E. *Equity: Theory and research.* Boston: Allyn and Bacon, 1978.

Walster (Hatfield), E., Walster, G. W., Piliavin, J., & Schmidt, L. "Playing hard-to-get": Understanding an elusive phenomenon. *Journal of Personality and Social Psychology,* 1973, *26,* 113–121.

Walster (Hatfield), E., Walster, G. W., & Traupmann, J. Equity and premarital sex. *Journal of Personality and Social Psychology,* 1978, *36,* 82–92.

Walton, R. E. How to counter alienation in the plant. *Harvard Business Review,* 1972, *50,* 70–81.

Warnick, D. H., & Sanders, G. S. The effects of group discussion on eyewitness accuracy. *Journal of Applied Social Psychology,* 1980, *10,* 249–259. (a)

Warnick, D. H., & Sanders, G. S. Why do eyewitnesses make so many mistakes? *Journal of Applied Social Psychology,* 1980, *10,* 362–366. (b)

Watson, R. I., Jr. Investigation into deindividuation using a cross-cultural survey technique. *Journal of Personality and Social Psychology,* 1973, *25,* 342–345.

Weary, G., & Arkin, R. M. Attributional self-presentation. In J. H. Harvey, W. J. Ickes, & R. F. Kidd (Eds.), *New directions in attribution research* (Vol. 3). Hillsdale, N.J.: Erlbaum, 1981.

Webb, E. J., Campbell, D. T., Schwartz, R. D., Sechrest, L., & Grove, J. B. *Nonreactive measures in the social sciences* (2nd ed.). Boston: Houghton Mifflin, 1981.

Weber, R. J., & Price, J. M. Knowledge of energy consumption. *Bulletin of the Psychonomic Society,* 1980, *15,* 267–268.

Weidner, G., Istvan, J., & Griffitt, W. Beauty in the eyes of the horny beholders. Paper presented at the meeting of the Midwestern Psychological Association, Chicago, May 1979.

Weidner, G., & Matthews, K. A. Reported physical symptoms elicited by unpredictable events and the Type A coronary-prone behavior pattern. *Journal of Personality and Social Psychology,* 1978, *36,* 1213–1220.

Weigel, R. H., Loomis, J. W., & Soja, M. J. Race relations on prime time television. *Journal of Personality and Social Psychology,* 1980, *39,* 884–893.

Weinberg, H. I., & Baron, R. S. The discreditable eyewitness. *Personality and Social Psychology Bulletin,* 1982, *8,* 60–67.

Weiner, B. A cognitive (attribution) emotion-action model of motivated behavior: An analysis of judgments of helpgiving. *Journal of Personality and Social Psychology,* 1980, *39,* 186–200.

Weiner, B. et al. Perceiving the causes of success and failure. In E. Jones et al. (Eds.), *Attribution: Perceiving the causes of behavior.* Morristown, N.J.: General Learning Press, 1972.

Weiner, N., Latané, B., & Pandey, J. Social loafing in the United States and India. Paper presented at the Joint Asian Meetings of the International Association for Cross-Cultural Psychology and the International Council of Psychologists, Taipei, Taiwan, August 1981.

Weis, D. L. Reactions of college women to their first coitus. *Medical Aspects of Human Sexuality,* 1983, *17* (2), 60CC, 60GG–60HH, 60LL.

Weiss, R. F., Buchanan, W., Alstatt, L., & Lombardo, J. P. Altruism is rewarding. *Science,* 1971, *171,* 1262–1263.

Weiten, W. The attraction-leniency effect in jury research: An examination of external validity. *Journal of Applied Social Psychology,* 1980, *10,* 340–347.

Wener, R. E., & Kaminoff, R. D. Improving environmental information: Effects of signs on perceived crowding and behavior. *Environment and Behavior,* 1983, *15,* 3–20.

Werner, C. M., Brown, B. B., & Damron, G. Territorial marking in a game arcade. *Journal of Personality and Social Psychology,* 1981, *41,* 1094–1104.

West, S. G., Whitney, G., & Schnedler, R. Helping a motorist in distress: The effects of sex, race, and neighborhood. *Journal of Personality and Social Psychology,* 1975, *31,* 691–698.

West, S. T., Gunn, S., and Chernicky, P. Ubiquitous Watergate: An attributional analysis. *Journal of Personality and Social Psychology,* 1975, *32,* 55–65.

Wetzel, C. G., & Insko, C. A. The similarity-attraction relationship: Is there an ideal one? *Journal of Experimental Social Psychology,* 1982, *18,* 253–276.

Wexley, K. N., & Pulakos, E. D. Sex effects on performance ratings in manager-subordinate dyads: A field study. *Journal of Applied Psychology,* 1982, *67,* 433–439.

Whalen, D. H., & Blanchard, F. A. Effects of photographic evidence on mock juror judgement. *Journal of Applied Social Psychology,* 1982, *12,* 30–41.

White, D. Pursuit of the ultimate aphrodisiac. *Psychology Today,* September 1981, pp. 9–10, 12.

White, G. L. Inducing jealousy: A power perspective. *Personality and Social Psychology Bulletin,* 1980, *6,* 222–227. (a)

White, G. L. Physical attractiveness and courtship progress. *Journal of Personality and Social Psychology,* 1980, *39,* 660–668. (b)

White, G. L. A model of romantic jealousy. *Motivation and Emotion,* 1981, *5,* 295–310. (a)

White, G. L. Some correlates of romantic jealousy. *Journal of Personality,* 1981, *49,* 129–146. (b)

White, J. W., & Gruber, K. J. Instigative aggression as a function of past experience and target characteristics. *Journal of Personality and Social Psychology,* 1982, *42,* 1069–1075.

White, L. A. Erotica and aggression: The influence of sexual arousal, positive affect, and negative affect on aggressive behavior. *Journal of Personality and Social Psychology,* 1979, *37,* 591–601.

Whobrey, L., Sales, B. D., & Elwork, A. Witness credibility law. In L. Bickman (Ed.), *Applied social psychology annual 2.* Beverly Hills, Calif.: Sage, 1981.

Wicklund, R. A. Objective self-awareness. In L. Berkowitz (Ed.), *Advances in experimental social psychology* (Vol. 8). New York: Academic Press, 1975.

Wicklund, R. A., & Brehm, J. W. *Perspectives on cognitive dissonance.* Hillsdale, N.J.: Erlbaum, 1976.

Wiggins, J. S. A psychological taxonomy of

trait-descriptive terms. The interpersonal domain. *Journal of Personality and Social Psychology,* 1978, *37,* 395–412.

Wiggins, J. S., & Holzmuller, N. Further evidence on androgyny and interpersonal flexibility. *Journal of Research in Personality,* 1983, in press.

Wiggins, J. S., Wiggins, N., & Conger, J. C. Correlates of heterosexual somatic preference. *Journal of Personality and Social Psychology,* 1968, *10,* 82–90.

Wilder, D. A. Perception of groups, size of opposition, and social influence. *Journal of Experimental Social Psychology,* 1977, *13,* 253–268.

Wilder, D. A., & Thompson, J. E. Intergroup contact with independent manipulations of in-group and out-group interaction. *Journal of Personality and Social Psychology,* 1980, *38,* 589–603.

Wilke, H., & Lanzetta, J. T. The obligation to help: Factors affecting response to help received. *European Journal of Social Psychology,* 1982, *12,* 315–319.

Williams, K., Harkins, S., & Latané, B. Identifiability as a deterrent to social loafing: Two cheering experiments. *Journal of Personality and Social Psychology,* 1981, *40,* 303–311.

Williams, K. B., & Williams, K. D. Social inhibition and asking for help: The effects of number, strength, and immediacy of potential help givers. *Journal of Personality and Social Psychology,* 1983, *44,* 67–77.

Williams, S., Ryckman, R. M., Gold, J. A., & Lenney, E. The effects of sensation seeking and misattribution of arousal on attraction toward similar or dissimilar strangers. *Journal of Research in Personality,* 1982, *16,* 217–226.

Williams, T. M., Zabrack, M. L., & Joy, L. A. The portrayal of aggression on North American television. *Journal of Applied Social Psychology,* 1982, *12,* 360–380.

Willis, F. N., Jr., & Hamm, H. K. The use of interpersonal touch in securing compliance. *Journal of Nonverbal Behavior,* 1980, *5,* 49–55.

Wills, G. Measuring the impact of erotica. *Psychology Today,* 1977, *11* (3), 30–31, 33–34, 74, 76.

Wilson, T. D., & Capitman, J. A. Effects of script availability on social behavior. *Personality and Social Psychology Bulletin,* 1982, *8,* 11–19.

Wilson, T. D., Hull, J. B., & Johnson, J. Awareness and self-perception: Verbal reports on internal states. *Journal of Personality and Social Psychology,* 1981, *40,* 53–71.

Wilson, T. D., & Linville, P. W. Improving the academic performance of college freshmen: Attribution therapy revisited. *Journal of Personality and Social Psychology,* 1982, *42,* 367–376.

Wilson, W. R. Feeling more than we can know: Exposure effects without learning. *Journal of Personality and Social Psychology,* 1979, *37,* 811–821.

Wimer, S., & Kelley, H. H. An investigation of the dimensions of causal attribution. *Journal of Personality and Social Psychology,* 1982, *43,* 1142–1162.

Winer, D. L., Bonner, T. O., Jr., Blaney, P. H., & Murray, E. J. Depression and social attraction. *Motivation and Emotion,* 1981, *5,* 153–166.

Winslow, C. N. A study of the extent of agreement between friends' opinions and their ability to estimate the opinions of each other. *Journal of Social Psychology,* 1937, *8,* 433–442.

Winter, R. *The smell book—scents, sex, and society.* New York: Lippincott, 1978.

Wishnoff, R. Modeling effects of explicit and nonexplicit sexual stimuli on the sexual anxiety and behavior of women. *Archives of Sexual Behavior,* 1978, *7,* 455–461.

Witkin, H. A., Mednick, S. A., Schulsinger, F., Bakkestrom, E., Christiansen, K. O., Goodenough, D. R., Philip, J., Rubin, D. B., & Stocking, M. Criminality in XYY and XXY men. *Science,* 1976, *196,* 547–555.

Wolchik, S. A., Beggs, V. E., Wincze, J. P., Sakheim, D. K., Barlow, D. H., & Mavissakalian, M. The effect of emotional arousal on subsequent sexual arousal in men. *Journal of Abnormal Psychology,* 1980, *89,* 595–598.

Wolf, S., & Latané, B. Majority and minority influence on restaurant preferences. *Journal of Personality and Social Psychology,* 1983, *45,* 282–292.

Wolfe, B. M., & Baron, R. A. Laboratory aggression related to aggression in naturalistic social situations: Effects of an aggressive model on the behavior of college student and prisoner observers. *Psychonomic Science,* 1971, *24,* 193–194.

Wolfle, L. M., & Robertshaw, D. Effects of college attendance on locus of control. *Journal of Personality and Social Psychology,* 1982, *43,* 802–810.

Womble, P., & Studebaker, S. Crowding in a national park campground: Katmai National Monument in Alaska. *Environment and Behavior,* 1981, *13,* 557–573.

Wood, W. Retrieval of attitude-relevant information from memory: Effects on susceptibility to persuasion and on intrinsic motivation. *Journal of Personality and Social Psychology,* 1982, *42,* 798–810.

Wood, W., & Eagly, A. H. Steps in the positive analysis of causal attributions and message comprehension. *Journal of Personality and Social Psychology,* 1981, *4,* 246–259.

Worchel, S. The effect of three types of arbitrary thwarting on the instigation to aggression. *Journal of Personality,* 1974, *42,* 301–318.

Worchel, S., Andreoli, V. A., & Folger, R. Intergroup cooperation and intergroup attraction: The effect of previous interaction and outcome of combined effort. *Journal of Experimental Social Psychology,* 1977, *13,* 131–140.

Worchel, S., & Brehm, J. W. Direct and implied social restoration of freedom. *Journal of Personality and Social Psychology,* 1971, *18,* 294–304.

Word, C. O., Zanna, M. P., & Cooper, J. The nonverbal mediation of self-fulfilling prophecies in interracial interaction. *Journal of Experimental Social Psychology,* 1974, *10,* 109–120.

Wortman, C. B., & Dunkel-Schetter, C. Interpersonal relationships and cancer: A theoretical analysis. *Journal of Social Issues,* 1979, *35* (1), 120–154.

Wortman, C. B., & Linsenmeier, J. A. W. Interpersonal attraction and techniques of ingratiation in organizational settings. In B. M. Staw and G. R. Salancik, *New directions in organizational behavior.* Chicago: St. Clair Press, 1977.

Wurtele, S. K., Roberts, M. C., & Leeper, J. D. Health beliefs and intentions: Predictors of return compliance in a tuberculosis detection drive. *Journal of Applied Social Psychology,* 1982, *12,* 128–136.

Wyer, R. S., Jr., & Gordon, S. E. The recall of information about persons and groups. *Journal of Experimental Social Psychology,* 1982, *18,* 128–164.

Yaffé, M., & Nelson, E. *The influence of pornography on behavior.* London: Academic Press, 1982.

Yagoda, B. How Hollywood manipulates film ratings. *Saturday Review,* 1980, *7* (12), 39–42.

Yandrell, B., & Insko, C. A. Attribution of attitudes to speakers and listeners under assigned-behavior conditions: Does behavior engulf the field? *Journal of Experimental Social Psychology,* 1977, *13,* 269–278.

Yarmey, A. D. *The psychology of eyewitness testimony.* New York: Free Press, 1979.

Yarmey, A. D., & Jones, H. P. T. Accuracy of memory of male and female eyewitnesses to a criminal assault and rape. *Bulletin of the Psychonomic Society,* 1983, *21,* 89–92.

Yarnold, P. R., & Grimm, L. G. Time urgency among coronary-prone individuals. *Journal of Abnormal Psychology,* 1982, *91,* 175–177.

Yates, B. T., & Mischel, W. Young children's preferred attentional strategies for delaying gratification. *Journal of Personality and Social Psychology,* 1979, *37,* 286–300.

Yinon, Y., & Bizman, A. Noise, success, and failure as determinants of helping behavior. *Personality and Social Psychology Bulletin,* 1980, *6,* 125–130.

Yinon, Y., Dovrat, M., & Avni, A. The reciprocity-arousing potential of the requester's occupation and helping behavior. *Journal of Applied Social Psychology,* 1981, *11,* 252–258.

Yinon, Y., Sharon, I., Gonen, Y., & Adam, R. Escape from responsibility and help in emergencies among persons alone or within groups. *European Journal of Social Psychology,* 1982, *12,* 301–305.

Young, J. E. Loneliness, depression, and cognitive therapy: Theory and application. In L. A. Peplau & D. Perlman, *Loneliness: A sourcebook of current theory, research, and therapy.* New York: Wiley, 1982.

Younger, J. C., Walker, L., & Arrowood, A. J. Post-decision dissonance at the fair. *Personality and Social Psychology Bulletin,* 1977, *3,* 284–287.

Yukl, G. Effects of the opponent's initial offer, concession magnitude, and concession frequency on bargaining behavior. *Journal of Personality and Social Psychology,* 1974, *30,* 323–335.

Zajonc, R. B. Social facilitation. *Science,* 1965, *149,* 269–274.

Zajonc, R. B. *Social psychology: An experimental approach.* Belmont, Calif.: Wadsworth, 1966.

Zajonc, R. B. Attitudinal effects of mere exposure. *Journal of Personality and Social Psychology Monograph Supplement,* 1968, *9,* 1–27.

Zajonc, R. B. Compresence. In P. Paulus (Ed.), *The psychology of group influence.* Hillsdale, N.J.: Erlbaum, 1980. (a)

Zajonc, R. B. Feeling and thinking: Preferences need no inferences. *American Psychologist,* 1980, *35,* 151–175. (b)

Zajonc, R. B., Heingartner, A., & Herman, E. M. Social enhancement and impairment of performance in the cockroach. *Journal of Personality and Social Psychology,* 1969, *13,* 83–92.

Zajonc, R. B., & Markus, H. Affect and cognition: The hard interface. Unpublished manuscript, University of Michigan, 1983.

Zajonc, R. B., Markus, H., & Wilson, W. R. Exposure effects and associative learning. *Journal of Experimental Social Psychology*, 1974, *10*, 248–263.

Zajonc, R. B., & Sales, S. M. Social facilitation of dominant and subordinate responses. *Journal of Experimental Social Psychology*, 1966, *2*, 160–168.

Zajonc, R. B., Shaver, P., Tavris, C., & Kreveld, D. V. Exposure, satiation, and stimulus discriminability. *Journal of Personality and Social Psychology*, 1972, *21*, 270–280.

Zehner, H. The secrets of sexual chemistry. *Cosmopolitan*, November 1981, pp. 250, 258–259, 340.

Zellner, M. Self-esteem, reception, and influenceability. *Journal of Personality and Social Psychology*, 1970, *15*, 87–93.

Zelnick, M., & Kantner, J. F. *Family Planning Perspectives*, 1980, *12*, 230–236.

Ziegler, M., & Reid, D. W. Correlates of locus of desired control in two samples of elderly persons: Community residents and hospitalized patients. *Journal of Consulting and Clinical Psychology*, 1979, *47*, 977–979.

Zillmann, D. Excitation transfer in communication-mediated aggressive behavior. *Journal of Experimental Social Psychology*, 1971, *7*, 419–434.

Zillmann, D. *Hostility and aggression*. Hillsdale, N.J.: Erlbaum, 1979.

Zillmann, D. Transfer of excitation in emotional behavior. In J. T. Cacioppo & R. E. Petty (Eds.), *Social psychophysiology*. New York: Guilford Press, 1983.

Zillmann, D. *Connections between sex and aggression*. Hillsdale, N.J.: Erlbaum, 1984, in press.

Zillmann, D., Baron, R. A., & Tamborini, R. The social costs of smoking: Effects of tobacco smoke on hostile behavior. *Journal of Applied Social Psychology*, 1981, *11*, 548–561.

Zillmann, D., & Bryant, J. Effects of massive exposure to pornography. In N. M. Malamuth & E. Donnerstein (Eds.), *Pornography and sexual aggression*. New York: Academic Press, 1983.

Zillmann, D., Bryant, J., & Carveth, R. A. The effect of erotica featuring sadomasochism and bestiality on motivated intermale aggression. *Personality and Social Psychology Bulletin*, 1981, *7*, 153–159.

Zillmann, D., Bryant, J., Comisky, P. W., & Medoff, N. J. Excitation and hedonic valence in the effect of erotica on motivated intermale aggression. *European Journal of Social Psychology*, 1981, *11*, 233–252.

Zillmann, D., & Cantor, J. R. Effect of timing of information about mitigating circumstances on emotional responses to provocation and retaliatory behavior. *Journal of Experimental Social Psychology*, 1976, *12*, 38–55.

Zillmann, D., Katcher, A. H., & Milavsky, B. Excitation transfer from physical exercise to subsequent aggressive behavior. *Journal of Experimental Social Psychology*, 1972, *8*, 247–259.

Zimbardo, P. G. The human choice: Individuation, reason, and order versus deindividuation—impulse, and chaos. In W. J. Arnold & D. Levine (Eds.), *Nebraska symposium on motivation, 1969*. Lincoln: University of Nebraska Press, 1970.

Zimbardo, P. G. *Shyness: What it is, what to do about it*. Reading, Mass.: Addison-Wesley, 1977.

Zimring, C. M. Stress and the designed environment. *Journal of Social Issues*, 1981, *37* (1), 145–171.

Zuckerman, M., Amidon, M. D., Bishop, S. E., & Pomerantz, S. D. Face and tone of voice in the communication of deception. *Journal of Personality and Social Psychology*, 1982, *43*, 347–357.

Zuckerman, M., DeFrank, R. S., Spiegel, N. H., & Larrance, D. T. Masculinity-femininity and encoding of nonverbal cues. *Journal of Personality and Social Psychology*, 1982, *42*, 548–556.

Zuckerman, M., Klorman, R., Larrance, D. T., & Spiegel, N. H. Facial, autonomic, and subjective components of emotion: The facial feedback hypothesis versus the externalizer-internalizer distinction. *Journal of Personality and Social Psychology*, 1981, *41*, 929–944.

Zuckerman, M., Schmitz, M., & Yosha, A. Effects of crowding in a student environment. *Journal of Applied Social Psychology*, 1977, *7*, 67–72.

Name Index

A

Abbey, A., 579
Abbott, A.R., 226
Abelson, R., 91
Abelson, R.P., 116
Abrahams, D., 222
Abramson, L.Y., 28, 509
Abramson, P.R., 585, 595, 598
Ace, G., 237
Ackerman, P., 300
Ackerman, P.L., 20, 225
Adam, R., 291, 293
Adams, C.A., 469
Adams, J.S., 264, 395
Adams, N., 103
Adelman, H.F., 73
Adorno, T.W., 184, 185, 534
Agosta, W.C., 575
Ahlering, R.F., 150
Aiello, J.R., 455, 457, 469, 470
Aiello, T.DeC., 455
Allen Guttmacher Institute, 483, 572, 601
Albany Times-Union (1981), 305
Albert, R.D., 336
Albin, R.S., 502
Aldag, R.J., 518
Alder, N.T., 575
Allen, A., 533
Allen, B.P., 134
Allen, J.G., 548
Allen, V.L., 251, 254, 255
Allgeier, A.R., 601
Allgeier, E.R., 572
Allman, L., 334
Alloy, L.B., 28, 509
Allport, F., 12
Allport, G.W., 533
Alpert, R., 201

Alsatt, L., 294
Altman, I., 461–463, 485, 486
Amidon, M.D., 41, 52, 53
Amoroso, D.M., 590
Andersen, S.M., 222
Anderson, A., 504
Anderson, C.A., 94, 474, 475
Anderson, D.B., 20, 225
Anderson, D.C., 475
Anderson, J., 588
Anderson, N.H., 114
Andreoli, V.A., 191
Anisko, J.J., 575
Antill, J.D., 203
APA Monitor (1980), 548
Apple, W., 41, 138
Archer, R.L., 299
Argyle, M., 42, 79
Arkin, R.M., 66, 68
Armogida, R.E., 548
Arms, R.L., 345
Aron, A.P., 236
Aronoff, J.R., 389
Arons, S., 588
Aronson, E., 158, 191, 500
Aronson, V., 222
Arrowood, A.J., 157
Asa, C.S., 577
Ascani, K., 269
Asch, S.E., 114, 250–252, 254
Asher, S.R., 542
Ashton, N.L., 457, 458
Asimov, I., 484
Associated Press (1976), 483
Associated Press (1981), 308
Augenstein, D.G.
Augenstein, J.S., 471
Aunis, A.B., 469
Auslander, N., 542, 543
Austin, W., 311, 397, 401, 496

Averill, J.R., 236
Avis, W.E., 224, 225
Avni, A., 302
Axelrod, R., 294
Azjen, I., 162

B

Babad, E.Y., 509
Back, K., 213, 214
Baer, R., 152
Bailey, S., 298
Baker, M.A., 472
Bakkestrom, E., 351
Ball, R.L., 349
Balling, J.D., 479
Baltes, M.M., 513
Bandura, A., 278, 329, 334, 338, 351
Banikiotes, P.G., 229
Barash, D.P., 328
Barden, R.C., 296
Barefoot, J.C., 460
Bargh, J.A., 94, 97, 99
Barkowitz, P., 178
Barlow, D.H., 587, 588
Barnhart, S.A., 578
Baron, R.A., 17, 28, 34, 266, 329, 333, 334, 337, 338, 343, 344, 349, 352, 353, 356, 359, 360, 362, 431, 459, 474, 514, 525, 577, 578
Baron, R.M., 469
Baron, R.S., 418, 419, 437, 438, 494
Barry, T., 476
Bar-Tal, D., 289, 300, 302, 557
Barton, E.M., 513
Barton, J., 506
Bar-Zohar, Y., 557
Basow, S.A., 203, 207

Bassett, R., 272
Batson, C.D., 269, 291, 295, 296, 298–300
Batten, P.G., 546
Baum, A., 469–471, 486, 504, 513
Baum, C.S., 470, 471
Baumann, D.J., 41, 296
Baumeister, R.F., 499
Baumrind, D., 28
Baxter, J.C., 80
Bayless, S., 492
Bayton, J.A., 180
Beaber, R.J., 138
Beach, L.R., 368
Beaman, A.L., 308–310, 426
Beane, W.E., 553
Beatty, P.A., 460
Beck, A.T., 544
Beck, J.G., 588
Beck, K.H., 505
Beck, P., 513
Beck, S.B., 224
Becker, F.D., 517
Becker, J.D., 591
Becker, L.J., 373, 375, 516, 517
Becker, M.A., 491, 554
Beckhouse, L., 441
Beggs, V.E., 587
Belgrave, F.Z., 222
Bell, A.P., 580
Bell, D., 476, 520
Bell, P.A., 337, 343, 473, 474, 486
Bellack, A.S., 360
Bem, D.J., 71, 72, 78, 533
Bem, S.L., 116, 199–201, 203, 222
Beninger, J.R., 517
Bennett, J.V., 513
Benton, A.A., 383
Ben-Veniste, R., 593
Berg, J.H., 546
Berger, C.J., 518
Berger, S.M., 419
Berkowitz, L., 28, 329, 333, 334, 338, 345–347, 596
Bernard, Y., 477
Berndt, T.J., 300
Berne, E., 343
Bernikow, L., 540
Bernstein, S., 201, 202, 349
Berrenberg, J.L., 516
Berscheid, E., 175, 212, 224, 226, 235, 395, 402, 578, 589
Bickman, L., 14, 31, 309, 490, 505
Bieber, I., 581
Biederman, M.F., 296, 298
Biggers, T., 480
Birch, K., 300
Birrell, P., 107
Birsky, J., 467
Bishop, S.E., 41, 52, 53
Bizman, A., 296
Black, J.B., 91

Black, J.S., 162
Black, T.E., 374
Blake, R., 191
Blanchard, F.A., 495
Blaney, P.H., 217
Blascovich, J., 380, 511
Blass, T., 532
Bleda, P.R., 476
Bleker, E.G., 559
Blosser, J.L., 296, 298
Blot, W.J., 475
Bluestone, B., 508
Blum, S.R., 513
Blumenthal, J.A., 552
Blochner, S., 225
Boffa, J., 513
Bohannon, W.E., 500
Bohm, L.C., 509
Boice, R., 458
Bois, J.L., 221
Bond, M.H., 373, 397
Bonner, T.O., Jr., 217
Bonsall, R.W., 575, 576
Boone, R., 229
Boorman, S.A., 319
Boothroyd, P., 236
Borden, R.J., 460
Bordens, K.S., 500
Borgida, E., 162
Bornewasser, M., 325
Bornstein, H.G., 479
Bornstein, M.H., 479
Borys, R., 176, 177
Bouska, M.L., 460
Bowen, D.V., 575
Bower, G.H., 91, 99, 353
Bowers, R.J., 438
Bowman, T.F., 478, 479
Bracey, D.H., 502
Brady, J.J., Jr., 419
Brauer, D.V., 229
Bray, R.M., 191, 262, 263, 417
Brehm, J.W., 151, 152, 166
Brehm, S.S., 548, 553
Brennan, T., 542, 543
Brenner, M.H., 508
Brewer, M.B., 89
Brickman, P., 373, 375
Bridgeman, D.L., 191
Brief, A.P., 518
Brigham, J.C., 102, 178, 179, 222, 493, 494
Brinberg, D., 368, 369
Bringle, R.G., 239
Brinton, L.A., 475
Britell, J.K., 314
Brock, T.C., 144, 355
Brockner, J., 215, 382
Brodt, S.E., 75, 544
Brody, J.E., 548–551
Broll, L., 302
Brooks, D.K., 462
Brothen, T., 224

Brown, B.B., 462, 463
Brown, B.R., 387
Brown, C., 588
Brown, C.E., 460, 461
Brown, E.R., 294
Brown, J.L., 294
Brown, M., 590
Brown, M.A., 517
Brown, P.L., 302
Brown, R., 335
Brown, R.A., 539
Brown, S.D., 294
Brownstein, P.J., 232
Bruggink, J.B., 437
Brunault, M.A., 456
Brundage, L.E., 229
Brunson, B.I., 552, 553
Brunton, M., 351
Bruun, S.E., 422
Bryant, J., 28, 333, 343–346, 360, 597
Bryant, S.L., 60
Buchanan, W., 294
Buck, R., 42, 52, 53, 79
Buck, R.W., 48
Buckhout, R., 492, 493, 525
Buckley, T., 300
Bunker, B.B., 260
Burger, J.M., 272, 273
Burgess, J.W., 456
Burgess, K.L., 213
Burgess, M., 355
Burgess, R.L., 516
Burggraf, L., 588
Burnam, M.A., 509, 551
Burns, L.B., 398, 400
Burnstein, E., 115, 118, 119, 434, 438
Burt, M.R., 502
Bush, M., 266, 270
Buss, A.H., 333, 334, 349, 424
Bussey, K., 199
Butterfield, F., 567
Buunk, B., 239
Byers, J.A., 575
Byrne, D., 134, 185, 214, 217, 226–228, 233, 236, 264, 290, 293, 316, 483, 501, 535, 536, 549, 554, 561, 578, 579, 583, 585–587, 595, 599–601, 604

C

Cacioppo, J.T., 127, 142, 143, 146, 147, 152, 153, 166, 228, 272
Cafferty, T.P., 491
Caldwell, D.F., 74
Calesnick, L.E., 469, 470
Calhoun, J.B., 465
Callero, P.L., 294
Camino, L., 338
Campagna, A.G., 583
Campbell, B., 162

Campbell, D.J., 518
Campbell, D.T., 134
Campbell, N.A., 162
Cann, A., 269, 270
Cannon, L.K., 472
Canter, D., 454, 477, 480
Cantor, J.R., 357
Caplow, T., 214
Capon, N., 491
Carifio, M.S., 456
Carli, L., 258
Carli, L.C., 419
Carlinsky, D., 588
Carlsmith, J.M., 48, 474
Carlsmith, L.M., 156
Carlston, D.E., 68, 70, 92, 115
Carmen, B., 52
Carnevale, P.J.D., 387
Carr, E.G., 356
Carter, W.B. 368
Cartwright-Smith, J., 46
Carver, C.S., 66, 70, 75, 100, 101,
    291–293, 302, 348, 398,
    419, 424, 430, 548, 553, 554
Carveth, R.A., 28, 345
Cary, M.S., 249
Case, T., 499, 501
Cash, T.F., 226, 229
Castell, P., 368, 369
Castle, S., 373, 375
Catalan, J., 269
Catlin, E.C., 501
Cattell, R.B., 591
Caulkins, R.S., 20, 225
Cavoukian, A., 467, 497
CEN SENIC Planning Committee,
    513
Chance, J.E., 556
Chapin, J., 598
Chapko, M.K., 476
Chassin, L., 505, 506
Check, J.V.P., 346
Cheney, A.B., 559
Chernick, L., 533
Chernicky, P., 28
Cherry, F., 134, 185
Chester, N.L., 510
Cheyne, J.A., 460
Chilstrom, J.T., 262, 263
Christensen, D., 174, 175
Christensen, H.T., 567
Christiansen, K.O., 351
Christie, R., 392, 393, 407
Christy, P.R., 342
Churchman, A., 462
Cialdini, R.B., 41, 152, 236, 269,
    272, 296
Cimbalo, R.S., 237
Clarke, M., 117, 118, 296
Clark, M.S., 116, 296, 302
Clark, R., 300
Clark, R.D., III, 295, 319
Clark, R.N., 516

Clayton, J.P., 600
Cleary, P.D., 548
Clore, G.L., 50, 191, 217, 299
Coale, A.J., 484
Cochran, P.J., 296, 298
Cochran, S.T., 329, 345
Cohen, C.E., 96
Cohen, J.B., 470
Cohen, J.D., 548
Cohen, M.E., 355
Cohen, R.L., 394, 395, 397, 403,
    408
Cohen, S., 471, 472
Cohn, N.B., 232
Coke, J.S., 291, 299
Colamosca, J.V., 290
Coleman, A.E., 553
Coleman, R.M., 520, 521
Coles, M.G.H., 236
Collett, P., 49
Collins, B.E., 72
Collins, C., 553
Comfort, J.C., 501
Commission on Obscenity and Por-
    nography (1970), 593
Condry, J., 198
Conger, J.C., 225, 278
Conner, R., 306, 307
Connolley, E.S., 254
Conroy, J. III, 464
Constantinople, A., 199
Contrada, R., 553
Converse, J., Jr., 157
Cook, M., 579, 604
Cook, S.W., 516
Cook, T.D., 139
Cooley, S.J., 441
Coombs, L.C., 519
Cooper, A.J., 575
Cooper, H.M., 258, 557
Cooper, J., 151, 157, 158, 160, 175
Cooper, M., 552
Corah, N.L., 513
Corballis, M.C., 146
Corliss, R., 579
Corty, E., 505, 506
Costa, F., 571
Costantini, E., 442, 443
Cottrell, N.B., 416, 417
Counselman, E., 137
Covey, M.K., 335
Cowan, C.L., 296
Cowen, E.L., 459
Cox, L., 223
Cox, V.C., 465
Coyne, J.C., 217
Cozby, P., 469
Craig, K.D., 278
Craik, K.H., 442, 443, 454
Cramer, C.C., 229
Crana, W.D., 306
Crandall, V.C., 556, 557
Crane, M., 200–202

Crane, W.D., 163, 164
Crews, D., 575
Critchlow, B., 160, 161
Crocker, J., 107
Cronbach, L.J., 537
Crosby, F.J., 404
Cross, H.J., 599
Crouse, B.B., 219
Crowne, D.P., 557
Croyle, R., 160
Crutchfield, R.A., 252, 253, 256,
    282
Cummings, L.L., 518
Cunningham, J.D., 203, 225, 232
Cunningham, M.R., 266, 294, 296
Curran, J.P., 222, 544, 570
Curry, W., 579
Cutrona, C.E., 540, 541, 543
Cvetkovich, G., 572
Czeisler, C.A., 520, 521

D

Dabbs, J.M., 299, 455
Daher, D.M., 229
Damron, G., 462
Daniel, H.D., 30
Daniels, R.A., 294
Darby, B.L., 269
Darley, J.M., 261, 289, 290, 295,
    305, 499, 516, 517
Darley, J.McC., 517
Davidson, E.S., 340, 362
Davidson, W.S., 356
Davis, A., 387
Davis, D., 229, 437
Davis, G.E., 469, 470
Davis, H., 509
Davis, J.D., 226, 579
Davis, J.H., 429, 449, 502
Davis, K.E., 55, 56, 63, 236
Davis, M.H., 299
Davis, R.W., 335, 358
Davis, W.L., 556
Davidson, J., Jr., 152, 553
Dawes, D.M., 376
Dayson, K., 552
Deaux, K., 193
de Carufel, A., 233
Deci, E.L., 72, 283
DeGregorio, E., 66, 553, 554
DeJong, W., 20, 266, 306
Dellinger, R.W., 472
Demerest, M., 480
Dembroski, T.M., 141, 547, 561
Dempsey, C.B., 268
Dengerink, H.A., 334, 335
Deni, R., 219
DeNisi, A.S., 196, 444
DePaulo, B.M., 229, 302
Derlega, V.J., 226, 229, 319
Dermer, M., 148, 589
DeSoto, C., 533
De Soto, C.B., 229

de Tocqueville, A., 540
Deutsch, M., 251, 387
De Young, G.E., 591
Diamond, E., 588, 589
Diamond, W.D., 439
Diaz-Loving, R., 299
Diehl, M., 256, 257
Diener, E., 424–428, 449, 537
Dienstbier, R.A., 314, 315
Dill, C.A., 506
Diller, L., 513
DiMatteo, M.R., 50, 51
Dion, K.K., 222, 226, 235, 578, 579
Dishman, R.K., 505
DiTecco, D., 505
Ditzian, J.L., 294
Dobrzynski, M., 514
Doherty, W.J., 559
Dollard, J., 331
Dollinger, S.J., 229
Donnell, S.M., 197
Donnenwerth, G.V., 368
Donnerstein, E., 28, 41, 332, 333,
      337, 346, 347, 356, 359,
      362, 363, 472, 593, 604
Donnerstein, M., 337, 356
Donovan, D.M., 538, 539
Donovan, J.E., 571
Doob, A.N., 497
Doob, L., 331
Dorfman, D.D., 150
Doty, R.L., 576
Dougherty, L.M., 44
Dovidio, J.F., 173, 295, 319
Dovrat, M., 302
Dow, D.D., 294
Downey, L., 571
Downing, L.L., 426
Drabman, R.S., 340
Drachman, D., 233
Dreilinger, E.A., 492
Driscoll, R., 236
Druckman, D., 80
Drukman, O., 289, 302
Dryer, A., 53
Dubé-Simard, L., 405
Duck, S., 34, 213, 241, 243
Dull, V., 89
Duncan, B.D., 300
Duncan, S.W., 296
Dunkel-Schetter, C., 511
Dunlap, R.E., 516
Dunn, A.J., 146
Dunnette, H.D., 400
Dutton, D.G., 176, 236
Duvall, S., 297
Dyck, R., 336
Dyer, M.A., 20, 225
Dyer, S., 198

E

Eagly, A.H., 126, 139, 140, 193,
      258, 259

Earley, P.R., 437
Earn, B.M., 557, 558
Easterlin, R.A., 483
Ebbesen, E.B., 92, 214, 438, 458
Ebbesen, E.G., 355
Eberly, B.W., 316, 549
Eberly, C.C., 316, 549
Edgerton, R.B., 462
Edmunds, M., 601
Edney, J.J., 462–464
Edwards, J.D., 505
Efran, M.G., 460, 499
Ehret, C., 521
Eidelson, R., 220
Eilenfield, V.C., 223, 226
Eisen, S.V., 65
Eisenberg, N., 319
Eisenberger, R., 316
Eisenman, R., 583
Eiser, J., 66
Eiser, J.R., 507, 525
Ekman, P., 42–44, 49
Elderton, E.M., 227
Elkes, R., 269, 270
Ellis, P., 480
Ellis, S., 229
Ellison, C.W., 546
Ellison, K.W., 492, 525
Ellsworth, P., 302
Ellsworth, P.C., 48
Elting, E., 553
Elverum, J., 553
Elwork, A., 494
Embree, M.C., 329, 345
Endelman, J.R., 230, 231
Enzle, M.E., 336, 375
Epstein, J., 456
Epstein, M., 219
Epstein, R., 536
Epstein, S., 532
Epstein, Y.M., 457, 468–470, 509
Erber, R., 99
Erkut, S., 299
Eron, L.D., 339, 340
Ervin, C.R., 227, 578
Espe, H., 480
Essock-Vitale, S.M., 577
Evans, D.E., 294
Evans, G.W., 454, 471, 472, 476
Evans, M., 96
Evans, M.C., 214
Evans, R.I., 504, 506, 511
Evensen, J., 464
Ezrachi, O., 513

F

Faletti, M.V., 511
Faling, V., 237
Falk, J.H., 479
Faraone, S.V., 515
Farquhar, J.W., 548
Faucheux, C., 262, 263

Fazio, R.H., 72, 73, 127, 129, 130,
      151, 157, 159, 160, 261,
      517, 552
Feen, R.H., 482
Fehr, R.S., 74
Feinberg, R.A., 229
Feingold, J., 343
Feinleib, M., 547, 561
Feldman, M.P., 580
Feldman, M.S., 500
Feldman, R.S., 44, 53
Feldman, S., 224
Felipe, N.J., 458
Felman, Y.M., 573
Fenton, M., 152
Ferguson, G., 462
Ferguson, T.J., 58
Feshbach, S., 340, 343
Festinger, L., 13, 151, 156, 213,
      214
Festinger, L.A., 260
Fiedler, F.E., 444–447, 449
Field, F.H., 575
Figler, M.H., 464
Finch, W.H., 20
Findley, M.J., 557
Fine, M., 490, 525
Finkelman, J., 553
Firestone, I.J., 290
Fisch, R., 30
Fischer, J.D., 486
Fish, B., 221
Fishbaugh, L., 258
Fishbein, M., 162, 505
Fisher, C.D., 518
Fisher, E.B., Jr., 548
Fisher, J.D., 302–304, 470, 471
Fisher, R.J., 490
Fisher, W.A., 579, 595, 599–601,
      604
Fiske, S.T., 14, 60, 65, 73, 80, 87–
      89, 91, 99, 101, 114–116,
      121, 171
Fitzgerald, H.E., 225
Fitzpatrick, M., 476
Flacks, R., 253
Fleming, I., 27
Fleming, R., 469
Flessas, A., 549
Foa, E.B., 368
Foa, U.G., 368
Fodor, E.M., 441, 442
Folger, R., 73, 176, 177, 191, 404,
      405, 502
Folkes, V.A., 222, 233, 238
Follingstad, D.R., 598
Foltz, D., 491
Fong, G.T., 496
Fontana, A.M., 501
Ford, K., 604
Ford, M., 576
Forest, D., 296
Forman, R., 214

Forsyth, D.R., 157, 253, 282, 449, 468
Foss, C., 462, 463
Foss, R.D., 268, 432
Foushee, H.C., 299
Fowler, F.J., Jr., 502
Fox, J., 377
Frances, R., 518
Franck, K.A., 480
Frankel, M., 496
Frankenhaeuser, M., 472
Fraser, S.C., 265, 266, 426, 427
Fraumeni, J.F., Jr., 475
Frautschi, N.M., 229
Fredrickson, C., 478
Freedenberg, T.G., 464
Freedman, D.G., 225
Freedman, J.F., 516
Freedman, J.L., 265, 266, 465, 467
Freeman, H.E., 513
Freeman, J.A., 472, 541, 546
Frenkel-Brunswick, E., 184, 185, 534
Freud, S., 298, 319, 327, 328, 343, 362
Frey, J., 476
Friedenbergs, I., 513
Friedland, N., 313
Friedman, H.S., 50, 51, 512
Friedman, L.N., 471
Friedman, M., 547
Friesen, W.V., 42, 43
Frieze, I.H., 192
Frodi, A., 349
Fromkin, H.L., 230, 231, 243, 355
Fuguitt, G.V., 478
Fuhr, R., 586
Fulcher, R., 490
Fulero, S., 96, 107
Funder, D.C., 532
Furman, W., 279
Furnham, A., 79

G

Gaertner, S.L., 173, 295, 319
Gaes, G.G., 134
Gallup, G., 313, 314, 316
Gallup, G.G., Jr., 580
Gange, J.J., 416
Ganzer, V.J., 278
Gara, M., 12
Garber, J., 296
Garcia, J.E., 446
Garcia, L., 536
Garcia, R., 419
Garland, H., 387, 441
Garner, B., 581
Garstka, W.R., 575
Garwood, S.G., 223
Gastorf, J.W., 549, 553
Gatchel, R.J., 469, 509
Gebhard, P.H., 569

Geen, R.G., 41, 280, 332, 334, 335, 338, 340, 355, 362, 416, 419
Geer, J.H., 583, 585, 586
Geffner, R., 191
Geis, B., 601, 602
Geis, F.L., 392–394, 407
Geis, G., 306, 307
Gelfand, D.M., 299, 309, 342
Geller, D.M., 233
Geller, E.S., 516
Gelman, R., 229
Gentry, W.D., 334, 504
Gerard, H.B., 158, 251, 254
Gergen, K.J., 302, 373, 393
Gerrard, M., 595, 599, 601, 602
Gershoni, R., 229
Gerson, A.C., 541
Gescheider, G.A., 501
Geva, N., 115
Gibbons, F.X., 75, 100, 297, 398, 400, 599
Gibson, R.H., 192
Gilbert, S.J., 277
Gillen, B., 223
Gilliland, M.A., 548
Gillis, A.R., 465
Gillis, J.S., 224, 225
Gillis, R., 66
Gillmore, M.R., 512
Gilmore, R., 439
Gilmour, D.R., 456
Gilmour, R., 34, 213, 243
Ginsburg, G.P., 380
Giuliani, G.A., 478, 479
Glass, D.C., 348, 471, 548, 550, 551, 553
Gleason, J.M., 66
Glenn, N.D., 569, 570
Gochman, I.R., 469
Goethals, G.R., 157, 261, 437
Goethals, G.T., 64
Gold, J.A., 228, 230
Goldband, S., 553
Goldfoot, D.A., 577
Goldstein, A.P., 356
Goldstein, J.H., 335, 355, 358
Goldstein, M.J., 593
Gollwitzer, P.M., 299
Gonen, Y., 291, 293
Gonzalez-Intal, A.M., 404
Good, S., 556
Goode, E., 581
Goodenough, D.R., 351
Gooding, K.M., 575
Goodman, G.S., 494
Goodstein, L., 233
Goodwin, M., 575
Gordon, S., 588
Gordon, S.E., 92, 102
Gordon, W.A., 513
Gormley, F.P., 469
Gormly, A.V., 227, 228
Gormly, J., 313, 317, 533

Gormly, J.B., 227
Gorsky, J., 316, 549
Gosselin, C., 582
Gossop, M., 505
Goswick, R.A., 472, 541, 546
Gotay, C.C., 302, 381, 382, 553
Gotestam, K.G., 278
Gottesdiener, A., 477
Gottesman, D., 511
Gottlieb, A., 306
Gottlieb, J., 293
Gottman, J., 541
Gouaux, C., 217
Gould, R., 65
Gould, R.J., 232
Graen, G., 441
Graham, J.A., 79
Granberg, D., 228
Grasley, D., 600
Graves, J.K., 501
Gray, R.A., 299
Graz, J.L., 225
Graziano, W., 224
Graziano, W.G., 173
Green, R., 580, 583
Green, S.K., 309
Greenbaum, P., 48
Greenbaum, P.E., 463
Greenbaum, S.D., 463
Greenberg, A., 336
Greenberg, J., 66, 67, 176, 177, 394, 395, 397–400, 403, 408, 430, 495
Greenberg, M.S., 31, 309, 492
Greenberger, E., 511
Greendlinger, V., 316, 549
Green, D., 72
Grether, J., 299
Grev, R., 296
Griffen, L.M., 469
Griffitt, W., 217, 227, 236, 469, 473, 536, 582, 589, 590, 595
Grimm, L.G., 549
Grisso, T., 492
Groner, N., 469
Gross, A.E., 27, 302
Grote, B., 572
Groth, A.N., 361
Grove, J.B., 134
Grube, J.W., 230
Gruber, K.J., 335
Gruder, C.L., 139, 293
Grumet, J.F., 64
Grusec, J.E., 294
Grush, J.E., 150, 215
Grzelak, J., 319
Guile, M.N., 458
Guimond, S., 405
Gully, K.J., 334
Gundlach, R.H., 581
Gunn, L.K., 240
Gunn, S., 28
Guthrie, R.D., 225

Guthrie, T.J., 506
Gutierres, S.E., 225
Gutkin, D., 300
Gutmann, M., 548
Guyer, M., 377
Gyllenhammer, P.G., 518

H

Haber, L., 581
Hage, J.N., 471
Hakel, M.D., 48
Halal, M., 117, 118
Haley, R.W., 513
Hall, E.T., 455, 457, 485, 486
Hall, J., 197
Hall, J.A., 203
Hall, J.V., 148
Halpern, P.L., 471
Hamburg, D.A., 504
Hamill, R., 108, 109
Hamilton, D.L., 90, 92, 102, 103, 114
Hamilton, P.A., 216, 222
Hamilton, T.P., 390
Hamilton, V.L., 280
Hamilton, W.D., 294
Hamm, H.K., 459
Hammen, C., 510
Hammersmith, S.K., 580
Haney, T., 552
Hannson, R.C., 223
Hansen, R.D., 59, 375
Hansford, E.A., 375
Hansson, R.O., 546
Hare, H., 294
Hargis, K., 296
Harkins, S.G., 420–422
Harmon, D.L., 501
Harper, D.C., 509
Harrel, W.A., 498
Harries, K.D., 475
Harris, J.R., 553
Harris, M., 308, 314, 316
Harris, M.B., 225, 335
Harris, R.J., 225, 395
Harris, R.T., 576
Harrison, B., 508
Harrison, C.L., 302
Harry, J., 580
Hart, H., 266
Hartman, J.J., 593
Hartmann, D.P., 299, 309, 342
Hartup, W., 279
Harvey, J., 486
Harvey, J.H., 41, 80
Harvey, J.M., 99, 559
Harvey, M.D., 336
Harvey, O.J., 182
Haskins, C.P., 575
Hassett, J., 311–313
Hastie, R., 14, 88, 92, 96, 106, 432
Hastorf, A., 121

Hatch, J.P., 585
Hatfield, E., 213, 235, 237, 243
Hathaway, S.R., 531
Hatvany, N., 494
Haynes, S., 547
Haynes, S.G., 561
Healy, J.M., Jr., 510
Heath, M., 221
Heaton, T.B., 478
Heberlein, T.A., 162
Hechinger, F.M., 314
Hecker, M.R., 576
Heiby, E., 591
Heider, F., 54, 204
Heilbroner, R., 484
Heingartner, A., 148, 417
Heisler, G., 314, 316, 317
Helmreich, R.L., 192, 203, 553
Hemstone, M., 183
Hendee, J.C., 516
Henderson, A.H., 506
Hendrick, C., 311, 511
Henley, N.M., 52
Hennigan, K.M., 139
Hensley, W.E., 302
Hepburn, C., 183
Herman, C.P., 84, 85, 166
Herman, D., 335, 358
Herman, E.M., 417
Hermann, T., 509
Herr, P.M., 127, 129
Herring, R.D., 515
Hersen, M., 360
Herskovitz, L., 571
Herzog, T.R., 479
Heshka, S., 457, 465
Hesley, J.W., 65, 533
Heslin, R., 144
Hibbard, M., 513
Hicks, R.A., 548
Higbee, K.L., 141, 374
Higgins, E.T., 60, 84, 85, 104, 105, 166
Hildebrandt, K.A., 225
Hilderbrand, M., 223
Hilgard, E.R., 353
Hill, C.T., 229, 237, 241, 512
Hill, P.C., 506
Hillery, J.M., 417
Hilton, W.F., 553
Hilltrop, J.M., 391
Himmelfarb, S., 126, 140, 306
Hinde, R.A., 213
Hinkle, S., 152
Hobbs, S.A., 546
Hochreich, D.J., 555
Hockenbury, D., 546
Hodge, G.K., 557
Hoffman, L.R., 441
Hoffman, M., 580
Hoffman, M.L., 294, 297
Hofman, J.E., 229
Hogan, R., 312, 533

Hokanson, J.E., 355
Holahan, C.J., 511
Holding, D.H., 472
Hollander, E.P., 262, 263, 441
Hollander, S., 226
Hölldobler, B., 461, 575
Holzmuller, N., 203
Hong, G.K., 469
Hood, W.E., 182
Hoon, E., 587
Hoon, P., 587
Hoople, H., 460
Horn, J., 300
Horn, N., 296
Horner, M., 198
Horowitz, I.A., 500
Horton, R.W., 340
Horvath, T., 224, 225
Hotch, D.F., 505
Houlden, P., 456, 503
Houston, B.K., 553
Hovland, C.I., 139
Howard, J., 107
Howard, J.L., 596, 597
Howard, M., 224
Howard, W., 306
Huebner, R.R., 44
Huesmann, L.R., 339, 340
Huggins, G.R., 576
Hulin, C.L., 518
Hull, J.B., 72
Hull, J.G., 61
Humphries, C., 553
Humphries, S.A., 349, 350
Hunt, M., 569, 571
Hunt, P.J., 417
Hunt, R.G., 515, 518
Huston, T.L., 213, 306, 307
Hwang, W.T., 567

I

Ibrahim, Y.M., 484
Ickes, W., 505
Ilgen, D.R., 192, 518
Imada, A.S., 48
Imai-Marquez, J., 595, 598
Infantino, A., 236
Innes, J.M., 417, 426, 427
Insko, C.A., 58, 64, 180, 181, 230, 233, 439
Instone, D., 260
Isaacs, S.L., 486
Isecke, W., 553
Isen, A.M., 117, 118, 121, 296
Ishii, S., 302
Istvan, J., 236, 582, 589, 590
Itkin, S., 50
Itkin, S.M., 191
Itzhak, S.B., 302
Ivins, B., 417
Izard, C., 42, 44, 45
Izzett, R.R., 500

J

Jackson, J.M., 289
Jacobs, P.A., 351
Jacobs, S.V., 476
Jacobson, R.S., 301
Jacquette, D.S., 299
Jaffe, Y., 343
Jakibchuk, Z., 278, 279
James, W., 531
Janda, L.H., 578
Janis, I.L., 139, 511–513
Janoff-Bulman, R., 513
Jarvik, L.F., 351
Jaspars, J., 183
Jazwinski, C., 238
Jeaw-mei, C., 129, 130, 159
Jellison, J.M., 226, 437
Jenkins, C.D., 546, 549, 550
Jensen, C., 107
Jensen, N.F., 482
Jessor, L., 571
Jessor, R., 571
Johnson, B.L., 556
Johnson, C.D., 313, 317
Johnson, D., 262, 263
Johnson, G.A., 236
Johnson, J., 72
Johnson, J.A., 312
Johnson, K.G., 289
Johnson, M., 552
Johnson, P.B., 192
Johnson, R.D., 426
Johnson, V.E., 585, 603
Johnston, S., 66
Jones, C.R., 104
Jones, E.E., 55, 56, 63–65, 133, 186, 264
Jones, H.P.T., 493
Jones, J.W., 312
Jones, W.H., 223, 472, 541, 546
Jordan-Edney, N.L., 462
Jorgensen, R.S., 553
Jorgenson, D.O., 400
Josephson, W., 567
Joy, L.A., 341
Judd, C.M., 136, 506
Julian, J.W., 441
Jung, J., 34
Jurow, G.L., 501

K

Kabatoff, R.A., 289
Kagitcibasi, C., 536
Kahle, L.R., 314, 315
Kahn, M.L., 229, 232
Kahn, R.L., 518
Kahneman, D., 108, 110
Kaiser, D.L., 595
Kalb, L.S., 196, 522
Kalb, D.F., 312
Kalle, R.J., 134
Kaminoff, R.D., 470

Kandel, D.B., 229
Kannel, W., 547
Kant, H.S., 593
Kantner, J.F., 601, 604
Kantola, S.J., 162
Kaplan, J., 502
Kaplan, M.F., 115, 500
Kaplan, R., 479
Kaplan, S., 479
Kaplan, V., 223
Karabenick, S., 221
Karlin, R.A., 469
Kassin, S.M., 496, 497
Katcher, A.H., 343
Katkin, E.S., 551
Katkovsky, W., 556
Katz, L.B., 102, 103
Katz, P.A., 207
Katzell, R.A., 515
Kaufman, M.T., 235
Kawash, G.F., 591
Kaye, H.E., 581
Kayra-Stuart, F., 226
Kazdin, A.E., 360
Keane, S.P., 278
Kearney, K.A., 230
Keating, J.P., 469
Kehoe, K., 553
Kelem, R., 426
Keller, K., 299
Kelley, H.H., 55, 57–63, 139, 237, 368, 387, 388
Kelley, K., 221, 222, 290, 293, 316, 465, 468, 535, 549, 561, 579, 583, 585, 597, 601
Kelley, S., 471, 472
Kelman, 27
Kendzierski, D., 159, 162
Kenney, D.A., 99
Kenny, C., 477
Kenrick, D.T., 41, 225, 236, 296, 533
Kent, G.G., 226
Kepner, C.R., 356
Kerber, K.W., 236
Kernis, M.H., 223, 225, 226
Kerr, N.L., 422, 429, 431–433, 449, 500
Kersting, R.C., 437
Ketcher, C.M., 342
Keverne, E.B., 575, 576
Keys, A., 546
Kidd, R.F., 417
Kiesler, C.A., 72, 137
Kiesler, S.B., 137
Kilham, W., 276, 280
Kilmann, P.R., 556
Kim, Y., 482
Kinder, D.R., 116
King, G.A., 104, 105
King, M., 228
Kinsey, A., 569, 580
Kinsley, M., 491

Kinzel, A.S., 456
Kirker, W.S., 91
Kirkevold, B.C., 312
Kirkland, K.D., 229
Kirsch, K., 266, 270
Kjos, G.L., 214
Klapper, J.T., 338
Kleck, R.E., 46
Klein, D., 511
Klein, K., 511
Kleinhesselink, R.R., 230
Kleinke, C.L., 48, 225, 229, 232, 579
Klentz, B., 308–310
Kleugel, J.R., 116
Klodin, V., 351
Klorman, R., 46, 47
Knapp, M.L., 49
Knight, G.P., 229
Knight, J., 148
Knowles, E.S., 457–459
Knowlton, W.A., Jr., 522
Knox, R.E., 434
Koenig, K., 253
Kohl, J., 266
Kohlberg, L., 298, 319
Komorita, S.S., 377–379, 385, 386
Konečni, V.J., 214, 355, 458, 472
Korda, M., 224
Kornhaber, R.C., 278
Krakoff, L.R., 553
Kramer, B., 484
Kramer, M., 555
Krantz, D.S., 471, 472, 513
Krasner, L., 517
Krasner, M., 517
Krauss, R.B., 138
Krauss, R.M., 41, 387, 516
Kravitz, D.A., 385
Kremer, J.F., 356–358
Kreveld, D.V., 150
Krosnick, J.A., 136, 506
Krulewitz, J.E., 228
Krupat, E., 282, 477
Kuhlman, D.M., 374
Kuhn, D., 491
Kuiper, N.A., 91
Kulik, J.A., 335
Kumar, P.A., 96
Kupferberg, S., 519
Kuralt, C., 217
Kutchinsky, 593

L

LaFong, C., 48
LaFrance, M., 52
Laird, J.D., 117, 118, 266
Lake, R.A., 176
Lamar, R., 575
Lamberth, J., 227, 578, 583
Lamm, H., 434
La Morto-Corse, A.M., 302

Landers, A., 237
Landy, D., 500
Lang, E., 382
Langer, E., 513
Langer, E.J., 48, 469, 513
Lanni, J.C., 464
Lanzetta, J.T., 46, 302
LaPiere, R.T., 159
Lapworth, C.W., 377–379, 385, 386
Larrance, D.T., 46, 47
Lasater, T.M., 141
Latané, B., 263, 289, 290, 292, 293, 299, 395, 420–422
Lavrakas, P.J., 224
Lau, R.R., 66
Lau, S., 238
Laufer, W.S., 312
Laughlin, P.R., 429, 437
Lavrakas, P.J., 476
Layton, J.F., 334
Law, L., 201
Lawler, E.E. III, 519
Lawton, M.P., 214
Lazarus, R.S., 470
Leary, M.R., 157
Lebras, C., 518
LeCompte, W.A., 471
Lederer, L., 588
Leeper, J.D., 505
Lefcourt, H.M., 555, 557, 561
Lefkowitz, M.M., 340
Legant, P., 501
Leginski, W., 500
Lehrer, P.M., 468
Leirer, V.O., 102, 103
Leiser, T., 300
Lenehan, G.E., 497
Lenney, E., 230
Lennox, V.L., 176
Leonard, J., 236
Lepper, M., 72
Lepper, M.R., 94, 112
Leshner, A.I., 577
Leung, K., 373, 397
Levenkron, J.C., 548
Leventhal, D.B., 334
Leventhal, G., 469
Leventhal, G.S., 395, 396, 401, 403
Leventhal, H., 141, 548
Levin, I.P., 114, 515
Levin, P.F., 296
Levine, J.M., 254, 255
Levine, L., 513
Levine, M.P., 553
Levine, S., 509
Levinger, G., 213, 240, 241
Levinson, D.J., 184, 185, 534
Levitan, D., 237
Levitt, L., 469
Levitt, M.J., 213
Levitt, P.R., 319
Levy, A., 465

Levy, S., 536
Lévy-Leboyer, C., 477, 486
Lewin, K., 13
Lewin, T., 500
Lewinsohn, P.M., 539
Lewis, M.S., 511
Lewis, S.A., 390
Lewis, S.K., 269
Ley, P., 512
Leyens, J.P., 338
Libuser, L., 458
Lichtman, C.M., 290
Liden, R.C., 441
Lieb, R., 229
Liebert, R.M., 338, 340, 362
Light, L., 226
Lightner, J., 99
Linder, D.E., 236
Lindskold, S., 389
Lingle, J.H., 115
Linn, R.T., 557
Linneweber, V., 325
Linsenmeier, J.A.W., 265
Linville, P.W., 77, 78, 88, 89, 91, 186, 187
Lipetz, M.E., 236
Lipkins, R., 513
Lippincott, E.C., 340
Lippitt, R., 13
Lippold, S., 222
Lipsitz, A., 439
Lipson, A.L., 226
Liptzin, M.B., 596, 597
Litowitz, D.L., 20, 225
Littlel, L., 216
Liverant, S., 557
Livingston, J., 509
Lockard, J.S., 312
Locke, E.A., 518, 519
Locksley, A., 183
Loeb, M., 472
Loftus, E., 192, 492, 494, 495
Loh, W.D., 492
Lombardo, J.P., 294
Long, G., 401
Loo, C.M., 465
Loomis, J.W., 185
Lord, C.G., 94
Lorenz, K., 328, 362
Los Angeles Times (1981), 476
Loschper, G., 325
Lott, B., 193
Lotyczewski, B.S., 459
Lowe, C.A., 375
Lowman, J., 579
Lucido, D., 513
Lucker, G.W., 553
Lueger, R.J., 316, 317
Lui, L., 89
Lumsden, C.J., 461
Lund, A.K., 505
Lundberg, U., 472
Luyben, P.E., 516

M

Maas, A., 102, 178, 179
Maas, A., 493, 494
McAbee, T.A., 491
McAlister, A.L., 548
McArthur, L.A., 58
McArthur, L.Z., 97, 99
Macaulay, J., 349
McCain, G., 465
McCallum, R., 469
McCandless, B.R., 355
McCann, L., 601, 602
McCarthy, B., 213
McCarthy, P.J., 464
McCauley, C., 480
McClay, D., 460
McClelland, D.C., 504
McClelland, L., 469, 516
McClintock, C.G., 373, 387, 388
McClintock, M.K., 575
MacCulloch, M.J., 580
Maccoby, N., 506, 548
McDavid, J.W., 258
McDavis, K., 299
McDonald, P.J., 223, 226
McDonel, E.C., 129, 130, 159
MacDougall, J.M., 547
McDougall, W., 12
MacFadden, L., 509
McGillis, D., 56
McGinley, H., 229
McGinnes, G.C., 44
McGlynn, R.P., 492
McGovern, L.P., 294, 299
McGowan, J., 533
McGraw, K.M., 20, 225
McGuire, W.J., 153, 154
Machlowitz, M., 238
McIntosh, M., 580
Mack, D., 495
McKee, D.C., 552
McKeough, K.L., 150
McKinley, J.C., 531
McLane, D., 237
McLear, P.M., 224
McMillan, L., 298
McMullen, L.M., 289
McNett, I., 491, 592
McTavish, J., 376
Macy, S.M., 517
Madar, T., 223
Maddux, J.E., 139
Major, B., 260
Malamuth, N., 343
Malamuth, N.M., 346, 363, 593, 604
Mallick, S.K., 355
Mandel, D.R., 469
Mann, J., 596
Mann, L., 276, 280, 426, 427, 455, 466, 467
Manning, A., 574–576

Mannucci, E.G., 553
Manstead, A.S.R., 307
Marber, S., 306
Margolese, M.S., 580
Marks, E.L., 300
Marks, G., 228
Markus, H., 91, 116, 118, 148, 200–202, 417
Marlatt, G.A., 538, 539
Marlowe, D., 393
Marsh, P., 49
Marshall, G., 513
Marshall, G.D., 75
Marshello, A.F.J., 374
Martens, R., 416
Martin, C., 404, 405
Martin, C.E., 569, 580
Martin, G., 300
Martindale, D.A., 464
Maruyama, G., 138, 228, 426, 427
Marwell, G., 402
Maslach, C., 75, 302
Massey, A., 465
Masters, J.C., 296
Masters, W.H., 585, 603
Masterson, F.A., 316
Matarazzo, J.D., 504
Mathews, K.E., 472
Mathewson, G.C., 158
Matlin, M.W., 416
Matsuyama, S.S., 351
Matter, C.F., 458
Matthews, K.A., 300, 550, 552, 553
Matthews, R.W., 469, 470
Mavin, G.H., 104, 105
Mavissakalian, M., 587
Maxwell, S.E., 506
May, J., 590
May, J.L., 216, 222
Mayer, F.S., 297
Mayo, C., 52
Mayol, A., 510
Mednick, S.A., 351
Meecham, W.C., 472
Meeker, F.B., 48
Meeker, R.J., 375
Mehrabian, A., 49, 219
Melamed, B.G., 513
Melin, L., 278
Melville, M.M., 351
Messé, L.A., 376
Messick, D.M., 396
Metcalf, J., 470
Metts, V., 229
Mewborn, C.R., 141, 142
Meyer, A.J., 548
Meyer, J.P., 229, 297
Michael, R.P., 575, 576
Michela, J.L., 57, 63
Michelini, R.L., 499
Michelli, J.A., 494
Middlekauff, R., 514
Middlemist, R.D., 458

Milavsky, B., 343
Miles, M.E., 20
Milgram, S., 28, 274–277, 280, 283, 477, 480
Miller, A., 238
Miller, C.T., 599, 601
Miller, D.T., 66
Miller, F.G., 229
Miller, J.A., 272
Mifller, L.C., 106
Miller, L.E., 500
Miller, N., 72, 138, 228, 297, 331, 426, 427
Miller, R.C., 260
Miller, R.S., 254, 255
Miller, R.W., 157
Miller, S., 469
Miller, S.S., 573
Millham, J., 316
Milligan, M., 476
Mills, C.J., 500
Mills, J., 158, 222, 296, 302
Mills, M., 309
Minge, M.R., 478, 479
Minkler, M., 513
Mirels, H.L., 232
Mirvis, P.H., 519
Mischel, W., 316, 532
Mita, T.H., 148
Mitchell, H.E., 134, 501
Mitchell, T.R., 196, 518, 522
Moe, J.L., 180, 181
Moehle, D., 439
Monahan, J., 492
Monson, T.C., 65, 533
Moon, T.H., 393, 394
Moore, B.S., 471, 553
Moore, D.L., 418, 419
Moore-Ede, M.C., 520, 521
Moos, R.H., 511
Moran, G., 218, 501
Morasch, B., 469
Moreault, D., 598
Moreland, R.L., 215
Morell, M.A., 551
Morency, N., 41
Morgan, B.B., Jr., 491
Morgan, C.D., 531
Morgan, C.J., 291
Morgan, W.P., 505
Moriarty, T., 20, 311
Morris, D., 49
Morris, J.H., 74
Morris, N.M., 576
Morris, W.N., 221, 254, 255
Morton, H., 458
Moscovici, S., 262, 263
Mosher, D.L., 595, 598, 599
Moskowitz, D.S., 532
Moss, M.K., 294
Mousaw, P., 237
Mouton, J., 191
Mowday, R.T., 519

Mowrer, O.H., 331
Mueller, C., 359
Mueller, H.S., 548
Mulherin, A., 297
Mullen, B., 510
Mummendey, A., 325
Munoz, R.F., 539
Munson, R., 469
Münsterberg, J., 492
Murakami, M., 225
Murphy, P., 191
Murray, D.M., 493
Murray, E.J., 217
Murray, H.A., 219, 531
Murstein, B.I., 226, 235
Musilli, L., 266
Myers, D.G., 429, 434, 436, 437, 449

N

Nacoste, R.W., 180, 181
Nadler, A., 238, 289, 302–304
Naficy, A., 157
Nagao, D.H., 502
Nagy, G.F., 238
Nahemow, L., 214
Narayanan, V.K., 518
Nash, J.D., 548
Nash, J.E., 228
Nash, R.F., 380
Nath, R., 518
Near, J.P., 515, 518
Neimeyer, G.J., 229
Neimeyer, R.A., 229
Nelson, D., 227
Nelson, E., 585
Nelson, Y., 457
Nemeth, C., 373
Nemetz, G.H., 278
Nerenz, D.R., 464
Neumann, P.G., 553
Newcomb, T.M., 204, 228, 242, 253
Newman, J., 480
Newsweek (1983), 305
Newton, J.W., 426, 427, 455
New York Times (1980), 305
Nezlek, J., 223, 226
Nicosia, G., 469
Nisbett, R.E., 65, 70, 87, 98, 108, 109, 113
Nocera, J., 572
Nock, S.L., 518
Norman, J., 314, 316
Norvell, N., 191
Nossiter, B.D., 483
Novaco, R.W., 539
Nowicki, S., Jr., 557

O

O'Connell, R.J., 575
Odbert, H.S., 533

Offir, C.W., 604
Ogden, G.D., 491
O'Grady, K.E., 223, 578, 595, 598
Ohbuchi, K., 348
O'Leary, D.E., 538
O'Leary, M.R., 538
Oliver, D.F., 226
Olsen, M.E., 516
Olshavsky, R.W., 505, 506
O'Neal, E.C., 456
O'Neill, P., 497
Orebaugh, A.L., 516
O'Reilly, C.A. III, 74
Orionova, G., 567
Orlick, T.D., 302
Ornstein, S., 400
Ortiz, V., 183
Orzech, M.J., 513
Osgood, C.E., 389
O'Shaughnessy, M., 49
Ostling, R.N., 588
Ostrom, T.M., 92, 115, 144
Ostrove, N., 499
Ota, S., 550
Otten, M.W., 557
Ovid, 579
Owens, D.D., Jr., 517
Ozer, D.J., 532

P

Page, B., 309
Page, R.A., 294
Pallak, M.S., 157
Palmer, J., 228
Paloutzian, R., 546
Pancer, S.M., 289
Pandey, J., 420
Pandy, J., 299
Pantin, H.M., 291, 292
Papageorgis, D., 153, 154
Parade (1981), 224
Parham, I.A., 532
Parish, E.A., 546
Park, B., 186, 187
Parke, R.D., 338
Parker, D.R., 334
Parsons, J.E., 192
Patchen, M., 207
Patterson, A.H., 463, 469
Paulhus, D.L., 235
Paulus, P.B., 13, 408, 449, 465, 468–470
Pearce, P.L., 295, 478
Pearse, R.W., 441
Pearson, J.A., 221
Pellegrini, R.J., 548
Pendleton, D., 512
Pendleton, M.G., 269
Penk, W., 558
Pennebaker, J.W., 20, 225, 455, 509, 551
Penner, L.A., 300
Penrod, S., 432, 503

Peplau, L.A., 237, 241, 540, 541, 544–546, 561
Pepper, S., 229
Peraino, J.M., 237
Perkowitz, W.T., 229
Perlock, D., 467
Perlman, D., 20, 540, 541, 561, 567
Perri, M., 226
Perry, D.G., 199
Perry, L.B., 585
Perry, N.J., 510, 521
Personnaz, B., 262, 263
Pervin, L.A., 532
Peters, J.M., 476
Peters, L.H., 518
Peters, M.D., 116
Peterson, E.A., 471
Peterson, I., 508
Peterson, L., 300, 511
Pettigrew, T.F., 557
Petty, R., 152
Petty, R.E., 127, 142–144, 146, 147, 152, 153, 166, 228, 232, 272, 273, 421
Pfaffmann, C., 575
Phares, E.J., 555, 556
Philip, J., 351
Philips, C., 505
Phillips, A.L., 223
Piaget, J., 298, 319
Pilchowicz, E., 579
Piliavin, I., 302
Piliavin, J., 239
Piliavin, J.A., 294, 295, 319
Pilkey, D.W., 590
Pilkonis, P.A., 545
Pineau, C., 480
Pines, M., 508, 510
Pisano, R., 334
Pittner, M.S., 553
Playboy (1981), 494
Pliner, P., 266
Poe, D.B., Jr., 517
Pomazol, R.J., 299
Pomerantz, S.D., 41, 52, 53
Pomeroy, W.B., 569, 580
Pond, C.A., 289
Pope, K.S., 243
Porter, J.W., 509
Powell, M.C., 127, 129
Powers, P.C., 280
Poythress, N.G., Jr., 492
Prakash, A., 299
Pratt, G., 477, 480
Prentice-Dunn, S., 423–425, 427, 428
President's Council on Environmental Quality (1978), 475
Presson, C.C., 505, 506
Prestholdt, P., 500
Preston-Martin, S., 476
Preti, G., 576

Preuss, G.G., 465
Price, G.H., 455
Price, J.M., 516
Price, K.H., 441
Price, R.A., 226
Prince, L.M., 50, 51
Pritchard, M., 580
Pritchard, R.D., 400
Proctor, J.D., 509
Pruesse, M., 590
Pruitt, D.G., 387, 390, 408
Pruitt, D.J., 58
Pryor, B., 480
Pryor, J.B., 115
Przybyla, D.P.J., 226, 236, 316, 536, 549, 572, 583, 586, 587, 599, 600
Pulakos, E.D., 193, 197
Pursell, S.A., 229
Putallaz, M., 541
Pyszczynski, T., 66, 67, 495
Pyszczynski, T.A., 589

Q

Quade, D., 513
Quattrone, G.A., 64, 186
Quigley-Fernandez, B., 233, 234
Quintanar, L.R., 146, 147

R

Rabin, R., 491
Rachman, S.J., 505
Rahe, D., 279
Raine, A., 557
Raines, B.E., 506
Rajecki, D.S., 126, 127
Rajecki, D.W., 166, 417, 464
Ramirez, A., 141, 588
Ramirez, J., 333, 343, 360
Ransberger, V.M., 474
Rau, L., 201
Raven, B.H., 513
Raviv, A., 300
Ray, C., 513
Read, S.J., 94, 95
Reardon, R., 579
Redd, W.H., 513
Reddy, D.M., 469
Redler, E., 294
Reeder, G.D., 64
Rees, K., 480
Regnier, F., 575
Reich, J.W., 35, 490
Reid, D.W., 513
Reifler, C.B., 596, 597
Reimanis, G., 559
Reinhold, R., 506
Reis, H., 283
Reis, H.T., 66, 223, 226, 397, 398, 400
Reiss, B.F., 581
Reiter, S.M., 516, 517
Reith, G., 278

Renfrew, P.D., 542
Research and Forecasts, Inc., 219
Relvenson, T.A., 546
Reyes, R.M., 99
Rheaume, K., 494, 405
Rhodewalt, F., 152, 553
Rholes, W.S., 104, 298
Rice, R.W., 515, 518
Richardson, D., 29
Richardson, D.C., 349, 350
Richins, M., 550
Riess, M., 156, 460
Riggiero, J., 190
Riggio, R.E., 50, 51
Riordan, C.A., 233, 234, 236, 237
Riorden, C., 190
Risser, D., 44
Rittle, R.H., 266, 267, 417
Roberts, M.C., 229, 505
Robertshaw, D., 558
Robinson, J.P., 514
Rodgers, J.E., 493
Rodin, J., 292, 293, 470, 509. 511–513
Rodrigues, A., 228
Roe, K.V., 301
Roesch, R., 492
Rogel, M., 311
Roger, D.B., 557
Rogers, M., 297
Rogers, R.W., 29, 139, 141, 142, 296, 334, 342, 353, 423–425, 427, 428
Rogers, T.B., 91
Rogoff, B., 229
Rohner, R.P., 470
Romer, D., 293
Rook, K.S., 544, 545
Roper, G., 438
Rorschach, H., 531
Rosen, H., 319
Rosen, L.S., 469
Rosen, R.H., 571
Rosenbaum, D.P., 309
Rosenbaum, M.E., 114, 374
Rosenberg, S., 12
Rosenfield, D., 73, 176, 177, 185, 404, 405
Rosenfield, H.W., 48
Rosenhan, D.L., 296, 496
Rosenman, R.H., 300, 547, 550
Rosenthal, R., 174, 175
Ross, D., 338
Ross, G.A., 229
Ross, L., 70, 87, 94, 98, 109, 112, 113
Ross, M., 66
Ross, S., 338
Rossbach, J., 469
Rothbart, M., 96, 107, 186, 187
Rothblatt, A.B., 585
Rotter, J.B., 316, 531, 532, 555, 560

Rottman, L., 222
Rotton, J., 476
Roundtree, C.A., 221
Rozelle, R.M., 80, 506
Ruback, R.B., 31, 309
Rubin, D.B., 351
Rubin, J.Z., 382, 390, 391
Rubin, Z., 229, 232, 237, 241, 541, 542
Ruble, D.N., 192
Ruggiero, M., 306, 307
Rule, B.G., 336
Rusbult, C.E., 240, 469
Rushton, J.P., 319
Russ, R.C., 228
Russell, D., 66, 540, 541
Russell, G.W., 345
Russell, J.A., 477 480
Rutkowski, G.K., 293
Ryan, M.J., 296, 298
Ryan, T.J., 549
Ryckman, R.M., 230

S

Saari, D., 266
Sabatelli, R.M., 53
Saegert, S., 469
Safer, M.A., 548
Safford, R.K., 434
Sagar, H.A., 92, 93, 180
Sakheim, D.K., 587, 588
Salazar, J.M., 490
Sales, B.D., 492, 494
Sales, S.M., 416
Salovey, P., 296
Saltzer, E.B., 505
Salzer, S., 460
Samaha, G.M., 221
Sampson, E.E., 531
Samuel, W., 516, 517
Sanders, G.S., 197, 228, 418, 419, 437, 494, 511
Sandman, P.H., 476
Sanford, R.N., 184, 185, 534
Sarason, I.G., 278, 537
Sarrel, L., 572
Sarrel, P., 572
Satow, K.L., 299
Saulnier, K., 20
Saxe, L., 490, 525
Schaar, K., 502
Schachter, S., 71, 74, 75, 78, 116, 213, 214, 221, 227
Schaeffer, M.A., 509
Schaie, K.W., 532
Scham, M., 573
Schank, R., 91
Scheier, M.F., 70, 75, 100, 101, 398, 419, 424, 430
Scherer, S.E., 456
Schiavo, R.S., 458
Schiffenbauer, A., 458
Schill, T., 598

Schkade, J.K., 469
Schlegel, R.P., 505
Schlenker, B.R., 156, 157
Schlosser, B.S., 437
Schmidt, G., 567, 572
Schmidt, L., 239
Schmidt, T., 197
Schmitt, D.R., 402
Schmitz, M., 469
Schnedler, R., 299
Schnedler, R.W., 335
Schofield, J.W., 92, 93, 180
Schopler, J., 469
Schorr, D., 103
Schriesheim, C.A., 444
Schroeder, H.E., 278
Schubert, H.J., 581
Schul, Y., 115, 118, 119
Schulsinger, F., 351
Schuster, E., 227
Schwartz, G., 509
Schwartz, M.F., 296
Schwartz, R.D., 134
Schwartz, S., 600
Schwartz, S.H., 306
Schweder, R.A., 532
Scitovsky, T., 317
Scott, K.D., 518
Sears, D.O., 138, 233
Sears, R.R., 201, 331
Sebastian, R.J., 226, 338
Sebba, R., 462
Sechrest, L., 134
Seeley, D.M., 585
Seeley, T.T., 585
Segal, M.W., 214
Seilheimer, S.D., 387
Seipel, M., 302
Sekerak, G.J., 417
Sekaran, U., 519
Seligman, C., 266, 270, 516, 517
Selzer, M.L., 510
Semin, G.R., 307
Sensenig, J., 152
Sentis, K., 91
Sentis, K.P., 396
Seta, J.J., 418, 469
Severy, L.J., 456, 503
Shabecoff, P., 516
Shaffer, D.R., 173, 499, 501
Shaffer, O.R., 311
Shaklee, H., 376
Shanab, M.E., 274, 276
Shanteau, J., 238
Shapiro, D.A., 226
Shapiro, N.R., 458
Shapiro, S., 193–195
Sharabany, R., 229
Sharon, I., 291, 293
Shaver, P., 150
Shaver, R., 306
Shaw, J.S., 203
Shaw, M.E., 457, 458

Shea, J.D.C., 455
Shearer, L., 504
Shelton, M.L., 296
Shemberg, K.M., 334
Shenker, S., 232
Shepherd, D.H., 500
Sheppard, B.H., 496
Sherif, C.W., 182
Sherif, M., 13, 182
Sherman, S.J., 129, 130, 159, 269, 270, 505, 506
Sherrod, D.R., 471
Shields, J.L., 561
Shigetomi, C.C., 299
Shimmin, S., 514
Shipley, R.H., 506
Shomer, R.W., 387
Shope, G.L., 355
Shovar, N., 68, 70
Shribman, D., 313
Shuntich, R.J., 336
Shure, G.H., 375
Sidera, J.A., 142, 143
Sidman, J., 596
Siegal, F.P., 573
Siegel, D., 496
Siegel, J.M., 553
Siegel, L.J., 511, 513
Sigall, H., 65, 133, 499
Sigusch, V., 567
Siladi, M., 201, 202
Silver, M., 233
Silver, R.L., 511
Simons, L.S., 334
Simonton, D.K., 22
Singer, A.G., 575
Singer, J.E., 74, 470, 471, 481, 486, 504
Singer, R.D., 340
Sinha, Y., 299
Sistrunk, F., 258
Sivacek, J., 163, 164
Sivacek, J.M., 376
Skevington, S.M., 183
Skolnick, P., 144
Skrypnek, B.J., 174, 175
Slater, E., 580
Sloan, L.R., 500
Slovic, P.,. 108
Smedley, J.W., 180
Smeriglio, V.L., 278, 279
Smith, E.E., 103
Smith, E.R., 116
Smith, F.J., 518
Smith, G.F., 150
Smith, H.G., 472
Smith, K., 152
Smith, M.P., 518
Smith, R.E., 537
Smith, R.J., 458, 475
Smith, R.W., 581
Smith, S., 29
Smith, T., 442

Smith, T.G., 546
Smith, T.W., 548, 553
Smith, V., 229
Snodgrass, S.R., 499
Snow, B., 553
Snyder, C.R., 230, 231, 243
Snyder, L.D., 102, 178, 179, 494
Snyder, M., 65, 159, 162, 174, 175, 266, 299
Sobel, D., 230
Sogin, S.R., 157
Soja, M.J., 185
Sokol, M., 510
Sokolov, J.J., 576
Solano, C., 533
Solano, C.H., 546
Soler, E., 476
Solomon, H., 476
Solomon, M.R., 439
Solomon, R.C., 235
Solomon, S., 66, 67
Solomon, S.K., 470, 471
Sommer, R., 454, 455, 458
Sorrentino, R.M., 319
Southwick, L.L., 160, 161
Sox, H., 511
Spangenberg, S., 255
Spaulding, K., 102, 178, 179, 494
Spence, J.R., 203
Spence, J.T., 192
Spiegel, N., 226
Spiegel, N.H., 46, 47
Spielberger, C.D., 502
Spinner, B., 346, 541
Spiridigliozzi, G., 553
Spitzer, L., 513
Sprafkin, J.N., 340, 362
Srinivas, K.M., 519
Srull, T.K., 104, 105
Stack, J.M., 571
Stadler, S.J., 475
Staneski, R.A., 225, 579
Stapp, J., 490
Starr, S., 596
Staub, E., 299, 509
Stech, F., 387, 388
Steck, L., 237
Steele, C.M., 160, 161
Steffen, V., 193
Stein, G.M., 403
Stein, R.T., 441
Steinberg, J., 296
Steinberg, L.D., 511
Steinberg, R., 193–195
Steinmetz, J., 112
Stephan, W., 589
Stephan, W.G., 185, 190
Stephens, L., 356–358
Sterling, F.E., 512
Stern, G.S., 553
Stern, J.A., 74
Sternberg, W.C., 233
Sternglanz, S.H., 225

Stetson, D., 518
Stevens, G.E., 196
Steward, J.E. II, 499, 500
Stewart, A.J., 510
Stinner, W.F., 482
Stock, W.E., 583
Stocking, M., 351
Stokes, L.D., 500
Stokols, D., 468, 471, 472
Stone, A.V.W., 300
Stone, B.J., 475
Stone, L., 235
Stone, W.F., 228
Stoner, J.A.F., 434, 435
Stonner, D., 355
Storms, M., 76
Storms, M.D., 459, 581
Stough, R.R., 462
Strack, F., 99, 112, 494
Straker, G., 301
Strand, P.J., 516
Strassberg, D.S., 232
Streeter, L.A., 138
Strentz, T., 502
Stringfield, D.O., 533
Stroebe, W., 256, 257
Strom, J.C., 48
Strube, M.J., 20, 446, 548, 550
Studebaker, S., 470
Stull, D.E., 229
Suarez, S.D., 580
Suchner, R.W., 193
Sue, D., 583
Suedfeld, P., 542
Suer, S.F., 575
Sugarman, R., 417
Suls, J., 300, 491, 510
Suls, J.M., 260
Sulzer, J.L., 223
Sundstrom, E., 464
Swann, E.B., 106
Swann, W.B., Jr., 94, 95
Swap, W.C., 215, 390
Syme, G.J., 162
Szegda, M., 117, 118

T

Tajfel, H., 183
Tamborini, R., 334
Tanford, S., 503
Tanis, D.C., 471
Tanke, E.D., 175
Tannenbaum, S.I., 549
Tanur, J., 441
Tavris, C., 150
Taylor, D.A., 232
Taylor, F.W., 515
Taylor, M.C., 203
Taylor, R.B., 229, 462, 464, 465
Taylor, R., 65
Taylor, S.E., 14, 60, 73, 80, 87, 88, 99, 101, 107, 121, 153, 171
Taylor, S.M., 192

Taylor, S.P., 294, 334, 336, 349
Tedeschi, J.T., 134, 233, 234, 236, 237
Teevan, R.C., 553
Terborg, J.R., 192, 198
Tesser, A., 147, 235, 579
Thalhofer, N.N., 460
Thelen, M.H., 229
Thibaut, J., 368, 387, 388
Thibaut, J.W., 439
Thomas, G.C., 291, 459
Thomas, M.H., 340
Thomas, T.L., 567
Thome, P.R., 349
Thompson, D.E., 457, 469
Thompson, J.E., 183, 191
Thompson, M.E., 572
Thompson, N., 588
Thompson, R.A., 297
Thompson, S.C., 99
Thompson, W.C., 99, 296, 496
Thornton, B., 500
Thornton, J.E., 577
Tilker, H.A., 280
Time (1980), 516
Time (1981), 476
Timnick, L., 472
Toch, H., 348, 356
Toi, M., 300
Toney, M.B., 482
Touhey, J.C., 193
Town, J.P., 99
Traupman, J., 213
Traupmann, J., 401
Tripathi, R.C., 299
Triplett, N., 414
Tripett, F., 478
Trivers, R.L., 294
Troutwine, R., 456
Tucker, D.M., 146
Tumonis, T.M., 385, 386
Tunnell, G.B., 314, 315
Turner, C.W., 334
Turner, J., 183
Turner, T.J., 91
Tursky, B., 509
Tversky, A., 108, 110
Tyler, T.R., 502

U

Udry, J.R., 576
Ugwuegbu, D.C.E., 500
Ulrich, R.S., 479
Unger, R.K., 223
U.S. Census (1980), 479
U.S. Department of Commerce, 515
Uranowitz, S.W., 266

V

Vacino, J., 219
Valins, S., 469
Valone, K., 138

Vandenberg, R.J., 349, 350
Vandenberg, S.G., 226
Vandenbergh, J.G., 465
Van Der Pligt, J., 66
Van Egeren, L.E., 380–382
Van Liere, K.D., 516
van Wagenberg, D., 517
Vaux, A., 511
Vecchio, R.P., 441
Veitch, R., 217, 227, 469, 590
Venables, P.H., 557
Vidmar, N., 496
Vincent, J.E., 269
Vinokur, A., 438, 510
Vinsel, A., 462, 463
Viscusi, D., 28, 509
Vogt, B., 296, 298
Von Eckardt, W., 480

W

Wachtler, J., 137, 221
Wack, D.L., 417
Wack, J., 513
Wack, J.T., 509
Wade, N., 568
Wagener, J.J., 117, 118, 266
Wagner, G., 583
Wagner, M.E., 581
Walden, T.A., 468, 469
Walder, L.O., 340
Walder, P., 309
Walker, J.W., 460
Walker, L., 157
Walkey, F.H., 456
Wall, J.A., 264
Wallach, M.A., 437
Wallis, C., 573
Walster, E., 226, 235, 401, 578, 589
Walster (Hatfield), E., 222, 239, 395, 401, 402
Walster, G.W., 226, 235, 239, 243, 395, 401, 402
Walton, R.E., 518
Wan, C.K., 316, 549
Wan, K.C., 373, 397
Ward, L.M., 477, 480
Ward-Hull, C.I., 224
Ware, E.E., 590
Warnick, D.H., 494
Warwick, D., 253
Wasserman, N., 223
Watson, R.I., Jr., 426
Weary, G., 41, 66, 68, 80
Weaver, C.N., 569, 570
Webb, E.J., 134
Weber, R.J., 516
Wehr, P., 356
Weidner, G., 552
Weigel, R.H., 185
Weiler, J., 441
Weinberg, H.I., 494
Weinberg, M.S., 580

Weiner, B., 77, 196, 297
Weiner, N., 420
Weinman, C., 513
Weinstein, E., 441
Weinstein, N., 471
Weinstock-Savoy, D., 510
Weis, D.L., 571
Weiss, R.F., 294
Weiss, S.M., 561
Weiss, T., 401
Weissberg, R.P., 459
Weiten, W., 499
Wells, G.L., 58, 493
Wells, K.S., 511
Wener, R.E., 470
Wentzel, A.A., 496
Wenzel, C., 41
Werner, C.M., 462
West, S., 596
West, S.G., 61, 299, 338
West, S.T., 28
Wetzel, C.G., 230
Wexley, K.N., 193, 197
Whalen, D.H., 495
Wheeler, D., 269
Wheeler, L., 223, 225, 226, 283
Whitcher-Alagna, S., 302, 303
Whitcup, M., 516
White, B.J., 182
White, D., 576, 577
White, G.L., 22, 226, 238, 239
White, J.W., 335
White, L.A., 345, 595, 599, 601
White, R.K., 13
Whitney, G., 299
Whobrey, L., 494
Wicklund, R.A., 99, 100, 151, 166, 297, 398, 400
Wideman, M.V., 513
Wiggins, J.S., 203, 225, 536
Wiggins, N., 225
Wiggins, N.H., 50
Wilder, D.A., 183, 191, 251, 254
Wilhelmy, R.A., 254
Wilke, H., 302
Williams, K., 420–422
Williams, K.B., 302
Williams, K.D., 302
Williams, L.J., 239
Williams, R.B., 552
Williams, S., 230
Williams, T.A. III, 496
Williams, T.M., 341
Williamson, N.L., 178
Willis, F.N., 459
Willis, K.A., 314, 315
Wills, G., 588
Wilmoth, G.H., 456, 503
Wilson, C.E., 309
Wilson, D.W., 472
Wilson, M., 214, 439
Wilson, T.D., 70, 72, 77, 78, 108, 109

Wilson, W.R., 148, 149
Wimer, S., 62, 63
Wincze, H., 587
Wincze, J.P., 587
Winer, D.L., 217
Wing, C.W., 437
Winslow, C.N., 227
Winter, R., 576
Winton, W., 41
Wishnoff, R., 591, 592
Witenberg, S., 300
Witkin, H.A., 351
Witmer, J.F., 516
Wolchik, S.A., 587
Wolf, C., 513
Wolf, S., 263, 420, 421
Wolfe, B.M., 334
Wolfer, J.A., 513
Wolfle, L.M., 558
Womble, P., 470
Wood, D.L., 575
Wood, W., 139, 140, 144, 145,
    153, 258, 259
Woolfolk, R.L., 468
Worchel, S., 64, 152, 191, 221,
    335, 496

Word, C.O., 175
Worsham, A.P., 457, 458
Wortman, C.B., 265, 511
Wright, S.L., 221
Wrightsman, L.S., 495–497
Wurtele, S.K., 229, 505
Wyer, R.S., 92
Wyer, R.S., Jr., 92, 102, 104, 105

Y

Yaffé, M., 585
Yagoda, B., 569
Yahya, K.A., 274, 276
Yandrell, B., 64
Yankelovich, D., 515
Yarkin, K.L., 99
Yarmey, A.D., 493
Yarnold, P.R., 549
Yates, B.T., 316
Yonin, Y., 291, 293, 296, 302
Yosha, A., 469
Young, A.W., 573
Young, J.E., 544, 545
Young, R.F., 417
Younger, J.C., 157
Youngren, M.A., 539

Yu, M.C., 476
Yukl, G., 383, 384

Z

Zabrack, M.L., 341
Zajonc, R.B., 116, 118, 145, 148,
    150, 215, 414–417, 419
Zanna, M.P., 84, 85, 114, 129, 166,
    175, 437
Zehner, H., 576
Zeiss, A.M., 539
Zellman, G.L., 192
Zellner, M., 144
Zelnick, M., 601, 604
Zembrodt, I.M., 240
Ziegler, M., 513
Zillmann, D., 28, 329, 333, 334,
    342–346, 353, 357, 360,
    363, 576, 588, 597, 604
Zimbardo, P.G., 75, 424, 544, 545
Zimring, C.M., 470
ZPG National Reporter (1977), 483
Zuckerman, M., 41, 46, 47, 52, 53,
    283, 469
Zuiches, J.J., 478
Zyzanski, S.J., 549, 550

Subject Index

A

Achievement
  female, devaluation of, 195–196
  and locus of control, 557
  need for, in leadership, 442
  and Type A behavior, 551
Acquaintance, and reduction of
    prejudice, 190–191
Actor-observer effect, 64–65
Adversarial legal system, 496
Affect, and social cognition, 116–
    117
Affective response
  and attraction, 216
  to environment, 476
Affiliation
  and attraction, 219
  and density effects, 469
  need for, 219, 220
Aggression, 321–363
  and arousal, 341–343
  control of, 352–361
  and crowding, 345
  definition of, 325–326
  direct provocation of, 335–336
  drive theories of, 328–329
  and excitation transfer, 341–343
  and frustration, 330–331, 334–
    335
  and heredity, 351–352
  individual determinants of, 345,
    348–353
  and intention, 325
  laboratory measurement of, 332–
    333
  and pain, 345
  and personality, 345, 348
  prevention of, 352–361
  punishment as deterrent to,
    352–353

reduction of, 357–359
  role of attribution in, 335–337
  sex differences in, 348–350
  and sexual arousal, 343–345
  situational determinants of, 341–
    345
  social determinants of, 330–341
  and temperature, 473
  theoretical perspectives on, 326–
    330
  and XYY chromosome syn-
    drome, 351–352
Aid, reactions to, 302
Air pollution, 475
Alternatives, and bargaining, 385–
    386
Altruism, 285
  and attribution, 296
  factors affecting, 298
  and sex differences, 299
Androgyny, 202–203
Anxiety reduction and social com-
    parison, 221
Appraising job performance, 520
Approval, need for, 299
  social, 144
Arbitration, 390. *See also*
    Bargaining
Arousal
  and cognitive dissonance, 160–
    161
  effect of, on cheating, 317
  role of, in aggression, 341–343
  sexual, 585
Asch procedure for studying con-
    formity, 250–252
Attention, 97–100
  effects of, 99
  and salience, 97–99
  self-focused, 99–101
  and vividness, 97–99

Attitude, 123–166
  and behavior, 162–164, 195
  change, 135–159
    and cognitive dissonance, 150–
      159
    effect of repeated exposure
      on, 145, 148–150
    and forced compliance, 154–
      157
    and persuasion, 135–150
    resistance to, 152–154
  and conformity, 256–257
  formation, 127–130
    role of modeling in, 128
    role of social learning in, 127–
      129
  measurement of, 130–135
    scales, 131–132
  similarity
    and attraction, 226, 227
    in courtroom, 500
  strength, 152, 162
Attitude-behavior link, 159, 162–
    164
Attitude-discrepant behavior,
    effects of, 154–157
Attraction, 209. *See also* Physical
    attractiveness
  and attitude similarity, 226
  and conformity, 253–254
  definition of, 212
  and functional proximity, 214
  and height, 224
  and physical attractiveness, 221
  and reciprocity, 233
  in reinforcement theory, 218
  and repeated exposure, 214
  and self-disclosure, 229
  sexual, 574
  and similarity, 226
  and smell, 575

Attraction (*cont.*)
  suffering-leads-to-liking effect,
    157–159
Attribution, 54–78
  and altruism, 296
  causal, 57–62
  and cooperation, 375–377
  and correspondent inference,
    50–51
  discounting and augmenting in,
    60–62
  error in, 64
  and job performance, 520
  key dimensions of, 62–63
  major theories of, 55–63
  role of, in aggression, 335–337
  self, 70–75
  self-focused, 99–101
  sources of bias in, 63–70
  as therapy, 76–77
  underutilization of consensus in,
    60
Audience, effects of, 413–419
Authoritarianism
  and prejudice, 184–185
  and jurors' response, 500
  measurement of, 535
Availability heuristic, 110

B

Balance theory, 204
Bargaining, 382–391
  and alternatives, 385–386
  and communication, 386–388
  and extremity of initial offer,
    383–384
  failure of, 389
  and interpersonal conflict, 389–
    391
  and mediation, 390–391
Baserates, underutilization of, in
    social inference, 107–108
Behavioral medicine, 504
Bias. *See* Self-serving bias
Bobo doll studies, 337–338
Body language, 48–50
Bogus pipeline, 133–134
Breaking up a relationship, 237
Bystander
  calculus, 295
  effect, 289, 305
  intervention, 285, 304

C

Cataclysmic phenomena, and
    stress, 470
Category accessibility, and person
    memory, 104–106
Catharsis, and aggression, 354–355
Causal analysis of emotions, 297
Cheating, 313

and arousal, 317
and interpersonal trust, 316
prevention of, 314
role of delayed gratification in,
    316
Chromosomal abnormality, and
    aggression, 351–352
Chronic self-destructiveness
  and cheating, 316
  and Type A behavior, 549
Cigarette smoking, prevention of,
    505
Circadian principles, 520
Cities
  creating desirable, 480
  crime rate, 479 (*See also* Crime)
  positive effects of, 476
  size of, 479, 483
Cognition, and response to erotica,
    586. *See also* Social cognition
Cognitive dissonance, 13, 150–159
  and arousal, 160–161
  and attitude change, 150–159
  and effort, 157–159
  and forced compliance, 154–157
  and social drinking, 160–161
  theory of, 151–154
Cognitive interventions, and reduc-
    tion of aggression, 357–359
Cognitive therapy, 544
Commitment, 307
  prior, 311
Communication
  and bargaining, 386–389
  characteristics of, and persua-
    sion, 140–142
Communicator characteristics, and
    persuasion, 136–140
  attractiveness, 136–138
  credibility, 138–140
  style, 138
Companionate love, 234
Competence, and response to
    crime, 307
Competition. *See* Cooperation
Competitors, 379, 380
Compliance, 264–271, 272–273
  "door-in-the-face" tactic, 268–
    269
  forced, 154–157
  and multiple requests, 265–271,
    272–273
  and reciprocal concessions, 269
  role of self-presentation in, 269
Computer simulation, in studying
    social cognition, 87
Conditioning
  of emotional responses, 217
  of homosexual preferences, 581
  instrumental (operant), in atti-
    tude formation, 127–128
  second-order, 218

Conformity, 249–263
  Asch procedure for studying,
    250–252
  and attraction, 253–254
  bases of, 260–261
  Crutchfield procedure for study-
    ing, 252
  factors affecting, 252–260
  and idiosyncrasy credits, 262–
    263
  methods for laboratory study of,
    250–252
  and private attitudes, 256–257
  role of social comparison in,
    260–261
  and sex differences, 256–260
  sexual, 572
  and social support, 254–255
Construct validity, 535
Contingency model of leader effec-
    tiveness, 444–447
Contraception, 572, 601
Contrast effect, and attraction, 225
Control
  of aggression, 352–361
  locus of, 555
  loss of, over events, 508, 510
  perceived, 509
  and stress, 508–511
Conventional level of moral judg-
    ment, 298
Cooperation, 370–382
  and attribution, 375–377
  and group size, 377–379
  laboratory method for studying,
    371–373
  and personality, 379–382
  and reciprocity, 374–375
  situational determinants of, 373–
    379
Cooperators, 379–380
Coronary-prone behavior pattern,
    546
Correlation
  and causation, 23–24
  illusory, 109–110
Correlational method, 19–24, 537
  and causation, 23–24
  strengths of, 22–23
Cost-benefit analysis, and resisting
    temptation, 313
Courtroom
  accuracy of testimony, 492
  behavior of defendant in, 498
  behavior of judge in, 494, 496
  behavior of jurors in, 498, 500
  jurors' response to egalitarian-
    ism, 500
  social psychology in, 491
  physical attractiveness in, 499
  race, as factor in, 500
  role of similarity in, 500

Credibility of communicator, and persuasion, 138–139
Crime
  neighborhood, 502
  nonviolent, 312
  and population size, 468
  pornography, 346–347, 585, 588
  preventing, 502
  rape, prevention of, 360–361
  response to, 307
  sex, 592
  shoplifting, 308
  tax evasion, 313
Cross-cultural comparisons of personal space, 455
Cross-group recognition, 177–179
Crowding, 465, 482
  and aggression, 345
  reduction of, 469
  sex differences in, 469
Crutchfield procedure for studying conformity, 252

D

Death instinct, 327
Debriefing, of research subjects, 28–29
Deception of subjects, in social research, 26–29
  problems of, 27–29
  purpose of, 27
  safeguards, when used, 28–29
Decision-making, in groups, 428–438. *See also* Groups
  process of, 429–433
  and risk, 434–438
  and social decision schemes, 429–432
Defendant, behavior of, 498
Deindividuation, 423–438, 430–432
  causes of, 424–425
  evidence on, 425–427
  response to suicide threat, 467
  techniques for countering, 430–431
Delay of gratification, and cheating, 316
Demand characteristics, 20–21
Density. *See* Crowding
Dependent variable, 16
Deprivation, relative, 404–405
Destructive obedience. *See* Obedience
Devaluing female achievement, 195–196
Dichotic listening procedure, 586
Diffusion of responsibility, 290
Direct experience, role of in attitude formation, 129–130

Discrimination, 168–207. *See also* Prejudice
  definition of, 172
  and reluctance to help, 172–173, 176
  subtle forms of, 172–173, 175–179
  and tokenism, 176
  toward females, 194–197
Display rules, 44
Dissonance. *See* Cognitive dissonance
Distraction conflict theory of social facilitation, 418–419
Divorce, 237
  as stress, 509, 510
"Door-in-the-face" tactic, for gaining compliance, 268–269
  and reciprocal concessions, 269
  and self-presentation, 269
Drive theories
  of aggression, 328–329
  of social facilitation, 414–416
Driving while intoxicated, and personality, 538
Dominance, and leadership, 442

E

Economic disruption as cause of stress, 508–509
Effort justification, 157–159
Egalitarianism, and jurors' response, 500
Ego-defensive function of self-serving bias, 66
Egocentrism, in perceived fairness, 395–396
Electroencephalogram (EEG), in studying persuasion, 146–147
Emblems, as nonverbal cues, 49–50
Emergency, response to, 288
Emotions
  and altruism, 296
  and attraction, 216
  causal analysis of, 297
  loneliness, 540
  Schachter's theory of, 74–75
  shyness, 544
  and stress, 508–512
Empathy
  development of, 300
  dispositional, 299
  hereditary factors, 300
Environment. *See also* Crowding
  and behavior, 451
  creating desirable, 480
  ideal, 478
  institutional, 513
  interpersonal, 455
  initiating improvement of, 516

noise, 471
  and stress, 508–512
Environmental psychology, 454
Equal Rights Amendment (ERA), 204–205
  factors affecting defeat of, 204–205
Equality, role of, in perceived fairness, 397
Equity, in social exchange, 395–405
Erotica
  behavioral effects of, 588
  effects of images of, 583
  interpersonal effects of, 589
  modeling effects of, 590
  motivating effects of, 590
  repeated exposure to, 596
Erotophilia, 594
Erotophobia, 594
  behavior and, 598, 600
Evaluation apprehension, 416–418
Evaluation of acquaintances, 221
Excitation transfer, and aggression, 341–343
Expectancy, 555
Experimental method, 15–19
  basic nature of, 15–17
  essential conditions of, 17–19
Experimental research, 537
External locus of control, 555
Eyes, in nonverbal communication, 46–48
Eyewitness testimony, 492

F

F Scale, 535
Facial expressions, 42–45
  development of, 44–45
  universality of, 42–44
Facial feedback hypothesis, 46–47
Fairness. *See* Perceived fairness
Fantasies, sexual, 583
Fear. *See also* Phobias
  of being apprehended, 315
  of embarrassment, 299
  of social blunders, 290
  of success, 198
Fear appeals, and persuasion, 141–142
Female roles. *See* Sexism
Field research, 20–21
First-shift rule, 430
Flexitime, 518
"Foot-in-the-door" tactic for gaining compliance, 265–268
  and positive view of helping situations, 267
  and shifts in self-perception, 266–267
Forced compliance, and attitude change, 154–157

Forewarning, and resistance to persuasion, 152–153
Free-rider effects, 422
Friendship, 209
Frustration, and aggression, 330–331, 334–335
Functional proximity, and attraction, 214
Fundamental attribution error, 64

G

Gazes, as nonverbal cue, 46–48
Generalized expectancies, 555
Gender schema theory, 199–200
Genital herpes, 573
Gestures, 48–50
Gratification, delayed, and cheating, 316
GRIT approach to resolving conflict, 389–390
Groups
  decision-making in, 428–438
    process of, 429–433
    risky shift, 434–438
    and social decision schemes, 429–432
  effects of, on individual behavior, 409–449
  homogeneity of, and prejudice, 186–187
  polarization in, 434–438
    and persuasive arguments, 437–438
    and social comparison, 436–437
  random assignment of subjects to, 17–18
  reference, 253
  and risky shift, 434–438
  size of
    and conformity, 253–254
    and cooperation, 377–379
Guilt, 315

H

Habituation effect, 596
Heat
  and aggression, 345
  behavioral effects of, 473
Height, and attraction, 224
Helping, 285, 302
Heredity, and aggression, 351–352
Herpes
  genital, 573
  simplex, 2
Heuristics, and social inference, 110–111
Home-field advantage, 463
Homophobia, 580
Homosexual behavior, 580
Hospitals, 513
Hypotheses, 25

I

I–E Scale, 555
Idiosyncrasy credits, and conformity, 262–263
Illusory correlation, 109–110
Imagination, 583
Impression formation, 111–119
  elaborate encoding in, 118
  information-processing view of, 115–119
  initial encoding in, 115–116
  weighted-average model of, 113–115
Impression management, in perceived fairness, 397
Incompatible responses, and control of aggression, 358–361
Independent variable, 16
Individual differences, 527
  in use of nonverbal cues, 50–54
Individual rights, in social research, 26–29
Individualists, 379, 380
Inequity, in social exchange, 395–405
Informational social influence, 251
Informed consent, 28–29
Ingratiation, 264–265
Initial encoding, in impression formation, 115–116
Initial offer, in bargaining, 383–384
Inoculation, and persuasion, 153
Institutional environments, 513
Instrumental (operant) conditioning, in attitude formation, 127–128
Intention, and aggression, 325
Intergroup conflict, as a cause of prejudice, 182–183
Intergroup contact, as a tactic for reducing prejudice, 190–191
Internal locus of control, 555
Interpersonal conflict, 389–391
Interpersonal environment, 455
Interpersonal trust, and cheating, 316
Intervention, 285
  cognitive, and reduction of aggression, 357–359
  to stop wrongdoer, 304
Intimate distance, 457
Intrinsic motivation, 72–74
Item analysis, 535

J

Jealousy, 238
Jenkins Activity Survey, 550
Jet lag, 521
Jigsaw method, for reducing prejudice, 191

Job
  commitment to, 519
  enlargement of, 518
  performance of, 520
  psychological aspects of, 514
  satisfaction in, 518
Judge, behavior of, 494, 496
Jurors, behavior of, 498, 500

L

Laboratory research, vs. field research, 20–21
Language, nonverbal. *See* Nonverbal communication
Leadership, 438–447
  and need for achievement, 442
  contingency model of, 444–447
  and dominance, 442
  effectiveness of, 444–447
  by females, competency of, 196–198
  great man/woman theory of, 439–441
  and need for power, 442
  and personality, 442–443
  relations-oriented, 445
  situational theory of, 440
  task orientation in, 445
  transactional view of, 441
  and vertical dyad linkages, 441
Legal system, and social psychology, 491. *See also* Courtroom
Less-leads-to-more effect, 157
Likert scaling, 131–132
Locus of control, 555
Loneliness, 540
Loss of perceived control, 508
Love, 209, 234
  companionate, 234
  at first sight, 236
  passionate, 234
"Low-balling," and compliance, 272–273

M

Machiavellianism, role of, in social exchange, 392–393
Majority-wins scheme, 429
Matching hypothesis, 226
Mate selection, 575
Measuring personality variables, 533
Mediation, 390–391. *See also* Bargaining
Medical specialist, reactions to, 511–512
Memory, 86. *See also* Person memory
  and persuasion, 144
  and schemata, 95–97
Mere-exposure effect, 145, 148–150

Message content, and persuasion, 142–143
Minority influence, 261–263
Modeling, role of, in attitude formation, 128
Moral judgment stages, 298
Motivation, intrinsic, 72–74
 self-motivation, 505
Multiple requests, and compliance, 265–271, 272–273

N

Need for achievement, and leadership, 442
Need for affiliation, 219
 as response to situation, 220
Need for approval, 299
 and prosocial behavior, 299
 social approval and persuasion, 144
Need for power, and leadership, 442
Need for social approval, and persuasion, 144
Needs, relative, 397
Negotiation. *See* Bargaining
Noise, 471, 509
Nonaggressive models, and control of aggression, 356
Nonverbal communication, 41–54
 and body language, 48–50
 emblems in, 49–50
 and expressiveness, 50–51
 eyes in, 46–48
 and facial expressions, 42–45
 and gender, 51–54
 individual differences in, 50–54
 practical effects of, 53–54
 staring, as cue in, 46–48
Normative social influence, 251
Nursing homes, 513

O

Obedience, 271, 274–277, 280–281
 basis for, 276–277, 280
 in laboratory, 274–276
 reduction of, 280–281
Objective self-awareness, 100–101
Objective tests, 531
Organizational behavior, 514
Outgroup homogeneity, illusion of, 186–187
Overjustification effect, 72–74
Overpopulation, 482. *See also* Crowding

P

Pain, and aggression, 345
Penile plethysmograph, 585
Perceived control, and stress, 509–510

Perceived fairness, in social exchange, 395–405
 and distribution justice, 395
 and egocentrism, 395–396
 and equity, 395
 and impression management, 397–399
 and relative deprivation, 404–405
 and relative needs, 397
 tactics for restoring, 400–403
Performance appraisal, 520
Permissive attitudes, 569
Person memory, 101–106
 contents of, 101–102
 and instructions, 102–103
 and priming, 104–106
 and social cognition, 101–106
 and visual imagery, 106
Person positivity bias, 138
Personal distance, 457
Personal space
 cross-cultural comparisons of, 455
 norms, 455
 privacy, 462
 sex differences in, 456
 situational effects of, 457
 violations of, 458
Personality, 527
 and aggression, 345, 348
 and cooperation, 379–382
 and driving while intoxicated, 538
 measuring variables of, 533
 and similarity, 228
 tests, 531
 traits, 531
Persuasion
 and attitude change, 135–150
 brain activity during, 146–147
 and communicator characteristics, 136–140
 and inoculation, 153
 and need for social approval, 144
 and reactance, 152
 role of self-schemata in, 142–143
 and recipients' characteristics, 143–145
 resistance to, 152–154
 and speed of speech, 138
Persuasive communications, 135
 and group polarization, 437–438
Pheromone, sexual, 574
Phobias, *See also* Fear
 erotophobia, 594, 598, 600
 homophobia, 580
Physical attractiveness
 and attraction, 221
 and being asked for help, 302
 components of, 224
 in courtroom, 499

Physical proximity, and attraction, 214
Physician, interaction with, 511–512
Pornography
 and aggression, 346–347
 effects of, 585, 588
Postconventional level of moral judgment, 298
Power, need for, and leadership, 442
Preconventional level of moral judgment, 298
Predicting behavior, 537
Prejudice, 168–207
 and authoritarianism, 184–185
 in courtroom, 500
 definition of, 120–122
 discrimination, 172
 and early experience, 185
 equality and perceived fairness in, 397
 explanations of, 181–185
 and illusion of outgroup homogeneity, 186–187
 and intergroup conflict, 182–183
 and intergroup contact, 190–191
 jigsaw method for reduction of, 191
 measurement of, 179–180
 reduction of, 188–191
 sexism, 191–205
 questioning the competency of female leaders, 196–198
 and social categorization, 183–184
 and social competition, 183–184
 in stereotyping, 174–175, 193–194
 and stigmatized groups, 175
 subtle forms of, 172–173, 175–179
 and tokenism, 176
Prevention of aggression, 352–361
Preventive medicine, 505
Primary territory, 461
Prior commitment, 311
Prior residence effect, 463
Prisoner's dilemma, 371–373
Privacy, 462
Private attitudes, and conformity, 256–257
Problem-solving orientation, and reduction of conflict, 390
Projective tests, 531
Propinquity, 213
Prosocial behavior, 285
 definition of, 287
 and need for approval, 144, 299
 in reinforcement theory, 294
 and religious values, 299
Proxemics, 457
Proximity, and attraction, 214

Public distance, 457
Public territory, 461
Punishment, as deterrent to
    aggression, 352–353

R

Race, in courtroom, 500. See also
    Prejudice
Random assignment of subjects to
    groups, 17–18
Rape, prevention of, through in-
    compatible responses, 360–
    361
Reactance
    and resistance to persuasion, 152
    role of, in defeat of ERA, 205
Reaction time, as technique for
    studying social cognition,
    86–87
Recall, 86. See also Memory
Recipients of persuasion, charac-
    teristics of, 143–145
Reciprocal concessions, in compli-
    ance, 269
Reciprocity
    and attraction, 233
    and cooperation, 374–375
    and receiving, 303
Recognition, 86
Reference groups, 253
Reinforcement-affect model, 218
Reinforcement
    role of, in conformity, 260–261
    value placed on, 555
Reinforcement theory
    and attraction, 218
    and prosocial behavior, 294
Rejection, 238
Relations-oriented leaders, 445
Relationship, deterioration of, 240
Relative deprivation, in social ex-
    change, 404–405
Relative needs, in perceived fair-
    ness, 397
Reliability, 535
Religious values, and prosocial be-
    havior, 299
Reluctance to help, and prejudice,
    172–173, 176
Repeated exposure
    and attraction, 214
    effect of, on attitude change,
    145, 148–150
    and response to erotica, 596
Representativeness heuristic, 111
Research, laboratory vs. field, 20–
    21
Resistance to persuasion, 152–154
Resisting temptation, 285, 311
Responsibility
    assumption of, 290, 307
    diffusion of, 290

Rights of individuals, in social re-
    search, 26–29
Risky shift, in decision-making,
    434–438

S

Salience and attention, 97–99
Schachter's theory of emotion, 74–
    75
Schemata, 88–97
    event (scripts), 91
    impact on social cognition, 92–
    97
    and memory, 95–97
    nature of, 89
    and perception, 92–95
    person, 90–91
    self-schemata, 90–91
Scientific management, 515
Screeners, 469
Secondary territory, 461
Self-attribution, 70–75
Self-awareness
    in deindividuation, 424–425
    objective, 100–101
Self-destructiveness
    and cheating, 316
    death instinct, 327
    suicide threat, 467
    and Type A behavior, 549
Self-disclosure
    and attraction, 229
    response to, 232
    sex differences in, 232
Self-effectiveness, 505
Self-esteem, and receiving aid, 302
Self-focused attention, 99–101
Self-help, 303
Self-motivation, 505
Self-perception
    Bem's theory of, 71–72
    and intrinsic motivation, 72–74
    shifts in, and compliance, 266–
    267
Self-presentation
    in compliance, 269
    and self-serving bias, 66–67
Self-schemata
    in persuasion, 142–143
    theory of, in sex typing, 200–
    201
Self-serving bias, 65–70
    effects of, 67–70
    ego-defensive function of, 66
    self-presentation and, 66–67
Sex crimes, 592
Sex differences
    in aggression, 348–350
    and altruism, 299
    in conformity, 256–260, 572
    and personal space, 456
    in response to density, 469

in roles, 199–203
    in self-disclosure, 232
    as stereotypes, 193–194
    and typecasting, 199–203
Sexism, 191–205
    questioning the competency of
        female leaders, 196–198
    reactance, in defeat of ERA, 205
    in stereotyping, 193–194
Sexual arousal, 585
    and aggression, 343–345
Sexual attraction, 574
Sexual fantasies, 583
Sexual Opinion Survey, 595
Sexual pheromones, 574
Sexual revolution, 566
    negative consequences of, 572
Sexuality, 563
    changes in, 566, 570
Sexually transmitted disease, 573
Shoplifting, 308
Shyness, 544
Similarity
    and attraction, 226
    attitude, 227
    behavioral, 228
    explanation of effects of, 228
    in courtroom, 500
    personality, 228
    and social comparison, 228
Situational determinants of behav-
    ior, 531
    on aggression, 341–345
Smell, and sexual attraction, 574
Sociability, 544
Social categorization, and preju-
    dice, 183–184
Social cognition, 81–121
    and affect, 116–117
    basic processes in, 97–111
    methods for study of, 86–87
    and person memory, 101–106
    role of schemata in, 88–97
    and social inference, 106–111
Social comparison
    and anxiety reduction, 221
    as explanation of similarity ef-
        fect, 228
    and group polarization, 436–437
    role of, in conformity, 260–261
Social competition, and prejudice,
    183–184
Social decision schemes, 429–431
Social determinants of aggression,
    330–341
Social distance, 457
    scales, 180–181
Social drinking, and cognitive dis-
    sonance, 160–161
Social exchange, 365–408
    and bargaining, 380–381
    basic nature of, 368–369
    and cooperation, 370–382

encouraging positive outcomes in, 403
inequity in, 395–405
laboratory method for studying, 371–373
perceived fairness in, 394–405
and threats, 387
unfairness in, 400–403
Social facilitation, 413–419
distraction conflict theory of, 418–419
drive theory of, 414–415
early research on, 413–414
and evaluation apprehension, 416–418
Social impact theory, 420–422
Social inference, 106–111
biases in, 106–110
errors in, practical effects of, 112–113
and heuristics, 110–111
overemphasis of extremity in, 107
and typicality, 107–108
Social influence, 246–283
informational, 251
normative, 251
Social learning
in attitude formation, 127–129
as theory of aggression, 329–330
Social loafing, 420–422
Social perception, 36–80
Social psychology
definition of, 6–11
emergence of, 11–13
future of, 14–15
growth of, 13–15
history of, 11–15
justification for, 8–9
research methods in, 15–29
role of theory in, 24–26
Social skills training, 544
Social support, and conformity, 254–255
Social transition schemes, 429, 432
Sociobiology, 327, 328
Socioeconomic differences, in remembering medical information, 512

Sociopathy
and cheating, 316
and empathy, 299
Speed of speech, and persuasion, 138
Staring, as nonverbal cue, 46–48
Stereotypes
about women and men, 193–194
self-confirming nature of, 174–175
Stigmatized groups, 175
Stimulus-response relationship, 537
Strangers. *See also* Bystander
in distress, 288
reactions to, 213
Stress, 470, 508–511
events and, 470
reducing effects of, 510
Structural equations, 87
Suffering-leads-to-liking effect, 157–159
Suicide threat response, 466
Superego, 298
Systematic observation. *See* Correlational method

T

Task-oriented leaders, 445
Tax evasion, 313
Televised violence, effects of, 337–341
Temperature, behavioral effects of, 473
Territorial behavior, 461
Testimony, accuracy of, 492
Tests
attitude scales, 131–132
item analysis in, 535
Likert scaling, 131–132
objective, 531
personality, 531
projective, 531
UCLA Loneliness Scale, 540
validity in, 535
Theory, role of, in social research, 24–26
Therapy
cognitive, 544

group, 548
social skills training, 544
Thermograph, 585
Third-party intervention, in conflict, 390
Threats
of medical institutions, 511
and social exchange, 387
Tokenism, as discrimination, 176
Truth-wins scheme, 429–430
Type A personality, 546
and achievement, 551
and cooperation, 381–382
development of, 547
Type B personality, 546
Typicality, and social inference, 107–108

U

UCLA Loneliness Scale, 540
Unfairness in social exchange, 400–403
Uniqueness theory, 230
Unobtrusive measures of attitudes, 134–135
Urban environment. *See* Cities

V

Vaginal photoplethysmograph, 585
Validity, 535
Value placed on reinforcement, 555
Variable
dependent, 16
independent, 16
Violence, televised, effects of, 337–341
Violent pornography, and aggression, 346–347

W

Work, psychological aspects of, 514. *See also* Job

X

XYY chromosome syndrome, and aggression, 351–352

1961 *Intergroup Conflict and Cooperation: The Robber's Cave Experiment,* a major source of insights into the nature and elimination of prejudice   Sherif, Harvey, White, Hood, Sherif

1962 Development of cognitive labeling theory of emotion, which emphasizes the key role of cognition in emotional experiences   Schachter, Singer

1963 Innovative and controversial research on obedience   Milgram

1964 First volume of *Advances in Social Psychology*   Berkowitz

1965 *Journal of Personality and Social Psychology; Journal of Experimental Social Psychology*   Katz; Doob

1965 "Social Facilitation," outstanding illustration of power of theory to explain diverse research findings in social psychology   Zajonc

1953 *Communication and Persuasion* describes classic research on persuasion and attitude change   Hovland, Janis, Kelley

1954 *A Theory of Social Comparison Processes,* the first systematic treatment of this key social process   Festinger

1957 *A Theory of Cognitive Dissonance,* one of the most influential theories in the history of social psychology   Festinger

1958 *Interpersonal Relations,* played a key role in development of attribution theory and research on person perception   Heider

1959 *The Social Psychology of Groups,* a major theoretical contribution to the study of social exchange   Thibaut, Kelley